PIERRE
BERTON

PIERRE BERTON

A BIOGRAPHY

A.B. McKILLOP

McCLELLAND & STEWART

Library and Archives Canada Cataloguing in Publication

McKillop, A. B., 1946–
Pierre Berton : a biography / A.B. McKillop.

ISBN 978-0-7710-5757-1

1. Berton, Pierre, 1920–2004. 2. Historians – Canada – Biography.
3. Journalists – Canada – Biography. 4. Authors, Canadian (English) –
20th century – Biography. I. Title.

FC151.B48M34 2008   971.007'202   C2008-900886-3

We acknowledge the financial support of the Government of Canada through the Book
Publishing Industry Development Program and that of the Government of Ontario through
the Ontario Media Development Corporation's Ontario Book Initiative. We further
acknowledge the support of the Canada Council for the Arts and the Ontario Arts Council
for our publishing program.

Typeset in Garamond by M&S, Toronto
Printed and bound in Canada

This book is printed on acid-free paper that is 100% recycled,
ancient-forest friendly (100% post-consumer recycled).

McClelland & Stewart Ltd.
75 Sherbourne Street
Toronto, Ontario
M5A 2P9
www.mcclelland.com

1 2 3 4 5   12 11 10 09 08

To
George James McKillop
(1921–2008)

whose Chilkoot was the Second World War

In Memoriam

I had what I can only call an intuition that there was in the soul of that boy some confused striving, whether of half-thought-out ideas or of dimly felt emotions I could not tell, which filled him with a restlessness that urged him he did not know whither.
– Somerset Maugham, *The Razor's Edge* (1944)

If you want me you'll have to take me as I am instead of trying to turn me into some lah de dah with a cane! I'm no stuffed shirt writing peanut ads. . . . God damn it – I'm a newspaper man.
– Ben Hecht and Charles MacArthur, *The Front Page* (1928)

In a story you had only to wish, you had only to write it down and you could have the world.
– Ian McEwan, *Atonement* (2001)

CONTENTS

—

Preface   *xi*
Prologue   *I*

PART ONE: ROMANCING THE NORTH

1.   The Family Bible   7
2.   The Telephone Call   24
3.   The House Below the Hill   42
4.   Beyond the Midnight Dome   63

PART TWO: NEWSHOUND

5.   Craigdarroch   85
6.   Get Me Rewrite   103
7.   Wunderkind   126
8.   Marking Time   149
9.   Citizen Straight's Boy   172
10. Headless Valley   196
11. Irwin's Recruit   219
12. The Allen Influence   242

PART THREE: CELEBRITY

13.   Writer, Editor, Author   271
14.   Arrival   301
15.   Star Crusader   327
16.   The Drop on this World   355
17.   Just Add Berton and Stir   389
18.   The Elsa Factor   415
19.   The Pulse of the Times   449

PART FOUR: ICON

20.   National Dreamer   483
21.   Astride the Summit   516
22.   A Wake of Whispers   549
23.   On Guard for Thee   584
24.   Iconoclast and Icon   626
25.   Last Words   660

Sources   *678*
Notes   *682*
Acknowledgements   *767*
Index   *771*

PREFACE

—

In the summer of 1961, freshly graduated from grade nine at Winnipeg's Cecil Rhodes School, I selected a book to take along on a family fishing trip, thanks to the advice of Mr. Alward, my history teacher. That book was Pierre Berton's *Klondike*, and it was the first work of history I encountered that was shelved in the "adult" section of the Winnipeg Public Library main branch. The name of the author meant nothing to me, but after reading that book on Lake Rozena near the Lake of the Woods (no fisherman, I), I knew that Canadian history was certainly not dull.

Berton's life intersected with my own in several ways, although I did not know this at the time. At home in Winnipeg, each Monday I delivered the *Star Weekly* magazine, utterly unaware that in the very weeks and months I did so, Berton was writing the most popular and influential column in Canadian newspaper history for its host newspaper, the *Toronto Star*. (For that matter, I was unaware of the existence of the *Toronto Star* itself: in those days, I believed that Don Mills, a name often encountered on cereal boxes, was so important that the post office did not require him to provide a street address: it was enough to write "Don Mills, Ontario.") A lengthy profile of Berton that appeared in the pages of the *Star Weekly* in 1959, "What Makes Pierre Tear?" failed to register on me, if I read it at all. At home, like so many other Canadians, my family and I settled in front of the television with a devotion not afforded to the United Church behind our house and watched *Front Page Challenge*, the quiz program featuring a glamorous panel that included a man in a bow tie; it seemed to be he who had the most fun identifying the hidden guests and the stories they represented.

A decade later, I entered a doctoral program at university to train as a Canadian historian, just as Berton captured the stern gaze of my professors by encroaching on their territory with the first volume of his history of Canada's first transcontinental railway. I defended my M.A. thesis, a narrative history of civic politics in interwar Winnipeg, within days of the release of this book, *The National Dream*, in the fall of 1970, and was puzzled when the external examiner began the questioning with the query, "What is history, Brian?" I was too stricken, or perhaps simply too gormless, to recognize at the time that Tom Peterson, the gentlest of political scientists, wanted me to ask myself a simple question: Is history a story to be told or a problem to be solved? This tension was soon to become central to Berton's relationship with the academic community. It helped shape my attitude toward the discipline that became my profession and affected my practice of it.

During Pierre Berton's final years, it struck me that when he eventually died, he risked being remembered primarily for his contributions to Canadian history: as Mr. Canada, the popular historian. Certainly the phase of his career taken up by writing history was important. For more than thirty years he had been in the public eye as the premier chronicler of Canadian history. But measured against the backdrop of his times, his life was of much greater canvas and significance than this. In my judgment, the most important and revealing years of his life were those between his arrival in Toronto in 1947 and his publication of *The National Dream* in 1970. These twenty-three years witnessed his rise to eminence and the transformation of his reputation from that of a coming author and local celebrity to a controversial national figure known to virtually every Canadian. Berton began to make his name when the very idea of a Canadian "celebrity" was repugnant to the arbiters of cultural standards. He established his reputation during the decades when an American-inspired culture of celebrity swept over popular taste, and he rode that wave, sometimes against the current, until his name held the status of a cultural brand. He accomplished this not simply through his omnipresence in the media, but because during these years the causes he supported and the values he held dear and defended came to be associated closely with the aspirations, the desires and fears, and the social values of his fellow Canadians. Mary Pickford, Stephen Leacock, and Mackenzie King had been well known, but

Pierre Berton became Canada's first modern celebrity and eventually its most celebrated native son and iconic figure.

Cultural historians sometimes employ the term "cultural moment" as a way of isolating a period of time – a day, year, or decade – that is marked by a flurry of artistic activity so intense that it helps define and lends coherence and consequence to an idea or a movement. A "moment" in this sense is as much connected to the Greek word *kairos* – a special point in time – as it is to *chronos*, chronological time. Pierre Berton was at the very centre of what might be called "the Canadian moment," the group of years between the mid-sixties and the early eighties marked by the rise and fall of the "new nationalism." Before then, Canada was a timorous nation, uncertain of its capabilities and its future, and as the eighties moved us toward the promised land of a globalized, market-driven, and privatized world, the nation lost its way once again. But during the Canadian moment, the country sloughed off the last traces of colonial inferiority and came to believe that all things were possible, whether in politics, the economy, or the realm of arts and culture. No figure stands more boldly in the forefront of this special moment, or did more to help bring it about, than Pierre Berton.

In 2001 I decided to undertake a biography of Berton, because I could think of no Canadian figure from whose life one might learn more about Canada's social and cultural transformation in the twentieth century, and especially about that culture in its elevated and popular forms of expression. I asked Berton for his full co-operation and that of his family, and for permission to use materials bearing his copyright both in public archival collections and in private hands. He agreed. He imposed no conditions except that my work should be candid and that I should tell such truths as I discovered. His family and close friends have been unfailingly encouraging and helpful.

This biography is the result of their unqualified generosity. It is a sympathetic and affectionate, but not uncritical, account of its subject. It is not a tale of tragic abuse, self-destruction, or recovery; nor is it one of overwrought self-absorption. It is a story of the incessant self-invention of a boy and a man, and of the boy in the man, and of a journey conducted over nine decades on the taut skin of life. It is perhaps trite to say so, but what Berton may have lacked in brooding artistic intensity, he more than made up for in his exuberant love of life and in his resolve to grasp as much of it as he could. In *The Razor's Edge*, Somerset Maugham, a novelist who affected Berton deeply, wrote this: "And however superciliously the highbrows carp, we the public in our heart of hearts all like a success story; so perhaps my ending is not so unsatisfactory after all." It is for readers to judge whether this is so, both for this book and for the man whose life it explores.

A.B. McKillop
Ottawa, Ontario / Messines, Quebec
April 2008

PROLOGUE

—

ON THE DAY PIERRE BERTON DIED, George W. Bush, president of the United States of America, made his first state visit to Canada, wanting to thank Canadians for the support they had provided after September 11, 2001, and hoping to repair a serious breach in Canadian-American relations, strained after the American-led invasion of Iraq. That night, Tuesday, November 30, 2004, *The National*, the flagship television news program of the Canadian Broadcasting Corporation, devoted sixteen of its twenty-two minutes to one man. That man was Pierre Berton.

The Canadian author's death completely overshadowed the American president's visit in the days and weeks that followed. The next morning, on the front page of the *Vancouver Sun*, a photograph of Berton wearing his Order of Canada pin and his trademark bow tie filled a twenty-four-column-inch rectangle over the accompanying story, "Canadian Icon Dies at 84." The Bush visit, occupying less than half this space, was relegated to a bottom corner of the page.

The public outpouring of respect and affection for Pierre Berton was unprecedented in Canada for a non-political figure, and it reflected the unique status he held in Canadian life. In newspaper and magazine columns, in letters to the editor, on radio and television, and in Internet blogs, Canadians from every walk of life spoke of the many ways he had left his mark on their lives. Some recalled, usually with unadulterated enthusiasm, his many television shows, especially the CBC program *Front Page Challenge*, on which he had appeared weekly for thirty-seven years. Others remembered him as a prolific writer of magazine articles. People drew attention to the controversial column he wrote for the highest-circulation daily newspaper in Canada, and the many times they had heard him on radio commenting on topical subjects.

Canadians praised him as a defender of the weak and as a champion of civil liberties; as a nationalist and as a conservationist; as a crusader for consumers and as an advocate of causes that were sometimes unpopular but that proved necessary. Finally, they spoke about his many books, especially those on Canadian history, and they expressed gratitude that Berton had made them aware and proud of their country's past.

Some regarded Pierre Berton as a self-centred and arrogant man, a repudiation of the stereotypes for which Canadians are best known: being nice and being boring. Those especially close to him knew instead an essentially shy man and a loyal, generous, and abiding friend. Few people have no secrets, and Pierre Berton had a few of his own. But for the most part his life resembled an open book – or perhaps, more accurately, an open newspaper or general-interest magazine. For he was not essentially a man of depth but one of breadth and range, inhaling the crisp air of the vast country from which he arose and then dedicating his life as a wordsmith to its service.

He was all these Bertons and more, for he had descended from the Canadian north like the north wind itself, determined not to be ignored. Like the nation's conscience, in the second half of the twentieth century and at the first gasp of the twenty-first, he variously coaxed, goaded, cajoled, warned, informed, entertained, and at times infuriated millions of his fellow citizens, using all the major media of the day – media that he came to master and dominate like few others.

No one in Canada, or for that matter in North America, managed to take hold of the full range of mainstream media with the same kind of commanding presence and authority. One searches in vain for an American or British equivalent. It is as if he somehow carried the DNA of Edward R. Murrow and Jack Paar, Vance Packard and Michael Harrington, Bernard DeVoto and Studs Terkel, with more than a little Garrison Keillor sprinkled into the mix.

Each of these figures – a war correspondent who spoke truth to power; a host of the most watched and enduring television interview program of its era; a muckraking crusader in the age of the consumer; a left-wing critic of North American society; a popular and respected historian of nation and empire in North America; a collector of the kind of folklore that serves as the first draft of history; a folksy, storytelling humorist of nostalgic bent – was or is a man of exceptional accomplishment in his own arena. The magnitude of Berton's achievement was that in this remarkable range of interests and accomplishments he spanned them all and became more than their sum. For half a century, he exhibited an uncanny knack for tapping into Canadian fears and desires at key moments in national life. He was the prophet of the middlebrow, a cultural observer who, in the words of the television producer Mark Starowicz, "sensed our national yearning long before anyone else and unearthed our overriding dramatic arcs."

In his final decades, Pierre Berton was often called a "Canadian icon," a term that he found silly. He made fun of his status in old age, but he was proud to have transformed himself in a long and varied life from journalist and author into iconic brand. And when he died, the rank and file of Canadians recognized something else: that someone utterly unique had gone from the scene, and that something of the country had been lost with his passing. They were saddened, of course; but, even more, they felt bereft. They knew they would not see his like again. Prime Minister Sir Wilfrid Laurier said that the twentieth century would belong to Canada. Instead, in myriad ways, Canada belonged to Pierre Berton.

PART ONE

ROMANCING THE NORTH

THE FAMILY BIBLE

—

NESTLED IN A RURAL SETTING on the fringe of Kleinburg, a pleasant village not quite blighted by Toronto's northern sprawl, lies a rambling house slung low to the ground, overlooking a carefully landscaped
garden and the rolling countryside beyond. Home to the Berton family
for half a century and more, it quickly disarms its visitors with the evidence of lives fully lived. Inside, it is filled with all kinds of memorabilia. Works by Canadian artists adorn its walls, Canadian books fill its
shelves. A convocation of academic hoods lines the stairwell, forming a
ghostlike academic procession that bears witness to the many honours
bestowed on the owner for his contributions to the nation. But of all
the mementoes in this museum of a home, one of those most prized is
the family Bible – an oversized omnibus volume containing not only
the text of the Christian canon but also a calendar, a Book of Common
Prayer, a concordance, and an index to the Scriptures, along with tables
of biblical weights, measures, and coins.[1]

The dates of births and marriages and baptisms and deaths so carefully recorded for posterity on the pages of this family heirloom mark
the passage of generations. They provide a sense of continuity, hinting
that blood courses through centuries no less than through veins.
Continuity confers security and comfort, a sense of one's bearings. Life
itself is a whirl or a disappointment, but the past, at least, holds a steady
course. Vital statistics, however, can only hint at a recognizable family's
history. Genealogical records often account for the full tide of family
circumstance, but they do not always chart the ebb of family fortunes.

The first names and circumstances noted in the Berton family Bible
speak to the flux of eighteenth-century European religion and politics,
and to the fluidity of borders. Above all, they draw attention to a wave

of transatlantic migration in the early modern era that became one of the most momentous episodes in human history. The Bible had been purchased in England by a native of America, but one of French Huguenot descent. In 1763, Peter Berton, a New York merchant and shipowner then visiting London, had acquired it and made the first entries.

The great European wars of religion in the seventeenth and eighteenth centuries that pitted Protestant against Catholic had been responsible for Peter Berton's place of birth, his faith, his political loyalties, and even his name. He came from a French Huguenot family – that is, from a Protestant one. His grandfather, Pierre Berthon de Marigny, had been born (probably in the 1670s) in Poitou, a border region of west-central France that was long a meeting ground between northern and southern cultures and the site of religious battles even before Charles Martel defeated the Muslims at Tours in 732. In the seventeenth century it held several sizable pockets of Huguenot population.

By the time Pierre Berthon was a child, the religious wars of the Reformation and the Counter-Reformation had ebbed and flowed in France for more than a century. Henry IV's Edict of Nantes had guaranteed Huguenots their religious and political freedoms in 1598, and a royal proclamation in 1643 had reconfirmed their rights. Yet the resistance of the Roman Catholic clergy to this toleration was such that toward the end of 1685 – when Berthon was likely still a boy – the French king, Louis XIV, revoked the document proclaimed on his behalf forty-two years earlier, during his infancy. Fed up with the political repression, forcible conversion, and general harassment that threatened once again to become outright persecution, thousands of Huguenots, many of them dedicated to commercial ventures, fled France for lands more tolerant of Protestantism. Pierre Berthon de Marigny and his wife, Marguerite, became part of this exodus.

Their immediate destination had been England, a country that those of a more enlightened French generation – most notably Voltaire – would soon praise as a land of unprecedented religious, economic, and political toleration, compared with France at least. But for Berthon de Marigny, England proved only a stopping point. America became his destination, and one of his first acts after arriving in the colony of Rhode Island was to anglicize his name. He appears in subsequent historical records as Peter Berton.

Virtually nothing is known of Peter Berton's son, but the family Bible acknowledges the birth of one grandson, and he bore the grandfather's name. Born in 1729, this Peter Berton purchased the Bible when he was thirty-four years old. By then, the Bertons had become a family of anglophiles – not only proudly Protestant but also fiercely loyal members of the Church of England and of the British Empire. The family had prospered in British North America, but the year 1763 was not a propitious one for British loyalists in colonial America. This was the year when – through the Treaty of Paris, which ended the Seven Years War – England took possession of most of the French colonies in North America, including all of Canada, Florida, and the territory east of the Mississippi River. But the English administration set in train a rising colonial discontent that a decade later precipitated the American Revolution.

Matters of commerce became central to that revolt against imperial control, and throughout the years leading up to the revolution Peter Berton remained a loyal colonial sea captain and merchant working out of New York. His situation became impossible, however, after the outbreak of hostilities between the American militia and British troops at Lexington and Concord in the spring of 1775. Because he did not hide his political sympathies, he found himself by early 1776 in flight with his family to Long Island, where he established a store. In August that year, a month after the American Declaration of Independence, it was plundered by rebels. This was a time for a loyalist to Britain to lie low, so he purchased a twenty-two-acre farm near Newtown, Long Island, a little north of the town of Brooklyn, and stayed there until war's end in 1783.[2]

Not one to trim his sails, Peter Berton lived by his allegiances. Earlier, he had been called upon to take a commission in the revolutionary forces, but he refused. In June, in command of his own vessel, *Free Briton*, he led one of three companies of British Loyalists out of the port of New York, northward to New Brunswick, a colony still faithful to king and empire. Two weeks later, on June 29, the ship reached the mouth of the Saint John River. It was a vessel full of refugees, but scarcely destitute ones. Of the 132 men, women, and children aboard ship, 30 were servants.

Although many of his charges no doubt disembarked at the port of Saint John, Berton and his own family settled farther up the river at

Oak Point. There he helped sustain the local Church of England, donating some of his land to build St. George's Church. This much is known of Peter Berton because in 1787 he testified before the Loyalist Claims Commission, seeking redress for American properties he had lost during the colonial revolt. He had paid a high price: Berton claimed ownership of five-sixths of the sloop *Commerce*, commandeered early in the war first by the British and later by the rebels; one-quarter of the sloop *Ranger*, scuttled and sunk by the British; one-eighth of *the Dolphin*, on her passage to England from a whaling expedition to Brazil in 1776 when it was overtaken by His Majesty's Ship *Argo*; and £100 interest in the whaling company, lost when the British navy secured its six vessels and cargo.

The amount of compensation Peter Berton received for these losses is not known, but testimony before the claims commission established his credentials as a United Empire Loyalist. Testifying on his behalf, a witness of unchallenged commitment to the British Empire spoke of him as "a man of integrity and very loyal and a decided Loyalist from the first."[3] Now fifty-eight, he had lived a full life and, given his time and circumstances, a long one. Following his appearance before the commission, he retired to Saint John. Predeceased by his wife, Ann, in 1790, he died on December 15, 1791, two weeks before the British Crown consolidated and strengthened its North American territories, giving shape to a future Canada by means of a Constitutional Act that divided the old Province of Quebec into the provinces of Upper and Lower Canada and granted it the rudiments of parliamentary institutions.

Peter Berton's family inherited not only his wealth but also his Loyalist pedigree, and they took both into the nineteenth century. Over the four generations that spanned the years between the eighteenth and the twentieth centuries, the family's trajectory reflected that of British North America itself. Berton fate, like Berton fortune, became inextricably linked to the shaping of legal and political institutions, the expansion of commerce, and the quest for the main chance.

Peter's son, George Duncan (1774–1828), became high sheriff of York County, New Brunswick, and cemented Berton ties to the provincial oligarchy through his marriage to Ann Street (1779–1832), daughter of the prominent army officer, lawyer, and politician Samuel Denny Street. In a life too short by half, George Duncan Berton's son, George

Frederick Street Berton (1808–40), consolidated the family position in the political and social order, becoming a barrister and serving – with the Honourable George Frederick Street – as a master of the Court of Chancery. He was also responsible for preparing an important "Revision of the Laws of the Province" in 1836.[4] In short, a Huguenot family that had fled a war of religion in France and a war of empire in New England had woven itself successfully into the Loyalist fabric of British North America.

As a kind of family Pentateuch, a record of beginnings, the entries on the early Bertons in the family Bible have held great pride of place. That the family tree can be traced backward to seventeenth-century France and then forward into colonial British North America lends the early forebears an attraction generated by their very distance in time. There is more than a whiff of the exotic in the French origins of this North American family, and something of the foreign, of the allure of retrospective transgression, in the New Brunswick Bertons' proud and unrepentant linkages to a pre-democratic age.

The Victorian Bertons are different, and less vivid to modern eyes. Closer to personal memory, they are not without emotional freight. But the authority of pedigree and the degree of interest in the family tree, with the Bertons as with other families, have focused on the beginning rather than the middle of the line of descent. Even as a young child, Pierre Berton knew the story of his French and American ancestors; but as an adult he knew so little about his paternal grandfather that in his autobiography he noted only the fact of the man's death. Yet the death of that grandfather, like a snowball misdirected by the wind, triggered a chain of events that radiated outward to affect others in momentous ways.

Following the mid-nineteenth-century commercial revolution ushered in by the British acceptance and practice of unfettered free trade, the Berton line took a direction away from the legal profession. For, like so many other families, it had become buoyed and carried along by the rising tide of transatlantic commercial life. William Street Berton – George Frederick Street Berton's only son – turned not to the world of law but to business. Born in Fredericton on December 19, 1835, he became an accountant. Little else is known of his life, except what the family Bible records: that he married Lucy Fox, daughter of William Lansdale Fox of Philadelphia, on December 12, 1870, in Saint John; that he had sons named Francis George and John Fitzgerald; and that he died in Milwaukee, Wisconsin, on March 31, 1874. He was thirty-nine years old when he was interred in the Freemasons' plot in Forest Hill Cemetery, Milwaukee.

What prompted William Street Berton, born in Saint John and son of a Loyalist, to assume residence in Wisconsin, the heart of the American midwest, remains unknown. Nor can we be certain that his family was with him, although there is no reason to suspect they were not. Perhaps he was there because Lucy had been born in the United States and had relatives there; certainly, more opportunities knocked in America than they did in New Brunswick. Of significantly more import, however, are two stark and foreboding facts: that upon his death William Berton left virtually no estate and that his children were at the time still infants. Jack was only a year or so old and Francis, known as Frank, had just turned two.

A corner of the Berton family had failed to catch the wave of western development in North America, perhaps lacking a knack for business or the pluck to take a risk. Perhaps that propitious moment of unexpected luck that the British champion of "self-help," Samuel Smiles, believed so essential for success in life simply eluded William Street Berton.

Frank, the elder of the boys by nineteen months, was to become Pierre Berton's father, and in the course of a long career as writer and historian, the son wrote lovingly of him. Yet Berton's accounts of his father's life, filtered through family memory rather than personal research, are curiously vague. In *Starting Out*, a memoir of his early years published when he was sixty-seven, Berton noted that when he was a boy he "knew very little" about his relatives "and even less about the Berton family history. . . . My ignorance, I think, was a reaction against my father's obsession with his ancestors. He talked so much about them."[5]

The ancestors in question were the distant ones, the Huguenots and the Loyalists, the persecuted, heroic, and successful forebears, not Frank's own immediate family, a study in the tragic failure of a life caught short. This helps account for the story Berton provides in his autobiography about his father's first twenty or so years, a passage so brief that its two sentences suggest more questions than answers. In them, the father, William, dies of a heart attack; the sons, Frank and Jack, are raised by their paternal grandmother in Saint John. Somehow she finds the means to send Frank to university, where he graduates as a civil engineer. Lucy Berton, Frank's mother and Pierre's grandmother, is nowhere mentioned.[6] This is all, and the account suggests the willed silence of the father and perhaps even a glance away by the son.

Historical records indicate that William Street Berton did indeed die at the age of thirty-nine, but of pneumonia rather than a heart attack. Lucy Berton and her children were likely in Milwaukee at the time of his death; if so, in the dark days that followed, she pulled up stakes and made her way back to Canada, restive infants in tow. Like so many other young Victorian widows, she depended on whatever charity her extended family was able or willing to offer. Lucy had blood relatives in the Fredericton area, and her mother-in-law, Delia (a Hooke before marriage to George Frederick Street Berton in 1833), widowed for more than thirty years, lived in Saint John. To which city and which branch of the family Lucy and her children first returned is not known, but in 1878, now herself a resident of Saint John, she had occasion to declare that she had become entirely dependent on the charity of relatives.

On February 16, 1878, Lucy left the children with her mother-in-law and reluctantly presented herself at 155 St. James Street, an imposing two-storey brick building with a square central tower topped by a Second Empire Mansard roof, popular in the Boston area at the time. The main roof was also in the Mansard style, and its flat top and steep sloping sides made possible what in effect was a third floor beneath it, likely used as dormitories for the thirty boys the institution accommodated. This was the Wiggins Male Orphan Institution, also called the Wiggins Male Orphan Asylum. Founded by the wealthy Saint John merchant Stephen Wiggins,[7] and incorporated in 1867 as if to declare that needy boys in a new nation deserve a new life, its purpose was to care not only for male orphans but also for destitute and fatherless children born in Saint John County. When Lucy Berton sized it up, she had walked to it through acres of utter devastation, for the previous year the fire of "Black Wednesday," June 20, 1877, had destroyed much of the city, caused an estimated $28 million worth of damage, and left thirteen thousand Saint John residents homeless. For acres all around the Wiggins, almost everything had been reduced to rubble. In the distance, the stern grey sky could be seen through the windowless holes in the walls of distant structures. Remarkably, the Wiggins Orphan Asylum had somehow escaped the worst of the inferno's wrath, suffering instead mainly smoke damage, outside and in.

With the kind of vacant numbness any loving parent would feel under her personal circumstances, made worse by the surrounding wreckage, Lucy Berton answered the questions about her son required for the institution's "Application for Admission" form. Place and date of birth: Saint John, December 12, 1871. Baptism: St. Paul's Church, January 31, 1872, by the Reverend William Deveber. Denomination of parents: Anglican. Pecuniary sources: none except the charity of relatives. Any other children: "one son aged five years." Health problems: none except whooping cough; vaccinated: in 1872. And so, in the middle of a New Brunswick winter and in this way, almost Dickensian in its emotional costs, Francis George Berton came to be boy number twenty-eight registered at the Wiggins institution.[8]

He did not immediately become a permanent resident. A place was not available for him until the fall. And in the meantime – what? Did the boy know what would soon happen? Did his mother prepare him gently for the separation, or did she let Frankie simply play throughout the spring and summer in blissful ignorance, free to do the things ordinary six-year-old children did? Did he cotton to her sadness, sensing that something, deeper than words could convey, was troubling his mother? And for her part, did she summon her fragile dignity and make the rounds of family and friends in one last attempt to keep her family intact? The relative who lived closest was her mother-in-law, Delia. But Delia was well past middle age, and how many women past sixty could take on such young boys?

Tears of hurt and fear and love and regret flowed freely on September 18, 1878, when Lucy took Frank to St. James Street, left him there, and then returned home to care for Jack. Her situation was uncommon but scarcely unique in a century of high mortality and impoverished widows. Even so, it remained a dilemma of biblical proportions, this choice of one son over another. When the decision reluctantly came, she had opted to continue nurturing the younger one, the one, she sensed, who needed her more. Perhaps she recognized a mental resourcefulness, an inner compass, in Frank even at six that would help him find his way. No doubt Frank learned something, too: that when the time had come for his mother to choose between sons, he was the one who had been sacrificed. Even if this intelligent little boy recognized that the sacrifice had been on the altar of his mother's grief, it could not have lessened the needlelike pangs of abandonment and the swelling sense of loss.

Frank Berton spent ten of his most formative and impressionable years under the roof of the Wiggins Male Orphan Institution. On his first night there he slept in the company of about two dozen other boys, but he was very much alone. When he arrived, he was three months shy of his seventh birthday; when he left he was almost sixteen.

The Wiggins institution was an orphanage, not a school. For their education, the more promising boys were sent to the Saint John Grammar School – after the Great Fire of 1877 a school in just about name only, for it had been an old and decrepit wood-frame building and it had fed the flames. So, as if his life were not precarious enough, Frank Berton, along with his classmates, spent his years of public education shunted from one cold and dreary Saint John building to another.[9]

The personnel of the Wiggins institution kept a record of how their charges fared, and the school log of examinations suggests that however fragile his emotional equilibrium may have been, Frank Berton's precocious mind seized on his studies. In 1885, aged thirteen and at the level called Standard V, his marks read: reading, 100 per cent; writing, 90 per cent; arithmetic, 95 per cent; algebra, good; geography, good; grammar, good; history, good. A year later, in April 1886, and now in Standard VI, his grades remained high: 100 per cent in reading, writing, and arithmetic; fair in grammar and history; good in geography. He matriculated from the Saint John Grammar School in October 1888. And with this rite of passage settled, he closed the door to the Wiggins Male Orphan Institution one last time and never looked back.[10]

In his memoirs, Pierre Berton stated his belief that Frank's paternal grandmother somehow put her grandson through university but that perhaps the Masonic Lodge paid his tuition fees.[11] Both are possibilities and he did find the means, for Frank Berton enrolled at the University of New Brunswick in the fall of 1888 on the heels of his matriculation. A more pressing question is one his son did not think to ask because he did not know about his father's years at the Wiggins institution. Where was Lucy, Pierre's grandmother, in all this? Given Frank's ten years at Wiggins, it seems unlikely that he had much regular contact with his mother or grandmother. Surely, periodic visits to the orphanage would have left a wake of sad and possibly bitter farewells, difficult for mother or child to bear. Less painful for her, perhaps, was the clean break. If this was the choice Lucy Berton made, by force of circumstance, six-year-old Frank would surely have experienced a deep sense of loss and abandonment. Even if his mother did visit him as often as she could, reassuring him of her love, would this sense of abandonment not have deepened when she left him again and again and again?

Still, there is no indication that Frank Berton left the Wiggins home embittered at his mother. It is likely, in fact, that after bidding farewell to St. James Street he paid his loved ones at least a visit before leaving for university in Fredericton. Perhaps by the age of sixteen he had come to understand that his mother's preference for one son over another had not been that at all, but a choice of the least damaging of two bleak alternatives. His letters to his mother a decade later would show few signs of emotional distance, so the likelihood is that during his Wiggins years, mother and son had maintained a degree of contact. The question is whether Frank Berton's years at the Wiggins school left him with any emotional scars and, if so, how deep and of what consequence.[12]

The University of New Brunswick had been founded in 1785 as the Provincial Academy of Arts and Sciences to educate people like the great-great-grandson of Peter Berton, UEL. Inspired in the wake of the American Revolution by the perceived need to provide "a virtuous Education" and to counter American ideas and values – "Principles contrary to the British Constitution" – it had come into existence by provincial charter in 1800 as a college dedicated to the liberal arts and sciences, although no instruction was offered by the institution, now called King's College, until the 1820s. Formally open to all denominations but in practice very much an Anglican institution, the college became secularized for reasons of provincial politics and by 1859 was transformed by charter into the University of New Brunswick.

By the time Frank Berton enrolled in 1888, the institution was well established and offered instruction in the arts and sciences to men and women alike. In grammar school Frank had been a good all-round student, but his strengths and interests lay mainly on the scientific arm of the arts and science scale. As a freshman, his course load maintained the sort of balance typical of the nineteenth-century liberal arts curriculum: mathematics, science, French, English, German, and history. He was to have taken Latin, an obligatory arts course, but could not resist putting a finger on one of the balance arms. He applied to be exempted from the Latin requirement so that he could enrol in a course in engineering. The request was granted.[13]

Pierre Berton's own account was that his father graduated from university as a civil engineer.[14] Understandably so, since Frank Berton later portrayed himself this way; it was as "Civil Engineer" that he declared his "Trade or Calling" on the attestation papers necessary to enlist in the Canadian Armed Forces during the Great War. But for all that he had taken engineering-related courses including hydraulics, economics, and masonry construction in his senior year, it was with a bachelor of arts degree – not one in engineering – that he graduated in 1892.[15] His alma mater did not offer an undergraduate degree in science until 1891, too late for Frank to meet its course requirements. And the professional faculties of law, forestry, and engineering were at the time just below the horizon at the University of New Brunswick; they appeared only with the dawn of the new century.

Engineering was a profession that his father "never actually practised," the son wrote in the same passage. The implication, given other things Berton's memoirs say about his father, is that so varied were his interests that other pursuits secured his attention. Frank Berton's interests were indeed many, but the more plausible explanation is that because engineering was then being transformed from craft to profession, and apprenticeship increasingly displaced by the academic credential, Frank Berton simply did not have the qualifications to find formal employment as an engineer.[16]

The autumn following Frank's departure, the University of New Brunswick's monthly magazine took note of its recent graduates. "Last but not least," said the writer, "we come to F.G. Berton. Berton holds the record for the half mile walk and managed to carry off the medal every time." His best subjects had been botany and chemistry, yet in his second year he had won the medal in French. And then a prophetic note: "Berton was a clever fellow but procrastination proved too much for him. He is now at his home in St. [*sic*] John waiting, like Mr. Micawber, for something to turn up."[17]

That once free he chose to return to his place of birth suggests his intention to stake a long-postponed if temporary claim on the childhood bedroom he could scarcely now remember. It was probably only then, when he became reacquainted with his mother and grandmother, that he learned of the two hundred years of Berton ancestry. Before his exile to Wiggins at six, the connection to the family past would scarcely have registered; and near the end of the decade he was to enter another kind of exile, although in family lore it became an adventure and at times no doubt was one. He would return to Saint John only once more, after the Great War, but by then he already carried the burden of his ancestral past with him.

Frank Berton was but one among many New Brunswick boys from circumstances modest or worse who developed a powerful sense of nostalgia for the heritage and land of their youth. James Dunn of Bathurst and Max Aitken of Newcastle, later business magnates of immense wealth, come immediately to mind. What seems to have separated Frank Berton from others was that he appears to have lacked, at least at this stage in his life, the ways and means of escaping the environment that limited his advancement.

So if it was an athletic-looking but rather uncertain and hesitant young man his mother and grandmother found on their doorsteps in the summer of 1892, they likely concluded that it was time at last to provide him with the only inheritance they could offer. At the end of the nineteenth century the Bertons lacked wealth but at least they possessed a pedigree, and a Loyalist one at that – forged of sacrifice, steadfastness, commitment to tradition. This, at least, was something in which Frank could take pride. However modest, the patrimony was a legitimate one that would compensate, if imperfectly, for blank memories of the young father he could not remember and of the middle-aged mother he scarcely knew.

Frank Berton's course in life was yet to be settled when he returned from Fredericton, bachelor's diploma fresh in hand, but his newly recovered family past offered a special kind of security, a mooring in time, and this was more than many people could claim. He assumed the burden of a family heritage while creating Micawber-like expectations that helped distance himself from his almost Dickensian childhood. Preoccupation with earlier generations of Bertons, and the Berthons before them, became central to Frank Berton's sense of self, and the family story remained in his kit for the rest of his life. Telling it, as he did so often, satisfied a deep personal craving and gave stability to a life whose otherwise sad poetry had been, to paraphrase the words of a bank teller turned poet he came to know, the rhymes of a rolling stone.

⁔ ⁕

In the early 1890s, Canada remained under the weight of an economic depression that had already lasted the better part of a generation. And nowhere was this more severe than in the Maritimes, whose "golden age" of sail lay in the past and whose rate of unemployment was among the highest in the nation. Elsewhere in Canada, the twin engines of industry and commerce chugged along unevenly, but the New Brunswick economy continued to languish and, if anything, was fast losing what little industry it possessed – an ironic but direct consequence of Canada's "national" economic policy.

Frank Berton became one of the casualties of that policy, and as with so many young men of the day who lacked either property or a profession, history in these years catches only fleeting glimpses of his coattail. He appears for a time to have apprenticed as a cabinetmaker. He is said to have spent a year in Quebec to learn French. For several years between 1893 and 1898 it is certain that he served in the military with the Third Regiment, Garrison Artillery, in Saint John.[18] There, at least, a fit young man with an aptitude and appetite for practical science could be put to good use.

Then, in the late summer of 1897, the event occurred that became the fulcrum of Frank Berton's life. Word reached Saint John that gold had been discovered in the Yukon. On Rabbit Creek near the junction of the Klondike and Yukon rivers on August 17, 1896, tipped off by the prospector Robert Henderson, California-born George Carmack and his Native brothers-in-law, Skookum Jim and Tagish Charlie, had stumbled upon a rich lode, and they began to spread the word. For a thousand miles up and down the Yukon, seasoned miners and men as green as spring willow, workers and gamblers and dreamers, rushed to stake claims. Carmack renamed his creek "Bonanza."

In January 1897, there had been only four houses on the townsite laid out on the marshy land at the junction of the Yukon and the Klondike by the merchant trader Joseph Ladue, who had quickly recognized that there could be as much gold in boom-town real estate as in gravel beds. Rippling white waves of tents ran up the slope of land to the forested hill that was Dawson City's northern and eastern boundaries. By April, fifteen hundred people lived in its shadow.[19]

Word did not reach the "outside," as northerners labelled the rest of the world, until the ice on the Yukon River broke the next May. Only then could the Klondike's instant millionaires travel out, first by stern-wheeler downstream to the delta of the Yukon at the Bering Sea and then down the Pacific coast to Seattle and San Francisco. Practising the sensational yellow journalism then nearing its apogee, the *Seattle Post-Intelligencer* chartered a tug, filled it with reporters, and chugged north-ward to meet the steamship *Portland*, southbound from Alaska. Before the disembarking passengers could reach their Seattle hotels, the first of several newspaper extras proclaimed: "Gold! Gold! Gold! Gold! 68 Rich Men on the Steamer *Portland*. STACKS OF YELLOW METAL." The story inside reported "more than a solid ton of gold aboard."[20] Instantly picked up by the wire services and sent out on transoceanic cables, those words grabbed the world's attention, and Frank Berton's too.

The stampede to the Yukon began immediately and Frank, along with hundreds of other down-on-their-luck New Brunswickers, decided to be a part of it. The Yukon gold rush exacerbated even further the great out-migration from the Maritimes between 1871 and 1901, when an estimated 264,000 people left the three Maritime provinces out of a total population of 894,000. This migration south and west hit New Brunswick hardest in the 1880s and 1890s, when over half of its young adults departed.[21] Frank had months to prepare, for late summer in New Brunswick was autumn in the Yukon, and soon the snows would come and the Yukon River would freeze and the region would be cut off to outsiders until the ice broke again the next May.

How he financed his trip across the continent and then to its far northern reaches remains unknown. Perhaps he had savings from working since graduation, and just possibly he borrowed the money. But the amount he needed was no pittance. Travel costs from Saint John to Vancouver were not excessive, since stiff competition between the Canadian Pacific Railway and the fledgling but ambitious Grand Trunk Pacific kept fares at bargain levels. But beginning early in 1898, desperately trying to cope with thousands of men yearning for gold but ill equipped to reach the goldfields, the North-West Mounted Police insisted that no one enter the Yukon Territory without taking with him a year's supply of provisions. Somehow, Berton found the means to purchase them.

Along with 550 other men, Frank Berton left Saint John in the third week of March 1898. In Montreal he visited friends of the family, worshipped at the Anglican Christ Church Cathedral, and outfitted himself with "sleeping bags, blankets, rubber boots, waterproof sheets, tent, camp outfit, etc." Then he rushed to the railway station and began the long trip to the west coast, first through the rugged Shield territory north of Superior, then across the endless expanse of prairie, and finally through the foothills and mountains of the Cordillera, the very spine of the continent. While hundreds of other men whiled away the hours aboard the train dreaming and gossiping and playing cards and snoozing, Frank was as often as not at the window or on the open platform of the carriage, eyes like a child's, closely observing and then meticulously jotting down in his journal almost everything that caught his eye. Not even the twenty tunnels and fifty-three snow sheds that peppered the mountain passes escaped his notice.[22]

On July 22, he stood at the summit of the Chilkoot, thirty-five hundred feet high, but he may as well have been at the top of the world. Behind him for sixteen endless miles, hemmed in on either side by rugged mountain slopes, the Taiya River forced its way south to the Alaskan port of Dyea and the ocean beyond. His back knew those sixteen miles. It had carried his gear northward along the Taiya, crossing it several times and following its rough banks to the encampment of Canyon City with its bustle of outfitters and freight provisioners; then past the more level ground of Pleasant Camp to Sheep Camp, a year back just that but now boasting more than a dozen jerry-built hotels, saloons, and supply houses to serve up to seven thousand transient residents.

Most men made it that far. The test came at "the Scales" and the steep climb to the summit. Frank had seen more than one man defeated before he could start the ascent, beaten when the packers reweighed the goods and refused to climb further without double the fee. But he was hauling most of his own gear and a year's worth of supplies, more than a thousand pounds of it. For this his reward had been to climb the "Golden Stairs" and its impossible thirty-five-degree slope to the top. He would need to do this, like all the trail, not just once but ten, twenty, maybe thirty times more, caching his goods in stages along the way. But he had done it once, and that was what counted.

From where he stood, Frank could see the long snake of men, backs bent like jackknives, heading up toward him. Moments ago he had been one of them, head down to block the harsh wind, neck and shoulders straining to take the sixty-pound load.[23] This may have been the best moment of his young life. Behind him on the trail, he had left good but spent men, and had passed dead and dying pack horses abandoned by their owners, and he had forced his will on a mountain. Now what he saw was like nothing he had seen before. The stark splendour of the panorama was enough to knock the remaining breath out of him.

The summit marked the international border, controlled by the North-West Mounted Police, who had staked out the peak earlier in the year and who brought something resembling order to the excited throng of men eager to protect their supplies. But his journey north was by no means over. He still had half the Chilkoot Trail to hike, another fifteen miles past Crater and Deep and Lindeman lakes, to the trail's end at the town of Bennett. Beyond that lay several hundred more miles of mountains and wilderness before he would reach Dawson City. From the level ground of the summit, the north slope would still be treacherous but it was downward, and after that most of the route from Lake Bennett to the goldfields would be on water. There were more dangers to come, he knew, unseen eddies and submerged boulders and white-water rapids. But much of his journey would be on the current of the majestic Yukon River, racing northward for another two thousand miles to the Bering Sea. And he would be riding it.

The murderous climb now lay in the past, like the life he had left behind. At the top of the Chilkoot, Frank Berton likely felt he had shed Wiggins boy number twenty-eight on Dead Horse Trail. He was twenty-six years old and strong and hard and resourceful, and he had proven to himself that he was a man willing to take a chance and face the unknown. Possibly at this moment he felt for the first time truly worthy of being a Berton. So, like Peter Berton setting sail on the dark swells of the Atlantic at the dawn of family memory, Frank Berton carefully readied his gear, steeled his resolve, and set his gaze to the north, heading away from his past.

THE TELEPHONE CALL

—

LAURA THOMPSON WAS AT HOME and had just begun to stir one morning in the spring of 1907 when she was asked to take a call from a Miss Currie, superintendent of kindergarten for the Toronto School Board. Would she be willing to accept a teaching position in Dawson City, in the Yukon Territory?[1]

The twenty-nine-year-old Toronto teacher was taken aback, but she found the offer intriguing. She knew very little about the Yukon, not even the location of Dawson City, but the salary of $2,100 was more than four times what she was currently being paid. Besides, Miss Thompson itched for new vistas. Her artistic elder sister, Florrie, had already travelled extensively in the United States and had studied in London and Paris, learning to paint miniatures; her religious sister, Maude, who had been a deaconess in the Anglican Church, aspired to be a missionary in the Canadian northwest. Laura herself had spent the summers of 1901 and 1905 visiting English relatives, and had toured great houses, museums, and art galleries; they had even taken her to Paris.[2]

But Laura had spent most of her time in the same kindergarten since passing her qualifying examinations back in 1895.[3] At the time she had been seventeen, but now, at twenty-nine, willowy and prim and handsome rather than beautiful, she was fast approaching the very model of the Edwardian spinster: bidding farewell to her youth and living at home with her parents, no beau in sight. It was time for a change.

Her father and stepmother professed horror at the prospect of losing a daughter to the wilds of the Canadian north, as she knew they would. Friends and acquaintances gave conflicting advice. "Why on earth are you going to Dawson?" a friend who had been to Dawson City with her husband asked. "Why, my dear, it's all over. They're all leaving. There's nothing new now." Laura had tried to convince herself that she intended to spend only a year away from home, and that this could do her no harm; but deep inside, she sensed, as she would later put it, that "I would see very little of this room or of my family in the years to come."[4] Faced with a determined daughter, her father relented and offered his best wishes. So the hot Toronto summer found her purchasing warm winter clothing, and almost before she knew it she had said her farewells, shed a few tears, and was on the train bound for Vancouver.

In late August 1907, the ss *Princess Beatrice* headed northward to Alaska with Laura Thompson aboard. The vast expanse of the Pacific ran to infinity on her left while foreboding coastal forests and mountains loomed on her right. Ahead lay the unknown. That the vessel's name was also her middle name surely was a good omen, yet she did not know what to expect. Back home, friends had warned her that it was mainly women of loose morals who made their way north, and then had advised that she must make sure she had a fine evening dress in her wardrobe. But she could still recall the thrill she had felt when, a few years earlier, she had read the journalist Faith Fenton's vivid reports in the *Globe* of her own trip to Dawson City. "Come up to the Yukon, O artists of our country. . . . Let our people know the rare summer beauties of this much-maligned land . . . our beautiful northern Canada!"[5] In the end, it had been the romantic dreamer as much as the experienced teacher who left for the Far North.

She knew where that part of her makeup came from, for her father, too, was a dreamer, and she was proud of him. Born in Newcastle-upon-Tyne in 1843, he had left England with his parents for Canada at sixteen. He was admitted to the Ontario provincial bar in 1865 as a solicitor, but he had never practised law. Thomas Phillips Thompson dreamed of changing the world. The idea of justice had led him to study the law, but he had soon recognized that the legal profession did not satisfy his wide-ranging interests. Instead, he began to write for newspapers, first in St. Catharines; by 1867 he had moved to Toronto to work for the *Telegraph*.

On February 3, 1872, Phillips Thompson married Delia Florence Fisher, the twenty-two-year-old daughter of a Guelph family of German background. Four years later, following the offer of a position with the *Boston Traveller*, he and Delia moved to the United States with their first-born, three-year-old Florence Clara (known as Florrie). Laura Beatrice was born there on March 13, 1878, but was back in Toronto with her peripatetic family within a year.[6]

At one time or another in the 1870s, Phillips Thompson wrote for most of Toronto's newspapers, including the *Mail and Empire*, the *News*, the *Telegram*, and the *Globe*. The police court column he wrote under the pseudonym "Jimuel Briggs" regularly poked fun at both the law and its victims, he was a favourite platform lecturer, and he became well known throughout Ontario as a humorist. All this changed when the *Globe* sent him to Ireland as a special correspondent, to report on the land reform agitation of 1880. There he heard Michael Davitt, an evicted tenant farmer's son, demand land reform, and Charles Stewart Parnell, the fiery Irish nationalist, preach the necessity of "home rule" for Ireland, under British control since the 1800 Act of Union. Thompson followed their speeches avidly. Their impassioned ideas fired up his sense of natural justice, especially when a tour of Ireland allowed him to witness directly the desperate poverty and living conditions of its tenant farmers. He returned to editorial positions with the *Globe* (1881–83) and then the *News* (1884–88). But his experience in Ireland had radicalized him. His final dispatch to the *Globe* from Ireland reflected this change: "And so, in spite of blunders, and crimes, and defeats – in spite of the greed of the self-seeking and the ambitions of the demagogues – through bloodshed, and tears, and suffering, the cause of the people will prevail by slow degrees, and the accumulated and buttressed wrongs of centuries be overthrown."[7]

Henceforth, as an early twentieth-century account of the family's history chose to put it, he became "closely identified with the Labor Reform and subsequently the Socialist movement . . . and wrote for several Labor and Socialist publications."[8] This was a masterpiece of late Victorian understatement, because Phillips Thompson, whom some knew only through his pseudonym, was the best known political satirist, socialist intellectual, and champion of labour in the country. His book *The Politics of Labor* (written after his return from Ireland and published in 1887), had become nineteenth-century Canadian labour's most sophisticated critique of the emerging industrial capitalism of the day. He was a major voice of the politically active Knights of Labor and had founded and edited several magazines and newspapers dedicated to the cause of the worker, including the *Labor Advocate*. For a time he advocated the land reform policies that the popular American reformer Henry George had put forward in his bestselling book *Progress and Poverty* (1879), and he became the Canadian champion of George's idea of the "single tax," a tax on economic rent, for such rent made landowners wealthy while impoverishing the landless. Thompson favoured workers' political involvement and action, but rejected strikes. He led the attack on monopolies and corruption, especially in municipal politics, and he was at the forefront of the battle for community ownership of public utilities.

By the turn of the century, he had moved beyond land reform and was an outright socialist. A year in Europe with his family in the 1890s had allowed him to investigate the social conditions of workers in France, England, and the Scottish highlands, and his graphic reports home to the *Globe* and the *Mail* had criticized and alarmed. Nationalization of the land by the state, he argued, would not do; needed now were "reforms in the commercial system, under which, at present, capital is made the means whereby one class lives in idleness, condemning the other to double toil."[9]

Perhaps because of his reputation as one of Canada's leading radical intellectuals, Phillips Thompson found it increasingly difficult to find steady paid work with mainstream newspapers, invariably steadfastly Liberal or Conservative. As a result, the family's life became one of genteel poverty. In the mid-1890s, they lived in a house on Toronto's Indian Road. It looked pleasant enough, with a veranda facing water and one side looking down upon one of the city's ravines. But looks were deceiving. The place lacked running water, the poor exterior lighting outside made it "unpleasant to come home to after dark," and the cold winds penetrated its rooms. Writing to her English cousin Fanny in 1895, Delia Thompson admitted that "it was a dreadful winter fearfully cold at times, and we were very poor, but we were all well, and it passed quickly."[10] It may be that all this proved too much for her, for she died in 1897 at the age of forty-seven. Within two years Laura's father married Delia's sister Edith, thirteen years her junior. Most of the family, especially Florrie, thought the marriage to be indecently hasty and opposed it; besides, the Church of England forbade the marriage of a man to his deceased wife's sister. But by then Phillips Thompson was an avowed atheist. Born in 1862, Laura's stepmother was only sixteen years older than she was. Whether she initially disapproved of the marriage remains unknown, but by 1901 it was she who urged reconciliation between Florrie and her father. The same year, Phillips and Edie Thompson had a son, Phillips Whitman. A half-dozen years later, Laura and her two sisters left home – Laura for Dawson City, Maude for the Northwest, and Florrie to the United States.[11]

After almost a decade in Dawson City, Frank Berton's life had been one long series of disappointments. Not that his trip down the Yukon River after conquering the Chilkoot had lacked adventure. He had nearly come to disaster with his supply boat on the dangerous Thirtymile section of the river. The vessel's bottom was damaged by a submerged rock and the supplies got drenched, but he had made it to the town that, in a letter home, he called "the miners' mecca."[12] It soon proved to be no mecca for him.

Frank always seemed to be just one step behind life's promise. By the time he reached the Chilkoot, gossip held that the rush to riches was already over, that there was little if any gold left to be had for new-comers, and that men had begun to leave Dawson by the dozens. And this proved true. The main flotilla of hundreds of boats had reached the town in early June 1898, but thanks to a false start (when he tried a route to the Yukon through northern British Columbia's Stikine River valley), Frank got to Dawson only on August 4. By then, some of the thirty thousand or so men who had arrived earlier were beginning to pull up stakes.[13]

Rabbit Creek merited its change of name to Bonanza, but by the time Frank arrived, the creeks for miles on either side of George Carmack's original strike had been staked out and claimed, especially Bonanza and its rich tributary, Eldorado. So Francis George Berton became one of the thousands of men who found themselves ambling along Dawson's Front Street that August, wondering what to do next. The street was so new that it was still rough with tree stumps, but strings of hotels, restaurants, barbershops, saloons, and dry goods emporia lined both sides, each showing signs of false-front bravado and hasty construction. Along the Dawson waterfront all manner of smaller craft – more than fifty sternwheelers, a score of barges, a couple of tugboats – and hundreds of tons of freight vied for space at water's edge, while dozens of hastily erected tents peppered the riverbank.

That September, when word reached Dawson that gold had been discovered at Anvil Creek near Nome, the first of thousands of men headed downstream, eager to make it to the new goldfields before the Yukon River froze. Again the stampeders looked north, this time to Alaska.

Frank was not one of them, for he had wasted little time in exploring the nearby creeks and gulches in the search for gold. He lacked experience, but as someone who had studied science and engineering he was not naive about mining, like many others who dreamed of riches in the Yukon. Yes, gold could be found by patiently sifting gravel in a pan on the creeks. But this merely hinted at where the seams might be. Klondike gold was river-borne placer gold, deposited millennia earlier in beds of sand and gravel. Millions of years of relentless erosion by water had released minerals from the hills and mountains, sweeping them to lower ground in streams and rivers. At nineteen times the weight of water, the gold sank to the beds of the streams that fed the rivers.[14] Frank knew that those primeval creek beds often lay deep below the surface. That was where the main gold deposits – the pay dirt – would be found, if a fellow was lucky enough.

In late September 1898, Frank Berton staked his claim. It was a 250-foot section of Quigley Gulch, which ran from the south into the Klondike River about halfway from Bonanza and Hunker creeks.[15] But after a luckless winter of miserable work thawing ground rock-hard from permafrost, breaking and removing it, and digging his way fifteen, twenty, thirty frozen feet down to the ancient formation, he had nothing to show for his efforts but the calluses on his hands. If gold was there at all, it clearly lay much deeper. So Frank called it quits and looked for other work. One of the great ironies of the Klondike gold rush was that men keen for an independent life too often became wage labourers, working the claims of others from dawn until dusk, moiling for gold belonging to other men. Sometimes Frank was one of them. Once again he waited, Micawber-like, for something worthwhile to turn up. Meanwhile, he shovelled gravel, washed dishes, collected bills, sold magazines.[16]

From the outset, Dawson City was a community of rigid class divisions. Government officials and professionals formed a close circle at the upper end of the social gradient; the miners, labourers, transients, and prostitutes occupied the lower levels. Between the two extremes stood the merchants.[17] So when Frank Berton, B.A., drifted around town from job to job, he was caught between the middle-class status his education and interests warranted and the semitransient working-class reality he lived. He failed to be recorded in the Dawson Post Office ledger as a resident of the town.[18] But he was nearby. A census taker found him in the area of Upper Hunker and Gold Bottom creeks, along with seventy-six other men living in bunkhouse #39, giving his occupation as "miner" but employed as a cook for a salary of $225 per year.[19]

This was not likely what Frank had had in mind when he left New Brunswick to seek his fortune. Above all, it seems, he wanted to assure his family in New Brunswick that he could – and would – do well for himself. He wanted others to believe that he was a man of worth. Berton family lore has it that just before Frank Berton crossed the Chilkoot Pass, at Dyea, he received a letter from Queen's University in Kingston offering him a "faculty post," but he declined it because to do so he would have had "to give up the struggle."[20] His quest, the lesson seemed to be, was of more importance to him than a secure position.

The story of sacrifice of a life of comfort for one of risk and adventure is significant, for it was to become central to Pierre Berton's view of his father and would help shape his own sense of the meaning of the Klondike gold rush. To Pierre Berton, his father's decision to forgo a secure future in order to complete his arduous adventure was an event pivotal to the family's journey through the twentieth century. "He had gone too far to turn back," he would write of his father, "and so he put the letter back in his pocket, forgot about it, and climbed his Chilkoot and thus, by a conscious decision, changed the pattern of his life."[21]

Indeed he did, once Frank Berton began the descent from the summit, heading north. But what of the comfortable position he rejected in doing so? It is not clear that the Queen's offer ever was made, for what kind of professorial academic position would Frank Berton have been qualified to assume? It is true that some who held only a bachelor's degree won professorial appointments at the time; certainly, Oxbridge undergraduate degrees still carried weight in Canada. But by the end of the nineteenth century such appointments had become rare, especially in the sciences.[22] In 1898, Frank Berton's six-year-old bachelor of arts degree from New Brunswick was no ticket to entry into anything but the most junior of academic positions, if that. In any event, no evidence appears to exist either that Berton applied for an academic post or that he was offered one.[23] The story of the letter that came too late is a good one, but it appears to be just that – a good story.

Something similar occurred in early 1901, when the University of New Brunswick's *University Monthly* magazine reported that "F.G. Berton, '92 of St. John, who went to the Klondyke, has obtained a lucrative position, being appointed principal of the Dawson City School."[24] This, too, was not so. Late in his life Charles McLeod, a pupil at Dawson Public School in 1900–1902, wrote of the male teachers he remembered. Frank Berton was not among them.[25] Nor does Berton's name appear on the one extant list of the Dawson Public School's teachers and principals. Like the academic offer from Queen's, the school principalship in Dawson appears to have been a projection of Frank Berton's desires, one made necessary to preserve his sense of self-worth. His career as a teacher was confined to a single year, and he did not teach in Dawson City. Instead, his name came to be listed as one of three people (the others female) teaching in the 1910–11 school year at the town of Granville on Dominion Creek.[26]

For his first dozen years in the Klondike, Frank Berton seems often to have lived hand to mouth, doing whatever jobs came his way, none for any significant length of time. He wrote regularly to his mother on the 1898 journey "in," but his correspondence home appears to have ended once he reached Dawson.[27] Soon he was one of the teamsters and lumberjacks employed by the lumber company of the trading post and sawmill owner Joseph Ladue, surveyor of the Dawson townsite.[28] The truth seems to be that after licking the Chilkoot, Frank Berton had very little by way of accomplishment to write home about.

Yet he had his restive mind. Berton was a man of boundless curiosity, a man who seemed to know something about everything and was intensely interested in it all. Perhaps this accounts in part for his inability or unwillingness at that time to stick to a job once he found one. Too much else was going on in this endlessly fascinating town, filled with the most colourful and larger-than-life characters imaginable and with a constantly altering townscape. New and revolutionary mechanized mining technology and the massive power dredges it made possible now worked the surrounding creeks, and it was clear that machines and corporations, not the individual miner, would be the gold diggers of the future, a future close at hand.

Just beyond the tailing piles left by the electricity-powered dredges, devices that could do the work of a hundred men, lay an untapped wilderness with hundreds of species of plants and animals Frank was keen to discover. And then there was the great and dangerous river that had so fascinated him on his way downstream from Lake Bennett in '98. A man could spend a lifetime here in this amazing land, hiking and observing and collecting and recording, and still not nearly exhaust the wonder of it all.

In July 1909, T.G. Bragg, superintendent of schools for the Yukon Territory, reported on the state of its educational institutions. He boasted that Dawson City not only provided instruction for all ages up to honours matriculation into the University of Toronto, but had a kindergarten room "in charge of an expert directress from Toronto."[29] Miss Laura Thompson had just completed her second year teaching in Dawson, and she had adapted quite well to the rhythm of the town.

Laura remembered vividly the remarkable journey she had made to reach it two years earlier. After the *Princess Beatrice* had docked at the rambunctious town of Skagway, the Alaskan gateway to the Chilkoot and White passes at the head of the Lynn Canal, Laura had lunched with others at the Golden North Hotel. Fortunately, it was no longer necessary for travellers to the Klondike to brave the Chilkoot Trail. Instead, she took the new narrow-gauge railway over the 2,800-foot White Pass to Lake Bennett and then to Whitehorse. Along the way, the train chugged past Dead Horse Gulch, where three thousand horses had perished in the mad rush of 1897. Her party stayed overnight at the White Pass Hotel, a place with "dejected-looking men" and rooms without keys.[30]

The next day, like most of the others, she boarded the sternwheeler *Casca* dockside on the Yukon. It managed to shoot the rapids and avoid the ever-dangerous Five Fingers (rocky projections from the river, fingers of death to the unwary or unlucky) and reached Dawson City safely. The regular forty-hour trip took twice that time after the *Casca* became mired on a sandbar at a spot called Hell's Gate, and it took the crew two days to float it again. But from that point in the river, Laura recalled later, "romance in many forms lay just around the corner."[31]

By the time she reached the City of Gold, she had already met a good number of people from Dawson. Aboard the *Casca* had been three of the town's schoolteachers, several nuns and nurses, and four clergymen – one of whom was Isaac O. Stringer, the new Anglican bishop of the Yukon, on his way to his next charge. Superintendent Bragg, a widower, met and welcomed the contingent of teachers at the dock, among them the demure new kindergarten teacher from Toronto. He accompanied them along dirt roads and down plank sidewalks to the boarding house he had chosen, since single female teachers were not allowed to live by themselves. Its haughty name was Kenwood, but it remained a house built of logs.

Laura's initial impression of Dawson was of the drab grey of its larger buildings and of the hordes of men, in costumes of every sort, crowding around the dock. (The 1911 national census revealed that men constituted 77 per cent of the population of Dawson, down from 81 per cent in 1901.)[32] From the outset it was a place of contrast and contradiction: "If the town itself was drab, this scene was alive with colour. If Dawson was dead, I asked myself, what must it have been like when it was alive?"[33]

She did not know it then, but the town had already changed from its unruly early days. Back in 1898, at the height of its population, Dawson had momentarily been the largest city west of Winnipeg. Within a year it boasted two banks, two newspapers, five churches, electricity, and telegraph and telephone lines. When a dance hall girl dropped a lantern in 1899 and fire destroyed much of the town, a rather more sophisticated, more properly Victorian community look took shape in the rebuilding. One symbol of the architectural bridge between the old

Dawson and the new was Charlie Meadows's lavish Palace Grand Hotel. Better known as "Arizona Charlie" because of his stint with the Buffalo Bill and Pawnee Wild West shows, Meadows soon created a venue through which passed some of North America's most popular entertainers and best theatrical troupes, from vaudeville to opera.[34]

Gradually Laura Thompson began to notice the way the town was working to shed its earlier "Good-Time Charlie" image, symbolized by the saloons and dance halls. The fifteen thousand or so Dawson and area residents of 1900 had dwindled to somewhat over eight thousand near the end of the decade; but it had become a relatively stable town, since much of the more transient population had moved on. White picket fences now surrounded modest wood-frame houses.[35]

Dawson City was one of a hundred resource towns that studded Canada's northern reaches like pins on a map. Usually founded with the discovery and exploitation of one staple or another – historically fish, fur, timber, and minerals – places like Timmins and Cochrane, Iroquois Falls and Rouyn-Noranda were almost always one-industry towns and therefore among the most unstable and precarious of Canadian communities. They attracted people from a wide variety of backgrounds, with the result that social divisions existed just beneath the surface of daily life. Community identity rested as much on hostility to the south and what the historian Kerry Abel has called "an imagined sense of northern uniqueness" as on the shared experience of a hard lot in life.[36] Stories and scandal rested silently in the shadows of such towns, ready to be drawn upon should the need arise.

As the years passed, Laura absorbed Dawson's many contradictions. This was a mining town in which false-front wooden stores sold the finest of Parisian gowns and the most exotic of goods and foodstuffs, from lobster to caviar, and where you could live in a rude log hut but order a posh six-course meal at any one of several local dining lounges. It was a town that placed restrictions on the sale of liquor in its many saloons but openly tolerated prostitution in the shacks lining the narrow alley behind Front Street and in Lousetown, a clutch of red-light cabins that had sprung up just across the Klondike River. This was a place made by tough men but where strong women like Belinda Mulroney could arrive as hash house operators and leave as duchesses.

"It was not a beautiful city," Laura recalled in old age, "but it certainly had character."[37]

◄►

Proprieties well observed do not restrict: they liberate, and they do so because they define and clarify boundaries of social and moral behaviour. Laura Thompson was ever one to observe proprieties, and from the moment she walked down the gangplank of the *Casca* and onto Dawson's Front Street, she conducted herself in ways designed to do an Edwardian school principal proud. In this way, like many white "European" women before her, she performed an essential role as importer of the standards of British civilization into one more colonial environment.[38] Her skirts remained the appropriate length, below the ankle, and she was seldom without a bonnet and a stiff white blouse. It did not occur to her to use the Christian names of those with whom she shared a house, even after she had lived in close quarters with them for several years, and she was genuinely taken aback when someone did. Familiarity was something one earned with respectful effort.

Yet she was no prude. Compared with some in Dawson, her big-city background had lent her a cosmopolitan outlook. Her father's parental attitude was a liberal one for its day, and his influence instilled in her a broad-mindedness unusual for the time – a view of the world her wry eye and dry sense of humour hinted at. She enjoyed the company of others. Very soon after her arrival she joined in the popular Dawson custom of holding at-homes, weekly afternoons during which visitors could pay their respects and, in the case of gentlemen, leave their calling cards. Several days a week, when school was not in session, she went to the at-homes of others. As a teacher, she occupied a place as part of Dawson's high society (although in its lower reaches), so she found herself with a broadening circle of acquaintance. She was, as she put it, one of the "crowd who went out" walking along the shoreline, skating on the river, and dancing at the annual (and formal) St. Andrew's Ball. A young banker who had recently arrived in town escorted her to the one held in 1908. His name was Robert Service, and he would soon be known around the world as the Bard of the Yukon.[39]

At the same ball, Mrs. Henderson, the federal commissioner's wife, asked her if she would like to accompany her and her husband to Granville, a mining community of about eight hundred in the Hunker Creek valley, about sixty miles away. Mr. Henderson had to open a curling rink there; would Miss Thompson be willing to play a few tunes on the piano? Laura jumped at the opportunity. Not long afterwards she found herself at a concert held in the town's Bachelor's Hall, with dancing to follow. Then and there she met Frank Berton.

A thin man a few inches taller than her, looking to be in his mid-thirties, he cut a raffish figure as he came across the dance floor and, to her surprise, sought her out. Soon she was in his arms, dancing, and trying to gain a sense of this man in the dark rumpled suit, stiff collar, and white tie, his long face dominated by a light-coloured but full moustache curled at the ends and a blond Vandyke beard that threatened to get out of hand. She had heard about this fellow before, the miner who solved problems in algebra for the fun of it and read Shakespeare to the children at the local school. When he spoke to her, he did so in a quiet, cultured manner. To the locals, she knew, he was known simply as "Doc," because in the absence of a dentist he was known to pull teeth.[40]

What had struck Doc's fancy about this woman? Perhaps it was her height and stately bearing. Perhaps it was her big brown expressive eyes or her face, handsome but not "cute." She seemed feminine without being prissy, serious but not solemn. She looked proud but also open to the world around her. This woman would not be easy to forget.

Even so, after the last dance that night Frank did not contact Miss Thompson for a year, and even then he did so only through an intermediary, who asked whether one of a "legion of admirers" might visit her some time. She immediately guessed it was Doc, and acceded to the request – but not before she consulted Miss Holtorff, another teacher, with whom she shared a bungalow. The visit took place, a diffident Frank accompanied by his chaperone, T.D. MacFarlane. Did she speak French? Would she like to learn? He would like to help her. Laura soon found herself, with others, taking lessons from him in a cabin he rented in Dawson for the purpose. At the end of each session Frank walked her home, even though his cabin was almost next to her bungalow. That year, 1909, she accompanied him to the St. Andrew's Ball, and by the next spring they had reached "an understanding." To Laura Thompson, Frank Berton had become less eccentric than intriguing.[41] Still, he was a strange bird, more interested in the taxonomy of a flower or the conjugation of Greek verbs than in the source of his next dollar. A man capable, it seemed, of doing just about anything, yet strangely adrift; a conservative man, yet one who appeared to lack an anchor in life.

Laura became that anchor. With marriage firmly in mind, Frank Berton worked the summer of 1910 on Bonanza Creek as a labourer for the Yukon Gold Company, saving what he could. By the fall he had managed to land a position teaching at the school in Granville. Laura chose to think of him as the school's principal and, as the sole male teacher, in effect he was; but the status was not official, if conferred at all.[42] Since his duties would keep him in Granville most of the time that school year, Laura arranged to visit her parents in Toronto. She had not seen them for more than three years.

She left in October and returned at the beginning of March 1911, moving back in with Miss Holtorff. Of the trip home, her memoirs say almost nothing except to note, in a self-consciously elliptical way, the strenuous arguments of friends and family alike urging her not to return to the north. The self-censorship suggests that the words were more heated than in 1907. The first trip meant a season or two of experience and adventure; the second more than suggested a permanent separation from home, family, and friends, and perhaps marriage to a man the Thompsons thought not entirely suitable because of his unsettled life. Yet return she did, and when her overland stage coach neared Dawson, Frank was there to intercept her with horse and cutter. That summer, and continuing into the fall and winter, Frank laboured once again on the creeks. For whatever reason, he did not return to the Granville school.

It turned out to be politics, not toil, that made his anticipated marriage financially possible. In the summer of 1911, Liberal prime minister Sir Wilfrid Laurier, in office continuously since 1896, called a federal election. The central issue was free trade with the Americans – championed by the Liberals but fiercely contested by the opposition Conservatives under the able leadership of Robert Borden. By the time the ballots were counted on September 21, much of English Canada had rallied to the anti-American thrust of the Conservative campaign.

"Continentalism is Treason!" went one Conservative campaign slogan. "A vote for Laurier is a vote for the Kaiser!" proclaimed another, echoing Sir John A. Macdonald's famous assault on the idea of free trade with the line "A British subject I was born, a British subject I will die." As traditional in his politics as he was in his dress and manner, Frank Berton did not hide his loyalties. His fervent hope was that if the Conservative cause triumphed, he might benefit from one of the many patronage positions that would follow.

Borden and the Conservatives won the election handily and, steeled by Laura's insistence, Frank immediately reminded the power brokers in Dawson's small Conservative inner circle of "his own past efforts in the cause." Dawson lore has it that Laura intervened directly with Mrs. George Black, whose husband had been rewarded after the election with an appointment as commissioner of the Yukon. However the deal was arrived at, Frank Berton was promised a government position.[43]

The security thus attained was enough for the couple to plan their wedding for the following summer, as soon as school was out. They married on Saturday, June 29, 1912, in a quiet ceremony at St. Paul's, Dawson's Anglican church. Because she was now a married woman, Laura forfeited her teaching position, in keeping with the practice of the day. After some discussion the couple moved out to Sourdough Gulch, near Bonanza Creek, until the anticipated government appointment materialized. "Mrs. Berton for the last five years has been in charge of the kindergarten in the Dawson school, where she won the hearts of scores of Dawson tots," proclaimed the brief notice of marriage in the *Dawson Daily News*. "Mr. Berton is well known to all old timers. He is one of the hardy ones, who conquered Chilcoot in 1898, and has been constantly in the country since that date. Mr. and Mrs. Berton will make their home in Dawson, after they return from the creeks, where Mr. Berton is employed by the Yukon Gold Company."[44]

It was a measure of Frank that he chose to live in a tent on the creeks, and a measure of Laura that she brought a roll of green oatmeal wallpaper to her new canvas home. In this way, while Frank spent his twelve-hour days on Bonanza with a sledgehammer, driving lengthy hollow steel rods (or "points") filled with steam into the ground to melt the permafrost, Laura papered the rough-hewn board walls that lined the inside of the tent and painted their few sticks of rude furniture.

Most of the time spent alone she felt terrified: of the silence, of the wild animals, of the strange men.[45]

In September 1912, Frank received an appointment as mining recorder, registering and maintaining mining claims in the Dawson City office of the federal Department of Mines. At forty-one, it was possibly his first truly steady job. He and Laura purchased a furnished house in Dawson for $700, and it became their home for the next four years. Frank settled into the new routine, his own fortune now that of recording the claims of others. The irony in this could not have escaped the former miner, and he may well have brooded about it, but he was not a man to complain. And so he stuck to his daily tasks, intending to remain.

The coming of the Great War in the summer of 1914 tested Frank Berton's loyalties to family and empire. As patriotic as the next Canadian anglophile, he wished to serve the Allied cause, but his marriage was still fresh and at forty-three his age stood against him for military service. He continued to work as the mining recorder, but the brief little adventure expected in July and August 1914 had turned by the summer of 1916 into a prolonged and entrenched war of attrition. The Battle of the Somme that dragged on from July through November became a horrendous slaughter with more than a million casualties. Disenchantment led to a drastic decline in enlistment, and conscription by federal legislation was a distinct possibility.

No one enlisted out of adventure, not after the Somme, with almost twenty-five thousand Canadians dead and missing and hundreds of thousands of casualties on both sides of the battle lines. Duty or a deep-seated need to prove oneself or demonstrate loyalty now summoned men to serve. This was especially so in Dawson, for George Black, granted leave from the position of commissioner, had raised a Yukon Expeditionary Force. On October 5, 1916, Frank took himself to the Dawson City recruitment office and signed up. As a "civil engineer," he declared.[46]

Before the month was out, he had said farewell to Laura and accompanied the Yukon Expeditionary Force from Dawson to Vancouver. There he transferred to the Royal Canadian Engineers and served with that regiment for the remainder of the war. Meanwhile, Laura stayed with her parents in Oakville, the small town, not far west of Toronto, to which they had moved. Early in 1917, Frank was stationed in Quebec, training for the Canadian Expeditionary Force. That February, his mother travelled from New Brunswick to visit him, and she died, of causes that remain unknown. She was buried in Ottawa, home of her second son, Jack. Frank left for the front in May, aboard the SS *Justicia*. Later, his daughter chronicled his war record: "In March 1918 he was assigned to the Second Field Canadian Engineers as a sapper and saw action at the battle for Arras. He was promoted to sergeant in May and in July returned to England to train as a commissioned officer. He received his Lieutenant's commission on Nov. 30, 1918, but the war was over."[47]

When Frank returned from overseas at war's end, he rejoined Laura in Oakville. As they renewed their marriage, the couple had lengthy discussions about where their future should lie. Should they stay in Ontario, perhaps on the fertile farmland near her aged parents? Or should they move to Vancouver Island, with its verdurous climate? In the end, they chose neither. "We both knew, deep down inside ourselves," Laura later recalled, "that the Yukon was in our life and we could not give it up."[48] Each had spent too many seasons in the North, and it held them in its grip.

For Laura, one special moment in the Far North remained clear. "We had struggled for hours up a steep, tangled gulch, our feet deep in wet caribou moss and our legs and ankles bruised by sharp rocks. Then, suddenly, we broke out on to a sunlit hillside. On its upper reaches, fairly dancing with the joy of life, was a grove of young white birches. Lower down, towards the valley, lay acres and acres of wild flowers – clumps of blue lupins, larkspur five feet tall, monkshood and great feathery bunches of white Baby's Breath. We never spoke of that scene to each other again, but it was one of the reasons why we were returning."[49] For Frank, perhaps the motivation was less romantic. What prospects did he have, in middle age, in the Canadian south? They returned to the North.

But not to Dawson, not immediately. When he sought to regain his former position, Frank found himself transferred instead to Whitehorse as a kind of government jack-of-all-trades, recording claims or fighting fires or inspecting weights and measures.[50] For the next two years, the Berton home was this typical small northern company town sustained by the White Pass & Yukon Route railway. They soon found that it lacked the complex fabric of Dawson's social life and even the curious charm of its slow decline, as gold became scarce and the number of adventurers waned. Residents of Whitehorse resented the privileges and attention they believed Dawson received from the government, and they snubbed people from the gold rush town to the north, so Frank and Laura socialized mainly with transplanted Dawsonites. One was Dolly Orchard, a former dance hall girl recently made respectable by marriage.

Late in 1919, Laura unexpectedly became pregnant. Now in her early forties, she had all but given up hope of becoming a mother, not least because at some point earlier she had experienced a miscarriage.[51] And so the months of anxiety began. She worried about medical care because Whitehorse doctors were even more transient than the town's prostitutes, seldom remaining for more than a month or so. She worried, too, that her age put her and her child at greater risk. Not that being young was any assurance: the two kindergarten teachers who had followed her at the Dawson Public School, much younger than her, had both died in childbirth. In July, confined in hospital and awaiting labour pains, she overheard two Whitehorse matrons discussing her imminent death.[52]

While Laura was still in the hospital, her third doctor left town – but not before delivering a healthy baby boy on July 12, 1920. Laura was of course deeply relieved. And Frank? At almost forty-nine, just about old enough to be the infant's grandfather, what did this man think and feel? Pride, obviously. Satisfaction, likely. Perhaps even a sense of fulfillment or completion. The child's birth may even have rekindled, if it needed a spark, his sense of the great unfolding of family lineage. Another Berton generation had made its appearance, the latest in a long line of descent and one born into a new century. Their miracle child had arrived, and his name would be a proclamation. He would be Pierre Francis de Marigny Berton.

3

THE HOUSE BELOW THE HILL

—

IN THE SUMMER OF 1921, when their son, Pierre, was a little over a year old, Frank and Laura Berton returned at last to Dawson. To their great delight, Frank had been recalled to the mining recorder's office there. Before the first winter snows fell, they purchased a small house on Eighth Avenue in the south end of town. It cost them $500, and it sat directly across the street from the log cabin in which Robert Service, then Dawson's most famous former resident, had lived a dozen years earlier while writing his first novel, *The Trail of '98*.[1] Immediately behind the Service cabin, the steep forested slope of the Midnight Dome began its ascent.

Their home was a small wood-frame bungalow with a parlour, a dining room, a kitchen, and one bedroom. Standing on the porch that ran along the front of the house they had a fine view of the town below. To the west, beyond the front yard, the slope eased and levelled out as it neared the Yukon River. Only a couple of hundred paces ahead, above the neighbouring cabins, rose the handsome two-storey municipal building where Frank once again worked. To the northwest, just beyond where Fifth Avenue bisected the town, stretched its commercial centre; and to the southwest they could see the woods poking up from the junction of the Yukon and Klondike rivers and had a clean line of sight to the great bulge of forested hill rising precipitously from the water on the Yukon's far shore.

Laura was struck by how much Dawson had changed in the five years they had been away. It was dying, its population shrunk to under a thousand residents. Ninth and Tenth avenues, once carrying traffic above the Service cabin, had been reclaimed by the forest and the hill; downtown, buildings had become derelict, homes boarded up. Many of the hotels near the waterfront were empty, including Belinda Mulroney's establishment, the Fairview, once the grandest in the town. Old machinery, scraps of iron, and pieces of discarded mining equipment lay rusting on the streetsides and in weathered sheds all around town. What the end of the gold rush and economic decline had not destroyed in Dawson, other disasters did. Toward the end of the decade, a memorial cairn erected to the dead of the Great War in Commissioner's Park would display the names of seventy-one Dawson men. (For the Second World War, there would be eight.) Lacking any memorial at all, but certainly not forgotten, were the 125 Dawson residents (including some of its most prominent) who in October 1918 had gone down with the Canadian Pacific steamship *Princess Sophia* in the Lynn Canal off the Alaska coast, with the loss of all on board.[2]

The whole town seemed to be stuck in time. Elsewhere, on the "outside," Laura knew the pre-war world and its lingering Edwardian remnants had begun to give way to what people called the "New Era."[3] The past seemed to have been discredited, its nineteenth-century values and complacency now questioned in ways her father had done a generation earlier. The months after Frank had returned from the war, when he and Laura were staying with her parents in Oakville, had been ones of great social and political unrest. A violent general strike had broken out in Winnipeg in May and June 1919 and was ruthlessly put down. One man had died and several strike leaders – including elected municipal politicians – were arrested and imprisoned. Farmers in western Canada and Ontario had begun to organize to oust old-style politicians. Earlier codes of belief and behaviour were under assault. People were impatient with the old ways: impatient with old-fashioned novels and poetry, impatient even with time-worn songs and dances. New musical fads had shoved aside the tango, the craze that just before the war had itself displaced the waltz as the dance of choice.[4]

But Dawson? Dawson, in its own diminished way, seemed to go on as if frozen in time. Laura and her genteel friends continued to host elaborate dinner parties and at-homes to maintain the decorum and tone of Dawson society; as before, gentlemen callers placed their cards in bowls discreetly left out for the purpose. In Dawson, the minuet still prevailed. The difference, unavoidable when one looked at the town with outside eyes, remained with Laura for the rest of her life. "I can still see the lined faces of the old men lighting up when the minuet was played," she recalled in her memoirs. "When I hear it today, my mind goes back to the Arctic Brotherhood Hall . . . and that incongruous spectacle of the sourdoughs gamely pirouetting and bowing as the snow swept down outside and the huskies howled to each other across the empty cabins."[5]

With the arrival of their new baby, however, things had certainly changed for Laura, and for Frank. Gone were the carefree country walks near the Thompson home in Oakville and on the boardwalks of Whitehorse. And then, when Pierre had barely reached the toddler stage, Laura discovered she was pregnant again. Shortly after they returned to Dawson, a mere fifteen months after Pierre was born, she gave birth to a daughter in the Roman Catholic St. Mary's Hospital. They named her Lucy, after Frank's mother. At forty-three, Laura knew that once again she had beaten the medical odds.

Laura and Frank Berton could not quite believe they had become parents at such a late stage in their lives.[6] Their greatest fear was that they would lose their children to illness. This fear became a near reality when in May 1922 Pierre came down with a menacing case of pneumonia. For several weeks the two-year-old remained in St. Mary's Hospital, desperately ill with delirium and fever. After he recovered, Laura made certain he was confined to bed whenever he showed any signs of an ailment. Both parents kept an extremely close watch on their children, sometimes for sustained periods, at the slightest cough or sneeze.

The Bertons took Pierre and Lucy with them almost everywhere they went, for help was hard to come by in postwar Dawson. A rare exception was church. The couple regularly went to services at the Anglican St. Paul's, where Lucy had been baptized. Laura went in the mornings and sang in the choir while Frank minded the children; Frank walked alone to the evening service. Although both parents attended, Frank was the more dedicated in religious matters. Throughout his life, he remained a High Church Anglican who not only respected but also strictly observed church ritual and litany. For her part, Laura went mainly as a matter of family and parental responsibility and to socialize and take part in the musical activities she so loved. She played the piano at services, at Sunday school, and on special occasions. The devoted daughter of a proud socialist, Laura held no special brief for God.

Inwardly, she may even have been an unbeliever.[7] But there was nothing harmful and maybe much that was good in the possibility that He existed, so it can scarcely be doubted that each Sunday she walked the few blocks from her home, down Church Street to the morning service, without the slightest hint of a troubled conscience.

Headed as it was by older parents who had reached adulthood when Queen Victoria was still on the throne, the Berton home perhaps adhered more to convention than those of the Dawson children with whom the Berton children came to play. Laura, ever the dominant parent, may have been broad-minded but she was also supremely conscious of proprieties. Lucy would later describe her childhood home as "Edwardian Victorian," a place where the children were raised with essentially Victorian values and not encouraged to speak up. To be seen but not heard, and "not to express" – which meant, one suspects, not to give voice to one's deeper feelings.[8]

Yet this was by no means a dour home. To Pierre, his mother seemed constantly to be singing something or other, everything from beloved church hymns to music hall ballads.[9] She was energetic, not afraid to speak her mind, more than willing to teach her children games and to play the piano. Frank, for his part, was rather more subdued – "a quiet man," as Lucy later recalled.[10] But he was full of the kinds of surprises that made children marvel. One of Pierre's closest childhood friends remembered Mr. Berton making a croquet set for the front yard and then coaching the children in the basics. But beyond that, John Gould's strongest memory of Pierre's father was of the man often sitting in the corner of the parlour, quietly reading in his Morris chair.[11] As often as not, the books were on botany or works of popular science.

Despite Dawson's shrunken population, the postwar baby boom meant that there were quite a few children the age of Pierre and Lucy around. As he approached school age, Pierre often played with John Gould, the miner's son who lived a few blocks north,[12] and Alex McCarter, who lived about the same distance south with his mother and grandfather, a former postmaster. (Alex's father had deserted the family.)[13] They became best friends. Boys and girls mixed relatively well in Dawson, so the usual children around the Berton house were Pierre and Lucy, Alex and his sister, Helen, and John and his sister, Lenore. But there were others, like John's close friend Ronnie McCuish, son of a Mountie, who lived two or three blocks away.

Fun was had in many ways and was close to hand. Sometimes Pierre, Lucy, and their friends found adventure simply by crossing Eighth Avenue, running past the old Robert Service cabin, and roaming the hill behind it. Their enjoyment was heightened by the sense of transgression, since Pierre and Lucy knew they were forbidden to be on the dangerous slopes of the Dome. In the summer they went swimming in the Dawson Amateur Athletic Association pool, a five-minute walk away, and in winter they skated on the rink set up near its clubhouse by the same organization. At home they sometimes played "gold miners" in the yellow sand on the side of the road or "doctor and nurse" on their front porch.[14] Invariably the boys were the doctors and the girls the nurses, and they took turns serving as the patient. One time when Johnny Gould was about eleven and the whole gang was there, it was Johnny's turn to be treated. His duty, of course, was to lie still on the big old steamer trunk on the porch and submit to their ministrations. The next day he felt desperately ill and ended up spending a month in St. Mary's Hospital with a serious case of appendicitis.[15]

Another time Pierre and Alex McCarter turned entrepreneurs. Frank Berton, McCarter recalled, "had a fondness for mushrooms," and the boys knew where the mushrooms grew around Dawson. One of the best places was right behind Mr. Berton's hollyhocks, so the two boys harvested a crop, put them in a tin, and took them to his office, where they tried to sell them to him. They should have known better. Mr. Berton recognized his own mushrooms and bawled them out, less for the fact of the picking than for the attempt at the sale.[16]

The children who ran with Pierre and Lucy were of like mind in their perceptions of the Berton children's father, but differed when it came to their mother. In Frank Berton, both John Gould and Alex McCarter saw a reserved figure who pretty much kept to himself. Nonetheless, Alex marvelled, like Pierre, at all the neat things he seemed able to do. Here was a man, after all, who not only recognized his own mushrooms but had an authentic dentist chair set up in his study and filled and pulled the town's teeth in the winters.[17] The gentle and studious McCarter took piano lessons for a while from Mrs. Berton and came to see her as a "very kindly person" who sat next to him at the keyboard and sought patiently to get him to read the music, not memorize it.[18] But John Gould, who spent more time outside than inside the Berton home, saw another aspect to her. He scarcely recognized it as such, but this had to do with class and social pretense.

Alex McCarter's family, with grandfather the breadwinner, occupied a position in the Dawson social register not much different from that of his friend Pierre, the son of the mining recorder. Both their families aspired to gentility. Music lessons were a symbol of this, and Mrs. Berton struggled as hard to teach Pierre the key of G as she did with Alex. Johnny Gould, however, looking like a cherub with his wavy blond hair but with a toughness absent in Alex and Pierre, was different. His father had come to town as a miner early in the century, and a miner he had stayed, although he had opened a blacksmith shop in Dawson with a partner. John still spent much of his time at the family cabin at Nugget Hill, near their claims. His family was therefore distinctly lower on the social ladder than either the McCarters or the Bertons. Mrs. Berton was nice to him, but he always sensed a certain distance. The warm and generous person Alex McCarter knew, the lady who gave "nice parties," was unknown to John Gould.[19]

To an extent, Gould's perceptions came from his own direct experience of the Berton home, but they were shaped also by those of his parents. His mother's view was that Mrs. Berton was a snob, "too hoity-toity."[20] Despite her husband's modest occupational rank, Laura Berton was not one to shirk from reminding others that she was friends with Mr. and Mrs. George Black. He was now member of Parliament for the Yukon, and his wife had been Dawson's leading matron for nearly a quarter-century. That Laura Berton had also taken upon herself the responsibility of providing reports on social and cultural events to the *Dawson Daily News* was likely another source of envy or resentment, at least for some.

It is by no means clear whether Laura and Frank Berton held the kind of status within the community they may have thought they possessed. Certainly the former kindergarten teacher was well known. Many of the young adults of Dawson were those Laura had taught before the war, and in the 1920s she gave their children music and

Sunday school lessons. She held at-homes until the day she left the town, and her uncredited pieces for the *News* continued to appear for most of that time. But in a small place like Dawson, she was about as anonymous as an author as she was as a hostess.

Frank had his own circle of acquaintance and association. As the mining recorder and one of the generation of '98, he was widely known. In 1919, he had been inducted into the Yukon Order of Pioneers' No. 2 Lodge, and in the 1920s he became an active member of the local branches of the Great War Veterans' Association, the Royal Canadian Legion, and the Loyal Order of Eagles (the American fraternal organization responsible for the advent of Mother's Day). He uncomplainingly supported Dawson's causes and even logged its library books, for he worked nights at the town's Carnegie Library.[21]

Yet Frank Berton never did quite fit in. In what was still a rough frontier town, his was an academic sensibility, his interests intellectual. He was not one of the gang who frequented the hotel beer parlours or the saloons, certainly not after he met Laura. To other men of his generation he appeared diffident, standoffish. On the creeks, out of gratitude, the men had called him Doc; in town, they called him the Professor. The nickname could convey either respect or ridicule. In Dawson, Alex McCarter noted ruefully as an adult, Frank Berton seemed "a misfit."[22] And not only this. The old-timers had a name for him quite unlike the image of the quiet family man he projected in the 1920s. With the kind of petty cruelty that life in a small town can muster, they called him "the French pimp."[23]

Except for telling about his adventures scaling the Chilkoot or paddling up the Stikine or down the Yukon, Frank Berton did not speak much about the details of his early life. It is almost surely a sign of the shame he felt that he went to his grave leaving his wife and children unaware of his years in the Wiggins institution.[24] He did later admit to having gotten drunk once during his first months in Dawson but, understandably, he remained silent about whatever other wild oats he had sowed.[25] Whether he had frequented Lousetown or come to know the girls in the cribs of Paradise Alley can be only a matter of speculation.

The old-timers' slanderous insult likely had nothing to do with sex. It was probably a simple put-down of a university-educated eastern Canadian who could speak a cultivated French, and with the manners and dress of a gentleman and the vocabulary to go with them. But if the '98ers' crude moniker threatened to resurrect a half-buried truth, it must surely also have been a source of wry amusement for the old-timers. After all, it spoke to a secret the men from the creeks shared, and of which even the town's self-appointed recorder of society events and cultural activities remained blithely unaware.

In 1886, the English author of children's stories Frances Hodgson Burnett published a modest little novel called *Little Lord Fauntleroy*. Her tale was of a fatherless but angelic little American boy named Cedric who unexpectedly inherits an English title and with it all the status and privilege that membership in an aristocracy can bestow. By the early twentieth century the book had become a classic. Mothers loved and bought it; their sons tended to hate it.

The story, or at least the image of Burnett's rags-to-riches hero, was not unknown to the Gould household in Dawson. It tended to pop into Mrs. Gould's head where young Pierre Berton was concerned. Said her son John, "We called him Little Lord Fauntleroy, you know. A goody-goody, always nicely dressed." This resentment came in part from Pierre's attitude, too eager to please by half, and in part from the special attention Laura Berton paid to her only son. "I think it was a result of his mother," Gould said. "I think she was quite firm in the way he dressed and the way he acted."[26]

No doubt Frank and Laura loved their children equally, and they saw both as exceptional because they had come along so late. But it is clear that they invested most of their energy and expectations in Pierre. In Laura Berton's published memoirs, *I Married the Klondike*, Lucy makes an appearance, but only to be born. An afterthought or – as her brother was to put it – "an accident." When Laura began to put thoughts about her life on paper, years earlier, she had called the manuscript "It's a Boy." Lucy was always good at school, often at or near the top of her class, but it was her brother to whom her parents gave books. As if to reinforce how special he was, his father told Pierre time and again about the long line of his French and Loyalist Berton ancestors. His mother spoke with pride about his grandfather the famous journalist.[27]

Laura Berton was well acquainted with *Little Lord Fauntleroy*, and it influenced her enough that she gave it to her son to read.[28] But by then, Burnett's book had transcended the printed word within the popular imagination of the day. It had become a cultural sensation, not unlike Harriet Beecher Stowe's *Uncle Tom's Cabin* in the 1860s. It was beloved by England's prime minister William Ewart Gladstone and American president Theodore Roosevelt, and had been adapted for the stage in London, Boston, and New York, where it played for nearly four years. *Fauntleroy*'s central theme – how the innocence and charm and natural nobility of a boy child can tame and redeem a harsh world and in doing so gain favour beyond measure – was widely known and treasured around the English-speaking world, as was the visual image of the boy himself. By the early 1890s, *Little Lord Fauntleroy* could be found in 72 per cent of American public libraries, second only to General Lew Wallace's epic novel of the early Christian era, *Ben-Hur*. Mary Pickford, "America's Sweetheart" but Toronto-born, played the endearing little hero in a 1921 movie adapted from the book, to be followed in the era of sound by Freddie Bartholomew, Shirley Temple, Mickey Rooney, and others.[29]

So Laura Berton dressed her very special boy in a very special way, one that would set him apart from other boys in the rough-and-tumble of Dawson. In a family photograph taken when Pierre was five, he sits on the front lawn, Lucy on her mother's lap and Frank on one knee behind his son. Pierre seems all legs in his short pants and knee socks. His hair is carefully trimmed in a "Dutch" cut, and he wears a white blouse with a frilly collar and a huge bow tie. The straps of his black shoes circle his ankles, further subverting the costume as that of a boy. In a studio photograph taken the same year, he wears a nervous smile and a sailor suit, complete with a middy blouse with the obligatory three white stripes on the blue collar and back flap. Reproduced in his autobiography next to one of sister Lucy, the photo shows a child whose hairstyle looks identical to that of his sister.[30]

Outside, the fashion for Fauntleroy and sailor outfits had declined in the postwar years, not least because the original association of Fauntleroy with the Victorian mother's perfect son had given way to that of Fauntleroy the sissy. Reinforcing this new interpretation was the fact that in silent movies and on stage, little Cedric was usually played by a woman. Even sailor suits, which had come into fashion in the late nineteenth century as a way of taking into account fathers' preferences for their sons' dress, were often now called "Fauntleroy suits," symbol of the effeminate mama's boy.

Still, a young middle-class boy on the outside dressed in such a way in the 1920s would scarcely have stood out, for such outfits remained relatively common. Dawson, for all its genteel pretension, was very different. On the streets the few Native children in town wore long pants and many of the other young children wore short ones, plus-fours, or bloomers – "shit catchers," as John Gould called them.[31] In the early 1970s, when Berton's closest childhood friend, Alex McCarter, revisited a photograph of Pierre as a boy, wearing a pale blue outfit, he had to admit that it was "a picture of a boy who is . . . well, a little bit sissified."[32] The photograph was taken at a performance of Mrs. Humby's dancing class, with Pierre playing the part of Thomas Gainsborough's "Blue Boy," complete with borrowed locks of long golden hair.[33]

The Fauntleroy story gained resonance and power in part because it was not just about a charming boy; it was also the story of a son's devotion and a mother's influence. Laura Berton seems to have relished both the devotion and the influence where Pierre was concerned. Dressing Pierre in a Fauntleroy outfit advertised his family's middle-class aspirations and perhaps helped Laura persuade herself that she had overcome the genteel poverty of her own upbringing. Whatever the motivation, having waited so long to have a child, she acted as if she wished her first-born to remain one. "I really don't think my parents wanted me to grow up," Berton wrote.[34] For the most part, Pierre complied with the way his mother dressed him. His one act of outright rebellion came at the age of five. He hated his Dutch cut so much, he later said, that when the time came to have his studio photograph taken he tried to cut his hair off.[35] It may be significant that, just after this, Pierre imagined a club into existence. He called it "Be-a-Boy."[36]

In the detested haircut and the velvet shorts, Pierre became a prime target for Dawson's bullies. "I was often called a sissy and beaten up by older and larger boys," he recalled. Pierre was short for his age, Alex McCarter remembered, not vigorous but easily excitable and full of nervous energy. "He was in a town of bullies," McCarter said, "and they bullied him. He didn't exactly fight back, but on the other hand he never ran away either." Sometimes his tormentors would mock his clothing, at other times his "foreign" name: *Pee-Air, Pee-Air*, they would chant, hands near their nether regions. They would attempt to make him angry, to goad him to fight, by daring him to sing "Au Clair de la Lune." Pierre did not rise to this bait with his fists. The only known instance of fisticuffs took place when his best friend John Gould gave him a bloody nose in a scrap on Fifth Avenue. When it came to bullies, the boy with the red hair and bangs instead disarmed his first critics with a remarkable memory and quick wit, through song and recitation. From a very early age, this boy remembered his lines.[37]

In the late summer of 1925, the year before Pierre was due to start school, Laura decided to take the children to Ontario to meet her parents. Unable to take an extended break from work, Frank stayed behind. So began Pierre's first adventure on the outside. Every revolution of the *Casca*'s paddlewheel south of the bend of the Yukon River where it met the Klondike took him farther into the unknown, and as the boat drew nearer to Whitehorse he began to gain an understanding of the length and power of the river. The train ride from Whitehorse to Skagway provided him with his first sight of a steam locomotive, fascinating yet frightening. The trip down the coast to Vancouver on the *Princess Louise* gave him his first glimpse of infinity beyond the ship's rail. The rail journey through the Rockies and the plains and the Shield country north of Superior on the way to Toronto was enough to grant even a five-year-old a sense of the vastness of the world beyond Dawson. And then, finally, he saw the bustle of Toronto's Union Station and, on Front Street, the panorama and din of the big city and its steady rush of motor cars and pedestrians, thousands of them, caught in canyons of brick and stone and concrete.

"For both children," Laura later recalled, "the outside world was like a fairyland. They had never seen coloured lights or animated signs, for instance." The marvellous could be found even in the mundane. In the orchard on their grandparents' property in Oakville, Pierre and Lucy discovered where apples came from and what a snake was. A terrifying encounter with a bulldog convinced them that not all dogs looked like huskies. "They were," Laura said, "like children from another world and the Outside was a huge continual carnival to them."[38]

A photograph captured Pierre and Lucy with their grandfather and his family on the front lawn of Phillips Thompson's Oakville home. Uncle Phil, born to Phillips Thompson's second marriage and now in his early thirties, stands in the rear in suit, tie, and waistcoat, sporting a Chaplinesque moustache. Beside him stands his mother, Edith, bonnet on head, eyes to the ground. She allows no hint of a smile. In front, the others sit on a wood-and-iron park bench, with Lucy on the lap of her great-aunt Allie. Beside them, the focus of the picture, is Phillips Thompson, dressed like his son. With a head of pure white hair and a full beard to match, and staring directly into the camera lens, he appears decidedly less like yesterday's committed radical than like the lingering Victorian patriarch. He has a cane in his hand, and cataracts cloud his eyes. But this is the very lion in winter, still writing and still fully capable of entertaining his grandson and others by belting out songs of the labouring classes such as "Drill Ye Tarriers Drill" and "One More Battle to Fight." His grandson, now six, sits to his left in his Dutch cut, short pants, knee socks, and ankle-strapped shoes. Pierre's left arm covers the top of his head, as if to prevent a sudden breeze from blowing away a wig.[39]

Laura and her children returned to the Yukon in early June 1926, and Frank was there to meet them in Whitehorse. He had purchased a poling barge, and for the next two weeks the Bertons made their way down the river with their two small children, much to the consternation of people in both Whitehorse and Dawson. Only two years earlier, they had lost their family doctor to its treacherous waters, but they survived the Thirtymile and ran the Five Fingers without capsizing and pulled up to the Dawson waterfront early one morning. The timing was at Laura's insistence, since her family's khaki clothing was soiled and she wanted as few people as possible to witness their base appearance. Her bloomers were baggy and her children looked like "unkempt Indians without being half as picturesque." Only later did she come to realize that those weeks on the river, "drifting with the current through that silent, wild country, with my children young and my husband in his prime," had been one of the happiest experiences of her life.[40]

With his family reunited, Frank began to expand and rearrange their home, adding a kitchen and bedroom and bath. He converted the old kitchen into a bedroom for Laura and himself. The old bedroom became Frank's den and dental office. The new bedroom was for the children. He also added stairs to the root cellar, previously accessible only by a trap door. Once when it was open, Laura was in the cellar and the children were upstairs playing blind man's bluff with paper sacks over their heads. "Suddenly," Lucy recalled, "Pierre wasn't there." He had fallen into the cellar, unhurt but startling his mother. "Pierre all gone, Pierre all gone," Lucy cried.[41]

Pierre entered grade one at Dawson Public School in the fall of 1926. From the outset he was a good student, precocious enough that after his first year the principal sent him directly into the third grade. "My mother pushed me," he would later write. She made certain he took part in school plays, reviewing his lines with him until they were letter-perfect. From at least the age of seven, she "urged" him to give recitations at school concerts, including one from James Whitcomb Riley's popular poem "Little Orphan Annie," with its recurring line "And the goblins will get ya if ya don't watch out!" The kind of line capable of bringing down the house, it received a spooky enough performance from young Pierre that sixty years later he still remembered the exact inflection he had given it. Lucy, barely of school age at the time, vividly recalled the moment she knew her brother was a ham at heart.[42]

John Gould, two years older than Pierre and a year ahead of him at school, remembered him later as "an excellent student. He did very well in school – a hell of a lot better than I did."[43] In part, this was because both of Pierre's parents, in their own ways, expected him to excel, and he knew it. At home, they led by example. His mother seemed always to be writing – occasionally her pieces for the *Dawson Daily News*, but most of the time a romantic novel, "Then Alice Came Home," the story of a southern Ontario farmer's daughter who falls in love with a young member of the nobility and marries him. This imagined life, a romance involving the triumph of love over class differences, was a plot line that would have furrowed the brow of her father the radical. Perhaps, however, it reflected the life she had hoped to lead with Frank. "We lived with it day in and day out for a decade," Berton recalled. He could remember lying in bed at night listening to his parents discuss the story and read chapters aloud. His, he later came to realize, was "a writer's environment."[44]

Telling stories and writing them down seemed a natural thing to do, not at all unusual. Pierre's father was an avid reader; his mother was an aspiring writer. Jack London, author of *The Call of the Wild*, had been in Dawson at the outset of the gold rush in '97. Robert Service's cabin was right across the street. The extended families of most of Dawson's residents lived thousands of miles away, so the town became almost by nature a place of colourful stories intended to invoke good memories and the silences necessary to keep bad memories at bay.

Frank Berton's encouragement of his son reflected his own more intellectual interests. He subscribed to *Scientific American*, copies of which he would leave conveniently accessible. He bought Pierre a microscope and a steam engine and explained how they worked, and why. He was a walking encyclopedia of the names of wildflowers and insects, rocks and stars, and took Pierre and Lucy for long country hikes, making notes of what they saw as they rambled on. If his mother nurtured Pierre's imagination, his father impressed upon him the endless fascination of the natural world.[45]

The children understood that their parents' ambition was fixed mainly on Pierre. As they advanced through the grades, they accepted that their mother and father hoped they would both attend university, but that Pierre was the one who was to have a career. In this respect, Laura and Frank Berton were little different from the vast majority of other parents of the 1920s who expected their daughters to "settle down" and marry after they finished school. Pierre was constantly pushed for better grades, especially by Frank, regardless of the marks the boy received. At his mother's insistence, he could be found front and centre in plays and concerts, and he was a frequent finalist in essay contests as they came along. "My parents clearly wanted me to be an achiever," he said.[46]

Encouragement is to be expected of good parents. The kind Pierre received went rather beyond this, and it is difficult not to think that it sprang from the thwarted ambition of a man who had failed to find his Eldorado and a woman who, like the mother of Mackenzie King, loved her husband but sensed that she had not married well. And so, as if to convince herself that at least one of her family would rise above

Dawson, Pierre's mother took every occasion to tell him that he was a marked child. "My mother used to say to me regularly, 'You're not the same as the other little boys, you know.'"[47] The incessant refrain, a vicarious projection of parental aspiration but with more than a hint that life on the "inside" was somehow hollow, confused rather than reassured its target. Not until much later did he recognize how odd it was that his mother did not say similar things to Lucy; but from a very young age he knew that his parents' ambitions were aimed at him.

Life had already told Pierre that he was special, all right. He dressed like no other child in Dawson, and the price of the distinction was ridicule and taunting. From the time he started school he longed, in fact, for nothing more than to fit in, to be accepted, to belong. He was desperate to wear long pants like the other boys. Yet his parents' inspiring words did not go unheeded; they shaped his sense of self and fed his needs in these formative years. There was satisfaction in being the centre of attention, even for the bullied. By the time he turned seven, Pierre Berton had come to recognize that if there was anything worse than being mocked or criticized, it was being ignored.

Eighteenth-century aestheticians, especially the philosopher and politician Edmund Burke, reflected a good deal upon what they called the "sublime." For Burke, the sublime was different from the merely beautiful. An ordinary waterfall might be beautiful, but the mighty Niagara Falls was sublime. Whereas beauty merely attracted, the sublime consisted of a fusion of attraction and repulsion, of wonder and terror.[48] In this sense, Pierre Berton's childhood in the Yukon was sublime indeed.

From his earliest days, Pierre found much about his town and the hills and woods around it worrisome and at times deeply frightening. The long winter months without sun ensured an atmosphere of perpetual dusk, the most dangerous time for those at risk from predators. From the side porch he could see the great rock-slide gouge in the side of the Midnight Dome to the north, looking as if earth had been scooped out by the thumb of an angry God. Peril loomed even in town. At any time, fire could consume one or another of its buildings, and over the years it did: the hockey rink, the school, the theatre. "Nothing was safe," he wrote.[49]

He had a hyperactive imagination. He told his sister stories about little animals that lived underground but drove automobiles or flew airplanes. Later, he made up variations on *Alice in Wonderland*. His father built the new bedroom when he was six, so for the first time he had a lair; it was a mixed blessing because while it gave space to his energies, it also heightened his fears. Nights seemed darker, their silence leading his thought to dangerous places. Each sharp crack of a tree in the frozen stillness was a creature stealthily approaching. *And the goblins will get ya if ya don't watch out!* From his bed he could hear the shriek of the dredges on the creek, working without breaks to scoop out the gold. "I believed the dredges were alive – monsters chewing away at the valley, whining in the distance like lost souls, and probably coming for me in the night."[50]

Wolves were a particular terror. A lone husky in town would begin to yelp, joined first by a few others, then more, until every dog seemed part of the bay. And then, from the river and the hills, he would hear the wolves. "The howl became a moving sound, a wave moving slowly across the community and on down the river like a soul in torment."[51]

"I could feel the shivers up my spine," he said. "The wolves both fascinated and terrified me."[52] This and similar experiences of heightened emotion – jagged and raw and simultaneously attracting and repelling – sparked and then fed the flame of a nascent romantic sensibility. The aesthetic tension took his imagination to uncharted regions; it made his mind almost vibrate with danger and dissonance. But it also afforded him his own share of the transcendent, for fear expanded his curiosity. Baying wolves and screeching dredges were just some of the ways Pierre Berton would experience the Arctic sublime, where life was lived on the jagged edge of the world.

In stark contrast to the frightening things that sometimes threatened to engulf him stood that part of his world that was familiar, especially his home. Outside, harsh winds and bitter cold; inside, warmth and security like that of the amniotic sac. He was comforted by the way his mother would sometimes sit on his father's knee, her arms around his neck. He loved watching his father busy at practical tasks, one day planting canary vine all along the back of the house, the next burning bones saved from the family meals to make fertilizer for the garden.

One of his great fears was that his parents might suddenly die when he was still a boy and he would be left alone in this hostile world. Existence seemed harsh and precarious enough even with a warm home and a loving family. It was the very security his family provided that aroused the fear that he might lose it. And so the sight of his mother and his sister and his dogs frolicking on the Yukon ice gave rise not to contentment but to anxiety verging on outright panic. And he prayed: "Oh, please God, don't let her die! She mustn't die! I couldn't bear it if she died. Please wait until I'm old enough to cope with it."[53]

He was afraid most of all of being left alone in the wilderness. One summer, even before he could read, he got lost while on a picnic on the hill behind his home. "Suddenly, I was surrounded by the terrible silence of the North. . . . I called for my father but there was no answering call. For all I knew he had been devoured by a wolf. I called again: silence. The forest began to press in on me and for the first time in my life I felt all alone and lost in the immensity of the wilderness." He ran around frantically, reciting the Lord's Prayer over and over, until at last he reached a clearing and saw his mother and sister readying things for the picnic. He never wanted to be alone again.[54]

Except during the dark of night, he found refuge from these fears in his wonder at nature's more benign elements. He found serenity in winter's silence and in the vast white blanket of snow that covered everything from October through April, capable of insulating a person against the freezing north wind. He relished the summer rambles with his father along the trails on the hill and the long walks with his mother and Lucy along the frozen river in the depths of winter. For him, the first steamboat whistle each spring signalling the arrival of exotic goods and strange people from the outside was as much part of the rhythm of the seasons as the annual freeze-up a few months later. Dimly aware of the uniqueness of his vantage point, he accepted the shimmering colours of the northern lights as simply one more element in the nature of things. For Berton the child, they were just clouds. Above all, he loved and embraced the Yukon River itself, the very lifeblood of his town.

Until he experienced the outside, Dawson was simply Dawson. It was all he knew; he had no sense that the city had a past that made it unique. For him, the past was yesterday, just as the northern lights were Klondike clouds. He knew of course that Dawson was built on the search for gold, but his knowledge of this was more or less confined to what little he gleaned from his father. Nothing in his experience set Dawson apart from whatever he knew about other small northern towns. His friends thought the same way. Asked whether, as a child, he thought Dawson was a special place, John Gould simply said: "Never gave it a thought. It was Dawson City."[55]

Pierre returned from his sojourn in Ontario still with little sense of the past, but he now possessed at least a little perspective. As he travelled upstream in 1925, the outside was all but unknown; coming downstream the next year was like returning from some magic kingdom, a realm that seemed to exist in some separate astral plane. Coming back traversed the boundaries of the real and the unreal. But which was which?

What accounts for a consciousness of history, a sense that the recollection of past time is of value? What is it that begins to give historical memory weight and authority and meaning for some people but not for others? Gradually dawning on Pierre, at a level more subliminal than conscious, was the radical disjunction between Dawson and elsewhere. In Toronto, even in Oakville, time moved forward to the future. The past was built upon. Old houses gave way to new. Paths became roads and roads became highways. People were constantly going somewhere, and with a sense of purpose. Life in this modern world was a neverending act of improvement.

But nothing improved in Dawson. Outside, people clamoured for more buildings to house new commercial and industrial ventures. In Dawson, there were always more than enough buildings to meet the town's needs. Fire and decay erased whatever sense of permanence the town once possessed, demonstrating on a daily basis how precarious life was. Pierre found a certain charm, a style, in Dawson once he could compare it with other communities. But it was the charm and style to which one bears witness when standing in the midst of a ruin. Before the age of twelve, Pierre stood in his own town like a latter-day Gibbon in the ancient rubble of eighteenth-century Rome, bearing witness to progress in reverse.

Dawson was a museum of intriguing things, but Pierre came to think of it as a junkyard. He and John Gould liked nothing more than to roam the streets in search of discoveries, and invariably, finding something new meant uncovering and dusting off something old. Shells of buildings were everywhere, abandoned by occupants after bankruptcy or quick decisions to head south. As often as not, inventory had been left behind, for it would have been far too expensive to ship out. The two chums had a field day one time on Third Avenue, rummaging in the old Kaiser Hardware Store next to Biggs' Blacksmith Shop. "There was hardware there – tons of it," Gould recalled at eighty-six. "I remember the small gold scales that the prospectors or some of the miners would carry . . . complete sets of scales and weights, hundreds of them lying around in there."[56]

The town was full of such treasure for curious kids. For Pierre, the fascination came not because the junk was old, but because it was there. "Here were mysterious knobs and wheels, levers, gears, and gauges that moved and jiggled and delighted a small boy's imagination." It was fun just trying to figure out what these peculiar pieces of junk had once been used for. Sometimes he went across the river to the tracks of the long-defunct Klondike Mines Railway and played on its abandoned locomotive and in the passenger cars behind it. Or he would explore the wrecks of paddleboats, each forlorn cabin its own graveyard of broken dreams. "They were the artifacts of history," Pierre later wrote, "but I didn't know that."[57]

History was something that happened somewhere else. That is what school taught him. History was the kings and queens of England and the story of dynasties and empires, wars in the Old World and exploration in the new one. He learned about Columbus's discovery of America and La Vérendrye's journey to its interior, but Pierre remained oblivious of George Carmack's strike at Bonanza. In this respect, his experience differed little from that of young Wallace Stegner a decade earlier, growing up in the town of Eastend, in southwestern Saskatchewan. Stegner the boy had been surrounded by those who had witnessed Louis Riel's North-West Rebellion in 1885, yet he had no awareness that his was a life lived in the very hub of the last great plains frontier.[58] Many years later, the remembered scent of the shrub called "wolf willow" would lure Stegner, by then a distinguished novelist and historian, back to the place of his childhood. For Berton, the call of the Yukon River was just as evocative of memory, and he would return not once but again and again in order to learn and then tell the stories of the men and women who risked their lives on it.

The realm of the exotic is the land of the unknown, and nothing about Dawson in the 1920s seemed exotic. Pierre had tasted the unknown when outside at five, but as those memories faded to fleeting images and impressions, he attempted to revive them by embracing fugitive fragments of the popular culture of the day. He was allowed to go to movies at the Eagle Hall, until it burned down, and then to the clubhouse of the Dawson Amateur Athletic Association. That the movies he saw were old ones meant nothing: he happily rode the range with Tom Mix and battled rustlers with Ken Maynard. "I saw myself in a white ten-gallon Stetson, mounted on a pure white horse, riding at the head of a posse of vigilantes, saving the entire Dawson community from some dreadful fate – but from what? I could never fantasize a catastrophe suitable to that peaceful community."[59]

Books transported him. He read everything that came his way, from stories of fairies and gnomes and trolls living under bridges to Lewis Carroll's Alice books, with their distortions of time and space and their inversions of the real and the fantastic. He discovered L. Frank Baum's book *The Land of Oz* at the age of nine, and fifty years later he recalled vividly starting to read it in the stillness of an early Sunday morning. "There were Tip and me running away from that old sorceress, Mombi, with a pocketful of bread and cheese and Jack Pumpkinhead beside us."[60] Even at the age of thirty-nine he returned often to Frank Baum and the Land of Oz. "Once again I am a small boy, crouched over the kitchen table longing for bread and cheese, following the yellow brick road to the Emerald City, not knowing what's good but only what I like."[61]

Some stories alarmed him because they seemed too close to home – for example, the Russian tale about a family fleeing in a troika from wolves, "tossing out their children to appease the pursuing pack"; and a Canadian saga about wolves closing in on a trapper huddled near his failing campfire.[62] So he yearned for journeys of adventure elsewhere. The only books that made a greater impression on young Pierre Berton than *The Land of Oz* were *Treasure Island* and *Tom Sawyer*, novels that allowed him the safety of vicarious escape, whether searching for treasure on a distant island or running away to become a pirate.

Quite often as a child, Pierre received a thick package from Oakville containing comic strips Grandfather Thompson or Uncle Phil had clipped from daily newspapers. To the consternation of his parents, Pierre would lie around on weekend mornings absorbing the antics of Tailspin Tommy, Toots and Casper, Barney Google, and Little Orphan Annie, supplemented later by watching the adventures of Oswald the Rabbit at the flicks. There was nothing subtle or coy or discordant about the comic and the cartoon: their humour paraded on page and screen for all to see. Caricature was larger than life, and anything larger than life appealed to Pierre. Gradually, he came to associate the outside not only with the march of progress and civilization but also with the wild and wacky adventures of Felix the Cat and Mickey Mouse. Thus began a lifelong fascination with the comics. It would not be long before his greatest ambition was to be a cartoonist.[63]

Still, the North had made its mark on him as surely as if he had been seared by a branding iron. By grade six, his interest in Dawson and its untold stories had been sparked. The subject of his entry in the school essay contest, sponsored that year by the Imperial Order Daughters of the Empire, was the discovery of gold in the Klondike. The North was not yet much in his head, and he knew little history, but the compulsion to tell a story was already in his blood.

4

BEYOND THE MIDNIGHT DOME

—

BILLY LOWE WAS ONE OF THE boys Pierre liked least. He seemed to know everything that was happening in the larger world: the new movies and the new gadgets, the places where there was actually no snow and where people bought pre-cut Christmas trees from lots. It was Billy who had told him that in the cities down south nobody ever said hello. "I remember thinking," Pierre later said, "how strange that was, how weird. A place where nobody knew anybody else."[1] His own recollections of the outside were no longer reliable, and to make things worse, Billy seemed to delight in exposing Pierre's ignorance. "Billy Lowe made me feel like a rube," he said.[2]

By the time Pierre turned eleven, he had become desperate to escape the confines of Dawson, to get out. Fortunately, his greatest desire coincided with the plans of his mother and father. After a decade of writing and typing and talking, Laura had at last finished her novel. Frank had accumulated enough time and savings from holidays not taken that the family was in a position to spend the better part of a year in Ontario. He had not been south since returning from the war, and Laura was eager to take her manuscript to Toronto publishers and to visit her father, now in his late eighties, in Oakville. Besides, both parents recognized the necessity of introducing their children, especially Pierre, to the things Dawson could not offer. Laura recalled fondly that when she was about Pierre's age, her father had taken the family to Ireland and England, and the experience had expanded her awareness beyond measure. So it should be for Pierre. As much as she and her husband had come to love the Klondike, they had no intention of allowing her son's horizons to be obstructed by the scarred face of the Midnight Dome.

This time the memories stuck for both children. Clearly, they were intent on remembering the trip, because Pierre declared it necessary to record their experiences in a notebook portentously titled "Diary of the Berton Family on their Journey 'Outside.' Begun by Pierre."[3] On the page facing the initial recto the young author had practised his signature: *Pierre Berton Pierre Berton Pierre Berton Pierre Berton*, each stroke of the pen more bold and confident and larger than the one before, the tail of the *n* wrapping up and back and then rushing down and around to become the stroke of the *t*, a stroke that became more cheeky with each repetition. He kept to himself the promise that he would try to account for every day. With the exception of a handful of entries contributed by Lucy, the journal's words are his – from the first ones on September 1, 1931, heading upriver the day they left home, to those of April 29, 1932, when the family was preparing to leave Toronto.

The journey out differed only in minor ways from that of 1925. Sternwheeler to Whitehorse. Train to Skagway. Then a steamer to Seattle (not Vancouver as in the first trip), followed by the brief voyage back up to Victoria and then to Vancouver. Pierre dutifully noted the rhythm and activities of life on board the steamer: the food he ate, the games he played, the scenery he saw. He wrote of going on deck for the moment the ship passed over the grave of the *Princess Sophia* (September 10). He took note of the interesting church he saw in an old Russian town, and of the many totem poles he observed along the shore (September 9). Later, in Vancouver, he recorded his visit with Alex McCarter, who had moved to Vancouver with his family (September 17).[4] A few days later, travelling through the Rockies in a Canadian Pacific coach, he made a brief entry that spoke unknowingly to his future: "There was wonderful scenery all of to-day. We passed by a monument telling where the last spike had been driven in finishing the CPR" (September 21). Four days later, after a brief stop in Winnipeg where they rushed to the Eaton's and Hudson's Bay Company stores and took in an Oddfellows parade (September 23), they arrived in Toronto. Pierre's uncle Phil, his mother's half-brother, met the family at the station. He took them to Aunt Florrie's.

The depression that had hit Europe and North America two years earlier had pummelled Toronto, and it showed no signs of letting up. Unemployed men roamed the streets, and Salvation Army soup lines in the city's core stretched down the sidewalks. But if a man managed to keep his job in these drab years, his family could very well be better off than before, for prices had dropped drastically. Those in the affluent Rosedale and Forest Hill districts who could not afford a maid in the twenties could sometimes do so now. And of those who earlier had only aspired to live in Rosedale, more than a few now walked its streets as residents. Florrie was one of them.

The Bertons' savings went significantly further in 1931 and 1932 than they would have six years earlier. Of the two parents, Frank especially viewed the time in Ontario as a way of exposing Pierre to the many educational and cultural opportunities a large city provided. Besides, he had missed out on a good deal himself. For this reason, and because Laura needed to be near prospective publishers, they had decided to stay not in Oakville with her parents but with Florrie in her modest two-storey home at 98 Huntley Street on the southern fringe of Rosedale. Pierre had never seen a brick house before.

Things utterly mundane to others made the greatest impression on the children. Many years later, Lucy could still recall the sight of neon lights.[5] For Pierre, the adventure was a feast of sight and sound and taste – a "smorgasbord of novelties," he called it.[6] The feel of pennies, dimes, and nickels: new, because in Dawson nothing cost less than a quarter. The sight of milk bottles: new, because in Dawson milk came in recycled beer bottles. The first sweet taste of Coca-Cola. Street signs and traffic lights. Elevators and escalators. Taxis and their horns, streetcars and their bells. Milkshake makers, popcorn machines, and roller skates.[7]

So intent was Frank on making the most of their time outside that, although he enrolled Pierre in the equivalent of grade seven at Rosedale Public School, on South Drive, he did not allow the boy, or Lucy, to attend until the beginning of October. He also informed the principal that he intended to keep them from classes at other times. Then he began to organize the family's life in a manner worthy of the retired lieutenant he was, creating a mental list of places he wished to take them and arranging for others to accompany the children on sightseeing excursions whenever he could not do so.

Frank marshalled them along to the talking pictures at the Uptown and the Orpheum, and Laura took them by streetcar to the Scarborough

Bluffs east of town. They saw a football game at Varsity Stadium, a skating show starring Sonja Henie at Maple Leaf Gardens, and the animals at High Park Zoo. During the year they visited Niagara Falls and rode an elevator to the top of the Bank of Commerce building, then the tallest in the British Empire. They heard the Hart House Quartet perform, saw performances of *As You Like It* and *The Mikado*, and viewed the Group of Seven paintings at the Grange. All things considered, Pierre would much rather have gone to see more movies.

For him, the highlight came when the family went to the Royal Winter Fair and saw Zacchini, "the Human Cannonball." Pierre's diary entry for November 21 was the longest he recorded. "First the cannon came out on a car. Then Zacchini jumped up on the cannon," he wrote, the image still imprinted on his retina. "He put on a cap and mask and long things on his arms and climbed into the cannon. . . . As soon as Zacchini got in there was a huge flood of light and a whole bunch of smoke and Zacchini sailed right up to the roof of the Coliseum and then gracefully dived down again into the net. He took off the mask, cap and long armlets, jumped slowly down from the net and ran off." He had found his trump card. "Now I will have something to tell Billy Lowe,"[8] he later recalled thinking.

Life with Aunt Florrie was decidedly less thrilling. Five years older than Laura, she was eccentric and set in her ways. To the children, she and Laura seemed always to be arguing. Florrie delighted in assuming extreme positions. Some, such as her tirades against war and the military, politicians and dogs, were of the kind that her father would have championed, except perhaps for the dogs; others, for example her notion that radio would lead to the decay of civilization, seemed plain silly. Laura invariably acted as Frank's defence counsel. Lucy remembered her parents being "horrified" at Florrie's harangues; Pierre mainly recalled his aunt's peculiarities, but he too noted the domestic tension.[9]

Not long after the Bertons arrived, Florrie afforded her sister and brother-in-law some privacy by moving into a small flat on Avenue Road, not far from the modest antique shop she operated on Bloor Street.[10] Frank enrolled in a University of Toronto lecture course in physics, and Laura gave talks on life in the Yukon to a variety of women's groups. He and Laura took advantage of the availability of Florrie and Phil to mind the children while they attended concerts together, or went places separately. Playing Boswell to their Johnson, Pierre dutifully recorded each event and venue, including a particularly intriguing one on November 4. "This evening Mamma and Daddy went to the Barrets of Wimple Street [*sic*] at the Royal Alexandra. Uncle Phil came. After the play Daddy went to the hospital for an operation on his nose." Just how Frank's nose came to give him such serious trouble after seeing Rudolf Besier's play about the love affair between Elizabeth Barrett and Robert Browning remained beyond the eleven-year-old's ken. Frank did not return from hospital until two days later.

Early in February 1932, Frank took Pierre to Ottawa, where his brother, Jack, lived with his wife, Maud (not to be confused with Laura's sister Maude), and daughter, Beth. While Frank attended the opening of Parliament, Pierre went across the river to Hull with Beth. The next day, February 5, Frank took his son to observe the House of Commons in session. There they saw George Black in ceremonial dress, doing his duty as Speaker of the House of Commons.

Pierre found all this impressive, but not nearly so memorable as his first taste of french-fried potatoes. Just as he preferred a cartoon or comic book over an art exhibition or a concerto, he would have awarded a prize to Aunt Maud's fryer over Mr. Black's tricorne hat and silk gloves any time. From his earliest days, he had little use for anything or anyone with an air of pretension. Earlier, his parents had taken him to see a passion play at Massey Hall. "I didn't like it," he recorded. "It was all in German" (October 12). A few days later, when his parents went to hear the Hart House Quartet, Pierre stayed home with his uncle Phil. "I drew some pictures from the funnie [*sic*] papers" (October 16).

The school curriculum in Dawson was ahead of that of Toronto, so both Berton children did well at Rosedale Public School. Pierre stood at or near the top of his class throughout the year, but both he and Lucy found themselves without friends and were bored.[11] Almost all he noted about school in the family diary was the progress he made in manual training class on his key rack and teapot holder.

Pierre readily became involved in various kinds of public performance, and Laura made certain that he knew his parts well, using the training she had received in elocution to help him project his voice.[12] He memorized a godawful poem his aunt Sarah had written to honour the King and recited it, to great family plaudits. He entered a public speaking contest at school and made up a story based on a picture his teacher gave him. He garnered only second place, but he relished the laughter and applause that came his way. "I was not yet hooked," he would later say of this, "but the hook was out and baited."[13]

Other events also proved noteworthy: for example, the measles Pierre came down with over Christmas. The family was put under immediate quarantine, and a big red warning sign was posted on the front door. It stayed up into the new year when Lucy took her turn nursing itchy spots and was confined to her bedroom. Another major occasion for Pierre was the November excursion when the family travelled to Oakville to be with Grandfather Thompson on his eighty-eighth birthday. While there, he reacquainted himself with his aunt Maude, whom he found even more eccentric than Aunt Florrie. The Berton family diary that day recorded a celebration, complete with "chicken and ginger ale and rice pudding and for tea we had grandfather's cake." A second dessert was served a little later in the evening, when Pierre gave his recitation of "Little Orphant [sic] Annie" (November 25).

Of all his Ontario relatives, Uncle Phil was Pierre's favourite. A journalist like his father, during the Depression Phil Thompson became one of the thousands out of a job and dependent on family for his room and board. He had time on his hands, some of it spent retyping his half-sister Laura's novel (February 5 and 6); but he had more than enough to spare for Pierre. It was Uncle Phil who got Pierre to pay serious attention to newspapers. The Bertons already subscribed to the *Mail and Empire*, as conservative and loyal as its masthead suggested. But Phil brought Pierre copies of the *Star* and the *Telegram*, significantly more liberal and adventurous in style and reportage. Pierre loved the singular devotion to newspaper cartoon strips that all male members of the Thompson family seemed to share, and he especially cherished his uncle's sense of the ridiculous.

Soon Pierre became addicted to newspapers. The comics section was the one he turned to first, his favourite strip being that of Mickey Mouse in the *Telegram*; but he delighted at others, such as George McManus's strip, "Bringing Up Father,"[14] featuring Jiggs and Maggie, the henpecked husband and his wife the social climber. For a boy about to enter his teens with an active imagination and a desire for adventure, the early thirties were the perfect years to discover the comics. The golden age of the adventure comic strip had arrived. Tarzan and Buck Rogers, introduced in 1929, had hit their stride: a boy could give himself over equally to the jungle exploits of the King of the Apes and the space missions of the twenty-fifth-century military man. Or to the first comic strip detective, Chester Gould's square-jawed, trench-coat-wearing Dick Tracy, sworn enemy of mobsters and goons and other villains with names like Stooge Viller, Doc Hum, Boris Arson, Littleface Finny, and – most notorious of all – Flattop. He began to draw cartoon figures in the margins of school notebooks, and they came to adorn the occasional page of the Berton family diary. At home he won applause for his renderings of characters from the comic strips.[15]

He soon discovered the more exotic and at times salacious side of the day's newspapers. They were not only, as he had thought, about politics and business dealings like the stories covered in the staid *Globe*. In the *Star Weekly*, he encountered "wild tales about dinosaurs, bizarre murders, and the antics of Hollywood stars," and the down-home humour of Gregory Clark. "I devoured them all," he later wrote.[16] He had yet to come across a model or depiction of a crusading journalist, but that time was not too many years away.

The fall and winter outside passed all too quickly. In early summer of 1932, the Bertons said their farewells to their Ontario families and friends. But before heading west, Frank took his children on one last adventure, to Sunnyside Amusement Park, where he treated them to every ride possible. Laura remained at home, for she was in no mood for light amusement. She had shopped her novel around to a number of Toronto publishers, but none proved interested in publishing it.

The Canadian National Railways train took them from Toronto to Vancouver, where they checked into the Sylvia Apartment Hotel, a pleasant accommodation on English Bay. It had been decided that Laura and the children would stay there for a week or two while Frank made his way north. He had arranged for the *Bluenose*, the twenty-six-foot-long, round-bottomed riverboat he had built in rented space in an abandoned hotel in Dawson, to be shipped south and to be waiting for them in Whitehorse. He wanted to take his son downriver with him, but Laura nixed that. So he went on alone, while Laura took the opportunity to enjoy Vancouver's beaches and the sights of English Bay with Pierre and Lucy.

When Laura and the children reached Dawson a few weeks later, Frank was at dockside to greet them. They knew immediately that something was wrong. From the moment she saw the expression on her father's face, Lucy said later, it "felt like a crisis."[17] Frank took Laura aside. "There were whispers, exclamations, long faces," Pierre recalled.[18]

Could the walk from Front Street to their bungalow under the hill have been anything but an anxious and silent one? It was only when they reached home that the children learned the reason for their parents' gloom. Their father had lost his job. Later they discovered why. By the spring and summer of 1932, the Depression's unemployment rates had reached new and unheard-of levels. The Conservative government of R.B. Bennett could think of little to do but retrench in all areas. One consequence was that the government of Canada did away with the office of the Yukon gold commissioner and reduced the commission's staff. Despite the fact that Canadian gold production increased dramatically between the mid-twenties and the mid-thirties and resource towns like Kirkland Lake began to prosper, Dawson's boom was minor.[19] At the age of sixty, Frank Berton, resident of the most famous gold rush town in the world, had become redundant.

He would receive a monthly pension of about $50,[20] but this was nowhere near enough to meet the high cost of living in town. Clearly, the family had to sell up and leave Dawson. Like their mother, the children were shocked at the news. It had never occurred to Pierre that his father would be without his position in the mining recorder's office or that Dawson would not remain his home. Yet at the same time, the restive part of him welcomed the news that the family would be forced to move away. He had gorged on life outside, and he wanted more of it.[21]

Frank and Laura decided to make Victoria their new home. A mid-size city conservative in tone and in politics, it had its share of former military men and a good number of retired Yukoners. The Bertons likely thought that Frank would feel comfortable settling down there in a way he would not elsewhere. A dedicated Conservative, he might just find a job somewhere in the provincial bureaucracy. For her part, Laura no doubt looked forward to Victoria's hospitable climate and to meeting other women who shared her literary interests. Its social scene was very British and proper, and it supported a chapter of the Canadian Authors' Association.

It seemed they had no sooner returned to Dawson than they were aboard the Yukon sternwheeler again, this time heading upstream for the last time as a family. They sold their little bungalow for about what Frank had paid for it a decade earlier, and took with them only a few possessions, including Laura's piano, Frank's beloved Morris chair, and a pair of rugs of wolf and bear skin. Frank had sold the *Bluenose* and given away Spark, one of the family's two pet dogs. The older one, Grey Cloud, half wolf and with them for as long as Pierre could remember, just disappeared one day. Only later did he and Lucy learn that his father had put the old friend down.[22]

About all Pierre rescued that was tangible from his life in Dawson was Terry, the pet turtle his mother had bought him in Vancouver's Chinatown. Terry was his companion all the way up the Yukon and most of the way down the Pacific coast aboard the *Princess Louise*, perhaps easing the pain of other losses. But one day while he was playing on deck with Terry, a heedless woman in high heels stepped on the turtle, crushing its shell and killing it. The dam burst. This one final loss released all the others. "I couldn't stop sobbing," he recalled. Even after they reached Victoria and booked into an old and run-down boarding house near Beacon Hill Park, he remained inconsolable.[23]

Nostalgia, one might say, is memory minus the pain. When it creeps into the mind of a historian who writes about his own life, it risks becoming self-indulgent treacle. Late in his life, Pierre Berton was too practised a writer to surrender entirely to the sugar content of life, including his own. But the fact remains that his temperament was essentially a romantic one, so his first choice of a title for a memoir of these early years was "Sweet Memories."[24] We should therefore be aware of the possibility that in the accounts Berton wrote about his earlier self, the balm of nostalgia served at times to mask some bitter truths. There had been nothing sweet, after all, in the loss of Terry the turtle.

As a title for his memoir, "Sweet Memories" did not survive the editing process. He wished to be candid, of course, for this was an important element of his mature self-image. But the discerning reader of his life and work will notice that all too often his autobiographical writing manages to avoid anything that threatens to become deep reflection, a trick made possible by Berton's skill in transforming a moment of high personal drama into yet another entertaining anecdote. In doing so, he distances himself from painful memories and at times avoids them altogether. He does not wish to reveal, so instead he tells. As a writer, Berton lacked the capacity and perhaps the will to explore the ambivalences and ambiguities, the longing and the pain, that were the stock-in-trade of his novelist friends.

"I look back on my years in Victoria with great nostalgia," Pierre Berton wrote in 1987.[25] And there were moments during his teenage years when life did seem full and contentment reigned. Some of his fondest memories, at least in retrospect, are of time spent with his father. On one occasion Frank insisted that Pierre come with him to the local Carmel Crisp Shop, the neighbourhood soda parlour, to see a neat new machine. It turned out to be a Silex coffee maker, something unknown to father and son alike. So there they stood, looking through the store window and marvelling at the way the machine sucked up the clear water and sent it back down, a rich golden brown. A few minutes later, they found themselves inside the shop tasting the result at the cost of a nickel the Bertons could not afford. Then there was the time when Frank took Pierre on a two-week camping trip, giving his son lessons in natural history and botany and astronomy as they explored the forest and the shoreline.[26]

These occasions were exceptional. By the time he reached his early teens, the distance between Pierre and his father had widened. Frank was nearing sixty-two when Pierre turned thirteen, a gulf of half a century. Shy enough with his peers, Pierre found that too broad a gap existed between himself and his father for him to be able to unburden his soul, even if he wanted to. This was "too intimate a contact," he said.[27] His reticence was something he later came to regret, for to the end his father remained something of an enigma to him.

Some of this was of Frank's own making. The loss of his job had devastated the man – "hit him with sledgehammer force," the son said.[28] At first he had tried to find employment, making desperate phone calls to his local member of Parliament and to a distant cousin, asking whether there was any work to be had.[29] To no avail. It irked him that he, a veteran of the Great War, had been discarded in such a way. He felt betrayed. Over the years, he slowly retreated into himself, becoming increasingly morose, perhaps the victim of self-recrimination. He attempted to maintain a cheerful demeanour, but often he was now just plain silent, except when talking about his ancestors, his early days in the Klondike, or the sour hand life had dealt him. He had spent most of his life's savings on the trip to Ontario, and he likely resented those who had let him do so when they probably knew that he would not have a position to return to. Fifty dollars a month was not much, but it was enough to ensure that his family would survive the Depression.

In Victoria, Frank should have been in his element, and his son came to conclude that he was, on the grounds that the former lieutenant and member of the Royal Canadian Engineers could now fraternize with any number of other former military men.[30] But Frank knew he was not an engineer, just one more man on a meagre pension. More and more of his days he spent tending the family garden; later, he took up weaving. Frank Berton's self-respect was likely not as rock-solid as his family believed. He had kept his childhood secret to himself; even less than his son could he share the depths of himself with others.

Although the Bertons had a hard time making ends meet, it was important to them to maintain dignity of appearance. They managed to purchase a two-storey frame house at 2365 McNeil Avenue in Oak Bay. Located on a double lot, it was a pleasant house, with a kitchen, a dining room connected by sliding double doors to the living room (which featured a fireplace), and three bedrooms and a bathroom upstairs. Oak Bay was a middle-class district, but they were house poor, for the mortgage consumed most of the family income.[31] Bones nominally purchased for a family pet instead made soup for the family. They scavenged firewood from driftwood salvaged at Shoal Bay, and kelp thrown up on the beaches became their garden fertilizer. Candy was a rare luxury. The family played its own version of Monopoly, the highly popular Parker Brothers game, with markers and a board Pierre made that featured local street names. At Frank's insistence, items Laura purchased at an auction during a reckless moment went back to the auctioneer. Eighteen cents Laura and Pierre miraculously found one day on a Victoria sidewalk seemed such a princely sum that it became a family story told for years. The Bertons got by on "very little indeed," Alex McCarter recalled.[32] But they managed. Movies may have been an extravagance, yet they somehow found the means to go to them.[33] The gramophone Laura had bid on and purchased found a place, along with a few records, beneath the Christmas tree. Not long after, they purchased a small Philco radio for the family and a second-hand bicycle for Pierre.[34]

Laura's pretensions would have sent her son to a private school for boys, but that was far beyond the family's means. Pierre spent his first year in Victoria in grade eight at Monterey Public School. Fortunately, when he reached the age of twelve, just after returning from Ontario, his mother at last let him wear long trousers. Bullies still plagued him, long pants or not, often because of some smart remark he had made.[35] But words also got him out of trouble, for he continued to deflect taunts and accusations with the only weapons he had on hand: a quick wit and an ability to entertain.

He did not fit in at Oak Bay High School any better than he had at Monterey Public School. Having skipped grade two, he was a year younger than most of his classmates, still small and skinny and decidedly awkward when it came to anything athletic – just "no good at sports," he said. At Monterey, he recalled, if a boy "didn't play sports you were a nobody."[36] His classes interested him little,[37] and Monterey had no extracurricular activities to speak of. The one activity that caught his attention was a little news sheet started by two other grade eight students. Pierre was desperate to be involved but was left out because he could not afford the nickel for his own copy.[38] His grades dropped, and he now stood nowhere near the top of his class. "I lazed through without effort or enthusiasm," he later admitted.[39]

Pierre's record as a student was undistinguished, but his mind was prompted less by intellect than by imagination, and throughout his life whenever these faculties clashed within him, imagination gained control. At thirteen and fourteen, when other classmates were at home doing arithmetic or studying Latin declensions, Pierre daydreamed about nightclubs. He imagined them to be the most glamorous places in the world. "I waited impatiently for the day when I myself would be part of the gay cabaret throng, sipping my champagne at a corner table, surrounded by women in spangled dresses."[40]

During the Depression, Hollywood's emphasis on glitz and glamour provided a temporary escape from worry and want, and the nightclub became a subject Pierre studied with rabbinical devotion. A series of popular movies starring the handsome crooner Dick Powell and the Halifax-born actress Ruby Keeler provided Pierre with a rich portrait of filmland's version of nightclub life. How could a curious thirteen-year-old boy ever forget the fantastic Busby Berkeley chorus lines of *42nd Street* or the suggestive lyrics of "Lullaby of Broadway," sung by Powell in *Gold Diggers of 1935*? When Broadway babies said good night, it was early in the morning; they didn't go to sleep until the dawn, with the milkman on his way.

After Boy Scouts on Friday nights, he hunkered down at home under the covers in bed with the radio turned very low. These were magical moments he never forgot, and when he described them later he had to use the third person – as if an older, more worldly Berton did not dare sully the innocence of his earlier self: "He would listen wistfully to Carl Ravazza and his orchestra playing sentimental music from the Hotel St. Francis, 'overlooking beautiful Union Square in downtown San Francisco,' or Mart Kenney and His Western Gentlemen 'from the beautiful Spanish Grill of the Hotel Vancouver on the shores of Burrard Inlet,' or Louis Prima . . . or Clyde McCoy or half a dozen others, all playing at famous night clubs. . . . And he would see the dancers on the spacious floor drifting about to the music; and he would see the waiters sliding from table to table with drinks and food; and he would wish with all his heart that he, too, could be there, preferably with Alice Fay or maybe Kay Francis."[41]

Unable to compete with such a rich fantasy life, his academic performance and social isolation got worse during his four years at Oak Bay. He hated the school and continued to feel on the sidelines of student life. The one exception was his history class, taught by a white-haired man nearing his seventies and on the verge of retirement. The students called him Doc Robinson. His pedagogy was unorthodox, but he made history come alive. One day, when talking about Stone Age hatchets, he said abruptly: "Boys – you've never tasted the cream of life, until you have known a woman." The remark became a classroom sensation, and Berton later regretted that when Doc Robinson left the school at the end of the year, nobody gave him a present.[42]

Not many classes captured Pierre's interest, and certainly none in the way Doc Robinson's did. Throughout high school his grades remained

middling. One of his weakest subjects was, ironically, English composition, for his teacher dismissed what he wrote as "too journalistic." He
did not really care for his teachers, he would later admit, and they did
not greatly care for him.[43] Socially inept and academically indifferent,
he began to act out in small but significant ways – for example, by conspiring with some classmates to organize a PEST club. Its purpose, he
noted, was "to pester everybody,"[44] including the spinster teacher on
whose desk they unleashed two matchboxes' worth of tent caterpillars.
For Pierre, this was likely the very opposite of "anti-social" behaviour.
Perhaps for his chums, PEST was a way of lashing out at authority, or
simply at teachers, and Pierre was by no means immune from the urge.
But for him the greater satisfaction came from his discovery that the
transgressive act secured attention just as effectively as the obedient one.
In PEST, a member rose in rank the more often he was caught. He had
come to realize that if one's aim in life was to be noticed, there truly was
no such thing as a bad review.

In 1935, the very middle of the Great Depression, the mining recorder
in Dawson died suddenly, and a telegram arrived offering Frank Berton
his old job back. At age sixty-four, life had handed him one of its few
reprieves. No doubt he had misgivings, but this was his duty – to his
wife, his children, himself. Returning to Dawson meant an end to their
years of want and the means of sending his children to university. His
pride and his self-respect were at stake, so he grasped that telegram as if
it were the thumb-sized nugget that had eluded him in the frozen pay
dirt back in Quigley Gulch.

Turning down an offer of employment in the midst of the Depression was unthinkable, so he made his preparations to leave – by himself.
Relocating his family would mean great domestic disruption and would
diminish whatever opportunities now existed for Pierre and Lucy.
That, too, was unthinkable. Yet the prospect of losing Frank to the
Yukon devastated his loved ones. The children did not understand why
he had to go away, and Laura worried at the thought of Frank's absence.
The plan had been for the couple to have a brief holiday in Vancouver
before he headed north, but as the day of departure drew near, suffering

from the flu and quite distraught, Laura took to her bed and could not raise herself from it.

Retrospect can sweeten memory, and these were not the "sweet memories" Pierre later thought might serve as the title of the memoir of his youth. These were confusing and bitterly sad days for him, and they became the most painful ones he was to suffer in a very long life, searing deep and leaving an emotional scar that never did fully heal. Yet when the time came, many years later, to take stock of his father's life and of this moment of leave-taking from Laura, for once he managed to plumb depths in his own dark waters. The scene he describes in *Drifting Home*, a book very much about Pierre's understanding of his father, is raw with love and despair, possibly the closest he could come to an emotional self-reckoning:

> On the day he left, Bob Allen, his old Dawson colleague who had been superannuated at the same time, was waiting in his Model A Ford to take him down to the CPR dock to catch the boat to Vancouver. My father went into my mother's room, sat down beside her on the bed and quietly closed the door and I could hear them talking in low tones for some time until Bob Allen honked his horn. Then the door opened and my father came out and his eyes were red and I could see my mother crying softly into her pillow and I felt that I had never in my life been so miserable.
>
> We helped him with his bags and climbed into the back seat of the car, my sister on one side and I on the other, with our father's arms around our waists. And as Bob drove slowly down Fort Street, my sister began to cry and I had to fight back the tears for, having turned fifteen and now being the man of the house, I was determined not to cry then or ever again. I can remember my father saying, over and over again: 'They're good children, Bob; they're good children,' and Bob answering: 'Yes, they *are* good children, Frank,' and then we were at the dock and he was going up the gangplank, waving back at us, and the boat was whistling and he was gone and nothing was ever quite the same again.[45]

This passage was one to which, once written, he could not bear to return. A dozen or so years later, writing his autobiography in the mid-

1980s, he could not bring himself to do other than gloss over the incident. The tension between the storyteller and the boy in him was too palpable. "I found it difficult to write then; I cannot bear to read it now," he wrote, by this time thinking also of the many love poems his mother sent to his father over the winter that followed.[46] Twenty-five years after this, when an interview touched again upon the subject of his father's departure, tears welled up in his eighty-two-year-old eyes and words failed him.[47]

Puberty came late to Pierre, at fifteen, just when his father headed north again. The awkward distance that had grown between them remained. By tacit agreement, they left things, some important things, unsaid. Pierre could not manage to bridge the distance in years, and his Victorian parent would not break down the barrier by trying to be a pal. And so they had parted, a father and son bonded mainly by blood.

School continued to be tedious, "a washout for me," Pierre said. He was still useless at sports. Instead, he liked doing nothing better than speeding wildly around town on his bike with a gang of neighbourhood buddies. On occasion he got into trouble, although nothing serious. His friend Dick Holden, who lived down the street in Oak Bay, and with whom Pierre went to school, Scouts, and college, noted this, ascribing Pierre's shenanigans to the fact that he was "bright and irrepressible."[48]

At school he shrank. He did not really see himself as one of the lads and he was painfully shy and ill at ease around girls, who intrigued but terrified him. When a chance came to play post office with the first girl he really liked, he could not bring himself to deliver the message: "I felt like an impostor," he said.[49] Throughout his high school years he had a crush on Wanda Ross, but could demonstrate his ardour in no better way than by pedalling his bicycle furiously past her, eyes averted, as she walked home from school. He thought about taking her to the dreaded Christmas Dance, but could not bring himself to start a conversation. In four years at Oak Bay High School, not once did he manage to exchange a word with this girl of his dreams even while both attended dances that involved an exchange of partners.[50]

The boy did make an effort. He took dance lessons with some other students every Friday night starting in grade ten, when the prospect of school dances loomed and everyone was talking about a new style of jazz called "swing." Violet Wilson taught Pierre the continental, the tango, the rumba, the barn dance, the waltz, and the foxtrot, but all but the last two eluded him. Dance class also brought other embarrassments, such as the night when the prettiest girl in class fainted while dancing with him. "She dropped like a stone to the floor," he later wrote, "and I stood there, gaping, feeling like a criminal and hoping for a secret wall panel to slide open allowing me to escape." For weeks thereafter, he imagined scenes in which he came dramatically to his dance partner's rescue. "I saw myself issuing crisp orders for cold towels, hot towels, ice, boiling water, smelling salts, etc., while holding back the crowd and feeling the young woman's pulse." The cold truth was that he had stood there helplessly while "a smooth, brilliantined youth" helped revive her and took her out to the balcony for fresh air. They returned three-quarters of an hour later. Pierre thought this was "excessive."

Berton came to look forward to high school dances, but invariably with the predictable apprehension of adolescents at social events organized by their teachers. He was one of the boys huddled in clusters on one side of the school gymnasium while the girls sat, giggling, on the other, both groups trying to look anywhere but at the other sex. In grade ten, Berton differed little from any other boy in the flux of hormonal change, but even in this circumstance of such natural self-absorption, the need to bear witness remained active. He could sense, even then, the ritualistic nature of the event. The whine of the saxophone playing "The Song of the Islands," the rustle of lavender taffeta, the sandwiches without crusts – all this and more remained with him for decades. He never forgot the sight of Mme Sanderson-Mongin, his college French teacher, "a small, wrinkled gnome of a woman, Parisian to the fingertips," confronting the line of boys and pointing to the waiting girls, yelling, "Fools! Fools! You have so little time! Dance! For God's sake, *dance!*"

Academically, he drifted. To Lucy, he seemed lethargic as a student. Mr. Hartness, the principal of Oak Bay High School, thought him plain lazy. During Pierre's final year, the man went out of his way in front of the entire class to announce that young Berton would never amount to anything. The next year he singled out Lucy. "You're lazy, lazy just like your brother," he charged. When her mother discovered this, she was furious and marched to the school, telling the man in no uncertain terms that never again should he compare one of her children to another in such a way.[51]

As at Monterey, the only school activity that really engaged his interest was the student newspaper. Thanks to his uncle Phil and the Toronto dailies he had begun to read at twelve, Pierre's interest in newspapers had by 1939 turned into a love affair.[52] In an act almost as clandestine as creating PEST, he started his own. At first handwritten and called the *Daily Totsman*, it soon morphed into the *Schoolboy*, typed out on his mother's old Remington. The hand-lettered masthead, the cartoon, the gossip, and stories with titles like "Crowds Swarm around Airflow Chrysler" were all by Berton. Students could purchase a copy for a nickel or rent one for a cent. The paper was a hit, not least because the teaching staff generally frowned upon it.

The experience gave him what students of high schools, those petri dishes of subcultures, invariably desire: to be distinctive and yet to belong, to be part of a group and yet win attention. And Pierre craved this more than most, especially the attention. As editor of the upstart newspaper, he gained instant status and influence. He loved the feeling. "I revelled shamelessly in my new-found power."[53]

The *Schoolboy* made its first appearance when his father was still in Victoria, there to help at times with the late-night typing. After Frank left for Dawson, Pierre felt a kind of emptiness inside that no homemade newspaper could fill, more in the pit of his stomach than in his head. He did not delude himself into thinking that had his father stayed in Victoria the distance between them would have narrowed. He did not miss an intimacy between father and son, because there had been little to begin with. Instead, he missed the things he had taken for granted: the reassuring sight of his father tending his garden or at his loom; the camping trips; the reliable stream of instruction on just about anything. Above all, he missed the fact that his father was simply no longer around to be the steadfast anchor. Without him, he felt quite adrift.

Membership in the Boy Scouts did much to add ballast to his life, and to provide him with a rudder. It brought him somewhat out of his shyness and provided him with a father figure, Lucy later said.[54] It reconfirmed the turn of the Bertons toward all things British, and steeped him in the facile masculinity of Baden-Powell's *Boy's Own* version of muscular Christianity. In Dawson, Pierre had been a Wolf Cub in a pack that included Johnny Gould, and he had enjoyed the experience. So when he became old enough to graduate to Scouts, he had joined with relish. Scouts, not school, became the core of his social life and the source of his closest friendships; and after Frank headed north the troop became more important to him than ever. He "lived and breathed the movement," he said.[55] He loved its outdoor life and its range of activities and the hierarchy of achievement required of its members. He was at ease with the Scouts' patriotic devotion to the King, and implicitly to the empire, for at this stage in his life he fully intended to be a Conservative like his father. Very likely he also found himself put at ease by the way the movement afforded a sense of fraternity without the risk of intimacy. "Because of the Scouts," he later said, "the awkward period of adolescence was for me a kind of idyll . . . the mingled feeling of mystery, friendship, and approaching adulthood stirring in me like the night wind in the pines."[56]

With his fellow Scouts in the lodge and on the trail, he could rise above himself and gain the badges, aspire to leadership. He felt confident as a Scout.[57] Around the campfire he could expose himself as the remorseless ham he knew himself to be. Of the many badges he earned, one was for "Entertainer," and he demonstrated how he earned it by playing the role of radio reporter, "rapping out news from a fake microphone in the style of Walter Winchell," the New York celebrity gossip columnist.[58] Even in the Scouts he felt impelled to found a newspaper, the *Seagull Special*, named after his patrol. It grew into the *Saint Mary's Special*, the name of his Scout troop, and lasted for a winter.[59]

While still sixteen he came down with scarlet fever. For a month or so he was laid up in bed and in pain, but when he recovered he seemed, in Lucy's eyes at least, to have gained a kind of energy that earlier he had not possessed, or at least had not let loose. The fever seemed to have burned out something in him, she said. "He started to move and then just never stopped."[60] In the same year, he gained height; by the time he turned seventeen, while still reedy and hollow-chested, he stood over six feet tall.

Pierre graduated from Oak Bay High School with his grade twelve diploma in June 1937, with an overall average of 76.2 per cent. In English, he was better at composition (84 per cent) than grammar (70 per cent). He did equally well (76 per cent) in English literature and social studies (history). He excelled in algebra (94 per cent). He had proven to be a good student, but a student memorable to a circle of friends as primarily the unchallenged master of movies and comics. His mother was intent on sending him to university, but he did not yet know what he wanted to study. His father wanted him to become a chemist, he knew, and thanks to the encouragement of Alex McCarter it was a subject that interested him. But his chemistry grade – at 64 per cent – was mediocre.[61]

Like the rest of his family, he had not seen his father for two years, but thanks to the monthly sums Frank sent back home, a trip north was now financially possible. Early that summer, which marked Laura and Frank's twenty-fifth wedding anniversary, he and his mother packed their luggage for one more journey to Dawson. The family could not afford to take Lucy, so she stayed with friends as a paying guest. Then mother and son made their way to Vancouver and the Klondike. It occurred to them along the way that, five years after leaving it, they still thought of Dawson as home.

PART TWO

NEWSHOUND

CRAIGDARROCH

—

THE IMPOSING OLD MANSION named Craigdarroch, in Victoria, seemed as far removed from the gold creeks of the Klondike as the mind could imagine. Yet it, too, was a symbol of fortunes that came from the ground. Local legend had it that the miner Robert Dunsmuir, an orphaned Scot of working-class origins, had found his Eldorado when on a fishing trip, the pay dirt not a boatload of salmon or trout but an outcropping of coal. The discovery made him British Columbia's first millionaire. By the 1880s, he possessed his own railway and had wrestled from the federal government a concession of fully one-fifth of the land of Vancouver Island, with rights to just about everything below its surface. Like other late-Victorian captains of industry, the West Coast coal baron built himself a castle.

Located in the prime residential district of Rockland, Craigdarroch Castle seemed not only to survey its surroundings, but also to look down upon them. With its high-pitched roof and tall chimneys, and with gables that aspired to be turrets, the castle seemed intent on reaching upward to the heavens rather than outward to the streets and houses beyond its grounds. Only the veranda, like a gallery running along its front and down one side, appeared to welcome visitors. This was the place where Pierre, fresh from the muck of the goldfields, calluses on his hands and dirt under his fingernails, began his higher education. It was the site of Victoria College and had been since 1921, a year after it affiliated with the six-year-old University of British Columbia.

The summer he had just spent in the North had changed him. By 1937, two years had passed since he had seen his father and five since he had left his hometown, and both seemed different. On the trip down the Yukon aboard the *Casca*, he had passed all the familiar landmarks of his childhood, conceding to himself that he had missed them more than he had been willing to admit. Initially Dawson had looked as it always did, aged and run down; but he no longer took it for granted. Here, after all, was a place capable of affording its visitors all the excitement of a visit to the set of a Hollywood movie. "For the first time I saw Dawson as a ghost town. . . . That impressed me. I realized it wasn't quite what I thought it was."[1] He could appreciate it as the unique community it had always been, and the work of mining and dredging especially intrigued him. At last his hometown truly piqued his interest.[2]

His father, too, had changed. Frank Berton no longer appeared as the larger-than-life figure of Pierre's childhood. He looked older, somehow diminished, while Pierre had matured to stand almost half a foot taller than his father. But there was more to it than that. Now his father looked like the sixty-six-year-old man he was. The spring in his step had gone.

Pierre needed to make money to help pay for college tuition, so he had submitted his name to the Yukon Consolidated Gold Company for seasonal work. He stayed with his mother and father at the house Frank had rented on Seventh Avenue and waited to see if his name would appear on the company bulletin board. At last, on July 12, his seventeenth birthday, there it was on the list. He was to go to Middle Dominion Camp, on Dominion Creek. He had been full of apprehension, and his insecurity was scarcely relieved when the local jeweller, looking at Pierre's soft hands, asked Frank pointedly whether he thought the boy "would make it" on the creeks.[3] But he had resolved not to let his father down, so he showed up for work, kit bag and leather boots in hand. He looked so green that the Yukon Consolidated truck driver assigned to take the recruits to their places of work simply hung a tag on him. "Berton – Middle Dominion," it read. The incident became legendary in the Dawson area.[4]

Pierre had not arrived in the Yukon until high school was out at the end of June, so not many weeks remained of the Yukon summer. Making $4.50 for a ten-hour day, he was not able to save much for tuition fees. But he had endured. He had served as a labourer, digging postholes, carrying lumber, fetching tools, and doing whatever else he was told to do. At nights in the Middle Dominion bunkhouse, when conscience told him he should be studying physics and chemistry, he could barely manage to wolf down his grub before surrendering to the oblivion of his cot. He had become a bunkhouse man but had little in common with his bunkmates, many of them immigrants from Norway, Austria, or Germany. After a while the inevitable razzing grew thin and his skin a bit thicker, his hands and his body hardened, and he knew he would last the season. When it came time to return to Victoria with his mother in early September, he regretted only that his father remained behind. He had not particularly enjoyed his time on Dominion Creek, but he gained satisfaction from the experience and knew he would be back the next year.

Approaching Craigdarroch Castle that fall to begin his studies at Victoria College, Berton was at first charmed. The sandstone structure, like "a fairy castle," appealed to the romantic nature.[5] An inscription from *Troilus and Cressida* on the entrance hall fireplace greeted everyone sweetly: "Welcome ever smiles and farewell goes out smiling." This place, offering lectures in history and English and French in a double drawing-room, those in physics and chemistry in a huge billiard room, and others in classics in the former kitchen, was where he was to spend the next two years readying himself for two more years at the University of British Columbia. He would receive his degree from UBC. Victoria College might boast of a fourth-floor ballroom, but with its limited curriculum, two hundred or so students, and worn parquet floors, Berton soon acknowledged it as little more than "a glorified high school."[6]

Victoria College was not the provincial university, but it was all the Bertons could afford. Pierre continued to live at home and bicycle to college. He remained an ungainly redhead, and he was still the restless sort of person his college-mate Dick Holden remembered from high school.[7] But he had returned from Middle Dominion Camp with a degree of manly confidence that only a few months earlier he had lacked. In Dawson that summer he had witnessed for the first time his father's mortality, his fading strength, and he seemed to gather his own as surely from this as from the long hours of hard labour on Dominion Creek. Doing the kind of work his father had tackled forty years earlier lifted at least some of his adolescent sense of inadequacy; in a minor way, sticking it out, "making it," and proving the Dawson jeweller wrong had been quite an accomplishment. For a boy who liked best to read comic books and watch movies, that season on Middle Dominion had served as his own personal Chilkoot.

Victoria College offered general courses in the arts and sciences as preparation for the senior undergraduate years at a university, and Pierre fully intended to obtain a higher education. Still, his performance during his freshman year scarcely proved stellar. With an overall average of 62.7 per cent, his marks were pulled down by a failure in physics (43 per cent) and a bare pass (58 per cent) in French. In English, he had hovered around the 75 per cent mark in the two courses he took. His father wanted him to be a chemist and had even managed to find the money to buy him a chemistry set. With a 68 per cent grade in the subject, this remained at least a possibility, if an unlikely one.[8] Earlier, he had experimented with different mixtures of elements in his basement, including one failed attempt to make gun cotton out of nitric acid and glycerine. But try as he might to follow his father's wishes, the only thing chemistry proved good for in high school was the entertainment value of setting up a stage in the garage, charging a nickel, and putting on an Oak Bay version of an alchemical magic show for the neighbourhood kids. He had changed the colour of water, blown up beakers and paper bags, and created bursts of coloured smoke and clouds of falling ash.[9]

One subject he did take very seriously, but it was not on the curriculum. This was the vast arena of popular amusement, and he did not need to force himself to pay attention. Eager to embrace all he had missed in the Yukon, he absorbed everything he could about movies and comic books and radio shows and the stars and entertainers that went with them, as if they were the very air he breathed. He became a voracious reader of pulp fiction and comic books, and he purchased them in job lots from second-hand magazine stores, traded them with friends, and carted home the ones discarded from people's basements. At the breakfast table he used fake covers to ward off parental disapproval, and at school he hid them under his history textbook.

This became more than an adolescent hobby; it resembled the obsessions of others with the makes and models of automobiles or the statistics of baseball players. It reflected Berton's need to gather together and learn everything he could about the wonderful world outside, compensation for a life in the North without benefit of radio or current news, and with very few movies – and old ones at that. "I was like a dehydrated desert traveller who suddenly encounters an oasis and laps thirstily at the beckoning pool," he later said.[10]

Radio had been a vital part of his life ever since his parents had bought their little Philco radio following the move to Victoria, and in the absence of a reliable national broadcaster, they listened to American programs beamed northward. Radio was to their new urban life what the campfire had been on the Yukon River island where they had once summered, a locus for family gatherings from which radiated an equally welcoming kind of warmth. In the Berton home, friends would gather around the Philco on Sunday afternoons and listen straight through the evening, fortified by Mrs. Berton's sandwiches and tea.

The small box stuffed with tubes brought into the living room the great entertainers of the era, like Eddie Cantor and Bing Crosby and Jack Benny. Laura Berton proclaimed Benny a fool, but Pierre noticed that she did not miss a program.[11] The tag lines of comedy shows and soap operas became part of the lingo, with a lexicon the teenagers could share with others at school and on the streets, a secret language that nurtured pockets of mutual interest and a community that their parents and teachers often spurned.

Even before he had finished high school, Pierre was known as a font of knowledge about all things related to radio, movies, comic strips, and comic books. Others could rattle off Lou Gehrig's batting average since joining the Yankees in 1923; young Berton could and did tell anyone who would listen everything they wanted to know about the story lines and stars of radio programs like *Amos 'n' Andy* or *The Shadow*, the latest dope from Walter Winchell about the goings-on in Hollywood or on Broadway. He knew the contents of the latest issue of *Bill Barnes, Air Adventurer* or *Nick Carter, Detective* by heart. Lots of teenagers around Berton followed the same passion, but few kept detailed records and notes. On the comic book version of *The Shadow* alone, Berton's notebook listed the titles of seventy-two issues he had read. Fewer still would have known, as Pierre did, the name of the show's ghostwriter (Maxwell Grant), the number of words in each issue (forty-five thousand), or the number of words (eighty thousand) Grant wrote each month. Berton later estimated that as a teenager he read more than 3.5 million words about "this scourge of the underworld" alone.[12]

Expertise is built on knowledge, but its by-product is authority and with it comes power. With all the earnestness of a Boy Scout, and with a mind like a sponge and a determination never to find himself in a cultural wilderness again, Berton took his burgeoning knowledge of popular entertainment into the halls of Craigdarroch and made his mark on his friends as surely as he engraved his initials into the panelling in one of its upstairs window wells. He may have arrived there with all the diffidence of a freshman, but he soon threw himself into college affairs. The impression he made on others was not always a positive one. At the beginning, he was not at ease with his classmates and did not get along with them particularly well. To some, he appeared brilliant but brash, full of himself and with ready opinions on any issue.[13]

What others accepted as simply part of the general zeitgeist of modern life, with its array of gadgets and advances in technology, Berton encountered as exotic phenomena. Since arriving in British Columbia, he had become his own unbidden and solitary experiment in the transformation of perception. He came to be thoroughly familiar with the culture and folkways of urban North America, but his roots in remote Dawson gave him a degree of detachment from that larger world, and a freshness of perspective that set him apart. In British Columbia and later in Toronto, at the epicentre of the country's publishing and entertainment industries, he would view his environment with the observant eyes of a cultural outsider. In 1932, he had thought the world outside was one great big circus,[14] and to the end of his life there would remain something in him of the innocent but curious boy in the big tent, endlessly fascinated with the strange but magnificent carnival of life.

Pierre returned north in early May 1938, arriving in Dawson with a queasy stomach after flying the last stage of the journey in a Ford tri-motor single-wing aircraft of the sort that had begun to transform the North by reducing the tyranny of distance and the isolation that went with it. The ice had not yet broken on the Yukon River. He spent three weeks with his father, awaiting instructions from Yukon Consolidated about the camp to which he would be posted. Word came that he should return to Middle Dominion. His work was more varied than it had been the year before, and he enjoyed it more. He spent the summer as a labourer on the mud flats, helping build roads and dams and driving pipe. Nap Mailey, a camp worker who became a good friend, remembered him that summer as a lad eager to dash in whenever he or the straw boss needed help.[15] Berton spent much of the time with shovel or sledgehammer in hand, working in deep muck. "My muscles are aching & my fingers are sore," he wrote to his mother on June 2, "but they are beginning to toughen up. I couldn't move the fingers of my left hand without exquisite pain this morning."[16] He had begun work at Middle Dominion on June 2, and it was the beginning of July before he had his first bath.[17]

Exquisite pain? Perhaps only because he was getting closer to doing the kind of work he knew his father had done twenty-five years earlier. Hammering together the network of pipes that fed water to the hollow steel points, he could watch the older men driving the points themselves into the ground. In his father's day, they had been filled with steam, but miners had long since discovered that cold water worked just as well to thaw the permafrost. "In my father's day the work was wet, hot, and filthy. For me it was wet, cold, and filthy."[18] Hot or cold, it was an affinity, a bond of experience that father and son now held in common. This was a hard way to earn a year's tuition, but it was a satisfying way of meeting expectations.

The grizzled men in the bunkhouse treated him well. To them he was "Pete" or "Point-hole Pete," except for one young fellow who was polite but insisted on calling him "Peterkin."[19] Berton wanted to punch the man in the face. He did not, but the teasing managed to put him into a sour mood for the rest of the summer. His letters to his mother more than hint at this, for their tone is generally one of irritability mixed with impatience and at times an attitude of superiority. He signed off his first letter by telling her not to use his radio too much.[20] In another, he took his aunt Florrie's side in a dispute she and Laura had had over surveying. "You were as much off the track as she was," he wrote. "I can picture the fight you had."[21]

His irritation surfaced again a few lines later, in a response to what his mother had written about some of her stories. "Am tired of hearing about detectives, judges son's [*sic*], sergeants & 'crooks' with ridiculous names such as 'Classy' Carson (hah! hah!)," he wrote. "If you can't pick a better handle than that you better write Sunday School Stories; Just because a man is a crook, he doesn't <u>have</u> to have a nickname. I am afraid that the reader will be too muddled to want too [sic] finish the tale." Then he admonished her still further for failing to locate the kind of camera film he had requested earlier. Such blunt words with either of his parents would have been unthinkable a year earlier.

Other letters to his mother that summer mixed gratitude for parcels received with petulant complaints at not being sent what he wanted. Her letters, he fretted, contained little news and not enough photographs. She sent clippings; he wanted the full newspaper.[22] "Your letter not very interesting," he griped. "You said aunt Caro came but didn't say how she looked or how she liked Victoria. You didn't say how you left the poor cat & her two little kittens. . . . You gave a very detailed description of your tea, including the exact clothing, food, programme, flattering remarks, etc – all of which I don't give a hoot for."[23]

The tendency toward irritability and impatience in letters home that summer likely had several causes. The ring of "Peterkin" still in his head; the ache of his body; the starvation for information and amusement. And also the beginnings of a declaration of independence by an eighteen-year-old young man who still addressed his letters to "Mamma" and "Daddy." Yet the thanks for the Life Savers received on his birthday was as genuine as his concern for the welfare of the family cats, which ran as a leitmotif throughout the correspondence. "The kittens should be a nice size by the time I get back," he wrote, in his last letter home. "You will have to call the one with the twisty tail 'Piggy.'" Then, only a few lines later, his concern took a more mature turn. "It is absurd for Daddy to stay here till he is over 70. He should quit within a year or two of his own accord. I can tell that he is getting tired of it and it is time he finished with the Yukon."[24] He resolved to tell his father exactly that.

In his second and final year at Victoria College, Pierre blossomed, although not in a direction that would ever make a chemist of him. His professors were in part responsible, for they tended to view students as the young adults they were and not, as did his high school teachers, as potential troublemakers. He told himself that he had to pick up his grades, even instructing his mother at the beginning of summer to ask the college registrar what books he was supposed to read and to send his chemistry and physics texts to him.[25] But not far into the fall, he dropped physics and picked up a course in history instead. It was a wise decision: in history, his final grade was 78 per cent. His chemistry textbook gathered dust like the Florence and Erlenmeyer flasks in his basement laboratory. He could no more resist moving toward a life with the printed word than his father had been able to resist the lure of the North.

Pierre was fortunate in having at last some teachers who seemed to recognize this. Mme Sanderson-Mongin, tiny and white-haired, with her stoop and pince-nez, took the time to introduce him to her "Continental philosophy of life." He appreciated that broad outlook as much as he did her eccentricities, although he proved no better at the language than he had the year earlier. His final grade in French remained the same: 58 per cent. He also liked Mr. Savannah, his chemistry professor, and felt comfortable enough with him to mention the fact that his father wanted him to become a chemist. A wise man, Savannah listened and encouraged, but he did not push the boy, and awarded him a final grade he probably deserved, a bare pass of 52 per cent.

No teacher, however, influenced Berton more than his English professor, Jeannette Cann. She, too, wore a pince-nez on what Berton later described as "a beak of a nose"; it seemed a perfect complement to the no-nonsense swept-back grey hair and academic gown. Miss Cann must have noticed something special in him, because she took him under her wing and became his mentor.[26] She knew of his interest in drawing, so she tried to expand his interests by introducing him to modern art and the works of Georgia O'Keeffe and Emily Carr. "You must buy an Emily Carr," she told her class. "You can get a big canvas for a hundred dollars. If you have to borrow . . . or steal the money, do it!" Alas, even $10 was beyond his means.[27]

Miss Cann encouraged her students to write, and to write about something they knew well. So he drew upon what had most imprinted itself on his mind, and it had nothing to do with Victoria. His first essay for her was on the departure of the last steamboat heading upriver from Dawson before freeze-up in the fall, chock full with the kind of detail that paints pictures in a reader's mind. Many years later, he could still recall what his mind's eye conjured: "the starkness of the Yukon hills"; "the river cold and grey, hissing past the town"; "the crowd on the dock, doomed to the prison of an eight-month winter, wistfully waving goodbye to those friends and relatives who were departing for warmer climes." She rewarded his effort with a grade of A+ and praised him in front of the class. "From that moment on," Berton later said, "she encouraged me constantly to write and, basking in the warmth of that approval, I wrote."[28] Miss Cann's standards were high. In spite of her interest in Pierre's work, his final grade in English – 73 per cent – was a little lower than that of the year before.

One short story he submitted to Miss Cann was called "Interior of a Trapper's Cabin." Blithely unaware of Edward Bulwer-Lytton, he began: "It was bitterly cold that night when I knocked on the cabin door, and as it opened, the glow of heat from the pot-bellied stove in the corner seemed to reach out and grasp me. . . . As the old trapper shut the door, I hung my parka and muffler on the wall, beside his snowshoes, and seated myself in the rocking chair by the stove." The light of an oil lamp casts a glow over the old magazines and "tattered calendars" that litter the place, and the boy narrator and the trapper settle down and play a game of checkers. They share coffee and "baking powder biscuits," and then it is time for the visitor to leave. "As I stepped outside, walking under a pair of huge horns over the door, my feet crunched in the snow. The cold had me in its grip once more. I looked back longingly at the lighted window, and then set out through the forest."[29]

Miss Cann awarded Pierre a grade of A rather than A+ for this paper, perhaps a sign of her reading of Bulwer-Lytton. The sole comment she wrote in his notebook was: "Good." This was probably all that needed to be put to paper; the true praise would have been offered in spoken words. Miss Cann had taught him well. The promise is there on the page: the active verb, the concrete detail, the fluid cadence, the fully realized paragraph – and the horns, clearly drawn from Pierre's indelible memory of the antlers he had seen hanging at the pitch of the roof of the Robert Service cabin across the road from home.

The effect of seeing his own words on paper, and knowing that others would appreciate them, was like a drug. He needed more, and classroom writing assignments were not enough. So he found himself one day staring at the college bulletin board, where two particular sheets of paper, typed in column format and with headlines, had been posted. However amateurish, they drew him like a moth to flame. The pages represented a full issue of the *Microscope*, a fledgling school newspaper founded by two members of his class. He had already been editor of papers at Oak Bay High School and in the Scouts, and had been excluded only for want of a nickel from the one at Monterey Public School. He felt excluded once again and resolved to rectify the situation. He went home, created his own mock-up of a newspaper page, and posted it on the board next to the others. Within days, the editorial board of the *Microscope* had become a troika, and its new editor had his own column, "Craigdarroch Comment."[30] The paper proceeded to offer wholly uninvited opinions on all manner of school affairs and did what just about every student newspaper needs to do to prove its mettle: lampoon the student council president mercilessly. Berton found his days with the *Microscope* deeply satisfying, even thrilling, and the interest and encouragement of his professors spurred him further away from his father's dreams for him.

He threw himself into other college activities. He became a member of the editorial board of the yearbook and vice-president of the glee club. He even helped found a short-lived club called the Anarchophiles – short-lived because at its first and only meeting the person designated to be its chairman refused on principle to assume his post. But it left one important consequence. Berton had been strident in supporting the campaign of one of the Anarchophiles' founders, Bruce Mickleburgh, for student council president. During one of the "heated discussions" that followed, someone asked the gawky and loud anarchist with the red hair just who he thought he was and what he intended to make of himself. Backed into a corner, Berton replied: "I'm going to be a journalist."[31]

It was less a decision than a reckoning with cloistered desire. But it was also a reckoning with destiny, and the words gave it voice, made it real. *Be a journalist.* From that moment on, the idea settled in him like gold dust in a rocker box. He went home and proclaimed to his mother that he intended to be a journalist, not a chemist. The prospect alarmed her. She recalled her own journalist father's near poverty and warned Pierre that he would be poor for the rest of his life, that he would be throwing a good future away. But he remembered the wisest words he ever heard from his old scoutmaster, a man who had held a job he disliked intensely all his working life: "Boys, if there's one thing I want to leave with you it's this: never, under any circumstances, no matter what the pay, take a job you don't like doing. It just isn't worth it."[32] So he stood firm.

The route from desire, through intention, toward decision had been no road to Damascus. It involved no conversion to a new faith but the recognition of an old one. From his earliest days in Dawson, Pierre's grounding had been in books and the stories to be found in them. He had always been an avid reader, and even in the shallow months walking the halls of Craigdarroch with his chemistry text prominently under his arm, he spent his time reading not science but fiction. In childhood, he had read all of E. Nesbit and Jack London and had devoured H.G. Wells, Dickens's *Pickwick Papers*, and Conan Doyle's Sherlock Holmes, along with Doyle's medieval romance *The White Company*. In college, he read his way through Stendhal's *The Red and the Black*, Turgenev, de Maupassant, Maugham, Dostoevsky, and Tolstoy, then Dos Passos, Fitzgerald, and Hemingway.[33] By the time he graduated from Victoria College in the spring of 1939 and prepared for a final season in the Yukon, he had thrown scholarly ambition aside. He would still proceed to university, but there would be no room for chemistry.

The summer of 1939 found Pierre back at Middle Dominion. The strictures of the Bertons' finances precluded a reunion of the entire family in Dawson, so it was decided that Laura would stay at home. Pierre left for the North as soon as college examinations ended in May. Lucy followed a month later, once high school was done for the year, in part to see her hometown again and also to keep house for her ailing father.

It did not take Frank's children long to recognize that his health had declined. Earlier, he had reported some chest pains to one of the few local physicians; he was informed that he suffered from angina pectoris. The sixty-eight-year-old took this diagnosis quite literally to heart. Told he was incurably ill, he convinced himself that it must be so, for such was his respect for the authority of science. Yet perhaps, too, the doctor's words seemed to validate a long-standing sense of unease with himself. At the back of his mind may have lurked the feeling, implanted in childhood, that this unhappy news was, after all, what he deserved. Besides, he was well aware from the family Bible that few in the male Berton line lived past their mid-fifties. By the time Pierre and Lucy arrived, gone were the forest hikes and the river excursions, and filling the void was an attitude of full-blown defeat. The son's main image of his father during this last summer of the Great Depression was, and remained, that of "a shrunken man, moving like a snail down the boardwalk of Fifth Avenue on his way to work, his thinning hair almost white."[34]

At nineteen, Pierre was among the youngest of the workers at Middle Dominion, but in this, his third season, he felt like a veteran. And he almost felt at home. While the Scandinavian and German labourers in the bunkhouse remained strangers, others like Percy de Wolfe and Alex Van Bibber had once been his Dawson playmates. Alex's sister, Helen, had been in Pierre's classes at school, often besting him academically. Another old chum, Charlie Mills, was also in camp; his father, Charlie Sr., owner of Dawson's Central Hotel, held a permanent place in Pierre's memory for his vocal rendering, on stage, of "Alexander's Ragtime Band."[35]

Driving points, hauling muck, and preparing ground for the dredges on the creeks was as onerous as ever, but he was used to it. The labour was satisfying and no longer left him drained at the end of the day. If anything, his tasks fuelled his ambition and topped up his energy level, for one of the first things he did was to establish a camp newspaper, *Pipeline*. Typed laboriously on foolscap in the mess hall, it resembled the news sheets he had produced at school and college, with hand-ruled columns, an editorial page, serialized fiction, a social calendar, gossip, and cartoons – all by Berton. He even gave it a motto: "Keep the Water Running." It was corny, overwrought, and juvenile, he later admitted. "In short, it was everything that a paper of this kind should be."[36]

The paper found a readership in the tough-minded but bored men who gathered around the mess hall bulletin board, at once amused and impressed by what they read. *Pipeline* boosted Berton's status among them, although he scarcely needed such bolstering to produce a second issue, then another and yet more. His self-styled position as "Editor" encouraged him to pursue the social life he had done without over the two previous summers.

Signs of his greater ease with people had been evident during his last term at Victoria College, when he had taken his first drink – a cheap rye whisky – and had engaged in some hijinks in downtown Victoria with fellow students. But in the camp, away from the risk of public exposure, he indulged himself rather more substantially. Gold was one of Canada's few hot industries in the Dirty Thirties, and there was once again good money to be had in working the creeks.

Had his eclectic reading told him that "sowing one's wild oats" was a well-worn literary expression, dating (in English literature) to the sixteenth century? Had the founder of the Be-a-Boy Club yet encountered Louisa May Alcott's *Little Women* (1869)? "Boys will be boys," Alcott had written, "young men must sow their wild oats, and women must not expect miracles."[37] Thus informed or not, Pierre began to sow some of his own during the month or so before he had to return to face his mother's very different ambitions.

Summer solstice in the Yukon, the day of maximum sunlight, brought with it a great excuse for northerners to let loose. Dawson residents headed for the top of the Midnight Dome to see the sun set and rise in quick succession on the twin edges of midnight. But on June 21, 1939, Pierre and a gang from Dominion Creek headed instead to the nearby King Solomon's Dome. The drinking began on the bed of a truck that happened along, swigs of Scotch whisky taken straight from the bottle they shared. All this was mere preparation for a stop at the roadhouse run by Joe Fournier, well known as the local bootlegger. There, plans were hatched for a trek to the crest of the King Dome. Already half drunk before he reached Fournier's place, Pierre found himself throwing billiard balls around the man's poolroom not long after arriving.

Word spread of a dance at another roadhouse, this one at Gold Bottom, down the Hunker Valley, and all thought of climbing the King Dome was for the moment put aside. The lingering odour of whisky gave way to a desire for the scent of perfume, and before Pierre knew it he and a few other boys had "borrowed" Fournier's pickup truck and pointed it in the direction of Gold Bottom. More swigs from the bottle. Arrival to the sound of a schottische played on an accordion. A slurred request for a dance. Rejection. The solace of the bottle.

Later, Pierre did manage to recall some features of that night. He remembered being back in Fournier's truck in the early hours of the

morning, heading for the summit; remembered the sharp turn and the
grate of tires as the truck slid across gravel on the way down; remembered jumping just before it hit the bush, then seeing it on its side and
at rest. No one had been injured, and most of the other men headed for
home, bunk, and hangover. No reporting to work the next day for
them. But all Pierre could think of, however clouded his thoughts, was
that the night's adventures could get him fired and would then surely
bring shame upon his family. His worst fear was that his own disgrace
would discredit his father in the eyes of the company officials, the men
who mattered in Dawson. So he headed downhill, stomach churning
but empty, for the long hike to camp and the seven o'clock shift. Not
long afterwards, perhaps that very night, he dutifully wrote up the
incident of the borrowed truck for *Pipeline*.[38] Nothing proved better
grist for the mill of this journalist than stories drawn from life –
including his own.

The incident should have sobered Pierre in more ways than one, but
he had not reckoned on the second major Klondike holiday – August
17, Discovery Day, when the boys from the creeks often headed to
Dawson for a good time that could last a week. He knew he should
avoid temptation, knew he should save his money for university, but
into the truck he went, with the others. Filled more with attitude than
with booze, he briefly reported to the rented north end house his father
shared with Lucy. He railed against the foreign workers who curried
favour with the bosses, and he declared bluntly that he would not
accompany his father and sister to the Discovery Day community
dance. He was going out on the town with his friends from camp.

One of the more polite names Dawsonites reserved for the Central
Hotel was the Bucket of Blood, and Berton's night out began there, in
Charlie Mills Sr.'s bar, drinking a concoction of gin and lemon meant
to resemble a Tom Collins. He downed more than a few. The boys
arrived, and soon they were all ambling unsteadily down Second Street
on their way to pay their respects to two women from Juneau who had
rented a cabin especially for the Discovery Day celebrations. Berton
recalled the moment:

> I joined the mob of men seated on stuffed couches in the tiny parlour.
> As the men engaged each other in a kind of artificial badinage, the two

girls bustled about with drinks and then indulged in a ritual. Each would sit on a man's knee for a few moments, fluff his hair, whisper in his ear, and drag him off to one of the two bedrooms. Five minutes later the man would emerge, looking sheepish, and the girl would follow shortly after to sit on a new knee. Finally, the moment came when one sat on my knee.

I can't remember much about it because it all happened so quickly. One moment she was sitting on my knee, the next she was scrubbing my genitals in a china basin in the bedroom. I flung myself at her, more to cover my own embarrassment than to display any lust. "Not that way, sport," she said, and showed me the proper way. Two minutes later she was calling her associate, who arrived with a fresh basin and towels, and I was back in the parlour with my friends.[39]

He did eventually appear at the town dance, but the only offer of a lingering embrace that night and for some time later came from the gin.

These were moments generally out of step with Berton's last season in Dawson. Nap Mailey, at camp again that year, recalled that except for admitting that he snuck in a few belts before heading home to Victoria, Pierre did not drink. Because of his father's position, Mailey said, Pierre had to live the riotous life vicariously.[40] He was more concerned that summer with putting *Pipeline* to bed than with bedding women or with propping up the bar at the Bucket of Blood. But, true to form, he hinted at his dalliance in print, apologizing in *Pipeline* for not giving "an accurate account of the Crowning of Miss Dawson," in part because he "had important business elsewhere."[41]

Pierre's brief career as a mineworker ended abruptly late in August, when he and others received notice that they were being laid off. He welcomed the news. He had enjoyed this last summer at Middle Dominion, but as he stood on the Hunker summit, ready to leave and looking down on the gold creeks, he knew he had had enough of the cold, the damp, and the muck, and that he had driven his last point. He was eager to enter university and stake his claim on life. Back in Dawson, Pierre helped Lucy prepare for departure. They were taking their father with them on the final trip outside. Henceforth, the retired mining recorder would live on a small government pension.

Before they left, however, one of Pierre's misadventures caught up with him. One day, their evening meal was interrupted by a knock at the door. It was an RCMP constable with a summons for Pierre to appear in court. Joe Fournier had charged him with the theft of his truck. Frank greeted the incident without comment but soon hired Charlie McLeod, Dawson's leading and only lawyer. His advice to Frank Berton was to get Pierre out of town. Tried in the absence of the defendant, the case nevertheless became part of Dawson lore. John Gould never forgot its details, few as they were.[42] As soon as the judge (a man named McCauley) noticed that the plaintiff was the local bootlegger, he dismissed the case and left Joe Fournier with the court costs. This much Pierre himself later recounted in his memoirs. But in 2004, Gould had more to say. He recalled that when Pierre and the gang returned to Fournier's roadhouse after they had partied at the Hunker summit, they found themselves out of money. "So they were writing cheques," Gould recounted, "and they were signing [them] 'Bob Hope,' 'Bing Crosby,' and such. And Joe was cashing them, because he was illiterate."[43]

The Bertons took their leave of Dawson toward the end of August. Much had changed in the world since Frank Berton had first stepped off the riverboat in search of himself, not least the arrival and the romance of the aircraft and automobile. Lucy flew with her father to Whitehorse on September 2, a trip memorable to her less because it was her first plane ride than because the fried egg sandwich that had served as her breakfast "did not sit well" during the rough flight.[44]

Pierre left Dawson by the river he had come to love. When he boarded the *Casca* in 1939, he began a journey that had scarcely changed since his father had braved the rough waters of the Yukon more than forty years earlier, a journey that had become as familiar and as ritualized for residents of the town as anything a church could offer. Pierre later judged the experience a leisurely and "dreamlike" one,[45] and so it must have seemed as the *Casca* made its way slowly, even majestically, past the natural landmarks the Bertons knew so well. It took almost a week to reach Whitehorse, still a sleepy town of three hundred, and at a pace unhurried enough to allow passengers to pick wildflowers along the banks of the Yukon. This was "northern time," dictated not by the needs of man but by the dictates of nature, including the unseasonably low water level of a great northern river. Life's heartbeat would quicken when he rode the White Pass railway to Skagway, where he would meet up with his sister and father; later they would gather at the rails of the *Princess Louise* on the journey down the coast. But for a few days, days without news, time almost stood still, punctuated only by the hypnotic sound of water being lapped up and hurled back toward the past in the slow rotation of the stern wheel.

At Whitehorse, as they waited for the early morning train in an autumn mist that could chill to the bone, a stranger emerged from the White Pass station with news from outside. He told Frank that the Krauts had invaded Poland and that Britain had declared war on Germany. The mother country was once again at war. It was September 3, 1939, and Canada too would very soon be involved in the fracas. To Pierre Berton, all this seemed a world away.[46]

GET ME REWRITE

—

SETTLED INTO VANCOUVER'S BEAUTIFUL Point Grey district on the city's western border, the University of British Columbia had been established in 1908 and by 1939 had already become known nationally for the strong loyalty of its graduates and the social and political commitment of its student body.[1] Its setting remained intimate, for it consisted of little more than a handful of unpretentious buildings, a football field, and lawns still in competition with the surrounding forest. Registered in third-year arts in September of that year, Pierre did not regard himself as a UBC freshman.

He lived in the only residence on the university grounds, Salisbury Lodge, a three-storey building built on the campus in the mid-1920s. He worried about how he would meet the costs of his room and board, which threatened to exceed his budget, even with some assistance from his parents. He wrote home dutifully, although at first not regularly enough, and a letter that did not arrive when his parents expected it brought a telephone call from Victoria. "When I heard about the long distance call, I had all sorts of unpleasant forebodings," he wrote his mother in September. "I pictured Daddy passing out after his 10th cigarette, or Lucy abducted by some daring college boy, or Mamma swallowing a bit of pork by mistake, or the cat having another litter, or some equally tragic occurrence." He was relieved to learn the only problem was that "my long expected missive had failed to make the deadline. I hope this one arrived in time to nip any more useless (and costly) phone calls, in the bud. Never fear, I am quite capable of taking care of myself."[2]

He craved independence, for the summers working in the North had given him a taste of personal autonomy. When he and Lucy returned from Dawson with their father, he had stayed not with the rest of the family at the Grosvenor Hotel in Vancouver but with some of his friends at the more economical Dunsmuir. They introduced him to the Cave, his first experience of a nightclub. Later, when he did visit home in Victoria, he brought along a woman several years his senior, a waitress he had met at the mess hall at Lake Bennett.

Her name was Agnes, but Pierre called her Aggie. At tea, Laura and Aunt Florrie greeted her with an arch politeness that chilled the drawing-room; the snob in them bristled at the thought that Pierre de Marigny Berton should apparently set his sights so clearly below his station. He liked being with her; she made him "feel grown up."[3] Yet he, too, was more than capable of acting like a snob, and he did so with Aggie. In the social whirl of UBC, he felt, a mess hall waitress would be out of place. Their relationship, he later claimed, was warm but platonic. When they returned to Vancouver, Aggie began to look for work and he settled in at Salisbury Lodge.

For all that he held third-year status, he still felt the freshman's disorientation. "I find it extremely difficult if not impossible to get down to work and concentrate on studies," he wrote early in October. "I hate to stay indoors, my mind is constantly wandering and I am restless and always wanting to be doing something else. I can't stay at the same thing for ½ hour."[4] He had enrolled in courses in English, history, and government, but it was all he could do in letters home even to mention academic work. Perhaps he had begun to succumb to the allure of the university's atmosphere, more relaxed and informal than that of eastern campuses[5] and assiduously dedicated to cultivating a healthy social calendar. The late thirties, wrote the university's official historian, was "the golden age of student clubs" at UBC.[6]

The war did not especially occupy him, for it had yet to make much of an impact on this faraway but very "British" province of the British Empire, much less within the cloistered grounds of the provincial university. Enrolment in the Canadian Officers' Training Corps (COTC) at UBC that autumn saw an increase from 98 to 219 student cadets, but the political ethos of the university tended to be that of a "breezy liberalism" critical of war in general.[7] Still, Berton did enlist in the campus branch of the COTC, with a mind to join the infantry. That, at least, determined what he would be up to on Tuesday and Thursday nights.

He enjoyed the military training but found it, like just about every-thing else, a distraction from the single-minded attention he wished to devote to the "Pub," the affectionate nickname for the student-run Publications Board, which coordinated the activities of student writers and journalists. "I am a cub reporter," he told his parents in the first letter home that September, mind racing far enough ahead that he dated it "yesterday."[8] At Victoria College, Pierre had read the *Ubyssey* regularly, and he knew that "guys who worked for it generally get a job" with one of the Vancouver newspapers.[9] The University of British Columbia student newspaper had appeared regularly since 1918, and it had produced a number of prominent Canadian journalists. It had long since become the best way of finding out what was happening on the UBC campus, and in the fall of 1939 it published twice a week, on Tuesdays and Fridays. The duties he was first given were meagre, but he was as enthusiastic about running errands, sharpening pencils, and fetching Coke and potato chips as he would have been if given an assignment.

He was confident this would come soon enough, and it did after two weeks' servitude to the senior editors. They told him to write about the week's library acquisitions. Pierre Berton's first headline as a recog-nized journalist was "New Books Grace Library Shelves," and the opening sentence of his first story read, "The following six books were purchased this week by the library." He read those printed words over and over again, and was thrilled each time. "I thought it was beautiful," he later wrote.[10]

Quite in step with the eager Boy Scout in Berton was the dogged sleuth. In the spring of the year, when he had announced his career intentions to his parents, he went around trying to find out how to become a newspaperman. University calendars were of no assistance, since no journalism program existed at a university in Canada. Instead, he devoured everything he could lay his hands on about the newspaper game, from practical journals such as *Editing the Small City Daily* to true-life accounts like *City Editor*. His encounters with Stanley Walker's tales of his days as city editor of the *New York Herald Tribune* and with the American journalist Emile Gauvreau's *Hot News* were like reading a newsman's Shakespeare.[11]

Walker and Gauvreau became his muses. "This is the story of a grotesque, fantastic world of impatient people," wrote Gauvreau in *Hot News*, "a world as large or as small as you want to make it; a world of emotions and sensations. . . . In this new world, you do not have to wait for exciting things to happen. You can *make* them happen."[12]

Intent on puncturing the romanticized world of the city editor in his autobiographical works, Walker had nevertheless furthered the image of the reporter as buccaneer. "The ordinary American newspaper reporter, not many years ago, in the O. Henry era and later," Walker had written in 1934,

> was identified in the popular mind as a low and irresponsible rake with misshapen and unnatural images in his head, a flask of gin on his hip, scant carfare in his pocket, dandruff on his coat-collar, a leer in his eyes, and headed straight for Hell or Seattle. . . . Today the reporter is supposed to smash all furniture in sight when invited to a home. He prefers to climb the chandelier before beginning an interview with the Chairman of United States Steel. He gets his greatest scoops while sleeping off a drunk in some boozy haven in the red light district. He writes best on twelve Scotch highballs. He insults everybody in earshot and is rewarded handsomely for his bad manners. He is happiest and most heroic when he has been thrown down a flight of stairs. He has one wife whom he rarely sees and always mistreats, an ex-wife in Peoria who has never been able to collect alimony, and a honey in Brooklyn Heights who regards him as a misunderstood Zola. Quite a lad.[13]

Cub reporters came to their craft already equipped with a well-stocked bank of images of the reporter and the newspaper. Often, like Berton, they had devoured the memoirs and novels of retired journalists like Walker and Gauvreau, but all they needed to do was go to the movies, and Pierre did that too. For, apart from the cowboy, perhaps no figure attached to a line of work received more attention in the popular culture of the day than the newspaperman.[14] Wire services and the faster presses of mass circulation papers were revolutionizing newspaper reporting, dispatching news from around the world with ever-increasing efficiency to readers. But while technology changed the delivery of news, rank-and-file reporters continued to conform to the popular stereotype of newspapermen. Films about newspapers and newsmen portrayed glamorized versions of their foibles and desires; Pierre Berton was an eager consumer of the image.

Hollywood produced a dozen or more movies about newspapers and reporters during the 1930s.[15] Often they starred America's most popular actors and were shaped by the fertile imaginations of its finest directors. Some of these films would become classics. Frank Capra's *It Happened One Night*, starring Clark Gable and Claudette Colbert and released in 1934, was one of nine pictures he directed between 1928 and 1951 on the newspaper life, invariably featuring "big-city smart-alecky journalists and their greedy bosses."[16] Four newspaper pictures, including *Five Star Final* with Edward G. Robinson and Marian Marsh and *Scandal Sheet* starring George Bancroft and Kay Francis, had appeared in 1931 alone – a year when Pierre had seen a good many movies as an eleven-year-old in Toronto. Such pictures attracted the leading ladies of the screen, including Claudette Colbert in *I Cover the Waterfront* (1933), Bette Davis in *Front Page Woman* (1935), and Carole Lombard in *Nothing Sacred* (1937).

One film, however, put virtually all other newspaper flicks of the era deeply in its debt. It starred the veteran actor Adolphe Menjou and a young Pat O'Brien, who made his film debut after beating out James Cagney and Clark Gable for the leading role. One of the four journalism movies of 1931, *The Front Page* stood out because of its sardonic humour, its unforgettable characters, and a dialogue and pace as rapid and as staccato as the *clack clack clack* of typewriter keys. Moreover, it owed its literary intelligence to a faithful adaptation from the stage play of the same name, a smash hit on Broadway in 1928. In writing *The Front Page*, the story of an ambitious ace reporter named Hildy Johnson who risks the ire of fiancée, boss, and colleagues to secure a scoop on the fate of a condemned murderer who has escaped from jail, Ben Hecht and Charles MacArthur had drawn upon their own experience of the same frenetic rough-and-tumble world of Chicago newspapers that Berton read up on during his final term at Victoria College.

In the world of his own imagining, Pierre was no cub reporter. He saw himself as Scoop Berton, clearing away coffee cups in the Pub offices today but writing lead articles for the *Ubyssey* tomorrow, and working for one of the Vancouver dailies the day after that. Three weeks into October, he wrote home to report the first *Ubyssey* article to carry his byline.[17] He did not mention its subject, but the piece explored a theme that would become one of Berton's primary motifs as a writer. It was on "College Spirit" and its importance.

> It is the spirit that impels red-sweatered Sciencemen to chant their lusty incantations upon the slightest excuse; it is the urge that prompts usually sober scholars to dash madly across the football field and rip the goalposts from the ground; it is the force that motivates frail little co-eds to sell apples on street corners for the good of the Cause. It is the power behind student publications, pep meetings, and every type of voluntary college activity. . . . Vague and intangible though it may be, College Spirit is the life blood of every great university. With it, a university lives, moves, and breathes; without it, it can only be a life-less institute, useful merely as a medium for turning out students prepared, perhaps, for technical positions . . . but not for life.[18]

The distance between this encouragement of college spirit and Berton's later cultivation of national spirit existed in time only; the dis-position toward a robust patriotism was already there in his head, although he scarcely made the connection then, if at all. Present, too, was the impulse to nurture a sense of community by drawing attention to acts done and shared in the past. "College Spirit was the driving force that impelled a band of U.B.C. students in 1922 to march in protest from the old Fairview shacks to the spot where the Cairn now stands," he reminded his fellow students. The students of UBC's early years had stood together in 1922 to insist that, after years of delay, the provincial government provide funding for much-needed university buildings. "College Spirit built the Stadium, and is erecting the Union Building. And College Spirit motivated the great Student Campaign in 1937." The student lobby of that year had resulted in construction of Brock Hall, the Student Union building. Pierre knew he was on to a good lead. The next issue of the *Ubyssey* carried another Berton byline, this atop a longer story about the small ivory-covered cairn in front of the science building, a marker, he said, that commemorated the students of the Great March. "Around this memorial to the 'Great Trek' of '22, a great university has sprung up. Student bodies come and go, but the Cairn remains."[19]

In one breathless letter to his folks, written after he had stayed up until four in the morning working on a history essay, he noted with pride that he had three front-page stories in the latest issue. In addition, since he wrote the news for CJOR, the privately owned campus radio station, he had auditioned as a newsreader and won the position. He also contributed cartoons to any publication that would accept them, and they soon found places in *Films on Parade*, the magazine of the Varsity Film Society, in the *Ubyssey*, and in *The Totem*, the university's yearbook.[20]

Near the end of his first term, he noted in a letter home that he was "writing like a demon" for the *Ubyssey*, keeping his eyes peeled "for interesting, out-of-the-way stories." His curiosity often rewarded him.[21] One such story unfolded when a slightly built young Norwegian asked him for directions to the office of John Irving, a philosophy professor. Berton soon learned that the man's name was Thor Heyerdahl, an archaeologist, and that he and his wife, Liv, had just returned from spending more than a year living in Tahiti and observing its ways. Before Heyerdahl got a chance to speak to Professor Irving, Berton had him in the student cafeteria for a lengthy interview. He discovered that the Heyerdahls had wanted "to see if two civilized people could revert to the native state and live in such a manner indefinitely."[22] (The answer was no.) He also learned that twenty-five-year-old Heyerdahl was convinced from studying Polynesia's prevailing winds and currents that immigration to the islands had come not from Southeast Asia, as school textbooks claimed, but from the west. The Kwakiutl Indians of the western coast of Vancouver Island, he said, were related to the Polynesians.[23]

Berton's two articles in the *Ubyssey* on the little-known Heyerdahl, his life in Tahiti, and his controversial theories scooped the Vancouver dailies. Within the decade, when the Norwegian explorer's book *The Kon-Tiki Expedition* (1948) was published and came to be translated into forty-eight languages, Heyerdahl was one of the best-known explorers in the world. But in the fall of 1939, he was conducting research quietly in the Provincial Museum. Thanks to the offer of a campus cub reporter, he also spent several evenings in the Victoria home of a retired miner who seemed to know a great deal about all manner of plants and animals around the world. He, Liv, and their young child were served tea by the old man's genteel wife, who said she was a writer like her son, Pierre.[24]

Pierre had little time to spare for classes, but by working late into the night he managed to meet all his deadlines, even the academic ones. His grades that term were respectable enough for a student who relied more on native intelligence than on acquired knowledge. "I got 10 out of 15 on my English . . . book review," he reported in December, "which was pretty good seeing as I did not read the book. It was on Pepys' Diary. Remarks by prof. 'You show a very good knowledge of the Diary.'"[25] Tuesday and Thursday nights continued to be taken up by COTC, and he now spent all day Mondays and Wednesdays in the printing plant, helping prepare the paper's Tuesday and Friday editions. Meanwhile, he had managed to get himself appointed publicity chairman of the Canadian Student Assembly,[26] an association of Canadian university students founded in 1937 under the auspices of the Student Christian Movement, a transdenominational network of student groups dedicated to spirituality and social justice. In this position, he helped to organize its annual conference, held in Montreal.

Thanks to the resignation of another student, Jim McFarlane, he had also secured a beat as the UBC correspondent for one of the city's dailies, the *News-Herald*. It was a job he had coveted for some time, for he knew it would take him one step closer to his ultimate goal: to be a full-time newspaperman. "I lost no time in going after it," he wrote. "It will take quite a bit of work . . . however I should be able to make in the neighborhood of 40 bucks a month which will be something. Also the experience will be invaluable."[27]

Readers of the *News-Herald* thus enjoyed an increase in short articles without bylines on all manner of goings-on at the local university: students cramming for exams; the CSA conference in Montreal; the COTC regimental dinner; a speech by the head of the art school.[28] The paper paid 40 cents per column inch, so editors wanted their news items short. Berton responded by linking paragraphs together in such a way that, as he put it, "each depended on the preceding and following ones."

When his editor caught on and insisted that his copy occupy no more than a page, he used a machine with smaller type and did away with margins.[29] Within a month he was earning enough to pay his board.

By the end of his first term at UBC in the fall of 1939, he had been appointed a *Ubyssey* assistant editor and was writing headlines as well as articles.[30] He took more and more responsibility for the *Ubyssey*'s actual production and layout, and felt himself a big step removed from the *Microscope* and the *Pipeline*. Still, there were similarities. "I believe I sent the last Ubyssey," he said in a mid-December letter. "I wrote most of it as everyone else was studying for exams."[31]

"I got demoted back to reporter on the Ubyssey last week," he informed his mother in mid-January of 1940. "I was running out the door and tripped over a chair which broke. As it was a new chair I was demoted."[32] The incident was a minor one, but it suggests Berton's frantic pace. He had returned to Victoria for Christmas but had not written home since. Rather than fret over the demotion, he went to a movie.

His Girl Friday had just opened across North America. Starring Cary Grant and Rosalind Russell, it was *The Front Page* remade for the age of Rosie the Riveter – a movie with the same frenetic energy as the stage play but with one important twist: Hildy Johnson was now a woman.[33] Vancouver newspapers had their own "sob sisters," as critics called the ambitious female journalists of movies; but while Berton had seen and liked Joan Blondell's performance as the reporter Timmy Blake in *Back in Circulation* (1937), his ideal newsroom remained a lair for lads, a place where "shirt-sleeved men hammered away at typewriters" and "others in green eye-shades sat at a big desk in the background, shuffling through mounds of copy."[34] Any movie that featured Cary Grant in the role Berton aspired to was bound to cheer him up.

Berton seems to have told his parents about his demotion not because he was upset but because it would serve to weaken the force of parental disapproval – "Daddy's somewhat stern letter yesterday" – of his apparent prodigality. A week later he was still on the defensive. "I believe I detect a note of bitterness . . .," he wrote, "the genuine impression [between the lines] that the male heir of the Berton household has not been conducting himself in his usual dutiful manner." He was working long hours downtown, he said. "After a tough session with the News-

Herald's painfully inadequate typewriter, I would drop exhausted into bed, soothing my conscience by promising it that I would write tomorrow." Then, to clinch his parents' sympathy, he reported that his "all-important marks" were "really quite satisfactory": 72 per cent in his two history courses. "So you needn't hide your face in shame anymore."[35]

He kept up a relentless schedule for the rest of the term, playing the part of Abe Lincoln's father in a radio drama on CJOR and writing several short pieces on local controversies for the *News-Herald*. He interviewed dozens of "prominent campus personalities" for a much-talked-about *Ubyssey* piece critical of the Canadian Student Association for passing an anti-conscription resolution. He found that controversy suited him. "I am afraid I am not very popular with the C.S.A. now, especially after the cartoon. I am supposed to be their publicity manager. Well, they can't say I haven't given them publicity." The cartoon was one of Berton's own. Entitled "Representing Student Opinion," it featured a giant hand labelled "vocal minority" manipulating a puppet.[36]

He enjoyed himself so much that early in February 1940 he suggested gently to his mother that he thought he might stay at UBC for two years more, rather than the one needed to graduate in 1941. "There is no need to rush through for a degree. You must realize that the degree alone is worse than useless and an extra year will not hurt me in any case." Besides, Lucy was about to finish her first year at Victoria College and could not afford to go away to university. Perhaps the family should move from Victoria to Vancouver? That way, Pierre suggested, both he and Lucy could live at home and thanks to his *News-Herald* work he could easily pay board of $20 a month. "By the way," he added, "I am assistant editor again."[37]

For all his devotion to journalism, Berton did not lack a social life. Like other Canadian campuses, UBC not only served as an institution in which to teach and learn; it also helped to forge middle-class values and facilitate the creation of friendships leading to marriage and careers.[38] Whatever their backgrounds, compared with most other Canadians they were children of privilege, and many of them were out for a good time. So there was an abundance of dances, socials, formals, and nights on the town, organized or sponsored by student clubs. No amount of work caused Pierre to miss many of them. He loved the excitement of the social scene and he found himself drawn to women. Berton was more than capable of being "one of the boys" if occasion warranted, and it often did; but he felt more comfortable in the company of women and gave them the impression that, unlike other young men, he was genuinely interested in what they had to say. He remained fundamentally shy, but this was soon overcome by his new-found persona as a cub reporter.

Judged by his dating patterns and other evidence, in Pierre's first year at UBC, women were often on his mind. When he was supposed to be taking notes about squad drills and organizing work parties during his COTC training in the fall of 1939, he found himself daydreaming. Sometimes he doodled in his notebook or sketched cartoons. Once, clearly thinking back to his final summer at Middle Dominion Camp, he flipped to a blank page and played at being Robert Service:

> There's a salmon scented girl
> And she's set my heart awhirl
> And she lives up in the Yukon far away
> And by the campfire bright
> We

This was lousy, so he started again, inspired by a phrase he had jotted down, "the venus of the squaws."

> Ah yes I like the white girls
> Oh they surely do look nice
> But then a man can't live
>   On looks
> Unless he's got the price.
> They always want a permanent
> Some powder or some rouge
> But my little squaw needs nothing
> At all except some mulligan stew.[39]

It did not take him long to abandon this poetic misadventure and return to lessons on the duties and knowledge expected of an officer. Perhaps his train of thought returned to the treatment of venereal disease, the subject of his notes on the previous page; perhaps it had shifted to Aggie, and to how shabbily he had treated her. In October, he wrote that she was thinking of going home to Victoria. "Delighted Looks from Assembled Family," he added parenthetically, likely reflecting his own relief. By the following March he had lost track of her, or so he wrote home.[40]

Whatever feelings lingered for Aggie did not prevent him from taking girls to clubs and dances and movies. His letters home are punctuated with the names, usually first names only, of young women he dated. In one sentence Rosalie accompanies him to the frosh reception at the Happyland; in the next, he is with Aggie again to see *The Wizard of Oz*.[41] He takes a girl named Mary Woodsworth to the Homecoming Dance early in November during his first term, and has his first date with the campus stringer for the *News-Herald*, a girl named Janet Walker, shortly afterwards, when Salisbury Lodge holds what he calls "a swell dance" at a club called the Peter Pan.[42]

Janet Walker had been almost the first girl he had met at UBC. The moment he stepped into the Pub offices in September 1939, there she was at a big typewriter near the entrance, a pretty girl in a yellow sweater, and she gave him a welcoming smile. "That girl is in love with me," he recalled of this moment twenty years later, "and I am in love with her." But this was the perspective of a man married to a woman who had once owned a yellow sweater. The truth is that Cupid's bow took rather longer to place its arrows than this little Valentine suggests.[43] Pierre recognized Janet Walker's name from reading the UBC student newspaper back at Victoria College, but he knew little else about her. For her part, this boy named Pierre Berton seemed at first far too opinionated. Not only that; he wanted to do everything at once, and *right now*.[44]

Janet Walker was a girl from the Fraser Valley. Her father sold fine clothing at the family's general store in Haney, a small town about thirty miles from Vancouver. In the thirties, the Walkers had moved there from Fernie when Janet was in grade eleven. She and her brother helped out in the store and delivered groceries to customers.[45] She was a spirited and buxom bundle of energy with an enthusiasm that radiated in all directions, at ease with others and concerned for them. To meet her was to like her. "She always seemed to be laughing – a very bubbly person," recalled an older schoolmate who used to pass her in the hallway.[46] She had arrived at the University of British Columbia in the autumn of 1938, fresh from completing grade thirteen (senior matriculation) at MacLean High School in Haney, and had gone straight into second year,[47] one of more than two thousand undergraduates.

A former vice-president of her high school's club for budding journalists, and the person principally responsible for putting out the yearbook, Janet enrolled in arts at UBC, rooming at a local boarding house with several other students. Her major subjects were English and philosophy, supplemented by a minor in history; but she was soon involved in a wide range of extracurricular activities. In the autumn of 1939, when Pierre met her at the front desk of the Publications Board office in the old gymnasium building, she was on the *Ubyssey* staff.[48] Among her courses were ones in advertising, so she assisted with advertising and sales in addition to writing articles. She was editor of the annual student directory and had become a member of the Alpha Delta Phi sorority and of the executive ("Publicity and Historian") of Phrateres, a group of 250 young women dedicated to promoting "friendship among all university women."[49]

Janet Walker's message as president of the student council in the year she graduated from high school had been, in part: "Don't go around criticizing what others do – go ahead yourself and help make conditions better."[50] So when she later joined the *Ubyssey*, she was not entirely impressed by the lanky redheaded student journalist with the French name, the loud voice, and the strong views. Like other students at UBC that fall, she initially had mixed feelings about Pierre Berton. It did not take her long, however, to discover that his apparent rudeness masked a social awkwardness. He did not dress to impress, for he seemed to have little fashion sense. As often as not his attire consisted of a tweed jacket, a pair of rumpled green checked trousers, and a maroon shirt with yellow tartan tie. Janet disliked the way he exaggerated for effect, talking for example about the "man-hungry co-eds" of UBC. She also found irritating his posturing as a "hotshot reporter" obsessed in his pursuit of the story. Still, everybody else seemed pretty dull by comparison.

That, she said, was the problem. And the reason she decided to go out with him.[51]

That fall, two days after a friend of Janet's named Virginia (Ginny) Galloway took him to a co-ed dance, Janet and Pierre went together to the Junior Prom at the Commodore. Later, when the *News-Herald* gave him tickets to the University Theatre to review the alumni presentation of a British farce of the 1920s called *Tons of Money*, they dated again.[52] They liked each other but felt no special commitment. "It wasn't a beautiful love, or anything," she said later.[53] Besides, they sometimes found it difficult to coordinate their schedules.

The gregarious Janet was, if anything, busier than Pierre. Now an associate editor of the *Ubyssey*,[54] she also penned the popular fashion and gossip column nominally written by the mysterious "Mary Anne."[55] Its main purpose was to make money for the *Ubyssey*, since it charged companies each time it mentioned a product. "The gossip stuff," Janet said, "was just shoved in to sell the stockings, or whatever."[56] In polite but at times breathless prose, Mary Anne revealed to readers not only which accessories would go perfectly with a white chiffon period gown but also who among the blond freshettes had gone out with which football player.[57] A member of the Radio Society and of the Student Christian Movement, of the Big Sisters and the Social Problems Club, Janet seemed to know everybody, and by name. The majority of *The Totem*'s club photographs each year featured her face. Invariably, it wore a smile.

Pierre might have wished to take the relationship further but, as he conceded in his memoirs, "Janet knew how to keep a man at arm's length in those critical moments on the doorstep when one did one's best to stretch the goodnights into a passionate embrace."[58] Less charitably, he would add that she "was everybody's sister, nobody's girl friend." In March 1940, he informed his parents without further comment that Janet was getting married the following month, and that her boyfriend was a policeman. (Late in life she would find this claim puzzling since, to her knowledge, she had not known any policemen and certainly was never engaged to one.)[59] The relationship between Janet and Pierre remained platonic. "We were best friends for years," she recalled. "Janet was not a girlfriend at the time," he later said, "she was 'one of the gang.' We did things as a group."[60] That spring, Pierre danced to the music of Mart Kenney and his orchestra at the Co-ed Ball with Ginny.[61]

As he neared the end of his first year at the University of British Columbia, Berton's nervous energy became more evident. The *News-Herald* had given him his first byline on Saturday, March 16, and he was over the moon.[62] His story had commented on a *Ubyssey* editorial on fraternities written by its editor-in-chief, John Garrett, a Victoria lad who had been a year ahead of him at Oak Bay High and who had managed, since then, to acquire a pseudo-English accent and a haughty attitude to match. Berton had interviewed "a lot of fraternity men" for his article, and by quoting them carefully and exposing their attitudes he had scarcely made himself popular. "It has, of course, wrecked any chances I may have had of ever joining a frat," he wrote. "However it was worth it." He loved controversy and the attention it brought, so he immediately submitted another contentious story. "Very hot stuff," he declared. "If the *Herald* prints it, my life won't be worth much tomorrow. However that's a problem all reporters meet up with."[63]

He felt almost part of the reporters' close fraternity, and was intent on earning a place in it. In the first two weeks of March 1940, *News-Herald* pieces had earned him $22.[64] Confident that the newspaper would hire him full-time for the summer, he could barely wait for classes to end. Meanwhile, he remained relatively indifferent to other issues of the day, whether the lingering Depression or the war in Europe. Military life held little attraction. He wrote home that he would likely quit the COTC because work on the *News-Herald* had made him miss the last five training lectures. "I hardly know there's a war on," he told his mother. "The whole thing is a big joke with both sides sitting underground in their impregnible [*sic*] lines waiting for an attack and probably playing poker."[65]

For many Vancouver residents during 1940 and most of 1941, the war that had broken out in Europe seemed very far away. Only after the Japanese attack on Pearl Harbor on December 7, 1941, and the fall of Hong Kong later that month did Vancouverites come to share the sense of danger and urgency that already existed elsewhere in the country. Before long, encouraged by scaremongering politicians, the federal government forced Japanese Canadians to report to Exhibition Stadium in Vancouver for removal to camps in the interior of the province or to farms on the prairies. Those unable to sell their property before they left Vancouver had it placed under the "protection" of a federal agency called the Custodian of Enemy Property, which proceeded to sell most Japanese properties and chattels for significantly less than their assessed value.[66] Berton wrote nothing about this at the time, but the treatment of Japanese Canadians registered with him.

For a while that term, his views assumed a pose: the undergraduate as cynic. It is tempting to suggest that this was because at the time he was struggling through Somerset Maugham's *Of Human Bondage* and Virginia Woolf's *Mrs. Dalloway*. Or because that term he had written a 750-word essay for another student on the question "Is Necking Immoral?" and although it had taken him only two hours, it received the respectable grade of 70 per cent.[67] But perhaps he had caught an intimation that while journalism could bring much satisfaction, it could also corrode the soul. "Journalism is not a career," a jaded journalist in David Graham Phillips's novel *The Great God Success* had said at the opening of the century: "It is either a school or a cemetery."[68]

Tradition holds that Diogenes, archetype of the philosophical cynic, once took up his lantern in the light of day to search for an honest man. It is known that throughout his life he assaulted social convention. No classicist himself, Berton nevertheless had begun to take up his own lantern, and at times when he looked around he did not like what the light exposed. He said little about the world beyond the campus, and wrote even less. The thought of returning to Victoria made him gloomy. "I'm afraid I shall never be able to stand Victoria again," he complained to his mother. "You have no idea how ghastly it appears from over here. . . . Every time I think of those bare Victoria streets on Sunday morning with a solitary Hindu leading his horse home, I shudder."[69] Perhaps to raise his spirits he tried attending a Roman Catholic Easter Mass a few weeks later. To no avail. "It was a beastly service. A lot of hooey with incense and chanting. . . . It's like giving your religion to you in sugar coated pills. How people can stand all that mumbo-jumbo is beyond me. It may be alright to feed a bunch of savages with that glittering hocus pocus but it's a bit thick for intelligent or supposedly intelligent people. Everybody crossed themselves on the slightest provocation – that is, all except me. I'm damned if I will."[70]

Academically, Berton survived his first year at UBC easily, even with his sporadic attendance in classes. His overall grade was 64 per cent, and his parents were likely not very pleased. Government was his best subject (76 per cent). English, ironically, was his worst: he barely scraped through one of his two English courses with a grade of 50 per cent. He averaged 65 per cent in two history courses.[71] But the calibre of his grades concerned him far less than whether Robert T. Elson, managing editor of the *News-Herald*, would choose him from among the dozen or so aspiring reporters he had decided to audition for a summer job. Elson hired Berton at the end of the second week: $50 a month, for twelve-hour days and six-day weeks. He also hired Ralph Daly, a young man almost as enthusiastic as Pierre, and just as entranced with the lore of the newspaperman.[72]

The location and offices of the *News-Herald* were as modest as its status among the city's newspapers. The paper was housed in a small two-storey building at 426 Homer Street in the warehouse district. Reaching the newspaper's editorial department involved a climb up a set of outside stairs. By any measure, its newsroom was, as Berton later stated, "small, dingy, and overcrowded."[73] But when Pierre began to work full-time with the *News-Herald* in the summer of 1940, it was as if he had stepped onto a familiar movie set and into a role he had been rehearsing for as long as he could remember.

Although some journalists turned novelists found the conditions and atmosphere of the modern large-city newsroom nightmarish and bleak, to Pierre, ever the romantic, "it was glamorous beyond description." The cynicism of the past few months seemed to have been put in his trouser pocket, to be pulled out, like his notebook, only when it served his new persona as reporter. In that cramped second-floor newsroom, Pierre Berton did not see people and positions. He saw characters and roles and scenes. He was his own rendering of Hildy Johnson, the epitome of the obsessive newshound who thought nothing of putting his story ahead of his woman, a variation on the archetypal flawed hero who would do anything to achieve his ends. He saw Robert Elson reprising the role of Hildy's tough managing editor, Walter Burns, characterized by Hecht and MacArthur as "that product of thoughtless, pointless, nerve-drumming unmorality that is the Boss

Journalist – the licensed eavesdropper, trouble maker, bombinator and Town Snitch, misnamed The Press."[74] He saw jaded columnists with neglected wives at home and female reporters who survived the chauvinism of the newsroom by either developing thick skins or wearing their hearts on their sleeves. The place reverberated with echoes of those movie staples, "Stop the presses!" and "Get me rewrite."[75]

On his first day on the job, Pierre found himself assigned to the waterfront and told to find out whether anyone was bootlegging gasoline, which was in short supply. Before he was done, he not only had found the bootlegger but was also on the trail of a local professor who claimed he had a new kind of gas that would sustain a car for 150 miles on a single gallon. "I will make this letter short, as it mainly concerns one question," he wrote his mother at the end of the month. "That is, shall I go back to UBC or not?"[76] His family's response isn't recorded, but Scoop Berton was in the game at last.

Part of the white noise of the newsroom was the ongoing clack of the British United Press teletype machine. In the United Press office that summer of 1940 was a baby-faced young New Brunswicker named Charles Lynch, paid $25 a week to live in a city he found inhospitable, insular, and "slapped together," just so he could feed newswire items out of San Francisco to the local United Press subscriber, the *News-Herald*. Lynch soon found out that in the pecking order of Vancouver newspapers, the conservative and lordly *Province* held sway. Owned by the powerful Southam newspaper chain, it boasted a circulation of a hundred thousand or more. Considerably beneath it in dignity and size were the family-owned *Sun* and the *News-Herald*, an upstart founded in 1933. A person reading the *Province*, Lynch said, was expected "to read it in reverent silence, something you could never do with the raucous *Sun* or the half-baked *News-Herald*."[77]

Lynch came to conclude that the Vancouver newspaperman was a unique and eccentric breed. "Everyone who worked at (or owned) the *Sun* was crazy, and the *Sun* itself reflected it. The morning *Herald* wasn't much different." Irreverence was the weapon of choice used by *Herald* reporters to counter the gravitas of the *Province*. At the *News-Herald*, said Lynch, "nobody gave a damn."[78] This devil-may-care attitude befitted a newspaper that could not afford to view any story as beneath itself. The *News-Herald* was by far the smallest of the Vancouver dailies, with a circulation of about twenty thousand. And because its salary scale was a miserable one, its staff was "a motley group."[79]

The *News-Herald* staff of the day, in fact, did constitute a farrago of memorable individuals, and many years later Berton described them with relish in his memoirs.[80] T. Harry Bruce, a veteran newsman, seemed to know so much that the paper ran a front-page feature offering readers a prize if they could stump him with a question. The prize was seldom awarded. The reporter Evelyn Caldwell, the paper's resident sob sister, wrote under the name "Penny Wise" and was so tough that on one occasion she chased a copy editor into a washroom, climbed into his cubicle, and hit him with a Coke bottle. The golden rule and constant refrain of the entertainment reporter Christy McDevitt, once a carnival press agent, was "When in doubt, lose the elephant." The reporter Al Williamson, debonair in his thin Gable-like moustache, was privy to all of Vancouver's scandals and secrets, but he refused to tell all for fear of losing his invaluable contacts. Benny Pastinsky, a former jeweller turned police reporter, was so dedicated to writing from the victim's point of view that he would dictate such improbable copy as: "I am a corpse. I am lying in a cheap room in the Niagara Hotel with a knife in my gullet."[81]

Pierre's reporting assignments were for the most part minor ones, covering events at the university and the luncheons of service clubs. But he sucked each occasion dry of whatever news value it held. At the end of some days, he would file half a dozen or more news stories, heedless of showing up his fellow reporters in front of Robert Elson.[82] To those at the *News-Herald*, but perhaps especially to Berton, Elson was a combination of God and Lucifer, a man with the power to bestow either blessing or damnation. Berton later recalled the image Elson projected: "a burly man with a bold, pugnacious face"; "a mass of nervous energy"; a figure who, in tense moments, "chewed copy paper as if it were lettuce."[83] The truculent former editor of the *Province*, hired away by the *News-Herald* for the princely salary of $6,000, was such an office gauleiter that he ate copy pencils when one of his unpredictable and uncontrollable rages consumed him.

For the most part, Berton managed to stay clear of Elson's wrath that summer. He had begun with such a burst of energy that the city editor had praised him with a wry smile for having written half the paper. But one time around midnight in the middle of May, Elson burst into the cramped newsroom and saw his cub reporter lounging at his post, feet on desk, paying rapt attention to "Terry and the Pirates," one of his favourite comic strips. Elson fired him on the spot. A few minutes later, the editor stumbled upon a story buried in his in-basket that scooped the other dailies by revealing the identity of UBC's gold medallist that year. He demanded to know who had written it. Someone told him it was Berton. Elson rehired him on the spot.[84]

Such characters served up a parade of amusing anecdotes and re-inforced the romantic stereotypes Berton already possessed. Only two, however, directly influenced his personal development as a print jour-nalist. The first was Bruce Hutchison, whose work Pierre had followed ever since he came across Hutchison's "Loose Ends" column in the Victoria *Times* during his high school days. Bruce Hutchison was a one-man journalism school. His hallmark as a writer, as the newsman Vaughn Palmer later noted, was his "rhythmic style and gimlet eye for detail."[85] Berton fast became one of Hutchison's legion of admirers.

Ontario-born and British Columbia–bred, Hutchison had spent his first years in Cranbrook, but his ne'er-do-well father moved from job to job, and the boy led a life of uncertainty, sometimes with his mother alone or with Victoria relatives. He found stability in his schooling, read widely in the classics, and discovered favourite writers in Shakespeare, Dickens, Carlyle, Conrad, and others. At sixteen, following perform-ances as Shylock in a production of *The Merchant of Venice* and as a member of his school's debating team, he was offered a column in the Victoria *Times* by its editor, Benny Nicholas. The year was 1918, and from there he never looked back. Throughout the twenties he covered federal and provincial politics, and the run of "Loose Ends" in the *Times* lasted for thirty-five years, continuing even when Hutchison moved to the Vancouver *Province* and wrote for magazines such as *Maclean's*, *Collier's*, and the *Saturday Evening Post*.

One Hutchison column in particular caught Berton's attention in the spring of 1939: not the one about the civil strife in Spain or the threat of war that could engulf all of Europe, nor about the creation of the National Film Board or the first royal visit of King George VI and Queen Elizabeth to Canada in May. Instead, the column had been about an ugly stucco-covered lighthouse that Victoria's civic leaders had erected in the heart of the city. The column delighted Pierre with its vituperative outburst. The lighthouse, Hutchison wrote, was "a simple abortion." Suitably inspired, and more than a little tipsy from cheap rye whisky, Pierre and some friends attempted late one night to paint the lighthouse red. They settled for a rather unsteadily drawn swastika, and the next day counted themselves lucky they had not been found out.[86] At nineteen, in short, Pierre Berton was scarcely an engaged citizen of Canada or the world. He was a college kid looking for a good time. Hutchison helped change this attitude.

Although Hutchison had his quirky hobby horses – ridding Victoria of the Pandora Street lighthouse was just one – it was the Hutchison of penetrating intelligence and liberal temperament who first tweaked Pierre Berton's interest in the serious side of newspapers. Hutchison had been an astute and wry observer of the Canadian political scene since his posting to Ottawa as a reporter in 1925. He had been in Washington to cover the ascent of Franklin Delano Roosevelt to the American presidency in 1933, had been in London to report on the Imperial Conference and the coronation of King George VI in 1937, and had spent time observing Hitler's Germany on his way home. The following year the Liberal Party loyalist and insider joined the staff of the *Vancouver Sun*. "I read Bruce Hutchison every single day," Berton later said. "I read everything he wrote. I thought he was brilliant."[87]

Berton admired not only the insights of Hutchison's observations but also his dry wit and his literary versatility. Here was not only a fine political journalist with a formidable knowledge of Canadian history but also a Canadian writer who had written pulp fiction in the 1920s and whose 1935 *Saturday Evening Post* story "Park Avenue Logger" had been turned two years later into a Hollywood movie.[88] Like the story, the flick told the tale of a young man whose wealthy New York father thinks he is a pantywaist and sends him to work in a lumber camp in order to make a real man of him. But the father little knows that his son is in fact a famous wrestler, the Masked Marvel. By the movie's end, the lad has exposed corruption at the camp, defeated the wayward loggers, and rescued the logging company for a beautiful young woman who, of course, falls head over heels in love with him.

This was exactly the kind of melodramatic stuff Berton loved. In Hutchison, Pierre found an inspiring range of writing, from middle-brow general entertainment to highbrow literary art, that began to channel his romantic temperament along more serious lines. Five years after *Park Avenue Logger* hit the screens, Bruce Hutchison travelled to Ottawa to be awarded a 1942 Governor General's Literary Award for non-fiction. *The Unknown Country*, his prizewinning book, was an attempt to explain Canada to Americans and to themselves.[89] The award was the first of three the West Coast journalist was to win for works of non-fiction, a feat that in the second half of the twentieth century Berton alone would equal.

The second newspaperman who influenced Berton during the first months of his apprenticeship did so in a more immediate way. Jack Scott, like Pierre, had printer's ink in his blood. His father worked as a desk editor at the Vancouver *Province*, and in June, when Robert Elson relinquished the managing editorship and promoted the city editor Reg Moir to the position, he hired Scott to fill Moir's old job. Being city editor meant days of twelve-hour shifts or more, but that did not stop Scott from writing his own column, "Our Town." Appearing five days a week, it quickly became one of the *News-Herald*'s most popular features.

A handsome young man with swept-back wavy brown hair, Scott at twenty-six was only a half-dozen years older than Berton. But he already had a decade of newspaper experience behind him and he seemed wise beyond his years. He was an intense man, yet one who enjoyed unwinding over a bottle and a game of poker. His columns, which could cover almost any topic from political and social contro-versy to birdwatching and family life, were folksy and unadorned. Scott's prose looked effortless, but he agonized over each word and phrase. At one moment, Berton would hear him yelling across the city room with an urgent assignment, and in the next, see him silently brooding at his desk over a troublesome sentence.

Long before he had a column of his own, Berton learned how to write one by reading Jack Scott and taking him as a mentor. He admired Scott's quick wit and the simple grace of his prose, the way his columns exhibited "the common touch."[90] It was from Scott he learned that just about any subject, however mundane, could make a good column.[91] One day Scott might write about the inscrutability of Chinese restaurants, followed the day after by his enjoyment of a very fine book. The best advice he ever received about writing a column, Scott said, came from the editor who told him, "A columnist is just an opinionated guy who lives down the block. If you ever aspire to be anything more we'll find a replacement for you."[92] Such lessons from a master of his craft were not lost on Berton.[93]

The city editor and the cub reporter grew quite close that summer. It was an exciting time to be at the *News-Herald*, for the ambitious Elson had decided to turn the paper into a cheeky tabloid and everyone had their part to play, large or small. The transformation took place with the issue of June 21, 1940, when the newspaper's pages gained in height but became narrower, reduced to five columns from eight, and with many more pictures. The newspaper's readers, said Elson in a full-page announcement of the change, "haven't time for long-winded Editorials and news. They want to be able to read it all over the breakfast table or on the way to work." He promised at least a page of pictures every day, "and when pictures tell the story better than text, we'll use them. This is the modern method."[94]

Elson very likely saw in his hyperkinetic cub reporter someone suitable to this "modern method." So, perhaps, did Scott. But Scott detected something more than this. Despite his more introspective nature, Jack Scott glimpsed in the young Pierre Berton certain characteristics of himself as a journalist – something of the newshound endlessly curious about his surroundings; of the reporter who saw a story in anything, anywhere; of the unabashed idealist eager to take up a cause and with the courage and the will to be blind to critics. It was Scott, above all, who that summer tried to convince Berton to abandon university for a reporter's life. He knew a man with a calling when he saw one.

WUNDERKIND

—

"IN THE SUMMER OF 1940 something happened to Canada." So wrote one of the UBC student journalists in the university yearbook, *The Totem*. The essay, a lengthy one on the COTC, chronicled the early impact of the Second World War on one institution of higher learning five thousand miles away from the European battlegrounds. In a single year, the dominant colour on the University of British Columbia campus had switched from the bright green of peace to the flat khaki of war. "It was on the last Saturday of September," the writer noted, "that the residents of the University Area first heard the thud of 1,750 student boots on the pavement of the University boulevard – 1,750 undergraduates and graduates, learning to be soldiers."[1] The author of the piece, "P.B.," was one of those students. He was, of course, Pierre Berton.

With the benefit of hindsight it seems inevitable that "P.B." should have been the author of an article documenting the brief history of the university's preparation for war. More than likely, the essay was his idea in the first place, for in the fall of 1940, when he entered his second year at UBC, Berton was the acknowledged wunderkind of campus journalism.

Still, during the summer he had found himself wondering whether he should even return to university – not because he had given much thought to enlisting for war service (his memoirs are silent on the issue) but because he so thoroughly enjoyed working at last for a big-city newspaper.[2] At the end of May, his first month at the *News-Herald*, Berton wrote to his mother that Jack Scott said he was "the best man he had in the office and would be treated as such." Young men have been known to present gilded lilies to their mothers, but judging by Pierre's record at the paper that month, there is no reason to treat his claim as suspect. Berton added that Scott had pressed him to stay, promising his own beat and more money.[3] Robert Elson could not have helped Pierre make up his mind, for at one moment the mercurial editor would praise his talent and speak of the future, and in the next he would berate him for some minor error and threaten to fire him if he weren't already a short-term hire. In the end, it was several veteran reporters who helped him decide. To a man, they counselled him to return to UBC for his degree. The piece of parchment, they said, "counted a lot."[4] His parents no doubt said the same thing. This was likely not what he wanted to hear, but he acted on the advice.

At the instigation of their children, Frank and Laura Berton moved to Vancouver late in the summer of 1940. Pierre was eager to remove himself from the noise and distractions of Salisbury Lodge and to cut down on expenses, and Lucy had determined to enrol in arts at UBC. For the first year, the Bertons rented a house on West 13th Street, but a year later, with Pierre's help, they found a pleasant stucco home at 4649 West 9th Avenue in Vancouver's Point Grey, not far from the university gates. The family was together once more.

Berton returned to a campus that was beginning to show the influences of a country at war. In his annual report, President L.S. Klinck offered to render "all possible assistance" to the federal government and to put the university's facilities, equipment, and personnel fully at the nation's disposal. The result was that while the number of students at UBC increased in 1940–41 to the unprecedented total of 2,600, they arrived to a campus depleted of faculty.[5] For many professors who were veterans of the Great War, memories of battle remained stark and bloody and fresh; they viewed the course of the first year of this new conflict with the alarm its events merited. Able to take into account the escalation of German militaristic aggression in the thirties, members of faculty like Berton's history professor, the distinguished historian F.H. Soward, could see that Hitler was a worse enemy than the Kaiser, that he had to be stopped, and that this war too would be a long and deadly one.[6]

The first issue of the *Ubyssey* in the fall of 1940 appeared on Tuesday, September 24, and it ran to a fat twelve pages rather than the usual lean four. Berton's was the lead article. "Students Pledge Full Support as Second War Session Opens" was a variation on the previous year's "school spirit" theme, serving in this case the cause of the COTC. In the shadow of war, Varsity's men, it proclaimed, had given up their blue and gold football stripes for khaki uniforms. The alma mater song was now "a marching theme for hundreds of student soldiers." The article did not urge readers to sign up, but since it began by noting that "the men of the University" had "quickened their step with the rest of the nation," there could be little doubt of what the author thought his fellow male students should do.

The year's inaugural issue was sprinkled with other stories about how the war was touching university life. A well-placed photograph beneath the article "Khaki Clad Students Bring War to Campus" featured two young men in uniform, co-eds on their arms. "When a uniform makes a man out of Joe College," its caption read, "it's a case of 'All this, and freshettes, too.'"[7]

Striking, in retrospect, is the complete absence of any coverage of events of the war itself. Over the spring and summer the "phony war" had ended. France had fallen and Denmark and Norway had been subjected to the Nazi blitzkrieg. During Berton's first month at the *News-Herald*, the British army had barely escaped annihilation at Dunkirk. While their campus newspaper reported that the university president wished them to curtail "frosh rites" and that *The Totem* had a glamorous new editor, UBC students would have learned only from relatives, radio, or city newspapers about the Battle of Britain being waged in the skies over England. No more than his fellow university students did Berton either seek to glimpse the larger picture or try to escape sophomoric pleasures.[8]

His move from the *News-Herald* back to the *Ubyssey* that fall involved an abrupt and radical shift of status. On campus, he was no upstart cub reporter but the new editor of the *Ubyssey*'s Tuesday edition. Janet Walker edited the Friday edition and would continue to do so until promoted to news manager in November. Jack Margeson, a classics major and the previous Friday editor, had replaced John Garrett as editor-in-chief, with the sanction of the university's senior administration. Berton was probably disappointed that the position had not gone to himself, but he later came to recognize that the mild-mannered Margeson – described in the *Ubyssey* as "the only scholar" on its staff – was exactly the kind of responsible and moderate editor the administration wanted during the national crisis.[9] Besides, the easy-going

Margeson, unlike Garrett, would give his editors a lot more leeway in putting together their editions. Berton took "all the rope" Margeson gave him.[10] The fat first issue was merely one sign of changes to come.

President Klinck's decision was no doubt the correct one, for Pierre Berton was all ego and no diplomacy. To Margaret Reid, who began to work on the student newspaper in the fall of 1940, Berton was less an editor than an experience. "He used to terrify me when I first met him out there at the 'Pub,'" she said. The Berton she encountered was a great tall fellow with a disconcerting habit of closing his eyes and swaying back and forth while she spoke. She could not always tell whether he was listening, but she recognized immediately that "he was terribly talented." Even Lionel Salt, who had been promoted from sports editor to news manager that fall, found the Tuesday editor an "overpowering physical presence."[11] Berton treated fledgling student journalists with the same disdain he felt had greeted him a year earlier. On at least one occasion, his ill-tempered criticism brought a young female reporter to tears. And when his sister, Lucy, joined the staff of the *Ubyssey* as a reporter that year, he treated her, by his own later admission, "with lordly condescension," as "just another of the several bobby-soxers who hung around the Publications Board offices . . . drinking Cokes and waiting hesitantly for an assignment."[12]

Nevertheless, most *Ubyssey* staff came to like him, as the ego and impatient outbursts were more than balanced by his outgoing personality, obvious gifts, and inexhaustible font of ideas. He had, said Salt, "a desire to learn about everything."[13] His enthusiasm, like the greasepaint of the class clown, rubbed off on everyone around him.

The war had not yet depleted the staff of the student newspaper as it had the university, thereby allowing lesser actors to step into the spotlight. Quite the contrary. Among the contributors Pierre Berton and Janet Walker edited and published were two whose literary lives would later rival Berton's own. One was an honours French major nearing graduation, but so shy that as often as not he would sneak his copy into the *Ubyssey* office without anyone spotting him. The other was a loquacious honours student majoring in mathematics, but also an aspiring young playwright and a critic of great promise. Eric Nicol and Lister Sinclair would, with Berton, make the 1940–41 edition of the *Ubyssey* more than merely memorable. The newspaper that year would become the datum, the established standard by which later student journalism at the University of British Columbia would be measured.[14]

While still at Victoria College in the autumn of 1938, Pierre had fallen under the spell of a new but ongoing *Ubyssey* feature. At first appearing under a variety of titles containing the name "Chang Suey," the column was a hilarious send-up of popular attitudes and undergraduate culture: imagine Fu Manchu in a college setting. At the outset, in 1938, "Chang Suey" had consistently sparkled; but, unsigned, it had declined after the original author surrendered it to other hands. Two years later, ever on the prowl for talent, the newly appointed Tuesday editor managed to find out that the genius behind "Chang Suey" was the ever-so-diffident Eric Nicol. Berton asked him to return with a new column, to run weekly.[15] Nicol's consent to do so is testimony to Berton's power to persuade, even at twenty.

"The Mummery" made its debut in the first issue under Berton's editorship, and Nicol signed it with the pseudonym "Jabez." No doubt he donned the cloak of anonymity to protect his privacy and maintain his personal space; but he chose the name, he said, because it translated from the Hebrew as "he will give pain."[16]

Instead, Nicol offered laughter. "Once upon a time, long, long ago," Jabez's first words ran, "before anyone had ever heard of Hitler, or Mussolini, or Lifebuoy, there lived a very plump man named Emperor Concertinus the Colossal, who commuted between Rome and Cleopatra before she gave him the old barber shop brush off in favour of one Marc Anthony, the answer to a maiden's phone number."[17] So began a lifetime of Eric Nicol laying bare the foolishness of the powerful, the foibles of the average guy, and the absurdities of everyday life. "The Mummery" could be farcical or satiric or serious, sometimes all at once. ("Mummery" is, after all, contemptuous play-acting.) But it never failed to amuse.

At his best, Jabez served a witty feast of satiric farce elevated to art by clever observations and turns of phrase worthy of the American humorist Robert Benchley, one of Nicol's heroes. Whatever the scene, outrageously exotic or maddeningly mundane, readers found themselves witness to a carnival peopled with the cockeyed timber of humanity, goofball and schlemiel alike: as Jabez might say, Damon Runyan and James Thurber in a Mixmaster. By October, followers of Jabez had met

Mrs. Gilder Spoonfedder, who had named "her four genuine daughters" Bertha, Bunty, Boop, and Benito; Mr. Merciful Honk, lustful for Miss Funga Claxon, expert at dancing La Conga; and Miss Panky Whoof, "who was observed wearing one of those new strapless gowns and a nervous expression."[18] "The Mummery" rapidly became the most eagerly anticipated item in the *Ubyssey*.

Lister Sinclair, mathematician-cum-playwright, was clever and witty in a very different way. "I met him at UBC when we were in our junior year," Berton said of him, "I was nineteen and he was eighteen, but I thought he was about eighty-five. He's the only man I know who's aged backwards."[19] The erudite Bombay-born polymath seemed wise beyond his years. He appeared to know everything about literature and music, his knowledge was encyclopedic, his memory photographic. His interests were at once eclectic and catholic. A member of the UBC Players' Club, in the fall of 1940 he had already triumphed as Mr. Bennet in a dramatized stage version of Jane Austen's *Pride and Prejudice*. At his insistence, the Iago he played in a staging of Shakespeare's *Othello* wore a moustache just like Hitler's. He starred in the club's noon-hour radio play "A Scienceman's Lover," written by Jabez.[20]

As with Nicol, Berton cornered Lister Sinclair for a *Ubyssey* column. Called "Pearl Castings," it appeared less frequently than "The Mummery," but it raised the newspaper's tone to a level not seen before in the *Ubyssey*. Where Jabez threw disdainful but amusing barbs in all directions, Sinclair cast his pearls from heights occupied earlier by Matthew Arnold's astute criticism and Bernard Shaw's barbed wit. If the biblical allusion (Matthew 7:6) of its title is anything to go by, the author of "Pearl Castings" did not expect plaudits from those he sought to elevate. A measure of the degree to which Sinclair saw his multitude of readers as swinish can be gauged from the denouement of his first casting: "There is nothing quite like the stinging denunciations of Dorothy Parker; her works are like coruscating beacons illuminating the follies of this confused, incoherent age. They are unique commentaries on the current eccentricities in man's behaviour."[21]

Berton brought other promising writers to the pages of the *Ubyssey* that term. Pat Keatley was one of them, contributing an eclectic column of personal anecdote and campus gossip called "Fruit Salad." Transformed from "Pat" to "Patrick" upon graduation, he would go on to a distinguished career as an international affairs correspondent with the *Guardian* in London. But Berton himself was the paper's mainstay and driving force. Janet Walker came to marvel at how, "in no time at all, he'd practically taken over the paper. He was doing twenty-eight stories to everybody else's one. You know, just bang, bang, bang." Lister Sinclair was not easily impressed by his peers, but the *Ubyssey*'s Tuesday editor was an exception. Many years later he recalled, "Pierre could sit down and write an article, . . . put another piece of paper in the type-writer, and go on to the next article. And do that, maybe write five or six, in an afternoon. I can't do that."[22]

By the end of 1940, the earnest Berton had written countless unsigned *Ubyssey* stories plus major bylined features. One story reminded readers of the generation of students whose march to Point Grey and presenta-tion of a petition containing fifty-six thousand names had shamed the provincial government into developing the campus on its present site; another admonished them for their poor attendance at the annual cairn ceremony commemorating the march. The goofy Berton had warned all "campus lovebirds, cuckoo-doves, lally-gaggers, sentimental smoochers, neckers, petters, lip-entwiners, and others who still have a hangover from the cupid-infested spring term" of the lurking presence of the psychology department's over-eager researchers.[23] Berton the car-toonist had peppered the *Ubyssey*'s pages with sketches of campus char-acters. Berton the Tuesday-edition editor represented the male of the species in a "Battle of the Sexes" quiz presided over by "Captain Query," Professor A.F.B. Clark. His opponent, naturally, was the editor of the Friday edition, Janet Walker. The *Ubyssey* reported the final score – 195 to 194 in favour of the men – in the Tuesday edition.[24]

Berton was now the chief announcer of the Radio Society (Janet Walker was secretary) and wrote scripts and took roles in radio plays broadcast over CJOR from the society's cramped quarters in the agricul-ture building. He created and produced a parody of the popular radio news show *The March of Time*, which used actors to dramatize the major events of the day. He called his version *The March of Slime*, and tried his best to capture the foreboding voice of the CBC announcer Westbrook Van Voorhis while lampooning goings-on at UBC and else-where. In a more serious *Varsity Time* broadcast, he told the story of the Canadian diplomat and UBC alumnus Hugh Keenleyside. In the new year he took his microphone to the Players' Club production of Shaw's *Candida*, where he described the scene behind the scenes and interviewed cast members, including Lister Sinclair.[25]

During the Christmas break, he redesigned the newspaper's layout, beginning with his own edition. The first Tuesday issue of 1941, on January 7, bore a clean, streamlined look. Its pages had been shorn of margin rules and with each issue its masthead floated from one spot to another on page 1. Now the de facto personification of the newspaper, toward the end of January he was chosen by the Publications Board as its spokesman when a student political group of considerable earnestness, Parliamentary Forum, challenged the Pub to justify the *Ubyssey's* wild activities and its expenses. He rose to the occasion, promising to "roll on, sweep on . . . to the glacial heights of victory." The debate was one of the biggest events of the year and played to a packed audience. "'I challenge any other fifteen students to equal the job now being done by the *Ubyssey* staff,' declared Pierre Berton, holding up copies of local and eastern university papers for comparison. 'This campus newspaper would be failing in its duty if it failed to criticize or report the activities of the students themselves.'" Berton carried the day: the audience rejected the Parliamentary Forum decisively. So, at least, said the *Ubyssey* report.[26]

Then, as if all this and becoming features editor of *The Totem* failed to challenge him, he started his own weekly column. He called it "Behind the News," and its purpose was delve below the surface of recent events to reveal the backstory. In fact, it allowed him to play the role of campus crusader. He urged student clubs to hold their dances on campus, and he praised the Greek-letter societies for publicizing events like the Red Cross Ball with pep rallies, in both cases to encourage "college spirit." He challenged the traditional requirement for formal wear on social occasions; the expense, he said, prevented many students from attending their own class parties. He sang to the success of Sid Poulton and his Varsity Orchestra, and chided the Phrateres women's group for saying that the campus band was not "classy" enough to play at their events. The column's life ended with an attempt to deflect the ire of a phalanx of Phrateres who in the previous week had come into the office, "waving their knitting needles angrily, and pin[ning] him verbally to the wall."[27] It may be that before the knitting needles were withdrawn, Pierre saw another side of the ever-sunny Janet Walker.

The long hours spent at the Pub in the basement of Brock Hall sometimes created a giddy atmosphere not found elsewhere on the UBC campus. Lifelong friendships developed, such as those among Janet and Pierre and Lionel Salt, Margaret Reid, Lister Sinclair, and Eric Nicol. The *Ubyssey* crowd dated one another. They went to movies en masse. They commandeered the same table at the cafeteria. The gang would go to dances at the Commodore Club, ending up devouring early morning meals in Chinatown. At restaurants they would hide their brown-bagged bottles of rye and sloe gin under the table. Or bring them to the relaxed "Pub Parties" held in the flats or apartments of those fortunate staffers with their own space. Pierre dated various young women, but at least one journalist colleague perceived an attachment that seemed slightly stronger than the others. "To spare the feelings of one of our feminine editors," wrote a *Ubyssey* columnist, "we have been forced to delete all mention of his love life."[28] The subject of the article was Pierre Berton, but the editor in question was Janet Walker.

Bonds were formed and barriers broken down in such ways. One night, Berton was reading galleys with Margaret Reid at the Jolly Roger, a café that offered supper for 50 cents. Pierre had put a nickel into the jukebox to play a big band number. Sitting on the counter, he asked her, "Do you know that song?" She did. It was "The Wood Chopper's Ball," by Woody Herman and his orchestra. "Okay, do you know this one?" he tested as he selected another disc. She recognized that one too. It was "The Fur Trapper's Ball," Herman's self-parody. Berton was impressed. At that moment, Margaret Reid recognized that he had accepted her as a friend and an equal.[29]

Forty-five years later, Reid and her husband, Lionel Salt, could still recite the lyrics of the mildly risqué "official song" Berton penned for the Pub during his year as Tuesday editor. "The Illegitimate Children of the Publications Board" began:

> John Garrett was an editor
> Drank whisky by the tub,
> He's the guy who made the Georgia
> An annex to the Pub.
> Jack Margeson's of different stock,
> Teetotalling's his boast

So while we called John Garrett "God"
Jack's called "the Holy Ghost."

Refrain:
There's a thriving kindergarten
In the depths of old Brock Hall,
They feed the kids on bottles
From the time that they are small.
They sleep on beer-soaked *Ubysseys*,
And Margeson is lord,
Of the illegitimate children
Of the Publications Board.[30]

This was the kind of inspired silliness emanating from the Pub that year that became the stuff of student legend at UBC, and it is a reminder of how psychologically distant were the students living in the ivory tower of Point Grey from the desperate goings-on in continental Europe. The columnist Allan Fotheringham was not at UBC or on its newspaper's staff until the 1950s, but the *Ubyssey* collective memory told him that back in these early war years "Pierre Berton was a terror."[31] But this was the terror of the carefree campus prankster, not the horror experienced by the persecuted and dispossessed of Europe.

Toward the end of Berton's graduating term, he was profiled in one of a series of occasional columns called "Revelations of the Writers." It began: "Sensational writer; radio announcer; fugitive from Victoria College; Tuesday's senior editor; debater; drama critic; and modern lover – that's Pierre Berton. To go still farther, the Orson Wells [*sic*] of the Pub – that's Berton. Pierre is the sort of journalist you see in Hollywood productions." It ended: "Drop into the Pub some day and see Pierre. It will be worth your time. He'll be the one standing on a table with red hair (his, not the table's) pulled over his face and doing his impersonation of an orang-utang during the mating season. One of the *Totem* editors claims it isn't an act."[32]

The caricature was not far from the mark. Above the *Ubyssey*'s masthead on March 28, the final issue of that academic year, a bold front-page headline screamed "Beast Stalks Campus." Beneath it was a photograph of the university library, and looming over the library's roof, thanks to the inspiration of a famous monster movie and a doctored photograph, was a crouching and menacing Berton – teeth clenched, hair pulled over his eyes, hands outstretched, as if to snare any campus Fay Wray who emerged from the stacks.

⧯ ⧮

Pierre Berton and Janet Walker graduated from the University of British Columbia on May 15, 1941, with freshly minted bachelor of arts degrees. That year, Pierre was closest to Virginia Galloway – sufficiently close that when Ginny got married a few years later, her mother told Laura and Lucy Berton in the receiving line that she had "hoped it would be Pierre standing there."[33]

Pierre owed the COTC a summer at training camp, but he was desperate to launch his career as a full-time newspaper reporter. Janet, too, was eager to begin a career. One weekend, she convinced her father, Andrew, to drive her to the summer home of Rita Myers, the rather intimidating editor of the social page at the *Province*, to ask for a job. She had done some volunteer work for Myers, writing copy about the many wartime weddings then taking place, but remained fearful of annoying a prospective employer by presuming to visit her home with such a request. She need not have worried. Myers was impressed with the young woman's spunk and offered her a position in the social department. For the rest of the war Janet lived in Vancouver, in boarding houses or sharing rented flats with roommates, some of whom remained lifelong friends. It amused Janet later that at the *Province* she found more ways of describing the colour blue – powder blue, sky blue, sunset blue – than she ever thought possible.[34]

Pierre's university degree was "Class II." Unlike Eric Nicol or Lister Sinclair, there was little of the scholar in him. He would have had to sit still too long for that, and he was not the contemplative type. Berton could be thoughtful when a subject seized his attention, but he was not one to brood or to engage in the kind of introspection that would allow him to explore emotional or intellectual depths, whether in himself or others. Like a water spider, he tended to skitter over the glistening surface of life, covering as much territory as possible in search of whatever the world had to offer.

That was why journalism appealed to him. A choice between spending precious time on a newspaper beat or in a lecture theatre had been no choice at all. He read voraciously but promiscuously, with no expectation that his study of the world might inform his reporting of it. His attendance during his second year at UBC remained as hit-and-miss as during the first – symptomatic of a disregard for disciplined learning that would have been unthinkable in his hero, Bruce Hutchison, had Hutchison attended a university. Yet Pierre managed to pass his courses. In fact, his overall average at graduation was 72 per cent – eight points better than the year before.[35]

Almost immediately after classes ended, Berton joined other COTC members on an obligatory two-week training camp on Vancouver Island. Because he had not yet turned twenty-one, he was not allowed to do any actual training; instead, he served as an orderly in the officers' mess, managing to spill soup on Lieutenant-Colonel Dr. Gordon Shrum, leader of the university's COTC unit and head of its engineering school. Apart from this, he claimed, the experience was not memorable. But he did form a distinct view of life in the armed services. "After seeing the army and the way it is run," he wrote to his mother from Nanaimo on May 27, "I could hardly imagine anyone joining it voluntarily or for patriotic reasons. I believe it is the worst possible thing a person could do. All sense of responsibility & individuality is lost. Besides this there is an unparalleled caste system which would be extremely bad. It's OK for 2 weeks but no longer."[36] The day Berton wrote these words, the British sank the German battleship *Bismarck*, having three days earlier lost their own ship, HMS *Hood*, and all but three of its crew of 1,418 to its guns. A month later, Germany attacked the Soviet Union, and the Nazi SS Einsatzgruppen program of mass murder began. Yet Pierre seemed to view army training as if it should be Boy Scouts for adults.

Berton joined the staff of the Vancouver *News-Herald* soon after he came back from camp, but his reputation had preceded him. A copy of the *Ubyssey* with the photo of a Kong-like Berton towering over the university library had circulated in the office, to everybody's great amusement.[37] Junior reporter he may have been, but he came back to the *News-Herald* with a whisper of notoriety. Berton felt as if he had returned to his second home. Jack Scott was there, still city editor and still writing his "Our Town" column. So too was the sportswriter Ray Gardner, the front-page editor, Barry Mather, and the editor-in-chief, Robert Elson, who gave Berton responsibility for covering religious news and for helping the social editor put together her page.

He gained valuable experience from these assignments, but they were probably more important for confirming and entrenching his views on religious and social issues in general. The contrast between the piety he heard from the pulpits of mainstream churches and the failure of those in the pews to address the poverty and desperation he witnessed on Vancouver's mean streets galled him. He found the same smug self-satisfaction in politicians, content to mouth platitudes about social inequality and social justice. "I came to realize," he later wrote, "that what the establishment really meant was that its own members did not intend to curtail their own comfortable existence in any way, to give up a single luxury in order to spread the wealth or give a boost to the wretched."[38] He was beginning to move to the left in politics and away from any connection with a religious institution.

This was in part a reaction against his father's conservative views on politics and religion, likely spurred by the fact that he lived at home, a strong-willed young man with opinions on everything, under the roof of a seasoned old man who seemed to know everything. Simply to annoy his father, Pierre announced during the summer that he was a communist – a word chosen purely to shock (like *anarchist* earlier), not to signal conviction. Frank Berton was no fool and did not rise to his son's bait.

Not that Frank or Laura saw much of their son. He worked a six-day week and more or less lived at the *News-Herald* office, either pursuing his own stories or writing headlines on the news desk. Even on his few days off he succumbed happily to the lure of the newsroom. His experience on the *Ubyssey* gave him the confidence to think he could do just about any job the *Herald* might ask of him; certainly if energy and enthusiasm could predict success, those around him witnessed a young man with promise.

Wartime was good for promotion, if a man or woman could keep out of uniform. The *News-Herald* was beginning to lose men to enlistment in the Canadian armed forces, but joining up was just about the last thing Berton had in mind for himself that summer. His mother told him she worried about his overwork, but he knew he was having the time of his life working the beat and just hanging out with his colleagues after hours.[39] He soon found himself designated night editor, with a raise from $50 a month to $85. He bought a car with Bill Grand, a photographer friend, even though he did not know how to drive.[40] Grand took the 1929 Essex to work and then parked it in the direction of Point Grey; Pierre steered it home in the wee hours of the morning. Berton behind the wheel was an experience that those who sat next to him never forgot.

The newspaper office was very much a "grace and favour" environment. A man could be an editor one day and a reporter among others the next. That the highly combustible Robert Elson was in charge at the *News-Herald* made promotions and demotions even more unpredictable. Berton had no sooner settled into his position as night editor than he was reassigned. The veteran newsman Reg Moir had just moved to the Vancouver *Province*, so Jack Scott became managing editor. Scott appointed Berton the new city editor. It was mid-July and Pierre had just turned twenty-one.

As far as he was concerned, the *News-Herald* was simply the *Ubyssey* writ large. His ideas for city news tended to run along the "Beast Stalks Campus" line and he saw almost any event as a potential news story. The angry woman who walked into the *Herald* office with a custard pie and a story about shoving it into her boss's face merited a two-column box on the city page. The intention of the reporter Les Bewley to protest the commercialization of Christmas by celebrating with only a glass of water resulted in a published photograph of Bewley, glass in hand.

Every night, Berton did battle with Barry Mather, a political left-winger who wanted to save page 1 for real news. With Jack Scott's connivance, Pierre managed to convince Mather to place at least one human interest story on the front page each morning. Then he went about finding Mather that story. At the time, Helena Gutteridge, a veteran urban reformer, member of the Co-operative Commonwealth Federation, and Vancouver's first alderwoman, was spearheading an effort to rid Vancouver of its rats, especially those that infested the city garbage dumps in east-end neighbourhoods. Covering city council, Berton wrote a story of a half-dozen paragraphs about the health risks. He made the issue his own and soon led the *News-Herald*'s campaign to save Vancouver from rats, plague, and pestilence. One photograph for which Pierre was responsible featured the bespectacled Gutteridge, looking every bit the stereotypical busybody, alongside a huge dead rat. Ray Gardner recalled that Berton "was happy as a pig in shit."[41]

Berton and others were granted even more licence when J.L. Burton Lewis of the *Province* replaced Robert Elson, who left for the United States to join the Luce newspaper empire. Where Elson was an ambitious editor always with a bee in his bonnet, Lewis (brother of Hunter Lewis, Pierre's English professor at UBC) was an eccentric fellow, "a short, wiry man with a neatly clipped moustache and a pair of pale blue eyes that popped but never seemed to blink." Seldom was he without a bottle of Canadian Club in his desk drawer. In the winter of 1941–42, when he wanted to show the *News-Herald*'s readers what winter was like on the Russian front, Lewis used a panoramic shot of snow on Vancouver's North Shore mountains.[42] Nobody twigged to the trickery.

One Sunday morning in December, Berton was having breakfast in the west-end apartment of two women from the newspaper's art department when the phone rang. The news editor, Al Williamson, summoned him to the office. The date was December 7, 1941: the Japanese had bombed Pearl Harbor. The newsroom that day was hectic, with everyone scurrying around, intent on putting out at least two extras. For the first time Pierre witnessed a newspaper at work on a breaking story of momentous consequence, serving the purpose for which newspapers existed. And for the first time, too, he recognized just how limited was his range of skills, and how marginal to the effort in the newsroom that day. Still, he was part of it, and he felt a deep sense of satisfaction at the thought. "For me, journalism had come alive," he later wrote. "I'd been involved with the real world and real news, something far more pertinent than the puffed-up threats of plague-carrying rats infesting the city dump. A real plague was raging in the world."[43]

The war had come to Vancouver. As a defence against Japanese bombs, the city was immediately blacked out. Politicians and editors urged residents to remain calm, but a day after the Japanese attack, authorities impounded more than a thousand fishing boats of Japanese Canadians and closed their Japanese-language newspapers and schools. Two days later, December 10, sudden noise from the British United Press teletype interrupted a late-night session with a bottle of rye Berton was sharing with Lewis in the quiet of the *Herald* offices. The British battleship HMS *Prince of Wales* and the cruiser *Repulse* had been lost to the Japanese in the South Pacific. The war now seemed far more immediate than it had only a week before. That night, as Lewis pounded out an editorial telling readers that the world they knew had come to an end, Pierre sat with him and two volunteer air-raid wardens from the Chamber of Commerce, polishing off whatever rye and scotch was still around. He sensed that his fledgling newspaper career would soon be overtaken by forces beyond his control.[44]

At twenty-one, Berton relished being part of the "press gang" at the Empire Café on Hastings Street, scoffing down grub chased with rye and schmoozing until three or four in the morning. He had looked forward to lazy Sundays on Jack Scott's veranda, talking newspapers. "I didn't want to become a soldier any more than I wanted to become a steam fitter or a shoe salesman," he wrote later. "I had found my niche in life and I was supremely happy. I wasn't even ambitious; if I could just stay as city editor for the rest of my career I would be more than satisfied – or so I thought."[45]

Thought, however, is seldom master of the man; he has other needs. Berton did indeed volunteer for war service in spite of the civilian job he loved, one that arguably contributed to the war effort. In this respect, he differed very little from thousands of other Canadians. By early 1942, the consensus among the boys in the office was that they would have to join up and do their bit. In January alone, a German U-boat offensive began along the American eastern seaboard, and in northern Africa Rommel led a counteroffensive against the British. Before the end of the month, the first American soldiers had arrived in Great Britain. And while Berton and his chums did not know it, SS-Obergruppenführer Reinhard Heydrich had held a conference in Wannsee to discuss and coordinate a "final solution" to the Jewish Question. Near the end of his life, reflecting on Canadians in the Second World War, Berton wrote, "English Canadians certainly wanted Canadian volunteers to join the fray, not so much for imperialistic reasons or sentimental patriotism, though these were present, but simply because *it was the thing to do*."[46]

It is difficult not to conclude that this was his own motivation for signing up more than half a century earlier.

On Thursday, February 5, 1942, twenty-five years after his father had done so, he found himself at a recruitment office. He wore 175 pounds on his six-foot-three frame and had twenty-one months of COTC training under his belt. Later, he would claim that he did not join the army; the army joined him. But at the time, conscription existed only as a possibility and in rumour was to be the subject of a national plebiscite in April. He would also write that while others rushed to enlist in the air force or navy ("anything to keep out of the army"), he did not, because his one experience of flight, on a triplane into Dawson in 1938, had been a miserable one. He was worried about being sick and the object of derision in the air or at sea. So he "opted for the army."[47] The evidence, however, suggests otherwise. His answer to question number 13 of the National Resources Mobilization Act Enrolment Form states that Pierre Francis Berton, occupation "editor," wished to join the Royal Canadian Air Force.[48]

"I knew at once that this was a turning point in my life," he wrote, "and determined to make the best of it. I tried to think of it, in Burt Lewis's term, as an adventure, but that didn't prevent a certain queasiness." His thoughts ran back to being on the bed of the truck a couple of years earlier, heading out to his first summer of work at Middle Dominion Camp.[49]

Whether it was Pierre or the recruitment officer whose mind changed is not known. But when Berton signed his attestation paper, he had joined the Canadian Army, regimental number K601753, rank private. Certainly, after his COTC experience in Nanaimo he harboured few if any romantic notions about army life. But his friends, Jack Scott and Reg Moir among them, were headed for the army. So was Burton Lewis. He may well also have had his father's army enlistment in mind. Pierre knew he was not as robust as his father had been, nor had he climbed the Chilkoot or survived a winter on the creeks. His father had joined the army when he was forty-five: could the son who had spent his first years wearing Dutch bangs and short pants measure up?

He left Vancouver for basic training in Vernon, British Columbia, early in March. His family was of course there at the train station to bid goodbye, pride and worry on the faces of his parents, their protected child now about to face life-threatening danger; Lucy's words of counsel were "to beware of strange girls." Janet Walker scurried to the platform, a little late but with a going-away present and an assurance that she would make certain his parents got home safely. This was the first of many such train station farewells for Pierre during the war, for he was often told to report for training only to have the order cancelled at the last moment. Lucy remembered the occasions well: each time there were fewer friends on the platform until eventually, when Pierre at last boarded the train for Vernon, "Janet was the only one there, other than family."[50]

If being bloodied in combat is the true test of the military life and of one's manhood, then Pierre Berton had a lousy war. Between March 1942 and March 1945, he found himself posted from one army base to another, constantly preparing for the war but never in it. His record of service reads like the work schedule of a long-haul trucker. In 1942 he was shipped from Vernon to Chilliwack, then to Nanaimo, and back to Chilliwack; in 1943, he found himself sent first to Gordon Head in Victoria and then to Currie Barracks in Calgary, where he spent the last six months of the year. By then the private had become a lieutenant.

He wrote home regularly, and his letters bore the marks of dutiful son and faithful reporter in just about equal measure. "Dear Folks" was the salutation he used in his first letter, written from Vernon at the beginning of training camp, but almost all the rest bore the greeting "Dear Mamma." That, at least, is what the Berton literary archive reflects. Of more than seventy of his letters that survived the war years, only two are addressed to his father and one to his sister. It is possible that some letters to Lucy have gone astray, but unlikely that any addressed to his father would have. Pierre's mother saw to that. These were the years, after all, when Laura Berton wrote "It's a Boy."

Training camp at Vernon lasted until late spring. "I am enjoying myself very much," he wrote, but that was only four days after he enlisted. Soon he was under the weather, complaining about the poor medical attention given to recruits. His uniform was military, but a reporter wore it. His first letter home described camp life in general: the duties he was given and the meals he ate; living quarters; the ages of his companions. "I am the only University graduate here, I believe, most of the boys being grade 8 or 2nd year high school."[51] They tended to fall into two groups, one of age twenty-one or twenty-two and another closer to twenty-five, with the latter predominating. That made him one of the younger lads in the hut. But he did not mention everything, did not mention witnessing his first two war casualties, fellow recruits – a gregarious truck driver named Harry, who came to believe that "they" were out to get him and who threw himself under the wheels of a Coca-Cola truck; and a sensitive, chess-playing youth named Wilson, who dropped his rifle one day on the parade square and began to wander around aimlessly. Neither was seen again. "We were changed by army life," he wrote on a Remembrance Day many years later.[52]

Berton's ambition was to have an active war, but on his own terms. He joined the Royal Canadian Artillery, because it was "the only unit I could think of at the time and seemed as good as any." That March he began a non-commissioned officer instructor's course. He found it tough going. Most of the other students had been in the army for more than two years, whereas he had only five weeks' experience. But he persisted. "My ultimate goal is, of course, to get into Intelligence from the Artillery and apply for a commission. . . . Then maybe I can get a Press Liaison job."[53]

Meanwhile, he kept close tabs on his corner of the newspaper world. Lucy sent him copies of the *Ubyssey*, and he read the *News-Herald* regularly. He was not impressed with the current state of the latter. "The paper has been completely rotten since I left if outward looks mean anything. However I notice a decided change for the better in the last issue which means that Scott must be at the helm. I recognize his touch."[54] This hubris was not entirely unwarranted, since Pierre had spent a good deal of time before he left the *News-Herald* plaguing editors and typesetters with suggestions about the paper's layout, and with some success. When he made a weekend visit to Vancouver near the end of March, he asked his mother to arrange a dinner party for his next weekend furlough, with Jack Scott and Ralph Daly and their wives as guests. He suggested that they be joined later in the evening by other friends from the *News-Herald* and the *Ubyssey* – among them Lionel Salt, Les Bewley, and Pat Keatley. When the party took place, he no doubt thanked Janet Walker for the "big package of chocolate cake" she had sent him earlier in the month.[55]

By this time he began to feel "cooped up . . . like a trapped animal," desperate for "some sudden and drastic change."[56] He had already transferred to the Seaforth Highlanders of Canada, figuring that if his aim was to be an instructor, he may as well be in the infantry because there, he had heard, it was easiest to advance. "So I joined the best regiment and am now a Scotchman, at least in name," he wrote. He knew the Highlanders were "a crack outfit," so concluded that they would be sent overseas first. "Besides, I like the hats they wear."[57] He spent much of his life at camp either in the classroom or on the parade square. "I thought when I finished UBC my examination days were over, but it looks like they've only started," he complained. Still, there was some satisfaction. His platoon – number 24 – won the Grand Aggregate Trophy and two other cups in inter-platoon competition. "I am enjoying the training very much," he found himself saying. "I like the bayonet fighting best."[58]

It had not always been so. At the outset of training, Berton and most of his fellow recruits lacked much enthusiasm or interest and thought of themselves as "zombies" – the derogatory term army volunteers used for conscripts.[59] After a week of training, Berton and two other recruits decided that they might just as well sign up for active service; they were the only men in the unit to do so. "And so we signed up and put up 'Canada' badges and then ran the 'gauntlet' of 75 men in the hut all yelling 'Sucker.'" Loyalties among the men lay not to the empire or to ideals. "A decade of Canadian isolationism, anti-militarism and black depression had done its work," he later reflected. "The real loyalties were to home towns, families and girl friends." Only with the advent of the platoon competition did the men begin to bond as a unit, now desperate to win. Pride replaced indifference and "perfection in close order drill became an obsession." The day Berton's unit won the gold cup and had their photograph taken together, they "swore eternal loyalty to one another." The next morning they broke up, often never to meet again.[60]

Joining the Canadian armed forces did not diminish Berton's appetite to perform and entertain at centre stage. Within days of arriving in Vernon he had helped a friend from Vancouver, a teacher who had taken a radio course, with a script. He cheerfully volunteered to participate in camp concerts, and produced and starred in new versions of his

UBC *March of Slime* radio skits. That winter and spring, he performed at concerts in Vernon, Kelowna, Penticton, and elsewhere. He combatted boredom by reading a lot, whether pocketbooks sent from home in what he called "Bundles for Berton," or books lent by acquaintances. He asked Lucy to send him his copy of *The Rubaiyat of Omar Khayyam*, along with his "little cartooning brush." He reported home that he found John Steinbeck's novel of the struggle of California migrant workers, *In Dubious Battle* (1936), "very good." He read the American novelist John P. Marquand's satire of New England gentility, *H.M. Pulham, Esquire* (1941), in which romantic love is surrendered to duty, and Phyllis Bottome's blistering anti-Nazi bestseller, *The Mortal Storm* (1938), adapted and released in June 1940 as a movie starring Margaret Sullavan, James Stewart, and Robert Young. He noted that he had eight more novels, lent by the niece of a friend, to read, but still asked his mother to send him *I Found No Peace* (1936), the autobiography of the United Press war correspondent Webb Miller.[61]

Berton was beginning to feel physically fit. His weight rose to 187 pounds, a good dozen more than ten weeks earlier. In May, he wrote home to say that he had been talking to some commandos who had just returned from overseas, and that he now hoped to train as one in Chilliwack. "They do all their training with live rounds and fire all weapons from the hip. There are 40 per cent casualties in training alone, which shows you how tough it is. But they say it is a lot better than lying around in Canada."[62] He concluded the letter by wishing his mother a happy Mother's Day and noting that he had sent her a potted plant.

One can only guess at the concern with which his parents greeted the news. Their Pierre in the army was one thing. But a commando? No correspondence from family members appears to have survived, but Laura and Frank Berton could only have been alarmed that their son should be willing to place himself in harm's way more than was absolutely necessary, and no doubt said so. A couple of weeks later, Laura received a letter from him. It began on an even enough keel, with chatty words about how he was keeping himself busy with the camp paper and a "long string of concerts." But Pierre's thoughts almost immediately spun out of control. "I am quite at [a] loss to understand why Daddy thinks I am not fitted for Commando training," he wrote. "Certainly if anyone is, I am." He pointed out that he was one of the few men in his unit who held "Category A" status – "which means perfect physical health." Both his weight and his height, he added, gave him a constitution more hardy than most other men.

The dam so carefully maintained for so long had cracked. Now it began to collapse:

> Apparently the idea back home seems to be the archaic feeling that for some inexplicable reason Little Rollo here is "different from the other boys."[63] This is the idea that has been drummed into me from early childhood – that I am weaker, need more care, can't stand up as well as the rest. It is the feeling that kept me from attending scout camps in the Yukon and from doing so many of the things that other boys were allowed to do – and consequently felt capable of doing. It is the feeling that kept me from attending movies on my own until the idea of doing anything on my own, going anywhere on my own without the support of my parents never occurred to me. Now, just as I thought I had completely rid myself of a clinging inferiority complex, I find that I am not even considered capable of standing up under three weeks of battle drill.
>
> It is not very heartening to find that one has not got even the confidence of one's own parents.

He stood firm in his intention to attend commando school and to go overseas as soon as possible. It was obvious, he said, that all Category A men would soon be shipped to Europe, and when that time came he wanted to be trained properly. "When I go I want to know the score." "Commando work," he added, was "damned interesting work and the sort of thing I would enjoy doing even though it is tough. As far as not being able to take it, that is ridiculous."[64]

The outburst ended as quickly as it had begun. The chit-chat resumed, this time about the UBC Players' Club's visit to town the previous night and backstage gossip that Lister Sinclair was about to leave for the University of Toronto. But Berton had at last confronted and given voice to a wound that had clearly festered in him since he was a child. What to Laura and Frank was simple parental concern and kindly advice had been to him the latest slight in a long history of overprotectiveness, disapproval, and lack of confidence.

Very seldom in his life would Pierre Berton loosen, even for a moment, the layers of protective armour he built around himself to keep self-doubt at bay and out of public view. This was one of those times, and it provides a rare glimpse of an inner life significantly more fragile than the persona of hearty self-confidence and *Boy's Own* bluster that impressed or put off others. However disturbed he was on this occasion, he avoided further confrontation or reflection on the matter. If his parents answered in defence of themselves, he did not respond in kind.

Of the two letters Pierre is known to have addressed specifically to his father during the war, the second one followed the outburst over commando school. A month went by, with it Father's Day, before he sat down to write the words "Dear Daddy." Gone is the question of his father's lack of confidence in him or anything else that had prompted the earlier flare-up. The armour is back in place, the emotions once again kept in check. Or so he thinks. He notes that his colonel wants to start a newspaper and that he has been elected "to do the dirty work." He asks how Lucy is making out in the job she had just taken. But then, as if he can't resist, he also asks whether she has joined a union. The contrived segue allows him to fly the radicalism of his own political colours in the face of his father's conservative beliefs. "Surely people have ceased to believe the old bogey about unionism being communistic," he writes. Lucy was no longer the subject of concern. "Anytime people want to discredit anything progressive, to serve their own ends, they label it red. Of course that doesn't work anymore."[65]

This was a volley to the flank, not to the heart. But, in the circumstances, it was still a volley, intended to protect himself against further hurt from that direction. The new posting, to Chilliwack, came through at the beginning of June, and he spent most of the summer helping set up camp at nearby Vedder Crossing. In mid-August, he took a weapons training course, but he never did become a commando.

8

MARKING TIME

—

LATER, TONGUE IN CHEEK, HE would claim that by the end of the Second World War he was "the best-trained soldier in the Canadian Army." During the war, however, nothing grated on him more than the endless delays in being shipped overseas. By September of 1942, a number of his colleagues had already left for Europe. Pierre went to Chilliwack. The posting required him to revert to the rank of private. One step forward, two steps back.

Boredom had begun to take hold even before the move. Restless as ever, he searched for something to engage his mind and channel his ambition. He contacted the father of a UBC graduate he knew. Les Barber, Chilliwack's long-time mayor, owned the *Progress*, the town newspaper. Having reported to his mother with some satisfaction that Barber was "a progressive journalist," he enjoyed swapping stories with the older newspaperman. The rapport proved comfortable enough that Pierre returned to the barracks with Barber's copy of Aldous Huxley's *Chrome Yellow*. As the first autumn winds blew across the parade grounds of the new Basic Training Centre at Vedder Crossing, Pierre read Huxley's satire of a jaded and fading postwar English aristocratic class. He already had the French cleric Arthur Dimnet's *The Art of Thinking*, number one on the *Publishers' Weekly* bestseller list for 1929, on the go.[1]

Berton had begun to take his training courses seriously, consistently scoring grades of 80 per cent or more. This put him at the top of his class.[2] Early October brought promotion to acting corporal. On December 10, a runner ordered him to report to the regimental sergeant-major on the double and he figured he was to be reprimanded or demoted for sneaking out of camp at night without a pass. Funny thing,

149

he thought: the previous night, scrambling back from town at four in the morning, had been the only time he had ever managed to tackle the obstacle course properly.

He expected to have his stripes taken away; instead, after "a queer look," the sergeant-major told him to report to the colonel, who leaned across his desk and said, "Congratulations, Mr. Berton." He had been promoted to the rank of second lieutenant, with the princely salary of $4.25 a day minus tax. "You have no idea how strange it sounds to be called 'Mister' after a year in which you'd been called everything else," he wrote. "It left me bewildered."[3]

While still in Vernon he had started a camp newspaper, the *Rookie*, with Dorwin Baird, a former *Ubyssey* editor. But with the assignment to Chilliwack he never did see its first issue. This scarcely disappointed him since the paper more or less existed in his head. He simply took the idea with him and started another, the *Torch*.[4] Like the *Rookie*, it was no bulletin board post-up; it was hand-set and printed by letterpress, not mimeographed. Still, it did not take itself too seriously. In one issue it sponsored a contest to select the "Army's Sweetheart" from among the four young hostesses who worked in the canteen. The caption to their picture went, "Who would you share your beer ration with?"[5]

It also published serious journalism, such as Berton's piece on Private Gene Llewellyn, who had served in the Spanish Civil War but was now training in camp. At times the paper was close to a one-man operation, with Berton the author of most articles, cartoons, and editorials, plus the overall design. It proved a great hit among the officers, but less so among the men: too much like a community newspaper, they said, not enough racy stuff.[6] Meanwhile, he had become a mainstay of camp concerts – for which he wrote and performed. "We put our show on for the Rotary club Thursday and Friday nights," he wrote to his mother in December, "and had an extremely good reception. Chilliwack audiences have the reputation of being very poor with applause. But this one reacted all right."[7]

A posting to Chilliwack had some advantages, one being its proximity to Vancouver and home, only 60 miles away rather than Vernon's 250. On weekends he would take the ninety-minute ride to the coast by electric tram, and seek out family and friends. At other times, Jack Scott and his wife, Grace, or Janet Walker and old university friends would travel to Chilliwack. Once, when Janet made the trip alone with food she intended to give to Pierre, hunger got the better of intent and by the time they met at the station she had consumed most of her gift.[8]

Pierre and Janet continued to maintain, even to themselves, that they were "just good friends," but others sensed something more. Not intensely romantic, the relationship had nonetheless begun to warm, for they thoroughly enjoyed each other's company. Janet's aunt Margaret appears to have played Cupid. A schoolteacher who lived in an apartment in Vancouver's west end, she often invited Janet and Pierre to dinner. "She would feed Pierre enormous steaks," Lucy recalls, "which he seldom got at home, and then, I expect, tactfully disappear."[9]

One Saturday night in Chilliwack, Pierre managed to separate Janet from the rest of the crowd and took her out on Cultus Lake in a rented canoe. There he kissed her for the first time. "What was it, I wonder," he later mused, "that prompted this first embrace? Was it the moon, dappling the waters, and the wind sighing in the frieze of conifers beyond? Was it the music of the 'Anniversary Waltz,' wafting across the lake from the roller rink? Perhaps. I think it more likely that it was the canoe itself." Lovemaking in this most Canadian of inventions required deft and subtle choreography, not sudden or spontaneous aggression.

The tactic worked on Cultus Lake that summer of '42. The careful caresses helped break down reserve, and perhaps made them more directly aware of their feelings toward each other. At that moment it was likely the woman and not the moon or the music or the canoe that drew him to her. Yet in the hourglass of memory it was the canoe and the country to which he gave credit. "A Canadian," Berton is believed to have proclaimed, "is somebody who knows how to make love in a canoe."[10] The quip perhaps hints at something more strenuous than a lingering kiss and a warm embrace, but theirs was not yet a full-blown romance. When they returned to Vancouver, their relationship had deepened but they continued to go out with others.

The legendary observation concerning the canoe first appeared in 1973, when the writer Dick Brown attributed it to Berton. Berton did nothing to dispel the notion. Janet, however, came to hold another view. She acknowledged the first kiss at Cultus Lake, and that it may have taken place in a canoe, but as far as she knew, the author of the "love in a canoe" quip was not Pierre but Ma Murray, the outspoken

British Columbia newspaperwoman people variously dubbed "the Rebel Queen of the Northwest" or "the Salty Scourge of Lillooet." Her daughter, Georgina, worked for a time at the CBC – and this, Janet thought, helped the quotation circulate.[11]

Surrounded by forest-clad mountains in the eastern Fraser Valley about fifty miles from Vancouver, Cultus Lake was a favourite destination for servicemen stationed at Chilliwack during the war. Its lures were nature's beauty, sockeye salmon, and a roller rink. On the parade ground by day, Berton often hiked the few miles to the lake by night. Not that he had been given leave to go. He was not the only soldier attracted by that roller rink, the blare of big band music, and the arm of a young woman, so army officials initiated a system of keeping tab on soldiers by issuing them with numbered disks that had to be turned in on leaving camp. "Just a short letter to let you know that I am not in the guardhouse as expected," Pierre confided to his mother in September. "I know of a little path out through the woods which I am using." One of the other lance corporals covered for him.[12]

On weekends, if he got a pass, he usually headed to Vancouver. He tried to keep tabs on his buddies, but Jack Scott of the *News-Herald* and Himie Koshevoy of the *Ubyssey*, like Berton, had enlisted. "Everybody seems to be getting called for service or is joining up," he complained. So he would settle for visiting his parents and chum around with Janet, Ginny Galloway, or Marion Macdonald. Whenever Marion visited Pierre from New Westminster, she would stay with Janet, sharing the single bed in her boarding house room on 5th Avenue, in Point Grey.[13]

Generally, however, Pierre kept himself very busy at Chilliwack: parade-ground drill; instructors' courses; work on the *Torch*; variety show preparation and performance; evenings at the roller rink. His mid-December letter consisted mainly of an announcement and a complaint. The announcement was that he would not be home for Christmas; the complaint, that he had no ribbon for his typewriter and could not "think with a pencil." Not much else than filial piety would make him send handwritten notes, but he did so. He apologized for his "scrawl," and explained that he found it "impossible . . . to write any way and extremely painful to write longhand at all."[14]

Berton's recalcitrant typewriter was a Hermes Baby, and it added a full eight pounds to his already heavy kit. He hated it. The keys jammed, the space bar jumped, the upper-case keys misaligned. Yet he carried it everywhere. Problems with the Baby pepper his correspondence home. "Will write again when typewriter is fixed," he later wrote his mother. By then, he was helping edit her Yukon memoirs and, as if to discipline his Hermes as he would an unruly pooch, he began to write again for the *News-Herald*. The army would have frowned on this, so he did so under the pseudonym "Joe Fraser."[15]

Mr. Fraser proved to be a valuable friend. The *News-Herald* paid $5 – about a cent a word – for each of the short pieces. "They sent me a check for $20 last week which is a great help," he wrote home in April. "I shall continue to supply them as I am able. Please say nothing whatever about it to anybody."[16] The extra cash came in handy. Unexpected costs were attached to rank, such as increased laundry bills and more rounds at the mess. "Being an officer seems to cost as much as being a Lt-Governor," he complained.[17] But in March he had sent money to his mother for her birthday, insisting she "spend it all at once and on yourself," and in April he enclosed $2 to buy his friend Marion a corsage of spring flowers.[18]

By then he was writing home no longer from a bell tent at Vedder Crossing but from officers' quarters at Gordon Head on the outskirts of Victoria. He had made enough of a mark on Chilliwack that the town's newspaper ran an article headlined "Lieut. Berton Leaves Camp," noting that he had "founded and directed the camp's bi-weekly newspaper, Torch, and also presented a 'March of Slime' broadcast at last year's Rotary show."[19] Only the Strait of Georgia now separated him from friends and family. The move was welcome because it lessened his unease at becoming an officer.

In Vernon and Chilliwack, as in the *News-Herald* newsroom, he took great pleasure in being one of the boys, a member of the crew, their sense of camaraderie fuelled by having officers and editors to complain about. The Yukon upbringing, the straitened family circumstances of his teenage years, the gravitation toward the left in opposition to his father's innate conservatism – all of these led to his identification with the ordinary joes around him. But once he became an officer, there were uncomfortable moments. He could not get over the difference in the conditions and treatment of officers and ordinary ranks. In his last hours as a corporal, he had awoken in a crowded hut on an iron cot

with two blankets and had eaten in a cafeteria; that night, as a lieutenant, he slept in a bed with sheets, had an aide to shine his boots and
polish his brass, and dined well at a linen-covered table in the officers'
mess. His colonel instructed him explicitly not to associate with the
men who had been his friends the previous day. This riled him, for he
knew from well-informed camp talk that Private Jack Arding, the camp
barber, had scored much higher on the army intelligence tests than had
the colonel. On the night of his promotion, Berton went to the movies
with Arding and some chums anyway, but everything had changed.
Men who in the morning had been his buddies suddenly became deferential; superior officers became his evening companions. The perks of
the officer class were his to enjoy, but he was uneasy with privilege. He
felt like a renegade and a fraud. "I got over it, of course," he later
recalled. "Indeed, I was surprised to discover how really easy it was to
be an officer." Even so, this experience attuned him to the harsh realities and costs of social class in a way that no university reading of *Das
Kapital* would have done.[20]

On July 10, Canadian soldiers landed in Sicily, part of the largest sea
invasion in history. The Italian campaign had begun, and among its
troops was a scrub-faced kid named Farley Mowat. Pierre Berton had
shipped out to Alberta a month or so earlier for yet more training. Over
the next few months, while Mowat and the Seaforth Highlanders
encountered some of the fiercest combat of the Second World War,
Berton, chafing for action, found himself at the Calgary home of Lord
Strathcona's Horse. He was impressed by the luxury of the officers' mess
at the Currie Barracks: it was "like some huge residential hotel, with its
magnificent drawing rooms, sumptuous bar, huge dining room, stuffed
mooseheads, long glass covered verandah and huge billiard room, etc."
Mess fees, he reported home, were only 30 cents a day.[21]

Not that he spent much time in the mess, for each night his unit hunkered down in tents several miles outside Calgary, between "desolate
foothills" next to the Bow River. Training was intense. "There is no
fooling around here." All exercises were done with live ammunition and
real explosives. It was stiff "but quite exciting" – the last training, he
wrote, before seeing action. "The chances are that we will be sent straight
to headquarters which has been moved from England to Africa."

It did not happen. For the next six months, the Alberta foothills, not the dunes of the Sahara, were the theatres he saw. He went on a fifty-three-mile map trek (through "wild uninhabited prairie"). He practised amphibious assault landings on the Bow River (his boat sank halfway across). He read and offered criticism of something his mother had written ("perhaps a little too wordy and gee-whizzy in spots"). He was chosen to organize and emcee the entertainment at the mess dinner ("some said the best that had been put on here"). At midsummer, he graduated as a first lieutenant and was chosen as platoon commander for the graduation ceremony.[22] By autumn the officers' mess was alive with men from Pacific Command battalions waiting to be drafted overseas, Berton among them. He was optimistic that he would be among the first to go, since his commission dated to the previous December and he was therefore near top of the list.

In late August he went to hear the Co-operative Commonwealth Federation leader M.J. Coldwell and did not doubt that the party would win the next federal election. And he had been heartened, too, by a letter from Jack Scott in Ottawa, saying that he expected to be in active service soon. He had received a first-class grade in yet another course (for which he thanked his mother for her "early child training with its no-pork policy etc."). But he seemed no closer to seeing action. Politics was the problem. In April 1942, a national plebiscite on whether conscription of troops should take place showed 70 per cent support from English Canada and 80 per cent opposition from Quebecers. Prime Minister W.L. Mackenzie King's hesitant policy, captured by his masterpiece of ambiguous phrasing "conscription if necessary but not necessarily conscription," sent as few troops overseas as possible. Many of Canada's soldiers continued to train at home.

A fall draft was cancelled in both September and October, and there was not much to do except work on the Victory Loan campaign. Berton put on a half-hour radio broadcast from a regimental dance at Halloween, complete with "impromptu interviews and Victory Loan plugs," but for Berton, military life consisted mainly of taking one more course – this time on rifles. "The possibilities of getting overseas," the dejected first lieutenant wrote one Friday in December, "seem to be fading day by day."[23]

He kept the gloom away by offering to read his mother's manuscript on her early days in the Klondike, now finished and in the hands of a stenographer, and by occupying himself with non-army activities. In Calgary, he saw Mart Kenney and his band give one of their weekly radio broadcasts and attended a "very entertaining" vaudeville show. He felt satisfied after mastering the "particularly effective style" of the American cartoonist Lawrence Lariar, on display in *Best Cartoons of the Year*. The collection was a gift from his mother the previous Christmas. He featured in a number of local radio programs, including an amateur show and a quiz show, and he took yet another course – this time on rifle coaching.[24]

Just after the new year, he was sent for instruction on health and sanitation, but at least this course would take him to Toronto, the provincial capital of childhood memory, and with a new friend, Harry Filion. The pair had met at Gordon Head early one morning while shaving, when the barrel-chested recruit had suddenly looked up from across the wash bench and said to Berton, "I'm getting married on Saturday. Do you think I should?" Berton's response went unrecorded, but the question marked the start of one of the great friendships of his life. Harry Xavier Filion's conversation turned from his fiancée, Veryl, to the *New Yorker*, and soon they found they had a great deal in common: an appetite for good books and almost any kind of food, some experience in journalism, an irreverent love of life, a fascination with the foibles of humanity, and "an abiding belief in the healing properties of rye whiskey." Pierre attended Filion's wedding but went alone.[25]

In early January 1944, the pair shared a room with two other servicemen at the Royal York Hotel, ready to paint Toronto red. "I must say I am pretty disappointed in this town," he wrote from the hotel room on his second weekend in the city. "We walked up Yonge to Bloor [last] Sunday and if Yonge is the main street it is a pretty shoddy showcase. It is composed of filthy pink stores and fish and chip shops. The town itself, streets and buildings are very dirty. There are a few nice shops on Bloor but nothing to compare to Granville Street. There are few smart stores. The people here look either very wealthy or very poor. The men all dress the same in black coats and hard hats giving them a drab and melancholy appearance. The women do not know how to wear clothes and show little imagination." The luxurious Royal York on Front Street had a special rate for servicemen, and with four men to a room it proved the cheapest place to stay. But it was the city, not the room, that disappointed. "Toronto on a Sunday is worse than Victoria," he wrote. "Nothing is open. It seems little changed from 1930."[26]

Camp Borden north of Toronto was another story. Originally set up in 1916 on twenty-seven acres of tree stumps and drifting sand near the town of Fergus, Ontario, about fifty miles northwest of Toronto, it was headquarters to the Commonwealth Air Training Plan, a scheme inspired by Prime Minister King's faith in "the power of the airplane in determining ultimate victory" in war. It was an inspired vision, for it trained thousands of Allied airmen over the course of the Second World War and became what the historian Jack Granatstein later declared Canada's most important military contribution to the war effort.[27] When Berton reported for duty, he found himself at a base with a population he estimated at twenty-five to thirty thousand people. It was "the size of a large town," he wrote his mother, with three good-sized movie theatres, a bowling alley, an indoor swimming pool, and other amenities.

When the health and sanitation course was done, he was assigned as an instructor in advanced training, involving matters of leadership, intelligence work, tactics, and logistics. For two months he was posted to Brockville, Ontario, to take a refresher course. It was dull, and seemed intended as much to keep idle troops occupied as to train them, but it did give Pierre a chance to visit his uncle Phil, who was also in the army. Pierre observed that Phil looked worn and thin and was "strongly CCF" in his political leanings. Any new posting served as grist for Berton's mill, and he used his time in Toronto to write a series of amusing articles called "Weekend Leaves in Toronto"[28] with Phil Calder, soon to become a CBC news correspondent in Europe. One article he wrote for the camp newspaper, the *Brockville Blitz*, called "The Long Road Back," was bought outright by the magazine section of the *Montreal Standard*. It brought him a cheque for $30.[29]

His impatience to be overseas was a constant itch. Back at Calgary's Currie Barracks that April, he complained about the weight he had gained in Brockville (he was now at 196 pounds) and found nothing much to report home about. Harry Filion had gone overseas. All the members of his officers' class, he claimed, exaggerating perhaps only slightly, had "married Calgary girls and settled down to family life." And then, as he wrote those words to his mother, came a telling if unintentional segue, "How thoughtful of Janet to send you the Mothers Day card," followed by a quickstep away from the implication, to a mention of Ann, the wife of his friend Bill Grand. "Must also look up Grace Scott and Veryl Filion. That makes three service wives I am supposed to see and presumably console."[30]

Berton spent the summer and fall of the Allied Normandy invasion safe in Canada, still instructing, and as restless as ever. He began night training. He applied to take a five-week battle course in Vernon and two months' instruction on security at the Royal Military College in Kingston. He told his mother that on an upcoming forty-eight-hour leave he would travel to Edmonton and try to hitch a plane ride north. He forgot his parents' wedding anniversary. Life had become an endless holding pattern.

In July he was bivouacked in a grubby camp twenty-five miles outside Calgary when word arrived that he had been ordered to the Royal Military College for military intelligence training. It was the break he had longed for. If he did well in these classes he would qualify as an intelligence officer, one step closer to the work of a journalist. Founded in 1874 by an act of the fledgling Canadian parliament and located at Fort Frederick, a small peninsula on the eastern fringe of Kingston, RMC was the heart of military training in the country. Closed to cadets a year earlier, in 1943 it was populated almost entirely by officers, either in training or providing instruction. By mid-month Pierre was firmly established in his studies. "It is a stiff course," he wrote, "all work and no play and we study every night until midnight or later." The place was a running contradiction, hallowed by tradition yet run by full colonels who looked "like boys of 26." Most of the majors, he noted, were younger than him; his twenty-fourth birthday had been marked by a card and a box of chocolates from Janet, with whom he kept in touch. "He used to write great letters," Janet said.[31]

Throughout that summer, word filtered through the ranks about the heavy casualties Canadian troops were taking in Normandy and Italy.

Berton wrote home that the Seaforth Highlanders had lost "every one of their officers" crossing the Liri River in central Italy. Perhaps the grim reality of war finally hit home, because for the first time in his life he became a dedicated student, working sometimes as late as four in the morning. He stood near the top of his class, helped by his talent for drawing maps and field sketches and by his speed at the typewriter. More than a few hints at his desperate need to serve overseas punctuate his letters in these months. In August he wrote, "There seems to be a pretty strong feeling here that we won't have time to get over to Europe and will probably be in the Pacific. Indications are that the European war is about washed up."[32]

His intelligence training at RMC ended in mid-September 1944. He felt exhausted but topped his class and received the only "Distinguished" grade.[33] Expecting to report back to Calgary, he took some time to visit his aunt Maud in Ottawa. Now, with the authoritative bearing of the commissioned officer he was, he found himself designated as adjudicator of a heated family squabble over just where on the eastern seaboard the original Berton had landed. Having no idea of the answer, he resolved the dispute by proclaiming that "the original record had been swallowed up by a quirk of history and that the hallowed spot had never been definitely established."[34]

Women especially liked his company, and he enjoyed theirs. No sooner had he cancelled plans to go to New York to meet Ginny because of a polio scare than a woman named Deane in Kitchener wrote to invite him to a graduation dance. He said he would go, but then received a letter from a girl in Regina asking him to spend his leave in that city. He was still considering this when Ginny reached him to say she was now in Montreal. "This necessitated me wiring Deane that I couldn't make it and tearing up a tentative reply to the girl in Regina. By now," he conceded to his mother, "I was beginning to see some truth in your remark about a girl in every port." Meanwhile, a package arrived from Janet. It contained clippings of the *News-Herald* columns written by "Joe Fraser."[35]

He chose to visit Ginny in Montreal and was struck by how steeped the city was in religion. "Every four steps you bump into a monk or an abbot or a nun praying or telling beads or merely mumbling to themselves." Montreal reinforced his distrust of religion and his disgust at inequality. "You forget for a moment you are in Canada," he wrote. "A little depressing to see so much splendour and richness side by side with the filth and squalor of the surrounding tenements." The only church he liked was the one overlooking the St. Lawrence River where the sailors prayed before sailing.[36] Still, he left Montreal in good spirits. Ginny had presented him with a gift, Somerset Maugham's *The Razor's Edge* – "an excellent book, quite serious, though Maugham's restrained bystander style prevented it from becoming as warm or intense as I thought it well might be."[37]

His return to Calgary came accompanied with a small measure of renown. News of his stellar performance at RMC had already reached the men. He found the congratulations "more or less gratifying," but revelled in the cab driver who had told him about a column he had read in a Vancouver paper by one Joe Fraser, a piece that had "attracted considerable favorable comment. 'Did you read it?' he asked me. 'Read it,' I answered. 'Hell, I wrote it.'"[38]

By Halloween he was back at RMC, now acting captain and on staff, with a room to himself in Fort Frederick, the only bachelor in the former cadet residence. He considered returning to the infantry in order to get overseas, but this would have meant losing rank and he wanted to be there as an intelligence officer. Meanwhile, he was receiving a major's pay. All this was "very satisfying." But the work involved more courses – on the German and Japanese armies and their tactics and weapons, security intelligence, air liaison photo interpretation, and more. This time, however, he was teaching them – organizing information and preparing lectures when not writing Joe Fraser's column for the *News-Herald*, keeping tabs on the whereabouts of his old friends from Vancouver, reading *Crime and Punishment*, or sending letters home detailing his latest weekend in Toronto and commenting on politics.

In November Berton shared his thoughts on King's shocking dismissal of Defence Minister J.L. Ralston in the middle of a cabinet meeting on October 31. The minister's insistence on increasing troop strength through conscription, Berton said, had instantly made the previously unpopular politician "suddenly akin to a tin god." Berton's fellow officers had "even cheered him in a movie the other night." On the "reinforcement issue" he sided entirely with Ralston. Unreleased documents would later reveal that the majority of the King cabinet believed Canada had sufficient troop strength to carry its army to victory, but in Berton's mind there was "no doubt at all" that the situation was in fact desperate. "Men whom I trained in Currie went overseas after four months, spent a week in England and went right into battle. This is, of course, outrageous because it is unnecessary. Infantry casualties have been terrific and they are combing the other services for reinforcements. I'm afraid politics has sunk to a new low."[39]

Perhaps it had, but politics certainly fascinated Berton and he did not shrink from expressing strong opinions on a range of issues. He cheered at the victory of the Democrat Franklin Roosevelt over the Republican Thomas Dewey in the American presidential election: "The results . . . were most gratifying, I thought. I could never imagine little Dewey at a peace table." He was harsh on the British Conservative prime minister: "I should rather think that Churchill's infamous dealings with the semi-Fascist groups in Greece, Belgium and Italy would pretty well wash him up before long. He is, I consider, an extremely dangerous man to have around at this time and as [Harold] Laski put it 'a gallant, romantic but outmoded 18th century imperialist' or words to that effect." The outlook was bleak. "What a disillusionment our dealings with the so-called 'liberated' peoples has turned out to be. It will have a long range disastrous effect on England which is already rapidly sinking in the diplomatic sphere even as Russia is rising. The world is rapidly turning socialist and only the Churchills and the U.S. seem to be oblivious about it."[40] The long hours poring over intelligence files on matters of strategy had begun to serve him well. His native intelligence had gained an analytical edge.

Berton's critical antennae pointed at the same time in the direction of literature and the arts. He had enjoyed *Crime and Punishment*. He was pleased that Bruce Hutchison's novel *The Hollow Men* had won acclaim and that the war correspondent Matthew Halton's book *Ten Years to Alamein* was a sold-out success. His letters home often asked for books, but only if they were worth keeping. The popular historian Will Durant's *Caesar and Christ*, though expensive, was one Pierre wanted. But not the work of the bestselling novelist Lloyd C. Douglas. "He nauseates me and never seems able to get out of the pulpit. His Magnificent Obsession gave the impression that he was trying to camouflage religion under a new guise. If that was his purpose he did it rather badly."

His mail must at times have resembled the stuff of a lending library. Books would arrive, books would leave. The latter included Frederick Bodmer's *The Loom of Language* (sent to his father as a birthday present) and Ginny's gift, *The Razor's Edge*. He enjoyed its story of a man's search for enlightenment. He also passed along Maugham's *The Moon and Sixpence*, based on the life of Paul Gauguin; some Homer; and *Van Loon's Geography: The Story of the World We Live In* ("which you may find good reading"). "Yes, The Well of Loneliness is quite a well known book," he responded when Laura mentioned Radclyffe Hall's notorious 1928 novel in a letter. "I didn't know it was still banned in Canada. . . . There are quite a few copies around though I've never gotton [*sic*] round to reading it. Deals with homosexualism."[41]

He pronounced the stage adaptation of Daphne du Maurier's best-selling novel *Rebecca*, playing in Toronto and starring Diana Barrymore and her husband Bramwell Fisher, to have been "very well done . . . and most enjoyable." The production had managed to sustain suspense even though all the action took place on one set. *Errand to Bernice*, also playing in Toronto and starring Gertrude Lawrence, "stunk to high heaven. An obscure and improbable plot and a wooden male supporting cast of two. Lawrence of course, was extremely good, and struggled nobly with a very poor vehicle."[42]

For most of 1944, Berton kept a commonplace book to help ward away boredom, the only time he ever did so. Its entries reveal Berton's quirky mind at play. On one page we find these lines: "Christ is the head of this house / The unseen guest at every meal / the silent listener at every conversation." Then the following note: "Sign on living room wall of bootlegger's place, Brockville, Ont." On another page, he copied down a list of telegrams sent to the company commander by private soldiers who had overstayed or intended to overstay their leave: "WANT 3 DAYS TO BEAT HELL OUT OF A MAN WHO PUT MY SISTER IN A FAMILY WAY AND WOULDN'T MARRY HER." Each request had been granted. Favourite quotations peppered the notebook, as if from a well-schooled vaudevillian: "We must not, like monks and old women, invoke the finger of God every time the cat jumps." "In the eyes of all the women I have loved I have remained invariably a little child. This accounts for my lack of success with women." "Democracy is free speech plus groceries." These one-liners from Anatole France, Stendhal, and the

American politician Maury Maverick, respectively, were noted and preserved like the best material of stand-up comics.[43]

By January 1945, no kind of diversion – political or cultural – any longer satisfied him. He needed to get overseas. Everything else, he said, was just "marking time."[44] In December, Jack Scott had written from Belgium, on his way to Paris. Harry Filion had done so from a field hospital where he was recovering from a machine-gun bullet in the right forearm. Pierre described Harry's story with *Boy's Own* relish: "His platoon was caught in a German counter attack in the Antwerp sector and he lost 12 men immediately. The positions were overrun and he still doesn't know how he got out alive. A couple of grenades blew up in his face but only stunned him. Later on the bullet got him. He also described killing his first German. The Jerry was walking along a dyke right into his arms."[45]

January 7: "I failed to get on the 1st draft which went out last night."

January 23: "If they don't hurry up the Russians will be in Berlin."

Every day now was agony, for it was becoming clear that the war would soon end. There was little for him to do, he said, except eat and help with the entertainment for mess night – teaming up with two girls, for example, to do a song-and-dance sketch. The song was "Don't Fence Me In"; he was part of the horse. He read John Gunther's *Inside Asia* and started Edgar Snow's *People on Our Side* and bought a chess book and – and then, in March, came the call.

Berton reached Halifax, ready to ship overseas, after a few days in northwestern Nova Scotia at Debert, a transit camp about twelve miles from Truro. "I cannot say that I'm deeply impressed by this bleak, barren country," he wrote. "Why anyone would live here by choice I do not know. The houses are all the same but rather pretty in a stereotyped way."[46] Six days later he left Halifax aboard the *Aquitania*, a First World War troop carrier saved from the scrapyard by the start of the second. Pierre shared a cabin with two other officers and slept on the floor. Just over a week later he reported from Britain. The trip over had been smooth and he had not been seasick. "England is beautiful and the weather magnificent. . . . How neat it all is after the vast unruly spaces of Canada." He had earned the nickname "Bugs Bunny" from the boys on board because his moustache bore so much wax that its drawn points made him look like a cartoon rabbit.[47]

From Liverpool he headed to Sussex and the Canadian Infantry Training Centre near Petworth, the landed estate of Baron Leconfield. It was a place of strange contrasts. Deer roamed grounds that hosted miniature Greek temples, yet the once immaculate lawns had been all but destroyed by army boots and slit trenches. He had read a fair amount on the trip over: *Ariel*, André Maurois's study of Shelley, a little book in the orange and white cover that distinguished it as one of the first Penguin paperbacks (1935); *The Young Joseph*, a Thomas Mann novel of 1934; and eleven hundred pages of *Jean Christophe*, a multi-volume novel sequence about the attempt of a musician (based in part on Beethoven) to live up to his ideals, observing and criticizing modern civilization in the process, by the Nobel laureate man of letters and musicologist Romain Rolland.

His setting was different but not his situation. He was put in charge of training infantry platoons of between twenty-five and forty men, offering instruction identical to what he had taught three years earlier as a lance corporal. None of his pupils had any advanced military train-ing: it was "a case of starting from scratch."[48] Still, he had made tele-phone contact with Jack Scott, who was with the Canadian army paper, the *Maple Leaf*, and the two made plans to get together in London at the Canadian Legion Officers' Club. He had hoarded two mickeys of Canadian rye for the occasion.

Pierre Berton's first experience of London, on the weekend of April 7–8, 1945, was not unlike that of most well-read, middle-class tourists. It overwhelmed him. From the moment he stepped off the train at Waterloo Station, its every edifice and intersection seemed to hold his-torical, literary, and cultural resonance, from Dick Whittington to Charles Dickens. Its architecture, classical and Romanesque, gothic and romantic, brought his reading of Hendrik Van Loon's book *The Arts* vividly to life. Like so many others, he searched out London Bridge and mistook Tower Bridge for it. The first sight of Westminster Abbey hit him "with the force of an electric shock." During his entire ramble up Whitehall and along Fleet Street his stomach churned with excitement.

"Every building seemed to leap from a picture postcard or from the pages of an illustrated book."[49] But Jack Scott and those two bottles of rye remained foremost in his mind.

The two met, as agreed, at the Canadian Legion Officers' Club and repaired to the room Pierre had taken. While Scott waited, Berton went to the front desk for glasses, ginger ale, and ice. He was greeted by a tall, dark, and pretty woman who gave her name as Frances, and after a little banter he invited her to join them. When her shift ended she did. The three finished most of the rye, then went out to dinner, followed by a pub crawl. At closing time, Scott returned to his flat and Pierre suggested to Frances that he accompany her home. She demurred, saying that she lived in the country and that there would not be a train back. Then, after a little hesitation, she said that a friend getting married that very day had a room in the Russell Hotel in Bloomsbury and that since he would not likely require it, she could stay there. "Would you see me to the door?"[50]

As they approached the hotel, she suggested that Berton, in his lieutenant's uniform, ask for the room key of a Captain Harding. The room clerk handed it over, no questions asked. Outside the room, Frances suggested that they use the rye in Berton's back pocket as a nightcap; inside, she said, "I don't really want your rye, I want you." Pierre left the hotel around noon the next day, April 8, still not knowing Frances's last name.

Berton had other encounters that spring and summer. The dangerous times encouraged them. Psychological defence mechanisms protected servicemen from believing that they would be the ones killed in action; yet each knew that it could happen. Hence the wild living, the sense of abandon, the careless and at times callous behaviour. Berton well knew that officers commanding infantry platoons had the highest casualty rate in the army. "As for sex," he later wrote of those days, "everybody sought it."[51]

One weekend evening at a carnival in Chichester, Pierre met a young woman. She was "plain and rangy and worked in a shop," but they went on a few rides and then for drinks in a pub. Afterwards they wandered into a park near the town square and settled onto the grass. Their coupling was interrupted by the town clock striking midnight. Near panic at the prospect of missing the last ride back to Petworth (he was to be the orderly officer the next day) and fearing demotion or court martial, he began looking for any sign of a military lorry. He promised to contact the girl again, but she countered with shouts of "It's cruel, it's cruel." The next day, when he phoned to apologize, she insisted on coming to Petworth despite his protests. They failed to find a room to rent, so once again settled for a grope in the great outdoors – this time, in a copse of trees outside town. Later, Berton remembered mainly the cold and the damp and the sound of a cuckoo.

The brief fling ended badly. The girl asked him to take her to Canada and he said he could not. "I felt a chill and then a rush of compassion, mingled with guilt," he wrote. "There she was, a prisoner of her class, her only route of escape through one or other of the soldiers from overseas – Canadians, Australians, Yanks – who had invaded her island and who represented a freedom and, presumably, riches she could never know in England. In that moment I felt for her more strongly than I had in those earlier hours of transport. But I did not see her again."[52]

That Sunday he wrote home, noting that he had been in London the weekend before and had spent "most of the time" with Jack Scott. (The rest of it, of course, had been spent with Frances, but that was a subject Berton was not prepared to broach.) Scott's hair was turning white after six months on the continent, "up and down the line." His roughest time had been at Antwerp, where he had been "badly mortared" but managed to escape injury. On his return to London, Scott concentrated on writing scripts for radio shows. Pierre's own activities consisted mainly of sightseeing: Number 10 Downing Street, he said, "looked like any other damn doorstep"; still, he had found "some good Chinese in Soho."[53]

The news that month from the theatres of war was good. In the Pacific, Americans had landed on the Japanese island of Okinawa and sunk the battleship *Yamato*, while in western Europe the Allies had begun to liberate prisoners from German death camps. It rankled Pierre that the war was winding down and he had not done anything but train and instruct. Men with whom he had paraded in Canada were being killed in battle, yet he was still studying the makeup of the German army. He expected to be sent to one of the regiments in western Europe before returning home, for the general opinion was that there would be a lot of "mopping up" to do over the next six months.

The notion may have occurred to him then that he had some mopping up of his own to do on a closer front. The train of thought in one letter goes from reconstruction in Europe to the superiority of British newspapers over Canadian ones, to a set of decidedly undomestic images: "One English woman has already proposed and asked me to take her back to Canada (I've only been out with two). . . . Girls here seem desperate for some kind of security – preferably in a country of opportunity and riches." Did he feel better or worse when these words hinted at, yet cloaked, his deeds? He returned to safe ground. People expected "V-Day" to happen any day now, and the whole nation was readying itself. "I think most people here badly want to celebrate something and V-Day is being designed to blow off steam which has been pent up for some time. Papers are full of preparations. A rather hollow victory in the opinion of many but general opinion [is] that some sort of whoopee is in order. I badly need socks."[54]

In the third week of April, Canadian military headquarters summoned Berton to London for an interview on possible intelligence work. Had he spoken German he might have been sent to the Continent right away, or so he thought. Instead, he found himself en route to the British military training centre at Aldershot in Surrey, thirty-five miles southeast of London. There he studied what he already knew. The course, he soon discovered, was "badly planned and badly taught," but he learned one important lesson he would draw upon in later years: that "the army could never rid itself of the belief that anything done in Britain was superior to anything done in Canada."[55] Even in 1945, in his mid-twenties, he resented the Canadian inferiority complex.

Training as an officer had reinforced Berton's inclination to assume command of just about any subject and not to equivocate about it. Ambivalence found little place in Berton's personality. His letters home in the spring and summer of 1945 reverberate with stark observation and judgment. "Everyone here seems to draw a sharp line between Churchill's war and home leadership and, strangely, enough, George VI is NOT popular although the Queen is. Labour stands to gain strongly . . . in the next election." This on April 23, and on May 16: "Despite your remarks about the 'glorious victory' I must persist in regarding it as rather hollow. It was crushing, but its very devastation will make it extremely costly to the following generation for, make no mistake, it is we, as much as the Germans, who will, in the long run, have to pay for every ruined building, every smashed industry, every damaged city. For they are as important to us as to the other side."

Berton had formed especially strong views on the winding down of the war, the prospect for peace, and the likely role of an international organization then being formed, the United Nations:

> The present security council is not one whit better nor more effective than the poor doddering old League. As long as the present veto system remains in force any single member of the big five can spike any attempt of the great powers to stop war. Nay, the Security Council can under this system, quite legally look the other way without fear of the recrimination that came to Britain and France when they looked the other way, somewhat illegally, during the Ethiopian episode. The present land grab . . . bodes very ill for peaceful settlement of land disputes, the refusal of Britain to abandon her colonies to a central authority coupled with the expressed desire of US and Russia to found colonial Pacific empires, and the shameful admittance of Fascist Argentina into the council are all most disturbing, as is Russia's blunt attitude . . . and our own inexcusable coddling of Nazi war criminals from Goering and Donitz down.[56]

By "our own," he meant the victorious Allies.

Russian and American troops had blasted their way into Berlin, defended ferociously but largely destroyed. On April 30, the day Hitler committed suicide in his bunker just south of the city's Brandenburg Gate, Berton reported home that, along with many others in Britain, he had seen newsreel photographs of Nazi atrocities.[57] A week earlier he had noted that people were "horrified by the latest atrocity stories" and that the newspapers had printed "some shocking pictures." Now he had seen them for himself – frightening pictures taken at Buchenwald. "People are very angry about the food rations to German prisoners which far exceeds the civilian ration. . . . A discussion is still raging as to whether VE day should or should not be celebrated." England was bitterly cold, with few fires because of the fuel shortage. The only warm place, he said, was in a movie house or in a bar "heated by human bodies."[58]

VE Day came on May 8, a Tuesday. London was nominally out of bounds for Canadian servicemen, but few were about to follow that order. Thousands of people in Trafalgar Square and Parliament Square had heard Prime Minister Winston Churchill broadcast the official end of the war with Germany from 10 Downing Street. An informal victory parade accompanied Churchill when he made his way to Whitehall. (The formal parade would be held two days later.) People of all ages gathered in the tens of thousands at Buckingham Palace to cheer the royal family. Red-white-and-blue bunting was everywhere. Late into the night, swirling celebratory bonfires lit the sky over parks and street corners everywhere.

The crowds were the most dense he had ever seen, packing central London and extending well into the suburbs. The cheering kept up for more than twenty-four hours. When he travelled back to Aldershot in the early evening, he listened to the sounds of merrymaking the entire way; "there seemed to be a mammoth bonfire every quarter mile or so." All of this he recounted with a reporter's eye in a letter home the next day, adding that if a British movie called *The Way Ahead*, starring David Niven, came to town, the family should not fail to see it. "It is the best military film I've yet seen. You will thoroughly enjoy it and it will give you a completely accurate idea of exactly what I do in the army."[59]

But how to mention Frances? To his mother she existed only as a parenthetical allusion in his letter of April 15. Yet he had sought her out on VE Day at the Canadian Legion Officers' Club, under circumstances he would never forget. He had made his way to the club through the mad London crowds with a friend, Wayne Ems. He found her serving food. In his later account of the episode, Frances looks at him coolly and hesitates before agreeing to go to a pub to celebrate the victory. And when they settle down for a drink, she gives him "a strange look." Berton invoked the scene forty years later. The dialogue is his:

"I want you to go over to the bar and bring back two very large Scotches," she said. He soon returned, drinks in hand.

"Drink it up. Drink it all."

"What's up?" Berton cupped his ear.

"Well, this is the first time I've ever had to tell a man he's about to become a father." The words, he later recalled, "hit me like a blow to the solar plexus. I couldn't even gulp."

"Look," Frances said. "It's not your concern, is it? You didn't seduce me. I seduced you. You're not responsible."

"But . . ."

"No! It's nothing to do with you. There's a nice man wants to marry me. He's an old friend. I'm comfortable with him, and I intend to go through with it. He knows all about it, incidentally."

"Yes, but . . ."

"I don't want you to get involved. Can you understand that?"[60]

In his memoirs, Berton wrote that he felt numb. No doubt he did. Almost all his recorded memories of VE day precede the encounter with Frances. Thereafter, the festivities and bonfires along the train route back to Aldershot scarcely registered, and Wayne Ems sat with a silent companion.

The story is affecting yet puzzling. There can be little doubt that the affair with Frances did occur. Berton would not have invented the tryst, which scarcely reflected well on him, simply for dramatic effect in a memoir. This woman may still be alive somewhere, yet she exists only as a character in the recorded memory of a former lover, and his sketch of her has not been consistently rendered. At first encounter, the cadence of the few words he gives her clearly seems intended to suggest an Irish background. "And what would you be wanting that for?" he has her ask when she first sees his bottle of rye. And as if to reinforce the Irish stereotype, he immediately lets his reader know that he "had never seen a woman put away so much booze and with so little effect."[61] Yet regarding the second encounter, the reader is told that Frances had "an upper-class accent," that she had been born in the United States, and that she was still an American citizen.[62]

In a portrait this thinly drawn, such inconsistencies seem significant; yet their meaning remains elusive, and perhaps this was Berton's intent. At the very least, they lead anyone wondering about Frances's background and identity in several directions: Ireland, England, America. But just as telling is Berton's own lack of curiosity about Frances herself. He does wonder in print about the mysterious – and improbable – Captain Harding, and asks why a Canadian lieutenant would be allowed the hotel room key of a captain and why Captain Harding did not use the room on his wedding night. But of Frances he has next to nothing to say. At the end of his story, he places himself on that train back to

Aldershot, and writes: "I still didn't know her full name and I don't know it to this day."[63]

Frances remained Berton's secret until he revealed their brief affair in *Starting Out* in 1987. His family learned about her only when they read the book. Even when he had the means to do so, he made no attempt to determine her identity, to locate her, or to find his first-born child, whether at the time of birth or later.[64] Berton had the ability to put his emotions in a box, to compartmentalize feelings, when necessary.[65] It became necessary to do so on that train to Aldershot, and it was evident when he drafted the passage describing the episode in *Starting Out*. The final sentence of one paragraph says that he never did learn Frances's last name; the first sentence in the next reads: "Meanwhile it was business as usual at Aldershot."[66]

Still, the pain was probably quite real at the time, for it is by no means certain which party had been the worse victim of this sad affair. Words he sent home on May 9 mention Frances not at all, but she is there, a silent witness to the masculine images he insists on invoking. This is the second letter Pierre chose to write to his father rather than to his mother during the Second World War. The decision gave him licence to confine the narrative to VE Day celebrations and to political events. Writing to the parent from whom he was more distant helped still the turmoil inside him.

A letter to "Dear Mamma" would have risked invoking them anew. His mother, the rudder of the Berton family, the dependable but judgmental kindergarten teacher who kept her brood on the straight and narrow, would have had questions to ask. His father's reticence would keep them at bay. Frank Berton would have understood Pierre's situation at the Russell Hotel, and perhaps he had experienced something like it himself. So a son wrote to his father that lonely day in May 1945. It was the only letter, of almost eighty extant from the war years, in which he felt the need to sign "Love, Pierre."

CITIZEN STRAIGHT'S BOY

—

"Hurry up and wait." Berton knew the description of army life well. With the war winding down, the tedium of the soldier in training threatened to be worse than ever. He had not yet seen action, and by the summer of 1945 it looked as if he never would, unless in Asia. He felt impatient with life. The frustration of years of preparation without the experience of combat was one reason, but it dawned on him that with his return to Canada, all manner of opportunities would be lost: the museums, the theatres, the limitless range of cultural experience in "this great museum of a country."[1]

His months in England had brought home to him just how little he knew. His decision to skip lectures in order to put out the *Ubyssey* now appeared foolish. He could distinguish Impressionism from Expressionism and baroque from rococo, but he had little acquaintance with classical music despite Lister Sinclair's efforts at UBC to get him to listen to Mozart and Beethoven. He had been interested, as he put it, "in the Duke and the Count."[2] He may not yet have heard Beethoven's Ninth, but he had already seen Disney's *Fantasia* five times and was crazy about the *Nutcracker Suite*.

He resolved to soak up as much of London's cultural life as possible. When his intelligence course at Aldershot finished, toward the end of May, he headed again to London and Jack Scott's flat in Chelsea. While Scott was at work putting out the *Maple Leaf*, now a full-sized daily, Berton haunted the used-book stores in Charing Cross, picking up Gilbert Murray's *Five Stages of Greek Religion* along the way. He caught midday piano recitals in the National Gallery and an all-Beethoven concert in the Albert Hall. He wrote home to his mother enthusiastically about Thornton Wilder's "strange new play" *The Skin of Our Teeth*, featuring Vivien Leigh in the title role. Since its Broadway debut in 1942, critics and audiences alike had either acclaimed or detested the play for its heavy allegory and jumbled chronology, its actors who insisted on stepping out of character, and its cosmic scale inspired by (some said stolen from) James Joyce. Berton loved it – not least, one suspects, because Wilder had described it as "the history of the world told in comic strip."[3]

While on leave, he travelled north to York, Edinburgh, and Aberdeen. He attended a service in the minster, walked the Royal Mile to Edinburgh Castle, and found himself struck by Aberdeen – "a town built entirely of granite," which gave it "a very clean appearance." But by the second week of June, London had drawn him back. He wanted, needed, to experience everything – "to gobble as much as I could before the plate was snatched from me." He went to exhibitions of Flemish and Dutch art, and of Picasso. He visited Madame Tussaud's. He saw the Tower of London (it was closed, as was the British Museum). He saw Laurence Olivier's movie version of *Henry V*; although "a magnificent performance," it failed to move him.[4]

Berton wrote home in mid-June that he expected to be back in Canada early in July before beginning to train with the Far East force. Tourist pursuits, meanwhile, had begun to pale. "I don't quite know what to do with myself," he wrote. He had just returned from thirteen days' leave and was about to embark on nine more. He sent most of his army pay home, and without money he could not do much; besides, the army granted leave only at short notice, so it was difficult to plan. "I am, candidly, getting a little tired of sight-seeing. One can stand just so much peering at ancient buildings and breathtaking scenery and then the whole thing begins to wear rather badly."[5] Perhaps, he said, he would go to Liverpool to see his mother's cousin; then again, maybe he would just stay with Jack. If he had any money, he would head to Scotland to buy some good tweed.

In the event, he spent his remaining leave with Jack Scott in Chelsea, and by cutting down on booze and women he found the means to haunt London's theatre district, taking in *Rigoletto* at the Sadler's Wells. He went to a performance of *A Midsummer Night's Dream*, saw *Hamlet* with John Gielgud in the title role, and watched Michael Redgrave play the lead in Franz Werfel's *Jacobowsky and the Colonel*. Set early in the war, the play hinged upon a resourceful Polish Jew who helps a Polish colonel flee from occupied Paris to London. Berton, too, aspired to art. He reported to his mother that he had finished a short story (subject unmentioned) and thought he might send it to the *American Mercury*, the magazine of Baltimore's cynical social critic and satirist, H.L. Mencken. He also contributed cartoons regularly to the *Maple Leaf.*

Toward the end of June, two disturbing letters arrived from home. His father had been hospitalized and was gravely ill and not expected to recover. "What a terrible strain the whole thing must be for you," he wrote his mother in the last of his letters from England. "I admire your fortitude and I think the kindest thing to hope is that it will be all over soon." He hoped that his mother would be able to find a nursing home and regretted that he had no money to send her. "Poor Daddy," he concluded. "The greatest tragedy of all, I think, is his inability to read."[6]

Within days he was with thousands of other men ready to board the *Queen Mary*, shuffling along narrow gangways and down crowded stairways to the troop quarters below.[7] Sleeping arrangements proved a nightmarish choice: either bunks only six feet long and about the width of a man's body or hammocks slung in tiers six and eight high. Days on board seemed endless, with the troops packed into quarters that became stifling and ripe with the sweat of a thousand men. The latrines overflowed and meals were barely edible, consisting of greasy beef stews and boiled vegetables, devoid of taste and nourishment. In peacetime, the *Queen Mary* was a stately ship of luxurious chandeliers and majestic staircases, but troops were kept away from the well-appointed areas. Each morning at 9:45 the men had some fresh air with lifeboat drills on deck. Berton did not especially enjoy the trip home, but he did find life aboard ship full of interest. Observing men living in such close quarters, along with reading, helped pass the time, while American cigarettes (Berton himself did not smoke) and limitless supplies of free chocolate reminded him of life's simpler pleasures.

He had been overseas for less than five months and had seen no action, so the welcoming crowds in New York after arrival made him feel like a phony. That and his father's ill health soured his spirit. Yet to others it did not show. Ray Gardner, who had left the *News-Herald* for the *Vancouver Sun*, had gone east to meet the troops returning home; much to his surprise he chanced upon Berton aboard a troop train heading west. The two newspapermen repaired to the smoker. They had a lot of catching up to do. "I got a good story," Berton told him. Then he proceeded with great relish to reveal details of troop life aboard the *Queen Mary*. Years later, Gardner remained struck at Berton's minute description of the troops, including how they felt and how they were managed – like the way the men had been given different-coloured cards to make certain they reached and could be confined to their assigned places on ship. It amazed Gardner that Berton "could see something interesting in everything." He recognized in Pierre an inversion of himself; not a "downer" given to depression, but a man of "tremendous enthusiasm" all the time. "It used to kill me," Gardner said.[8]

When Berton arrived in Vancouver in mid-July, it was as if his overseas experience had never taken place. Long-time friends had not even known he was out of the country, and he could not think of anything he had accomplished as a military man while away. Meanwhile, the house in Point Grey had "become a hospital."[9] The dining room was a makeshift bedroom because Frank Berton was far too weak to climb the stairs. Pierre found a man who looked "haggard and skeletal, staring at the ceiling, clinging to life." Lucy, who had a position at the weather office, assisted her mother, and the two women provided round-the-clock care in separate shifts. Frank himself did not respond much, even to Pierre's overseas stories. At night he would sometimes become delirious. Nothing specific seemed to be the cause of this deterioration beyond advanced age. To his son, he seemed to have lost the will to live. His mother's health, too, had been affected. She had lost weight, looked exhausted from the strain, and felt guilty at wanting her husband's ordeal to be over. Little that summer provided much cheer.

On evenings when he was not helping to care for his father, Pierre would walk to the officers' leave centre to meet Janet. One night she told him that at last she had fallen in love – with a New Zealand airman named Bill Hamilton. The short courtship had taken place while Hamilton had been posted to Vancouver. They had met at a dance near Deep Cove, and for a half-dozen weekends or so, they went out together. "It was a beautiful love," she said.[10] Then he was gone, sent to the Burma campaign. The news of Janet's engagement no doubt saddened Pierre, for while she was his "closest woman friend and confidante," he may have wished their relationship had become something rather more than that.[11] He offered Janet his best wishes and his support, and the two picked up as they had left off – more than chums and less than lovers.

Janet Walker learned of her fiancé's death in the skies over Burma when her roommate, Muriel Griffiths, phoned Reg Moir, city editor of the *Province*, to send word that a telegram had arrived from Bill Hamilton's mother in New Zealand. Her son had been shot down. It was the wedding day of Marg Reid and Lionel Salt, buddies of both Janet and Pierre from their *Ubyssey* days.[12] It was entirely characteristic of the young woman that the happiness of her friends seemed more important than her own grief, so she went to the wedding. Pierre, who was an usher, recalled that she was as cheerful as ever, despite the circumstances. They did not stay for the post-wedding party. Instead, they took a long, quiet walk around the seawall in Stanley Park. For a while at dusk they sat together on a park bench, alone in their shared misery. No tears, few words, only the languid waters of Lost Lagoon and hungry ducks and Janet turning to him. "Thank you," she said.[13]

The dropping of the atomic bomb on the Japanese city of Hiroshima on August 6, 1945, put an end to Berton's hope that he might see active service in the Pacific theatre. The war was effectively over. Pierre Berton had spent almost four years in the army and all his training seemed to have gone for naught. His thwarted ambition would need to be channelled elsewhere, and he knew exactly in which direction. He wanted his old job back as city editor of the *News-Herald*. But when he went to the Little Mountain Barracks to obtain his discharge papers and clothing allowance, he was informed that because the war had not yet formally ended he should report immediately to Brandon – for jungle training. This seemed absurd to him even then, and more so as the years passed. "Brandon, Manitoba? Jungle warfare?" he wrote in his memoirs. "Surely this was a ghastly error or an equally ghastly joke."[14]

On the evening of August 15, while revellers with whistles and sirens celebrated VJ Day downtown, Berton boarded the train heading east. For the next two days he shared the men's smoking car with Harold Bell, a soldier he had met aboard the *Queen Mary* on his return to

Canada. All the way from Vancouver to Brandon, the two veterans prepared for the jungles of Manitoba by downing a fierce concoction of ethyl alcohol and grapefruit juice Bell had brought with him.

In Brandon, Berton found camp life surreal. "Nobody would admit the war was over," he wrote.[15] Bayonet training seemed meaningless, since the men wielding the bayonets knew that the Japanese had already surrendered to General Douglas MacArthur on an American battleship. Toward the end of August, a month of listlessness and waiting as endless as the prairie horizon, Berton received a telegram from his mother. His father had been hospitalized again and the prospects looked bleak. Granted compassionate leave, he headed back to Vancouver.

Too late. When he picked up a copy of the *News-Herald* at the Vancouver train station, there it was: his father's name at the top of the obituary column. He had died on August 29, at the age of seventy-two years. For the rest of his life, Pierre insisted that Frank Berton had died not of the heart condition his physician identified in 1939, but of the sad withdrawal from life that had begun with his final return from Dawson. He remained convinced that when that doctor warned his father to take life easy because of his bad heart, "that's when he gave up."[16]

The funeral service was held at a Vancouver funeral home. It was plain but conducted according to Anglican practice, which called for the casket to be closed and a pall draped over it. This was clearly what Frank Berton, a High Church Anglican "strict for proprieties," would have wanted.[17] So when an attendant came to the family's pew and suggested the casket be opened, the son was livid. "I thought my brother would hit him, he was so provoked," Lucy recalled. The casket stayed closed. When the organist played Frank Berton's favourite psalm, "Unto the Hills around Do I Lift Up My Longing Eyes," no one who knew him, or who knew Dawson, could have doubted which hills he had longed for. Janet Walker did not attend, but she wrote Frank Berton's obituary for the *Province*.[18]

Later came the farewell for the Berton son, and Pierre left again for Brandon. He remained there until the end of October. By then, no one was interested in training, not least because the radio broadcast of the first game of the World Series from Briggs Stadium in Detroit on October 3 focused attention on the only battle by this time worth fighting. The series became an epic seven-game struggle between the Tigers and the Chicago Cubs. Like MacArthur, the Tigers prevailed. Berton listened so hard that fourteen years later he distinctly recalled "*seeing that game.*"[19]

Berton's discharge from the army took so long because the army had misplaced his documents – for the fourteenth time – and it took until the end of October to locate them. So he whiled away his time that autumn walking around Brandon. He went to the local movie theatre three times to see *A Song to Remember*, with Cornel Wilde and Merle Oberon playing Frédéric Chopin and George Sand. At local cafés he listened to the crooner Perry Como sing "Till the End of Time" on the jukebox. Later, whenever he heard Doris Day singing Les Brown's song "Sentimental Journey" (a number one hit in 1945), his memory went back to "that lackadaisical, useless fall" and "the sere leaves of wolf willow and cottonwood drifting across the scrub prairie."[20]

At last back in Vancouver, he settled into his old bedroom at home on 9th Avenue and soon enough found his way to the *News-Herald* office, hoping to regain his former job as city editor. The paper had declined. The perky little tabloid of Berton's memory was no more. As if to return to the status quo ante bellum, the *News-Herald* had reverted to its original, larger size. Most of the men who had put the paper together were gone. Jack Scott was still overseas, Ray Gardner and Robert Elson had left. Ralph Daly and Evelyn Caldwell had gone over to the *News-Herald's* rival, the *Vancouver Sun*. Berton found only a couple of faces in the city room from the old days. The new city editor was a veteran newsman named Bill Bell, a few years from retirement. He gave no indication that he wanted to relinquish his position before then. The *News-Herald* rehired Berton the returned soldier, but from his perspective it did so more out of duty – governments had promised veterans their jobs back – than from enthusiasm. He found himself assigned to the city desk, but in a junior position. Others had warned him that the *News-Herald* had changed, and not to go back. Now he knew why.

It is not difficult to see why men who feared losing their jobs might have looked upon Pierre Berton with suspicion. Bill Bell saw a brash twenty-five-year-old with a limitless reserve of energy and enthusiasm. More than likely, he had heard stories of Berton's earlier stint at the *News-Herald*. But there was a difference that only those who had known him before would have detected. Gone was the tall and gangly shallow-chested youth; in his place stood a two-hundred-pound army officer almost six feet four, with the bearing and authority of command. The young man had acquired a distinct presence. When he spoke, people listened.

His attitude toward the paper continued to sour; he liked nothing about it and his memoirs probably reflect his view at the time: "The headlines were puerile, the writing flat, the columns unreadable. It lacked zest and personality."[21] From Berton's perspective, Bill Bell went out of his way to scupper his career. "He skewered me neatly," Pierre said. He later recalled that one time Bell had told him to edit some copy but not to send it to the composing room until Bell had okayed it after his coffee break. He did as he was told, but the coffee break lasted for hours and the paper was put to bed late. So he absorbed the blame, concluding that Bell had used the incident as a way of taking him off the city desk and demoting him. Berton was once again a reporter on the street, like the cub he had been. As a result, he took his situation to a government arbitrator. Had the government not guaranteed returned soldiers the jobs they had left? He lost the decision because even in his demoted position his salary exceeded the one he had left when he enlisted.[22]

There he was, walking the pavement that fall, drumming up stories about returned soldiers and municipal events. Yet on occasion he received assignments of a more serious nature. The most noteworthy of these was to witness the execution of a man named Prince at Oakalla Prison in the Fraser Valley, about an hour's drive from Vancouver. "It will be an experience for you," the city editor told Berton.[23]

He could not sleep the night before the hanging, scheduled for six in the morning; and at the prison he refused the stiff drink offered to witnesses. The banter beforehand reminded Pierre, in an odd way, "of the stag line at a high school dance before the orchestra strikes up or of the conversation among the first guests at a cocktail party before the bar is opened." The scene of the execution was a disused elevator shaft. The executioner, "a small round, faceless little man" who used the name "Arthur Ellis" by Canadian tradition, wore a tuxedo. From the ceiling hung a huge noose; its presence recalled the hangman's knot he had learned to tie in Boy Scouts to win a proficiency badge. When the condemned man entered the room with the warden and two guards, he gave Pierre and the other witnesses a self-conscious, "twisted little grin." It reminded Pierre of the looks on the faces of performers at amateur theatricals. With the witnesses at the railing, the execution proceeded with industrial efficiency. Hood on the head of the condemned. Guards at attention. Priest reading. Noose taut. Lever pulled.

Later that day in Vancouver, Berton dutifully wrote up the execution, using the dry, objective style of the professional journalist. Still, the spectacle scarred him. A dozen years later, not long before a murder that resulted in the sentencing of a fourteen-year-old Canadian boy to death by hanging, Berton described the impact of the execution at Oakalla on him. "I have never been able to put that scene from my dreams," he wrote. "Sometimes I am the man to be hanged, and sometimes I am the hangman, and sometimes I am the witness and sometimes I am all three at once. But the dreams return, again and again, to haunt my nights and to keep me tossing on my troubled bed, waiting for 6 a.m., waiting for the alarm to ring."

The late fall of 1945 was the only time in his life when Berton suffered from something approximating acute depression. His father was dead, his mother's health was precarious, his sister's job had been put at risk now that so many men had returned from overseas, and he had just witnessed judicial murder: all this and the knowledge that not only did the *News-Herald* underutilize him, it didn't want him. Berton's plight was real enough, but like all the episodes in his life it was also becoming a story that even then he was beginning to craft in his mind for later use. It was not false, but neither was it the rounded truth. While others might have viewed the assignment to Oakalla as a vote of confidence in his ability, he chose to see it as a form of punishment. In somewhat different circumstances, the larger story would have played differently in his head, with his return to the beat as liberation from the drudgery of the city desk. But at the time he was feeling sorry for himself, so the story took the shape it did: the soldier returns, only to find himself unsettled at home and unwelcome on the job.

Every story needs an ending, and over the years the story Berton told about his return to the *News-Herald* after the war came to acquire an upbeat turn. In his memoirs it went like this: A week before Christmas

1946, he had an unexpected scoop. The press had reported a missing nurse and speculated that she had been kidnapped. Berton quickly discovered that she had run away from home – what kind of story was that? He wrote about the kidnapping of the nurse anyway. By the end of the year, however, he concluded that he had had enough of the *News-Herald*, so he quit and began to look for work elsewhere.

Others knew better, and one of them was Wilf Bennett, a *News-Herald* editorial writer at the time. Years later, Bennett recalled the night early in 1946 when Berton joined him for coffee in the Pall Mall Café. It was the day after Bell had demoted him. "He was a pretty sad looking guy," Bennett recalled. "The stricken look in his ambitious eyes almost brought tears to my own." From Bennett's point of view, the clash between Bell and Berton was part of the age-old struggle within any news organization "between the 'big idea' men and the guys who have to get the paper out. All of us in the business know it well; and each type is highly suspicious of the other." The Berton that Bennett knew was positively "effervescent with ideas and ambitions." He had "no dearth of imaginative ideas. Every story had to have an angle and everything had to be a 'big deal.'" The problem was that unfinished stories piled up at the city desk under Berton's watch. "Pierre's brain was working like a bee-hive, but the linotype machines were sitting idle." This had been enough to drive Bill Bell to distraction. The composing room waited for copy while Berton, "the big operator" at the city desk, "kept three phones busy" in search of the sensational story or big scoop. "Every deadline became a headache as most of the city-side copy remained in the process," Wilf Bennett recalled. "Finally this drove Bill to the point of no return, and he bounced Pierre."[24]

Bill Bell begged to differ. In a response to Bennett, he denied that Berton had been fired because his bumptiousness and effervescence had alienated those above him. Rather, it was because in an article he had written concerning the federal budget, released in mid-October 1945, Berton raised the ire of powerful business interests by saying that proposed taxes on alcohol would have little effect on the cheap gin distilled by B.C. companies. "Now, as an editor, you know," Bell wrote, "you cannot insult B.C. gin with immunity. The result was, of course, to fire the party responsible no matter who he was, and Mr. Berton, despite the offer of another position, preferred to be considered 'fired.'"[25]

Whatever the circumstances that led to Berton's dismissal from the *News-Herald*, the fact most noteworthy was that being fired from the newspaper was not part of the story he chose to tell in his memoirs. In his view, he quit to go on to better things. Memoirs, after all, involve acts of concealment as well as revelation, for whether of saints or sinners they are sketches of an acceptable self.

〰

In the staid Vancouver of the 1940s, the Sun Tower, at the corner of West Pender Street and Beatty Avenue, lived an architectural double life. By day, it was a perfectly respectable seventeen-storey building in the Beaux Arts style, sporting a three-storey faux copper dome atop a hexagonal tower that rose from a larger, more conventionally shaped office building. It was said that at the time of completion in 1912 it was the tallest building in the British Empire, and it attracted attention from the outset. Thousands had watched Harry Gardiner, the "Human Fly," crawl up its exterior in 1918 and Harry Houdini suspend himself from atop its summit two years later. No one could deny that the building had flair: high above the street, nine Greek figures could be seen supporting its cornice line. Vancouverites dubbed them the "nine maidens."

In the dark of night, the Sun Tower commanded notice like no other structure in downtown Vancouver. After dusk its dome sported a large and dazzlingly lit globe, and down the full length of the six corners of the building's tower ran twin narrow-gauged tracks of red and white neon lights. The nine maidens now revealed themselves shamelessly as the nine naked Greek muses the good burghers of Vancouver refused to acknowledge in daylight. Near the top of the building, large neon letters spelled "THE SUN," with lightning bolts extending from each end of the name. Against a pitch black sky, the tower's neon outline resembled nothing so much as a bottle of booze topped by a blazing cork. Vancouver's Freudians knew better.

The day after Bill Bell fired him, Pierre Berton headed to the Sun Tower, headquarters of the *Vancouver Sun* since 1937, when a fire had forced it from its offices across the street. He wanted to see Hal Straight, the paper's managing editor, a man he had met through Harry Filion, who had signed on with the *Sun* at war's end as a photographer-reporter.

Harry and his friends, including Berton and Straight, would frequently meet over a bottle of rye and not much else at Filion's apartment in the basement of a Shaughnessy Heights mansion. Berton knew that Straight had already sized him up because every once in a while Straight would hint that Berton should ship himself over to the *Sun* – that maybe, just maybe, there might be a job for him.[26]

The *Vancouver Sun* came from the tradition of crusading journalism that launched the progressive era in the late nineteenth and early twentieth centuries, decades of moral and social reform. At the end of the Second World War the Cromie family of Vancouver owned the paper, and the brothers Sam and Don ran it. Their father, Robert, once a Winnipeg bellhop who became private secretary to the railroad construction magnate John William Stewart, had acquired it in 1917 through one of those mysterious transactions, central to the myth of the self-made man, in which a penniless young fellow miraculously secures the asset that generates success in life. The *Sun* was a five-year-old, money-losing morning paper in 1917, with a circulation of seven thousand and a near-worthless stock. Robert J. Cromie knew nothing about newspapers. But Stewart knew a steal when he came across one, and Cromie had enough pluck and luck to make Samuel Smiles, the best-selling Victorian author of books such as *Self Help* – well, smile. For whatever reason, in an instance of largesse as inexplicable as it was remarkable, Stewart more or less gave the *Vancouver Sun* to Cromie. Within a generation, the ambitious ex-bellhop had transformed it into an evening paper that gave the Vancouver *Province* serious competition in the circulation wars.

Under Cromie in the 1920s the *Sun* had made the cause of discriminatory freight rates – a long-standing western grievance with the railways and the East – its own. Its allegiances were fierce: to Vancouver, to British Columbia, and to western Canada, in that order. It boosted its hometown, took the great American muckraker Lincoln Steffens (a house guest of Cromie) as its patron saint, and delighted in attacking the tycoons of the East and the politicians of Ottawa.

Then, in 1936, Robert Cromie died of a heart attack. His children were still in their teens, so staff members superintended by a board of directors ran the paper. In 1942, when a majority of board members decided to sell the *Sun* to a rival, the Winnipeg-based newspaper chain controlled by the Sifton family, twenty-six-year-old Don, a minority shareholder who had worked as a reporter for the *Sun* and on the news desk of the *Toronto Star*, was disconsolate to the point of panic. His salvation proved to be the *Sun*'s sports editor.

An all-round athlete in his youth, Hal Straight, born in Vancouver, had been a member of the 1932 minor league city baseball champions, the Vancouver Athletics. He was a good enough pitcher to be granted a try-out with the Seattle Indians of the Pacific Coast League, but as the sportswriter Jim Coleman delighted in pointing out many years later, his friend Lefty Straight was good but he was also a one-pitch wonder with "a dinky little curve."[27] Fortunately, Straight liked writing about sports just about as much as he did playing them. He had been a UBC stringer for the *Vancouver Sun*, and when a football injury put an end to any prospects of a career as a professional athlete, he turned to the newspaper life for good. He became a staff writer in the *Sun*'s sports department in 1933.[28]

When he heard young Cromie's lament, Hal Straight knew exactly what was required: the unopened bottle of rye in his desk drawer. He also knew what to do. Before the day (but likely not the rye) was done, Straight had telephoned Don Cromie's brother Sam in Edmonton and instructed him to contact his mother and convince her to use her shares to maintain family control. (She had been left 50 per cent ownership of the paper.) Then he dispatched Don to his mother's Vancouver home to secure power of attorney. The deal with Sifton fell through. Those on the board of directors responsible for the original negotiations resigned. Don Cromie became publisher. Hal Straight declined the offer of the city editor position on the grounds that he lacked experience, but added that he could certainly fill the managing editor's position. When Don Cromie asked him how, the sports editor's answer was simple: "I'll hire a good city editor."[29]

❧❦

When Berton entered the Sun Tower early in January 1946, Hal Straight was in charge and the newspaper had a good city editor in Himie Koshevoy. Straight hired Berton to assist Koshevoy at the salary he had left at the *News-Herald*. Like everyone who worked in it, Berton soon discovered that the Sun Tower was a triumph of pizzazz over practicality, all but given over to an elevator shaft and the stairway that wound around it. Offices ran off into nooks and crannies like hasty afterthoughts. The eight-storey base was little better. Supporting columns turned the floor space into an obstacle course. Departments were scattered, and in open office areas the desks vied for space under indifferent lighting. Editorial supposedly occupied the fourth floor but in fact was "all over the place."[30] The composing room was on seven and eight. The presses were in the basement.

The setting meant nothing to Berton because it was the actors on the stage that captivated him. He could scarcely believe his luck. Life at the *Sun* truly was just like stepping into a production of *The Front Page*; every newsman knew the play and the movie. With the *Ubyssey*, he had acted out his own variation of its script, but with a supporting cast of the earnest and the shy. He alone had been the gorilla atop the library. But working at the *Sun* was something else again. Here everyone seemed drawn from Ben Hecht's rough-and-tumble Chicago newspaper world. Moreover, all the players at the *Sun* remained in character. In the absence of a professional code of journalistic practice, the Broadway and Hollywood versions of newspaper life took its place, and the *Sun*'s reporters and editors did their best to live down to it. No one at the *Sun*, and few elsewhere in the newspaper world, excelled in the role better than Hal Straight.

True to the silver-screen image, the man was larger than life. Barrel-chested, with youthful looks and big blue eyes, Straight resembled Babe Ruth in his prime at one moment and the brilliant young Orson Welles at the next. When Straight's daughter Beverley first saw Welles's cinematic portrait of the publisher William Randolph Hearst, *Citizen Kane*, she was immediately struck: "That's so much like my dad."[31] She was not the only person to draw the comparison. Upon Straight's death from cancer in 1989, Denny Boyd, a veteran *Sun* columnist, wrote that watching *Citizen Kane* made him giggle. "I giggle because every time I see a padded Orson Welles playing newspaper tycoon Charles Foster Kane, it seems to me that Welles is actually doing a pale version of a genuine newspaper giant, Vancouver's Hal Straight."[32] When Straight's friends and colleagues celebrated his sixtieth birthday with a spoof newspaper – the creation of Straight's wife and the editor Ralph Hall –

in 1969, the three words of its front-page headline, emblazoned in red, were "'Citizen' Hal Straight."

From the moment he became managing editor of the *Sun*, all in its universe revolved around him. When Pat Terry, the city editor at the time of Straight's big promotion, balked at taking orders from a former sportswriter and was about to throw a paperweight at his adversary, Straight's response had been to upend him into the office wastebasket.[33]

Straight had a narcissistic streak and was intent on converting people to his way of thinking. Like the pitcher he had been, he sized you up and then did what was needed to accomplish his objective. His huge physical presence either impressed or intimidated, or both. "He never walked in a small way," his daughter recalled. "He could be really over-bearing" yet "also really be your biggest cheerleader." He was a compulsive man, "a compulsive drinker, a compulsive eater, a compulsive everything. Everything he did was 'more, more, more,' so sometimes his words would get beyond his tact."[34]

No one could remain indifferent to Hal Straight. A restless man who could not stand hanging around the office for long, he was always on the lookout for an excuse to escape the office, usually in the company of a crony. He admired imagination and daring, and rewarded those who showed it. The team of journalists he had put together alternately "feared, hated, respected, and loved" him. Some called him "Pappy"; others called him "that sonofabitch" or worse. He coaxed and provoked, goaded and inspired: anything to get the story. Janet Walker thought of him as "scary . . . I was always glad I didn't have to work for him," acknowledging his authority at the *Sun* and the iron hand with which he ran the paper. She admired the way Pierre stood up to him.[35] For Pierre, Straight played true to the kind of newsman he admired most. In short, Straight was Berton's kind of newsman and Pierre Berton was Citizen Straight's kind of boy.[36]

Whenever he was in the Sun building, Berton spent his time in the newsroom, usually chasing stories at the city desk or writing headlines and editing copy at the edge of the horseshoe-shaped universal news desk. Straight took to him from the start. He liked his energy, even his self-promotion. Straight once told his daughter how he had noticed that Berton knew from the moment he started at the *Sun* that, as she put it, "the gig was to get on the front page. And so he'd come racing in with some story, and he'd go, 'Stop the press, stop the press. . . . I've got a headline story, I've got a front-page story.'"[37] Like his managing editor, he wore his fedora in the office; it went with his trench coat[38] – the uniform of the iconic foreign correspondent.

Under Straight's watch, no headline was too corny, no story too lurid: anything to scoop the competition. Midgets from the Clyde Beatty Circus, along with their agent, merited the attention of the editorial office. The *Sun's* lingo was as exaggerated as its stories. Suicides did not fall, they hurtled; prices did not go up, they soared. People over fifty were aged and women under forty were always pretty. Fires were mysterious blazes; business figures were tycoons and moguls. Dogs were always faithful. Holdups were always daring. *Wild* was the word applied to any police chase. "I soaked up all this verbal lore," Berton later recalled, "and felt proud that I was able to write the language so skillfully." Even at the time he recognized how trite this overheated prose was. He loved it anyway.[39]

Love had overtaken Pierre in other ways, too. For some time, Berton had resisted pressure from family and friends to do the obvious thing and marry Janet Walker. But by February 1946, he and Janet had come to what he described in his memoirs as an "understanding." He had proposed a few times when drunk, and she had sensibly told him to try expressing the same sentiments when sober. Now that the war was over and he had a steady job, the time seemed right. His mother was delighted when he told her he intended to marry Janet, and he took from this that she expected the stability of marriage would settle him down and allow him to fulfill whatever destiny was in store for him. He half believed this himself, so he went down to O.B. Allan's jewellery store and spent five weeks' pay on a diamond ring. Smart enough not to give it to her at the boxing match they attended at Hastings Park, he took Janet later that evening to Stanley Park, found a bench, and, there under the moonlight, proposed to her. "Few troths," Harry Filion said later in his inimitable way, "have ever been plighted to greater applause."[40]

They knew that when they married, household finances would be tight. Company policy at the *Province* was that female employees quit their jobs as soon as they married – in Janet's case, much to Hal Straight's delight since, as Berton later noted, "she was a first-rate reporter who often single-handedly beat out the *Sun*'s platoon-coverage."[41] They would live in her small apartment in Stanley Park Manor, in Vancouver's west end. Rent was $45; Berton's monthly salary was about $200. Still, they would manage.

That spring, Harry Filion was best man at the Bertons' "newspaper wedding," held on March 22, 1946, in Canadian Memorial Church, a congregation of the United Church of Canada. Muriel Griffiths, Janet's roommate, was maid of honour, and Himie Koshevoy and Ralph Daly served as ushers, along with Janet's brother Donald. Janet's bridesmaids were her friend Dorothy Menzies of Haney, and her fiancé's sister, Lucy. The bride's party wore pink, cream, and yellow.[42] Jack Scott was still overseas, but Hal Straight and most of the rest of the *Sun* crowd as well as friends from the *News-Herald* were there, along with chums from the *Ubyssey* days. When the nuptials took place, Laura and Lucy Berton sat proudly on the groom's side of the church and Janet's mother, father, brother, and other Walker relatives on that of the bride. Laura's health had gradually improved after the toil and worry surrounding Frank's final days.

After a brief honeymoon in Seattle, Berton returned to work with a new assignment: to interview visiting celebrities. The trouble was that the interviews had to take place before 9:30 in the morning in order to meet the *Sun*'s 10:00 a.m. copy deadline. As a result, whether the subject was the actor Basil Rathbone or the musician Oscar Peterson or the ventriloquist Edgar Bergen or the "Hubba Hubba Girl," Evelyn West, he or she was usually in some state of undress. He loved these contacts with the famous. The lion tamer Clyde Beatty refused Berton's plea to be allowed to go into the cage with him, but the reporter did get a role as a spear carrier in Egyptian costume for the touring San Carlo Opera Company's production of *Aida*.

The celebrity beat was his morning work; afternoons he covered the Vancouver waterfront, a district that fuelled his imagination even more than underclad actresses. Berton revelled in the phrase "I cover the waterfront," the title of a book, a movie, and a popular song. In 1932, the former *San Diego Sun* reporter Max Miller had published a best-selling novel about a young reporter who aspires to book authorship but must first pay his dues on the rough waterfront beat of a daily paper. A year later, the movie *I Cover the Waterfront* was released and Mel Tormé took Johnny Green and Edward Heymans's theme song to the night-clubs and airwaves, followed later by Billie Holiday. Little wonder that Berton loved the waterfront assignment; he repeated the catchphrase to anyone who asked what he did at the paper.

Everywhere he looked on the Vancouver shoreline he saw potential front-page material. The harbour was a gumbo of fishermen and dock-workers, drunks and con artists, smugglers and – for all he knew – spies. This was early 1946, and the Gouzenko spy scandal, in which a Russian cipher clerk in Ottawa defected with a cache of documents proving the existence of a Soviet spy ring in Canada, had just ushered in the Cold War. To Berton the Vancouver waterfront was "the cross-roads of the world," so he hired small boats and headed out with Janet to the ships in the harbour to fish for the news. One day he netted seven separate waterfront stories.[43] No catch was too small to be stretched into a big one.

That year the *Sun*'s editorial core consisted of Hal Straight, Himie Koshevoy, Harry Filion, and Pierre Berton. The club automatically embraced Jack Scott as soon as the returned veteran realized, as Berton had, that the *News-Herald* was a home no more. They were an odd-looking lot. Straight lived large – in girth as well as manner – but Harry Filion outsized him. He was the only man Beverley Straight could recall who was bigger than her father. Koshevoy, short and thin, played Stan Laurel to Straight's Oliver Hardy. Berton, too, stood out, with his ruddy complexion, his height, and his unruly red hair. Even when they got together in later years they reminded Straight's daughter of nothing so much as a troupe of sideshow carnies.[44]

They drank hard and played hard. The venue of choice, when not a downtown hotel bar, was the Filions' flat, where the boys would be joined by others such as Evelyn Caldwell, who had defected from the *News-Herald* and taken the shopping columnist "Penny Wise" with her. There was always music, often jazz (especially Dixieland), and plenty of cheap booze, practical jokes, and corny gags. Harry and Himie and Hal would do their Mutt and Jeff soft-shoe. Pierre would bellow out his party staple, "The Shooting of Dan McGrew," the Robert Service poem memorized in childhood, or he would pound the piano if one proved handy. Filion would dazzle all and sundry with his sleight of hand and his amazing ability to tilt, somehow, to an angle of almost forty-five degrees.[45] The man seemed to possess no angle of repose, no tipping point at which his vast bulk had, by the laws of nature, to come crashing to the floor.

Professional duties scarcely interrupted the carnivalesque atmosphere, as long as the boys filed their copy on time. On one occasion when a group of schoolchildren came into the newsroom, Straight, with a snap-brim fedora atop his oversized head and trademark wide suspenders stretched across his broad frame, shouted to Ray Gardner from across the floor, "Axe murder – 4th and Vine – go over and cover it!" Both men grabbed their hats, ran from the room – and went for a cup of coffee.[46] One Easter, a friend of Straight's, a Roman Catholic named J.C. Maclean, received a gift of Band-Aids and a nail puller.[47] He immediately knew who had sent it. "He and I got along like a house on fire," Berton said of his relationship with Straight. "Between editions we'd drink a bottle of rye together in Stanley Park and go right back and do the rest."[48] Sometimes between editions they just shared the bottle in Straight's office. How could he not worship a man who loved the movie *Gone with the Wind* so much that he swore his wife looked just like Scarlett O'Hara and he named his champion retriever Rhett?[49] Straight's aura drew out the best in people, everyone labouring in its intense heat for the scoop that would bring the *Province* to heel.

The return of peace brought Canadians a welcome security, but also, for some, a distinct sense of drift, a slow withdrawal from the excitement of the uncertain outcome and the adrenalin rush of the war years. Men returned to their jobs, and women for the most part left offices and factories for homes and children. As if to compensate, they readily consumed the over-the-top news coverage in which the *Vancouver Sun* specialized. In the first year after the war, the *Sun* reached a circulation of 100,000. The circulation of the *Province* was at the time about 125,000, but the gap between the two rival papers was closing at a rate of 1,000 a year.[50]

Then, that summer of 1947, came what Berton called "an act of God." Hal Straight must certainly have thought it so. The International Typographical Union and the Southam newspaper chain, which owned

the *Province*, found themselves at loggerheads, and the result was a protracted printers' strike at the grande dame of Vancouver newspapers. It
began on June 5, 1947, and continued throughout the summer and well
into autumn, with union and non-union workers pitted against each
other in a struggle that at times became violent. Under such conditions,
the *Province* was able to publish only in a much-diminished form, and
only episodically.[51]

Straight seized the opportunity by giving his reporters even more
licence than usual – anything to gain market share. By this time, Berton
had established himself as one of the *Sun*'s leading reporters, often with
his own byline over stories of "passion and revenge, murder and suicide,
fire, flood, and accident."[52] Now he took full advantage of his elevated
status, Hal Straight's obsession, and the wild sense of humour they and
others at the *Sun* shared.

One of the men Berton teamed up with was Ray Munro, the most
flamboyant photographer at a newspaper that employed Harry Filion.
A pilot during the war, Munro drove the way he flew, often speeding
through city streets chasing ambulances with his fellow photojournalist
Art Jones, a *Ubyssey* alumnus. One time, teamed up together, Berton
and Munro decided to enrich the lives of the members of the Vancouver
Women's Press Club, including Janet Berton, by releasing a pig in the
lobby of the Hotel Vancouver, where the club's annual meeting and
ball were set to take place. Reporter and photographer would then
record, in word and picture, the scoop that was bound to follow. For
once, a scheme appeared too goofy even for the *Sun*, and higher-ups
nixed it. That was when Berton and Munro came up with Plan B: keep
the animal but change the location of its liberation. They decided to
release the pig, well greased, not in the lobby but in the hotel's
Panorama Roof ballroom.

On the morning of the day of the meeting and dance, two newspapermen turned up at an enormous pig farm in the Fraser Valley. Its
owner allowed himself to be convinced that he should lend the men one
of his piglets for twenty-four hours. "My paper has decided to grace its
front page with a formal portrait of a typical pig, suitable for framing,"
Munro had told the man. "Your piggery has been chosen above all
others for this honour." Soon the trunk of Munro's car contained one
of the several thousand squirming and squealing piglets. They hid the

oinker until evening, first in the attendant's hut on the *Vancouver Sun* parking lot and then in Munro's bathroom.

At ten o'clock that evening, with the dance under way and Munro in hiding near the dance floor with the pig, the agitated president of the Women's Press cornered Berton, who was present as the guest of his wife. The woman had heard rumours about an errant pig. Berton vehemently denied the story; Janet – a prominent member of the club's executive – knew the truth, turned white, and said nothing. A description of the "great moment" that followed must be left to Mrs. Berton's naughty husband:

> The argument had not ended when there was a dreadful roll of drums, a hush over the assembly, and Munro rushed in cradling our pig in his arms.
>
> "Ladies and gentlemen," he cried, breathlessly. "The first man or woman to catch this fine pig, which I now release, wins a full bottle of the finest UDL brand two-year-old rye whiskey."
>
> And with that he released the pig.
>
> The pig just stood there.
>
> Munro gave it a bit of a push.
>
> The pig's knees buckled slightly and it slid along the floor under Munro's coaxing.
>
> Then it lay down quietly and closed its eyes.
>
> George Young, the *Sun*'s chief photographer, picked up the pig gently and handed it to Munro.
>
> "Give me the cheap bottle of rye," said George Young.
>
> "That's not fair!" Munro shouted, "you didn't give the pig a chance."
>
> He retrieved the pig and gave it an enormous push along the floor.
>
> The pig slid obediently over the waxed hardwood, came to a slow stop like a curling stone, rolled over on its back and began softly to snore.
>
> I have never seen such an exhausted pig.
>
> "The poor little thing," said a sentimental girl reporter, and began to cuddle it.
>
> A buzz, half amused, half angry, began to rise from the multitude.

Munro looked about warily for the nearest exit, found it, and with the practiced movements of a man who has filched many a murder victim's photo from under the noses of his rivals, made his escape.

I pretended innocence, and more or less got away with it.[53]

Berton and Filion also made a team that would go to almost any lengths for a story, and Straight and Koshevoy played them like salmon in the Fraser, letting them run the line before reeling in the catch. That fall, Straight ordered the pair to Deep Cove on Burrard Inlet to cover an apparent murder. Sure enough, they found that a man named Teeporten, at work on a woodshed near his cottage, had been blasted with a shotgun and bludgeoned to death. His wife had been beaten up in front of her young child. A missing eighteen-year-old house guest became the prime suspect. The police had left the scene of the crime unattended, so Berton and Filion snooped around the cottage even though word had it that the perpetrator was still somewhere nearby. Berton noticed a collie crouching beneath the steps and a headline flashed through his mind: "Faithful Dog Waits Vainly for Dead Master." It was, he thought, a good follow-up story.[54]

Reporter and photographer thought nothing of pestering Mrs. Teeporten for an interview and a picture, and cared little for her battered condition or her tragic loss. To Berton she was just a story; he saw her as "a picture on page 1, the bandage on her head and the serious expression graphic evidence of her woe."[55] As Filion drove Berton back over the Lions Gate Bridge to the Sun Tower, Berton thought only of the leads for three stories taking shape in his head: one for the front page about the murder, a sidebar piece on Mrs. Teeporten's fear that the murderer might return, and a human interest item about a faithful dog.

For as long as it could get away with it, the *Sun* milked the Teeporten tragedy, reporting every sighting of the culprit and every rumour about his whereabouts. Berton briefed a cub reporter about how best to interview the alleged killer's mother. He questioned the chief of police about the motive for the crime. He returned to the scene with Harry, nominally to "interview" the dog. But when the police arrested the suspect, Pierre was having a swell time at the *Sun*'s annual staff party. The occasion was uproarious and memorable, not least because it was the night on which Evelyn Caldwell somehow broke her leg. "She was carried off in high style on a stretcher," Berton later reported, "preceded by three Highland pipers hired on the spot by Sam Cromie, munching on a gardenia garnished with French dressing."[56] The next day, a bleary-eyed Berton learned that the young man wanted for the Teeporten slaying had been holed up all along in a modest hotel just a few blocks from the Sun Tower and the office party. The end of the story had come close to recapitulating the climactic scene of *The Front Page*, when the escaped murderer is discovered hiding in a rolltop desk in the paper's boisterous newsroom.

In spite of the excitement of this kind of wild journalism, Berton felt "a tiny ember of discontent" nagging at him. The restlessness was enough that late in the year he applied for a Kemsley Scholarship in Journalism; if he won, he and Janet would be able to enjoy a year in England working for Viscount Kemsley's newspaper chain.[57] Meanwhile, in the Filions' kitchen, while Janet and Veryl pampered the Filions' baby daughter, Victoria, Pierre and Harry continued to concoct newspaper stunts.

The unexpected entrance of the veteran politician Gerald McGeer into the Vancouver mayoralty race of 1946 had suddenly transformed a lacklustre campaign into one of the most exciting in decades. When the colourful McGeer – who had already been mayor, a member of Parliament, and a senator – suddenly came down with an acute case of appendicitis, the Vancouver press scrambled to St. Paul's Hospital to interview and photograph him, only to be refused access. Years later, Berton delighted in picturing the scene as reporters and photographers from the three competing Vancouver newspapers milled around the hospital corridors: "In this group, complete with herringbone jacket and Windsor-knotted tie, was P. Berton, Eager Boy Reporter, and his faithful sidekick, Harry 'The Bomber' Filion, usually described in print as 'Ace *Vancouver Sun* Cameraman.'"[58]

Berton and Filion were desperate for a photograph of McGeer and considered masquerading as hospital attendants or having a friend pretend to be a nurse to gain access to McGeer's room, but Berton suddenly had a better idea. They rushed back to the *Sun*'s morgue and rooted through dozens of old photographs until they found one of Constable Bobby Cooper taken at St. Paul's a year earlier after the officer had been shot in the chest by a thug. Then they spread scores of photographs of Gerry McGeer in a variety of positions – "McGeer flaying, attacking, pointing in pride; McGeer in Indian headdress, miner's helmet, and robes of office; McGeer shaking hands, accepting cheques for charities, laying cornerstones, etc." – and found just the right pose: the one with the politician's head set to fit perfectly on the photo of Constable Cooper in his hospital bed. Harry rephotographed the montage and gave it proudly to his managing editor.

Hal Straight immediately recognized the stunt. "It's a fake," he said, and paused. "But it's a damn good fake," he added. "Page 1. Four columns!" Later, Janet's friends at the *Province* told her that when its city desk editor saw the *Sun*'s first edition that day he blasted his photographers for failing in their duty. Assisted by all the publicity, McGeer won the election by a landslide, swept into the mayor's office for the second time, and vigorously pursued his campaign promise to rid the Vancouver police force of corruption.[59]

By this time, the circulation of the Vancouver *Province* had dropped from 127,420 just before the strike to under 96,000 after it. The *Vancouver Sun*'s circulation, meanwhile, had reached 125,000 and it was still climbing.[60]

HEADLESS VALLEY

—

IN THE AUTUMN OF 1946, George Murray of Fort St. John, B.C., publisher of the *Alaska Highway News* and a stringer for the *Vancouver Sun*, printed an article in the *News* about a little-known tropical valley in the wilds of the Canadian north. Hal Straight immediately reprinted it.[1] Articles soon began to appear in the mainstream North American press about the remote terrain near the junction of the Northwest Territories, the Yukon Territory, and the province of British Columbia. This was the Nahanni River valley, a twisting river system some two hundred miles long and located between the Mackenzie and Selwyn mountain ranges.

Typical of these pieces was one by R.A. Francis and Margaret Francis, bearing the title "Nahanni . . . Valley of Mystery." "The tumultuous Nahanni tells no secrets," it began, "but the winds above the river are heavy with the breath of mystery, of terror, of nameless, fearsome death dealt swiftly by unseen hands."[2] The authors told a lurid tale of lost gold and missing people involving legends of "head hunting savages and pre-historic monsters." As often as not, men and women who went into the Nahanni Valley did not return. The body of one of its victims had been nearly decapitated, leading local old-timers and Native people to call the place "Headless Valley." Yet, wrote Francis and Francis, "in this valley, like a cloud-wrapped Himalayan Shangri-La, hidden among the frozen tundras, soft, fragrant breezes blow and tropical trees and flowers spring lushly from the fertile soil watered by hot springs."

Who, in that first year of the return to bland "normalcy," would not have been fascinated by a place in Canada's north that evoked images at once of paradise and of hell? Readers and moviegoers could still recall James Hilton's compelling description of Shangri-La in his 1933 novel,

Lost Horizon, and Frank Capra's evocation of it in the 1937 movie of the same name. Few Canadians had thought of the North as exotic. Shangri-La? The region in their minds was a remote land of Eskimos and igloos, tundra and polar bears. This version was different and dangerous – and, above all, exotic.

Newspaper editors deemed the story newsworthy. The *Globe and Mail* reported on the tale of Headless Valley on September 12. Not to be outdone, the more provocative and adventurous *Toronto Star* published Headless Valley stories on September 13, October 12, and October 21, and editorial and opinion pieces on October 21 and October 26. Other papers quickly picked up the lead of these two major Canadian dailies. That fall and winter, Headless Valley became a hot topic. It was great escapist reading for newspaper subscribers across the continent.

Hal Straight was a master at creating and exploiting hot topics. The flurry of breathless articles about Headless Valley aroused a frantic competition among adventurers, eager to be the first to lead an expedition to investigate its mysteries. Frank Henderson, nephew of the prospector credited with having started the Klondike gold rush, announced that he wanted to return to the Nahanni with a group of U.S. Marines to search for a partner who had gone missing there six years earlier. Canadian Major-General F.F. Worthington, a veteran of the Great War and champion of the use of heavy armour in warfare, declared that he intended to head a Canadian expedition to the Nahanni. The polar explorer Tom Carolan and the miner Hal Hendrickson, both of British Columbia, talked about organizing their own exploration parties. Within a week of placing a two-line classified advertisement for expedition members in a Vancouver newspaper, Hendrickson had received 154 applications, including one from a fourteen-year-old boy in Albuquerque, New Mexico.[3] By January 1947, the Headless Valley story had piqued interest around the world. It was then, as Hal Straight related the circumstances, that he placed a phone call to a northern bush pilot and aspiring airline entrepreneur, Russ Baker.

Straight had known Baker since the 1930s, and he was well aware of the fierce rivalry that existed between Baker (who owned Central British Columbia Airways) and Baker's friend and competitor, Grant McConachie (who had founded Yukon Southern Air Transport). In 1937, McConachie's company had won the government air-mail contract between Edmonton and Whitehorse; five years later, Yukon Southern was one of ten regional airlines purchased by the Canadian Pacific Railway to form Canadian Pacific Airlines.

Straight knew the two men well enough to describe McConachie as Baker's "old drinking jig-a-jigging and wrist-twisting friend," and he knew that Baker was "envious as hell" at his friend's new-found success. He also knew that Baker, still struggling to keep his small airline afloat, would do just about anything to promote it. So he asked Baker to do him and the *Vancouver Sun* a favour. Would the bush pilot take Pierre Berton and the photographer Art Jones to Headless Valley? Baker said he would.

Hal Straight knew very well that the stories about Headless Valley, especially those touting the lush tropical climate and the headhunters, were groundless to the point of being plain silly. He knew this because his brother-in-law, Len White, a mining engineer and prospector, had been to the area and "had documented proof that the story was nonsense." But as Straight put it many years later in a letter to a friend, "I felt it was my duty and a great story to try to uncover the disappointing truth." Citizen Straight knew immediately that he would give this assignment to the man who had posed as a beast on the roof of a university library. The decision marked a turning point in Pierre Berton's life.

Untroubled by the peculiar academic notion that the journalist should be "objective" or "disinterested" and should examine all angles of a story in the search for "truth," Berton held a simpler creed: that "news was not truth; it was what somebody claimed was truth."[4] He immediately embraced the story of Headless Valley, one he felt he'd been born to tell. A child of the North, he knew its freezing winters, and after four years of army life, he had bivouacked in many strange places under harsh conditions. Berton knew as well as Straight that the Headless Valley tale was a whole lot of nonsense built on a modest stock of fact. But exploiting it would allow Pierre the outsider to come in from the margins, to be at the centre of an adventure.

At Straight's request, Berton went to a shabby hotel on Hastings Street in Vancouver and interviewed a young man named Walter Tully, who claimed to have been to Headless Valley and seen its extravagant vegetation, breathtaking waterfall, and skeleton without a skull. His *Vancouver Sun* story, accompanied by a Harry Filion photograph, began: "The true story of the South Nahanni River's bizarre 'Headless Valley' was told today by a man who has actually explored its 200-mile length and lived to tell the tale." Shortly afterwards, when his mother told him she too wanted to go to Headless Valley, Berton recognized just how powerfully this story had gripped people's minds. It was straight out of the lurid pulp fiction of the day.[5]

Berton completed a *Sun* assignment to write about the various expeditions that were in the planning stages, and then one of those moments of serendipitous luck occurred that make or break a career. *Maclean's* magazine had asked the West Coast journalist Clyde Gilmour to develop an article on Headless Valley. Too busy at the time, Gilmour turned it over to Berton, who proceeded to do some library research, tone down his prose, and send a piece to the editors in Toronto.[6] Hal Straight did not object. By this time, rather to his surprise, Berton found that he was himself becoming enthralled by the story – not least for its mixture of history, myth, and bullshit. So – and this is *his* version of events – he rushed off to Hal Straight's office. "I felt reasonably sure in this dull month of January," he told a CBC radio audience five years later, "he would fall in with my plans to fly 1,500 miles into the North and discover – in the newspaper sense, that is – the Valley of Mystery. I wasn't disappointed. Mr. Straight was eating peanuts and he continued to eat them as I outlined my plan. 'Get a pilot' was all he said, between mouthfuls. I began looking for a pilot."[7]

In Berton's version, it was Jack Scott, who had flown with Russ Baker in 1942, who suggested the "mad pilot" for the Nahanni expedition, and it was Berton himself who contacted him. "By a fantastic coincidence," Berton claimed, Baker happened to be in Vancouver at the time, staying at the Georgia Hotel. What happened next strains credulity: "I went over to his hotel and he opened the door, a huge thick thug of a man with a broad brown face and penetrating eyes. And what do you suppose was lying on the floor of his room? A map of the Northwest Territories. And what do you suppose was circled on the map? Yeah. The Nahanni River. Like everybody else, Russ Baker, the mad pilot, wanted desperately to seek out that never-never land on the roof of the world."[8]

Whatever the truth may be about how Russ Baker came to join the *Vancouver Sun*'s expedition to Headless Valley, whether Straight or Berton had made contact, the fact is that both men believed that a great story invariably trumped fidelity to detail. Both believed that this was a great story, and they proceeded to tell it with gusto, adding garnish with each telling, whether to Straight's favourite airline stewardess or to Berton's fledgling radio audience. Straight authorized the flight on Wednesday, January 22.[9] Three days later, Berton, Baker, and Jones left on their adventure to the North. Hal Straight was relieved that Don Cromie, the *Sun*'s publisher, had not yet got wind of the scheme.[10]

⋈

Hal Straight and Pierre Berton estimated that the trip to Headless Valley would last a week. They guessed wrong. It lasted for two and a half weeks, and during that time the North experienced temperatures that were among the lowest recorded to that date. Unknown to Berton, those in charge at *Maclean's* followed his exploits closely. Arthur Irwin, the editor of *Maclean's*, liked the article Berton had submitted, so he read the reports that began to appear daily in the *Vancouver Sun* as much for the reporter as for the adventure.

Berton's plan had been to fly with Baker and Jones by commercial airline to Prince George, and then on to Baker's home near Fort St. James. The route to the Nahanni would take them east through the Rocky Mountain trench to Finlay Forks, located at the point where the Finlay and Parsnip rivers joined to form the Peace River. From there, they would fly through the Peace Pass in the Rockies to Fort St. John, then north along the Alaska Highway to Fort Liard on the Liard River in the Northwest Territories. The final legs would involve flying to the mouth of the Nahanni where it flows into the Liard, then north along the Nahanni into Headless Valley.[11]

Life soon overtook art. The Canadian Pacific commercial flight was forced to turn back because of hundred-mile-per-hour winds and fast-forming sheet ice, leading to a twenty-hour delay.[12] When they arrived at Prince George, one of Baker's crew was there to meet them with his airplane and they took off immediately for the big white house he had built above Stuart Lake.

Russ Baker was a pilot with more than ten thousand hours of flying time and any number of harrowing adventures behind him. His Junkers aircraft, designed in 1918, had a single low wing. It was about fifteen years old, had skis instead of wheels, and was frail but reliable. It had no instruments. "His weather gauge was a cabin's smoke," Berton reported, "and his barometer the sky at dawn."[13] Although the weather was deteriorating, Baker did not seem worried. "He figured, if we got snowed in somewhere we could set up the stove inside the plane, chop a hole through the roof for the smokestack, and be as snug as bugs in rugs," Berton wrote a few years later. "This made Art Jones and I feel just great."[14]

They took off laden with provisions and with a fourth man on board, Baker's mechanic Ed Hanratty. When the party landed at Finlay Forks to bivouac for the night, it was bitterly cold. Berton knew about Finlay Forks, because this was the place where Thomas Prince, the man whose execution he had witnessed at Oakalla, had murdered two trappers.[15]

Next morning found the Junkers buried to the wings in drifting snow and the skis frozen into the ice. (Just how cold it was at Finlay Forks remains unclear: Berton's report from the location gives −37 Fahrenheit, but handwritten notes he made at the time read, "Finlay Forks, BC. Temperature 18 below dew point −22 wind 40 mph gust up to 50 mph light snow now falling."[16]) The Junkers's engine battery was frozen solid, Pierre's typewriter was like a hunk of concrete, and Jones's yellow camera filter had cracked from the cold. They remained grounded for several days, digging out the plane, thawing the battery in an oven, and heating the engine with a blowtorch. The temperature outside dropped to −68 degrees. When it finally rose to between −30 and −40, they took off, but when they reached Fort St. John the authorities refused them permission to leave because of the frigid conditions. Baker took to the air in the direction of Fort Nelson without an authorized flight plan.[17]

At Fort Nelson, on the Alaska Highway, the Junkers's engine blew up when they tried to take off. They waited two days for a new one to be flown in, and Berton used the delay to develop a story about British cold-weather tests of military equipment then being conducted in the area, supposedly under a cloak of secrecy. Then they found themselves on an unexpected hundred-mile diversion north to Deer River to bring a Native trapper, Ed Gardner, and his expectant wife back to Fort Nelson. They landed on the river in four feet of snow, but when they tried to take off again, now with extra passengers, the Junkers would not budge. With Baker, Mrs. Gardner, and another member of the

Gardner family on board, they managed to dislodge the aircraft from the frozen snow and Berton, Jones, Hanratty, and Gardner ran along outside the fuselage until the Junkers gained enough momentum to take off. The next morning, when they tried to leave Fort Nelson for the Nahanni, they discovered that the RCAF had cleared the runways of snow, leaving bare asphalt. "So now," Berton later told his radio audience, "you had the spectacle of the four of us desperately shoveling snow *back* onto the runway so we could get into the air."[18]

Baker flew his crew to the trading settlement of Fort Liard in several hours of fog, diving the plane close to the ground at times to figure out where he was. Most of the time, Berton reported, the pilot could see nothing, "but occasionally there'd be a ragged hole in the fog and Russ would spot the corner of a lake or a piece of river that looked familiar and he'd know where he was. Just like a man going home on a crowded streetcar identifying his own corner by a hunk of the curb seen through a tiny section of the window."

They reached Fort Liard late in the afternoon, landing on the frozen river. "We had hardly set our skis down before the three symbols of the north country came down the bank on dog team to greet us: A Roman Catholic Priest, a Mounted Policeman, and the head of the Hudson's Bay Post: God, Justice, and Mammon were all represented. And there on the bank was the church, the police headquarters and the pink roof and white siding of the HBC. It was from this little settlement, fifty years before, that the two McLeod brothers, Frank and Willie, had headed for the lost mine of the Nahanni Valley, just over the horizon. They had never returned, and their murdered corpses had begun the legends that now hung like a pall over the region."[19]

Despite delays to the schedule due to bad weather, unexpected rescue missions, and broken equipment, Berton sent his reports to Straight with such regularity that only one of fifteen daily stories about the mystery of Headless Valley had to be delayed. The northern presence of Canadian Pacific and the Government of Canada telegraphic services made this possible, but the *Sun* needed the dispatches a few days prior to the publication date. Readers missed only the instalment of Saturday, February 8, the day Baker's aircraft blew its engine. By then Berton had already filed two stories over and above those promised for the series – one about the rescue of the trapper's wife and another about his discovery of the British navy's secret cold-weather experiments near Fort Nelson.[20]

At each stage of the saga, from Prince George to Bear Lake, Berton and Straight exchanged telegrams. Straight tried to keep his reporter's focus on the sensational, and Berton either telegraphed or radioed his stories to the *Sun*. The text he sent along did not consist simply of the story itself. For each instalment, Berton also wrote his own "precede," a brief preamble intended to grab the reader's interest. He also provided teasers to follow each day's story, hinting at the next day's adventure.

The one item of good news Berton received at Finlay Forks was Straight's telegram announcing the sale of the series to International News Service. People around the world would now read about the *Sun*'s expedition to Headless Valley. The Hearst newspaper chain and the London *Daily Express* were also eager to reprint the series.[21] The stakes had become very high, and Straight worried that the delay in reaching the Nahanni might harm the story's sensational nature. He sent Berton a telegram: "GET SOME DRAMA HEADLESS VALLEY INTO EARLY ARTICLES STOP GLOBE MAIL WANTS SERIES STOP GET SOME GOLD AND MURDER IN SOON STOP STUFF READING FINE STOP KEEP PUNCHING AND DON'T FORGET TO KEEP MENTIONING HEADLESS VALLEY."[22]

When Straight received the "precede" of Berton's first piece, he was surely pleased: "A daring expedition is enroute by ski plane to the mysterious 'Headless Valley' in the Canadian Northwest east of the Yukon – a weird valley where men have met strange deaths and where bizarre legends abound regarding head-hunting cave-dwellers, prehistoric monsters, etc." The teaser that day was "Tomorrow: The little ski plane expedition battles a 40 mile an hour blizzard to land in the tiny trading outpost of Finlay Forks, B.C." Berton even provided his editor with a "divisional" for each instalment, a page or two of attention-grabbing details for International News Service to use to attract readers. At times this became almost a separate account of the adventure. Straight scarcely needed to do anything except send Berton's copy to the composing room, calculate his profits from newswire syndication fees, and watch his subscription base grow.

Taken as a whole, the Headless Valley series was the bravura performance of a newspaper reporter who had begun to master his craft. Berton understood that journalism involved far more craft than it did art. Still, it was not without art. He and the *Sun* had promised they would reveal the long-hidden secrets of Headless Valley in daily columns; the problem was how to do this when unexpected delays continued to prevent the expedition from reaching its destination. The first instalment in the series appeared on February 3, but not until February 11 was he able to report that he had actually landed in Headless Valley. It took good craftsmanship to draw the reader's attention away from the fact that he had spent far more time travelling to the valley than exploring it. The trick was something every journalist must learn: find the real story and tell it, not the one you thought you would tell. And the heart of this story was not so much the mysterious valley as the intrepid reporter.

Berton kept faith with readers during the buildup, reminding them regularly of the danger surrounding the valley and retelling the stories with a skill and flair that others lacked. These tales he set against the immediate story being played out in real life. Moreover, he knew that these unexpected delays were a blessing in disguise, heightening the tension he was trying to create. "I knew from my researches," he later wrote, "that we would find very little, but I wasn't about to let out *that* secret yet. Instead, I concentrated on the colourful adventures of Russ Baker, the quintessential bush pilot, who had cheated death on various occasions and wasn't shy about retelling old tales."[23]

The story now held truly universal appeal, for it had become a saga of man against the elements, in quest of the unknown, set in the frozen Canadian Arctic. The third instalment, for example, told an exciting tale of four men who only a day or so before had put a blowtorch to a frozen airplane engine and used shovel, crowbar, and jack to pry the skis loose from the ice. Only then did Berton let the nominal subject of the series unfold:

> We began to wonder what we would discover when we actually reach "Headless Valley" – where 14 men have perished and the will o' the wisp of a lost gold mine still haunts prospectors' dreams.
>
> We are already in the heart of the badlands where the magic world "gold" makes the eyes glitter with a new brightness and lonely men die violently with their shoepacks frozen to their feet.

Here, hundreds of miles off the asphalt roads of civilization, the Nahanni (where "Headless Valley" is located) is still a faraway, legendary river to the prospectors and trappers whose life is a see-saw battle with the wilderness.

They know no more about it here than the white collar workers of Vancouver and Seattle, for although we have flown 700 miles across the rough, unruly face of the province we still have 700 more to go.

They have heard here of the strange, mysterious South Nahanni River, where men have met strange deaths.

They have heard of the hot springs and the stories of tropical growths, of the prehistoric beasts and the "bad Indians."

But no man here knows the truth about the Nahanni, because no man here has travelled up or even flown over the twisted river where, legend says, mists block the ground from sight.[24]

From this point on, the series became a rugged adventure story about the struggle to reach, penetrate, and survive the Nahanni – just as large and compelling a story as that of the valley itself. Instead of offering its readers escape, it offered involvement; not suspension of disbelief, but identification with the expedition and its members. That reference to "white collar workers of Vancouver and Seattle" was a stroke either of luck or of genius because it bridged the gap between city dweller and northern inhabitant. From bungalow or log cabin, readers bore common witness to this real-life drama. Perhaps Berton had this in mind from the outset, secure in the knowledge that most of the Headless Valley legends were groundless. Even so, he had found a formula that worked, a mixture of mythic quest and modern adventure, and readers around the world were riveted by it.

Report no. 5, for Fri. Feb. 7 release. Finlay Forks, B.C.
The dizzying mountain walls dwarfed our plane as we bumped through the Peace Pass in 68 below weather.

The cabin of our plane was like the inside of a refrigerator and cameraman Art Jones and I felt like the abused bananas of the singing radio commercial. . . .

Report no. 6, for Sun. Feb. 9 release. Fort Nelson, B.C.
Here, as everywhere, our expedition has been met by raised eyebrows
and widened eyes. At the Musquaw post office here, the postmistress
stared at us as if we were mad. . . .

"I hope you are both good bushmen," she said to me and to Art
Jones, our staff photographer.

We said we were just newspapermen on a story.

"I hope you come back with your heads," she said. . . .

Report no. 7, for Mon. Feb. 10 release. Fort Nelson, B.C.
Jones and I, the three Gardners and the baby, crammed into the tiny
cabin, jammed ourselves as far forward as possible to lighten the tail.

With only a quarter mile of bent river on which to take off, Baker
gunned the motor to the utmost and headed down the perilously
short runway. . . .

Report no. 8, for Tues. Feb. 11 release. Fort Liard, B.C.
Here on the outer rim of civilization we began at last to gather a few
morsels of facts about the Nahanni region and the Slavey Indians
whose superstition has helped to weave a mist of legend about the
valley. . . .

I talked today to Willie McLeod, nephew of that same Willie
McLeod who came out of the Nahanni in 1905 with an Eno Fruit
Salt bottle plugged full of coarse gold nuggets and who with his
brother went back to the valley and to his death. . . .

Report no. 10, for Thurs. Feb. 13 release. South Nahanni River. *Precede.*
The intrepid ski plane expedition to mysterious "Headless Valley" in
the wilderness of Canada's northwest territory has landed successfully
on the South Nahanni River at the entrance to the valley itself. . . .

Their first discovery – and an exciting one – was that a lone
trapper and his wife have been living on the edge of the valley in utter
isolation for five years and that the legends about the existence of hot
springs in the midst of this frozen wilderness are true.

The expedition members, however, have yet to penetrate the
valley itself where they will now explore the many legends that have

grown up regarding this faraway region where lone trappers and prospectors met strange deaths. . . .

Berton's report to readers about his chat with the trapper Gus Kraus and his Native wife, Maggie, carefully countered the intentionally overblown claims of his lead. "Nobody can convince Gus Kraus that this wild region in which his snug cabin is built is tropical," he reported. "As far as he's concerned it's just another valley with a few hot springs at the mouth."[25] Later that day, Baker, Berton, and Jones flew over the hot springs themselves. They could see half a dozen of them throwing mist off a creek that ran into the South Nahanni about forty miles upriver from the Liard. From there, the Nahanni twisted through a 1,500-foot-deep canyon. Beyond the canyon lay Headless Valley.

Berton filed the article from inside Headless Valley on February 8, 1947, by transmitting it over the expedition's portable radio. It appeared in newspapers around the world on Friday, February 14. Russ Baker aborted four landings before he was able to set down on the ice of the South Nahanni River, and even then, Berton reported, the aircraft "bounced twenty feet into the air, hit again, bounced again and skipped like a basketball down the ice."[26] Baker said that he wouldn't attempt a winter landing there again for $10,000, and would personally give $100 to any pilot who could repeat his performance in early February.

Having by this time recounted and embellished the Headless Valley stories as much as he dared, Berton now punctured the myths, one by one. "This was the spot," he wrote, "where the McLeod brothers had been murdered on the way out from their lost gold mine, the spot that Indians had declared was guarded by evil spirits, where head-hunters – great hairy men – were said to roam in bands and where weird mists rise from the ground." It was a mystery no more. The *Vancouver Sun* expedition had discovered that "the mystery of Headless Valley melts away when you reach it. It is just another lonely, silent valley . . . ominous only by virtue of its inaccessibility. It was cursed only by the silence of the tomb. No living thing, beast or human or head-hunter, roams its untrodden snows."

The single sign of civilization they discovered was on a riverbank a mile from where they landed. There, Berton said, they found two crumbling old cabins, and with them "a rubber boot, an old syrup can, a rusty tobacco tin," and "a pin-up photo of Rita Hayworth – these were the only signs that civilization had come briefly to this valley."

When Hal Straight read the reference to the pin-up of Hayworth, he knew that Berton had discovered gold of another kind. For once in the series, he needed to rewrite, and very likely he took on the job himself. On February 17, the following text – significantly expanded from Berton's original – appeared in the *Vancouver Sun*.

> In the heart of this weird valley, deep in the grim sawtooth Nahanni Mountains where men have died for their gold, we found, of all things, a pin-up girl. Are you listening, Rita Hayworth? More important, is your press agent listening?
>
> Miss Hayworth, let us be the first to tell you that you are the official queen of Headless Valley. For it was your pretty head and scantily-clad torso that we found staring right at us out of a tattered and crumbling cabin in the forbidden valley.
>
> Who placed you here in this empty, forgotten log shack in this dead and silent banshee wind we have no way of knowing, but very nice you looked smiling at us from a sun-soaked California beach as you adjusted the zipper on your white-necked bathing suit. Believe us, Miss Hayworth, you brought the only breath of the tropics that has ever kissed the snow-locked wastelands that stretch across the 10 miles of this valley of dead men.[27]

Accompanying the article was an Art Jones photograph, taken in the run-down cabin. In it, a scruffy-looking, wide-eyed Pierre Berton, mouth open and gap-toothed, leers at a photograph of a beautiful and smiling Rita Hayworth.

Berton had fun in this, the eleventh and climactic column of the series, by taunting the half-dozen other parties still preparing to explore Headless Valley. The *Sun* expedition, he said, had left mementoes. "Just to make everybody feel at home we have laid out a section of the valley in streets, and roads, avenues and boulevards, so that those who follow will get their bearings."[28]

The next day Berton reported that he and his companions had returned with their heads from Headless Valley. They had dispelled its ghosts and exposed its secrets. The valley was not a single valley at all, but a two-hundred-mile stretch of rivers and valleys into which men poured very tall tales. Two of the men reported dead – Ernest Savard and Andy Hays – had been found alive. The "valley" was tropical only "if you call a handful of hot springs a tropical valley, . . . but personally I kept my arctic parka on." No treacherous mists got in the way of Art Jones's cameras, and the odd "wisp of vapor coming off the hot springs . . . didn't look very mysterious." Headhunters? "Nix. The place is deserted. Besides, there haven't been enough heads missing." As to assorted ghosts: "Sure, and we saw Santa Claus riding a winged salmon over Virginia Falls."[29]

The trip home proved uneventful, so Berton reported from Watson Lake about an experience Russ Baker had during the war. In February 1942, three American bombers on a training exercise went missing in the Watson Lake area; a million dollars worth of aircraft, twenty-four men, and top-secret Norden bomb sights had mysteriously disappeared. (The Norden sights, used over Hiroshima, featured a computer that calculated the point at which the bombs should be released over a target.) It turned out that the aircraft had landed safely after getting lost, but could not get airborne again. The American army pilots insisted that if a rescue plane landed, it too would be stranded. Baker disagreed, and said that for $10,000 he would bring the men and the bomb sights out. It took him several trips, but Baker rescued the men and the equipment.[30]

Berton and Jones got back to Vancouver safely enough, much to Janet's relief. She had telephoned Hal Straight almost every morning to check up on her husband's safety and whereabouts, and had calmed her nerves by painting the kitchen. Pierre himself had been made aware of the risks involved, since his insurance company had used his imminent departure for the Nahanni region in mid-winter as an excuse to double his life insurance premium.[31] Hal Straight telegraphed Berton earlier that he had "paid off prospectors" to "keep [their] mouths shut"[32] about the phony tales surrounding Headless Valley; now he wanted Berton himself securely out of town and away from reporters until the wire service newspapers had published the last instalment in the series.

Janet and Pierre promptly headed for a brief holiday in Seattle courtesy of the *Vancouver Sun*, but not before Straight proudly showed Berton a telegram he had received from Hollywood:

AM THRILLED AT BEING NAMED QUEEN OF HEADLESS VALLEY
BUT WON'T LET IT GO TO MY HEAD STOP SERIOUSLY BELIEVE MR
BERTON AND HIS EXPEDITION HAVE DEMONSTRATED EXTRA-
ORDINARY COURAGE IN THEIR EXPLORATION OF THIS UNKNOWN
AREA OF THE CANADIAN NORTHWEST STOP WOULD COME TO
VANCOUVER TO CONGRATULATE THEM MYSELF EXCEPT THAT
ORSON WELLES AND I ARE BUSILY TRYING TO FINISH NEW FILM
LADY FROM SHANGHAI WHICH WE ARE MAKING TOGETHER AND
REALIZE IT IS IMPOSSIBLE TO GET AWAY STOP WOULD LIKE TO
TAKE A LOOK AT BATHING SUIT PHOTOGRAPH THOUGH IF ONLY
TO SEE HOW I MADE OUT WITH THAT ZIPPER.[33]

The telegram ended: "Very best to you all, Rita Hayworth."

The *Sun's* Headless Valley series had been a smashing success, and
Hal Straight, for one, thought they all deserved an award. Never shy
about such things, he was soon on the telephone to Seymour Berkson
of International News Service. "Some kind of scroll saying this was
the greatest newspaper adventure since the war," he suggested. By the
end of February, the handsomely framed, hand-lettered scroll had
been hung in the managing editor's office. Its inscription read in part:
"In commemoration of the Vancouver, B.C., Sun's ski-plane expedition to 'Headless Valley' – the greatest real life adventure story since
the end of the war and an outstanding example of modern journalistic
enterprise."[34]

Berton was also pleased that *Maclean's* had accepted his earlier
Headless Valley article without revision. With near-perfect timing, it
appeared under the title "Valley of Mystery" in the March 15 issue.
Immediately, he suggested two other stories, and the magazine gave
him the green light to work on them. Arthur Irwin had now seen
enough of the quality of Pierre Berton's work, and of his imagination,
exuberance, and drive, that he dispatched an assistant editor, Scott
Young, to Vancouver to meet with him.

Berton and Young got together early in April at the Hotel Vancouver.
The meeting produced an anecdote Berton – like Young – never failed
to delight in telling. "I remember sitting with him in a Vancouver hotel
having a drink and talking about the old days," Berton related decades
later, "and I said, 'Isn't this a beautiful city? Look at this city. Look out

the window. Look at those mountains. Look at the sea. A man would be a fool to leave Vancouver.' And Scott said, 'Well that's too bad, I was here to offer you a job.' I said, 'I'll take it.' And so I packed up and we moved to Toronto and I went to work for *Maclean's*."[35]

❧

Berton leaped at the opportunity to work for *Maclean's*; the forty-five-year-old magazine was the best in the country. The novelist Thomas B. Costain had been one of its early editors, Robert Service and Lucy Maud Montgomery had written for it, and members of the Group of Seven had provided illustrations. Still, it was difficult to put his recent adventures behind him. He had enjoyed the limelight afforded by the exploits and loved repeating the tall tales only to debunk them. But he was not sure he wanted to be remembered as Mr. Headless Valley. "If one more person comes up to me and says 'Gee – I see you still got your head,'" he said at the opening of a *Vancouver Sun* radio broadcast, "I think I'm going to impale him on a sharpened copy pencil. That's the sort of thing I've been getting, ever since I returned from the South Nahanni River, which is better known to you as Headless Valley."[36] He was being coy, of course; the rest of the radio talk delivered a rollicking good account of his adventure. He readily admitted that it had been a stunt, but it had been *his* stunt, involving a daring Canadian on a dangerous mid-winter trip into one of Canada's most inhospitable wildernesses. He had survived, but so had the Headless Valley myth, despite the debunking.

He had reached a readership not simply of the *Sun*'s hundred thousand or so, but of millions. The U.S. Marine veterans conceded that the Canadians had beaten them and sent their congratulations. Jack Benny cracked jokes about Headless Valley on his radio program. The American reporter, newscaster, and world traveller Lowell Thomas, the first reporter into Germany following the First World War and the first to interview T.E. Lawrence in Jerusalem, dramatized Berton's expedition into the Nahanni in one of his network radio broadcasts. *Time* magazine reported on the Canadian expedition to Headless Valley. A movie company expressed interest in the legend. A large New York paper editorialized on the international competition to reach it.[37]

Headless Valley taught him a lot, and not only about Headless Valley. The whole experience made him realize how crucial it could be to a fellow's career to seize an opportunity and run with it. After the series had appeared, the International News Service general manager, Seymour Berkson, sent a personal letter. "I don't mind telling you," Berkson wrote, "that we were all delighted with the splendid expert feature writing you put into this series from the beginning to the end. It was a magnificent job and we got a great kick out of handling such beautiful copy."[38] A month later, Chester Weil of King Features Syndicate forwarded a letter he had received from James Henle, president of the Vanguard Press in New York. "Here is an idea that I got out of reading the material on Headless Valley," Henle wrote. "One of the most interesting gents I have met in print in a long time is this chap Russ Baker. I wonder if there wouldn't be a book in him. Perhaps this chap Pierre Berton would be the man to write it."[39] The idea was a sound one, and Pierre determined that he would write just such a book even without a contract from Vanguard. He knew what he would call it, too – "Snowball in Hell" – because, as he later put it in the introduction to the completed manuscript, "if a man keeps on flying, season in, season out, winter and summer, breakup and freezeup, year after year, he has, in the long run, about as much chance of dying with his boots off as a snowball in hell."[40]

Upon his return to Vancouver, Berton found that almost overnight he was a local celebrity. The public now viewed him as an expert on the Canadian north. Even with the series done, people clamoured to hear him speak or ask his advice or tell him their own stories. A clerk at the Larocque Department Store in Ottawa wrote to let him know how much he had enjoyed his lecture on mines in Alaska. A man from Oregon wrote to say that he wanted to move to Headless Valley to get away from city life. A resident of Revelstoke expressed appreciation for the talks Berton was giving on CBC radio in Vancouver. An employee of the federal Department of Transport's Radio Range Station in Yellowknife wrote in frustration to complain that newspapers continued to locate Headless Valley in British Columbia rather than the Northwest Territories, and to lay the blame on Berton. A couple of months after the series had ended, a man representing a group staying at a lavish California resort, the Hotel del Coronado, wrote to tell him that their local paper had carried just two of the articles. "About 15 of us are waiting for more news," he wrote on April 25. "What became of your expedition?"[41]

What indeed? In a way, it had not really ended. Public interest in Headless Valley persisted long after Berton had solved its mystery. This intrigued and puzzled him, and taught him the enduring power of myth. "I hated, really, to have to dispel the legends of Headless Valley, they were so good, and people wanted so much to believe in them," he told his Vancouver radio audience. "I feel like a bit of a heel, in a way, for debunking this particularly engaging fairy tale."[42] Nevertheless, over the next six years he exploited the fantasy shamelessly. He wrote a number of magazine articles about it and, by his estimate, delivered dozens of lectures and gave "radio talks by the score" over both the CBC and the BBC. "The fact is," he was to tell a radio audience in 1953, "that Headless Valley is an indestructible legend."[43]

All the Nahanni hoopla had fuelled his ambition. He had already begun a book about his wartime experiences and had also acquired enough stories about Russ Baker to fill the volume Vanguard Press seemed to want. Unfortunately, the possibility of writing either work in England on the Kemsley Scholarship had evaporated: the award had gone to his *Vancouver Sun* colleague Ray Gardner. A story lay behind that. Hal Straight was to have written letters of recommendation for both Gardner and Berton, but Berton found out that his boss had allowed Gardner to write his own. When Pierre marched to Straight's office and asked why he hadn't let Pierre write his own letter, too, Straight's reply was simple: "Because I didn't want to lose you."[44] The story was Berton's, but the tale rings true. This was the kind of mischief Hal Straight thought of as fun.

━━

Like H. Joseph (Joe) Miller, the lead character of *I Cover the Waterfront*, Berton aspired to be more than a newspaperman. He wanted to test his literary mettle, to experiment with other media. The Canadian Broadcasting Corporation was the obvious forum. He managed to secure an on-air commentator's contract for July 27, 1946, to January 31, 1947, and a fee of $12 for three cartoonlike sketches he drew "to illustrate

Women's Programs" (presumably for advertisement purposes: this was radio, after all). Berton's radio play *By-Line Story* was produced by the CBC in the Vancouver Theatre. It aired over the CBC Western Network late in the evening of January 23, 1947, and for his bit part in it he received a fee of $50.[45] At the same time, he began to expand the scope of his newspaper work by contributing feature pieces to the *Sun*'s magazine section.

Late in the war, and continuing until his move to Toronto, he tried his hand at other forms of creative writing. The first experiments did not stray very far from real life. They drew from his experience in the North as a youth and involved characters he felt he knew well, whether real or imaginary. The short story "Mystery Men," published as the leading piece in *Reading: A Canadian Magazine* early in 1946, told the stories of two unrelated individuals. One was Old John, a hermit who had gone north for gold and stayed forty-four years. "Surely, I reasoned," says the narrator, "there must have been something more to hold him here for a lifetime in this solitary valley – some other motive than gold?" Old John's answer was slow in coming, but "simple and all-embracing": "I like it here."

The second character in "Mystery Men" was Joe Rosenbaum, a clothing salesman from the city, who appeared to like being wherever "anything was doing." Rosenbaum was worrisome, because he seemed to follow the narrator everywhere. "He is the reflection in the department store window, the shadow on board promenade [*sic*] by the beach, the echo in the corridors of the arena." He was, for the most part, a stranger, yet the narrator felt he knew Joe Rosenbaum better than some of his own relatives. The story ends with an ironic twist, when Rosenbaum accuses the narrator of following *him*. Unnerved, the narrator stays home from work for a week, "hermit-like, reading soothing books, listening to the radio." Eventually he pulls his study curtains to face the outside world, only to see Joe Rosenbaum walking past the window.[46]

It is not difficult to see in this story certain hints of the contrasting strands in Berton's colourful makeup: one is the thoughtful man who relishes the silence of the North, the man who craves its stillness and is caught by its lure; another is the man of insatiable curiosity, the investigator of urban bustle, the raconteur of the carnival of life, the child who needs always to be the centre of attention, the lad from the North who has found himself drawn into the vortex of life outside and who now senses he may not easily escape its grasp.

One short piece Berton wrote just after the war drew upon his knowledge of local lore but claimed to be a true tale. "Magic in Their Souls" appeared in *British Columbia Digest* in July 1946, tagged by its subtitle as "The First Original Story of Vancouver's Jubilee." It sketched the lives of some of the characters who had helped to make Vancouver "tick," from Skaalch, an Indian of legend, to Louis Taylor, a well-known newspaperman, to Matt Nystrom, the old logger who busked on the city's streets with his two-dollar fiddle. Vancouver, said Berton, was full of such characters – "the famous cat man," "the mad Chinaman," and all manner of others. "Theirs is the sort of tale," he said, "that helps to add spice to the history books. . . . We ought to pay some sort of homage to their memory, even if their monuments lie only in our hearts."[47]

Pierre liked the prospects of this idea so much that he drew a mock movie poster. The words "Magic in Their Souls – by Pierre Berton" appeared on a scroll, and the illustration behind it showed ghostlike heads rising from a campfire. A line at the bottom of his sketch reads, "A Full-Length Feature."[48] He was developing the knack of harnessing his imagination not only to story, but to its conversion to other media and to the promotion of everything he did.

Later ventures into fiction portrayed thinly veiled refractions of himself. The pieces made little if any attempt to construct character, and the plots were contrived, striving for the kind of trick ending perfected by O. Henry. Quite apart from whatever literary merit they hold, the stories are of considerable value because they provide insight into a man not much given to sharing his interior life. The manifest content of these stories tells one tale; the latent content says something rather different. Together, they lay bare some of the emotional tremors and ambivalences on which Berton's memoirs remained resolutely silent.

In "The Waiting Room," which Berton wrote while still living with his parents and sister just after the war, a group of people gather in the antechamber of Heaven, just inside the Pearly Gates. They expect the arrival of dead loved ones. Two men are annoyed to discover that they are the first and second husbands of the same woman. Their jealousy evaporates, however, when the woman enters and – looking decidedly more aged than either man remembers – does not seem to notice her former husbands. Instead, she and an old man who has also been in the waiting room greet each other warmly. He is her third husband.[49]

In "Water Hazard," a war veteran tells his story to another, a bartender. A month out of the army, the vet has just got married to a woman named Lydia despite the fact that an earlier relationship had once turned him "sour." He had been with that first woman in Seattle, but they "didn't quite click." He joined the army, in fact, because he "wanted to put some space between this woman and me." He was suspicious. "I don't know if you ever had a gal – you figured she was your gal – but all the same you knew there was another guy somewhere in the background. Know what I mean? Yeah, well that's the way it was with me and her."

In a manner that seems to reflect the war service Berton wished he had had, rather than the one he experienced, the unnamed veteran talks about his "best friend," Harry. Pierre Berton had seen no combat during the war, and Harry Filion had seen hard action and been badly wounded in the process. But here the narrator and the fictional Harry are together in Holland, crossing the Maas River in assault boats and helping take out German pillboxes. "I covered Harry and he went up to the pillbox yelling to the Krauts to come out. Three of them came out waving a piece of rag and looking badly shook up. Everything might have been okay but one of them had a grenade in his belt." The narrator shoots all three Germans with his Sten gun, three Germans more than Berton had met taking courses overseas, but the grenade goes off. Harry receives a stomach wound. Shrapnel nicks the narrator in the arm, but he manages to help swim back across the Maas with Harry in tow. On shore, Harry pulls an envelope out of his pocket and asks his buddy, "Will you go and see my girl?" Inside the envelope is a photograph of Harry's girl. She is the girl from Seattle. Harry didn't make it. The girl in the picture was Lydia, "the same Lydia I'm married to now."[50]

The story "Past Imperfect" sees its protagonist, a war veteran named Phelps, stepping into the Granite Theatre on March 7, 1947, to see a revival showing of the movie *It Happened One Night*, Frank Capra's romantic comedy about a gruff and out-of-work reporter (Clark Gable) who helps a snobbish runaway heiress (Claudette Colbert) only because he sees a good story, and then finds himself falling in love with her. Phelps enjoys the movie, for it has taken him back to the middle of the

Depression, which in retrospect appears much better than it did at the time. He wonders what his life might have been like had he married Sally instead of Florence. He is musing on the fads and fashions of his own day when he notices that the date on the newspaper is March 7, 1936. At first he is incredulous, but all the papers on the street bear this date. Somehow he has stepped back eleven years in time, to the day when he first saw *It Happened One Night*.

At first he is disoriented, flashing back to his first operational flight over Germany on a night when he lost his squadron. "Then Phelps suddenly realized that he was a free agent. He had no wife or family. . . . In 1936 he was still a single man. . . . A feeling of freedom caused a slight tingling sensation, a curiously happy feeling which he at once repented." He realizes he can predict the future. He can make a fortune on the stock market. At work at the life insurance company, he encounters Sally and tells her that Joe Louis will be next heavyweight champion of the world. She tells him he is crazy, only to make him realize that he no longer needs to marry Florence. "He was free. He could, if he wished, teach history a lesson. He could change it." He could marry Sally. He proposes and she instantly says yes, and he tells her that they will be secure because he has put all his spare cash into Crimson Mountain stock that morning.

He marries Sally the next day, confident in the knowledge that, "in one small respect, he had changed the course of the world. He had, in a sense, routed fate." Then Crimson Mountain begins a steep decline. A little later, Jim Braddock knocks out Louis in the first minute of the first round. Something has gone "very, very wrong." The large events of history, like Mussolini's victory in Ethiopia, occur as predicted. "It was just the small details that didn't tally." He warns the Defence Department of the certainty of a war that would begin in September 1939, but it takes no heed. He lectures widely on the dangers of Hitler and Mussolini. Near penniless by this time, he wagers his last $100 that Vivien Leigh will be chosen to star in *Gone with the Wind*. He loses his bet: the studio chooses Betty Grable.

He is now derided even by his friends as a crank and an eccentric. Sally has long since left him. Even he has come to think himself demented. He hopes in vain for some event to happen that has already taken place. At last it does, on March 7, 1947, when he notices a revival showing of *It Happened One Night* at the Granite Theatre. "At last – a link with that other existence. He *hadn't* dreamed it: it *was* true." He takes the show in, and thoroughly enjoys it. Afterwards, outside, he buys a newspaper. Its dateline reads: "March 7, 1936."[51]

All three pieces seemed to anticipate the strange twists the screenwriter Rod Serling would take with time in *The Twilight Zone*, when it began to air on CBS television in 1959. They more than hint at their author's fears and desires, and the interplay of past, present, and future in his overworked imagination. They also suggest a man confused by his relationships with women and uncertain about marriage itself. In the latter respect, so does "A Study in Tweed," at seven hundred words very much the "vignette" its subtitle records, written from 1915 Haro Street in Vancouver, the Bertons' first marital abode. Here, a university student believed to be the "scion" of a prominent and wealthy family makes a big impression on campus by always appearing, even at formal balls, in his brown tweed suit. This makes him stand out and gets him attention – and girls. His unusual attire makes him seem distinctive. In the end, however, the man in tweed turns out to be penniless. Gossip about his summer vacations in Florida turns into the hard truth of work in a logging camp.

The brief sketch could be drawn from Berton's own experience at Victoria College in the fall of 1937, fresh from the mining camp at Dominion Creek. The lesson the character from the logging camp and the author from the mining camp seem both to have learned is that clothes make the man. In this case, the most revealing sentence occurs not at the end of a Berton short story, but at its beginning: "You can say what you want about a tight collar and starched shirt being like a straitjacket, but looking back on it all, there is something intriguing about white ties and tails, and all they connote."[52]

It was time to pack for Toronto.

IRWIN'S RECRUIT

—

FROM THE STIFLING CONFINES of the one-room flat they had sublet on the northwest corner of Bloor and Spadina, Mr. and Mrs. Pierre Berton had a view only of the building's tiny inner courtyard. The place had little natural light, reminding Janet of a cave, and the lack of windows opening to the street meant no refreshing lake breeze.[1] Instead, in the hot June of 1947 they were treated to the screech of Toronto streetcars. To the young couple, the battleship grey walls of the flat suited the city to which they had just moved. Vancouver and Toronto: what a world of difference there was between the wild farewell party the *Sun* had thrown for them and the silent greeting of their dreary new surroundings. Had Ray Munro and Art Jones really called an ambulance and had Pierre and Janet trussed up in straitjackets and marched around the block, with Evelyn Caldwell telling total strangers they were having epileptic seizures?[2]

Toronto just after the war was a city that threatened to outstrip Montreal in population, industry, and wealth, and was fast becoming the nation's financial capital. Still, it remained the "Toronto the Good" of yesteryear. During the war it had produced Lancaster bombers and boasted of eighty-seven industrial plants, but until 1947 its residents could not attend a commercial sporting event on a Sunday or buy liquor by the glass at any time. As soon as war veterans such as Berton returned home from overseas, they had made certain the politicians changed that law.[3]

More than a million people lived in metropolitan Toronto by war's end, but few seemed to love their city the way Vancouverites worshipped Vancouver or Montrealers stood loyal to Montreal. Toronto was a city with a skyline punctuated by church spires, yet it seemed dedicated to the almighty dollar. The year Pierre and Janet Berton arrived in Toronto, a CBC radio skit featured a ditty called "We All Hate Toronto":

> Sing a song of moola
> Pocket full of scratch
> Piling up mazuma
> Watching nest eggs hatch![4]

The skit had been written by Lister Sinclair, who had left Vancouver in 1942 to study mathematics at the University of Toronto. No one who knew him was surprised that he had found himself drawn away from mathematics and into the city's blossoming arts community. Thanks to the producer Andrew Allan, Sinclair's plays, skits, and sketches, often featuring him in the cast, aired regularly on CBC radio broadcasts.

Toronto was certainly no Vancouver, but Pierre and Janet Berton were not the sort of people to harbour loneliness anywhere they might be. In the one extant letter Pierre wrote to his mother in the summer of 1947, he describes the couple's social life just after they reached Toronto in June. Within a few weeks they had visited Oakville and played bridge with Pierre's uncle Phil and his wife, Louise. They had travelled to Fort Erie with Gerald and Elizabeth Anglin, old friends from Vancouver (Gerry had been hired to work at *Maclean's* before the war broke out), and stayed at the cottage of Betty Anglin's family. At Crystal Beach, Pierre insisted on riding out over the water on the roller coaster. Later, they all went to Niagara Falls, then drove to Buffalo and took a lake steamer back to Toronto.

Their life in the city that month was a whirl. The Bertons saw John Gielgud's production of *Love for Love*, fresh from Broadway (its run in New York had ended on July 5). It was an old Congreve play, and Pierre thoroughly enjoyed it – "a completely perfect production." They also saw Lucille Ball in Elmer Rice's *Dream Girl* – "also very enjoyable, tho somewhat pale, I thought, after Gielgud." Hal Straight telephoned that month, asking Pierre to find him some reporters. Berton hired three, one from the *Globe* and two from Canadian Press.

Quite early on, he discovered that social life in Toronto could at times be like that of a small town. Late that July, Brenda McDougall, an old flame of Pat Keatley's, invited Pierre and Janet to her home. The actor Tommy Tweed and his wife, Jean, who worked at the CBC, were there. Tweed, it turned out, had been the first blind date of one of Janet's ex-roommates. In his letter home, Pierre professed not to be surprised at this; even Scott Young's wife, Rassy, had been a friend of another former roommate.[5]

The previous April, Berton had received a letter from Arthur Irwin, confirming his appointment to the staff of *Maclean's* under the terms Scott Young had laid out at the Hotel Vancouver a few weeks earlier. "All of us here are looking forward to your arrival and I hope that the new venture will turn out to be both stimulating and profitable to you."[6] Berton was just as eager to report for work. "Even in 1947," he later confessed, "Toronto was the place to be" as far as newspaper and radio work was concerned. The city itself did not particularly attract him. "I comforted myself with the knowledge that Montreal, New York and, of course, Buffalo, were just around the corner." His sights had been set on New York City and *Life* or the *Saturday Evening Post*. Still, Toronto was a stepping stone. Buffalo, with its nightclubs and bars, was "an oasis of gaiety just two hours from Hogtown."[7]

Pierre knew that with the Nahanni article published and another well advanced, he had made a good start even before his first day on the job. Still, he was nervous about his first contact with Arthur Irwin. From what he had heard, Irwin was a tough-minded editor-in-chief and a stern taskmaster, at times abrasive and testy. The meeting came soon after he reached Toronto. It began in Irwin's office in the nondescript Maclean Hunter building at University Avenue and Dundas Street. The man who greeted him was soft-spoken, genteel, and impeccably dressed. Balding, and with a grey moustache and owlish eyeglasses, Irwin looked like a professor who had embraced the world of business.

Berton's first encounter with his new employer did not go well – it seemed all long silences and vacant small talk, something for which Irwin had little use. "What do you think of Norman Corwin?" the editor of *Maclean's* asked, without warning. Berton knew that Corwin was a popular American writer and radio producer equally adept at handling light entertainment or serious social issues, so he said that he thought the man was "pretty good." Wrong answer: he was superficial, Irwin said. Later, he took Berton to the posh University Club. While

Irwin picked at his meal, Pierre launched himself at a plate of oysters and lamb chops.[8]

By the time he hired Berton, Arthur Irwin had garnered a lot of experience in the magazine business. Born in 1898 and a native of Ayr, Ontario, Irwin had arrived at *Maclean's* at the age of twenty-seven. A veteran of the Great War, the experience of which had deepened his attachment to Canada, he had earned his place at *Maclean's* with stints at the *Mail and Empire* as a reporter from 1920 to 1923 and at the *Globe* as a feature writer from 1923 to 1925; he quit late in 1925 when he came under attack from within the paper over his criticism of the Conservative Party's intimate connections to business interests. At the beginning of April 1926, he was appointed the magazine's associate editor, and by the age of twenty-eight he was second at the magazine only to the magazine's editor, H. Napier Moore, himself new to *Maclean's*.[9]

Napier Moore made a point when joining *Maclean's* that under his leadership, as he later recalled, it would "seek out, stimulate and develop Canadians" who were "striving for expression and who have talent." The arrival of Arthur Irwin certainly met this aim, but by all accounts it was Irwin rather than Moore who gave the magazine a nationalist mission, ensuring that its contents were not only written by Canadians but about Canadians, their lives, their struggles, and their attitudes.

Born in Newcastle-on-Tyne and a devotee of the British Empire, Napier Moore loved American show business and British pomp in equal measure, and he revelled in the part he played each year in the annual Arts and Letters Club variety review. His imperial disposition and love of the theatrical did not wane. Canada became important to him, but primarily for its place within the orbit of the empire and Commonwealth. As late as 1956, two years after he retired to the Bahamas, he entertained the Empire Club of Canada with a hearty defence of Britain's military intervention in Egypt to seize control of the Suez Canal. Life at *Maclean's* during the Moore-Irwin years came to involve a constant battle between the two men, not least over the nationalist issue.[10]

Like the great *Winnipeg Free Press* editor J.W. Dafoe, Irwin believed instead that Canada was a North American nation and that its values arose out of the North American environment and experience.[11] If

Canada's central historical circumstance at mid-century placed it geographically, politically, and culturally between Britain and America, Napier Moore represented the past and Arthur Irwin the future.

Those in charge of the large Canadian magazine company Maclean Hunter, the owner of *Maclean's* – notably the executive vice-president, Floyd Chalmers, and the president, Horace T. Hunter – sensed this during the Second World War. Despite the continuing involvement of the company founder, Colonel J.B. Maclean, a pre-war, empire-loving Canadian businessman, they made Irwin the managing editor of *Maclean's*. The position allowed him to shape the magazine's content and slowly shift its direction toward Canadian subjects. At the beginning of November 1945, he became editor-in-chief. Napier Moore found himself relegated to the margins. From Berton's perspective, even in his first weeks at the magazine, this was progress. Moore, he said years later, "was a pompous fool. . . . He really had no sense of the country and no idea how to put out a magazine. He was an embarrassment . . . a silly-ass Englishman . . . who took all the credit but did little of the hard work."[12]

Berton's first years at *Maclean's* coincided with Arthur Irwin's ongoing recruitment of the best young writers in the country. Before the end of Irwin's first month as editor-in-chief, Hal Masson, born in Ontario and a former air force man, had become assignments editor, specializing in short fiction. At the beginning of December, Scott Young arrived. The twenty-seven-year-old navy veteran and London correspondent for Canadian Press became the magazine's articles editor. After three years at war, Gerald Anglin came back to the magazine in January 1946 to handle production. The former war correspondent John Clare left the *Toronto Star* soon afterwards to be a *Maclean's* staff writer.

Arthur Irwin's prize catch, however, had been Ralph Allen, appointed as assistant editor in 1946. Born in Winnipeg in 1913 but raised in Oxbow, Saskatchewan, where his father was a CPR station agent, Allen left Oxbow as soon as he could. Before he turned seventeen he had found a job as a sportswriter with the *Winnipeg Tribune*. In 1938 he headed east, to Toronto and the *Globe and Mail*. During the war, his evocative and compelling reports of military action for the *Globe* confirmed his reputation as one of the best war correspondents in the business.[13]

One thing about Arthur Irwin: he looked for writers with talent, not for extensions of himself. Irwin was university-educated and urbane, a moderate man, and a reticent intellectual. Allen was shaped by the school of hard knocks, blunt and every ounce the hard-bitten newsman. Irwin was a man to whom bartenders offered sherry; everything about Allen suggested that he was made for stronger stuff. The two men were opposites in many ways, but both had the ability to recognize the truly gifted and to draw out the best in the people they employed. Both also shared a heartfelt commitment to Canada and Canadians and felt compelled to tell the country's stories.[14]

Jack Scott and Hal Straight, Arthur Irwin and Ralph Allen, filled out the quincunx of extraordinary men – with Bruce Hutchison at its centre – whom Berton credited for making him a craftsman in his trade and shaping his commitment to Canada. Berton grew to admire both men, but it was the courtly Irwin rather than the world-worn Allen to whom Berton looked for mentorship. Twenty-two years older than Pierre, Irwin was a wise father figure, whereas Allen, seven years Pierre's senior, was more a worldly older brother. Berton liked the way Allen "didn't stand for any nonsense," and understood that his tough stance toward staff writers was a sign of respect.[15]

With time on her hands and in a strange city, Janet did most of the housework and the packing and unpacking when they moved from one place to another. Pierre may have done his fair share of the work, but it certainly did not affect his rate of production for *Maclean's*. His first byline after reaching Toronto was for an article he had begun with Charles Lynch on Brazilian Traction while he was still in Vancouver. Called "The Light," it appeared in the August 15 issue. By the end of 1947, his byline had appeared in six more feature articles in the biweekly magazine – two in September, two in November, and two in December. In fact he had written more. Arthur Irwin's policy was that no writer could have two bylines in one issue; a second article would require a pseudonym. On September 15, Berton contributed one such piece – about tugboats – because the issue already carried his byline over a feature on Stanley Park and its value to Vancouver.[16]

The subject of the September 15 item was predictable, given Berton's recent arrival from the Pacific coast, but readers of the magazine soon came to expect the unexpected from him: a tornado that tore through Windsor; a resourceful Vancouver entrepreneur and his dream to build a city aquarium; the brilliant scientist in charge of the Chalk River atomic energy station; a crisis in the music business over performance rates and royalties. Berton missed having a major article in every issue between the end of August and the beginning of the new year only because Irwin sent him to Manhattan in September to cover the "World of Tomorrow" conference at the United Nations. He was just gearing up.[17]

He warmed to Arthur Irwin in spite of a second awkward meal together. That fall, the Bertons decided to ask the boss over to dinner. Pierre inquired what he liked to eat and Irwin said he enjoyed duck, but the duck Pierre purchased in Chinatown proved to be "as tough as nails." Conversation once again faltered. The whole evening, Berton recalled, was "weird." Yet a few months later, when Berton risked bringing Irwin home yet again, the evening was filled with delightful and animated discussion. "Janet couldn't believe that this was the same man who had sat so silently and glumly at the previous meal," Berton later told Ralph Allen's son, Glen.[18]

Despite Berton's obvious talent, Arthur Irwin and Ralph Allen put him through the same tough apprenticeship served by all the other recruits. Irwin was not much of a writer, but he was a first-rate editor and his employees lived in fear of the cramped notes he always left in the margins of their typescripts. Possessed of a systematic mind, he insisted on firm logic and factual accuracy. His marginalia became the stuff of legend among magazine writers. "Evidence?" "Who he?" "What is a lobster?" With Irwin, Berton said, "you had to prove everything."[19]

While Irwin emphasized substance, Allen tended to dwell on style. (His war novel, *Homemade Banners*, was published in 1946.) Irwin lived by the Methodist work ethic; Allen possessed a Presbyterian's conscience. Allen's marginal notes were as caustic as Irwin's, and at times personally brutal. Berton recalled that if Allen received a second-rate story submission he would say, "Somebody's written this with their foot." Berton heard him once tell Max Braithwaite, a freelancer who contributed to *Maclean's*, "Your article is so bad, we have to rewrite it before we throw it in the wastepaper basket."[20]

None of Berton's early copy hit either Allen's round file or his own, but more than once it was sent back heavily marked up by one or both editors. Arthur Irwin taught Berton that the heart of the good non-fiction article lay in its research. "Have you done your homework?" he would ask. Everyone at *Maclean's* heard those words at one time or another. The average article took Berton two days to write but a month to research.[21] This became the ratio of his writing life.

In his early days at *Maclean's*, Berton was a handful and quick to show his western chauvinism. Irwin encouraged free and open discussions at his Thursday morning editorial meetings. At times they became boisterous, and Berton did little to temper the tone or volume. "We've never *heard* of that in B.C.," Scott Young heard him bellow. "Nevertheless, Pierre, it exists," went John Clare's sardonic retort.[22] Irwin once took Berton aside and told him, in his restrained way, that there were "less blunt ways" to express his opposition to ideas. Instead of shouting "I don't agree with that!" Irwin suggested, Berton should word his opposition in the form of a question. "It was good advice," Berton said many years later, "and I've taken it ever since."[23]

As at the *Ubyssey*, and probably at the *Vancouver Sun*, Berton did not leave everyone at *Maclean's* with a favourable first impression. Arthur Irwin hired him because, as he once said, "I thought this boy was a comer." Yet the wunderkind who arrived, fresh from the coast, struck him as someone "pretty brash, very cocky." Irwin liked the young man's "enormous, fantastic energy," but found that it came in an abrasive package.[24] The Pierre Berton that June Callwood and her husband, the *Maclean's* writer Trent Frayne, met in 1947 almost alarmed them – too loud, too big, too much the smart aleck. He seemed "too young and sure of himself," Callwood said. Like so many others, when she thought of Berton she thought immediately of *The Front Page*.[25]

Born in 1924, Callwood was herself larger than life. By the time Berton arrived in Toronto, the native of Chatham in southwestern Ontario, as bright as she was beautiful, had put a half-decade of news-paper experience behind her with the *Toronto Star* and the *Globe and Mail*. Most of her childhood had been spent in a francophone enclave near Detroit named Belle River, where her father, Byng, a plumber by training, had managed to open a tinning plant. In 1936, June was sent to a Roman Catholic boarding school and thought for a time about becoming a nun, but she returned home the following year because her parents could not afford the tuition. That same year, deeply in debt, Byng left his wife, Gladys, and his daughters, June and Jane, to seek work in the Canadian west.[26]

Gladys and her girls joined their husband and father in Regina for most of 1940, but when he signed up for the Royal Canadian Engineers and was shipped overseas, the family returned to Ontario and took up residence in Brantford. June excelled in school and made many friends. One was a fellow high school student, Ross McLean, who shared her love of the newspaper and entertainment industries. At school she wrote for the student newspaper of Kitchener Collegiate, the *Grumbler*, and soon found herself the *Kitchener Record*'s stringer for high school news.

After her mother forced her to quit school at sixteen to help support the family, she parlayed acquaintance with a member of the newspaper's board of directors (he had officiated at a ceremony at which June had won a short story award) into a letter of introduction to the editor of the *Brantford Expositor*, and secured a full-time job with the paper. It paid $7.50 for a six-day week.[27] Two years later, the city editor of the *Toronto Star* hired her, sight unseen, as a reporter at the newspaper, so she moved to Toronto.

One look at the stunning but very young woman in high-heeled shoes, and the *Star*'s city editor demoted her to secretary. As a girl Friday, she was willing but not content to do work unworthy of either her talent or her ambition, but she answered mail and wrote the required photo captions. After two weeks on the job, she was fired when a Camp Borden sergeant took issue with her caption on a photo of an army tank. She refused a job at the Toronto *Telegram* when offered a secretarial rather than reportorial position, and after trying unsuccessfully to enlist in the RCAF as a fighter pilot, she found the office of Bob Farquharson, managing editor of the *Globe and Mail*, and was granted a three-day trial as a reporter.

She struggled at first but soon found her stride, and with it, confidence. Before long she was a regular staff reporter covering everything from criminal trials to the Miss Toronto pageant. In 1944, still only nineteen, June married a fellow *Globe* journalist, Trent Frayne – a westerner whose friends in his hometown of Brandon, Manitoba, called him

"Billy" despite his Christian names, Trent Gardiner. Callwood found in him the dependability and stability her father had failed to provide.

June and Trent met the Bertons at a welcoming party for Pierre thrown by either Gerry Anglin or Ralph Allen – years later they could not recall which – and the Fraynes found they shared a good deal with Janet and Pierre beyond the common newspaper background: a similar progressive political and social outlook, for example. As months and years went by, they dined at each other's homes, became close friends, and swapped stories about the joys and woes of parenting.[28] Like Janet Berton, June Callwood quit her salaried position when she married. While her children were young she turned to freelance magazine work. By the 1950s her pieces were regular features in *Maclean's* magazine.

No one who wrote for *Maclean's*, except the team of Frayne and Callwood, could match Berton in his first years at the magazine. Abrasive and cocksure though he was, the man nevertheless produced. In 1948, *Maclean's* published fifteen feature articles with the Berton byline. Their themes point to his interests and concerns. One preoccupation was injustice, past and present, and two remarkable Berton features gained particular public attention that year. The February 1 issue carried a piece with the short but gripping title "'They're Only Japs.'" It was Berton's account of the seizure of property and internment of Japanese Canadians during the Second World War. The title of the second article was equally short and blunt: "No Jews Need Apply." Appearing in the November 1 issue, it described employment practices that discriminated against Canada's Jews. Both were inspired in part by the disjunction Berton detected between the vaunted "human rights" rhetoric he had heard at the United Nations "World of Tomorrow" conference and the realities of ethnic relations he had experienced in Vancouver during the war.

Neither article dwelt on abstract struggles for a principle called justice. Instead, they told stories of great drama and actual discrimination, stories that no reader could forget. Ken Kitamura had been one of the richest men in Vancouver, with a nice Packard car and a $50,000 house on the fringe of affluent Shaughnessy Heights. Berton found him running a lunch counter on Toronto's Yonge Street. "I'm just a dishwasher," said the Japanese Canadian who had once owned a large merchandising business. From this beginning, Berton proceeded to tell Canadians about other fellow citizens, "12,000 ghosts" swindled by a panicked state and victimized further by a thinly veiled racism.

In a similar vein, Berton began "No Jews Need Apply" with the story of Norman Lyons, a young Toronto accountant who had been told constantly during the war that there were no jobs for him, and to whom an employee of a prominent accounting firm had once said, "There's no use beating about the bush. We don't employ Jews here." The idea for the article arose from Pierre's research on the Japanese Canadians, but it took flight at the first party Pierre and Janet attended in Toronto, when conversation among his old friends from the Royal Military College turned to talk about Jews as "these people."[29]

Armed with the blessing of the weekly editorial meeting, Berton had burrowed into the subject of anti-Semitism in Canada. To test its prevalence, he went to the Maclean Hunter stenographers' pool and found two experienced "girls" with similar backgrounds; he instructed them to answer newspaper advertisements for stenographers, typists, bookkeepers, and filing clerks. He chose these occupations because, as he put it, "they cut right across the industrial and business field – from insurance companies to truck manufacturers." One woman gave her name as Greenberg, the other as Grimes. Each telephoned forty-seven prospective employers. "Grimes" received forty-one immediate interviews; "Greenberg" (who had telephoned first) was informed twenty-one times that the job had been filled. In nine other cases, either the telephone was slammed down in her ear or she was told, "You wouldn't want the job anyway."

Then Berton went directly to the offending firms to ferret out the truth. His interviews with employers revealed the stark face of discrimination. To illustrate his point further, he shifted the article's attention to the banning of Jews from Ontario's summer resorts. A woman calling herself Marshall made twenty-four reservations for a two-week holiday, but another who gave the name Rosenberg was not able to book more than twelve. "We are tending toward a ghetto society, Canadian style," he wrote.[30]

Berton supported his findings with figures from studies done by the Canadian Jewish Congress and from a wartime Gallup poll. Then he proceeded with a detailed social and demographic analysis, bolstered by the 1941 Census of Canada. "The wall of segregation which today keeps the Greenbergs estranged from the Peabodys is as high as ever," he concluded. "And like all walls, it can cripple the freedom of men on both sides of it. Until it comes down, it stands in the way of both Jew and Gentile – a stubborn and ugly barrier blocking the pathway to the good life." This was scarcely the sort of journalism characteristic of North America in the early years of the Cold War, when even the brash new medium of television, in the judgment of Erik Barnouw, its premier historian, learned "caution and cowardice."[31]

During his research, Berton learned from the director of the Maclean Hunter stenographers' pool that the company's own policy was not to hire Jews. This sufficiently shocked him that he bolted into Arthur Irwin's office to accuse *Maclean's* of anti-Semitism. Irwin angrily denied the charge. Faced with the choice of resigning, asking to be taken off the story, or continuing with his research, Berton chose to charge ahead. It was, he later said, "the line of least resistance." In his memoirs, he would note that Irwin made no attempt to monitor progress on the piece or restrict its scope. Still, although the piece ran as a lead article, it remained silent on *Maclean's* policy on the employment of Jews.[32]

Linked to Berton's concern for social justice was a second set of articles in 1948 focused on contemporary social problems. "The House of Lost Weekends" (March 1), a story about life at the unnamed Homewood Institute in Guelph, dealt with mental health issues, especially alcoholism.[33] "Nightmare Pills" (May 1) drew attention to the use and abuse of sleeping pills such as Nembutal. The article "Benzy Craze" (June 15) continued the theme, exploring the shadowy world of drugs in Vancouver, where even "upstanding citizens" sniffed Benzedrine inhalers – nominally to beat a cold but in fact to get "a jolt that rivals cocaine."

One can almost hear Berton ask questions of himself during the research for these articles on alcoholism and substance abuse. What makes men and women take these drugs? What is it about life today that interferes with their ability to cope? Why do people get caught up in such fads and fancies, dangerous or not? What ever happened to our free will? Clearly, such questions came into play, for between these features on drug abuse he published two others that revealed the way modern social research techniques had been used not simply to analyze but also to shape public consciousness.

"Quiz on Your Doorstep" (April 1) appeared a month after the piece on alcoholism. It told the little-known story of Gallup polls and described how pollsters could predict both political and consumer preferences. Determine the preference, Berton suggested, and you can create and profit from the habit. But the profits, he warned, might well come at the customer's expense. The article "Want to Be a Boss?" (June 1) followed "Nightmare Pills." In it, Berton noted that prospective executives were subjected to psychological tests to evaluate their potential. Almost every Berton article carried with it some kind of historical narrative that helped explain its context, and this one was no exception. "Want to Be a Boss?" contained a comprehensive overview of the way social research, with its origins in clinical and medical health settings, had come to penetrate the contemporary marketplace. Businesses now had ways of getting inside people's heads, whether of corporate executives or of ordinary citizens and consumers, in order to maximize profits.

Much of this perspective came from the Berton who wore tweed, the one with left-leaning political convictions and unabashed compassion. The course of moral concern tends to flow toward those lacking power, and with Berton it came accompanied by a torrent of words. But another line of inquiry came from that part of him intrigued by white tie and tails. Berton may have thought of himself as an outsider; indeed, in temperament and outlook, he remained one. Nevertheless he was drawn, like a northern moth to a campfire flame, to stories of people on the inside – to what the author Peter C. Newman, following Berton's lead, would later call "the flame of power."[34] Berton's third set of articles in 1948 dealt with men of influence.

Berton came to pride himself on the way he was able to mine his own life for good material, so he chose the moguls he knew best: the Cromie family, that remarkable team of father and sons who had taken the near-bankrupt, low-circulation *Vancouver Sun* and made it into one of the most remarkable and successful newspapers in the country. His account was affectionate but knowing, a story that revealed intrigues and squabbles within the Sun Tower. The first of a number of articles he would write on the rich and powerful, especially those in the newspaper business, it appeared as "Vancouver's Rising Sun" on July 1, 1948.

That summer, Arthur Irwin sent him to the Yukon. Janet was expecting their first child early in August, but Berton could scarcely turn down the assignment: after all, he was the one voice of the North at *Maclean's*, and Irwin was offering a free trip to his childhood home.

Having had enough of staring at their building's empty courtyard, and with Janet several months pregnant, the couple had moved in midsummer from busy Spadina Avenue to an apartment at another Toronto intersection. This one was in a fairly new building above a hardware store near the corner of Donlands and O'Connor in East York. On August 5, not long after they moved in, Janet gave birth to a daughter. They named her Penny. Like Spadina, the new place had only one room, to be shared with a baby and crib, but it had some advantages – a balcony where the baby could be given fresh air, and around the corner a drugstore with baby supplies and a druggist's daughter, twelve years old but responsible, who did babysitting. ("We didn't know any better," Janet Berton later recalled.) The apartment was also next door to the Donlands Theatre but, strapped for cash, the Bertons could seldom afford the 25-cent cost of admission.[35]

Parents in the early postwar years stood in awe of science in general and of medical authority in particular, and family doctors kept husbands well removed from matters related to pregnancy and childbirth. Fathers as often as not were at the office or in a waiting room, cigar at hand, when their wives gave birth. The book that would help generate a fundamental shift in such attitudes had been published just two years earlier, when Dr. Benjamin Spock's 25-cent pocket book, *The Common Sense Book of Baby and Child Care*, appeared in stores throughout North America. In it, Spock suggested that mothers and fathers who took an active role in raising their children would find it an experience of great joy. Berton would come to be such a parent, but in the summer of 1948 this expectant father went north with no great reluctance, uncertain whether he would be present at the birth of his first child. Fortunately, by the time Penny arrived, he had returned home, and he was with Janet when she left the hospital with the couple's new baby.

Three articles came out of Berton's northern trip: one about his experience travelling up the Alaska Highway, another on the enduring enticement of gold in the Klondike, and a third describing life in Dawson City.[36] Part travel writing, part history, part reminiscence and reflection, the series was written by the Canadian best equipped to tell other Canadians the story of the North in all its richness. Berton was the one writer who could make it appear not merely a quaint land of Mounties and trappers and lynx but a geographical region of great relevance to a rapidly expanding postwar nation – a part of Canada that now seemed to reflect the country's future as well as its past. The title of the inaugural article, "Let's Drive to Alaska," invited Canadians in the south to get into their cars and explore the highways heading north. "The Alaska Highway is now open to tourists," ran its subhead. "And they'll find crazy rivers, covered wagons, six-bit beer and 1,500 miles of scenery."

This was Pierre Berton as Canadian development agent, not simply an observer of consumer culture but an advocate of it. "You can buy anything in Fairbanks from an electric toothbrush to a set of falsies – if you have the money. . . . This is what the highway was created for and this, too, is what it is creating: the New North, wide-open and raucous as ever, free-spending, armed to the teeth, full of all the hopes and despairs of a new kind of gold rush, as tough and hard and ruthless and beautiful as the fancy women who walk Fairbanks' streets. This is the 1948 model of the frontier and perhaps it isn't very different from the earlier models, underneath the gloss."[37]

The visit to Dawson moved him deeply, and no reader of the two articles he devoted to it could have missed the fact. On one level, the trip north helped him rediscover aspects of his early life; on another, it allowed him to recognize something of what he had become. Berton made no attempt to conceal his emotions with a cloak of objectivity or to discount the appeal and power of nostalgia. Nostalgia was in fact his means of drawing people into the past, engaging their emotions along the way. "An old home town," he began, "is many things to many people: faces, memories, old buildings and vacant lots, climate and history and low blue hills, dust and gravestones and old, old men – a shifting montage of sound and impressions that sometimes stray through your dreams like the sound of an ancient schoolbell or the bark of a dog, long dead."[38] A dog like Grey Cloud, he might have added.

Berton the professional researcher delighted in providing fascinating concrete detail about a ghost town that somehow remained very much alive – the names of long-gone gold rush hotels, like the Greentree; the seltzer bottles and the ashtrays made from sardine cans in Eddie Rickard's second-hand store; a Scottish bride's wedding presents, unwrapped for thirty years because she did not intend to stay. This strange dance of life and death, of present and past, of lure and lament, fascinated him, and he wrote of it from stale memories but with fresh eyes. The people of Dawson had asked him whether he noticed great changes in his hometown; the greatest change, he said, had been in himself. Crumbling buildings, once ordinary to him, wore the patina of old romance. Still, Dawson's glory had long gone, and he sensed "a strange restlessness" about the town.[39] Perhaps he acknowledged a link between change and restlessness, the need for reinvention, and saw it in himself.

He and Janet moved again before Penny was two years old, this time to a basement room at 19 Kingsway Crescent in Toronto's west end. The house was quite elegant, but the Bertons' room was damp and gloomy and – at $100 a month – expensive; but it was large enough for the new baby and perhaps one more. Neither parent was pleased with the new place – for one thing, the bathroom was icy cold and Janet found it impossible to toilet-train Penny. But they decided that this was where they would stay until they could afford a house. Before long, chats with a neighbour led Janet to become involved with a group dedicated to the care and treatment of troubled children and their families.[40]

The possibility of liberation from their subterranean existence on Kingsway came even before they moved there, and Lister Sinclair was their liberator. Since the Bertons' arrival in Toronto, he and his wife, Alice, had been their closest friends. A fixture at the CBC, with scores of plays and radio documentaries already to his credit, Sinclair had bought three acres of land in Kleinburg, a small village about twenty-five miles north of Toronto. One of his friends had purchased forty acres from a local farmer, with the idea of turning it into a colony for writers and artists. The Sinclairs' lot ran up from the bank of the meandering Humber River and was next to the property and house of the Toronto writer and poet Ron Hambleton and his wife, Jean.

In the early summer of 1948, Pierre and Janet drove to Kleinburg with the Sinclairs to look around. They had given little thought to moving from the city, but the picture-postcard main street of the village, with its frontierlike buildings of clapboard and false fronts, and the Humber River valley, with its gentle meadows and rolling hills, changed their minds. "As the hillside rose we found ourselves in an orchard of wild apple trees mixed with hawthorn," Pierre recalled. "Above we could see a strip of pastureland, the grass more than ankle high. We reached the top, sat down, and looked due west into the setting sun. The wooded valley stretched off below us for miles, with the tinsel sparkle of the river winking through. On the far ridge we could see a single barn, nothing more."

"I think we should buy it," he said to Janet. She immediately agreed.[41]

Almost before they knew it, they were the proud owners of three acres of land in the Humber Valley. All they had to do was arrange water and electrical services to the property, raise the money to build a house, and find a way of getting between work and home. Neither Pierre nor Janet had a driver's licence. All this took time. Meanwhile, the pleasure of life with little Penny more than compensated for the indifferent surroundings of the basement on Kingsway Crescent. It was there that Janet sometimes cared not only for Penny but also for Scott and Rassy Young's little boys, Bob and Neil.

Pierre's work at *Maclean's* continued to go well. In September 1948, he had turned his attention to one of Canada's most successful politicians, Ontario's Conservative premier, George Drew, rumoured to be a candidate for the leadership of the Progressive Conservative Party of Canada. The title was stark, "George Drew" (October 1), but the content proved rich, providing a thoroughly researched and highly distilled biography of the public and private man some people called "Canada's Churchill." Blair Fraser, Ottawa editor of *Maclean's*, wrote to Berton from the House of Commons Press Gallery as soon as he finished reading the piece: "That was a swell job on Gorgeous George. I thought you hit it just right – a recognizable portrait, friendly without being gooey, frank without being hostile."[42]

After the serious features in October and November on Drew and on anti-Semitism, Berton filled out the year with a couple of articles on light-hearted subjects and a final one of more sober bent. The first was on the return of university students to campus, with a focus on McGill and its social life. The second, carrying the salacious title "He Was a Love Slave," profiled a colourful ex-boxer named Thomas P. Kelley who regularly showed up at *Maclean's* trying to sell stories. Kelley was a whopper of a story in himself, and he became exactly this under Berton's byline. Few Canadians had heard of him, yet he was Canada's most prolific writer of pulp fiction – a man with thirty *noms de plume* and almost three million words in print.[43]

Jack Scott sent praise that December. "Hello, white boy," he began. "Just finished your 'He was a Love Slave' and thought I'd better write quickly to say it was a lovely job . . . strictly boff. Also to thank youse for giving the fine goose to Cromie."[44] The chatty letter retailed the latest *Vancouver Sun* gossip, including "the usual sagas of the imbibing bouts" involving Hal Straight.

Berton ended the year with an article on a gang of Toronto teenagers who hung out in the city's west end and whose criminal exploits had been the subject of much attention in the daily press. Written in collaboration with the war veteran and social work professor C.G. Gifford, "The Beanery Gang" carefully blended human interest, ethnographic description, and social analysis. Written for a mass audience, it nevertheless resembled the accessible genre of sociology involving participant observation made popular by the sociologist William Foote Whyte in his 1943 book on Boston gang culture, *Street Corner Society*.[45]

Berton was becoming comfortable with the demands of writing for magazines and meeting their deadlines. But much of his effort at more literary work had gone nowhere. The recognition brought a bittersweet end to an otherwise satisfying year. True, the CBC had broadcast his radio play *Water Hazard* back in January, when he and Janet still lived on Donlands, and he had received a cheque for $35 in payment. But at the end of October Raymond Whitehouse, the CBC's drama producer, rejected five of his other plays, including *The Waiting Room* and *Past Imperfect*. CBC drama scripts, Whitehouse noted, aimed at being either entertainment or Canadiana; "your scripts swing so completely on the fantastic motif that I feel they would not fit into the over-all tone of the series." This was especially so with *The Waiting Room*, which Berton had converted from short story to radio play. It was "a clever satire," Whitehouse said, but "so involved that . . . a radio audience would wind up in a complete state of bewilderment and would call it quits before we would." Whitehouse suggested that Berton abandon the "abnormal motif" and write him "a drama based on the normal every day human existence problems which we all have to face." To make matters worse, Vanguard Press had expressed no further interest in his completed book-length manuscript on Russ Baker. In November, the New York publisher Farrar, Straus and Company rejected it outright.[46]

Berton would have had as much difficulty finding a publisher in Canada, even if his manuscript on Russ Baker had been better. The state of publishing in the nation was worse than it had been at the beginning of the century, when more than a dozen publishing houses existed in Toronto alone, soon to launch such bestselling authors as Ralph Connor (the Winnipeg clergyman Charles W. Gordon), Mazo de la Roche, and Robert E. Knowles. In 1897, the Methodist Book Room and Publishing House alone released thirty-seven Canadian titles. By way of contrast, in 1948 English Canada's publishers published only fourteen works of fiction.

Much seemed to conspire against the project of being a successful writer in Canada at mid-century. Canada's book industry, like the country in general, suffered from a postwar "mini-depression"; the home market was small; media coverage was negligible. The frayed cloak of colonial inferiority, whether in the universities, the national press, or the publishing houses, cramped the national imagination and sapped its vitality. Many who counted in the literary establishment thought Canada to be "a people without a literature,"[47] even as novels of mid-century by established writers such as Morley Callaghan, Hugh MacLennan, and Thomas Raddall and those by younger writers such as W.O. Mitchell exposed such a view as false, at least as it applied to fiction. Original works of trade non-fiction by Canadians on Canadian subjects rarely interested publishers, and Canadian readers seemed to prefer books written by American and British writers. For one prominent Canadian publisher at mid-century, the reason for the weakness in domestic book production rested "with the failure to date of any large group of Canadian authors to express this country to the Canadian people in a really arresting way."[48]

The year 1949 no sooner began than *Maclean's* gave Berton an assignment unusual even by his adventurous standards. For the better part of a week he found himself on a DC-4 aircraft accompanying a Royal Winter Fair champion, Glanafton Laurel Heather, and twenty-three other purebred Holstein dairy cattle on a six-thousand-mile flight from

Toronto to Montevideo, Uruguay. Berton the new cowhand accompanied his herd not from waterhole to waterhole but from airport to airport – in Florida, Colombia, Ecuador, Peru, and Uruguay. The published article, "Git Aloft, Little Dogie" (March 1, 1949), introduced *Maclean's* readers to the crew of the DC-4 and their adventures, not least during a flight through the Andes between Chile and Argentina at seventeen thousand feet with a failing engine and no oxygen.

Except for a threat of jail in Santiago due to the improper visa of one of the crew, Berton survived his days as a cattle wrangler without major incident. Pungent with the aroma of cow dung by the time the last of the herd was dropped off, he enjoyed a flight back from Palm Beach to New York that was surreal, one lone passenger on a plane loaded with nine thousand pounds of gladioli. "How lucky can you get?" he later wrote, thinking of the remarkable improvement in air quality between the two flights.[49] The record of the *Maclean's* editorial conference that followed was less sanguine: "Berton left here with our camera and light meter, half a dozen rolls of film and an English-Spanish dictionary. He returned, two weeks later, with a bad sunburn, a tin of Chilean crab meat and a tendency to pepper his conversation with the word 'manana.' Of the camera there was not the slightest trace."[50]

Berton was shocked to discover on his return that Ralph Allen no longer worked for *Maclean's*. He had resigned as its managing editor to become a sports columnist with the Toronto *Telegram* in order to have more time for his fiction. Arthur Irwin did not rush to fill the managing editor position; instead, he made John Clare the magazine's associate editor. Berton became articles editor, the post Clare had left. After a year and a half on the job, he was now a member of the *Maclean's* editorial staff.

Not everyone welcomed this news. He was still a brash and opinionated fellow from Vancouver, and these characteristics made him abrasive to others as an editor, especially to those who worked for him. He was insensitive, Trent Frayne said – like a little boy who was not aware of other people's feelings. Ralph Allen told writers that they were capable of producing better work; Berton would yell that they were hopeless. "Jesus Christ, Frayne," he once barked, "third edit and it still smells as if you wrote it with your feet." This to Trent Frayne, senior to Berton in the magazine's pecking order, and an unmistakable appropriation of one of Ralph Allen's favourite remarks. Berton's editorial technique at the time, June Callwood said, "had all the subtlety and charm of a sledgehammer."[51]

Still, no one denied that Berton was a superb articles editor. Frayne and Callwood agreed that what he lacked in polish he more than made up for in editing skill. His stock of ideas for possible articles seemed limitless, and he could tease stories from his writers that they did not know they had. His acute editorial eye had been noticed in 1948, when an unsolicited twenty-four-page manuscript on an unlikely subject by an unpublished author from Kitchener showed up on his desk. Berton was taken immediately with its distinctive and graceful style and trumpeted its virtues to Scott Young, then the articles editor. Edna Staebler's article about sword fishing in Cape Breton appeared in *Maclean's* as its lead article on July 15, 1948. It was her first publication. In 1949, through the fiction editor W.O. Mitchell (whose first novel, *Who Has Seen the Wind*, had been published by Macmillan of Canada two years earlier), she met Berton in person. He suggested that her next subject should be her hometown and its Mennonite heritage.[52] She took his advice and the article won the Canadian Women's Press Award for Outstanding Journalism.[53]

Blunt though he was, Berton told writers precisely what they should do and in what direction to take an article. With time, his early roughness in handling people wore down, and on occasion he could be positively charming as well as helpful. Sidney Katz, who joined *Maclean's* in the early 1950s, said that when he came away from sessions with Berton he felt stronger than when he had entered them.[54]

Berton held the position of articles editor for the next three years. At the same time, his influence was being felt in other areas. He advised associate editor John Clare in March 1949, for example, of the way the *Saturday Evening Post* handled certain design issues, in particular the symbiotic relationship between an article's title and its layout. He suggested that, as at the *Post*, *Maclean's* heads should be written before the layout was decided: "In this way the layout is made to fit the title and not the title the layout. In my opinion this is far preferable to our way."[55] Whenever Berton had an idea – any idea – he made it known; he never hesitated to reach beyond his responsibilities as articles editor to offer advice on any number of matters to those above him.

This expansive interpretation of his editorial duties likely affected his personal output in 1949. While he gave ideas, advice, and direction on articles to Clyde Gilmour, Isabel LeBourdais, June Callwood, Sidney Katz, Ray Gardner, McKenzie Porter, Jock Carroll, Gerald Anglin, Eva-Lis Wuorio, and other writers, only five articles other than the one covering his South American bovine adventure appeared with his byline. It was a perfectly respectable record by almost anyone's standards, but it paled beside the tally of sixteen pieces he had published in 1948.

His chosen themes echoed those of the previous year. In "The Amazing Career of George McCullagh," he wrote on the prominent newspaper tycoon who had in 1936 folded Toronto's two main newspapers, the *Globe* and the *Mail and Empire*, into a powerful new organ, the *Globe and Mail*, and who had just acquired the *Telegram*. He profiled another Canadian city, this time Edmonton, booming from the new Alberta oil economy. He provided his own singular perspective on the latest developments in popular culture and its effects on ordinary people. In a hilarious piece, "Phooey on Freud!" – which used Alfred Hitchcock's 1945 thriller *Spellbound* and its dream sequence sets by Salvador Dali to hook the reader – he lampooned the North American infatuation with pop psychology. He satirized contemporary courtship rituals and sexual mores and took a swat or two at mindless conformity and McCarthyite demagoguery in "The Life and Loves of a Queen Bee" – as related by a queen bee named Agnes. In "Make Way for the One-Eyed Monster," he described his first encounter with television while on a trip to New York. "When we twist the familiar knobs to tune in the familiar programs," he wrote after returning to his Toronto apartment, with its two small radios, "we feel rather as Henry Ford must have felt when, after taking the first whirl in his new horseless carriage, he was reluctantly forced to step back into a buggy and jolt off down the rutted road."[56]

In mid-September 1949, Floyd Chalmers sent Arthur Irwin a memo he had received from Maclean Hunter's president, Horace Hunter. It began: "We are not developing in the minds of our people a sufficient feeling of pride in Canada." Hunter went on to opine that Canadians were not properly aware of their advantages or opportunities, and that as a result they might well acquire "an inferiority complex" because of their proximity to the American behemoth next door. "Could we not make this the keynote of a continuous campaign in Maclean's Magazine?" Hunter asked Chalmers.[57]

Irwin was devastated. His entire approach to *Maclean's* for more than two decades had been to make it a truly Canadian magazine, written by Canadians for Canadians. A few days later, he sent a wounded letter to Chalmers. "I've slaved my guts out over more than a million dollars worth of the printed word in a never ending battle with mediocrity in an effort to get power, and drama, and emotional conviction into the singing of the story of Canada," he wrote. "I've coddled and wheedled writers by the hundreds to make them reveal this country and its people in singing prose, persuaded artists to hold up the mirror, spewed out ideas for other men to wrestle with and taught them how to wrestle, built a Canadian staff where there was no staff, transformed a tenth-rate American dress into a Canadian dress whose origins are unmistakable, built a great property which is as unmistakably Canadian as the smell of the autumn forest in Timagami and is recognized as such from one end of this country to the to the other." The company's president, Irwin said, did not seem to see what was happening right under his nose.[58]

Irwin readily admitted that he had been caught with his "emotions down" and that Chalmers should tear up the letter and forget that he had read it. But the man was thoroughly crushed. What more could he have done to make *Maclean's* an authentically "Canadian" magazine? What more could he personally have written or said about his nation? Just a few months earlier had he not given a lengthy speech in Buffalo called "What It Means to Be a Canadian"? His first words had been, "I come here today as a Canadian to try to tell you something about my country and its people."[59] Here I stand, he might have said; I can do no other.

Irwin left *Maclean's* without fanfare at the end of the year, having accepted an offer from Norman Robertson, clerk of the Privy Council in Ottawa, to take charge of the National Film Board. But he did not do so until he had coaxed Ralph Allen to return to *Maclean's* to take his place, and until he gave Allen one last instruction: to publish the text of his Buffalo speech. It appeared on February 1, 1950. Allen found its title in the one phrase that captured the author and his subject: "The Canadian."

12

THE ALLEN INFLUENCE

—

RALPH ALLEN'S NAME APPEARED on the masthead of *Maclean's* as its editor at the beginning of the 1950s and it remained there until the decade drew to a close. To some, *Maclean's* in the 1950s *was* Ralph Allen, so closely was its success associated with his tenure at the helm. During those years, the magazine emerged from the shadow of mass-circulation American competitors such as *Life*, the *Saturday Evening Post*, and *Time* to become a central institution in Canadian life.

The achievement was certainly Allen's, but it arose from ground Arthur Irwin had already broken and cultivated. Allen's earlier stint at the magazine, working closely with Irwin, had made him an enthusiastic agent of his mentor's nationalist vision, and for the next ten years he extended it, developing the pool of young, brash, and inventive writers Irwin had recruited, and hiring more like them. *Maclean's* witnessed the blossoming of that immediate postwar core, such as Trent Frayne, and the appearance of fresh faces – W.O. Mitchell, David Macdonald, Jim Coleman, Barbara Moon, Hugh Garner, Fred Bodsworth, Hugh MacLennan, Peter C. Newman, Christina McCall (who married Newman in 1959), Peter Gzowski, Farley Mowat, and other writers – drawing them in from the margins of Canadian cultural life and onto a large stage that made them into figures of national stature.

The transformation of *Maclean's* also came about because Ralph Allen brought with him an important change of sensibility. Irwin had encouraged and supported the people around him, but he was not easily approachable – "a dry stick of a guy," according to Gerry Anglin.[1] Irwin was a man of probity; he was self-contained, his integrity evident to all. Allen was more complex, and those who came to admire and even to love him found it difficult to put the heart of that complexity into words. In some ways, he was an island unto himself, easy to love but difficult to know. There was a depth about this man with the red hair and the freckles, and it gave him a manner that suggested confidence and accomplishment, yet also vulnerability and a deep-set angst. "He was burdened," Christina McCall noted of him. "He felt *responsible* to every human being he met."[2] In the words of another *Maclean's* writer, "What made him rare and important to so many people was a quality of personal goodness that's very nearly impossible to describe." He was the kind of person whose words and actions held the power "to illuminate other men's lives and authenticate other men's experiences."[3]

Berton's work at *Maclean's* in the year of Allen's return consisted mainly of developing and editing other people's articles instead of writing his own. At Thursday morning editorial meetings he threw himself into heated discussions over stories, and he coaxed and cajoled and encouraged and berated staff writers and freelancers alike. His personal output of articles diminished significantly in 1950, but his contributions were groundbreaking ones: six articles on power and influence in the Canadian media – a two-part series on the life and empire of the business tycoon E.P. Taylor, a three-part series on the family that owned the Southam media empire, and a year-end inversion of the free enterprise theme, called "Everybody Boos the CBC."

Notoriously private and eager to avoid public scrutiny, mid-twentieth-century Toronto's business and financial community lived in Rosedale mansions and worked in Bay Street office towers. Like a latter-day medieval guild, it conducted its affairs well away from public scrutiny. A century earlier, Upper Canadian political reformers had their own name for the tight oligarchy that controlled the economic and political fate of the province and dominated its legal profession. They called it the Family Compact. At the dawn of democratic politics in Canada, such privileged influence had been a matter of great public attention and heated debate. But in the freewheeling, open society that was Canada in the 1950s, the public glimpsed business leaders mainly when they attended charity balls or raced horses. Berton made it his business to end this.

A year earlier, his article on the newspaper tycoon George McCullagh had painted an intimate and compelling portrait of the public and private man. McCullagh had insisted that he would grant an interview only if he was allowed to vet anything Berton wrote. Supported fully by Irwin, Berton refused the deal. Then he spent three weeks interviewing every McCullagh friend or acquaintance he could find, and he pored over the *Globe*'s clipping files. His experience writing the piece and the success of its reception taught Berton that the subject's co-operation was not essential when writing about a "big shot."[4]

Since the technique had worked with McCullagh, he thought it would work with Edward Plunket Taylor. Once again Berton interviewed widely, friends and enemies alike. He even corralled Taylor's daughter after class at McGill University. She refused to talk, but word got back to Taylor, as Pierre knew it would, that a reporter named Berton was in hot pursuit of a story about him. Three weeks after the McGill encounter, he received a telephone call. E.P. Taylor wanted to know when this persistent reporter would be coming to interview him.[5]

"To most Canadians he is an anonymity concealed somewhere in the dark labyrinth of interlocking directorates behind the façade of a bewildering number of familiar brand names," Berton wrote early in the first of his two instalments. Then he proceeded to peel away the layers of mystery surrounding the man and his empire. Readers learned that the financier had been so concerned with balance sheets as an undergraduate (also at McGill) that his fellow mechanical engineering students called him "Overhead Taylor." They learned that he went horseback riding at 6:30 a.m.; that his father and his uncle, both brewery executives, had died of heart attacks; that he took dancing lessons at Arthur Murray's and that he suffered from "stomach trouble"; that his favourite movies were those with happy endings, "racy detective stories and fast musicals"; and that during the Second World War he had spent nine hours in a lifeboat with the federal minister of munitions and supply, C.D. Howe, after their ship was torpedoed.[6]

E.P. Taylor, Berton stated, was "the embodiment of the common conception of the North American businessman carried to the end point." But he made it clear that Taylor's claim transcended his three Cadillacs, his racehorses, and his patrician lifestyle. This businessman's vast wealth reached into Canadians' lives in untold ways, from the Honeydew Restaurants they frequented to the soybeans they ate. When they put gasoline in their automobiles or pitch on their roofs, if they had a bottle of beer or a spoonful of sugar in their coffee, if they took out life insurance or sipped on a bottle of Orange Crush, chances were that E.P. Taylor, president and presiding genius of Argus Corporation, profited from it. This was what Berton dubbed "Taylor-Land," and he devoted the second part of his examination of Taylor's life to its geography, illustrated by a large chart listing just under a hundred companies in which Taylor had an interest. No one who finished Berton's articles on E.P. Taylor could have remained unaware of the vast reach of "big business" or the myriad ways it touched Canadian lives.[7]

Berton's three-part series "The Southams" ran in June and July 1950 and told the tale of "Canada's ranking newspaper dynasty." E.P. Taylor's reach extended to scores of Canadian business firms; that of the Southams had spread to a number of the nation's major newspapers and several of its radio stations. "A prolific, individualistic and sometimes eccentric family group, the Southams have, in about 80 years, made themselves as ubiquitous as Eaton's catalogue,"[8] Berton wrote. The Taylor story had been about a single brilliant financier; the Southams' was the saga of a family dynasty and its rise. Not since Mazo de la Roche had published her hugely popular series of novels about the Whiteoak family in the 1920s and 1930s had Canadian readers encountered such sustained attention to an Anglo-Canadian variation on the theme of gentry turned patricians. The difference was that, within his more general account of the family's many foibles, Berton revealed the origins and impact of four generations of Southam wealth.

He moved from an overview of the Southam clan in his first instalment to a detailed treatment of the family's history in the second, complete with a graphic depiction of the family tree since the 1860s. In both, he provided a seamless account of the family's business success (the Southam Company's profit in 1949 was a record $1.2 million) and of its antics – the sixty-yard drop kick Gordon Southam once made for the Hamilton Tigers in the last fifteen seconds of a football game; the $1,000 bet that Bill Southam placed at Dufferin Racetrack on whether it would rain by three o'clock.[9]

Berton's third instalment dwelt on the unpredictable blend of Southam benevolence and Southam penny-pinching that inspired loyalty and resentment in employees. The company's tolerance of strange behaviour on the part of its employees, he wrote, "can perhaps be explained by the fact that the family has produced some of the country's most engaging eccentrics from its own blood lines." The family patriarch, Wilson Mills Southam (1868–1947), had produced a lineage of one daughter and six sons. Of these, Richard Southam, who managed the family's Toronto printing plant, was known to knock on the doors of total strangers in the wee hours of the morning with the story that his car had broken down. Then he would produce an assortment of liqueurs, liquors, and cocktail mixes, handing cut flowers to irate wives when he left with their husbands to party on.

The second-eldest brother, Bill, made Richard's escapades seem tame. Naturally, Berton gave him a lot of attention. Bill Southam sent X-rays of his stomach to the wife of a friend when she suspected that he had taken her husband one evening on an alcoholic adventure – perhaps to demonstrate that the man had at least consumed a little food. Publisher of the *Hamilton Spectator*, Bill would instruct his reporters to write ribald stories about its most prominent citizens, have a single copy of the paper printed, and then put it on their doorsteps in place of the regular paper. In 1935, he converted the living room of his summer home into "a cockfighting arena, complete with sawdust ring and three-tier bleachers." He paid the fines of about a hundred spectators after the police raided the party. He liked to wear an admiral's uniform. Once he showed up at a funeral in bedroom slippers. Another time he appeared at his own dinner party as a waiter complete with goatee.[10]

After the series ended, Clyde Gilmour of the *Vancouver Sun* wrote to tell Berton something he had learned from a fellow journalist, Charles Woodsworth, about the reaction of Harry Southam. "Old Harry LOVED the stuff," Gilmour related, "although he professed to tut-tut-tut over one or two racy bits. HOWEVER . . . and this is what we got such a hell of a bang out of . . . Harry wasn't the least <u>bit</u> taken aback by your fabulous yarns about his screwball brother Bill. Instead, he merely looked up from the advance copies which you people had sent him, and remarked to Charlie: 'For goodness sake! I haven't heard HALF these stories about Bill! Wonder where on earth Berton dug them up?'"[11]

Pierre was no doubt amused at this, but he had made clear to his readers, even as he entertained them, that the quirky affability of the Southam family rested on a fortune dependent on a fiercely competitive and at times ruthless business empire: his subtitle for the third instalment was "Papers, Pickets, and Profits." Here he wrote from personal experience, since "pickets" referred to the lengthy and bitter Vancouver newspaper strike involving the *Province*, the main competitor of his old paper, the *Sun*. The strike was a consequence of Southam's poor labour relations and supreme care of the bottom line.

Like his articles on racial discrimination and anti-Semitism, Berton's lengthy treatments of the Taylor and Southam empires reflected a less strident and judgmental version of the kind of journalism not much seen in North America since the days of the "muckrakers" a half-century earlier, when Ida Tarbell exposed the practices of Standard Oil in an eighteen-part series in *McClure's Magazine*. Unlike the work of these pioneering crusaders against injustice and inequality, Berton's early investigative pieces did not take the form of a moral crusade directly inspired by Christian values or Protestant righteousness. He did not preach as much as inform, leaving to his reader's intelligence and conscience the conclusion as to whether the businessmen whose stories he told were captains of industry or robber barons. Berton had buried his former *News-Herald* habit of bending facts when necessary to sell the story: Irwin would have fired him for that. He felt passionately for society's victims, whether groups or individuals. But as befitted a feature writer for Canada's premier magazine, he sought now to give at least a semblance of balance, so he laid out the facts for all to see.

His stories were about people as much as justice. Behind the curtain of "Taylor-Land" was a man called "Eddie," whom people either loved or hated, feared or admired. Taylor had become a target of their passions, Berton said, because he represented middle-class aspirations. Similarly, beyond the saga of the Southams lay the details of a host of stories, many yet to be told, of history and commerce and the mass media; above all of Canadians themselves, ordinary and extraordinary. Each article Berton worked on for *Maclean's* made him more aware of how many such tales there were and how little Canadians yet knew about themselves and their country. It would be difficult, he recognized, to accomplish such a task within the confines of a magazine feature.

⬥⬥

In the fall of 1950, Pierre and Janet moved to Kleinburg.[12] Their second daughter, Pamela, had been born in May, and Penny, pretty as a china doll and beginning to show an independent streak, had just turned two years old. They could not abide the prospect of living in the damp basement on Kingsway Crescent any longer and decided to start construction on their Kleinburg property. Not without difficulty they managed to obtain a mortgage, for most moneylending firms balked at their decision to build in Ontario a house designed for the benign climate of the west coast. Finally a branch of Victoria and Grey Trust in Lindsay, Ontario, lent the Bertons $8,000, enough for a first mortgage, and it went into a pool of capital established by Bill McCrow, the set designer turned building contractor who had come up with the idea of constructing inexpensive homes for a colony of arts people.[13]

McCrow now organized the construction, while the prospective homeowners met to organize their colony and set rules for communal living. Each family would pay $25 a month for shared services, including a baker who agreed to deliver to the community's homes.[14] The rules worked at first, but eventually the undercapitalized and overidealistic project dissolved in acrimonious disputes. As a consequence, house-building took place only when the contractor's cash flow permitted.

The Bertons moved not to the idyllic rural property of their dreams but to an abandoned construction site that shared the name of the communal undertaking, Windrush: Jalna in the age of the bungalow. The wood frame of the modest 1,450-square-foot Berton house (less than half what McCrow had wished) had been erected and sheathed, the interior walls laid out, and the subfloors poured and set. The rest of the work was up to them, for the $8,000 loan had not gone far. The house lacked doors and windows, gravel was scattered all over the floors, and fibreglass insulation threatened to dislodge from between the studs. Through a large hole where a picture window was to go, Janet and Pierre could see an ocean of mud that had once been pastureland. In twenty years, they told themselves, they would laugh about this.[15]

Despite the mosquito bites and the mess, they enjoyed themselves and treated the first few months as an adventure. The centrepiece of their unfinished home was a large fireplace of Port Credit limestone, an incongruous sign of permanence in the half-finished house. Lacking a stove, they cooked their meals in it. For furniture they had a couple of wingback chairs and a number of empty wooden orange crates. Pierre spent his two weeks of holiday putting up wallboard and ceiling board.

Years later, Janet recalled how, day after day, she would use one arm to hold up the T-bar long enough for Pierre to nail the board to the ceiling joists; with the other she nursed Pamela. Eventually, Pierre stapled burlap to the walls and sprayed them green.

Gerry Anglin once had the idea of writing an article called "The House That Built Pierre." Over the years, he and his wife, Betty, visited the Berton homestead often and witnessed the enlargement of the house as the family expanded. "Like Topsy," he said, "it kept growing." Anglin was aware of the financial pressure Berton was under to finish construction, furnish the place, and meet the cost of commuting to and from Toronto. Part of Berton's ambitious drive, Anglin said, was that "he needed money for that darned house."[16] He was correct. "A big factor in my working so hard," Berton later told June Callwood, "was that I didn't want to lose the house."[17]

Pierre pursued a range of activities outside *Maclean's* to augment his salary, which was about $5,000 annually. Despite the earlier rejections, he had continued to churn out radio plays. Andrew Allan produced a new one, *King of Diamonds*, for the Vancouver Theatre, and it aired to a radio audience on February 28, 1949. He reworked rejected plays and several came to be produced. *Past Imperfect* was broadcast on February 23 and again on November 11, and *The Waiting Room* on June 10. Each performance earned a cheque for $75. Early in 1950, through the agency of the Canadian Broadcasting Corporation, he recorded ten four-minute talks on Canadian subjects for the BBC, and took strong exception when the CBC's Elspeth Chisholm tried to reduce his $20 per-talk fee to $17.50 because of rewrite costs. The fee remained $20.

From the CBC's perspective, he was a hard and insistent bargainer. The fee schedule was as much his as the broadcaster's: $20 for each original four-minute item; $35 for fifteen-minute pieces (plus a $15 step-up fee if used by the BBC). "I don't know at what point we agreed on a payment of $30.00 for an 8-minute item," Chisholm wrote. "We usually pay $25.00. . . . If, however, this was your understanding, we will pay that fee."[18]

Whenever he was not editing and helping craft articles by others for *Maclean's*, or researching and writing his own, Berton bombarded the CBC, the BBC, book publishers, and corporate in-house magazines with ideas for plays, talks, scripts, and stories. Most initiatives paid off,

sometimes more than once. In March, Peter McDonald, a drama producer for CBC radio, accepted a Berton script, *Sharp Edges*. Single-
performance rights at the time were $100, with additional income
forthcoming whenever the CBC assigned broadcast rights to the BBC. So
the hustler from *Maclean's* quickly drew up a list of eight programs with
subjects that recycled his life and his work at *Maclean's*: Dawson City;
work on the gold creeks; Russ Baker and his adventures; Edmonton's
airport as gateway to the North; a hoax that hoodwinked the town
council of White Rock, B.C.; Dr. David Keys and the politics of nuclear
energy in "Atomic City"; Carl Hannawals, a retired fur trader; and the
ghost town created by falling mercury prices at Pinchi Lake, in central
British Columbia.[19] In early May, with the CBC as his conduit, he sold
an eighteen-minute (2,600-word) school broadcast for children titled
"Life in the Yukon" to the British public broadcaster for its program
Round the Pacific. The CBC accepted his true story "Beefsteaks by
Airplane," based on his earlier South American adventure. He received
the CBC fee plus an additional step-up fee for rebroadcast on the BBC
program *Eye Witness*.[20] The $65 cheque became one of many that pro-
vided a healthy supplement to his income.

In July, in advance of placing it with the CBC, Berton sent a script
based on his articles of the year before on drug use and abuse to the
Department of National Health and Welfare. E.S. Hallman of the
CBC's Talks and Public Affairs section announced the corporation's
intention to air the piece on August 15. Misgivings about Berton's comparison of the Benzedrine craze to "Coke and Aspirin" delayed the
airing. He contacted Smith, Kline & French Laboratories for a check of
factual accuracy on its racemic amphetamine sulphate (Benzedrine)
inhaler and was informed that the company had changed the name of
its product to Benzedrex. "You certainly seem to have all the facts concerning this drug at hand," the company spokesperson wrote, while
beseeching the author to phrase his talk in a way that "any of the 'evils'
would not be considered applicable only to our brand of the drug."[21]

That month, Pierre appeared on the CBC game show *Beat the
Champs* and won a set of *The Book of Knowledge* from the Grolier
Society of Canada. Most likely it went into one of the family orange
crates.[22] He sent letters to the Ford Motor Company's house magazines,
the *Lincoln-Mercury Times* and the *Ford Times*, suggesting articles on

Dawson City, Alaska, and Edmonton.[23] He submitted a dramatic piece, *Creeping Green*, to the CBC for its *Summer Theatre* series. When the Toronto script editor rejected it on August 1, he peddled it to the CBC's Winnipeg drama producer. The play broadcast in the *Prairie Playhouse* series on September 7. By then he had already cashed the corporation's $75 cheque.[24]

Attempts to find a foothold in British magazine publishing went unrewarded. In October Berton wrote to the London literary agent Rupert Crew to inquire about work as a feature writer, but Crew informed him that his stable of feature writers was already full. He also tried to place a 2,500-word article on the extraordinary Lister Sinclair with Odhams Press for its *John Bull* magazine. Lawrence Earl of Odhams held out a hint at publication with one hand and offered faint and condescending praise, of the sort that often infuriates Canadian authors, with the other. "You did a smack-dab North American job on it," Earl wrote, "but British tastes are a bit different." Then he quoted three readers, including the editor of *John Bull*, who panned the piece. "It's a fascinating example of a personality which is so much favoured by transatlantic writers," the editor wrote, "and which is supposed to carry pep, punch and conviction, but which usually succeeds in making the British reader disbelieve in the character altogether. . . . Nor is one impressed to learn that 'He springs out of bed, book in hand, and gets through 11 pages while brushing his hair.' This is, I suppose, a North American way of conveying that he's a speedy reader and only makes one feel that he must be ambidextrous or something." Earl concluded by saying that he hoped the writer would still feel his piece "worth toying with." Berton had been offered a cruel lesson: literary art required more than cartoonlike characterization.[25]

He could handle such rejection, although he usually tried several publications before giving up. After the exchange with Lawrence Earl, for example, he sent the Sinclair piece to *Everybody's* magazine.[26] But he would not brook unfair treatment over fees. He complained to the CBC when it offered only $35 for his profile of Robert Service, written for its *Canadian Success Stories* series, and then expressed his annoyance that someone else had suggested an item on E.P. Taylor. He insisted that the BBC explain tax deductions from his reproduction fees, and he received an apology from the broadcaster when it inadvertently rebroadcast his four-minute talk on Dawson City without his approval. "The editor of 'London Calling,'" wrote the BBC's Canadian representative, "now clearly understands that you must be consulted in future before any of your material is used."[27] This insistence on control became a hallmark of Berton's relationship with the entertainment industry.

Berton conducted most of his freelance work from the office at *Maclean's*. That he managed this speaks to his powers of concentration, to his ability to fix upon the task at hand yet maintain command over the full range of things to be done. As articles editor, he was responsible for all the pieces that appeared in the magazine. He annotated the margins of every draft article with comments and suggestions and then appended a memo on its strengths and weaknesses to be sent up the editorial line – first to managing editor John Clare and then to Ralph Allen.

His responsibilities included handling the slush pile, the hundreds of unsolicited manuscripts *Maclean's* received every month. He read every submission and wrote to each author. He dealt with writers who walked in off the street to try to sell their literary wares, and some of his assessments came close to cutting literary careers short. One young man, the son of a truck driver, had quit school at fourteen but in his early thirties still wanted to be a full-time writer. When Berton met him, he was contributing pieces to a Maclean Hunter sister magazine, *Bus and Truck*. Berton told him that the humorous articles he had written were awful and that he should find some other line of work. Arthur Hailey's weak self-confidence eroded further, and in 1953 he quit writing and took a job as sales promotion manager for a trailer firm.[28]

Three years later, after psychological assessment, Hailey changed his mind. On a Trans-Canada Airlines flight one day in 1956, the plot for a television drama suddenly came to him. He wrote the script for it in ten days. *Flight into Danger* – the televised drama that invented the airplane disaster film genre – aired to high acclaim on CBC television later that year, and the play turned novel called *Runway Zero-Eight*, published in 1958, made the man's reputation. Arthur Hailey's next novels, *Hotel* in 1964 and *Airport* in 1968, were runaway bestsellers and made him a wealthy man. Over the years, Hailey and Berton became close friends and often vacationed together.[29]

All the people at *Maclean's*, Berton said late in life, were "buddies of mine."[30] The staff of writers Irwin pulled together and that Allen expanded and inspired were young and ambitious. In these golden years, almost all of them came to believe that *Maclean's* was not only the best magazine in Canada but one of the best in North America. This confidence rolled over into their embrace of the magazine's mission. They fully imbibed the Irwin-Allen obsession with Canada – its geography and history, its values, its people and politics.

In this they found themselves ahead of public policy. *Maclean's* became a voice of Canadian nationalism several years before the landmark Royal Commission on National Development in the Arts, Letters and Sciences issued its 1951 report. Led by Vincent Massey, former high commissioner to Great Britain, and Georges-Henri Lévesque, dean of the Faculty of Social Sciences at Université Laval, the commission members included the Saskatchewan historian Hilda Neatby and the president of the University of British Columbia, Norman Mackenzie. Their eloquent report urged greater government aid for the arts and sciences and more protection against the intrusions of American culture.[31] For the remainder of the decade, and well beyond, *Maclean's* served as a major forum for those who supported the nationalist principles, propositions, and ambitions of the Massey Commission.

Berton's year-end piece for *Maclean's* in 1950 drew direct attention to the Massey Commission and more than hinted at the need to prevent erosion of the CBC's public mandate by private broadcasting interests. The otherwise upbeat article, "Everybody Boos the CBC," provided a case for the defence. It told the story of the rise of public broadcasting in Canada, explained why it was needed, and detailed the many ways in which the CBC informed Canadians of all regions about themselves and others. It noted that the corporation's "strong influence on the Canadian mosaic" came about, in part, because close to seven thousand Canadian writers, actors, newsreaders, and producers got cheques from it each year.[32]

Most of Berton's hard-earned extra income in the 1950s went into his house, but some of it found the tills of hotel bars and public houses in downtown Toronto. Ralph Allen "liked to drink at noon," Berton said, but sometimes a *Maclean's* noon lasted until quitting time. The Westminster Hotel was a favourite haunt, but the day's venue could as easily be a nearby Chinese restaurant on Elizabeth Street or the Horseshoe Tavern on Queen Street near Spadina Avenue. Allen would find himself surrounded by a half-dozen or more of his staff writers and editors, Berton included, fortified with what seemed to others like an endless parade of martinis.[33]

Alcohol, like cigarettes, remained central to the self-image of newspaper and magazine writers. They all knew about the bibulous lunches of the acerbic Dorothy Parker and the other New York literary wits at the Algonquin Hotel in the twenties, for this was the lore of the trade. Phrases like "hard-drinking" and "hard-working" were inseparable. Reporters depicted in movies often had drink or fag in hand; within a year, Humphrey Bogart would appear as a big-city editor in *Deadline USA* (1952) doing just that. Aware of the stereotype but enamoured of it for its reckless glamour, reporters and writers continued to play true to type.

During the Irwin and Allen years, *Maclean's* at lunch resembled a floating version of the Toronto Press Club at 99 Yonge Street. Both groups lived by their own rules, ignoring provincial liquor laws like the one requiring patrons to be seated while drinking. The Toronto Press Club's patrons were for the most part reporters from the daily papers, but *Maclean's* people, especially Trent Frayne, were known to haunt it. "All the men," June Callwood said of her husband and his colleagues, "were big, big drinkers." Back in 1947 Arthur Irwin was overheard saying to Blair Fraser over the telephone, "My whole staff got drunk today." Around the corner at the Horseshoe Tavern, they didn't get around to ordering lunch until four o'clock.[34]

⋈

Berton flourished under Ralph Allen's second coming. The new editor of *Maclean's* gave him a good deal of leeway and he turned a blind eye to the freelance work his articles editor did on company time. Allen's house rule was that writers could do freelance work as long as they avoided magazines in direct competition with *Maclean's* and maintained their productivity for the home team. He was adamant, however, that none of his writers express any public views that suggested a conflict of interest. When Berton joined the Canadian Radio League, dedicated to public broadcasting, Allen made him choose between remaining a member and staying at *Maclean's*. Berton chose *Maclean's*. The issue created a degree of ongoing tension between them.[35]

Allen certainly did not want to lose the man. He knew that he could rely on Berton to come up with first-rate articles and – crucial to any editor – to meet his deadlines. He received twelve major features in 1951 under Berton's byline, each bearing the mark of intensive research on an interesting subject and written in a lively style. Even so, Allen had to decline a request from the American magazine the *Nation* for the articles editor to write an 1,800-word piece on the Korean War along the lines of some remarks Berton had made in the *Toronto Star*. "Hated to do this," Allen said in a handwritten note to him, "since the Nation so obviously is <u>not</u> a competitor. But I'm still afraid that if we started tinkering around with this particular house-rule, we'll end up setting precedents we can't follow."[36] Allen's use of the word *still* suggests that this was not the first time the matter of freelance work had arisen.

By 1951, Berton had established three main avenues to extra income: the CBC, Ford Motor Company publications, and the National Film Board. The difference between this year and 1950 in this respect was that as often as not these clients now solicited his work. He was reliable and co-operative, he submitted material when he promised, and he made revisions without complaint.

The CBC, more than any other non-salaried source, helped the house in Kleinburg down the slow road to completion. The corporation sent him a $50 cheque for rebroadcasting his talk "Life in the Yukon" to schoolchildren, another in the amount of $35 a piece on the Canadian north for Radio Ceylon, then thirteen more, totalling $520, for a series on Canada for CBC International and an additional $156 in step-up fees. He made $12 per script when the CBC produced several of his true-life stories, one called "I Found the Lost Valley," and more when he contributed to the broadcaster's national radio series on public affairs, *Citizens' Forum*, an earnest attempt to give neighbourhood discussion groups access to the airwaves. At year's end he did a four-part *Canadiana* spot on the Yukon gold rush.[37]

The hustling paid well. *Ford Times* sent him $150 for his article on "The Living Ghosts of Dawson City," and the *Lincoln-Mercury Times* forwarded $200 for the one promised earlier on Edmonton. Meanwhile, Donald Mulholland, director of production for the National Film Board, wrote to express his delight at discovering that Berton was interested in writing for film. Mulholland was eager to receive two proposed scripts, one on private enterprise called *Away Back in 1951*, the other titled *The Decline of the Small Town*. About the former, he warned Berton that the government agency he worked for was "not encouraged to be cynical at public expense," and of the latter he noted that Arthur Irwin did not accept Berton's conclusion that small-town Canada was in a state of decline. No sooner had Berton received a contract from the NFB for the film *Quebec Industrial* than he submitted a proposal for another, called *The Monsters That Mine the Klondyke* (*sic*).[38]

Somehow amidst this frenzy of activity he found time to read. On at least two occasions in 1951 he gave talks on books for the CBC's program *Critically Speaking*. One dealt with three books: E. McCall Gillis and E. Myles, *North Pole Boarding House* (1951), by a housewife who spent a year in the Arctic; Judith Robinson's *As We Came By* (1951), about an auto trip the author had taken through England, France, Italy, and the Netherlands; and Richmond P. Hobson Jr.'s *Grass Beyond the Mountains* (1951), a larger-than-life story of an American rancher who left Wyoming in the 1930s for the wilds of British Columbia, and later created the Frontier Cattle Company. Despite Hobson's obvious penchant for tall tales, Berton said, he was a "cracking good story teller." He liked Hobson's work so much that he convinced Ralph Allen to serialize the book in *Maclean's*.[39]

On a second program he reviewed two books, amusing but helpful, by the English humorist Stephen Potter: *The Theory and Practice of Gamesmanship* (1947) and *Lifemanship* (1950). The first, Berton noted, was about "the art of winning games without actually cheating," while the second told how to take the technique and apply it to everyday life. "There is a neat section on Drinkmanship," Berton noted: "how to make your opponent pay for all drinks and not realize it until he gets to the crucial point of the subsequent golf game." He professed surprise, however, that Potter had not "seen fit to pay some small tribute to the work of L. Sinclair of Kleinburg, whose Birdsmanship never fails to put him 'one up' or *Bitzleisch*, as Rilke calls it, and his opponent 'one down' . . . ah . . . *Rotzleisch*. In the midst of a serious conversation, especially if he is pressed, it is Sinclair's gambit to suddenly cock one ear, place finger to lips and say: 'Quiet, just a moment. I think . . . yes – hear that! – purple winged Godwit! – pretty late for these parts – shouldn't be surprised if that isn't a *first*.' At which point Sinclair produces an enormous pair of binoculars, stares out the window with them for the briefest instant, then exclaims 'Godwit alright. The teal variety. Just a moment while I note this – it's rather important.'"[40]

◄►

The Korean War disrupted Berton's focus on Canada and Canadians. Jockeying between the Soviet Union and the United States for geopolitical influence during the early years of the Cold War meant mutual suspicion between the superpowers over influence in Southeast Asia. On June 25, 1950, about 135,000 soldiers of the North Korean People's Army, with support from the Soviet Union, moved south across the 38th parallel into the Republic of Korea. Three days later they had captured its capital, Seoul. This was the first incidence of serious international aggression since the formation of the North Atlantic Treaty Organization a year earlier, and when the United Nations Security Council called on UN members "to render every assistance" to South Korea, Canada obliged on the grounds that its mission was to assist the United Nations through its membership in NATO, but not to be part of an American operation. A consensus of the House of Commons held that support of the United Nations might help moderate American policy.[41] The Royal Canadian Air Force did transport duty and on July 12, 1950, the Royal Canadian Navy sent the destroyers *Cayuga*, *Athabaska*, and *Sioux* into Korean waters under the UN flag.[42]

At first, when the American army led by General Douglas MacArthur forced the invading army back to the 38th parallel, it appeared that no Canadian ground troops would be needed. But when MacArthur continued to advance north beyond the 38th parallel, the Chinese began to assist the North Korean army with men and *matériel*. American forces were pushed south. "An entirely new war" had begun, MacArthur declared in late November. By the end of the year, the Second Battalion of the Princess Patricia's Canadian Light Infantry, the first "citizen volunteers" of the Canadian Army Special Force, were on the ground in Korea. Canada was at war again.

Berton was eager to interview leaders of the Canadian military effort, and with Ralph Allen's blessing he did. Early in 1951 he travelled to Fort Lewis in Washington State, where the Canadian troops at the service of the United Nations Special Force were in training before deployment. First he profiled the leader of the CASF, an Australian-born former sheep farmer and power company lineman, Brigadier John Rockingham. The article appeared under the plain title "Rocky" in early February 1951. The story of a courageous veteran of the Second World War who had a Distinguished Service Order to his credit within a month of seeing action, it wove Rockingham's army and private lives together in a manner intended to assure Canadians that their lads would be trained and commanded by the kind of dedicated veteran who, in other circumstances, would rather be digging holes for power poles.[43]

Berton's piece in the next issue of *Maclean's*, "The Crisis and the Colonel," was on Lieutenant-Colonel Jacques Alfred (Jimmy) Dextraze, recipient of two Distinguished Service Orders by the age of twenty-five, and commander of the French-Canadian Royal Twenty-second Regiment, the Van Doos, in training since November 1950 at Fort Lewis.[44] Dextraze was another example of the civilian-soldier, a man whose life, as Berton characterized it, had moved "in fits and starts . . . from crisis to crisis, from civilian to soldier, soldier to civilian and back to soldier again" for a decade. Dextraze's background was positively Bertonesque, for the man had variously been a shipping clerk, a lumberjack, and a company executive, and "only a man with a strong sense of purpose, a prodding conscience and a toughness of spirit and body could do these things." The article showed how these attributes were central to Dextraze's strict training method, to his almost obsessive dedication, and to his sense of responsibility to the men under his command.[45]

The Cold War was heating rapidly in North America, and the fiercely anti-Communist senator from Wisconsin, Joseph McCarthy, was near the peak of his demagogic power. The colour of the enemy had been transformed from Nazi grey to Communist red, and Americans had begun to hunt down Communists wherever they could find them. To this end, the United Steelworkers of America had launched a campaign to gain control of a renegade local of the International Union of Mine, Mill, and Smelter Workers at Trail, British Columbia. The main influence on the Mine-Mill union was Harvey Murphy, a leading Canadian Communist, and the Steelworkers were bent on getting rid of him. The issue became one of international significance because Trail was the location of a heavy-water hydrogen plant. It was a "nuclear town."

Berton recognized the Cold War–atomic energy connection. In an article published in April 1951, he drew attention to the interest the Canadian Communist Party took in work on nuclear energy in Canada and with no hint of disapproval he quoted the assertion of the *Pacific Tribune*, the party's organ, that "the atomic products at Chalk River and Trail can be made to serve the interests of humanity."[46] But the striking feature of Berton's almost forensic investigation of the labour struggle was the sympathetic and even-handed treatment he afforded Murphy, a graduate of Moscow's Lenin Institute. Despite the anti-Communist fervour of the times, Berton was no red-baiter.

At the opening of Alfred Hitchcock's 1940 espionage thriller, *Foreign Correspondent*, set on the eve of the Second World War, a dedication scrolls down the screen: "To those intrepid ones who went across the seas . . . To those clear-headed ones who now stand like recording angels among the dead and dying . . . To the Foreign Correspondents – this movie is dedicated." Berton had seen the movie on release, and more than once he had expressed a desire to be a foreign correspondent, if not to break a spy ring, as the actor Joel McCrea had done in the role of the reporter Huntley Haverstock in Hitchcock's film.[47] The Korean War gave him just such an opportunity, the kind of work he had longed for between 1942 and 1945.

Berton's chance to be a war correspondent in a battle zone had come at last. His lobbying of Ralph Allen to cover the Korean War, if indeed he did so, remains unrecorded, confined as it is to the void between two chapters of his memoirs.[48] Allen certainly knew experienced Canadian war correspondents. He was one of them. But he could scarcely leave for a stint in Asia so soon after assuming the editor's chair at *Maclean's*. Over at the Toronto *Telegram*, the humorist Greg Clark, all five feet two of him, had been decorated at Vimy in the first war and had reported the blitzkrieg in France, the disasters at Dunkirk and Dieppe, and the struggle for dominance in Italy and northwestern Europe in the second; but he was almost sixty years old.[49] Matthew Halton had won his spurs in Italy as a CBC war correspondent reporting from the front lines when the Canadians crossed the Moro River on their way to liberate Ortona in 1943, but after the war he had remained in England as the corporation's senior foreign correspondent for Europe. Peter Stursberg had reported on the liberation of Holland

and the final victory in Europe for CBC radio and remained with the corporation.

Berton, not yet thirty-one, was young and available, and his training camp interviews with Brigadier Rockingham and Lieutenant-Colonel Dextraze had prepared him well for an assignment to Korea. So desperate was he that when Maclean Hunter insured his life for $25,000 instead of the promised $100,000, he remained unperturbed.[50] What else could Allen do but give the man the assignment he so coveted?

On the day he left for Korea, Pierre stopped by the *Maclean's* office to pick up his portable typewriter. "It was one of the funniest mental snapshots," his colleague Barbara Moon recalled. "He had it all – a belted trench coat with all the tabs and loops and aura around him . . . canteens and kit bags and a snap-brim hat. He had already thrown himself into the role of foreign correspondent."[51]

In early March 1951, Berton left McChord Air Force Base in Washington State and reached Korea by way of Alaska and Japan, flying with the Military Air Transport Service on an RCAF supply plane under the command of a twenty-two-year-old, curly-haired flying officer named Dean Broadfoot. He was accompanied by Jock Carroll of the *Montreal Standard*, Bill Herbert of the CBC, and eight bottles of Canadian Club whisky. The long trip, which included a blizzard at an American military base called Shemya on a small island in the Aleutians and a night on the town in raucous postwar Tokyo, naturally became an article, "Milk Run to Korea" (May 15). In it, he did not divulge that after the hard landing on a South Korean runway heavily damaged by artillery fire, Herbert refused to leave the aircraft and returned immediately to cover the war from Tokyo.[52]

Berton was determined to report from as near the battlefront as possible. So, armed with a dunnage bag containing his Canadian Club, he took off by Jeep with Jock Carroll in search of the Second Battalion, Princess Patricia's Canadian Light Infantry. Somewhere south of the 38th parallel he found the battalion in disarray: "The colonel, Big Jim Stone, had fallen ill and had been invalided back to Tokyo. A dozen private soldiers had died from drinking the wrong kind of alcohol. Three more were in the guardroom charged with raping and killing a Korean woman."[53] The shocking situation served as a stern reminder never to sentimentalize army life.

His earlier profile of Rockingham, leader of the Canadian Army Special Force, might have led *Maclean's* readers to expect coverage of the Korean War from the vantage point of the generals; if so, they were sorely disappointed. From the PPCLI camp amid war-scarred hills, he set his gaze steadfastly on the conflict as ordinary soldiers and civilians experienced it. In "Corporal Dunphy's War" he portrayed the war from the perspective of a leader of a nine-man section (the smallest unit in the army), and at the level of the slit trench. He travelled to the crowded port city of Pusan, explored its slums, and wrote "The Long Ordeal of Mrs. Tak," about a refugee who had fled from her home near the Manchurian border to a hovel in war-torn Pusan. Back at army head-quarters, assisted by interviews with officials and army records, he wrote lengthy case histories of three captured Chinese soldiers – Chong, a former Nationalist, Li, a former Communist, and Wu, a young recruit – enemies who proved to be captives of their own propaganda. The experience became the story "This Is the Enemy."[54]

In Tokyo at the beginning of July, about to head home, Berton encountered and interviewed a Japanese-Canadian former teacher named Marie. She too had a story to tell. After Pearl Harbor, the Canadian government had sent the family to a tarpaper shack in the Kootenay Mountains, and the federal Custodian of Enemy Property had seized and sold her family's property and possessions. After the war, faced with moving either east to work the sugar beet farms or back to Japan, Marie and her parents (both in their seventies) felt they had no choice but to emigrate to her father's former home, the fishing village of Aikawa. "My gosh," she told Berton, "it was just like what I used to teach the First Graders about prehistoric times": the fire in a pit; the constant squatting; the stench of the fields; the laundry done in the town gutter; above all, the utterly servile position of women. Even later, after Marie married a businessman and moved with her parents to a small Tokyo apartment and began living comfortably, the treatment of women continued to irk her. Men often referred to their spouses as "my stupid wife." Some kept concubines. Others, like one family friend, made the women of his family "squat at the rice pot in the corner, acting as servants," rather than dining at the family table.[55]

In developing feature articles on each of these subjects, Berton took extensive field notes, battered out on the Hermes Baby he had carried around since enlisting in 1942. Of Seoul, for example: "2nd OCCUPA-TION: . . . When [UN] troops moved in found Red posters in streets but no pix. English signs told Americans lay down arms. There was no civil control of city only military. Only time people left house was for markets. Didnt travel at nights. SK agents left in city murdered single soldiers. Used to tamper with phone lines and when man came out fix wires garroted him." He spent much of his time interviewing civilians: Charlie Hong, a university student; Dr. Park Chai Bin, a researcher in social hygiene; Mr. Li, Seoul's mayor; Mrs. Han Yung Sook, a war victim in Seoul. Notes on Mrs. Sook: "North Korean Communists killed her son. Shot him because he wouldn't join army. Found him in house. Now she has nothing. No spoons, no plates. 9 yr old daughter. Wrinkled gray haired. Gold teeth. White dress and fur vest. Old purse. She had been a cook. Ate at mother's house across river but now can't cross. 'How can we live day by day.' 61 yrs old. Hand grenades broke her house in street fighting thrown by NK. She came back to Seoul one month ago."[56]

From such raw material – seven single-spaced pages of small type on Dunphy, four on Mrs. Tak – Berton fleshed out the urgent anthropology of an ugly war.[57] "Corporal Dunphy's War" begins as a real-life parody of war movie cliché. Berton portrayed the men of Dunphy's section as a disparate group of boys with nicknames like Wandering Willie and Trigger Jim and Chicago Bill, who called themselves "the Leper Colony." Strangers to one another at first, their ordeals in battle had forged a fiercely loyal fraternity.

Even in war, life could imitate art. Berton recognized the cliché as one of the unit's own making, for the name the Lepers gave themselves came from the 1949 movie *Twelve O'Clock High*, starring Gregory Peck.[58] A tough general (Peck) takes command of a battered bomber group badly depressed from heavy losses. With good reason it called itself the "Hard Luck Unit." By the movie's end, through stern discipline and calculated distance from his men, the general has driven them to test themselves in battle, and they regain their confidence and rise to heroic heights.

Berton let the Hollywood-style notion of platoon life as a "band of brothers" that Dunphy's men had constructed for themselves take hold in his readers' minds, and then gradually went about deconstructing it with glimpses of war's true face. Kerry Dunphy was well educated and affable and a good leader of his men, but he and his soldiers were also crude and fearful. "I'd like to get my hands on one of them Chinks just so I could choke him and know he exists," one of them said. The Chinese, their hated enemy, at least had their respect; the South Koreans, their allies, garnered none. The Canadians referred to them as "gooks." After killing a Chinese soldier, one of the Lepers broke down completely and was sent home traumatized. They saw the bodies of sixty black American troops, slaughtered in a night attack. "Killed in their sleeping bags with their boots on" is what Berton's copy originally said, but at the request of a federal government censor Ralph Allen decided to delete those details.[59]

"In many movies about war," Berton told his readers, "there is usually a point toward the last reel when the ordinary soldier stands up and makes a little speech about what his particular war is all about. There are no such speeches in the Leper Colony." These Canadian soldiers, including the new Leper who thought he was fighting Chiang Kai-shek's troops, were scornful of talk of a United Nations "police action." No one had become more cynical than their leader, Dunphy: "He can see no evidence that the war has benefited the people on whose land it is being fought. 'No schools, no churches, no progressive farming – nothing,' he says. 'Why, they're still tilling the farms with little sticks. . . . They don't know or give a damn who runs the country,' he says, and his buddy Denne adds: 'To them we're just the white race fighting on their ground to save our own face.'"

Dunphy and his men came to hate the Americans more than they did the Chinese invaders. All the Lepers heaped scorn on the notion that their war was fought for freedom. "It seems you always got to take somebody's word for it that the Korean people are 'liberty loving,'" Berton quoted Dunphy as saying. "I haven't met a gook yet who was."

Toward the end of March, Dunphy's PPCLI battalion moved to a new location in a bean field thirteen miles northeast of Seoul. Berton now had an opportunity to spend time in Korea's capital, so with a borrowed Jeep, a public relations officer named Joe Levison, and a correspondent from New Zealand, he took the deeply rutted mud road into the city. They entered an eerily silent Seoul ten days after it had been "liberated" for the fourth time in nine months. The city had been devastated, "inert along the broad, debris-strewn Han River," Berton reported, "a lifeless metropolis without food, without power, without water, virtually without people, and almost without hope."[60]

Berton returned home in July 1951 a troubled man.[61] He had trudged through the rubble that was Seoul and seen "a carcass of a city."[62] He had accompanied Canadian troops on patrol and discovered that they had little understanding of why they were there. He had spoken with the enemy and found not a rapist or a looter or "a political intellectual who goes into battle with the phrases of Marx and Engels ringing in his ears," but an illiterate peasant under thirty who cared little for world revolution or imperialist Wall Street bankers but much for "the simpler and more pressing business of getting two bowls of rice a day." Berton had worn khakis and the blue beret of the United Nations, and he came to the conclusion that they represented little more than a smokescreen to mask a foolish American imperial adventure.

Ralph Allen was clearly moved by Berton's unvarnished portrayal of the war in Korea, but the war correspondent himself felt that his reports had been too restrained and self-censoring. "I wanted to squirm out of the straitjacket of the 'objective' reporter," he wrote, "and say, as bluntly as possible, how I felt and what I thought."[63] Once home, he likely conveyed this frustration with no little passion to his editor, for the August 1, 1951, edition of *Maclean's* contained a rare signed editorial, "The Real War in Korea," with Pierre Berton its author.

"Can you win a war in this tragic year of 1951 as you win a prize fight, by brute force in the fifteenth round?" the editorial asked. The answer, Berton suggested, required people to recognize that its nominal objective, to resist aggression, was "a negative objective." What, he asked, had been positive about the Canadian mission to Korea? "Sure, we're winning the old-fashioned war of brawn. But what about the new-fangled war for men's minds? Have our actions in Korea made more friends for the western world? Have we been able to convince the Koreans themselves that the phrase 'our way of life' is something more than a slogan? Have we succeeded in selling our brand of democracy to this proud but unhappy race? It is terrifying to report that the answer seems to be a flat, unqualified 'No!'"

Instead, he had seen misery and destitution arising from a war with "beasts on both sides."[64] A wretch dying of gangrene, refused medical attention because he was Korean. A Canadian private emptying his machine gun into a Korean grave. Drunk and arrogant troops "dispensing the largesse of democracy – a piece of gum here, a piece of chocolate there – to the ragged hungry children begging on the curb." "The great lesson of the new decade is already clear," the editorial read:

> That the ends of military expediency are not enough, that you can't burn away an idea with gasoline jelly but can only destroy it with a better idea. But this lesson hasn't been put into practice.
>
> Our soldiers are sometimes referred to as "the ambassadors of democracy" but the painful fact is that they lack both training and talent for ambassadorship. They have been taught how to fight and they fight well. They have not been taught how to act and they act badly.
>
> It seems to me that there are two basic principles we must accept. . . . These days it is as important to teach a soldier how to get along with other people as it is to teach them the first and second stoppages on the Bren gun. This will take more than just the odd lecture and the occasional pamphlet. The idea needs to be drilled into the troops as surely as the manual of arms.
>
> The other thing we must understand is that we all share some of the responsibility for what has happened to the Korean people and their land. No matter who is to blame it is we who must rebuild this wretched country, for victory will rest in the end with the side that gains the trust of the people.
>
> I believe this is the only practical aim we can follow in Korea if we are to come out of this business with our heads up and our ideals unsullied. The fact that it is also the moral course is perhaps an added argument in its favor. If we succeed with it we may yet make "our way of life" seem worthwhile to the people who've had it inflicted on them for the past twelve months.

Berton knew that there was nothing romantic about war: Harry Filion's combat wounds and his own waiting around to see action bore witness to that. But his experience in Korea taught him that all war was folly. The idea of a "just war" was to him "pious hypocrisy," and men and nations learned little from the experience. The cost of "liberation" often vastly exceeded limited and ambiguous gain. The Korean War hardened Berton's view of the United States. Seven years before the journalists William J. Lederer and Eugene Burdick published *The Ugly American*, their bestselling and highly controversial fictionalized account of American adventurism in Southeast Asia, Berton had outlined the gist of their argument. He was not to change his mind. America gained little if any understanding from its adventure in Korea, he would write near the end of his life, and the consequence had been disastrous instances of miscalculated aggression in Vietnam and elsewhere. Canada in Korea, Berton wrote, was little better. "In its headlong rush to follow the American lead and get into action as quickly as possible, the Canadian Army had made no effort to tell the troops who signed up anything about the Koreans, their history, or their society."[65]

"The Americans continue to fight imperialistic wars," he wrote. But this stark observation lay in the future. In the summer of 1951, his editorial on America in Korea noted cynically that Korea had been "liberated," and asked "At what cost?" As Lederer and Burdick were to say near the end of the decade: "We believe that a nuclear cataclysm is unlikely, but that our free life well may be lost in a succession of bits and fragments."[66]

Following the evening news on the Sunday after his editorial appeared in *Maclean's*, Berton gave a CBC radio talk on the subject. "Wars are fought with more than guns these days," he said. "They're fought with ideas and concepts, and it's precisely these things that seem to have been forgotten by the people who drew up the army syllabus of training."[67] The idea that in Korea democracy was being saved from dictatorship was mere cant. "South Korea," he informed his listeners, "is little more than a police state."

Such views annoyed at least some listeners and readers. "I often listen on short-wave radio to Moscow," one Albertan wrote to the editor of *Maclean's*, "and want to congratulate you and your Pierre Berton on doing so much more effective, or at least more subtle and dangerous job of furthering the Red line of lies and slander."[68] Yet this was the view of a distinct minority; *Maclean's* published several excerpts of letters from those who agreed with its guest editorial. "I have discussed this piece with many friends," wrote one reader, "and their reaction is: 'Somebody *had* to say it, somebody at last makes sense out of the whole confused mess.' I'm glad *Maclean's* takes the lead!" "The best thing yet done about Korea," a British Columbia reader wrote. "Thank you, thank you indeed, for having the courage to print such sturdy, soul-searching stuff," went a letter from Toronto.[69]

The Korean War did not end: it hardened into a stalemate that was to last into the next century. An armistice signed in 1953 divided the country at the 38th parallel, reflecting the American and Chinese spheres of influence. By then, the Canadian military budget was ten times that of 1947 and the nation had remilitarized. The influence of Great Britain, greatly weakened by the Second World War, lessened while that of the United States grew. Generals and procurement officers came to recognize the magnitude of American military power and the quality of its military hardware. Meanwhile, Canadian diplomats and politicians began to turn their attention to finding ways, in the words of the political scientist Denis Stairs, "to moderate the exercise of American power."[70]

For ordinary Canadians, Korea had been a rotten little war that claimed 1,543 casualties. For Pierre Berton, it had been an example of human folly writ large. His weeks as a war correspondent had convinced him that some wars – like the war against Hitler – gave a nation no choice but to fight, but that few wars were necessary and all wars transformed the nations engaged in them. The Korean War did not make Berton a pacifist, but it did convince him that people could ignore the lessons of history only at their peril.[71]

PART THREE

CELEBRITY

13

WRITER, EDITOR, AUTHOR

—

AFTER THE ADRENALIN RUSH of Korea, Berton was happy to settle back into life as writer and editor, husband and father, but his pace in the late summer of 1951 remained as frenetic as ever. The Massey Commission had filed its well-publicized report and the Canadian middle class had begun to take an interest in Canadian culture. Princess Elizabeth and her husband, Prince Philip, were set to make their first visit to Canada in the fall. And Janet delivered what amounted to an ultimatum: no more children until the kitchen was done.

Berton returned to *Maclean's* his usual ebullient self, and the blunt but effective direction he provided left time for other projects. The editorial team decided that given the Massey Commission's high media visibility, Berton should do a profile of the commission co-chairman, Vincent Massey, and his family. The thinking around the editorial table was that since the Masseys were almost Canada's indigenous royalty, the piece would serve as a nice complement to the official royal visit. With an early fall deadline, Berton set out to do his research.

"There'll Always Be a Massey" appeared in the October 15 issue, its title inspired by "There'll Always Be an England," the patriotic song Vera Lynn made popular during the Battle of Britain. The attention-catching brief description accompanying the article, known in the trade as the deck, would alone have disarmed any Masseys disposed to take exception: "Canada's most famous family started on the road to wealth from a tiny implement forge near Port Hope. From gilded mansions where 'theatre' was a naughty word rose a remarkable clan whose sense of showmanship and history produced Abe Lincoln on the stage, the country's greatest music hall, a traffic-stopping Bible class, a headline-making report on culture, and perhaps even our first native governor-general."

The first sentence of the piece would have delighted them: "No Canadian family, past or present, has had a more profound impact upon the nation than the great House of Massey, whose monuments are graven out of enduring clay."

Having duly acknowledged the family's importance, Berton knew he could apply his formula – three parts family fortune, two parts personal foible, and one part each of civic pride and Canadian history – as he had done with E.P. Taylor and the Southams. Toronto's Fred Victor Mission, Massey Hall, the Massey-Harris agricultural implement plant, and the University of Toronto's student centre, Hart House, epitomized the family: "the heady brew of showmanship, culture, old-time religion, hard business sense and national spirit which has made the Masseys a moving force in Canada for five generations." With those words Berton introduced the story of five generations of a family whose "twin themes" were "showmanship and sanctity . . . blended into a masterly counterpoint" with impunity. Could its scion Vincent possibly object when he read of himself that "approaching him . . . is like entering a Gothic cathedral," or that employees of the family firm described him as "Lorenzo the Magnificent plus Henry Ford," or that his favourite role as an actor at Hart House had been that of a pope?[1]

The article's denouement returned to the deck's whiff of political revelation. During his research, Berton discovered that because Vincent Massey had insisted that certain meetings of his royal commission be conducted entirely in French and without translation, he had become the most popular English-speaking Canadian in Quebec. *Le Devoir* had touted him as Canada's next governor general. Exported from the pages of this influential but low-circulation French-language newspaper to those of English Canada's most popular magazine, an idea that might have been stillborn took on new life. Vincent Massey was appointed Canada's first native-born governor general in 1952.

Berton pursued his media and publishing contacts beyond *Maclean's* as if he had never been out of the country. His radio appearances on such programs as the CBC's current affairs show *Citizens' Forum* and the quiz show *Beat the Champs*, and on both radio and television versions of *Court of Opinion*, in which a moderator called upon panellists to provide instant opinions about controversial subjects, had increased to the point that listeners now expected to hear his voice. He felt himself so much a regular that he began to associate his children's birthdates with these programs. When his third daughter was born in October 1952, almost nine months to the day after the Kleinburg kitchen was finished, Penny and Pamela dubbed her "Catherine Ann New Doll," but their father thought of little Patsy as his *Court of Opinion* child, not least because his fees from the show helped complete the renovation in time for the new baby's arrival.[2]

Constantly fearful of the spectre of privatization, the CBC tended to cultivate and stay with those contributors who were reliable and loyal; provocative perhaps, but not sufficiently so as to put the corporation at risk of public or government censure. Berton was among them, in spite of the listener who claimed that his radio talk on Korea had been "biased, prejudiced and non-factual."[3] Kate Aitken, champion of Canada's homemakers and a hugely popular fixture on Toronto's CFRB, the country's most listened-to radio station, was another. For those on the inside, work at the CBC could be positively clubbish. Often Berton found himself sharing the *Court of Opinion* studio with Lister Sinclair and the *Beat the Champs* microphone with Ralph Allen.[4]

Berton's Korea articles and broadcasts increased the value of his currency with those on whom he relied for freelance income. "Your series of articles in *Maclean's* on Korea, have made darn fine reading," wrote Maurice Crompton, chief of the CBC's Commercial Division. "Obviously, you have written your stuff 'a la Gunther' – at some bar in Tacoma – but it makes mighty fine reading."[5] "I heard your Korean report the other night and thought it was excellent," CBC talks producer Elspeth Chisholm said, adding that she intended to rebroadcast his *A Canadian Looks at Europe* series in the U.K. and Europe.[6]

Berton rose to the challenge of the feature article as he had earlier to the newspaper scoop. He enjoyed both but, like radio plays, the work no longer offered much exhilaration. He had graduated from writing for a newspaper to editing a magazine; now he wanted to be the author of a book. John Farrar had spurned his story of Russ Baker as jejune, and Pierre recognized that it was just that – the sort of adventure, he later admitted, "that might have appeared in *Chums Annual* – the kind I had devoured as a boy."[7] Perhaps a niggling fear of failure, however uncharacteristic of the man, helps account for the fact that he somehow lost a book-length manuscript about his wartime experience. He took pride in the fact that he was a writer, but he felt driven to publish a book. In the early fall of 1951 he had no idea what it would be about.

That October, Ralph Allen assigned him to cover the cross-country tour of Princess Elizabeth and Prince Philip. Berton took unusually detailed notes as part of the press entourage that followed the royal couple from Saint John in New Brunswick to Eaglecrest Lodge on Vancouver Island, but he found time for three nights of hard drinking in the Saint John home of Ian Sclanders (*Maclean's* Maritimes editor) and more moderate tippling at a lavish Vancouver party. Rapturous crowds greeted the princess and the prince in Halifax, still very much an outpost of empire. Astonished guests watched the royal couple square dance at Rideau Hall, the governor general's Ottawa residence. When they arrived at Vancouver's Shaughnessy Hospital to visit the elderly and the veterans of three wars, mobs of children met their convertible, all polished black and gleaming chrome. The nation's enthusiasm for the heir to the throne and the possibility of a revived British international reputation seemed to capture a swelling national self-confidence, and Allen and *Maclean's* were proud to promote it in a series of reports from the road. Before his coverage even began, Berton decided that his first book would be on the royal family.

He returned from Vancouver with the shape of two other *Maclean's* articles in his head. Vancouverites' self-absorption with their city became one. Compared with it, he said, "Tristan's passion for Isolde pales and Dante's infatuation with his Beatrice seems pretty shabby." On the other hand, the city's aura was enough to make a visitor "from some less favored corner of the globe grind his teeth in envy and frustration." He had fun with the themes of local pride and national resentment, even as he touted Vancouver's fine sights and scenery and drew a portrait of its lively civic history and character.[8]

Reinforcing the notion that his articles in *Maclean's* were mere extensions of the Berton persona, his final piece of 1951 was an account of that splendid party he had attended in October at the opulent home of Ronald and Helen Graham, Vancouver's most active and popular socialites. The retired financier's house, an architectural mix of English Tudor and Pacific Coast contemporary clad in shocking pink stucco, boasted a kitchen equipped to serve six hundred and a swimming pool that each Monday hosted hundreds of children from nearby University

Wiggins Orphan Asylum.

Frank Berton was a resident of the Wiggins Male Orphan Institution in Saint John, New Brunswick, from the age of six until he was sixteen.

Before her marriage in 1912, Laura Berton (centre) entertained gentlemen callers in the Victorian fashion at weekly "at-homes."

Dawson City Museum (image number 1999.12.1.43)

Frank Berton was a champion walker, an inveterate hiker, and an accomplished amateur naturalist.

All his life, Pierre Berton had family pets. Here, Grey Cloud helps him gain his footing in life.

William Ready Division, McMaster University Library

The Bertons of Dawson City
lived in their Eighth Avenue
bungalow until 1932, when the
family moved to Victoria after
Frank Berton lost his position as
mining recorder.

Pierre got to know his grandfather,
Thomas Phillips Thompson, during
two trips "outside," from Dawson to
Ontario, in 1925 and 1931–32.

Pierre spent the summers of 1937 through 1939 working in the Klondike gold fields, as his father had done thirty years earlier.

At the University of British Columbia student newspaper between 1939 and 1941, Berton rose from cub reporter to editor.

Berton gained legendary status at UBC with the "Beast Stalks Campus" issue of the *Ubyssey* on March 28, 1941.

During the Second World War, Berton's fellow *Ubyssey* editor Janet Walker was an affectionate friend. She and Pierre married in 1946.

Berton was close to his mother, Laura, seen here strolling with him down a Vancouver street in the early 1940s. She initially titled her memoirs "It's a Boy."

In the immediate postwar years, Berton excitedly followed his mentor, the *Vancouver Sun* managing editor Hal Straight, on the carousel of life, in this instance while Jack Scott bore witness.

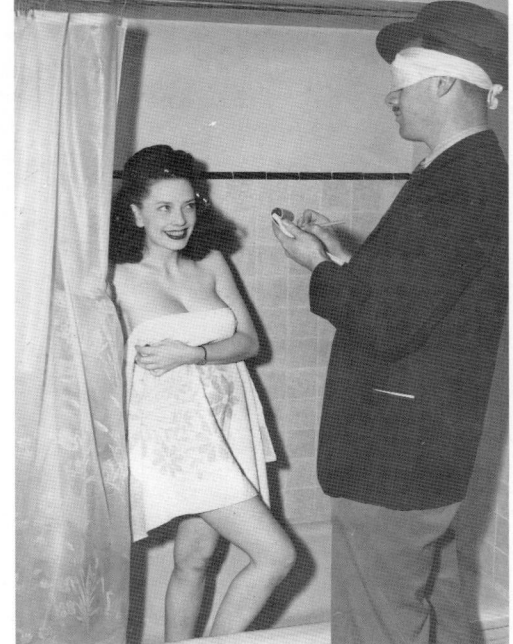

In 1947, as a *Vancouver Sun* reporter, Berton interviewed Evelyn West, better known as the Hubba Hubba Girl. In his memoirs, he noted that her hubbas had been insured by Lloyds.

Shortly after this photo was taken at a Women's Press Club evening gala, Berton and a fellow prankster, Ray Munro, let loose a pig in the Hotel Vancouver ballroom.

Perhaps the most unexpected find of the 1947 Headless Valley adventure was the grizzled Berton's discovery of a pin-up photo of the actress Rita Hayworth in a trapper's cabin.

Berton's sensational Headless Valley series caught world attention, and also the eye of Arthur Irwin, editor of *Maclean's*. A few months later, Berton was working for him in Toronto.

In 1950, Ralph Allen took over from Irwin as editor of *Maclean's*. The magazine flourished under his leadership. So did Pierre Berton, who became its managing editor in January 1953.

Berton's 1961 children's book, *The Secret World of Og*, was written for his own children, who appeared as its main characters. Left to right: Pamela, Patsy, Pierre, Paul, Peter (standing), Peggy Ann, and Penny.

Hill school. Assisted by eight servants and four gardeners, the Grahams were known to hold six parties a week, sometimes two a day.

Berton's piece made no pretense to any Veblenesque criticism of conspicuous consumption or social inequity; it was simply a good yarn about the Point Grey adventures of the idle rich, to whom Berton now had access, and – this was the key point – thanks to him, so too did readers of *Maclean's*. Its thesis may have been fuzzy but its message was clear: Pierre Berton was Canadians' window on the world. The role was enhanced when, in an affectionate story that became his first *Maclean's* article of 1952, he revealed to readers that the *Vancouver Sun's* "food and household hints" columnist, previously known only as "Penny Wise," was in fact his volatile former colleague Evelyn Caldwell, an unflappable world traveller whose extraordinary exploits merited a story by Pierre Berton.[9]

Berton's work at *Maclean's* began to assume a trajectory dictated by personal ambition and a hope that it coincided with the magazine's needs. Writing a book would require large blocks of time that he scarcely enjoyed as articles editor. Ralph Allen was aware of this, and in February 1952 he created the position of associate editor specifically for Berton. Pierre now had more overall responsibility but less need to pore over every sentence the magazine's writers churned out. Still, excluding editorials, fiction, and his own pieces, during his year as articles editor, then as associate editor, he was responsible for the care and nurture of a total of 173 articles, including a series of photo essays on Canada and Canadians by Yousuf Karsh that continued into 1953.[10]

The idea for a piece to follow the profile of Evelyn Caldwell came from his life in the countryside. The Berton property opened out into a valley with a vast horizon, but the grounds surrounding the house were still not landscaped. Penny's view from the home as a small child, she recalled, was of "a barren wasteland."[11] That March, Berton wrote about the Dominion Seed House, "A Garden in Your Mailbox." Home life had made him an expert on the catalogue of the country's largest mail-order seed business. "Reading it the novice gardener is transported into an exotic world where radishes grow to twenty-five pounds and watermelons shrink to eight inches," he wrote, "where cucumbers wriggle like serpents and morning glories come out in the afternoon."[12]

This was the kind of stuff Pierre could write in his head, and did, from information absorbed over breakfast, one more hint to readers that this was a chap whose life was an open book in which ordinary Canadians could discover variations of their own experience. The man, it seemed, could take the most mundane material and make it fascinating. Headless Valley had been a captivating tale by anybody's standards – but seed catalogues? In Berton's hands, absolutely.

After the Dominion Seed House story came a major two-part profile of the *Toronto Star*, as if inspiration had followed Berton down the highway from the fields around Kleinburg to the pavement of downtown Toronto. (The paper's masthead actually carried the name *Toronto Daily Star* until 1971.) Like the sagas of the *Vancouver Sun* and the empire of the Southams, the extraordinary story of the Toronto newspaper founded by Joseph E. Atkinson ("half radical, half Bourbon") and presided over in the 1950s by his "sphinx-like" son-in-law, Harry Comfort Hindmarsh, reminded Berton of how picaresque the media world could be. The story of the *Toronto Star*, his title read, was "The Greatest Three-Cent Show on Earth."

Berton's engaging account ran in the March 15 and April 1 issues of *Maclean's* in 1952. As usual, his research was extensive, and it included material gleaned from several interviews with Hindmarsh. The profile balanced information with intimacy. It was a fully rounded portrait of Canada's largest mass-circulation daily and its remarkable cast of characters, from the defrocked Presbyterian minister turned novelist Robert E. Knowles and the young American reporter Ernest Hemingway, early in the century, to the volatile Gordon Sinclair and the inscrutable Harry Hindmarsh himself in its middle decades. "The Toronto Star," went Berton's subhead, "got to be one of the loudest, craziest and most successful papers in the world by unleashing an army of reporters on stories and stunts carefully calculated to please – as well as infuriate – some of the people all of the time."[13]

The upper echelon of the *Toronto Star* seems to have concluded that Berton, a resident of Toronto for fewer than five years, knew more about their newspaper than they did themselves. After the second part of the *Star* profile appeared, someone at the *Star* contacted Berton to ask him to prepare an essay on the life and career of Hindmarsh for the paper's own archives. When the man died four years later, Berton's piece began on the front page and took up all of page 4.[14]

The *Toronto Star* story rounded out Berton's treatment of newspapers and newspapermen in Canada. Collectively his articles on the subject could have become the scaffold for a social history of the Canadian newspaper business. But as if to signal that fresh winds beckoned, Berton chose as his final *Maclean's* article for 1952 a story about a different medium. Always a step or two ahead of the zeitgeist, he turned his attention to the dawn of the age of television. The new medium, he knew, was in its infancy, but he could sense the revolutionary influence it would have.[15]

The scientific theory behind television had been in place since the 1880s, and the technology to convey pictures was developed by the British scientist John Logie Baird in the 1920s. The British Broadcasting Corporation transmitted the first experimental television images in 1926, six years before its television service was launched. In Canada, the Montreal radio station CKAC became the first to broadcast television signals, and in July 1931 viewers at the twenty or so locations in Montreal with television sets witnessed Canada's first live television program, consisting of a violinist, a singer, and a cartoonist.[16]

Television became available to the mass market in North America at the end of the Second World War, when factories previously geared to wartime *matériel* turned to the manufacture of domestic appliances. In 1945 the American Federal Communications Commission began to issue television broadcasting licences. Radio manufacturers and private broadcasters such as the Radio Corporation of America (RCA) and the National Broadcasting Company (NBC) joined forces to provide electronic goods and services. Stars of stage and screen like Jack Benny and Lucille Ball began to consider second careers in television. American viewers saw the heavyweight fight between Joe Louis and Billy Conn on the small screen in June 1946 and the opening of Congress the following January. "The tube," said the television historian Erik Barnouw, "was suddenly alive with activity."[17]

"No one knows yet what the exact shape of TV will be in Canada," Berton wrote in May 1952, but by then he had already made himself an expert on developments inside the old Victorian mansion on Jarvis

Street that housed the CBC. With Montreal, Toronto was one of the two Canadian cities with CBC television studios (Ottawa and Vancouver would obtain them the next year). On September 8, two days after the CBC's first television broadcast was aired in Montreal, those few Torontonians with television sets saw the first CBC broadcast in their city. It was a news announcement about the capture of Toronto's notorious Boyd Gang.

Pierre Berton was as prepared as anyone to exploit this new medium of communication. At ease in the radio studio, he eagerly grasped the opportunity to appear on television. Four days into the history of CBC television in Canada, he was part of it. On September 9, he appeared on a televised version of *Court of Opinion* with his fellow panellists Kate Aitken and Lister Sinclair and the moderator, Neil LeRoy. The experience was a disaster. No one knew quite what to do or where to look, everyone was self-conscious, and opinions offered spontaneously on radio appeared contrived in a television format, especially when the panellists had to offer them immediately after actors had dramatized the issues of the day.

"I left the studio that night," Berton later said, "resolving never again to let myself be put through such an ordeal." But the next day, when a taxi driver who had watched the broadcast identified him by name, he changed his mind. "I had written scores of articles for the largest magazine in the country, but nobody knew me. I realized that, in spite of my lofty attitude and my abject terror, I would have to come to terms with the new medium. It was the greatest marketing tool yet devised, and since I was now determined to write best-selling books, I would have to make use of it. Television was not an end in itself, but it would be the means to publicize my real work."[18]

The "real work" was writing books. This dictated all else. Virtually everything Berton wrote for *Maclean's* from the spring of 1952 until he left the magazine in 1958 consisted of serialized material from books in progress. The grand success of the Headless Valley series had taught him that the financial principle of "leveraging" – the use of borrowed capital to increase the potential return on an investment – could work in publishing as well as in business. It was certainly worth a gamble. Publishers might fear that serializing material from a book before publication detracted from its originality or appeal and that sales would fall, but

Berton thought otherwise. After five years of his recycling the same Nahanni stories, interest remained as strong as ever. Serializing was like priming the pump: give readers a taste of good material and they will want more. Besides, had Robert Weaver, in charge of talks and public affairs at CBC, not offered him $50 per talk for a series, *North to the Nahanni*, earlier in the year?[19]

Berton had scarcely begun to enjoy his position as associate editor, which placed him third in the editorial pecking order (below only Ralph Allen and managing editor John Clare), when he found himself promoted once more. On January 6, 1953, Allen circulated a memo to the editorial staff announcing that Berton had been appointed managing editor. The taciturn Clare was shuffled aside, reluctantly accepting the editorship of *Chatelaine*, Maclean Hunter's women's magazine. Berton knew that the promotion would be his last at *Maclean's*; in his own mind, at least, he was far too left-leaning for Floyd Chalmers, now president of Maclean Hunter, ever to hand him the editorship.[20]

"Mr. Berton," said Allen's directive to the editorial staff, "will continue to be responsible, under and in consultation with the Editor, for all editorial activities." In creative matters, the art director and the articles and fiction editors were to report to the new managing editor – "working definition of a creative matter: anything connected with the initiating, obtaining and approval of editorial matter from the idea stage to the stage of approved body text and approved layout." Where production was concerned they were to see the new associate editor, Leslie Hannon, who reported to the managing editor.[21]

The promotion relieved Berton of the daily chores of the associate editor: the coordination of production schedules, the regular briefing of department heads on deadlines and space allotments, the liaison with the press room and the advertising department. But he was expected "to edit, title and blurb most of the copy for the magazine," which by the end of 1952 had as many as ninety-six pages per issue. His own contribution of articles diminished considerably as his responsibilities increased and his mind gravitated toward the writing of books. An output numbering thirteen *Maclean's* articles in 1951 had been reduced to five in 1952, fewer than most other staff writers.[22] He was in pursuit of different and larger quarry.

⋈

The promotions of 1952 and early 1953 allowed him time to travel. After his *Toronto Star* profiles appeared in March and April of 1952 he was able to spend almost a year tracking down material and stories about the royal family, and then give them shape. The first in the series appeared in *Maclean's* on March 15, 1953. The popular writer had been absent from its pages long enough that Allen felt obliged to account for his whereabouts. "For eleven months," Allen's "In the Editors' Confidence" column revealed, "Pierre Berton, a tall man with reddish hair, has been wandering around asking questions about the Queen from Halifax to Victoria in the wake of the royal tour, gathering anecdotes and impressions. He also spent two months in England. In between hundreds of interviews he read ninety-seven books on British royalty."[23]

Berton had flown to London in October 1952. He found a flat near Piccadilly, spent a good deal of time in the British Museum Reading Room, and then interviewed English aristocrats close to the royals in England and Scotland, including Edward Hardinge, private secretary to Edward VIII, and Lady Brabourne, cousin to Prince Philip. He managed to annoy the Queen's press secretary, Lieutenant-Commander Richard Colville, by giving the impression that he thought the man was a public relations flack and not a palace official. Colville was aghast when Berton suggested a tour of Buckingham Palace. "See around the palace? . . . See around? My dear chap – nobody sees around Buckingham Palace!"[24]

The lieutenant-commander had not reckoned on the ingenuity of a colonial journalist whose hunt for his story had already included an interview with the postmaster at Crathie,[25] the village just outside the grounds of Balmoral Castle. Rebuffed but not perturbed, Berton located a book on Buckingham Palace, found out that the Royal Philatelic Collection was located in a remote section of the second floor, and then telephoned Sir John Wilson, keeper of the royal postage stamps, to say that a fellow from *Maclean's* wished a viewing. He left unsaid whether *Maclean's* was a philatelic magazine. "If he got that impression," Berton admitted later, "I didn't correct it." The next day he took in much of the palace on his way to and from the stamp room.

The downstairs world of Buckingham Palace remained closed to him, but through a newspaper friend he managed to secure an interview with a palace servant at a nearby pub.[26] The clientele seemed to consist entirely of palace servants and the newspapermen interviewing them. Berton's own confidant appeared nervous. After a quick pint, fearing the two were being watched, the man suggested another locale. The intrepid Canuck followed him through a side door, down an alleyway, and into a second pub – only to have the whole business repeated a second pint later. The intrigue, bordering on farce, reminded Berton of nothing so much as "those interviews we read about with Igor Gouzenko."

Berton eventually stumbled onto the one key that got him past the secretaries and into the confidence of high officials. The magic password was "Beverley Baxter." Early in the century, Baxter, born in Canada, had aspired to a literary career, and as a young man he had gained two powerful champions. The publisher J.B. Maclean had accepted his early writings for *Maclean's*, and the tycoon Baron Beaverbrook had secured him a position in 1920 with the London *Daily Express*, which Beaverbrook controlled. By the mid-1950s, Arthur Beverley Baxter, long an intimate of the great men of the British Empire, had been a fixture of the journalistic establishment and the London correspondent of *Maclean's* for many years. It was he who first provided its readers with details of the abdication of Edward VIII in 1936.

Baxter's regular column, "London Letter," continued to hold pride of place near the front of the magazine. "To introduce Mr. Baxter is a difficult job," the man introducing him to a joint meeting of the Toronto chapters of the Canadian Club and the Empire Club of Canada in 1941 had said, "because no introduction is necessary. He is known on both sides of the Atlantic, not as 'Mr. Baxter,' not as 'Mr. Beverley Baxter,' but just as 'Beverley Baxter.'"[27]

The line "I'm a friend of Beverley Baxter's" therefore carried with it the charismatic aura of influence, and for Berton it opened doors and unsealed lips. For this he was grateful, even though Baxter was exactly the kind of pompous agent of empire he could not stand and did not care to meet. In this way, assisted by a Scottish postmaster, a royal philatelist, a paranoid palace servant, and others, a clever and persistent Canadian author crafted a portrait of the royal family in a book like no other on the subject.

The first of the seven parts of "The Family in the Palace" appeared on March 15, 1953. The series was carefully planned to culminate in the June 2 coronation of Elizabeth II. The previous fall, Berton had sent a seventeen-page book proposal to a New York agent, Willis Kingsley Wing, whose Canadian clients included his *Maclean's* colleagues Ralph Allen, Scott Young, and Eva-Lis Wuorio. The respected firm of Alfred A. Knopf immediately expressed an interest, so Berton took two weeks of holidays, set up an orange crate desk and an orange crate filing cabinet in his Kleinburg bedroom, and expanded the thirty thousand words of his articles into the eighty-thousand-word manuscript Knopf called for. This was relatively easy, since the articles had been intended all along as chapters for the book.[28]

As preparation, Berton had read other authors for inspiration and for literary style. Inevitably, given his subject, he had fixed upon English writers, especially the anti-Victorian modernists of the Bloomsbury Group, whose privileged and eccentric lives fed their art. Books by Harold Nicolson and Christopher Sykes, Edith Sitwell and Margot Asquith, but especially those by Lytton Strachey, fuelled Berton's own.[29] Strachey's unsentimental iconoclasm and mordant wit, on brilliant display in *Eminent Victorians* (1918) and *Queen Victoria* (1921), had eviscerated Victorian pretense and proved instrumental in making the word *Victorian* synonymous with prudery and hypocrisy. His style was the inspiration Berton needed to write an account of the English royal family unlike the hagiographical and fawning tomes that so dominated the book market and delighted groups such as the Canadian organization Imperial Order Daughters of the Empire.

The series began with a historical survey of the Saxe-Coburgs and the Hanovers, the two royal houses that had united to form the House of Windsor. It continued with articles on the Duke of Windsor and the abdication crisis, the means by which Elizabeth was taught to rule, the Canadian royal tour of 1951, and a minute-by-minute account of one day in the life of the new queen. The seventh and climactic piece came in the special coronation issue of *Maclean's* released for sale on May 27, a week before the event. To satisfy readers' appetites, Berton's contribution to the special issue was in effect two back-to-back instalments: one on the heavy publicity the new queen had to endure and the traits of character she possessed to endure it, and the other on the strange rites of royalty.

The prose of "The Family in the Palace" was crisp, witty, and attuned to the ironies and disjunctions of the lives of his subjects. But Berton did not share Strachey's corrosive intent. Canada in 1953, for all that it fell under the growing shadow of America, remained a kingdom as well as a dominion, and Berton well knew that neither the Canadian public nor the magazine John Bayne Maclean had founded would tolerate a hatchet job on the monarchs who presided over the fledgling British Commonwealth of Nations.

Only a few weeks before the coronation, following the death of Queen Mary (wife of George V and grandmother to Elizabeth) on March 24, a lead editorial in the *Globe and Mail* had concluded: "It is difficult to explain the emotional power which marks the attachment most Canadians feel for the Royal Family." In the coronation issue of *Maclean's* the title of Ralph Allen's editorial on the Commonwealth was "The Free World's Greatest Asset." On the day of the coronation itself, adjacent to editorials on "The Queen" and "The Commonwealth" filled with rapturous commentary on the young monarch and her kingdom, the *Globe* published a dedicatory poem, "Canada to Her Queen, 1953," by Sir Thomas White. Its text, set against a background of rays of light emanating from a queen's crown and brightening the earth below, began: "Queen of our hearts and of our realm, / This day we pledge to thee / The homage of a people's love / A Nation's fealty."[30]

Berton wanted to attract the wide North American readership that a book published by a New York publisher such as Knopf made possible. To do so, he had to write about the royals in a way that would appeal to Canadian readers, yet went beyond their parochial loyalty to the monarchy. But where was the sure path between fawning and ridicule? In the end, while attention to the writers of Bloomsbury made him carefully hone each turn of phrase, his strategy was not much different from the one he used when writing about the Southams and the Masseys. He did not need to demean his subjects' accomplishments to make them interesting, only show readers that they were human, that despite their lofty place in the world these important people possessed the same flawed humanity as the average man or woman.

Berton had discovered that quotidian detail breached the gap between the vaunted and the mundane – Queen Victoria's son Edward VII didn't like rare beef but he was king for all that – and that while people looked up to the powerful and the famous, something inside them wanted to bring the mighty down. So he acknowledged the mystique and the mythic proportions of royalty, revealing as he did so that those who sat on thrones had warts and foibles just like the rest of us. He offered readers something more than a book on the British royal family. An indifferent monarchist at best, he was an accomplished expert when it came to movie stars: "The Family in the Palace" was a pioneering case study of the culture of modern celebrity and a handbook on how to write about it.

From the outset, the series on the royals – and the book that resulted from it – fixed upon the ambivalence with which ordinary British subjects treated those who reigned over them. Canadians expected their royals to possess something of a common touch, yet expressed surprise when they did. "A cataract of newspaper trivia," Berton began, "brings home every day the point that the people in the palace are mortal: that a fairy prince likes to drink pink gin and drive a sports car ninety-two miles an hour; that a fairy princess can wink at a soldier and go mad about Danny Kaye records; that a fairy queen plays a mean game of canasta and is crazy about as plebeian a pastime as square dancing. And yet, when a middle-aged Prince Charming rejects a throne for the most fundamental of mortal emotions, the shock to his subjects is so great that it must be cushioned by the daily repetition of the phrase that 'after all, he is human.'"[31]

A man who drinks gin, a girl who winks at a soldier, a woman who plays canasta – these ingredients were crucial to the Berton recipe. They humanized royalty even as they maintained mystery. The overarching theme of his series on the royal family became the extraordinary tension arising from the psychological traits of the dynasties that together constituted the House of Windsor: the Hanovers and the Saxe-Coburgs. The Hanovers, who had given Great Britain four Georgian kings, were hot-blooded and impetuous but could be brave, cruel, and passionate. Coburg blood, in contrast, ran chill and blue, befitting a family that over the centuries had proven to be almost obsessive in matters of duty.

The resulting mix, in Berton's complex portrait of the Windsors, was a psychodrama of mythic proportions and "astonishing human contrasts":

> Edward VII with his love for plovers' eggs, baccarat, professional beauties and Duminy triple sec '83; Edward VIII with his tastes in night clubs and his propensity for playing the drums in jazz bands; the fashionable Princess Margaret who likes to read racy French novels, drink pink champagne and dance until dawn – how can these be equated with George V, that most domestic of monarchs, who preferred his stamp collection and his morning bowl of soup to more esoteric pursuits and was always in bed by 11:10 p.m.; or George VI whose heart lay in the pheasant and grouse coverts at Sandringham and Balmoral; or Elizabeth Regina, that consecrated young Queen whose serious, preoccupied face bears the Coburg stamp of duty?[32]

This passage from the first instalment of "The Family in the Palace" played with the themes of duty and excess in ways to which readers could directly relate. In crisp phrases and concrete detail, and with an interpretive framework sustained by narrative power rather than analytical assertion, it showed a prose style, charged but "cool," not often found in *Maclean's* and rare in Canada. During the two weeks holed up in his Kleinburg bedroom, Berton had discovered his métier. He had written a book; serialization was merely a means to that end.

The readers of *Maclean's* soon let him know what they thought of his treatment of the royals. In the issue of June 1, on the eve of the coronation, most of the magazine's regular "Mailbag" column was devoted to reaction to Berton's series. A New Yorker, Alan Feld, thought it "the best, most informative and most human writing on the Royal Family" he had ever seen, and Kenneth Macleod of Antigonish, Nova Scotia, concluded that it demonstrated the superiority of monarchy to republicanism. Christy McDevitt of North Vancouver praised Berton for producing "an outstanding job of work," and Maude Leopold of Castleton, Ontario, found the royal articles highly interesting. "There is a vast improvement in *Maclean's* generally," she added.

Then came the objections. "With many others I was shocked and horrified," Alice L. Fairweather of Saint John wrote. "Why did Mr. Berton have to drag out the skeletons of history and rattle their bones for the public? He has dug up all the nasty little things, . . . and aimed to detract from the dignity of monarchy whom an older generation were taught to admire and respect." Gertrude Pringle of Victoria had one word for the series: "revolting." "What's the matter with Berton?" Mrs. Margaret Yeoman of Lloydminster, Saskatchewan, asked. "Does he really believe your readers are gullible enough to take the tripe he has written about some members of the Royal Family?"[33] Such divided reaction seemed promising for the book already in production: nobody seemed indifferent to Berton's treatment of the royals.

The Royal Family: The Story of the British Monarchy from Victoria to Elizabeth appeared early in 1954 in New York, under the Knopf imprint. Berton's contract gave Knopf North American rights, which meant that the Canadian publisher had to be McClelland & Stewart, Knopf's Canadian distributor. This was disappointing, since he preferred Macmillan of Canada with its distinguished list of Canadian authors. Still, the brash young head of McClelland & Stewart, Jack McClelland, a sandy-haired veteran from the Royal Canadian Navy two years Berton's junior, seemed positively keen on the book. Son of the founder of the firm, McClelland was a man brimming with ideas and never lacked for an opinion – a man much like Berton himself.

At their first meeting they jousted with each other over how best to publicize *The Royal Family*. Berton wanted to launch the book with a cocktail party; McClelland, mindful of the criticism from some *Maclean's* readers, felt that his controversial portrayal of the royals as ordinary people required something less expensive but more dramatic – "a special gimmick," perhaps a poster featuring some of those read- ers' harshest words. "It may be a lousy idea," McClelland wrote to his vice-president, Hugh Kane, "but it may be novel enough to make it interesting. . . . Even if it doesn't sell, it should be a lot of fun, and it may sell very well. I think it is particularly important that we do a good job on this one, promotion-wise, if we want to keep Berton as an M&S author. I am not absolutely sure that we do, but a lot of people . . . think that he has a tremendous future ahead of him. All I am asking for is a couple of million dollars worth of publicity for an expenditure of about ten bucks."[34]

Unorthodox promotional efforts notwithstanding, *The Royal Family* did not find a readership as large as Berton had expected. The book, he later admitted, was "a flop." His explanation was that the overblown attention to Elizabeth II's coronation gave Canadians "a bellyful of royalty."[35] But other factors also led to the disappointing sales. Alfred Knopf's choice of the Bauhaus designer Herbert Bayer proved only that Bayer had little idea of how to design an effective book jacket. That was a matter on which Berton and McClelland had immediately agreed. Its royal coat of arms, in red over a royal blue background and with a blurb in tiny type, seemed to promise a dull book on heraldry rather than the lively saga of a family dynasty.

The American reviews were favourable. The *New York Times* touted *The Royal Family* as "unsurpassed in our day for its grave and gay stories of the lives of kings" and the *New York Times Book Review*, describing Berton as "an energetic, far-from-sycophantic Canadian," called it "a little classic of pioneer research." The *Chicago Herald Tribune* proclaimed it "the most entertaining book about Royalty since Lytton Strachey wrote his *Queen Victoria* thirty years ago." A review in the *Christian Science Monitor* dwelt at length on Berton's twin themes of spontaneity and duty, but felt obliged to warn that in spite of the author's "underlying respect" for the British royal family, "the frankness of Mr. Berton's style may sometimes disconcert readers used to the greater caution of press writers in the British Isles." Berton's former English correspondent Lawrence Earl, of Odhams Press, penned a paragraph-long note in *Kirkus Reviews*, a periodical twenty-one years old but still typed, not typeset. The book, he wrote, offered readers "absorbing reading," a "superior assemblage of majesties as people and rulers." For Lawrence Earl, damning with faint praise was an English art form.[36]

In the kingdom of Canada, book review editors all but ignored *The Royal Family*. The *Globe and Mail* several times noted that it was one of the new books most in demand in the Toronto Public Library, but did not choose to review it. Neither did the *Toronto Star*. Berton had managed to offend many who held the royal family in great respect while failing to pull other readers into the bookstores. He was disappointed but not deeply perturbed. By almost any other Canadian writer's expectations but his own, *The Royal Family* had in fact been quite a success.

In the year of its release, Knopf sold 6,448 copies and McClelland & Stewart a further 3,173. Berton's net royalties came to $2,251.53.[37]

Yet the very existence of this book, his first, brought deep satisfaction and added a new dimension to his self-image. "Now I was more than a mere writer," he wrote. "I was an author, with all that word's connotations – the pipe, the smoking jacket, the finger lightly touching the forehead."[38]

❦

Late in 1953, Canada's future caught up with Berton's past. On December 8, Prime Minister Louis St. Laurent, the mild-mannered and gentle successor to Mackenzie King, moved second reading of Bill 6, creating a "Department of Northern Affairs and National Resources" out of the wreckage of earlier departments that had administered Canada's north. It was time, proclaimed the man Canadians called "Uncle Louis," for the nation at last to pay the North serious attention. "Apparently we have administered these vast territories of the north in an almost continuing state of absence of mind. I think all honourable members now feel that the territories are vastly important to Canada and that it is time that more attention was focused upon their possibilities and what they will mean to this Canadian nation."[39]

A number of circumstances converged to make the Canadian government pay belated attention to Canada's northern regions. The Cold War left North America vulnerable to attack by Russian bombers and missiles. Postwar Britain, victorious but impoverished, had no capacity to come to Canada's aid in times of threat. This, along with the fear of nuclear attack by the Soviet Union, led to Canadian co-operation with the United States in the construction and financing of the DEW Line and the Pine Tree Line, strings of radar stations along Canada's northern coast from Alaska to Ellesmere Island and across the 50th parallel.[40] Instead of easing Canadian anxiety, the American presence simply added another worry. What would become of Canadian sovereignty over its northern reaches?

In addition, Canada's growing industrial needs after the war placed increasing demand on the mining sector for domestic and export purposes. With the discovery of gold, nickel, lead, zinc, and uranium, the

North began to be associated less with fur traders than with economic development – the modern equivalent of the "last, best west," Minister of the Interior Clifford Sifton's description of the prairies in the late nineteenth century.

Radio, television, and prosperity made Canadians of the 1950s slowly aware of the disparity of wealth and condition between those in the south and those in the North, and it was becoming impossible to ignore decades of government mismanagement and neglect. Newspaper editorials of the day predicted the possibility of a flowering of Canadian life, but one in seven Inuit were in southern hospitals, northern life expectancy at birth was less than a third of the Canadian average, and the rate of infant mortality was five times higher. In 1952, Farley Mowat's account of his experience in the North, *People of the Deer*, had accused governments and missionaries alike of destruction of the traditional Inuit way of life and sparked a storm of controversy, including the charge that his account was as much fiction as fact.[41] In the south, where millions of Canadians in cities enjoyed the comforts of new suburban bungalows and family time in front of the television, the federal government's promise of a full and fair share of Canadian life to northern peoples played equally to social responsibility and to national guilt.

The North had scarcely been very far from Berton's mind in spite of the attention he had paid to the royals. The CBC remained interested in almost anything he offered on northern Canada, and he continued to earn extra money with radio talks on the subject. "If you like true adventure, with a touch of the zany and wild, give a listen tomorrow," the entertainment writer Gordon Sinclair advised readers of his Saturday *Toronto Star* radio column in September 1952.[42] The occasion was – what else? – a rebroadcast of Berton's Headless Valley series. One of those who heard the broadcast was John Gray, Macmillan of Canada's cultivated president, who then approached Berton to write a book on the gold rush for his Great Stories of Canada children's series. Using mainly the history and lore in his head and whatever published sources proved handy, Berton wrote the thirty thousand words of *The Golden Trail* in a week. It did very well. Over the years, Macmillan sold 100,000 copies.[43] There was gold in the Klondike still.

The St. Laurent government's sudden discovery of the North became a matter of discussion at *Maclean's* editorial meetings early in 1954.

Berton scarcely needed prompting to schedule a fall issue devoted to the region, and no discussion was necessary to decide who would craft the lead article. That summer, Allen sent Berton on a lengthy trip across the Arctic, from Baffin Island to the Mackenzie Delta. Pierre was ably assisted in his preparation by information Blair Fraser had gleaned from George Jacobsen, who travelled extensively around the Arctic supervising military construction projects for his firm, Tower Construction Company.[44]

The southern concept of northern apparel was blue jeans and heavy woollen shirts, but Berton knew that for the right occasion northerners liked to dress up. The one journalist wearing a suit and tie and fresh white shirt to an Arctic cocktail party in honour of Jean Lesage, the new minister of northern affairs and the first cabinet minister to visit the region in years, Berton, still on his own tour, became the only member of the press invited to accompany Lesage on his fact-finding trip across the North. The pilot of the single-engine Otter was an ambitious young flyer named Max Ward.[45]

That spring, with details of the trail of '98 still fresh from writing *The Golden Trail*, Pierre decided that if his seventy-five-year-old mother were ever to see the story of her life in the Klondike in print, he would need to assist her without delay. For years Laura had worked and reworked her story, but it remained "It's a Boy," with her son always the central character. Whenever he had a chance, whether in Vancouver on business or when his mother visited the family in Kleinburg, he sat down with her, gradually drawing out those traces of her life she took for granted as mere background. Mother and son talked it through. Then he took her manuscript, stripped it of almost all references to himself, and wrote anew about her life in the North, trying as best he could to capture her voice. His version of her tale may have lacked the intimacy only Laura herself could have provided on her relationship with the man she had married, but what the story lost in emotional power it more than gained in what the *Globe and Mail* reviewer William Arthur Deacon called "these bizarre elements" in Dawson's history. Unusual detail and eccentric characters had become staples of Pierre's own literary repertoire – the famous poet across the street, the set-piece description of the interior of a miner's shack, the gold dust under the floor of the bank.[46]

Publication of *I Married the Klondike* very nearly came posthumously for mother and son. On Wednesday, October 6, 1954, when Berton read the *Toronto Star*, as he did every day, the "Buzz Sawyer" comic strip seemed innocuous enough. Its first panel featured Buzz on the telephone to the skipper of a ship of hurricane hunters in Florida. "Hey, Chic! I need the latest fix on 'Howlin' Hazel'. Where is she?" When the *Star* briefly noted a real hurricane named Hazel on its entertainment page that day, it appeared next to Louella Parsons's Hollywood gossip column. Like other Torontonians, Berton could not have anticipated that the comic strip hurricane would soon engulf Toronto.[47]

In the week that followed, Hazel's ferocity led to the evacuation of a thousand women and children to hurricane shelters in Guantanamo; then it devastated Haiti and raged into the Carolinas. The Toronto press gave it little attention. The *Star* reported on October 9 that the storm had become "very dangerous" and was moving in a northwesterly direction, but its editors chose to place this short item on the social notices page. The *Globe and Mail* ignored its existence until October 12, when it merited a brief page 8 notice.[48]

Serious attention came only with the arrival of the storm itself. Strong winds and heavy rain reached Toronto on Thursday, October 14. On the following day, when the *Star* at last gave front-page coverage to the storm, well subordinate to banner headlines about a strike at the Oakville Ford plant and confined to small boxes with heads that read "Hazel Hurls Huge Waves on U.S. Coast, Moves Inland" and "Fear Hurricane May Hit Toronto Around Midnight," Berton became worried. That day, his entire family was in Toronto on a shopping expedition in search of children's shoes.

Late Friday afternoon, Laura and Janet, along with five-year-old Penny, three-year-old Pamela, two-year-old Patsy, and a family friend named Ethel Post, fled from the harsh downtown wind and rain and packed themselves into Pierre's second-hand Ford for the trip home. With Berton behind the wheel, they crawled along the streets northward, the water at times up to the hubcaps and the brakes threatening to fail. They were heading directly into the area where Hazel was doing its worst damage: the Humber River watershed, a hundred-kilometre-long area that ran from Georgian Bay past Kleinburg and Woodbridge, through Toronto, and into Lake Ontario. The hurricane intensified as they plowed through sheets of rain. When they reached Highway 27, the road north to Kleinburg, they found it awash in floodwater. The highway had become part of the river; fields looked like lakes, and underpasses were filled with submerged vehicles. Cars were stranded or abandoned as far ahead as they could see. Forced to turn around at one flooded underpass, they slowly made their way by another route along the swelling Humber, past the villages of Weston and Thistletown, toward home.

At the crest of the Humber summit above the village of Woodbridge, Pierre could see nothing but "angry water, waves with white caps on them and a Niagara pouring from the bank above, roaring down what had once been a road. In the foreground, like black puppets against the wild waters, danced the tiny figures of men." Three hours on the road and still seven miles from home, they turned back and wound their way along country side roads.[49] By ten o'clock that night almost four inches of rain had fallen on Toronto. Winds of seventy miles an hour had beached yachts at the Royal Canadian Yacht Club. More than twenty feet of water covered the junction of Muskoka Road and Long Branch Avenue. Automobiles had been swept into the Don River with passengers clinging to their vehicles. At one point Laura Berton, tired and exasperated, tried without luck to convince her son that they should stay the night in a motel she noticed.

They reached Kleinburg after dark, only to find the road from the village to their house half a mile away blocked by a collapsed hillside. Determined to reach home, ex-Lieutenant Berton led his drenched platoon through rain and rubble. That night he and his family slept in their own beds. On its knoll, the house was safe and dry, but the forest below had become a swamp. The next day he learned that the motel his mother had seen was beneath eight feet of water.[50]

The Bertons had been lucky, for Hurricane Hazel took the lives of eighty-one people in and around Toronto, including Penny's little friend from dance classes, Dallas Reid, who drowned with his family when their car was pulled into the raging Humber. The torrent also claimed two children of Don Radley, a family friend, when a wall of water capsized their rescue boat in Woodbridge. Like their neighbours, the Bertons went for several days without power, telephone, heat, or water. Pierre took a week of holidays to help clean up debris.[51]

⋈

By the time Pierre returned to *Maclean's*, the special issue devoted entirely to the Canadian north was ready for the newsstands. It appeared in the second week of November. His lead story, "The Mysterious North," took pride of place and a quarter of the magazine's editorial space. *Maclean's* had taken Prime Minister St. Laurent's challenge to Canadians to heart. It was indeed time to focus more attention on the North and its possibilities. The title of Ralph Allen's editorial made the magazine's position clear: "We Haven't Done Right by Our North." In it, he chided his fellow Canadians for their complacency.

> Most of us take the same fierce and unearned pride in the Canadian north that we take in Jacques Cartier's voyage to Tadoussac or Marilyn Bell's swim across Lake Ontario. Every time we think of it our red corpuscles multiply by proxy and our stature soars by associ-ation. Just to be in the same general precincts, historically and geo-graphically, makes titans of us all.
>
> The fact is that, as a nation, we Canadians have put less heart, brain and muscle into the development of the north than we've put into any common undertaking in our lifetime. . . . The chief qualities brought to the north by government – and that means by the Canadian people as a whole – are timidity, parsimony, indifference and sloth.[52]

Allen and *Maclean's* drew special attention to the question of Arctic sov-ereignty, an issue the prime minister had mentioned often over the past year. Perhaps, the editor wrote, St. Laurent had learned a lesson that Canada should have learned fifty years earlier: "the inescapable fact that history detests the absentee landlord and always catches up with him and leaves him dispossessed." Blair Fraser's hard-hitting contribution to the issue, "The Truth About Our Arctic Defence," advanced a simple argument: "We Have None."[53]

Allen's editorial reflected the tone of the issue's lead article. Other contributions drew readers' attention to the harshness, the poor medical conditions, and the few amenities of northern life.[54] But Berton's feature oriented readers to the region as a whole, his canvas as expansive as the North itself, and as varied. This was a land so vast as almost to beggar comprehension, a terrain into which the British Isles could be dropped many times over and with more lakes than the rest of the world put together. "It rolls endlessly on," Berton wrote, "a great jigsaw puzzle with half the pieces missing. Our neglect has almost lost it to us. Now we can't take it for granted any longer. Here's a report on the half of Canada few people really know."[55]

Canada's Everyman had been on the road again. "The Mysterious North" was no ordinary report: it was an invitation for Canadians to come along with Pierre Berton on an educational but arduous twenty-thousand-mile trip across the top of Canada. It began with the indefatigable reporter on the Mackenzie River, aboard a tugboat called *Radium Yellowknife*, hauling sulphur for a leaching plant and whisky for its men; it ended with his landing in a Beaver aircraft at Yellowknife, almost at the North's geographical centre. There, with the man from *Maclean's*, readers could enjoy their "last real view of the north before returning to the land of traffic lights and parking meters."

Berton tipped his hat to the fur trade and the gold rush, but his gaze remained firmly set on the North of 1954, not that of a century earlier. Colourful figures could be glimpsed along the way, but nostalgia was not on the bill of lading. This was a north far less known to most Canadians than that of the legendary coureurs de bois. It was the north of Northern Affairs Minister Jean Lesage, not of the missing Franklin expedition; a north "still waiting for the white man's moccasins"; a land at once of lonely men in parkas leaning into swirling snow and of isolated but busy industrial communities extracting lead and zinc from frozen tundra. "The greatest misconception, of course," wrote Berton the Arctic tour guide, "is that *the north* is all of a piece from the Klondike to Ungava. You might as well lump Scotland and Serbia together because they both belong to Europe."

This extraordinary "frontier on the top of the world" remained mysterious because for the most part Canadians had long taken the land and its people for granted. Fur and minerals remained its staples, as they had for centuries. But such single-resource communities were subject to cycles of boom and bust that led to lives of feast and famine. "Our neglect of the north," Berton wrote, "besides bequeathing us a native problem that will take generations to untangle, has on several occasions all but cost us sovereignty of the Arctic. Indeed, as one historian has pointed out, 'our concern about the north in the past can be correlated with the fear of losing it.'"

The *Maclean's* special issue on the North found the magazine's largest readership since the abdication of Edward VIII in 1936. For Berton, the timing of its appearance along with the attendant publicity could not have been better. *I Married the Klondike* appeared in 1954 under the Little, Brown imprint in Boston and Toronto, and in London under that of Hutchinson and Company a year later. (The first Canadian edition was published under the McClelland & Stewart imprint only in 1961.) The prose was Pierre's and the title was his – or almost his, since he later admitted lifting it "shamelessly" from the American writer Osa Johnson's 1940 memoir, *I Married Adventure.* He had pressed his American agent, Willis Kingsley Wing, to find a prominent American publisher, and with success. Berton himself had made certain the book received good advance notice by arranging three lengthy excerpts in successive issues of *Maclean's.* Less than a week after the special issue renewed readers' interest in the North, William Arthur Deacon's glowing review of *I Married the Klondike* appeared in the *Globe and Mail.* Mrs. Berton, he wrote, had "produced an engrossing record of a unique and now vanished episode in Canada's social history." "What a motley throng mingled in that isolated community!" he exclaimed.[56]

Laura Berton enjoyed the media attention, and Pierre had the good sense to keep his distance while his mother appeared on radio and television and at women's clubs, telling her story and publicizing her book. Toronto readers who went off to Britnell's or Eaton's to purchase *I Married the Klondike* were unaware that they were buying Pierre Berton's second book in all but name, but they knew it was part of his story.

Beginning with his Headless Valley scoop, continuing with many talks on radio and in person, and culminating in his lengthy set piece in the most popular issue of *Maclean's* in many years, Berton was beginning to shape a professional self that powerfully linked author and subject. The combination of "Berton" and "North" was forming a cultural equation of some strength. Many who purchased *I Married the*

Klondike no doubt did so because it was an interesting new book about a woman's life in the North; others bought it because it was about Pierre Berton's mother. And the "Mysterious North" magazine series was the synoptic fair draft of his next book.

❦

He worked on the manuscript for the next several months, writing from six in the morning until it was necessary to drive to Toronto. The process was simple enough: he simply fleshed out the articles he had written for the special northern issue of *Maclean's* – *articles* in the plural because another feature in the issue, called "The Yukon's Coming Alive Again," had been his. Its author, Grattan Gray, was the house pseudonym used to accommodate the one-byline-per-issue rule.[57] Berton reworked and blended these articles, adding material gathered earlier on the Nahanni, the Alaska Highway, and the Klondike as he went along. Then he sent the manuscript to Knopf in New York, trusting that the publisher would like his second book as much as it did his first one.

The letter of response he received from Harold Strauss, his editor, was polite but merciless. The subject held little interest for the reader, Strauss wrote. Its style was awkward; it lacked "positive attractiveness." The Knopf editor continued: "Surely a writer of your gifts can make his style much more inviting than it is in this manuscript." The manuscript was full of all sorts of errors, from misspelled names to grammatical lapses, and required a "stylistic polishing which only you can provide." In short, its shortfalls were beyond rescue by an editor.

Berton had submitted what amounted to hack work to one of the most prestigious literary presses in North America, and he got precisely what he deserved by way of reply. The care he had taken with the style of *The Royal Family* was absent from *The Mysterious North*. Even the area that was usually Berton's strength – his research – was deficient: "Some of the book," Strauss admonished, "sounds like small town journalism operating under the old rule of including as many names as possible." What Berton had thought was a unique section of the book – the chapter on Headless Valley – fell short. "While the story undoubtedly made wonderful newspaper and magazine copy," Strauss wrote acerbically, "the more or less sensational aspects of the Headless Valley story seem overplayed for the purposes of a book." Finally, he asked, how could Berton claim to be writing about the Canadian north when he had almost nothing to say about northern Quebec, Labrador, or the eastern Arctic?[58]

Deflated but unbowed, Berton initiated a practice that was to become an important feature of his writing life: he turned to a trusted woman to help him out.[59] In this case the woman was Barbara Moon, one of the most accomplished writers at *Maclean's*. She had joined the magazine fresh out of university in the late fall of 1948, starting in the steno pool. After a stint as front desk receptionist, an experience she found humiliating, Moon returned to the steno pool but soon rose to become secretary to Berton and John Clare. They quickly recognized that she was not only an excellent researcher but also full of story ideas. In 1951 Allen made her the magazine's western editor, but after an unhappy couple of years in Vancouver and Edmonton she returned to Toronto. By the mid-1950s she was contributing pieces regularly from Vancouver, Edmonton, Calgary, Washington, and Wawa, Ontario.

A month before Berton's "Mysterious North" feature, the latest of Moon's articles had appeared in *Maclean's*. She no longer worked for the magazine, having recently been appointed assistant editor of *Mayfair*, but Ralph Allen had commissioned her to write a piece on Montreal's posh Ritz-Carlton hotel. So she booked herself in – only to be sent to a less tony hotel, the Mount Royal, by a staff suspicious of a single young woman arriving on her own. "Even after she did win a room at the Ritz," Allen wrote of her experience, "it was three days before the management found out what the brunette in 603 was up to. From then [on] she had to move like lightning to light her own cigarettes."[60]

By the mid-1950s Moon possessed a sterling reputation as a magazine writer. When she returned to *Maclean's* in 1956 (she would stay until 1964), Berton was delighted to have her back, although much to her annoyance he tended to treat her as his assistant of old.[61] Knowing how bright she was, however, he asked her to read his rejected book manuscript and to give him a detailed, line-by-line critique of it. She did just that, producing what he recognized, then and later, as a "first-rate report on the book's many failings."[62]

One of Berton's characteristics as a writer, whether of articles or books, was that he did not often let his ego control his judgment. His

ambition to become an "author" rather than remain a "writer" may
have involved a false and pretentious distinction, but he approached
the actual work of writing as craft, not art. For more than a decade he
had earned his keep as a professional writer, yet he had just learned a
valuable lesson. The first draft of a book was less writing than typing,
at least for him; the writing came with revisions, and for this he often
needed guidance.

Pierre had been an obedient child, almost always heeding his
parents, and as an adult he did not often ignore the counsel of men and
women whose opinions he respected. He took Strauss's criticism to
heart and spent his vacation time in 1955 travelling through the eastern
Arctic, from the southern tip of Baffin Island to the iron mines of the
Ungava Peninsula. Supported financially by *Maclean's*, the trip provided
him with the balanced geographical coverage of the North he had
lacked, at the same time producing two articles almost as a by-
product.[63] Then, having absorbed Moon's detailed critique of the original manuscript, he completely rewrote it. Near the end of June 1955, he
received another letter from Harold Strauss. "I've read through THE
MYSTERIOUS NORTH again. . . . I think you've done a fine job. The style
is now up to your excellent standards, and the book is all of a piece."[64]

Berton's name was scarcely a household word in Canada in the mid-
1950s; still, as managing editor of *Maclean's* he was not unknown or
without influence. So he had used it to secure the attention and assistance of a number of experts on the North whose doors would have been
closed to authors less well connected. Frank B. Walker of the Hudson's
Bay Company, who had helped arrange his 1954 northern trip, sent him
material on the Coppermine settlement. Gordon Robertson, deputy
minister of northern affairs and national resources, offered the services
of several officers of his department, including Graham Rowley, coordinator of government activities in the North, and Svenn Orvig of the
Arctic Institute of America in Montreal. Cyrus S. Eaton, chairman of
the board of the Chesapeake and Ohio Railway Company, responded
enthusiastically and in detail to Berton's request for material on iron ore
deposits in Ungava.[65]

The Mysterious North, dedicated to his wife with the plain words
"For Janet," appeared on bookstore shelves in February 1956. Its four
parts – on the legend of Headless Valley, the Alaska Highway's road to

resources, the barren landscape of the eastern Arctic, and the "feast and famine" nature of northern life – reflected Berton's own journey of discovery since 1947. Written in a distinctly more matter-of-fact style than *The Royal Family*, it nevertheless possessed one priceless virtue: the way it blended the account of the North with the experience of the author into one seamless story. Berton on the royals had read like the notes of a gifted armchair anthropologist who had stumbled upon a tribe at once exotic yet strangely familiar; Berton on the North was the voice of the North itself, a voice of undeniable authenticity. "I suppose this book was really begun a quarter of a century ago," its first sentence read, "when I was a boy living in the Yukon and the north was the only land I knew."[66]

The *Toronto Star* and the *Globe and Mail* reviewed *The Mysterious North* soon after its publication, focusing on Berton's lifelong connection with the region: his birth in the Yukon, his adventure in Headless Valley, his drive down the Alaska Highway. "Thus, knowing the mysterious north from childhood," stated the *Star*'s piece on the book (more author profile than book review), Berton had produced "not only a factual but an interpretive book, doing for the Canadian North what Bruce Hutchison has already achieved for 'The Unknown Country' as a whole." Here, said the *Star*, was an author as "responsive to the land's magic" as he was "adept at conveying it to the reader."[67]

William Arthur Deacon's review in the *Globe and Mail*, placed strategically beneath a photograph of "Old Permafrost himself – Mr. Pierre Berton," clad in a hooded parka and waving goodbye as he left for the North – also emphasized Berton's Klondike origins. This gave him a distinct advantage over other writers on the Canadian north, for it handed reviewers a ready-made interpretive "hook" for their pieces: the subject was in this author's very lifeblood. "In the sense that Spinoza was 'God-intoxicated,'" Deacon wrote, "Mr. Berton is intoxicated with that 40 percent of Canada that is covered by the Precambrian Shield." The author, he added, seemed to be "an impulsive fellow, who delights to hurl his readers without warning to some distant spot in the million and a half square miles covered by the narrative."[68]

Deacon was not entirely uncritical. He found *The Mysterious North* "disorderly" and without a sense of direction or much "logical progression from point to point." The book, he said, read like "a chatty, folksy encyclopedia." The *Globe* reviewer had a point: despite Berton's attempts to address what Harold Strauss had labelled "small town journalism," *The Mysterious North* was crammed with so many names and so much information that at times it threatened to tax a reader's capacity to absorb it all. Not every reader, however. A Dartmouth College geography professor named Trevor Lloyd, reviewing the book for the *New York Times Book Review*, praised Berton for not letting his Toronto location interfere with his love of the North, concluding: "His book is an astonishingly comprehensive and thoroughly reliable account of northern Canada today, and it is very entertainingly written."[69]

Pierre Berton was beginning to acquire the kind of authority his work as a journalist had not afforded, for all that it had given him something of a national presence. He had, as yet, no formula for success, and knew not at all that in fact he was in the process of stumbling upon one. But in his "God-intoxication" with the history, geography, and mythic power of the North, he had tapped into one of his country's most deeply felt myths of identity – that of the "true north strong and free."[70] As he did so, his own work became increasingly linked to Canadians' collective anxieties and desires and their need to hear stories about themselves as a means of self-understanding and expression.[71] This was the first step toward the creation of what would make Berton not only a bestselling author but also a cultural brand and, following upon it, an iconic figure in Canadian life.

ARRIVAL

—

BERTON LEFT THE KLONDIKE when he was eleven years old, but at the age of thirty-seven, despite his salaried duties at *Maclean's*, his child-like marvel at life's unexpected turnings still energized him. Ambitious but unknown young men like his father had gone north to seek their fortunes; the son would find wealth and glory in the Canadian south.

Pierre's weekdays were full, eight hours or more, not counting the long commute to and from Kleinburg. But as managing editor he spent most of his office time handling the work of others. Berton's own pres-ence in the magazine as the author of feature articles had all but dis-appeared. In 1956, his byline was on display only once, and it was above a slight piece on a Christmas theme.[1] It did not appear at all in 1957. Only one Berton article was published in May 1958, but it was a sub-stantial one: "A Native's Return to B.C." Warning of the perils of pros-perity and of the conflict between industry and environment, it also served as Berton's affectionate farewell to the province of his youth.[2] When his name reappeared beneath the title of a *Maclean's* piece later in the year, it was as the author of excerpts from a new book.

The critical acclaim garnered by *The Mysterious North* was more than enough to draw Berton's attention away from magazine work and toward the book trade. Even before its publication, he knew he would write another book on a northern theme. But this would be a different project, one not written against the grain of his instinct to tell stories. In his attempt to write a "serious" book, he had produced a work that read in parts like an academic monograph shorn of footnotes, and crammed with as much research as he could pack into it.

On the other hand, *The Golden Trail*, his brief account of the Klondike gold rush written for juveniles and published in Canada by

Macmillan in 1954, had been an adventure story worthy of *Boy's Own* or *Chum.* The steady stream of royalties it generated, along with those from *Stampede for Gold* (the Macmillan book expanded by two chapters for Knopf and the American market), prompted him to consider the possibility of a gold rush book for the adult market. The *New York Times Book Review* had called *Stampede for Gold* "a bonanza for adventure lovers."[3]

The sales of the juvenile books, not the critical success of *The Mysterious North*, convinced Berton that if he told the story of the Klondike as an adventure story for adults, using novelistic techniques, the book might find a large readership. His mother doubted that others would be interested in the subject, but he persisted, and in the spring of 1956 he sent Willis Kingsley Wing a detailed proposal. The New York agent sent it to Knopf. "Merely looking over your memorandum regarding the Klondike madness dizzies me," Alfred A. Knopf himself wrote. "How in God's name have you been able to do all this research, hold down your job and write books as well? You are a miracle man." Knopf added a handwritten exclamation point to his typewritten final sentence.[4]

The book that became *Klondike* was scarcely a new project in 1956. Off and on, Berton had been doing research on the gold rush for years, and by the time he wrote *The Mysterious North* he already had thick files of material, including many letters he had solicited in print and over the airwaves from anyone who had been in the Far North in 1898 or with relatives who had been there. Scores of men and women responded, including a man from Emporia, Kansas, who was on the Chilkoot Trail at Sheep Camp on Easter Sunday morning, 1898, when avalanches took the lives of some sixty prospectors. Sourdoughs of '98, old friends from his Dawson days, employees of the Vancouver Yukoners' Association, and strangers who had heard one of his Klondike radio talks sent him letters with their stories.[5] To all this he added information gleaned on the trip north for *The Mysterious North*. At night he worked assiduously through the books in the lengthy bibliography Janet had compiled at the University of Toronto Library and the Toronto Public Library.[6] On days when Janet went into Toronto with Pierre, the children were cared for by Mrs. Dukes, a Kleinburg woman about the same age as Janet whose blue-rinsed hair seemed to fade to white as the day progressed.[7]

In May 1956, Harold Strauss responded formally to Berton's outline and sample chapters. "You are a very good writer whom we want to publish for a long time to come," he wrote. He found one of the chapters "really exciting," but the other, on Soapy Smith – the ruffian dubbed "the dictator of Skagway" until he was unceremoniously murdered – did not quite convince the editor that Smith was a real person. Strauss was also worried about the pace of the book. "In both chapters, your narrative moves with express train speed. But over a long book, I wonder whether your writing won't seem a little breathless."[8]

Strauss's main concern, however, was Berton's prolixity, which threatened to produce a book of over two hundred thousand words. Wing had warned Berton that excessive length would drive up the list price.[9] Strauss, however, told the author that the problem lay in Berton's intention to write a "definitive" work. "We think it is a singularly inappropriate word for a book of this kind. Definitive books are usually dull. . . . There is no doubt that you have dug up a vast amount of new material. But you yourself point out that [the] Klondike is not the most important historical subject in the world. Let's not kid ourselves. People will read your book – and I hope many of them will – primarily for entertainment, rather than for enlightenment. I do not deny that there will be a good deal of enlightenment in the book, but if you ask yourself how many people feel that they simply must have a new book on the Klondike, you will see my point." A book of two hundred thousand words, Strauss added, would be "quite an impossible project for us," for it would necessitate a list price over $10 – more than double the cost of most clothbound books at the time – and consequently a very small print run. "You're a professional writer, and I should not have to go into too many details with you. You simply have fallen in love with your research, and let the job get out of hand."

These were chastening words, but not discouraging ones. If anything, Strauss's admonition reinforced Berton's determination to approach the new manuscript differently than he had *The Mysterious North*, by letting story rather than research take command. Clearly, he had not yet succeeded in doing so.

In the summer of 1956, Pierre and Janet Berton went on a busman's holiday to the West Coast. The gold rush had taken place almost sixty years earlier, and if he was to interview its survivors he had to do so without delay. So he flew ahead by plane, Janet and the children followed by rail, and the family reunited in Vancouver. The couple looked for Klondike material in West Coast libraries – Janet with the children in tow. Pierre, as ever, was indefatigable, but Janet was the force that steeled his resolve. "As a former journalist, and a good one," Pierre later admitted, "she was an expert on the care and feeding of authors." Janet understood the kind of research her husband needed, and it was Janet who did much of the library and archival grunt work, hunting down "personal accounts, background information, and social histories of the era."[10]

Janet in fact was the one responsible for their most important find that summer. The Bertons had spent an exhausting day in Seattle, on the trail of the Klondike legend Belinda Mulroney, the woman who arrived in the goldfields a washerwoman's daughter and left as the proprietor of Dawson's best hotel. Pierre had learned from Lulu Fairbanks of the Sourdough Association that Mulroney lived near Seattle, but on that evening he wanted nothing more than a good steak. Janet suggested he look up Mulroney in the phone book under her married name, Carbonneau. No luck. Pierre concluded that she must be dead, but Janet insisted they consult the Seattle city directory. One entry for "Carbonneau" existed, but the address was outside the city. Pierre's priority was dictated by his stomach, but Janet managed to contact a neighbour and discovered that Carbonneau had indeed lived in the Yukon. Pierre had little choice but to take a taxi to meet her. She was indeed Belinda Mulroney, and a lengthy and informative interview ensued with a feisty old gal whose memory remained as sharp as a knife blade.[11] Janet stayed behind in their hotel room.

In the spring of 1957, Berton received word that *The Mysterious North* had won the 1956 Governor General's Literary Award for Non-Fiction. A year earlier, the University of Toronto historian Donald G. Creighton had won the prize for *John A. Macdonald: The Old Chieftain*, the second and concluding volume of his magisterial biography of Canada's founding prime minister. Berton now stood with Creighton, Bruce Hutchison,

Hugh MacLennan, and other writers who had won the nation's highest literary honour for their distinguished works of non-fiction.[12]

He was quick to recognize that *The Mysterious North* had given him an asset far greater than whatever income the book's modest sales generated: what he called an "identifying tag" for public appearances, something he recognized as essential for media success. Journalists and producers could now call him an expert on the North, whatever his knowledge of it, and a bestselling author regardless of his sales figures. He liked the resonance of the term *bestselling*, he said. "It suggested I had my feet firmly planted on the financial ground." The aura of success, he knew, not proof of it, was all that counted. He had acquired cachet, and he intended to exploit it.[13]

Throughout 1956 and 1957 Berton kept up a steady stream of television and radio appearances. He wrote skits and songs for *Spring Thaw*, the highly successful comedy revue Mavor Moore had produced annually since 1948. He fed articles to magazines other than *Maclean's*, wrote radio plays for the CBC, and contributed a major entry on the Canadian north to the *Britannica Book of the Year*. At the request of the filmmaker Frank Radford (Budge) Crawley, he wrote a script for a promotional documentary called *The Future Lies North*, featuring C.D. Howe, Prime Minister St. Laurent's powerful minister of trade and commerce, and aimed at promoting American investment in Canada.[14] Berton's involvement in this project was ironic. The report of the Royal Commission on Canada's Economic Prospects, by the accountant and public servant Walter Gordon (he later became Lester B. Pearson's finance minister), was at that moment in the final stages of preparation, and when released in November 1957 it would express concern about American control of Canadian businesses and resources. Berton himself, influenced by the "Canada first" orientation of *Maclean's* under Irwin and Allen, was coming to similar conclusions. His days of yearning to write for the *Saturday Evening Post* had ended.

The National Film Board sought Berton out on more than one occasion, and invariably he answered the call. He wrote and narrated a three-part series directed by Douglas Tunstell called *Women on the March*, on the advancement of women in the twentieth century. The first and second reels, concerning turn-of-the-century suffragettes and women's struggle for equality through the vote and in factory work, went into production. The third, on changing standards of morality, was never produced because Ellen Fairclough, appointed minister of citizenship and immigration after John Diefenbaker's landslide victory of March 31, 1958, did not want moral issues included in the film. Perhaps she had read Berton's script, for not many years would pass before he was to run afoul of traditionalists for his outspoken views on morality. In response to Fairclough's intervention, Berton refused to have his name listed in the film credits of the first two parts of *Women on the March*.[15]

Far more enjoyable was his contribution to the NFB documentary *City of Gold*, the story of Dawson City and the stampede to its gold fields. Remarkably, the film became possible when Dawson yielded gold of another sort. In 1949, while trawling through an old sod-roof house pegged for demolition, a Dawson jeweller named George Murdoch uncovered several hundred glass-plate negatives depicting Dawson in 1898. Recognizing their quality and historical significance, he arranged to deposit them in the Public Archives of Canada in Ottawa. Six years later, the NFB filmmaker Colin Low discovered them. Most were by the American photographer Eric Hegg, and they were extraordinary.

Low persuaded his superiors that these still photographs could form the heart of a documentary, and that a film crew should travel to Dawson City – dauntingly expensive at the time – to shoot live-action footage to accompany the photos. When they reached Dawson, they found a decrepit town of four or five hundred souls, its buildings far advanced in decay. After the crew's return to Montreal, the editing process began, using techniques drawn from the film board's experience in animation to manipulate the camera in such a way that the still photograph provided a dramatic moving image. History had been brought miraculously to life. Many years later, the American filmmaker Ken Burns, the presiding genius behind such acknowledged documentary masterpieces as *The Civil War* (1990), *Baseball* (1994), and *Jazz* (2001), acknowledged that *City of Gold* had been "a seminal influence" on his work.[16]

Berton was asked to write and provide the voice of the film's narration only after *City of Gold* had been filmed and was well into production. The principal figures behind the project, apart from the cinematography specialist Colin Low, were its producer, Tom Daly, its director,

Wolf Koenig, and its co-writer, Roman Kroitor. Still, as a prizewinning writer who spoke with the voice of authority on his hometown's story, Berton had a not insignificant role.

His involvement gave *City of Gold* an authenticity it might otherwise not have possessed, and his firm voice reinforced the power of its images. Pierre travelled to Montreal to develop the script with the veteran NFB writer Stanley Jackson and – in the midst of consolidating his research for *Klondike* – went to Dawson to film the narration on location. "This was my hometown, and my father's town before me," his first words intoned, while in the soundtrack a cello and clarinet brought to life the wistful score of the Canadian composer Eldon Rathburn. This first scene set the mood for the remaining twenty-three minutes of the film.

Berton's remuneration was $300, but his reward was greater than this. During his conversations with the NFB people in Montreal follow-ing the Dawson filming, he discovered, as he put it, that "we all [shared] an attitude towards the Klondike experience of life, man's search for himself as much as for gold."[17] He now had the heart of the argument for his book, a thesis borne out not only by the history of the gold rush but also by the story of his father's involvement in it.

City of Gold was nominated for an American Academy Award and a British Academy of Film and Television Arts Award, named Film of the Year at the Tenth Canadian Film Awards, and awarded a Golden Mikeldi award at the Bilbao International Festival of Documentary and Short Films.[18] It became the most successful short documentary film in the history of the National Film Board, winning more awards and viewed by more people to that date than any other moving picture in its category. Berton had not been responsible for the genesis of *City of Gold*, but he was its face and its voice.

As successful as he was coming to be, Pierre needed all the outside income he could earn. With the birth of Peter in August 1955, the Berton clan had expanded from three children to four, and the house seemed to require an additional room with every new arrival. In the late fifties it continued to change shape and size, never quite looking finished – rather like the family that inhabited it with such gusto. The orange crates had disappeared, but the house still lacked baseboards, and Berton came to regard the exposed joists as architectural "texture."

He called the structure his dream house and made it the subject of a CBC radio talk called "Our House." Sometimes, he admitted, "I think of my house as a nightmare house, but only sometimes." Visiting friends, he added, were inclined to say that it would be a "lawvley place" when it was finished. Still, over the past half-dozen years, the place had come together, in a "faltering and erratic sort of way." Every improvement had cost far more than the Bertons had anticipated, but the house and its surroundings held the potential under the right circumstances to appear in an issue of *Better Homes and Gardens*. Berton had landscaped the property, creating an apple orchard by dint of will. Hills rose where flat grassland had dominated. From the knoll on which the house sat, one could look down the slope, beyond the orchard, and see the cedar forest that ran along the banks of the Humber River.

The Berton homestead had grown to six rooms, plus a utilities room and bathroom, and had neither basement nor attic. In the West Coast style, its roof was flat and hung out over the house by four feet. The living room was twenty feet long, with a sixteen-foot-wide window that reached from floor to ceiling. Picture windows were one of the striking features of the house, which was built on two levels separated by a drop of a few feet. Heating was by hot-water pipes in a concrete floor. The structure was anchored by a central stone wall that continued to the exterior, where it formed a windbreak. Inside, the wall turned a right angle to form a twelve-foot-wide fireplace, open on two sides and incorporating a built-in wooden bookcase. The firebox was set about two feet off the floor, easily accessible for laying a fire and highly efficient in throwing heat. Logs burned directly on the bare stone.

No doors were installed in the main living area, because none were needed; in the early years even the bathroom stood open, and the washing machine was a distinguishing if unusual feature of the sparsely furnished living room. Perhaps discomfited by the absence of a bathroom door when visiting his daughter and son-in-law, Janet's father bought a door for them. The $8 purchase served its purpose for the rest of the Bertons' married life. The kitchen opened into the dining room, one corner of the L-shaped living room. The burlap-covered walls were adorned with custom-built storage units. The result was a look that may have seemed expensive but was half the cost of plaster. The spacious front hall gave visitors the impression that the house was larger than it was. As Berton told his radio listeners, "We've got a nice new house and an empty pocketbook."[19]

By 1957, the place was a busy den of perky pipsqueaks, each bearing a first name beginning with the letter *P*. The family tradition had begun simply enough. The first-born of the Bertons of Windrush came to be called Penny because Pierre and Janet liked the name and it was fashionable; besides, Pierre insisted that no child deserved the name Penelope. "Pamela" was Janet's choice because she once had a doll of that name with brown eyes like those of her second daughter. By the time the couple's third child came along in 1952, four-year-old Penny and two-year-old Pamela could participate in choosing a name for their baby sister. The alliteration became a game. Thus Patsy. And three years later, when the Bertons had their first boy, "Peter" seemed obvious. It was all but inevitable that their second son, born in 1958, would be called Paul.

The parade of *P*s was not a homage to Pierre Berton's vanity, as some thought then and later. It was, instead, a joyful family rite, the inadvertent product of an anarchic domestic democracy assisted at times by the well-intended conspiracy of friends. Barbara Gilmour, Clyde's wife, wrote the Bertons a letter containing all the *P* names she could find in the naming books. "Everybody was helping us along," Janet Berton said. "We had enough *P*s in the pod."[20]

Much of the drive at this stage of Berton's life came from genuine insecurity about how he would support and maintain this burgeoning family and house. He had received an increase in salary at *Maclean's* in 1956, but it was not enough for the addition the house desperately needed, so he took every job that would bring in extra money and commissioned the builders anyway. Meanwhile, he carefully tracked royalties from *The Mysterious North*. He was disappointed in its sales, but this reflected his lack of knowledge of the book trade at the time. Knopf's first print run had been 7,500 copies – a more than respectable size for an American publisher of a little-known Canadian author; 2,500 were sent to Canada. Sales were adequate enough that the book went into a second printing of 2,500 copies, 1,000 intended for Canada. Still, between November 1956 and April 1957, returns (152 copies) exceeded sales (137), and in May and June only 24 copies were sold. Like most book authors, Berton initially found his royalty statements mystifying. He complained to Harold Strauss that he appeared to be receiving royalties of only 2 cents a copy for Canadian sales. Strauss acknowledged a problem but cited export discounts and suggested that his author may have misread a decimal point: "You must have gotten at least twenty cents a book if not more."[21] Such is the precision of accounting in the book trade.

Berton managed to complete a first rough draft of *Klondike* on thirteen consecutive weekends amid the din of construction and the domestic distraction of a home with four children under the age of ten. He chose not to hammer out the manuscript by typewriter but to dictate it, and immediately regretted the decision because corrections and rewriting consumed as much time as typing a draft would have taken.

Fortunately, he had organized his research material well, using an idiosyncratic cross-indexing method he had developed on the fly when working at *Maclean's* and fine-tuned for *The Royal Family*. His practice was to number each paragraph of his typed notes or photocopied material; when a critical mass of research notes developed, he would file them in a workable sequence in thick loose-leaf binders. Each binder covered a specific subject, and he gave each numbered paragraph a subheading. Any given binder could contain hundreds of sections, separated by tabs. By mid-December 1957, the manuscript was revised and sent to Harold Strauss at Knopf.[22]

Berton's activities ranged so broadly and his pace was so frenetic during 1956 and 1957 that late in life even he marvelled at his hustle.[23] The pace quickened as 1957 waned. Already active writing film scripts, editing a national magazine, giving radio talks, and writing books, he now ratcheted up his involvement in television.

❦

The presence of Ross McLean at the CBC, which he had joined in 1948 fresh from the University of Toronto, had brought Berton fresh opportunities to work in the medium. A native of Brantford, Ontario, captured early by the pizzazz of show business, McLean had edited the town's high school newspaper back when June Callwood was a student reporter. Following the war, the bespectacled and youthful McLean had worked as a producer for several years in radio, brimful of ideas for lively programs and capable of turning cocky or reserved in a moment. By 1957 he had become an important presence around the Jarvis Street studios of the CBC, and he was responsible for two hit programs, *Tabloid* and *Close-Up*.

McLean's role within the CBC went well beyond his work as a producer of television programs. As Peter Gzowski later observed, he served as "a bridge between two widely separate facets of the CBC's corporate personality: on one side the flamboyant, brassy dispenser of entertainment, a sort of civil-service song-and-dance man; on the other the tweedy, pipe-smoking Brahmin of information." In short, McLean brought "the flair of show-biz to the often-dull realm of televised talks and public affairs."[24]

Fighting Words, the program in which the erudite host Nathan Cohen asked an assortment of panellists to identify and discuss quotations and their authors, reflected the "Brahmin of information" side of CBC television programming. Cohen was colourful and controversial, but the Maritime-born theatre critic was merciless in his condemnation of the second-rate, leaving some viewers feeling undereducated and nationalists feeling slighted, if not betrayed. The program, in the words of the historian Paul Rutherford, was "a game of wit and words for highbrows."[25] Ross McLean was a self-confessed "lowbrow."

Tabloid and *Close-Up* reflected this orientation, and McLean did his best to meld the elevated standards of the British Broadcasting Corporation with the glitz and glamour of Hollywood. The anglophiles responsible for the CBC regarded the BBC as public broadcasting at its finest, and with good reason when compared with the idiosyncratic individualism of American radio and television. McLean's introduction of distinctive American-style "personalities" to the airwaves, along with the format of an interview program, had the effect of turning the on-air casts of these public affairs and interview shows into celebrities. Between March 1953 and September 1960, *Tabloid*, popular and eclectic and broadcast daily during the workweek, made its host, Dick MacDougal, its weatherman, Percy Saltzman, the interviewer Elaine Grand, and their guest interviewers some of the best-known faces on Canadian television.

From the outset of his career as a CBC producer, McLean saw in Pierre Berton the mixture of informed intelligence and natural showman he liked. "He was 32, and suffered no shortage of convictions," McLean recalled. "I found his self-certainty intimidating." He sensed the kind of "journalistic thrust" he wanted, so he assigned Berton the interviews he knew would be tough. Soon Berton was a regular contributor to *Court of Opinion*, *Tabloid*, and *Tabloid*'s spinoff, *Close-Up* – which McLean described as "'Tabloid' with a fattened budget and a furrowed brow."[26] The CBC poured considerable resources, human and financial, into the program.[27] As a result, McLean was able to deploy its interview team around the world.

Hosted by the veteran radio broadcaster J. Frank Willis, whose trademark was his walrus moustache, the program's probing interviews presented a who's who of the era, including Bertrand Russell, Anthony Eden, and Evelyn Waugh. But at times McLean's choices as interviewers also resembled a who's who of Pierre Berton's colleagues at *Maclean's*, including Blair Fraser, Barbara Moon, Dorothy Sangster, and others. Grumbling could occasionally be heard that public affairs programming at the CBC was too incestuous, with the same handful of Toronto journalists constantly on air. So close was the *Maclean's* connection that in 1958 the CBC's assistant controller of programming, Alphonse Ouimet, sent a memorandum to the director of TV programming in Toronto complaining about "the excessive use of *Maclean's* men" on *Close-Up*. The point was certainly valid, but as Rutherford has noted: "The trouble was that such men as Blair Fraser and Pierre Berton proved very impressive on television, unlike all too many of their fellow scribblers who weren't able to shine in the new medium."[28]

Close-Up debuted at ten o'clock on a Sunday night in the first week of October 1957. North America's first weekly television magazine program was born, and Pierre Berton was part of Ross McLean's stable, helping the producer find and interview guests such as the nuclear scientist Leo Szilard and the author of *Lolita*, Vladimir Nabokov.[29]

While Berton struggled to complete his Klondike book and to meet his commitments to *Maclean's*, Ross McLean dispatched him to distant places for *Close-Up* assignments. One time he found himself on a British Columbia highway near Salmon Arm, filming the colourful minister of highways, Phil Gagliardi, whose driver's licence had been suspended for speeding. Berton ended the interview by presenting him with a bicycle. On another occasion, after Pierre discovered that Robert

W. Service was still alive and living in Monte Carlo, he flew to France with the associate producer, Patrick Watson, and a camera crew to interview the venerated poet. Watson never forgot the hair-raising ride along the Mediterranean coast from Nice with Berton at the wheel of a rental car, "driving the oncoming motorists into horn-jamming rages as we careered along that dizzying road." The interview with the Bard of the Yukon took place over several days in the spring of 1958, with Berton at times reminding the man who had once dated his mother of the details of his own life and the lines of his best-known verses. Service died on September 11, 1958, not long after the interview aired.[30]

Television work gave shape to Pierre Berton's public image, and he took everything on offer. He had come to understand, as Patrick Watson put it, that television "was not primarily a vehicle for informing people . . . but was something closer to theatre." In the new medium, personal aura was king. To stand apart, right from the outset of his television career, he made a bow tie the signature of his public persona. Hal Straight had inspired the idea. On a trip to Vancouver in the early fifties, Pierre had teased Straight for wearing one, perhaps thinking that it was an outmoded affectation. In heavy downtown traffic, Straight abruptly double-parked his car in front of a haberdashery store, pulled a bow tie off the rack, charged it to his account, and on the way to Stanley Park showed Berton how to tie it. For Straight, a bow tie was a mark of distinction.[31]

Personality was as crucial as wardrobe in the development of a public presence during the early years of television and in a decade absorbed by psychology and psychiatry. Berton had long since shed any lingering youthful diffidence. His voice was confident and loud, its tone at times caustic. Ross McLean sought him out for precisely these traits. "We were well aware Pierre would not be the most charming and lovable interviewer on television," he observed. "We needed his digging and abrasive qualities." McLean had the CBS interviewer Mike Wallace in mind as a model. One of Berton's most memorable early interviews for *Close-Up*, in fact, was with Wallace, well known for his confrontational interviewing style. But their encounter was a disaster. "Pierre was gauche and easily out-manoeuvred," Ross McLean told June Callwood in 1959.[32] It took some time for Berton to become comfortable on *Close-Up*. At first he appeared ill at ease – "anxious and awkward," in Callwood's estimation.

Still, his all-embracing enthusiasm and his social concern were evident in his interviews – the former with Robert Service, for example, and the latter with "Mom" Whyte, a controversial foster parent in Bowmanville, Ontario. Whyte and her staff of four had been responsible for the care of sixty-seven children at her farm, Whytehaven, when one of them choked on his formula and died. On *Close-Up*, Whyte appeared frail and humble and God-fearing, but Berton was his usual aggressive self. He questioned her about a damning fire marshal's report to which she had not responded, and exposed the contradiction of her claim to have no money for improvements, while spending $50,000 to expand the facilities for her burgeoning "orphanage empire."[33] Berton's onscreen presence captured viewers' attention, and few remained indifferent to it. Some saw him as the abrasive villain of the show; by the end of the decade, he drew more hate mail than anyone else.

In the summer of 1957, when Berton was dictating and then editing the text of his gold rush book for Knopf, the CBC aired a new television panel show, the brainchild of the writer John Aylesworth, as a summer replacement for *The Denny Vaughan Show*, a variety series. (At the end of August, Vaughan's show was cancelled and he complained that the CBC was "selling out Canadian talent to the Americans" by drastically cutting variety entertainment.) Panel and quiz shows were ubiquitous on television at the time. They were informative, entertaining, and – most important – inexpensive to produce. With its title adapted from the American game show *The $64,000 Challenge*, and its basic idea borrowed from the BBC program *What Happened Last Week*, the show first aired on Monday evening, June 24, 1957. Guided by a moderator, three regular panellists and a guest questioned and identified a person hidden behind them to discover the news story from past or present to which he or she had a connection.[34]

That evening, led by the moderator Win Barron, the panel of *Front Page Challenge* consisted of the veteran newspaper columnist Gordon Sinclair, the twenty-one-year-old actress Toby Robins, and the American-born entertainment writer Alex Barris. The former *Maclean's* journalist Scott Young rounded out the group of interrogators. Together, they managed to identify a man who had survived a mine disaster at Moose River (Alfred Scadding), a woman who had been present at the birth of the Dionne quintuplets (Madame Legros), and the mayor of Montreal (Jean Drapeau), whose story was the investigation of criminal vice on his city's streets.[35]

Berton did not see the program because he did not own a television, but he knew about it. Stories had circulated in Toronto media circles during the early summer about the auditions that its producer, Harvey Hart, was holding in the basement rec room of his Willowdale home. "Everybody, it seemed, was being tested except me," Berton wrote. He need not have worried at the lost opportunity. A month into the summer run of *Front Page Challenge*, the CBC confirmed that the program would continue into the fall. Hart decided that two changes of personnel were necessary. Win Barron, the show's "managing editor" (as the moderator was initially called), had proven to be hesitant and uncertain on air, and Alex Barris tended to be too flippant to pursue the hidden stories.[36] On July 25, CBC management announced that the managing editor of *Maclean's*, Pierre Berton, would be a *Front Page Challenge* guest panellist on August 5. (The contract called for Berton to receive a fee of $100.)[37] When the day of the show came, Berton drove down from Ogopogo Lodge in the Haliburton Highlands to make his appearance. He never did audition for the role.

The first weeks were by no means easy. On the day after Berton's guest appearance, Gordon Sinclair noted in his *Toronto Star* radio and television column that while its ratings from the Toronto-based polling firm Elliott Haynes placed *Front Page Challenge* first among Canadian-made programs, ahead of *Holiday Ranch* and *Country Hoedown*, fourteen American shows scored above it. By the end of the month, its producers had stirred up a good deal of consternation and resentment within the Toronto entertainment community by announcing that Barron would be leaving and by restricting the search for his replacement to a handful of well-known entertainment figures – thought to be Berton, the veteran broadcaster Austin Willis (brother of J. Frank), the actors Paul Kligman and Barry Morse, and the musician and television host Fred Davis. To make matters worse, the CBC brass inexplicably replaced Harvey Hart, a decision that upset both the producer and the panel.[38]

Near the end of September 1957, word leaked out that Davis had won the competition for moderator and that Barris had "lost his seat on the panel." A month later, in his *Star* column, Gordon Sinclair revealed two secrets about the program. "Pierre Berton will be a semi-regular three out of four on 'Front Page Challenge,'" he wrote, "and apparently granddad that I am, I was the last of the whole crew to notice why Toby Robins no longer does a walk on."[39] Just as no married couple in a television situation comedy could be seen in the same bed without one foot on the floor, no visibly pregnant woman could be allowed on-air exposure.

Few journalists in Canada had proven better at pursuing a story than Berton, but that was only one contribution he could make to the show. Its producers quickly recognized that the program's appeal lay more with the panel's personalities than with the hidden guests or their elusive stories. No less than a prime-time soap opera, *Front Page Challenge* had a cast of characters. Playing variations on themselves, Sinclair became the blunt and grizzled columnist, Robins the beautiful and perky young actress, and Pierre the chippy reporter. The mix was perfect: an old curmudgeon viewers grew to like, an aspiring career woman they immediately admired, and a smug know-it-all they loved to hate.[40]

June Callwood captured Pierre Berton, panellist, as viewers saw him in the early days of *Front Page Challenge*: "When moderator Fred Davis cried, 'Pierre, you're right again!' the studio audience begins to applaud and there is a swelling of orchestral jubilation but Pierre's expression remains stern, unsmiling, unsurprised. He blinks a few times to indicate indifference, all but yawns and, in general, displays the characteristics of a boy riding no-hands past his girl friend's house."[41]

Berton could bring to the program a detective's instinct, needed for tough stories, and so to some viewers he was "the aloof inquisitor, the very epitome of a hard-nosed reporter, who tracked down a story and grilled a victim with a cold zeal." But they knew too that on another level he served as a foil to the accommodative instinct of Canadians that made this northern breed of former colonials at once nice but boring, even to themselves. This was an ingredient missing on *Front Page Challenge* at the beginning, and in Berton its producers found an antidote to "nice." This was a man viewers could detest for his cocky detachment yet admire for his breadth of knowledge. "He's a marvellous villain," John Aylesworth proclaimed with a note of satisfaction.[42]

Even the cast and crew found it difficult to warm to Berton at first. Fred Davis found him "a cold fish." "I can't get close to him," Davis told Alex Barris. A studio director thought that Berton's arrogance was real:

"Pierre was probably the most unpopular with the crews," Steven Hyde said, "because they found him very snobby, very aloof. He was all for the working man but he didn't want to rub shoulders with them."[43]

Arrogant or distracted? Aloof or shy? Perceptions of Berton varied, and a case could be made for each. The one truth universally acknowledged, however, was that Pierre Berton made *Front Page Challenge* a show to talk about from the moment of his first appearance. In November 1957, the *Toronto Star* media columnist William Drylie wrote, "Pierre Berton, said by some at CBC to be the hottest interviewer on tap . . . may be inviting over-exposure on TV. We've seen him on Tabloid, he's on Close-Up, and now on Front Page Challenge three out of every four weeks." But in the spring, when the program was bumped from its usual place in the television lineup to accommodate (what else?) the hockey schedule, Drylie wrote: "The Front Page Challenge show that was wept about was one of the tamer turkeys in the series and would never have been missed. Only Pierre Berton was worth his salt."[44]

In 1958, *Maclean's* approached the height of its quality and influence under the stewardship of the editor Ralph Allen and the managing editor Pierre Berton. With each issue, the two editors and their writers assessed the state of the nation and canvassed almost every corner of its political, social, and cultural life. In January alone, Sidney Katz wrote about mental illness in new immigrants and about the question of who owned outer space in the era of Sputnik; Peter C. Newman provided a profile of "the second most powerful Tory" (the forty-one-year-old federal justice minister, E. Davie Fulton); and Christina McCall described one apparent solution to the national housing problem – "the brave new world of trailer living." A self-mocking Mordecai Richler produced "How I Became an Unknown with My First Novel."[45]

In Berton's final year as managing editor, *Maclean's* was a storehouse of articles about issues of great but as yet unrealized import, examples of social and political history on the run. Bruce Hutchison wrote about "the coming revolt against leisure" (March 15). Katz asked, "Is there a drug to cure cancer?" McKenzie Porter contributed "The Great Back-to-School Boom" (March 15), and Janice Tyrwhitt filed "Are Our

Children Growing Up Too Fast?" (April 12). Blair Fraser reported on the uneasy state of Canadian-American relations (March 1) and in a piece called "The Pipeline Uproar: How Much Smoke? How Much Fire?" provided a sober assessment of the reasons for nearly nine years of debate over a trans-Canada pipeline. "Here is what is known about gas pipeline profits and political tie-ins – and the tough questions still to be answered," went its tagline (July 5).

Lighter fare was to be had, such as Barbara Moon's profile of the "fiery godmother" of Canadian theatre, Dora Mavor Moore (February 15), and McKenzie Porter's portrait of the Canadian boxer Yvon Durelle (April 26). In July, Moon wrote about Canada's best-known comedians in "How Wayne and Shuster Took New York" (July 19), and in August the magazine reported that colour television had been a "flop." Only 350,000 sets had been sold in the United States and 300 in Canada over the previous five years. Reception was bad and sets, at $500 to $1,000, were too costly (August 2).

In retrospect, one can see that the magazine was charting the approach of a revolution driven by demographic change, scientific research, and technological advance, by generational revolt and an incipient reorientation in relations between the sexes. In June, Katz promised *Maclean's* readers "the truth about teen-age drinking" (June 21); in July, Callwood asked, "How good is the birth-control pill?" (July 19). In August, a Newman story proclaimed, "Women Are Equal – Especially Ellen Fairclough." History was to demonstrate that the significance of "the pill" was not as a solution to the long-feared "danger of over-population," as Berton's deck for Callwood's article claimed, and Ellen Fairclough was certainly not a "liberated woman" by the standard of a decade later. Viewed with historical distance, the pages of *Maclean's* in the late fifties bear witness to the birth of the turbulent sixties.

August 1958 was the last month in which Berton's name appeared in *Maclean's* above a piece of original journalism during the decade. His multifarious activities had sparked a mixture of discontent and expectation among the magazine's staff. Some writers had come to resent the range of Berton's freelance work and the size of his income, yet saw in his success a model for grasping such opportunities themselves. The disgruntlement crystallized in the form of a memorandum that the senior writer Sidney Katz sent at some point to Maclean Hunter's president,

Floyd Chalmers, indicating that he was thinking of doing television work and asking for clarification of the company's rules on salaried employees who engaged in such ventures. From Berton's perspective no such rules existed, at least not written ones, and when he found out about Katz's memo he suggested to Katz that "when there are no rules you don't rock the boat by asking for them." Besides, he reminded Katz, Maclean Hunter employees such as Blair Fraser and Ken Wilson of the *Financial Post* appeared regularly on CBC public affairs programs. Did they ask for rules?[46]

Berton had tried to be careful that his television work did not interfere with his responsibilities. *Close-Up* was filmed on Sundays, and he prepared for it on Saturdays. Out-of-town interviews, such as the one with Robert Service in France, he did on holiday time. He recorded *Court of Opinion* for radio on his Thursday lunch hours. *Front Page Challenge*, recorded live on Monday nights, took little time or effort: he simply walked to the CBC Jarvis Street studios after work at *Maclean's*. Asked later by Alex Barris why he even did *Front Page Challenge* when he was so busy, an exasperated Berton responded: "It's easy money. And it doesn't take any work. . . . For Christ's sake, I go down there every other Monday for three hours and I get a lot of dough." Television and radio, he insisted, took no more than five hours a week.[47]

Whatever the degree of separation between Berton's salaried and freelance careers, the Katz memorandum forced management at *Maclean's* to address the issue of moonlighting by staffers. The ruling from the executive suite was that whenever any of its employees appeared on a television program, the magazine for which he or she worked had to be clearly identified. This was already the case with Berton on *Court of Opinion* and *Front Page Challenge*, and he thought Maclean Hunter should be satisfied with the free publicity. At the CBC, *Close-Up's* producer, Ross McLean, bristled at such blanket online credit. "In my mind," he wrote, "the CBC was paying Berton good money for the work he did for Close-Up. I did not feel he owed *Maclean's* the plug."[48]

What irked Berton most about the whole affair was that he was the only Maclean Hunter employee likely to be affected by the new rules, and he told Chalmers so. The Maclean Hunter president remained firm, and Berton concluded that Chalmers now expected him to confine himself to *Maclean's*. He found the situation impossible, in part as a matter of principle and in part because his house devoured outside income the way old Dredge number 4 sucked up the gold and silt of Bonanza Creek. He had not once considered leaving *Maclean's* in his eleven years there; he loved the job and its creative environment. But now the possibility entered his mind. Why not strike out on his own?[49]

The idea was easier for Berton to countenance than for most others at *Maclean's*. A few months earlier Beland Honderich, editor of the *Toronto Star*, had sounded him out about working for him as an "adviser," with the status of associate editor. Berton figured Honderich might have had him in mind as the *Star's* next managing editor. He had resisted the overture, but early in August he called Honderich to say he was now available. Without specifying any precise role, Honderich offered him a $15,000 yearly salary to come to the *Star*, a thousand dollars more than he was receiving at *Maclean's*. Berton accepted without haggling. He suggested a daily column, running Monday through Friday. Agreed. Within days, with his wife in a Toronto hospital in labour with their fifth child, Pierre Berton walked into Ralph Allen's office and told him he was quitting.

"Oh, shit!" Allen said.

Janet, in the hospital, simply giggled, and suggested that it was not the best time for her husband to be without a job.[50] Later that day, she gave birth to the Bertons' second son, Paul.

Berton had arranged that his first column for the *Toronto Star* would run on September 16, so during the family holiday at Ogopogo Lodge he began to list ideas for columns as they came to him. Before the two weeks were up he had forty items in his notebook; eventually, he used all of them.

He was also preoccupied with the publication of his Klondike book, set to be released in mid-October by McClelland & Stewart in Canada and Knopf in the United States. With the exception of a difference of opinion with Harold Strauss at Knopf over use of the definite article in the American title – the publisher suggested "Klondike Fever" and the author insisted on "The Klondike Fever" – the road to production and release had gone smoothly.[51] "You're the boss," Strauss wrote. "Let me have your final decision." *The Klondike Fever* it became, with *The Life and Death of the Last Great Gold Rush*, a subtitle of Berton's devising, used for both editions.[52] Berton agreed with Jack McClelland that for the Canadian market, simply *Klondike* would suffice.

In June, Alfred Knopf had written to say that he had read the galleys with considerable pleasure. "I certainly marvel at your energy and skill," he added. "What a man!" Just as important, at the Knopf summer sales conference, the salesmen had been enthusiastic. "They really expect to do a job on the book," Harold Strauss reported. At the end of August Berton received even better news. *The Klondike Fever* was a Book-of-the-Month Club alternate selection for December. "Some alternates do very well indeed," Strauss wrote. "We have one of which the Book-of-the-Month Club has used over 100,000. On the other hand, some alternates do only 5,000 to 10,000 copies." Either way, it seemed to Berton that by Canadian standards he would have a bestseller.[53]

Before the summer was done, he had begun to think about what major event of Canadian history he might turn to after *Klondike*. What could possibly trump the greatest gold rush of them all? It occurred to him that a good subject was the building of the country's first trans-continental railway, the Canadian Pacific.[54]

His first column for the *Toronto Star* appeared, as agreed, on September 16. Berton himself had yet to show up. He had contracted the mumps. His face and neck were swollen, and he quite literally did not dare show his face at the *Star* offices. So each morning during his first week at the *Star*, Janet, with Pamela and Patsy in tow, and nursing baby Paul, accompanied her husband into the city. While he and the children waited in the car, she took his copy into the *Star*'s King Street offices.

The newsroom occupied most of the fourth floor, beginning at the west end. Off to the east was a wide corridor that some staffers called Peacock Alley – because that was where the bylined columnists and critics worked. At one time or another during Berton's stay at the *Star*, Ron Haggart, Lotta Dempsey, Wendy Michener, Robert Fulford, and others could be found there. The critic Nathan Cohen had his own private office near the end of the corridor, and two or three yards beyond it was another – one with a secretary stationed outside. That was where Janet's husband would report to work once the mumps had run their course. Leaving the building, Janet may have noticed that the walls were devoid of the usual cheap artwork, clippings, stale jokes, photographs, and other paraphernalia that usually adorned newspaper office walls. Beland Honderich, reserved in manner in his pinstriped suits and in his third year as editor-in-chief, had banned such clutter and monitored the walls for infractions. Members of the *Star*'s staff didn't call the relentlessly hands-on chief "the Beast" for nothing. Janet Berton could be forgiven for thinking that with or without decorated walls, the place would become a whole lot livelier when her husband arrived.[55]

On the morning of September 16, above the *Toronto Star* masthead, a large heading read: "'By Pierre Berton' First Page, 2nd Section." Those of the three hundred thousand and more subscribers to the *Toronto Star* who turned to the opening of the section saw the piece immediately: two columns in width, it took up almost the length of the page and was capped by a photograph of the columnist, a man approaching early middle age, sporting a receding hairline, an Errol Flynn moustache, and a gap-toothed smile. Readers would have recognized him even without the column's eponymous title. Apart from Lester B. Pearson, the Nobel Prize–winning Canadian diplomat newly elected as leader of the Liberal Party of Canada, Pierre Berton seemed to be the only public figure in Canada who sported a bow tie, and there it was in the picture.

Berton's premiere column was most unusual. Headed "A Binding Agreement between Two Interested Parties," its twelve hundred words of legalese peppered with "hereinafters" and "party of the second parts" appeared to be a contract between the columnist and his editor. It would not have taken readers long to recognize the spoof. The columnist promised to produce "a daily column . . . on matters of national and local importance, and sometimes on matters of no importance whatsoever." His opinions would be "his own and not necessarily those of the Editor, or the Editor's wife, or the Editor's bridge partners." As the party of the second part, the Editor was not to censor the Columnist's work "even when it appears to him to be excessively foolish." Whenever the columnist wrote something that conflicted with "the cherished views" of the newspaper's directors, their wives, or their bridge partners, the Editor was to "grit his teeth and stare glumly out of the window." Moreover, "should the Columnist be so heretical as to raise his tiny voice against certain Interests who are also advertisers (such as the Quislings who push instant 'coffee' or the brigands who manufacture bread that tastes like library paste), the Editor will grin and bear it." Berton went on to promise that he would not accept gifts or bribes, not write "sentimental columns about his family or funny columns about his wife, except on those terrible days when he can think of nothing to write about," or interview animals or reprint columns by request; he would, however, make certain predictions and publish readers' vicious letters, in return for which he was on occasion to "be permitted to get away with a lousy column." It was, Berton declared, "an iron-clad contract."[56]

In this way, Pierre Berton began another stage in his career, this time reinventing himself as a roving columnist committed to providing the *Toronto Star* with twelve hundred words a day on any subject that piqued his interest. It was bound to be gruelling but also liberating, freeing him to devote time entirely to his writing.

A quotation attributed to the American actor Denzel Washington goes: "I say luck is when an opportunity comes along, and you're prepared for it." Berton's first appearance on television had been preceded by years of radio work and other kinds of performance going back to skits around the campfire with the Boy Scouts. His curiosity had driven him to New York to investigate the new medium and to write about it. In the same way, when Prime Minister John Diefenbaker stood before a packed civic auditorium in Winnipeg on February 12, 1958, and announced his "northern vision" for Canada – with its promise of "a new hope! A new soul for Canada!" – Berton had already submitted to his publisher a book that told the story of the most treasured of all Arctic resources.

Diefenbaker, elected the previous year with a minority government, sought a solid majority in the federal campaign of 1958. The Progressive Conservative Party, he declared, was to be "the party of vision and courage," and he appealed directly to the generation whose grandfathers had climbed the Chilkoot. "To the young men and women of this nation I say, Canada is within your hands. Adventure. Adventure to the nation's utmost bounds, to strive, to seek, to find, and not to yield."[57] Canadian voters responded to the insurgent westerner by awarding his party 208 out of the 265 seats in the House of Commons.

Diefenbaker had turned to the final line of Tennyson's poem "Ulysses" to find the inspirational closing words for his influential "northern vision" speech. Berton had ransacked the quotation books for something that would capture the meaning of the Klondike gold rush. By the end of his search he possessed the exact passage he wanted, and it became his book's opening epigraph:

> "All my life," he said, "I have searched for the treasure. I have sought it in the high places, and in the narrow. I have sought it in deep jungles, and at the ends of rivers, and in dark caverns – and yet have not found it.
>
> "Instead, at the end of every trail, I have found you awaiting me. And now you have become familiar to me, though I cannot say I know you well. Who are you?"
>
> And the stranger answered: "Thyself."

The attribution beneath the passage read "From an old tale," but this was a conceit and a deception. Unsuccessful with *Bartlett's*, Berton had concocted the passage himself. The "tale" was about as old as his need for the next idea. Such a ploy would have been unthinkable for a university-based historian, for this kind of misrepresentation was an academic high crime. But it gave the saga the aura of universal appeal.

Published in October 1958 with a Canadian title as stark as a lone pine, *Klondike* complemented and reinforced the popular will to believe in Diefenbaker's invocation of "a transcending sense of national purpose" rooted in an engagement with the North. Diefenbaker's "northern vision" positioned the development of the North as a form of national duty, in the tradition of the transcontinental railways given life by Macdonald and Laurier. Dief believed northern development, like the nation's historic east-west communications axis, would serve as a counterweight to the increasingly heavy American influence on Canadian life. In writing *Klondike*, Berton reached similar conclusions about the role of the North in forging a national identity and a sensibility distinct from that of the United States.[58]

Berton primed the pump of potential book buyers with a four-part serialization of *Klondike* in *Maclean's*. The excerpts, which were substantial but by no means scooped the contents of the book, ran from mid-September to the end of October.[59] By that time the first of the American reviews had appeared. They were rapturous. "Mr. Berton's scholarly approach, his intimate familiarity with the region through boyhood memories, his eloquent and dramatic style give the narrative a ring of authenticity," wrote the *Christian Science Monitor*. "Drama and humor lurk on every page and there is a beautiful vein of anecdote running through the entire account," said *Library Journal*. "A comprehensive and absolutely first-rate history," proclaimed the *New Yorker*. "In his orbit of the Yukon, I'll accept Berton's word on everything," confessed the reviewer for the *Saturday Review*.[60]

The most influential review of all, no doubt, was that of the *New York Times Book Review*, written by Senator Richard L. Neuberger of Oregon. Neuberger conformed to the template of the typical review of a Berton book. He drew attention to Berton's pedigree as "the son of a Klondike nugget hunter," a background that made possible not only "a meticulous but lively saga of the great gold rush" but also "the most authentic" work he had come across, despite having "read just about everything on the subject. . . . It leaves very little to be told by anybody else."[61]

Newly liberated from office routine, Berton poured his energies into promotional schemes, spurring Jack McClelland to market *Klondike* the way he thought it should be – not that Jack was short of ideas of his own. Using Berton's northern contacts, McClelland arranged to have three hundred caribou-skin pokes, filled with a handful of sand and a pinch of gold, distributed to reviewers and media types. Roy Minter of the White Pass & Yukon Route railway coordinated the project and the Yukon Consolidated Gold Corporation of Dawson City provided sand from Bonanza Creek. Every twenty-fifth poke contained twelve nuggets.[62] "In the comfort of your kitchen pour some water in a small frying pan," the accompanying instructions told the lucky recipients, "pour in your poke of gold and start mining. Fortunately you won't have to suffer the hardships and heartbreaks of mining that Pierre Berton describes so dramatically in his new book 'Klondike.'"[63] The nuggets cost Jack McClelland $150.

A highly coordinated media blitz, unprecedented in the history of McClelland & Stewart, unfolded with military precision. Media figures across the country received copies of *Klondike* accompanied by a personalized letter. The group included fifty-one newspaper literary editors, five literary columnists, forty-six outdoor columnists, and well over two hundred others. The news editors of 117 small-town newspapers in Alberta alone received review copies of the book. In Toronto, Berton appeared at the Park Plaza hotel bookshop to sign copies and spoke at the Women's Press Club. McClelland & Stewart prepared expensive window displays and door signs that quoted Neuberger's rave review in the *Times Book Review*. The signs were highly visible at a "Klondike party" held for thirty key movers and shakers of the Toronto media guild, including William Deacon, principal *Globe and Mail* reviewer, Beland Honderich, editor-in-chief of the *Toronto Star*, Alex Barris of the Toronto *Telegram*, Gordon Sinclair of CFRB, and Isabel Craig, bureau manager of United Press International.[64]

Writing a newspaper column, making weekly appearances on television, and publishing another major book still did not satisfy Berton's need for a public life and the recognition that went with it – whether acclaim or notoriety did not seem to matter. That autumn, Berton and the Toronto radio station CHUM agreed that he would provide eleven one-minute commentaries per day, running twice an hour, fifty-five a week, on whatever subject he chose. In this way began a rivalry and eventually a friendship, because the Canadian-born former evangelist Charles Templeton had just returned to Canada from the United States and had struck a similar deal – ten commentaries a minute long, five days a week – with the All-Canada Radio syndicate. Berton's gig paid $125 per week. By 1961 his views were heard on thirty of CHUM's affiliate stations in addition to CHUM itself.[65]

Toward the end of 1958, what she later called "the horrible truth" began to dawn on Janet Berton. "I was married to a public figure," she told *Chatelaine*, Canada's premier women's magazine. "In the first twelve years of our marriage . . . my husband and I lived more or less like any other couple. Then . . . all this changed." He was now a mainstay of *Front Page Challenge*, with two and a half million viewers per week. Hundreds of thousands of people read his *Toronto Star* column daily. Even greater numbers heard his capsule comments on CHUM and its affiliates many times a day. He continued to appear on television's *Close-Up* and radio's *Court of Opinion*, and his new book, *Klondike*, was a great success.[66] Janet Berton's husband had suddenly become famous.

STAR CRUSADER

—

ON THE DAY PIERRE BERTON wrote his first column for the *Toronto Star*, June Callwood and Trent Frayne sent him a congratulatory telegram: "TO WISH YOU LUCK WOULD BE FOOLISH AND TO WISH YOU SUCCESS REDUNDANT HOPE INSTEAD YOU HAVE MOMENTS WHEN SATISFIED TODAYS SUPERB BEGINNING MUST SURELY BE ONE."[1] Callwood and Frayne knew well that Berton's move to the *Star* involved about as much luck as Maurice Richard finding himself in front of an opponent's net, ready to pounce and score. Berton and Richard shared this: they could sniff opportunity and instinctively knew how to take advantage of it. At the *Toronto Star*, Berton would be able to range freely in pursuit of his interests. It would not have escaped the comic book connoisseur that he was now employed by the very newspaper that had inspired the artist Joe Shuster to create the *Daily Star*, where Superman, disguised as the mild-mannered Clark Kent, was a hard-working reporter.[2]

For most of its existence, the *Toronto Star* had been on one crusade or another. Started in 1892 as a strike sheet by typographers of the *Toronto News*, the struggling newspaper initially called the *Evening Star* gained stability and direction in 1899. In that year a number of wealthy supporters of Prime Minister Sir Wilfrid Laurier purchased the newspaper in order to provide a Liberal voice in otherwise Conservative Toronto. The man they made its publisher was thirty-four-year-old Joseph E. Atkinson, formerly a reporter with the Montreal *Herald* and the *Globe*. In January 1900, Atkinson changed the paper's name to the *Toronto Daily Star*.[3]

Almost immediately, Atkinson – who, with Elmina Elliott, his wife and a fellow journalist, was a fervent advocate of the social gospel brand

of Christianity – harnessed the newspaper to the cause of social justice
and reform. "Holy Joe" Atkinson remained at the helm of the *Star* until
his death in 1948. Over the decades his newspaper kept faith with
Canadian liberalism and its party, and as often as not its progressivism
was farther ahead than that of the politicians. The *Star* championed all
manner of causes, from the Fresh Air Fund and the Santa Fund (providing recreation and gifts for needy children), clean water, pasteurized
milk, and workers' rights early in the century, to federal relief programs,
mother's allowances, and social welfare legislation in the 1930s and
1940s. Along the way, Atkinson and the *Star* exposed the conditions of
Toronto's slums and defended civil liberties, including those of Japanese
Canadians interned by the federal government during the Second
World War.

The *Toronto Star* trumpeted itself as the newspaper of ordinary
working people, and those people became its readers. Within a year the
7,000 subscribers of 1899 became 10,000. In 1905, with a circulation of
37,000, it moved from Adelaide Street to King Street West and into the
largest newspaper quarters in the country. By 1909 its 65,000 subscribers gave it the largest newspaper circulation in Toronto. Skip two
decades: boasting 175,000 subscribers on the eve of the Depression, it
moved into a new office tower on King Street West, where it was to
operate until 1971.

When Pierre Berton joined the *Star* it was still steadfastly committed to its liberal and progressive past. In 1942, six years before his death,
Atkinson had created the Atkinson Charitable Foundation and transferred ownership of the *Star* to it; the Conservative provincial government countered by passing a law that prevented charitable organizations
from owning more than 10 per cent of profit-making businesses. The
legislation was a clear attempt to sever the *Star*'s connection to the
reform principles of the Atkinson tradition. For a decade, the five
liberal families behind the foundation struggled to maintain the legiti-
macy of their ownership of the *Star* in the face of determined political
opposition from Conservatives in the Ontario legislature and in their
social arm, the Albany Club.

Finally, early in 1958, the trustees of the Atkinson Charitable Foundation arranged to purchase the newspaper themselves, a matter

requiring the approval of the Supreme Court of Ontario.[4] In testimony before the court, they declared that the *Toronto Star* would subscribe to what they chose to call the Atkinson Principles: "a strong, united and independent Canada; Social Justice; Individual and Civil Liberties; Community and Civic Engagement; the Rights of Working People; and the Necessary Role of Government."[5] In securing Berton for its stable of columnists, the *Star* had acquired a journalist whose newspaper background reflected its engaged and at times provocative approach to news coverage. Moreover, his views on social issues and his willingness to speak out on them coincided almost exactly with the Atkinson Principles.

Beland Honderich likely had more than Berton's political outlook in mind when he lured him to the *Star*. After the war, under the direction of Atkinson's son-in-law and successor Harry Hindmarsh, the paper had become increasingly sensational, regularly featuring strange incidents, awful train wrecks, horrifying crimes, riveting trials, and bizarre human interest stories. Few issues lacked at least one tear-jerker in which readers' emotions were manipulated by a heart-wrenching tale of an impoverished widow, a dying child, or a neglected pet.

In ways that Hal Straight and the Cromie brothers would certainly have approved, the *Star* went out of its way to trump the coverage of its chief rival, the Toronto *Telegram*. After John Ross Robertson founded the *Telegram* in 1876, the newspaper had claimed the loyalty of the Conservative and Protestant working class of Toronto. However different in politics, both papers declared the common man as their own and fought for his allegiance, along with his subscription. Competition for readership became especially fierce in the 1950s. On the extraordinary day in early September 1954 when Marilyn Bell became the first woman to swim across Lake Ontario, both papers flooded the waterfront. Reporters tried desperately to scoop one another, hiring boats and ambulances aimed at obtaining an exclusive interview. Each paper put out extra editions throughout the marathon swim. The whole scene, June Callwood wrote in *Maclean's*, was "bizarre and hectic."[6]

The fact was that at the time of Berton's arrival, the *Star* was struggling. The new owners, trustees also of a charitable foundation, proved timorous about the over-the-top sensationalism of the past, an approach inspired by the American Hearst newspaper chain. This, together with an increase in the *Star*'s price from 5 to 10 cents in 1957, had sent circulation figures plummeting from 387,000 in 1957 to 320,000 in 1958. Sales dropped even further, to 316,000, in 1959.[7] Beland Honderich's coup in securing Canada's most controversial journalist for the paper was clearly intended to help stop this financial hemorrhage.

Berton proved more than willing to meet the challenge. Over four years, beginning in September 1958 and continuing to November 1962, he wrote almost a thousand columns on an astonishing range of subjects. Yet at the outset, haunted by the fear that he might run out of ideas, he resolved to stay at least three columns ahead. He remembered Jack Scott, agonizing at the *Vancouver Sun* over "Our Town," his own daily column, so trenchant in observation and yet so graceful in style. To Berton's mind, Scott and Bruce Hutchison remained without question the best columnists in the country.

The inspiration and example of Scott and Hutchison heartened him, as did his experience in handling a wide array of subjects day by day at *Maclean's*. Its editorial board had constantly struggled to achieve the right mix of articles, and Berton saw no reason why he couldn't apply the same technique to a daily newspaper column. "I wanted to achieve a sense of surprise," he wrote, "to put my readers off balance, so that they would be asking what that son-of-a-bitch was going to do next." This, too, was the ploy of Gordon Sinclair, the old curmudgeon of *Front Page Challenge*, by turns lovable or spiteful.[8]

Columnists of the late fifties and early sixties often chose a specialty such as politics, sports, entertainment, or fashion. Blair Fraser confined himself to politics, Gordon Sinclair to entertainment. Berton's column was radically different. Its hallmark was its eclecticism, in subject, style, and mood. On any given day, he might profile a celebrity or review a consumer product; defend civil liberties or report on his experiments in the kitchen; comment on civic architecture or expose corrupt officials. He warned about scams and fraudsters, provided lessons in history, and condemned injustice and discrimination. Sometimes, the column would simply be one of Berton's surreal fantasies invoking the lives and times of the zany extended family he named the "Grebes," satirizing the fads, fashions, and foibles of the day.

The subjects of "By Pierre Berton" in its inaugural week provided ample evidence that this column would be out of the ordinary: a sarcastic poem dedicated to the United States Air Force, ridiculing an American general's proclamation that small nuclear weapons could be "humane"; the verse of Robert W. Service; the Hollywood scandal prompted by the actress Elizabeth Taylor's "theft" of Eddie Fisher, husband of her friend Debbie Reynolds. "Well now, nothing's really changed much. Eddie loves Liz and Liz loves Eddie and Debbie loves Eddie, too. No, there's one change: Eddie doesn't love Debbie."[9] To Berton, this Tinseltown tempest reflected the infantilization of American society and culture.

The next week, Berton penned a tongue-in-cheek ode to Toronto's invasive new Gardiner Expressway. He drew attention to the "coincidence" of *Time* magazine's constant and adulatory coverage of Prime Minister Diefenbaker and the Diefenbaker government's elimination of the 20 per cent tax on advertisements imposed by the previous Liberal government on foreign magazines like *Time* and *Reader's Digest*. He wrote a scene for a play on the interests of teenagers. He took issue with a statement by the president of the Chrysler Corporation of Canada that advertising dollars should not be directed to publications criticizing his company's products. To round out the week, the Friday column exposed the sales tactics of "the grisly business of modern funerals."[10] Very often during Berton's four years of columns he was well ahead of other journalists in discerning and writing about important issues hidden beneath the surface of life. His topics changed radically from day to day, but over the months readers began to sense his core values and major preoccupations. Each concern – consumer society, crime and punishment, and social justice – was a glance into his kaleidoscope of interests.

His chosen themes suggested an instinctive sense of natural justice and a principled alliance with the man on the street and the woman in the home. Along with his Klondike origins, these became central to the formation of what would become the Berton brand. Over the next four years, his column proclaimed the thoroughly populist outlook of a champion of ordinary people. Almost everything Berton wrote made evident, sometimes forcefully, that he had not forgotten what it was like to be on the fringes of society or to hear the yell of the bully. The unsettling shades of Little Lord Fauntleroy stayed with him still.

❦

Berton began to write his column for the *Toronto Star* at a time of momentous change. The Soviet Union's surprise launch of an unmanned satellite named Sputnik sped up the Cold War and heightened the sense of continental apprehension one historian dubbed "nuclear fear." The baby boom that followed the war ushered in a child-centred society, the social norms of which followed the life cycle of children's development and needs, whether in education, health, or shelter. New housing developments came to be built well away from places of work, the result of the North American commitment to the single-family dwelling, an inadequate supply of affordable housing within city limits, and a romantic view of suburban living. All of these factors challenged and changed the rhythm and requirements of family life: the suburb increasingly became the site of a Canadian variation on the American dream.[11] Men and women craved the domestic stability of the nuclear family and its commitments even as their attitudes in matters of sexuality, marital fidelity, and gender relations started to shift. Allegiance to mainstream organized religion, strong in the immediate postwar years, showed signs of confusion and the first hints of spiritual disarray.[12]

Still proud of their British heritage and monarchical connection, English Canadians nevertheless could not help but notice – especially in the aftermath of the Massey Commission and the warm glow of the television age – the degree to which their country was coming to resemble America's attic. "Few Canadians realize the extent of this dependence," the authors of the Massey Commission's report wrote. "Our lazy, even abject, imitation of them has caused an uncritical acceptance of ideas and assumptions which are alien to our tradition."[13]

Propelling these economic, social, and cultural changes was the reorientation of North American capitalism and the continental economy away from producing goods and toward consuming them. Economic strain and uncertainty instilled by a decade of depression and a long war had caused people to defer their material desires in the years immediately after 1945, but this soon changed. Sales of automobiles in Canada numbered 78,000 in 1946 but rose to 159,000 a year later. Jobs became plentiful. Enrolment in Canadian schools increased by almost two million pupils between 1945 and 1960.[14]

The Cold War, imperial loyalty, and demographic change did not escape the attention or concern of Canadians, but in 1959 these matters hovered like gathering clouds above daily life. At ground level, a lot more Canadians were preoccupied by the deaths of the singers Buddy Holly and Ritchie Valens in a plane crash, and with whether to buy their children the new Bic ballpoint pen or the new doll called "Barbie," than by satellites in the sky or the next royal visit. The Wham-O novelty company sold twenty million hula hoops in the first six months of their release in 1958. With the advent of the credit card and the instalment plan, consumer debt in the United States rose at a rate triple that of the growth in personal income.[15] As a suburban husband and father of five youngsters, Pierre Berton lived in the heart of Consumerland, with all the anxiety of affluence it entailed.

The abundance of goods and choice of products delighted people, but they also confused them as an older culture of constraint rooted in Christian asceticism gave way, in the words of the historian Gary Cross, to "the power and appeal of an ever-advancing consumerism."[16] The flood of new products onto the market brought with it a vast increase in advertising. American companies had spent $2 billion on advertising in 1939; by the late fifties, expenditures were $12 billion annually.[17] What car should we buy? What salesman can we trust? What brands are the best? Is this new drug safe?

In the Canada of the late fifties, sources of accurate information or credible advice about goods and services were scarce. The American magazine *Consumer Reports* had existed since 1936, but it remained on the margins of Canadian awareness and was found on few magazine stands. A number of women's groups had banded together in 1948 to form the Canadian Association of Consumers, and its members tried to lift the ban on margarine and championed the idea that "advertising should serve as well as sell"; but its main accomplishment by the late 1950s had been to put an end to the practice of issuing trading stamps at grocery stores. Not until the early sixties did the Canadian Association of Consumers test products or publish its findings.[18] Meanwhile, with the largest Canadian newspaper base at his disposal, Pierre Berton became – to use the title he gave a number of his columns – "my own one-man Consumers' Report."

Throughout his four years at the *Toronto Star*, Berton devoted many columns to consumer issues, helping his readers make informed choices, warning them about misleading ads, fraudulent charities, service industry scams, high-pressure sales campaigns, phony contests, and much else. He wrote about the best and worst of fireworks and about Bromo-Seltzer and the kids' fad in 1957 for "Fizzies," the tablets that made instant effervescent soft drinks. He provided comparisons of supermarket prices and noted the variations in cost between brand-name and generic drugs. Exorbitant charges for concrete in Toronto, real estate promotions that promised more than they delivered, and misleading appliance ads did not escape his notice. The title of one column alone indicates the range of subjects to which he gave critical scrutiny: "My Own Consumers' Reports – Drugs, Flats, Mags & HP Sauce."[19]

"The woods are full of bad guys," he wrote, in a column that outlined "the Berton system" for survival in a world of "sharks" and "suckers."[20] This was his antidote for gullibility, free to all, and complete with a detailed set of instructions on how to detect and stop a shark at the family door. If by chance you found the shark inside your living room wielding a contract, Berton advised you to read the fine print. Beware of attached promissory notes called "negotiable instruments," for they allowed the vendor to sell the contract at a discount to a third party not responsible for the goods you'd bought. When you phoned the company to complain, you would be out of luck.

Berton warned readers of the "hard-sell" tactics used by vacuum cleaner and encyclopedia salesmen and reported on "the racket in hot furs."[21] He described the sales routine taught to a teenaged door-to-door sales force by the Consolidated Circulation Agency, which sold *Liberty*, *Saturday Night*, *Chatelaine*, and *Maclean's*, among other magazines. The pitch was for a few pennies a month to help send a boy on an educational tour of Europe, but the "ballot" that "approved of the tour" was in fact a long-term subscription to the magazines, signed for by the unwitting customer.[22]

Berton also devoted a number of columns to the well-honed techniques of mass persuasion that were based on research in depth psychology. Vance Packard, Berton's contemporary as a crusader for consumer protection, had written on the subject in his controversial 1957 bestseller, *The Hidden Persuaders*, with particular emphasis on the way advertising agencies used social science motivation research to influence people's buying decisions. Berton was aware of Packard's work, but he had explored the use of depth psychology to alter consciousness almost a decade earlier in his *Maclean's* article "Want to Be a Boss?"[23]

From the outset, Berton was assisted by individuals he called his "operatives" – each identified only by a number. To understand door-to-door sales of stainless steel cookware, he sent "Operative 26" to take a course offered by World Wide Distributors & Co., and then told his readers to be alert – because the salesmen were trained to appeal to the customer's avarice and vanity.[24] To learn about encyclopedia sales, he sent "Operative 81" to answer a newspaper advertisement that paid "college men" $90 weekly for a summer job. As the weeks and months went by, readers started to think that Berton employed dozens of such "operatives," part researchers, part spies; all the while, he was poking subtle fun at the public fascination with Ian Fleming's James Bond, whose seventh fictional adventure, *Goldfinger*, appeared in 1959.

At any time at the *Star*, Berton had little more assistance than a secretary and a part-time research assistant, but as his controversial column claimed greater attention, the mail brought any number of tips about scams and fraudsters and matters to investigate. Unlike the reaction to his *Maclean's* articles, where it sometimes took a month for a "letter to the editor" to appear, response to his *Star* columns was immediate. Almost as soon as copies of the paper hit the pavement, Berton's phone would begin to ring, both at the office and at home. On one day in June 1959 alone, he logged thirty-seven incoming office calls from informants and complainants.[25]

Berton's first "operative" at the *Star* was a male secretary named Lee Rathlou. Rather studious, extremely efficient, and deferential to the point of embarrassment, Rathlou was by nature a reticent man. Whenever asked by his boss to do something out of the ordinary, he would be reluctant and at times appear worried. This made him less than suitable for some of the unusual missions Pierre had in mind. Shortly after

Berton returned from a holiday in Mexico and described to Rathlou
the wonders of a Mayan ruin he had visited, Rathlou told him he was
quitting to take photographs in the jungles of Yucatán. He left in
December 1959.

Berton looked around for a replacement, and found one in thirty-
nine-year-old Ennis Halliday, a woman with a good deal of office experience. "She had all the right qualifications," Berton later wrote, "a fast
typing speed, an efficient executive ability, and she looked after me like
a sister." Discreet and unflappable, Halliday remained with Berton as
his private secretary for almost twenty-five years.[26]

Berton's research assistant was equally adept at her work, but quite
unlike Halliday in other ways. His secretary looked and acted like the
dedicated and capable office manager she was, trustful of others; he
found Marilyn Craig, his researcher, "chameleon-like" in the way she
could make herself "look dowdy one day and glamorous the next." He
also found that she possessed two other qualities essential for the work
he wanted her to do: the first was that she pursued any investigation
with the zeal of a hound on the hunt; the second, as Berton put it, was
"her unshakeable belief in the cupidity of almost everybody; she was
convinced that the entire world was populated by crooks and con men."
He had discovered the perfect spy, and had no intention of bringing her
in from the cold.[27]

Marilyn Craig went undercover as "Operative 67" for a series of
investigations. Under the guise of an innocent and gullible housewife
in need of a product or service, she helped Berton expose the shady sales
tactics, financing, and warranty schemes of the automobile business.
Titles of his columns on these subjects indicate his careful mix of cus-
tomer warning, industry exposé, and consumer assistance: "How to
Turn an Automobile into an Obsession"; "Harrowing Experiences of an
Honest Used Car Dealer"; "Things I Didn't Know till Now about the
Car Business"; "Why There Are No Bargains on Bernard Hurtig's Car
Lot"; "How the Used Car Business Can Be Cleaned Up."[28]

Operative 67's cases of consumer espionage became the stuff of
legend, at least around Toronto. They helped make Berton's run at the
Star so distinctive that for decades afterwards readers could recall
certain favourite columns. Craig did the sleuth work that uncovered TV
repairmen who overbilled or charged for non-existent repairs, and it

was she who helped expose the "bait-and-switch" scheme of a Dupont Avenue appliance company that offered a brand-name vacuum cleaner for only $12.95. After the disappointed customer was told that the advertised cleaner was "temporarily" out of stock, she was then harassed until she purchased a much more expensive model.[29]

One of Operative 67's most memorable undercover operations began when Berton told Marilyn Craig, a good dancer, to take lessons from the Arthur Murray Dance Studio and step all over the instructor's feet. He had more than a hunch what would likely happen, and Operative 67 proved him right. When she arrived at the studio, wearing a cheap blouse, a wrinkled skirt, well-worn shoes, and stringy hair – in short, looking insecure and vulnerable and open to advice from her "betters" – she found herself assigned a well-groomed "private tutor" named Wallace. The pair worked through the steps of several dances, and Craig contrived to stumble as much as possible without forcing her partner to quit with bruised feet. Finally came the tutor's assessment: his delightful partner was a "fast learner," full of promise. Operative 67 reported the conversation to Berton, who conveyed it to his readers. "'Why,' said Mr. Wallace, 'I remember Alva Gooch. You remind me of Alva. When she came here she was terribly shy, but now she's the life of the party.'" Dance lessons, Mr. Wallace added, would increase Craig's confidence and help make friends in a cold city like Toronto.

Then, of course, he suggested she sign up for their "special introductory offer" – if he could convince his hard-boiled boss to let her enrol. Now Operative 67's steadfast champion, Wallace disappeared to plead with the man, who resisted but at last gave way, saying that perhaps something could be worked out, but only if the young lady signed on the spot. Stating that she wished to think the matter over, Operative 67 took her leave – much to the consternation of the manager and Mr. Wallace. Marilyn Craig's subsequent research on the dance studio industry revealed that many people fell for the kind of high-pressure sales tactics she had just experienced, sometimes paying thousands for the privilege.[30]

Craig enrolled in the basic course and supplied enough juicy material for a half-dozen more columns. She returned to the studio, and into the arms of Mr. Wallace. He praised her. He suggested they dance closer. He said she would learn her steps best if she took as many lessons in as short a time as possible, perhaps as many as two hundred. Operative 67 calculated that this would cost her a thousand dollars or more. She already knew of a couple eager to obtain their Arthur Murray Bronze Medals, and willing to fork over about $3,500 for them. She also knew that the Arthur Murray Lifetime course cost $15,000, and that in Toronto a hundred students had enrolled. Berton reported it all, including the story of one local woman who had signed up for four Lifetime courses: $60,000 for dancing lessons.[31]

At the dance studio, a hunt began to uncover the identity of the mysterious Operative 67 who was doing so much damage to its reputation. "Everybody is looking at everybody else with marked suspicion," Berton wrote. "The idea that there is a traitor in the ranks has made them all a little uneasy." So he announced that Operative 67 had decided to quit. "They keep asking about her bank account," he reported. "They want to know how much money she makes. Operative 67 would rather dance the samba."[32]

Gradually, through other undercover work, Berton discovered some of the dance studio's darker strategies, including the key to what the company called "emotional selling": find the weakest point in a person's character and exploit it to sell more lessons. Instructors were taught about "post-selling" (obtain a small commitment in order to secure a larger one) and "assumptive selling" (always assume a student is going to take more and more lessons). They learned how to maintain students' enthusiasm through constant praise and encouragement, and they were told to maintain personal contact by telephone. At staff meetings, the instructors discussed the studio's "balkers" – those reluctant to take more lessons – and ways to overcome their resistance.[33]

Somehow Berton obtained lengthy and highly confidential scripts of the instructors' sales pitches, and he published excerpts. He wrote about the gimmicks used to open wallets: make the lessons appear glamorous and desirable; cultivate insecurity in the student by suggesting she lacks talent or commitment; tell her she has been granted the chance to purchase a Lifetime membership and immediately present her with the application form. On it, the student is asked to list all personal assets. Berton quoted from the studio's documents: "Most pupils rarely have $9,000 sitting idle in the bank. They usually have stocks and bonds, matured insurance policies. . . . These things are for something special. What could be more special?"[34]

Three years later, Berton was pleased to report: "In July 1960 the U.S. Federal Trade Commission issued a cease and desist order against Arthur Murray, Inc., the licensor of 450 franchised dance studios, barring them from making bogus offers designed to 'lure the innocent' into signing up for dance lessons."[35]

Pierre's initial fear that he might run out of ideas for columns proved baseless. Newspaper advertisements alone provided an inexhaustible stream of work for his hard-working "operatives," and like a pair of Klondike prospectors he and Marilyn Craig dug through classified sections and trade magazines for any hint of the hard sell or the scam. As a result, "By Pierre Berton" continued to expose hucksters who promised housewives successful songwriting careers (at the right price) and financiers who offered mortgages (at exorbitant costs), along with a host of other shady offers and dodgy opportunities.[36] But when Berton encountered a pamphlet of the Wilbert W. Haaze Company of Forest Park, Illinois, manufacturers of burial vaults, he knew he had discovered pay dirt a mere six feet under.

The discovery resulted in a series of notable columns on the North American funeral industry. These went beyond exposé and became penetrating examples of cultural observation and criticism little seen in Canadian newspapers at the time. As he told his readers, "The cult of the dead is the cult of the twentieth century." Men and women, seduced by the good life of an abundant society, placed so much faith in technology and its promise of never-ending progress that it had become the balm that now accompanied mourning, and the funeral industry took full advantage of the connection. The United Church of Canada advised its congregants that funerals should be kept simple and that "elaborate and costly devices to restore a life-like appearance to the body" had no place in a Christian burial, for a person's worth was not measured by such means. But according to Berton, the funeral companies of a consumer society had reinvented the Egyptian cult of the dead and were willing to provide any device or service money could buy. The Wilbert W. Haaze Company promised its customers "The Ultimate in Peace of Mind Protection," because, its pamphlet said, after the hymns are still . . . the fond words softly spoken . . . the living find quiet comfort in the knowledge that the ultimate in care and affection has been accorded their loved one. . . . The scientifically engineered combination of quality-controlled special pre-cast asphalt fused with quality-controlled steel-reinforced concrete provides the maximum of peace-of-mind protection.

The contemporary funeral industry hawked its wares to the grief-stricken, preying on the bereaved and their feelings of inadequacy and loss. "When you use Scientist Series fluids," the Kellogg Chemical company told its mortuary clients, "you take the family into the slumber room, feeling certain that they will be impressed and more than pleased by what you have accomplished." Modern life as reflected by the funeral industry, Berton said, denied the very idea of death, as their treatment of bodies and graves testified. Dearly departed Dad should be buried in a "men's burial suit," and Mum should be put on display in "the new gold brocade strap pump." The industry catalogue told undertakers to insist that families dress the deceased in "practical burial footwear." Theirs were "the finest for those who care enough," the catalogue declared.

"There is no longer, at the graveside," Berton wrote, "any suggestion that the body is being returned to the earth, to nourish that earth and serve some useful purpose after life has ceased." The modern gravesite sported false grass, and painted boards covered the grave. "No one doubts the benefits in peace of mind the sealed casket has brought to the general public," a coffin manufacturer assured its customers.[37]

In subsequent columns, Berton drew attention to the dubious ethics of the Memorial Gardens Association, a United States corporation that declared there was "nothing illegal or immoral in making business enterprise out of death." He informed the public that (to use the title of one column) "the cost of dying doesn't have to be so high." To dramatize his case, Pierre used a ploy that had worked for him back at *Maclean's* when he wanted to write about anti-Semitic attitudes and practices. He assigned Operative 67 the task of telephoning thirteen undertakers with the news that her mother would soon die of cancer and asking what they would charge for an arrangement – "no funeral, no embalming, no service, no death notices, the cheapest available casket." The answers Craig received were for the most part evasive and ambiguous. Several undertakers insisted she visit the funeral home "to sign papers and talk the whole matter over."[38]

People should be wary of these ploys, Berton wrote. Then he offered "the correct dope about burial, cremation, costs and the law" for people who would rather spend money on the living than on the dead. Don't make your decisions about funerals based on what the neighbours will think, he advised in one column; don't use the funeral as a status symbol, he warned in another.[39]

Just as Berton had anticipated the work of Vance Packard on the connection between psychology and sales, so he became the first reporter to expose the modern funeral industry for the manipulative commercial enterprise it was, a business that nevertheless reflected some of the basic assumptions of contemporary life. Three years after he wrote the last of his columns on the high cost of dying, the expatriate daughter of a talented but highly eccentric British family wrote a best-seller on the exact same subject in the United States. By the time Jessica Mitford published *The American Way of Death* in 1963,[40] Berton had long since explored the meaning of the "slumber room" and moved on.

In his *Toronto Star* column, Berton wrote about the consumer society more than any other subject. After all, with a large family and an ever-expanding house, he was a consumer himself. He was the father who complained in an open letter to the president of Eaton's one Christmas that he would need a Ph.D. to assemble the store's "Ranch Wagon Pedal Auto." Besides, he asked, "what's a knurled centre pin?"[41] The tenor of his advice to readers was less to curb their consumption than to consume wisely; he intended to warn people about exploitation and protect them from it.

On matters related to consumerism, Berton's situation was an ambiguous one, for he had to reconcile in his own mind his simultaneous roles as consumer and critic. But on issues related to crime and punishment, discrimination and inequality, or freedom of expression, the distinction between justice and injustice was sharp and clear. The man from the margins of Canada needed no coaxing to take up the cause of the victimized and downtrodden. Within weeks of starting his column, he drew public attention to the sentencing of teenagers to lengthy terms in adult prisons, to the difficulties such prisoners had in adjusting to life "outside" once back on the streets, and to the state of Canada's prisons and the sordid conditions within them.

A firm believer that even the hardest criminal could be rehabilitated and find redemption under the right circumstances, he told the story of John (Bugs) Brown, released from Kingston Penitentiary on Thursday, September 25, 1958, after spending most of the years since 1931 in prison. Once dubbed "the Terror of Jarvis Street" for his armed robberies in Toronto, Brown had turned to educating himself behind bars, matriculating and then taking a host of university courses in classics, ancient and modern languages, political philosophy, and English literature. Released in 1947, frightened and insecure, he got caught up in a Toronto gang war and spent another decade in jail. But he continued to study, and aimed at becoming a journalist. His final release looked promising: he had a wife and daughter, an apartment, and a good job waiting for him with a Toronto businessman named Harold King. He spent his second day of freedom with King, and the next one shopping for books. The volume he bought, but kept secret from his family, was called *How to Live with a Bad Heart*. On his fourth day of freedom, he died of a heart attack. His last words were: "I'm not going to die. I've done so many bad things in my life, I've got to have some time to do some good ones." For Berton, this was "a tragedy in three acts" that deserved public scrutiny.[42]

Berton devoted a number of columns to the question of punishment within the prison system. One, provocatively titled "A Report on Torture as Practiced in Modern Canada," described in detail the brutal treatment of four mentally challenged inmates in Kingston Penitentiary using a device known in the institution as "the machine." Stripped and blindfolded and strapped face-down on a V-shaped contraption resembling two long ironing boards, the prisoners were then beaten with a heavy, perforated leather strap. This method of torture, Berton said, reminded him of the rack and thumbscrew of the Middle Ages. "I oppose the torture of human beings, sane or demented, not because of what is done to the tortured, but because of what is done to the torturer.

And we are all torturers, each one of us in this free democracy, as long as we condone torture and maintain it as law on our statute books." The practice, he declared, dehumanizes us all, just as it did the guards in Kingston Penitentiary. Berton's revelations resulted in the abandonment of this barbarism.[43]

Over the months that followed, and throughout 1959, Berton wrote a number of columns pointing out other instances of cruel punishment or terrible institutional conditions. One concerned the 1954 death of an eighteen-year-old boy named Ralph Jacobs at the Guelph Reformatory – another example of "legal torture," he said – in which, at the outset of ten days of close confinement, four guards savagely beat the boy with "strap-like instruments . . . about 18 inches long, four inches wide and an inch or more thick." Aware that another ten lashes would be his on the final day and taunted by his guards, Jacobs hanged himself with a cloth belt. Prison officials pointed out that the lad had not been beaten for over a week, and the coroner's jury assigned no blame to anyone.[44]

On January 21, 1959, Berton reported on facilities for solitary confinement at the Ontario Reformatory at Millbrook and at Collins Bay Penitentiary in Kingston that would better be described as dungeons. At Collins Bay, meals consisted of one bowl of water and about two slices of bread per day, and the only heat in winter was in the immediate area of the steam pipe. The mental discomfort was even worse, a fact Berton demonstrated not only with prisoner testimony but with reference to brainwashing experiments at McGill University in 1954, sponsored by the Defence Research Board, in which student volunteers were paid $20 a day to undergo almost complete sensory deprivation. "Of the 46 students who took part in the experiment," Berton reported, "only one was able to stick at it for more than five days. Everyone, in fact, pleaded to quit after 24 hours."[45]

Early in February, he told the story of an Ontario government ward who at sixteen was sentenced to ten years' imprisonment in Florida's Raisford Penitentiary for stealing $160. He escaped, was captured, and then was chained in a solid steel cell called "the Cage." The slightly built teenager from a broken home was then placed in a cell with seventeen others and subjected to sexual assault. Lacking the financial means for an appeal, he could not hope for release until the age of forty-eight.[46]

The problem, Berton argued, was not that of the justice or penitentiary systems alone. All of society was in some respects to blame for such
cruelty and harsh punishment. Two Progressive Conservative members
of the Ontario provincial parliament had attacked him publicly, accusing him of "pouring out sympathy for the criminal" and wanting to
"mollycoddle" wrongdoers. But Berton was making a larger point; he
believed "that as long as we continued to condone the use of the lash
and the strap we bear the marks of a sadist society."[47]

Sometimes Berton simply stumbled upon stories that demanded to
be brought into the light of day. In the last week of 1959, he and Janet
drove to Orillia with their old friends Gerry and Elizabeth Anglin and the
Anglins' mentally challenged twelve-year-old son, Mark. The boy had
been with his parents during the Christmas holidays, but otherwise was
a patient who lived in the Ontario Hospital School in Orillia. Berton was
greeted by staff and patients like a visiting rock star; they surrounded
him, at least one person with an autograph book in hand.[48] But he was
just as interested in them, and the hospital visit turned into a reporter's
investigation. He was shocked by what he witnessed. More than two
thousand patients were crowded into facilities which, he reported,
"would be heavily taxed if 1,000 patients were removed." Many of the
buildings were old and decrepit, little more than fire traps. Signs of
neglect were evident everywhere he looked. The stench of human waste
was inescapable, absorbed into wooden floors. One area contained a
single washbasin for 64 patients; another housed one bathtub for 144
people. Ninety beds were crammed into a room designed for seventy. The
overcrowding grew worse year by year, with no signs of relief in sight.

"Remember this," Berton wrote. "After Hitler fell, and the horrors of
the slave camps were exposed, many Germans excused themselves
because they said they did not know what went on behind those walls;
no one had told them. Well, you have been told about Orillia."[49] The
column, published in January 1960, caused a sensation. The next day,
the Ontario CCF leader, Donald C. MacDonald, toured the institution
and declared its conditions "intolerable." Confronted with Berton's
words, Ontario Health Minister Dr. M.B. Dymond admitted that the
charges were true. In reporting the story on its front pages the *Star*
quoted from Berton's column: "Orillia's real problem is one of public
neglect. It is easier to appropriate funds for spectacular public projects

such as highways and airports than for living space for tiny tots with clouded minds."[50]

The public outcry was such that in its next Throne Speech, the Ontario government announced that it would provide an increase of funds for more hospitals. Four months later, after Janet Berton read a report in one of the Toronto dailies about the death of a child at the Orillia hospital, she wrote to the Ontario minister of health and enclosed a clipping of the story. She also noted the lack of improvement to facilities, the shortage of staff, and the overcrowding. Dymond replied that her letter had been "the subject of a discussion" between the premier and himself, apologized for the circumstances, and thanked her for her "very keen personal interest in the matter of these unfortunate children." That month, patients began to be removed from the older Orillia hospital buildings and sent to better facilities elsewhere.[51]

Pierre Berton's hard-hitting pieces about crime, punishment, and social conditions were all the more effective because readers came upon them unexpectedly. So it was on October 5, 1959, the day after a column on the Arthur Murray Dance Studio, when Berton weighed in on the case of Steven Truscott. Five days earlier, a judge and jury had sentenced fourteen-year-old Truscott to death by hanging for the brutal sex slaying of twelve-year-old Lynne Harper. On entirely circumstantial evidence, the boy had been found guilty of her murder. A *Toronto Star* editorial on October 2 called the verdict "a travesty of Canadian justice,"[52] but its measured prose appealed only to the reasoning mind, not the compassionate heart, and its message was blunted by a flat concluding paragraph about prison reform and industrial schools. In contrast, Berton's column three days later consisted of a stark poem titled "Requiem for a Fourteen-Year-Old":

> *In Goderich town*
> *The sun abates*
> *December is coming*
> *And everyone waits;*
> *In a small, stark room*
> *On a small, hard bed*
> *Lies a small, pale boy*
> *Who is not quite dead.*

The cell is lonely
The cell is cold
October is young
But the boy is old;
Too old to cringe
And too old to cry
Though young, –
But never too young to die.

It's true enough
That we cannot brag
Of a national anthem
Or national flag
And though our Vision
Is still in doubt
At last we've something
To boast about:
We've a national law
In the name of the Queen
To hang a child
Who is just fourteen.

The law is clear:
It says we must
And in this country
The law is just.
Sing heigh! Sing ho!
For justice blind
Makes no distinction
Of any kind;
Makes no allowance for sex or years,
A judge's feelings, a mother's tears;
Makes no allowance for age or youth
Just eye for eye and tooth for tooth –
Tooth for tooth and eye for eye:
If a child does murder
The child must die.

. . . .

In Goderich town
The trees turn red
The limbs go bare
As their leaves are bled
And the days tick by
As the sky turns lead
For the small, scared boy
On the small, stark bed
A fourteen-year-old
Who is not quite dead.[53]

Berton composed this emotionally charged verse in what he later called "a black fury," and he did not address the question of Steven Truscott's guilt or innocence.[54] What outraged and sickened him was the simple fact that a statute existed in Canada allowing the execution of a child, and that "the authorities had no intention of carrying out this grisly sentence. They didn't intend to kill him, only to torture him by pretending."

Berton's condemnation of the Truscott sentence unleashed a firestorm of reaction in a province already divided over Truscott's culpability, the fairness of the trial, and the question of capital punishment. Normally unflappable, he was taken aback by its ferocity. One man phoned to say that he hoped one of Berton's daughters would be raped by a sex fiend. A woman said that if she had been Truscott's mother, she would have killed the boy herself. Berton was accused of attacking the judicial system, the Queen, and the town of Goderich.[55]

On the Saturday following Berton's "requiem" for Truscott, the *Star* published a lead editorial insisting that action was needed to initiate an appeal of the sentence of capital punishment. A few days later, he answered his critics. "I am past being angered by this kind of response," he wrote, "only saddened by its violence and lack of reason." No one seemed to have grasped his argument: "We have reached a point in time where there are other solutions than the noose."[56]

Berton sympathized, however, with one group of correspondents – those who, "in honest bewilderment," asked why he had written his requiem for the fourteen-year-old boy and not for his victim. There could be no doubt that the original crime was horrific, he said; but about "the second crime, the Truscott verdict," there existed great public debate. That was why he had taken his stand. "The murder of one child by another, in hot blood, is horror enough," he wrote. "The murder of a second child by society, in cold blood, is horror piled on horror. And the cheerful agreement that this second murder is only a sham – a ghastly little game of cat and mouse – is horror unspeakable."

One reader of Berton's "requiem" and its attendant publicity was the Toronto writer and social activist Isabel LeBourdais, whose own son was fourteen in 1959. She obtained a copy of the 2,500-page transcript of the Truscott trial and became convinced the boy was innocent and wrongfully convicted. In a letter to Jack McClelland in 1963, LeBourdais wrote, "My effectiveness in freeing Steven will be directly related to the amount of public opinion I can arouse on his behalf."[57] A magazine article she planned to write became instead a book, *The Trial of Steven Truscott*, published in March 1966. It was a strongly argued case for the defence – "a moral duty," she wrote, "that would involve my life until the duty was done."[58]

The Trial of Steven Truscott went on to become a bestseller. The original printing of 15,000 copies was immediately snapped up. On April 19, 1966, a press release from McClelland & Stewart, the book's Canadian publisher, announced the fifth print run, bringing the number of copies in print to 100,000. Only a day earlier, the solicitor general of Ontario had announced that a formal review of the Truscott case would take place. A year later the Supreme Court of Canada upheld the lower court's conviction, but by then public opinion across the nation reflected the belief, widespread and growing, that Truscott's trial had been flawed and unfair. In 1969, after a decade in prison, he was placed on parole.

The penultimate chapter of *The Trial of Steven Truscott* is called "Requiem," and it gives credit to Pierre Berton for having first drawn public attention to the fate of Steven Truscott, reproducing "Requiem for a Fourteen-Year-Old" in full. Truscott's struggles were far from over, and for many people justice had not yet been done. But because of a poem and the book it helped inspire, the Truscott case was not to fade from Canadian memory. The hanging Pierre had witnessed at Oakalla in the late forties was something he had not forgotten, and the notion of hanging a boy in his mid-teens repulsed him. So too did the trend to view capital punishment as just another variety of spectacle, a development he had satirized in an early work of fiction in which execution by hanging had become entertainment perfect for the age of television.

Berton also drew attention to the issue of racial discrimination. He informed his readers of an Ontario government form that parents of newborn children received – number 68(4)13-1691 – that asked them to identify the racial origins of their child in order to register the birth, and threatened them with a fine or jail time if they failed to comply. This made filling out the form rather difficult for Berton's friend Ray Silver, whose grandparents hailed from the United States and Alsace-Lorraine, whose wife was Irish on her mother's side and English on her father's, and who knew that his own body contained "a fair amount of Semitic blood . . . from one side of the Urals or the other." Quite apart from the repugnance he felt at the nature of the request, Berton objected because attributing racial origin on the basis of the country from which the male parent came made no sense. His own ancestors had lived in North America since 1681, and before that hailed from France and Germany. "What, then, is my racial origin? I say it is Canadian. . . . After eleven generations am I still a Frenchman, rather than a North American? Are my children, who are half Scottish, to be listed as French because 300 years ago one of my ancestors was a Huguenot?" The time had come, he insisted, to end such misleading and dangerous practices based on long-debunked notions of racial purity. Racial origins? "Mammal" was good enough for him.[59]

The *Front Page Challenge* host Fred Davis and his wife, Jo, ran up against discrimination of another sort when they convinced some neighbours in their Port Credit subdivision to provide financial sponsorship for one of the fifteen thousand Europeans who, fifteen years after the war, still lived in camps for the dispossessed. Refugee and welfare agencies were keen on the idea, but red tape in Ellen Fairclough's Department of Immigration, involving the length of sponsorship and the religious affiliation of sponsors, imposed insurmountable barriers. As Berton pointed out, it was easy to sponsor a strong immigrant for your farm or a skilled one for your factory, but for "the truly unselfish sponsor" Canadian Immigration had no place. "If you are a small community which believes that you *are* your brother's keeper," he wrote, "that you want nothing out of it except the knowledge that you have helped your fellow-man, that you are willing to take anybody at all as long as the need is there – then the problem is much more complicated." Meanwhile, with World Refugee Year half over at the end of 1959, Fred and Jo Davis and their neighbours waited for their refugee to arrive.[60]

Berton told the story of an Italian immigrant named Ange D'Angelo, a man with a good education and work experience but whose Italian accent marked him as a "DP," the derisive postwar term for displaced persons. His life in Canada had been a litany of discriminatory acts against him.[61] Other columns recounted the political discrimination faced by a Finnish woman because of an earlier affiliation with Communist organizations, and the colour bar enforced in the Avenue Road clubhouse of the Overseas Visitors' Association, a club run by white South Africans. Yet more dealt with a Toronto landlord's refusal to rent apartments to black people and the CPR's failure to promote a black Canadian from sleeping car porter to sleeping car conductor because of his colour.[62]

"The time has come for this country to take a stand on the subject of South Africa," Berton wrote a few weeks after South African police shot and killed sixty-nine black men, women, and children in Sharpeville in March 1960. "I mean a forthright and ringing statement from the prime minister of this country, announcing to the world that the Commonwealth is no longer big enough to embrace both South Africa and Canada and that one of them will have to get out." Canada protested atrocities in Hungary and refused to deal with Communist China and other countries outside the "so-called Free World," but with respect to South Africa and its system of apartheid it remained utterly silent, thanks to "the myth that the Commonwealth [was] sacred and must be held together at all costs." The reality, he said, was that the Commonwealth's only current value was that it preserved "the illusion of a long-dead British Empire."[63]

The following Sunday, he attended a rally at Massey Hall to raise funds for victims of the Sharpeville massacre and appeared on stage as a member of the Committee of Concern for South Africa. The next day his column called for a national boycott of South African goods. He condemned the Ontario government for expressing little concern about apartheid and violence. He criticized the editorialists of the *Star* for "pretending that the Commonwealth is a sort of Little League U.N." The whole situation reminded him, he said, "of the what-we-should-or-shouldn't-do-about-Nazi-Germany discussions that raged on the campus back in 1937 when I was a college freshman." It would be shameful, he added, if Canada, "the oldest and most powerful member of the Commonwealth," failed to provide serious leadership.[64]

Berton also tackled the issue of anti-Semitism, which he knew existed at all levels of Canadian society. He revealed, for example, some "interesting political associates" of Watson Kirkconnell, president of Acadia University, one of Canada's most distinguished scholars and co-editor of the 1947 book *The Humanities in Canada*.[65] Kirkconnell may have been an Arnoldian humanist of purest spirit – he was indeed – but he was also a virulent anti-Communist who was a member of the Freedom Association of Canada, a group that claimed that fluoridation of the water supply was a Communist plot to addle the brains of North Americans and whose organ, the *Canadian Intelligence Service*, distributed free to members, preached a militantly Christian and anti-Semitic gospel. The United Nations, in its view, was "evil." Brotherhood Week was "the brainchild of organized Jewry," as was racial integration in American schools and the idea of a bill of rights for Canada. The magazine Kirkconnell received did back some causes: it firmly defended apartheid in South Africa, and it numbered among its heroes U.S. senator Joseph McCarthy and the Quebec fascist Adrian Arcand.[66]

If a conspiracy existed in Canada or elsewhere, Berton suggested, it was not one organized by Jews. He pointed out that the editor of the *Canadian Intelligence Service*, Ron Gostick of Flesherton, Ontario, was a member of a right-wing branch of the Social Credit movement. This group, called the National Federation of Christian Laymen, believed in the world conspiracy of Jews and accepted the truth of the well-known and infamous anti-Semitic forgery the Protocols of the Elders of Zion. One proud publication by the leader of these "Christian Gentlemen," Gary Carr, was a pamphlet called *The Synagogue of Satan*. Perhaps it was a coincidence, Berton noted, but the Toronto premises of the Freedom Association to which Kirkconnell was so devoted just happened to be the former premises of Social Credit – of which, until 1958, Alberta premier E.C. Manning was an executive member.[67]

Berton continued his attacks on anti-Semitism in Canada into the 1960s. He drew attention to a sixteen-part series called "The Abrahamic Covenant," written for the *Gospel Witness and Protestant Advocate*, by Dr. G.B. Fletcher, professor of theology at Toronto Baptist Seminary and circulated by the Jarvis Street Baptist Church. The columnist quoted typical passages: "Communism is a modern version of the Jewish world state. . . . There is only one group of people whose overthrow would affect every merchant on the face of the earth, and that is the international banking system which is controlled by World Jewry. . . . Zionism [is] an international militant Communist organization with a religious name. It is strictly a Jewish organization . . . dedicated to the establishment of one vast world kingdom, with the Jews as 'a new Aristocracy of spiritual grace.'"[68]

Several columns in 1960 took inspiration from the article Berton had published a dozen years earlier in *Maclean's* on anti-Semitism in the job market and in the resort industry. This time, he sent two sets of letters to 106 resort owners, requesting two weeks' accommodation for four people, including two children. Some letters were in the name of "Mr. Sol Cohen," others bore the name "Mrs. D.M. Douglas." To ensure that "Mr. Cohen" should have the advantage, Berton mailed the Cohen letters a day before those of Douglas.

Had anything changed since 1948? Not much. Eight resorts did not answer Mr. Cohen's letter, and Berton named them. Seven more informed Cohen that they had no accommodation, but offered it to Mrs. Douglas. Berton named those resorts, too. They included the Holiday Inn at Picton and the Kawartha Lodge in Lakefield. Quotations from the letters sent to Mr. Cohen and Mrs. Douglas indicated clearly that Cohen received what Berton called "the small, small hello."[69] This column stirred up so much discussion and consternation that Alan Borovoy, executive secretary of the Toronto and District Labour Committee for Human Rights, wrote to all the resorts in question except the one to which Berton had given "a clean bill of health" – Green Gables, in Muskoka – requesting clarification of their policies. Only a dozen resort owners replied, so Borovoy conducted his own investigation and demanded that Ontario's Anti-Discrimination Commission take further action.[70]

Berton's investigation of Jews, Gentiles, and jobs, making the same use of telephones, yielded rather better results. The Fair Employment Practices Act of 1950 had made questions about race and religion illegal, and in almost every instance both "Weinburg" and "Craig" received the same courteous treatment. In one case, however, Miss Weinburg was told the job was a junior one that would not interest her, while Miss Craig was encouraged to learn that she could "work up to a senior position." Discrimination still existed, but it had moved from the application form to the interview.[71]

The connection between journalism and the cause of social justice was in the Berton family genes. At the end of his first year as a *Star* columnist, Pierre wrote a tribute titled "The Best Known Columnist of His Day." Its subject was Phillips Thompson and his life as a writer and social activist. A tribute it certainly was, and a touching one at that. But equally unmistakable was the way Berton crafted the column to enhance his own public image.

At the end of the piece, he quoted from what he called the best epitaph offered by the press upon Thompson's death in 1933 – that of the *Toronto Star*: "The late Mr. Phillips Thompson was in his day a clear-sighted and just-minded journalist. He was one of the gentlest of men, but utterly incapable of pretending to agree in a matter of opinion with you or with the King of England if he did not so agree. There was a mild but firm force in him. . . . He spoke for the inarticulate, he was on the side of lost causes, he could show you that minorities, although outnumbered, were usually right."[72] Only at this point, at the column's conclusion, did Berton reveal that this good man, now "forgotten," had been his grandfather. The tactic connected the grandfather's life and virtues in the mind of readers with the persona of the grandson, also saying, in effect, *I am not a man to be forgotten*.

We should not conclude from this not-so-subtle manipulation of his readers that the views expressed in Berton's *Star* column were insincere; it was only that he was too canny about his own career and concerned for success to be content to wait for Fortuna's graces. The presentation of self Berton so carefully constructed later in his memoirs mimicked the cheerful spawn of Horatio Alger, portraying an earnest man, candid in manner and with a nose for news, to whom good things happened thanks to a little luck. But this was a man who organized his professional life such that he was always several columns and a couple of books ahead of schedule. It would be naive to think that Pierre Berton did not bring something of the same degree of calculation to the trajectory of his career.

The subjects of his columns constantly highlighted this ability to identify with others. The marginalized immigrant, the confused citizen, the conned customer, the powerless voter, the victimized inmate – these and others who lacked power and resources became the people to whom Berton devoted his time and interest. All this, along with the zany antics of a devotee of *Mad* magazine, he served up in the frenetic delicatessen that was "By Pierre Berton." After some two hundred weeks of daily columns, involving more than a million words, his image would be enlarged, his public persona given depth and moral resonance. The arrogance people suspected on *Front Page Challenge* was now, as often as not, viewed as confidence; the "know-it-all" attitude, the sign of a man not embarrassed to show that he understood what he was talking about and that he preferred straight talk to phony diffidence.

His colleagues in what he once called "the newspaper game" may have envied his success and at times found him irritating, but they could scarcely deny the extraordinary success of his newspaper work. In 1959, a jury awarded him the J.V. McAree Memorial Award for the best daily newspaper column in Canada. Holy Joe Atkinson would have approved.

16

THE DROP ON THIS WORLD

—

In September 1958, when Jack Scott learned that Pierre Berton was leaving *Maclean's* for the *Toronto Star*, his column "Our Town" had expressed his delight. Pierre's years at Canada's leading magazine had certainly been rewarding, he suggested, but the newspaper was where his friend belonged. "In terms of vitality a newspaper is a shout of urgency while the magazine is a murmur of introspection," Scott wrote; his hunch was that "this is what brought Pierre home." As a sort of "welcome back" gift, Scott sent his friend a copy of an essay by the journalist George Murray of the *Chicago American* – tips for Murray's son, who was thinking of following his father into the newspaper trade. Don't be bored or cynical, went Scott's summary, for the former is suicide and the latter "can dull a newsman's sensations." Above all, "live consciously," Scott quoted Murray as saying. "Consciousness isn't just a matter of being out of bed, dressed and walking. It's a trick of having the eyes, ears and mind in focus. Once this yoga-like concentration is mastered, newspapering becomes simple. Everything in life becomes grist for the newspaperman's mill, . . . he sees things hidden from other men. He's more enthusiastic, laughs more readily, excites other men's envy."[1] Scott had written the column out of affection, not worry, for he knew very well just how fully his protégé epitomized Murray's ideal.

Over the four years that followed, Berton's column in the *Toronto Star* made an impact unique in Canadian journalism. Himie Koshevoy was the *Star*'s city editor for a brief period, and he had a chance to observe Toronto newspaper readers on the subway. "I watched the people open their papers," he told Berton. "They all skipped page 1 and turned to your column."[2] Politicians and civil servants flipped to "By Pierre Berton" even before visiting the editorial pages.

This was especially the case early in 1959, when the column accused politicians in York Township, at the northwest edge of Toronto, of corruption. Public land was being sold under suspicious circumstances to private interests for amounts substantially less than their actual value. Beginning with "Some Questions about Sales of Real Estate in York Township," Berton provided a detailed forensic analysis of the relationship between politicians and developers, supplying in the process the names of suspect individuals along with a series of questions for which he hoped the authorities would seek answers.[3] Indignant local politicians vented their spleens over the accusations. Letters to the editor took extreme positions on the controversy and the muckraker who had started it. Soon, the government of Ontario found itself forced by Berton's evidence and highly charged public opinion to appoint a judicial inquiry. On May 5, 1960, Judge Joseph Sweet released his 266-page report. That day the lead headline in the *Toronto Star* read: "York Township 'Fertile for Corruption' – Judge."[4]

The Sweet report concluded that Berton's charges were accurate and justified. Individual misconduct existed, attitudes and practices were irregular, and the council had been "inept" and "negligent" in the sale of land. Within days, one York Council member had resigned, and he and three other men were under arrest. On May 12, a meeting of 750 township ratepayers demanded the resignation of the entire council. A *Star* editorial supported the irate citizens.[5]

The column also influenced its readers in less dramatic ways. Following an affectionate piece Berton wrote about the joy of owning a Siamese cat, Janet tried to buy her husband a second one, only to discover that Toronto pet stores had suddenly sold out of the breed.[6] When three precocious teenage boys from Forest Hill Collegiate wanted publicity for their favourite social cause, they sought out Berton at his office. One of them, Rick Salutin, had stumbled upon Berton's column in the *Star* on the very day it debuted and became hooked on its eclectic mix of subjects, among them the Peter Pan statue on St. Clair Avenue, not far from where he lived. "It never occurred to me that you could write lovingly, and read absorbedly, about streets you live on," he later wrote. Berton proceeded to interview the three students as if they were from some strange and exotic tribe. They maintained a tone of high seriousness, but he was more interested in finding out what they did for fun. When Salutin said he liked *Mad* magazine, Berton looked up from his notepad as if thinking, "Maybe there's hope for this kid." It was the discovery of Berton's extraordinary output that gave Rick Salutin a role model for engaged journalism. Berton, of course, turned their encounter into a column.[7]

It was characteristic of "By Pierre Berton" to take its readers seriously, offer them a forum of their own, and provide a sense of empowerment. Quite regularly the column consisted of readers' reactions and views on a range of subjects, pro and con – in this sense, Berton may well have invented the first routinely "interactive" newspaper feature. Titles convey something of their flavour. In the column's first few months: "Audience Reaction: About Soup, Radio, Dick and Jane" (October 22, 1958); "In Which Readers Discuss Beans, Bay Leaves, Spam and Coffee" (November 18, 1958); "In Which the Readers Take Over Almost Completely" (January 9, 1959). At the midpoint of its life: "Beefs – My Readers versus the Sacred Cows" (January 18, 1960); "My Readers Respond with Meals They Can't Forget" (November 2, 1960); "Readers' Comment: Can't Kids Make Their Own Fun?" (December 26, 1961). Near the end of its run: "Letters – to and from the Columnist" (June 4, 1962); "Please Don't Stop Writing Those Angry Letters" (August 21, 1962).

In 1961 and 1962, the crusading themes of the first two years continued. He remained the consumer's champion. He turned a column warning against "let me be your friend" financial ads into a three-part series, "The Moneylenders," attacking finance companies for their outrageous rates of interest. He criticized the United Appeal for its emotional manipulation: "its overworked symbol of the outstretched hand," he said, masked the fact that only one dollar in nine went to agencies dedicated to protecting children. He revealed that gangsters had brought the protection racket into the world of Bay Street stockbrokers. He spent a day on Toronto's skid row, writing about the harsh and dreary life of the "shifting, shabby throng" that lived on it, and he provided an update on the high cost of dying.[8]

One story in 1961 made front-page headlines. It told in detail of the brutal way Toronto police officers had broken up a Yorkville house party, and then, at the Don Jail, forced a number of women to strip, lie on a table, and undergo intimate examination. Charges of the illegal sale of liquor and of drunkenness were later dropped, but not before one woman lost her job thanks to the lurid publicity. As a result of the story, both the provincial government at Queen's Park and City of Toronto authorities became involved. Mayor Nathan Phillips, the Civil Liberties Association, and others demanded a full investigation. "Probe Don Jail 'Indignities' on Innocent Party Guests," blared the *Star*'s banner headline. Later in the month, the Metropolitan Toronto Police Commission suggested that "police use more restraint in handling house party raids."[9]

In his final year with the *Star*, Berton's column reflected his increasingly radical outlook. He stepped up his attack on the finance industry with a hard-hitting six-part series on the high cost of money – in the form of undisclosed charges added to the purchase price of certain consumer products and high interest rates for automobile financing and mortgages. He explained that he would not cross a picket line at the Royal York because the hotel considered certain of its workers to be "extra help" and therefore not worthy of regular benefits.[10]

A few days before the federal election of 1962, Berton declared that he intended to vote for the New Democratic Party, founded a year earlier to take the movement for social democracy, represented by the Co-operative Commonwealth Federation of the depression-laden 1930s, into the 1960s and a new era. This federal election was the first contested by the New Democratic Party and the first in which poll results were to be analyzed and predicted by the IBM 1401 computer. At the remarkably compact size of five feet high and three feet across and with a memory equal to a full fourteen kilobytes, it was, the CBC broadcaster Bill Murphy reported on the eve of the election, an "amazing machine."

Berton used his column to declare that the Diefenbaker government had left a trail of political and financial disillusionment, while the opposition Liberals had failed to come up with adequate policies on "the two great national issues – unemployment and health insurance." The NDP had no chance of forming a government, he admitted (as the CCF, it had been reduced to only eight members of Parliament in 1958, down from twenty-five a year earlier), but he insisted that he would not be wasting his ballot. "I shall vote for it because this nation desperately needs a substantial radical vote to stiffen the backbones of the

Progressively-More-Conservative-Liberals and goose them into some kind of bolder action. The old CCF was Canada's conscience, and without the presence in Parliament of that dedicated band of idealists we would barely be in the twentieth century. Does anybody really believe the old parties would now be talking about a national health scheme if the CCF hadn't led the way?"[11] Three days later, on July 18, John Diefenbaker's Progressive Conservative Party, which had been returned to office in 1958 with the largest majority in Canadian history, was reduced to a precarious minority government of 116 members. It had been blamed for the downturn in the Canadian economy, the cancellation of the program to build the Avro Arrow airplane, and the decline in the Canadian dollar.

Over the four years in which "By Pierre Berton" appeared – 1,200 words a day, five days a week – newspapermen across the country marvelled at the achievement. For most columnists, this alone constituted a full-time job. How did the man do it, along with everything else he produced? The Berton phenomenon itself became the hook in a mounting number of profiles. "Here's Pierre . . .," went the title of a March 1959 piece by Gordon Minnes in Montreal's upscale *Mayfair* magazine. "As recently as eight months ago," Minnes wrote, "few people would have recognized the Berton name. . . . Its bearer was still a virtual unknown tucked securely behind the scenes as managing editor of *Maclean's Magazine*. Since then the Berton face, the Berton voice, and the products of the remarkably prolific Berton typewriter have become known to millions not only in Canada but in the United States and overseas as well." Toronto's *Park Plaza Magazine* drew attention to what it called "the Berton syndrome." The man had become ubiquitous, it said; but the title of its profile reflected not criticism but pride: "Pierre Berton – Dynamo of Many Talents." Talent Berton possessed, in spades; the man showed depth as well as range. Had the Governor General's Awards committee not announced in May that he had won his second award in the non-fiction category, for *Klondike*?[12]

Later that year, June Callwood wrote a lengthy profile of Pierre Berton for the *Star Weekly* magazine. "A haughty, embarrassed, arrogant and shy redhead," she began, "Pierre Berton is currently a greater Canadian phenomenon than the Maritimes' Reversing Falls or the meteor crater in Ungava."[13] Perhaps her inspiration for the piece came from the unsatisfied curiosity of a friend who had worked with Berton for years but who continued to wonder – as did so many others – about the source of the man's relentless drive and his limitless energy.

Throughout his years at the *Star*, Berton showed no signs of tiring, much less losing his zest for life. In the fourth year of writing his column, he continued to appear weekly on *Front Page Challenge* and eleven times a day on CHUM radio with *Pierre Berton Speaks*, his short commentaries on hot topics. He also continued as a fixture on *Close-Up*. When the *Vancouver Sun* columnist Barry Mather visited Toronto, he was astonished at the degree of Berton's visible presence in the city. His mug was everywhere – on streetcar ads, billboards, newspaper boxes, and of course five times a week at the head of his column. "This is Pierre Berton's town," he declared.[14] Berton was no longer simply a first-rate columnist or a prizewinning author: he had become, in name and image, an identifiable commodity, and a highly valuable one at that.

Did any of his journalistic colleagues think back to Budd Schulberg's 1941 novel, *What Makes Sammy Run?*, whenever their thoughts turned to Pierre Berton's sudden fame? In the book, the veteran newspaper columnist Al Manheim, agonizingly conscientious, tries to figure out his young co-worker Sammy Glick, a crass opportunist one step removed from a street hustler, ambitious without bound, and always on the go. "Sammy Glick was teaching me something about the world," Manheim confessed. "Of course, I hadn't found out what made him run, and, lucky for him, I had no idea just where he was running. . . . It looked as if Sammy Glick had the drop on this world."[15]

Few if any would have called Pierre Berton an opportunist, at least not since his earliest days in the newspaper business. Careerist perhaps, but not opportunist: Berton's rise to eminence had come about at no co-worker's expense, and he had assisted many. Writers of the day attempted to describe the Berton magic, but none did better than Callwood in capturing the curious mix of braggadocio and sensitivity:

> No dervish ever whirled with a greater display of Roman rockets, water guns, tambourines, cries of "Eureka!," clouds of itching powder and flappings of gaudy cloth. He is part ticker-tape parade, with a drunken brass band, and part detached, cold machine operating an

assembly line with time-study precision. He is a galaxy of attitudes, the result of trying to superimpose toughness and boldness, which he admires extravagantly, over a self-conscious and flinching interior.[16]

The nation's journalists could write about the Berton phenomenon all they wanted, and they did. But no more than Al Manheim with Sammy Glick could any of them, even close friends like Callwood or Charles Templeton, explain what drove the man. "What makes Pierre tear?" Templeton had asked, rhetorically, thereby giving Callwood her title. Only one thing was clear to Berton's colleagues across the country, whether they admired or resented him. The veteran *Maclean's* columnist Sidney Katz stated it plainly in October 1962: "Berton makes all other Canadian columnists look like amateurs."[17]

Despite his great success at the *Toronto Star*, Berton did not want his reputation to rest on his work as a newspaper columnist. The main reason he had left *Maclean's* in the first place had been to find more time to write books. But he soon discovered that "By Pierre Berton" was as demanding as the managing editor's position at *Maclean's*. Still, Berton was a relentless, even joyful recycler of his life and works, so he continued the practice, once again working with Jack McClelland. From 1959 to 1963, they published four books together, each of which had its origin in Berton's columns for the *Toronto Star*.

Just Add Water and Stir, published late in 1959, provided a confection as eclectic as it was rich, self-described as "a random collection of satirical essays, rude remarks, used anecdotes, thumbnail sketches, ancient wheezes, old nostalgias, wry comments, limp doggerel, intemperate recipes, vagrant opinions, and crude drawings." On the title page, a photograph of Berton had him standing in a business suit and bow tie – eyebrows raised, arms and legs crossed – looking puzzled and leaning against the five words of the title stacked like blocks, as if propping himself up against the office water cooler. The book reflected his playful side. It included profiles of his friends and of celebrities he had met – Russell Baker, Glenn Gould, Charles Templeton, Milton Berle, Robert Service, among others – and profiles of a variety of magazines, from

Time and *Mayfair* to *Playboy*, *Mad*, and *Justice*. For good measure, *Just Add Water* also contained a number of Berton's favourite recipes, including those for tomato soup, baked beans, corned beef hash, and clam chowder.[18]

Jack McClelland's editorial staff consisted primarily of sharp-minded and skilful women, usually unmarried, and they did not quite know what to think or say about the collection of Berton columns. A well-researched and vivid history of the Klondike gold rush was one thing for these editors, usually with backgrounds in literature and language, to consider. But this kind of cheap grab bag? Some editors, and not only the women, had significant reservations about the content and sales potential of a seemingly random collection of newspaper pieces that half the people in Toronto had already read. But Berton was intent on seeing this collection into book form and Jack McClelland was eager to keep him as a regular M&S author. He was quite willing to let the two-time Governor General's Award winner have his way. From a commercial point of view, McClelland and his editors need not have worried. *Just Add Water and Stir* went into a second printing almost immediately, and reached a sixth printing within a year.[19] Still, disapproval lingered, like the ink of a new typewriter ribbon on an editor's fingers.

When a second collection, *Adventures of a Columnist*, appeared in the fall of 1960, its jacket copy bragged that Berton's newspaper column was "one of the most popular, one of the most controversial and one of the most widely-read daily columns ever written in this country" and that *Just Add Water and Stir* had been "an immediate best-seller."[20] The new Berton book, it suggested, was even better than its predecessor. *Adventures of a Columnist*, the blurb promised, offered a highly personalized, behind-the-scenes look at the business of writing a daily newspaper column. Berton admirers would learn the sources of his facts and ideas and the identities of his secret operatives, while those "less enthusiastic about Mr. Berton" would find "many controversial opinions that won't lower their blood pressure." The back cover featured a photo of the author, this time in the role of intrepid reporter. He now leaned against a brick wall at the corner of a dodgy downtown alley, the brim of his fedora down and the collar of his trench coat up – and with a frown worthy of George Raft – secure in the knowledge that he was safely costumed in the visual clichés of his trade.

Despite the campy playfulness of the photograph and the presence of the word "adventures" in its title, this book was more serious in content than *Just Add Water* had been. It contained several of Berton's most controversial columns, along with background commentary. The collection included his "Requiem" for Steven Truscott; a section on "the hard sell," including "Operative 67's Adventures in Arthur Murrayland"; another on fads and foibles of life in the twentieth century; one on "unsociable social comments" – for example, his reactions to the hospital in Orillia; and another on the power of nostalgia, with abundant evidence of Berton basking in it.[21]

As with *Just Add Water and Stir*, Jack McClelland made the author's celebrity, more than the book's content, the basis of his marketing strategy. On the front jacket of *Adventures of a Columnist*, the book's title was in a script that appeared handwritten above the author's name. The name itself occupied the bottom three-quarters of the cover, and the word "Berton" was in such large type that B E R spanned the full width of the cover, forcing T O N below it. The design gave the impression that this was not merely the name of an author but an abstraction, an important entity unto itself. This was the first Berton book designed by the graphic designer Frank Newfeld, and it marked the beginning of a decades-long association in which Newfeld, working closely with the author, helped create a look that shaped the distinctive visual appeal of a Berton book.

As each new collection of Bertoniana came along, members of the McClelland & Stewart editorial department struggled to reconcile uneven content with potential sales. Each year the author submitted a selection of his columns organized by theme, and each year McClelland's editors laboured to choose the best ones to publish. When they had received a copy of Berton's second collection for evaluation, they were already inclined to be skeptical. The senior editor Claire Pratt, daughter of the poet E.J. Pratt, liked the personal nature of "Twelve Hundred Words a Day," the original working title of *Adventures of a Columnist*. She thought this gave it an advantage over *Just Add Water and Stir*. Still, she wrote to McClelland, some of the selections were "over-Bertonized."[22]

Another editor, Ellen Stafford, was less charitable. "The fault," her reader's report began, "is not in our stars, but in the Star – or rather, in a daily stint of 1,260 words for instant publication. 'Just add Berton

and stir' – it's an extremely good deal for the Toronto Star, but ultimately, I think destruction for the writer." Still, she concluded that
after a careful culling of contents, this second book should be published. *Just Add Water* had, after all, sold 6,700 copies the previous fall.
At times the constant shuffle of columns and ongoing search for the
best title seemed to make the editors giddy, as when Stafford wrote in
a memo to Jack McClelland, "Here's Berton. Hey! Title! Seriously!
Here's Berton – and could go on *More Berton* for next book, *Still More
Berton*, and so on. . . ."[23]

Beneath the obvious desire to have McClelland & Stewart publish a
money-making book there existed within the editorial group an underlying tone of disappointment that the company for which they toiled
was willing to publish such apparent froth when works of greater literary or intellectual merit risked too little editorial attention and publicity. M&S vice-president Hugh Kane, for one, believed that his boss had
lavished too many resources on *Just Add Water and Stir*, especially after
Berton and McClelland held an expensive promotional party featuring
a cooking contest between the author and rival columnists.[24] So much
for the *gravitas* of a serious publisher, some thought.

Others questioned whether readers would tire of these books, so
similar in origin and content. "I hate to admit it," one editor confessed
in an internal memo about *Adventures*, "but these columns do look
pretty good. I just wonder though whether we won't run into the law of
diminishing returns." A book following so soon after *Just Add Water*
would likely not sell in the same numbers, complained another editor
to Claire Pratt. "It would be a case of going to the well too quickly. . . .
I have read so many of his columns they seem to have lost some of their
novel freshness." Pratt herself shared the view about a possible decline
in sales of the second Berton collection, although she did note that *Just
Add Water* had done well in western Canada, where few people had
access to the *Toronto Star*. In a handwritten note at the bottom of one
of her reports, Pratt wrote: "From what I have picked up at random
talking to people, many would buy another Berton to give next
Christmas to the same people they gave *Just Add Water* to last year. Can't
see it myself."[25]

Sales of *Adventures of a Columnist* were respectable in the year of its
release, but not as good as *Just Add Water and Stir* the year before. This

was not the breakthrough book McClelland had hoped for, but the record was good enough to keep him interested in more Berton collections. By the end of the decade, sales of *Adventures* reached 12,000 copies, but by then *Just Add Water* had reached 26,000.[26]

Despite the respectable sales record of both collections, Berton turned to another kind of project in 1961. He decided to write a book for youngsters like his own. Pierre the father detested children's books that patronized their readers, and he had no use for "pallid little tales about goody-goody moppets named Dick and Jane, or their dreadful cat, Puff."[27] Berton goofed around with his own children a good deal; no aloof fifties-style dad, he. The forty-year-old father, quite willing in his youth to be King Kong on a library roof, enjoyed telling them scary stories. The child in him knew that in the right circumstances children like to be spooked.

The Secret World of Og began as adventure story tailor-made for his own brood. "There were five children, counting the Pollywog, and their names all began with the letter P," the book began. "Why that should be no one was quite sure but Father said it was done purposely so that it would be easier to divide up the silverware when they all got married." The book identified each of its characters – Penny, Pamela, Patsy, Peter, and Paul ("the Pollywog") – and as the tale progressed, each character developed traits that distinctly resembled those of the five children to whom the story had originally been told.

The "Og" of the title was a member of a mysterious subterranean race that Pamela stumbles upon one day when a "tiny little saw" appears mysteriously from the floorboards in the playhouse the children share in the woods near their home. But "Og" was also an affectionate Berton nod in the direction of Frank Baum and *The Wizard of Oz*, one of his childhood favourites. Before long the children are off, like Dorothy, on their adventure – not down a yellow brick road but into the pit beneath the trap door of the playhouse to a secret world populated by little green people, some nice, some not.[28]

Berton wrote the book during two vacations in Mexico and sent it to Knopf in New York, where a female editor declared its emphasis on the stuff of popular culture – "comic books, series books, and TV programs" – to be offensive, as if such references tainted any literary quality the book might have. When Pierre sought Jack McClelland's advice, both a New York children's editor McClelland turned to and his own editorial staff responded in a like manner. The New York editor thought the book in "very bad taste" because it appeared to be "spoofing the attitude of teachers and librarians." Some M&S editors were no less critical. Responding to a passage revealing that the Pollywog liked "gum drops, steak, licorice cigarettes, and Dr. Kleeb's pet food," but not Pablum, one reader declared: "This will certainly not endear us to the manufacturers of Pablum and, after all, it is the accepted baby food." Others at McClelland & Stewart were less harsh. One thought the book had potential, "because of the author's name," but "had it been written by an unknown it couldn't be given very serious consideration without substantial revision. I hope Mr. Berton will revise because it is not calculated to enhance his reputation as it stands." Only one editor liked the book as it was, finding it "a charming story which would have a great appeal for children."[29]

Despite the editors' mixed reviews, Berton stood firm in the conviction that his book, written *about* real children *for* real children, marked a departure from conventional juvenile fiction and would find a strong readership. The stiff-backed guardians of children's imaginations had closed rank, Berton told McClelland in an angry letter, because they were "engaged in a vast conspiracy to take the guts out of juveniles." In short, they underestimated the complex minds of children, and in the spring of 1961, Berton, with five children thirteen or younger and another baby on the way, had done his research.

Jack McClelland half-heartedly defended his editors' verdict, telling Berton that in his personal view "the weakness of the book" was "that you grind a lot of private axes and prejudices." This was a curious charge. The book certainly contained opinions and themes, but they concerned such subversive notions as the sanctity of childhood innocence and the thrill of mischievous sibling adventure, the high worth of comic books and the futility of learning by rote, the waste of war, and the dangers of judging creatures by their colour. The author refused to revise or soften it. McClelland decided to publish the work anyway, but continued to express reservations about content and sales potential to Hugh Kane. Nevertheless, he told his vice-president to "indulge" Berton "as much as possible" and to treat the book "as a priority item."[30]

McClelland & Stewart published *The Secret World of Og* in the fall of 1961, and Little, Brown quickly picked it up in the United States. McClelland had conceded to Berton in his letter of February 14 that his success as an author had come because he had been right far more often than he had been wrong. The sales figures confirmed Berton's judgment once again. Customers purchased 8,284 copies of the book between its release and midsummer 1962. Reviews were fine, but word-of-mouth enthusiasm spread unexpectedly by schoolteachers was better. By 1970, sales of *The Secret World of Og* would reach 14,000, climbing by the mid-1980s to well above 70,000.[31] Inspired by the story and by the pictures by the veteran Canadian magazine illustrator William Winter, hundreds of children over the decades would write to the book's author to express their love of *The Secret World of Og*, thanking him with drawings of scenes from the book. These letters gave Pierre Berton more satisfaction than any others he received, and he tried to respond with a personal note to each young fan.

Berton spent as much time with his family as he could, given his hectic schedule, but this was not easy. His crusades for the *Star* kept him at the office for long hours, and his work as a lead interviewer for *Close-Up* took him away on a number of overseas trips. When he first joined the *Star*, he had requested an annual five-week holiday. Beland Honderich agreed, but suggested that two of the weeks should be "disguised as an assignment."[32] As a result, Berton's travels produced several multi-part series of columns and *Close-Up* interviews. Janet accompanied him on these busman's holidays whenever circumstances permitted. The CBC and the *Star* saved money by splitting costs. In 1959 and 1960, Pierre escaped from the office and travelled to the Middle East and Russia, England and continental Europe, the United States and Japan. The experience broadened his perspective and in significant ways began to alter his outlook, especially toward the United States.

He flew to Cairo with a four-man CBC *Close-Up* film crew in April 1959 with the intention of interviewing Gamal Abdel Nasser, the controversial president of Egypt. They waited, but Nasser proved inaccessible and they found themselves instead making a documentary about contemporary Egypt. In a series of incidents, Berton noticed something significant about the direction of modern life outside of North America. It began when he was offered "refreshments" in the office of a high Egyptian official. The drink turned out to be Pepsi-Cola – surely, he thought, a most unusual choice of beverage for Middle Eastern officialdom. He learned that the best restaurant in Cairo was called the St. James, a name so terribly British in resonance. Sure enough, it was the very replica of a Pall Mall club. But at an outdoor theatre visible from the restaurant's balcony, the film on the screen was a Hollywood monster movie starring Alan Ladd, called *Invaders from Mars*. Near the end of the trip, he and his crew went to a nightclub they had heard about, located beyond the pyramids. There it was, complete with restless camels, Nubians in Turkish dress, delicious-smelling kebabs and strange tents. Yet the live music they could hear turned out to be saxophones playing "Deep in the Heart of Texas."

On his return to Toronto, Berton wrote two columns about the misconceptions people held about the Middle East, and another called "Some Notes about the Spread of Coca-Colism." Hotels around the world were becoming indistinguishable, he lamented. Employees wore the Hilton version of native dress, not the real thing. "I have an awful feeling," he wrote, "that in the One World of the future the band will always stand ready to play 'Deep in the Heart of Texas;' that Alan Ladd and Vistavision will be just around the corner; and that every drug store will have a doughnut-making machine in the window."

"The old imperialists of the 19th century," he added, had been "turned in," but in their place stood "the new models who represent the Cultural Imperialism of the 20th. The new models are often pleasant enough young couples from Wisconsin," people who – as one of Berton's more cynical colleagues quipped – "'insure themselves with Mutual of Omaha, read *Holiday* magazine and keep a set of International Silverware in their dining-room table.'" These people were "nice enough to know," Berton concluded. "But in their own way they are just as dangerous as those cloistered pukkah sahibs who lived, walled off from the real Egypt, in a dream hotel of their own contrivance – a little bit of old England which, on a certain January day, was ravaged, looted and utterly destroyed by the people who had for generations been on the outside looking in."[33]

A month later, the *Star* sent him abroad again, this time to the Soviet Union. Stepping off the plane, he found that the producer of *Close-Up*, Ross McLean, had already arranged for the cameraman Erik Durschmied to photograph his arrival. The Cold War seemed to be thawing under Nikita Khrushchev, Stalin's eventual successor, and Berton wanted to find out whether life in the Soviet Union had improved since the brutal dictator's death in 1953. He found Moscow's thousand-room Hotel Ukraine a larger and more ornate version of Ottawa's Château Laurier, but at a bargain-priced $4.50 a day for two. At an upscale Moscow café, Durschmied introduced him to a beautiful young woman who worked at the perfume counter of the famous GUM Department Store. She had not yet tasted Coca-Cola, but swooned at the mere mention of Sinatra and had become a Sarah Vaughan fan from listening to The Voice of America on radio. She knew the lyrics of "Blue Moon" and was trying to master the hula hoop.

"It occurred to me then," Berton later wrote, "as it was to occur to me again in other foreign climes, from Tokyo to Budapest, that no political system, no ruthless dictatorship could withstand for long the creeping tide of American pop culture. . . . Some would see it as a dream come true; others might view it as a nightmare."

Gorky Street shops had the full range of American-style consumer goods, but few Russians could afford them. Still, the signs of Coca-Colism were there to be seen – even, improbably, in Moscow, when a Chevrolet Impala driven by a black American man rounded the corner at ten o'clock one night. The *Holiday on Ice* show from the United States had been giving nine shows a week for eight weeks, with twelve thousand people attending each performance. "Indeed," Berton wrote, "this ice show is to Moscow what the Bolshoi Ballet has been to New York."[34]

After his week in Russia, he shut himself in his Kleinburg bedroom, which still doubled as his office, and in an afternoon wrote three columns for the *Toronto Star* and twenty-two items for CHUM, and then drove into Toronto for his appearance on *Front Page Challenge*.[35]

A trip to Western Europe in September 1959 came as a relative disappointment. Of London he had little to say, except that Madame Tussaud's waxworks gave tourists just what it advertised: "dolls, slightly overpainted." The figures could not compare with those in the mausoleum at Red Square, where visitors could view "every pockmark on

Stalin's face" and "every tiny hair at the fringe of Lenin's goatee." The art reproductions peddled by "little men with pencil-thin moustaches" outside the Louvre in Paris were a distinct improvement over Tussaud's, but these colourful artisans seemed a dying breed.

On the glamorous Côte d'Azur, the playground of princesses and aristocrats, Berton learned that the most sought-after place for a rendezvous was a coastal resort called Juan-les-Pins. He went there: "What a let-down! Here was Coney Island, Miami Beach, Broadway and 42nd all rolled into one. The air was filled with music all right, but it was Rock and Roll. The streets were jammed with teenagers. Coca Cola flowed like tears and the friendly Pharmacie had been replaced by a Drug Store." The town's casino featured a dance marathon of the sort popular in North America in the thirties, and its "cultural festival" turned out to be devoted neither to film nor music but to "Festival Sex," a nightly event at which contestants stripped before a panel of judges.

Italy proved unremarkable. Berton kept running into Canadians and couldn't buy a pizza, even in Pisa. Outside the Sistine Chapel, he encountered "an unending river of tourism"; inside, the crowd gesticulated and shouted. "It was Babel," he later told readers of the *Star*; "it was Grand Central Station; it was the Toronto subway at 5 o'clock." But once he raised his head toward the ceiling, "the Babel faded, the words of the guides grew dim, the hubbub ceased . . . the throngs of tourists vanished, and only the silence of four centuries remained. I had been right after all. When you gaze upon Michelangelo's great ceiling, you are always alone."

Aboard the aircraft on his way home he began to compose the next few columns in his head, as he did each day on the hour-long commute from Kleinburg. After sampling the on-board meal, he had one more idea. The final column of the series on his European holiday featured his open letter to the president of Trans-Canada Airlines, complaining about the "handy-dandy, pre-cooked, pre-chewed, half-warmed TCA dinners."[36]

In July 1960, Berton went to Los Angeles, heartland of the new America, to cover the Democratic Party leadership convention. At his hotel, miles from the site of the convention, Duncan Macpherson was there to meet him. It had been at Berton's urging, first, that Beland Honderich had lured the brilliant if inflammable cartoonist away from

Maclean's to the *Star* and, second, that Macpherson had agreed to cover the convention with him. When they met in Los Angeles, the artist was already well fortified. Later, in the lobby of the Biltmore Hotel, crowded with delegates, Macpherson told Berton that the scene reminded him of "the crowd leaving the Food Products Building at the Canadian National Exhibition."

At the convention itself, Berton was especially interested to see how television was changing presidential politics, and he soon discovered that at this political event, the first beamed to American homes in colour, just about everything was pre-scripted for the tube. In the absence of hard news, the 950 working journalists had turned to rewriting each other's stories. Berton and Mike Wallace commiserated over this. "Journalistic incest" was the phrase Wallace used.

The political speeches had an air of irrelevance about them. The keynote address by Senator Frank Church of Idaho had been leaked to the press before it was delivered, leaving only the gullible to think that the editorial speculations of the *Los Angeles Times* about what he might say possessed any prescience. In Berton's view, Church's speech was "a flabby piece of propaganda," ordinarily unworthy of coverage, but in L.A. that week, it was hot stuff.

Berton was not especially impressed either by the debate between the candidates Lyndon Johnson and John F. Kennedy or by the battle on the convention floor between the camps of Kennedy and Adlai Stevenson, Kennedy's main opponent. Berton's view was that Kennedy won the debate with Johnson mainly because of the "star status" the media lavished on him. The professionalism of Stevenson's organized hoopla reminded Pierre of the Hitler Youth. The Kennedy clan, meanwhile, stood stoically in their box, confident in the knowledge that Stevenson had few delegate votes. When Kennedy gave his victory speech, he did so without emotion, speaking crisply, and "with the air of a man who had it in the bag from the beginning."[37]

On one dull day during the last week of the Democratic convention, Pierre paid a visit to the Hollywood studios of Ziv Television, which had purchased the television rights to *Klondike*. The studio had produced such popular series as *Highway Patrol* (1955–59, starring Broderick Crawford) and *Sea Hunt* (1957–61, featuring Lloyd Bridges), and was a pioneer in television syndication. Under the leadership of founder

Frederick W. Ziv, the company had marketed its products by passing over the networks and selling directly to regional sponsors which then placed the shows with local stations. For the proposed Klondike series, Berton was a paid consultant, ready to answer any questions the film-makers might have of him during his visit to California.

What about foliage? a member of the production team asked. Mainly birch and aspen, dominant in the deciduous forests of the North, he answered. Pines? Maybe. Oaks? No. Too bad, said the pro-duction man. All southern California could offer was pines and oaks, so pines and oaks it would be. Not many scenes would feature snow; too expensive. So was mud, although it had been used in the pilot film. The production man asked whether Sweet Caporal was the cigarette of choice in the Klondike. Cigars, not cigarettes, were in vogue back then, Berton replied, especially in gold-rich Dawson. Production Man nixed the idea: the show was sponsored by a cigarette company.

Berton reminded him that to be authentic, the series should feature actors from various ethnic and racial backgrounds, since the Klondike gold rush had drawn people from around the world. "The sponsor was very firm," said Production Man. "No Negroes. . . . No coloured people at all." Pierre suggested that all the male actors should sport handlebar moustaches, because that was the fashion in the 1890s. This, too, Production Man rejected. People would think the show was a comedy, a western with a bunch of Groucho Marxes. At the end of the session, Berton was informed that his technical advice had been absolutely invaluable. He was not invited back.[38]

Later, he learned that the script for the first episode had been written by Sam Peckinpah, the director was William Conrad (later star of the detective show *Cannon*), and one of the actors was James Coburn, aged thirty-one. Still, the series, which began its run in the fall of 1960, was poor, very much the American horse opera one might have expected from the producer of *Tombstone Territory* and *Bat Masterson*. After a few episodes it faded from sight.[39]

Within a month Pierre was with Janet in Japan. The trip produced a six-part series for the *Star*, along with a half-dozen side stories. He had not been to Tokyo since the Korean War, and found that with the country's headlong rush to modernize its social and cultural life had come an uneasy combination of the old and the new, of centuries-old tradition and rapid innovation. He investigated the Japanese economy and its seemingly contradictory mix of low wages and generous company benefits, a strange marriage of capitalist parsimony and almost medieval paternalism. According to the management expert Peter F. Drucker, Berton noted, Japanese industrial benefit packages were the equivalent of three times the wages paid. On a visit to Tokyo's huge Takashimaya Department Store he noticed that almost every window mannequin wore a traditional kimono, yet bore a white Caucasian face and blond hair – "no more Japanese than Toby Robins," he observed. This took him to the crowded office of a plastic surgeon whose clinic performed a hundred operations a day, many on women who wanted to have their eyes westernized. He interviewed its director on the conflict between the traditional geisha and Western styles of beauty.

Janet and Pierre visited Hiroshima, and discovered that a large new industrial city of half a million people had risen from the ruins of the atomic conflagration that in 1945 had left only forty-five structures intact. Most of its residents had come from other parts of Japan. Pierre found the city's Peace Memorial Museum disturbing. Its exhibit of artifacts and photographs, he wrote, "for sheer horror outdoes every-thing save the relics of Belsen and Buchenwald." Perhaps it was only his imagination, he conceded in the column that inevitably followed, but "I seemed to feel the eyes of the little Japanese boring into my back as I stared at those terrible pictures of heaped and peeling human bodies." The rising tone of outrage in his column would have escaped few readers. "The Germans, we are told, were stunned by motion pic-tures showing the horrors of the extermination camps. No sensitive Westerner can escape the same sense of guilt in the museum of Hiroshima. We roasted people to death over a slow fire. . . . We tortured them as surely as the Nazis tortured the Jews."

Later, in the beautiful city of Kyoto, the Bertons arranged through city officials to visit the home of a "typical Japanese family" to learn about Japanese domestic life. The man who greeted them turned out to be a mine owner and most of his house boasted Western-style furniture. "This typical Japanese family," Berton wrote, "was about as typical as John David Eaton's would be in Toronto." Still, he found the family tea ceremony enchanting – its "every movement formalized" and its purpose "the enjoyment of all the senses." The aesthetic side of Japanese culture appealed to him. He delighted in Japanese meals, "where every morsel of food is arranged like a brush stroke on a palette, and where every dish is a miracle of craftsmanship and taste," and he found himself almost overwhelmed by the beauty and serenity of Japanese gardens.

At the stone garden of the Ryoanji Temple in Kyoto, laid out centuries earlier by a Zen Buddhist monk, he committed a faux pas. Mesmerized by the way the Zen artist had grouped the stones perfectly, creating an atmosphere of harmony, he gazed out at the garden for some time and then looked at his watch and remarked to the guide that if he did not leave immediately he and Janet would miss their lunch. "Ah, yes. Of course, the stomach must come before the soul," said the accommodating guide. "It was a stupid thing to do," Berton admitted to his readers, an embarrassment that troubled him for the rest of his visit.

Everywhere Pierre went in Japan, signs of the uneasy juxtaposition of West and East, modern and traditional, struck him, and he took advantage of every opportunity to experience both. One night he and Janet stayed at a traditional Japanese inn, bathing in a beautiful room, complete with steaming hot pools. The next morning they enjoyed a succulent seven-course breakfast, followed by tea. "I wouldn't have missed it for the world," he wrote.[40]

Nor would he have missed playing armchair anthropologist in this foreign culture. He took note that, as a nation of "enthusiasts," the Japanese exulted in every fad that came along. In 1960, it was "Winkie," a black inflatable doll. Earlier, it had been the hula hoop. Chocolate was another obsession – including chocolate makeup, face powder, and lipstick. Black performers such as Harry Belafonte and the Mills Brothers were very popular. Latin music dominated nightclub acts; not long before it had been rockabilly. A young man Berton encountered knew Canada as "the land of Paul Anka." Hip Japan seemed to be a place where genuine Japanese beatniks patronized a host of coffee houses, where people came to tears listening to "Auld Lang Syne," and where the monk at the Shinto shrine called the sacred deer home to the tune of Beethoven's Sixth Symphony.

Once home himself, Berton took the measure of his experience. Is Japan going Western? he asked. He thought not. "Japan has a habit of taking the customs of foreign lands and making them her own," he wrote. Some fads would be forgotten, others would take on "a Japanese flavour." He recalled the words of a Japanese friend: "We arouse easily. We forget easily too. After all, that's how it was with the war."[41]

Berton's attitude toward popular culture and the homogenization of culture – for which he had coined the term *Coca-Colism* – was ambivalent and at times contradictory, and it would remain so. The Canadian nationalism he had acquired during his days with Ralph Allen had gradually weakened, and in various columns on the Canadian identity he admitted that the future of Canada depended on its relationship with the United States.[42] His sojourns abroad reawakened the nationalist impulse in him. He now recognized the phenomenon of American-led globalization (although he did not use the term), and he witnessed the baneful effect it had on indigenous customs and traditions. There was more than a streak of anti-modernism in him, and very often his *Star* columns were given over to nostalgic evocations of old customs or artifacts in the face of the new and often alarming world of planned obsolescence and disposable tradition in which he lived. It was as if, when he greeted each new social or technological advance, he felt compelled to imbue it with the authenticity of the tried, the true, and the familiar.

Berton was a man driven to invoke the past and to gain a glimpse of the future. Disneyland fed both the need and the desire. A few weeks after he returned from the Democratic convention in Los Angeles, he confessed to his editor and readers that at the moment Jack Kennedy was entering the packed Coliseum in triumph, their faithful correspondent was "actually in Frontierland taking a mine train to the painted desert." Pierre Berton spent twelve hours at Disneyland that day, and claimed to have been "the only visitor to ride every single ride and take in every single event in the space of one day." Everything in Disneyland was new and clean and bore "the touch of a master hand," he wrote. "Disney has understood the way to a small boy's heart; and perhaps more than any man in history he has understood that, at heart, we are all small boys."[43]

Berlin in August of 1961 was no Disneyland. The *Star* sent him there as soon as the Soviets began to erect a wall between the Soviet and western sectors of the city, and Janet went with him for companionship. They flew into Hamburg, rented a Volkswagen, and took the autobahn through the Soviet zone into Berlin, entering through the checkpoint at Helmstedt. For a full day they drove around the entire perimeter of the city, staying as close as they could to the border, and observing.

The wall had divided the city in ways that seemed surreal. Tenements that fronted on the western sector held their residents captive. The wall ran directly through the vestibule of a church in one locale and through a farmhouse in another. Pierre and Janet drove their Volkswagen to Checkpoint Charlie, and, on edge, entered East Berlin. Berton felt "detached from the real world in a way [he] had not felt in Moscow," experiencing "a small shiver of apprehension" as the car sped them past the site of Hitler's bunker. Stalinallee, East Berlin's prime boulevard, reminded Pierre of the cheerless sterility of the buildings on Toronto's University Avenue. They found the central core of Berlin "silent as a tomb," and they passed "shattered cathedrals, gutted department stores, smashed government buildings, and courtyards still heaped with mossy rubble after sixteen years of peace – block on block of age and decay, mould and desolation, spectral in the gathering dusk." He wondered why this held for him "a chilling familiarity." Then he knew: the streetscape reminded him of the Dawson of his childhood.[44]

Still, the couple thoroughly enjoyed their trip to Berlin. On their first morning they took an excursion by steamer on the Havel, a large lake near the western outskirts of the city. They spent leisurely evenings in sidewalk cafés, "toying with an aperitif and watching the world saunter by." They enjoyed memorable meals, including a Chinese dinner and a Danish lunch. One evening they went to the Resi, a large "dance palace" where by custom people arrived alone and wrote notes to the dance partners they desired. Both Bertons received one. The next day they had the messages translated. Janet's: "You're looking wonderful tonight, darling. It's too bad you are not alone!" Pierre's: "Isn't it about time you asked your wife to dance?"[45]

Later, after the cafés and an interview with a West Berlin city planner and any number of "odd sights and strange discoveries," the Bertons left for Vienna. This, Pierre said, was a city that seemed "to understand the art of living," a city on "one long coffee break," with fine restaurants, abundant pastry shops, and perfect hot dogs. A side trip into Switzerland afforded him an opportunity to offer "Berton's Laws for Tourist Behaviour." He warned his readers about the exorbitant compulsory tips charged by "the bandits who run the tourist industry," in the process drawing attention to Pierre Berton, the Seasoned World Traveller.[46]

Impressions of East Berlin and Disneyland jostled in his mind, one evoking images of isolation and neglect, the other a sense of community and abundance. Like Canada itself, Berton wished no return to the past, yet occasionally he glanced longingly backwards. He looked forward to what the future might bring but stepped hesitantly toward it. For him, Disneyland was not the future, it was the past made perfect – a past purged of want, decay, and imperfection – and of the untidy complexities of ordinary life.

In the context of his other travels, he could not have failed to notice that the Disneyland responsible for bringing out the boy in him was also the supreme expression of the economic and cultural imperialism – the Coca-Colism – he had come to fear and resent in a world Marshall McLuhan would soon dub the "global village." Yet the more he expressed himself publicly on this cultural contradiction, the more he consolidated and strengthened, rather than weakened, the Berton brand. For in doing so, he reflected and articulated the ambivalence of Canadians themselves on such matters, thereby naturalizing the contradiction, making it seem less problematic. Canadians, he told his countrymen, could embrace the future without rejecting their past. They could be loyal to the Queen, yet toast her with Coke.

Berton published only *The Secret World of Og* in 1961, but he had another collection of columns in hand. At McClelland & Stewart, however, Jack McClelland was aware of the reluctance of his staff – veering toward resistance – to publish a third collection of Berton columns in as many years. Instead, other projects began to take priority for both publisher and author. Berton started a novel in 1961, working at it in his rare spare time. Fiction was the one area of writing where success had eluded him, and he kept his subject to himself.

The idea for another non-fiction book came quite literally as a gift from the streets. One day, a young Swiss photographer named Henri Rossier walked into his office with a portfolio and asked for help in turning its contents into a book. The portfolio contained documentary-style photographs, taken during Rossier's two years of residence in Toronto. Collectively, they documented the remarkable transformation of Toronto from a repressed and austere city of WASPs into a vibrant and at times even bawdy multi-ethnic metropolis. Berton liked the idea, and wrote a text that explained the significance of the photographs. Macmillan of Canada expressed interest in the project, so he placed it there. *The New City* was born.[47] Its sales proved disappointing, in Berton's view because Torontonians did not wish to read about themselves, and outsiders did not want their stereotype of staid and boring Toronto exploded. Yet *The New City* was in some respects a project ahead of its time. In the era of the Internet, the book would come to be reassessed. In the words of the photographer Sean Waisglass, it had been a pioneering enterprise – "an old photoblog" that spoke to "the power of street photography."[48]

By the early sixties, the financial strain on Berton's life had lessened. He had incorporated Pierre Berton Enterprises in 1958, and the company grossed $37,000 within a year, at a time when the average annual salary of a worker in the Canadian manufacturing sector was $5,817. Throughout the sixties his income steadily rose. The Kleinburg home now possessed some charming touches, including a large swimming pool in the back garden, an indoor tropical garden, and a Berton-built hillside sown with a thousand tulip bulbs.[49] The family had grown once again, with the birth of Peggy Anne in May 1961. Penny was about to enter her teens and continued to marshal the morning inspection line before her brothers and sisters went to school, assisting Janet in other ways around the house. Their father was usually present at breakfast, reading the newspapers, and with them on weekdays from seven o'clock or so, when he returned from the office, until they went off to bed. The Berton children did not suffer from a distant or absent father, busy as he was.

The annual summer vacation with the whole family and the occasional pet became a sacrosanct Berton event, and he seldom failed to write about them. One of the first of these began on Dominion Day, 1961, when the eight Bertons, their Siamese cat, the Princess Sari, and its kitten, the Prince of Kowloon, navigated the full length of the Trent-Severn Waterway, some 240 miles long with only 33 miles of artificial channels. In April, Berton had written to a marine rental company inquiring about a houseboat that would sleep eight, dangling hints of advantages to the firm along the way. "I hope that the idea intrigues you," he wrote to the company's production manager, "as, quite apart from the usefulness of it to myself and to my newspaper it would provide good publicity for your own projects in the future. We would probably assign photographers at various points to take pictures of the trip and do other promotional work on it." Within days, the man offered Berton a deluxe thirty-five-foot houseboat the company had been building for its own use. It came equipped with barbecue, bunk beds and divans, a fridge and stove, a flush toilet, and running water. The manager told Berton he would be pleased to pay him a personal visit to iron out the details.[50]

It proved fortunate that proprietor and client were on such good terms, because on the first day of the trip the houseboat's steering cable snapped in the channel near Sparrow Lake.[51] The Bertons were marooned there until a company employee arrived to rescue them with a stronger cable. Berton the sailor proved to be as erratic and hapless as Berton the motorist. In a scene that resembled a madcap Jerry Lewis movie, reversed cables caused the rudder to turn in the wrong direction, and all the way to Lake Couchiching Berton had to steer the boat by turning it opposite to the direction he wanted to go.

With each day, he recorded the adventures of the Berton clan in the pages of the *Star*, and curious readers waited for them along the lengthy route. Janet began to think of the trip as "like a royal tour, only less organized." People demanded to see the new baby, Peggy Anne, and the Princess Sari. Three-year-old Paul fell into the canal, as did the Prince of Kowloon. Pamela rescued her brother, and the kitten, too, survived. Crowds of Berton-watchers sought his autograph, and even nine-year-old Patsy joined the lineup – after all, she told her father, "everybody else was getting one." The vacation had become an adventure in a gold-fish bowl, and at times it put the children on edge; but it remained an adventure. When people hoisted banners saying "WELCOME BERTON FAMILY," Patsy felt special.[52]

The family survived the sometimes arduous voyage and Berton used the experience to muse on various topics along the way: Champlain's voyage into the interior of Canada and his encounters with Native people; the threat to the property of the Canadian humorist Stephen Leacock from subdivision by developers; the luxurious estate on Balsam Lake owned by the descendants of the railroad baron and financier Sir William Mackenzie; the way the Langton family had somehow endured as pioneers in Upper Canada's Kawartha country; "the curiously gifted, oddly stubborn, quaintly snobbish crew" that were "the Literary Stricklands" of Suffolk; how Catharine Parr Traill and Susanna Moodie forged a life in the Canadian bush; the delicate natural balance between the waterway system and its surrounding hinterland and the difficulties in maintaining that balance; the sad fate of the Cobourg-Peterborough Railway, "one of the great white elephants of the age of steel."[53]

Toward the end of this "voyage of discovery," variously marooned and feted, water-soaked and secure in their bunks, Pierre was drawn back to another family voyage thirty-five years earlier, when he and his mother, father, and sister had drifted four hundred miles down the Yukon River. Already his mind was at work converting family events taking place around him into instant nostalgia. "Remember the weeds and how Peter pulled them off the propeller? Remember the shad flies? Remember how the mosquito got inside Peggy Anne's net and bit her all over the head and how good she was about it? Remember the time the air mattress fell off and we fished it out with a boat hook? Remember the first fish Patsy caught and how she insisted on cooking and eating it even though it was only 6 inches long? Remember how Paul kept saying he saw Indians in the woods? Remember the games of *Careers* and the readings from *Ozma of Oz*?"[54] Nostalgia helped him fend off a personal sense of loss, of endings, and it was central to his drive to tell stories.

Sunday nights in front of the television, watching Ed Sullivan's variety show, was another Berton family ritual, as it was for millions of North Americans. Television was also taking on a greater importance in Pierre's professional life. He scarcely needed reminding that his appearances on TV, not his articles or books, had been responsible for making him an instant celebrity. So in 1961 he made a rough pilot for a television series based on his *Toronto Star* column, another forum in which he would speak on subjects that struck his fancy. *By Pierre Berton* the television show was only five minutes long, but Berton shopped it around within the Toronto media community.

One of the contributors to *Maclean's* at the time was a freelance writer named Judith Krantz (who with the publication of her second novel, *Princess Daisy*, was to become a multimillionaire within the decade). Berton knew her husband, Steve, general manager of the Canadian branch of Screen Gems, a subsidiary of Columbia Pictures. Steve Krantz took charge of the project, found several television stations willing to broadcast the show, and signed up a sponsor – Independent Grocers. From his office in New York, the Screen Gems producer Herbert Sussan helped develop and pitch the program.[55] Berton became co-producer and co-owner. On the grounds that no publicity was bad publicity, he made himself intentionally provocative – suggesting on one occasion that Prince Charles should marry a black African to prove that "the Commonwealth meant something." Some royalists wanted to lynch him after that.

Airing daily over a four-month period in 1961, at different times established by each station, the program gained a 17 per cent audience share in the Nielsen ratings, respectable enough to encourage those backing it.[56] The experiment had been a success, and Screen Gems started to plan a full-scale *Pierre Berton Show* that was to feature interviews with a wide range of people, from international celebrities to complete unknowns, whose lives were of interest – in short, anyone its host found intriguing. Berton jumped at the prospect, and began to clear time for a headlong leap into a television career.

In June 1962, he made his final appearance on *Close-Up* in an episode that became unintentionally controversial. Berton's interview was with Lester B. Pearson, leader of the opposition in the House of Commons. Unaware that only ten seconds remained before the show was to end, he asked Pearson, in effect, whether he would not rather be dead than Red. The politician's hurried response was: "Well, I want to do what I can to make that choice unnecessary, but if I have to make it, I would rather live under Mr. Khrushchev than die, and do what I could to throw him and his type out of power." The program ended before he could elaborate. Pearson was subsequently assailed by his opponents for being "soft on Communism," and Berton was pilloried for asking the question in the first place.[57]

He spent much of June and July combining business and pleasure at the first Dawson City Gold Rush Festival. The eight Bertons flew to Edmonton, rented a large station wagon (a 1962 Pontiac Laurentian V8) and a tent trailer, and headed up the Alaska Highway on an 1,800-mile trip to Dawson City. Most of the roads were gravel and they camped all the way. It had been fourteen years since Pierre had last been on the Alaska Highway, and more than twenty-five since his camping days with the Boy Scouts.[58] The adventure provided him with enough material for most of his columns that July, along with articles on "the wackiest festival of all" and "how to go camping with six kids," pitched earlier to the editor of the *Star Weekly*, John Clare.[59]

The Dawson City Gold Rush Festival was the brainchild of the theatre promoter Tom Patterson, the energetic founder of the Stratford Festival. The idea came to him when he read Berton's *Klondike*. In 1959, he met with officials of the Department of Northern Affairs and Natural Resources who were in Stratford to set up an "Eskimo exhibit." They were enthusiastic about the festival concept. Patterson flew to Dawson that fall and became captivated by its geography and its history. The Canadian Government Travel Bureau took to the idea as a way of preserving Dawson's historical character and encouraging tourism, and before long plans were afoot for a historically accurate restoration of Arizona Charlie's Palace Grand dance hall and theatre and for the staging of a lively Broadway-style musical called *Foxy*, based on a free adaptation of Ben Jonson's *Volpone* and starring Bert Lahr of *Wizard of Oz* fame.[60]

In a November 1961 "preliminary report" on the proposed Dawson City festival, Berton, a member of the festival's board of directors, promoted the idea in his *Toronto Star* column, announcing that he thought it "highly likely that Dawson City may become to Canada what Disneyland is to the United States" – a prospect that later, as an environmentalist committed to historical conservation, he would have found appalling.[61] On the whole relationship between development and preservation, Berton was as ambivalent as his fellow Canadians in the 1960s. While he promoted his hometown as a future Canadian Disneyland, he raised funds from the forest industry by citing the failure of Canadians to protect historical sites to the extent Americans had done.[62] A fine balance existed between encouraging tourism for Dawson and turning it into a northern version of Frontierland.

While in Dawson, the Bertons panned for gold on the famous number 30 claim, "staked by Russian John and sold to Big Alex McDonald for a bag of flour and a side of bacon." They went to Hunker Creek and climbed aboard Dredge number 11, built during the summer of 1939 when Pierre had worked the creeks himself. He took his family to Discovery and Bonanza creeks, an excursion that was at once a history lesson and an act of homage. After their week in Dawson they drove south, following the Yukon River, toward White Pass. On the way, Penny and Pamela declared that seeing *Foxy* at the Palace Grand had been their favourite part of the trip. For Patsy, "something of a tomboy" to her father, the highlight was spotting a moose and its calf in a swamp. Peter, almost seven, liked the overturned transport truck on the side of the highway, and Paul, three, said without hesitation that his was the helicopter ride to the top of the five-thousand-foot Midnight Dome. Peggy Anne, only thirteen months old, said nothing, and her father chose to regard her introduction to some Siberian husky puppies as her warmest memory.[63]

This was Berton's first time in Dawson with his full family, and any number of moments were special; but one in particular stood out when he reflected on the trip. It occurred when he was sitting alone in Dawson's Occidental Hotel and struck up a conversation with a stranger. The man, in his early forties, turned out to be the American composer and lyricist Johnny Mercer, whose great songs, including "Ac-cen-tchu-ate the Positive" (1944), "Laura" (1945), and "On the Atchison, Topeka and the Santa Fe" (1945), had "haunted" Pierre's courting days. He had a languorous chat with this southern gentleman from Savannah, reminiscing about the golden days of the American songbook and musing on postwar changes in popular taste. Whether the conversation turned at any point to Mercer's song "Arthur Murray Taught Me Dancing in a Hurray" (made popular by Betty Hutton in the forties), or to the fact that Murray himself had been Mercer's instructor, remains unknown.[64]

Returning home, the Bertons left Skagway on the ss *Princess Louise* and travelled through the Inside Passage from the Alaskan panhandle to

Vancouver; then they spent time on Gabriola Island, a twenty-minute ferry ride from Nanaimo, B.C. By then, plans for the expanded television show were well into development. Pierre had been a guest earlier in the year on *The Tonight Show*, hosted by Jack Paar on NBC, and he liked its format, anchored by lively interviews.[65] Berton's hour-long show was to run, like Paar's, five nights a week. He knew that he would not be able to continue writing for the *Toronto Star*, and he prepared to give the newspaper notice that his final column would appear some time in November.

Meanwhile, he readied a third collection of columns for publication. He had submitted the manuscript in early June, before leaving for the Klondike, telling Jack McClelland, "Haste is imperative. There is little sense in showing this to any of your readers since I am now satisfied with it and have no intention of changing it, deleting or adding anything. Besides, I am convinced that all your readers are idiots. You read it." He insisted on a "nice clean look . . . lively but not too arty" for the book's design. "I trust the cartel that runs the print shop are not going to bugger this book by closing shop during the most urgent period of book production," he added.[66] Undaunted, McClelland sent the manuscript to Diane Mew, perhaps his most skeptical editor, one with an admitted dislike of books of columns. He received a positive report. "All in all," she wrote, "the collection sparkles with wit, controversy, and good writing."[67]

In July, the galleys for the book found Berton on Gabriola. Over the remainder of the summer he corrected the page proofs.[68] *Fast Fast Fast Relief* reached bookstores in October, released to coincide with the publication of "Pierre's Adventures in Bertonland," a lengthy article by Sidney Katz in *Maclean's* about the Berton phenomenon. McClelland had met with Katz over lunch and had sent the writer copies and reviews of Berton's previous books, along with galleys of the new one. Later, at Katz's suggestion, the publisher and the magazine co-operated in promoting the work.[69]

Given Berton's well-known role as a watchdog for consumers, those who purchased *Fast Fast Fast Relief* may have thought it was an exposé of the pharmaceutical industry. Certainly, the George Feyer cartoon of a man walking away from a "self service" guillotine with his head under his arm and a bottle marked "pills" next to him would have suggested the idea. But the book was not about drugs at all, at least not of the pharmaceutical variety. Instead it was about the way Berton's writings arose out of his dream life. "Dreams," he wrote in a revealing foreword, "are our means of nightly escape from the vexations of the real world – a kind of fast, fast, fast relief, more effective, perhaps, than buffered aspirin or capsuled tranquilizer. Daydreams provide even faster relief since the dreamer himself controls them. They are a luxury that few can afford, but a columnist, almost by definition, is a daydreamer. Many of the pieces in this book have grown out of idle daydreams prompted by the question: *I wonder what would happen if . . .?*"[70]

At one level, *Fast Fast Fast Relief* was the usual eclectic mix that tended to sour Jack McClelland's editors. One section comprised Berton's own "sure-fire" lists, catalogues, and laws, whether of "realistic Christmas toys," "adult behaviour," or dust jacket blurbs. Another reprised Berton as consumer crusader, with pieces on the problems people encountered in getting married, adopting a child, dealing with automobile insurance, using credit card machines, or arranging "easy payment" financing. Still more sections dealt with the quirky character-istics of certain Canadians and the "seasonal reflections of a country dweller." But the central thread of the book remained Berton's dream life, the wellspring of his creativity as a writer.

He even dreamed in colour, or so he claimed. It was his rich imagi-native life that had seen him at the age of five wake in the dark to a scarlet devil seated at the foot of his bed, and at seven have a vision of himself floating over the landscape of Manitoba on a cigar-shaped airship. Berton's daydreaming created his "Carols for the Nuclear Age" (*"It came upon the midnight clear, / That glorious sound of old: / Of sirens howling near the earth, / To sound the Tocsin-Bold!"*). Dreams were the invisible force that sealed his commitment to what he called "the writing game" and to those who played it best – like Hal Straight, W.O. Mitchell, Thomas P. Kelley, and Lister Sinclair. Dreams made the satires involving Harvey Grebe and his oddball family Pierre's favourite columns to write.

All such stuff and more made its way into *Fast Fast Fast Relief*. The book's strong anti-nuclear-weapons stance and its consumer advocacy certainly put his liberal principles on display. One of Canada's most dis-tinguished scholars, J.M. Robson of the University of Toronto, a leading authority on the British philosopher and politician John Stuart Mill, pointed out in a review that the book – "muckraking of a high rake and low muck kind" – provided a "clearer personal outline" than any before it of Berton's system of values: "He helps to make the middle-brow high, and to keep the criminal low." Perhaps Robson saw in Berton what he admired in Mill: the clear grit of stalwart liberal conviction. A year later, writing about another Berton collection, he observed approvingly that "Mr. Berton knows and detests this surface-world [of confidence games], which is kept by crust from the underworld. . . . For those who want to strike back, Mr. Berton offers some suggestions at the end of the book. I've tried some of them, and they work."[71]

Jack McClelland took a great liking to *Fast Fast Fast Relief.* "I think you'll have a terrific book," he wrote Berton on Gabriola Island. And to Sidney Katz he confided: "I really do believe Pierre to be in total about the most talented writer-journalist-editor (not literary giant) that I have yet encountered." With McClelland's encouragement, Harold Strauss at Knopf had already begun to pitch the next Berton book to follow *Fast Relief* – "The Black Arts of Salesmanship" was its working title – to his sales managers.[72]

Berton was becoming as ubiquitous a presence within McClelland's publishing offices as he was outside, at the newsstand, or on the family tube. Rumours circulated within M&S that Berton was going to do a book on the Alaska Highway in collaboration with Henri Rossier, and that he had signed a contract with M&S to write "a major work on Niagara Falls." A draft press release of May 1962 announcing these projects noted that sales of *Klondike* had passed the 25,000-copy mark and that sales of *The Secret World of Og* had reached 10,000.[73]

The swan song of "By Pierre Berton" the column came in the week of November 5–9, and his pieces proved as unpredictable as ever. Monday's column mused on what book and theatre critics might have written about such tales as *The Odyssey* and "Jack and the Beanstalk." Tuesday's told of one man's struggle to get his pension money back from the company he had worked for. On Wednesday, in the spirit of a popular television program called *Target: The Corrupters* (which starred Steve McNally as a newspaper columnist on the crime beat), he told about his own uneasy encounter with two mobsters named Costello. On Thursday, he related the story of the financial and other woes of

Mrs. Tong, widow of a police offer shot to death in 1952 by the infamous Boyd Gang.[74]

On Friday, November 9, 1962, Pierre Berton surprised his faithful readers by revealing that the column that day was his last. Nearly a thousand columns, a million and a quarter words, seemed enough. He thanked readers for their interest, and the *Star* for its hands-off attitude, and then declared that although he was leaving the newspaper, a Berton connection would nevertheless endure. "It gives me great pleasure," he wrote, "to announce that Miss Patsy Berton, aged 10, has consented to remain with the organization. . . . Every afternoon at 4:30, come wind, hail or sleet, you will see her small figure struggling across field and stream, bowed beneath the crushing weight of the ever-expanding newspaper." And on those rare occasions when Patsy was forced to stay in school, he warned, "the man on your doorstep, collecting the weekly 60 cents, may easily be me."[75]

Life at the *Toronto Star* had been an experience as exhilarating in its own way as working at *Maclean's*. "In some ways," he had written as early as 1959, "this is the craziest newspaper I've ever worked on." Not crazy like the Vancouver *News-Herald*, which crammed its entire staff into one small newsroom; not like the *Vancouver Sun*, where the managing editor Hal Straight once rolled a fired employee into his ad department in a wastepaper basket. The *Toronto Star* was crazy because everyone at the paper, including Berton himself, "seemed to be several people rolled into one." Charles Templeton, the *Star*'s page 7 opinions editor, had his own daily radio show and moderated a TV panel and often found himself pilloried by the *Star*'s TV critic Max Braithwaite. Nathan Cohen, the newspaper's senior critic, received Braithwaite's lash for the way he moderated *Fighting Words*. For his part, Cohen often attacked Templeton, declaring once, when Templeton won a television award for being "an outstanding new personality," that it "demonstrated the paucity of real talent on Canadian television." Templeton, of course, used his radio program to comment on the "curmudgeonish pose" Cohen assumed in his *Star* column. Gordon Sinclair, the *Star*'s second TV critic, also delighted in goading Cohen, saying of one of his TV interviews that it was "aimed at a pink cloud audience . . . far removed from life . . . artsy dartsy . . . a snobbish show," thereby provoking Cohen to dismiss Sinclair in print as "a scissors and paste purveyor of gossip."[76]

All this was great fun, the self-serving sport of a group of very talented journalists, and for four years Berton had been glad to be among them. Each – Templeton, Braithwaite, Cohen, Sinclair and the book reviewer, theatre critic and broadcaster Robert Fulford – had at one time or another taken critical jabs at him: Fulford for Berton's "atrocious drawings," Braithwaite and Cohen for his interviewing techniques, Sinclair for the stiffness of his broadcasts, and Templeton for the joy of simply being contrary. These men of the *Star* needed each other. The banter of chummy infighting at once enlivened them and kept them in a spotlight they themselves controlled, prima donnas on a carousel of mutual promotion. For Berton, the time had come to dismount and try another ride.

17

JUST ADD BERTON AND STIR

—

THE NEW PIERRE BERTON TELEVISION show launched in the fall of 1962. CFTO, a Toronto affiliate of the CTV network, contracted to air the program for an hour each weeknight at 11:30, and private stations in Ottawa and Montreal soon signed up. Screen Gems appointed Herb Sussan as executive producer, but at Berton's urging Ross McLean produced the show in the studio. Pierre also insisted that, while its format was to be that of a program-long interview, its emphasis should be as much on entertainment as on journalism, with steady attention to well-known names from show business. And he rather liked Sussan's suggestion that the show be called *The Pierre Berton Hour*; that way, the star couldn't be fired.[1]

Berton was at first stiff and uneasy in front of the camera. The shift from hard-nosed interviews on *Close-Up* to a format largely given over to entertainment taxed his confidence; as he later admitted, the "goofy egotism" of his earlier television work was no substitute for good technique in front of the studio camera. He found it difficult to concentrate on air with all the behind-the-camera activity, and his nervousness led him to interrupt his guests. As the critic Bob Gardiner put it in the *Ottawa Citizen*: "The man's presence seems a liability unless he learns to shut up."[2]

A *Maclean's* contributor named Harvey Grebe, who just happened to share the name of one of the figures of comic fantasy featured in Berton's *Toronto Star* column, evidently agreed. In a lengthy review of the program for the magazine in October, he wrote that Berton was not as smart as Jack Paar, but clearly more intelligent. Inviting the reporters Charles Lynch and Douglas Fisher to expose the shallowness of the views of the Social Credit leader Réal Caouette had been a good idea, but, alas, the interview had "degenerated into banality" when Berton asked Caouette if he slept in pyjamas or in the raw. His interview with the pioneering television talk-show host David Susskind – for some reason Grebe called him "a creep from New York" – the reviewer found interminable. Grebe thought it astounding that Berton could have an hour-long discussion with three beautiful women – the CBC television personalities Elaine Bedard, Joyce Davidson, and Toby Robins – about sex, and not once mention morality, religion, or love. Instead, Grebe noted, the host had asked Robins whether men made passes at her, and Toby said yes. He had asked Davidson if "a young woman should stay a virgin for long," and she had replied: "If she waited until she was thirty-five, what has she been saving it up for?"[3] Her remark sufficiently offended the sensibilities of some viewers and CBC executives that Davidson was forced to leave the CBC. Rumoured to be already involved romantically with Susskind, who was separated but not divorced from his wife, she left for New York. Six years later, she and Susskind married. How many quick readers of Maclean's and the Toronto Star caught on to "Grebe's" prank remains unknown.

The fact that The Pierre Berton Hour was the first Canadian television show of its kind attracted viewers, and they grew to like what they saw. One Toronto letter writer confessed to Berton that he was "a slobbering Berton fan," and then urged him to interview an author named Rachel Carson about her new book on environmental degradation, Silent Spring, being serialized at the time in the New Yorker.[4]

When CTV began to broadcast the program early in 1963 over the full network, moving it to 11:00 p.m. in competition with Earl Cameron and the CBC national news, one of Janet's friends in British Columbia wrote to her: "Don't know what reception the Pierre Berton Hour is getting across the country but here in Ladysmith he's definitely replaced late movies." A by-product of the show, she added, was that "people who normally wouldn't ever watch a panel show with anyone above the intellectual level of an Ed Sullivan comedian, will now sit and learn . . . and find their minds stimulated for the first time in their lives."[5]

That spring The Performing Arts in Canada ran a profile of The Pierre Berton Hour called "Controversy Is Here to Stay," with the tagline "Sex, Sanitation, Politics, Religion, and Racial Discrimination – the Story of Bad Boy Berton or the Tale of a Journalist with a Social Conscience."

The magazine noted that Berton was at his best when doing interviews and at his worst when trying to be humorous. It praised the show's "hard-hitting, thought-provoking" format, noting that while it had won "a devoted following," many advertisers shied away because they did not want their products identified with any type of controversy. This was a shame, wrote the reviewer, since Berton was pioneering a "controversial-conversation" show much needed in "our TV wasteland."[6]

Berton often had attractive female guests on the program, and at times talk became risqué and glances appeared flirtatious, resulting in lots of mail – as when the model Ulla Moreland helped the host dress a turkey using the American writer Morton Thompson's turkey recipe, made famous in Berton's *Toronto Star* columns. Ross McLean, very much a ladies' man, ensured that such women regularly graced the set, very often in company with literary heavyweights. The Canadian television personality Denyse Angé appeared with Malcolm Muggeridge, the singer Joannie Somers with Ogden Nash, and Ulla Moreland with S.J. Perelman.[7]

But the most distinctive feature of *The Pierre Berton Hour* was its quirky variety, captured by the *Performing Arts* writer: "You want nostalgia? How about Berton and Al Capp or Rube Goldberg reminiscing on the old days as cartoonists? The national purpose? The perceptive Bruce Hutchison talked of it eloquently. June Callwood and Irving Layton clashed on Love and/or Marriage. There has been religion . . . racism . . . humour, both erudite and wacky. . . . The list is formidable, and all sparked by Berton's own expertise in this field, as reporter, editor, author." How could one not admire a host who might interview a prostitute and talk frankly about her work one night and play straight man to Kiddo the Clown on the next? Berton, proclaimed *The Performing Arts in Canada*, was "a great Canadian National Resource."[8]

In the fall of 1963, Berton submitted the manuscript of "The Black Arts of Salesmanship," his fourth book of columns, to McClelland & Stewart. Each of the three previous collections had sold over 10,000 copies, so Jack McClelland was enthusiastic. Not so his editors, who seem to have formed a united front. Berton's new manuscript differed from its predecessors in that it provided an expanded treatment of the many confidence games, rackets, frauds, swindles, and examples of unscrupulous salesmanship he had written about earlier in the *Toronto*

Star. McClelland's editors remained unimpressed, and recommended against adding another Berton collection of recycled *Toronto Star* columns to the M&S list.

Jack McClelland decided to publish the book anyway. He agreed with his editors' judgments about the quality of "The Black Arts of Salesmanship," but Berton had become a household name and he certainly possessed the all-important sizzle, if he didn't always deliver the steak. The title of one exposé in the new book suggested that its author was well aware of the benign hucksterism essential to successful marketing: "Don't Sell the Product: Sell the Story." McClelland changed the book's title, and M&S and Knopf released it later in the year as *The Big Sell: An Introduction to the Black Arts of Door-to-Door Salesmanship & Other Techniques*. It was an immediate success. The manager of the Ontario sales division of Canada Packers Limited became so convinced that something needed to be done to protect the "little citizen" that he wrote to William G. Davis, Ontario's minister of education, to suggest that *The Big Sell* be required reading for Ontario's schoolchildren. By the end of the decade, 32,000 copies of the book had been sold.[9]

A month before Berton's final column appeared in the *Toronto Star*, Ken Lefolii, Ralph Allen's successor as editor of *Maclean's*, approached him with the offer of his own page in the magazine every two weeks. Berton accepted, thinking he could simply take his approach at the *Star* to his new space in *Maclean's*. In doing so, he failed to heed the advice Jack Scott had provided four years earlier – that while vitality in a newspaper is "a shout of urgency," a magazine requires "a murmur of introspection."

Under Lefolii, experienced *Maclean's* writers like Blair Fraser, June Callwood, Barbara Moon, and Ralph Allen continued to publish substantive, thought-provoking articles on important subjects. Peter C. Newman and Robert Fulford held forth in columns of their own. Newman offered readers a backstage look at political deal-making at the seat of power, a sure sign that the genteel and discreet journalism of Blair Fraser's generation was passing. Fulford's coverage of cultural matters treated the arts as seriously as Newman did politics. In 1962 and

1963, Fraser wrote about life in a divided Berlin, and Allen provided "a calm report" on the Cuban Missile Crisis, while Shirley Mair contributed an article titled "Abortion Mills and the Law" and Christina McCall Newman exposed "Canada's class system."[10]

When "Pierre Berton's Page" made its appearance on January 26, 1963, half of its space chided the National Council of Christians and Jews for promoting "Brotherhood Week" instead of meaningful anti-discrimination legislation. The satirical American songster Tom Lehrer had recently lampooned the same target with his song "National Brotherhood Week" on the NBC revue *That Was the Week That Was*. But the rest of the column was a rather jejune update of Robert Service's verse "Clancy of the Mounted," intended as a political spoof. This was the kind of fluff Berton produced each year for *Spring Thaw*, and to some it seemed out of place at *Maclean's*, which held a distinct sense of its own national significance. Subsequent Berton columns also suffered from this bifurcated attention, flitting from topic to topic and from light banter to high dudgeon. On March 9, Ken Lefolii and Blair Fraser drew attention to "the nuclear mess," and June Callwood wrote about the emotion of anger, but the subject of "Pierre Berton's Page" was lonely hearts ads, a topic he had written about in the *Star* in 1961.[11]

The uneven quality of the Berton's pieces puzzled and disappointed the *Maclean's* staff. Robert Fulford could not understand how almost overnight the best columnist in the country had become its worst. By May, he, Peter Gzowski, the managing editor, and others on staff had concluded that the column was an embarrassment to the magazine. "After a few issues," Fulford wrote many years later, "we began to wonder how we could gracefully get rid of him."[12]

Berton was at his most effective when he focused on serious matters. He wrote with insight about the "real issues" of yet another federal election and he spent election night (April 8) with the victorious Lester Pearson, bearing witness to the politician's transformation from leader of the opposition to prime minister. But "Pierre Berton's Page" all too often reflected a journalist who no longer seemed to differentiate between substantial and ephemeral subject matter. A frivolous and self-indulgent Berton article in the June 9 issue, "Confessions of a Hotel Fancier," scarcely enhanced his reputation. Readers of his *Toronto Star* column had found the eclectic mix of themes delightfully unpredictable and at times even titillating, but subscribers to *Maclean's*, especially in the months following the Cuban Missile Crisis when the magazine published ominous articles with titles like "We Can Do Something about Fallout," preferred introspection to titillation. The times were unpredictable enough.[13]

On May 18, "Pierre Berton's Page" dealt with only one subject, and it caught everybody's attention. "It's Time We Stopped Hoaxing the Kids about Sex," the title ran. Berton had recently read an article by a psychiatrist named Elliott Markson on adolescent sex, and it made him examine his own views on the subject. Markson had pointed out that of the 9,600 patients in Ontario psychiatric hospitals, an "astonishing" 4,000 were under the age of sixteen. The great hoax of the twentieth century, Berton wrote, following Markson, was that "every adolescent is taught that sex is the key to everything – but he can't enjoy it for another ten, fifteen or twenty years." Why, then, Berton asked, should people be surprised that so many teenagers reached a state of emotional upheaval requiring psychiatric treatment? He blamed popular magazines for emphasizing the sanctity of virginity and for insisting that premarital sex would only "lead to disaster." At the same time, sexual popularity was "the foundation on which the great postwar Teen Market has been built," the very premise of "the Going Steady syndrome."

He criticized magazines such as *Teen Life*, aimed at twelve-to-fourteen-year-old girls, for devoting themselves almost entirely to "the sexual philanderings of adult hero figures." He attacked them for using starlets such as Beverley Washburn, Tuesday Weld, and Annette Funicello as models for sexual behaviour, offering advice about "how I snared Johnny" (Washburn) or "on and off romance" (Weld) or bragging about "the men in my bedroom" (Funicello). In *Hit Parader* magazine, the singer Connie Francis instructed preteen children on how to date.

Like it or not, Berton wrote, the drive of the marketplace and the manipulative nature of popular culture meant that adolescent sex was a reality; attitudes had to change to reflect this truth. "Having goaded the infants into a state of emotional and romantic frenzy," he wrote, "to which intercourse, rather than cold baths must be the obvious release,

we are going to have to accept teenage sex as matter-of-factly as we now accept the other facets of togetherness. . . . Premarital sex isn't always a bad thing; what *is* bad is the sense of guilt, shame and sin which keeps young people at arm's length from their parents and in a state of constant emotional tension. Further we must make much less fuss about virginity and continence and realize that, while they're okay for some people, they are not necessarily okay for all.

The church, he wrote, should lead the way in rethinking attitudes toward sex; after all, this was the institution responsible for equating sex with wickedness in the first place. He saw evidence that this was beginning to happen, since both a prominent Toronto Anglican archdeacon and the Archbishop of Canterbury had recently recommended that the church restate its position on sex. A Quaker pamphlet had gone even further: "The insincerity of the moral code may well be the cause of the widespread contempt of the younger generation for society's rules and inhibitions," it stated.

When Berton reached this point in the column, he reflected on the certain public reaction it would arouse. Here he was, condoning premarital sex, but would he condone it for his own children? He was the father of four daughters, two of whom – Penny, almost fifteen, and Pamela, a couple of weeks from turning thirteen – had reached puberty. To avoid the accusation of hypocrisy he knew would follow, he had to address the matter, and he did:

I fancy I hear a Greek chorus of well-intentioned old women carolling their slogan: "Would you want your daughters, etc. . .?"

Well, I have several daughters, Mesdames, and I must tell you that this is not a question that haunts my slumber. They are pretty levelheaded girls and if, in a moment of madness or by calculated design, they find themselves bedded with a youth (and I trust it will be a bed and not a car seat) I do not really believe the experience will scar their psyche or destroy their future marriages. Indeed I would rather have them indulge in some good, honest, satisfying sex than be condemned to a decade of whimpering frustration brought on by the appalling North American practice called "petting."

Be that as it may, I pray one thing is clear to them: whatever occurs, they will always have the full sympathy of their parents. They will not be banished into the snowstorm with their little bundle, nor will they be made to suffer shame for acting out, to its ultimate conclusion, the latest Hit Parade ballad or fan-magazine fantasy. Neither will they be condemned to the hell of an incompatible shotgun marriage simply because, for one evening, they decided to learn for themselves what all the adult shouting was about.

As for my sons, I fully expect that by the age of seventeen they will know, from experience, something about life and that when they finally wed they will be wise enough in the ways of the world to make their wives physically content, and tolerant enough, by reason of previous experience, to make their marriages compatible.[14]

Berton sent the finished column to his editors at *Maclean's* and no one objected to its contents. When he asked Peter Gzowski whether the column might cause trouble, the editor responded by saying, as Berton later put it, "We got rid of all *those* subscribers some time ago." Robert Fulford suspected "it might stir up some arguments" but sent the piece off to be typeset. "No one in the office," as far as Fulford knew, "considered it scandalous." Shortly after the article appeared, Larry Mann, warming up the *Front Page Challenge* audience, told them that the Berton article was just "good common sense."[15]

Nevertheless, church groups, parent-teacher organizations, and school boards rose in indignation. Roman Catholic associations, including the Knights of Columbus and the Catholic Women's League, issued their objections. An Edmonton university group called Berton a "sexual deviant." The principal of Knox Christian School in Bowmanville, Ontario, proclaimed that Berton's ideas "were more to be feared than nuclear bombs or Communistic betrayal." A prominent Toronto architect said that he hoped Berton's daughters "would be pregnant by the age of fifteen."[16]

The controversy struck close to home. A neighbour wrote to Janet informing her that she would not let her offspring play with the Berton children any more. At school, unaware of her father's controversial column, Penny became subject to catcalls and snide comments. What annoyed and disappointed her was not so much the schoolyard words as her father's lack of thoughtfulness in not forewarning her.[17]

Berton was unaware that Floyd Chalmers, president of Maclean Hunter, had found his piece offensive, lowering the tone of a magazine intended for family reading. Management began to shun him. "The first hint that something was really wrong," he wrote later, "came when I walked out the front door of the Maclean Hunter building on University Avenue and noticed that Donald Hunter, the vice-president, and several executives were pointedly turning their backs on me."[18]

On a weekend stay with Janet at the Muskoka cottage of Jack and Elizabeth McClelland, Pierre received a telephone call from Ken Lefolii, informing him that management had decided to put an end to his column. Widely respected by his writers and editors but viewed as uncooperative by those above him, Lefolii had been placed in a difficult position. The overall weakness of "Pierre Berton's Page" made it difficult for him to defend his writer on journalistic grounds, and Berton had few supporters even among his *Maclean's* colleagues. Under such circumstances, Lefolii had little choice but to bow to Chalmers's demand to suspend the column – thereby surrendering the key principle of editorial independence.[19]

Berton soon learned that his name was not to be associated with *Maclean's* magazine in any way and that he was not wanted even in the Maclean Hunter building. By any yardstick, these were draconian measures, directed as they were toward someone who had been an important contributor to the success of *Maclean's* during the Irwin and Allen years. But Berton accepted Lefolii's explanation that "Pierre Berton's Page" had not been very good and concluded that Maclean Hunter had capitulated to those who had put pressure on the magazine's subscription and advertising departments.

Perhaps, however, more was involved in the decision to banish Pierre Berton from *Maclean's* than the adolescent sex column alone. Historical explanation is grounded in context, and here the broad context of Berton's firing has not sufficiently been established. What else did he write about around the time the column was cancelled?

Only a couple of weeks after the Canadian federal election of April 8, 1963, Berton tackled the issue that had stood near the centre of the campaign and was of major concern for ordinary Canadians: socialized medicine. The New Democratic government of Saskatchewan, inspired by former premier Tommy Douglas, had passed a medicare bill in 1961. It had received royal assent in November and took effect on July 1, 1962. On that day, physicians in the province went on strike in protest, deepening the public divide over the issue of health care – in Saskatchewan and throughout the country.

During the federal election campaign of 1963, the Liberal Party under Lester Pearson promised that, if it won, the first "60 Days of Decision" would usher in a new flag, state-supported health care, and a national pension plan. When the Liberals did win, falling just short of a majority government, they gave every indication that they intended to fulfill their election promises. In short, from the vantage point of the medical profession and the health insurance industry, April 1963 was no time for a journalist with Pierre Berton's high profile and power of persuasion to weigh in on the issue of medicare. On April 20, Berton's column did just that. Its subject was "the grave flaws in private medicare." "In the raging battle over a national health scheme," he began, "the opponents of state medicine marshal a powerful argument: Most Canadians, they say, already have available to them some private form of insurance. Why duplicate it needlessly?" Then he set out to show how misleading and misguided this argument was.

Thousands of Canadians did not possess such insurance, he wrote, and loopholes galore existed in the fine print of the policies of those who did, allowing companies to avoid coverage or to cancel policies at their whim. Mentioning insurers like Continental Casualty, British Pacific, and Mutual of Omaha by name, Berton backed up his charges with specific examples, using information gathered once again by Marilyn Craig. "A British Pacific salesman," he said, "told my Operative 67 that its Community Health Services Plan was 'just like Medicare – only private.' Actually, it's as full of holes as a colander." The sales pitches of the industry, he insisted, were full of misleading gimmickry. Health insurance salesmen emphasized broad coverage, but they glossed over the exceptions that narrowed it. A policyholder badly burned when a kitchen stove exploded could not make a claim because the entire home had not been in flames. Another, injured when his motorcycle hit a truck, could not collect because the motorcycle was not covered.[20]

Condemnation of such practices by the best-known journalist in the country, at a time when public attitudes over medicare were so volatile, did not sit well with Canada's insurance industry, the medical establishment, or a good number of senior politicians. Equally alarming was the fact that Berton seemed unlikely to let go of the subject. Indeed, his final column in *Maclean's* was not on "hoaxing the kids about sex": it was "The Big Lie about Medical Insurance." In this second assault on private medical insurance, he did not mince words. "How soon," he began, "will the general public understand that it is being duped and deceived by the medical profession, the insurance companies, and the politicians on the subject of health insurance? How soon will they cotton on to the Big Lie, told over and over again – that the vast majority of Canadians are now adequately protected against sickness and accident by the existing private health plans?"

The deception perpetrated by the insurance industry, he stated, "must surely be purposeful." The Ontario minister of health, Dr. Matthew Dymond, was merely a propagandist for the status quo. He noted that while Dymond insisted that the public demanded voluntary and private health insurance, only 47.2 per cent, not 70 per cent as Dymond claimed, had some form of private health insurance. And of those who did, only 18 per cent held policies that included comprehensive coverage for "in hospital" treatment, surgery, and home and office calls.

People did not want charity, Berton asserted; they wanted security where their health was concerned. Yet, he charged, the premier of Ontario, John Robarts, had introduced a medical insurance scheme in the legislature that amounted to "little more than a minor amendment to the insurance act." It was time to end the fraud and the delay in providing adequate health coverage. "If the medical profession can come up with a privately administered scheme that gives the kind of coverage that the British people enjoy, well and good," he wrote. "If they can't, then we ought to get on with the business of socializing medicine as quickly as possible. You can't manipulate statistics forever. You can't maintain day in and day out the pleasant pretense that everything is grand when it obviously isn't. Let the doctors and their friends put up or let them shut up. But let them stop hoodwinking the public."[21]

At one of the most sensitive points in Canadian political history, and over what would come to be recognized as among the most controversial issues of the twentieth century in Canada, Pierre Berton had seized hold of the dragon's tail. In addition to having offended religious moralists, he now threatened the interests of the medical profession and the insurance industries while at the same time making enemies of the premier of Ontario and his minister of health.

There cannot be much doubt that if Floyd Chalmers received complaints and threats from members of the religious community on teen sex, he also received complaints, and possibly threats, from the medical and insurance communities on medicare. The advertising department at *Maclean's* was already fearful of giving offence to anyone – "especially," as Fulford notes, "anyone connected with a potential advertiser." An article by Sidney Katz in December 1962, "Your Health and the Almighty Pill," carrying the teaser "Overmedication: An Important Report on How We Endanger Ourselves with Drugs," had annoyed the drug companies and shocked the management of *Maclean's*.[22] The charge of "hoodwinking the public" over private medical care and insurance, as much as "hoaxing the kids about sex," explains why Pierre Berton disappeared from the pages of *Maclean's* magazine in June 1963.

His greatest disappointment in the *Maclean's* fiasco was the lack of support from Ken Lefolii. He understood and accepted that the overall weakness of "Pierre Berton's Page" made it difficult for the editor to defend his writer against pressure from above, but he believed that the decision to fire him should have been made at the editorial level. Berton concluded that Lefolii's capitulation to management over the suspension of his column was a harbinger of worse times to come at *Maclean's*.

In mid-June, Leslie Hannon, a contributing editor at *Maclean's*, sent him a letter of support: "Quite a lot of people have written me concerning the disgusting turn of affairs at Maclean's," Hannon wrote. "Following earlier events, this kind of thing was pretty clearly predictable." In August, Hannon wrote again. "You probably know from local rumblings that I am now a member of that distinguished band of ex-Maclean's editors." He had "resigned" at the end of July. Based in England, he had been given the choice of a six-month job in Canada or severance where he was. The magazine paid the equivalent of his fare home but refused him any pension benefits. "So, after 13½ years, the comfy paternalism of the dear old Colonel turned out to be a thinly covered doorstep of best Steep Rock granite."[23]

The relationship between the magazine's editors and writers and Maclean Hunter's executives continued to deteriorate. Floyd Chalmers had all but lost confidence in Ken Lefolii, especially after Lefolii published Berton's second piece on medicare. When Chalmers put *Maclean's* under the control of a new vice-president, Ron McEachern, formerly editor of the *Financial Post*, relations between the editorial staff and management reached their nadir. Peter Newman, who had worked with McEachern at the *Post* and would soon leave *Maclean's* to become the Ottawa columnist of the *Toronto Star*, warned his colleagues that McEachern would be impossible to work with. He was correct. In July 1964, McEachern decided that a short article by Harry Bruce on a Toronto newspaper strike would do little more than "stir up animosities" and, bypassing Lefolii altogether, ordered the printers to drop the piece. Only from the printers did the editors discover it had been killed.[24]

Ken Lefolii had no choice but to resign, and his decision was followed by what Peter Gzowski called "the Big Quit." Without meeting formally to talk about the situation, managing editor Gzowski and four of the magazine's most senior writers – Harry Bruce, Robert Fulford, Barbara Moon, and David Lewis Stein – submitted their resignations. A few days later, management called a special meeting at which Floyd Chalmers tried to persuade the writers to stay. "We all noticed that Lefolii was not there," Fulford recalled, "and someone asked about his future at the magazine. Chalmers said his resignation had been accepted. . . . I left the room wondering if perhaps the whole incident had been perpetrated as a way to get rid of Lefolii."[25]

During the summer of 1963, mail arrived from friends and strangers alike expressing their shock at Pierre's sudden departure from *Maclean's*. Robert E. Krug, of Tavistock, Ontario, reported that those most strident in declaring the offending teen sex column "nauseating, naïve and obnoxious" just happened to be the people who most often asked to borrow his copy of *Maclean's* so they could read it. "If you were dismissed . . . merely because of public repercussion and in an attempt for them to protect themselves and to regain the good graces of their subscribers by so doing, my ideals of Maclean's have been lowered to the bottom rung." A woman named Judith Young wrote to Janet to say that she had lived vicariously with the Bertons on their trip to the Yukon, had "caught many glimpses" of the family in other articles and in the Og book, and had been "terribly moved" by some of Pierre's television interviews. "You Bertons have made a real mark on the land, not from the Social Service desk, pulpit or parliament. . . . Because of his constancy & sincerity in writing, I am proud your husband is a Canadian. Our country is wide open, in desperate need of [a] leader, strong & clean clear through. . . . I wish you two unlimited strength and health . . . and thank you for passing on to us, and our youngsters, much needed facts."[26]

Such letters of support were nice to receive, but as the summer unfolded Pierre had more important matters to worry about. His mother had injured her hip and was immobilized for a time during the spring, but she still intended to travel from Vancouver to Kleinburg for her annual summer holiday. Early in June, CTV announced that his television show would not continue beyond the summer unless several stations took it from Screen Gems on a syndicated basis. The loss of the show would mean a substantial reduction in his income. The year 1963, as he later admitted, was not a very good one. "The critics hated my TV show. The network refused to renew it. My readers called me a dirty old man. *Maclean's* fired me. It had been a bumpy ride."[27]

He needed to escape, if only for a while, so in July he joined George Feyer, the cartoonist who had illustrated *Fast Fast Fast Relief*, in his native Hungary. Small in size and raunchy by inclination, Feyer delighted in entertaining people with his felt pen. At parties he would draw breasts on women's bare backs, and once he drew large elephant ears on the abdomens of Pierre's boys, Peter and Paul, making their penises appear to be trunks. Berton loved Feyer's irreverence as much as his cartoons, and they became close friends.[28]

For several weeks the two men lived it up in Budapest, and Feyer introduced his friend to what the Hungarian chose to call "the simple entertainment of the people" – not only folk songs and dances but also Hungarian nightlife. At the Budapest Tancpalota, a dance hall that was turning people away at the door, they gained access when Feyer told Berton to say something, anything, in English. Once the doorman heard the magic words "A bunch of the boys were whooping it up in the Malemute saloon," he flung open the door and let them through.

Later, Berton and Feyer drove through the countryside to a holiday resort at Lake Balaton, encountering some hitchhikers along the way. Through Feyer, Pierre asked one of them why he and his friends would not want to live in the "free world." "You Americans work too hard," came the reply. To the hitchhiker, it was Berton and his fellow North Americans, not those living behind the Iron Curtain, who were the prisoners of an oppressive political system. The discussion got Berton thinking about whether he was himself a workaholic and whether a distinction should be made between work and toil.[29]

Berton returned to Canada reinvigorated and ready to make a decision on a most interesting proposal from the Anglican Church of Canada. In the previous spring, the Reverend Ernest Harrison, secretary of its General Board of Religious Education, had asked him to write a book on the state of the church in Canada to be read by congregations and discussed during the 1965 Lenten season. The idea puzzled but intrigued Pierre.

As a child, he had been drawn to the exotic nature of church ritual and had taken his confirmation instruction in the Anglican Church seriously. But during his mid-teens, like so many others, he began to find the services boring. Covering churches as a reporter had made him skeptical; obligatory army church parades had made him disaffected and angry. As a new father, he had intended to have his first-born, Penny, baptized in the Anglican Church, but he found the assertion in its "Publick Baptism of Infants" service that "all men are conceived and born in sin" something he could not accept without being a hypocrite. Penny was christened, instead, in the United Church of Canada, the church of Janet's upbringing, and Pierre had had little contact with the Anglican Church since then.[30]

Still, Berton found Harrison's overture refreshing. The Christian churches needed to reassess their beliefs and their function in a society undergoing major social and cultural transformation. He met with Harrison after returning from Budapest, and asked whether the invitation still held after all the "hoaxing the kids about sex" uproar. When Harrison said yes, Berton agreed to undertake the project as long as he could broaden its scope to include the other mainstream Canadian churches.

The agreement was a gamble for both men. Harrison had asked for a frank and honest assessment of the church in Canada in order to encourage "dialogue" – and he risked commissioning a book highly critical of his own institution. The prospective author risked time that might more profitably be spent on projects that guaranteed immediate income. The Anglican Church offered no advance for the book, and Berton and Harrison confirmed their agreement over a handshake.[31]

In the early fall, Berton was as busy as ever. He now did two five-minute commentaries each weekday for a second Toronto radio station, CHFI, and Screen Gems had found enough private television stations, including John Bassett's CFTO in Toronto, to continue *The Pierre Berton Hour* through the 1963–64 season. After a rough start, the show had gained a respectable audience share in its first season, and its host had spoken in Toronto and New York with 406 very different individuals in over 195 hours on air. The range of guests had been as varied as the subjects of his *Toronto Star* column. One night might feature Farley Mowat and the next, Jayne Mansfield.[32]

For the 1963–64 season, the show was scheduled for broadcast at 11:30 p.m., and its format was cut from sixty to thirty minutes, necessitating a change of name to *The Pierre Berton Show*. The season launched at the end of October, with another lineup of wide-ranging guests. This made the program difficult for TV critics to judge. "His show varies so much," wrote the *Calgary Herald*'s Bob Shiels, "that it has to be one of the tougher ones to pin down, pro or con." Nor did the entertainment reporter know quite what position he should take on Berton himself, since other critics had called the man "everything from an inept Buddha to Canada's top television personality." Only one thing was certain: the Berton show was never dull. In its first year, Shiels noted, "the dust never settled. He seemed to start a controversy almost every time he appeared on the screen." One show, featuring Helen Gurley Brown, author of the controversial 1962 bestseller *Sex and the Single Girl*, was axed by the stations before it could be aired. "It may be I'm just not for a mass daytime audience," she told Berton, "although I can't believe there aren't plenty of 'enjoyers' as well as the always vocal, outraged dissenters. If I hadn't taken an outrageous stand to begin with, I wouldn't be in a position to talk to anyone now – nobody would ever have heard of me."[33]

The first-season cancellation of Gurley Brown came about at the suggestion of nervous station managers. But there was more to it than this. In the months leading up to publication of Berton's "It's Time We Stopped Hoaxing the Kids about Sex" column, *The Pierre Berton Hour* had tongues wagging. As the TV columnist Jon Ruddy put it in the Toronto *Telegram*: "The show has turned again and again to tender areas of public opinion. Berton has unearthed some disturbing facts about burial costs and customs. He has probed drug addiction, organized crime, penal institutions, abortion, and prostitution, in a manner guaranteed to offend the sensitive, and antagonize all manner of organized groups."[34] By then, the range of guests included the Communist leader Tim Buck, the supermarket magnate Sam Steinberg, and the advice columnist Ann Landers – and that was in one week alone.

Early in 1964, Berton sparked even more controversy when he taped a series of interviews in Montreal, a move designed in part to convince the English-language station CFCF to carry his program. His interview with the Quebec minister of natural resources, René Lévesque, was spirited. Lévesque admitted that he was "a Quebecer first, a French-Canadian second, and a Canadian third," and he was forced to declare for the first time publicly that Quebec had to become "something that we can feel as a nation state for the French-Canadian people."[35] In February, the show sparked a debate over bilingualism when Berton's guest, Trans-Canada Airlines president Gordon McGregor, complained that the airline's progress in becoming bilingual was hampered by a lack of qualified French-speaking managers and workers. McGregor's words made headlines across the country, highlighting the issue of bilingual recruitment in the corporate sector.[36]

The unpredictable parade continued unabated into spring. In March, Rabbi Abraham Feinberg claimed on the show that Hitler's rise might have been prevented if Pope Pius XII had excommunicated him. Other guests during the month included the American syndicated columnist Art Buchwald; the putative "greatest con man of the century," eighty-nine-year-old Joseph Weil; and the controversial psychologist Dr. Joyce Brothers. In April, his guests included Jack Ruby's lawyer, Melvin Belli, Canadian finance minister Walter Gordon, and the folksinger Oscar Brand. A CTV mail poll at season's end revealed that, of all the guests, the most popular was a man who had admitted he could read two thousand words a minute if he had to. The guest was Lister Sinclair.[37]

Toward the end of the 1963–64 television season, Berton was able to report that he had interviewed over two hundred guests that season. He was proud most of them (120) had been Canadian, but admitted that "big names from outside Canada are still the raisins in the cake." For this reason, he proposed extensive travel for 1964–65, beginning with a trip to London in the fall to tape forty shows. He was irked by the 11:30 p.m. slot scheduled by the network, preferring 7:30 p.m. He told Jon Ruddy that CFTO's even later placement of the program, at 11:40 p.m., following forty minutes of news, weather, and sports, was "a monstrous injustice."[38]

The critics, however, had been turned. They, along with most viewers, had decided that *The Pierre Berton Show* was a hit. "Pierre Berton, whose TV interview show will return next fall, has developed a new way to relax. . . . For years the big (6-feet-4), red-headed journalist, who . . . makes his living talking on TV and radio as well as writing, has been quick to join an argument and generous with his opinions, but now he finds it pleasant to relax and listen," wrote *TV Guide*. "The advent of the Pierre Berton Show to this area," wrote the *London Free Press* columnist L.N. Bronson, "is something nearly every viewer has been wanting."[39]

Canadians were taking notice of the program, and they were also beginning to see themselves in a new light. Berton had not found it easy to convince Screen Gems that it should produce a show "with Canadians of international character who would say what they think." The producers thought it impossible to find Canadians of stature who would speak their minds in a colourful and entertaining fashion. But his show had proven him right, and Berton himself, columnists admitted, was the prime evidence.[40]

Berton had made a rough but successful transition from newspaper and magazine columnist to television host and provocateur. The conquest of another medium lent force and authority to his celebrity status. He was increasingly well known – and no longer mainly for his role on *Front Page Challenge*. *The Pierre Berton Show*, proclaimed the *Chatham News* at the end of May 1964, had "sparked countless controversies and debates in the realm of social reform." Any time a public squabble involved him, chances were that it would be picked up by the wire services and flashed to newsrooms across the nation. People held him to be both a herald of the new and a throwback to the old. "Often described as a man 50 years before his time, Mr. Berton closely resembles more than any other 20th century journalist, the crusading muckrakers popularized in the early 1900s by Lincoln Steffens," the *Chatham News* declared.[41]

While some took offence at the frequent banter about sex on his show, Berton was in steady demand as a speaker on contentious social and political issues, especially those involving social equality and justice. In April, for example, he took part in a three-day meeting sponsored by the B.C. Corrections Association in Kelowna. In his address, he imagined what a historian of the future might say about justice, crime, and punishment in 1960s Canada. Such a historian, he told the audience, would no doubt conclude that "the system of justice favored the upper classes over the lower; and he would of course point to a very definite class system. He would note that there was a whole series of crimes which virtually went unpunished while at the same time the police spent an enormous amount of time persecuting members of the lower classes for crimes which the people of 2010 wouldn't consider crimes at all."[42]

From the early 1960s on, stories written about Pierre Berton in newspapers and magazines began to appear ever more frequently. Between January 1958 and February 1963, the *Globe and Mail* mentioned the name "Pierre Berton" sixty-four times on thirty-one pages; but between 1963 and 1968, the numbers jumped to 614 mentions on 283 pages. At the *Toronto Star* between 1958 and 1962 Berton's name appeared 2,774 times on 810 pages, not counting the 930 times it stood at the head of his own column. After Berton left the *Star*, his name maintained a constant visibility in the press. Between December 1962 and January 1969, it appeared 3,824 times on 923 pages.[43] Wire copy stories made the Berton name ubiquitous, permeating the country. An important plateau had been reached in the transition from familiar name to established brand.

To become a successful brand, a product must have more than a recognizable name, for name, trademark, and design are empty markers, lacking meaning, until certain "authors" begin to tell stories about that brand. In essence, a product's markers must be imbued with positive customer experiences. "Advertisements, films, and sporting events," says the marketing expert Douglas B. Holt, "use the brand as a prop. Magazines and newspaper articles evaluate the brand, and people talk about the brand in conversation. Over time, ideas about the product accumulate and fill the brand markers with meaning."[44]

In Berton's case, among the "authors" of brand meaning were Berton's own writings and self-promotion, his Canadian publishers McClelland & Stewart and its publicists, the culture industries and all the intermediaries they supported – book reviewers and booksellers, television and radio critics, newspaper and magazine columnists. Talking among themselves and to the larger world about Berton's books and articles, his radio and television programs, and the man himself, they provided his brand with the element most essential for its making: narratives that circulated and collided within the public sphere, stirring debate, arousing curiosity, feeding anticipation, and dwelling on what this man meant to his fellow Canadians. They invested the Berton name with personal as well as social meaning, and drew from it a sense of their own identity. As Holt puts it: "Acting as vessels of self-expression, the brands are imbued with stories that consumers find valuable in constructing their identities. Consumers flock to brands that embody the ideals they admire, brands that help them express who they want to be."[45]

The 1960s became a key decade in forming the Berton brand. First, Berton and McClelland conspired to find ways of publicizing Berton as an author, and the media fell in line, dazzled by lavish parties and sacks of gold dust. Coverage of his *Toronto Star* collections helped provide focus and coherence to the multi-faceted image Canadians held of him: Berton as the tall and gangly boy from the Klondike who had struck it rich in central Canada; Berton as the historian and champion of the North; Berton as the media wunderkind who had mastered newspapers, magazines, radio, and television; Berton as the crusader for social justice, protector of the innocent consumer, the poor and the oppressed. Berton Berton Berton Berton.

Reviews of his books in the 1960s almost always lauded the man. The *New York Times Book Review* praised the "cynical wisdom" of the "expert on human gullibility" who had written *The Big Sell*. "Mr. Berton has done his worthy best to save the fool from his folly," wrote the reviewer.

"The author of *The Klondike Fever* here examines another type of gold rush: the way of the door-to-door salesman and the mail-order shark, plus . . . $36,000 dancing lessons," said the *Saturday Review*. "Every easy mark (and who isn't?) should read it."[46]

In a three-paragraph review of *Just Add Water and Stir* in *Saturday Night*, Arnold Edinborough provided a textbook example of brand-building endorsement. First came the idea of a man larger than life both figuratively and literally ("Pierre Berton is a giant in the newspaper industry – he stands well over six feet"); second, emphasis on his extra-ordinary productivity ("He turns out more wordage in a day than most people do in a week"); third, acknowledgment of authority, benign and benevolent ("This undoubted eminence sometimes leads him to sound a little like God, but he still manages . . . to please all comers"); fourth, provision of some general criticism, turning this awesome deity into the flawed hero of the coffee shop ("His intemperate recipes for Tomato Soup, Baked Beans, Corn Beef Hash, and Clam Chowder . . . betray a gluttonous and greedy gourmand, rather than a gourmet"). Finally came reinforcement of the original "larger than life" motif, but now – with attention drawn to the man's background and his abundant talent and accomplishments – a motif given full-bodied resonance through the link of obligation made between the man and those who "bought" him. "Berton is still the best newspaper columnist in the country and his collected columns should be studied by every journalism student. They show what true journalism should be – probing, factual, tightly written, sometimes jolting and always interesting."[47]

Notices like Edinborough's were a marketer's dream, for they were meaning-makers, not simply reviews. They assessed the content of Pierre Berton's articles, columns, books, and television programs, but they also forged links between Berton's beliefs and values and those of his readers and viewers. In doing so, they became instrumental in trans-forming *Berton* from a familiar surname into an enduring brand.

Berton wore such praise and criticism well: the praise pleased but did not surprise him, and he conceded that the criticism was more accurate than not, where his collections were concerned. The words that opened one review of *Fast Fast Fast Relief* – "There are two types of Canadians. Those who love Berton and those who hate him" – he would have found flattering. But what no doubt gave him pause were comments made in another review of the same book, a mixed one, which criticized Berton's heavy-handed satire but admired his reflections on the natural environment. "Here," wrote H.R. Percy in *Canadian Author and Bookman*, "Mr. Berton shrugs off the hard veneer of the columnist and becomes the true man, the true writer. Cynicism, superiority and all the other poses which inspire hate, together with the inevitable superficiality of the columnist, falls away: we find Mr. Berton warm, sincere, writing not to impress but to express; writing not out of a newspaperman's hard head but out of an artist's feeling heart; writing, I suspect, as he dreamed of writing before the modern Grub Street exerted its merciless pressure upon him; and writing, I hope, as he will write increasingly in the future, now that the pressure is off."[48]

Percy's thoughtful admonition reflected a truth about Berton's professional life at the time. His commercial success as a muckraking journalist had drawn him away from the kind of writing that earlier had brought him critical renown. True, he was now doing research on a serious subject, the state of religion in Canada, and his commitment to social justice and writing about it was genuine. But Percy had been correct about the "merciless pressure" of New Grub Street – whether in print or on the tube.

The tension within Berton between the desire to be seen as clever and the need to tell enduring stories surfaced early in 1964, when on one hand he delivered the completed manuscript of his novel to McClelland & Stewart and, on the other, he and Jack McClelland began to explore the possibility of a history of the Canadian Pacific Railway. The latter was a work to be undertaken – they hoped – with the co-operation of the company. "It's a centennial project," McClelland wrote to D.B. Wallace of the CPR Public Relations and Advertising Department, "that could be used for a long time as evidence that the Canadian Pacific hasn't entirely turned its back on the past. I think we are agreed that it's a great story; that Berton is probably the best person to write it; and the best person who is likely to be available to write it for some time." McClelland emphasized the "total public relations potential" of the undertaking. "This would not be a Company book," he pointed out, "but it would be the story of the dramatic origin of the Canadian Pacific. I don't think Berton would write a company history

– any company history – for any amount of money. This book he is willing and anxious to write."[49]

The overture got nowhere. "You have presented an interesting case for consideration of such a book," went Wallace's stilted prose. "However, the Company is in the position of having to evaluate, on the basis of Centennial requirements and promotion expenditures, a number of proposals related to its participation in the 1967 activities." In short, thanks, but no thanks. McClelland's response was brief. "I would be less than honest if I didn't say that I am astounded by your decision."[50]

Berton succeeded little better with his novel, which he called "72 Wedgewood Crescent: A Tale of Free Enterprise." His typescript, complete with jacket copy and author biography for the back flap, had been waiting for Jack McClelland when he returned to the office after New Year's at the beginning of 1964. "In this exciting tale about the cut and thrust of the world of big business," went Berton's blurb, "the author, a long-time supporter of the Free Enterprise system, tells the heart warming story of a one hundred percent Canadian girl and her rise to a position of power and prestige in her chosen Profession. On a secondary level the book is a moving tribute to the high principles of Quality and Service without which no business enterprise, no matter how ancient, can long survive. Thrill-seeking adventurers, eager for another Fanny Hill, are warned that this is a moral story about moral people, in the best Horatio Alger tradition, happily free of those suggestive scenes which have marred our literature of late." McClelland immediately circulated it without the cover page, providing only the title in his covering memo.

It would have taken McClelland's in-house readers no time at all to figure out the identity of the author, for the manuscript – a promiscuous mix of comedy, farce, and satire – held up to ridicule just about every sacred cow Pierre Berton had lampooned in his *Toronto Star* column from 1958 to 1962: moralistic hypocrites, the rich and powerful, commercial radio and television, hucksters and advertising agencies, newspapers, new technological fads, and countless other features of contemporary urban life. Within the McClelland & Stewart editorial department, the high hopes for the first original Berton book since *The Secret World of Og* turned to shock and then dismay. The latest product of the Berton writing machine was a novel about a bordello of industrial proportions in Toronto's affluent Rosedale district in which worker and client were matched by computer punch card.

The novel's characters possessed Bertonesque names of the sort deployed in his *Toronto Star* fantasy columns starring the Grebes, inspired perhaps by Dickens and Runyon but reminiscent of the *Mad* magazine school for authors: G.O. Sleed, a prominent and respectable Toronto tycoon, known by those who count simply as "G.O." – a single, middle-aged man whose fortune rests on his secret ownership of the one and only bordello in a Toronto purged of vice by the sanctimonious Urban Renewal and Social Reform League, of which Sleed is president; Judy Gilpatrick, a beautiful young woman of brains and ambition with an impeccable private school education, who is a Novice Pet in Sleed's establishment; Danny Drivel, the ex-convict who sets up a rival establishment – not a high-tech one like Sleed's, but one of the old-fashioned sort, complete with plush upholstery, soft lights, sweet music, and personal selection; Aggie Perlmutter, Sleed's long-time secret mistress.

G.O.'s business is patronized by the most eminent figures in the land, including the governor general and his aide-de-camp, the upper echelons of the Roman Catholic Church, leading politicians, businessmen, and other highfalutin figures. The *Playboy*-like Pets in the firm's employ are carefully selected from the very best Canadian families, and many of the young woman have become famous through television or other notable pursuits.

The plot of the novel hinges upon the competition between Sleed and Drivel, paralleled by the rise of Judy Gilpatrick in Sleed's enterprise. Through some clever manoeuvres, along with a little blackmail, she gains a controlling interest in G.O.'s business and soon is the company vice-president. Drivel leaks word to the police that his competitor Sleed has a shocking secret life with a mistress. Officers watch Sleed visit his old flame one night – a night when he tells Aggie that he knows about the child she once gave up for adoption, only for Aggie to tell him, "Not *the* child, Gerry-O. You mean our child" – and then they arrest her for unlawfully keeping a common bawdy house.[51]

The entire nation, fed by newspapers with names like the *Scream* and the *Moan* and the *Murmur*, is outraged at such blatant moral turpitude and calls for Aggie's blood. Sleed saves her by insisting in court that

Miss Perlmutter is not a call girl, that she is a woman of upstanding character, and that she has been his steadfast mistress for many years. The case against Aggie is dismissed, but Steed's reputation is in tatters. Steed confronts Judy Gilpatrick and tries to get her to acknowledge that she is his long-lost daughter. She denies it but volunteers to become his heir. "After all," she says, "I really am a chip off the old block."[52] She takes over the business after claiming that she will double the firm's profits, and the book ends in the same way it begins, with interviews of prospective Pets – except that under Judy's non-sexist management half of the Pets will be Pals.

Of Jack McClelland's staff, only one editor held out any hope for the novel. "Some people may be very annoyed by the book; others may consider that it is of questionable quality but I think there is a market for such a book written by Pierre Berton," he wrote. The manuscript seemed to him "vaguely reminiscent" of Mordecai Richler's novel *The Incomparable Atuk*. Three other editors were not so charitable. The author is "totally lacking in subtlety, the all-important quality necessary for successful satire," wrote the first. The manuscript's greatest weakness "lies in the author's inability to decide whether he is writing comedy, farce, or satire," judged another. "It is difficult to think of any constructive criticism of a novel that is so uniformly slick, bland, and second rate," wrote the third.

All agreed that the manuscript reflected poorly on Berton himself. "It seems that Mr. Berton is the victim of his own propaganda," number three concluded, and in doing so she spoke an editor's truth to this author's power: "Satire is all the rage; poking fun at cherished Toronto institutions is always good for a laugh; to keep the P.B. image of fearless exposure before the public, there must be a provocative book a year; and above all there must be Sex. Push all the buttons, and the Berton machine disgorges 72 Wedgewood Crescent. Ideal for Berton fans, the despair of struggling writers with creative ability who find it impossible to get published. For the majority of discerning readers, I suspect, a bit of a bore."[53]

Despite such excoriating comments, Jack McClelland had "72 Wedgewood Crescent" copy-edited, and in early March of 1964 it was ready for typesetting. The company lawyer, Robert I. Martin, had vetted the manuscript for libellous content, found none, but weighed in with his personal opinion: "The book is in very poor taste." It would be of no credit to McClelland & Stewart, and "would do Mr. Berton a great deal of harm."[54] McClelland read the manuscript one last time, and then sent a letter to his author. The book was based on a good idea, well written, and "moderately amusing," he wrote. Some readers and reviewers might find it "brilliant, devastatingly witty, and sharp," but others would find it "a crashing bore." The great majority would view it as merely adequate. McClelland told Berton that from his point of view as a publisher, the book was "a good publishing proposition . . . eminently promotable" and certain to sell between 5,000 and 10,000 copies. But looking at the project as a friend, he said, his view was different. "I have a hunch that a substantial element of the press will use this book as an excuse to crucify you. It's not a brilliant book and you are expected to write brilliant books." McClelland reiterated his willingness to proceed, but left the ultimate call to his author, a "personal decision" for Berton to make.[55]

Pierre Berton was publication-mad, but no fool. The 313 pages of "72 Wedgewood Crescent" eventually took their place among his personal papers in Kleinburg, along with "Snowball in Hell," the Russ Baker story – extant but not to be published. Although this failure as a novelist rankled, his ambition to write a successful work of fiction did not disappear, even after Peter Israel, editor-in-chief of Putnam's, also rejected the book. "In the end it is a case of our feeling a book just isn't as good as it ought to be," he wrote, adding that he would be "most curious to follow its career in the future."[56] For the rest of 1964, Berton concentrated on his television show and his work on the church in Canada. He had no inkling that he was about to write the biggest-selling book of his career.

THE ELSA FACTOR

—

BY THE MID-1960S, JACK MCCLELLAND, who prided himself on publishing authors, not books, had built up a stable of successful writers, most notably Farley Mowat, Peter C. Newman, and Pierre Berton. Thirty thousand copies of *Renegade in Power*, Newman's path-breaking book on the Diefenbaker years, sold in the two months following its publication late in 1963. McClelland's ambition to publish the best Canadian books expanded accordingly; he wanted McClelland & Stewart to surpass companies like Gage, Macmillan, and McGraw-Hill in volume as well as quality.[1] One way of doing so was to corner the market on books that exploited Canada's forthcoming centennial in 1967, and he enlisted Berton in the effort, inviting him to become the editor-in-chief of a new venture called the Canadian Centennial Library.

McClelland had already launched multi-volume projects such as the Carleton Library Series (which reprinted works of Canadian history) and the Canadian Centenary Series (a projected seventeen-volume narrative history of Canada), but these works were predominantly academic in appeal. What he had in mind for the more popularly pitched Canadian Centennial Library was a mail-order operation (complete with negative billing) run in concert with *Weekend Magazine*, which would take care of marketing and advertising. Berton accepted McClelland's offer, which included a downtown office, a secretary, and an editorial staff. The project was set to be announced at the end of October 1964.

Berton also became involved with a second group linked to Canada's hundredth birthday, a business venture called Centennial Celebration Consultants. This was a small consortium of experts with impressive credentials in the communications and culture industries; for a fee, they would "help industries plan and execute their part in the 1967 Centennial Celebration." A former Ontario provincial cabinet minister, Robert Macaulay, was the prime mover of the project, and he recruited the independent filmmaker Budge Crawley, the Toronto architect John C. Parkin, and the popular CFRB newscaster Jack Dennett. McClelland and Berton capped the list. The group talked up the approaching centennial with great enthusiasm, for across the country many projects, large and small, were in the planning stages. How could such eminent consultants fail to make money?[2]

Between assignments to write an original article on the Yukon and Northwest Territories for *Grolier Encyclopedia* and to address "the measure of morality" on the CBC television program *Horizon*, Berton worked away in the spring and summer of 1964 on the church project, reading books on religion and society ranging from Lewis Mumford's *Faith for Living* (1940) and Robert and Helen Lynd's *Middletown* (1929) to Dietrich Bonhoeffer's *Letters and Papers from Prison* (1953) and Paul Tilloch's *The Eternal Now* (1963), as well as works by Gunnar Myrdal, Vance Packard, Charles Templeton, and others. One morning each week, in the home of the Toronto professor and alderman William Kilbourn and his wife, Elizabeth, a devout Anglican, he engaged in a series of discussions with clergy and laity, social workers and others. At these meetings, Ennis Halliday, still Berton's secretary and office manager, took shorthand notes.[3]

By the end of May, Jack McClelland and Rev. Ernest Harrison had reached an agreement on the terms of a contract between M&S and the Anglican Church for a book of fifty thousand words to be written by Berton, submitted to the publisher by September 1, and published within five months. Sixteen thousand copies were to be printed. The Anglican Church would take 7,000 copies at a discount of list price less 40 per cent; M&S would sell the remaining 9,000 through regular bookstore channels. McClelland & Stewart was to pay the General Board of Religious Education of the Anglican Church a royalty of 25 per cent of the net price on all copies sold in the trade.[4]

This was an unusual arrangement. Berton initially agreed with Harrison to supply the book to the Anglican Church so long as McClelland & Stewart published it; Berton said he "wanted nothing from the church, except, possibly, some help with the research." But

this three-party agreement sacrificed the control that author and publisher would ordinarily possess. As Jack McClelland explained the situation to Willis Wing: "The position of the Church, not unreasonably,
has been that this is their book; that they must make their normal
margin of profit out of it; and if we, as the commercial publishers, can
accommodate ourselves to that scale and still make money out of the
market beyond their normal Lenten quota, all well and good. . . . I
would not say that their terms were easy. They established the discount,
plus a large royalty to be paid to them (25%), plus the terms of the
royalty agreement with the author." Berton himself was to receive an
advance from M&S of $1,000, a 10 per cent royalty on the first 5,000
copies sold, and 12 per cent thereafter. Author and church stood to
make good money from the book if it sold well; not so the publisher.[5]

Berton delivered the manuscript of *The Comfortable Pew* to
McClelland & Stewart on September 1, 1964, as promised. The title was
Arthur Hailey's, suggested when the Berton family spent part of August
at his cottage on Kennisis Lake in the Haliburton Highlands. Pierre
responded in kind the following spring when he proposed the single
word *Hotel* as the title for Hailey's next novel.[6]

Jack McClelland read Berton's typescript immediately and wrote to
Willis Wing in New York, proclaiming the book "superb" and adding,
"I think it's going to be one of the most important Canadian books that
we have ever published." McClelland was certain that once Berton provided examples appropriate for British and American readers, Wing
would have "a very controversial and very saleable property" to offer in
those markets. M&S sent a copy of the typescript to Harrison in mid-
September, and a week later he responded on behalf of the Anglican
Church. "We are delighted with Pierre's book and feel that it will tee off
some really interesting debate."[7]

Berton now prepared for the new television season. Screen Gems had
renewed *The Pierre Berton Show* for a third year, taking thirty-five weeks
of thirty-minute programs, with five airing each week. They also made
him co-producer – a duty for which he was paid $90 for each group of
five shows, in addition to his other compensation.[8] This would be a

crucial year because he intended to make the show and its guests more international in flavour.

After CTV had dropped the program at the end of the first season, he and Screen Gems had steadily built a market for it by making arrangements with individual stations, including some affiliated with the CBC. By 1964, stations in Toronto, Montreal, Calgary, Regina, and Halifax carried it, while the CBC affiliate CHSJ-TV in Saint John and CFPL-TV in London (Canada's second private station) had signed up to do so in the near future. To whet viewer appetite in late August and early September, CFPL broadcast the best of previous shows, including interviews with three Canadian "elder statesmen": the CCF politician M.J. Coldwell, the Group of Seven painter A.Y. Jackson, and the anthropologist Marius Barbeau.[9]

By mid-September, Berton had thirty shows "in the can." CFCF-TV in Montreal received a telephoned bomb threat warning that Berton's life would be in danger if he proceeded with a planned program on terrorist activity in Quebec. The show went ahead anyway. It began with a story and pictures of Sergeant-Major Walter (Rocky) Leja, badly injured while disarming a bomb planted by members of the Front de libération du Québec. A journalist from La Presse provided background on Quebec separatism, explaining that it took inspiration from the independence movement in Algeria. Finally, Berton interviewed Pierre Elliott Trudeau, a law professor at the Université de Montréal. While acknowledging that Quebec had received "a raw deal" within confederation, Trudeau rejected outright any comparison between Quebec and Algeria. At one point, Berton asked Trudeau whether it was true, as separatists claimed, that President Kennedy had said he favoured a State of Quebec. "Why shouldn't he favour it?" Trudeau replied. "It will be a banana republic run by Washington."[10]

Later in September, Berton flew with a Screen Gems production staff to London, England, to tape fifteen more shows. By the time he returned to Toronto, he had interviewed Bertrand Russell, Noel Coward, Roy Thomson, Vivien Leigh, Douglas Fairbanks Jr., and others, including a gaggle of mods and rockers, two British counterculture youth groups. All the London interviews were interesting and informative, but one proved especially compelling. It was with a woman he had not previously heard of, but whose name had become household currency. Honor Blackman, the beautiful actress starring with Sean Connery in the James Bond film *Goldfinger*, was the cause of long lineups in front of Leicester Square theatres that fall.

Blackman had been a starlet at the age of twenty-two, but she sank into relative obscurity until, in her mid-thirties, she acquired the role of black-leather-clad Cathy Gale in the hit television action series *The Avengers*. In her half-hour chat with Berton, Blackman talked as much about failure as about success, and was candid about her problems. After returning from a year with Jupiter Theatre in Toronto, she had been so depressed, she admitted, that she "could not face the milkman in the morning." She spoke of her mental collapse and the reasons for it, and of her months of confinement in an institution where patients "moaned and cried like animals." Blackman's struggles, and her eventual triumph, Berton suggested in an article for the *Telegram*, was a salutary reminder of the price of fame and of the danger of believing one's own press clippings.[11]

Canadian TV critics were astonished at how much Berton managed to accomplish in London, and they were not alone. "Pierre Berton is back from England," the *Telegram*'s Bob Blackburn wrote, "where he taped – hold tight – 16 shows in two days, astounding the British crews. This is iron-man stuff, and I'd be skeptical of the report if I hadn't seen him perform a roughly equal task – 12 hours in three days – in New York a couple of seasons ago, when at least he admitted at the end that he was getting tired." In his off-studio time, Berton had researched the background of each program and filmed an introductory show about the British scene. He returned to Toronto just in time for the season debut of *Front Page Challenge*, and on the following day taped two more *Pierre Berton Show* episodes, one with the journalist and former war correspondent Quentin Reynolds. So much for the notion, commonly held two short years earlier, that Berton "was no TV personality" and "that Berton, that leg man in seven league boots, had overstepped and would stumble."[12]

The first show of the 1964–65 season featured only Berton himself, along with a cup of coffee. "He didn't come back exactly mellowed by a summer holiday," wrote the *Montreal Star* television and radio critic Pat Pearce. The talk show host took swipes at the flag debate, the "ponderous approach" Prince Edward Island was taking to its centenary, and the controversy over topless bathing. "What he did come back with . . . was a certain freshness, an easing of the strains that can make a commentator say too much, belabor an issue too long. . . . Berton's TV show last night was a kind of capsule of his writing when it was at its inquisitive, descriptive and critical best." The assessment of the critic L.N. Bronson of the *London Free Press* was similar. Far from belittling Canada, "it would seem this is more the work of the canny performer seeking to bring out every detail of a guest's views, and to keep the continued attention centred upon him which the show demands."[13]

That fall, the show made headlines across the country. In October, Berton's interview with a former prison inmate named Alvin Gunn revealed the brutal conditions in Montreal's St.-Vincent-de-Paul Penitentiary. Gunn described deplorable living quarters, rat-infested cells without toilets, homosexual attacks on prisoners by guards, and the presence of "criminals" aged twelve to fourteen, at least one of whom had tried to commit suicide. Two prison psychologists treated the many inmates. "Prison Brutality in Montreal Penitentiary Revealed Last Night," ran a headline in a P.E.I. newspaper.[14]

In mid-November, Berton interviewed Prime Minister Lester B. Pearson in a full-hour special uninterrupted by commercials, filmed at Ottawa station CJOH and aired from 9 to 10 p.m. on November 22. He had scooped the CBC, and not for the first time. This was in fact the latest of several interviews with Pearson. His *Close-Up* interview in 1962 had been informal and personal. In 1963, a relaxed Pearson had answered questions with ease, and the interview proved so successful that the Liberal Party of Canada used a clip in its television ads.[15]

This interview was different. Pearson remained composed, but the session was a "no-holds-barred" event, with probing but polite questions (made sharper by Ennis Halliday's fine research) and candid if sometimes cagey answers by the diplomat turned politician. The prime minister announced that Canadians could expect "O Canada" to become the official national anthem by the summer of 1965. He admitted that French and English Canadians had different concepts of the word *nation* and said that he hoped to have medicare in place by 1967. But the most startling revelation of the show came when the prime minister confirmed a *Toronto Star* story of early October that the

Seafarers' International Union — taken over by the government a few months before when its leader, Hal Banks, skipped the country after federal charges were laid against him — had indeed contributed cash to the election campaigns of several Liberal members of Parliament.[16] The show, wrote Bob Blackburn, "was a joust, a treat, a spectacle, an education, a tribute to both protagonists, one thing that *couldn't* happen on the CBC, a marvellous hour of television which must be repeated."[17]

For the rest of the year, *The Pierre Berton Show* maintained its variety and quality. The session with British young people, recorded in September, aired at the end of November and made clear the contemporary teenager's beef with the adult world. As part of the same theme, Berton interviewed the lead singer of a new rock group called the Rolling Stones. "I don't feel morally responsible for anyone," twenty-one-year-old Mick Jagger told Berton.[18]

Canadian watchdogs, however, remained resolutely on duty. A week after the mods and rockers interview, CBC's Ottawa headquarters blocked its affiliates' broadcast of a *Pierre Berton Show* in which he interviewed homosexuals in California and New York about their lifestyles and their haunts. The cancellation, said the *Toronto Star* TV columnist Frank Moritsugu, reflected the extreme nervousness of the CBC brass arising from "the sensational excesses of its own program, 'This Hour Has Seven Days,'" which had begun to broadcast on October 4. The hard-hitting show had already dealt with the assassination of John F. Kennedy and the Hal Banks affair, threatened to spoof the Queen during her royal tour, featured John Rock, the Roman Catholic physician who had developed the birth control pill, and interviewed George Lincoln Rockwell, the leader of the American Nazi Party.[19]

That December, *The Pierre Berton Show* came to Kleinburg and into the Berton home. Sylvia Fraser wrote an account of the event in the *Star Weekly*, and its title and tagline captured the moment: "Bedlam at the Bertons' — or what happened when one busy husband decided to bring some of his work home from the office." The hook for Fraser's story was how a "Canadian housewife," who happened to be married to "a well-known TV personality and writer," needed always "to be ready for anything." Put another way, it described how Janet Berton handled the encounter between a production crew of ten, plus twenty technicians with "half a house full of equipment" and a family of "six children, two Siamese cats, five poodles, one collie, two tanks of goldfish, one horse and one mouse," all in a home now expanded to ten rooms.[20]

Shortly after nine in the morning, a woman arrived to groom the family pets, followed at 9:30 by a crew that proceeded to lay two thousand feet of cable in the house. "By noon," Fraser wrote, "the Berton premises resembled a mob scene from Ben-Hur," with twenty-one vehicles parked outside. Pierre, "an island of apparent calm, almost boredom," played *Largo* on the piano, while Janet searched desperately for her children's socks. When something resembling order prevailed, Berton took a seat on a plush striped chair in his living room, plucked a few of the Princess Sari's hairs from his navy blue suit, and calmly "launched into a spellbinding summation of 1964 . . . separatism, the flag, the world's horror threshold."

Throughout the day, backstage, Janet Berton remained the unflappable hostess, a natural role for her. She had coffee for forty constantly available, assisted the athlete Bruce Kidd (whose knee operation kept him on crutches), found time to prepare a gourmet meal for the gourmand James Barber (who explained to her husband the television host the perfect way to boil a potato), and tried to mollify an impatient and "discomfited" Rudy Vallee (who arrived late and with four poodles, all yapping). While the Berton children sang Christmas carols to the television cameras, down the hall in their father's office Vallee, not often kept waiting, decided he would not do the show and wanted a cab to take him away. It took the combination of Pierre, Janet, and the show's newly appointed producer to convince Vallee to proceed with the interview – which was accomplished without a hitch. "And off, in an impatient puff," wrote Fraser, "went the man who once told the world: *My Time is Your Time.*" Fifteen minutes later, with Berton in the middle of his interview with Bruce Kidd, the front door flew open. "Who," Rudy Vallee demanded, "forgot to give me my briefcase?"

Berton ended the year on a decidedly less hectic note. He interviewed Chatham's own Sylvia Fricker and her husband Ian Tyson, who together constituted the folk singing duo Ian and Sylvia, about how to balance both a career and marriage.[21]

The fall season had been a great success. The show was so popular that promoters could put a monetary value on its commercial influence. "If one of my clients slips in his pitch for just one minute on the Pierre Berton Show," one publicist declared, "that's right away worth 8,000 bucks." A quick plug Quentin Reynolds had given to a sports program was worth $5,000, he said.[22] During the season, Berton had made one gaffe he especially regretted. While in London he had been at the Pickwick Club when a member of a well-known British rock group entered the premises. Berton was so amazed that no crowd formed around the musician that he forgot to get the Beatle George Harrison's autograph for his daughters.[23]

At the beginning of December, Screen Gems had quietly announced the appointment of the producer who helped the Bertons deal with Rudy Vallee. She joined the show as "program organizer" at a time when its production staff was in flux. Ross McLean had left to return to the CBC as the producer of *Telescope*.[24] The show's associate producer left not long afterwards in order to be part of the team building the CBC's *This Hour Has Seven Days*. The executive producer, Herb Sussan of Screen Gems in New York, had departed some time earlier to pursue other projects. By the fall of 1964, the show's execution depended on Sussan's successor and on one researcher, one unit manager, and the new program organizer.[25] She was Elsa Franklin, described by the *Winnipeg Free Press* television critic Bob Noble as "a former protégé of Lorne Greene, dancer, actress and public relations girl."[26] She had no experience with television, but Berton immediately recognized that she was the person he needed and wanted.

Born in Ottawa in 1930, Elsa Shaffer had longed to be an actress and dancer. The Jewish daughter of a Russian mother who was the eldest of ten children and of an athletic Austrian father whose Montreal family was in the manufacturing business, she went to Lisgar Collegiate like her mother before her. At the high school, the one with the most demanding standards in Ottawa, she put on solo song-and-dance acts as she had in earlier grades. Elsa's parents wanted her to earn a university degree, but as their strong-willed daughter later put it: "I didn't give a damn about a B.A. I just wanted to act." She did enrol at Queen's University but abandoned the institution after fewer than six months.[27]

Elsa knew that Ottawa-born Lorne Greene, the Canadian CBC announcer and actor, was a friend of her father, so the rebellious young woman managed to convince her parents to let her move to Toronto to study at the Lorne Greene Academy of Radio Arts, located across from the CBC building on Jarvis Street. There, Greene, Lister Sinclair, Mavor Moore, and Andrew Allan were her teachers. But Elsa Shaffer was too driven, too vivacious, too much the natural performer to let her ambition rest there. Encouraged and assisted by Greene, and having won the reluctant acquiescence of her parents, she spent a year in New York at the Neighborhood Playhouse, the acting studio that had produced such stars as Marlon Brando and Julie Harris. Working at Bloomingdale's during the day, she once sold a lampshade to Greta Garbo.[28]

On a visit home, however, she met and fell in love with a British-born journalist named Stephen Franklin, a drama critic for the *Ottawa Journal*. They married in 1950, and she followed her husband as his career took them from one city to another. After a two-year stint in Edmonton, they moved to Vancouver when Stephen became the western editor of *Weekend Magazine*. They stayed there from 1957 to 1962. By then they had three children – a son, Havoc, and two daughters, Jodie and Melissa. Even so, she regularly read thirty-five or more newspapers and magazines a day in search of story ideas for Stephen.

In Vancouver, Elsa gave free rein to her abundant energy. For a while she assisted her brother, Ivan Shaffer, a business writer who owned a Toronto public relations firm, helping his company promote M&S books and authors in Vancouver.[29] Then she and Stephen opened a small bookstore, Pickpocket Books, specializing in paperbacks. Elsa ran it. She also did some acting for the CBC because, as she later put it, "I only had three kids."[30]

Pickpocket Books soon became a chain of four stores, including a large outlet in Burnaby. It was at one of the Pickpocket stores that she first met Berton, hustling his latest release. Overexpansion and under-capitalization led to the closure of the small chain. Elsa blamed the publishers for ending what, for her, had been an exciting venture in the book trade.[31]

The Franklins moved to Toronto in 1962, when Stephen took up an appointment as the first Southam Fellow in journalism at the University of Toronto. It took Elsa little time to find freelance work with a Toronto publisher. Jack McClelland's publicist had fallen ill and he asked Franklin if she could help out. He allowed her to work from her home on Bin-Scarth Road and gave her a company car. During the 1962–63 publishing seasons, she handled the promotion and publicity campaigns for all of M&S's trade books. The list included Berton's *Fast Fast Fast Relief.*

Franklin let it be known that she wanted to be Jack McClelland's assistant, but between her abrupt, no-nonsense manner and her habit of bypassing the hierarchy at M&S to deal directly with McClelland, she had made an enemy of Hugh Kane and no doubt annoyed others. Beverley Slopen, who in 1964 was in her first year at M&S as an editorial assistant, found Franklin volatile and bullying.[32] Perhaps to mollify Kane and his staff, McClelland suggested to Franklin, with characteristic charm, that she was "too good-looking" and energetic for the book trade and would become bored. She was made for television, he told her.[33]

Elsa Franklin has said that she met Pierre Berton for the second time at a party, not long after she arrived in Toronto. Berton remembered the encounter vividly. "She wore her jet-black hair down to her shoulders and parted in the middle like a model for a Renaissance painting," he wrote. "That, coupled with her high cheekbones and long, bridgeless nose, accentuated her startling appearance. She might easily have sat for Modigliani." Cynthia Kelly, a writer for the *Telegram*, described Franklin thus: "She looks one-third Italian Renaissance, one-third Mona Lisa, and one-third Hayden Street urchin." When Jack McClelland reintroduced her as his new publicist at that party, she immediately commandeered his most prolific author's attention. As Berton noted of the incident: "She came up to me and gave me hell about what was wrong with my television program."[34]

It had been some time after their move to Toronto that the Franklins bought a television, but once they did, Elsa watched *The Pierre Berton Show* with more than passing interest. "I just couldn't believe that anyone could be so awkward," she recalled. She felt almost embarrassed for the man. In the early days, Ross McLean had brought in all sorts of Hollywood comics and celebrities to enliven the show, but what Franklin saw was a "big hulk" of a host who "really didn't connect at all." Elsa told Pierre that he was at his best when dealing with serious matters, and should concentrate on that. Berton agreed. "I figured this was a pretty smart cookie."[35]

Given the turnover at Screen Gems, Berton lobbied hard to have Franklin appointed as his producer. The company resisted. Television production was very much a man's world, and female producers were unknown and unwanted. At Screen Gems, women did not occupy even menial positions. Still, with the star of Berton's show supporting her, the head of Screen Gems granted Franklin an interview. Feet up on his desk, he asked: "Why should I hire you?" "Because I have infallible taste," she answered.[36] He hired her to put the shows together, but initially gave her the underwhelming title "program organizer" – as if to draw a gendered line in the studio sand. Soon she was not only hard at work organizing the Berton show at Screen Gems but also taking an active part in the promotion of *The Comfortable Pew*.[37]

Franklin began her new job, by her own reckoning, "nervous and scared." She found her first months "terrifying" but put up a tough front, learning on the job.[38] That year, her self-assured and aggressive manner led to conflicts with the new American executive producer, Dan Enright, and the program's studio director. In the director's view, Franklin interfered too much in the show's operations – the placement of the audience, the comfort and quality of set furniture, for example – and he wanted her gone. So, for that matter, did Enright, in self-imposed exile from the United States after scandalizing the television industry by rigging *Twenty-One*, the popular game show he had produced.[39]

Berton remained adamant, insisting on a change of director and the appointment of Franklin as producer. Enright agreed to a change of directors, so long as the new producer was a man. But after a few weeks of stalemate, he relented. Elsa Franklin was officially designated producer of *The Pierre Berton Show* early in December 1964.[40]

Eventually Franklin and Enright reached a modus vivendi, although she continued to find him "very difficult" and he likely thought the same of her. But he allowed her to do anything she wanted with *The Pierre Berton Show*. Sometimes he made suggestions but her response would be, "Look, if you don't like it, I'll get out. Otherwise, this is what I'm doing." Later, she attributed her boldness to the fact that she had a husband who worked.[41] For her the job was a matter of choice, not survival.

In this way, a very close working relationship began between Berton and Franklin that was to last for the rest of his life. Franklin handled everything about the Berton show except the hosting of it, and she continued to do so until production stopped in 1973. It is not too much to say that from this point on she managed almost all aspects of Berton's life, beyond Kleinburg and his family. Berton had acquired more than his pick of producers. He had found a second helpmate.

More than a year before publication of *The Comfortable Pew*, word leaked out through a persistent *Globe and Mail* reporter that the Anglican Church had asked Pierre Berton, fired from *Maclean's* magazine for condoning premarital sex, to undertake a book about Canadian churches. Irate congregants began to telephone church headquarters. The *Canadian Churchman*, an official Anglican publication, reassured readers that the book would be recommended but not required for Lenten reading.[42] Before Berton had put a word on paper, *The Comfortable Pew* had begun to stir up controversy. Was the decision to commission Berton foolish or courageous? The tide of advance publicity was almost enough to make Pierre Berton and Jack McClelland believe in Heaven.

While author and publisher remained resolutely silent, Anglican clergy and laity, already worried over a decline in church attendance and divided over the wisdom of a possible union with the United Church of Canada (under discussion since the 1940s), kept Berton's unpublished book in the public eye by feeding the very debate they hoped for yet feared. In March, faced with deeply divided responses to the project (forty-eight messages "violently opposed" to publication and twenty-eight in favour), the executive of the General Board of Religious Education reaffirmed the decision to go ahead with publication. The executive committee of the Diocese of Calgary issued a strong protest against church sponsorship of the book, while in a "gloves-off debate," delegates to the Synod of the Diocese of Ottawa quashed a motion criticizing the GBRE.[43]

Berton watched the controversy brew and at the end of November sent Jack McClelland some of the more sensational headlines – "Fear Berton Will Harm Anglicans," "Berton Book Bothersome," "Anglicans

Shy from Berton" – for use on the book's back jacket. McClelland
agreed to the idea. Meanwhile, he had sent copies of the edited manuscript to Eric Hutton at *Maclean's*, John Clare at the *Star Weekly*, and
Hugh Shaw at *Weekend Magazine*, inviting their bids for excerpt rights.
He also met with Anglican officials concerned that their bishops
wouldn't have a chance to read the book before being called upon to
comment on it and fearful that prepublication leaks of passages from
the book might hurt sales.[44]

After McClelland assured Hugh Shaw that the Anglican Church
would not withdraw sponsorship of *The Comfortable Pew* and that he
would do his best to prevent any breach of the publication date embargo
by newspapers and other magazines, *Weekend Magazine* offered $3,000
for a 3,500-word excerpt, a very generous sum at the time. "There is no
doubt about it," McClelland told Shaw, "interest in the book is beginning to swell. It's going to be highly controversial and probably blow up
a fair storm. We won't try to minimize the storm in any way."[45]

This was a truly laughable understatement, and McClelland knew it,
for Elsa Franklin was already hard at work readying promotion of *The
Comfortable Pew*. Hugh Kane warned McClelland that "if we are to
avoid trouble we must make it very clear to Elsa what her duties and
responsibilities will be," and McClelland did so. By mid-September, he
had ironed out an agreement with her, providing a budget of $3,000,
of which $300 was to be her fee. M&S would send out mailings and
posters, but the responsibility was hers "to both develop and implement
the program for both trade and public areas" and to provide clean copy
and determine the dates for mailings. McClelland's deal with Franklin
effectively marginalized his own publicity department.[46]

From the Screen Gems office, the Franklin-Berton juggernaut
bombarded McClelland & Stewart with promotional strategies that
resembled a military plan of engagement. Elsa sent newspaper clippings
for a *Comfortable Pew* display banner to an advertising agency; she
organized a "literary tea" for Pierre a few days before the publication
date.[47] Together, they drew up a highly detailed itinerary for a cross-
country author's tour set to begin on the eve of the book's release and
designed to maximize media coverage in Montreal, Toronto, Winnipeg,
Saskatoon, Calgary, Edmonton, and Vancouver.

The Comfortable Pew was launched on January 23, 1965, as scheduled. By then, McClelland knew the book was going to be a huge success. "It looks like we have a runaway best-seller on our hands," he had written to Ernest Harrison. "The books printed, or on order, now total 53,000." At *Weekend Magazine*, Hugh Shaw was delighted. "Obviously, *The Comfortable Pew* is getting to be the biggest thing in church literature since the Gutenberg Bible," he wrote to McClelland. In the context of Canadian publishing, Shaw was not far off the mark. Jack McClelland's long-time assistant Marge Hodgeman wrote to her counterpart at Willis Wing's agency in New York that five days before publication M&S held orders for 55,000 copies, and that six days after it appeared, the book was in its fourth printing, bringing the total to 72,000. "It won't surprise me to see the sales go up to 100,000," she added.[48]

In Toronto, Franklin arranged for Berton to pitch the book on his television show and also on the CBC television programs *This Hour Has Seven Days*, *Front Page Challenge*, and *Take 30*, on CTV's *Telepol*, on CFTO's *Toronto Today*, and on the CBC radio programs *Spectrum* and *Court of Opinion*. On January 25 alone, Berton appeared on the Toronto radio programs of Betty Kennedy, Gordon Sinclair, and three other private station show hosts.[49]

Franklin accompanied Berton to each city on the cross-country tour and coordinated the local schedules. The whole trip was hectic. In Winnipeg, Berton discussed *The Comfortable Pew* at the University of Manitoba one morning, had an interview with the CTV broadcaster Bud Sherman at noon, and hosted a press conference at his hotel in the afternoon. The next morning, in Calgary, he held forth on television for two hours, presided at a press conference at the Palliser Hotel at eleven, taped five half-hour segments of *The Pierre Berton Show* in the afternoon, dined with the Anglican chaplain of the University of Calgary, and discussed the book in the evening with students.[50]

Berton had almost no free time during the tour, and the days of grilling on the hot seat made him irritable. More than once he lost his patience with student questioners and snapped at them; in interviews with colleagues his responses could be mean-spirited. Word of this spread, and for some time afterwards interviewers exhibited a certain wariness with him. He came to regret having acted so unprofessionally.[51]

Still, a year's prepublicity, the welcome controversy, and the gruelling tour paid dividends. The country was abuzz, and lay and church groups alike debated the book. In February alone, Berton's clipping service sent him over six hundred newspaper stories, articles, and reviews. Thirteen weeks after publication, *The Comfortable Pew* reached its eighth printing, with 145,000 copies sold. A survey by the marketing company Telepoll provided respondents with excerpts and a review critical of the book: 47.6 per cent of those surveyed said they planned to read it. Only 7.6 per cent believed it would harm the church, while 37.9 per cent thought it would help. Telepoll concluded that *The Comfortable Pew* would be read by two million Canadians.[52]

"The Pew: Phew! It's a Gold Mine," ran the headline of a *Toronto Star* story estimating that Berton would make $25,000 on sales of 100,000 copies. In a Ben Wicks cartoon, the wife of a distraught clergyman who has taken to bed tells him, "There, there dear. . . . It was just a nasty dream. The Bible is still a bigger seller than The Comfortable Pew." In the *Globe and Mail*, the columnist Dennis Braithwaite declared the arrival of "the Berton Era":

> Virtually every media outlet was preoccupied with Pierre Berton and his new book. We get Berton in the morning and Berton at night. He is in the book section, the religious section, the TV section of our daily papers; he is the subject of feature articles and gossipy items in our national magazines; he is interviewed by every disk jockey, advice to the housewife dispenser, numerologist and pitchman on every radio station in the land; he is on every television program, on every Canadian channel, not just once in a while or two or three times a day, but all day, every day – or so it seems. Our children lisp his name; our teen-agers take his advice on sex; our wives curtsy to his image.

Men, Braithwaite insisted, now spoke of the olden days, when "the Yukon was but some vague spot on the map, when Kleinburg was a sunny rural seat, when the talk show was unborn and Screen Gems hugged the coast."[53]

The Comfortable Pew sold more copies than any other book Pierre Berton would ever write. Total sales in Canada (mainly of the $2.50 paperback) eventually passed 175,000, and in the United States

Lippincott sold 130,000 copies of an edition that included critical responses. At Elsa's insistence, *Weekend Magazine* increased payment for excerpt rights from the original $3,000 to an unheard-of $8,000, and at Berton's request Jack McClelland increased his royalty on each book sold above 16,500 to 15 per cent. At a conservative estimate, Berton earned royalties of at least $59,000 on Canadian sales alone – the equivalent of $391,000 in today's dollars.[54]

Berton's latest book drew attention to certain realities that no thoughtful Canadian could now avoid. It painted a stark picture of the church's isolation from contemporary society and social thought. It criticized the church for cozying up to the business and professional communities; for its inability to communicate and use the new media effectively; for its long delay in confronting the issue of racism; for its treatment of homosexuals as if they were lepers; for its alienation of Native communities through a message that was Western but not necessarily Christian; for its indifference to what he declared to be a sexual revolution. Berton insisted that church leaders wake up to the new attitudes toward questions of chastity, premarital sex, birth control, and divorce. He took the church establishment to task for its complacent portrayal of Christ and for its lack of welcome to the nonconformist in pew or pulpit.

Berton called for a return to the principle of "Christian love, in all its flexibility, with all of its concern for real people rather than for any fixed set of rigid Principles." He wished to see a church that would revolutionize society and revolutionize itself. "Once the Church becomes the most uncomfortable institution in the community, only those who really matter will stick with it. At this point, one would expect the Church to come back to those basic principles of love, faith, and hope that have made martyrs out of men."[55] In making his case, Berton allied himself with John A.T. Robinson, the Anglican bishop of Woolwich. He quoted from Robinson's controversial 1963 book, *Honest to God*, which called on readers to abandon the notion of a transcendent God "out there" in favour of a God located within themselves. Robinson, in return, drew attention to *The Comfortable Pew* in the preface of his next book, *The New Reformation*.

The fury over *The Comfortable Pew* continued unabated. Clerics preached sermons with titles like "The Blindness of Berton" in the spring of 1965, and lay people published books called *Termites in the Shape of Men: Common Sense versus Pierre Berton* and *Just Think, Mr. Berton (A Little Harder)*. But copies of *The Comfortable Pew* continued to fly off bookstore shelves, and requests arrived for translation rights into Danish and Norwegian. The Anglican Church held a symposium to discuss the book, and then commissioned William Kilbourn to edit an anthology based on the presentations. Inspired by Berton's success, Ernest Harrison released two books of his own, *Let God Go Free* and *A Church without God*. The result was that G.B. Snell, bishop of Toronto, barred him from preaching and officiating at services in the diocese.[56]

Over the years, Berton gained a kind of visionary authority for having written *The Comfortable Pew*, and the phrase became part of the English lexicon. Fifty years after its publication, Michael Creal, who had been general secretary of the Anglican Church's Department of Religious Education in 1965, would say that Berton's "report card" had raised important social and ethical issues, including the mass killing of civilians as a means to an end and the role of the church with respect to Canada's First Nations.[57]

The Comfortable Pew and the controversy that surrounded it once again illustrated Pierre Berton's uncanny knack of fixing upon a subject that reflected collective Canadian anxieties and desires at a critical juncture in the country's history. In writing about the place of the church when he did, he acted as a cultural mediator – part stern prophet, part family counsellor, part observant bystander at a church parade, willing to shout that the bishop wore no clothes. Performing this role, he extended a reputation already earned as a crusader for the unwary consumer and the ordinary joe, and for equality and justice. By criticizing the complacency of those sitting in Canada's pews, he played directly to the generation gap of the sixties – for polls had indicated that those who objected to *The Comfortable Pew* tended to be over fifty years of age. In doing so, Berton allied himself with the baby boom generation and its situational ethics, and lent credence to both. For many of that generation, the church needed to become "relevant," to engage in "dialogue" with others, to be open to fresh ways of assessing life's meaning and the values of others, especially those of the young, thereby providing parents with a pathway to understanding their own children. The times, they were a-changin', and Pierre Berton was rolling along with them.

Like other successful cultural brands, Berton had made an emotional connection with his customers. The hundreds of profiles that tried to explain him and the incessant attention to his "product" gave Berton's brand layers of significance that went beyond his role as controversialist and author. All this – the personal and social values attributed to him and the interpretive directions taken by his books – established links between the brand and important aspects of the social mythology and cultural identity of English-speaking Canadians, along with the tensions inherent in myth and identity.

The most successful cultural brands address such tensions and seek to ease them. During the 1940s and 1950s, for example, Coca-Cola built upon its extraordinary reputation as a product synonymous with the myths of suburban comfort, patriotic zeal, and the American way of life. But in the face of sixties counterculture, an unpopular war, and youthful social protest, Coke's association with patriotism, militarism, and suburbia worked to its disadvantage; America's beverage risked falling out of favour. The company's marketers came up with a campaign that reattached Coke to American values, this time to the values of youth, and to the ideals of peace, compassion, and brotherhood. "I'd like to teach the world to sing in perfect harmony," the young men and women in Coke's new flagship commercial sang, gathered on a hilltop and gazing upward. "I'd like to buy the world a Coke and keep it company."

Overnight, Coke's brand had been reconstituted and revived. It had tapped into the idealism of youth culture with a humanistic plea for understanding and tolerance. "Things go better with Coke," its best-known slogan promised. "The right identity myth, well performed," Douglas B. Holt writes, "provides the audience with little epiphanies – moments of recognition that put images, sounds, and feelings on barely perceptive desires." This has the effect of lessening social tension by helping shape and nurture a sense of identity and purpose that provides stability in periods of social or cultural stress.[58]

Berton's criticism of the state of the church in Canada, at a time when its authority and relevance were seriously questioned, performed a similar function. *The Comfortable Pew*'s unstated assumption was that the churches were out of touch with a Canadian ethos that was compassionate, equitable, and caring. This is what many Canadians wanted to believe about themselves, and Berton helped validate the desire. In this process, the Berton brand became more than simply a well-known entity. It had taken another step toward becoming iconic.

❦

After the cross-country promotional tour for *The Comfortable Pew*, Pierre took a brief vacation with Janet in Mexico and then returned to his office – actually, to his offices, for he now worked out of three. Sometimes he laboured at home in Kleinburg, especially when writing his books, where he now had the luxury of a main-floor study at one end of the house. He had begun gathering material on the Canadian Pacific Railway and was also waiting for Doubleday New York to publish a compilation of satirical pieces, many written earlier for the *Toronto Star*. He called the volume *My War with the 20th Century*. It was a mixture of fantastic tales and warm nostalgia. One story, a recycled 1958 *Star* column, was "Memories of Jack Benny in the Days of the Radio Craze." When Benny read the manuscript for Doubleday, he wrote Berton: "I think it has some of the funniest articles I have ever read. I was alone while reading the book and I laughed out loud which, of course, is not an easy thing to do." In a note of thanks to Benny for agreeing to write a short comment for the book jacket, Berton told the comedian that he had been a fan since 1932.[59]

Berton also had a second-storey office at the corner of Simcoe and Richmond streets in downtown Toronto, home to the Canadian Centennial Library. One of his first acts as editor-in-chief had been to hire Ken Lefolii as managing editor and Frank Newfeld as art director.[60] In consultation with Jack McClelland, they projected eight books spanning Canada's first hundred years, including volumes on eminent Canadians, art, literature, sport, and food, to be published by Canadian Centennial Publishers, a creature of McClelland & Stewart and *Weekend Magazine*. It was at one of the organizational meetings in 1964 that Jack McClelland had agreed to appoint Pierre Berton to the McClelland & Stewart board of directors. By this time, as Roy MacSkimming has noted, "Berton's sales were so important to the company that he owned a small percentage of M&S."[61] As if to demonstrate his worth as an M&S series editor, Berton assembled the initial volume for the Canadian Centennial Library himself. *Remembering Yesterday: A Century of*

Photographs appeared under his name in 1965, followed a year later by Claude Bissell's *Great Canadian Writing: A Century of Imagination* and *Great Canadian Painting: A Century of Art*, with illustrations chosen by Eric Hutton but not attributed to him.

Berton's third place of work, the one where he spent most of his time, was the Screen Gems offices at the corner of Carlton and Church streets. There he worked alongside Elsa Franklin and Ennis Halliday and the assistants Franklin employed to do research and perform other duties. It was in these cramped quarters that they dealt with the abrupt cancellation of a show on hypnotism after a viewer complained that a recent Ontario law prohibited exhibitions of hypnotism as entertainment.[62] It was also where they planned Berton's interview with the Black Power leader Malcolm X.

The interview, conducted only a few days before Berton launched *The Comfortable Pew*, proved to be a momentous one in which the articulate and thoughtful guest belied his public image as an outspoken demagogue and fiery orator. Berton quizzed him about his views on the assassination of President John F. Kennedy. When Malcolm X answered that, to him, "the whole matter was a case of politics, hate, and a combination of other things," the host's retort was: "There seems to me to have been a fair amount of hate in the Black Muslim movement itself." Malcolm made no denial. Berton asked whether his god was white or black and what he meant when he said that black Americans would do "whatever is necessary" to secure equal protection under the law. Colour was irrelevant where God was concerned, Malcolm said, and he evaded the latter question. Berton quizzed him about his recent suspension from the Black Muslim movement, and asked whether he still believed in the creation of a black state. He admitted that he did not. "I believe in a society in which people can live like human beings on the basis of equality," he said. Such views were heresy among the more extreme elements of the Black Muslim movement. Within a month, Malcolm X fell to an assassin's bullet.[63]

The Pierre Berton interview was the last substantive one Malcolm X gave on television, and it aired shortly after his death. "There has been nothing I know of to show how a man such as Malcolm X might . . . appeal to, or get through to, people of thought and intelligence" in addition to Black Muslim or Black Nationalist gatherings, the *Montreal*

Star columnist Pat Pearce wrote after viewing the show; "nothing to explain why his followers might not just be outraged by his murder but grieve for him. The Berton interview did."[64]

That winter and spring, with *The Comfortable Pew* tempest still raging, Elsa Franklin lined up interviews with the Stratford Festival founder Tyrone Guthrie, the artist Harold Town (on two consecutive evenings), and the American writer Merle Miller, whose 1964 book, *Only You, Dick Daring: Or How to Write One Television Script and Make $50,000,000*, told of his struggles with CBS to make a TV series, thereby exposing the power politics and petty intrigues at the network. "Pierre had a lot more rapport with him," wrote Adelaide King in the *Toronto Star*, "than with those clergymen, actors and interracial couples who've been on the show lately."[65]

Elsa Franklin's first season with *The Pierre Berton Show* had been a demanding one, but it was a success. By the summer, she had plans well under way for the production of 140 new shows for the 1965–66 season. The five stations that carried Berton's initial five-minute commentaries in 1961 had become a committed group of thirteen channels carrying the thirty-minute program in 1965. The show, wrote a TV critic for the *London Free Press*, had become "a Canadian television fixture." Outlets aired it at various times, and Berton could now be seen in the afternoon, in evening prime time, and late at night. Stations sometimes ran the show twice a day during the summer months. Most of the 1965–66 season was to be filmed in Toronto, but fifteen shows would be done in London, ten in Paris, ten in New York, five in Washington, fifteen in Hollywood, and an unspecified number in Montreal. Franklin usually travelled to each location in advance in order to ensure that arrangements were in place. Only then would Berton arrive.[66]

Viewed as a cultural moment, "the sixties" began not at the start of the decade but a few years into it. Until 1964, what one writer called an "illusion of innocence" held sway in the United States and Canada.[67] In the United States, the interventionist liberalism of Roosevelt's New Deal seemed intact, and the Kennedy White House projected a youthful energy and idealism. In Canada, Lester B. Pearson, winner of a Nobel Peace Prize for his diplomatic work during the Suez Crisis, showed signs of ushering Canada into an era dedicated to the welfare of all. Cold War rivalry and the threat of the bomb still existed, but Nikita Khrushchev visited Disneyland and the Soviet Union blinked after its ill-fated attempt to ship ballistic missiles into Cuba. Race relations in America were uneasy but remained peaceful overall. The institutions of marriage and family, depicted by TV programs like *Leave It to Beaver* and *Father Knows Best*, seemed stable. The early raunchiness of rock and roll stars like Little Richard, Chuck Berry, and Jerry Lee Lewis had given way to pop stars like Fabian, Pat Boone, and Ottawa's own Paul Anka; the sanitized songs of the latter preferred puppy love and adolescent yearning to the earlier themes of sexual tension and social rebellion.

Then, with Kennedy's assassination on November 22, 1963, everything changed. Those in search of an explanation for Kennedy's murder had a choice between a deranged gunman or a sinister conspiracy. The May 1964 "Great Society" speech of Kennedy's successor, Lyndon B. Johnson, emphasized the widespread discrimination and poverty in America, but many found his promise to end them a form of cynical opportunism. Congressional passage of the Gulf of Tonkin resolution provided a convenient rationale for full-scale American military intervention in Vietnam. The idealism of Martin Luther King's "I Have a Dream" speech in 1963 gave way to race riots in Rochester, New York, the murder of three civil rights workers in 1964, and a violent confrontation in Montgomery, Alabama, between black protesters and police the following year. The American "family," represented metaphorically in such popular TV shows as *Gilligan's Island* and *The Beverly Hillbillies*, began to be portrayed as dysfunctional. Millions of women had opted to use the birth control pill and found a new sense of independence and agency. In both the United States and Canada, the children of the baby boom started to enter colleges and universities, and to voice their opposition to the Vietnam War and the values of their parents' generation. Their behaviour became increasingly associated with drug use and sexual licence.

As their nation's centennial approached, Canadians participated vicariously in these predominantly American events, milestones that became part of a shared cultural transformation. Berton – the Canadian with an opinion on everything – was a leading interpreter of events as they unfolded, constantly contrasting the past with the present, the personification of a curious contradiction. On one hand he was Canada's nostalgia king, constantly reminding others of the good old days of

family commitment and an innocence now lost; on the other, he projected the image of a hip celebrity who embraced the swinging sixties.
This ambivalence, mirroring the traditional Janus-like face of Canada
itself, coveting both order and freedom, innocence and experience,
became evident not only in his television show but also in his private life.

In the 1965–66 television season, he interviewed the fighters Jack
Dempsey and "Two Ton" Tony Galento about the old days in the fight
game, talked with the bandleaders Artie Shaw and Guy Lombardo
about the era of the big bands and "the sweetest music this side of
heaven," and shared stories with Jack Benny's sidekick, Dennis Day,
about the golden age of radio. In a Remembrance Day solo show, he
reminisced about his life in the army and the friends he had made
during the Second World War. He interviewed his long-time friend
Yukon (Bud) Fisher about panning for gold and the way things used to
be in the frozen north, and he used photographs from *Remembering
Yesterday* to show what Canada had looked like in the 1860s, the days of
Confederation. He continued the practice of filming a Christmas Eve
show at home with his wife and children, this time with some special
guests: Uncle Bobby and his animals, along with the folksinger known
only as Joso. Surrounded by a world in flux, the sanctity of hearth and
home appeared very much preserved in Kleinburg.[68]

At the same time, those who liked the Berton television show for its
controversial subject matter were scarcely disappointed. Guests in
1965–66 included a woman with three children whose father had
deserted them, a nineteen-year-old unmarried mother determined to
keep her baby, and a former newspaperman who had become a barbi-
turate addict when he tried to stop drinking. Berton interviewed
Thomas Davis of the American right-wing John Birch Society and
Norman Thomas, whom some in the U.S. called "Mr. Socialist." Isabel
LeBourdais told her story of the injustice done to Steven Truscott, a
former inmate named Wayne Lonergan spoke of his twenty-two years
in prison, and the Native activist Fred Kelly explained why Aboriginal
people were restless in Northern Ontario.

Themes arising out of the *Comfortable Pew* imbroglio found a steady
presence on the show in the year following the book's publication.
Roman Catholics debated the issue of birth control, with Bishop James
Pike – a Catholic turned atheist turned Episcopalian – explaining his

heretical views. Dr. Anne Biezanek, a Roman Catholic convert and psychiatrist, told about how her church forbade her to take communion once she set up a home-based birth control clinic.

Certain shows proved to be especially memorable, signposts of the sixties. Tom Wolfe, standard-bearer of the "New Journalism," analyzed the contemporary scene, and the eccentric twenty-six-year-old music producer and millionaire Phil Spector rambled about his psychiatrist and the generation gap. The comedian Bob Hope gave a rare interview and revealed a serious side. The historian Arthur Schlesinger Jr. told the inside story of his years in the Kennedy White House, as did Evelyn Lincoln, Kennedy's secretary. Mrs. Ian Fleming, whose husband died in 1964, revealed that she was quite indifferent to James Bond, as either character or cult. The Canadian novelist Hugh Garner described his poverty-stricken early life in a Toronto slum, and the eighty-seven-year-old American novelist Upton Sinclair made one of his last media appearances. Berton interviewed Lester Pearson for a record fifth time and talked at length with the political newcomers Jean Marchand, Maurice Sauvé, Pierre Elliott Trudeau, and Gérard Pelletier. The "New Wave" Liberals explained why they did not believe Quebec should have any special status within the Canadian confederation.

Increasingly, Berton's show demonstrated a preoccupation with the revolutionary aspects of the decade. McClelland & Stewart's collection of Berton's transcribed television interviews in 1966 was called *The Cool Crazy Committed World of the Sixties*, a title that McClelland thought exciting but that Berton disliked.[69] "The youth revolution, the Negro revolution, the sexual revolution, the religious revolution, the pop culture revolution – these form the threads of our time, and all are intertwined," went the text Berton provided for the book's back cover. In one way or another, Berton identified and supported each of these "revolutions," for he trumpeted the interests of youth, the cause of social justice, the modernization of religious belief and practice, and the preoccupations of popular culture – including sex.

Berton's attitude toward sex often exhibited an adolescent prurience. At the *Toronto Star* in the late fifties and early sixties, he had compared the breasts in *Playboy* magazine with those in its sixteen competitors and measured degrees of exposure in each publication. He interviewed *Playboy*'s founder, Hugh Hefner, about the magazine's success and asked him who read it. "What we've successfully reached is a young influential guy – the kind we always had in mind," Hefner answered. Berton wondered whether the notion that "flat chests mean more brains" was really true. The ongoing presence of "predatory females" in men's adventure magazines fascinated him, as did the "hypermammalian development" of the stripper Cupcake Cassidy. During a trip to London in 1960 he proclaimed the city the "Mecca of the striptease industry," having taken the trouble to do research in Soho.[70]

Berton revelled in the liberated ethos of the sixties. He explored Toronto's after-hours watering holes, such as the Calypso Club on Front Street, the Peppermint Club on Bay, and the Cellar on Avenue Road – thick with music and dance and a sexual undercurrent as strong as the cigarette smoke. When Yorkville became the trendy place to be, Berton was there, too, sometimes reciting his own poetry. While most reviews of *The Comfortable Pew* dwelt on the author's critique of organized religion, Arnold Edinborough's in *Saturday Night* saw a close connection between Berton's rejection of the church and his support for the sexual revolution.[71]

During the first flush of Elsa Franklin's presence, *The Pierre Berton Show* often featured guests and topics linked to sexual issues. Early in the fall of 1965, Jayne Mansfield, billed as "the bosom queen of Hollywood," explained her philosophy of sex. Two so-called "older women," Nancy Phillips, who wrote "One Woman's Column" for the Toronto *Telegram* between 1957 and 1971 (the year of the *Telegram*'s demise), and Gladys Taylor, a writer whose novels of pioneer days spoke to the ennobling influence of good people, discussed Stephen Vizinczey's daring novel *In Praise of Older Women* with its author.[72] The burlesque queen Ann Corio talked about her career as a very successful stripper. Dr. Eustace Chesser, a British version of Alfred Kinsey, spoke in London with Berton about his best-selling book, *Love without Fear*, stating that "nature is not concerned with chastity." In 1966–67, Jacqueline Susann plugged her salacious work, *Valley of the Dolls*, a Las Vegas showgirl named Dartie Minsky gave advice about how to handle stage door

Johnnies, and the Irish novelist Edna O'Brien explained why she believed women should have as many lovers as a man has mistresses.

Berton scarcely escaped this sexually charged milieu when he was with his friends at M&S, for McClelland & Stewart in the sixties was as different from John Morgan Gray's staid Macmillan of Canada or Lorne Pierce's upright Ryerson Press as could be. Jack McClelland was a night owl who enjoyed women and vodka in equal measure. Girls and hockey had been his main interests as an undergraduate at the University of Toronto, and he readily told the writer Marika Robert in 1963 that he "would rather discuss beautiful women or sailboats" than the books he published.[73]

The atmosphere around the office was an extension of Jack's ways. Allan MacDougall, in charge of the M&S sales force, admitted that he had been "captivated by the climate of licence at M&S: the raucous editorial meetings, the long beery lunches, marathon sales conferences that ran on alcohol and sexual intrigue."[74] Mordecai Richler and Farley Mowat, central to Jack's stable, had a roguish quality to them, and both liked to party. Irving Layton and Leonard Cohen were well-known Lotharios. But Pierre Berton was the leading figure among McClelland's hard-working, hard-drinking, hard-playing boys.

In the very early sixties, Berton and McClelland formed what they dubbed the Sordsmen's Club, a name they came to regret. Only men could be members, but meetings regularly featured a sampling of bright and vivacious women ranging from secretaries to well-known public figures, usually in publishing and broadcasting. On the few occasions when they were asked about it over the years, both men tended to be vague or disingenuous. Berton attributed its name to McClelland, and McClelland said he had heard of it, but that it was Berton's club. Despite such coyness, it is clear that together they were the institution's driving force. Jack McClelland's papers at McMaster University include desultory Sordsmen's Club financial records, a fugitive menu, and a mysterious wall mount inscribed "Sordsmen 1st Prize" – presumably intended for a plaque commemorating a singular achievement of one lucky member or another. One of them, the multi-millionaire businessman, race-car owner, hot-air-balloon captain, big-game hunter, Canadian bobsled team manager, and all-round bon vivant Charles

(Chuck) Rathgeb, described his friend Berton as the group's "master of ceremonies and general factotum."[75]

For its first few years, the Sordsmen's Club was known mainly to members, guests, and leading figures of Toronto's media community – a close-knit and influential group that in 1965 the journalist Jon Ruddy dubbed "the Gnat Pack."[76] But in 1963, Berton's former *Maclean's* colleague McKenzie Porter outed the Sordsmen in the *Telegram*. On Tuesday, October 15, he wrote: "Tomorrow in a private den off the Franz Josef Room another monthly luncheon will be held by the most wistful little secret society in Toronto. I speak of the Sordsmen's Club." He went on to describe feasts of five hours' duration, and the exclusion of wives, and the club's main purpose. "Although they conduct their proceedings with a Gilbertian degree of ceremony and decorum," he wrote, "the underlying aspirations of these middle-aged gallants are not difficult to perceive. The braggartry implicit in the name Sordsman, even though it is spelled without a 'w,' is palpable to any psychologist." Porter then named names.[77]

McKenzie Porter's heresy was as much that he held up some of Toronto's best-known men to ridicule as it was that he embarrassed them by revealing a closeted aspect of their private lives. Moreover, he had shown up at the Franz Josef Room with a photographer and then written about the way those readying for lunch scuttled "like frightened scandal-case witnesses" to a secret exit. The next day a copy of the Sordsmen's lavish menu appeared in the *Telegram*. "In my column," he wrote two years later, "I likened the Sordsmen to corner boys who have to gang up before they can summon enough courage to whistle at girls."[78]

Porter's exposé set Toronto tongues briefly a-wag, but its main effect was that the Gnat Pack's "second tier of writers and broadcasters" – among them "Marika Robert, June Callwood, Farley Mowat, Charles Templeton, Lister Sinclair, Elsa Franklin, and Fred Davis" – closed ranks around its innermost circle, refusing to comment about the club but using every opportunity to badmouth McKenzie Porter. In his memoirs, Berton provides an anecdote about an incident during which Charles Templeton, at a bar, shook an angry fist at the *Telegram* columnist. Porter "was in his cups and sneering at me," Berton wrote, so Templeton threatened to slug the fellow. Porter's exposé may have prompted this confrontation; it may also help account for uncharitable comments Berton makes about Porter – "an oddball Englishman . . . the master of the low-profile character sketch . . . a self-declared snob" – in an autobiography otherwise generous in its assessment of others.[79]

In 1986, *Saturday Night*'s editor, Robert Fulford, commissioned the biographer Elspeth Cameron to write a detailed profile of Pierre Berton. As preparation for it, Cameron conducted over forty interviews, and a number of respondents spoke freely about the Sordsmen's Club, confirming Porter's account and adding flesh to rumour. The twenty or so members, artists and writers, publishers and businessmen, would arrive for a lavish luncheon, indeed accompanied by women not their wives. Spouses could be guests, but only if their husbands were not present.[80] The club's core consisted of Pierre Berton and Jack McClelland, as well as Harold Town and John C. Parkin. Other members included Berton's friends Arthur Hailey, George Feyer, and Chuck Rathgeb, along with a former figure skating champion, Ralph McCreath, and a Maclean Hunter trade magazine editor, Bill Forbes. William Kilbourn appears also to have participated.

The location of meetings varied, but hotel restaurants were the venue of choice, especially the Franz Josef Room in the Walker House hotel on Front Street. Women invited to dine at one time or another included the broadcaster Adrienne Clarkson, the journalist Barbara Moon, Joan Taylor (wife of the sportswriter Jim Coleman), the socialite and columnist Nancy Phillips, the broadcaster Joan McCormack (later Frankel), the singer Dinah Christie, and the artist and gallery owner Dorothy Cameron. Some guests arrived not knowing who had invited them and expecting no more than a highly charged luncheon; they soon became disabused of the notion. "We had an idea that we shouldn't go home alone, let's put it that way," said Nancy Phillips, who also said she did. According to Cameron's notes, when one particular afternoon "dissolved into innuendo and disappearances," Barbara Moon overheard another guest, Jean Lewis, remark: "It somehow seems appropriate that I'm wearing my made-over wedding dress." Another woman that afternoon asked, "When are we supposed to burst out of a cake?"[81]

Members treated those they entertained to meals of smoked salmon, fried shrimp, fine cheeses, and ample supplies of vintage wine and champagne, as long as they agreed to stay for at least five hours. The first time Joan Taylor attended, she was introduced to shark's fin soup. The food was matched by bons mots, bright ideas, and witty speeches. "Raconteurs all," wrote one woman, "a sidesplitting aspect of the lunch was for any one of them to rise at random, glass in hand, and insult a friend of theirs. When practiced by this band of sports, insult was raised to a boffo art. . . . High-flying insult, like exquisite repartee, is unreportable, and often unprintable, as it was at these lunches with the performer hammering away at his target's idiosyncrasies, a barrage of hambone oratory and off-colour language delivered over howling, jeering, and comeback insults from the audience. Pierre did hilariously well in the insult contest. But he was too nice to win." On at least one occasion in 1963, William Kilbourn recalled, buns pummelled the speaker. Her subject was feminism.[82]

For some who attended, the monthly gatherings involved interesting conversation, fine food and wine, and nothing more. Their afternoons ended with a taxi ride home, courtesy of the Sordsmen. For others, lunch was followed by desserts not on the menu. Halfway through the meal, Cameron notes Joan Taylor as saying, the men would get up and take seats beside different partners. Late in the afternoon, couples would disappear, sometimes upstairs or to one madcap adventure or another. Harold Town's first flight in an airplane took place on what his mistress Iris Nowell called "a Sordsmen's caper," when he, Berton, Parkin, and companions flew to New York on Chuck Rathgeb's refurbished B-52 bomber. Given Nowell's account of Town's behaviour, it appears to have been a rather raucous flight: "Here I am running up and down the aisle in this plane, crazy over what I'm seeing, yelling 'Jesus, you guys, look down there at the fields. Look at the lakes! It's such a gas!'"[83]

"Certainly things happened," Cameron's interview notes for Taylor read in part: "When I went I had a hell of a good time"; "O.K. go jump in bed with [the] guy if you wanted." If Pierre wanted you, the notes record, he would be serious on a short-term basis, taking the attitude "Let's have a good time for awhile." For Taylor, McKenzie Porter's newspaper article messed up a good arrangement – "a rotten thing to do."[84] William Kilbourn, too, confirmed that guests routinely went off with Sordsmen at afternoon's end. The "heart and soul of it," Cameron recorded him as saying, "was male chauvinism. 'Boys will be boys.'" At least one marriage, between a judge and a professor of sociology, resulted from these liaisons.[85] The divorce rate among Sordsmen and guests remains uncalculated.

Elspeth Cameron's profile of Berton duly appeared in *Saturday Night* in 1987, and it portrayed him as the perpetual Boy Scout whose adolescent enthusiasms helped explain his life and career. The lengthy article briefly mentioned the Sordsmen's Club but said nothing of Berton's philandering. Yet some people Cameron interviewed made clear that his circle knew a good deal about it but had remained discreetly silent, not least out of respect and concern for Janet Berton and Elizabeth McClelland. Cameron's notes indicate that Janice Tyrwhitt (Berton's colleague at *Maclean's* and later editor of his books) told her that she knew Berton had affairs but that he was discreet about them. But *womanizer*, Tyrwhitt said, was not the right word to describe him. Helen Simpson, who had known the Bertons for over forty years, claimed at one point early in her interview with Cameron that Pierre was "not what you'd call a ladies' man," but later spoke of him as just that: "a ladies' man – always has the velvet glove, [if you] know what I mean."[86]

Joan McCormack Frankel had been a CFTO television journalist and Sordsmen's Club guest on more than one occasion, and had come to know Berton quite well. On the outside, she told Cameron, Berton appeared supremely self-confident, outspoken, and a womanizer; yet "inside he was still – is still the gawky overgrown teenager with acne."[87] Women saw in Berton what Helen MacLean, one of the characters in W.O. Mitchell's 1962 novel, *The Kite*, saw in the fictional celebrity journalist David Lang. "The thing she liked most about him was his willingness to listen: 'I'm listening and I value what you say even though you are a woman.' It was all the more flattering from a man who was frank, who obviously did not suffer fools gladly. It inspired an answering frankness." They could sense Berton's well-hidden shyness and the vulnerability. He was the kind of man who wanted mothering as well as loving and was in some ways more needful than they were. While they were attracted to his reputation and his power, they did not feel threatened by this large, ungainly man. Instead, they appreciated the gentleness, the kindness, and the respect with which he treated them.[88]

Pierre Berton's appetite for women was a facet of his prodigious appetite for life. At *Maclean's*, an editor once said in jest that the magazine should do a feature called "The Girlfriends of Pierre Berton: A

National Survey"; another quipped that the accompanying illustration would be so large it would have to be published as a foldout. Jack McClelland told Cameron he was saving "the real story of Pierre Berton – the other side" – for his memoirs. It was Pierre, McClelland confided to Elspeth Cameron, who "told me to go after" a woman named Helen Visser. "A lady-killer. I'd like to get the ones he throws away," Chuck Rathgeb told Cameron, laughing. Cameron heard Joan Taylor describe him as "a wonderful lover, very tender and loving," and Taylor was a woman who knew Pierre well enough to be aware that when he was about to travel for more than three days, his suitcase would carry French safes.[89] Cameron also recorded the views of a Toronto writer and socialite who spoke of his "rather varied sex life," of his belief that you can love more than one person, and of the fact that the women in his life remained close friends.

In every other aspect of his life, this was a man who grasped opportunity when it came his way, and he greeted women with the same energy and enthusiasm he threw into the quest for a story. Both involved forms of seduction, aimed at breaking down barriers to reveal a hidden truth in order to satisfy desire. The quest to know, whether involving information or people, is arguably a highly eroticized act. In the case of Berton's relations with women, by the 1960s any seduction appears to have been mutual, meeting the needs of both parties. Like David Lang, Berton believed that life came with a short string, its only touchstone one's own mortality, so the string had to be played out to the full. For their part, women found in Berton attention, courtesy, and understanding; perhaps, for some, a trophy. Almost without exception, like his circle of close friends, they were discreet, protective of him and of themselves. The Toronto media were not much different. Berton's amorous exploits were common knowledge and the subject of Toronto cocktail party chatter and newsroom gossip for decades, but the stories seldom strayed from such venues. As the *Globe and Mail* reporter Sandra Martin wrote years later, in a carefully worded sentence, "A lover of cats and women, he both inspired and demonstrated loyalty."[90]

Thinking back on Berton's relations with women many years later, Joan Frankel noted that he embodied all the attributes of Mars – power, competence, efficiency, and achievement – in the Mars-Venus characterization of male-female differences in approaches to relationships.

(Certainly, as far as sex roles were concerned, he was quite traditional in his attitudes into the 1970s, when his daughters embraced the feminist movement and helped channel their father toward it by calling him on his male chauvinism.) To Frankel, he had a great capacity for sympathy, going out of his way to help those in need, but he lacked the ability to fully empathize, to comprehend a woman's "life and soul." Besides, his sheer presence tended to suck the air out of a room, and this exacted a toll on those close to him.[91]

Janet and Pierre's close friends sometimes worried about the state of the couple's marriage and wondered about Elsa Franklin's influence. "One of most difficult problems – Elsa – Pierre – Janet," Elspeth Cameron wrote down during her interview with Jack McClelland. McClelland found Janet Berton remarkable for putting up with her husband's peccadilloes over the years. "J *has* to know about Elsa," Joan Taylor is quoted as having said, suggesting that the relationship involved more than business. Notes from one Cameron interview indicate that their friends believed Pierre and Janet had reached "some sort of agreement." Taylor opined that Elsa had created "the perfect set up" – a genuine business association that involved dining together regularly and extensive foreign travel. "Not too subtle – a way of letting you know," the notes read. They also record Taylor's view that Franklin had "moved in on" Berton – insinuating herself even into his family life as a means of protecting herself; that Berton had wanted to "break it off," but that she "clung to him"; that older members of his inner circle worried among themselves about the relationship. Charles Templeton said that it was one involving "a lusty man" and a woman for whom sex was "the main thing." Templeton, however, was no admirer of Elsa Franklin. He saw her as "gauche" and "nasty."[92]

In fact, far more motivated this female powerhouse, both in the 1960s and later, than sexual pursuit and pleasure. Elsa knew there was gossip about the nature of her relationship with Berton; she chose to ignore it, and no one made accusations to her face. In a lengthy interview with this author, she freely conceded that she had had affairs, but added: "You look at the CBC. You look at anybody in this kind of work. Somebody's screwing somebody, somewhere. . . . [Pierre] may have screwed a hundred women – probably more, but what has that got to do with –? It's not the sex, you see. It's got to be something else." Asked directly if she and Pierre ever became lovers, she would neither confirm nor deny. "I would never answer that question," she said. "The most important thing was that we worked well together and that we were good friends and I was loyal."[93]

Whatever the nature of the relationship between Pierre Berton and Elsa Franklin, their working partnership was brilliant. Berton and Franklin became a highly efficient and effective media, marketing, and publication team, unrivalled in Canadian life and capable of functioning separate and apart from their marriages. Franklin conceded that the time she spent with Berton did trouble her husband, Stephen. "Steve certainly knew," Cameron's notes record Joan Taylor saying, "& would drop the odd bitter comment about it."[94]

If Pierre's close liaison with Franklin disturbed Janet, she did not let it show. Franklin and others Cameron interviewed were unanimous in the view that, all else aside, he remained devoted to his wife and children. Janet's friends were at times concerned for her, but they marvelled at how easygoing and lacking in jealousy she remained.

In the fall of 1965, McKenzie Porter found himself forgiven. He was invited to appear on *The Pierre Berton Show*. Until he had exposed the Sordsmen's Club two years earlier, he had received more television work from Berton than from anyone else. Then, suddenly, he was persona non grata. There would be no more poolside "splash parties" at the Bertons' for him. But Porter was chuffed that he was once again on Pierre's guest list for the show, and duly made his appearance.

This may have been a sign that Berton held no permanent grudge. His renewal as a Berton television guest seems to have been intended as something between a practical joke and gentle revenge. The pre-broadcast publicity said as much: "McKenzie Porter, English snob par excellence, the most prejudiced, outrageous newspaperman in Canada, tries to explain why he thinks he knows what's right for everybody."[95] All was forgiven, if not quite forgotten. It was time for Pierre Berton to turn his energies to Canada's centennial, puncture even more sacred cows, and build a railway to unify the nation.

19

THE PULSE OF THE TIMES

—

IN SEPTEMBER 1966, THE *Toronto Star* television columnist Roy Shields wrote a piece to which he gave the title "Why Everybody Hates Berton."[1] The reason, he claimed, was the simple one that Pierre Berton was "the most successful Canadian journalist in this country's history." Shields made it clear that by *hate* he meant a blend of envy, jealousy, and resentment, stirred by awe.

Berton had just celebrated the fifth season of his television show, and the previous summer's schedule had been exasperatingly full – exasperating, that is, for Shields to recount. Berton, Franklin, and crew had spent a week on the Rhine and Mosel rivers, followed by another in Kenya and Tanganyika, in both cases shooting film for the show. He had finished two books, *The Cool Crazy Committed World of the Sixties* and *The Centennial Food Guide* – the latter an anthology of a century of writings about food and drink, complete with original recipes – for the Canadian Centennial Library, researched for the most part by Janet in the few spare moments of her hectic life. (Fletcher Markle gave the Bertons a half-hour plug for the food anthology when he profiled the couple and their book on the CBC television program *Telescope.*[2]) He had helped Jack McClelland launch an illustrated book series with M&S (this enterprise would become a division of M&S in the 1970s) and had cut a long-playing record for Arc Records, *Pierre Berton Reads Robert Service*. His treatment for a one-hour television drama series built around automobile racing, developed with Fletcher Markle and Elsa Franklin, was being circulated in Hollywood (it did not find a producer). He had invented an optical illusion toy with Frank Newfeld, contributed to a satirical map of Canada concocted by Jack McClelland, John Richmond, and Ken Lefolii, and taped twenty-seven episodes of

The Pierre Berton Show in New York and Toronto. "All right, Berton, that's about enough," Shields concluded, seemingly exhausted by simply enumerating the man's accomplishments. The year 1966, Berton later wrote, he had found "remarkably gentle."[3]

Elsa Franklin, of course, had been the person who provided Shields with the list of Berton's activities, since she coordinated all aspects of his professional life. By the end of 1966 Berton had decided that he no longer needed the services of Willis Kingsley Wing in New York to represent his publishing interests in Canada. He and Franklin, not Wing, had secured the record serial rights fee for *The Comfortable Pew*. "As you know it is very valuable for me to have an agent elsewhere, but the fact of the matter is, I know as much about the publishing and magazine business here as anyone and it is usually simpler and more effective for me to do my own negotiating with publishers and magazines."[4]

At the cramped and sometimes chaotic Screen Gems office, the legwork behind *The Pierre Berton Show* depended very much on the team of talented women that surrounded its host. Ennis Halliday continued as his secretary, Elsa Franklin drew up most of the guest lists for interviews, and two or three assistants hired by Franklin on a yearly basis did the research and assisted in other ways. Berton's practice was not to pre-interview, on the grounds that "no one likes to tell the same story twice." Instead, he relied on carefully prepared questions, deliberately crafted to elicit informative responses. Guests never knew in advance what questions might be asked, but, having reviewed the background material, Berton could in most cases predict what their responses would be. He never asked a question he did not think would be answered.

For some time, Franklin had made a point of improving his appearance and on-camera demeanour; his hair, now white, featured fashionable mutton chop sideburns, and he wore pastel-coloured shirts and matching hand-sewn pocket handkerchiefs – a Carnaby Street influence. She helped him relax, encouraging him to simply be himself, and the coaching worked. After one London interview near the end of the decade, the septuagenarian composer and film director Dimitri Tiompkin turned to Berton's assistant Dawn MacDonald and proclaimed, "*That* is a great man. Never before in my life have I made such a request, but send me a photograph of him with his signature." After an interview in New York the same year, the Yippie and Chicago Seven member Jerry Rubin told MacDonald, "I like that man. He is a man of the revolution." When she relayed the comment to Berton, he smiled and said, "Rubin is a part of *my* revolution, not the other way round."[5]

Franklin worked her researchers hard, variously inspiring, coaxing, and badgering them – always demanding full attention to the job at hand. Some found her impatient and overbearing. "I was terribly hurt and terrified by her," said one, "even though she toughened me up." Others, like Ruth Ellen Soles, saw beyond the abrasive manner. At different times Franklin's researcher, secretary, and production assistant, Soles came to appreciate her for her exacting standards and for a warmth and generosity not always evident to others.[6]

Berton's "all feminine entourage" (as the *Windsor Star* journalist Bert Steel put it) went with him whenever the show went abroad. What Soles called "the drill" began as soon as they found their hotel. Franklin would go to her room while Soles ordered the local daily newspapers for the length of the stay and checked to make sure the Smith-Corona typewriter Berton took everywhere had arrived. (She always carried a pencil sharpener for the soft lead pencils he used.) Franklin's room became command central, and after Soles had clipped everyone's room number to a lampshade, her boss would issue marching orders for the tapings to come. "She made me a professional," Soles said in 1982. "To this day, I think 14 steps ahead."[7]

Later, Berton told one of his former researchers that on trips to New York or Los Angeles or London, he would sometimes think about them typing away in their hotel rooms while the life of an exciting foreign city beckoned. "I would say to Elsa, 'Oh, let them go,' and she would always say 'No, they have work to do.'" Most assistants burned out or simply left after a year or two, but out of the experience came the careers in television production of a number of successful women, including Eva Nagy Innes and Eva Czigler Herrndorf. Marilyn Craig, retired as Operative 67, joined the staff in 1966.[8]

While Pierre chatted in New York with Johnny Carson, host of *The Tonight Show*, and the writer Jimmy Breslin or in London with the historian Arnold Toynbee and Dame Edith Evans, Janet Berton took care of her brood, grown to seven by 1966. From the outset of her life in Kleinburg she had been an active community member, whether leading

Explorers at the local United Church, attending school council meetings, or joining social service organizations. So when her friend Helen Margeson telephoned her in 1965 to ask whether she would serve on the Toronto Children's Aid Society's Committee for the Adoption of Coloured Youngsters, she agreed.

The Children's Aid Society had difficulty placing multiracial infants for adoption, for people seemed to prefer fully white or fully black babies. To counter this attitude, Janet and other committee members gave slide shows and talks in Toronto-area schools and church basements, trying to convince people to take multiracial children into their homes. "Mommy's out selling babies" was the way one of her kids explained her absence on nights she was away from home. On a number of occasions, she and Pierre discussed the problems of mixed-race children in the Toronto area. Then one day he suggested they adopt one. The couple had been talking about having another child, Pierre was well known for his outspoken criticism of racial discrimination, and the two agreed they should act on their beliefs. In consequence, a representative of the Children's Aid Society, initially suspicious of the couple's motives, showed up unannounced at the Berton home one Saturday morning and saw the children happily playing with friends, and the adoption went forward. The only stipulation the couple made was that the child be of mixed colour.[9]

The whole Berton family travelled into Toronto in the summer of 1965 to the adoption agency to pick up the newest member of the family. They designated Peggy Anne, now almost four, to accompany the social worker to the backroom nursery and bring back "her" baby. When they returned, the social worker was carrying a tiny brown moppet with big eyes and curly black hair, and Peggy Anne was holding her new sister's hand. She had been given the name Robin, but at home that soon changed. Pierre's suggestion of Prudence met a chorus of condemnation; instead, they called her Perri.

Warm and welcoming and without pretence, the Berton residence had long been a second home for neighbourhood children and sometimes their parents. Almost always, there were visitors for dinner on Sunday nights, sometimes guests of Pierre such as the New York publisher Alfred Knopf, sometimes those of Janet such as their neighbour

Dr. Peter Granger, the local Scoutmaster who had become Pierre's personal physician. So frequently did friends come for supper that in her mid-teens Patsy wondered whether there would ever be a time when she would sit down to a meal with just her immediate family. Only later did she come to appreciate her mother's natural generosity and understand the grace of her example.[10]

The Bertons seemed to pick up wayward children the way they picked up wayward pets – without much thought to background or behaviour. One such child was eighteen-year-old Victoria Filion. Very much the progeny of her father, the exuberant and comic Harry, Vicki had proven by her late teens to be more than her father and mother, Veryl, could handle. She found high school a real challenge, and had trouble concentrating on any one thing for long; so she quit. A strong-willed only child, she seemed impervious to guidance – at least from her parents. In 1965, Pierre and Janet agreed to take Vicki into their home, hoping that a change of environment and the company of other teenagers would give the wild child from the West Coast a sense of direction.[11]

Vicki's exposure to the boisterous Berton home came as a shock for the only child. "All those people under one roof (eight children, two adults, and many, many animals) scared me half to death," she later recounted. She spent the next six months with the Bertons, sharing a downstairs bedroom with Penny, two years her junior. The adjustment was hard for Penny at first, but she did not complain and the two girls became fast friends. Vicki registered in high school, and for a while, with her new-found family and its non-judgmental parents, everything went as Harry and Pierre had hoped. She soon discovered what she later called "the beauty of this family." There were few arguments and little backtalk. This alone was something new to her. "Homework was done with dispatch, as were the dishes – my jaw agape. Pierre and Janet rarely had to raise a voice to scold. . . . It was a well-run unit and I became an improved person." Improved, perhaps, but not controlled. That summer Pierre became involved in a Kleinburg charity event for the Voice of Women where the entertainment was provided by a small travelling circus. Vicki fell for the assistant lion tamer. Nothing could keep her from pursuing her beau from this point on, and soon she and

Michel Gabereau were wed. This scenario had not been in the Filion-Berton playbook.[12]

Another unexpected visitor to the Berton home was a young woman Pierre interviewed for television during the 1966–67 season. Mary Carpenter was a twenty-three-year-old Inuit woman from Sachs Harbour, Northwest Territories, newly arrived in the Canadian south. Berton had met her father, one of the wealthiest Native people in the region, when traversing the North for *Maclean's* years before. Her appearance on *The Pierre Berton Show* was a memorable one, for she broke the stereotype of northern Native people as silent and self-effacing and wearing a perpetual grin. Mary Carpenter was outspoken – "a born shit-disturber," as Berton put it – and she spoke frankly about racism and class in Canada's north. When she told Berton on air about the humiliation of being slapped in the face by a white woman who asked why she wasn't grateful for everything white people had done, she broke down in tears, and he cut to a commercial, reassuring her that it was important for Canadians to hear such things. Later in the interview, her composure restored, she said of Canada's whites, "They took away my language, they took away my parents, and they made me a Twilight Eskimo."[13]

Of all Berton's guests that year – and they included the comedian Mort Sahl, the singer Petula Clark, and the black activist Stokely Carmichael – Mary Carpenter impressed him most. He invited her to spend Christmas with his family, and she appeared with his children on the annual Christmas show from Kleinburg. Carpenter was happy to be there, since her landlord had asked her to leave days before, following a boisterous party with friends from home; besides, the flatmate she had advertised for earlier turned out to be a call girl. "Honestly," she wrote Berton, "my phone never rang so much."[14]

That Christmas, Berton discovered that Carpenter dreamed of a higher education, so he contacted a professor who had seen her on television and had offered to help raise funds to send her to university. Pierre also spoke to friends at *Maclean's*, suggesting a first-person article by Carpenter, accompanied by a sidebar of poems she had written that reflected her bitterness toward white people. Like so many others, Mary Carpenter was made welcome by the Berton family – and maintained contact with Pierre over the years to come.[15]

≫≪

A transcontinental railway and a world exposition helped refuel Pierre Berton's nationalist commitment in the mid-1960s. In 1966 he gave his project on the building of the Canadian Pacific Railway serious, if episodic attention. For the first time, he hired a researcher to gather documents. Norman Kelly, with a freshly minted M.A. in Canadian political history from Carleton University, had heard that Berton was looking for a researcher, made contact, and found him easy to talk to. Kelly, later to become a Toronto city councillor of long standing, was at the time enrolled in Queen's University's Ph.D. program in Canadian history.[16]

Located in Ottawa, Kelly began work for Berton in May 1966, preparing a detailed index of primary and secondary sources available in the Public Archives of Canada and elsewhere. Then he began to compile a comprehensive bibliography that assessed the sources. With the help of an article he suggested to the *Ottawa Citizen*, indicating that Pierre Berton was seeking historical material on the CPR and its construction, information began to arrive about construction songs, diaries, and hitherto unknown correspondence. Berton provided Kelly with an overview of how he thought his book would unfold – the West as it existed before the CPR; surveying, politics, financing, and construction; subsections on minor figures, the importation of Chinese workers, the Riel Rebellion, and completion of the railway with the driving of the last spike.[17]

Kelly completed his bibliography in late fall. He was surprised at how little had been written on the CPR and the 1880s and how scattered the primary sources were. "At first I thought your venture to be little more than the journalist's imaginative reworking of a well-known subject (you should hear the digs I receive from historians); but my research has convinced me that your book will mark a significant advance in our understanding of the later 19th century."[18] At Ennis Halliday's suggestion, Berton asked for a progress report each Monday, and Kelly received payment on a semi-weekly basis, at the rate of $100 per week. This continued into 1968.[19]

Berton was pleased with Kelly's work and congratulated him on its excellence; but he kept pushing his researcher toward new sources of material, whether the Canadian Railroad Historical Association or the granddaughter of the assistant to Sir Sandford Fleming – the latter a key figure in the history of the transcontinental railway. For while thorough, Kelly's research lacked an essential ingredient. Berton hinted at it in the letter to Kelly in which he outlined the book. "As an aside in all these instances I need the very smell and feel of the times. A feeling of what Winnipeg, Ottawa, Montreal and the other major cities were like. What people wore and ate, their habits, fads and fancies and popular songs of the day. On specific days I need to know what the weather was like."[20] The analytical and intellectual nature of Kelly's training in history, in short, neglected the senses – touch, taste, sound, and sight. Berton appreciated Kelly's assistance, but he knew that for this book to engage readers he would need to coax an evocative recreation of people and places out of the source material.

One striking feature of the general outline Berton sent to Norman Kelly in October 1966, was the absence of any reference to the Canadian Pacific Railway as a vehicle for nation building. The notion of its role in the east-west integration of Canada was inherent in the very idea of a transcontinental railway, but the theme of the railway as an embodiment of national ambition and spirit was not yet dominant. He had read Donald Creighton's magisterial two-volume biography of John A. Macdonald, which all but made the CPR the product of Macdonald's mind and will; but at this stage Berton was just as interested in the building of the railway as in the ambitions of Canada's first prime minister. He wanted to write about coolies more than Conservatives. The inspiration for fusing concrete achievement with national vision came less from his reading or research than from his own life. For in 1967, while Kelly doggedly tracked down historical sources, Pierre Berton witnessed contemporary Canada's national dream directly.

Berton went to Expo 67, the "Universal and International Exhibition" held in Montreal, no fewer than five times in the summer of 1967. Initiated by Montreal mayor Jean Drapeau in 1962 after Moscow cancelled its plans to host the fair, Expo – with its theme "Man and His World" – marked Canada's entrance onto the world stage, and constituted a grand climax to the hundreds of centennial projects in every town and city in Canada. At Expo, Canadians' ambitions and achievements were put on display, among them the Toronto architect Arthur Erickson's pyramidal structure "Man in His Community," built out of Douglas fir, and the Montreal architect Moshe Safdie's revolutionary housing design, Habitat 67. Each was easily as remarkable as Buckminster Fuller's geodesic dome, which housed the American pavilion.

Opening day, April 27, 1967, marked by fireworks and speeches and hoopla, became a peacetime symbol of national pride equivalent to the taking of Vimy Ridge in war fifty years earlier. On the front page of the *Toronto Star*, Peter C. Newman wrote on April 28 that Expo's opening day was perhaps "one of those rare moments that changed the direction of a nation's history . . . the greatest thing we have ever done as a nation." Berton was present at the opening ceremonies, combining business and pleasure. He, too, recognized the import of the moment, and savoured it. Listening to the band playing and the thousands of proud Canadians singing and watching clouds of balloons rise slowly into the air, he was moved beyond measure. "I tried to fight back the tears in my eyes and failed. My friend the witty Bill Forbes . . . stood with me, and I saw that his eyes were damp, too. It was a glorious moment. . . . It was impossible . . . not to sense the feeling in the crowd. *We did it!*"[21]

Berton saw this as a great "romantic moment," one of the best of his life – the kind Somerset Maugham had said were so elusive and difficult to recognize. Even as the balloons continued to ascend, he began to convert the occasion into instant nostalgia – imagining himself, as he so often did, looking back as an old man, glimpsing the Berton of 1967 "through the inverted telescope of the future." It was a poignant moment, too, with a sense of loss intruding into that of gain, and there can be little doubt that during the ceremonies his mind went back to other aspects of his own past – to the West Coast, to Dawson, and to his mother. Laura Berton, almost eighty-nine, had died earlier in the year, after a descent into dementia; she was placed in a nursing home when she was no longer able to recognize even Lucy, who had been caring for her. Pierre and his mother had always been close, but working on *I Married the Klondike* had drawn them closer. It troubled Berton that one more link to the past, his past, had been severed.[22]

Special moments in a life are fleeting, and once gone, they left deep pangs of loss for Berton that only an evocation of history could alleviate. The uniqueness of Expo 67, with its radical casting away of national diffidence and modesty and its embrace of pride of country and accomplishment, was one such instant. This sense of the constant erasure of the past, part of his makeup since he had witnessed Dawson's gradual but inevitable decay as a child, led Berton to treasure the existential moment. He resolved that his family would not miss Expo, so he took Janet to the fair for a week in May as a kind of reconnaissance mission, and while there the couple planned a Berton family adventure for midsummer.[23] Nineteen-year-old Penny was already working at the fair, so Pierre arranged to lease a twenty-six-foot boat to take the rest of the Berton gang from the Rideau Canal and Kingston to Montreal. It was Janet who took the Power Squadron courses on boating and navigation.

As often as not, the advice Janet Berton gave her captain went unheeded at the helm. On the way to Montreal, Pierre was stopped for speeding on the Rideau Lakes, and coming back via the St. Lawrence Seaway he managed to lose control of the boat as it entered a lock, damaging the hull enough that water began to flood the head. The family abandoned ship while still in the lock, following a moment of panic when no one could locate Perri. They found her in the galley, stuffing herself with jelly doughnuts. Later, they made their way home in the dry comfort of a station wagon.[24]

The opening of Expo 67 and the family's summer adventure became the highlight of Pierre Berton's centennial year, topping receipt in Montreal of an award from the Canadian Authors Association as its "Man of the Century" – a designation he deemed plain silly, given Canadian writers of the quality of Stephen Leacock, W.O. Mitchell, Gabrielle Roy, and Donald Creighton. Other centennial-related activities proved equally anticlimactic.[25] Centennial Celebration Consultants had been a bust. Few agencies or groups believed that such a lofty set of experts would do any actual work, so Berton and his partners used their meagre earnings to throw a party for themselves. His musical, *Paradise Hill*, commissioned by Mavor Moore for the Charlottetown Festival, was another flop. Set in the Klondike, it was based on a supposedly true story about a miner who "rents" a dance-hall girl one winter with an offer of her weight of gold. "An outlandishly turgid and lifeless concoction" was Nathan Cohen's verdict.[26]

Still, the year held some very special moments beyond that of Expo 67. One was the experience of organizing and taking part in his own community's celebration of the national centennial. The first Binder Twine Festival, of which the Bertons were principal organizers, evoked Kleinburg's days before suburban encroachment, when the blacksmith of the rural village hired townspeople to help tie up the sheaves of wheat, and music and dancing followed a hard day's work. The event was so successful, with Pierre and Janet and others dolled up in old-fashioned garb, it became an annual event.[27]

In the autumn, *Front Page Challenge* entered its second decade. Fred Davis, Gordon Sinclair, the broadcaster Betty Kennedy (who had replaced Toby Robins in 1962), and Pierre Berton were now such fixtures in Canadian living rooms that their personalities and weekly presence brought the comfort of the predictable. *The Pierre Berton Show* began its sixth season as explosive and controversial as ever. In October, the separatist leader Pierre Bourgault told viewers that his group, the Rassemblement pour l'indépendance nationale, would block traffic and even sink a ship in the St. Lawrence Seaway, if necessary, to strengthen its bargaining position with the federal government. At the beginning of November, Secretary of State Judy LaMarsh charged that the CBC was plagued by "rotten management" and was then called to appear before the House of Commons broadcasting committee to explain herself. Within a month, J. Alphonse Ouimet, president of the CBC, announced his resignation.[28]

The Canadian Centennial Library proved to be a great success, with each of its ten titles, including the Bertons' *Centennial Food Guide*, selling print runs of 100,000 or more. Berton was now in charge of the entire McClelland & Stewart Illustrated Books Division, launched at a lavish reception at the King Edward Hotel in June 1967, to which three hundred guests were invited.[29] Berton brought Leslie Hannon back from England when Ken Lefolii left, and commissioned individual titles like *The Taming of the Canadian West* and *Remember Expo*. Planning began on a new series, the Illustrated Social History of Canada, to include one volume for almost every decade of the nineteenth and twentieth centuries. The first books, available upon subscription and sent out by mail, would be released in the mid-seventies. Margaret Atwood and June Callwood were among the authors and the University of Toronto historian Michael Bliss was the senior editorial adviser. M&S paid Berton an annual salary of $24,000, half of which was in the form of shares in the common stock of the company. Eventually, this amounted to more than 2.5 per cent.[30]

Pierre also had two other new projects under way. One was a television program developed for Screen Gems, the brainchild of the ever-inventive Elsa Franklin. She called it *Under Attack*. Less a program than a happening, the show reflected the commitment she and Berton shared to give youth a public voice. Prominent public figures in politics, the arts, and the entertainment industry would be grilled by a panel of three university students, with Pierre as moderator. One of Franklin's favourite enterprises, the show travelled to campuses in Canada and abroad, taking the pulse of the baby boom generation and allowing them to confront their elders. It was picked up and broadcast by television stations across the country. Some guests, such as the cartoonist Al Capp and the TV producer David Susskind, proven veterans of *The Pierre Berton Show*, gave as good as they got with student critics who could at times be shrill or strident. Others, such as Nathaniel Branden, follower and lover of the right-wing novelist and libertarian Ayn Rand, became rattled by the experience – in Branden's case, to the extent that he walked off the set when a youthful panellist, drawing attention to Branden's trembling hands and his white knuckles, asked him why he was so afraid of three students. Franklin convinced Branden to finish the show by agreeing not to air his petulant exit.[31]

With two television programs in production, both involving extensive travel, Pierre and Elsa worked long hours and spent a great deal of time away from home. They travelled to Hollywood and New York and taped thirty-six half-hour shows, then went to Italy, Japan, and Australia. Abroad, Franklin frequently encountered long-standing chauvinism and deep-seated resistance to a woman in charge of a television show. Angry but persistent, she produced dozens of shows under trying conditions by sheer force of will, including eight in one afternoon in the Australia studio. The effort was exhausting but had its rewards – not least, accommodation in fine hotels around the world, great food and wine in splendidly appointed restaurants, and an intense companionship born of mutual attraction and respect.

Berton's second new project was a book for M&S inspired by the startling success of *The Comfortable Pew*. Once again, a Canadian institution had approached him to investigate a pressing matter. This time the issue was nothing less than the state of Canadian society. The institution that suggested the topic was the New Democratic Party of Canada.

In the second half of the 1960s, Canada, like other western industrial countries, was in the throes of social and political ferment due in large measure to the friction of generational change and the last gasp of nineteenth-century imperial authority. Young people, women, anti-nuclear and anti-war protesters, socialists and nationalists, anti-imperialists and anti-colonialists – all demanded change and a voice in the process. They wanted social and political transformation, and they wanted it without delay. Underlying their discontent was the gulf separating the values of baby boomers and the political and economic elites of their parents' and grandparents' generations, one marked not simply by differences in attitude toward modern life but by mutual incomprehension. Key words to the ethos of the day were *relevance* and *now*.

Nineteenth-century nostrums about the inherent superiority of unfettered free enterprise and an individualist ethic that preferred equality of opportunity to equality of condition continued to be spouted by a dominant elite that had survived depression and war and had finally been rewarded for its struggles with unprecedented stability and prosperity. For this generation, the traditional social, political, and economic values had proven their worth and were not to be hastily discarded. But to those born and bred in the postwar affluent society and caught up in the social revolution of the times, such values were an impediment to personal growth and the kinds of change attendant upon it. *The Comfortable Pew* had caught fire in part because it unmasked this generational divide. For the well-educated baby boomers, the first generation in history to attend colleges and universities en masse, older values should at least have been put to the test of critical scrutiny. The more these young people did so, the more they recognized the discrepancy between parental rhetoric and contemporary reality, between anodyne words about freedom and equality and the persistence of social injustice.

By 1967, leading members of the New Democratic Party acknowledged that these and similar issues desperately needed to be addressed, if only for their party's own survival. John Diefenbaker, Lester B. Pearson, and Tommy Douglas, the earnest leaders of Canada's three major parties, had been born in the Victorian era, and by 1967 it was apparent to many that these were not the men to lead Canadians into its second century. Early in the year, Berton and Charles Templeton covered the Progressive Conservative Party leadership convention for CTV, scooping the CBC by slipping a walkie-talkie to a scrutineer, who sent them results of the voting from the counting room.[32] Diefenbaker lost the party leadership through what was, in effect, a palace coup engineered by the party president, Dalton Camp. Former Nova Scotia premier Robert Stanfield took Diefenbaker's place. In December, Pearson announced that he would retire before the federal election expected in the new year. Members of the New Democratic Party were well aware that Tommy Douglas, in charge of the party since its formation in 1961, would not lead them much longer, and that David Lewis, a former labour lawyer and current MP, was waiting patiently for the call.

Of the three mainstream national political parties, the New Democrats were at once best equipped to deal with the issue of social class and most vulnerable to internal division because of it. Inequality had been an inherent target of the CCF since the early 1930s, and class interests remained the enemy after the "farmer-labour-socialist" CCF allied itself with organized labour to create the New Democratic Party in 1961. But by 1967, its younger members – who considered it as much a social crusade as a political party – had begun to ally themselves with the international New Left movement. Increasingly, they criticized the NDP for its hierarchical and bureaucratic structure, urging it to pay more attention to decisions made at the grassroots and to support women's liberation and national freedom movements. The party brass responded by deciding to ask Pierre Berton to do for the question of class and equality what he had done for institutional religion. This would at once calm internal dissension and place the NDP's main issues on the national stage, and do so during the crucial lead-up to a federal election featuring at least two new party leaders.

Berton accepted the offer from the New Democrats without reservation, stipulating the same basic arrangements that surrounded *The Comfortable Pew*. The book was to be published by a trade publisher who would pay him royalties. He was to receive no fee from the party, and it was to be involved only to the extent of facilitating discussions between Berton and people that he and the party thought would provide insight into social issues and problems. With these conditions agreed, he worked on the project intermittently in the spring and summer of 1967, reading as widely as time and circumstance permitted.

Jack McClelland, of course, was eager to repeat the success of *The Comfortable Pew*. It pleased him that with the new book a third party would not demand royalties, as the Anglican Church had done. He hired John Robert Colombo as the freelance editor for the manuscript, and Berton delivered it early in October. Then began the engine of what was becoming a well-oiled two-stroke publicity machine. The first stroke was the M&S publicity and advertising infrastructure, and the second was Elsa Franklin. As soon as McClelland glanced over the manuscript, he decided that its print run would be 100,000 in paper and 3,500 in hardcover – the former a number new in Canadian trade publishing. So too was the promotion budget. Instead of the normal 10 per cent of anticipated net revenues, the budget for the Berton book (called *The Smug Minority* after much in-house debate over titles like "Call It Tomorrow," "The Comfortable Illusion," and "The Freedom Myth") was set at an extraordinary 25 per cent. Franklin's advertising budget for the book eventually reached $20,000, beginning at $8,000 and increasing in steps as sales reached new levels. Franklin's fee came to 10 per cent of the total.[33]

Once Colombo had finished editing and Franklin had hyped the book to the editors of the major national magazines, McClelland formally offered first serial rights to a 3,500-word excerpt, again specifying the conditions that applied to *The Comfortable Pew*. Peter Gzowski of the *Star Weekly* magazine was the first to respond, by telephone and then by letter, with the proposal of at least four such excerpts, along with a feature article on Berton. Late in November, Jack McClelland notified the magazine editors that M&S had decided against a sealed bid or auction. Rights would instead be granted to the magazine that offered the best combination of money and "collateral promotion help," including cover treatment plus radio, newspaper, and TV advertising backup. Options now included the possibility of three 2,500-word excerpts.[34]

The offers came rolling in. W. Borden Spears of *Maclean's* offered $2,500 for a 2,000-word excerpt, to be accompanied by a revised version of Sidney Katz's earlier Berton profile. Hugh Shaw of *Weekend Magazine* offered $5,000 for three instalments and vaguely promised "prominent mention" on radio and television. Denis Harvey of the *Canadian* offered $7,000 for three excerpts and reminded McClelland of his magazine's presence in 2,139,969 homes across Canada. But Gzowski offered $7,500 for three excerpts, along with a week-long teaser campaign in the *Toronto Star*, dedication of at least 50 per cent of the *Star Weekly*'s advertising space to the book, point-of-sale exposure, and promotional support (carefully itemized) outside his magazine to the value of almost $82,000. As his pièce de résistance, Gzowski promised a cover devoted to Berton and his book, along with a feature article by Sylvia Fraser of the *Star Weekly* staff – a writer in whom, Gzowski and others knew, Jack McClelland held a strong personal interest.[35]

The Gzowski offer was easily the most thorough and best of those received, and Jack McClelland accepted it; but not before convincing the *Star Weekly* editor that the serialization merited a flat $10,000. *Maclean's* received second serial rights, which allowed the magazine to excerpt the book, but only after the *Star Weekly* did. From McClelland's point of view, the round figures of 100,000 and 10,000 for print run and serial rights, respectively, would in themselves produce a wealth of publicity and buzz and therefore be well worth the price. He was correct, but he forgot that publicity could work against a book and its publisher as well as for them.[36]

McClelland gave Elsa Franklin full responsibility for the *Smug Minority* publicity tour, and she became heavily involved in all aspects of its promotion. For the first time, M&S sent a sales representative, David McGill, across the country for the sole purpose of selling a single book and soliciting orders in time for its release in early 1968. McGill's prepackaged pitch was that Berton would not endear himself to the business and political leaders "who run our country and line their own pockets," holding back Canadian development.[37]

In concert with M&S, Franklin arranged to send promotional material and review copies to media personalities and outlets, union leaders, bankers, educators, social workers, psychologists, and outspoken figures such as the mayor of Ottawa, Charlotte Whitton. An elaborate accordion-fold brochure played up the many facets of the Berton persona – Pierre the family man, Pierre the author, Pierre the interviewer, Pierre the editor, Pierre the contrarian. As a promotional gimmick, small bags of chocolates were sent to select members of Canada's "smug minority," such as bank and trust company executives. Press releases went out en masse to bookstore managers, book review columnists, and radio and television producers and personalities. While noting Berton's controversial argument, the publicity material emphasized the publishing phenomenon itself: the unprecedented 100,000-copy print run; serialization in the *Star Weekly* and *Maclean's* "for the highest prices ever paid for a Canadian manuscript"; major profiles; extensive radio and television coverage; U.S. publication of a book "designed solely for Canadian readers" by Doubleday in New York; a thousand review copies. Canadian book marketing had met Marshall McLuhan: the Berton name, and the aura created by the attendant publicity and packaging, had become at least as important in selling the book as its contents.[38]

The Smug Minority, for all its brevity at 160 pages, marked the zenith of Berton's career as a crusading journalist. It was a fierce polemical attack on class and social inequality in Canada. Written for ordinary Canadians in the language of ordinary Canadians, from its first pages the book took issue with the unexamined assumptions about progress and improvement that were reflected in the clichés of Gordon Sinclair, Berton's *Front Page Challenge* colleague. His notion of freedom for the individual, the author charged, had helped delay the fluoridation of Toronto's water supply by several years. Sinclair constantly spoke of money-making as a calling and of work as evidence of sanctity. Berton challenged this gospel and dismissed Gordon's conclusions that poverty in old age was the result of laziness and that "do-gooders" and "bleeding hearts" were social leeches. In the twentieth century, the lingering traces of seventeenth-century Puritanism remained entrenched in social attitudes, reduced as often as not to what Berton chose to call "a subtreasury of great Canadian myths" that needed to be exploded – myths embedded in such self-interested bromides as "A woman's place is in the home," "Too much security kills initiative," "Government planning is the denial of freedom," "Higher taxes will wreck the nation," and "Private property must be sacrosanct."[39]

Berton completely rejected traditional Horatio Alger–style nostrums about the inherent value of work. He harked back to his summers as a student in the Klondike on the thawing crew. Friends and relatives had admired his callused hands, and the job had raised his status to that of a young man working his way through college. But the labour itself was relentlessly exhausting and hopeless, and accomplished little more than shifting the location of gold from frozen permafrost in the Yukon to subterranean vaults in Fort Knox. By 1968, Berton had come to recognize the environmental effects of the mining to which he had been party. All traces of plant life were destroyed, all topsoil sluiced away; by the time the thawing crew arrived, "the sinuous valley, misty green each spring, flaming orange each fall, had been reduced to a black, glistening scar."[40]

As a desultory university student, Berton had not likely read a word of Adam Smith's classic eighteenth-century treatise, *The Wealth of Nations*, much less its famous passage on the way the new industrial division of labour dehumanized workers. But he drew from his research for *The Smug Minority* a similar conclusion. He was no social theorist, but his native intelligence and instinct took him in this and other fruitful directions.

Reviewers criticized him for concentrating on the very poor and the very rich, ignoring the vast middle class. But he had no quarrel with the middle class beyond its complacency; his concern as a polemicist was with the victimization of the poor by means of the maxims and policies of the very wealthy. He could also have argued that a good polemic requires stark juxtaposition and calculated simplification. Berton did give ammunition to his critics, however, by opening his book with "Conversation for the Twenty-first Century," a brief invented dialogue between a father and son looking back to the old days of the 1960s. Its style was reminiscent of some of his more fanciful *Toronto Star* columns: "What was it like in the olden days, Pop?" "Gee, Pop, that sounds like the Middle Ages. Were those people really like serfs?" The comic book vocabulary and Berton's breezy tone made the book accessible but diminished the authority of his argument and made some critics dismiss the book outright as a waste of Berton's talent.

Yet in two and a half pages of seemingly jejune dialogue that some judged unworthy of a serious book about social class, Berton provided a succinct and accurate, if intuitive, tutorial on the idea of hegemony and how it operated. This despite the near certainty that he had never heard of the obscure Sardinia-born Marxist and social activist who had developed a theory of cultural hegemony while languishing in an

Italian prison in the 1920s. Antonio Gramsci had been incarcerated by Mussolini for his radicalism throughout the 1920s and into the 1930s. He managed to smuggle his notebook of writings on the role of intellectuals and the nature of hegemonic control out of prison, but they did not become available in English translation until the early 1970s. Ultimately Gramsci's work inspired Noam Chomsky and Edward Herman to explore what they dubbed in 1988 "the manufacture of consent" – control without resort to coercion. But here is Berton in 1968:

What was it like in the olden days, Pop? I mean around the 1960's . . .
Was it like they show it on TV?
Well, now, son – you know TV tends to glamourize history out of all recognition, sometimes. Things weren't all that good, you know, back then . . .
Then why do they always talk about "the good old days," Pop?
People tend to view the past through a fog of nostalgia, son. You know – lovers spooning in the quaint drive-ins and whole families sitting around the bar-b-q. But don't forget that for most people life was composed of equal parts of boredom and drudgery. It was, in essence, a serf society run by a smug minority of well-entrenched overseers.
Gee, Pop, that sounds like the Middle Ages. Were those people really like serfs?
They would have resisted the name; but in our terms they were. . . . Historical evidence makes it clear that the masses of the people who lived in Canada in the Sixties were chained to tedious and degrading jobs which they despised; that between one-fifth and one-third of them were prisoners of a poverty so grinding we can scarcely contemplate it; and that only the wealthy had the freedom to enjoy a proper education.
And this smug minority you mention that ran things . . . who were they, Pop?
A small, in-bred, establishment of business and political leaders who had a vested interest in maintaining the status quo.
But gosh, Pop, why didn't the people revolt if conditions were as bad as all that?
Because the minority convinced the majority that life was wonderful.
Oh, come on, Pop. That's stupid.

Read your history books. You'll find that's what happened. Of course the big establishment had the help of the minor establishments – religious, educational, journalistic, judiciary – in this brainwashing.

You mean they convinced people that serfdom was an okay thing?

Oh, quite easily. The most menial and wretched toil was held to be highly honourable. It conveyed a magical thing called "status." People preferred it to happiness. . . .

But hold it, Pop. They didn't have any freedom?

That's right. But the minority boasted so loudly about this non-existent freedom that they convinced the majority they had more of it than any people in history. . . .

This minority you talk about, Pop: they must have been a real bunch of hypocrites to fool the people that way.

Not at all, son. All the available evidence show that they honestly and sincerely believed all those things themselves. You see that's what made the minority so smug.[41]

The French thinker Pierre Bourdieu would not publish his theory of "cultural capital" and its production until the early 1970s;[42] but Berton stumbled upon this notion, too, and cottoned to its significance. He argued that instead of equating leisure with idleness we should regard it as a form of capital – as a way of measuring national productivity other than by the gross national product alone. "When we talk about natural resources," he wrote, "we think again in material terms: pulp and paper, wheat and hydro power, oil and mineral wealth, fish and lumber. Yet people are also a natural resource; physical health, brain, talent, artistic genius – all these things are part of our true Gross National Product. . . . It would not be easy, but neither would it be impossible to measure the Gross National Product of our literature, music, and painting and stack it up against that of other countries. For these things, along with dollars and cents and the production of bicycles and farm machinery, are part of our real wealth."[43]

The most important and influential chapter of *The Smug Minority* was the one titled "The Shackles of Poverty." The poor, he stated, were caught in a "vicious cycle of want" from which they could not hope to extricate themselves unless aided by the state. The New Democratic Party in 1968, like Berton, may have been unaware of the theoretical ruminations of a long-dead Italian radical who had written from a prison in fascist Italy, but it was intensely interested in poverty, for many Canadians understood want. As Berton pointed out in the chapter's opening, the 1961 census revealed that almost five million urban and rural Canadians lived in poverty. Of these, "at least three million were living in destitution, a condition of poverty so abject that the purchase of a ten cent newspaper becomes a luxury." In short, one-third of the nation had little share in "the affluent society" and had little real freedom, if any.[44]

The Canadian Chamber of Commerce campaign against public assistance to the underprivileged, "Operation Freedom," had been nothing more than a Canadian variation of the Big Lie, he insisted, without drawing attention to the fact that the phrase "Big Lie" was of Nazi origin. Freedom to such groups meant "freedom from taxes, freedom from the necessity of paying pensions, relief, family and mothers' allowances, and freedom from national health insurance." Where was the legislation that restricted individual freedom? On this the Chamber of Commerce was silent. Berton suggested that it likely included legislation such as the Combines Act, which "restricted the freedom of individuals to get together in hotel rooms and arrange for identical bids on public contracts or to fix prices on everything from photo supplies and cement to bakery products and false teeth."[45]

Myths about the evils of public assistance to the poor abounded, whether in the canard that those who received it were leeches or in the claim that the country could not afford more welfare. The Canadian Manufacturers' Association magazine, *Industry*, had warned that "these parasites living upon the strong will destroy the strong and the direction of our lives will be taken over completely by political regulation," but who and where were these "parasites"? Berton disaggregated the 970,000 Canadians receiving public assistance at the end of 1966 in order to find out: 92,000 received aid because they were blind or disabled; 118,000 lived in institutions; 200,000 were destitute widows or single mothers with small children. Were these people parasites? Of the remaining 560,000, 210,000 were heads of families, and the rest were women and children. And of those 210,000 family heads, almost 110,000 were in some way disabled. Were they parasites, too? This left about 100,000 "able-bodied men," and most of them were seasonal and unskilled workers. As to the government assistance that people like Trevor Moore, vice-president of Imperial Oil, called "handouts" and "treats," what exactly were they? Old age pensions? Mothers' allowances? Welfare payments "to the sick, the lame, and the blind"? It was impossible to know, since "the brave statements" of men like Moore were cloaked in generalities. "Anyone who examines the facts will know that this is claptrap," Berton wrote, "but as long as the poor remain faceless these myths will persist."[46]

In *The Smug Minority*, Pierre Berton allied himself not only with the poor and the downtrodden, as he had in his days at the *Star*, but also with the disaffected youth of the sixties. In this respect, the book was as much about the clash of generations as about class conflict. He described an August 1967 encounter in Toronto City Hall between Comptroller Allan Lamport and a delegation of hippies from Yorkville village. Called by Lamport in a genuine attempt to understand this strange new breed of youngsters, the meeting degenerated into a dialogue of the deaf. Lamport could not understand why his questions about the hippies' "aims and objectives" were met with groans, or why one young man responded to his insinuation that they were not productive members of society with the curt words, "That's the very attitude I resent."[47] For their part, the hippie delegation made little effort to understand why work and accomplishment were so important to Lamport's generation, the values of which had been shaped by decades of war and depression.

The hippie generation, in Berton's view, was on the front lines of the struggle against lingering Puritan values. In his younger years, Allan Lamport had done the same, for he had been largely responsible for the elimination of Toronto's Lord's Day blue laws. Confronted with a generation that wished to opt out of a social system emphasizing productivity and wealth in favour of a search for life's larger meaning, the Toronto comptroller did what Gordon Sinclair had done. "Lamport's iconoclasm, like Gordon Sinclair's," Berton wrote, "dies away when faced with those who would smash the real idols. He cannot stomach the terrible vision of the barefoot hippies sauntering about Yorkville, engaged in nothing more productive than conversation with their friends. Surely they must need *something*: 'recreational facilities,' perhaps, and one can see the vision appear as a balloon over Lamport's head: well-scrubbed, crew-cut hippies in clean, pressed shorts vigorously attacking the parallel bars or leaping about on the tennis court."[48]

Making this "generation gap" worse was the way resentment and fear of strangely dressed, long-haired youngsters resulted in restrictions on civil liberties aimed at youth. It had disturbed Berton when his daughter Patsy was sent home from Woodbridge High School one hot summer day for nothing more than wearing a dress that exposed her bare midriff. No laws existed in the country regulating the length of one's hair, but in 1966 a twenty-three-year-old guitarist had been ordered by a Vancouver magistrate to have his hair cut. A Canadian Press report revealed that in Montreal the same year, a judge "made it clear that young men with shoulder-length hair have two strikes against them when they appear in court before him." These were not idiosyncratic judgments. In July 1967, the *Ontario Magistrate's Quarterly* stated: "The longhairs are not just beatniks; they're dead-beats, and if growing their hair long is going to be the prevailing fashion . . ., we will be seeing more and more of them all the time in magistrate's courts. There is just no future for them outside the beneficent confines of the excellent penitentiaries and reformatories that are ready and willing to receive them. They will get a haircut there, all right, and very fast."[49]

Education, Berton wrote, was the main road to a more just, equitable, and compassionate Canada – for in education lay emancipation. And it should be free at all levels, whether public schools or colleges and universities. He reminded readers that Ontario educators of the nineteenth century, men like Egerton Ryerson, had recognized this. They had struggled against opposition to a state-sponsored public school system and prevailed. As to higher education, John Porter's 1965 book, *The Vertical Mosaic*, in Berton's view "perhaps the most important Canadian work of the post-war years," had destroyed the comforting myth that Canadian universities were open and accessible to all who wished to attend. Porter had demonstrated empirically that the country's universities were indeed "pastures for the privileged." No reader of *The Vertical Mosaic*, Berton insisted, could "help but be outraged and scandalized by the short-sightedness of a WASP-dominated power elite so in-bred in its composition and so narrow in its attitudes that it has seriously stultified the spirit and potential of the nation."[50]

Canada had shortchanged its youth, and in so doing had short-changed itself. The country had invested in markets and industry but continued to underinvest in human beings. "The idea that education can be treated as an investment," he wrote, "is a new and intriguing concept" – and it should be acted upon. He pointed to the work of the American economist Theodore Schultz, who had written in 1961 that "much of what we call consumption constitutes investment in human capital," and that education and leisure time served to increase that capital by improving the value of human life.[51]

"The march of social progress" in Canada, Berton concluded, had to change course. It would be led by those whom society preferred to view as clowns and dismiss as "wild-eyed idealists," but who nonetheless advocated progressive measures like the end of capital punishment, free education, liberalized divorce laws, and a guaranteed annual wage. Behind them would come the artists, poets, and the occasional novelist – having "caught the echo of the nuts and the goofballs" ahead. Next would be radical labour leaders and independent local politicians, along with "way-out teachers and assistant professors," outspoken radio show hosts and sociologists and philosophers, and militant housewives carry-ing no placards but "laden with thick briefs, committee reports, studies, polls, texts on parliamentary procedure, and minutes of the last meeting." In this populist parade of Berton's fantasy, it is the rank and file of ordinary Canadians who lead solemn lawyers and bankers, entrenched labour leaders, and holier-than-thou editorial writers listen-ing "to the dronings of the Q.C.'s and to the judges and bishops who march along behind them." Trailing at the rear are the political leaders of the nation.[52]

The Smug Minority had been keenly anticipated by Toronto's journal-ists and critics. Robert Fulford reported that in the Park Plaza roof bar, the Ford Hotel, the Press Club, and the Four Seasons – favourite watering holes of the media – there was a good deal of chatter about the book in the days before its release, and not only because of its content. *Maclean's* had decided to run an original article on Berton to accompany its excerpt from the book, and had assigned Jon Ruddy to write it. But Ruddy had recently written pieces to which Berton had taken exception. In the *Telegram*, his article "The Comfortable Few" had discussed Berton and his cliquish circle of friends in an unflattering manner, and in *Toronto Life* magazine he had gone further, criticizing the "family compact" of the Toronto media. Ruddy's depiction, Fulford wrote, was of "a kind of sinister network of interlocking talents on the journalistic scene."[53]

This, a skeptic might have observed, was the hegemonic function of the Berton splash party, a genuine family affair that just as genuinely reflected Berton's much-admired loyalty to his wide network of friends (except, obviously, for McKenzie Porter). Twice each year, old acquaintances and stars from the newspaper, magazine, radio, and television communities gathered at poolside in Kleinburg to frolic and relax, swim, and tie one on. But ritualized social observances are not without important functions. There, near the pool and in the sprawling house, the media elite maintained long-standing friendships and cultivated new ones, smoothed rivalries and talked shop. In this relaxed atmosphere, they knew they could risk exposing sides of themselves in an environment where risqué behaviour and indiscreet confidences could be left behind with the wet towels, to disappear with the wash. It was an environment that nurtured the mutual sympathies of their class and cemented their common bond as purveyors of information, strengthening loyalties buried so deep they seemed the very order of things.

Berton was well aware that he had become a figure of influence as well as controversy, and he was not beyond exercising the former to protect his interests. So when Ruddy telephoned to request an interview, Berton declined; then he called the editor of *Maclean's*, Borden Spears, and asked him to replace Ruddy with another writer. Spears quite properly pointed out that, should this happen, the whole media community would know about it within a day and would scoff at Canada's most prominent defender of press freedom trying to interfere with editorial decisions at his former magazine. Berton backed off and granted Ruddy the interview. He also objected, more wisely perhaps, to a *Star Weekly* proposal for a large poster of himself posing nude in the manner of Rodin's *Thinker*, on the grounds that it would make *The Smug Minority* seem frivolous. As Fulford and others noted, the objection came from the writer who until that moment had been the hungriest in the country for publicity. Undeterred by Berton's veto, the *Star Weekly* hired the Vancouver artist Roy Peterson to draw Berton in the buff à la Rodin.

The Smug Minority was released on February 10, 1968, and launched three days later with a party at the Press Building in Ottawa, attended by politicians, senior civil servants, professors, businessmen, and media people. Among those invited were some members of Parliament, Walter Gordon, Paul Martin Sr., Stanley Knowles, and John Turner, as well as the poet Al Purdy and professors R.L. McDougall and David Farr of Carleton University.[54] A French edition, published by Éditions de l'Homme in Montreal and bearing the title *La minorité suffisante*, was set to follow.

Critical reaction was swift, severe, and divided. Two letters Jack McClelland received from a book club in which subscribers received advance copies suggested how explosive the book was to become. The first was from Charles E. Hendry, director of the School of Social Work at the University of Toronto. "The uncomfortable few who have tried desperately to communicate the facts and the meaning of poverty, with very limited impact or success, at long last have found a voice that is bound to be heard. . . . What Michael Harrington did for the United States in his arresting *The Other America*, Pierre Berton, in his own inimitable style . . . has done, and not without profoundly disturbing effect, in his *The Smug Minority*."[55]

The second letter was from a man named Ian H. McNish, an Ontario lawyer and future judge, and it could scarcely have been more different: "I must confess that either Mr. Berton has all the sophistication of a wild-eyed campus freshman politician or this book is the put-on of the year. I suspect the latter. . . . Mr. Berton may be at home writing about the Klondike, the robber barrons [*sic*] of the Danforth or cooking turkeys, but I would respectfully suggest that he save further embarrassment to himself, to McClelland & Stewart and to the general reading public by keeping his analysis of society as a whole a deep dark secret."[56]

To a good number of Canadian book reviewers in the mainstream press, the moment for which they had long waited had come. At last Pierre Berton had exposed his left flank and had faltered, and it was time for his comeuppance. Long-deferred *schadenfreude* fuelled outraged reviews by journalists who earlier had treaded carefully when approaching Berton's work. As often as not, Canadian reviewers and columnists attacked the man as much as his book, having forgotten the fallacy of the argument ad hominem. "Pierre Berton bugs me," wrote William C. Heine of the *London Free Press*. "Not in any way he intends, though. In all he writes and says there is the underlying attitude of a man who was once a crusader and still considers himself one . . . and that's what bugs me. Because he's not a crusader at all. He's a professional dissenter and doing very well at it indeed." The income he would earn from the book made him part of the smug minority itself, Heine concluded. "About the only thing that went into *The Smug Minority* were scissors and paste-pot," thirty-six-year-old Allan Fotheringham decided in the *Vancouver Sun*.[57]

Michael Barkway, publisher and editor of the *Financial Times*, ignored the argument of the book, and remained content to suggest that with *The Smug Minority* Berton had unearthed a vein of richness not seen since the gold rush of '98. People at dull parties, he suggested, should try to predict the title of the man's next books. "'Hippy through Fifty'? 'The Perils of Pierre'? 'How to Sympathize without Really Suffering'?" Berton, he said, "writes like a retarded teenager who discovers that the law is on the side of the propertied establishment and thinks it an awful shame. The book is as shallow as that." Barkway's unbecoming language indicates clearly that the author had touched on matters of real sensitivity to those who fit the smug minority profile. As Jack McClelland wrote in his short response to Barkway, "Migod! Berton really stirred up your adrenalin gland."[58]

In the *Globe and Mail*, the columnist Dennis Braithwaite ridiculed Berton for continuing to believe in 1968 the ridiculous notion that laissez-faire capitalism caused social problems. "The welfare state," he said, was not "the anteroom of heaven." Berton himself, he declared, was the true Puritan in the Canadian parlour. Braithwaite had never been a Pierre Berton devotee, but it is likely that he became especially riled when he came across the passage in *The Smug Minority* in which Berton quoted one of Braithwaite's own *Globe and Mail* columns: "'We don't want any more handouts, thanks a lot,' cries Braithwaite, a former left-winger who long ago turned his coat."[59]

Hardly ever did a Canadian reviewer directly engage Berton's assessment of inequality and class in Canadian society, except with clichés that dismissed his ideas as old hat or discredited. "The young – and not only the young –," Braithwaite pontificated, "have advanced far beyond Berton's faded formula of simplistic Marxism."[60] In fact, little was formulaic or even Marxist about Berton's argument, and although his book simplified issues for the sake of polemical effect and was written in plain language, it was by no means as shallow a work as its detractors claimed. As a social critic of problems associated with class, Pierre Berton was an autodidact, very much as Phillips Thompson had been. Where Thompson had become radicalized by reading Henry George's *Progress and Poverty* and by witnessing the plight of the Irish, Berton had read and reviewed with approval Michael Harrington's searing 1962 indictment of poverty in *The Other America*, had assimilated the argument and evidence of Porter's *Vertical Mosaic*, and had spoken to scores of Canadians about the relationship between wealth, class, and poverty in Canada.

David McGill of M&S tracked national sales of *The Smug Minority* carefully and reported to Jack McClelland that, overall, the book was doing very well. McClelland wrote to Gzowski at the end of February that all the stock had been shipped to stores, and that while reviews at first glance "appeared to be about 90% nasty, a more careful analysis indicates that it is about a 50-50 pattern." "Some of the cons," he added, "have been very violent." McClelland's problem was not low sales: it was that everywhere he went, people asked whether the much-hyped 100,000 copies had sold out yet, implying that anything less would constitute a publishing failure. Unsold copies were fully returnable to the publisher, and McClelland could find a large portion of the print run back in his warehouse within a few months. At one point a frustrated McClelland felt obliged to clarify the matter with Scott McIntyre, a bright young member of his advertising, promotion, and publicity department. *The Smug Minority* was "selling very well indeed thank you." In fewer than five weeks, readers had purchased 65,000 copies.[61]

A copy of McClelland's memo to McIntyre found its way to Robert Fulford, and the next day he used it in a *Toronto Star* column on *The Smug Minority*'s critical reception and sales record.[62] He reported on reviewers' wild reactions, including one in the *Sherbrooke Record* that began: "Pierre Berton is the Mother Gerber of the literary world. He masticates McLuhanistic thought-thumps into the platitudinous pabulum precious to the plebeian palate."[63] Reviews, said Fulford, fell into three general categories: "Apoplectic" (Michael Barkway of the *Financial Times*); "Ho-Hum" (Shaun Herron of the *Winnipeg Free Press*); and "More-in-Sadness-than-in-Anger" (Allan Fotheringham in the *Vancouver Sun*). Was the book the bestseller McClelland & Stewart had hoped for? Fulford's answer drew upon McClelland's memo, which reported that in Canada's largest cities, sales were only fair. But in the nation's secondary cities, towns, and rural areas, the book moved briskly. *The Smug Minority* did very well in the Maritimes and the Prairies. In cities such as Halifax, Edmonton, Calgary, Regina, and especially Winnipeg, sales were strong. Perplexed by the phenomenon, Fulford asked Hugh Kane why sales were disappointing in Toronto, Montreal, and Vancouver, and provided Kane's simple explanation: "Those three cities are really the Establishment. The smug minority live there."

The book went on to sell almost 100,000 copies in its first few years of issue, a bestseller by any measure.[64] Yet the myth that it had been a publishing failure became sufficiently entrenched that when McClelland & Stewart began to run into financial difficulties *The Smug Minority* was rumoured to have been responsible. Berton came to regard this book as one of those that had given him true satisfaction, for he had spoken forcibly about a key issue of the day. Jack McClelland viewed it not only as an important book, but also as one that reflected Berton's self-imposed mission. "It is a book for the masses," he wrote in his explanatory memo to Scott McIntyre, and he quoted Robert Fulford: "Unlike almost everyone who writes on social questions in this country, Berton wants to speak, not to a community but to the nation; not to a few thousand people but to hundreds of thousands."

"If that is commercialism," McClelland concluded, "I plead guilty and if everything that Berton says in the book is old-hat and trivial, why have I been receiving abusive letters including one from the head of a major trust company who has also made it his business to try to prevent broadcasters from praising the book. Perhaps the Establishment has been stung a little."[65] Judged by the success of *The Smug Minority* outside the major centres, ordinary Canadians – the citizens who understood poverty and inequality because they had often experienced them

– were decidedly less shocked by the severity of Berton's indictment than those in positions of power and influence. Instead, they bought the book in droves.

So supportive of Berton's message were members of the New Democratic Party that with his encouragement its MPs began to use the book's notoriety as leverage in their campaigns in the federal election called for June 1968. The journalist and NDP leadership candidate Douglas Fisher, who praised *The Smug Minority* in three separate newspaper columns, was the first to ask Berton's permission to use it as a campaign tool. Pierre agreed. "I wrote the book to stimulate political discussion and political action," he announced, saying that he would lend his support to any candidate, regardless of party, who promised "to work for the reforms in the fields of education, social welfare, work and leisure" he advocated. He offered to send copies to the first candidates in any riding who convinced him that the book would be used "as a political manifesto" and promised to relinquish all royalties on copies they distributed. To separate genuine from spurious interest, he devised a questionnaire interested candidates had to complete.[66]

As a result, *The Smug Minority* became an issue in the 1968 federal election. More than a hundred New Democratic Party candidates, including Tommy Douglas, based their campaigns in part on the questions it raised, and they began to hand out copies to voters. In a May 27, 1968 memo to David McGill, Jack McClelland expressed his worry that the care he had always taken to avoid any association of M&S with a political party might be compromised by Berton's offer. He personally deplored Berton's action, he said, but concluded that any harm done by the author's alliance with the NDP would be outweighed by the benefits of attendant publicity – such as a scheduled national free-time television discussion between Berton and Tommy Douglas on issues addressed in the book.[67]

Other benefits accrued from this alliance between author and political party. M&S had agreed to supply copies of *The Smug Minority* to NDP candidates and supporters at a discount, and by mid-June the party had ordered 5,000 copies. The cost to members was 75 cents. As the biographer James King has noted, McClelland's strategy was brilliant. He had turned a possible public relations disaster into a marketing success story: the heavily discounted bulk sale to the NDP allowed him to get rid of most of the remaining stock.[68]

On balance, *The Smug Minority* had enriched Berton's reputation. Despite the harsh critiques from big-city critics and Bay Street barons, the book had exposed the discrepancy between the myth of Canada as a land of equality and justice for all and the harsh realities of class and poverty for many, and had linked this situation to the clash of generations. Vast differences in wealth and the rebellion of youth against their elders constituted some of the deepest tensions in Canadian society. By encouraging national debate on poverty, youth, and education, *The Smug Minority* helped convince Canadians that these issues had to be addressed in the open. To this extent, the book eased the way for Pierre Trudeau's first-term commitment to the "Just Society." Its success in mid-sized cities and small towns ensured that Berton became a household name everywhere in the country, a name now fully associated with national aspirations for social equality and justice.

PART FOUR

ICON

20

NATIONAL DREAMER

—

PIERRE BERTON'S SECOND EXCURSION into serious social analysis coincided with reflections on a career of almost thirty years. *The Smug Minority* was his fourteenth book, not including those he had edited for the Canadian Centennial Library, but how many of them would be memorable? He knew that the very timeliness of his latest effort, for all its notoriety, would date it very quickly, as with *The Comfortable Pew* once the controversy subsided. His collections of reworked newspaper columns and television interviews had a similarly limited shelf life, although he thought they might be useful one day as windows into the era. Clearly, much of what he had written would not endure. Who would remember *The Big Sell* or its author?

But then there was *Klondike*, the book that a decade after publication remained the definitive work in its field. It served as an implicit rebuke of his ephemeral journalistic writings. Berton recognized that he had not simply an interest in history but a real flair for it, and that, apart from Donald Creighton and W.L. Morton, scholars nearing retirement, few historians any longer seemed either able or willing to tell Canada's story. "I had known what I should do ever since writing *Klondike*," he later acknowledged. "I should produce another odyssey involving the movement of large numbers of people through time and space."[1]

In 1968, he made a decision that once again changed his professional direction. His problem was one of scarce time, not scarce ideas, so he began to reduce his professional commitments significantly in order to devote more energy to the Canadian Pacific project. He quit as host of *Under Attack* (Fred Davis became the show's moderator), and in mid-August he met with Jack McClelland and told him that he couldn't continue his intense editorial involvement in M&S's various series; to do so, he said, would keep him from producing the kind of book he wished to write. They agreed that Berton would remain a director of the company and a member of the editorial policy committee. Since McClelland owed Berton over $20,000 in back salary, Berton suggested it be paid at the rate of $1,000 per month. These moves meant a substantial reduction in annual income – $20,000 for *Under Attack* and $30,000 for editorial work at M&S – at a time when his eldest two daughters were at university and the house desperately needed renovation to accommodate the nine Bertons who now lived in it.[2]

Berton's resolve to work on the railway book more or less full-time was firm, and during the spring and summer of 1968 he threw himself into the research, travelling with Norman Kelly to the Public Archives of Canada. There he gained access to the original correspondence of John A. Macdonald and struggled to understand the letters of CPR president George Stephen (Baron Mount Stephen), whose handwriting rivalled that of the politician Edward Blake for its illegibility.[3]

He had two advantages that academic historians, for all their freedom to engage in research, lacked. As a celebrity he had connections to smooth his way, and as a literary entrepreneur he had a personal secretary to serve his needs: either Ennis Halliday, who after remarriage changed her surname to Armstrong, or Anne Michie, her successor.

As a celebrity, he had become acquainted with N.R. (Buck) Crump, the CPR's current president. A career railroader and an amateur railway historian, Crump had developed a personal interest in Berton's project, despite his company's rebuff of the earlier Berton-McClelland proposal for a centennial history of the CPR. As a result, Travers Coleman, supervisor of news services at Canadian Pacific in Montreal, and J.C. Bonar, company archivist, were more than willing to forward books, bound copies of company reports, and other materials from the company archives to Berton and Kelly.[4]

In Toronto, Ennis Armstrong helped organize and file the incoming material, and she and Berton gave Kelly detailed instructions about passages of Hansard to copy, railway route maps to locate, people to contact and interview, photographs to identify, and railway and exploration records to consult. "Have you looked at the material on Marcus Smith in the National Archives?" Berton asked Kelly in one letter. "His granddaughter Mrs. A. Elizabeth Smith . . . tells me that [Dominion Archivist]

Kaye Lamb has fifteen pages by Smith in his own handwriting, plus a scrapbook of newspaper clippings."[5]

In July 1968, the CPR flew Kelly to Vancouver, put him up at the Hotel Vancouver, and sent him by train – "surrounded by divisional engineers and superintendents" – along the railway's main line, stopping at Kamloops, Calgary, and Winnipeg, with a side trip to Edmonton. With Crump's blessing, Coleman placed the company superintendent's business car at Berton's disposal so the writer could take in the transcontinental trip west himself.[6] This level of research assistance was not the sort that Canadian historians could expect from cash-strapped universities or from the earnestly accountable Canada Council, almost their only source of funding. (And it helps explain the churlish reception some historians gave Berton's CPR saga.) Berton began his railway trip in mid-July, and by the end of the summer much of the research was complete. He and Kelly then shared the long and laborious task of reading sixteen years of newspaper accounts, from the *Globe* to the *Inland Sentinel* of Yale, B.C.[7]

The co-operation of the Canadian Pacific Railway reached its limits when Norman Kelly requested permission to examine the company's financial records for the 1880s, located in the president's vaults. He was politely refused. A concerned Berton wrote to Crump: "It seems to me that this is of the highest historical importance since the financial story of the company – especially the efforts of George Stephen to obtain adequate financing from the government – is essential to any understanding not only of the actual construction and incorporation of the railway itself, but to [an] understanding of the 1880s in Canada with which the book substantially deals." The request was denied, despite Berton's emphasis on the company's essential role in Canadian history. N.R. Crump delighted in providing Berton with free rides on his trains and details about the maximum grade and curvature of the roadbed, but the CPR's key financial records remained locked up.[8]

The exciting story that had unfolded during research had by 1969 seized Pierre's imagination, and he was desperate to begin writing. But *The Pierre Berton Show* continued to impose heavy demands, especially with its time-consuming annual sojourns to Los Angeles, New York, and London. The latter part of the 1968–69 season saw Berton and Franklin filming in Berlin, where he interviewed Hans Popper of Munich (leader of the Association of Anti-Zionist Jews), Daniel Cohn-Bendit ("Dany le rouge," leader of the 1968 French student revolutionary movement), the lord mayor, and the sole German-raised rabbi of the city.

Screen Gems celebrated the thousandth episode of *The Pierre Berton Show* with a banquet on February 3, 1969. Berton spoke briefly on the state of the Canadian television industry. Jack McClelland enjoyed himself and wrote Elsa Franklin – the perennial organizer – a note of congratulations. "It was great! A real tour de force whatever that may be . . . another major Franklin success." He signed the note, "Love and kisses."[9]

The show continued to be the successful and familiar mix of showbiz, sex, celebrities, and interesting people, together with airings of personal problems and society's ills. As far as Berton was concerned, to be a good interviewer a host had to be part seducer, part con man, at once putting his mark at ease and boosting self-confidence while seeking the moment of self-revelation.[10] Shows in the 1968–69 season featured the legendary stripper Gypsy Rose Lee, the actors Sharon Tate (murdered by the Charles Manson gang within a year) and Charlton Heston, the *Playboy* "playmate novelist" Alice Denham, the publisher Robert Guccione (*Penthouse* magazine), and Rachel Jones, airline stewardess turned co-author of the 1967 bestseller *Coffee, Tea, or Me*. Berton asked Father Gregory Baum whether birth control should be a matter of conscience or creed for Roman Catholics and spoke with two black psychiatrists about the roots of rage in American streets.

Canadian figures remained a strong presence on the show. Guests at the end of the decade included Laurier LaPierre, who talked about his controversial broadcasting career; Jean Drapeau, who revealed Mob attempts to bribe and threaten him; and Peter C. Newman, who hyped his new book about the Pearson years, *The Distemper of Our Times*. The newsman Norman DePoe and his son David, a Yorkville hippie activist, described how they spanned the generational divide. June Callwood, arrested in Yorkville while trying to break up a confrontation between young people and police, told viewers about her experience with law enforcement and the legal system. (Berton needed no research for that interview: he had been Callwood's character witness in court.) The musician Bobby Gimby, "Canada's Pied Piper," revealed how his centennial theme song "Ca-na-da" came to be written, and Scott Young's son,

Neil, a rock star, suddenly famous and wealthy, spoke candidly about his experience in what he called "the Hollywood jungle." The American humorist Alan Abel talked about his career as a professional hoaxer, and Gordon Sinclair talked about the travails of being Gordon Sinclair.

In the wake of *The Smug Minority*, the emphasis on issues of social justice became more pronounced, and Berton and Franklin used the show to raise public consciousness. In the fall of 1968, they developed a hard-hitting five-part series, "The Shame of the Prisons," in which Berton interviewed inmates about conditions and rehabilitation and grilled the commissioner of penitentiaries alongside an ex-inmate, an architect, and a criminologist. Early in 1969, another five-part series, "The Indian Revolution," provided a forum in which Aboriginal spokesmen voiced their grievances, while clips from motion pictures laid bare the racial stereotypes white people held about the Native population. One of the episodes, "The Rape of the Language," provided the first hard evidence that Aboriginal people had been "beaten, starved and otherwise punished by church and federal schools."[11]

Once the 1968–69 television season ended, Berton was finally in a position to devote most of his attention to the railway book, and he blocked out the month of July in which to start writing. He had the telephone removed from the house, an annoying hardship for its other inhabitants, and told friends and acquaintances he was leaving for Mexico. Then he sat down at the typewriter. Ennis Armstrong had organized his binders of evidence, and all his notes had been sorted, annotated, and placed in legal-size loose-leaf folders. His almost photographic memory stood him in good stead as he reviewed the material until he could visualize, not merely recite, the events conveyed in his notes.

The story in his mind had moved beyond the successful construction of a railway. As he put it in his memoirs: "I saw the building of the railway as the great epic story in our history. Every nation has one – usually a civil war, a revolution, or a bloody victory. But this, our seminal epic, was a unique historical adventure – not a struggle of brother against brother but of man against nature. . . . Our major battles have been against the environment. That would be my sub-theme."[12]

The theme of a transcendent nationalism made possible by a railway line had taken hold slowly, but was in place by early 1968 when Berton had complained to Crump after being refused access to the CPR's crucial financial records. "We would have no country without it. . . . There is no way to untie Canadian history from company history. The two are identical."[13] In some ways, Berton's views reflected and extended the "Laurentian thesis" developed earlier by Harold Innis, J.M.S. Careless, and Donald Creighton. The argument went that a combination of transatlantic metropolitan economic and political ties between Canada and the French and British imperial heartlands, along with the waterway communications system penetrating the continent from the St. Lawrence River and the Great Lakes, had forged an east-west political and economic axis that helped thwart first American annexation and later the forces of continental integration. In Creighton's two-volume biography of Sir John A. Macdonald, the building of the CPR was the virtual embodiment of Macdonald's national vision.[14]

Berton attacked his first draft in a day-and-night creative binge that began at eight each morning and sometimes continued past midnight. He began on the last day of June 1969 and was done by the end of July.[15] Only a week or so into the writing, it became clear that the story of Canada's first transcontinental railway could not be told in one volume: it needed two, something that Norman Kelly had suggested earlier. The story really began before Confederation, with entrepreneurial and imperial dreams of western expansion and more than a decade of political debate and intrigue. Kelly had also told him that the Canadian west should not be treated as a monolithic entity. Perhaps the enormous scope of his project did not fully strike Pierre until keys hit paper. He already knew that the title of poet E.J. Pratt's epic poem, *Towards the Last Spike*, contained the perfect words for the title of his second volume, but the title of the first – *The National Dream* – came only when he remembered that he had used the expression in the first draft and then discarded it.[16]

That manuscript – Berton called his approach to first drafts the "Slash-and-Burn School of Composition" – was very rough, for the objective was simply to get the words on paper.[17] There would be, as usual, three more drafts before submission to McClelland & Stewart. The real secret of literary craftsmanship as far as he was concerned lay in the process of revision. He relied heavily on his desire to convey feeling and emotion, and he gave it free rein, playing interpretive variations on Creighton's main themes along the way. The manuscript also reflected Creighton's approach to history in that it conceived the past as a combination of character and circumstance.[18] He deployed a large cast of colourful people – entrepreneurs, politicians, railwaymen, and workers who lived extraordinary lives – and rendered them vividly, bringing history alive in the process. A gushy sentimentalism ran from his sentences like so much treacle from a sap bucket.

Over the next three months, in hours cadged from other assignments and between television interviews while out of the country, he rewrote his manuscript completely.[19] Satisfied near the end of the year that he had a reasonable draft, he gave copies to Norman Kelly and to Michael Bliss, the young Canadian business historian at the University of Toronto, for their comments. Kelly, schooled in academic history but lacking professional experience, was "stunned" by the high quality of the draft he read; probably he was also relieved that his own hard work had paid good dividends. Bliss was wary of Berton's request for feedback: as he later told Elspeth Cameron, he had found *The Smug Minority* "a real turkey" of a book.[20]

Nevertheless, Bliss read the manuscript in January 1970, and late in the month, for a fee of $10 an hour, provided Berton with comments. In his covering letter he apologized if his words seemed impatient or arrogant; this, he said, happened naturally when grading. "Actually, I admire the manuscript very much," he wrote. But this was mere prelude to a range of criticisms provided in a five-page overview and a thirty-nine-page report. In the latter, he took issue with Berton's view of Macdonald's intentions and motives; with the lack of evidence to support the claim that (as Bliss put it) "the construction of the railway meant a great adventure to many a Canadian, or a new freedom for the nation"; with the inexplicable absence of Louis Riel from the story; and with much else. These comments covered only the first chapter, which Bliss said "should be rewritten, drastically."[21] Many other suggestions and corrections followed.

More generally, Bliss criticized the manuscript's breezy, "gee-whiz and gosh-and-golly" approach to history, especially in its early chapters, and for its tendency to "drum up the drama as it were" by means of various stylistic devices. He cautioned Berton about letting his enthusiasm carry him away. "There are too many artificially contrived crises, too many larger-than-life heroes, and wicked villains, too many 'famous' this's and 'notorious' that's. Many of these conventions went out with Victorian prose style, and I don't think attempts to revive them in the 1970's will be well received either by academic people or literary people."

Above all, he took exception to what he called Berton's "nationalist bias," evident in the attempt "to integrate the book around John A. Macdonald's 'vision' of building the Canadian nation by the all-Canadian railroad." Even Creighton, Bliss said, did not go this far, at least not explicitly; besides, "no historian under 55 would dare follow Creighton all the way in his portrait of Macdonald." The over-the-top rhetoric and the extravagant claims, he warned, would "seriously affect the book's public reception."

Despite such harsh judgments, Bliss's overall assessment was positive. Macdonald's struggle to build the Canadian nation was not the real story, he said; it resided, instead, in the human relationship with the physical environment: "the struggles of men against nature," the stories of ordinary people in extraordinary circumstances, and Berton told this well. The research that had gone into the book, he said, was "prodigious," much of the evidence new, and its presentation accurate and impressive. With *The National Dream*, he concluded, Berton had come near achieving "one of the great ideals in historical writing – a book that is entirely suitable for the layman and yet definitive for the professional historian." Only Bernard DeVoto in the United States had achieved this, Bliss said; Donald Creighton had "come close."[22]

Berton thanked Bliss for his thoughtful and thorough report and arranged for Ennis Armstrong to send him a cheque for $250. Then he sent a copy of the professor's memo and report to Jack McClelland.

McClelland recognized that the assessment was intelligent and valuable, but he warned his author that it was "so typically that of a frustrated academic that it really troubles me. I think you should take care not to be too confined by the inhibitions of the academic historian." He found the comments about the unwillingness of younger historians to follow Creighton's views on Macdonald amusing but sad, since it was "precisely because Creighton had more guts than most of our historians that his Macdonald book was important and useful and widely accepted." As for Bliss's preference for the theme of man struggling with nature over that of the struggle to make a nation, McClelland had essentially only one word: "To that I say horseshit. It's all very well for a historian to tell an amateur historian that his most important contribution is 'the first good account of the role of the people who really did the physical work' so that you will be known as the man who glorified the working man, but migod, Pierre, this is arrogant nonsense." To counter Bliss, McClelland urged Berton not to "water down" his main themes.

As to the view Bliss held that Berton's nationalist theme was too narrow and simplistic, and that it reflected the view of "a generation of insecure nationalists" who had begun "to rewrite our history to provide themselves with an emotionally satisfying past," McClelland had nothing but scorn. "I for one would be very reluctant to heed the advice of a man who could write such tripe. He may be a sound, academic historian, but I think he is somewhat lacking in practical judgement."[23]

Berton's romanticism was not the only impulse at work in shaping his story of Canadian history in the 1870s and 1880s. He could not escape the influence of the contemporary scene. By the end of the 1960s, expressions of nationalism in Canada, so innocent and inspiring when the historian Frank Underhill said in 1964 that "a nation is a body of people who have done great things together in the past and who hope to do great things together in the future," and so unabashedly evident during the centennial, had begun to wane among supporters. Most Quebec nationalists wanted a better deal for their province, and some argued for Quebec's outright independence. But at least this view sprang from hope. Nationalism in the rest of Canada had come to be rooted in fear – fear of the separation of Quebec, fear of American economic and cultural domination, fear of the "Americanization" of Canadian higher education, fear of American imperial and military aggression. English-Canadian nationalists found it difficult to express themselves in ways that were unambiguously positive.

This was Canada's "new nationalism," and it gained support and momentum in the late sixties and early seventies.[24] But divisiveness became one of its principal characteristics. The radical wing of the NDP called itself "the Waffle" yet was determined to do anything but vacillate, a sure sign that Canada was on the cusp of the age of irony. Led by the Toronto economist Mel Watkins and a Queen's doctoral student, James Laxer, the Waffle insisted in its founding manifesto on Canadian ownership of Canadian businesses and institutions. Blending a militant socialism with a strident nationalism, it championed the independence of Quebec and liberation movements throughout the world. It condemned the United States for the Vietnam War, which had escalated radically since the election of a Republican president, Richard Nixon, in 1968 – a year of student revolt in Paris, Berlin, London, and to a lesser extent North America.

Meanwhile, the stridently nationalist Carleton University English professors Robin Mathews and James Steele and their allies mounted a crusade to "Canadianize" universities populated overwhelmingly by British and American instructors, many of whom were extraordinarily patronizing toward the country in which they had come to live. The radicalism of historians and English professors, but especially of economists, disturbed moderates within the political left and the academic community. This divisiveness made the inner workings of the NDP and the universities turbulent, and was seen by some as an attempt to destabilize Canadian society and culture and to discredit measures for workable reform.

The years when Berton researched and wrote *The National Dream* and *The Last Spike* were paradoxical, for the rise of nationalism in English-speaking Canada occurred in an atmosphere of national dread. From the mid-1960s to 1970, the year *The National Dream* was published, a spate of books and anthologies with alarmist titles and dire themes appeared, such as *Lament for a Nation: The Defeat of Canadian Nationalism* (1965), *The New Romans: Candid Canadian Opinions of the U.S.* (1968), and *The Struggle for Canadian Universities* (1969). Each in its own way addressed the crisis in Canadian nationhood and the problem of maintaining the country's sovereignty and culture. When Berton's first railway volume appeared on bookstore shelves, Ian Lumsden's edited collection, *Close the 49th Parallel Etc.: The Americanization of Canada* (1970), and Kari Levitt's book *Silent Surrender: The Multinational Corporation in Canada* (1970) were already there. Two years later, Margaret Atwood would give her study of Canadian literary identity a stark one-word title: *Survival.*[25]

Lament, struggle, surrender, survival. In the months when Berton assembled the Canadian nation in his mind and put the story of one of its greatest ventures on paper, he was aware of the culture of fear in the Canada of his own day, and set out to do something about the problems that fuelled it. Berton later noted in his memoirs that in 1969 he had lunch at Toronto's King Edward Hotel with Peter C. Newman, then the editor of the *Toronto Star*, and gave his full support to Newman's proposal for a new organization that would rally citizens to the nationalist cause. The initiative was set to be backed financially by the former Liberal cabinet minister and economic nationalist Walter Gordon, closely connected to the left-of-centre *Toronto Star*. A more important midday meeting, which Berton did not apparently attend, took place on February 3, 1970, also at the King Edward Hotel, when Newman, the Toronto political economist Abraham Rotstein, and Gordon made the decision to establish the Committee for an Independent Canada. Berton became an active and vocal founding member of the association.[26]

His deepening commitment to Canadian history did not dilute his left-leaning opinions. He had opposed the Vietnam War since the mid-sixties and continued to do so into the seventies. His television show in 1969–70 featured Robin Mathews on the dangers of appointing too many American professors; George Thayer, author of *The War Business*, on the profit-driven arms race; Jessica Mitford on the political persecution of Dr. Benjamin Spock; and Robert McClure, moderator of the United Church of Canada, on the legalization of marijuana. A group of students from Everdale Place, one of the country's first free schools, debated the principal of Upper Canada College on whether high schools should be less structured. The highlight of the season proved to be a five-part series on the women's movement. Inspired in part by Franklin's experience with male chauvinism overseas, "The New Suffragettes" examined social and economic discrimination, "man the enemy," and the question "Is woman's place really in the home?"

Berton went to the inaugural convention of the Committee for an Independent Canada in February, joining Mel Hurtig, Earle Birney, Judy LaMarsh, Al Purdy, W.L. Morton, Harold Town, Adrienne Clarkson, Thomas Symons, Beland Honderich, and many others in a gesture of nationalist solidarity. Jack McClelland not only became a member but was appointed CIC co-chair, with the editor of *Le Devoir*, Claude Ryan.[27]

McClelland was as dedicated a Canadian nationalist as anyone in attendance; at Elsa Franklin's suggestion, he had branded McClelland

& Stewart with the tagline "The Canadian Publishers."[28] Yet in a year of great success, with three books on the bestseller list, including Farley Mowat's *The Boat Who Wouldn't Float*, he nevertheless faced serious financial trouble – not least from cutthroat competition from subsidiaries of American publishers and from changing reading habits. As McClelland's biographer James King noted: "It was the age of trash, specifically Jacqueline Susann and Harold Robbins." The M&S revenue stream and profits were rising – $107,325 in 1970, up from $83,750 a year earlier – but the company carried a heavy and increasing debt load, 30 per cent of which would come due in March 1971.[29]

Ironically, McClelland's year of greatest nationalist visibility ended with his ready acceptance of the sale of Ryerson Press, one of Canada's oldest and most distinguished indigenous publishing houses, to the American publishing giant McGraw-Hill. Late in the fall of 1970, he appeared as a guest on *The Pierre Berton Show* and stated that Ryerson had declined over the years, and because it was "no longer a serious competitor," the United Church of Canada had good reason to sell it to whoever made the best offer. Government subventions were not the answer; nor, he said, were they desirable. In fact, if more companies like Ryerson Press fell into American hands, "we would put an end to American domination in a hurry." At the end of the year, perhaps sensitive to the contradiction between his "Canada for Canadians" public role and his commitment to unfettered free enterprise, a tired and dispirited McClelland indicated that he would likely quit the publishing business. On February 18, 1971, he announced to his stunned staff that he intended to sell the firm. This was as much a sign of despondency as intent, for in the words of his biographer he had become "physically and emotionally drained." Like his authors, McClelland was convinced that Canadian books and magazines were essential to a Canadian identity, yet M&S was in serious financial trouble despite its stellar stable. For Jack, the sad fact was that not enough Canadians cared to "buy Canadian," including Canadian books.[30]

McClelland's asking price for "The Canadian Publishers" was $1.5 million, and his own personal financial commitment to the firm was closer to $2 million. But despite the firm's reputation, interested purchasers failed to materialize. American publishers balked at the heavily Canadian backlist. Canadian investment companies viewed publishing as a game of high risk and low return. The federal government waited for offers from the private sector. The Canadian Book Publishers' Council, dominated by foreign-owned publishers, showed little sympathy for the company's plight. Finally, aware that a sale of M&S was unlikely, the Ontario Royal Commission on Publishing weighed in on the matter. Formed in 1970 in the wake of the sale of Ryerson Press and led by the lawyer and writer Richard Rohmer, along with Marsh Jeanneret, publisher of the University of Toronto Press, and the political guru Dalton Camp, the commission recommended a $961,000 interest-free loan, to be paid back over ten years. The government of William Davis accepted the recommendation in April 1971.[31]

The near-death experience of M&S reinforced Berton's belief in the need for state protection of fragile cultural industries, as it did McClelland's. The two men remained heavily involved in the Committee for an Independent Canada, the overt aim of which was to encourage federal policies that would "significantly diminish the influence . . . exerted by outside powers – their citizens, their corporations and their institutions – on Canadian life."[32] The cloaked intention of the CIC, at least for Gordon and Rotstein, was to provide a workable nationalist alternative to a Waffle extremism deemed unacceptable to most Canadians. Berton was part of a CIC delegation that met that year with Prime Minister Trudeau and Revenue Minister Herb Gray to urge the federal government to adopt such nationalist legislation.

In April, as a member of the Association of Canadian Television and Radio Artists, he was one of a delegation of forty-six who flew to Ottawa to address the Canadian Radio-Television Commission on the troubled state of the nation's television industry. "The tragedy today," he told the CRTC, "is that our Canadian broadcasting philosophy . . . has become an American broadcasting philosophy, which sees the medium simply as an extension of the market place. . . . The Canadian broadcasting philosophy has to be bound up with the Canadian dream of an independent nation in North America . . . a nation with its own mythology, its own heroes, its own songs, its own character, and its own idiom."[33] Such contemporary anxieties about the fragility of Canada as a nation-state were very much on Berton's mind while he wrote and revised *The National Dream* and *The Last Spike*. They became the subtext of his story of the national railway.

On Christmas Eve, 1969, Marge Hodgeman sent a memo to two M&S editors informing them that Jack McClelland had received Berton's long-awaited manuscript of the first volume.[34] Having escaped from her native Hungary in 1956, twenty-seven-year-old Anna Szigethy had recently joined the firm with the title "editorial coordinator" after a university education in New Zealand and positions at Cassell Publishing and Collier Macmillan. More junior in status, Judith Turnbull was expected to have a role, if a minor one, in seeing *The National Dream* through to publication. Everyone in the company, from Jack on down, knew that much of the editorial, marketing, and production departments' attention and energy in 1970 would be devoted to *The National Dream*. The Berton Year had begun.

Szigethy read the manuscript as soon as it arrived, and immediately wrote to the prospective copy editor, Janet Craig, enthusiastically: "There is no doubt in my mind that this is going to be a really great book. It is astonishingly vivid throughout; for me, it has achieved what no other 'history' has ever achieved: planted bandied-about historical figures firmly on the ground. Names that have never been any more than names (with dates) emerge as live raucous human beings."[35] With these words of praise, and some minor suggestions – for example, that Berton be asked to reduce the level of detail on construction contracts but to add material on the results of a royal commission appointed to inquire into them – the manuscript awaited Craig's attention.

McClelland set about securing endorsements of the manuscript from Canadians of stature, mainly for use as jacket blurbs. He contacted the historian W.L. Morton of Trent University, co-editor (with Donald Creighton) of McClelland & Stewart's Canadian Centenary Series and author of *The Canadian Identity* (1961), *The Kingdom of Canada* (1963), and many other works. Early in March, McClelland reported to Berton that Morton was "tremendously enthusiastic" and found it "not only a readable and interesting book but a most important contribution to Canadian history." Not long afterwards, Berton and his publisher met over lunch to map out a plan of action on jacket design, marketing, and promotion. Berton insisted on scrutinizing all details, from copy-editing to distribution. McClelland's memorandum to the senior members of his editorial and production staff early in April began: "THE NATIONAL DREAM by Pierre Berton is by long odds the most important book on our Fall list." The memo made it clear that the success of the company as well as the book would depend on "the care and attention" they gave "to all aspects of the programme from this point on." Publication was set for the second week of September.

McClelland's plan called for a first printing of 10,000 copies, but he anticipated sales of at least 40,000 – 50,000 to 60,000 if the Book-of-the-Month Club (which had already expressed an active interest) adopted *The National Dream* as its October offering. If so, it would be the first time the New York-based BOMC selection committee had chosen a Canadian title. The final manuscript was to go to the production department on April 8, be on press by July 7, and be warehoused by August 21. Promotion had already begun and would become more intense as the publication date drew closer. Among McClelland's sales tools was a sixteen-page excerpt sampler to be used as a giveaway at the Canadian Booksellers' Association Convention in early summer and distributed widely thereafter. Its cover, McClelland suggested, would have a heading along the lines of "Who said that Canadians are dull?" Catherine Wilson, McClelland's director of promotion, publicity, and public relations, was to coordinate the process and take care of details.[36]

The version of *The National Dream* Berton submitted to McClelland & Stewart was his fourth draft: he had rewritten the manuscript twice more between sending Kelly and Bliss their copies and digesting their comments. Bliss's comprehensive report had proven very helpful, and as Berton revised, and revised again, he tried to steer a middle passage between a professor's constructive criticism and a publisher's bluff advice to ignore it. While the book was in production and the marketing campaign took shape, he continued with volume two; now his subject was the railway's construction and completion. He was not able to write at the Screen Gems office, since most of his time there was devoted to plotting the 1970–71 television schedule with Franklin, especially the annual blitz of Hollywood set for August. He and Franklin arranged interviews with eighteen guests, including the creator of Woody Woodpecker, Walter Lantz, the *Andromeda Strain* author

Michael Crichton, the boxer Sugar Ray Robinson, and the actor Jack Lemmon. Franklin's workload was as heavy as his own, if not more so, since she was producing *Under Attack* as well as *The Pierre Berton Show*. As the summer wore on, she became heavily involved in the promotion of the new book.

The National Dream was launched to great fanfare with a party for the press on September 9, shortly after Berton and Franklin returned from an extended filming trip to California. The event was a disaster, at least from Berton's perspective, and likely from Franklin's.[37] The next day he wrote an angry letter to McClelland, expressing his dissatisfaction and blaming the M&S promotional staff. "You will recall that, at the outset, I urged that Elsa be given the responsibility, at a small fee, of running the opening party. I think you will have to agree now that she should have been." He held Catherine Wilson responsible for what he regarded as a fiasco. "Even simple things, like handing the guests tapers, or making sure they got a cake box, seemed beyond her; Elsa even had to do that. If Elsa hadn't come in as a volunteer several days ago the affair would have been even more disastrous than it was."

Berton went on to complain that it was Franklin, not Wilson, who had arranged the feature stories that Lotta Dempsey and Bob Blackburn had written. The litany of accusation hardly ended there: Wilson could not write copy, she hadn't been able to attract newspaper photographers or TV cameramen to the launch event, and she did not seem to follow up contacts with the working press. Berton claimed that when he telephoned Wilson about her arrangements for a Montreal appearance, she said that nothing had yet been done. "Ye God! I suppose what is angering me most is what seems to me to be a very casual attitude to the promotion of what is clearly your biggest money making book this fall. It angers me not just as an author but also as a director and a shareholder in the company."[38]

The blow-up had been in the making for years, since the production, marketing, and publicity machine Franklin had created for Berton ran at cross-purposes to that of McClelland & Stewart. This led to garbled communications, action expected but not taken, and general frustration at the perceived incompetence of M&S employees and agents. Almost certainly, any level of performance by the company's staff would have been found wanting, as it had been before and would be later.

This was Berton and Franklin at their most imperious, requiring perfection of all who served them. Both were on the M&S board of directors, Berton since the mid-sixties. McClelland & Stewart continued to owe him a good deal of back salary and royalty money, and this stiffened his attitude of proprietary entitlement. In the summer of 1971, two years after he left M&S to become vice-president of Macmillan of Canada, Hugh Kane, in a conversation with the *Toronto Star* books columnist Peter Sypnowich, assured the journalist only half facetiously that "there's no truth to the rumour that Pierre Berton owns McClelland and Stewart."[39]

On the other hand, clearly there had been serious problems in organizing the book launch, some of them of Jack McClelland's own making. He was the one who had insisted that *The National Dream*'s 10,000-copy print run be celebrated with a cake the size of a pool table decorated with 10,000 very large candles. Every restaurant M&S contacted, including one in the Royal York Hotel, had refused to hold the event because of the fire hazard. When Berton and Franklin returned from Hollywood early in September, they were appalled to discover that a week before the launch no venue was booked, no posters made, no invitations issued. "At this point, thank God, Elsa entered the picture," Berton told McClelland. "But Elsa felt it necessary to defer to Cathy at all times and this caused a split in the executive handling of the affair." In a final and petulant expression of anger and frustration, he said that he would rather have no promotion of his next book than "the kind of bungling" experienced with this one.[40] It was an outburst unworthy of the man and quite unfair to Catherine Wilson, whose side of the story he had not sought to learn.

In the week after his return from California, Berton was the star attraction at no fewer than eight functions, delivering the opening speech at the Binder Twine Festival, emceeing the Opera Ball, making corned-beef hash on the CBC series *55 North Maple*, hosting a large "wet lunch" and press preview of the new season of his TV show, sitting for an interview with the broadcaster Don Sims and the actor and television personality Bruno Gerussi, attending a big bash hosted by the radio station CKEY in honour of its acquisition of *Dialogue* (the show he did with Charles Templeton), and presiding at the season opener of the show itself. Bob Blackburn followed him around all that week and confessed that he lacked the stamina to keep pace.

The "wildest" event by far, Blackburn said, had been the book launch for *The National Dream*. At the last minute, Elsa Franklin had managed to convince Pierre Moreau, manager of Les Cavaliers, a restaurant on Church Street, to host the event. Berton and McClelland arrived several hours early, and the two helped with preparations in their own way – to use Blackburn's coy words, "making sure the bar wasn't serving any inferior whiskey." He reported that the pair went through so many dry runs of the candle-lighting ceremony that when the guests began to arrive "they couldn't see past the ends of their noses and the room smelled like a fire at Madame Tussaud's."

McClelland began handing out tapers to arriving guests, telling them to light the candles. As they did so, more smoke filled the restaurant. Moreau was simultaneously trying to prevent some of the guests from fleeing to the sidewalk with their drinks – an act not allowed by liquor control authorities – and to stop guests with tapers at the ready from lighting any more candles. But whenever one person withdrew, another stepped up to the cake. Blackburn witnessed the ensuing chaos: "Moreau then resorted to throwing wet tablecloths over the fast-spreading firestorm, which by now looked like the aerial photographs of the bombing of Dresden, and barely managed to keep the whole thing from going up."[41] Fortunately, the waiters soon regained control and doused the conflagration. Probably as embarrassed as annoyed at the fiasco, Berton looked for someone to blame. Moreau, the restaurant manager turned firefighter? Elsa, event manager extraordinaire? McClelland, the enthusiastic sponsor of the launch? Himself, for joining Jack at the bar before noon?

A week after the book launch, Berton sent a sarcastic letter to McClelland. "Before your brilliant designers and genius P.R. people commit any advertising for THE NATIONAL DREAM to print, I should like the opportunity of looking it over and making suggestions." He wanted lots of books in the cities where he would speak, and insisted on assurances that Catherine Wilson would set up press conferences, alert the local radio and television stations, and arrange for booksellers to sell autographed books before and after his speeches.[42]

The anger over the bungling of the book launch faded with the success of *The National Dream*, but not the underlying resentment or the need for a scapegoat. A firestorm of another sort was brewing, but it would take another year, and another launch, for it to ignite.

The National Dream received immediate critical acclaim, both in the press and from grateful readers. One of the first to offer congratulations was Michael Bliss, who on the day after the launch wrote its author to say that he had produced "a splendid book that more than lives up to everyone's expectations," with just the right combination of scholarship and readability. Bliss was particularly delighted that Berton had heeded his advice so closely. He had purged the extravagant adjectives, and his prose was far less breathless in tone. Bliss now found Berton's portrait of Macdonald and his motives to ring "absolutely true." Enormous improvements had been made between the first and final drafts. "More than anything else," Bliss noted, "it's the rewriting that tests the author's skill, resourcefulness, and tolerance." Howlers of fact and interpretation had been exorcized, thanks not only to Bliss but also to advice from the historians P.B. Waite and W.L. Morton. But it was because of Bliss that Louis Riel came to hold pride of place in a central section of the first chapter, called "The Struggle for the North West."[43]

Newspaper reviewers were ecstatic. In the *Vancouver Sun* Berton's old mentor, Bruce Hutchison, called it "one of the finest historical works ever written in Canada, a genuine masterpiece." Hutchison, along with Hugh MacLennan, had already praised the book extravagantly in reports to the Book-of-the-Month Club, as Jack McClelland knew they would.[44] In the *Toronto Star*, Peter Sypnowich declared that it was "a book that almost certainly will confirm Pierre Berton as Canada's writer No. 1." In the *Calgary Herald*, Jamie Portman said that it was a book that belonged "permanently on the shelf of anyone who cares about Canada." McClelland & Stewart made public the words W.L. Morton had provided in the letter Jack McClelland had solicited before publication: Berton had "made more vivid than any other writer the tremendous drama of the decade of attempts to build the Pacific railway. More yet, he recalled without chauvinism, the great reasons why Canada is Canada. It is a fine and timely book."[45]

Such high praise drove *The National Dream*, slowly at first, up the ladder of the bestseller lists. Magazine excerpts played no role, since *Maclean's*, *Weekend Magazine*, and the *Canadian* had all declined to make an offer for serial rights on the grounds that the tale of political and business intrigue was too complicated for their readers, and was after all only the first instalment of a larger saga. For similar reasons, Knopf opted not to publish the book in the United States, preferring to wait until Berton could write a one-volume condensed version.[46]

The near-fatal book launch, the absence of prepublication excerpts, and a black book jacket that quickly looked shopworn all contributed to disappointing sales in September – steady but slow; that, at least, was Berton's view. In Toronto, Britnell's had sold only 100 of 500 in stock, and Vancouver's Duthie Books only 68 of 500; in Montreal, Eaton's had sold 27 of 150 and Morgan's, 75 of 100.[47]

Working around his television schedule, including a trip to Australia during which the *Australian Women's Weekly* hailed him as the "Canadian champion of women's rights,"[48] Berton organized and consolidated the research for *The Last Spike* and readied himself to write as soon as he could find a solid block of time. Early in the fall, he began to consider what his next project would be, and wrote to Michael Bliss to ask whether he knew of a good researcher. "I am planning to do my next book on the opening of the Canadian West and the western boom roughly between the years of 1900 and 1912," he wrote, "and I need somebody with a good history background [who] knows his way around archives," preferably someone who also had "a journalist's eye as well as an historian's." This was an attribute he found lacking in Norman Kelly, for all his archival skills.[49] Not long afterwards, Bliss recommended one of his fourth-year undergraduate students, a young man from Scarborough named Glenn Wright.

In October, Berton launched into a two-stage book tour to western Canada to publicize *The National Dream*, travelling to Winnipeg, Vancouver, and Victoria over a four-day period early in the month, and to Calgary, Regina, and Edmonton a month later, speaking to clubs, appearing at book signings, and giving media interviews each day, as usual. In November, when he returned from the second trip west, he sent Jack McClelland another angry letter. Once again, he attacked Catherine Wilson. She had no itinerary ready for him when he returned from Australia, and arrangements for press conferences and autographing sessions, he said, remained vague when she did produce one. M&S representatives in each city received information only at the last minute. Autographing sessions had been a shambles because Wilson had inexplicably told the reps that he would not sign books. A detailed three-page report followed on screw-ups in Calgary, Regina, and Edmonton.[50]

By then, however, sales of *The National Dream* had taken off. McClelland announced publicly in the late fall that the book was a "phenomenal success." Booksellers had taken 25,000 copies, and another printing of 10,000 had been ordered, making the anticipated sales of at least 35,000 a record for a book selling at a price of $10 – expensive for the day. *The National Dream* now topped the bestseller lists.[51] Finally, in December, Berton had time enough to write. Before the new year, his first draft of *The Last Spike* was complete and reworked enough to send to Michael Bliss.

Berton later claimed, however, that the most significant event of that fall had nothing to do with writing or publishing. It concerned an unexpected addition to his family. That fall, Peter Granger, his Kleinburg physician, had found out from a truant officer that a teenager, Eric Basciano, estranged from his family and not going to school, was about to turn sixteen. He arranged to take the boy to the Bertons' for his birthday, thinking perhaps that the sheer number of young people was bound to help any celebration. Basciano was rather quiet that night, but the party went well. The family and Basciano became sufficiently comfortable with each other that he stayed over. One night's sleep turned into another, and another. Plans to place him in a foster home fell through, and he took a permanent place in the Berton home, staying until he was in his twenties and studying music at the University of Western Ontario. Pierre and Janet regarded him as their third son, although he was never formally adopted. Eric later told Pierre that he had been so silent on the day of his first encounter with the Bertons because it had been the first time he had celebrated his birthday.[52]

⋈

That year, on the annual Christmas Eve episode of *The Pierre Berton Show*, three of his daughters turned the tables and interviewed their father. There had been a turnabout of another kind, too. Only four years earlier depicted as the overexposed bad boy of Canadian journalism for the strident polemics of *The Comfortable Pew* and *The Smug*

Minority, Berton almost overnight had become the keeper of Canada's memory. Critics who not long before had dismissed him as a huckster of the trite now portrayed him as a nationalist saint and one of the nation's greatest writers. A range of articles about him appeared in the fall and into 1971, and the promise of a second and perhaps even finer Berton volume within the year kept him in the national spotlight. Profiles invariably praised *The National Dream* for its fresh look at the building of the transcontinental railway, its lively prose style, and its attention to social as well as political history. But in retrospect, what is most striking is the connection made between the national vision of the 1870s and early 1880s and its equivalent a century later.

The critics began to associate Berton himself with Canada's aspirations, past and present, even before *The National Dream* was published. "Pierre Berton's National Dream," ran the headline above a profile written by the *Toronto Star*'s Peter Sypnowich. Journalists like Sypnowich remained essential to the reinforcement of Berton's cultural brand; they were the opinion makers, the people who told the brand's own story, thereby affording it meaning. Just as a half-decade earlier they had written about Berton as the ordinary Canadian's champion, as perhaps the country's leading crusader against inequality, so now they added to their stock of distinguishing attributes his role as cataloguer, interpreter, and guardian of the nation's past. In the *Vancouver Sun*, John Rodgers wrote that the restored Canadian Pacific locomotive at Kitsilano Beach was a reminder of an older Canada, a nation with "a great dream" that did not "vanish into airy nothings." Berton told Canadians how a newly founded Canadian nation had built not just a transcontinental railway but "a workable alternative to the United States."[53] Surely, went the implication, the larger, stronger, and wealthier Canada of the 1970s could resist the United States once more. Berton's railway saga was not only about trains and spikes; it was also about the courage and resolve of a people.

In *Renegade in Power* and *The Distemper of Our Times*, Peter C. Newman had portrayed Canada's modern leaders as ineffectual and its politics variously scandal-ridden and disappointing and, above all, lacking true vision. So when Arnold Edinborough wrote in the *Financial Post* that, "as Berton's book brilliantly shows, our political forerunners were . . . a bunch of grafting, self-serving, greedy, place-seeking money-grubbing rogues as ever ran the business of any country anywhere," he drew attention implicitly to the parallels between the politics and politicians of the 1870s and those subject to Newman's wrath in the 1970s.[54]

In *Saturday Night* Harry Bruce also compared the political ethos of the two epochs, and he invoked Berton's story of resolve and endurance as if it were a vitamin supplement needed to strengthen the national will. Despite parliamentary debates that had "seethed with hatred, betrayals, festering grudges and incidents of personal viciousness that exceeded anything that has occurred in the Commons in our own time," Canada had survived and struggled on. Bruce's fellow Canadians could therefore take heart. Canada's story as Berton told it, Bruce wrote, was "nothing less than the great shapely drama of How We Won the West and Saved Canada From a Fate Worse than Death. That fate, of course, was absorption by the United States of America." Surely, in the era of Pierre Elliott Trudeau and his much publicized "Just Society," and of the Committee for an Independent Canada, the Canada Council, and a rising national-ist movement, there was hope for Canada still.[55]

Bruce Hutchison, too, drew attention to the way *The National Dream* linked past and present. In a lengthy piece called "Old Tomorrow versus Young Today" – for which the subtitle read: "The Same Conundrum" – Hutchison's concern was whether Pierre Trudeau could offer Canada the level of leadership and vision Macdonald had provided. *The National Dream* was now the historical litmus test of national vision for all Canadians. The book, Hutchison said, "raises grave questions" about the state of modern Canada. "In a word . . . does modern Canada, with all its wealth, technology and sophistication, still have those qualities that made it in the first place? . . . Do not dismiss these questions as merely retrospective speculation irrelevant to our current dilemma. Nothing could be more relevant and contemporary." Trudeau faced the same conundrum as Macdonald: "the American presence beside us, the mouse-and-elephant parable in Mr. Trudeau's imagery, the rapacious Yankees in Macdonald's nightmare." The question, Hutchison said by way of conclusion, was "whether the Canadian people have the permanent lifestuff of nationhood in them, the will to surmount new obstacles of the spirit unknown when the physical task of the CPR was done."[56]

The National Dream resonated with Canadians far beyond its explication of their history, significant as that was. In a time of confusion, uncertainty, and fear for the future, Berton gave them hope. Canadians had tackled impossible tasks before, and had prevailed. They had repelled American influence, and built a railway with little American or British financial support. They did so when their political system was in as much turmoil, and was even more corrupt, than in their own day. The title of Arnold Edinborough's *Financial Post* article had captured the possibility of building a nation regardless of circumstance: "Dream, Nightmare or Insanity? All Three – But It Built a Nation." All that was needed was national will.

The reception accorded to *The National Dream* by Canadian opinion makers realigned the image Canadians held of Pierre Berton. His association with progressive social causes remained, as when a Queen's University student newspaper early in 1971 called him "the conscience of the nation" for having championed youth, condemned the Vietnam War, opposed Trudeau's imposition of the War Measures Act, encouraged a greater understanding of Quebec, and supported government legislation to limit American foreign investment in Canada.[57]

In becoming Canada's new-found Homer, spinner and interpreter of the nation's myths, he had acquired the stature of paterfamilias. The unnamed author of one extended review of *The National Dream* made the connection between the message and the man: "*The National Dream* reminds us that Pierre Berton also happens to be one of the most brilliant journalists Canada has produced, and that his entire career has been dominated by a profound love for this country and its people." In a *Telegram* review, John Bassett wrote that he did not make "the mistake of some historical writers by treating the narrative as if it happened a long, long time ago and had no relevance today." Read it carefully, Bassett said, and you will see not only the roots of contemporary western alienation but also that for Macdonald "the price was worth the prize." The title of the *Toronto Star* review was "Pierre Berton Creates a New Canadian Mythology."[58]

Congratulatory notes from friends and acquaintances inevitably followed. Mavor Moore declared that *The National Dream* was "superb history, lucid and gutsy writing and exciting literature." Tommy Douglas wrote from the House of Commons to say that he and his wife had finished the book and that it was "a monumental piece of work and tremendously good reading." He also congratulated Berton on "a humdinger of a speech" he had recently given. Laurier LaPierre wanted to turn the book into a television series. Berton wrote back with thanks, but told LaPierre that "preliminary talks" had already taken place with Lister Sinclair at the CBC and with Fletcher Markle about such a series.[59]

Berton promised Jack McClelland the manuscript of *The Last Spike* in January 1971, and he delivered on schedule. Cover and interior design was well in hand by then, using those of *The National Dream* as templates. *The Pierre Berton Show* went to Mexico in March, and while there he made a personal tour of Mexico City with David Alfaro Siqueiros, one of the country's pre-eminent painters and revolutionaries. Berton of course wanted to interview him on camera. Elsa Franklin and her girls had also lined up Ivan Illich, the radical priest and exponent of educational reform, and the movie actress Isela Vegas, just as radical in her rejection of marriage to her lover and her support for women's rights in a Hispanic society hostile to the concept. But when the owner of the television station told him that a government censor would sit in on the interview sessions, Berton refused to soften his line of questioning. He wanted to ask a panel of students what they thought of the Mexican government, responsible a few years earlier for the death of three hundred students at the hands of the Mexican army, but after he discovered that the student panel would not be allowed, he refused to do any shows. Instead, he flew to Acapulco for a holiday with his family, and Franklin went off to Zihuatenejo.[60]

Berton had left a clean copy of the manuscript of *The Last Spike* with M&S in January, but let it be known at M&S that editorial work should not begin until after he heard from Michael Bliss. Meanwhile, he continued to revise. Twenty-one pages of comments from the Toronto historian arrived early in February, as thorough as before. Once again, Bliss apologized for his "scolding professorial tone." Some familiar problems existed – a weak first chapter and too many anecdotes, for example. But Bliss found far less overwriting in the new manuscript, and its level of expression was much better. Much of the material, especially about construction, was new. He urged more clarity in the role Americans played in finance and engineering and about the nature of Macdonald's "vision." In volume one, Berton had emphasized Macdonald's vision of nation, but in volume two this was much less evident. More sympathetic attention, he wrote, should also be paid to western grievances. "In general we might as well all realize that Canada hasn't been a very united nation and Eastern claims for the good effects of John A. and his railway may simply increase disunity. We do want Western schoolboys to read the book." Finally, Bliss suggested that somewhere Berton should incorporate Hollywood's portrayal of the story of the CPR in the 1949 movie *Canadian Pacific*, starring Randolph Scott as a construction boss, and with CPR vice-president and general manager Cornelius Van Horne reduced to the role of "a rather weedy manager."[61]

Much of the University of Toronto historian's commentary was aimed at protecting *The Last Spike* from the wrathful pen of the York University professor H.V. Nelles, who in a lengthy review in the December issue of *Canadian Forum* had attacked the central premises of *The National Dream*. Nelles had praised the diligence of Berton's "research assistants," who had "toiled valiantly in the archives turning up fresh material," but condemned him for not being abreast of recent research and for adopting Donald Creighton's impassioned prose style. Berton had produced an important book, he wrote, at least judging "from its rapid ascent of the best seller list"; but it was an old-fashioned one, "a much expanded edition of the received version" of Canadian history. In his drive to tell an exciting story about nation building, the author had not thought to ask some simple but essential questions. Were the threats to Canada – especially those of American competition and control – ultimately worth the huge cost of the CPR? Did the harnessing of transcontinental railway building to Macdonald's National Policy serve Canadian or merely eastern interests? For a westerner, Nelles noted, "it is ironic that the central Canadian nationalists regard the CPR as an instrument of national unity; he can think of few other institutions that divide the nation more." Harold Innis, he added, had seen that Macdonald's impetuosity had led to eastern dominance over the West. "Western Canada has paid for the development of Canadian nationality, and it would appear that it must continue to pay."[62]

It was strange, Nelles had observed, that "the dazzling reappearance of the CPR as nationbuilder" took place just after the publication of

Donald Creighton's pessimistic account of modern Canadian history as political tragedy in *Canada's First Century*. "Did the country pay too high a price for a transcontinental railway?" the review asked by way of conclusion. "One can still be a nationalist and say yes."[63]

"Keep in mind," Bliss warned, "that Prof. Nelles will undoubtedly review this volume for the *Forum*. If you grant that this was by far the most penetrating and formidable criticism of vol 1, however annoying, then it is useful to see most of my remarks as an attempt to head him off the second time around."[64]

A grateful Berton, recovering from a midwinter bout of the flu, replied a few weeks later, enclosing a cheque for $275. "Believe me, your comments were well worth it. I have taken almost all of them into consideration." Indeed he had. The final paragraph of *The Last Spike* dealt with Randolph Scott and *Canadian Pacific*. The $525 Berton paid Bliss for his comments on *The National Dream* and *The Last Spike* was very likely the best investment he ever made.[65]

By mid-April, Berton had his blissfully improved draft ready and in M&S hands. The Book-of-the-Month Club picked the book as a fall reserve selection, promising an advance of $10,000 against royalties. Anna Szigethy had met with Berton before he left for Mexico in March, and informed McClelland that Franklin already had preliminary plans for promotion: a black-tie dinner in Ottawa, a possible cover story in *Time*, miniature last spikes as giveaways, and a quick trip to the West with a four-day stay in the Vancouver area, where he would deliver a major speech. Berton pitched the obvious follow-up, an illustrated version of the railway saga, and Szigethy – now executive editor – recommended to Jack McClelland that the project go ahead.[66]

The frenetic cycle of packaging and selling Berton and his railway began anew. Jack McClelland had contacted Bruce Hutchison and Hugh MacLennan to request assessments for book club purposes once again, and the grand old men of Canadian letters accepted the offer and the promise of $500 that went with it. Toward the end of May, Berton was a featured speaker at the Canadian Booksellers' Association convention, and McClelland sang Berton's praises in a letter to the author. "It is one of the best talks on the subject of being Canadian that I have ever heard," he wrote. Even the booksellers had been won over. "Although the retailers have sold a helluva lot of your books through the years, it is clear that you would never have won a popularity contest with them, but that is changing and an amazing number of booksellers came up and said how impressed they were with your honesty, sincerity, etc."[67]

In a letter to McClelland written in early May, Berton reported that he was well advanced in his abridgement of the two railway books for an illustrated omnibus volume, *The Great Railway* (the phrase Berton had used in the subtitles of *The National Dream* and *The Last Spike*), and he provided detailed suggestions about its desired size and layout, down to the width of the margins. He promised that the manuscript would be ready by mid-February 1972. It was. *The Great Railway: Illustrated*, with text reduced to 336 pages, appeared later that year, and so did its 574-page American equivalent under the Knopf imprint, *The Impossible Railway: The Building of the Canadian Pacific*.

"While I'm on the subject of promotion," he told McClelland, "I think it would be well to make a deal with Elsa Franklin as soon as possible so that she can get working on some of the long range problems of promotion, including my own availability in the fall which can be integrated with my television schedule and also things like press parties, dinners, etc. which are too often left to the last moment." Berton's suggestion was no doubt intended as a clear signal to McClelland that he wanted no repetition of the unpleasantness of the promotion of *The National Dream*.[68]

In June, Berton arranged a meeting with his prospective new researcher, Glenn Wright, whose graduation in history from the University of Toronto was only days away. When Wright arrived at Berton's Carlton Street office, he was introduced to Michael Swift and Robert Taylor, a pair of historians who worked at the Public Archives of Canada, and the four men talked about archival sources for a history of immigration to the Prairie west. Berton sent Wright almost immediately to Ottawa and the archives, where he met Dominion Archivist Wilfred I. Smith and went about establishing the location of primary sources. That summer, Wright visited archives in Winnipeg, Regina, Saskatoon, and Calgary, and he spent the better part of 1971–72 compiling a bibliography and sampling old newspapers, especially the *Manitoba Free Press*. Wright enrolled in a master's degree program in the winter of 1972, taking courses with Michael Bliss and Carl Berger, who taught the history of western Canada; but by then, he later recalled, thanks to his year of paid research, he'd already had "a bit of a graduate education." Berton, he said, "was very good at explaining archives."[69]

By the early summer of 1971, Elsa Franklin had a grab bag of ideas for *Last Spike* promotion: an author tour by private railway car if N.R. Crump would provide one; reproductions of old CPR railroad tickets as invitations to press receptions; mementoes such as genuine railway spikes imprinted with the book title and author's name; a marathon radio broadcast from the rolling railway car, during which Berton would talk about the history of the railway and passing points of interest. Franklin had plans for posters, flyers, route maps, a Last Spike song, special dinners in the grand Railway Committee Room of the House of Commons and in the old Ottawa Union Station, and autographed ex libris. Franklin's estimate of the promotion budget was a whopping $20,000: $15,362 to cover Elsa's promotion management fees ($3,000) and print materials, publicity tours, and newspaper advertising; and another $4,838 for unspecified "special projects."[70]

Throughout the summer, but especially during August, a flurry of memoranda and press releases sped from the Franklin-Berton offices to M&S, the press, and booksellers – including a general notice that Jack McClelland was in search of "an inspired bartender" to concoct a Last Spike cocktail, one different from the existing Rusty Nail. The first suggestion McClelland received, stated the release, was "vodka and Geritol, stirred not with a plastic swizzle stick but gently with a railroad tie."[71]

The launch of *The Last Spike* took place at Toronto's Westbury Hotel late on a Sunday morning, September 12, 1971, the day after publication. The elaborate brunch was a carefully organized blend of flair and nostalgia. Guests mingled, Last Spike cocktails in hand, to the recorded sounds of a chugging steam locomotive. Later, they sat down to a repast of wheat cakes, Winnipeg goldeye with Niagara grape sauce, sourdough bread, New Brunswick fiddleheads, wild blackberry pie, and "pioneer coffee." While Alderman William Kilbourn, W.L. Morton, former premier Leslie Frost, Jack McClelland, and Berton himself toasted and told anecdotes about such CPR luminaries as Cornelius Van Horne, George Stephen, and Sir John A. Macdonald, guests refreshed themselves with Last Spike coolers – the cocktail diluted with soda water.[72]

Later in the month, Berton, Franklin, and McClelland together kicked off a series of book promotion breakfasts and radio and TV interviews. Crump had declined to provide a private railway car on grounds of cost, but Franklin was undeterred. Her itinerary called for a late September trip to Montreal, Edmonton, and Calgary over a span of eight days. From November 8 to 10 they were in Vancouver and Victoria. They spent November 30 to December 2 in Regina and Winnipeg, followed by a promotional excursion to Ottawa. By Berton's account, "a mass of people" descended on him at Bolen's Bookstore in Victoria for autographed copies. In every city, Pierre occupied a suite and McClelland a room at the local CPR hotel.[73]

The gruelling tour worked, for sales of *The Last Spike* were strongest in those cities Berton visited. McClelland had shipped 25,000 copies to bookstores in late August, the prepublication demand helpfully goosed by a review in *Time* magazine three weeks before the release date. (The pre-emptive review thoroughly annoyed book review editors across the country.)[74] The first print run was 40,000 copies, plus 25,000 for Book-of-the-Month Club members. By the end of September, a print order for 20,000 more was in place. McClelland estimated that bookstore sales would reach at least 50,000 copies, and he was betting on more.[75]

On the Saturday of *The Last Spike*'s official release, when he might have been expected to spend the day in Toronto celebrating, Pierre Berton was instead in Kleinburg, presiding with Janet over the fifth annual Binder Twine Festival. That day, feature stories about the book and its author appeared in newspapers across the country. One was by Margaret Daly of the *Toronto Star*, who recorded his Kleinburg activities and then wrote: "Also as you read this, he may be quietly taking his place in Canadian history – along with Walter Gordon, Mel Watkins and a handful of others – as one of those whose efforts ignited and fanned the spark of a new Canadian nationalism in the 1970s." Daly's piece nicely joined the published book and the nationalist mission of its author. Twentieth-century issues had been brought to bear on nineteenth-century history, and they looped, like the Möbius strip of a past master, back into the present, somehow making everything seem better. Berton, she said, was "the Captain Marvel of the Canadian communications field."[76]

"It's no longer a case of who is Pierre Berton?" wrote Reg Vickers, books editor of the *Calgary Herald*. "Rather, it's more like what is Pierre

Berton? Has he become another national institution like Saturday night hockey and *Maclean's* magazine? Is he merely a prepackaged commodity for the benefit of book publishers and TV networks? Or, is he perhaps Canada's best salesman of nationalism and one of our most ardent figures for economic independence?" In this and in a host of similar tributes, Berton was placed atop the lofty pedestal where he would remain for the rest of his life. Two of Vickers's three Bertons were the straw men of a writer's conceit, and in his next paragraph Vickers threw them to the wind. "With the publication this month of *The Last Spike* . . . the Berton phenomenon reaches its peak. One Toronto columnist wrote that with the launching of the book, Berton was 'quietly taking his place in Canadian history.'" But it was more than this, Vickers suggested: "Is Berton merely writing about our history, or is he becoming an actual part of it?"[77]

Berton reckoned his latest book was perhaps the best he had written, better even than *Klondike*, and clearly superior to *The National Dream*. The saga of building the transcontinental railway was intrinsically more interesting than the hope and planning and conspiring about it, resulting in a story of rugged adventure told in prose that blazed like sunlight on a glacial lake. The implicit nationalist and political message of *The National Dream* had been to convince Canadians that they should continue to strive to achieve the nation's desires regardless of obstacles – political, economic, or personal. Following close on its heels, the sequel demonstrated that these desires could be fulfilled and the dream realized. As a consequence, the reception accorded *The Last Spike* later in the year seemed to confirm his instincts about the book's merit.

Friends and colleagues, the daily press, and national magazines greeted the book with high praise, proclaiming it more satisfying than *The National Dream*. "A rage-for-life Berton breathes life into a stormy, gutsy epic," went the title of Arnold Edinborough's rave review in the *Financial Post*. The tale was "truly epic," the story of great challenges met by great men through great effort – "the throbbing stuff of history," he said. "It is, in short, the basic story of Canada, and Berton makes it engagingly human and utterly absorbing." But the impact of the book, as with *The National Dream*, came less from its lively style than from its contemporary relevance. "The Great Railway is not simply narrative," wrote Donald Cameron in *Maclean's*; it was a recipe for resisting

American influence. This was its lesson for the present. "So Berton's book is no mere curiosity; the issues he talks about are with us still." The *Alberta Historical Review* assessment by Hugh Dempsey, curator of the Glenbow-Alberta Institute, concluded: "In these days of uncertainty about our Canadian identity *The Last Spike* sounds a timely reminder, 'Stand fast, Craigellachie!'"[78]

Bruce Hutchison had said as much in his report to the Book-of-the-Month Club. "Mr. Berton's book, appearing at exactly the right time, tells us that in human essentials, and in ever-recurring trouble, Canada has not changed at all. The endless gamble continues for the same old prize. Canadians will win it again if they understand their unlikely past. . . . The last spike at Craigellachie, a common steel spike so typical of our breed, was driven deep into the nation's memory and is still our great folk symbol."[79]

Academics and journalists alike picked up on the psychological significance of Berton's railway books for contemporary Canadians. In 1973, when the full effect of *The National Dream* and *The Last Spike* could be assessed, the Queen's University historian Donald Swainson concluded that "the enormous success of these books illustrates the deep desire possessed by middle-class English Canadians for national symbols and identity." The title of a report in the *Wall Street Journal* the same year spoke to its impact: "Canada's Pierre Berton Succeeds by Reinforcing a National Identity." The country's "most popular historian, its all-time best-selling author and . . . superstar of Canada's electronic media," the *Journal* stated, had all but become its resident therapist, "helping to solve a kind of national identity crisis."[80]

Pierre Berton served up *The Last Spike* as he did the cocktail named after it – to reduce inhibition and galvanize resolve. The story begun in *The National Dream* came to its conclusion, and the story it told of great national accomplishment over adversity gave English Canadians not simply a sense of the past, but a vicarious sense of personal satisfaction. In the transition from national dream to last spike, Berton's dialogue with Canadian readers shifted from alleviating their fear to fuelling their desire. Fear and desire: the very core of the ad man's world, and the psychiatrist's. This was the final stage of the imprinting of his brand. Everything after would be a matter of expansion and consolidation.

Between 1966 and 1980, first on CFRB and then on CKEY, Berton and Charles Templeton argued across the microphone on their controversial radio program, *Dialogue*.

The controversial columnist McKenzie Porter appeared a number of times as a guest on Pierre Berton's television shows, including once on *Under Attack* in 1965.

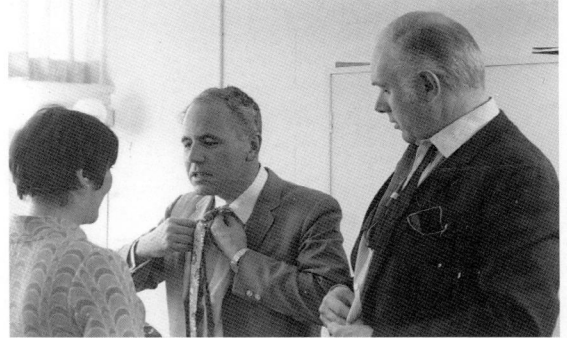

Berton's friends appeared often on his televised interview show, including the bestselling author Arthur Hailey, who prepared for his appearance under the watchful eye of Berton's producer, Elsa Franklin.

Berton obtained a rare interview with "the sick comic" Lenny Bruce during the 1965–66 television season. The comedian spoke of his lengthy struggle with police over his allegedly obscene act. Bruce died in August 1966 of a presumed morphine overdose.

The Bertons loved cooking and published two books on the subject. In 1966, Pierre and Janet published *The Centennial Food Guide*, for which this was a publicity still.

The appearance of David Susskind and Joyce Davidson on *The Pierre Berton Show* in the 1966–67 season resulted in a "prickly show" in which she attacked her hometown of Hamilton and he criticized "the Canadian personality."

The *Tonight Show* host Johnny Carson became Berton's guest during the 1966–67 season. In 1972–73 the show would feature Carson's ex-wife Joanne, speaking of life with Johnny.

The Liberal leadership convention of April 1968 was one of many Berton covered as a reporter. His interview with the eventual winner, forty-six-year-old Pierre Elliott Trudeau, was broadcast by the CBC.

Early in 1974, the CBC aired a popular eight-part series based on Berton's bestselling books *The National Dream* and *The Last Spike*. Earlier, the author and series narrator posed for an iconic publicity shot.

Moderator Fred Davis and the veteran *Front Page Challenge* panellists Berton, Betty Kennedy, and Gordon Sinclair celebrated the show's twenty-third season in 1979–80.

Radio listeners could hear Berton almost every day on any topic.

A bearded Berton returned home from hospital and began recuperating in July 1983. The press reported that he had pneumonia, but the condition was a pulmonary embolism.

Elsa Franklin and Janet and Pierre Berton celebrated his television program *Heritage Theatre* in June 1985 by having a picnic for its 157 actors.

Even Jack McClelland, publisher of the risqué work of fiction *Masquerade*, failed to guess who its author, Lisa Kroniak, really was – until Berton's publicity stunt at the King Edward hotel.

The year 1987 found Berton working at the slanted desk his son Peter had designed to protect him from muscle strain.

Berton joined other members of the arts community, including Liona Boyd, in April 1988 to show their support for Bill C-60, a federal measure expanding the rights of creators to display their work.

Beginning in New York, Berton travelled to an oil rig in the Arctic to launch *The Arctic Grail* in 1988.

Farley Mowat and Berton chat amicably at the Writers' Development Trust's "Great Literary Dinner Party" at Toronto's Sutton Place hotel in November 1989. Their relationship had not always been so jovial.

The singer Maureen Forrester and Berton share a laugh at the comedian Frank Shuster's funeral in January 2002.

Governor General Adrienne Clarkson was one of the hundreds who celebrated Pierre Berton's life in the Canadian Broadcasting Centre on December 7, 2004.

To destroy the brand, now mature, would require Canadians to repudiate not just Berton, but themselves.

The Last Spike became the stake that shattered the resistance of all but the most grudging of critics to Berton's place as a national institution and the nation's leading historian. The veteran historian George F.G. Stanley, who disliked Berton's television persona and public posturing and who had been critical of *The National Dream* for its rhetorical excesses, appreciated *The Last Spike*'s subdued tone and greater credibility and welcomed "the return of Berton of the *Klondike*." In *Saturday Night*, Harry Bruce admitted that Berton's attitude of superiority had often tempted him, like other journalists, "to bring the mighty low," and that he had taken the same attitude into his reading of *The Last Spike*. Berton, Bruce wrote, was not Alan Moorhead or Barbara Tuchman or "any other brilliant foreigner. He's Our Pierre and, for longer than I care to tell you, I wondered how in the world I was going to make a brilliant show of sticking the old needle into Pierre this time." But it was Bruce who was skewered. "Berton and *The Last Spike* have beaten me. I could find no way to attack him that bears any relation to this beautiful book."[81]

ASTRIDE THE SUMMIT

—

IN THE SUMMER OF 1971, Pierre Berton climbed the Chilkoot Trail, as his father had done before him. Thanks to his role as historical consultant for a project aimed at creating an international gold rush park in the North, he had been invited to accompany a group of Canadian and American experts exploring the site of the most memorable phase of the trek to the Klondike gold fields, the formidable Chilkoot Pass. In lieu of a fee for his services, he was allowed to bring along two of his children – Pamela, twenty-one, and Peter, not quite sixteen. They were flown by helicopter from Skagway to Canyon City Camp, where they stood at the beginning of the trail, face to face with Canada's past and their own.[1]

With the hemlock and spruce rainforest behind them, and reminders of the quest for gold everywhere – rusted steam boilers, remnants of discarded clothing, abandoned tools – Berton and his companions scrambled up the difficult boulder-strewn slope and its treacherous skin of loose shale. During the climb he thought of his father's arduous clamber to these heights in pursuit of his dream, and very likely the ruminations elided into thoughts about his own dreams over the years. When twenty-seven-year-old Frank Berton reached the summit seventy-three years earlier, he had not yet come close to realizing his ambitions; at fifty-one, the son had also arrived at the top, and all he could possibly have hoped for had come true. Before him now, in landscape and in life, lay the long level of the ridge, and then the slow descent.

With the success of *The National Dream* he had acquired a degree of national admiration and respect that surpassed any of his earlier accomplishments. The need to write and the joy of writing remained as strong as ever; but he no longer felt compelled to reinvent himself, time and again, as if to discover who Pierre Berton really was, and why. Those days had gone. He still possessed abundant creative energy, but the time had come to take stock, to look back, to dwell on a past that had always obsessed him, and to expand its canvas. At the summit, he took time to rest with Pamela and Peter and they talked about the family, its history, and its long connection to the North. Before they reached Lake Bennett, the end of the Chilkoot Trail, they had decided that the next year the whole family would drift north, down the Yukon River.

Earlier that spring, Jack McClelland had received a letter from a seventy-three-year-old Austrian-born woman named Ida Schneider, who had emigrated to Canada in 1927 and had corresponded with Pierre Berton a few times about problems experienced by her epileptic daughter. "I have read the book, 'The National Dream,' by Pierre Berton. It is a veritable Canadian Saga and to think, we are still brainwashed that Canadians have no identity." Schneider had likely known of Berton's reputation as a friend of the disadvantaged; now the man meant something more. Perhaps for the first time since she touched Canadian soil, someone had explained to her what it meant to be a Canadian.[2]

Berton's volume of personal correspondence increased exponentially in the early 1970s. Suddenly he had become everybody's Pierre, viewed as a man of integrity and concern who could be trusted to take care of the national memory as well as people's interests and needs. He also continued as a political activist. Early in November, he and Charles Templeton aired a *Dialogue* program from Washington, D.C. They were intent on presenting a petition to the White House, and they walked toward it pushing a wheelbarrow that held the document signed by 112,000 CKEY listeners, protesting against American plans to conduct a nuclear test on the Aleutian island of Amchitka. Only later, when the Watergate scandal broke, did they realize that the presidential aide who received them and rolled the wheelbarrow into the White House had been President Richard Nixon's counsel, John Dean. The two journalists thought the importance of the cause was worth the shtick of the stunt, but McKenzie Porter, Pierre's long-time critic, disagreed, accusing them of impudence and of damaging Canada's "reputation for moderation and protocol." In the same *Globe and Mail* column, Porter suggested that Prime Minister Trudeau should get his hair cut.[3]

Berton's mail came from perfect strangers and old friends, from national organizations and local clubs and businesses, from writers and teachers and politicians, from those who offered praise and others who sought advice or curried favour. All manner of groups and associations asked him to lend his name to their cause by joining their boards, and far more often than not he accepted. At the request of J.E. Hodgetts, he joined the board of directors of the Canadian Studies Foundation. He let his name stand for election as a director of the Canadian Writers' Foundation, a charity founded in 1931 to assist writers facing acute financial distress. The foundation, Berton wrote, was "essential to the literary well-being of Canada." He served on its board for more than twenty years.[4]

Since the 1960s, he had informally and quietly assisted authors. Usually they were unknown, even unpublished, and he provided them with advice and encouragement. Sometimes he asked Jack McClelland to look at their manuscripts. Those afflicted with disease or disability especially caught his eye. One was Susanne Moss, who suffered from cerebral palsy. He had interviewed her on his television show during the 1968–69 season and continued to provide support as she struggled to write about her difficult life, arranging for McClelland to read her manuscript once it was ready. In extensive correspondence spanning a half-dozen years, Moss came to see Berton as her guardian angel. Her requests, by telephone and letter, came often, and they were usually so insistent that he must at times have found them exasperating. But invariably he answered her pleas, at one point even buying her a television (she had wanted the hi-fi set she had seen in a Bad Boy furniture store). When M&S published her book, *Too Many Tears*, in 1976, he wrote its preface. He tried to assist another such author, Helen Maloney, who suffered from terminal cancer, but Anna Szigethy nixed the idea in a brief note attached to Berton's letter of support.[5]

He remained undaunted by failure to place such manuscripts. Early in 1972, McClelland received a Berton missive asking him to consider a manuscript from a man who was manic-depressive. The letter also suggested that McClelland consider publishing a collection of caricatures by Terry Mosher, a cartoonist whose work appeared under the name Aislin and who would soon join the Montreal *Gazette*. "He is, in my opinion, not only the best caricaturist in Canada (better than Duncan Macpherson) but one of the best in the world."[6] McClelland concluded that there would be little market for such a book.

As a result of unsolicited correspondence, Berton lent a young mother, a friend of the family, $600 to help with her child's tuition, politely declined an invitation from the Rosedale NDP to run in the next federal election, accepted the invitation of a Toronto schoolteacher named Laura Kinrade to visit her grade one class at King Edward School and watch the Apollo 16 splashdown, and provided advice to a northerner from Whitehorse on how to go about writing his autobiography.[7]

〰️

The Bertons started down the Yukon River to Dawson on August 3, 1972, as planned, three days before Paul's fourteenth birthday. His presence with them was little less than a miracle, for less than six weeks earlier he had undergone heart surgery. Eric was unable to go, but the rest of the family, along with Lucy's son, Berton Woodward, and Penny's friend Robert Holmes, flew to Vancouver and made their way to Lake Bennett via Whitehorse, where they collected their gear.

For eleven days, they floated down the river in two sixteen-foot Zodiac rubber boats and one eighteen-foot Avon, powered by three twenty-five-horsepower Johnson outboards. Skip Burns, who had been a guide on the Chilkoot Trail with Pierre the previous year, had gladly agreed to be their main guide and pilot, and he was assisted by Ross Miller, Scotty Jeffers, and his own new bride, Cheri. Back in Toronto, Jack McClelland, well aware of Berton's erratic habits behind the wheel of any vehicle or vessel, had insured his leading author with Lloyd's of London for $250,000; he tried for a headline-worthy million-dollar policy, but no insurance company would take the risk. For McClelland, the Berton family trip was another promotional opportunity. Their well-publicized arrival in Dawson was set to coincide with the release of a new and expanded edition of *Klondike*, on August 17 – the seventy-fifth anniversary of the discovery of gold in the Yukon. McClelland, of course, fully intended to get at least one new book about the adventure out of his author – a second if he could convince Pierre to write for the children's market.[8]

The trip did indeed produce a book, *Drifting Home*, which Berton wrote in the spring of 1973, while on holiday at a rented villa on Portugal's Algarve coast.[9] Arguably one of his finest books, it is easily his most personal. His work organizing and ghostwriting *I Married the Klondike* had been a gift to his mother. *Drifting Home* was a son's testimonial to his father.

Throughout the trip down the Yukon, he made notes on the family's adventures, the historic import of the water route and its geography and people, and the course of his parents' lives. The result became a book that knitted together many pasts and a single present, and he wrote it with an emotional intensity that was heartfelt and genuine.

Each day the voyagers floated farther north, away from a world of radio and television and newspapers. They drifted through Miles Canyon and its fearsome gorge, through the length of Lake Laberge with the ruins of the old Mounted Police post on its shore, around the dangerous hairpin curves of the Thirtymile River, past Hogan's Rock and Wolf Bar and Five Mile Bend and Seven Mile Bend to Little Salmon Village and the river for which it was named. They headed toward the roiling waters of Five Fingers Rapids, and ran its deceptive channel; and then they drifted still further, down the five hundred miles of river that bore them to Dawson City.

The eleven days of this trip into time marked the closest Pierre Berton would come to reckoning with the life of his father, for the shadow of Frank Berton strays throughout *Drifting Home*. He is the riddle at its core. In the book's final pages, when the family has reached Dawson and Pierre and his family visit the old Administration Building where Frank once worked, Pierre recalls a recurring dream, one he has had for many decades: "I am scampering and hiding between rows of tall wooden walls behind a familiar building I cannot identify. Now I realize that this is that building and those walls were high stacks of cordwood arranged in parallel lines and stretching out like fingers behind the back door of my father's office, where we children often played in the afternoons after school."[10] Is it too much to suggest that in this dream it is less the "familiar building" that cannot be identified than the father hidden behind wood and wall?

All his life, as child and man, Pierre Berton could never quite square the intelligent, "infinitely curious man" who was his father, a man who knew French and Greek and could make a telescope, with the long-serving, half-impoverished clerk he became and the "shrunken man" Pierre saw in Dawson in 1939, "moving like a snail down the boardwalk of Fifth Avenue on his way to work, his thinning hair almost white."[11] In the end, the nearest he came to understanding him was to conclude that Frank Berton's life had been a quest for adventure, not gold, and that the dream itself was what counted most. This explanation of his father's motivations, forced as it was in *Drifting Home*, had been the central thread of *Klondike*, and reappeared again in *The National Dream*, *The Last Spike*, *The Arctic Grail*, and much else in the subsequent Berton oeuvre.

Interspersed with these reflections on his father in *Drifting Home*, Berton gently laid in descriptions of his early life in the Yukon, and of his Kleinburg family in the large rubber rafts and their engagement with the surrounding flora and fauna, landscape and people. Back home in Kleinburg, life, as one journalist observed it that year, was "a chaos of kids, dogs, cats and birds in a menagerie loosely directed by his harried wife, Janet," while Berton, with his white sideburns, appeared "relaxed and serene" in orange shirt, black denims, and running shoes.[12] Life on the river likely mirrored this life at Kleinburg that August; but if so, it was a family scene with an important additional element. For with this family was the earlier one, that of Frank and Laura, to which the journey down the river paid homage: two families, separated by time but joined by a northern wilderness and the river that fed it. There they were, the whole Berton gang, having great fun camping out on the water and exploring the shoreline and calling each other the Deaners and the Wows as if they had just stepped out of an Arthur Ransome novel to the war cry, "Swallows and Amazons together!"

Like the whole trip and the book that came out of it, Berton's account in *Drifting Home* was a highly romanticized version of the experience from the observant imagination of Canada's best-known romanticist; yet in some ways the voyage resembled a frenetic operational exercise organized for badges at a Boy Scout jamboree. Patsy regularly kept up the boat's log, Berton Woodward took notes for prospective newspaper items, Penny carried along a Super 8 movie camera to make a family documentary, and her friend Robert took still pictures for a magazine article. Pierre, presiding over all and missing nothing, was already mentally outlining the book Jack McClelland wanted and, while at it, composing in his head the text to accompany the photographs for the article Robert had in mind. ("Floating Down the Yukon" appeared in

Maclean's that December.) "The Yukon gets under your skin as no other part of this country can," he wrote. "It has been under mine for more than 50 years. Part of the magic, I suppose, is the feeling that the river is eternal."[13]

The fall of 1972 was eventful in more ways than one, because it involved the publication of several new Berton books and a blow-up at McClelland & Stewart that raised questions about his influence and doubts about Jack McClelland's judgment, cost a highly valued employee her job, and alienated two of the firm's most valuable authors.

When Berton resumed work in September, he did so with a real sense of accomplishment. In March he had won his third Governor General's Award, for *The Last Spike*. Episode 1,500 of *The Pierre Berton Show*, now the longest-running daily program in the history of national television in Canada, was set to air in the fall. That July, the CRTC had granted the broadcaster and entrepreneur Al Bruner a licence to establish a third television network, to be called Global, and he met with Berton and Franklin about producing shows for it as competition for CTV and CBC. The Book-of-the-Month Club had adopted the updated edition of *Klondike*, and in the fall *The Great Railway: Illustrated* became available in bookstores, with a first printing of 20,000 copies. It contained 275 rare photographs, and Berton had exercised his blue pen so vigorously that the word count of the original two volumes had been reduced by 80 per cent – to 95,000 words from 500,000. A newly illustrated version of *The Secret World of Og* was in the works, with artwork by Patsy Berton, and shooting was about to start on an eight-part CBC series based on *The National Dream*, with dramatized scenes written by Timothy Findley, documentary segments by William Whitehead, and Berton in the role of narrator.[14]

In September, three books by Pierre Berton were on the national bestseller list. *The National Dream* had been there for a hundred weeks, and *The Last Spike* for fifty; *The Great Railway: Illustrated* had climbed to sixth place, and everyone expected the new edition of *Klondike* to be the fourth Berton title to join the list. One of Elsa Franklin's press releases proudly noted that combined sales of *The National Dream* and

The Last Spike meant that "Canadians [had] laid out two and one quarter million dollars to read about their own history." For these two titles alone, Berton's 15 per cent royalties came to $375,000 on the list price of $10. A one-volume abridged paperback, released when the televised version of *The National Dream* aired, sold 175,000 copies. Sales continued to be strong in subsequent years. Over 3,300 copies of *The National Dream*, 3,000 of *The Last Spike*, and 1,200 of a boxed set sold within a period of a few months in 1974, with expectations of a significant increase in 1975. *The Secret World of Og* sold 17,000 copies during the year, in part because it was on the public school curriculum in British Columbia. By then, Pierre Berton sales figures would have a combined retail sales value in Canada alone of more than $6 million.[15]

This explains in part why, in interviews dating from early in 1972, Berton began stating that he was "purposely arrogant," first as a Canadian nationalist and then in terms of his own achievements. He was tired of Canadian diffidence and false modesty. Canada, he insisted, was "bloody good," and so, for that matter, was he. "To instill confidence, somebody has to be a little over-confident," he told one reporter. "What I've been trying to show myself and everybody else is that we can make it here." The Canadian Press picked up the remarks, and soon his words became the core of articles in newspapers across the country, variously emphasizing Canada or Berton, sometimes conflating the two.[16]

The problem with an assumed attitude is that it can be taken for the genuine article, and sometimes it becomes as much. That is certainly how a good number of those who dealt with Berton interpreted his behaviour at the time. Assumed or not, the arrogance seemed real, and his continuing sense of disgruntlement with the way his books were treated at M&S fed the perception. His discontent in 1971 over the typeface and printing quality of *The Last Spike* had led an exasperated Jack McClelland to reply: "I consider your complaint about THE LAST SPIKE to be hyper-critical in the extreme. Great God man." Six days later, Berton was back at it, complaining of broken type, smearing, fading, and bad register. "Don't hand me horseshit about amateur and professional designers," he wrote Jack. "If either you or I – both amateurs – let the professional designers have their way I'd be out of business and so would you. This is especially true on the two railway books." The same day he insisted, against all commercial logic, that five hundred copies of the book be on hand for an autographing party in Kleinburg during the 1971 Binder Twine Festival, although no such event was to be held in Toronto. He had complained, too, about the accuracy of the guest list for the *Last Spike* launch. "I think this is sloppy work, Jack," he said. This kind of attitude, with its assumption of superiority and privilege, continued throughout 1972.[17]

In fact, it had been Elsa Franklin who had drawn up the initial *Last Spike* guest list, although Catherine Wilson at M&S was responsible for finalizing it and sending out the invitations. "Elsa will get the same snarly reaction from me that you usually get," McClelland wrote to Wilson. "I get more and more crotchety I guess, but when the names of the guests are improperly spelled, it absolutely drives me up the wall and I wonder if any part of it is right and will be handled properly. But to hell with it."[18] In Berton's eyes, however, Franklin could do no wrong, so the blame fell on the handiest victim – Wilson. A year later, little had changed, except perhaps for Berton's inclination to let his arrogance masquerade as a form of personal and national virtue.

When Catherine Wilson organized a party in the countryside on the weekend of September 16–17 in honour of John Newlove, winner of the 1972 Governor General's Award for Poetry and an M&S editor, without checking whether a competing event was planned for the same day, a clash long in the making began to play itself out. Franklin had arranged a gathering at the Berton home in Kleinburg for more than 180 members of the Toronto media glitterati, along with executives from the CPR and all the city's booksellers, to celebrate jointly the release of *The Great Railway: Illustrated* and the expanded version of *Klondike*. Invitations for both events went out at the same time from Catherine Wilson's office, and many of the same people were on both guest lists. Perhaps the mix-up occurred because in an August 1 budget estimate for the promotion of *Klondike* and *The Great Railway* Franklin had specified September 23 as the day for the celebration of the Berton books; in another such report, which did not give a date, she had indicated that the Kleinburg event would be "not too large" and "quite separate from the launching for *The Great Railway*." For reasons unknown, the party was moved ahead by a week.[19]

Berton, likely animated by Franklin's fury at the scheduling conflict, was beyond mere annoyance. Jack McClelland received the brunt of his anger at what he viewed as one more example of Catherine Wilson's carelessness. The author appears to have stopped short of calling directly for Wilson's dismissal, but clearly he thought that at the very least a severe reprimand was in order.[20]

McClelland's response was to overreact. Berton, after all, had accounted for 20 per cent of McClelland & Stewart's net profits in 1971, and the publisher continued to maintain – sometimes to the chagrin of his staff – that M&S's authors were far more important than its employees. At McClelland's insistence, Peter Taylor, director of advertising, promotion and publicity, fired Catherine Wilson at a breakfast meeting on Monday, September 18, asking her to leave immediately. Larry Ritchie, vice-president, general manager, and a shareholder in M&S, arranged to have her company car confiscated.[21]

Hearing of this, and of Berton's complaint, Farley Mowat, who for some time had believed that Berton had such a hold over McClelland and his firm that the interests of other authors suffered, fired off a letter to key members of the Toronto literary community. He assumed and therefore claimed that Berton had insisted on Wilson's dismissal. The CBC's Robert Weaver, one of those to whom Mowat sent his letter, wrote to McClelland: "We have known one another for a long time, and I kind of like your crazy firm, and how in the world could you have fired Cathy?" Book review editors and critics such as Robert Fulford, William French, and Kildare Dobbs, he said, would have named Wilson "without hesitation" as "the best book promotion person in the city."[22]

Any such intervention was too late: the damage had been done. Wilson, a divorced mother supporting three children, consulted a lawyer the day after her dismissal. In a state of shock, she was completely taken aback at McClelland's action. Only two days earlier, on Sunday, she and Jack had been in Montreal at an event celebrating the publication of Mordecai Richler's *Shovelling Trouble*, and he had made no mention of any difficulties with Berton. The phone call McClelland made to Wilson on Tuesday night, insisting that Berton had him by "the short and curlies," scarcely improved her state of mind or the situation. "You didn't have the decency to speak with me yourself," she wrote the next day. "I was deeply hurt that you place so little importance on my feelings – one of my problems in accepting it was that I still believed in you and what you stood for."[23]

"Jack McClelland's habit," Berton wrote late in life, "was to dictate his letters long after midnight, with a bottle of vodka at his elbow." McClelland, likely well fortified, justified the actions he had taken with respect to Catherine Wilson in a late-night letter he dictated but did not send to her. Even so, he later made certain that Wilson's salary was paid for the next six months and the company car returned to her for the same period. Subsequent legal advice indicated that these actions had been the appropriate ones to take. Toward the end of the month, he went about trying to dampen the discontent of another offended party. "Just a note to say I think the Kleinburg event was really great," he told Elsa Franklin. "In execution and in attention to detail, it was superb."[24]

That the matter had gotten so out of hand certainly troubled Berton, but he was far more annoyed by the way Farley Mowat had exacerbated the affair by rallying other writers against him. In a letter dated October 10, he demanded a written apology. "I point out to you that you have, in the most intemperate fashion, been phoning various McClelland & Stewart authors, some of them friends of mine, making charges against me which are not only untrue but which I've had no opportunity to answer." He chastised his old friend for not having spoken to him directly, instead choosing to telephone Janet, "again in the most intemperate fashion," causing her a sleepless night. "It is bad enough when my enemies slander me behind my back but I do not expect this of my friends. And the last person I would have expected it of would be you, since I've always thought that you were fair minded, and given to listening to both sides of any controversy. . . . The next time you want to take issue with me, I suggest you do it to my face."[25]

A couple of days later, Mowat replied. He admitted having spoken with friends who were authors, but they also happened to be authors "deeply concerned over the effects of Mrs. Wilson's firing on McClelland and Stewart, its president, and on a number of other people including both you and me. I assure you that, despite what you may have heard over the grapevine, the majority of the authors involved share common sentiments about this matter. It pains me to add that these sentiments are also widely shared by many people who are not directly associated with McClelland and Stewart." Mowat denied making any "derogatory charges" and refused to apologize, but offered to meet Berton to discuss the matter. "I value your friendship and in times past have, on many occasions, risen to your defence when you were being subjected to attack by your 'enemies' and detractors. However I also value the friendship which exists between myself and several other people involved in this affair and there is no way I will not defend <u>any</u> friend who has been unjustly treated. I really hope we can resolve this affair amicably and I am prepared to do anything within reason to achieve this."[26]

What Mowat said to McClelland the next month sang a different tune. "Someone has done a hell of a lot of lying about the whole mess," he wrote, "and I'm damned if I'll take the buck. . . . Well, chum, I won't initiate anything more (unilaterally), but neither will I grovel to Pierre. You might call it the Last Straw. As far as I'm concerned, any friendship I had with him is at an end. It now remains for him to decide whether we part on a basis of neutrality, or wage war."[27]

McClelland sought some way to reconcile his two prize authors. With Berton's letter to Mowat in hand, he wrote to Pierre, applauding him for phrasing it so moderately. "I now find myself in the cross-fire between two old and valued friends. Unless all three of us are extremely careful there will be three losers." He accepted much of the blame, but noted that the actions he had taken had been called for – by implication including Wilson's dismissal – and expressed his regret that it had resulted in Mowat's "emotional outburst." He added: "Partly because of that, and partly because I am now satisfied that Farley has been almost systematically poisoned by the myth of Berton domination over McClelland [that] clouds the whole issue to a very considerable degree." He concluded with the hope that the "mutual friendship" between the three men would not be destroyed because of the way he had handled the Wilson affair.[28]

To some extent, at least, Mowat's belief that M&S was under Berton's thumb was justified. Jack McClelland lived in fear that his most important author, essential to the financial stability of the firm, would bolt, and as a member of the M&S board of directors Mowat had ample opportunity to observe the tag team of Berton and Franklin at work. But Jack McClelland had done much to feed any jealousy. As early as the 1950s, he had found ways to fuel the competition between the two authors, at one time prompting Mowat to say to him, "You're such a depressing son of a bitch. There are times when I darkly suspect that you are too interested in making money."[29]

Berton and Mowat reined in their egos sufficiently that the next year they agreed to appear together at a proposed gala celebrating the release by each of his twenty-first book, an event which Governor General Roland Michener and Prime Minister Pierre Trudeau were expected to attend. The event never took place because of delays in confirmation that these luminaries would appear, but the two writers continued to see each other, amicably if with restraint, at gatherings of what those in the media community dubbed "the *Maclean's* gang," a group of writers and spouses among whom were numbered the Fraynes, Scott Young, Max and Aileen Braithwaite, Fred Davis, Arthur and Sheila Hailey, John C. Parkin, and Harold Town.[30] Favourite venues were the Hailey, Davis, and McClelland cottages.

Measured against Berton's usual productivity, the year 1973 was a fallow one. After the surfeit of railway books in 1972, only *Drifting Home* was due to appear, scheduled for fall release. *The Pierre Berton Show* was in its eleventh season, and Berton let it be known that this would be its last. He did not want to fall into a rut, he said; besides, he wanted the show to end on a high note, carried by twenty-two stations – the most ever. "I'm just going to lighten the work load," he told the *Globe and Mail*.[31] A skeptic might say that such a statement comes accompanied by an offer in the back pocket, and this was so for Berton and Franklin, since plans were already well advanced to produce two new shows for Global. Even so, the blitzkrieg pace of Berton's professional life was easing.

In its final year, Pierre and Elsa varied the approach of *The Pierre Berton Show*. It went abroad, as usual, to London and to Lebanon, and had its usual share of American celebrities – for example, Richard Bach, author of the runaway bestseller *Jonathan Livingston Seagull*, and the star of *A Clockwork Orange*, Malcolm McDowell. It also had its quota of notoriety, as when Berton exposed the censorship of his Lebanese shows by playing audio tapes of the pre-censored versions, which he had smuggled out of the country. But on five different occasions over the 1972–73 season he devoted a full week to a single topic: problems faced by the Canadian north (week of November 13); nostalgia (December 4); the Arab point of view (January 15); famous people's dreams (March 5); and famous childhoods (April 16). Interspersed between them was the normal range of guests, including the former

Teamster president and jailbird Jimmy Hoffa in October, the alleged
Soviet spy Alger Hiss in January, and the actor Trevor Howard in April.
The season itself had opened with the Super 8 home movies Penny took
on the *Drifting Home* holiday.[32]

The range of high-calibre talent appearing on the show's series on
human emotions alone spoke to the degree of international renown and
respect the program had acquired: Diana Dors, Rex Reed, Glenda
Jackson, David Niven, Patty Duke, Cornel Wilde, Lily Tomlin, and
Vivian Vance, veteran of the *I Love Lucy* show. All were drawn to the
program, like so many others before them, by Berton's promise of a rare
half-hour interview, unedited, by a journalist with a reputation for
being genuinely interested in his guests.

At the end of the final season, the Toronto dailies paid homage to the
accomplishment. In the *Globe and Mail*, Blaik Kirby praised the show's
"eleven years of increasing skill and success," and congratulated it for
being the first to range the world in search of guests. Bob Blackburn
wrote in the *Toronto Sun* that Berton had "brought a lot of class to talk-
show TV that will stand as a text-book example. No Cavett he, nor even
Carson. Indeed, the man is almost humorless. But he exhibited, to the
gratification of his fans, more enduring virtues, such as that of obviously caring, of being concerned with his subjects." Jack Miller, in the
Toronto Star, drew a breath of relief, reassuring the newspaper's readers
that plans afoot at Global meant that the demise of *The Pierre Berton
Show* would not mark the end of Berton's presence on television.[33]

Insecurity is the flip side of arrogance, and despite Berton's braggadocio, his massive public exposure, and his success as an author, something inside tugged at his sense of self-worth. He claimed that he did
not give a damn about what people thought of him, but he was by no
means as thick-skinned as he pretended. Since his days as a columnist
at the *Toronto Star*, he had subscribed to a clipping service, and he read
and preserved the clippings assiduously. He told people that he was
indifferent to the academics' criticism of his books, but attacks from
this quarter invariably drew his attention and sometimes his ire. He was
sensitive about his reputation as a historian, and when the Canadian

Historical Association invited him to its 1973 meetings to be part of a special session designed to assess *The National Dream* and *The Last Spike*, he agreed with alacrity.

By the time the conference took place at the Learned Societies' meetings at Queen's University in Kingston during the early summer of 1973, Canadian scholarly journals had reviewed both volumes. In later years, he would often tell reporters that "the academics" hated his books, and he had great fun chiding them for their patronizing poses and their disdain for the role of the historian as storyteller. Yet taken as a whole, the reviews of *The National Dream* and *The Last Spike* reflect as much admiration as criticism. George Stanley, who probably still disliked Berton's strutting persona, nevertheless now called *The National Dream* "exciting stuff . . . Berton at his most endurable and enduring," and suggested that it deserved to be read by layman and academic alike. Paul Rutherford noted Berton's flair for the dramatic, but said, "Nonetheless the book is a superb piece of work." He wrote that Berton's description of construction life impressed, in part, because he was "so concerned with chronicling the fears, hopes, and habits of Canadians." Dalhousie University's P.B. Waite had helped Berton improve his books when still in manuscript; still, he chided the author in published reviews of the railway volumes for minor errors of fact. Overall, however, Waite pointed to Berton's impressive achievement, drawing attention to "the fresh air" of *The National Dream*, "its sense of space; the reader is never allowed to escape from the clutches of the country. Its geography, its sense of being, are with him all the time. This is marvelous." *The Last Spike*, he declared, was "a first-class piece of work by any standard. He has done justice to it."[34]

Unlike Rutherford, a younger historian with an interest in the history of popular culture, Stanley and Waite were historians firmly rooted in the Creightonian tradition of grand narrative. A pioneer in western Canadian history, Stanley nevertheless brought to his work a framework drawn from the imperial history he had read at Oxford; Waite, a political historian who was a born storyteller and a master of the telling phrase, had been a student of Donald Creighton, and his work arose out of the Laurentian interpretation of Canada's past. Stanley and Waite were sensitive to the importance of region, but treated region within a larger national and imperial context.

This approach to Canadian history was under assault when Pierre Berton took part in the panel that discussed his books. For the baby boom generation of historians who had found positions in history departments in the late 1960s and early 1970s, transforming the profession in the process, Creighton's interpretation of Canadian history was looked upon with disdain, as too central Canadian, too dismissive of regional interests and needs. Indeed, his 1969 swan song at the CHA conference, an address called "The Decline and Fall of the Empire of the St. Lawrence," had been greeted with derision and outright hostility – and not only because of Creighton's churlishness and sarcasm and his angry denunciation of Quebec and Quebecers.[35] For many in attendance, the occasion marked Donald Grant Creighton's self-inflicted fall from grace.

Symbolic of the reorientation of the profession's approach to Canada's past were major changes in the demographic profile of the CHA, which now had much stronger regional, working-class, feminist, and "ethnic" representation. The president of the CHA in 1973 was the University of Alberta historian Lewis G. Thomas, a western Canadian specialist. Conference presentations on traditional political topics gave way that year to issues of social and regional history. Especially notable as part of this new wave were papers by Gerald Friesen on the western Canadian identity and by Gregory Kealey on shoemakers' responses to industrialization. Both scholars would eventually serve as the association's president.[36]

At the Berton plenary session, and with Berton present, two historians made formal commentaries: T.D. Regehr of the University of Saskatchewan, an expert on Canadian railways, and Albert Faucher, a Université Laval economist and historian who had once studied under Harold Innis. In Berton's treatment of Canadian history, Quebec was scarcely present, so Faucher concentrated on problems confronting the farmers of Quebec when faced with competition from western farm products. The national railway may have been a dream for the Montreal business community, but for the province's small-business owners, rural and urban, it was more like a nightmare. From the floor, Alfred Dubuc, a historian from the Université de Québec à Montreal, dismissed the entire CPR initiative on the grounds that the railway should have been constructed entirely with state money.[37]

Regehr had reviewed both Berton railway volumes for *Saskatchewan History*, and had criticized them for the romantic approach that turned Macdonald into "an economic nationalist before his time." His reviews, nevertheless, had been judicious and balanced, noting Berton's extensive research. Of *The National Dream*, in his view the weaker of the two volumes, he had concluded: "It is more accurate than the romantic versions of the past, and more interesting than some earlier academic works." Of *The Last Spike*, he had written: "Berton has an admirable knowledge both of the plot and the principal characters and writes in a very lively and exciting style." His remarks at the session began with an admission that as someone who grew up near the Crowsnest Pass, he was not hostile to Berton's history of the railway. His more substantive comments focused on the perspectives of western prairie grain farmers, who had become very critical of the CPR for its high freight rates and its failure to build the branch lines they needed; he also faulted Berton for his use of questionable sources in his account of Major Albert Rogers, after whom Rogers Pass was named.[38]

The audience of five hundred that packed the large and dimly lit lecture theatre reacted in different ways. Those swept up by the lure of social history had arrived already convinced that Berton's kind of history was merely warmed-over Creighton; for them, his books held scant analytical content and broke little interpretive ground. Everyone brought their own expectations to bear on the session, and they observed what those expectations had already framed. Allan McCullough, who worked for the National Historic Parks Branch, arrived expecting the session to be lively, "as the pros tried to show up the amateur," but found it "low key, almost anti-climactic, with Berton easily holding his own." Jim Miller, a few weeks short of having tenure as an assistant professor in the University of Saskatchewan's history department, didn't think the panellists were particularly rough on their guest. "When asked a picayune question by one of the panelists," the young University of Guelph historian Terry Crowley later recalled, "I remember [Berton] coming back with: 'There are five sources pertaining to . . .,' and then ably going through a thorough analysis of each primary source."[39]

When time came for questions and answers, members of the audience pulled apart Berton's footnotes and at times questioned the integrity of his research. The journalist Douglas Fisher was there that night.

"Berton handled himself with authority and ease," he reported. Fisher also noticed "an uneasy squirm and a group gasp" when Berton said that he had written the first draft of volume one in three weeks, while that of the second took three and a half. "It was a fascinating override by an outsider before a very critical group, well-salted with men with derisory or contemptuous views of such 'pop project' production."[40]

At least some in the audience noted that this session was decidedly unlike most others. Discussions at the CHA were almost always polite affairs, with comments and criticism intended to be helpful. This session was not. One Queen's doctoral student, Terry Cook, who had come expecting Berton to be lionized for having demonstrated to so many that Canadian history was not dull, was taken aback. "The tone of some questioners was definitely to show up this popularizer, to take him down a peg or three . . . betraying as it did a less attractive, whining, jealous side to the academic historic profession."[41]

The two historians who had been Berton's harshest critics in print were in the audience that night. Both had studied under Donald Creighton. H.V. Nelles of York University, the scholar who had torn apart the assumptions behind *The National Dream* in the *Canadian Forum* in 1970, also attacked *The Last Spike* for its "unqualified acceptance of the company point of view" and for its "wildly out of size, two-dimensional figures" in 1972. Donald Swainson, a Queen's University historian of western Canada, had taken the outsider to task for his central Canadian bias and for making the CPR into a national symbol. Neither historian spoke up.[42]

Terry Cook left the session sensing "a grudging admiration" for Berton, "as if Daniel had been tossed into the lion's den" and "after the roaring, emerged not only unscathed, but with the respect of even ever-cynical grad students." Yet he also felt disillusioned with the academic practice of history and embarrassment at this scholarly performance. It occurred to Douglas Fisher that no one had taken up the fundamental issues raised by Berton's popular books. "If our past and our historiography," he wrote, "is to have more and more worth as a heritage, where is the duty of the historian to write and publish for a mass audience? Is this to be left to the journalist popularizer? If not, what canons do the historians use in entering the act of revaluing and popularizing our past?"[43]

Fisher expressed himself poorly, but the point he tried to make was an important one. In their concern for thorough and up-to-date research and their infatuation with the most advanced – that is, the most recent – theoretical approaches applicable to their subjects, historians had stopped writing in a manner accessible or of interest to the general public. They had forgotten the most fundamental duty a writer has: the duty to engage the reader. Instead, they had come to write for themselves, their colleagues, and their tenure and promotion committees. On what grounds, then, could they criticize writers who published "popular history" and whose books sold, like Berton's, in the tens of thousands? If history was indeed essential to national well-being, as professional historians so often said, by what standards could they justify their own rejection of narrative history?

Such questions should indeed have been engaged, then and there, but the moment passed, and the profession narrowed, and historical practice fragmented into ever-narrowing gyres of specialized interest and an ever-diminishing readership. Many of the Young Turks present that night had rejected the old-fashioned idea of historical progress, but they believed with the righteousness of the converted that theirs was a new and superior kind of Canadian history. Little doubt most left the auditorium imbued with a sense of triumph; but this minor event in the history of Canadian culture may in retrospect be seen as the tipping point of a tragic capitulation – the willing surrender of their public audience in the interest of professional advancement.

Berton returned to Toronto with no good reason to think better of professional historians than he had before and disappointed that there hadn't been more questions.[44] The professors went back to their offices and for the most part paid little attention to either of Berton's books on the transcontinental railway or to others he produced, except perhaps for *Klondike*. One view of Berton as a historian that did endure was the notion that he was able to accomplish what he did because a team of researchers did much of his work, a myth fed by journalist and academic alike. Arnold Edinborough wrote of his "research team," and George Stanley of "Berton and his boys," and H.V. Nelles of his "research assistants," comments meant as tacit criticism, since the image of the historian as humanist, alone in his study with the sources, remained strong in English-Canadian letters.[45]

The facts were that at few if any points in his work as a historian did Berton employ more than one research assistant at a time, and whatever other help he received came from office staff when they sorted or organized material already collected. No more than his academic counterparts did he wish to stand in front of a photocopy machine or sit at a microfilm reader if assistance was available, and, unlike the professors so scornful of his ways, he paid for such services from his own pocket.

If the Kingston experience was not in some ways dispiriting enough, it was also the case that his work on immigration to western Canada was not going well. Unlike the history of the gold rush or the railway, that of the prairies yielded too few figures of mythic dimension and legendary significance. When Glenn Wright's material arrived, Berton had found the story it told too fragmented, lacking the single-minded pursuit of riches or the missionary zeal that led to the driving of the Last Spike. Instead, dispersed throughout the documents was a tale, epic enough, of unknown immigrants settling into the less-than-exotic landscape of the empty plains.

This project, he recognized, would take far longer than expected, and gradually his attention turned to other interests.[46] When Farley Mowat convinced a number of writers to appear at the proceedings of the Ontario Royal Commission on Publishing after the commissioners failed to invite a single writer or writers' association, he had Berton's full support. This group – which included June Callwood, Fred Bodsworth, Margaret Atwood, Graeme Gibson, and Ian Adams – became key figures in the founding of the Writers' Union of Canada in 1973. Berton became an active charter member, arguing that the group should expand its initial conditions for membership (restricted to published writers) in order to be more inclusive and increase its influence. In 1976, with Atwood, Gibson, and Callwood, he helped found the Writers' Development Trust of Canada (later renamed the Writers' Trust of Canada). He was among the authors who picketed the Coles bookstore chain at one of its Ottawa outlets for dumping U.S. editions of Canadian-authored books onto the market at rock-bottom prices; later, he refused to autograph at W.H. Smith bookstores for the same reason. Over the years, he continued to be active in helping protect and advance writers' welfare and interests.

The family trip down the Yukon to Dawson had heightened his awareness of the fragile ecology of the North and the threat posed to it by modern industry, so he joined the Heritage Canada Foundation, founded in 1973. He became heavily involved in the organization, helping it to acquire historic properties in Dawson City and St. John's, Newfoundland. Later he criticized the Trudeau government for allowing the prime minister's staff to use Sir John A. Macdonald's old office, and he chided Vancouverites for not forming the formal organization required by Heritage Canada before it could become involved with the city on heritage issues. Meanwhile, he broached the idea of another Berton anthology to M&S, a selection of his best occasional writing. The unanimous verdict of M&S sales representatives across the country was to reject the idea, and to urge him to wait at least a year. The clear message they conveyed to Jack McClelland was that his author was overexposed.[47]

The filming of *The National Dream* also consumed his time. Developed initially by Lister Sinclair with Berton's assistance, led by executive producer Jim Murray and director Eric Till, and spearheaded by Knowlton Nash, the CBC's director of TV information programs, it was broadcast by the CBC on eight consecutive Sundays, beginning on March 3, 1974. The series found an audience of three million viewers, a record for CBC drama. William Hutt, in the role of John A. Macdonald, was outstanding.[48]

Berton's two new shows for Global Television, *My Country* and *The Great Debate*, also debuted in 1974. Berton and Franklin worked at first from an office in the Lord Simcoe Hotel, then at the beginning of September 1975 moved operations to a house they purchased jointly at 21 Sackville Street in Toronto's Cabbagetown. For *My Country*, using the occasional prop, Berton related tales, unscripted, about unusual or little-known aspects of Canadian history, frequently focusing on a colourful individual: the champion sculler Ned Hanlon, the explorer Samuel Hearne, the First World War flying ace Billy Bishop, the assassinated politician D'Arcy McGee, the vanished Toronto millionaire Ambrose Small. Other episodes dealt with specific topics or events, such as the Cypress Hills Massacre, a sealing disaster, the mystery of the Franklin expedition, and the elusive Canadian identity. Ratings were meagre, since Global chose to launch the show in mid-season, but fifty-two episodes aired before the show stopped production in 1976.[49]

The Great Debate, which Berton moderated, was Franklin's idea. In it, two national or international public figures debated a major issue of the day in front of a live audience in a Yorkville studio. Guests included such luminaries as William F. Buckley, Ralph Nader, and Edward Teller, but for Berton the best debaters of all were the team from the Oxford Union. The show continued for an eight-year run, ending in 1981.[50]

When Berton turned back to history, it was to a subject that had long fascinated him: Hollywood's portrayal of Canada. He remembered well his experience at the Ziv Television studios in Hollywood back in early 1960, trying to convince the production man of the need to portray Canada in an accurate manner. His memories remained clear, too, of the Americanization of other cultures he had witnessed during working vacations in Germany, Italy, Japan, and elsewhere. The only way to combat this slant was through education, and how better to educate Canadians about the manipulation of their own sense of themselves than with a book about the distorted way Hollywood depicted their country?

He needed someone who could assist with the research, so approached an old friend from his days as articles editor at *Maclean's*. Janice Tyrwhitt had joined the magazine just after graduation from Trinity College in 1950, and he had become something of a mentor to her. By the mid-fifties she was a staff writer, and at times she partied with the rest of the *Maclean's* gang. For two years she had worked as a researcher at *The Pierre Berton Show* – the most strenuous job she ever had, she said. In 1974, she joined Berton and Franklin again, as assistant producer of *My Country*, the first of their programs for Global television. Her duties involved hiring stringers to do the research, but she prepared material for some programs herself. When Berton contacted Tyrwhitt to ask whether she would be the researcher for his book on Hollywood's depiction of Canada, she felt too exhausted from television work to accept. He asked her to suggest another candidate, so she called a young woman who could fill her shoes.[51]

Barbara Sears was a recent emigrant from England with a degree in political science from the University of Essex. She also possessed some background in film and at the time was working for the National Film Board.[52] Berton met with Sears and quickly discovered that she was intelligent and diligent, with a fine sense of the theatrical, precisely the kind of personality he had been looking for since Norman Kelly had worked for him. In June 1974, he wrote enthusiastically to Jack McClelland, requesting that his new researcher be paid a third of the royalties he was to receive. This reduced his share of the royalties from 15 per cent to 10. He also sent Janice Tyrwhitt a case of Scotch.[53]

The approach Barbara Sears took to documentary evidence was a visual one, and she had the knack of seeing in historical documents the movielike scenes they could project. She did the research for *Hollywood's Canada* and did it superbly, this time by examining old films for the way they distorted the documented historical record. After Berton finished his first and second drafts of the book, Janet Berton read the manuscript to root out awkwardness and infelicities and Janet Craig, who freelanced for McClelland & Stewart, did the copy-editing. Elsa Franklin handled contract negotiations and coordinated production, publicity, and promotion. A few years later, Janice Tyrwhitt became Berton's primary editor. Sears, Franklin, and Berton's "three Jans" – Janice Tyrwhitt, Janet Craig, and Janet Berton – this was the true Berton "team."

In the first stages, he and Sears would brainstorm, sometimes even in search of a topic to write about. Often she knew little about the subject, but Berton liked the fresh eyes she brought to the process. This early phase of a project was always fluid and seldom if ever involved a pre-established agenda for research or a set interpretive framework. "Projects grew and shifted shape according to what we found," Sears recounted. "I don't think that any of the books I worked on had a defined program which we established as viable and then set out to execute. . . . Flexibility – in both ideas and execution – was key."[54]

Once the viability of the project was settled, Sears would assiduously comb libraries and archives, collecting material. Sometimes this included interviews, depending on the book. They would discuss the available sources, and after Barbara did a preliminary reconnaissance they reviewed the results. If necessary, she pursued further leads and resources. Berton's secretary organized Sears's findings as they came in, grouping documents and notes in binders. Berton then read through the material, indexing as he went along, until he had full command. Only when this was done would he would hammer out a first draft, invariably relying too heavily on the index cards and as a result larding his manuscript with too much research. Several times, Sears saw him throw away an entire first draft and begin again.[55]

Working smoothly and efficiently, Tyrwhitt took each draft apart and showed him better ways to deploy the material. She read the copy twice, first for a general picture. On her second pass she made detailed notes on each page, cutting out clichés and substituting well-chosen words for Berton's less precise ones. She pinpointed what was dull or dead, and identified what was missing. For each chapter she prepared a memo outlining what worked and what didn't. Berton's role in this process was to heed her advice and, to his credit, invariably he did. Then Janet Craig went to work word by word, catching authorial errors and infelicities, at times making more substantive suggestions, refining the prose until she decided the manuscript was satisfactory.[56] This degree of highly skilled support by people dedicated to his work was a major reason why Berton was able to be such a productive historian in the years that followed. For that, he recognized, is what he had become – a historian – and he relished the role.

Thanks to the special skills of Barbara Sears, Berton made excellent progress on *Hollywood's Canada*. She tracked down every movie made by the American film industry that featured Canada, from the days of one-reel silent pictures to horse operas and musicals made in the 1950s. Then, together, she and Berton watched all 575 of them. Their print sources stretched from Ottawa to Hollywood and London. Before they were done they had discovered relevant files even in the records of the Department of Trade and Commerce and of the RCMP. Berton had a revised draft ready for final typing by mid-March 1975, production began in May, and Franklin fuelled her promotion machine with a budget pegged at $20,000.

That April, Government House announced that Berton was to be among those honoured by induction as an Officer of the Order of Canada, along with the actor Kate Reid, former senator Thérèse

Casgrain, the opera singer Louis Quilico, the editor of *Chatelaine*, Doris Anderson, and others. "I long ago decided to accept any award offered me," he wrote in 1995, "as long as I wasn't required to make a speech." In 1973, the first offer of an honorary degree had come, from the University of Prince Edward Island. The next year, York University and the University of Toronto followed suit.[57]

Hollywood's Canada was released in the early fall, but not before a minor crisis erupted when the M&S publicist Patricia Bowles released error-ridden galleys to *Saturday Night* and the *Globe and Mail*. Berton was furious. He would rather have a later review, he told McClelland, than a review based on incorrect galleys. "I swear on a stack of bibles that I will never, never, never again have anything to do with his promotion," Bowles informed her boss. In return, McClelland pleaded: "Don't be critical of Pierre, and don't, please don't, tell me that you want no part of future promotion of his books. . . . Pierre is a senior author and a valuable one. He is also a Director of the company. He is extremely demanding, but not unprofessional or unreasonable."[58]

This was so. McClelland was well aware that M&S did not run smoothly or efficiently – in fact it was perpetually in a state of crisis and near chaos. In a 1973 *aide-mémoire* (for his eyes alone) enigmatically titled "Gemstone," dictated to Marge Hodgeman after a collapse in his health and intended as reflections on the firm, he wrote of questionable managerial competence at M&S, and of his employees' sense of insecurity and his own. Despite the financial bailout by the Ontario government in 1971, the company's finances continued to be precarious, and he admitted that responsibility for its financial and editorial troubles were at least in part the consequences of his own decisions. Throughout the remainder of that long decade, McClelland had not merely Berton's discontent to deal with, for at one point or another he and his editors ran afoul of Margaret Atwood, Adele Wiseman, Margaret Laurence, Peter C. Newman, and others who variously felt neglected, ill-treated, or poorly served.[59]

That fall, Berton spoke about *Hollywood's Canada* and about the Americanization of the Canadian image to anyone who would listen. In September he travelled west from Montreal on a media tour to Winnipeg, Edmonton, and Vancouver, where he gave a *Hollywood's Canada* lecture at the Vancouver Institute of the University of British

Columbia and an extended interview to John Haslett Cuff of the *Georgia Straight*. In October, he spoke at a Montreal advertising and sales executive club lunch and to the Toronto University Women's Club. In November, he travelled extensively again, this time autographing books.[60]

Hollywood's Canada showed how over the decades the film capital had depicted a Canada that its citizens would never have recognized: a Canada without prairies; a Canada of "happy-go-lucky French Canadians, wicked half-breeds, wild trappers and loggers, savage Indians and, above all, grim-jawed Mounties." (A wistful telegram from a commissioner of the RCMP had pleaded with one producer, saying: "Mounted Police would appreciate being left alone.") Hollywood's Canada was a wilderness; a country with apparently only one city, Montreal, but with forests that began at the American border and extended to the Arctic Circle.

The major revelation of the Sears-Berton research was the discovery that in the late 1940s the Canadian government came close to legislating a Canadian film industry into existence by forcing U.S. producers and film distributors to invest some of their box office profits in Canadian films, and that the opportunity was lost after a specious American promise was made to Canadian officials that more Canadian references would be incorporated into movies.

Berton's choice of American flicks as his subject was an indulgence of sorts by a movie buff of long standing, but his decision to write the book held more import than this. It reflected his continuing fidelity to the nationalist cause. The problem was not simply that the portrayal of Canada in American films was a distorted one; it was also that Canadians had come to accept the misrepresentation. As he said in an interview with an Alberta journalist, "Canadians have seen themselves through Hollywood's eyes. We know the movies are wrong, but we don't know what's right. We don't have what the Americans have, which is a larger than life mythology. . . . That's our major problem – our identity. I think the image of the country as a whole to the world . . . is totally distorted."[61]

Most major reviewers immediately picked up on the book's nationalist message and its alarm about "the tidal wave of a foreign mass culture," as James Eayrs put it in the *Montreal Gazette*. For Roy MacSkimming, the *Toronto Star*'s reviewer, "The shock effect of Berton's massively detailed book comes from seeing ourselves as another ethnic group, like the Mexicans or southern blacks, whose history has been stolen or misrepresented." Writing in the *Globe and Mail*, a skeptical Martin Knelman spoke to the significance of the book's timing: "Could it be that this book . . . is meeting the public's psychological needs at a particular moment? Perhaps it's part of our cultural nationalism to need a persecutor. Perhaps we need to believe that the Hollywood version was a malicious plot to deprive us of our heritage." Such a tendency "to tell off outsiders for not being respectful of Canadian individuality and independence," he concluded, "borders on national paranoia."[62]

In an otherwise indifferent review, the *Globe and Mail* book columnist William French, probably the most influential reviewer in the country, wondered what all the fuss was about. Wasn't the manipulation of images of the past and present precisely what art does? "Do we care what others think?" Surely, he wrote, such anxiety was simply a manifestation of the age-old "Canadian inferiority complex."[63] Other reviewers, such as the poet Alden Nowlan and the film studies specialist Peter Harcourt, thought otherwise. Nowlan praised Berton for his intentions. "More power to Pierre Berton," he proclaimed. Harcourt agreed with French that factual distortion was the cost of art's transformative power, but he was more than sympathetic to the author's objective: "What the CPR did for Canadian geography, Berton has tried to do for the Canadian imagination: to unite us as a nation by inviting us to share in his image of the national dream. This image entails our recognition of ourselves as an actual nation, as a multifarious group of people who, whatever our cultural background and the physical distances between us, are a self-determining entity."[64]

By the mid-1970s, however, the tide had begun to turn against cultural nationalists. Irreconcilable differences on the issue of French-Canadian nationalism divided its anglophone counterpart. The OPEC oil crisis of 1973 triggered a downturn of international industrial economies, including Canada's. The federal government's implementation of the Foreign Investment Review Agency a year later, coupled with its creation of a state-owned oil company (Petro-Canada) in 1975, provoked a stiff backlash by oil companies, industry, and the business community to such protectionism. What seemed to nationalists such as the Edmonton book publisher Mel Hurtig a winnable battle in 1971 now began to appear a long, protracted struggle at best. The membership of the Committee for an Independent Canada, 7,000 to 8,000 strong in 1971, had waned to fewer than 4,000 by 1973 and continued to drop.[65]

Hollywood's Canada appeared in this context of economic and cultural uncertainty, with Canadians worried about jobs as much as identity. At first the book seemed to do well. M&S had shipped 35,000 copies in its first season, and Berton's royalty statements for the period showed total sales of 23,929 copies. But by the end of 1976, once returns were factored into the calculation, net sales proved to be only 12,753. As Jack wrote to Pierre, "It is an absolute disaster."[66]

Another disappointment, from Berton's point of view, was his failure to convince McClelland, Anna Szigethy (now Porter), and the M&S editorial staff to publish two proposed anthologies of original essays from various contributors: "The Failure of Free Enterprise" and "Coping with Widowhood." The former arose out of Pierre Trudeau's statements about the shortcomings of the so-called free enterprise system, and the latter was to consist of testimonials from people who had experienced the loss of a spouse. McClelland approved of the ideas as book subjects, but only if tackled by a single author, not a collective. He advised Berton, however, not to undertake them personally.[67] The projects went nowhere.

Meanwhile, during a winter vacation in Jamaica, Berton recycled research done for *My Country* the television program into *My Country* the book. It comprised stories of the Franklin expedition, Blondin crossing Niagara Falls on a tightrope, Bill Johnson, the pirate of the St. Lawrence, and Brother XII, leader of a mystic cult on Vancouver Island. The book, he later admitted, was "a lazy writer's book . . . a quickie," churned out "because it was easy and the money was good." Tuition loomed for six of his children and so did bills for the latest expansion of the house, now grown to 6,500 square feet from its original 1,450.[68] But what would he undertake of a more substantial nature?

The seeds of the idea had been planted during the research for *Hollywood's Canada*. Seeing a Yukon steamboat sequence slipped into an American movie about the Dionne quintuplets had annoyed him, but it had also sparked renewed interest in the famous babies, born during the Depression. Theirs was the kind of extraordinary tale he had fought to find back in Vancouver as a newshound hot on the trail of sensation, a human interest story of almost Shakespearean proportions. Besides, this was a subject that would allow him for once to write about the history of his own times. Elsa Franklin and Janice Tyrwhitt came to believe that the Depression had marked him as much as the North, and he likely thought so himself.[69] Berton and Sears had researched the story of the Dionne quintuplets for the *My Country* show but decided to hold this remarkable Canadian tale in reserve for a later time.

In 1976, that time had come. While initially she knew little of the Dionne story, Sears recognized that research on this project would be less onerous and expensive than that involved in tracking down the scattered sources used in *Hollywood's Canada*. Much of the material was held by the Archives of Ontario, conveniently located in the heart of Toronto's downtown hospital district. Berton arranged for Sears to receive an advance of $4,000 on 2.5 per cent of the revenue from the book, and in her usual efficient and exhaustive way she plumbed the resources of the provincial archives, the Metropolitan Toronto Central Library, and the township offices of northeastern Ontario, along with the files of the *North Bay Nugget* and the Toronto daily press. As research threw up new leads, she and Berton interviewed more than fifty people. Ennis Armstrong, who had returned as Pierre's secretary, transcribed the tapes and annotated the notes.

Jack McClelland signed the contract for the Dionne project, but he and his staff were decidedly less than enthusiastic even after they saw the finished manuscript. On one hand, he found it to be the typical "superbly well-organized, well-crafted and well-written Berton production," but he was not convinced that the subject matter merited book-length treatment. "To put it differently," he wrote the author in March 1977, "it contains more information about the Dionne years and the Dionnes than I personally care about." Linda McKnight, one of his senior editors, initially came to the manuscript with a similar view, but the manuscript had engaged and held her interest. She had heard about the Dionnes all her life, she told Jack, yet here was much that was new. "And it is a fascinating story, revealing what fools mortals be," she reported to Anna Porter.[70]

No one at M&S was at all certain of the book's audience. Would it appeal to young or old readers? Did Canadians of the 1970s care about the Dionne story? Would the book find a foreign publisher? Even Elsa and Pierre thought the book would need some special big "hook" to sell it. Once again McClelland gave Franklin a publicity budget of $20,000.[71]

For his part, Berton did little but gripe throughout the whole *Dionne Years* production process, not only about error-riddled computer typesetting but about M&S in general. "I am in a state of rage over the shoddy treatment that all my books have been receiving," he wrote, after delays with reprints and his discovery that the printer, T.H. Best, had supplied a thinner paper stock for reprints of *Klondike*, *The National Dream*, and *The Last Spike*, making slimmer volumes that did not properly fit their preprinted dust jackets. An exasperated McClelland acknowledged the problems detailed in Berton's letter, but added: "I filed it but only after carefully affixing my 'Bullshit' stamp for the benefit of some student in the future." The rubber stamp was one that McClelland had ordered especially for occasions such as this, likely with Pierre Berton in mind, among others. Unmollified, the author continued to complain about the lack of copies of *My Country* in stores and about having Diane Mew assigned to copy-edit the Dionne book instead of Janet Craig.[72] Dark mutterings like these from Berton quarters continued into 1978 and well beyond.

Worries about the market for the Dionne book proved groundless. The amazing story of the quintuplets sold itself, although the reviewer Jeff Greenfield, writing in the *New York Times Book Review*, exclaimed that it strained credulity.[73] Five baby girls born to a poor northeastern Ontario francophone family in 1934 had miraculously survived a backwoods birth. In a decade of misery and want, such heart-filling news was exactly the sort to make people feel better – a triumph over adverse circumstance at the most basic human level. The story made headlines around the world and the blessed babies became famous. Middle-class tourists by the thousands began to drive from southern Ontario and Quebec to see them, so many that with tourist dollars and a revival of the northeastern Ontario economy in mind, the provincial government of Mitchell Hepburn removed the girls judicially from the custody of their parents and set them up in a state-of-the-art facility with a medical staff armed with the latest child-rearing theories. The grounds also featured a zoo-like viewing area for the thousands of curious visitors. The quintuplets became wealthy from their share of entrance fees to their compound, but remained virtual prisoners – divorced from normal human interaction – until the age of nine. They yearned for their parents while in the facility, but lacking even elementary socialization they found life in the family home intolerable once they were allowed to return. The struggle between the provincial government and the children's parents was such that each child suffered incalculable psychological damage and their later lives were fraught with difficulties.

What strained credulity for Jeff Greenfield was instead "a thirties melodrama" for Pierre Berton, complete with stock heroes and cardboard villains, but with roles the opposite of those accorded them in the 1930s. Dr. A.R. Dafoe, admired earlier as the heroic and selfless country physician who delivered the babies, is seen in *The Dionne Years* to succumb gradually to the lure of financial inducement, making almost as much money as the quints – a "well-born misfit" turned into "a backwoods martinet," in the words of the *New York Review of Books*.[74] The children's father, Oliva Dionne, viewed in the thirties as a virile country bumpkin and callous parent willing to display his children like freaks in a carnival, is in Berton's hands a man desperate for the return of his children, pitting a family's resources against the power of the state.

The subtheme of government interference in private lives struck a resonant chord in a decade that welcomed Trudeau's admonition that the state had "no business in the bedrooms of the nation." But there was more to the matter than this. As Greenfield and others picked up, a central feature of *The Dionne Years* was its evocation of the culture of celebrity. For Greenfield, this offered a contemporary lesson. In the era of books by Watergate conspirators and tapes by the killer who called himself "Son of Sam," he wondered, how well had American society "coped with the power of the media machine to shape and ruin human beings by its sheer omnipresence." Margaret Atwood, writing in *Saturday Night*, commented along similar lines: "The book's real concern . . . [is] what causes the public, at any given time, to adopt this or that figure, this or that hero or heroine, as its symbol and totem?"

What accounts for fame? Atwood's question was one in which the most celebrated author in Canada, together with a public saturated with celebrity, happened to hold more than a passing interest. And the question seemed to be pointed at the Berton phenomenon as much as that of the quints. "'Pierre Berton,'" she wrote, "as the evidence makes clear, is really a set of identical quintuplets whose mother wisely concealed their birth to keep them from becoming unwitting public fetishes, as the Dionnes did. . . . This theory would explain Berton's (or Bertons') interest in the Dionnes."[75]

The historian Jack Granatstein, defender of academic standards and one of Berton's most dogged critics, had a less elevated theory. "How can we account for the extraordinary success that Pierre Berton has achieved as a chronicler of Canada's past?" he asked at the outset of a review of *The Dionne Years*. "How is it that this man, single-handedly propping up McClelland & Stewart, can produce a book for each fall season?" The answer, he said, did not lie in the writing, for while "clear and simple" it was "not brilliant or flashy." As a researcher, Berton was okay; he was "diligent" and had "an eye for the telling anecdote"; but these traits were part of the kit of every good writer. "The primary reason for his success," Granatstein revealed, "is that he is omnipresent in the media, that he is tough, shrewd, and combative, that he has the contacts and connections to get the maximum in publicity." With such advantages, and an aggressive publisher, the result was that "every non-reader in Canada has a shelf of Bertoniana right alongside the *Reader's Digest* condensed books."[76]

Despite the York University historian's churlish tone, Granatstein had a point. Berton fully exploited his celebrity to gain market share. Left unstated was the fact that Canadians bought his books not necessarily because they wanted to read what he wrote about, but because they wanted a part of him, like taking home pieces of the Holy Cross. Buying a Berton was not merely edifying, it brought comfort – for some, even solace. Granatstein had to concede that Berton possessed the knack of choosing topics that struck "a responsive chord in the Canadian consciousness." The CPR books, he noted, had appeared "at a time when the Centennial glow was fading and when Canadians needed a boost to their national ego." Their unabashed nationalism provided "a popularized and mythologized history to a people who want and need it and who have failed to receive it from their academic historians. Berton fills a national need."

Certainly, no historian in the country worked more diligently to become the new Pierre Berton than Jack Granatstein, and in the late 1970s the Berton publishing record was one that any author would envy. Little doubt Granatstein hoped that his own recent books, on conscription and on Canadian-American economic relations, would address the kind of need Berton's books met.[77] *My Country*, which McClelland had thought would do well only "in the long term," made the bestseller lists, and between its fall 1977 release and Christmas, sales figures reached 13,860 copies. When a follow-up, *The Wild Frontier*, was released a year later, it sold 38,100 copies. *The Dionne Years* found a steady readership over time and sold almost 100,000 copies in Canada and the United States, in hardcover and two paperback editions.[78]

Reviewers treated *My Country* and *The Wild Frontier* as what each was: a "Pierre Berton Christmas pot-boiler" from "the recycling king of Canadian writing." Neither book satisfied academic critics, one of whom found *My Country* so lacking in depth and analytical coherence and content as to portray the Canadian as "a frostier version of the American cowboy." Another questioned Berton's view that British paternalism shaped the frontier in Canada and his conception of that frontier, while conceding that "the 'academic' historian who would sell his wares to a wider audience has much to learn from the master." In general, reviewers could not deny that the Canadian history Berton wrote was far more interesting and accessible than that of his academic competitors. "*My Country* is not only mining the Canadian past," wrote one, "it's also Berton engaged once again in his personal attempt to popularize Canadian history. And because of that, the writing tends to preach – because it *is* his country. What else would you expect from the man who built the CPR?"[79]

As the decade of the seventies waned, the association of Pierre Berton's name with everything symbolized by the driving of the Last Spike continued strong and resonant. For his remaining years, many Canadians thought of him first and foremost as the man who wrote *The National Dream*. When the country began to experience the chill of the era ushered in by Margaret Thatcher and Ronald Reagan, with its commitment to commerce over culture and to the international marketplace over national boundaries, Canadians clung to the Berton brand with the tenacity of a goalie to his hockey stick.

22

A WAKE OF WHISPERS

—

BENEATH THE PHOTOGRAPH OF THE author in the blazer, white shirt, and bow tie, the caption read: "The man they call Mr. Canada had been talking books all day – and it was only 10 o'clock." The accompanying article in the Victoria newspaper began: "The trouble with being a national institution is . . ." There was no need in 1979 to identify the figure, for so well was he known that people could no longer review his books without also reviewing the man himself. As Lynda Hurst of the *Toronto Star* had put it the previous year: "They read him (or say they do); listen to him, watch him on TV. He's been a proselytizing fact of our lives for almost three decades now. And consequently, as his friend Charles Templeton points out, Pierre Berton can't go anywhere any more without 'leaving a wake of whispers behind him.'" It had been Templeton who first gave him the weighty moniker. A 1979 article in *Maclean's* called "The Berton Years" had quoted him as saying, "The truth is, Pierre Berton is Mr. Canada." The quip stuck like pine tar.[1]

Secure in the comfort that at last he had found his métier – that of chronicler and popularizer of the nation's past – Berton plied his trade in the 1980s with the confidence and dexterity of the master craftsman he had become, and with the assistance of his editorial team he produced a series of works of Canadian history any one of which would have secured an academic historian's reputation. Collectively, these volumes expanded the nation-building theme he had made his own. Leaving new ways of interpreting the past to the scholars, he concentrated instead on telling Canada's story to Canadians. Academic historians often accused him of repeating what they already knew. But Berton recognized what they seemed to have forgotten: that to others less schooled, historical events so "well known" might arrive as revelation, and that, besides, each generation encounters the past anew – just as they do Shakespeare. Much of Canadian history, when known at all, resided somewhere between remembering and forgetting, fact and folklore. It had lessons to offer, and Berton intended to make those lessons known and redress the understandable amnesia of a forward-looking North American people. Pierre Berton's reputation as the chronicler of Canada's "communal national mythology" was firmly in place, and he was content that, for the rest of his life, he would not deviate from this role.[2]

In the decade of life when most men choose to retire, Berton enjoyed some of his most productive years. He had nothing to gain by mastering new media or impressing critics and reviewers, or worrying about the state of his finances, but he did need to nurture and sustain his sense of self. He had reached the height of his power and influence, but he seems to have sensed that he would never again produce a work of history with the deeply felt passion of *Klondike* or the cultural influence of *The National Dream* and *The Last Spike*. Canadians needed to learn much more about their past, and he intended to offer it to them as often as he could; but each new book became an embellishment to his established body of work, one more title to add to the lengthening list. The books would continue to sell, although his name, now part of the national lexicon, had to be kept in the public eye, and this required a steady pace of production. To do anything less would put his brand at risk and jeopardize the livelihood of those who worked for him. More important, it would also take away his greatest source of satisfaction and fulfillment, which was to write.

As the eighties approached, people and groups across the country contacted Pierre Berton more than ever, asking him to speak at teachers' conventions, university conferences, media events, trade fairs, and literary gatherings. Health and legal associations, executive groups, educational meetings, Rotarians and Freemasons, heritage and conservation associations, student banquets, and other bodies, large and small – everyone seemed to covet his presence. The demand was so great in the late 1970s and 1980s that he had no choice but to turn down scores of invitations each year, often at the cost of lucrative speaker's fees. Event organizers wanted him not only at the Hog Day and Pork Fest in Winnipeg and the Miss World Canada contest in Ottawa, but also at the Heritage Canada Awards at Rideau Hall and the cultural festival of the Canada Games. In 1978, when Toronto mayor David Crombie invited him to be on the board of the Juvenile Diabetes Research Foundation, he replied: "I made a New Year's resolution to get off boards this year. . . . I'm on so many now that they are taking all my time away from writing, which is what I really want to do."[3]

Canadians from all walks of life felt a genuine need to make contact with him, to forge a link, any link, as if such a bond, however forced or fleeting, might in some intangible way lend meaning to their own lives. For a few, Berton's presence was not confined to waking moments. "Although our paths have never crossed, I did meet you in my dreams," the musician Carl Tapscott wrote, following the success of *The National Dream* and *The Last Spike*. In one reverie, Tapscott heard his wife telling him that she would rather watch Berton than Johnny Carson. The writer Barry Broadfoot had a recurring dream. Berton rides on horseback onto a ranch the western writer has fixed up in the Okanagan Valley. The Toronto media star proceeds to interview a boy Broadfoot grew up with. Berton the historical detective finds the only interesting passage in a pioneer's diary and, like an avenging angel, uses a .22 rifle to ward off a large and fearsome owl-like apparition. In his letter, Broadfoot asked Berton whether he had ever had such a dream himself.[4] These nocturnal fantasies appear to have sprung from the dreamers' fears and insecurities, yet Tapscott and Broadfoot felt bound to share them with Berton anyway, as if by doing so they might cause some kind of talismanic charm to do its work.

Old friends and acquaintances alike found pretexts by which to re-establish a connection. Pierre's old history professor at UBC, Fred Soward, wrote to say that he was pleased he had recommended his former student to Arthur Irwin back in 1947, thirty-one years earlier. Browni Joerin, a colleague from the *News-Herald* and from school days in Victoria before that, renewed her acquaintance – for no apparent reason beyond the desire to make contact. The journalist Peter Brimelow wrote to congratulate Berton on his *Maclean's* piece on E.P. Taylor – twenty-eight years after Berton published it. The poet Al Purdy wrote in praise of his nationalist fervour, saying "Long may you wave. . . . I think you're a necessary guy to have around." The *Maclean's* writer Roy MacGregor told Berton that he spent two days "transfixed" over the Dionne book. "When it was over I had learned something beyond the story of five sisters. I knew then how the very best handle their material." E.P. Taylor's brother Fred wrote to say that while he had been "very uncooperative" when Berton had interviewed him many years earlier about E.P., he would be "very glad" to get together. "I follow your work with great interest and admiration."[5]

Letters such as these arrived day after day and continued to do so for years thereafter. Some curried favour, but far more often they reflected the simple need to connect. Laura Kinrade, the schoolteacher who had continued to correspond with Berton since he visited her grade one class in 1972, regarded him as her mentor. In one letter she informed him that at last one of her articles had been accepted for publication. "I love writing as much as teaching and so to have someone else enjoy it is like the icing on the cake." A few years later she wrote to say that she had made him an executor of her estate. In 1978 Berton sliced the top of his finger badly while demonstrating a Cuisinart on Peter Gzowski's ill-fated CBC late-night television talk show, *90 Minutes Live*. Bleeding profusely, he continued to banter as if nothing had happened. Paul Hoffman of the Plasti-Fab Company sent along its safety-enhancing "Accessory Centre" for storing Cuisinart discs and blades. "This unit," he assured Berton, "was designed to prevent people of your mechanical aptitude from cutting their fingers. . . . Unfortunately, we have so far been unable to design a safety device to stop those who *want* to put their fingers into the blades." When Berton appeared on the show a second time, not long after the accident, the Canadian distributor of Cuisinart wrote to the man with the bandaged finger to tell him how well he had handled his mishap. Stephen Lewis congratulated him on the ACTRA Award he had won for public affairs broadcasting. "It seems to me that about all that's left is the Nobel Prize," he stated, calling Berton "a role model for humankind." He added that he and his wife, Michele Landsberg, were "crazy" about their Cuisinart.[6]

Prominent figures approached Berton on a number of occasions over the years to run for political office, usually at the federal level. Following publication of *The Smug Minority* in 1968, the NDP had asked him to run in the Toronto riding of Rosedale. He declined. A decade later,

Jack McClelland wrote to his friend on behalf of "a distinguished group of Canadians." The group included Peter Newman, Margaret Atwood, Mel Hurtig, and other eminent figures who wanted him to stand in the next federal election as an independent nationalist. "What they are saying," McClelland wrote, "is that the country is in dire straits and needs people like you in the House of Commons." In the letter, McClelland declared himself to be a "post-nationalist," an indication less that his nationalist sentiment had waned than that the financial troubles of M&S and the declining influence of the Committee for an Independent Canada had worn him down. Still, he affirmed his full support of the signatories of the letter, all of whom believed "that you could do a great deal to ensure that Canada has a future by trying your hand at politics." With the prospect of a minority government looming in early 1978, the idea of the leadership of Joe Clark, who scarcely inspired Canadians, or even of Pierre Trudeau, with whom many had become disenchanted, appalled McClelland. "I believe there is no Party now in existence that can pull Canada together. . . . I can tell you quite honestly, Pierre, that I can think of no other Canadian who has the public image, acceptance and ability to pull the whole goddamn thing together. . . . I will work with you and Elsa in devising the most brilliant political campaign of all time."[7]

Berton made it known that he was flattered at the offer but had no intention of seeking office, for a life in politics would constrict his independence of mind. He was not cut out to be a politician, he said; besides, he wanted to concentrate on writing his books. A month later, Peter Newman wrote to him about the group's overture. "I did want to write you regarding our scheme to make you Prime Minister of Canada. I quite seriously believe this would have been a marvellous opportunity for the many of us who have become so disillusioned with Canadian politics to re-enter the game. At any rate, I respect your decision and send you my very warmest wishes." Thereafter, Berton continued to support the NDP and refused overtures from other parties. When an irate citizen took offence at receiving mail that used Berton's name to solicit financial support for the NDP, an equally annoyed Berton responded: "What arrogant nonsense! . . . If parties can use bag men, why can't an author like myself help out the party of his choice? Are you saying that nobody but politicians should get involved in politics? . . . I don't do commercial endorsements and wouldn't want to accept money for anything like that, but I do endorse things I believe in, and I believe in the NDP. I find it odd that you should think any of this is in 'bad taste.'" A year earlier, when the Progressive Conservative MP Sinclair Stevens had invited the Bertons to his party's "Confederation Dinner," Berton thanked him for the invitation, but added, "In spite of what you say this is really a fund-raising gimmick for the next election. I wish you luck; but I ain't contributing."[8]

Politics was just one of the distractions that threatened to take his attention away from writing, and in 1978 he could not afford the lure, for he and Barbara Sears had settled on the next project. Coming up with ideas for books was never his problem; choosing among them was. People often sent suggestions. Justice Donald A. Keith of the Supreme Court of Ontario suggested that he consider writing about the Canadian contribution to the Second World War, and his old friend Ray Gardner sent him a clipping concerning a Saskatchewan madam of the 1930s named Lizzie Spedding – "an old bawd," Gardner said, who made "the Happy Hooker [look as] pure as the driven snow." Jack McClelland was keen that Berton write on the Canadian experience at Dieppe, for he believed it held serious potential "to make the heritage come alive." But after the thematic limitations of *Hollywood's Canada* and the down-home family saga of *The Dionne Years*, Berton positively longed for a story with the magnitude and grandeur of *Klondike* and *The National Dream* – works "in which large numbers of people move through time and space."[9] Among Canada's wars, the War of 1812 was an event that met these criteria.

He knew little more about this war than schoolboy lore surrounding the battles of Lundy's Lane and Queenston Heights, and Barbara Sears knew even less. The subject seemed to be of epic proportions; the question was whether enough good material was available to sustain a book. He and Sears discussed such questions over lunch, and he asked her to assess the project's feasibility. The report Sears produced, based on an examination of secondary works, proved encouraging. No general Canadian overview of the war appeared to exist, and Canadian military writing on it was "very boring." Battles might be exciting to watch or talk about, she wrote, but "they don't make for very exciting reading."

This, she warned, might pose a special challenge. Sears mentioned the "'peripheral' feeling" she experienced as she read about the war. It was essentially a British colonial affair, so most accounts reflected British rather than Canadian perceptions. Her report convinced Berton that the war had what he wanted – a broad geographical canvas and, as she encouragingly put it, "enough interesting characters . . . to be fun." Some accounts, she added, even held that the war had been "the 'birthplace' of Canada as a nation." Its colonial nature "certainly helped show Canadians who they were (if only to the extent that they were very definitely not American – or British either, for that matter)."[10]

Berton immediately recognized the connection between the historical subject – the British Empire at war in North America – and contemporary Canadian nationalism. He certainly hoped the book would make a contribution to military history, but thought of it primarily as "the story of the first stirrings of the new country, the beginning of a national identity, and the great conflict that helped define the nation." Sears had already discovered "some pretty interesting heroes" and some "astonishingly incompetent" American generals. In short, the subject was a perfect one to choose as Canada entered the 1980s, for it linked an early nineteenth-century war that was arguably the seedbed of Canadian nationalism to twentieth-century readers eager to discover their roots and affirm their identity. In the wake of the American involvement in Vietnam, it would also be the story of a costly conflict no nation had won, an indictment of the folly of all war.[11]

Initial enthusiasm quickly turned to a sense of dismay, as it often did when he began a difficult and lengthy book, for his supremely confident public face belied private worries. Launching into the War of 1812 took him back to the early days of working on *Klondike*. "I could not fight off the feeling of foreboding that kept me awake nights, the sense of depression that dogged me as I started to read and codify the early research." This is the account he later gave of his unease at the time, and there is a self-dramatized air about it, a sign that in this respect Berton differed little from other anxious authors absorbed in the first stages of a large work. "There has to be a legitimate reason for all those historians churning out boring stuff," Sears had warned. "I hope the lack of evidence isn't it." He knew from experience the one sure way to rid himself of this funk: throw himself into the research. "It is only when I begin to dig deeply," he wrote, "that I once again fully experience the joy of writing."[12]

Once Barbara Sears had completed her primary research in the Toronto Public Library, the national archives of Canada and the United States, and more than a dozen regional and state libraries, archives, and historical societies, Berton tackled the first draft. He found the work plodding and couldn't seem to establish an evocative style. His text lacked a much-needed note of immediacy, for he wanted to convey the momentous events of 1812 as if they had occurred yesterday. To this end, he had already planned a scene-setting thousand-word prologue in the present tense. About a hundred pages into the draft, frustrated and unhappy with what he had put down, it occurred to him to write the entire manuscript that way. It was a serious gamble, for if executed poorly over the course of a long book, the ploy would merely annoy readers. But he took the risk anyway, threw away what he had written, and found that, as he put it, "the story took on a thrust of its own." The fear that evidence would be too thin to sustain a book proved groundless; in fact he soon recognized that the story would require two volumes. He took the second draft of volume one to Jamaica on a family holiday and worked on it each morning until he felt he could let others read it.[13]

Jack McClelland received *The Invasion of Canada* on schedule, as usual, early in 1980. He was as delighted with it as he had been in 1976 with *My Country*. McClelland expected Berton's War of 1812 volumes to pump up the company's precarious finances, as the author's two recent collections had done. (By 1986, sales of *My Country* would reach 61,280, surpassing the 58,015 of *The Wild Frontier*, its successor.)[14] But he also wanted Berton's work to continue to serve the nationalist cause. The end of the seventies had not been kind to the movement in Canada, and signs could be seen of a troubled future for it. The Conservative Party leader Margaret Thatcher, the Iron Lady, had become prime minister of England in May 1979, intent on reversing her country's economic decline by reducing the level of state intervention. In the United States, Ronald Reagan, the Republican governor of California who had bid unsuccessfully for his party's presidential nomination in 1976, was rumoured to be about to enter the race again, with backing from wealthy industrialists. Reagan had promised during his California state campaign to send "the welfare bums back to work," and he and Thatcher attacked state social welfare programs with the fervour of evangelicals in a Victorian slum. Together the pair, whose names would soon give rise to the words *Reaganomics* and *Thatcherism*, preached the gospel of an unfettered marketplace where national borders were viewed as impediments to progress. So when Jack McClelland had written to Berton about *The Invasion of Canada* in August of 1979, his praise for the idea had contained more than a tincture of resignation. "I haven't any doubt that it will have a greater impact than the railway books. It is a pity that it probably comes too late to help Canada much in terms of identity."[15]

Berton's enthusiastic view of the War of 1812 as "the story of the first stirrings of the new country, the beginning of a national identity, and the great conflict that helped define the nation" gave McClelland a glimmer of new hope. At the beginning of the seventies, in a *Canadian Forum* piece called "Is There an English Canadian Literature?" another John McClelland had lamented the failure of Canadian writers to "construct a literature out of the historical events at [their] disposal." Whatever their faults, the instructor in French at Victoria College had written, Americans at least had created "the heroes of an important literature which is far from dead." But Canadians? "The War of 1812 . . . somehow remains a foreign war which happened to be fought here."[16] *The Invasion of Canada* held the potential to alter this mindset.

Berton submitted his manuscript in a state of elation, convinced he had written a masterpiece. "The critics would acclaim me. This wasn't mere scribbling, this was high art." Or so he thought. He would later write that at the time the M&S editorial department was short-handed and that as a consequence he asked Janice Tyrwhitt to edit his book as a freelancer. The editors at M&S were certainly overworked, but there can be no question that, for this author, one of the best would immediately have been assigned to the book. It is much more likely that Berton had Tyrwhitt in mind all along. Within a fortnight she sent the manuscript back, heavily marked up and accompanied by an eight-page letter of assessment. Parts of the manuscript she pronounced excellent, but other passages she deemed underwritten or lacking in "sureness of tone." She liked Berton's use of the present tense, but thought its deployment needed a lot more work. "Ideally, the historical present should be a living skin not a straitjacket. It diminishes your opportunity to reflect, compare, enrich, which is why those flashes of insight are so essential. To some extent this tense means trading off depth for surface, so the surface must glitter."[17] Chastened but grateful for such insight and constructive criticism, he went back into his study, started from the beginning, and worked his way through another draft.

Janice Tyrwhitt was delighted with the changes Berton made. "Bravo!" she wrote. "You've done all I hoped you would do, and more. The book works splendidly now."[18] *The Invasion of Canada, 1812–1813* was released in September 1980, the same week that *The Third Wave*, the futurist Alvin Toffler's announcement and analysis of a new age – that of post-industrial society – sat at number one on the *Maclean's* non-fiction bestseller list. Morton Shulman's *How to Invest Your Money and Profit from Inflation* and Peter Drucker's *Managing in Turbulent Times* occupied numbers two and eight, respectively. The eighties, a decade of excess in which winning meant everything, whether in international relations, in the stock market, or in sports, had begun. In a speech to the British House of Commons in 1982, President Reagan would declare that the Soviet Union was an "evil empire"; in 1987, in Oliver Stone's movie *Wall Street*, the actor Michael Douglas's character would insist that "greed is good." Use of anabolic steroids by athletes rose to epidemic proportions in these years. It was in the dawn of this day of triumph at any price that Pierre Berton's defence of Canada appeared.

Most reviewers rewarded *The Invasion of Canada*, the story of the origins and first stages of the War of 1812, with plaudits. The warm reception confirmed and reinforced the status Berton had won with his railway books as Canada's favourite and best popular historian. Critics praised the liveliness of his prose, the immediacy of his story, and the value of his effort to make Canadians better acquainted with their own past. For a nation deemed dull by others – and whose citizens tended to believe the canard – Berton offered up a history stitched together with outsized personalities: Sir Isaac Brock, the brave English martyr of Queenston Heights; Tecumseh, chief of the Shawnee, proud and loyal to the British cause; William Henry Harrison, the ambitious and ruthless governor of Indiana Territory, later an American president – figures from a war of which Canadians were generally ignorant.

Berton's melodramatic depictions of the main characters in his story were of the sort that had populated Hollywood B-movie blockbusters for years, and Elsa Franklin and Jack McClelland had some fun as they swapped memos about the publicity campaign for the book. "It's the greatest thing since sliced bread," began a press release Elsa sent to Jack, supposedly for his approval. "*Yes!* That's what Jack McClelland, former boy wunderkind of the publishing world, said when he saw the manuscript of Pierre Berton's THE INVASION OF CANADA. . . . You, too, will want to thrill with Berton as he describes the sex life of General Isaac Brock, the weird puberty rites of the Shawnee Indians and the maidenhead grabbing antics of General Roger Sheaffe. . . ." Jack, well aware that this year's bestselling works of fiction would be potboilers by James Michener, Robert Ludlum, Sidney Sheldon, and Judith Krantz, played along: "I don't think it is coarse or vulgar enough for the current marketplace. Try to make it a bit more disgusting."[19]

Franklin's mock memo nevertheless reflected the quandary she and McClelland shared. What could possibly be done to promote Pierre Berton that had not already been tried? What could trump cross-country train tours, pokes of gold, specialty cocktails, and launch parties that threatened conflagration? "What the hell can we do for an encore?" Jack asked Elsa. In his mind, the very real problem drifted into a flight of nationalist fancy. The British sack of Washington in 1814 filled his mind's eye. He visualized "a scene where we have a White House in every bookstore in Metro Toronto and by pre-arrangement we set them all on fire simultaneously by radio control." But why stop there? "Maybe burning the White House won't be popular in every part of Canada. Maybe in the West, they would prefer to burn Fort York. Perhaps we have to have a special model available for Western separatists and all Canadians who hate Toronto." Marketing Berton had entered the realm of the surreal, and McClelland knew it. "This is one of the sleaziest ideas we have ever had," he admitted to Franklin, "but from past experience we know that sleazy ideas are probably the most effective."[20]

The reception accorded to *The Invasion of Canada* when it appeared in early fall 1980 (and to its successor, *Flames across the Border*, a year later)

reflected the gulf that had come to exist between popular taste in history and the dominant scholarly approach to writing about the past. It also revealed divisions of opinion within the academy. Mainstream media loved the book. In *Maclean's*, Doug Fetherling pronounced *The Invasion of Canada* "probably Berton's best historical work since *Klondike*." The *New York Times Book Review* declared that it was "popular history as it should more often be written, exciting but carefully documented, in a clear, somewhat classical style." In *Saturday Night*, Michael Bliss, who had gained public notice with a prizewinning biography of the turn-of-the-century Canadian businessman Sir Joseph Flavelle in 1978 and would soon publish a breakthrough popular life of Sir Frederick Banting, pronounced it "probably Berton's best book."[21]

The reviews in academic journals were mixed. "Mr. Berton's lively and entertaining book rescues this seemingly insignificant and bizarre conflict and imparts to it the life it deserves," wrote a reviewer in the *University of Windsor Review*. In the *Canadian Historical Review*, Trent University's Keith Walden, author of a Queen's University M.A. thesis on Isaac Brock as a cultural symbol, assumed a reserved if at times patronizing tone. The book, he wrote, succeeded "rather well," even if its explanations were "conventional." Its author was "trying to explain" important events in Canadian history to Canadians, and he took "his responsibilities to history seriously," but was "caught between the need to be truthful and the need to provide a colourful and absorbing narrative to attract a wide readership."[22] Few examples better illustrated the reorientation of the Canadian historical profession since the 1960s than that Walden, one of the country's most imaginative young historians, could have reached the conclusion that fidelity to truth and lively prose were somehow mutually exclusive. Many of Walden's generation of historians had come to spurn narrative because, in their view, it did not lend itself to the use of theory for the purpose of critical analysis.

When it came to being patronizing, an elevated station helped; Colonel C.P. Stacey, dean of Canadian military historians, outdid himself. Clearly miffed at the effrontery of this journalist turned historian in marching onto his own parade square, Stacey began a *Books in Canada* review with the words: "Pierre Berton does not tell us just why he has undertaken to write what is clearly going to be quite a long book on the War of 1812." Permission, he seemed to imply, should have been obtained from command headquarters. The rest of the review consisted of a series of swats from Stacey's regimental baton. The author, he wrote, was "threshing old wheat," yet his publisher was convinced that he was engaged in "a considerable literary enterprise." As history, the book left "much to be desired"; its approach was merely storytelling and its author just "a skilful anecdotalist" who inundated his readers with Indians. A comment Berton made that Brock "despised democracy" Stacey found naive in the extreme – rather like attacking the general "for never having voted NDP." At 363 pages, the book was "long-winded," he wrote – forgetting, it seems, that his own study of Canada's war policy alone during the Second World War had required 681 pages. Then fell the colonel's intended coup de grâce: the book had been printed in the United States. "Is it a fair assumption," Stacey asked, "that this time the Great Canadian Storyteller and The Canadian Publishers are out to crack the Great American Market?"[23]

Stacey's review annoyed Berton and enraged his publisher. The opening salvo left Berton baffled, for scarcely any other Canadian book had been written on the war in a hundred years. Besides, writers of popular and academic history served different purposes and reader-ships. Academic historians sold their points of view to colleagues on the grounds that what they were saying was new and innovative. They ana-lyzed why events happened. Historians like himself sold their stories to the public by describing the very experience of those events. From his point of view the two tasks were different, and neither was more legiti-mate than the other. He found Stacey's other criticisms puzzling and irksome, especially the complaint about an "awful lot" of Indians in the book. The way their loyalty to the British cause was betrayed in the peace treaty following the war had been one of his subplots. He did not, however, challenge Stacey in print, for he knew Jack McClelland intended to do so.

McClelland was as furious at *Books in Canada* as at its reviewer. "To review a new book of broad general interest by Pierre Berton," went his letter to the editor, "you have chosen a specialist in military history. Did you invite a former Nazi to review *Sophie's Choice*? . . . C.P. Stacey is all too representative of a body of scholars who think Canadian history should be reserved for historians. His petty nit-picking makes clear not only his envy but also his concern that Berton might succeed in bringing the War of 1812 out of the dusty closet in which historians have enshrined it." The *Books in Canada* subhead for Stacey's review had suggested that Berton's face might turn crimson after reading it. McClelland now turned the tables. Only the specially bound "advance proof" copy sent to Stacey had been printed in the United States; the finished copies of *The Invasion of Canada* had actually been printed and bound in Canada, including copies destined for Little, Brown, the American publisher, and the Book-of-the-Month Club. "Colour Professor Stacey crimson," McClelland concluded.[24]

Amid its praise, the review in *Choice* made the academic point that while the book was exciting, it was also "somewhat old-fashioned," weak where "broader social, political, and economic considerations" were concerned.[25] This was so, presuming that readers wanted an explanation of such things. No doubt some did, but Berton's approach was never to aim at the mind or intellect; he targeted the heart and will of those readers for whom it was less important for history to explain processes than to convey meaning. In writing about the War of 1812, Berton intended to enlighten, but also to sear the reader's imagination with the horror of war and to galvanize national resolve. So even as he went about puncturing some Canadian myths, he did so in a way that heightened historical awareness and bolstered Canadian pride and spirit.

Those with a literary sensibility recognized this. In a review published in *Quill and Quire*, the writer and critic George Woodcock remarked that in *The Invasion of Canada* Berton avoided "the Creightonian myth of Canadian westering, with the CPR as the extension of the St. Lawrence," drawing instead upon the strengths of his railway books – their sympathetic portraits of workers. Once again, Woodcock wrote, Berton had shown himself to be "the most truly populist of Canadian historians in the sense of being aware constantly of the ordinary people whose view of the events they move through is often more earthily accurate than that of the 'great men.'" Moreover, he did so while challenging the hoary old Upper Canadian myth that the volunteer farmers and townsmen who constituted the Canadian militia were the ones primarily responsible for saving Canada from the Americans in 1812 (the British Army, American ineptitude, and Tecumseh's Indians did that). But the very way he exposed myths and humanized heroes – showing, for example, how the idea of military gallantry led Brock to his death – helped valorize the lives and significance of anonymous citizens.[26]

The assessment of Michael Bliss better reflected his own political desire than it did Berton's historical judgment. "Instead of being a prisoner or propagandist of our nationalist mythology," Bliss wrote, "Berton exposes much of its foolishness": the absurdity of the war itself, the farcical American invasion of 1812, the frightened soldiers among both American and Canadian ranks. "Those who expect Berton to perpetuate nationalist nonsense about the war of 1812 are quite wrong," he wrote. Even in the 1960s, Bliss had been critical of the nationalist politics of the left, which tended to equate economic protectionism with protection against foreign domination and control; by the 1980s he had gravitated toward the neo-conservatism of Thatcher and Reagan. For him the key to *The Invasion of Canada* was found in Berton's final sentence: "Thus, in a psychological as well as in a political sense, we are Canadians and not Americans because of a foolish war that scarcely anyone wanted or needed, but which, once launched, no one knew how to stop." Bliss chose to conclude from this that the absurd little war had led to the equally absurd little distinction Canadians made between themselves and Americans. Elsewhere in his review, he had noted that Berton was "alert to the silliness and ironies of the war," but here he ignored Berton's intent, which was to demonstrate that this war, however foolish, had instilled in Canadians for the first time a fundamental difference in Canadian political and social values from those of the United States, and that a reawakened awareness of this foundational moment in Canadian history could serve once again to keep the barbarians from the gates.[27]

This "absurd" war, as Doug Fetherling and others were careful to note, had in fact been one of great political, cultural, and educational moment, for it had made possible what Berton called "the viable democracy" Americans did not want to admit existed to their north. To make his own political point, Bliss had quoted Berton selectively. The sentence he chose dealt with consequences: a foolish war led to a foolish illusion of national distinctiveness. Yet the word *thus*, which Berton used to begin that sentence, implied antecedent conditions in a chain of cause and effect, fleshed out in the one that preceded it: "Out of [the war], shaped by an emerging nationalism and tempered by rebellion, grew that special form of state paternalism that makes the Canadian way of life significantly different from the more individualistic American way." In short, from this war, however ridiculous, had emerged a genuine sense of shared values that allowed British North Americans still loyal to the Crown to differentiate themselves from the American polity to the south. With it came the individuated frame of mind necessary for independent nationhood. Thousands of Canadians bought *The Invasion of Canada* and *Flames across the Border* and took away from them precisely this message. The books provided a means of fortifying their national commitment at a time of renewed assault from without and within.[28]

Flames across the Border, the concluding volume on the War of 1812, was found beneath many Canadian Christmas trees in 1981. At almost five hundred pages, it was significantly heftier than its predecessor, and it covered almost two years rather than the few months of *The Invasion of Canada*. But those who had read of Brock's death on Queenston Heights the year before would have revisited familiar terrain. Many among its cast of characters soldiered on, once more fixed, as if in aspic, in the present tense that the majority of reviewers enjoyed for its immediacy. Aficionados of book reviews would have noted that most of the reviewers of *Invasion* had also been redeployed, and that Fetherling, Bliss, Walden, Stacey, and Woodcock used much the same ammunition as before: the author's uncritical use of anecdote; the preference for descriptions of social conditions over analysis of social structure; the Ontario-centred point of view (ignoring, for example, the naval war in the Maritimes); the lack of a larger geopolitical perspective. Walden, grown bold, listed a series of subjects the Kleinburg warhorse had failed to address and approaches he failed to take – "which is only to say, perhaps, that he is a writer, often a good one, but not a historian." Brereton Greenhous, a historian with the Department of National Defence, echoed this refrain. Berton was able to provide his myth-busting account of Laura Secord's story, he wrote, only because "a real historian" had already done so in 1952. Colonel Stacey accused Berton of climbing "on the bandwagon" of public interest in war with a book containing little new information or fresh interpretation. "A person with a modicum of skill and intelligence and a PhD granted by a good graduate school might have produced a more balanced book," he wrote in summation, allowing that the professional historian "would be most unlikely to give us as good and lively a story."

Indeed, Stacey conceded more than this. He admitted grudgingly that the public "devoured" Berton's books, while few people except professional historians and their students read academic history. Stacey, too, had reservations about the short-sighted direction his profession had taken. Professional historians should "think twice before they denigrate Berton," he wrote, for "people read him because he knows how to communicate, an art the professionals have not troubled to cultivate. Writing is in danger of becoming a lost skill among them."[29] This was a point also made by Roger Hall, one of the few professional historians in Canada concerned with his colleagues' abandonment of the quest for a broad readership. But in Hall's view the problem could not be blamed on the historical profession alone. Had Berton lived in the United States or Great Britain, he wrote in *Books in Canada*, he "wouldn't be a problem" because in those countries the "serious but not scholarly historian" was popular and accepted. "In literary class-ridden Canada, however, to be popular is almost an epithet, to be commercially successful a wanton curse, to express oneself in a clear uncluttered prose without an overlay of protective notes, akin to crass exhibitionism. Too many Canadian professional historians . . . regard themselves as the sole certified guardians, explorers, and exhibitors of the country's past." To them, Berton was the outsider not to be trusted, made therefore to "run a critical academic gauntlet" despite the fact that as a historian, he was "careful, resourceful, and capable . . . with an eye for detail and a tendency to overemphasize the colourful" – not exactly heinous crimes. The problem, Hall noted, was that Canada lacked a cohesive and serious but not scholarly academic community, with the result that cultural criticism became an academic preserve. "In other words, there is no easily defined place for serious writers like Berton in this country and so he is raked continually by those who should really leave him to his self-defined task and get on with their own work."[30]

Doug Fetherling, Michael Bliss, and George Woodcock adopted just such a laissez-faire attitude. Fetherling wrote his review for *Maclean's* in the present tense, as a mark of critical appreciation, and the scene he invoked was of Berton in his study, struggling to bring the War of 1812 to life and his saga to a conclusion. "Only the living win," he wrote, "the author, the public. Berton has done it again." Bliss began with a warning to history department historians. "The condescending, nit-picking reviews Berton often gets from my academic colleagues are even more out-of-place than usual with this project. These are the books I hope my children will someday read about the War of 1812." He praised Berton for the quality of his research (duly noting the important con-tribution of Barbara Sears) and placed him in the front ranks of popular historians like Barbara Tuchman and Antonia Fraser. "If you or your friends like to read Canadian history, buy these books." Bliss's one lin-gering reservation was whether the War of 1812 held enough historical weight to warrant such extensive attention. "Should we be more inter-ested in the burning of York than Napoleon's retreat from Moscow, know more about the Battle of Lake Erie than the Battle of Trafalgar?"[31]

The reference to "Napoleon's retreat from Moscow" alluded not only to the event itself, but also to Tolstoy's *War and Peace*. Bliss had made the same remark in his review of *The Invasion of Canada*. It was a point well taken in the context of overall historical significance. George Woodcock too made the connection to the great Russian author and his masterpiece, but recognized a dimension of Berton's treatment that transcended the relative weight of historical events. What distinguished Berton's history from that of "most academic historians," he stated, was "his deep moralism." The fact that he had lavished such attention on the War of 1812, this "foolish and unnecessary conflict," chronicling in excruciating detail its great human misery and waste, led the reader to realize that, "as certainly as Tolstoy in *War and Peace*, Berton is making his judgements on the phenomenon of war and on the political preten-sions from which it emerges." The war had been the making of Canada, and this came at great cost. "Can anyone truly say," the author had asked, "that the game was ever worth the candle?" Berton's question, Woodcock wrote, was a rhetorical one. "What in our hearts can we say but 'no!' But that, it seems to me, is the answer Berton, as surely as Tolstoy, is intent we should make to war of any kind." Among academic historians in Canada, perhaps Donald Creighton alone "would lead us so firmly towards a moral conclusion," he said. "And this, I suppose, is what marks off . . . a man of imagination as distinct from a man of mere scholarship. . . . Facts become pictures, and pictures lead to a judgement implicit from the outset." The power of history, the critic concluded, lay in lessons people too easily forget, and "in the power to recreate a past that time has stolen from us." Pierre Berton had recreated circumstances that helped shape the world in which Canadians now lived; his was a past with little patience for heroics and posturing or "for men who think themselves great," but one that still had "room for true heroes," one that led to an altered view of the past, a past that is richer, deeper, truer.[32]

As the 1980s unfolded, Berton, now in his sixties, increasingly felt that his career had reached its zenith. "I began to be haunted by a growing feeling that things were winding down," he wrote in 1986. A first inkling of this may have come back in February 1979, when a group of his friends held a tribute dinner in his honour at the Royal York hotel. The idea had been Peter Newman's, and the organizing committee fluctuated from meeting to meeting. Jack McClelland, Charles Templeton, and Bill Forbes were key members, but Elsa Franklin became the driving force. Guests at one hundred tables, each set for ten, paid $50 – $35 if they were members of a writers' association – and the Writers' Union of Canada received one-third of the revenues. Over a lavish dinner, friends from the many chapters of Berton's life feted him with words: June Callwood, Trent Frayne, and Arthur Irwin; the authors Robertson Davies and Margaret Atwood; Eric Nicol, Lister Sinclair, and Bruce Hutchison; Hal Straight and Bill Forbes; Clyde Gilmour and Mavor Moore; Gordon Sinclair and Arthur Hailey; Stephen Franklin and Peter Newman; the journalists Larry Zolf and Scott Young; and, as court jesters, the cartoonists he so admired – Roy Peterson, Sid Barron, Terry Mosher (Aislin), Duncan Macpherson, and Ben Wicks. The organizers' original plans called for a giant backdrop of the Chilkoot Pass, with a staircase matching the slope of the hill, to rise about fifteen feet and then discreetly descend and wrap around the end of the backdrop, meant to convey the guest of honour's rise to fame, from brash and callow West Coast hotshot to confident and omnipresent national celebrity.[33] But practicalities melted the grandiose Chilkoot stage set, and the event went off perfectly well with a couple of plain microphones. Pierre found it touching. But occasions marking lifetime achievement can be unnerving, for they are conducted in the past tense.

The terrain of life seemed to have levelled out, the way the Trans-Canada Highway heading west sheds the stands of conifers and the granite of the Shield in southeastern Manitoba, then straightens and opens to the vast horizontal plain of the prairies. In 1980, after four years on CFRB and another ten on CKEY, *Dialogue*, the radio program he and Charles Templeton shared, went off the air. Jack Scott died that year of cancer. *The Great Debate* stopped production in 1981, after eight seasons. Politically, those in the passing lane seemed to have left Berton behind. In 1980, he had spoken in Quebec City for the No side of the debate over the first Quebec referendum on separation, but he felt that he had merely preached to the converted. Canada's identity and interests were under threat as much as ever from international influences, but the CIC disbanded in 1981, having declared that its goals had been accomplished. "That wasn't true," Berton wrote, "but the 'me' generation was more interested in profit than patriotism." The day of outspoken nationalism was on the wane. Whatever influence he had had with the federal government in lobbying for nationalist policies lay in the past, in the first flush of the Trudeau years. He remained as committed to heritage conservation as ever, but his final year as chairman of Heritage Canada ended in 1983. He had done much to help preserve some of the finest historic buildings in Canada, but his old home in Dawson was now in bad repair and its boardwalk was overgrown with weeds.[34]

A Canadian Press photograph captured him in 1982, sitting on the porch steps, hands on knees and looking morosely into the distance. He was there to record a half-hour documentary on his beginnings intended to run prior to the three-part TV adaptation of *I Married the Klondike* in the fall. The script called upon him to climb the porch steps to the front door, saying, "It's an uncanny experience, to come home again to Dawson City where the ghosts of the past still linger," and once he was in his old living room he was to add, "Some of those ghosts are here on these walls." The CBC aired the series in the fall. The backstory of his life had become history – in this case bad history, based on an English expatriate's script that conveyed little that was authentic about life in the Yukon. The CBC brass rebuffed Berton's offer to fix the screenplay, and he found the episodes "insipid, conventional, boring."[35]

What more could he strive to accomplish? He had won almost every available prize, from the Governor General's Award for Non-Fiction to the Stephen Leacock Memorial Medal for Humour (for *Just Add Water and Stir* in 1960), and they showed no signs of abating. The eighties brought the Canadian Authors Association Literary Award for Non-Fiction in 1981, the Canadian Booksellers Association Award in 1982, and induction into the Canadian News Hall of Fame in 1983. Honorary degrees continued to pile up. Home from one convocation or another, he would hang the hood beside the others on the wall flanking the stairs. In the early eighties, to those from P.E.I., York, and Toronto, he added more from Brock (1981), Windsor (1981), Athabasca (1982), Victoria (1983), McMaster (1983), Royal Military College (1984), Alaska (1984), and UBC (1985). Eventually, fourteen of the colourful garments adorned the wall.

The circumstances at McClelland & Stewart were decidedly less pleasant. Despite its distinguished backlist, the company struggled to remain afloat, and Jack McClelland was burned out and on the verge of collapse. Marge Hodgeman and Farley Mowat, both very concerned about his condition, insisted that he make way for someone else to lead the firm. Anna Porter, once the obvious successor, had left in 1982 to establish Key Porter Books, so in the spring of 1982 Jack announced that Linda McKnight would take over as president and publisher. He would remain as chairman of the board. McKnight, an M&S employee since 1969, was to oversee the company's day-to-day operations. She knew that strict economies were necessary if the company was to survive, and it became clear to all, including Berton, that the days of pampered authors and excessive launches were a luxury the company could no longer afford. McClelland encouraged McKnight to be tough-minded and run the house as she saw fit, but she soon discovered that Jack was incapable of putting economics ahead of authors. His incurable optimism helped keep the annual list too large for sales to match, and his ongoing behind-the-scenes meddling cut into her effectiveness. He remained, in the words of his biographer, "a backseat president."[36]

In 1982, McClelland received the Canada Council's prestigious Molson Prize for his contributions to Canadian culture, but M&S teetered on the brink of receivership. Within a year the Canadian Imperial Bank of Commerce called in its loan. A sale of almost the entire inventory did little to address the problem of ongoing indebtedness. Berton's investment as a shareholder in M&S had become a bad one. The golden years of his privileged and cozy relationship with M&S, like the days of the Last Spike cocktail, clearly lay in the past.

His own life was financially secure, and had been since the seventies. The *Wall Street Journal* had estimated as early as 1973 that his annual income was in the $400,000 range, and when Gary Ross wrote "The Business of Being Berton" in 1975, he observed that the author no longer seemed to be motivated by money to write. Still, Berton and Franklin readily admitted to squeezing every possible dollar from the work he did – whether recycling old material, charging a dollar a word for magazine articles, bargaining hard with M&S (the pair enjoyed playing the game of good cop/bad cop at the negotiating table), or demanding hundreds of dollars in reprint fees and several thousand for speeches given to high-powered groups like the Empire and Canadian clubs. By the eighties, he charged well-heeled associations $4,000 to $5,000; but for groups like the Boy Scouts or the Canadian Civil Liberties Association, Franklin told Gary Ross, "he wouldn't dream" of soliciting a fee and paid his own expenses. He gave heavily to the United Church in Kleinburg and to the New Democratic Party.[37]

In late November 1982, Pierre Berton stood in black tie in New York's Regency Hotel with the governor, the chief warder, and the gaoler emeritus of the Incorporated Ancient Order of the Beefeater and received the $10,000 Beefeater Club Prize for Literature, awarded for *The Invasion of Canada* and *Flames across the Border*.[38] The cash was handy, but he scarcely needed it to put food on the family table. His 1980 contract with McClelland & Stewart for the War of 1812 volumes had been a lucrative one. For the first time, the publisher ordered a first printing of more than 100,000 copies for a hardcover book. Seventy thousand copies of *Invasion* were shipped to bookstores before the publication date. Stephen Franklin estimated that with revenues from "15% royalties, book club and paperback sales, TV and film rights, translations, serialization and anthology fees," the two books could gross $1 million. At a $19.95 list price, Berton stood to earn close to $300,000 per volume on McClelland & Stewart's sales alone, exclusive of sales by Little, Brown in the United States.[39]

Over the years, Berton's titles had accumulated retail sales of more than $12 million, without counting mass-market paperback editions. *The National Dream* and *The Last Spike* had grossed $500,000 for Pierre Berton Enterprises (which handled all his non-television work). His earnings usually went first into short-term deposits, and then into a forward-averaging annuity, rolled over the following year. At the time *The Invasion of Canada* appeared, his net worth was estimated at $1.5 million – an amount equivalent to $3.7 million in 2008. He readily gave Stephen Franklin a rough breakdown: "$100,000 in downtown Toronto real estate; $50,000 in gold; $600,000 odd in stocks and bonds; $300,000 and $40,000 in pension funds (the ACTRA fund and one with my company) and my home and property in Kleinburg, which needs a new evaluation but must be nudging up to $500,000." In 1979, his company had grossed $339,696, split about 25 per cent each among books, radio, television, and investments. One year when he had no new book on the fall list, he made $100,000 on his backlist alone. He had come a long way since signing for *The Royal Family* with Knopf in 1954 for $300.[40]

At home in Kleinburg, Berton's parental responsibilities had waned, for most of his children had left the family nest. By the early 1980s, only Paul, Peggy Anne, and Perri (now a teenager) lived at home. Free-spirited Penny lived with her partner, John Hardy, on the island of Bali, Indonesia, where the couple designed jewellery and other artistic objects crafted by islanders. Patsy married Rico Gerussi, son of the Toronto actor Bruno Gerussi, in 1980 – the first of the Berton children to wed. (The wedding present they received from Mother and Father Berton was a sporty Subaru.) Peter had become an architect with the Thom Partnership, and was known to do well playing the stock market. Paul had begun a career in journalism. Soon enough, there would be only Pierre, Janet, and the cats.

But Pierre still had to support his other family. The headquarters of Pierre Berton Enterprises was his two-storey brick row house on Sackville Street – in the early 1980s still industrial, rundown, and unfashionable. From the window in the old master bedroom that served as his office he could see the automobile bumpers stacked in the Toronto Plating Company lot. My Country Productions, in which he and Franklin were equal partners, had purchased the eight-room house in 1975 for $41,000 cash. His office staff consisted of Ennis Armstrong and a part-time assistant, although additional help would come and go as required. Ennis marshalled his time, organized his files, and handled his correspondence. But at the centre of the enterprise was the team of women who made the efficient production of his books possible. The group became complete once he convinced Janice Tyrwhitt to work for him regularly after her involvement with the War of 1812 books, and it operated like a well-oiled machine.

That he had such a staff at his disposal may have seemed an unfair advantage to scholars used to lonely research trips and the editorial once-over of an underpaid copy editor at an underfinanced academic press; but the luxury brought with it a burden of responsibility the professors did not have. Sears, Tyrwhitt, and Craig did contract work for others, but a substantial portion of their steady income came from Pierre Berton Enterprises. Because they were so skilled, their services were in demand elsewhere, so if Berton wanted to keep his team intact he had to earn enough to provide them with regular work, and that meant always being one or two books ahead of the one in hand.

With success came expenses he would not otherwise have incurred. With the publication of *The Dionne Years*, Berton initiated an ongoing arrangement to sign over as much as a third of his royalties to Barbara Sears. (That book had earned the pair a cool $250,000.) He and Franklin had invested $100,000 in a second company, Eve Productions, formed to produce a feature film based on Constance Beresford-Howe's 1973 novel, *The Book of Eve*. (The book is about a married woman who, in a spontaneous act, leaves her husband after a lengthy marriage, builds a new life for herself in an unfashionable district, and finds happiness, independence, and – unexpectedly – love when her neighbour woos her with good cooking and sparkling conversation.) The screenwriter Charles Israel had come up with the script they had commissioned, but Elsa found it difficult to put the finances in place. Pierre had extraordinary expenses in Kleinburg, too. He estimated that in 1979 alone he had spent between $30,000 and $50,000 on the garden. Since his annual income could fluctuate by as much as $100,000, a book on the annual fall list meant financial security for those around him in both Kleinburg and Cabbagetown.[41]

Front Page Challenge celebrated its twenty-fifth anniversary in 1982, a milestone that evoked many memories. It had first aired two weeks after John Diefenbaker came to power, and it had weathered the vicissitudes of Canadian broadcast policy and tastes through 850 programs, reaching an average of about two million viewers per week. Fred Davis, Betty Kennedy, Gordon Sinclair, and Pierre Berton had helped make the show a national institution, and their faces were instantly recognizable to virtually every Canadian. Over the twenty-five years, the show had featured more than 1,800 guests representing wildly diverse news stories, and Pierre the nostalgia king could look back on many who had in fact touched his own life. Thor Heyerdahl's appearance in 1963, to describe his Kon-Tiki expedition, brought to mind the evening the adventurer and his wife had spent with the Bertons in the fall of 1939. The appearances of Al Capp and Lester Pearson had been like reprises of the memorable interviews he had conducted with them for his own show. Ellen Fairclough had been a mystery guest in 1959, the very year when Fred and Jo Davis were struggling with her federal department over their attempt to sponsor immigrants, and not long after Pierre's own squabble with her over the script for *Women on the March*. Jessica Mitford's appearance on the show in the early sixties, related to her probe into the high cost of dying in America, conjured up his own earlier exposé of the subject for the *Star*. Arthur Hailey's 1965 debut, to mark the $21,000 he had received from the CBC for *Flight into Danger*, brought to mind how ham-fisted and insensitive Berton had been at *Maclean's* in telling Hailey he had no future as an author; by the time Hailey made a second appearance, in 1974, to talk about Bahamian independence, Pierre and Janet had shared a number of vacations with the Hailey family. Herb Gray's report on his recommendations to cabinet for federal controls over foreign investment evoked the heady days of nationalism in the late sixties and early seventies. Pierre was proud that his mother had been a *Front Page Challenge* guest in 1959, representing the story of the Klondike gold rush, and he was as surprised as anyone when Janet and the spouses of the other panellists appeared as guests in 1972 to celebrate the show turning sweet sixteen.[42]

Even a near tragedy for the Bertons had become a *Front Page Challenge* news story. In 1977, in the wake of the Parti Québécois victory in Quebec the previous fall and with the prospect of a referendum on separatism looming, the federal government had sent a number of celebrities – Berton, the hockey broadcaster Foster Hewitt, Bruno Gerussi, and others – on an expensive junket across the country with their families, from Dawson City to Corner Brook, simply to promote being Canadian. Not far from Edmonton, the private aircraft carrying Pierre, Janet, Peter, Peggy Anne, and Perri inexplicably ran out of fuel and had to make an emergency landing. The only available spot was a nearby highway. At first the pilot had difficulty lowering the landing gear, but the dangerous touchdown went smoothly. The turn of events proved unnerving enough that after everyone had safely evacuated, Pierre and Peter – at the time twenty-two – climbed back aboard the twin-engine Rockwell Turbo Commander for a snort or two from Pierre's vodka bottle. Later that year, Peggy Anne and Perri became *Front Page Challenge* mystery guests.[43]

Whether or not his life was "winding down," the hectic pace scarcely slowed. The daily two-hour commute, the weekly spot on *Front Page Challenge*, the pressure for more television work, the host of keynote speeches, the constant slate of interviews, the incessant flow of letters – all this reached its peak in the 1980s. His health had generally been very good and he had worked out regularly with Charles Templeton at the Cambridge Fitness Club in downtown Toronto, running a few miles each day. But recently he had been experiencing severe weakness, hunger, and thirst. In 1981, blood tests had shown a blood sugar level of only eighty. At the time, the diagnosis was that he suffered from "emotional fatigue."[44] In June 1983 he felt especially out of sorts – ill enough to check himself into York Central Hospital. Dr. Granger had continued to monitor his glucose levels and also had him taking the anticoagulant drug heparin as a preventive measure against stroke or heart attack. But this illness seemed unrelated to the heart; it was more like pneumonia. So he spent his sixty-third birthday in a semi-private ward, with an IV needle in his arm, while doctors conducted various tests.[45]

Word began to leak out that he had been hospitalized for pneumonia, but the situation was worse than this.[46] After a scare in which he feared he might have cancer of the lymph glands, the medical staff discovered a pulmonary embolism. His lungs were so full of blood clots that they looked on the X-ray screen like Japanese bonsai trees. Transferred to the intensive care unit, he was administered the new clot-dissolving medication streptokinase. Released from intensive care, he remained in hospital, and his family resumed their pampering. Each morning, Janet brought freshly squeezed orange juice, and others arrived carrying everything from sushi and Peking duck to roast beef and Yorkshire pudding. Jack McClelland paid a visit even though he was himself checked into another hospital, for his health had been poor for a number of months.[47] He had a hard time leaving, once the York Central staff noticed his hospital wristband. Berton himself checked out, if his memoirs are to be believed, with the Beatles refrain "Will you still need me, will you still feed me / When I'm sixty-four?" running through his head.[48] Always the romanticist, this man; forever the fabulist.

Pierre's health as an adult had always been robust, but his experience of a serious medical condition forced him to face his own mortality. For the first time since he came down with scarlet fever as a child, he had found himself in a state of helplessness. Sidney Katz, his old *Maclean's* colleague, noticed that Berton came away from the experience chastened, and that for a while he gave up alcohol. Pierre's mother and father and maternal grandparents had lived full lives, but the man himself knew from the family Bible that his paternal grandfather had been laid to rest in a Milwaukee grave at thirty-nine. Jack McClelland's health remained unstable; Elsa's husband, Stephen, had incurred three separate strokes, and now suffered from numbness down his right side. The younger son of June Callwood and Trent Frayne had been struck by a drunk driver while returning on his motorcycle to Queen's University the previous year. Casey Frayne's tragic death at twenty years of age in April 1982 shook the Bertons badly, for it exacerbated the anxiety Pierre and Janet shared over the safety of their own children on the highway. They had offered what little support they could to the grieving parents but knew that words could scarcely allay their friends' grief. Instead, all they could give were gentle hugs, along with plenty of liquor for the funeral. The gesture was one the Fraynes never forgot. Betty Anglin sat next to Pierre at the memorial for Casey. "He streamed tears," she said.[49]

Elsa noticed that following his hospitalization Pierre stopped working as much in the evenings, preferring to watch the hospital drama *St. Elsewhere* and reruns of the cop show *Kojak*. Still, he seemed as determined as ever to maintain a steady rate of publication and appearances. Completing *Flames across the Border* had been an exhausting process, and he was reluctant to embark too soon on another highly ambitious project. Barbara Sears had herself vetoed a book on the 1837 Upper and Lower Canada Rebellions because she preferred not to read any more nineteenth-century handwriting if she could possibly avoid doing so; besides, she had come to loathe William Lyon Mackenzie, the red-wigged rebel with the scurrilous tongue. Meanwhile, Pierre continued to beat his nationalist drum in after-dinner speeches on the Canadian identity, and did so with such regularity that one wag called him "a one-man marching band on behalf of Canadian nationalism." His message had not wavered even when the nationalist movement faltered and faded. "I believe that the cultural explosion, which has already begun, will expand over the next two decades," he told the *Financial Post* at the beginning of 1982. A renaissance in Canadian arts and letters was about to take place, he predicted. One day when driving into town it occurred to him that he ought to turn the material he used in his "Canadian identity" speeches into a book. The result, churned out in about a week, was *Why We Act like Canadians*, published in the autumn.[50]

The brief book took the form of a series of letters, nominally by a Canadian to his American cousin Sam. In it he outlined the differences between their two nations and the frames of mind they had come to reflect. Berton wrote, however, for his fellow Canadians. In his view, they still needed to acquire a clear understanding of the distinct set of attitudes, beliefs, and priorities that had arisen out of Canada's founding moment – when, for a variety of reasons, a group of northern colonies in British North America had refused to join the revolt against the British connection. From this, the book said, had come the Canadian emphasis on liberty within the law rather than an open-ended "pursuit of happiness"; a polity based on allegiance to the Crown rather than commitment to a covenant; a social and ethnic mix that had gradually, if at times reluctantly, arrived at forms of accommodation rather than forming a crucible for assimilation. Unlike Americans, who had come to view rule by the British imperial state as a form of tyranny, Canadians had witnessed the protection of the British system of justice and the exercise of British imperial authority and therefore did not fear an interventionist state the way Americans did.[51]

Berton paraded all this and more in the short, chatty book. Those who had embraced the nationalism of the seventies found in *Why We Act like Canadians* a handy primer to help confirm and explain to themselves why they thought as they did and how their values fed into a sense of collective identity. The Alberta historian Hugh Dempsey proclaimed it "an excellent book which explains why Canadians are different from Americans." Clyde Gilmour, to whom Jack McClelland sent a preview copy, wrote that he had read the book with great pleasure. "I want to congratulate you on what I consider one of the best books you've ever done."[52]

The broad economic, political, and cultural forces of the eighties made conversions to the nationalist faith difficult. The Canadian economy had entered its worst recession since the Second World War. Oil prices were high, GDP was low, and per capita income was in decline. Prime Minister Trudeau, re-elected in 1980, had outraged many Canadians (especially in the West) with the National Energy Program – the dreaded NEP – that regulated oil prices in order to give Canada better control over its supply of energy. On another political front, the uncertainty accompanying constitutional reform set many Canadians on edge. Meanwhile, President Ronald Reagan – folksy, avuncular, smiling, and exuding confidence – had proclaimed that his countrymen had "every right to dream heroic dreams" and promised a new dispensation, an era of renewal and prosperity.[53]

In academic circles, studies of national character were coming to be seen as the stuff of the 1950s, a decade viewed as one of complacent consensus in North America. Life, scholars now said, was more complex and fractured than simple nostrums about national identity would allow. Toronto-based media sophisticates, especially those who equated a continental vision with a cosmopolitan outlook, dismissed *Why We Act like Canadians* as the puerile musings of an old-fashioned romantic several steps behind the times. What Canadian needs another sermon on national character, the *Globe and Mail* asked. "Those of us who ever give a thought to a national character are already aware of what makes us different. And those who don't care won't abandon their TV sets (tuned to NBC) long enough to acknowledge Berton's history lesson, let alone absorb it. . . . And who can blame them? As a lecturer, Professor

Berton can be just as boring as those academics who fancy they have a mission and confuse a harangue with enthusiasm."[54] This snide mix of superiority and cynicism was typical of criticism from such quarters. Past swipes had been aimed at Berton's brash effrontery and arose from a resentment usually born of envy; those of the later years would often carry an air of world-weary resignation and the self-satisfied ennui of minds captivated by the ironies of the postmodern condition.

For thousands of ordinary Canadians, however, the book served its purpose. Decades later, market research would reveal that consumer identity is forged as much from what people don't like as from what they do. The desire to avoid "dissociative reference groups," it turns out, is as powerful in identity formation as the wish to belong to groups more attractive. This "power of dissociative influence" works with consumers of products; what Berton's instincts told him was that a similar social psychology obtained with respect to the formation of national identity. It was shaped just as surely when Canadians examined and rejected American values as when they tried to articulate their own.[55] Berton's avuncular polemic led down both roads.

Pierre left the controversy of *Why We Act like Canadians* for others to fret over, for by then he was preoccupied with finishing his long-delayed saga about the settling of the Canadian west. This would round out a quartet of books on Canadian history launched by *Klondike* and continued by *The National Dream* and *The Last Spike* – the "epic story," as he later portrayed it, "that began with John A. Macdonald's dream of a continental railway." Since 1971, when Glenn Wright started research on the settlement of the prairies, Berton had struggled off and on to find some way to convey the magnitude of the scattered tale of western development, and he and Barbara Sears had resumed the project anew when *Flames across the Border* was done. In early summer 1983, he was convinced that at last he had a workable approach, but his sudden hospitalization in July put everything on hold. By then, he had drawn together "a lively cast of rogues," and he knew exactly how the book would begin and end.[56]

It was several months before his health fully stabilized. By early 1984 he had recovered strength sufficiently to trigger an acrimonious month-long dispute with Coles Bookstores over the importation and remaindering of foreign editions of *The Invasion of Canada*. The Writers'

Union of Canada came to his assistance, and soon the protest involved several branches of the federal government, including the Department of Justice, which was asked to investigate the matter. After much public and private bickering, an agreement (brokered by Jack McClelland) was reached. Coles agreed to put an end to its importation of any such books by Canadian authors, and a committee of members of the publishing industry was formed to resolve further issues.[57]

That spring witnessed the launch of Tour de Force, a quiz game Berton and Charles Templeton had developed after *Dialogue* came to an end. Playing on a board shaped like a racetrack, participants advanced by answering questions from fifty categories. Some, such as "Explorers," "Inventors," "Books and Authors," and "Space," were conventional ones; others made the game more distinctive: "Wicked Women," "Sex Symbols," "Famous Monsters," "Comics." Players sought to reach the goal of seventy points, and could gain a shortcut to winning if they successfully answered questions from five cards in a row – a feat deemed a "tour de force." The game company Waddingtons had bought into the idea for the game with the bilingual title, but Elsa Franklin handled the promotion. In Montreal, a press release issued prior to the launch of the game at Hôtel de la Montagne on February 9, 1984, boasted that pre-issue sales of "the Quiz Game for All Canadians" already approached 100,000 copies. In Toronto, Franklin organized a Celebrity Challenge at a pub-like Pat and Mario's restaurant, at which members of the public could play Tour de Force against such prominent figures as Ben Wicks, Fred Davis, Dinah Christie, David Crombie, the CBC broadcaster Mary Lou Finlay, Jack McClelland, and Bob Rae, leader of the Ontario NDP. Proceeds would go to Jessie's Centre for Teenagers, a shelter founded by June Callwood.[58]

The Promised Land appeared early in September 1984, at a time when M&S was in a state of disarray, especially with respect to its marketing and sales staff. M&S authors complained about the neglect of their books, but Berton was not among them. He had what others did not: he had the Elsa factor. Janet and John Foster's book for M&S, *Discovering Wild Canada*, sold about 6,000 copies that fall, and then all but disappeared from public view; Berton's new offering reached bookstore shelves and reviewers' desks in plentiful supply and with the predictability of back-to-school sales. The Americans had been repelled, the national railway built, the North opened up, and now the West was settled, always in time for the Christmas season.

The reviews were as foreseeable as the book's success. *Maclean's* proclaimed that no one had done more than Berton to show that Canada's history was "as exciting as that of any other country," leaving readers to figure out who else might have done so. Certainly it was not the scores of Canadian historians, for their reviews conceded the field. In the *Canadian Historical Review*, McGill's John Herd Thompson predictably and accurately complained that the book was "old-fashioned" in its Creightonian style, given over to "larger-than-life personalities," and had remarkably little to say about "the ordinary people who broke the plains" despite "his evident sympathy for them." He admitted that such criticism might simply appear to be envious carping, since Berton "gets read and we don't." In *Saturday Night*, Ramsay Cook chided Berton for selling subjects familiar to scholars as new interpretations – the career of Laurier's interior minister, Sir Clifford Sifton, for example – but he spent the first third of his review attempting to heal "the petty little war" between popular and professional historians. Professors "shouldn't carp when Pierre Berton and the popularizers awaken the memories of large audiences," he wrote. But they did have a duty to encourage a "better popular history," and Berton "could certainly do better."[59]

What was old hat to Cook and Thompson, prairie-born historians, was a story by no means familiar to many Canadians, including westerners themselves, for no more did the average person possess an informed or accurate overview of what their parents and grandparents had lived through than veterans did about the wars in which they had fought. *The Promised Land*, John Bemrose wrote in *Maclean's*, "offers western readers a better understanding of themselves" because it showed how "current western attitudes" came from the pioneer experience, forging in westerners a self-confidence and deep-rooted social cohesiveness, along with a political outlook anchored in a common set of grievances. Ramsay Cook, too, recognized the book's contemporary resonance. A long-standing critic of emotion-based nationalism, he was less sanguine than Bemrose: "The old master popularizer has done it again. He has fallen upon a good story and dressed it up as only an old *Star* man could. He knew when it was time to celebrate the national dream. He recognized the cultural nationalistic market when he wrote *Hollywood's Canada*. This book makes its appearance as a new version of western regionalism is passing from outraged infancy to the age at which it will want to read about itself. Westerners, a forgiving, long-suffering people, will doubtless agree that *The Promised Land* is a compelling act of contrition for all those nationalist effusions that Berton once heaped on the CPR, their national nightmare."[60]

The critical reception accorded to *The Promised Land* effectively marked the end of the academic historians' public struggle over Canadian history as a form of property to be controlled by a priesthood of the past – themselves. They could complain all they liked about how "largely derivative" Berton's new book was, but derivative to whom? Not to the rank and file of Canadians, or perhaps even to the readers of *Quill and Quire*, in which the York University historian Michiel Horn made the charge. For librarians and booksellers who read this book trade magazine, Horn's opening description of *The Promised Land* as "vintage Berton" was likely enough to bring the order form to hand. Hugh Dempsey admitted that being "attractive to the masses" did not necessarily mean there was something wrong with a book, and he found Berton on the prairies "thoroughly entertaining and informative." The business historian Duncan McDowall discovered a healthy mix of colour and veracity, praising the book's author for his vivid detail and his "dutiful archival research," as well as for bringing to the fore as a central theme "the tension between promise and disillusionment, between the expectation of prosperity and the grim reality of mud and crop failure," thereby disabusing the reader of "the heroic myth of western settlement." The reviewer for *Canadian Geographer* conceded that striking a balance between narrative and analysis was difficult for any historian, for emphasis on the former invariably came at the expense of the latter; but he also declared that compared with the superficiality of most other books on the Canadian prairie west, Berton's was "almost a model of scholarship."[61]

It proved more than this for David C. Jones, whose own book *Empire of Dust: Settling and Abandoning the Prairie Dry Belt* was in press. For Jones, *The Promised Land* pointed toward "a new form in the writing of Canadian history." The book may have lacked the magisterial scope and overarching analytical framework of the University of Manitoba historian Gerald Friesen's recently published survey, *The Canadian Prairies: A History*, but it had pace, energy, wit, and vivacity. "It is an artistic unity by a litterateur of many crafts," Jones wrote, "with the skill of a novelist, journalist, and historian combined." Berton's new book stood as a challenge to "the scholar's responsibility to the masses." The eighties had witnessed a decline in the awarding of degrees in history throughout North America, and Jones attributed the trend at least in part to how historians were trained. History students began their apprenticeship "with a fine feeling for public sentiment, with a story weaver's bent and with a deep understanding of the make-up of the common man," he said. However, "when they graduate they have become analysts, shorn of their sensitivity to the common people, with a language and a style as jejune as the Sahara," and "a perversity to keep them that way." For Jones, Friesen and Berton represented models of the academic and popular approaches to history, and what was needed was a history that incorporated the best of both. Berton's work, he said, was far more scholarly than Friesen's was popular.[62]

Before long, Jones predicted, academic historians would come to engage the masses. Their books might then have the wisdom of *The Canadian Prairies*, but the new form would very likely "resemble more the adjustment Berton has already made than the purer, but more constrained paradigm which has guided Friesen."[63] Jones would soon put his formula of an equal measure of Friesen and Berton to good use in *Empire of Dust*, but clearly one of its active ingredients was Alberta optimism, for he underestimated the degree to which academic historians were willing to abandon a readership for status within their guild. With very rare exceptions the career trajectories of Canadian historians of the eighties, especially those dedicated to social history, rejected the ordinary reader and the marketplace. But Jones's characterization of the migration of history graduates away from clear writing and references to person and place gained credence with each passing year – so much so that within a few years Friesen's scholarly book on the history of the prairies would seem positively Bertonesque by comparison.

Berton himself had concluded by the mid-1980s that he now had little to complain about where academic reviews were concerned; only rarely in the future would he comment on them, and even then mainly to help interviewers generate controversial copy. Besides, whenever reviews appeared for one book he was already preoccupied with the next. *The Promised Land* ended with the dreams of the Canadian west "shattered by the nightmare of the Great War." His next work was to be about that war, and he set Barbara Sears to the task almost as soon as she was done with the prairies.

Meanwhile he pressed on, attending convocation ceremonies at Royal Military College in Kingston and the University of Alaska at Fairbanks to receive honorary degrees, speaking at carefully selected events such as the annual general meetings of Pollution Probe and the Ontario Association for Mathematics Education, and turning down a host of other invitations – medal and decoration ceremonies, poetry sweatshops, genealogical societies, farmers' markets, and breakfasts with the stars. An advertising agency representing the Royal Bank attempted to promote the bank's image by linking it to Berton's own in a series of programs for television it proposed to call "Pierre Berton Starring in Canadians: The New Wave." The series tagline, "If You Succeed, We Succeed," was aimed at "the kind of men and women whose attitudes could bring this country out of its recession and into a golden era." Each commercial was to feature the success story of a member of Canada's "new wave." Pierre Berton should be the host and narrator. After all, went the agency's pitch, he was "Mr. Canada." Mr. Canada declined the offer.[64]

23

ON GUARD FOR THEE

—

IN NOVEMBER 1985, PIERRE CAME across the abstract of a paper given at an academic conference by Dr. Lorna Irvine, a professor of English at an American university. The paper was titled "The Real Pierre Berton." That he had become the subject of scholarly study rather than journalistic barbs was another bittersweet reminder that people were beginning to sense his day was done, his oeuvre more or less complete. Stephen Franklin's death in February (the consequence of his third stroke) and Gordon Sinclair's passing the previous spring, at eighty-three, reminded him that he was himself now a senior citizen and reinforced the nagging feeling that Mr. Canada had become yesterday's man.[1]

Irvine had not been the first to subject Berton to sustained scrutiny, or to try to. In 1979, the journalist Jay Myers, who had interviewed him for *Canadian Author and Bookman*, requested six more interviews for a biography he intended to write, entitled "I Just Call Myself a Writer." Berton demurred. He lacked the time for so many interviews, he replied, and further, "I don't think it is a very good idea, from my point of view, for this kind of book." In the same year, he did provide some assistance when Ken Porteus, a fourth-year history student at the University of Winnipeg, wrote a term paper on the academic reception of his historical writing.[2]

By the mid-eighties, as Irvine's paper indicated, scholars in English departments had also become interested in Berton's work. A University of Waterloo graduate student named Jennifer Wilson contacted him in 1985 to arrange a meeting to explore the literary dimensions of his books. Berton met with her on a February afternoon, and by the time he wrote to Lorna Irvine asking for a copy of her paper, he had at hand

Wilson's eighty-one-page study. It examined the literary dimensions of history, the relations between fiction and non-fiction, the structure and themes of romance, and the persistence of the "quest" theme in Western literature. "In a sense," her conclusion began, "we in the historical profession are suffering from our own identity crisis." It was in crisis, she noted, because "inflexible attitudes" and a "denial of the expressive implications" of their field blinded historians to the discovery of meaning – as distinct from explanation – in history. In contrast, an "inherent and persistent romanticism" allowed Berton to embrace a dictum he had encountered many years earlier in his reading of Somerset Maugham: that "only in retrospect" could "the true moments of romance be found." This, Wilson concluded, was Pierre Berton's life-long quest, and she was very close to the mark.[3]

He was no doubt pleased at the literary context Wilson afforded him, for in her paper his historical works stood side by side with Northrop Frye's theories. But he found Irvine's angle more intriguing than Wilson's, for the young Canadian-born professor at George Mason University in Virginia had written about him as a literary confidence man. She had fully explored how his writing revealed the rhetorical strategies of a man "able to persuade people to buy almost anything. . . . Like the characters in whom he shows such interest, Berton appreciates the New World tradition of living by one's wits and approves of the relative classlessness of the confidence mentality. . . . Berton recognizes opportunity; he well knows how to sell Canada – and himself."[4] He could scarcely disagree, for he had written a lot about confidence men over the years and he recognized the type in himself. Like Richler's Duddy Kravitz and Schulberg's Sammy Glick, he lived by hustle and wits, and was proud of it.

Earlier in the year, his actions as an author had provided Irvine with remarkable evidence for her thesis. On Thursday, July 11, 1985, a day before his sixty-fifth birthday, a special event had taken place at Toronto's King Edward hotel. At an elaborately staged media event, Paul Soles, as moderator, challenged a panel of three local celebrities – the politician and author William Kilbourn, the actor Dinah Christie, and the media gadfly Pierre Berton – to determine the identity of a neo-phyte author named Lisa Kroniak, author of the recently published M&S novel *Masquerade*, a collection of fifteen sexual fantasies centred upon the goings-on in an upscale brothel. In the May 25 press release for the book, Kroniak was quoted as saying, "When I meet someone I tend to act out what I consider to be that person's perception of me. Everybody does it. But it's especially true of lovers. Lovers definitely are into role-playing. A love affair is a masquerade in which each partner tailors his role to the other person's needs and desires."[5]

In the manner of the quiz show *To Tell the Truth*, the panellists questioned three masked women to try to figure out which among them was the novelist. When none appeared to be a suitable candidate, Soles adjusted the famous words to suit the occasion. "Will the real Lisa Kroniak please stand up?" he asked. Pierre Berton rose to full height.

An audible gasp filled the room. No one except Elsa Franklin, who had acted as Lisa Kroniak's agent, had been in on the hoax. Janet Berton and Jack McClelland had been left in the dark. If the press release entitled "A Sporting Proposition for Jack McClelland" is to be believed, when Kroniak learned that Jack McClelland decided to cease having book launch parties for reasons of economy, she decided to make him a sporting proposition: she would pay for a media party, but if her book went into a second printing as a result, McClelland would become responsible for the expenses. "I believe it's an offer you can't refuse," Kroniak was quoted as having written to the publisher.[6]

McClelland & Stewart's editors had been lukewarm about the submission, thinking it might be "too European" for Canadian tastes. Jack asked Janet Turnbull, in charge of Seal Books, to read the manuscript. "I hunted through this manuscript to find anything worthwhile in it," she reported, "but I'm sorry, Jack, MASQUERADE is one of the worst books I've looked at seriously in a long time. I have no problem with a book of straight sexual fantasy. . . . What I do have problems with is a book of boring sexual fantasy. . . . Ms. Kroniak isn't a bad writer, line-for-line. If she applied herself to something meaty, like a strongly plotted contemporary sexual novel, she might be worthwhile." Nonetheless, M&S president Linda McKnight, who may not have seen Turnbull's assessment, had taken a chance on the unknown emigrant novelist living somewhere in the West, with an offer of a $1,000 advance. This was a full $49,000 less than the lowest advance M&S had ever offered Pierre Berton. Upon release, the book languished on bookstore shelves. Major dailies largely ignored the book, but a few offered comments.

"Entertaining but somewhat flawed in execution," wrote Laszlo Buhasz, an assistant editor at the *Globe and Mail*. Writing in the *Gazette*, Michael Carin spoke of "an oily prose somewhere on the dipstick between Harlequin and *Penthouse*."[7]

On a day when the front page of the *Globe* expressed concern about the difficulties of getting at the truth behind the recent Air-India disaster, Berton made headlines. "Literary Masquerade Was a Ball for Berton," read the title above a William French story. The piece had legs enough that the newspaper ran the item almost word for word the next day in its Saturday edition. The stunt Berton and Franklin had pulled off was covered by newspapers across the country; a week later, the W.H. Smith book chain purchased all remaining copies of *Masquerade*. By then, M&S was considering a second paperback printing and a special hardcover edition.[8]

According to Elsa Franklin, Berton decided to mount the hoax as a lark, and very likely he did find it as much fun as releasing a greased pig in a Vancouver ballroom. But the book had been in the works for about three years. The idea had come to him in the middle of the night in London when, suffering from jet lag, he imagined a bordello in which all manner of sexual fantasies could be realized. Later, on a Caribbean vacation, he began to write it. Some of his motivation arose from questions that had lingered in his mind over "72 Wedgewood Crescent" and Jack's reluctance to publish it in the early sixties. Could he write a decent novel? Would readers buy a work of fiction by Pierre Berton? Would "72 Wedgewood Crescent" have sold well had it been published? Did people buy his books on their own merit or simply because of his name? The reception afforded to *Masquerade* helped answer these nagging questions; besides, this was his benign latter-day revenge on M&S for its earlier editorial timidity.[9]

Berton had great fun concocting the characters that featured in his "fifteen variations on a theme of sexual fantasy," even if they were rendered in cardboard remaindered from "72 Wedgewood Crescent": Erika the perennial schoolgirl; Candace, "antiseptic in her starched nurse's uniform"; Julio, the beautiful young man in mascara; Lara, the very model of innocence, who becomes Ilsa, "the Bitch of Berlin"; Andrea, queen of the jungle; Shana, "every woman's fantasy"; three nuns, named Flame, Lola, and Bibi; Alix, the schoolmarm in tweed suit and thick glasses, looking forty but only twenty-four; and Turk, in his truck driver's outfit.

Sexual fantasies that arise at three in the morning, as Berton's did in that London hotel, are driven not by ideas but by urges, and in his mid-sixties Berton still had both. But the Sordsmen's Club had slowly languished and then . . . well, petered out as its members aged, and Berton found he liked his recently acquired public image as respectable national paterfamilias rather than rakish rogue. His had always been a life rich in dreamscape and fantasy, and of course some of both were sexual in nature. His imagination gave body to his fantasies, and his affluence and style of life afforded him the luxury of indulging them should he wish to do so.

In *Masquerade*, refractions of Berton's longing made their way into the male "clients" he created. A customer named Marcus longs "to get away . . . for an adventure – any adventure – even if it [means] flirting with death."[10] Another, long-married Karl, loves his wife, Anna, but is no longer satisfied and seeks excitement in other ways. Hugo has never married, but he has a long-time married mistress as well as several casual girlfriends. Even so, he is bored and consults a psychiatrist, Dr. Virek, who encourages him to be more adventurous. "Society has become permissive, even blasé," Virek tells him. "What was once sinful has now become normal. What was once bizarre has become chic." Hugo's fantasies, in short, have not sufficiently kept up with the sexually liberated times, not enough to allow him "to continue to enjoy that delicious feeling of wickedness, of nonconformity." Psychiatrist and client agree that a homosexual encounter is in order. With the assistance of Andrea, Hugo hooks up with a beautiful young man named Julio. They attend a Beethoven concert and later share a bottle of wine in Julio's apartment. He is aware that Julio is impressed by his age and superior knowledge, and is drawn to him. "Will you take me to the movies again, tomorrow?" Julio asks. "Hugo nodded gently, feeling Julio's hand on his shoulder. The hand moved slowly down his arm, briefly touched his own outstretched palm, searched and discovered his inner thigh. Hugo felt a small tingle, took a deep breath, closed his eyes. A moment later, it seemed the most natural thing in the world to take the young man in his arms."[11]

It is beyond doubt that Pierre Berton was a heterosexual male, but it is equally indisputable that this was a man whose embrace of life was as capacious as possible. Curiosity was a lifelong trait; a preoccupation with varieties of sexual experience surfaced in *Masquerade*. At times when he needed advice, especially about his dreams, he consulted the model for Dr. Virek, a Willowdale psychiatrist he had known for many years. Whatever his personal experience, it's likely that Berton approved of the advice that his fictional therapist offers to his bored protagonist: "Think of it as therapy," Dr. Virek tells Hugo. "Everybody should try everything once."[12]

After three years as president and publisher of McClelland & Stewart, Linda McKnight had come to find her position an impossible one. The problem was Jack McClelland, whose pledge to give her free rein had proved an empty promise. On the one hand, he spoke often, whether in public or in private, of his intention to divest himself of the company and leave the publishing industry entirely; on the other, he had invested so much of himself in M&S that its fate seemed inextricably linked to his own. He could not let go, content to relish his emeritus position as McKnight suggested he should in 1984. As his biographer James King observed, Jack had become "trapped within the machinery he had invented."[13]

McClelland's relationship with those in charge of his own firm reached its nadir in mid-1985. The issue was Jack's willingness to sell paperback rights to M&S titles, from L.M. Montgomery to the core of the contemporary stable – including Farley Mowat, Margaret Laurence, Margaret Atwood, and Mordecai Richler – to Seal Books, a mass-market paperback imprint owned jointly by McClelland & Stewart and Bantam Books of New York, for far less than the properties' value. Even worse, he consulted neither the M&S editorial director Valerie Thompson nor Linda McKnight; the former heard about the apparent deal from the competition. With her authority undercut and important M&S assets about to be sold from under her, McKnight had little choice but to submit her resignation. McClelland returned to the presidency, and so did his combination of charm and bluster. But everybody in the industry knew that M&S was in a state of perilous disorder. At Queen's Park, in fact, McClelland himself had become a symbol of an industry that was capricious and therefore a bad investment. "There was always a feeling in the Ontario government," one senior official told the *Toronto Star* books editor and columnist Roy MacSkimming, "that Jack was a loser."[14]

McClelland had no sooner settled once again into his former role than the Royal Bank of Canada announced that it expected McClelland & Stewart's line of credit, recently expanded, to be repaid. Unable to meet the demand, Jack contacted a member of his board of directors for assistance, the real estate developer Avie Bennett, who had helped arrange the Royal Bank financing. Bennett offered more than assistance: he offered to buy the company. By the end of 1985, the deal was done. He paid McClelland $1 million for his shares and M&S investors another $1 million in order to assume full control of the firm. Bennett moved M&S from the old Maclean Hunter building to a property at the corner of University Avenue and Dundas Street, which he designated McClelland & Stewart House. He agreed to retain Jack McClelland in an advisory capacity for five years, and the two men settled into a somewhat uneasy relationship in offices at either end of the executive suite. Within a year, by mutual agreement, McClelland vacated his office and the company.[15]

Meanwhile, Elsa and Pierre remained as inseparable as ever. They now had another television show ready to air, this one produced by CHCH-TV in Hamilton but running on the CBC network. It was a drama series called *Heritage Theatre*, and they produced it on a very modest budget (initially $25,000 per show, raised by an incredulous Telefilm Canada to $30,000) and with equally modest costumes and simple sets. But they employed the best actors in Canada – Bruno Gerussi, Graham Greene, Eric House, Frances Hyland, Gordon Pinsent, Fiona Reid, R.H. Thomson, and others – and took pride in paying them above union scale. Altogether, they turned out twenty-six half-hour shows that dramatized scenes from Canadian history. Lister Sinclair wrote the scripts, and Berton edited the stories and acted as on-camera narrator, while Franklin coordinated all other details.[16] She also accompanied him whenever he was on tour. Their relationship was quite literally so close that in 1981 Pierre had Ennis Armstrong write to the management of Four Seasons Hotels to complain that its Ottawa establishment had not met his request for "two rooms either connected or adjoining."[17]

In June 1986, the first *Heritage Theatre* episodes aired on CBC television each Saturday night. On Canada Day, along with the politician Jean Marchand, Pierre Berton was elevated to Companion of the Order of Canada, the order's highest rank. (Ramsay Cook, Peter Gzowski, and Ben Wicks were among those named to the order the same day.) Throughout the summer, the Berton publishing juggernaut proceeded apace. *Vimy*, his fall offering, was being readied at M&S for its release, while Barbara Sears was researching his next work, on Arctic exploration. During five days of a holiday in Victoria in late summer, he churned out sixty thousand words of the first volume of his autobiography. When *Vimy* appeared early in September, his work schedule was such that he knew he would start to write *The Arctic Grail* the following April.[18]

Vimy was an obvious choice as the book to follow *The Promised Land*. Berton's story of the settling of the Canadian west had begun and ended with scenes, based on an actual historical figure, set at the Winnipeg railway station on a single day in the summers of 1895 and 1914. In the book's opening, a young Slavic professor of agriculture, dressed formally in "a neat, dark suit," dreams of a future of peace and prosperity in the promised land; at its conclusion, the same man, Josef Olekskow, clad in khaki, departs from the railway platform for Europe and war, ready to sacrifice himself for his new country. *The Promised Land*, as its first line stated, was "about dreams and illusions, escape and survival, triumph and despair," and about foolish optimism and eventual disenchantment; and of 1914, Berton wrote: "The dreamers themselves went off to the battlefields and were themselves shattered." The Great War epitomized such themes. Canada's greatest moment in the war had been the taking of Vimy Ridge on Easter Sunday, 1917. At that moment, Berton argued, Canada passed a critical test.[19]

When Elspeth Cameron interviewed Barbara Sears for *Saturday Night* early in December 1986, *Vimy* was flying off bookstore shelves, and material for the book still lingered in the researcher's mind. Sears had been skeptical about the subject. Not Canadian-born, she had not sensed Vimy's significance. It was not the Somme, or Passchendaele; as a battle, it lacked their length or complexity and held less interest for her. Further, she was not especially sympathetic to Berton's incessant blowing of his nationalist trumpet. But he had no doubts about his new subject, so she had undertaken the research. She gathered material from old accounts of the battle and read through the classic studies of Basil Liddell Hart and A. Fortescue Duguid and the recent work of Jack Granatstein, Desmond Morton, and Reginald Roy. Her final bibliography included over 150 such sources. To sixty-three interviews with veterans of the First World War conducted earlier by the CBC for the television series *In Flanders Fields*, she and Berton added more than seventy of their own, the vast majority of which she conducted. She found these interviews emotionally taxing, for it was difficult going into the homes of men in their eighties and nineties and raising a subject that in many cases they had avoided talking about for more than sixty years. Minds would wander, words would fail, but at times the exercise evoked memories that to Sears seemed "fresher than what happened yesterday." Often, the interview sessions yielded written documents – letters, diaries, memoirs – that had not seen the light of day. These became the core of the book's research.[20]

When Janice Tyrwhitt first read the manuscript of *Vimy*, she was horrified. It was full of guns and carnage – a real "gung ho," *Boy's Own* kind of story, she told Cameron. Likely with John McCrae's poem "In Flanders Fields" in mind, Berton had the action taking place in Flanders rather than in Artois, and he had larded his text with far too much undigested factual detail. The battle action proved impossible to follow, and the overall tone of the book was wrong. In short, he had produced a mess.

Her report on the manuscript went through his draft chapter by chapter, for more than sixty pages. The whole structure of the book needed to be changed, including its beginning and ending. Even the corpses needed character, and the characters needed continuity. The book, she said, should be for people with no relatives at Vimy, and especially for the generations who knew little about the First World War and felt war was wrong. "I said, 'You've got to understand [that] to someone young or to women, all this [is] meaningless and unsympathetic.'" He needed "to get more irony and ruefulness and caring" into the book. Try for "passionate engagement," she told him, "not the broad canvas of the War of 1812 books."[21]

Berton took Tyrwhitt's lengthy critique to heart and overhauled his manuscript completely. He cut away the overheated prose – enough, Tyrwhitt told Cameron, to turn "bad Kipling into good Kipling." He broke down the battle scenes into thirty-four sections, lending coherence to chaos. He produced the new opening and ending she wanted, readily adopting her suggestion to take a section from the middle of the manuscript, "Ten Thousand Thunders," and use it as the opening set piece. The earlier draft had concluded with the flower of Canadian youth going off to death and glory, but Tyrwhitt had warned him that this ran contrary to the ethos of the mid-eighties. The final passages of the new draft better reflected the values of the new day and Berton's own beliefs about war. In stark detail, *Vimy* in final form laid out the heroism and horror of the taking of the ridge and explained why Canadians in 1917 saw the battle as an important milestone in the making of the nation. It provided an abundance of evidence why Canadians who read the book should remain proud of their forebears, but it also reflected the anti-war views of the decade. "Was it worth it?" he asked. The generation of 1914 had said yes, believing that the Great War would end all war. The next generation had discovered otherwise, but clung to a second justification for the carnage. "Because of Vimy, we told ourselves, Canada came of age; because of Vimy, our country found its manhood. But was *that* worth it? Was it worth the loss of thousands of limbs and eyes and the deaths of five thousand Canadians at Vimy to provide a young and growing nation with a proud and enduring myth? Now that the Vimy fever has cooled, a new generation sees the Great War for what it was. . . . Was it worth it? The answer, of course, is *no*."[22]

This simple but firm answer echoed the one he had provided earlier concerning the War of 1812. The affirmation reflected his long-held beliefs. Years earlier, he had written about the futility of the UN intervention in Korea, the only war in which he had been near the sharp end of the stick, and he had been a vocal opponent of the disastrous American misadventure in Vietnam in the 1960s and early seventies. In the future, he would place himself on record as a strong opponent of the first and second invasions of Iraq. On the Second World War alone was he equivocal, for while he regarded his own experience of it as a waste of time and training, there remained the black perfidy of Hitler and the Nazi regime, and the searing images of the death camps – made more sickening because he had first seen them thanks to the magic of a silver screen in the comfort of a London theatre.

In examining the battle for Vimy Ridge, a Berton book once again took an important event in Canadian history, evoked its mythic dimensions, and then punctured and reconstituted the myth in such a way that it continued to hold enduring power. The war had not been worth the sacrifice, but Canada had indeed come of age. *Vimy* was very much, in Berton's view, "a new book for a new generation." When he wrote it, he had in mind a remark made in one of the reviews of *The Last Spike* – to the effect that "every generation gets, and in fact needs, its own version of the building of the CPR."[23]

Pierre had no intention of glorifying war, but he did want to draw attention to the heroic dimension of it. In at least one instance he ignored evidence in order to do so. Years earlier, an old friend from the *Maclean's* years, Dave Macdonald, had considered writing a biography of Billy Bishop but abandoned the idea when Bishop's son Arthur took up the project. By then, however, Macdonald had read through Billy Bishop's wartime correspondence. In a letter to Berton at the end of 1985, he quoted extensively from his notes, which suggested that Bishop was "a falsely modest blowhard – totally self-centred . . . and quite capable of any deceit to get whatever he wanted." For Macdonald, Bishop had been an obsessively self-aggrandizing seeker after fame, decoration, and glory in warfare, and many of his exploits seemed dubious. He quoted from one of Bishop's squadron-mates and friends, who summed up the man by saying, "Bish has the face of an angel, and the mind of a thief." He recounted that when Arthur Bishop was about sixteen, his father had "boasted to him of all the famous women he'd laid in his day, including Rita Hayworth. During his fatherly recitation, Billy's wife – Arthur's mother – was knitting in the next room. 'This may sound terrible,' Arthur told me, 'but he had absolutely no conscience.'" Macdonald provided several instances in the life of the war ace that demonstrated this, but when *Vimy* came out, the portrayal of Billy Bishop was the Bishop of legend, observing enemy attacks from the air, destroying enemy balloons, engaging in dogfights, and winning the Military Cross.[24]

The military historian Brereton Greenhous did his best in *Quill and Quire* to warn readers of Berton's overcharged imagination and errors of fact – that Berton got the colour on the ribbon of the Victoria Cross wrong, for example – and to let readers know that description is not the same as explanation. But the editor's title for the Greenhous feature review, "War Stories to Further Our Social Mythology," made the professor merely seem pedantic. In *Maclean's*, John Bemrose chided Berton for his effusive nationalism, and for his "unrestrained booster-ism," but noted the pride that lit the pages of his book. In *Books in Canada*, the military historian Desmond Morton pointed out errors, and twice referred to Berton's "researchers" – forgetting, perhaps, that his quip that "frequent repetition does not guarantee truth" applied as much to a reviewer as to an author under review. But Morton confirmed Berton's contention that Vimy had been the moment when Canada "was transformed from colony to nation," and that the Canadians who had been there on April 9, 1917, "had felt it in their bones." The subject, he said, was as natural for "the faithful chronicler of our national epics" to turn to as "the War of 1812, the building of the CPR, and the settle-ment of the Canadian West." *Alberta Report* found a contemporary message in *Vimy's* vivid account of "the battle that forged a nation," but also a certain sadness of tone that lamented the loss of a pioneer-ing spirit that had "found its finest expression on a French battlefield and then was submerged in the dross of 20th century urbanization and Americanization."[25]

Berton counted *Vimy* as his thirty-third book. It was his ninth major contribution to an understanding of Canadian history. He had more in him still. Moreover, the next ten years were flanked by volumes of auto-biography which marked the boundaries of a decade in which his country's past and his own became increasingly linked, so much so that his own causes and those of the nation seemed at times to be the same. So vaunted had his reputation become that he was able to frame

Starting Out, the story of his rough beginnings and dedicated to his sister, Lucy, against his image as a "Well-Known Personality," secure in the knowledge that the assertion would be regarded as understatement. "I hate to be called a personality," he told the journalist Paul Kennedy in 1986, but at no point in his career did he deny that he enjoyed being one. "There are no rules in this country that say you have to be a celebrity. But I think you have to enjoy it. Some people say that they hate it, but that's bullshit."[26]

Fame has distinct advantages. It means, for one thing, that when you have an autographing session at a bookstore, crowds show up. Gone were the days when Farley Mowat and Berton would idle away their time at a table in a Montreal bookstore, each signing his name to the other's books for a laugh. Berton had little doubt that his celebrity, as much as the subjects he wrote about, sold his books. "If they've read my books before," he told Kennedy, "they'll come out and buy one for someone else. They give them away at Christmas. People don't read books in this country, they give them away as presents." It was this kind of statement that, for Lorna Irvine, had exposed the confidence man in him. As he said to Kennedy: "I wouldn't be writing this stuff if there weren't the market for it."[27]

A good confidence man could use his skill to sell virtue, too, especially if he believed fervently in the justness of a cause. Throughout the 1980s, he used his public presence to publicize worthy causes he had always supported, and others. He drew attention to any infringement of civil liberties that came to his notice. In 1985, when Peggy Anne was a twenty-four-year-old art student living in New York City, she was removed from a bus at the Canadian border, accused of carrying illegal drugs, abused verbally, and strip-searched by a female Canadian customs officer. No drugs were found. Her angry father protested vociferously. "This was just a wild goose chase," Berton said.[28]

For a period early in the 1980s he tried half-heartedly to distance himself from claims that he was too preoccupied with Canadian nationalism, for he had quipped some time earlier that "Canadian nationalism is deader than a dodo." But the rise of the free trade issue in the middle years of the decade under a Progressive Conservative government that preached the neo-conservative gospel of unfettered market competition, together with government cuts in funding for the CBC, occurred while he was at work on *Vimy*. He found it grating to be writing a book about the sacrifice an earlier generation had made for the nation while the government of the day seemed ready to make the "silent surrender" to American interests and culture that Kari Levitt and Herschel Hardin had warned about in the 1970s. He detested Brian Mulroney's government and called its plans for free trade with the United States "an imminent threat" to Canada's future, as Macdonald had labelled free trade in 1891 and Borden in 1911.[29]

In the second half of the eighties, with the nation badly divided, he glimpsed a renewal in nationalist feeling and political engagement, and used his cultural authority whenever possible to support causes or oppose measures important to him. He was in Ottawa for the founding meeting of the Council of Canadians in 1985, when a number of prominent Canadians met to organize opposition to the policy initiatives of the recently elected Mulroney government. Along with other council members, he had expressed concern when the American icebreaker *Polar Sea* traversed the Northwest Passage that August without permission or protest from the Canadian government. His was the first name on the full-page public appeal the council placed in Canadian newspapers in September 1987 under the title "The Future of Canada Is on the Table." The public statement warned citizens about the "growing evidence that the so-called 'free trade' agreement our federal government is actively pursuing will, at best, seriously compromise Canadian sovereignty and could eventually force Canada into union with the U.S." The nation, it declared, was up for sale. Who would stand on guard for Canada? Berton, among others. He contributed to and helped promote *If You Love This Country*, a 1988 anti-free-trade book put out by McClelland & Stewart, with contributions from the progressive left – Mel Hurtig, Rick Salutin, Michele Landsberg, the labour leader Bob White, and the geneticist and environmentalist David Suzuki, for example. (Walter Gordon, an obvious contributor, had died in March 1987.) With essays as well by Margaret Atwood, Graeme Gibson, Jack McClelland, and Farley Mowat, the volume seemed very much like the campaign tract of "the Canadian Publishers" that it was.[30]

He also became a founding member of the Group of 78. The loose association, counting among its members Margaret Atwood, Tommy Douglas, Margaret Laurence, the diplomat and environmental activist

Maurice Strong, the broadcaster Patrick Watson, and John Polanyi, winner of the 1986 Nobel Prize in Chemistry, sought to integrate global priorities, including peace and disarmament, equitable international development, and a strong and revitalized United Nations. Specific projects included economic recovery for Africa, the famine in Ethiopia, and a formal response to the federal government's 1987 White Paper on Defence. Desmond Morton described that policy document at the time as "a compromise between defence advice, public opinion, and business and regional lobbies," each one insisting that the $10-billion defence budget be designed for its benefit. The white paper was also riddled with Cold War rhetoric. A year later, Berton teamed up with a group that included Atwood, Farley Mowat, David Suzuki, Peter Newman, June Callwood, and the folk musician Gordon Lightfoot to call for a national television debate on the "desperate environmental situation." An honorary chief of Alberta's Blood Tribe since 1971, as Chief Big Plume he helped raise funds for a cultural and religious centre on the reserve in 1987. He objected strenuously to the recommendation of the Nielsen Task Force that the federal Department of Communications remove the postal subsidy for library books sent by mail.[31]

While his reform spirit remained willing, his body slowed him down. Following the thrombosis scare of 1983 it became necessary to monitor his health more carefully. He suffered pain from muscle spasms and pinched nerves, and consulted Allan Knight of the Sunnybrook Medical Centre for treatment. Entries for therapy, blood tests, specialists, and dietitians vied with luncheon dates for time in his schedule. By 1986, he had conceded that his energy was on the wane, even for writing. In his prime, he had often written fifteen thousand words a day, working from morning to midnight; the half-dozen assignments handed to him at six in the morning would be done by noon. Now he was happy if he could produce fifteen typed pages a day. Perri, his youngest, had moved out, and the house – described by an observer as "somewhat reminiscent of a hunting lodge, with skin drums, native sculpture and tribal masks, an old stone fireplace, brimming bookshelves and family gifts" – was now peaceful during the week. On weekends, however, it came alive, for the children and grandchildren regularly headed north to its frenetic kitchen and its dining room table still regularly set for twenty.[32]

He had reached the obvious stage at which to write an autobiography and reflect upon the contours of a hectic life. Ross McLean had died at the beginning of June 1987, at sixty-two, and a legion of stories were gone with him. Word had it that Robert Fulford was writing his memoirs. So Berton pressed on to complete his own.[33] "Life was fast fading away," he wrote of his frame of mind at the time. Besides, he added, he wanted to write about his newspaper years. The reasoning is telling. The sense of urgency driven by intimations of mortality was there, but to what purpose? For him, it was not to reflect on the meaning of life, or to confront a past; instead it was to meet his need to tell the story of his days as a gonzo journalist on the West Coast. Berton was not motivated by this alone, but to the extent that writing an autobiography involves the presentation of a life that is inevitably a tale, Berton the autobiographer became captive to his role as exactly that: a lifelong teller of tales.

Berton had written so much about himself and had given so many interviews about his life and times since the late 1950s that he had come to possess a kind of mental Rolodex of set-piece episodes from the life of Pierre, ready to flip to whenever one was needed. Harried newspaper reporters, magazine writers, and book reviewers consulted clippings of past interviews in the company morgue before they arrived for their own interview with the grand old man. The result was frequent repetition of the same old questions, followed by freshly minted restatements of the same old answers, all serving the purpose of reinforcing the well-honed narrative of his life. Only after the session was over might the serious journalist recognize the lack of depth or revelation in the notebook or on the tape recorder. The lazy reporter scarcely cared: he had good copy. The one fruitful result was that the Berton legend lived on, each new decade of readers learning about its northern origins and its rapid rise to the heights in the centre of Canada.

Starting Out was written quickly, and largely from memory, with little recourse to the relevant personal documents. His motivation came less from inner necessity than from the needs of the fall list. He had promised M&S a book for the fall of 1987, but his volume on Arctic exploration was still in progress, so he hammered out the story of his life, from birth to the move to Toronto. Reviewers were ambivalent when the book came out in September 1987. No reviewer denied that

Berton's life was worth an autobiography, despite John Haslett Cuff's comment earlier in the year that the man had been "so aggressively ubiquitous" for so many years that "the tendency is to yawn when his name comes up." Indeed, most reviews gleefully repeated some of the book's best anecdotes. They also remarked on its lack of depth. "The lack of introspection is both intriguing and typical: for all his noted readiness with an opinion, Berton the man remains curiously opaque," wrote John Bemrose in *Maclean's*. William French and Al Purdy made similar comments. All the tales he told about himself had been put in sequence, life as anecdote.[34] The man had connected through words the oft-drawn scenes of his life, together with a few stories not yet told. His Klondike upbringing had been a staple of newspaper accounts since the 1940s, and very likely it was the best-known story of any Canadian childhood. He had so peppered the press with tall tales of his wild days as a Vancouver reporter that Allan Fotheringham (the old *Ubyssey* hand who had replaced Gordon Sinclair on *Front Page Challenge*) gleefully rehashed them over and over again in his own columns, first in the *Vancouver Sun* and then on the back page of *Maclean's*.

The signposts of Berton's life all went on display in *Starting Out*, like so many caches of pemmican on a fur-trade route: the isolated but magical childhood in Dawson; the remarkable and attentive parents; the exuberance of youth; the excited discovery of life on the "outside"; the hustling college reporter; the brash newspaperman with the brilliant scoop; the rise to national attention; and, finally, the move east with fame and fortune clearly on the horizon. The young self he chose to present to others was a natural romantic, in love with life and wanting it all, a boy with an insatiable hunger for facts and an equally limitless need to express himself; an awkward, sensitive, naive youth who only gradually became wise to the world. The mature self that is the autobiographer's voice in *Starting Out* is a narrator in firm possession of the facts of his own life, like the reporter he becomes as the book unfolds – a man at once self-deprecating and self-assured, who has not planned his life but who has missed few of the opportunities that have come his way. As narrator of this story, he is a man who can laugh at the foibles of his youth and not be afraid of lampooning his vaunted status as a "Well-Known Personality." He is an authority whom readers can trust and count upon to be frank when candour is required – revealing his fling with Frances in London, for example. A man, above all, who is a skilful storyteller with the capacity to be observant and objective, even about himself.

The story Berton told was indeed his story, as far as it went, and it contained remarkably few errors of fact, for his memory remained prodigious even in his mid-sixties. But *Starting Out* also revealed transparently that its author did not possess the kind of brooding introspection, often used for self-recovery, that increasingly characterized autobiography and memoir in the 1980s. "No one has ever accused Berton of being profound," wrote the *Globe and Mail* reviewer William French. "He's by turns nostalgic, zesty and benign, and obviously enjoyed recalling what he describes as the sweet summer of his youth. He seems bemused by the image of himself as the hot-shot young reporter, intent on scoops." The salient word here is *bemused*, for something within Berton required the security of distance, even from himself. "I'm not one of those people who goes into long periods of self-examination," he told a reporter over a beer. "That's why I'm not a poet, I guess." Then, raising his glass, he said: "My attitude towards life, basically, is that it's one hilarious joke."[35]

This degree of self-knowledge he possessed, but even here he might have tried to prod deeper. Instead, one reviewer did it for him. Writing in *Queen's Quarterly*, William Closson James, a professor of religion at Queen's University, noted Berton's unwillingness to engage in the autobiographer's "process of self-discovery as the wellsprings of the inner life are uncovered." His strengths were instead those of the reporter: objective detachment, an eye for detail, and recognition of the memorable and the unusual. But these very qualities worked against the grain of introspection, leading instead toward the most basic, descriptive kind of self-study. Berton, James wrote (following the critic James Olney), was the kind of autobiographer who bears witness rather than burrows within; the kind "who separates his former from his present self, tries to narrate the events of his life after the fact (but shows little awareness of that assumed point of view), attempts to get out of his own skin, and seems to have reached a point of development beyond which there will be no more change."[36]

The "bemused" Berton that William French observed, one who suggested an acquired ability to laugh at an earlier self, was for James a man whose seeming objectivity served as a defence mechanism. The preoccupation with his early days marked a certain detachment from it, despite its deep influence. The mocking of his celebrity status did not seem genuine, coming across instead as a "mock embarrassment or feigned self-consciousness." Berton paid a price for his candour, for it came, James observed, "at the expense of severing the connection between his past and present lives – the Well-Known Personality can afford to laugh at the awkward and insecure youth."[37] The older Berton, he might have noted had he known more of Berton's life, could afford to cast Frances in the role of seductress, thereby absolving himself of responsibility for his actions or for the child he likely left in his wake. "That stuff in England," he told one reporter, "well, I think it's illustrative not so much of me but of those crazy, bizarre times."[38]

As a literary work, *Starting Out* made for interesting reading, but it resembled something that might have appeared in the Victorian era, a latter-day mix of a character-building Dickensian childhood, lots of self-help in the manner of Samuel Smiles, and the late-imperial romantic adventure inspired by the Baden-Powell or Kipling of his youth: a life at once rough, plucky, and adventurous. As such, it stood in stark contrast with other books at the time. On the same page of the *Globe and Mail* where William French's review of *Starting Out* appeared, two other titles received notice. One was a history of Rochdale College, the failed experiment in co-operative student residential living on Toronto's Bloor Street that had gone from utopian vision through hippie haven to drug den within a few years in the late sixties and early seventies. The other was Sylvia Fraser's *My Father's House*, a searing memoir of sexual molestation.[39]

Measured against such works, one a tale of self-indulgent excess and the other a story of truth revealed through flashes of painful recollection, *Starting Out* appeared time-worn in tone, form, and content. The son of Laura and Frank reined in his candidness with circumspection just before reaching the point of meaningful self-awareness. He was no doubt engaged in a genuine search for his earlier self, but his storytelling deployed the kind of "superfluity of detail" that lends historical narrative the appearance of objectivity. The problem was that self-absorption and personal revelation were becoming key ingredients in new writing about the self. Mere anecdotal exposition without inner emotional

intensity was no longer in favour. Truth, toward the end of the twentieth century, was as fragmentary as memory. No form of narrative was
any longer to be trusted.[40]

Commentators on Berton's promotion of *Starting Out* noted that
release of the book seemed to have energized him. A disc problem in his
back continued to give trouble, and it affected the use of his arms, but
his only concession to it was that he walked more gingerly. His son
Peter designed a new office for him. A different chair and use of a pillow
lessened the stress on his back, and a desktop that sloped toward him
(designed by Peter from an idea by Charles Templeton) eased the ten-
dinitis caused by almost a half-century of pounding his typewriter. A
controlled and insulin-free diabetic, he monitored his weight and his
diet carefully. Salmon and broccoli replaced the steak and cocktail
lunches of yesteryear. In fact he had become a bit heavier, but with
regular workouts he looked leaner and showed no sign of the drain of
the book tour. A *Vancouver Sun* reporter, Doug Sagi, speculated that
perhaps this had something to do with the new book's subject matter.
"You really have to have a sense of what the public wants to read,"
Berton told Sagi. "That's why he chose Pierre Berton as the subject for
his latest book," the reporter suggested in his story.[41]

The revitalized Berton was an active chairman of the Writers' Union
of Canada in 1987–88. His example within the union had inspired many
authors over the years: William Deverell, for example. "I can remember
on many occasions, how he attacked milksop, overly tame resolutions,
particularly on political or civil rights issues, and almost invariably
swung enough people to see matters his way, with eloquence, yes, but
also unparalleled logic." Deverell recalled only two instances when a
union vote did not go Berton's way, such was his suasive power and the
respect with which he was held.[42] During his presidential year, Berton
went on what William French called "a coast-to-coast pilgrimage" to
improve the standards of book reviewing in the country. That year the
union initially visited three newspapers – the Halifax *Chronicle-Herald*,
the *Edmonton Journal*, and the *Vancouver Sun* – trying to coax book
review editors into providing better coverage. Later it conducted a
national survey of key book review pages, and provided a report card on
the results. Inspired by this initiative, and either smarting from a dismissive review William French had given *Starting Out* the week before or

determined to exact a little revenge for academic criticism over the years, Berton tore apart the impressive-looking new volume *The Illustrated History of Canada*, not for its content but for its writing. Of its six eminent academic authors, including Ramsay Cook, Desmond Morton, and P.B. Waite, only the third of these escaped his wrath. Waite's contribution, Berton said, was "a model of what the others should be. After the turgid style of the textbook prose [of some of the other contributors], his is positively breezy. He actually describes his people."[43]

Other new Berton initiatives were more positive. He led the Writers' Union lobby against the federal government's proposed pornography legislation (Bill C-54) and continued to be an active member of the steering committee of the Friends of Public Broadcasting, founded in 1984. The following February his was one of 1,284 names of prominent Canadians beneath an open letter in the *Globe and Mail* to Prime Minister Mulroney warning that his government's cuts to the CBC budget constituted the worst threat to public broadcasting since the founding of the corporation in the 1930s. He also claimed to be the president and sole member of the Society for the Preservation of the Word Unique.[44]

The renewed energy carried over into his writing. When *Vimy* neared completion, he sat down with Barbara Sears and mulled over ideas for a subject less onerous and taxing. They came up with a book intended to resemble *My Country*, a series of light profiles, this time of the Arctic explorers who had sought the Northwest Passage. "What I had in mind," he later confessed, "was another superficial book – something I could knock off in a few months."[45] He ought to have known better, and perhaps at some level he did, for he must have recognized that this subject would inevitably steer him toward his first and most instinctive theme. The idea that all of life is a quest arose from his need to understand the meaning of his father's journey to the gold fields almost a century earlier. That, surely, had been the personal meaning of the epigraph he had invented for *Klondike*: "'Instead, at the end of every trail, I have found you awaiting me. And now you have become familiar to me, though I cannot say I know you well. Who are you?' And the stranger answered: 'Thyself.'"

The quest theme had been central to Jennifer Wilson's paper. Following Northrop Frye and Frank Kermode, she had argued that the human search for identity was central to the structure of romance.

The object of any romantic quest is less to articulate what constitutes that identity than to achieve self-understanding as one encounters the descents and ascents of life. Invariably, this involves a fall from grace and a struggle to recover it, then deliverance and redemption. Wilson had charted in Berton's writings the presence of the idea of the quest in every historical work he had written. It ran like a rich vein through *Klondike*, for the search for gold was really a search for self. It resided in the railways of *The National Dream* and *The Last Spike*, heading off toward the Pacific but implying the prospect of return; in *The Invasion of Canada*, which ends not with the last gasp of war but with the beginnings of identity; in *Vimy*, a saga of descent, trial, and ascent worthy of Milton; in *The Promised Land*, with its opening epigraph from Exodus: "And I am come down to deliver them / out of the hand of the Egyptians, / and to bring them up out of that land / unto a good land and a large, unto / a land flowing with milk and honey." In fact, Berton's own life had epitomized the myth of deliverance.[46]

The quest for the Northwest Passage provided Berton with the broad span of time and vast canvas that could do full justice to this mother of all literary themes, for in a century of imperial rivalry it became what the search for the Holy Grail had been for medieval kings and knights. Barbara Sears soon located a wide range of primary and secondary sources on the subject, especially British and American ones, including diaries and journals in the Scott Polar Institute in Cambridge, England. Three years in the making and 672 pages in length, *The Arctic Grail* became the longest book Berton would write. Drafting it consumed most of 1987, but by midwinter 1988 it was done, revised, and in the hands of McClelland & Stewart. That March, a party of eighteen Berton family members left for two weeks in Antigua, thanks largely to shared royalties from *The Berton Family Cookbook*, published in 1985 by McClelland & Stewart and launched on October 20 with an "autumn luncheon." The volume was indeed a family affair: foreword by Pierre, introduced by Janet, edited by Paul, cartoons by Patsy, compiled by Penny, and with additional drawings by Peter and Peggy Anne. Janet toured to promote the book for the remainder of the month and into November.[47]

"Pierre Berton has the happy knack of finding subjects for his books that are ideally suited for his talents and his temperament," William

French's review of *The Arctic Grail* began. "Now, in this gripping tale of Arctic exploration, Berton has found his ideal subject." French repeated the accusation he had made of *Starting Out*, that this author lacked depth, but the story of a century of adventurism by British, American, and Scandinavian explorers, he wrote, nevertheless provided "enough rivetting reading . . . to last until spring breakup." The colourful book made for interesting newspaper copy.[48]

Even more, the story of the imperial struggle to be first through the Northwest Passage and the subsequent rush to reach the North Pole had a very obvious contemporary message. The issue of Arctic sovereignty, renewed with the voyage of the *Polar Sea* and kept in the public mind by the 1987 decision of the Conservative government to build a fleet of nuclear submarines and station them in the Arctic, was very much on Canadians' minds in the fall of 1988. The country was in the midst of the campaign for a federal election, set for November 2. In a televised debate, Liberal leader John Turner accused Prime Minister Mulroney of abandoning the east-west political axis created by Macdonald and maintained by Laurier and his successors in favour of a north-south trading zone that would reach from Mexico to the High Arctic. Liberal Party television advertisements showed an American trade negotiator telling his Canadian equivalent that only one thing was needed in the new free trade agreement: elimination of the Canadian-American border.[49]

The Arctic Grail made its appearance in this volatile environment, and the contemporary political message of its tales of high adventure became immediately clear. Unlike the usual Berton work of history, this book was populated largely by foreign nationals who had laid claim to Canada's land and waters. Berton spent the first half of the book focused on nineteenth-century British explorers who represented imperial interests, such as Sir John Franklin – heroic but foolish in his haughty refusal to adapt to Arctic conditions or ways, even for his own survival. In its second half he dwelt on the exploits of Robert Peary and Frederick Cook, Americans out to be the first to reach the North Pole – brash, self-promoting, egomaniacal men. And con artists. Berton's Peary was a liar, and his Cook an outright fraud. In fact, the whole search for the new Holy Grail, whether in the form of the passage or the pole, was in Berton's view little more than a glorious con game on a

grand scale. "What matter if the Passage was commercially impracti-
cal?" he asked. "England was about to embark on a new age of discovery in which it was the exploit itself that counted." The Americans "had
one thing in common – a desire to win at any cost. . . . In this obsession they were harbingers of the new century – the American century –
in which winning is everything and it matters not how you play the
game."[50] The crusader had resurfaced, warning of hucksters.

The lesson was obvious. Canadians needed to shed vestigial European
and American values and cultivate and treasure those adaptable to
Canada's cultural and political as well as natural environments. If
Canadians did not take preventive action, they, too, would find themselves victims of the politician as confidence man, ambitious and venal
enough to gamble with the country's future with a reckless throw of
the dice. Canada could be lost. "As our nation moves through the
second quarter of its second century, we have begun to realize how
much of our past and our future lies in that vast region, and that if we
don't claim it, other nations will," wrote a reviewer from resource-rich
Alberta. "If we have an identity at all, it lies in the true north." Berton's
"knack for events and personalities that reveal how Canadians came to
be Canadians," the reviewer added, "has made him an oracle of the
Canadian psyche." After a year in which he published only his memoirs,
the oracle, said the reviewer, was "back in the history game."[51]

Avie Bennett approved a promotional campaign for *The Arctic Grail*
the flamboyance of which had not been witnessed since the releases of
The National Dream and *The Last Spike* almost twenty years earlier. It
took place in stages: first a party in New York, then more parties in
Toronto, Calgary, and on the Mackenzie River delta. During a stopover
in Yellowknife, while Berton waited for the flight to Inuvik, his publisher set out to see the sights downtown. "Bennett is on his own personal quest for the imagined north," wrote a reporter who was with
him. "'Do you have a whorehouse here?' he politely asks the driver. No
whorehouse, but the driver says she can introduce the publisher and his
pals to the mayor, and pulling in to City Hall, she does."[52]

From Yellowknife, an entourage of about eighteen – Berton,
Franklin, Bennett, and what one scribe called "a herd of paparazzi" –
flew to Inuvik. A helicopter scooped them out over the Beaufort Sea,
where it eventually lowered them onto a rescue ship. Soon they reached

the Gulf Oil rig *Molikpaq*, ninety-six kilometres north of Tuktoyaktuk in the Northwest Territories. It was as near to the Northwest Passage as they could possibly get, an 11,265-kilometre-long quest for publicity. Presumably on the grounds that nothing succeeds like excess, the author, his publicist, and his publisher allowed themselves to be winched by cable onto a precarious platform and swung by crane seventy-five feet out over the frigid Arctic waters. Berton clung to a steel cable with one hand and held *The Arctic Grail* aloft in the other, while the camera shutters of frozen paparazzi whirred in the distance. Later, back aboard the rig, the group feasted on a lunch of roasted muskox. Given the morning's excitement and the non-alcoholic champagne with which they toasted *The Arctic Grail*, the meal seemed a distinct anticlimax.[53]

Within a week of its release, McClelland & Stewart had received orders for 30,000 copies of *The Arctic Grail*. Management expected sales to exceed 50,000 at a list price of $29.95. Berton stood to earn more than $225,000 in royalties before signing a third over to Barbara Sears. Franklin's extravagant marketing campaign gained widespread attention. This was a tale, Daniel Francis wrote, of "storybook heroes freezing their toes off in search of impossible dreams," a description that stood just as well for the publicity campaign as for the book.[54] Francis was one of the few Canadian authors devoted to popular history, and he was good at it. A less enamoured reviewer was Christopher Moore, the award-winning author of *Louisbourg Portraits*, a book lauded as possessing an enviable balance of popular and scholarly social history. Berton had singled him out in his review of *The Illustrated History of Canada* the previous year as one of the contributors whose prose "trudges stolidly forward, encumbered by box-car sentences, and the over-use of the passive voice," so Moore struggled to be judicious: "The Arctic Grail closes on a plea to include the Inuit in northern history. Sadly, Berton has been almost completely unable to do this himself. . . . There is an ethnographic literature, not wholly valueless, that documents Inuit worlds. Who better than Berton to lead Canadians into them? But that might have meant challenging his readers – and Berton is cautious about that." Then Moore drew back. "He has given us an adventure with colour and drama. Are we asking too much to ask for more?"[55]

Berton continued to flog his book on the road for the remainder of the fall and into the early winter. The "one-man band" seemed to have more energy than any three authors, the *Toronto Star* entertainment writer Sid Adilman marvelled. "He's three provinces ahead of us," Peter Gzowski told a crowd at the M&S launch of his own book at the Art Gallery of Ontario. In the midst of the flurry of excitement over *The Arctic Grail*, Berton also finished the scripts for *The Secret of My Success*, a twenty-part half-hour television documentary series he was to host, produced for Screen Gems by My Country Productions, and featuring interviews and profiles of the fashion designer Linda Lundstrom, the entrepreneurs Sam Sniderman and Frank Stronach, the publishers Anna Porter and Adrienne Clarkson, the cartoonist Ben Wicks, and others. Research was well under way on his next book, *The Great Depression*; he wrote and narrated fifteen videocassettes subsequently shown each day at the Canadian Aviation Museum in Ottawa; and he accepted an offer to become the first chancellor of Yukon College in Whitehorse.[56]

Adrienne Clarkson had become Berton's publisher early in 1987, when Avie Bennett named her president of M&S. At first, the appointment seemed a stroke of genius. Clarkson was a very well known media personality, was highly cultured and well spoken, and had just finished a term as Ontario's first official representative in Paris. The problem was that, as Roy MacSkimming has noted, "she had no more hands-on experience of the profession than Bennett." Moreover, she approached her employees with a combination of imperial condescension and cultural cheerleading. She lectured, but she did not listen, and she failed to gain the loyalty of the M&S editorial staff, many of whom had been with the company for years. She resigned the next year, succeeded by another Bennett hire, Doug Gibson, who in 1986 had left Macmillan of Canada for M&S, where he established an imprint bearing his name.[57]

Though these changes were unsettling, they did not seem to affect Berton's star in the larger world. Journalists struggled to find a way of describing the kind of status he now possessed. The words *personality* and *celebrity* no longer seemed adequate, for Berton saturated the fabric of Canadian life to a degree that even those as well-known and beloved as Peter Gzowski and Barbara Frum, another CBC host, did not. Toward the end of 1987, the print journalist Allan Gould called him "a Canadian icon," along with Gordon Sinclair. *Saturday Night* also used the phrase to describe his stature. Before long, the label took its place as the ultimate marker of his brand, a sure sign that basic myths of

English-speaking Canadians were firmly attached to his name. This iconic status became so fixed to his image that a Calgary interviewer could glibly ask, "Speaking of you, how does it feel to be called an icon?" He responded with his stock answer to questions about celebrity. "I don't want to be called a celebrity, personality or an icon; I want to be called a writer."[58]

The final year of the eighties began on a low note, with Hal Straight's death of cancer at age seventy-nine. The two old friends, along with the Vancouver columnist Jack Webster, a frequent *Front Page Challenge* guest panellist, had spent time together the previous August aboard Straight's fishing boat at Sechelt, B.C., recalling the crazy days of West Coast journalism, long since gone. There on the Strait of Georgia, three men in a boat lamented Harry Filion's death before he had a chance to see Vicki Gabereau's triumph as a radio and television broadcaster, marvelled at Jack Scott's way with words, and debated the intelligence of salmon.[59]

The year improved. *The Arctic Grail* was nominated for a Governor General's Award in February (Anne Collins won for *In the Sleep Room*, her chilling account of CIA-sponsored brainwashing experiments in Canada). Berton remained in demand to attend writers' festivals and support his favourite causes, from Amnesty International and the Writers' Trust to environmental and heritage-friendly municipal reform. More than thirty years after publication, McClelland & Stewart reissued a slightly updated edition of *The Mysterious North*.

Berton's relationship with McClelland & Stewart had gone well after Jack left. He could certainly not have expected better promotion of *The Arctic Grail* from any other publisher. He liked Bennett – liked his support of the arts, liked his left-of-centre political views and the way he had rescued M&S from almost certain collapse. In 1987, Franklin had brokered a deal with Bennett and Penguin Books Canada for mass-market paperbacks of four of Pierre's bestsellers: *Why We Act like Canadians* (with a new chapter on Canada-U.S. trade negotiations), *The Invasion of Canada*, *Vimy*, and *Flames across the Border*. Two years later, she made a similar arrangement for *The Dionne Years*, *The Wild*

Frontier, Drifting Home, and *My Country.* In August 1989, she received a $22,500 cheque for Berton's share of Penguin's advance. Pierre had meanwhile proposed no fewer than four books on Niagara Falls for M&S – a straightforward history, a coffee-table volume containing historical and contemporary photographs, and two others not yet outlined on paper but no doubt the subject of conversation between author and publisher. Bennett clearly saw huge sales ahead. He agreed to an advance of $300,000 for world rights to the package. Franklin received the first $100,000 before the end of the year, with the remainder to be paid in $50,000 instalments on delivery of each book. Berton finished the final chapter of his next work for M&S, *The Great Depression,* in March 1990.[60]

The eighties had witnessed major changes in the North American economy. The decade, given over to economic expansion and the gospel of free trade, had instead seen unprecedented takeovers and consolidation across a range of industries. As early as 1974 the economist Arthur Laffer had pitched his statistical model of tax elasticity, popularized as the "Laffer curve," to the Republican staffer Dick Cheney, then deputy to the White House chief of staff, Donald Rumsfeld. A repackaging of the age-old "trickle-down" approach to generating national wealth, it projected prosperity for all – once governments implemented a "supply-side" economics aimed at increasing the supply of goods through incentives to producers. Laffer's idea that lowered tax rates would produce higher overall revenue ultimately resembled the "voodoo economics" its critics called it. During the Reagan years, from 1981 to 1989, overall productivity increased and unemployment fell, but the rich became richer and the poor ended up worse off. Poverty increased, personal savings decreased. The American national debt tripled and the trade deficit quadrupled.[61]

There were parallels in the publishing industry, for by the end of the decade it was largely controlled by a half-dozen global corporations. Retailing witnessed the growth of "big-box" stores such as Wal-Mart in large strip malls on major traffic thoroughfares outside urban centres, selling new books at deep discounts that small independent bookstores could not match. Chain bookstores the size of warehouses, often located in the same suburban malls, did likewise. Such trends, beginning in the United States, soon extended to Canada. By the mid-1990s, two such chains, Chapters (a merger of Coles and SmithBooks) and Indigo, the brainchild of the Toronto businesswoman Heather Reisman, dominated the trade in Canada.[62] Corresponding changes took place in readers' purchasing habits. The leisurely browsing of walk-in book buyers in owner-operated bookstores started to become a harried beeline of suburban commuters heading for big-box discount stores on their way home. Book industry experts discovered during the decade that the best-seller lists had become almost completely the preserve of book-a-year writers like Robert Ludlum, Danielle Steel, Tom Clancy, and John Grisham, even when newspapers and magazines expanded the lists from ten to fifteen titles. At the beginning of the eighties, the sales levels of such authors sometimes hit 500,000 copies; by the end of the decade, American blockbuster sales reached the millions.[63] As in other sectors, publishing had come to be dominated by a few mega-brands that were imprinted on consumers' minds; that in publishing, these brands happened to be authors was almost beside the point.

The generous treatment Berton received in 1988 and 1989 from Avie Bennett reflected the era. If any M&S author could be predicted to hit the new sales stratosphere, surely it would be Canada's most prolific author of non-fiction. In the fall of 1990, when *The Great Depression* began to climb the weekly *Globe and Mail* bestseller list, rising to number three by the end of September and nipping at the heels of Wayne Gretzky's autobiography, the hopes of author and publisher seemed to have been borne out.[64] But there were signs of troubles over the longer term. When he took part in the Vancouver Festival of Authors, Berton had to compete for attention with an array of authors very different from those of an earlier day. Also seeking the limelight at the festival were the British bad-boy novelist Martin Amis, the investigative journalist Victor Malarek, and a former teen runaway, Evelyn Lau; they reflected an era disenchanted with politics, alienated from mainstream society, and smitten by postmodern cynicism. More than a decade of right-of-centre politics had done much to erode the idealistic and interventionist social policies of the 1960s. The age of *The Simpsons* and *Seinfeld* had dawned; the sensibilities that embraced the corrosive ironies put on display in these popular television sitcoms, one antic and the other laid-back, made Berton's straightforward liberal optimism seem artless and out of date.[65]

Undeterred, in 1991 he launched a twenty-two-volume history series aimed at a less jaded audience. To be published over the next couple of years by McClelland & Stewart, Adventures in Canadian History targeted preteen and teenage readers from grade four to high school. About a hundred pages in length and inexpensively priced at under $6, the volumes grew from well-tilled Berton ground, with titles like *Before the Gold Rush*, *The Death of Isaac Brock*, *The Men in Sheepskin Coats*, and *Steel across the Prairies*. A *Vancouver Sun* piece on Berton at a Vancouver event publicizing the series that fall suggested that the frenzy of renown could be only as enduring as the advent of the next generation: to younger Canadians he was now largely an unknown entity. The author of the brief article, a high school student named Sarah Goodman, clearly knew next to nothing about Berton or his track record until she conducted her interview. She did inform her readers that he wrote history "in an authentic yet exciting manner," but seemed breathless from having stumbled upon a person who had actually once interviewed Mick Jagger and Malcolm X. The headline above the article, "Berton Recounts History with a Story Teller's Flair," conveyed information second nature to her parents' generation; but to Sarah Goodman and Generation X, named that very year in Douglas Coupland's "tales for an accelerated culture," Pierre Berton himself was simply a curious blast from the past.[66]

The Great Depression told the story of Berton's own generation in its formative years. He had been nine when the stock market crashed in October 1929 and was leaving his teenage years behind when the Depression ended a decade later. In Victoria, his family had lived a life of genteel poverty. The tale of struggle, endurance, and survival that shaped the values of the parents of the baby boom generation was part of his own story. But at 560 pages *The Great Depression* was a lengthy book, and a laboured one at that. "There seems to be a lack of zest and enthusiasm that was so evident in *Klondike*," wrote Barry Broadfoot in a highly critical *Globe and Mail* review. The book overwhelmed the reader with detail, was riddled with cliché, and was "without feeling for people and places." In the seventies, he claimed, the Depression was "in," because the generation that had survived it had become affluent and could wear its hardship "as a badge of honour." But in the nineties things were different. The world was again failing, but the Depression

generation now wished to bid farewell to much that the decade represented.[67] A few weeks later, an exasperated Charles Templeton came to
his friend's defence. Broadfoot's review, he wrote to the editor of the
Globe, was "thinly disguised jealousy from a man who also writes an off-
brand kind of history; a so-called 'oral history,' that is essentially tape-
recording and arranging on paper other people's extemporized memories
of events . . . a hell of a lot easier than the sweaty, head-down digging
serious historians find it necessary to do in preparing a trustworthy
record of the past."[68]

Reviewers of the book divided along ideological lines. Writing in
Alberta Report, the free marketer Kenneth Whyte issued the conventional platitudes – good research, epic narrative – and then drew attention to *The Great Depression*'s "intensely political" nature, one that "tells
us much more of Berton's politics than it does of '30s politics." The
book, in his view, was a slanted, moralistic tale of "mindless optimism"
and greedy capitalists, a work critical of Canadian complacency in the
1920s and dedicated to extolling the virtues of the interventionist New
Deal in the United States. It demonized Prime Minister R.B. Bennett,
reeling and confused like all Western politicians by the sudden economic downturn; meanwhile, it portrayed leaders of the left such as the
Communist Tim Buck and the socialist Tommy Douglas as saints.
From Whyte's perspective – that of a regional political class alienated by
federal neglect of western Canada and favouritism toward Quebec, and
critical of federal centralization – Berton's history merely served to prop
up the tired old rationale for state intervention that had resulted in the
bloated welfare state.[69]

Supporters of the left applauded *The Great Depression* for its strongly
held and compassionate views. For the Winnipeg-based writer Heather
Robertson, the book was "bursting with energy and the confidence of
a man who's been there." She applauded Berton's treatment of women's
experience in the 1930s, particularly their exploitation at the hands of
Eaton's department stores. The decade was a violent one dominated
by the clash between business and the unemployed. "Canada," she
wrote, "wasn't born at Vimy Ridge, as Berton used to think, but in
Saskatchewan in 1933, when the Regina Manifesto made democratic
socialism in North America possible." *Canadian Forum*, once the voice
of those who inspired and wrote that manifesto, praised the book as

"altogether splendid, one of Berton's best." The academic journal *Labour/Le Travail* was well to the left of the *Forum*, and in it, the York University historian Paul Axelrod took issue with the book's form as "a melodramatic morality play" and with its failure to make an original contribution to scholarship. But he made an essential point: "At a historical moment when free enterprise ideology is being deified and reified around the globe, Berton's book is a timely reminder of the social costs of capitalism in collapse," resurrecting "the passions and struggles of the system's critics and casualties."[70]

Penguin hoped that *The Great Depression* would succeed, since its mass-market paperback of *The Arctic Grail* had sold very well – seeming proof that the new hegemony of book-a-year authors had arrived in Canada. After consulting Doug Gibson at M&S, Penguin decided to offer an advance of $60,000 for paperback rights, the same amount offered for *The Arctic Grail*. But the tone of the letter from Penguin Canada's associate publisher, Jeffrey Boloten, to Elsa Franklin hinted that this level of offer was unlikely to continue. The collapse of the American stock market in 1987 and the subsequent recession in the American economy had taken its toll in Canada, Boloten noted, and the combination of a decline in the numbers of booksellers, the "looming threat" of a federal goods and service tax, and predictions of serious sales losses from the new tax on books had created what he called a "chilling effect" on the book market. Nevertheless, the cheque for Penguin's purchase of rights to *The Great Depression* arrived with the letter. Elsa wrote "$75,000" in the letter's left margin, a sign perhaps that to her, where Pierre was concerned, no advance could ever reflect his worth.[71]

Niagara: A History was nowhere near as successful as Berton hoped it would be. The idea of writing a history of the awesome falls from physical formation to honeymoon haven had been on his mind since he had researched the War of 1812 in southwestern Ontario years earlier. He thought Niagara Falls held a story of universal appeal, for it inspired both wonder and fear and was also a symbol of North America's social and technological development, for good and for ill. But he had been unable to interest an American publisher. Reviewers acknowledged the fascinating nature of the falls and the people drawn to it over the years, but they found the book's formula rather tired – "a seamless book of anecdotes fleshed out with tiny distilled biographies, all written in the pedantic, scrupulous style so familiar from Berton's other books," John Doyle wrote in *Books in Canada*. Peeter Kopvillem at *Maclean's* noted that Berton brought his story to life, but that readers could be forgiven for concluding, from the author's cast of "adventurers and dreamers" and "visionaries and industrialists," that this was a story they had come across before. Academic reviewers played their old familiar tune: too little analysis, too much description. Even so, anyone who wished to pursue the confidence man leitmotif in Berton's thought could find a lot of evidence in his latest book. Those who simply wanted something to put under the Christmas tree, Lakehead University's Patricia Jasen suggested in the *Canadian Historical Review*, would find *Niagara* "as easy to consume as a box of Black Magic."[72]

Berton's relationship with McClelland & Stewart began to show signs of strain again in 1991. He had promised M&S the second volume of his memoirs, but early in the year, perhaps with the prospect of placing the book elsewhere already in mind, he agreed to repay his $40,000 advance by having it credited against the new juvenile series. A Native Canadian threatened to sue him, along with McClelland & Stewart, for his depiction of Native people in *Revenge of the Tribes*, one of the volumes in that series. The M&S accounting department mistakenly overpaid his royalties on Book-of-the-Month Club rights for *The Great Depression*, leaving him $2,210.36 in the company's debt, and it compounded the problem in 1993 when it failed to note that Berton had agreed to reduce his royalty on the book from 15 per cent to 10 per cent on a reprint of the cloth edition. As a consequence, more royalties had been overpaid and he owed M&S a further $9,044.90.[73]

As if to prove that he could still keep up with the tempo of the day, in March 1991 Berton arranged with his old friend Beland Honderich at the *Toronto Star* to return to its pages with a regular weekend spot on entertainment, charting, as the *Star* reporter Peter Goddard put it, "the far-reaching changes and enormous growth in show business and the arts." For the next three and a half years his pieces provided a mix of cultural, political, and social commentary. Those old enough to recall his *Star* column thirty years earlier may have looked forward to his return, but others might have been puzzled by Pierre Berton's new presence in the *Star's* pages. The column flitted from subject to subject in the manner of his earlier jibes at fads and foibles of the day. But the kitschy instant nostalgia and the *Mad* magazine humour, not to mention the ramblings of a seventy-one-year-old man on the meaning of Madonna and her sexual antics, must have appeared to some hopelessly dated in the context of the first Gulf War, economic recession, gangsta rap, and the now-toxic Mulroney administration. His 1993 attempt to lampoon political correctness in the women's movement with a spoof on James Bond's treatment of women, in which Pussy Galore takes Bond to court for sexual harassment, seemed to some readers insensitive and obtuse. "Young men transferring Bond's fantasy into reality may, and hopefully will, get summarily introduced to a better understanding of sexual assault and its consequences," wrote one angry male reader to the editor.[74]

Times enough there were during this stint at the *Star* when the Berton of old stood out, but not often. "In a land where most of our journalists operate comfortably from the centre of society, giving only slight glances to the marginal and minority issues," wrote one reader, "Berton reminds us of the true writer's worth." He once again took up an involvement with municipal politics, lending his support to a group of reformers dedicated to environmental and heritage issues – opposing condominium development around Fort York, for example. He came to the support of the former inmate Roger Caron, whose 1978 book of jailhouse life, *Go Boy!*, he had helped get published. In 1993, with Caron imprisoned again, this time for robbery, assault, and hostage-taking, Berton's renewed defence of the man seemed a matter of pigheadedness rather than principle. "I have great trouble explaining to my kids that crime does not pay," wrote an irate Willowdale mother, reacting to a Berton column on the matter. News that he would lead a group of tourists on a rail tour of the Rockies, stopping at Craigellachie to re-enact the driving of the Last Spike, threatened to turn him into a parody of his former self. Even his connection to the North had become awkward, for Yukon College announced in October 1993 that a local citizen would take Berton's place as chancellor. The reason given was the prohibitive cost of airfare. The more salient one was that members of the college community in Whitehorse found him arrogant, expensive, and aloof.[75]

He also came to be at the centre of an acrimonious dispute within the ranks of the Writers' Union of Canada. For most of its history,

Canadian literature had been dominated by white writers of European extraction. But the Canada of the 1990s had become as multiracial and multicultural a society as any in the world. The Writers' Union had actively worked toward a membership that reflected this sociological reality, but tensions existed between those who advocated the ideal that different cultures should hold certain Canadian values in common and others who believed it essential to maintain cultural difference. To stimulate debate on these and related issues, the Writers' Union undertook to sponsor a conference in Vancouver in late June and early July 1994. The federal Department of Canadian Heritage agreed to provide funding. Called "Writing Thru Race," the conference was to find ways of bringing non-white writers into the mainstream of Canadian cultural life. For some Writers' Union members, the very idea of "whiteness" – its nature, its meaning, its connection to power – was central to the conference's main theme; they believed that non-white participants should be free from discomfiting feelings arising from the "white gaze." As a consequence, the organizing committee decided that certain workshops would exclude whites.

For Berton and other long-time members of the Writers' Union, such as June Callwood, this decision was very troubling. The whole purpose of founding the union had been to eliminate discrimination within what their late friend Margaret Laurence had fondly called the "tribe" of Canadian writers, and to become more inclusive in membership and participation. At its founding in 1973, Pierre had urged the union to broaden its criteria for membership, and it irked him in 1994 that the organization was willing to use its own members' dues and the taxpayers' money for an exercise in reverse racism. Callwood, a leading feminist since the early 1970s, had written *Jim: A Life with AIDS*, a compassionate book about one of the early Canadian victims of the disease, and had founded Casey House, a hospice for those who suffered from the disease, as well as Nellie's, a hostel for women fleeing violence. Few Canadians had more deeply rooted experience as friends of the weak and the disadvantaged or as advocates and defenders of civil liberties in Canada than Berton and Callwood.[76]

The cultural atmosphere of Canada in the late eighties and nineties, influenced by the near-paranoid nature of the American "culture wars" of the day and by the country's own racial and gendered tensions, had pushed such commitment or accomplishment to the margins. The postmodern suspicion of history and tradition was reaching its peak, and no more than Berton did Callwood have much patience for the "politically correct" climate of the times. In 1988, while serving PEN International as the incoming chair of its Canadian branch, she helped organize a conference dedicated to helping imprisoned and oppressed African writers, raising funds to help writers from Ghana, South America, and India attend. The Tobago-born poet M. NourbeSe Philip claimed that too much attention had been afforded to white writers, and local black authors picketed Roy Thomson Hall, the conference venue. Harassed at one point, Callwood had only two words to say: "Fuck off." The response made news in the *Globe and Mail* the next day, much to her dismay and embarrassment. Similarly, in December 1991, she was stunned when, at a staff meeting at Nellie's, a black employee accused her of being a racist for challenging the speaker's wholesale accusation of racism against the staff in general. The charge was outrageous, since Callwood had been instrumental in the effort to make certain the staff of Nellie's came from diverse racial backgrounds. In the February board meeting, another staff member issued the alarming promise, "We're gonna get you, you racist!"[77] Callwood never did recover from the anger and hurt of that moment. Three years later it became Berton's turn to be on the receiving end of such sanctimony.

The 1994 annual meeting of the Writers' Union of Canada was held in mid-May at Ryerson University, and Berton attended, as he had done regularly since the union's founding. News of the "Writing Thru Race" sessions being closed to white participants had long since reached the press and politicians. The *Globe and Mail* columnists Michael Valpy and Robert Fulford had condemned the Writers' Union decision. (The titles of their columns more than hint at the volatility of the controversy: "A Nasty Serving of Cultural Apartheid," went Valpy's; "George Orwell, Call Your Office," ran Fulford's.) In the House of Commons, a Reform Party MP from Calgary, Jan Brown, called the conference racist, leading Heritage Minister Michel Dupuy to withdraw federal funding for it.[78]

The union's annual meeting tried to address the controversy directly by holding a forum on the "Writing Thru Race" conference. Support for the aims of the conference was unanimous, and some white writers, including one Jewish author, reminded others that prejudice and discrimination transcended even skin colour. But speaker after speaker supported the exclusion of whites from conference sessions. As Berton later put it, "A shroud of guilt hung over the proceedings." So he stood up to speak. Only one word would describe a union-sponsored conference that denied entrance to some of its members, he said. *Racist*. The whole exclusivity issue could have been avoided, he added, had the union simply chosen a different venue and not asked for taxpayers' money.[79]

His words met with a chorus of boos, hisses, and catcalls. He tried to remind those assembled that the union had made every effort in recent years to increase the number of women and minority writers in its midst. "It's true the Writers Union hadn't done enough," he said. "But we will not be tarred with this brush." A ripple of applause greeted his comments, at which point one of the panel members, Makeda Silvera, writer, editor, and publisher of Sister Vision Press, said, "I've had enough of this racist shit." She stood up, abandoned the panel, and sat with the audience. "The emotional muddle only intensified," wrote the *Globe and Mail*'s reporter, Val Ross, "as some white writers tried to distance themselves from Berton. Only one member stood up to remind listeners of Berton's long activist record." The conference itself proved to be an anticlimax, ignored by most of the media and attended in only modest numbers. Most of those who went to evening readings were white. "This conference was not primarily meant to educate the members of the Canadian public," Roy Miki, the conference organizer, told a press conference. Pierre Berton helped make up the shortfall in funding with a private donation.[80]

While his writing and actions threatened at times to diminish the lustre of his brand in the highly charged cultural and political atmosphere of the decade, Berton's relationship with McClelland & Stewart continued to deteriorate. Doug Gibson informed him early in 1994 that sales of *A Picture Book of Niagara Falls* were dreadful, with orders under 9,000 and returns outstripping sales. M&S sales people reacted to the release of his trade paperbacks, Gibson reported, with a chorus of "Oh, not another one." Sales of *The Great Railway* in a new format had yet to reach 4,000, and only 888 copies of the new printing of *Drifting Home* had left the bookstores with customers. As a result, plans to bring out *My Country* in trade paperback had again been postponed. Gibson stated that he was pleased Berton was "hard at work on the autobiography," but then rather gratuitously added that *Starting Out* had been "regarded as something of a disappointment" – except when judged by sales over the long term.[81]

Berton responded by expressing doubts that M&S had any intention of issuing the planned Japanese edition of the Niagara picture book or having anything more to do with Adventures in Canadian History. Eleven days later, Gibson informed him that the poor sales of the Niagara picture book made "drastic action" necessary and that not only its jacket but possibly the jackets of all Berton's books were to be completely redesigned. Furthermore, M&S had made a decision to cut the *Niagara Falls* list price from $35.00 to either $24.99 or perhaps even $19.99.[82]

Berton was no doubt disappointed at the apparent lack of interest and the likely reduction in revenue from royalties, but he became plain angry when he learned that on the matter of cover redesign, M&S had bypassed Frank Newfeld, who had been so instrumental in helping develop a distinctive look for M&S books, especially Berton's histories. For Berton, the issue was a matter of ethical conduct and professional courtesy. He phoned Gibson to express his concern and followed up the call with a letter: "I am very concerned at the ethics of having another designer produce an alternative cover [for *Niagara Falls*]. . . . Have you any idea of the insult that you have offered Frank Newfeld? He is one of the best designers in the country, and without any real consultation you have foisted somebody else's design on him. You have also, inferentially, asked him to pass judgement on another designer's work, something I am certain he will not do." He concluded by saying that he could not have his name associated with such dubious business practice and that he expected Gibson to resolve the issue.[83]

An acrimonious dispute followed over whether M&S had violated the Society of Graphic Designers' Professional Code of Conduct, which barred one designer from commenting about or competing with another designer's work. In a letter to Frank Newfeld, Gibson attempted to explain that a cover redesign was the only way of rescuing a situation in which 15,000 copies of the 20,000 print run for *Niagara Falls* seemed fated to remain on warehouse shelves. It was better, he said, to make the book look different than to remainder it. "Instead, we want to give the book a new life by giving it a new jacket. This is where you come in, as designer."[84]

Frank Newfeld, a highly sensitive man and not the easiest person to work with, found Gibson's letter troubling. He was especially annoyed by what he called "the petulant tone" of Gibson's first words: "Okay, my apologies, I didn't know about the Professional Code of Conduct preventing you from looking at something we've had mocked up in-house." In a letter to Berton, he complained that sending his design of *Niagara Falls* to another designer for overhaul had been insulting, especially when the company whose image and reputation he had done so much to mould was the one doing the sending. Newfeld had known about the possibility of a new jacket since the launch of the book, and no one had hinted that he would not be the one to redesign it; but he had suspected from the first that M&S had someone else in mind. A letter from Newfeld to Gibson failed to resolve the dispute, and in March 1994 he withdrew entirely from further involvement.[85]

Berton's own relationship with M&S was now close to the breaking point. He expressed a "wish" to remain involved with *Niagara Falls*, the illustrated volume, to attend any meetings about the new cover, help choose the new photograph for it, and examine the finished design for approval. But this was really an insistence. Franklin, who did not think Doug Gibson a "real publisher" – by which she meant a publisher whose primary interest was in his authors – agreed to a one-year postponement of the release of *Niagara: A History* as a mass-market paperback, but told him that she and Berton did not want to see any further delay. She also reminded Gibson of the dates for disbursing the advances on the book and on the booklets in the Adventures series.[86]

As if the winter and spring of 1994 were not stressful enough, given the deteriorating relations with M&S, the months were made worse by the fact that in February Peggy Anne developed a serious streptococcal infection in her arm. For a while this put her in real danger. In early March, after two operations, she was still in the hospital. Once released, she stayed with her parents while recuperating. That spring and summer, Pierre corresponded fairly regularly with Jack McClelland in Florida and Muskoka, offering advice about McClelland's memoirs. "Keep your own biographical material probably to a minimum," he wrote. "What people really want to read about is your adventures in the contemporary world with some of the best known literary figures of the last half-century. That is where you can get very personal and have a good deal of fun. The book should be fun to read when it's finished. That means a great many anecdotes – and you're not short of those." He suggested that the title should be something like "Wild Authors I Have Known."[87]

At the end of September, the *Toronto Star* abruptly cancelled Berton's column. Beland Honderich was no longer the publisher, having retired at the beginning of the year to make way for his fifty-seven-year-old son, John. "We feel the page three column should be more arts and entertainment-oriented to fit the focus of the Arts section," the younger Honderich informed Berton, adding that the *Star* would welcome any freelance articles and that the door would not be closed to Berton at One Yonge Street.[88]

Berton was disappointed, and he let it be known. "The *Star* has other uses for this space," he announced in his final column, pointedly titled "Leaves from a Minor Celebrity's Notebook." Some readers were dismayed. One was the Reverend James G. McDonald, of Scarborough, who wrote to the editor that any space "allocated to this truly magnificent writer by the *Star* or by any other representative of the media is, in my opinion, the best use possible." The journalist Pete McGarvey was also disturbed. Reminding the newspaper's executives as well as its readers that Berton's column of the late fifties and early sixties had won the circulation wars for the *Star* "single-handedly," he recalled that Berton had been the paper's "heart and soul." "Twenty years before 'consumerism' entered the language," McGarvey noted, "Berton was the acknowledged champion of that cause." He had exposed the hypocrisies of Moscow officialdom, defended the beleaguered Joyce Davidson, revealed the dreadful conditions of the Ontario Hospital School in Orillia, and much more. "What endeared him to a huge readership was his humor, as much as his crusading. Berton was a master of the comic essay, a satirist supreme, a true son of Stephen Leacock, with a bow, perhaps to S.J. Perelman." For this, he had received merely the ingratitude of a large daily. "In my books this minor celebrity is a giant, first last and always." McGarvey's column in the *Orillia Packet and Times* carried the title "Pierre Berton Deserved Better."[89]

Berton and Franklin thought he deserved better from McClelland & Stewart. Toward the end of 1994, Franklin noticed discrepancies in royalty statements for *Niagara*. M&S listed an author deficit of $21,138 for the hardcover, but once trade paperback royalties and Berton's share of the $25,000 Book-of-the-Month Club advance were taken into account, she claimed that Berton was in fact owed $2,326.92. Negotiations over the contract for *My Times*, the second volume of his autobiography, went badly. In 1987, the auction for Robert Fulford's memoirs had brought him $80,000, and M&S offered nowhere near this for *My Times*. Given all that had happened during the year, Franklin shopped the manuscript around to three publishers in addition to M&S; each offered several times more than Avie Bennett did. Finally, on December 2 she faxed Bennett a copy of a brief letter in which Berton stated his intention to take *My Times* elsewhere. He expressed disappointment at the lack of enthusiasm Bennett and Gibson had shown for the book, but held out the olive branch of the right of first refusal for M&S on his next book, to be on the year 1967, Canada's "turning point." He also indicated that he would continue to work on the Adventures in Canadian History series for the firm.[90]

In a letter to Franklin on December 8, Bennett showed no sign of a conciliatory mood; instead he voiced indignation as well as disappointment. He told her that M&S had been aware that she was shopping *My Times* around "to an embarrassing extent, since the chain buyers were amused to be canvassed and were asking us what was wrong with the book." Such canvassing by other publishers to suss out sales expectations for the work of a prominent author, he wrote, "reveals a lack of confidence." He found it ironic that Berton should have accused M&S of lack of confidence in his book, since both he and Gibson (each had read the manuscript) had said just the opposite. This may have been so, but the fact was that Berton's approach to autobiography was not exactly au courant, and Bennett knew it. The rage in the publishing industry, as ready to travel with the pack as run-of-the-mill writers, was what the trade called "recovery lit," described by the *Globe*'s publishing reporter, Val Ross, a few years earlier as "part pop psychology, part spiritual thought-for-the-day." Modern memoir tapped into this combination of self-absorption, self-reflection, and self-recovery. "Ideas for these books come up in editorial meetings," Bennett told Ross. "I guess it's a function of age; I say, 'You gotta be a moron to read a book like that,' but the younger staff all say, 'Great idea.'" Clearly, Berton's chirpy auto-biography would not have found much enthusiastic support among the rank and file of the M&S editorial or sales staff.[91]

But Bennett owned the company. He could have published *My Times* had he wanted to. For him, he reminded Franklin, the problem was financial: Berton's unearned advances on the Niagara books and the Adventures series added up to $271,000. "Since it is now clear that cash in hand is your main criterion in dealing with us, this marks a change in our relationship. In future we will have to make our decisions about the backlist of Pierre Berton titles on strictly business considerations." Berton's forty-year relationship with "the Canadian Publishers" had effectively come to an end.[92]

24

ICONOCLAST AND ICON

—

IN THE FALL OF 1995 the autumn leaves dropped, Quebec and the land known as the Rest of Canada were at odds, and Pierre Berton published a book. For Canadians, these events had come to seem the very order of nature. Doubleday Canada released the second and concluding volume of his autobiography, *My Times*, early in September, for which it had paid an advance of $152,000. "This book is for Janet, without whom . . ." read the dedication, the ellipses perhaps a sign of inexpressible gratitude. For the next few months his name and his image were on prominent display in Canadian newspapers and magazines. Such attention was not something he could take for granted anymore. Berton was no longer "a dominant public personality," the *Toronto Star* book review columnist Philip Marchand wrote. "It is easier to treasure him now, oddly enough, than in his heyday, when he bristled with confident opinions on the airwaves."[1] His heyday was indeed past, and gone with it much of the Canada he had known and written about. But the more it receded, the more venerable he became to the Canadian public.

In the spring, the CBC abruptly cancelled *Front Page Challenge* after thirty-eight years on the air. For the first time since the dawn of Canadian television, Berton was not a regular presence on TV screens. He knew the program would end – its demise had been predicted when Gordon Sinclair died – and in the late eighties it had been cut back from thirty-nine programs a year to eighteen. Still, he was disappointed that its long run was over. He was annoyed, like the other long-time panellists, that the CBC had shown so little sense of occasion in marking the end of a show with such remarkable staying power. "I heard about it in the usual classy CBC style – on a speaker phone," Fotheringham said. "The boss, George Anthony, was conveniently out of town."[2]

Back in 1969, the CBC had cancelled *Don Messer's Jubilee* after a highly popular decade on the air. At the time the targeting of specific demographic groups by the television industry was in its infancy, but the public broadcaster had clearly wished to project an image of a Canada that was hip and of a citizenry that was young and urban. Don Messer, Charlie Chamberlain, and Marge Osborne were unabashedly rural, folksy, and the very antithesis of hip. In fact, the comedian Don Harron had for years gently lampooned the stereotype whenever he played the grizzled, cardigan-wearing but likeable old yarn-spinner Charlie Farquharson, a sure sign of the rural according to the nation's cool urbanites. By the mid-1980s, demographic analysis had become central to television. It could differentiate markets for advertisers, and this drove everything from the placement of commercials to the content of programs. *Front Page Challenge*, with its aging white panellists and their nerdy obsession with newspaper stories, had become a hindrance to the CBC in its desire to attract a demographic of viewers across the racial groups and from the generation born in the age of the Internet. This is perhaps what the CBC meant to convey when, in a lifeless press release announcing the show's end, it referred to "the rapidly changing TV environment."[3]

Rick Salutin placed the cancellation in the kind of broad context that would have made Berton proud. "Sometimes it feels as if privatization is sweeping the land," he wrote in his column, "taking the firstborn of every public institution." For Salutin, the CBC's decision reflected its "endangered status," one more investment ready to be given over to the private sector in the interests of the "free market." "Nothing seems to be public any more," Salutin lamented. "Everything is seen as private stuff to buy or sell in the marketplace." Who, he asked, would now speak for the public?[4]

Long-time CBC viewers complained in legions about the demise of *Front Page Challenge*. Like Berton himself, the show had mellowed over the years; the public regarded its panellists as if they were members of the family. "The program lasted 38 years," Michael Valpy wrote, "because it was tribal, a fact recognized in Canadian cultural thought for at least the past two decades. It was wedded to national metaphor, national humour, the national looking glass." The title that accompanied Valpy's column was "No More Front Page Challenge. No More Canada?" In theme and sentiment, his column that day was an extension of the one he had published a week earlier. "What Canadians are doing," it had read, "is niche-consumerism, embracing selected bits and pieces of doctrine and dogma. . . . The question is: How much do they still believe?" The column, on the subject of religion, had been titled "Reflections on the Day of Crucifixion."[5]

My Times, Berton's account of his life since arriving in Toronto in 1947, was a picaresque tale, stitched together with anecdote. Its author, wrote Peter Buitenhuis, had been "a mirror of his times, . . . determined to hold up to his audience the image of itself." He was correct, for the book was far more mirror than lamp. For Lynne Van Luven, Berton was "too busy, too interested, and too passionate to ever really dwell on (or in) the worst of times." Berton depicted himself as having struggled for about a decade after reaching Hogtown, but thereafter, the narrative of *My Times* became a parade of unexpected triumphs, turning the book for one reviewer into "a sometimes tedious chronicle." Yet it also resembled George MacDonald Fraser's riotous novels about the adventures of the Victorian adventurer and bounder Harry Flashman, with their eponymous hero somehow always at the flashpoints of history, and at times the causal agent. "Again and again," Buitenhuis noted, "he was the right man at the right place at the right time."

Reviews of *My Times* frequently reflected gendered positions. Buitenhuis liked the anecdotes and gossip Berton provided about his "good friends and tough enemies," the way he was one of the boys and was willing to dish it out and take it, too. The theme unifying Philip Marchand's review was of how Berton challenged conservative belief in all forms – "a career made throwing snowballs at top hats," as he put it, following Berton's own view of himself. But Van Luven was little taken with Berton's "adventures with his drinking buddies," a hint at the clubby "old boys" atmosphere that had pervaded so much of Canadian life when Berton was in his prime. The Toronto author Anne Denoon, reviewing for *Books in Canada*, was more blunt: "The journalistic band Berton joined may seem . . . quaint to younger readers: an alcohol-fuelled, almost all-male, visible-minority-free milieu."[6]

On one characteristic of *My Times* the reviewers agreed. This was not the book for readers who sought self-examination: "short on introspection" (Denoon); "very little about the author's emotional life" (Marchand). In the climate of the nineties, agonized introspection made for lucrative sales. Faced with the public hunger for self-revelation, the this-is-what-I-did adventures of an author raised by Victorians and shaped by the Depression, a man who saw history as a set of essentially public acts, could impress only by sheer industriousness. Pierre Berton had been as busy as any Canadian beaver, no doubt about that; but as Lynne Van Luven warned, "Jaded young things might consider this book a snore." The book's epilogue "finds him in elegiac mode," Anne Denoon wrote. "For Berton, as for other liberal crusaders of his generation," she added, "being publicly called a racist during the brouhaha surrounding the 1994 Writing Through Race conference was an experience that seems almost to have broken his spirit."[7]

In this way, the year 1995 saw Berton at once celebrated and sent to Coventry. With the release of *My Times*, a major story on the forthcoming International Festival of Authors in Toronto announced that its sixteenth annual gathering would feature a celebration of Berton's life and times, with an onstage interview by Charles Templeton and tributes by Margaret Atwood, Alan Borovoy, Michael Bliss, Arthur Hailey, Lister Sinclair, and the Inuit writer Mary Carpenter. Five days before the event, the *Globe and Mail* ran a full-page feature by Val Ross, "Captain Canada at 75." Ross drew attention to the soon-to-be-held Harbourfront event, noting that "at 75, Berton is going to get his with more 'icons' and 'beloveds.'" Throughout Berton's career, Ross observed, he had always been "either in synch with his times or slightly ahead of them." Nice words, but the caption beneath the accompanying photograph of "Captain Canada" better caught the thrust of the profile: "Pierre Berton, the man who joined TV in its infancy and who . . . had the instinct for writing the right books for the times, is out of synch with his country."[8]

The timely "tribute" read all too much like Berton's literary obituary. It mentioned the failing health ("I have an old man's diabetes") and the absence of a bestseller since *The Great Depression*. It noted that generalists like him, once dominating the bestseller lists, were "going the way of the general interest magazine, network television and neighbourhood public schools." These disappearances reflected the shrinking of the public sphere in the era of privatization, Salutin could have added, because private interests had pushed the idea of the public good to the margins: more resistance like Berton's to such forces was needed, not shrugs of resignation. But Ross took a different tack. She had little doubt that the Canadian icon would continue to publish, to recycle, to question authority, and to criticize half-baked ideas and hidebound beliefs. But his time was past. "One senses he has already kissed off parts of the century. . . . And what you see is Berton, finally, out of synch. His epic prose, his lack of interest in matters psychological, his stout liberal humanism, his vision of Canada are not the values of the 1990s. He knows it."[9]

Indeed he did. He knew he was captive to his temperament and his generation and did not mind it a bit. *My Times* illustrated the advice he had given Jack McClelland, for it focused on the public act rather than the private man, an approach that reflected both his lack of interest in psychological bafflegab and his fixation on the revelatory capacity of surface detail. After recounting the coming-of-age romps of his youth and early manhood, any discussion of his private life ended; he did not mention the Sordsmen's Club; he said nothing about tensions that may have existed within his marriage as the working relationship with Elsa Franklin developed, intensified, and became one that to others resembled something significantly more than a business partnership. But given his long-held views as a civil libertarian it was unthinkable that he should reveal any arrangement he and Janet might have worked out to reconcile his separate lives in Kleinburg and Cabbagetown. Any other intimate relationships likewise remained his business. The account of family life in *My Times* carried nary a hint of any resentments his children may have had living in the Berton fishbowl and struggling for success in the shadow of such an unmatchable role model.

For a man so interested in the culture and trappings of celebrity, Berton proved singularly uninterested in assessing its effects on those around him. In truth, it was Janet who provided her brood with the kind of patient guidance and grounding they needed for lives that could at times be as difficult as they were privileged; it was she, despite her own heavy involvement in community affairs, who had always subordinated her life to his, from finding errant files or lost socks to driving to his favourite North Toronto dry cleaner to pick up and deliver his clothing.[10] Instead, in *My Times*, the Berton children appear fleetingly, reprising much the same roles their father the narrator assigned them in *The Secret World of Og*. Only in his brief epilogue did Pierre release himself to introspection, and even then it was the introspection of the public man. "I am painfully aware," he wrote, "that I am no longer with it. I can sing all the lyrics of every popular song written in the thirties and forties, from 'Barnacle Bill the Sailor' to 'Sweet and Lovely,' but I cannot relate to the MuchMusic channel on television. . . . My times are accelerating so fast that the world has started to pass me by."[11]

Even so, he persisted, kicking against the pricks of time. On the eve of the second Quebec referendum he stood on Nathan Phillips Square with the dancer Veronica Tennant and the singer Maureen Forrester (whose daughter Paula Kash his son Peter had married) to greet the twenty-five thousand Canadians on the "Walk for Canada," a crowd desperate to convince the people of Quebec that their Canada included and needed Quebec. The intensely emotional, even cathartic gathering brought tears to the eyes of many, and Pierre Berton was one of them. The next day, as the referendum ballots were being counted, he joined the hockey legend Ken Dryden and the celebrated scientist John Polanyi on CBC television to discuss the meaning and likely consequences of the vote. This was the final nationalist moment of the century for English-speaking Canadians, the greatest and most uninhibited release of collective pride since Expo 67 and the victory of Team Canada over the Russians in the Canada-Soviet hockey series in 1972. Pundits and columnists noted that this strange country was one that had a history of spurning such outbursts – this country, as Robertson Davies once said, which was "not really a place where you are encouraged to have large spiritual adventures." Its storied history had made Canada a nation united, if at all, by patriotic commitment to state institutions rather than by nationalistic fervour. Why was it, the columnist Lynda Hurst asked, that Canadians had "so rigorously denied themselves the emotions of nationhood?" She spoke to Pierre Berton, among others, in search of an answer, for she knew his next book was going to be on Canada in 1967. Perhaps, he said, it was because two world wars had taught Canadians what devastation patriotism had wrought; or maybe the northern environment simply made them taciturn.[12]

The Quebec referendum and the emotion-laden Montreal rally that preceded it caused a number of Canadians, not least Berton, to reflect upon the state of the nation and their place in it. Jack Granatstein, once a staunch believer in the superiority of academic over popular history, now proclaimed that his own scholarly tribe had helped destroy Canadian unity and the national history on which it rested. "You can teach about maids in 1890s Sudbury or unionism in the West," he told Hurst bitterly, "but you can't teach the national story." On the other hand, Maude Barlow, chair of the social democratic Council of Canadians that Berton had helped found, reached the conclusion that the emotional outburst in Montreal held potential dangers, for it "could flow into right-wing nationalism." Canada, in her view, was better off without it. Whatever the perspective, right or left, the consensus was that the country suffered from a "national malaise." A panic of books released that fall described its several guises, not least Richard Gwyn's *Nationalism without Walls: The Unbearable Lightness of Being Canadian.* Meanwhile, *My Times* rose to number three on the *Globe and Mail* national bestseller list.[13]

"Berton seems to be edging gradually but ever more inexorably into the shadow – there is a wistful, elegiac tone to his recent work," Philip Marchand wrote toward the end of 1997. This was true, as the titles of his two most recent books indicated. *Farewell to the Twentieth Century* appeared in 1996, followed by *1967: The Last Good Year*, not long before Marchand wrote his column. Both books appeared under the imprint of Doubleday Canada, for with the publication of *My Times*, the Canadian branch of the large American publisher had become his main publisher. Thanks to Franklin's negotiating skills and the enthusiasm of Doubleday Canada's president, John Neale, who had worked at M&S during Berton's heyday, Berton once again had a publisher eager to promote his books.

Pierre's commitment remained strong, but the fire was gone and he was slowing down. He kept his engagements to a manageable number, although to most others his calendar would have appeared impossibly full. He continued to support favourite causes. With Margaret Atwood,

Farley Mowat, the artist Robert Bateman, and others, he helped lobby Ontario's Conservative government at Queen's Park to rescind its decision to open the Temagami area, rich with old-growth trees, to mining and logging. He held to his unpopular civil libertarian view that in the interests of freedom of expression, the British author David Irving, a serious historian but also a Holocaust denier, should be allowed to enter Canada to express his views, however odious. Berton was one of a number of prominent Canadians, including the ever-involved Atwood, Avie Bennett, the singer Sylvia Tyson, the lawyer Clayton Ruby, and the Barenaked Ladies singer Steven Page, who sent an open letter to Prime Minister Jean Chrétien to protest the $291-million cut to the CBC budget; he and others warned of the "grave injustice" that would be done to writers should Bill C-32, the government's amendment to the Copyright Act, go through as planned. He opposed the way the CBC brass was assigning different roles to its AM and FM networks, but supported the award of Toronto's last FM frequency to the corporation. With the CBC under assault by government cost-cutters, the Stanley Cup increasingly resident in the United States, and the national health system at risk, he lamented that so many "key symbols of Canadian culture" were under threat or vanishing. "If we lose things like that," he said, "we don't have a viable nation. A nation has to be a community."[14]

His increasing alienation from contemporary life threatened to turn his commitment to history into a form of nostalgia, at least in the public mind. But he was willing to take the chance if it meant getting Canadians to embrace their country at an emotional level. He released a CD-ROM in which his familiar voice could be heard narrating the text of *Klondike*. He gave a talk called "The Shape of the Nation" to attendees at the Winter Cottage Country Show at the Toronto Congress Centre. He took the stage at Roy Thomson Hall in June 1997 with Elmer Iseler, the Toronto Mendelssohn Choir, and the Hannaford Street Silver Band to provide the narration for an Iseler concert piece, "Canadian Tapestry," a coast-to-coast tour in the imagination. To the accompaniment of the choir and band, "the sage of Kleinburg" (so said the *Toronto Star*) read from his books, about voyageurs, Vimy Ridge, Loyalists, and loggers. "It was as close as Canadians come to forsaking their natural reticence," wrote Christopher Hume, "taking their hearts out of their back pockets and wearing them on their sleeves." The pitch Berton made to the emotions was old-fashioned but it was effective and it encouraged others. That year, the popular historians David Cruise and Alison Griffiths published a work of history in the Berton mould. *The Great Adventure: How the Mounties Conquered the West* acknowledged its indebtedness to his pioneering work.[15]

In May 1997 the CBC announced that Peter Gzowski would retire from *Morningside*, in itself a national institution, at the end of the month. Critics worried about who could possibly take his place, for Gzowski had become as comfortable to Canadians as an old pair of slippers. Michael Enright? Too cerebral and snide. Ian Brown? Too self-absorbed. Stuart McLean? Now there was a man with possibilities, for he had honed his talent for storytelling on Gzowski's radio show, once reducing its host and himself to an on-air fit of uncontrollable giggles over the apparent demise of a cricket McLean had bought for a dime. Since then, Gzowski's sidekick had turned the manufacture of nostalgia into a combination of art form and revenue stream with his CBC radio program *The Vinyl Café*, and while some members of the metropolitan cognoscenti may have adjusted their dials at the sound of the elongated intonation of his sentences and their Eliot-like drone, small-town English-speaking Canada did not. Here was a folksy Canadianism that unabashedly, like Berton's histories, tugged at the heartstrings. Self-fashioned as the Canadian version of Garrison Keillor, an avuncular Minnesotan as Canadian as an American could get, McLean modelled his program on Keillor's popular variety show on Minnesota Public Radio, *A Prairie Home Companion*, complete with its signature monologue. He could do wistful with the ease with which Peter Gzowski could drag on a cigarette. Within a year, McLean would take his show on the road, playing in town halls across the country to audiences eager to connect to a common culture and shared values. Meanwhile, the media critic Geoff Pevere wrote, the nation seemed on a countdown to some kind of cataclysmic event. Entertainment writers treated Gzowski's imminent departure "as though it were a papal deathwatch."[16]

Berton's generation was fast passing. When the journalist Ron Collister retired from radio in June 1995, after eighteen years as an on-air host, Berton was among those who phoned in with congratulations; two years later, a mere pup of sixty-nine, Collister was dead of kidney failure. Fred Davis had passed away of a stroke in 1996, at seventy-four, a little over a year after *Front Page Challenge* was cancelled. Clyde Gilmour died in November 1997, and Berton took part in a public tribute to him in the Glenn Gould Studio at the Broadcasting Centre of CBC Toronto with, among others, Alex Barris, the CBC broadcaster Shelagh Rogers, and Elwy Yost, long-time host of TVOntario's *Saturday Night at the Movies*. Jack McClelland remained alive, but precariously so. He had been found in the swimming pool of his Florida condominium in 1996, having apparently suffered a stroke. For some time he remained in a coma, and his family and friends realized once he returned to Toronto that he would never fully recover. The house that Jack built turned ninety that year, and at an Art Gallery of Ontario gala many M&S authors celebrated the anniversary, along with the life of Jumpin' Jack Flash. Berton was there, but his generation existed largely as ghosts amid the guests. Laurence and Davies were gone, and Mitchell and Callaghan, both in their eighties, were too weak to be present. Jack was well enough to attend, slender and silver-haired and frail – "a larger-than-life figure from another, and more tempestuous era," Judy Stoffman wrote. A figure like himself, Berton may have thought.[17]

Berton's *Farewell to the Twentieth Century*, for which he received an advance of $15,000, was a makework project propelled into print by the simple need to publish and an eye on a benchmark as the sum of his backlist now approached the number fifty. *My Times* had appeared only a year earlier, and Stoddart Publishing had released *Winter* and *The Great Lakes*, coffee-table books of photographs by André Gallant and text by Berton, in 1994 and 1996, respectively. His manuscript for the book on 1967 was near completion and due to be published on the thirtieth anniversary of Expo 67. But this was not enough. He revisited *My War with the 20th Century*, a collection of *Toronto Star* columns Doubleday had published out of New York in 1965, substituted the phrase "Farewell to" for "My War with," shuffled the contents, added a few recent pieces, and published the new concoction. He even recycled his 1946 short story "The Waiting Room." This was the huckster in him at work, ready to peddle second-hand or out-of-date wares as the new and the fashionable, and getting a kick out of it. As if to warn his readers of this, on the title page of the book's first section he provided a brief epigraph from D.H. Lawrence: "Never trust the artist. Trust the tale. . . ."[18]

Doubleday Canada provided *Farewell to the Twentieth Century* with a fresh-looking cover that showed Berton wearing a tartan bow tie and a shrug, as if he were saying, "Don't blame me. . . . It's life that's absurd." To its credit, the collection demonstrated Berton's capacity to maintain the alien's view of an otherwise familiar world. Some pieces dealt with the great issues, like nuclear deterrence and capital punishment. But most involved the lesser ludicrousness of everyday life. Berton excavated the first technologically driven consumer society as if he were Howard Carter at King Tut's tomb. What would the future make of the objects embedded in this century's sediment? The barbecue. The Coke bottle. The apron. And what of the twentieth century's peculiar compulsions and rituals? To satirize his culture's obsession with the female breast, he invented the Snarfs, an Amazon tribe that worshipped the elbow. Those with underdeveloped elbows wore padding; those better endowed had "to carry their arms in special slings for support, but this seems to make them all the more desirable."[19]

The critical response was mixed. In the *Globe and Mail,* CBC radio's Bill Richardson – himself a wry observer of life's foibles – signalled his appreciation of the book's sardonic humour. He praised its introduction, specially written as a letter to Berton's grandchildren. "This, he tells them, was a century that fed itself on its own lunacy, a century defined by a kind of abiding the-king-has-no-clothes neuroticism that willfully embraced the patently absurd." At his best, Richardson said, Berton ranked with James Thurber, Greg Clark, and Stephen Leacock. The collection was uneven, he noted, but when people assessed the twentieth century "Pierre Berton's name [would] be invoked as one of the most reliable and sharp-eyed of our country's interpreters."[20]

Side by side with Richardson's gentle assessment of Berton in the *Globe* on June 22, 1996, was the review of a book that was all about Richardson's generation. The book was *Boom, Bust, and Echo,* and it provided a demographic explanation of the way baby boomers had come to dominate all aspects of society and had done so from infancy into late middle age, with no signs of letting up. The cohorts that followed them – the "bust" (1967–79) and "echo" (1980–95) generations – lived in the shadow of the boomers and they resented it. The reviewers Stephen Smith and Linwood Barclay numbered among them, and they did not find *Farewell to the Twentieth Century* funny. "I can't remember the last time I got to the end of a book feeling so vanquished," wrote Smith, a Toronto writer, "so much like the book itself – hilarity free." Barclay, a *Toronto Star* columnist and the author of his own book, *Father Knows Zilch*, found Berton "a bit like that guy we knew who, after delivering a punch line, would demand to know whether we got it." Neither reviewer, in the wake of the scandalous California murder trial of O.J. Simpson, found Berton's heavy-handed satires, whether of James Bond in the dock accused of sexual harassment or of Amazonians obsessed with elbows, remotely amusing.[21]

The final years of the twentieth century were sour ones. The count-down to the new millennium had an apocalyptic ring to it, symbolized by near panic that the world's computers would crash. Use of the short-hand "Y2K" indicated that 2000 was the year that dared not speak its name. Books published in Canada during the run-up reflected the nation's dour mood, and 1997 proved no exception. Anthony Hyde published *Promises, Promises*, a book about "breaking faith in Canadian politics." The work, Peter C. Newman wrote, quivered with Hyde's "almost religious longing for politicians who might, at least occasion-ally, talk truth." Wayne Skene's *Delusions of Power* lamented the nefari-ous consequences of deregulation and privatization in the energy industry. In *1867: How the Fathers Made a Deal*, Christopher Moore showed how a hundred years earlier the Fathers of Confederation had accomplished what contemporary politicians had failed to pull off at Meech Lake and Charlottetown. The story was a salutary one, Jeffrey Simpson wrote in his review, "in a country that seems frightened to admit success, and sometimes seems to believe that history began the day before yesterday." The federal election in June 1997 resulted in a second majority government for the Jean Chrétien Liberals, but it revealed deep fissures in the body politic and a feeling of public ennui and electoral dismay. The death of Diana, Princess of Wales, pursued by paparazzi in a Parisian road tunnel at the end of August, led to an out-pouring of grief not witnessed since the assassination of John F. Kennedy twenty-five years earlier. The pall it cast intensified the gloom.[22]

Into this publishing season Berton launched *1967: The Last Good Year*, for which he received an advance of $152,000, an amount identi-cal to that for *My Times*. Peter Newman greeted it with a rave – as was his wont; earlier, when Berton had told him of the project at a writers' luncheon, Newman's reply had provided him with the book's title: "Well, that was the last good year." Canada's centennial, Berton wrote, had been a watershed, the brief shining moment that became Canada's Camelot. It was the country's unabashed display of pride and independence, the last year of genuinely shared national experience. As Judy LaMarsh, secretary of state in 1967, later said, "We grew up to be one hundred together, and we all shared that experience. We learned to have our own style. We cast off the bonds of our conformity, and slipped out of our cloak of grey anonymity forever." To tell this story, Berton and Barbara Sears had done their usual thorough survey of available evidence, sampling the nation's newspapers and magazines and conducting over thirty interviews (mainly in Toronto). They also explored the Lesbian and Gay Archives, the Ontario Jewish Archives, and the Hockey Hall of Fame in addition to collections of government documents and unpublished doctoral dissertations.[23]

The result was a snapshot of a year that began when residents of the small Manitoba town of Bowsman embraced the future by making a bonfire of its outhouses and ended with the departure of Prime Minister Pearson and the advent of the Trudeau era. Berton readily admitted that Canadians in 1997 were healthier and wealthier than they had been in 1967, and that Canada was a more tolerant and less repressed nation. In 1967 the Toronto Maple Leafs won the Stanley Cup, the first volume of the report of the Royal Commission on Bilingualism and Biculturalism recognized Canada's cultural dualism, and a new Royal Commission on the Status of Women promised equality between women and men. But *1967* also drew attention to the harbingers of a troubled future, and this lent the book a degree of dramatic tension. In July, Charles de Gaulle made his "Vive le Québec libre" speech at Montreal's city hall, while the band played "La Marseillaise" in the background; by October, René Lévesque had quit the Quebec Liberal Party to form the Mouvement Souveraineté-Association. The independence movement in Quebec gained new confidence, while the rest of Canada reacted with a combination of dismay, hurt, and a timorous fear of giving offence on this and other matters. The CBC, for example, proved unwilling to air *Warrendale*, Allan King's prizewinning documentary about disturbed children, and it abruptly cancelled *This Hour Has Seven Days*, nominally because the program offended public morality and violated journalistic ethics. "Why, then, do we look back to 1967 as a golden year compared to 1997?" Berton asked. "If we are better off today, why all the hand wringing? There are several reasons, but the big one, certainly, is the very real fear that the country we celebrated so joyously thirty years ago is in the process of falling apart. In that sense, 1967 was the last good year before all Canadians began to be concerned about the future of our country."[24]

Those of Berton's generation, like Newman, were inclined to agree with his bleak assessment, and others who in their youth had witnessed the exuberance of the sixties at first hand appreciated his portrait of the decade. Judy Daniel of Dearfield, Ontario, was one. "I have just finished reading it & want you to know what it has meant to me," she wrote. At last she had a way of conveying to her children what those years were like, she said. But critics of the sixties had little sympathy with Berton's depiction of the "last good year." Marianne Ackerman, a Montreal journalist, decried the "bitter nostalgia" of his evocation of Canada's brief golden age. "Was 1967 Canada's last hurrah, or simply the last good year for Pierre Berton's folksy dream of razzle-dazzle, 19th-century nationhood?" she asked.[25]

1967: The Last Good Year did well enough to merit publication by Seal as a mass-market paperback, with its provocative subtitle changed to the more benign *Canada's Turning Point*. The clothbound edition sold 10,541 copies between its release in fall 1997 and April 1999, but it failed to crack the *Globe and Mail*'s national bestseller list. In the fall of 1998, the list was a testimonial to a self-absorbed age, for it was populated by titles such as *Dr. Atkins' New Diet Revolution*, *Feeling Good: The New Mood Therapy*, and *The Milkman Next Door*. Among the few Canadian books to make the list that autumn was the Toronto literary scholar Rosemary Sullivan's study of Margaret Atwood, *The Red Shoes*, which entered as number ten on October 3, only to be supplanted the following week by *I Am Jackie Chan*.[26]

With his valedictory to the country's centennial in readers' hands, Berton turned his attention to the century that was about to end. Anniversaries, after all, are the bread and butter of the timely book. So he embarked on a lively survey of the past hundred years, tentatively called "The Uncertain Century." Designed to be released with the advent of the new millennium, the project threatened to derail from the outset. Its sheer magnitude was daunting. Berton quickly discovered that the available evidence was uneven. Hundreds of scholarly works existed on the period prior to 1950, but not enough diaries, memoirs, and historical accounts dealt with the half-century since then. In addition, most government documents were not yet released to the public; the decennial national census, for example, was closed to public scrutiny for the foreseeable future. To make matters worse, Barbara Sears became seriously ill and could not undertake the taxing research and travel the endeavour demanded. Pierre did employ Joan Forsey, an experienced journalist on economic and political matters, followed by the freelance researcher George Dick, and they searched the libraries and archives for resources. But no one could replace Sears's discerning eye, her ability to gather together the raw materials needed to paint word pictures and to project and organize the overall shape of a book in a form that resembled a movie's storyboard. For this had become the necessary groundwork that allowed Berton to lay out his books as a series of scenes, enriched with descriptive "texture" and artfully stitched together by transitional bridges.

At a certain point as he mulled over his research, he recognized that the dominant theme of "Canada's century" had been that of war; it provided him with the key to organizing his unruly project. He decided to confine the book to Canadian military engagements, from those in South Africa in 1899 to the actions in Korea during the early 1950s. The result was *Marching as to War*.[27] The title was scarcely original: it came from one of the most popular Victorian hymns, "Onward Christian Soldiers," with the opening line "Onward Christian soldiers, marching as to war." Berton the joyful recycler had already used the phrase as the title of a chapter in *Starting Out*.

In January 1998, Pierre learned of the death of his old friend W.O. Mitchell. He had last seen Mitchell at the Winnipeg Art Gallery, when W.O. delivered the 1996 Margaret Laurence Memorial Lecture. Established by the Writers' Union shortly after Laurence's death in 1987, the lecture had become the highlight of each year's annual meeting. In 1996 it was Mitchell's turn to speak on a writer's life, clearly with little time left, since he had been undergoing chemotherapy treatments and was much weakened, delivering his lecture from a wheelchair. It was a courageous performance – evocative and poignant, memory faltering but not the heart, at some moments hilarious and at others deeply moving. When it ended, to a standing ovation, Berton expressed the gratitude of those present and bid what both friends knew was a fond farewell to the beloved author. Berton's eyes welled with tears as he recounted favourite stories and thanked Mitchell for finding the strength to rise from a hospital bed to entertain and edify others.[28]

Over the decades, Berton and Bill Mitchell had been close. Pierre had many friends in literary circles – Atwood, Mowat, Callaghan, Laurence, Davies, Findley, others – but a degree of ease and intimacy developed during the *Maclean's* years between the enthusiastic gadfly and the introspective humorist that marked their friendship as special. Bill Mitchell's view then was that Pierre's talents were wasted as a journalist, that he had something more substantial to contribute to Canadian life than magazine articles would allow. The fleeting nature of such work troubled both men.

Despite their difference in temperament, or perhaps because of it, when the two men got together, conversation tended to turn toward matters of deep significance. There was something about Mitchell, perhaps the dialectic of innocence and experience that marked his sensibility or the fact that both men saw the course of life as essentially a quest for meaning. Maybe it was just Mitchell's homespun voice, rasplike but comforting, that allowed Berton to open up to him. Berton had read and provided acute observations on the manuscript of his friend's second novel, "The Alien," for John Gray at Macmillan in 1953. Early in the summer of 1961, Pierre travelled to High River with a *Close-Up* film crew to do a feature on the author of *Who Has Seen the Wind*, and Mitchell subsequently appeared no fewer than three times on *The Pierre Berton Show*.[29]

For *The Kite* (1962) Mitchell had specifically used the Berton of *Maclean's* and the *Toronto Star* as his inspiration for David Lang, the highly strung but inquiring and attractive veteran reporter and television celebrity who arrives in the prairie town of Shelby to write a profile of its cantankerous 111-year-old patriarch, Dad Sherry, and instead gains a woman's love. The novel, which tells of one man's attempt to understand another, hints at conversations the two men held during and after their years at *Maclean's*. That Mitchell associates Lang's restiveness with a fatherless childhood suggests the possibility that at some point during his conversations with Pierre the subject had turned to Berton's own father. In *The Kite*, David Lang tries to get to know Dad Sherry, whose recesses seem impenetrable, and as he encounters this inscrutable man he begins to acquire a deeper understanding of life, of love and happiness, and of himself. When Mitchell later said, in his Laurence Memorial Lecture, that "we writers are travellers – all travelling through time from the time that we are born till the time we reach a common destination that all mortals have," no one in the art gallery audience would have identified more fully with the sentiment than his friend Pierre.[30]

Berton's spirits were buoyed in 1998 by his selection for the new Canadian Walk of Fame, as one of the inaugural group of Canadians whose names were to be engraved in granite stars set into the sidewalks of Toronto's theatre district. Despite some controversy over whether this was too American a form of commemoration, Berton and thirteen others saw their stars, in the shape of stylized maple leaves, set in concrete that June. Among the other honorees were the singers Gordon Lightfoot and Anne Murray, the actors Christopher Plummer and John Candy, the pianist Glenn Gould, the race car driver Jacques Villeneuve, and the figure skater Barbara Ann Scott. But against the more pleasant aspects of the year, which included hosting a seventeen-day tourist cruise from Hong Kong to Singapore in October, were decidedly less pleasant dealings with McClelland & Stewart, which still controlled his backlist. Berton complained early in the year when he could not find a copy of either *The National Dream* or *The Last Spike* in the CPR exhibit in the lobby of the Hotel Vancouver and was told by exhibit staff that the books were out of print. If this was indeed the case, he wrote to M&S's publisher, Doug Gibson, he wished to retrieve the rights to the books. Gibson assured him that the two railway volumes remained in print in the Penguin mass-market editions and insisted that, by the terms of the original 1970 contract, M&S retained the rights to the books in all formats.[31]

The tension between the parties did not end there, for Berton was quite concerned about the way McClelland & Stewart was handling his backlist, a source of a significant portion of his yearly income. He requested reversion of the rights for *The Arctic Grail* because, with only a few hundred copies remaining in the M&S warehouse, it was effectively out of print. He made the same request with respect to *Vimy* and the two War of 1812 books. Franklin believed all his major titles should remain in print, and of course he concurred. Doug Gibson retorted that the only Berton titles "out of stock" in the Penguin mass-market paperback format were *Vimy*, *Why We Act like Canadians*, *The Promised Land*, and *My Country*. Perhaps accounting details were so sparse because in a number of cases Berton had not earned back his advance, he suggested.

The dispute, inevitably involving Franklin, continued for more than a year. Finally, in February 2000, Avie Bennett confirmed that the rights to fifteen of Berton's historical works, from *Klondike* to *A Picture Book of Niagara Falls*, would revert to the author. From Bennett's point of view, and no doubt that of Doug Gibson as well, this was to M&S's benefit, since Berton's statements of royalty earnings for July 1 to December 31, 1998, showed that he had earned only $10,763.77 for all of his adult titles. Meanwhile, the unearned advance on the juvenile series now stood at $117,061.57, an average deficit of $5,321.00 for each of the twenty-two volumes, now all published. The unearned advances on the historical and photographic Niagara books stood at $59,656.13.[32] Eventually Doubleday would issue much of the Berton backlist in freshly designed trade paperback formats, ensuring that his main historical works remained on bookstore shelves.

The year, which began for Berton with a death, also contained "a literary resurrection," for this phrase became the subtitle of what proved to be his final collection of previously published articles. In May 1998, Doubleday brought out *Worth Repeating*. Dedicated to Elsa Franklin, it was a useful collection – not least for its $30,000 advance – because it contained many of his most memorable writings as a journalist. Some selections had been written for *Maclean's*, *Mayfair*, and the *Toronto Star*; others were drawn from previous anthologies and from *The Comfortable Pew* and *The Smug Minority*. The pieces included his 1949 article for *Maclean's* on television, "The One-Eyed Monster," his 1958 column for the *Star* on the practice of torture in modern Canada, the 1965 account in *The Comfortable Pew* of why he left the Anglican Church, and "The Car as a Cultural Driving Force," written for *Canadian Geographic* in 1989. In the preface to the volume, the broadcaster and columnist Geoff Pevere positioned Berton as perhaps the nation's greatest example of the journalist as generalist, writing not for posterity but for his times. "To read him on Toronto's Union Station during the fifties, on the *Star* newsroom during the twenties, or on returning with his family to his boyhood home of Dawson City, is to breathe the very aroma of a past moment in our country's history. . . . For a great many of us not even born when he wrote what follows, he made it impossible to think about Canada without thinking of him."[33]

Pevere's observations were prescient, for they suggested that in an unmoored age, increasingly stripped by global forces of a sense of history and collectively held national values and traditions, Berton was not as out of synch as some of his more cynical recent critics preferred to think. *Worth Repeating* reminded people that behind his rah-rah, heart-on-the-sleeve nationalism, which put off those young urbanites seduced by New York or London, was the man who for half a century had told one story above all: "the story of Pierre Berton's belief in Canada as a just and tolerant society, and of his conviction in his own practice as a way to police breaches of that fragile but honourable contract." Reviewers agreed with Pevere's assessment. This book by "a Canadian icon" was "truly worth repeating," the historian and novelist Allan Levine declared in *Books in Canada*. Levine drew readers' attention to Berton's powerful writings on issues of social justice – from his exposure of abuse in Canadian prisons to his angry requiem on the Truscott decision. "A carefully crafted selection . . . that shows a writer engaging with the world around him," one that demonstrates "the remarkable currency of Berton's spiritual, political, and cultural criticism," wrote the Toronto writer and poet Michael Holmes in *Quill and Quire*.[34] The brand retained its lustre.

On January 11, 1999, CBC television aired a documentary called *Pierre Berton: Canada's Arrogant Icon* in its *Life and Times* series. Produced by the Idea Factory! out of Edmonton, the hour-long profile, introduced by the novelist Ann-Marie MacDonald and narrated by the broadcaster Knowlton Nash, began with an outburst from its seventy-eight-year-old subject – "Goddamn right, I'm arrogant" – and then proceeded to lay out Berton's variegated career, demonstrating along the way that the arrogance was a pose intended to signify Berton's rejection of Canadian diffidence. To be arrogant, he said, is to be sure of yourself. Besides, as June Callwood noted on the program: "How could he help but be arrogant with all the things he's done? He can't pretend he didn't do them."

Other old friends appeared in the documentary. Berton "spoke truth to power," said Lister Sinclair; he was "the most aggressive spokesman of a liberal humanist tradition in Canada, then or since," he added. "No, he wasn't stubborn," Charles Templeton stated. "He believed what he believed." Overall, *Canada's Arrogant Icon* portrayed a Canadian who was self-confident, quite able and willing to mock his celebrity status, and well aware of advancing age. The most poignant moments in the televised portrait were those filmed in Dawson City. As the camera rolled, in scenes with the Administration Building and the old family bungalow in the background, he spoke fondly of his life in this town of collapsed buildings and discarded machinery, "rusty, falling away, like the rest of us."[35]

The broadcast prompted a surge of letters from friends and strangers alike to his Cabbagetown office. Having come across the documentary's title, Dave Sutherland of Victoria wrote even before he saw the show: "I am not certain what the O.E.D. says, but 'arrogant' is a term applied to the over-confident who have contempt for others. Rather, you should refer to yourself as 'self-confident,' a commendable quality." Sutherland had first encountered Berton when he read the Headless Valley series in the *Vancouver Sun* in 1947. Berton's discovery of the picture of Rita Hayworth in an abandoned northern cabin remained fixed in his memory. "It may have been that article that contributed to my spending the last thirty-seven years in the Northwest Territories, not a moment of which do I regret," he told Berton. "Thank you for being self-confident and good at what you do." Jeanne Hopkins of North York also took exception to the "arrogance" theme. "I disagree with many who describe you as aloof and not approachable." She had written to him years earlier, and had felt "honoured" when he replied. Dinah Christie had known Pierre since her stint as the satiric songstress of *This Hour Has Seven Days*, if not longer; later, she appeared on his television show. "You really are Canada to me, and I thank God for having been around to watch you grow and contribute so hugely to our National Pride," she wrote. "I think you're one of the all-time great Canadian writers and a real national icon!" wrote a fan. "It was obvious that you were not only an icon, but an approachable icon," wrote another, who had met him at a Writers' Union meeting.[36]

Toward the end of February, Pierre and Janet went on vacation and booked themselves into the Club Med resort at Varadero in Cuba. While there, Pierre had an attack of severe pain that was diagnosed as congestive heart failure, and he almost died. Following a few days in hospital he was transported back to Toronto by air ambulance (at a cost of $18,490). During his recovery over the following months, he lost forty pounds and developed an unsteady gait that failed to improve with time. Notes of concern arrived from friends shocked to learn that they had come so close to losing him. Janice Tyrwhitt wrote: "I'm only one among so many you've given a hand up the ladder at work, and a warm hug at your splendid parties." Timothy Findley sent a note from France. "Our time together at work on The Dream and with The Union are seminal – absolute centres of unforgettable comradeship and a sharing of convictions at every level. Besides which, you old devil, you taught me how to tie a bow tie! . . . You will not know what I owe you – but I do. And I thank you." Graeme Gibson also sent his regards from France, saying that he and Peggy (Atwood, his life partner) already looked forward to the annual sojourn to Pelee Island, where they all regularly went birding. Pierre appreciated his friends' good wishes but was worried at the loss of six months of work time.[37]

He curtailed his normal range of activities for the remainder of the year, and with Franklin he closed the offices of My Country Productions at 21 Sackville Street. From this point on, most of his business mail went to Kleinburg, the final home of Pierre Berton Enterprises. He answered correspondence from there, with some secretarial assistance; publishing matters and interviews were usually handled at Franklin's house on Hillcrest Avenue. The letters kept pouring in: notice from M&S that *Niagara* had been remaindered at $2.25; thanks from Canadians for Medical Progress for his support of animal rights; more thanks, this time from John Herbert, author of the controversial 1967 play *Fortune and Men's Eyes* (about homosexuals, attitudes toward them, and their treatment in prisons), for the "rich and thought-provoking word pictures" Berton had provided of "the past that has shaped us." He learned that he had won the Alliance of Canadian Cinema, Television and

Radio Artists' John Drainie Award for his contribution to broadcasting. The Canadian Club thanked him for the address he gave in November, "Did the 20th Century Belong to Canada?"[38]

One of the last letters he had written before going on his ill-fated vacation had been one of encouragement to Penny Dickens, since 1982 the executive director of the Writers' Union of Canada, urging her to persist in the important work she did for the organization despite problems she had experienced with its "late, lamented executive." Up and around and back at the typewriter in September, he maintained his outreach. He advised a nine-year-old aspiring author from Kleinburg that it might be better to write her book before contacting a publisher; he nominated Maude Barlow and Eric Nicol for induction into the Order of Canada; he reminisced at length with a war veteran about his experience in Korea; he sent the writer Heather Robertson a promissory note for $1,000 in support of her class-action suit against Thomson Canada over electronic rights for authors. At year's end he wrote an introduction for Rick Searle's book *Phantom Parks*, adding the weight of his authority to Searle's argument that Canada's national parks were under threat from the forces of industry, tourism, and development, and that action was necessary if the parks' fragile ecologies were to be rehabilitated.[39]

All this involved a good deal of work, but often enough a letter arrived that more than compensated for the effort. One such missive came in August, from Surrey, England. John May had first discovered Berton on television in 1967 while visiting Canada. Since then, married into a Canadian family, he had thoroughly explored Pierre Berton's Canada. He had travelled to Craigellachie and driven to Dawson City. "We made the pilgrimage to Vimy," May wrote, "and saw Niagara in a different light after reading your books. Of course the thirties on the Prairies were also made clearer to us. . . . Thank you for opening my eyes to Canadian history and life." Vivien Bowers of Nelson, B.C., also wrote to tell him how often his books had touched her life. She had been delighted and touched, for example, to discover Berton next to her father, Fritz, once Vancouver's city manager, in an old family photograph. Such signs that he continued to connect with people helped rebuild his strength.[40]

Pierre's former Dawson City home had once again come alive, for in 1989 he had learned that the old bungalow was available for sale and arranged for the Yukon Arts Council to purchase it, assisted by his gift of $50,000. Pierre and Lucy had opened it in 1996 after structural and other repairs were made. Russell Smith, a Toronto novelist and cultural commentator, became its first writer-in-residence. The thirty-three-year-old Smith had the memorable experience of a seven-hour drive with Berton from Whitehorse to Dawson City.

Between Smith's residency in 1996 and the beginning of 2001, thirteen other writers from across the country had lived and worked at Berton House, usually for three months each. Local organizations provided maintenance, members of the arts council acted as hosts, the Canada Council paid travel and living expenses, and a committee consisting of Pierre, Elsa, and others chose the residents from among a pool of applicants. Committee members at times hinted that applications should be open to writers of any stripe, and that they should be required to stipulate precisely what they intended to accomplish, but Berton disagreed. In a letter written in 2000 to a member of the Berton House committee he provided his conception of the retreat. First, it should be for professional writers who had published at least one commercial book. Second, the writers should not be obliged to produce anything. "My original idea was that they could have that time to reflect, to get to know the Yukon, and if they wish to write, to complete some writing. But the main purpose is not to let them write, but simply to give them time off from writing if they want it, or time off to think about writing or about the place they're living in. That's why I called it a 'retreat.' As I well know, writers do need time off away from telephones and other people in order to collect their thoughts. This is what produces great books."[41]

When asked to undertake one engagement or another, he now openly stated that he was semi-retired and interested in spending whatever energy was left to him in writing his books. But when Art Jones, his Headless Valley companion, asked him to write a note of appreciation for a celebration of the eighty-seven-year-old Canadian big band leader Mart Kenney, to whose music Pierre used to dance, he was happy to oblige. He kept up with old friends, as always. "Seems a long time since we played Monopoly at your home," he wrote to Cy Porter, a British Columbia friend from childhood. "I never forgot the way to win in business was to buy Park Place, and slap a hotel on it. Strange, isn't it, how a boyhood inclination can lead to a fierce acquisitive nature?" In another letter to "Hambone," his affectionate name for Porter, he returned to the subject: "You'll be interested to know that my grand-children (I have thirteen) are all made Monopoly players, much as we were in the old days. The damn game, however, takes too long for me, so I let the little kids struggle over it on a Sunday afternoon."[42]

The new century brought renewed celebration of his life. In the summer of 2000, he marked his eightieth birthday. The day became something of a media event, with reporters and photographers invited to witness his regular workout on a treadmill. That night, Janet staged a poolside splash party, attended by the Berton clan and about two hundred guests. Toronto dailies noted the occasion with major profiles. Canadian Press sent news of the birthday to subscribing newspapers across the country, reporting that Berton spent part of the day at his health club before downing a piece of coconut cream pie (his favourite) and a cup of coffee. In *Maclean's* Allan Fotheringham wrote his millionth column about him. "Pierre Berton, songster, partygoer, storyteller, star of stage, screen and radio, has written 38 books in 38 years. Or is it 1,381 books in 1,381 years? No one can remember."[43]

Each month another symbol of Canadian identity seemed to disap-pear or come under threat of doing so. In June, McClelland & Stewart literally gave itself to the University of Toronto. Donating 75 per cent of the company to the university and selling the remaining 25 per cent to Random House was the only way the venerable house could be kept intact and its survival guaranteed, said seventy-three-year-old Avie Bennett. Berton, like others in the publishing industry, was relieved that the firm lived on. He also became involved in efforts to preserve the *St. Roch*, the RCMP schooner that in 1944 had done what no ship had done before: traverse the treacherous waters and icefields that con-stitute the Northwest Passage. Over the years, the *Globe and Mail* reported, the old ship had been badly neglected through government cost-cutting and the "collective amnesia [of] Canadians who probably know more about *Old Ironsides* . . . than they do about the *St. Roch*." Berton had already lamented the disappearance of Eaton's, which had established so many connections with Canadians, from its bargain basement sales and mail-order catalogues to its store-sponsored Santa Claus parades and its special 1948 Christmas toy, Punkinhead, the teddy bear with the unruly tuft of hair.[44]

Ironically, the author of *The National Dream* was less disheartened when financiers split Canadian Pacific Limited into five separate companies. "The tradition of rail travel," he told the *Globe and Mail* business commentator Eric Reguly, "is in the past." From another perspective, the real sadness of the occasion was perhaps that Reguly, attention clearly fixed on the corporate bottom line, took such glee in ridiculing those who would be "weepy with nostalgia about the dismemberment of a cultural icon." Any cultural icon? M&S had survived, but barely. Commenting on the means used to ensure the survival of cultural institutions as central to Canada's cultural identity as the Canada Council, the CBC, or the Stratford Festival, the columnist Martin Knelman expressed alarm that Jack McClelland's great achievement had met such a strange fate. "I'm afraid the time has come," he concluded, "to admit the country McClelland once governed finally is on the verge of disintegrating." That summer, news came from the High Arctic that global warming was causing the ice packs of the Northwest Passage to disappear. Another Canadian touchstone was melting away.[45]

Canadians had been ground down by almost thirty years of attacks on national borders and the pride of nation that went with them, and the assault showed no signs of lessening. Russell Smith declared the romanticism of seventies-style nationalism, with its emphasis on cultural survival and "the myth of the wilderness," to be of little significance for the new Canada. (Bertonian nationalism had been important decades earlier, Smith told an interviewer in 2003. "I think it's over now. It's turned into provincialism, and I don't feel a part of it."[46]) Besides, he said, what meaning could it possibly have for the Portuguese teenagers or Vietnamese businessmen of Canada's large cities? (Perhaps more than Smith suspected, since he, born in South Africa, and his partner had made fifteen attempts to rent a summer cottage.) A fellow *Globe* columnist, Heather Mallick, signalled her agreement with the view of the philosopher Mark Kingwell that "nostalgic fantasy" was "structurally unstable, important for what it hides more than what it reveals" (Kingwell's words). She found Sinatra's song "It Was a Very Good Year" odious and confessed that she gagged when preparing to write "an affectionate review" of Berton's *1967: The Last Good Year*. To her, the year had not been good at all; nor was any other, except when viewed through nostalgia's distorting lenses. William Thorsell, cultural bureaucrat and former *Globe and Mail* editor-in-chief, suggested that the nationalist vision of "George Grant, Pierre Berton, Walter Gordon, Pierre Trudeau, Margaret Atwood, and the NDP" be replaced by Mordecai Richler's Duddy Kravitz and his incessant hustle. As a substitute for the brief cultural "moment" of unadulterated Canadian nationalist feeling in the sixties and seventies, a vision that clearly distinguished the nation's values and interests from those of the United States, Thorsell suggested the one articulated in *Here: A Biography of the New American Continent*, a book by a former *New York Times* Ottawa correspondent, Anthony De Palma. The new Canadian nation of Thorsell's longings, shaped by the North American Free Trade Agreement, would be (*pace* De Palma) "a space with no 'there' defined by national borders."[47]

Every such body blow delivered to Berton's kind of Canadian identity, whether struck by bluster, ridicule, or cynicism, in fact helped dust off and polish the Berton brand. Early in the year, the *Star*'s Sid Adilman reported that "the man dubbed Captain Canada" showed no signs of being finished. A couple of months later, in May, when Peter C. Newman abruptly announced that he had resigned from Friends of Canadian (formerly Public) Broadcasting because it had strayed from its original idealistic goals, Berton broke with his friend on the issue. "It's broadened its mandate to include concerns over what is happening in the private sector," he said, "and I think that's appropriate because public broadcasting is affected by private broadcasting." He refrained from speculating whether Newman's sudden announcement might have been linked to the fact that the private broadcaster CanWest Global, frequently attacked by Friends of Canadian Broadcasting for its low quotient of Canadian content, was about to broadcast a four-part documentary series based on Newman's book *The Titans*. Most members of the Canadian cultural community stood with Berton, not Newman. That fall, in a delicious irony, the editor of *Maclean's*, Anthony Wilson-Smith, on the occasion of excerpting *Marching as to War*, pronounced Berton "our king of convergence" – "a walking, talking human prototype of the media platforms that BCE, the Asper family and others are spending hundreds of millions to develop. . . . So we can thank Berton for teaching us more about our past – and also for serving as a role model for the media in the future." Little wonder that Judy Stoffman reported on "the adulation that now follows . . . Pierre Berton, former bad boy of Canadian media."[48]

He knew that he was no longer "at the centre of things," but delighted in recounting his fall into grace. The experienced newshound was well aware that newspapers across the country were already preparing his obituary. So, in more circumspect ways, were his friends and admirers, for the former organized events in his honour and the latter attended them in droves. On April 26, 2001, largely at the initiative of the indomitable Elsa, a Toronto fundraiser celebrated Berton's fiftieth year as a writer. (That his first paid journalism dated back almost sixty years and his first book – *The Royal Family* in 1954 – only forty-seven, did not seem to matter.) Four hundred guests paid $100 each to dine on a ten-course meal at the Imperial Gourmet Garden Restaurant, a Chinese establishment on Dundas Street, and to hear testimonials from writers, publishers, and old friends. In attendance were several former writers-in-residence at the Berton House Writers' Retreat, including Russell Smith and the literary critic Audrey Thomas. Proceeds from the event went to support the retreat and its operations. The next day Rick Salutin's *Globe and Mail* column took the form of a tribute to Pierre Berton and Eric Nicol for the role models they had been for him.[49]

"Timing can make a book or break it," Berton wrote when reflecting on what made some books popular and others not.[50] Settling on a date of publication was like spinning a kind of literary roulette wheel. An author had little control over the outcome. Yet it had not been mere chance that *Maclean's* experienced its "golden years" when Berton was writing for it and editing its pages, or that the subscription numbers at the *Star* had skyrocketed during his tenure as daily columnist. Too many of his books had been the fabled "right book at the right time" to reflect mere happenstance. *The Mysterious North* had appeared just when Canadians began to take the "new north" seriously, and *Klondike* coincided with the first flush of enthusiasm for Diefenbaker's "northern vision." Sales of *The Royal Family* had faltered only with the exhaustion of public attention following Queen Elizabeth II's coronation. *The Big Sell* appeared in the heyday of the consumer revolution, helping people understand it, and *The Comfortable Pew* and *The Smug*

Minority mirrored and stirred the flux of social change in the sixties. *The National Dream* and *The Last Spike* helped shape the newly discovered nationalism of the early seventies, and *The Invasion of Canada* and *Flames across the Border* appeared during the "first fine rapture" of the marketers of globalization as they campaigned to counteract the nationalist impulse in Canada.

So it was, too, with *Marching as to War: Canada's Turbulent Years 1899–1953*. Doubleday Canada launched the book on September 9, 2001. Less than forty-eight hours later, terrorists attacked New York and Washington, putting the world on alert that no place on earth was safe any longer and sending the United States on a path to war. In the aftermath of 9/11, and with Canadians concerned about their future international role, Berton's lengthy saga of a peaceable kingdom gone by necessity to war immediately resonated with readers. Whatever the critics might say about the merits of *Marching as to War*, people were keen to buy it. By Remembrance Day, 2001, it was number three on the *Toronto Star* bestseller list after eight weeks in the lineup; it continued to hold its own into the new year.

The success came despite the fact that the book had itself been the object of a sneak attack. In August, a month before publication, Jack Granatstein, using galley proofs, had published a blistering review in *Books in Canada*. Fresh from a stint as director of the Canadian War Museum, and with a history of the Canadian army just completed, Granatstein, like C.P. Stacey before him, was clearly not pleased to find this interloper on his turf. Berton's book, he wrote, was so "riddled with errors of fact and historical interpretation" that it was "completely unreliable." Apprised of the review, Berton admitted that the book indeed contained errors of fact, but suggested that Granatstein's chief grudge was over *Marching as to War*'s conclusion that Canadian soldiers had fared less well in the Second World War than they had in the Great War of 1914–18 and that the army might have done better under British instead of Canadian command. Granatstein had found this an extraordinary position for a nationalist to take, but Berton stood firm: "We didn't have a single trained officer with battle experience. Canadians had been badly trained in the Depression."[51]

Reviewers with less at stake in the success of Berton's book and its contrarian views than Granatstein were not as harsh. In the *Toronto*

Star, Hans Werner, an expert on the Winnipeg Mennonite community, confessed that Berton's style put him to sleep, but otherwise he took little issue with the book and its interpretations. Of particular interest to Werner was "the recurring sense of déjà vu" he experienced as the cultural, social, and political ramifications of the narrative unfolded, for he discovered that the interwar years in Canada had been ones of alienation and discord, rather like Werner's own day. In the *Globe and Mail*, Modris Eksteins, author of the Trillium-Prize-winning book *Rites of Spring: The Great War and the Birth of the Modern Age*, commended the book for its "narrative verve," while noting that its focus on "the drama of life and death" left the author little time or space to reflect or analyze complex issues. In a telling point, Eksteins wondered, too, whether Berton's "judgmental narrative," so reminiscent of the nineteenth-century historians Carlyle and Macaulay, moralistic believers in the providential unfolding of progress, was an approach to history suitable for the twenty-first century. "It is this progressivist vision of history and historians," Eksteins noted, "that the wars of the 20th century assaulted, along with so much else."[52]

Berton could have done little to meet this criticism: he would have had to alter his view of the world. Still, he knew his book would have been better had circumstances been different. Jack Granatstein had criticized him for ignoring primary sources in archives and writing instead from the secondary accounts of scholars. Guilty as charged, a verdict that reflected how crucial Barbara Sears had been to the success of his books. The two researchers who had taken her place had scoured libraries for sources on the subject, but they lacked Sears's intimate acquaintance with archival records. Given her unavailability for research and his advancing age, *Marching as to War*, all 632 pages of it, was the best book he could produce, and with these liabilities was perhaps even a significant achievement. Fortunately, the capable women around him once again served him well. Janet kept his home life stable. Elsa prodded him into persisting when his bad heart made him think about quitting. Janice Tyrwhitt provided her usual thorough critique (although in one instance he refused her suggestion to delete a section on three interwar fraudsters she thought irrelevant but he found fascinating: she was right). Barbara Sears was well enough to offer incisive comments and helpful suggestions, which he heeded. "I think of them as lifeguards," he wrote, "manning shore stations, ever ready to throw me an inflatable raft as I flail around in a literary ocean."[53]

Interest in Canada's history had begun to grow in the mid-1990s, out of concern for the "cultural amnesia" of the times. One sign of this was the founding of Canada's National History Society in 1994. Having inherited *The Beaver*, the magazine of popular history, from the Hudson's Bay Company, the society immediately created the Pierre Berton Award for distinguished achievement in the writing of popular history. Then it named Pierre Berton as the first recipient. The fiftieth anniversary of the end of the Second World War also increased interest in the nation's past, especially its military and political affairs. Jack Granatstein had been instrumental in stirring this revival of interest, commenting on Canada's military heritage, championing the idea of a new Canadian War Museum, and attacking academic historians, school administrators, and politicians, whom he held largely responsible for the death of Canadian history. Meanwhile, Charlotte Gray's dual biography of Susanna Moodie and Catharine Parr Traill, *Sisters in the Wilderness*, competed for pride of place on the bestseller lists with Frank McCourt's *Angela's Ashes*, the poignant memoir of the author's early life as an impoverished Irish emigrant to America. At the beginning of 2001, the number one spot on the *Globe and Mail* non-fiction list was taken up by *Canada: A People's History*, an illustrated volume based on the highly successful CBC television documentary series of the same name.

Berton himself had become pessimistic about the future of Canadian history. In an interview with Rudyard Griffiths, head of the Dominion Institute, an organization dedicated to combatting the loss of a common memory and civic identity in Canada, he lamented the "fading away" of Canadian nationalism and with it a sense of community and of stories held in common. To Griffiths's suggestion that the new century was witnessing a resurgence of Canadian patriotism – he cited Molson Breweries' unabashedly nationalist "I Am Canadian" television ads as an example – Berton replied: "I don't think average young Canadians give a damn about history." He expressed his worry about globalization and the anxiety that came with it. "What will protect our identity is our culture," he told Griffiths. "It will not be our economics or the fact that we have a lot of gold in the ground. But if we produce a distinctive culture, then we will remain an independent nation in that sense." The crisis of remembrance in Canada was real; in his view, it would be up to the writers and the poets to do something about it.[54]

The bureaucracy of the federal government demonstrated its degree of awareness of Canadian writers and intellectuals just before Christmas, 2001, when a branch of the Department of Canadian Heritage informed Berton that in order for the producers of *Canada's Arrogant Icon* to receive their tax credit, he would have to supply proof he was a Canadian. He refused to sign the document sent to him. Executives of the Idea Factory supported his stance, expressing their shock at the government's request. Berton found his situation ludicrous. His family, after all, had been in Canada for generations. "It's nationalism gone crazy," he said. "I couldn't believe they were asking me to say I was Canadian." Faced with citizens as incredulous as they were irate at this bureaucratic nonsense, a sheepish federal government backed down. No spokesperson of the Canadian Audio-Visual Certification Office returned journalists' telephone calls and Pierre Berton never did produce proof of citizenship.[55]

His health began to deteriorate significantly in 2002. Because of the unsteadiness on his feet, he had been using a cane since the late 1990s, but walking had now become painful and difficult. Diabetes meant the circulation in his legs was poor. He bitterly resented that cane, Patsy thought, because he didn't want to admit he was failing. A driver transported him to and from Toronto whenever necessary. He attended the comedian Frank Shuster's funeral at Holy Blossom Temple in January, and it was Pierre, photographed in a fit of laughter with Peter's mother-in-law, Maureen Forrester, who graced the pages of the *National Post* and the *Globe and Mail* the next day. He read from *Marching as to War* at the Words in Whitby reading series in April and banded together with Robert Bateman, the pianist Anton Kuerti, the singers Buffy Sainte-Marie and Bruce Cockburn, David Suzuki, Margaret Atwood, and others that September to denounce the anticipated war in Iraq. "Stick to your poetry and pianos," was Marcus Gee's response in a *Globe and Mail* column, the first words of which fixed upon "Pierre Berton, author." "If ever there were proof that brains and common sense don't always go together, this is it."[56]

Views like Gee's may have played well in Washington or in the Langevin Block or National Defence headquarters in Ottawa, but they found decidedly less favour among mainstream Canadians. The "glit-terati" Gee so heavily derided reflected the country's mood on military intervention in Iraq better than he did. The following day, in a full-page advertisement celebrating "green" Canadian book publishers, there was Pierre Berton, reclining in bed with a book, wearing only a robe and bow tie and petting a cat. "He's good between the covers," read the headline. At eighty-two, Pierre Berton was not only good: he was sexy good.[57]

The year 2002 witnessed the release of his affectionate little book *Cats I Have Known and Loved*, its title inspired by Jack London. Snap-shots of family felines peppered its pages, and his deft sketches provided a parade of cats for the endpapers. The cover featured Pierre holding Elsa's pet, Suki, "the last of the strays." The unpredictable goings-on of Berton family pets, especially the cats, had often enlivened Pierre's letters to his far-flung children – Patsy in London and Penny in Bali, for example. It delighted him to play armchair anthropologist one last time, categorizing their social types and recounting their adventures, naming them all in his dedication – "Potty, Happy, Pieface, Brownie, Sebastienne, Snowball, Punkoo, Marmalade, Sari, Simon, Paprika, Puss. . . ." The honour role of favourites went on for three more para-graphs. Editors at the *Globe and Mail* made him cover boy of its books section, cat in lap, in the week the paper reviewed the book. The heading for the photograph, "What's New? . . . Pussycats" harked back to the Swinging Sixties and the suggestive baritone voice of Tom Jones.[58]

By the fall of 2002, Berton's poor health was worrying his family and friends, not least because he continued to maintain too hectic a pace for his age and condition. Late that summer, he and Franklin were at work in the McMaster University Archives, which housed his papers. He had already drafted his next book, *The Joy of Writing*, and they were in search of key pages from his typed manuscripts to use as illustrations. In Berton's view, revision was the great key to good writing, and he often gave those who asked for the secrets of the writer's craft nine (or is it three?) simple words of advice: "Read read read, write write write, rewrite rewrite rewrite."[59] That August, while Berton and Franklin worked in an adjacent office, a prospective biographer sat in the archives reading room poring over the Berton papers. At one point Franklin, who was aware that Berton had consented to the biography, approached the researcher and quietly suggested that any interview with Mr. Berton should take place very soon, since his health was clearly failing. A few days later, the interview took place in his Kleinburg study.[60]

The Joy of Writing, published on January 28, 2003, was one of the few winter releases of a Berton book. Disregarding his frailty, he took to the road with Elsa. *Cats I Have Known and Loved* was on the *Globe and Mail* bestseller list throughout the month, perched incongruously with Margaret MacMillan's *Paris 1919*, Michael Moore's *Stupid White Men*, and Noam Chomsky's *9-11*. When it disappeared from the top ten at the beginning of February, *Marching as to War* promptly entered the paperback list at number 10. The latest book's subtitle – *A Guide for Writers Disguised as a Literary Memoir* – quite accurately indicated its nature. While it contained many handy hints about the technicalities of writing, it was basically an overview of his travails as a writer over the years. Aimed at the ordinary reader rather than the English major, it made no pretence of assisting in the art of literary expression. It was, instead, a book on craftsmanship – no theory, no meditations, just the nuts and bolts of putting thoughts to paper. No littérateur, he; just a writer. Reviewers warmed to the book immediately.[61]

When the Americans launched the war of "shock and awe" in March 2003, its first days marked by the protection of the oil fields and the looting of priceless treasures from the unguarded Baghdad museum, Berton spoke out. "What is the purpose of this war?" he asked an *Ottawa Citizen* reporter. "I think that Bush was in the doldrums until Sept. 11 came along, and then he invented a war which isn't a war, which seemed to go on forever and that gave him a good deal of political prestige. It's a political decision and we're going to have to be very careful that we don't suddenly become part of the American imperialistic hegemony. I think it's important that we go our own way, because we're quite a different kind of country." As Lister Sinclair had observed, speaking truth to power had always been one of Berton's hallmarks. The next day, to a packed lecture theatre at Carleton University, Berton spoke on the joy of writing when he gave the annual Kesterton Lecture at the School of Journalism and Communication. At the beginning of the new academic year in the fall, he was on hand to host the ceremony announcing the 2003 winner of Canada's National History Society's Pierre Berton Award, at a gala hosted by the Hudson's Bay Company.

"Charlotte Gray is a superb storyteller," he said of the winner that evening, "and that is what this country desperately needs now that our history has been so shamefully ignored by our educational system."[62]

Aware of Berton's rapid decline, in the summer of 2003 select Toronto journalists obtained the interviews necessary for lengthy final profiles. The *Globe*'s popular interviewer Sarah Hampson found him in May, relaxing in Franklin's back garden, bow tie in place. As the questions began, the Berton Rolodex spun smoothly, stopping at the required prompt cards: "Northern Childhood"; "Fun with Hal"; "The Researchers Myth"; "The Joy of Recycling." When Hampson's interview appeared, it naturally repeated the tales that had been in the *Globe*'s morgue for decades. The best insight of the column proved to be that the Berton bow tie was "part of his iconography, . . . an announcement that says he knows who he is, . . . a smile, too, placed there all perky and fresh at his neck, displaying both a mischievous sense of humour and a pleased self-importance."[63]

In midsummer, the *Globe* feature writer John Allemang obtained two lengthy interviews in Toronto and Kleinburg. The first of these started with a question pitched by the subject himself: "So, are you writing my obituary?" It was impossible for any interviewer to avoid falling prey to Berton's endless array of well-honed anecdotes, but Allemang at least tried to establish a new angle. His profile suggested that the tipping point of Berton's life lay in the role he had played, beginning in the late 1950s and 1960s, in helping an uncertain and equivocal nation gain a clear sense of identity under the influence of the American empire. "He was a nationalist and an iconoclast," Allemang wrote, "at a crucial time when you couldn't be one without being the other. His fervent brand of patriotism may not have aged well," Allemang admitted, "but without his history of badgering and campaigning, any national self-confidence we possess would be completely uprooted." The profile, "The Original Canadian Idol," appeared toward the end of August, accompanied by a full-page photograph of the idol himself, still larger than life but now looking drawn and weary. As Allemang put it, "He knows that his final front page spread can't be far away."[64]

25

LAST WORDS

—

IN MARCH 2004, AFTER MORE than twenty years in Bali and now
a successful designer of jewellery, Penny Berton returned to Canada.
Terrorism had reached even her exotic location a year and a half earlier,
when bombs killed more than two hundred people in a crowded entertainment district of Denpasar, the capital city. But this was not the
reason she had decided to come home. She did not quite know why,
only that the time had arrived to be near her parents. For the next few
months she stayed with them in Kleinburg; given their situation, it was
a stressful time for everyone. Her father could scarcely get around,
even with his accursed cane. Her mother's hip gave her a lot of trouble
and she wore a brace on her leg. Each worried about the other's condition. The Berton children in Toronto had begun to confer regularly on
how best to look after them. Peggy Anne was the official caregiver and
received a salary to make meals and manage the house. As the weeks
passed, Penny helped out when she could and saw first-hand how difficult her sister's task had been.[1]

The driver Elsa had found for Pierre was a reliable man who chauf-
feured him to and from Toronto, usually to her place, where they saw
to the business of Pierre Berton Enterprises. By the time of Penny's
return, her father's latest book was in press – profiles of five larger-than-
life figures of the Canadian north. The material came from research
completed much earlier, mainly for *Klondike* and *My Country*; otherwise, the project would have overtaxed him. Each month seemed to
bring another reminder of life's fleeting nature. Early January saw the
death of Doug Creighton, founding publisher of the *Toronto Sun*, fallen
to Parkinson's disease at seventy-five, and by mid-month eighty-one-
year-old Alex Barris was gone, of complications from a stroke suffered

a year earlier. The most difficult blow, however, came on June 14, when Jack McClelland, blind and deaf, also passed away, six weeks before his eighty-second birthday. Canadian Press immediately contacted Berton and Franklin for reaction. "He was a great promoter . . . , an energetic guy, and cared a lot about the country," Franklin said. "I divide the book industry into two parts – before Jack and after Jack," Berton declared. Before McClelland's arrival on the book scene, he added, authors would be lucky if their publisher invited them out for a glass of sherry. "Jack would laugh at a glass of sherry. It would be half a bottle of vodka, and from there on, it would be a roller-coaster ride as far as publicity was concerned."[2]

There was no law that said one couldn't stir a pot at home, so Berton continued to stir his. Like other writers, he had voiced his outrage that January when the RCMP raided the home of the *Ottawa Citizen* reporter Juliet O'Neill in search of the source of leaks of information concerning the detainment and torture of Maher Arar, who was suspected of terrorism. "They're trying to scare journalists," he said. "We can't let this kind of intimidation stop people from using confidential sources." In March, he joined the entertainers Bryan Adams, Sarah McLachlan, Stompin' Tom Connors, Susan Aglukark, and others in signing a petition urging the prime minister to keep Canada out of the proposed United States missile defence system. He did not protest in May when, without his permission, the Stanfield underwear company created racy billboard ads featuring a pair of red shorts draped over the side of a canoe on a beach, accompanied by the text of Berton's oft-repeated definition of a Canadian. "I don't want a stack of free long underwear; I wouldn't know what to do with it," he said. "A bottle of whiskey would be more important."[3]

After staying with her parents until June, Penny went to the West Coast and purchased a home on Saltspring, one of the Gulf Islands. Near the end of September, the day before Franklin's fundraiser for Berton House, now an annual event, she flew back to Toronto. Before leaving Vancouver she asked Vicki Gabereau, who had visited the Bertons during the summer, whether she should arrange a longer stay, given the health of her parents. Vicki said she should, and it was sound advice. Penny found them very frail. Her father seemed unusually tense, worried she thought about his appearance at the banquet and about getting around on his upcoming book tour, so she took him in hand and administered a relaxing massage. The whole family had become quite concerned. Clearly, he was in no condition for the rigours of cross-country travel. "He wants to die with his boots on," Penny thought, not "wasting away in some nursing home."[4]

The fundraising dinner the next evening proved a great success. Three hundred and fifteen people drawn from Berton's wide network of friends, the literary community, and ordinary readers of Pierre Berton books paid $150 each for an eleven-course meal at the Bright Pearl Seafood Restaurant on Spadina Avenue. Pierre made his appearance in a wheelchair, wearing a blue pinstriped shirt, dark suit with Order of Canada pin, and of course his trademark bow tie. He looked anxious and slightly embarrassed about the wheelchair when colleagues and strangers sought him out during the pre-meal cocktail hour. Vicki Gabereau, assisted by Franklin, acted as emcee for tributes, plugs for Berton House, and songs by Murray McLauchlan. During the multiple courses of Chinese food and the accompanying entertainment, he seemed preoccupied and for the most part remained silent at his table, alongside Janet and two of their daughters, McLauchlan and his partner, Denise Donlon, and a couple from Ottawa. Late in the proceedings, when Vicki called on him to come to the podium, he required assistance and grasped the sides of the lectern.

Wearing a fringed buckskin jacket that had been a gift years earlier, he drew his breath. Then the voice: "A bunch of the boys were whooping it up in the Malamute saloon, / The kid that handles the music-box was hitting a jag-time tune." The transformation was immediate. The voice was clear, the body erect. Berton delivered the fifty-eight lines of Service's "The Shooting of Dan McGrew" with the same gusto he had all his life, whether in Harry Filion's apartment with his fellow newshounds, at raucous parties with the *Maclean's* gang, or at home, hamming it up with his children and grandchildren. The voice gained strength and remained strong to the end, the final lines delivered in a confessional stage whisper, flush with melodrama: "I'm not so wise as the lawyer guys, but strictly between us two – / The woman that kissed him and – pinched his poke – was the lady that's known as Lou." It was a bravura performance, and a moving one. Those present that night knew that this could very likely be the last time they would hear this child of the North.[5]

Doubleday Canada's release of *Prisoners of the North* on September 28, 2004, coincided almost exactly with the flash of publicity related to the Berton House banquet. This was his fiftieth book in fifty years, and he made clear that it would be his last. "Fifty is enough," he told the *Ottawa Citizen* reporter Paul Gessell in a telephone interview from Kleinburg that became a scoop. "His writing days are over," Gessell wrote. "Berton is 84 and in poor health. . . . He needs 10 to 12 hours of sleep every night and simply does not relish the idea of spending two years or so dedicating himself to a book project." The piece went out via CanWest News Service to Asper-owned newspapers across the country. The news was not that Berton had written a book about his favourite subject, the North, and that it dealt with larger-than-life northern figures – the adventurer Joe Boyle, "King of the Klondike"; the explorer Vilhjalmur Stefansson, "the blond Eskimo"; Lady Jane Franklin, widow and protector of her husband's reputation; John Hornby, "the hermit of the tundra"; Robert Service, the bard of the Yukon. It was instead that Pierre Berton had written his last book. Almost everyone who commented on it, beginning with Gessell, linked its subject matter to its author. "In the end," Gessell wrote, "*Prisoners of the North* is really about six people. The sixth is Pierre Berton himself."[6]

Berton said as much in the preface to the book. Northrop Frye once described Canada as a nation of accountants, and eminent Canadians at times seemed bent on confirming the truth of the adage by balancing the double-entry columns of their lives: Glenn Gould, for example, recorded the *Goldberg Variations*, the music that had made him famous as a young man, only months before he died of a stroke at fifty; Frye himself summed up his life's work in a series of lectures at Victoria College, where he had spent his undergraduate years, just before he passed away. So it was with Berton. "Time and again my heritage has intruded into my literary output, occasionally without my realizing its presence," he wrote. "Like my father before me and the five remarkable characters that follow, I, too, in my own way am a prisoner of the North." Thus the triptych of his life: the inscrutable father, the remarkable son, the mysterious north.[7]

Reviewers passed lightly over the fact that Berton had spoken and written about these characters many times before and that the book lacked any documentation. They usually chose instead to note, as Pat Donnelly did in the Montreal *Gazette*, that Pierre Berton had produced one of his typical page-turners. The appearance of *Prisoners of the North*, Kim Hughes wrote in the *Toronto Star*, provided "another opportunity to say it loud and proud. Pierre Berton – towering Canuck icon, winner of a gazillion prestigious awards, confessed cat freak – is really, really cool." Enveloped in such affection for its author, the book became an immediate bestseller. It entered the bestseller lists as number five in the Victoria *Times-Colonist* on October 10 and number ten in the *Globe and Mail* on October 30, and remained in the top ten as Christmas approached.[8]

The diabetic lesions on his feet would not heal, despite regular dressings by a nurse, and he suffered from the occasional nosebleed, but while more or less confined to the house he remained busy. He launched a new monthly series of profiles of fascinating episodes and figures in Canadian history in the *Globe and Mail* – free publicity for *Prisoners of the North*, after all. It began on August 28, with a story of Arctic survival; another, on the amazing Joe Boyle, appeared on September 26. October's instalment, on Lady Franklin, had yet to be finished. He was also eager to begin his book tour. Among other appearances, he was set to open the Harbourfront International Festival of Authors, do a reading at the Canadian Authors Series in Port Colborne, and be the star attraction at a Nicholas Hoare "Books and Brunch" event at Ottawa's Château Laurier.[9]

First, however, he had an engagement at a new library in the city of Vaughan, near Kleinburg. He was to cut the ribbon and make a speech at the opening of the Pierre Berton Resource Library on a Sunday afternoon in mid-October. During the week preceding the event, he fell three times. He ended up with a number of bruises, but fortunately did not break any bones. After the Berton House fundraiser, Penny had decided to remain in Kleinburg to help Peggy Anne. "We were all – I was, at least – panicking," she said. Her father's hemoglobin count was down, he was sleeping a great deal, and yet he was still making plans and meeting commitments. He did a number of radio interviews and went into Toronto to give a speech. One day, the comedian Rick Mercer and a crew from his television show *Monday Report* arrived to tape a feature with Berton for the show. It took several hours.

Berton had always taken an interest in the goings-on in Vaughan and its surroundings, and in the past he had been a thorn in the side of its developer-friendly politicians. This had scarcely changed, for at a rally in September he had told people to "get mad as hell" and stop the construction of a road planned to run through environmentally sensitive Vaughan parkland. "I hope you'll all raise your voices and your pens – or your computers these days – and let the people at the council level know how we feel," he told the crowd. "They see this park as a thousand houses, each producing taxes." Later that day, the Mohawk leader Grey Eagle, David Sanford, also opposed to the road, honoured him at a Native cleansing ceremony. Now, on Sunday, October 17, the firebrand was to be honoured once more. Almost the entire Berton family was on hand for the opening of the new Vaughan library, which featured two computer labs, a business library, and an Internet café among its amenities. Although the organizers had promised a brief ceremony, the proceedings became long and drawn-out, with the guest of honour scheduled to speak at the very end. Franklin would likely have had something to say about that, but she was not there, for she did not drive often and was not about to risk the journey when the fall weather was inclement. For a couple of hours, Berton sat on a stage in a tent, while wind and rain swirled around it and its occupants. As time passed, he became increasingly uncomfortable in his wheelchair because of the bruises and sores. The inconvenience to her ailing father annoyed Penny.

When his time came at last, Berton duly thanked the people of Vaughan for the honour they had bestowed upon him. "It's a little staggering," he said; the only association he thought he would ever have with a library, he added parenthetically, was with its overdue department. His own early reading had been of pulp magazines like *The Shadow* and *Nick Carter*. Recommendations by adults intent on improving him had left him cold. "I tell you, I never read such moralistic crap in my life," he told a laughing audience. Parents should mind their own business and let their children read whatever they wanted to. "I don't necessarily look for a book to learn something. I look for a book to entertain myself. That's what great literature does. It entertains you."[10]

At home that evening, Janet took a fall in the kitchen, and Penny and Peggy Anne ran to her assistance. Their mother did not seem to be in any pain, but they were unable to move her to an upright position in order to get her to bed. Finally, they looked at each other and knew they had to call 911 for medical assistance. Soon Peggy Anne was with her mother in an ambulance on the way to York Central Hospital, while Penny stayed with her father. Janet had broken her hip and spent the next twenty-four hours and more in the hospital's emergency ward before she learned that she would be hospitalized for some time.

Penny noticed an immediate deterioration in her father's own condition after Janet's fall. She monitored his sleep several times that Sunday night, for his nose had begun to bleed again because of the blood-thinning medication he took for his heart condition. Around midday on Monday, Patsy suggested that he admit himself to York Central to attend to his bleeding nose and to have his hemoglobin checked. He was reluctant to do so because he had looked forward to seeing the Mercer show that night. But he knew that at York Central he could see Janet, so he consented. Accompanied by Patsy, he spent most of the day in the emergency ward, waiting like many others for attention. When, in frustration, she asked a physician whether he could treat her father's nosebleed immediately, he answered, politely enough, that Canada did not have a two-tier health care system and that Mr. Berton would need to wait in line like the others. Later, she spoke of that moment: "I said, 'Dad, don't you wish they had that two-tier system?' and he says, 'Nope, nope, that's not the way we do it.'" He was adamant, Patsy said, that he be given no preferential treatment.

Pierre would not allow himself to be admitted overnight to the hospital once a doctor had checked him over and treated him. He wanted to return home to his own bed; besides, he wanted to see the Mercer program. So did many other Canadians, for word had leaked out the previous Friday that in a two-minute segment called "Celebrity Tips," Pierre Berton was going to show the Newfoundland-born laughmeister how to roll a joint. The long-time critic of Canada's drug laws, especially as they concerned cannabis for recreational use, had readily admitted to reporters that he had begun to use marijuana in his forties; he did not reveal that the weed's distinctive fragrance could occasionally be detected at home in Kleinburg, and not always when he was around.

Television viewers that night saw the distinguished-looking old man in the bow tie sitting at his living room table. "Looking back on my career, you know," he said with a slightly patrician air, "I cannot count the number of times a young man or young woman has come up to me and said, 'Hey, Mr. Berton, what's the best way to roll a joint?'" After a young man at the table tries but fails to do so, Berton intervenes: "Well let me tell you, it's not that way. Come on, put that down. Let's start over." With copies of *The National Dream* and *Prisoners of the North* in front of him, he calls for "a good hard surface" and suggests that the books will serve this purpose just fine. He indicates his favourite variety of paper and his preference for the best way to distribute the mix – "firm but not too firm," he advises. "Remember, Canada, it's the loose joints that tend to fall apart, leaving unsightly toke burns on your chairs, or on your bow tie."

Asked later by a *Hamilton Spectator* reporter about the spectacle of the "establishment icon casually endorsing an illegal drug," eight of the city's police officers associated with its Clean Sweep program combating drugs in schools simply shook their heads. The *Spectator* reporter appears to have shared their astonishment: "The author of *The National Dream*, a pothead," he wrote. Contacted by Canadian Press about his appearance, Berton reaffirmed his support for the legalization of marijuana. Canada's current laws, he said, were dysfunctional and outdated. "I smoke about once a month to help me relax," he told the CP reporter. Asked whether he was worried that the television appearance might tarnish his reputation, Berton replied, "I've reached the stage in life where I don't give a damn what I say or what people think."[11] Penny didn't know whether her father ever saw his last hurrah on television.

The Mercer show appearance by no means hurt the venerable Berton brand; instead, it confirmed the brand's strength. Berton's little lesson on how to roll a joint reminded those Canadians aware of his early crusading zeal that the man remained as outspoken and as true to his principles as ever. In this case, his open endorsement of the recreational use of marijuana reflected the views of a majority of Canadians. Strong support existed within the country, police forces notwithstanding, for minimum punishment for marijuana use; most Canadians, in fact, wanted the drug legalized. But Berton's final television appearance also enhanced his public persona in another way. Part of his long-earned image had been that of the earnest teacher, not lacking wit but predominantly serious in the lessons he wished Canadians to heed. On Mercer's *Monday Report*, he played against the grain of that image. His campy performance, with its exaggerated know-it-all demeanour and his haughty tone of voice, caught Berton's sense of theatre; his self-mockery proved enough to disarm even the sternest of critics and reaffirmed Pierre Berton, professor of pot, as the lovable grand old man of Canadian letters. Almost immediately, his last few minutes on television made their way onto YouTube, thanks to a generation of young and media-savvy Internet viewers, there to circulate indefinitely, along with clips from *The Pierre Berton Show* featuring the final TV appearance of Malcolm X and the "lost" interview of Bruce Lee, the cultish Kung Fu teacher and actor who had instructed such macho Hollywood stars as Chuck Norris and Lee Marvin.

The wheels of justice revolve unmercifully slow in Canada as elsewhere. At the end of the month, the federal justice minister, Irwin Cotler, requested that the Ontario Court of Appeal review the Steven Truscott case to determine whether Truscott had received a fair trial or whether a miscarriage of justice had been done at the time of the original conviction in 1959. The *Toronto Star* took advantage of the occasion to reprint Berton's "Requiem for a Fourteen-Year-Old" in full. The conclusion of what the newspaper called "Berton's poetic crusade" was perhaps at last drawing near.[12]

As late as the third week in October, Berton remained fully alert, with a number of books on the go. They included A.N. Wilson's massive history *The Victorians*; Richard Barber's *The Holy Grail*; Margaret MacMillan's *Paris 1919*; Stephen Birmingham's 1981 biography of Wallis Warfield Windsor, *Duchess*; and Lynn Truss's bestseller *Eats, Shoots & Leaves* (which he found delightful). At his children's urging, he unhappily cancelled his book tour. One daughter or another took him to visit Janet in the hospital, but otherwise he remained at home. He had always been one for a good night's sleep, but now he slept for long periods during the day. On Saturday, October 23, following a visit to her mother in the hospital, Patsy drove to Kleinburg to check in on her father. She found that he had taken to his bed. He stayed there all weekend.[13]

It was obvious that he required full-time medical care, and the children agreed that the time had come to have their father hospitalized. An ambulance arrived to take him to York Central Hospital, where Janet still remained. In his earlier visit to York Central, doctors had done batteries of tests and spoken in vague terms about a pacemaker. "For the life of me, I can't believe that he didn't know, on some level, that this was it," Patsy said; yet he maintained what she called his "soldiering on" spirit. She remembers him saying, "I'll get the pacemaker, I'll be fine." The medical staff gave him transfusions for his hemoglobin problem, but his enlarged heart was still not able to get enough oxygen. He remained at York Central for the rest of October and almost to the end of November, visited often by Janet and by his sons, daughters, and grandchildren. Elsa also stopped in regularly.

He was still confined to York Central on Thursday, November 25, when Jack Granatstein, his fiercest and most persistent critic, was given the Pierre Berton Award at a ceremony at historic Fort York, in Toronto. It was a remarkable achievement for the retired York University historian. In a *Globe and Mail* column as early as 1977 he had lamented the success of "amateurs and journalists" whose sloppily researched works of history had come to hold pride of place in commercial publishing. "Pierre Berton has produced a shelf full of books over the last few years," he wrote, singling him out for particular scorn. Berton was "a good researcher," Granatstein had conceded, but he "consciously [made] his work 'interesting.'" Berton had taken great pleasure writing one of his rare replies to a review, a lengthy rebuttal to academic arrogance that included the words: "Well, professor, I sure as hell don't consciously make it dull." But in the years since that exchange, the meticulous scholarship of academic historians had been pushed to the margins, constricted to the small press runs and even smaller readership of university presses. In the 1980s Granatstein became tired of writing books that few people read and that made no money, so he began to write specifically for the marketplace. By 2004, with sixty books notched up, he was as fierce in his condemnation of academic history as he had ever been of the popularizers. Still, he could not resist another dig. "Canadian history is too important to be left to only Pierre Berton," he said at the award ceremony. In his pocket he carried a bow tie.[14]

Berton's absence from the Pierre Berton Award ceremony went unreported by the press, as did his hospitalization. He remained in York Central until Monday, November 29, four days after his long-time friend Arthur Hailey, a few months his senior, died in his sleep at home in the Bahamas. York Central medical staff transferred him that day to Sunnybrook Hospital – either for the pacemaker operation or, more likely, because they knew he did not have much more time to live: the family was never informed of the reason. An ambulance took him to Sunnybrook, while Peggy Anne drove her ailing mother and Patsy took her own car. They found him in a semi-lucid state, and spent the day at his side. He enjoyed a piece of Patsy's cranberry bread and a cup of tea, but couldn't keep it down. Later, Patsy drove her mother back to York Central.

That evening the attending physician warned Patsy and Perri, who had arrived to see their father, that the situation was "not good" and that members of the family should be called to his bedside. Janet had hardly settled into her bed at York Central when she had to leave again for Sunnybrook. Pierre's most fervent wish was for a cup of tea, but he was not allowed any liquids. Later, when he said "Good night Patsy," she realized he was bidding goodbye. He drifted off to sleep. The family stayed for a while, then left. The next morning Patsy returned and rubbed his feet to comfort him. In the afternoon she had to leave to attend a medical appointment for her daughter downtown. She was gone for only an hour, but it was in that hour – between and 4:00 and 4:15 p.m. – that her father died. Janet and Peggy Anne were at his bedside during the final moments.

Penny had stayed with her parents until about a week before her father's final trip to the hospital, but had returned to the West Coast to arrange some public showings of her jewellery in Victoria. On the after-noon of Tuesday, November 30, a showing had just started when her brother Peter called to let her know of her father's passing, afraid that otherwise she would learn it from the media. She thought of leaving the event, but stayed because that was what she thought her father would want her to do. She found the next few hours strange. At first, no one around her knew about Pierre Berton's death, but during the second half of the show she could hear clients speak about it, oblivious of her identity. That evening, on the way home, she stopped at a friend's house on Saltspring to watch the CBC's television coverage.

Shortly after Berton's death that afternoon, the family talked about how best to release the news. Peter had called Penny, and Berton Woodward, Lucy's son, had phoned his mother; he also wanted to telephone his sister, Paisley, who worked for the CBC. The public first learned of Berton's death on the six o'clock news. At CBC headquarters that night, the production team of the network's flagship television news program, *The National*, debated how much attention should be devoted to Pierre Berton's death, with an American president arriving in Ottawa to confer with the prime minister about peace in the Middle East, disputes over U.S.-Canada trade, cross-border security, and Canadian military involvement in Iraq and Afghanistan. Later that evening, the Berton family were touched to find that the radio and television news lavished so much attention on Pierre's extraordinary life as well as his sad death.[15]

Talk in the *Globe and Mail* newsroom that night was just as animated. At around quarter to six, Sandra Martin was at work with other arts writers and critics on the third floor of the *Globe* building when her phone rang. It was Elsa Franklin. Martin knew Berton was in ill health. "He's died, hasn't he?" she asked, her question in part a statement of assumed fact. She expressed her condolences, and then hung up and sent an email to her supervisor. She had recently moved from the Review to the Comment section of the paper to become the chief obituary writer, so she needed to find out the editors' plans for covering the Berton death. In the newsroom she found a circle of news editors gathered together, debating what to do about the two major events of the day. Fortunately, Martin had already written a draft obituary, and she told them it could run once she incorporated some quotes of the reaction of friends. After a little more conversation, the front-page editor declared, "This is bigger than Bush," and the scramble was on to put the paper to bed. "I was thrilled and proud," Martin later confided, "because I too thought the passing of Pierre Berton was bigger than 'Bush does dinner with Paul Martin' and I was glad that the hard news guys at my newspaper felt the same way."[16]

The next morning the *Globe and Mail* awarded President Bush two of the coveted top-right columns on the front page. Above the story stood a modestly sized head-and-shoulders shot of President Bush and Prime Minister Paul Martin, standing one in front of the other and looking in opposite directions. The shot clearly suggested the Janus-faced nature of Canadian-American relations. But next to the Bush piece, there was Pierre Berton staring beyond the camera in his buck-skin jacket, standing just above the precipice of Niagara Falls in 1991. The photograph alone consumed more column inches than the entire page 1 coverage of Bush and Martin's "cozy summit." Above Berton's photograph, the headline ran, "A Voice of Canada Is Gone," and below it, Sandra Martin's lengthy piece began with a simple four-word para-graph: "Everybody called him Pierre."

Other major Canadian dailies displayed similar coverage. Four of the six front-page columns of the *Toronto Star* went to Berton's death, and a photograph of Berton standing on the platform of a caboose, in a double-breasted winter coat, dominated the page. The entire above-the-fold front page of the *National Post* consisted of a photograph of Berton in his garden, captured in profile wearing a blazer and bow tie, hands atop his cane. In addition to its prominent page 1 coverage, Hal Straight's old paper, the *Vancouver Sun*, devoted two more pages inside, chronicling his life and exploits, especially the Headless Valley expedi-tion that had forged his reputation. At the *London Free Press*, where he was editor-in-chief, Paul Berton argued that the first official visit of the American president merited more comprehensive coverage than his father's death. He was outvoted by the other editors. "To you, he's just your dad," the managing editor, Joe Ruscitti, told him. "To the rest of the country he was a national icon."[17]

For more than a week, Canadians from all walks of life expressed their sorrow. Some had known Pierre Berton well and admired him deeply; many others recognized that he had been a reassuring or annoy-ing presence in their lives for as long as they could remember. Those who knew little about him came to sense with the outpouring of grief that something irreplaceable had been lost to Canadian life. In Ottawa the day after his death, the nation's leaders issued tributes to the man. Berton had "put a mirror to the face of Canada," said the government leader in the Senate, Jack Austin. The nation's cartoonists paid homage, too. In the *Gazette*, Aislin featured Berton wearing a bow tie, its wings shaped like maple leaves. In the *Globe and Mail*, Brian Gable showed a lineup of the recently deceased in the clouds, approaching Heaven, each carrying a heavy tome. A nearby sign reads: "Book signing today! *Eternity: A Popular History.* Pierre Berton." In the *National Post,* the Michael de Adder cartoon featured Berton wearing a loud suit and bow tie, with a cane in his hands and a halo over his head. He stands at the entrance to Heaven, where a wizened old angel sits at the check-in desk fiddling with some cigarette paper. Above Berton run the inevitable words, "Sir, that's not the proper way to roll a joint."[18]

Members of the Writers' Union of Canada began to post notes of remembrance and appreciation on the union's website, expressing thanks for the personal support he had provided, his constancy as a trade unionist, and his strength of purpose as the organization's leader. Letters to the editor debated his place on CBC television's recent contest to select "the Greatest Canadian," and more than a few of these wondered how the hockey commentator Don Cherry could possibly have made the list of top-ten finalists but not Mr. Canada himself. (Berton placed at number thirty-one, one spot behind the athlete Rick Hansen and three in front of Laura Secord: he very likely would have voted for the winner, Tommy Douglas.) Reporters apologized for having interviewed him about a new book without reading it, and for being callous in interviews. Farley Mowat wrote of his delight at the manner of his friend's departure. "Who but he, in taking leave of us, would have upstaged the arrival in Canada of the would-be Emperor of the World?" The *Toronto Star* proclaimed that while Berton had been missed when he left the paper, "now he will be missed by an entire nation." Six months later, the Canadian Journalism Foundation published an announcement that featured the familiar image of Berton at his typewriter. It announced that he would be the posthumous recipient of its Lifetime Achievement Award: "With eyes to see and ears to hear, and a will to write, he was the greatest journalist of his generation."[19]

Canadians grieved Berton's death, but not with cries of anguish; instead, they tried to convey to each other, and to themselves, their gratitude for his presence and how bereft they felt. Something ineffable had been irretrievably lost with his passing. "I felt a familiar, enduring light go out," wrote Iris Nowell. A man from Cambridge, Ontario, expressed the sentiments of many: "His prolific body of Canadiana will likely never be equalled either in scope of subject or richness of detail. . . .

Fiercely proud to be a Canadian, he had a wonderful awareness and ability to see great things among us while the rest of us sat quietly in awe of the exploits of our braggart neighbour to the south. . . . When we talk of our greatest Canadians, his passing should make us all pause to reflect and be thankful of where we live in this increasingly turbulent and troubled world." A resident of Pender Harbour, B.C., wrote: "Mr. Berton is the person whose long and consistent defence of this country has made him a father to my identity as a Canadian. I felt as if a close relative, one who had played a central role in raising me, was gone." An editorial in the *Gazette* concluded with the words, "To the end of his career, Pierre Berton loved Canada as he might his own daughter."[20]

Private and public memorials followed. On December 4, the Saturday following Berton's death, the family held a wake and open house at their Kleinburg home. It was intended especially for neighbours and close friends like the Fraynes, but everyone seemed to turn up to pay their respects. The turnout was heartwarming, of course, but Patsy later felt that the visitation should have taken place over the whole weekend, or at least at specifically designated hours. As matters turned out, Janet, wheelchair bound and still in a state of shock, sat in a receiving line that seemed to last for hours.

The following Tuesday, December 7, in the Barbara Frum Atrium of the Canadian Broadcasting Centre in Toronto, hundreds of people gathered for a two-hour celebration of Pierre Berton's life. Entirely planned and orchestrated by Elsa Franklin, who hand-picked the many speakers and gave them strict orders to focus on only one aspect of Berton's life and be very brief, the ceremony was a deeply touching love-fest. The entire Berton family sat in the front rows and wore bow ties in tribute, either around their necks or on their arms. Behind them were gathered what the *National Post* called "a who's who of Canadian publishing and broadcasting from the past half-century." By a wall-sized photograph of Berton in a white shirt, open collar, and untied bow tie, arms crossed in a self-satisfied manner, the eighteen eulogists gave their two minutes' worth. Among them were Adrienne Clarkson, governor general of Canada, and Harold Redekopp, senior adviser to the president and CEO of the CBC; Betty Kennedy and Allan Fotheringham; Lister Sinclair and June Callwood; Graeme Gibson and Margaret Atwood; Pierre's sister, Lucy, son Paul, and daughter Peggy Anne.

Dinah Christie offered her tribute in song, as did Linda Kash, who reprised a number from *Paradise Hill*, the Klondike musical Berton wrote for the 1967 Charlottetown Festival. Vicki Gabereau presided over the ceremony.

"He gave us our story; he gave us our narrative," said the governor general. "Wow! I had no idea Pierre Berton did all these things. I just thought he was an old guy who liked to get high every so often," said Rick Mercer. "He was the Wayne Gretzky of shit-disturbers," he added. When Berton agreed to appear on his program, Mercer related, he had said only "Bring the pot." When the television crew packed up to leave and Mercer thanked the Bertons for their hospitality, Pierre's farewell words were "Leave the pot." "You're gone, Pierre, but you'll never die," June Callwood said. Allan Fotheringham and Vicki Gabereau voiced their farewells with choked voices. After all the words had been uttered, the guests mingled and continued the act of remembrance in conversation assisted by free-flowing champagne, made available at the insistence of the deceased. That evening, Elsa looked back fondly at the early days of working with Pierre at the Screen Gems office on Carlton and on the road with *The Pierre Berton Show*, recalling their frequent shouting matches. "We yelled through all the major capitals of the world," she said. "Through all the yelling, Pierre became my best friend. But I won't stop yelling."[21]

On December 4, Berton's final profile of remarkable Canadians for the *Globe and Mail*'s Flashbacks series had appeared. It was about Laura Secord, and it ran true to the lifelong Berton formula for success: debunk a myth but extend and reaffirm another. In a thousand words, its author challenged the comfortable legend that in 1812 Secord warned British lieutenant James Fitzgibbon of an imminent American attack on Canada; yet at the same time, he managed to convey the importance of continuing to be vigilant of Yankee aggression. The last line of the article, "Save the Niagara Frontier for Canada," written about Secord's mythic significance, held Pierre Berton's final published words.[22]

At Thanksgiving the next year, family and close friends gathered in Kleinburg to dispose of his ashes. Pierre had expressed his preferences concerning his own death as early as the war years. "How wasteful and foolish the practice of plastering a person's grave with flowers is," he wrote to Lucy in 1942. "When I die I want to be cremated with no ceremony and no religious service of any kind – and NO FLOWERS. And I don't want them to play 'Nearer My God to Thee' either."[23] Almost everyone was there to honour his long-established wishes, except Penny's daughter Elora, and Lucy, who two days earlier had broken her ankle. But Vicki was able to make it, along with her partner Tom Rowe and her son Morgan. Janet's hip made a wheelchair her constant companion and she had chosen to live permanently in a well-appointed long-term-care facility in North York. But the rambling house remained very much a home alive with family members, since sons and daughters and granddaughters gravitated toward it as they had when Pierre was around. His presence lingered still, for the house remained crowded with all manner of Berton memorabilia trapped in time, from the hoods along the stairway to the art on the walls and the books on the shelves. Collectibles from world travel were scattered throughout. The corridor to the silent study somehow seemed longer. Outside, every mound, tree, and flower served as a reminder of the force of will of the man they still mourned.

They gathered in front of the house, on a hillock Pierre had created years earlier, known in the family as their own Paradise Hill. One day the Bertons would erect the sign Vicki had made bearing its name. That Sunday afternoon, assisted by a facilitator, they all paid their last respects to his memory, the adults standing around in a ragged circle and most of the smaller children seated near them on the grass. Perri recited a poem, and Patsy's children sang the Rankin Family song "We'll Rise Again," assisted by their father, Rico. Patsy read a piece she had written that dwelt on her father's mannerisms and habits of speech, including the broad inflection he gave to words like *orange, porridge,* and *curry* – a consequence, Patsy believed, of her grandmother Laura's early days in Boston. While Peggy Anne filmed the proceedings and people reminisced, in the background a boom box played some of Pierre's favourite tunes. One was "My Echo, My Shadow, and Me," sung by the Ink Spots; another was "Just a Closer Walk with Thee," performed by the Preservation Hall Jazz Band. Almost everyone that warm afternoon said a few words, including those few who usually remained silent. Janet, in her wheelchair, then read a passage, chosen not from Ecclesiastes but from *Drifting Home*. It was about the game Pierre used to play, made up when he first read Maugham on how the romantic moment crept up when least expected:

> Ever since reading those lines I have tried to see every day in terms of both the past and the future . . . to pretend, at any given instant, that I am an old man at the close of life thinking back to the days when I was in my prime and longing to relive them. Whenever I play this game the sky at once seems bluer and the grass greener. I am playing it now, lying back in the boat and looking over my family in the guise of an old man who has been given a brief reprieve to re-experience a moment from the past. I see my children, as I see the river, in terms of both the past and the future – as the toddlers they once were and as the adults they will soon become. I think of them as grandparents with children of their own and I wonder again which one of them will be the first to return to the river and whether these successive voyages by the third and fourth generations may become a kind of family tradition (for I have inherited my father's love of ritual). And I wonder again what the river itself will be like a generation hence.[24]

When Janet finished reading, loved ones blanketed her in warm words. "Oh well," she said, "I had a good script."

Then they dug some holes and planted daffodils and began to spread the ashes. Members of the family grasped some ashes from a large plate, and sprinkled them into the soil while the Ink Spots sang "If I Didn't Care" in the background. As they were doing so, Patsy's fifteen-year-old daughter, Michaela, became tearful. As her father consoled her, her mother scattered some remains and Michaela followed suit. Still distraught, she reached cautiously into the ashes. When she withdrew her hand, the remains in her palm contained a large crown for a tooth. The moment seemed surreal and the Bertons burst into laughter. The southwest breeze, up from Lake Ontario, lifted the ashes and blew them northward.

SOURCES

—

This book is based on materials in the papers of Pierre Berton, which are housed in the William Ready Division of Archives and Research Collections, McMaster University. In the early 1970s, the university's chief librarian, William Ready, considered writing a biography of Pierre Berton and contacted the Kleinburg historian. After he had recorded a number of interviews and collected some material related to Berton's life, Ready produced a manuscript; alas, it proved to be a digressive and largely undigested set of undocumented musings to which he gave the enigmatic name "Chanticleer." The title was characteristic of the work. That unpublished manuscript remains in the archives now named in his honour. Fortunately, as a result of Ready's interest and initiative, Pierre Berton agreed to deposit his private papers in the McMaster University Archives.

The Pierre Berton Fonds, as this collection is called, is a very substantial archival holding. The Berton papers went to McMaster University in a series of acquisitions that eventually reached thirteen in number. The McMaster archives received the first of these in 1974; the final one arrived in 2007, forwarded by the Pierre Berton Estate, whose literary executor is Elsa Franklin. Consisting of textual records, photographs, and audiovisual material, the collection occupies 110.9 metres of shelf space, a total of 450 archival boxes. Its finding aid has nearly five hundred pages, but fortunately it has been carefully prepared and is available electronically to researchers through the Internet.

Complementing the Berton papers at McMaster are the records of McClelland & Stewart, which include a collection of Jack McClelland's private papers. The M&S collection is understandably vast (415.8 metres), and letters, memoranda, and other materials related to Pierre Berton as an M&S author and a friend of Jack McClelland are extensive. Also in the McMaster archives, thanks to William Ready and his successors, are the papers of Jack McClelland, Farley Mowat, Robert Fulford, and other Canadian literary figures. The holdings of the Berton and M&S collections contain such a wide range of correspondence that travel to literary collections located elsewhere proved largely unnecessary.

Taken together, the Berton and M&S papers provide the means to give shape to Berton's professional life. The Berton papers are less helpful for constructing Berton's private or inner life. Berton appears to have kept virtually all of his incoming letters, and he corresponded with hundreds of people over the years. But except for about seventy letters home written during the Second World War, the Berton papers contain very few letters that deal with personal matters. Letters to literary friends tend to be businesslike and brief. One searches the collection in vain for a sustained literary exchange of depth or substance. Many of the boxes in the collection contain research materials and manuscripts of edited versions of his many published works. They shed light on his writing habits, but are less helpful in constructing his life.

Other possible sources either have been destroyed or proved unavailable. Janet Berton believes that her father destroyed her wartime correspondence and other papers at the time of her marriage. Penny Berton's letters from her father, written over the many years she spent in Bali, Indonesia, remain in storage there. Letters Berton wrote to his daughter Patsy when she lived and studied in England in the 1970s, and which she very kindly lent me, were almost entirely undated and concerned with his daughter's circumstances and the mischief of the family cats. Some original materials related to the Bertons in the nineteenth century remain in the possession of Lucy Woodward in British Columbia, while others appear to be held in the Berton home in Kleinburg.

Fortunately, when the biographer Elspeth Cameron prepared in late 1986 and early 1987 to write a major *Saturday Night* profile of Berton, commissioned by the magazine's editor, Robert Fulford, she conducted lengthy interviews with Pierre Berton, Janet Berton, Lucy Woodward, and many of their friends, colleagues, and acquaintances. Cameron's handwritten notes of these interviews, more than forty in number, are part of the Elspeth Cameron Papers in the Thomas Fisher Rare Book Room of the University of Toronto Robarts Library. I transcribed each set of notes verbatim, creating an electronic record of the full range of interviews. They have proved invaluable in the writing of this biography, since Cameron caught her subjects when (for the most part) they were in their sixties and had firm memories of the people and events they described. Moreover, as an experienced biographer and assiduous researcher, she asked probing questions based on a good deal of preparation.

When I began research on this book, a number of those whom Cameron interviewed had already died and most others were in their eighties, with fading strength and recollections that had become less reliable and at times confused. As a consequence, my approach to the use of interviews as a research tool was to conduct them sparingly and less to discover new information than to confirm or disconfirm events, recollections, and judgments already part of the historical (archival and print) record. At times, I spoke to people to obtain their views or opinions on specific people and events. By the time I interviewed Pierre Berton in 2002 and 2004, he had long since established in his own mind a set narrative of his life, suggested in this book, having spoken and written about it so often and at so much length over so many years. Words and phrases he used in interviews with me echoed those he had deployed in his two volumes of autobiography, *Starting Out* (1987) and *My Times* (1995), and in scores of interviews. Like her husband's, Janet Berton's memory, too, had begun to fade. It remained strong where her family circumstances were concerned. She could recall fifty-year-old telephone numbers and the colour of wedding dresses, but at times memory failed where more general matters of recollection were at issue.

For the family life of the Bertons at home, I concentrated on interviews with the three eldest Berton siblings – Penny, Pamela, and Patsy – and spoke with them at length. Clearly, these women had inherited their father's prodigious power of recall, for they provided many details of family life in Kleinburg and on holidays, and they gave me a number of insights into the dynamics and goings-on of their remarkable family. An interview with Lucy Woodward, conducted at her home in White Rock, B.C., helped clarify many otherwise confusing aspects of Berton and Thompson family genealogies. Beverley Straight, of Vancouver, shed the light of a close family friend on life with the Bertons, and provided valuable insight in other ways. During the years of preparing this book, I spoke with Elsa Franklin many times, and recorded one lengthy and revealing interview. Franklin kindly also let me borrow certain documents in her possession about *The Pierre Berton Show*.

This book is in part about the way those other than Berton himself have attempted to understand the man by constructing meaningful narratives about him. Over many years, he has been the subject of hundreds of articles, book reviews, and profiles. Of the major pieces, a number stand out for information and insights they provide into the man and his times and for journalists' attitudes toward him. They deserve to be singled out: June Callwood, "What Makes Pierre Tear?" *Star Weekly Magazine,* Oct. 10, 1959; Sidney Katz, "Pierre's Adventures in Bertonland," *Maclean's,* Oct. 6, 1962; Robert Fulford, "The Fantastic Adventures of Super Berton," *Toronto Star,* January 20, 1968; Dawn MacDonald, "Will the Real Pierre Berton Please Stand Up?" *Chatelaine* (Aug. 1970); Gary Ross, "The Business of Being Berton – It Isn't *All* Working on the Railroad," *Canadian* magazine, Apr. 5, 1975; Elspeth Cameron, "Once Upon a Time," *Saturday Night* (Aug. 1987); Val Ross, "Captain Canada at

75," *Globe and Mail,* Oct. 7, 1995; John Allemang, "The Original Canadian Idol," *Globe and Mail,* Aug. 23, 2003; Sandra Martin, "Obituary: Berton Was a Dominant Force," *Globe and Mail,* Nov. 30, 2004. It comes as no surprise that one of the most celebrated and influential Canadians has attracted the attention of the cream of Canadian journalists and writers.

In this book I have sought to remain true to the task of the biographer by maintaining a steady gaze upon the human subject while meeting the requirements of the historian by establishing a social, cultural, and intellectual context sufficient to flesh out that subject's life. In this respect, I have tried to follow Pierre Berton's dictum that a sense of place, as well as time, is essential in the act of historical narration. The balance between character and circumstance (to use a phrase that describes Donald Creighton's approach to biography and history) is a delicate one, and I have been assisted by a wide range of scholarly works on the theory and nature of biography and autobiography and on many aspects of the history of Canada, of journalism, of the radio, movie, and television industries, of popular and consumer culture in general, of publishing, and of much else. The length of this bibliography, which would add many pages to this book, has made it impossible for it to be included here, but bibliographical references to works used are provided in the notes.

For similar reasons, I have not included a full bibliography of Berton's writings, or even of his fifty books (over seventy if one includes his works for juveniles). Besides, to this number of book entries would need to be added over a hundred entries representing articles he wrote for *Maclean's* magazine, and over a thousand more for columns written for the *Toronto Star* between 1958 and 1962, and in the early 1990s. I would be pleased to send a bibliography of Berton's *Toronto Star* columns to any interested reader. Those who wish to locate and explore the book's sources will find them cited fully in the notes.

NOTES

—

ABBREVIATIONS

AC   *University of British Columbia Alumni Chronicle*

BPB   "By Pierre Berton" column in *Toronto Daily Star*, 1958–1962

DH   Pierre Berton, *Drifting Home: A Family's Voyage of Discovery down the Wild Yukon*, Twentieth-Anniversary Edition (Toronto: McClelland & Stewart, 1993 [1973])

ECI   Elspeth Cameron Interviews, Elspeth Cameron Papers, Thomas Fisher Rare Book Room, Robarts Research Library, University of Toronto

G&M   The *Globe and Mail* (Toronto)

IMK   Laura Beatrice Berton, *I Married the Klondike*, preface by Robert Service, foreword by Pierre Berton (Whitehorse: Lost Moose Productions, 2002 [1961])

JGM   John Gordon "Jack" McClelland, publisher, McClelland & Stewart

JMF   Jack McClelland Fonds, William Ready Division of Archives and Research Collections, McMaster University Library, Hamilton

M&S   McClelland & Stewart

MCK   A.B. McKillop Interviews, in possession of the author.

MM   *Maclean's* magazine, Toronto

MSF   McClelland & Stewart Fonds, William Ready Division of Archives and Research Collections, McMaster University Library, Hamilton

MT   Pierre Berton, *My Times: Living with History, 1947–1995* (Toronto: Doubleday Canada, 1995)

NAC   National Archives, Library and Archives Canada, Ottawa

NLC   National Library, Library and Archives Canada, Ottawa

PAO   Public Archives of Ontario, Toronto

PB   Pierre Berton

PBF   Pierre Berton Fonds, William Ready Division of Archives and Research Collections, McMaster University Library, Hamilton

SN   *Saturday Night* magazine, Toronto

SO   Pierre Berton, *Starting Out: 1920–1947* (Toronto: McClelland & Stewart, 1987)

TF   Thomas Fisher Rare Book Room, John P. Robarts Research Library, University of Toronto

TFF   Thompson Family Fonds – 1864–1895, William Ready Division of Archives and Research Collections, McMaster University Library, Hamilton

TS   *Toronto Daily Star*, abbreviated in text to *Toronto Star* or *Star*

WR   William Ready Division of Archives and Research Collections, McMaster University Library, Hamilton

WRF   William Ready Fonds, William Ready Division of Archives and Research Collections, McMaster University Library, Hamilton

CHAPTER I: THE FAMILY BIBLE

1   L. Beatrice Berton, "A Loyalist's Family Bible," undated letter to an unidentified newspaper, but most likely the *Victoria Times*, WRF, box 49: miscellaneous PB genealogical material.

2   Information about the life of Peter Berton (grandson of Pierre Berthon de Marigny) is drawn from three articles by "Observer" in the Saint John *Telegraph-Journal*, Mar. 1935, under the general title "Linking the Past with the Present – Captain Peter Berton, Loyalist, and His Family." Copy in WRF, box 49: miscellaneous PB genealogical material.

3   Observer, "Linking the Past." Observer indicated that the witness was likely Colonel George Ludlow, appointed in 1784 to the Supreme Court of New Brunswick. Later he became chief justice of the province.

4   See "Berton, George Frederick Street," *Dictionary of Canadian Biography Online*, vol. VII, 1836–1850; also "Street, Samuel Denny," *DCB*, vol. VI, 1820–1835.

5   *SO*, 233.

6   *SO*, 16.

7   Wiggins has been described as "the most successful of the bluenose merchants," and on his death left an estate of $704,000 to his descendants. See T.W. Acheson, *Saint John: The Making of a Colonial Urban Community* (Toronto: University of Toronto Press, 1985), 53.

8   The Wiggins Male Orphan Institution (Saint John) Records are housed in the New Brunswick Museum, Fredericton. The institution's geographical responsibility was expanded in 1895 to include the entire province. Later known as the Stephen Wiggins Home for Boys, it continued until its closure in 1982. My account of Frank Berton's years at the Wiggins institution is drawn in part from these institutional records, including its "Record of Examinations 1885–1913." The home's "minutes" unfortunately begin only in 1891, after Berton had left the institution.

9   A permanent new building, housing boys and girls, was not constructed until 1897, when it opened as the Saint John High School. A historical sketch is available on the Saint John High School website:http://www.sjhigh.ca/frames.php?page=http://www.sjhigh.ca/about/history.html.

10 Jennifer Longon (New Brunswick Museum) and Mary Flagg (Archives and Collections, Harriet Irving Library, University of New Brunswick) to author, June 2 and May 28, 2004, respectively.

11 *SO*, 17.

12 Lucy Woodward, PB's sister, was unaware of Frank Berton's years at the Wiggins school until she read this chapter in manuscript. She is strongly of the view that his experience at the school, separated from his mother, would have had no scarring effect on him. She recollects that "except for the darkest days of the Great Depression" her father was "a happy, confident and contented man." Lucy Woodward to author, June 5, 2007. This is not the man PB saw in the summer of 1939 or the one he portrays in his memoirs.

13 University of New Brunswick, Students' records, marks, and tests, UNB Archives, RG 24, book 9. Frank Berton's record of matriculation is recorded in the university's matriculation register, UNB Archives, RG 5, book 1.

14 *SO*, 16; see also PB, *Klondike: The Last Great Gold Rush, 1896–1899*, rev. ed. (Toronto: McClelland & Stewart, 1972), 409.

15 University of New Brunswick, Students' records, marks, and tests, UNB Archives, RG 24, book 10.

16 See R.D. Gidney and W.P.J. Millar, *Professional Gentlemen: The Professions in Nineteenth-Century Ontario* (Toronto: University of Toronto Press, 1994); A.B. McKillop, *Matters of Mind: The University in Ontario, 1791–1951* (Toronto: University of Toronto Press, 1994).

17 *University Monthly* (University of New Brunswick), vol. 12, no. 1 (Oct. 1892), 5–6.

18 *SO*, 17; also Attestation Paper, Yukon Infantry Company, CEF, for Francis George Berton, Oct. 5, 1916; available on the website of Library and Archives Canada on the page entitled "Soldiers of the First World War (1914–1918)."

19 PB, *Klondike*, 68, 82.

20 PB, *Klondike*, 98.

21 Patricia Thornton, "The Problem of Out-Migration from Atlantic Canada, 1871–1921: A New Look," *Acadiensis* (Autumn 1985), 20–23; Alan A. Brookes, "Out-Migration from the Maritime Provinces, 1860–1900: Some Preliminary Considerations," *Acadiensis* (Spring 1976), 28–29.

22 Frank Berton to Mrs. W.S. Berton, Mar. 21, 1898, PBF, box 306, file 2; *DH*, 12–13.

23 For a contemporary account of traversing the Chilkoot Trail, see Robert B. Medill, *Klondike Diary: True Account of the Klondike Rush of 1897–1898* (Portland, Oregon: Beattie and Company, 1949), 21–46; see also Carl L. Lokke, *Klondike Saga: The Chronicle of a Minnesota Gold Mining Company* (Minneapolis: University of Minnesota Press for the Norwegian-American Historical Association, 1965), 51–71; PB, *Klondike*, 236–60. Robert Kroetsch's novel *The Man from the Creeks* (Toronto: Vintage Canada, 2000) evokes splendidly the arduous journey of the gold seekers' journey north.

CHAPTER 2: THE TELEPHONE CALL

1 "I Married the Klondike. Comments on First Draft, Episode One. From Elsa Franklin and Pierre Berton," undated typescript, PBF, box 378, file 4; *IMK*, 13.

2 On Florence Clara Thompson ("Florrie") and Edith Maude Thompson, see manuscript beginning "William Thompson, son of Thomas Thompson of Liverpool," TFF, file 14. Background of the Thompson family history is provided in *The Thompsons of Morland in Canada* (White Rock, B.C.: privately printed, 2002), compiled and written by Lucy Woodward. This volume contains extensive correspondence, as well as excerpts from journals and genealogical information. Laura's trips abroad are noted at page 5.

3 Laura Thompson's qualification as a kindergarten teacher is noted in Delia Florence Thompson to "My Dear Fanny" (Frances Thompson, an English cousin), July 12, 1895, TFF, file 13.

4 *IMK*, 14–15. The friend in question was Mrs. Harry Ridley.

5 Quoted in Faith Fenton, *A Passionate Pen: The Life and Times of Faith Fenton* (Toronto: McClelland & Stewart, 1996), 255. Fenton (born Alice Freeman) lived in Dawson City from 1898 to 1904 and reported to the *Globe* on average twice a month.

6   The *Toronto City Directory* indicates that Phillips Thompson changed his place of residence seven times between 1881 and 1912.

7   Quoted in "The Best Known Columnist of His Day," BPB, Sept. 8, 1959.

8   "William Thompson," TFF, file 14. My account of the Thompson family and its background is also drawn from "Record of the Thompson Family," a thirty-one-page manuscript dated 1901; TFF, file 14.

9   Thompson quoted in Greg Kealey, *Toronto Workers Respond to Industrial Capitalism, 1867–1892* (Toronto: University of Toronto Press, 1980), 279. Kealey's discussion of Phillips Thompson's contribution to Canadian labour and intellectual life is extensive, as is the account in Bryan D. Palmer, *A Culture in Conflict: Skilled Workers and Industrial Capitalism in Hamilton, Ontario 1860–1914* (Montreal and Kingston: McGill-Queen's University Press, 1979).

10 Delia Florence Thompson to "My Dear Fanny," July 12, 1895.

11 Woodward, *Thompsons of Morland*, 4.

12 *DH*, 19.

13 Charlene Porsild, *Gamblers and Dreamers: Women, Men, and Community in the Klondike* (Vancouver: University of British Columbia Press, 1998), 4–5.

14 Samuel D. Holloway, *Yukon Gold: A Guide for the Modern Goldseeker* (Whitehorse: Outcrop, 1985), 15–18.

15 "Application for Grant for Placer Mining, and Affidavit of Applicant, Frank G. Berton," September 27, 1898. Claim number 544. Dawson City Museum.

16 These are Laura Berton's later recollections of some of the things her husband had done before they met. *IMK*, 95.

17 Porsild, *Gamblers and Dreamers*, 196–98.

18 See "Klondike Social History Project. Quantitative Database Indexed by Surname," compiled by Charlene Porsild, 1994, Dawson City Museum. See also "Clarence Craig Post Office Ledger, 1897–1906," in the same location.

19 See Census of Canada, 1901, section 206: "Unorganized Territories," subsection 38: "Upper Hunker & Gold Bottom."

20 PB wrote that his mother had told him of the letter and the offer; *DH*, 23. Asked by the author whether he had ever seen the letter himself, Berton replied that he had not. MCK, Pierre Berton, Sept. 15, 2004.

21 *DH*, 23.

22 The rise of the advanced academic credential such as the Ph.D. conveyed professional status and authority at Queen's as elsewhere. In engineering, by the early twentieth century the tradition of practical apprenticeship rooted in craft had given way to formal academic courses and degrees aimed at professionalism. See J. Rodney Millard, *The Master Spirit of the Age: Canadian Engineers and the Politics of Professionalism* (Toronto: University of Toronto Press, 1988), 7; see also R.A. Buchanan, *The Engineers: A History of the Engineering Profession in Britain, 1750–1914* (London: Jessica Kingsley, 1989).

23 In commentary on the original draft script of the documentary *City of Gold*, PB stated that his father "applied for a professorship at Queen's." See "Dawson City film: Commentary," PBF, box 159, "City of Gold" file. The story can be found in *IMK*, 84; *DH*, 23; *SO*, 17. A search of the Queen's University Archives failed to uncover any letters to or from Frank Berton; email exchange between author and Queen's University Archives, May 27, 2004. The author's similar search of

the PBF for a letter of application or an offer of employment at Queen's went unrewarded.

24 *University Monthly* (University of New Brunswick), vol. 20, no. 5 (Feb. 1901), 133.

25 Charles McLeod to Editor, *Klondike Sun*, July 20, 1999.

26 Typescript entitled "Teachers – Dawson Public School," Dawson City Museum, "Dawson Public School" file.

27 The author has been unable to locate any letters by Frank Berton written after summer 1898.

28 One photograph in the picture collection of the Dawson City Museum shows Frank Berton in 1898 or 1899 at the twenty-four-horse stable owned by the Ladue Lumber Company (record number 14203); another shows him as one of the twenty-three lumberjacks employed by the firm.

29 "T.G. Bragg, Superintendent of Schools for the Territory," *Dawson City News*, July 21, 1909.

30 *IMK*, 22.

31 *IMK*, 26–27.

32 Table A9, "Sex of Yukoners, 1898–1921," in Porsild, *Gamblers and Dreamers*, 208.

33 *IMK*, 29.

34 PB, *The Klondike Quest: A Photographic Essay, 1897–1899* (Toronto: McClelland & Stewart, 1983), 215–18.

35 Frances Backhouse, *Women of the Klondike*, rev. ed. (North Vancouver: Whitecap Books, 2003), 184–85.

36 Kerry Abel, *Changing Places: History, Community, and Identity in Northeastern Ontario* (Montreal and Kingston: McGill-Queen's University Press, 2006). I am grateful to Sandra Campbell for insight into northern communities such as Rouyn-Noranda.

37 *IMK*, 36.

38 See Sylvia Van Kirk, *"Many Tender Ties": Women in Fur Trade Society, 1670–1870* (Norman: University of Oklahoma Press, 1983); Adele Perry, *On the Edge of Empire: Gender, Race, and the Making of British Columbia, 1849–1871* (Toronto: University of Toronto Press, 2001).

39 *IMK*, 68, 49. See Service's preface to the book, 9–10.

40 *IMK*, 183.

41 *IMK*, 93–95. In *IMK*, Laura Berton disguised the identity of Miss Holtorff by using the pseudonym "Hamtorf." Lucy Woodward to author, June 5, 2007.

42 Frank Berton's name appears only as a teacher in Granville in the document "Teachers – Dawson Public School." *IMK* also states that Frank Berton was in Granville at the time (96).

43 *IMK*, 109; MCK, John Gould, June 26, 2004.

44 "Quietly Wedded in the City – To Remain Here," *Yukon Daily News*, July 1, 1912.

45 *IMK*, 111–16.

46 Attestation Paper, Yukon Infantry Company, CEF, for Francis George Berton.

47 Lucy Fox Berton's death on Feb. 10, 1917, is recorded on a loose sheet of paper containing genealogical material and interleaved within the Berton family Bible in the possession of the Berton family, Kleinburg. On Frank Berton's war service, see Woodward, *Thompsons of Morland*, 7–8.

48 *IMK*, 132.

49   *IMK*, 132.
50   *IMK*, 133.
51   MCK, Pierre Berton, Sept. 15, 2004.
52   *IMK*, 138–39.

CHAPTER 3: THE HOUSE BELOW THE HILL

1   *IMK*, 143–44.
2   On the sinking of the *Princess Sophia*, see William R. Morrison, *True North: The Yukon and Northwest Territories* (Toronto: Oxford University Press, 1998), 123–24. The cenotaph commemorating the Dawson dead in the First and Second World Wars was erected and dedicated in September 1927. MCK, Gould.
3   See J.O. Miller, *The New Era in Canada: Essays Dealing with the Upbuilding of the Canadian Commonwealth* (London: Dent, 1917).
4   See McKillop, *Matters of Mind*, 251–52.
5   *IMK*, 151.
6   ECI, Lucy Woodward, Dec. 31, 1986.
7   *SO*, 35–36.
8   ECI, Woodward. "My parents had strong rules for us," Berton wrote. See PB, "Beginnings: Pierre Berton," *Today Magazine* (*TS*), Sept. 19, 1981; copy in PBF, box 286.
9   *SO*, 36.
10   ECI, Woodward.
11   MCK, Gould.
12   For the family background of John Gould, see "About the Author," in John A. Gould, *Frozen Gold: A Treatise on Early Klondike Mining Technology, Methods and History* (Missoula, Montana: Pictorial Histories, 2001), 99–100.
13   Lucy Woodward to author, June 5, 2007.
14   ECI, Woodward.
15   MCK, Gould.
16   WRF, interview with Alex McCarter, July 3, 1972.
17   WRF, McCarter interview.
18   WRF, McCarter interview.
19   WRF, McCarter interview.
20   MCK, Gould. Late in life, both PB and Lucy (Berton) Woodward came to recognize their mother's snobbishness: "She was a bit of a snob, my mother. . . . She knew what her place was, or thought she did." MCK, Pierre Berton, Sept. 15, 2004. In this interview, PB recounted a conversation with his sister, who had visited him a week or so earlier, in which they agreed about this.
21   WRF, McCarter interview; "Oldtimers," appendix to "Clarence Craig Post Office Ledger, 1897–1906," Dawson City Museum; MCK, Gould.
22   WRF, McCarter interview.
23   MCK, interview with a long-time Dawson City resident who wishes to remain anonymous.
24   This information came to PB as a considerable surprise, as recorded in MCK, Pierre Berton, Sept. 15, 2004.
25   *SO*, 18.

26 MCK, Gould.

27 MCK, Pierre Berton, Sept. 15, 2004; *SO*, 14–15; ECI, Woodward.

28 MCK, Pierre Berton, Sept. 15, 2004.

29 *Little Lord Fauntleroy* is available on the Internet at several locations. See, for example, the "Page By Page Books" site at http://www.pagebypagebooks.com/Frances_Hodgson_Burnett/Little_Lord_Fauntleroy/. The quoted passage occurs in chapter 5, page 3 of 12.

30 *SO*, photograph section following page 160. PB's caption for this photograph mistakenly attributes it to the Berton visit of 1931. Great-aunt Allie died in May 1931, before the Bertons visited Oakville that year. I am grateful to Lucy Woodward for this information.

31 MCK, Gould.

32 WRF, McCarter interview.

33 *SO*, 47. With his sister, Lucy, Berton was a student at Mrs. Humby's dance classes. MCK, Pierre Berton, Sept. 15, 2004.

34 *SO*, 38.

35 *SO*, photograph section following page 160.

36 ECI, Woodward; *SO*, 43. His whole ambition at the time, he would later say, was "to wear long pants and get my hair cut." MCK, Pierre Berton, Sept. 15, 2004.

37 WRF, McCarter interview; ECI, Woodward; MCK, Gould; also Lucy Woodward to author, June 5, 2007; PB, "Beginnings."

38 *IMK*, 171–72.

39 The photograph is in *SO*, in the section following page 160. Some such songs Thompson had himself written and published in one of his books. See Phillips Thompson, *The Labor Reform Songster* (Philadelphia: Journal of the Knights of Labor, 1892). A microform copy is available in the NLC. See also *SO*, 64.

40 *IMK*, 190.

41 Lucy Woodward to author, June 5, 2007.

42 ECI, Woodward; *SO*, 41.

43 MCK, Gould.

44 *SO*, 21.

45 *SO*, 41.

46 *SO*, 38, 15. See Veronica Strong-Boag, *The New Day Recalled: Lives of Girls and Women in English Canada, 1919–1939* (Toronto: University of Toronto Press, 1988).

47 *SO*, 15. See Charlotte Gray, *Mrs. King: The Life and Times of Elizabeth Mackenzie King* (Toronto: Viking, 1997).

48 See Edmund Burke, *A Philosophical Enquiry into the Origin of Our Ideas of the Sublime and the Beautiful*, 6th ed. (Dublin: Graisberrty, 1766). The treatise first appeared in 1756.

49 *SO*, 26.

50 *SO*, 30.

51 *SO*, 29.

52 *SO*, 33–34.

53 *SO*, 35.

54 *DH*, 107–08. At the age of eighty-four, this childhood fear still haunted him. "I was just terrified," he recalled. "I was alone, and that was a big thing for me then. I still remember it." MCK, Pierre Berton, Sept. 15, 2004.

55 MCK, Gould.
56 MCK, Gould.
57 *SO*, 25.
58 Wallace Stegner, *Wolf Willow: A History, a Memory, and a Story of the Last Great Plains Frontier* (New York: Viking, 1962). Stegner moved from Saskatchewan to the United States while still a child. Winner of a Pulitzer Prize for fiction, he taught creative writing at Stanford University for many years. See Jackson J. Benson, *Wallace Stegner: His Life and Work* (New York: Penguin, 1996).
59 *SO*, 33.
60 "In Which I Make a New Journey to the Land of Oz," BPB, Nov. 5, 1959.
61 BPB, "In Which I Make a New Journey."
62 *SO*, 34.
63 MCK, Pierre Berton, Aug. 12, 2002.

CHAPTER 4: BEYOND THE MIDNIGHT DOME

1   MCK, Pierre Berton, Sept. 15, 2004.
2   *SO*, 58. See also 31, 48–49.
3   "1931–32 Journal," PBF, box 236, file 21.
4   WRF, McCarter.
5   ECI, Woodward.
6   *SO*, 60.
7   *SO*, 59–60.
8   *SO*, 62.
9   *SO*, 66; ECI, Woodward; MCK, Pierre Berton, Sept. 15, 2004: "There was that – I guess you could use the word 'tension' – it was certainly there."
10 MCK, Pierre Berton, Sept. 15, 2004.
11 ECI, Woodward.
12 Lucy Woodward to author, June 5, 2007.
13 *SO*, 67. It is possible that "aunt Sarah" was Hattie Sarah (Birdie) Thompson, daughter of Theodore Thompson, PB's uncle. See Woodward, *Thompsons of Morland*, table following 386.
14 See Roy Nuhn, "The Comic Strip Collecting World of Jiggs and Maggie," *Northeast Journal of Antiques & Art* (Mar. 2003), available online at http://www.northeastjournal.com/LeadingStories/March2003/ComicStripCollectingWorldofJiggsandMaggieMarch2003.htm.
15 *SO*, 68.
16 *SO*, 68.
17 ECI, Woodward.
18 *SO*, 72.
19 Donald A. Cranstone, *A History of Mining and Mineral Exploration in Canada and Outlook for the Future* (Ottawa: Natural Resources Canada, 2002), fig. 3.4: "Canadian Gold Production, 1858–2000," 9; Internet access at http://www.rncan.gc.ca/mms/pdf/hist-e.pdf.
20 ECI, Woodward.
21 *SO*, 73.
22 ECI, Woodward.

23 *SO*, 76.

24 "Sweet Memories," PBF, box 208, file 16.

25 *SO*, 77.

26 *SO*, 80–81.

27 *SO*, 81.

28 *SO*, 73.

29 ECI, Woodward.

30 *SO*, 89–90.

31 MCK, Pierre Berton, Sept. 14, 2004. Information concerning the layout of the house is from Lucy Woodward to author, June 5, 2007.

32 WRF, McCarter; *SO*, 78–80.

33 ECI, Pierre Berton, Sept. 13, 1986.

34 *SO*, 83, 85.

35 ECI, Dick Holden, Feb. 21, 1987.

36 *SO*, 77; PB, "Beginnings."

37 ECI, Woodward.

38 *DH*, 116.

39 *SO*, 78.

40 "Thanks, Folks, You've Been a Really Grand Audience," BPB, Sept. 29, 1959.

41 BPB, "Thanks, Folks."

42 PB, draft typescript for *The Pierre Berton Show*, attached to Steve Krantz to PB, May 26, 1961, PBF, box 104, "Business Correspondence, 1961–62" file.

43 PB, "Turning Points," manuscript prepared for *McGill Journal of Education*, n.d., PBF, box 99, "Turning Points in Education" file.

44 *SO*, 93.

45 *DH*, 136–37.

46 *SO*, 93.

47 MCK, Pierre Berton, Aug. 12, 2002.

48 ECI, Holden.

49 *SO*, 98; PB, "Beginnings."

50 "Some Memories of an Adolescent Tribal Rite," BPB, Dec. 22, 1960. Material in this and the following two paragraphs is drawn from this source.

51 ECI, Woodward; *SO*, 119. Exact recollection of the words of the principal varies slightly from sister to brother: PB adds an extra "lazy." Lucy Woodward recalls encountering Hartness around 1948, when Pierre worked for *Maclean's* magazine. "Oh Miss Berton," he said to her, "we are *so* proud of your brother. I always knew he would do well." Lucy Woodward to author, June 5, 2007.

52 *SO*, 94–95.

53 *SO*, 95.

54 ECI, Woodward.

55 *SO*, 95–96.

56 *SO*, 96.

57 PB, "Beginnings."

58 *SO*, 96. See Neal Gabler, *Winchell: Gossip, Power and the Culture of Celebrity* (New York: Vintage, 1994).

59 MCK, Pierre Berton, Sept. 15, 2004.

60 ECI, Woodward.

61 Copies of PB's academic records at public school, college, and university can be found in TF, Elspeth Cameron Papers, box 81, file 3.

CHAPTER 5: CRAIGDARROCH

1   MCK, Pierre Berton, Sept. 15, 2004.
2   MCK, Pierre Berton, Sept. 15, 2004.
3   *SO*, 104.
4   MCK, Gould; *SO*, 106.
5   PB, "Turning Points."
6   *SO*, 119.
7   ECI, Holden.
8   Elspeth Cameron Papers, TF, box 81, file 3. All grades reported in this chapter are from this source.
9   PB, "Beginnings."
10 *SO*, 87.
11 *SO*, 86; ECI, Woodward.
12 "Memories of the Pulp Era: Doc Savage and the Living Shadow," BPB, Mar. 17, 1959; *SO*, 87–88.
13 ECI, Himie Koshevoy, Feb. 20, 1987.
14 MCK, Pierre Berton, Sept. 15, 2004.
15 ECI, Nap Mailey, Feb. 21, 1987.
16 PB to "Dear Mamma," June 2, 1938, PBF, box 331, file 23.
17 PB to "Dear Daddy," July 4, 1938, PBF, box 331, file 23.
18 *SO*, 112.
19 *SO*, 116.
20 PB to "Dear Mamma," June 2, 1938.
21 PB to "Dear Mamma," July 11, 1938, PBF, box 331, file 23.
22 PB to "Dear Mamma," July 14, 1938, PBF, box 331, file 23.
23 PB to "Dear Mamma," Aug. 4, 1938, PBF, box 331, file 23.
24 PB to "Dear Mamma," Aug. 11, 1938, PBF, box 331, file 23.
25 PB to "Dear Mamma," June 2, 1938.
26 PB, "Turning Points."
27 PB, "Turning Points."
28 PB, "Turning Points."
29 PB, "Interior of a Trapper's Cabin," n.d., PBF, box 243, file 44. See also *SO*, 41. This short story appears to be the earliest extant example of PB's creative writing.
30 *SO*, 120–21.
31 *SO*, 122–23.
32 *SO*, 97, 123.
33 ECI, Pierre Berton, Sept. 3, 1986.
34 *DH*, 149; *SO*, 128.
35 *SO*, 130.
36 *SO*, 130–131.
37 The phrase occurs in part 2, ch. 41: "Learning to Forget." See http://xroads.virginia.edu/~HYPER/ALCOTT/ch41.html.

38 These events on the evening of the summer solstice, 1939, are drawn from *SO*, 136–38, corroborated by MCK, Gould.

39 *SO*, 141.

40 ECI, Mailey.

41 *SO*, 142–43.

42 Gould's story serves as the basis for PB's account in *SO*. He told it again, in similar detail, to me in 2004.

43 MCK, Gould.

44 Lucy Woodward to author, June 5, 2007.

45 *SO*, 144.

46 *SO*, 145.

CHAPTER 6: GET ME REWRITE

1 Paul Axelrod, *Making a Middle Class: Student Life in English Canada during the Thirties* (Montreal: McGill-Queen's University Press, 1990), 139.

2 PB to "Dear Mamma," Sept. 25, 1939, PBF, box 237, file 25; PB to "Dear Mamma and Daddy," n.d. (Sept. 1939?).

3 *SO*, 146–47.

4 PB to "Dear Mamma," Oct. 9, 1939, PBF, box 237, file 25.

5 See Axelrod, *Making a Middle Class*, 164.

6 Harry T. Logan, *Tuum Est: A History of the University of British Columbia* (Vancouver: University of British Columbia, 1958), 134.

7 Logan, *Tuum Est*, 138; Axelrod, *Making a Middle Class*, 164.

8 PB to "Dear Mamma and Daddy," n.d. (Sept. 1939?).

9 PB quoted in Robin Laurence, "Pierre Berton – Media Star in Training at UBC," *AC* (Fall 1990), 38.

10 "My Days as a Reporter on the Old College Rag," BPB, Mar. 30, 1959.

11 Stanley Walker, *City Editor*, foreword by Alexander Woollcott (New York: Frederick A. Stokes, 1934); Emile Gauvreau, *Hot News* (New York: Macaulay Company, 1931).

12 Gauvreau, *Hot News*, vii.

13 Walker, *City Editor*, 37.

14 This had been the case for some time, since journalism and the journalist had long been a staple of mainstream American fiction. Evidence suggests, as the historian Howard Good has noted, that "the youthful readers of newspaper novels who went on to journalism careers were the image made flesh." Howard Good, *Acquainted with the Night: The Image of Journalists in American Fiction, 1890–1930* (Metuchen, N.J., & London: Scarecrow Press, 1986), 93.

15 MCK, Pierre Berton, Sept. 15, 2004. In the forties, the number almost doubled.

16 Joe Saltzman, *Frank Capra and the Image of the Journalist in American Film* (Los Angeles: Norman Lear Center, University of Southern California, 2002). Saltzman provided an overview of the book in a luncheon address (Mar. 27, 2002, Doheny Memorial Library, University of Southern California): it is available online at http://www.ijpc.org/Capra%20speech.htm. See also Loren Ghiglione and Joe Saltzman, "Fact or Fiction: Hollywood Looks at the News," available in

PDF format on the website "The Image of the Journalist in Popular Culture," at http://www.ijpc.org/index.html.

17 PB to "Dear Mamma," Oct. 22, 1939, PBF, box 237, file 25.

18 PB, "College Spirit – That Certain Something We All Have – Or Have We?" *Ubyssey*, Oct. 20, 1939.

19 PB, "Cairn Ceremony Recalls College Spirit of 1922," *Ubyssey*, Oct. 31, 1939.

20 PB to "Dear Folks," Nov. 7, 1939, PBF, box 237, file 25.

21 *SO*, 150.

22 "Young Couple Goes Native But Tahiti Too Civilized," *Ubyssey*, Nov. 10, 1939.

23 PB, "Bella Coola Key to South Sea Riddle – Norse Student Solves Indians' Origin," *Ubyssey*, Feb. 23, 1940.

24 PB to "Dear Mamma," Nov. 23, 1939, PBF, box 237, file 25.

25 PB to "Dear Mamma," Dec. 3, 1939, PBF, box 237, file 25.

26 See Axelrod, *Making a Middle Class*, 130–31.

27 PB to "Dear Mamma," Dec. 3, 1939.

28 A set of *News-Herald* clippings on these and other subjects are enclosed with PB's letter of Dec. 14, 1939, to "Dear Mamma," PBF, box 237, file 25.

29 *SO*, 154.

30 PB was first listed as assistant editor of *Ubyssey* in the Nov. 14, 1939, issue. This was the issue immediately following the one containing PB's first Heyerdahl article.

31 PB to "Dear Mamma," Dec. 14, 1939.

32 PB to "Dear Mamma," Jan. 15, 1940, PBF, box 237, file 26.

33 *His Girl Friday* was released on Jan. 18, 1940.

34 *SO*, 153–54. For literary realism and the newsroom, see Good, *Acquainted with the Night*, 99.

35 PB to "Dear Folks," Jan. 21, 1940, PBF, box 237, file 26.

36 For the cartoon, see *Ubyssey*, Jan. 19, 1940. See also PB to "Dear Folks," Jan. 21, 1940. Throughout January 1940, the CSA's opposition to wartime conscription dominated *Ubyssey* headlines. The article immediately preceding PB's Jan. 21, 1940, letter home was: "Saskatchewan, Mount Allison Sever with C.S.A.," *Ubyssey*, Jan. 19, 1940. But see also "Conference Asks Amendment of B.N.A. Act; Commission Also Vetoes Canadian Conscription," *Ubyssey*, Jan. 9, 1940; "Dean Charges C.S.A. Subversive," *Ubyssey*, Jan. 16, 1940.

37 PB to "Dear Mamma," Feb. 4, 1940, PBF, box 237, file 26. *Ubyssey* announced PB's promotion to assistant editor on Jan. 5, 1940. His position is not noted again until the issue of Feb. 16, 1940, presumably the date of his reappointment.

38 See Axelrod, *Making a Middle Class*.

39 COTC *Journal* (Autumn 1939), PBF, box 237, file 22.

40 PB to "Dear Mamma," Oct. 9, 1939, and Mar. 11, 1940, PBF, box 237, files 25 and 26, respectively.

41 PB to "Dear Mamma," Sept. 25, 1939.

42 PB to "Dear Folks," Nov. 7, 1939; PB to "Dear Mamma," Nov. 23, 1939; MCK, Janet Berton, Feb. 2, 2007.

43 BPB, "My Days as a Reporter."

44 MCK, Janet Berton, Feb. 2, 2007; ECI, Janet Berton, Sept. 13, 1986.

45 Haney would later come to be incorporated into the larger community of Maple Ridge; MCK, Janet Berton, Feb. 2, 2007.

46 Marjorie Church (née Osmond), letter to author, Jan. 4, 2005.

47 Chris Hives (University of British Columbia Archives), to author, Jan. 6, 2005.

48 *Ubyssey* first listed Janet Walker as a "new reporter" on Oct. 4, 1938. See "Ubyssey Reporters Meet Friday Noon," *Ubyssey*, Oct. 4, 1938. The first of her few bylines was for Janet Walker and Bill Backman, "Utopia in Sight – Campus Personalities to Reform," *Ubyssey*, Jan. 6, 1939.

49 *The Totem* (1940), 203; also 56, 195. See Lee Jean Stewart, *It's Up to You: Women at UBC in the Early Years* (Vancouver: University of British Columbia Press, 1990), especially ch. 7, "Boys' Rules: The Masculine Institution and the Feminine Image," 91–96: "Phrateres took the shape of a vast, unlimited sorority which attempted to overcome the tendency of the Greek letter societies to fragment the female population into social cliques. Its name, the Greek word for sisterhood, and its motto, 'famous for friendliness,' had been the idea of the Dean of Women at UCLA in 1924." A chapter was established at UBC in 1934 (94).

50 Quoted in Sheila Nickols, "Looking Back: Janet Walker Berton's Roots in Maple Ridge," *Maple Ridge and Pitt Meadows News*, Dec. 8, 2004.

51 ECI, Janet Berton, Sept. 23, 1986.

52 PB to "Dear Mamma," n.d. (inscribed "Fall 1939" but internal evidence suggests a date after Dec. 3); also PB to "Dear Mamma," Dec. 14, 1939; MCK, Janet Berton, Feb. 2, 2007.

53 MCK, Janet Berton, Feb. 2, 2007.

54 *Ubyssey* first listed Janet Walker's name as associate editor on Sept. 22, 1939.

55 Janet Walker's "Shopping with Mary Ann" made its appearance in *Ubyssey* on Mar. 18, 1938. The column itself pre-dated her arrival at UBC. For Janet Berton's amusing recollection of her life as "Mary Ann," see Janet Walker Berton, "Shopping . . . with Mary Ann," *Ubyssey*, Dec. 10/11, 1948.

56 MCK, Janet Berton, Feb. 2, 2007.

57 ECI, Janet Berton, Sept. 13, 1986.

58 *SO*, 151.

59 MCK, Janet Berton, Feb. 2, 2007; PB to "Dear Mamma," Mar. 11, 1940, PBF, box 237, file 26.

60 MCK, Pierre Berton, Sept. 15, 2004.

61 PB to "Dear Mamma," Mar. 3, 1940, PBF, box 237, file 26; also ECI, Janet Berton, Sept. 13, 1986.

62 PB, "Student Newspaper Charges Campus Parties Seeking Political Control – U.B.C. Fraternities Under Fire," *News-Herald*, Mar. 16, 1940; see also "Editorial – Election Selection," *Ubyssey*, Mar. 15, 1940.

63 PB to "Dear Mamma," Mar. 17, 1940, PBF, box 237, file 26.

64 "Students Attend Farewell Banquet," Mar. 16, 1940. For typical unsigned *News-Herald* articles in March almost certainly written by PB, see for example "'Open House' Day at University," Mar. 1, 1940.

65 PB to "Dear Mamma," Mar. 11, 1940.

66 Patricia E. Roy, *Vancouver: An Illustrated History* (Toronto: James Lorimer & Company, 1980), 138.

67 PB to "Dear Mamma," Mar. 27, 1940, PBF, box 237, file 26.

68 David Graham Phillips, *The Great God Success* (1901; reprint, Ridgewood, N.J.: Reprint Edition, 1967), 11.

69 PB to "Dear Mamma," Mar. 3, 1940.

70 PB to "Dear Mamma," Mar. 27, 1940.

71 Elspeth Cameron Papers, TF, box 81, file 3.

72 *SO*, 155–56.

73 *SO*, 153.

74 Ben Hecht and Charles MacArthur, *The Front Page*, in *The Stage Works of Charles MacArthur*, edited with introduction and notes by Arthur Dorlag and John Irvine (Tallahassee: Florida State University Foundation in co-operation with the School of Theatre, Florida State University, 1974), 122.

75 Hecht and MacArthur, *The Front Page*, 155. The Chicago journalism of the 1920s that inspired *The Front Page* is evoked by William T. Moore, in *Dateline Chicago: a Veteran Newsman Recalls Its Heyday* (New York: Taplinger, 1973), and A.A. Dornfeld, *Behind the Front Page: The Story of the City News Bureau of Chicago* (Chicago: Academy Chicago, 1983). Moore provides several anecdotes about the reporter Hilding Johnson, the real-life inspiration for Hildy (59–60), and Dornfeld provides colourful material about Johnson and the editor Walter Howley, the model for Walter Burns (110).

76 PB to "Dear Mamma," "Sunday am" (but also marked "Summer 1940 May?"), and PB to "Dear Mamma," May 30, 1940, PBF, box 237, file 26.

77 Charles Lynch, *You Can't Print That! Memoirs of a Political Voyeur* (Edmonton: Hurtig, 1983), 33–34. Lynch does not hyphenate "*News-Herald.*"

78 Lynch, *You Can't Print That!*, 34.

79 *SO*, 156.

80 Only one letter PB wrote between June 1940 and September 1942 appears to have survived, or at least can be found in PBF. This is a letter of May 27, 1941, written while PB was on exercise with the COTC. As a consequence, my account of these months has had necessarily to rely on anecdotal material provided in *SO* and on interviews with PB.

81 *SO*, 156–58.

82 For example, for the four-day period May 6–9, 1940, PB appears to have been responsible for the following items in the *News-Herald*: "U.B.C. Faculty Head Honored," May 6; "Graduation Banquet and Dance Tonight," May 6; "Graduating Class to See 'The Patsy,'" May 6; "University Graduate Leaders of Tomorrow, Declares Dean," May 7; "Dean Invites Criticism of U.B.C. Teaching at Annual Class Day," May 8; "Orames Praises Rotarians' Work," May 8; "Young Student Best Orator," May 9; "Banquet and Dance Tonight Officially Welcomes New Members of Convocation," May 9; "University Student to Receive Fraternity Gold Medal Award," May 9. The pace did not slacken as the summer progressed.

83 *SO*, 160.

84 PB's friend Himie Koshevoy, a UBC graduate and *Ubyssey* veteran, recalled this incident in detail similar to that PB provided in *SO*, 161–62. See ECI, Koshevoy. PB himself first wrote of the incident in "A True Account of the Day I Was Fired," BPB, May 14, 1959.

85 Vaughn Palmer, "Bruce Hutchison," *Proceedings of the American Philosophical Society*, vol. 147, no. 1 (Mar. 2003), 88. The article originally appeared in the *Vancouver Sun* on Sept. 15, 1992, the day after Hutchison's death. Biographical information in the following paragraph is largely drawn from this source, at 87–88.

86 PB's friend Dick Holden was among the pranksters that night and recounted the goings-on in ECI, Holden. See also *SO*, 125–27.

87 MCK, Pierre Berton, Sept. 15, 2004. For Bruce Hutchison's political loyalties, and how they affected his reportage, see Patrick H. Brennan, *Reporting the Nation's Business: Press-Government Relations during the Liberal Years, 1935–1957* (Toronto: University of Toronto Press, 1994).

88 The movie version was directed by David Howard and distributed by RKO Radio Pictures. See also Bruce Hutchison, "Park Avenue Logger," *Saturday Evening Post*, Nov. 30, 1935.

89 Bruce Hutchison, *The Unknown Country: Canada and Her People* (Toronto: Longmans, Green, 1943; first published in New York by Coward-McCann, 1942). A second work of non-fiction received a Governor General's Award for 1942: Edgar McInnis, *The Unguarded Frontier: A History of American-Canadian Relations* (Garden City, N.Y.: Doubleday, Doran, 1942).

90 MCK, Pierre Berton, Sept. 15, 2004.

91 PB, "Foreword" to *Great Scott! A Collection of the Best Columns by Jack Scott*, edited and with introduction by Peter Murray (Vancouver: Sono Nis, 1985), 11.

92 Jack Scott, "The Blueberry Caper," in *Great Scott!*, 186.

93 PB, "Foreword," in *Great Scott!*, 12. A few months before he died, PB said of Scott: "He was very well known because he wrote the best column in town, which I think was one of the best columns written in the country." See MCK, Pierre Berton, Sept. 15, 2004.

94 "Answering Your Questions about the New Easier-to-Read News-Herald," *News-Herald*, June 21, 1940.

CHAPTER 7: WUNDERKIND

1 PB, "The Boys Dress Up in Khaki . . . and Become Men of the C.O.T.C.," *The Totem* (1941), 14–15.

2 *SO*, 155–56.

3 PB to "Dear Mamma," May 30, 1940.

4 PB to "Dear Mamma," May 30, 1940.

5 Logan, *Tuum Est*, 138. In September 1940, the *Ubyssey* reported "the largest registration of undergraduate students" in the university's history, more than 2,200 students. See "U.B.C. Enrollment Near New Peak Says Registrar," *Ubyssey*, Sept. 24, 1940; *The Totem* for 1941 reported student numbers for the 1940–41 academic year at 2,650 (54).

6 See "Loyalists Hear Warning against 'Defeatism'" and "Russian Bear Looks for Best Way to Jump, Says Professor," *News-Herald*, May 18 and May 22, 1940. PB reported on two patriotic speeches that Soward gave. That autumn, he enrolled in History 15, Soward's course in European history.

7 "C'est la Guerre," *Ubyssey*, Sept. 24, 1940.

8 Berton later admitted as much: "It was acknowledged that Hitler was up to no good, but the horrifying implications of what he was really doing escaped most of us living in our own little world of campus politics and campus gossip." *SO*, 169.

9 "Margeson Elected Editor-in-Chief of Pub for 40–41," *Ubyssey*, Mar. 20, 1941.

10 *SO*, 166.

11   ECI, Lionel Salt and Margaret Reid, Dec. 9, 1986. Salt and Reid, like several others on the *Ubyssey* who became couples that year, subsequently married.

12   *SO*, 165, 168.

13   ECI, Salt and Reid.

14   Public figures associated with the *Ubyssey* in the 1940s include the poet Earle Birney, Arthur Mayse of the *Saturday Evening Post*, the novelist John Cornish, the filmmaker Norman Klenman, Toronto Chief Librarian Henry Cummings Campbell, and Robert Elson of *Life* magazine; in the 1950s, the *Maclean's* columnist Allan Fotheringham; in the 1960s, the journalist Michael Valpy; in the 1970s, the politician Svend Robinson. See BPB, "My Days as a Reporter."

15   *SO*, 168.

16   Paul Grescoe, "Eric Nicol's Joys and Pains – of Humor," *MM*, Nov. 19, 1979.

17   Jabez, "The Mummery," *Ubyssey*, Sept. 24, 1940.

18   Jabez, "The Mummery," *Ubyssey*, Oct. 1, 1940. Nicol graduated from UBC (B.A. 1941, M.A. 1948), served in the RCAF (1942–45), and went on to a highly successful career as a newspaper columnist (Vancouver *News-Herald*, *Vancouver Daily Province*), playwright (*Her Science Man Lover* was performed at UBC for twenty-eight straight years), and all-round humorist. He won the Stephen Leacock Medal for Humour three times.

19   Quip by PB written to publicize "A Tribute to Lister Sinclair," *Ideas*, CBC Radio, Oct. 29, 2001; at http://www.cbc.ca/ideas/features/lister/index.html.

20   "Players' Club," *The Totem* (1940), 40; "Drama Thrives as Players' Club Enact . . .," *The Totem* (1942), 46; *SO*, 167.

21   Lister Sinclair, "Pearl Castings," *Ubyssey*, Nov. 8, 1940. Sinclair contributed a second column, one called (unaccountably) "Garlic in Hydrophobia." It was, in PB's words, "very lowbrow, containing nothing but off-color jokes." BPB, "My Days as a Reporter."

22   These recollections by Janet Berton and Lister Sinclair can be found in the documentary *Canada's Arrogant Icon: The Life and Times of Pierre Berton*, produced by the Idea Factory production company for CBC Television, 1999.

23   Each of these *Ubyssey* articles bore a PB byline: "Annual Cairn Ceremony to Be Held Tuesday," Oct. 9, 1940; "AMS Meeting, Cairn Ceremony Fail from Lack of Interest," Oct. 4, 1940; "Campus Cupid Has Little Peace from Psych's Class," Oct. 29, 1940.

24   "Student Savants in Brain Clash with Quiz King," *Ubyssey*, Nov. 15, 1940; "Men Eke Out Meagre Margin in First Battle of Sexes," *Ubyssey*, Nov. 19, 1940.

25   "Varsity Time Goes on CJOR tonight," *Ubyssey*, Feb. 28, 1941; "Backstage Broadcast First Night," *Ubyssey*, Mar. 14, 1941. "March of Slime" is mentioned in *SO*, 173, where PB doubly misspells Van Voorhis's name as "Wesbrook Van Voorhees"; "'Varsity Time' Is on the Air," *The Totem* (1941), 50. See also Sandy Kleinfeld, "From Lunch-time RadSoc to Big-time Radio," *AC* (Summer 1986), 15.

26   "Forum Challenges Ubyssey to Justify Its Existence," *Ubyssey*, Jan. 21, 1941; "Ubyssey Takes Up Forum Challenge to Debate," *Ubyssey*, Feb. 4, 1941; Les Bewley, "Dirty Work Afoot as Publications Orators Suck Pebbles in preparation for Wednesday's Word-Battle," *Ubyssey*, Feb. 18, 1941; "Ubyssey Cost Justified Debate Audience Rules," *Ubyssey*, Feb. 21, 1941.

27 The women's group had not, as he claimed, slighted the Varsity Orchestra because it preferred to hire a downtown professional orchestra for its latest fundraising event. The campus band had not put in a formal application for the gig. See *Ubyssey* issues of Jan. 7, 14, 21, 28, 1942, and Feb. 2, 1942.

28 "Revelations of the Writers," *Ubyssey*, Feb. 21, 1941. Comments on social life can be found throughout "Halcyon Days," ch. 4 of *SO*, 148–86. ECI, Salt and Reid; MCK, Pierre Berton, Sept. 15, 2004.

29 ECI, Salt and Reid; ECI, Janet Berton, Sept. 13, 1986.

30 ECI, Salt and Reid; Allan Fotheringham, "When You and I Were Young, Allan," *MM*, Nov. 2, 1998; *SO*, 166. For PB's reminiscence about the evolution of this doggerel, see PB, "The Berton Fathered It; Kindergarten Thrives On," *Ubyssey*, Dec. 11, 1948, 7, 9.

31 Fotheringham, "When You and I Were Young."

32 "Revelations of the Writers."

33 Lucy Woodward to author, June 5, 2007.

34 MCK, Janet Berton, Feb. 2, 2007.

35 PB's UBC transcript is in Elspeth Cameron Papers, TF, box 81, file 3. PB's final grades in May 1941: English, 66 per cent; history, 66 per cent; Philosophy 1, 77 per cent; Philosophy 9, 73 per cent; government, 80 per cent.

    In *SO*, PB states that in F.H. Soward's history class in 1940–41 he received a grade of 50 per cent because he did not attend class and tossed a coin to determine answers in the objective examination Soward had set. This is not the case. Berton's UBC transcripts record that he received a grade of 99 out of 150 (66 per cent) in History 15 that year. In neither of the history courses Berton took the previous year did he receive a grade of 50 per cent. He did, however, receive a final grade of 50 per cent in English 19, taken in 1939–40.

    The story, however, made for a good punch line: "'I did my best to flunk you, Berton,' he [Soward] said, 'but you just squeaked through. I mentally thanked the gods of chance.'" (*SO*, 170).

36 PB to "Dear Mamma," May 27, 1941, PBF, box 237, file 27.

37 ECI, Ray Gardner, Nov. 6, 1986.

38 *SO*, 176.

39 *SO*, 180.

40 *SO*, 177.

41 ECI, Gardner. For details on the career of Helena Gutteridge, see Susan Wade, "Helena Gutteridge: Votes for Women and Trade Unions," in Barbara K. Latham and Cathy Kess, eds., *In Her Own Right: Selected Essays on the History of Women in British Columbia* (Victoria: Camosun College, 1980); available online at http://ccins.camosun.bc.ca/~latham/inherownright/tableofcontents.htm.

42 *SO*, 181–83.

43 *SO*, 183–84.

44 *SO*, 185–86.

45 *SO*, 187.

46 PB, *Marching as to War: Canada's Turbulent Years, 1899–1953* (Toronto: Doubleday Canada, 2001), 327. Italics in original.

47 *SO*, 188.

48 Elspeth Cameron Papers, TF, box 81, file 3. Unless otherwise stated, references to Berton's military service are drawn from the official record of service to be found in this source.

49 *SO*, 189–90.

50 Lucy Woodward to author, June 5, 2007.

51 PB to "Dear Folks," Feb. 9, 1942, PBF, box 237, file 28.

52 "For November 11: Some Things I can't forget," BPB, Nov. 11, 1959.

53 PB to "Dear Mamma," Mar. 18, 1942, PBF, box 237, file 28.

54 PB to "Dear Mamma," Mar. 11, 1942, PBF, box 237, file 28.

55 PB to "Dear Mamma," PBF, box 237, file 28. Information in the second half of this paragraph is drawn from these two letters, marked only "Thursday" and "Wednesday" but clearly written in March or early April 1942. In these and other cases, I have determined the month and year through internal evidence – for example, by comparing locations noted in the letters or on the letterhead with postings listed in PB's official record of service.

　　PB originally dated more than twenty-five of his wartime letters (almost all of them typed) only with the day of the week. A number of these letters bear handwritten dates he added subsequently, likely when he wrote his memoirs in the 1980s. A comparison of the day and month noted on a letter with a perpetual calendar reveals, however, that more often than not this later dating is in error.

　　The following example illustrates the problem. One letter is marked only "Tuesday," and lacks date, month, or year. Internal evidence suggests that it was written in July 1944. PB has inscribed on it, by hand, "July 5, 1944." But in 1944, July 5 was a Wednesday. The letter states that his mother's most recent letter has reminded him that he has forgotten his parents' wedding anniversary (June 29). In later dating his own letter July 5, PB inferred, probably correctly, that it would have been the first one he wrote home that month. If so, and assuming that the "Tuesday" noted in the original letter is not in error, the correct date should be July 4, 1944. Wherever necessary and possible, I have dated PB's letters in this manner. Where doubt remains, I have appended a question mark to the citation.

56 PB to "Dear Mamma," "Wed." (probably early April 1942), PBF, box 237, file 28.

57 PB to "Dear Mamma and family," Mar. 31, 1942; and PB to "Dear Mamma," "Wed." (probably early April 1942), both in PBF, box 237, file 28. PB was not formally a member of the Seaforth Highlanders; he was merely, as he put it, "a reinforcement." But the affiliation, however tenuous, allowed him "to wear either the Balmoral or the Glengarry rather than the despised field service cap"; *SO*, 192.

58 PB to "Dear Mamma and family," Mar. 31, 1942.

59 *SO*, 191–92.

60 "Military Memoir No. 2874: The Man in the Bunk Above Me," BPB, May 5, 1960.

61 The Michigan-born journalist had covered riots in Ireland in 1917, in Morocco in 1925, and in India in 1930, and then the Italian campaign in Ethiopia in 1936; but it was when he fell from a railroad platform in London during a blackout in 1940 that he became the first correspondent to be killed in the Second World War. See Doral Chenoweth, "54 War Correspondents K.I.A. WWII," at http://www.54war correspondents-kia-30ww2.com/chapter1.html; Bosley Crowther, "The Mortal Storm," film review in *New York Times*, June 21, 1940; PB to "Dear Mamma," "Tuesday" (probably June 23, 1942), PBF, box 237, file 28.

62 PB to "Dear Mamma," "Wednesday" (probably May 6, 1942), PBF, box 237, file 28. Since the letter opens by noting that PB wished it to be received by Mother's Day (which fell on Sunday, May 10, in 1942), the letter must have been written on May 6.

63 Little Rollo Holiday was one of the best-known characters in American children's literature before the Civil War. He was the heroic main character of a series of school primers by the Boston school principal Jacob Abbott (1803–79). These not only taught children to read but provided them with a charming role model. The Little Rollo series ran to twenty-eight volumes, bearing titles such as *Rollo Learning to Read* (1835), *Rollo at Work; or, The Way for a Boy to Learn to Be Industrious* (1837), and *Rollo at Play; or, Safe Amusements* (1837). See "Nineteenth-Century American Children & What They Read: Some of Their Books," at http://www.merrycoz.org/BOOKS.HTM.

64 PB to "Dear Mamma," "Saturday" (late May 1942), PBF, box 237, file 28. This letter was posted from Chilliwack, so was likely written shortly after PB was posted there on May 26, 1942.

65 PB to "Dear Daddy," June 23, 1942, PBF, box 237, file 28.

CHAPTER 8: MARKING TIME

1 PB to "Dear Mamma," Sept. 11, 1942, PBF, box 237, file 28.

2 PB to "Dear Mamma," Aug. 27, 1942, and Sept. 11, 1942, PBF, box 237, file 28.

3 PB to "Dear Mamma," Dec. 14, 1942, PBF, box 237, file 29; "Army Memoir No. 2254: The Day I Became an Officer," BPB, Feb. 8, 1960.

4 "First Issue of Army Paper Published Here," *Chilliwack Progress*, n.d. (Nov. 1942); clipping in PBF, box 286, "Torch Newspaper 1943" file. This article noted "Corporal Pierre Berton" as editor and advertising manager and "Pte. Art Jones" as assistant.

5 "First Issue of Army Paper."

6 *SO*, 208.

7 PB to "Dear Mamma," n.d. (Dec. 1942), PBF, box 237, file 29.

8 MCK, Janet Berton, Feb. 2, 2007.

9 Lucy Woodward to author, June 5, 2007.

10 John Robert Colombo, *Colombo's Canadian Quotations* (Edmonton: Hurtig, 1974), 53a. Colombo notes: "Attributed by Dick Brown in *The Canadian Magazine*, Dec. 22, 1973." See also *SO*, 204–05.

11 MCK, Janet Berton, Feb. 2, 2007; Jackson House, "Ma Murray: The Salty Scourge of Lillooet," *MM*, Mar. 19, 1966, 18, 48, 50; Earle Beattie, "The Rebel Queen of the Northwest," *Chatelaine* (May 1952), 16–17ff.

12 PB to "Dear Mamma," Sept. 18, 1942, PBF, box 237, file 29.

13 MCK, Janet Berton, Feb. 2, 2007.

14 PB to "Dear Mamma," Dec. 14, 1942.

15 PB to "Dear Mamma," Sept. 21, 1943, PBF, box 237, file 30.

16 PB to "Dear Mamma," n.d. (Apr. 1943), PBF, box 237, file 30.

17 PB to "Dear Mamma," Dec. 14, 1942.

18 PB to "Dear Mamma," n.d. (Mar. 1943) and PB to "Dear Mamma," n.d. (Apr. 1943), PBF, box 237, file 30.

19 "Lieut. Berton Leaves Camp," *Chilliwack Progress*, Apr. 21, 1943.

20 BPB, "Army Memoir No. 2254"; *SO*, 212.

21 PB to "Dear Mamma," n.d. (July 1943), PBF, box 237, file 30.

22 PB to "Dear Mamma," "Sun." (July 1943), PB to "Dear Mamma," "Mon." (Aug. 1943), PBF, box 237, file 30.

23 PB to "Dear Mamma," undated letters of September to December 1943, PBF, box 237, file 30.

24 PB to "Dear Mamma," "Sun." (Dec. 1943), PBF, box 237, file 30.

25 *SO*, 213. Janet Berton did not later recall being present at the Filions' wedding; MCK, Janet Berton, Feb. 2, 2007.

26 PB to "Dear Mamma," Jan. 7, 1944, PBF, box 237, file 32.

27 J.L. Granatstein, *Canada's War: The Politics of the Mackenzie King Government, 1939–1945* (Toronto: Oxford University Press, 1975), 43.

28 "On the Prowl – with Betty MacDowell – More Recollections," *Brockville Recorder*, n.d.; copy in PBF, box 286, "Torch Newspaper 1943" file.

29 PB to "Dear Mamma," Apr. 20, 1944, PBF, box 237, file 32.

30 PB to "Dear Mamma," Apr. 20, 1944.

31 PB to "Dear Mamma," July 18, 1944, PBF, box 237, file 32; MCK, Janet Berton, Feb. 2, 2007.

32 PB to "Dear Mamma," July 18, 1944, and PB to "Dear Mamma," Aug. 2, 1944, PBF, box 237, file 33.

33 PB to "Dear Mamma," Sept. 14, 1944, PBF, box 237, file 33.

34 PB to "Dear Mamma," Aug. 9, 1944, PBF, box 237, file 33.

35 PB to "Dear Mamma," Aug. 2, 1944, PBF, box 237, file 33.

36 PB to "Dear Mamma," Sept. 21, 1944, PBF, box 237, file 33.

37 PB to "Dear Mamma," Sept. 21, 1944.

38 PB to "Dear Mamma," Sept. 21, 1944.

39 PB to "Dear Mamma," Nov. 8, 1944, PBF, box 237, file 34. PB also noted that General Andrew McNaughton (whom King appointed minister of defence in Ralston's place), previously very popular among the troops, had "suddenly dropped in prestige. The tacit admission that he did not favor conscription was stunning as it had always been believed that he was strongly in favor of it. The troops are not taking it well at all. King is bitterly hated."

40 PB to "Dear Mamma," n.d. (Dec. 1944), PBF, box 237, file 34.

41 Frederick Bodmer, *The Loom of Language: An Approach to the Mastery of Many Languages* (New York: W.W. Norton, 1944); Somerset Maugham, *The Moon and Sixpence* (London: William Heinemann, 1919), and *The Razor's Edge* (London: William Heinemann, 1944); Hendrik Willem Van Loon, *Van Loon's Geography: The Story of the World We Live In* (New York: Simon and Schuster, 1932); Radclyffe Hall, *The Well of Loneliness* (London: Jonathan Cape, 1928), all noted in PB to "Dear Mamma," n.d. (Dec. 1944).

42 PB to "Dear Mamma," Nov. 8, 1944, and undated letters of Nov. and Dec. 1944, PBF, box 237, file 34.

43 "Some Leaves from a Tattered Notebook," BPB, Jan. 14, 1960. Berton likely obtained the quip from Maury Maverick from his memoir, *A Maverick American* (New York: Covici, Fried, 1937). Maverick is credited with having coined the term *gobbledygook* to describe bureaucratic jargon.

44 PB to "Dear Mamma," Jan. 7, 1945, PBF, box 237, file 35.

45 PB to "Dear Mamma," n.d. (Dec. 1944), PBF, box 237, file 35.

46 PB to "Dear Mamma," Mar. 13, 1945, PBF, box 237, file 35.

47 *SO*, 240; PB to "Dear Mamma," Mar. 27, 1945, PBF, box 237, file 35.

48 PB to "Dear Mamma," Apr. 5, 1945, PBF, box 237, file 35.

49 PB to "Dear Mamma," Apr. 5, 1945; *SO*, 241–43.

50 *SO*, 244–45. This dialogue is PB's recreation.

51 *SO*, 246.

52 *SO*, 247–50.

53 PB to "Dear Mamma," Apr. 15, 1945, PBF, box 237, file 35.

54 PB to "Dear Mamma," Apr. 15, 1945; *SO*, 251.

55 PB to "Dear Mamma," Apr. 23, 1945, PBF, box 237, file 35; *SO*, 250.

56 PB to "Dear Mamma," May 16, 1945, PBF, box 237, file 35.

57 PB almost certainly saw *Nazi Murder Mills!* (Universal-International), released to theatres on April 26, 1945, and featuring the American actor and newsreel narrator Ed Herlihy. The nine-minute documentary contained footage taken at camps in Grasleben, Hadamar, Ohrdurf, Buchenwald, and Nordhausen. The same day Universal-International released another newsreel, *Nations Meet to Map World Security Plan*, about the conference to draft the charter for formation of the United Nations. Sample still photographs and the entire audio tracks from these documents can be seen, heard, and purchased at the commercial website BuyOutFootage.com.

58 PB to "Dear Mamma," Apr. 30, 1945, PBF, box 237, file 35.

59 PB to "Dear Daddy," May 9, 1945, PBF, box 237, file 35. Originally made as a training documentary, *The Way Ahead* was re-edited, expanded, and renamed *The Immortal Battalion*. Released in 1944, the movie also starred Peter Ustinov and Stanley Holloway. The novelist Eric Ambler wrote the original story for the film; Ambler and Ustinov collaborated on the screenplay. It was directed by Carol Reed and had a "Foreword" by the American journalist and war correspondent Quentin Reynolds.

60 *SO*, 252–53.

61 *SO*, 244.

62 *SO*, 253–54.

63 *SO*, 254, 246.

64 In an interview conducted on September 15, 2004, I asked PB about his encounter with Frances. He confirmed that he did not attempt to contact her again, at the time or later. He had nothing to add to the narrative he had constructed of the encounter in *SO*.

65 Provided with this assessment in 2007, Janet Berton responded, "I don't think it's [*long silence*] inaccurate, I guess." MCK, Janet Berton, Feb. 2, 2007.

66 *SO*, 254.

CHAPTER 9: CITIZEN STRAIGHT'S BOY

1 *SO*, 255.

2 *SO*, 255.

3 PB to "Dear Mamma," May 26, 1945, PBF, box 237, file 31.

4 PB to "Dear Mamma," June 8, 1945, PBF, box 237, file 31.

5 PB to "Dear Mamma," June 15, 1945, PBF, box 237, file 31.

6 PB to "Dear Mamma," June 25, 1945, PBF, box 237, file 31. See also *SO*, 256–57.

7 *SO*, 256–57. In "Hey, Pop, What Did You Do in the War?" BPB, June 29, 1959, PB states that his passage to North America was aboard the *Queen Elizabeth*. But the RMS *Queen Elizabeth* was not released from U.S. service to repatriate Canadian troops until October 1945. See historical accounts of the RMS *Queen Mary* and the RMS *Queen Elizabeth* at www.ocean-liners.com.

8 ECI, Gardner.

9 *SO*, 257.

10 MCK, Janet Berton, Feb. 2, 2007.

11 *SO*, 258.

12 MCK, Janet Berton, Feb. 2, 2007.

13 ECI, Salt and Reid; *SO*, 259.

14 *SO*, 260.

15 "Some Memories of Good Old V-J Day," BPB, Aug. 13, 1959.

16 MCK, Pierre Berton, Sept. 15, 2004. Lucy Woodward believed her father had had a stroke: "One morning he collapsed getting out of bed and could not get up again" (Lucy Woodward to author, June 5, 2007). Frank Berton's death certificate states that the immediate cause of death was a hemorrhage in the bowel from a benign tumour (papilloma) in the large intestine, likely brought on by coronary sclerosis and pulmonary edema. At the end, his lungs failed him, not his heart. A copy of Francis George Berton's death certificate is accessible through the Vital Statistics Section of the British Columbia Archives.

17 Lucy Woodward to author, June 5, 2007.

18 MCK, Janet Berton, Feb. 2, 2007; Lucy Woodward to author, June 5, 2007.

19 BPB, "Some Memories of Good Old V-J Day"; italics in original.

20 BPB, "Some Memories of Good Old V-J Day."

21 *SO*, 269.

22 *SO*, 270.

23 "The Hanging That Troubles My Dreams," BPB, Mar. 10, 1959. Information in the next two paragraphs comes from this source.

24 Wilf Bennett, "'The Day Pierre Berton Was Fired,' Recalled by Ex-editorial Writer," *News-Herald*, Nov. 24, 1962. This was a special commemorative issue occasioned by a reunion of former *News-Herald* staffers in association with the Newsmen's Club of British Columbia. The newspaper itself had ceased publication five years earlier.

25 "Good Morning – with Wilf Bennett," Vancouver *Province*, Jan. 27, 1963.

26 *SO*, 275–76.

27 Jim Coleman, "Dinky Curve Benefitted Newspaper Profession – Straight Might Have Picked Baseball Career," in "'Citizen' Hal Straight Celebrates 60th Birthday," Sept. 1969. In this article, Coleman mistakenly states that the team was the Seattle Rainiers, but it acquired that name only in 1937, when Emil Sick bought the struggling Indians and renamed the organization. See the entry for "Seattle Rainiers" in HistoryLink.org, available at: http://www.historylink.org/Slide_show/index.cfm?file_id=7123.

"'Citizen Hal Straight'" was an eight-page mock newspaper put together with loving care by Straight's irreverent newspaper colleagues in honour of their mentor and distributed to his friends and family. Contributors included Jack Scott (granted the front-page lead by his peers), Dick Beddoes, Jack Webster, Bruce Hutchison, Simma Holt, Himie Koshevoy, Penny Wise, Frank Rasky, PB, Jack Wasserman, Jim Coleman, Lee Straight (Hal's younger brother), and Pat Slatterty. The contributors were a veritable who's who of the Canadian newspaper world. The entire back page consisted of a Yousuf Karsh photograph of the Straight family at their cottage. I am grateful to Beverley Straight for the gift of a copy of "Citizen Hal Straight."

28 MCK, Beverley Straight, Feb. 22, 2005; John Armstrong, "Service Set for Colorful Ex-editor," *Vancouver Sun*, Feb. 14, 1989.

29 Details of the Cromie story are drawn in part from PB, "Vancouver's Rising Sun," *MM*, July 1, 1948.

30 This description is drawn Tom Ardies, "The Vancouver Sun," in "A Tale of Three Papers – Zany Days at the Dailies," *Vancouver Magazine* (Oct. 1980), 79. The article consists of excerpts from Walter Stewart, ed., *Canadian Newspapers: The Inside Story* (Edmonton: Hurtig, 1980).

31 MCK, Straight.

32 Denny Boyd, eponymous column, *Vancouver Sun*, Feb. 14, 1989. Boyd wrote: "Those of us with 30 or more years in the Sun newsroom – and that's four or five of us – don't just think of Straight as the big guy who once called the shots every day. We recall him as the man who took a weak, characterless paper and shaped it, put steel and boiling excitement and integrity in it."

33 MCK, Straight. Information here is from a one-page document prepared for the University of British Columbia School of Journalism. Ms. Straight read this text aloud during the interview. For the incident about the wastebasket, see also "Corn Plasters," by "Cub Reporter," in "'Citizen' Hal Straight Celebrates 60th Birthday."

34 MCK, Straight.

35 MCK, Janet Berton, Feb. 2, 2007.

36 MCK, Pierre Berton, Sept. 15, 2004. For PB, Hal Straight epitomized the whole environment and supporting cast in the Sun Tower. Part of his own self-image back then, PB said, "came from the style of the day from the movies," part "from some of the New York papers," and Straight seemed the very embodiment of this reading. "He was that kind of a newspaper man," PB said. "Hell-bent for leather and didn't give a damn for anybody, wore his hat in the office, and so on. I think we all thought of ourselves in those terms. The guys I worked with did. . . . We thought it was a glamorous business because the movies had made it a glamorous business."

37 MCK, Straight.

38 ECI, Gardner.

39 *SO*, 280–81.

40 *SO*, 286–87.

41 *SO*, 287.

42 MCK, Janet Berton, Feb. 2, 2007.

43 *SO*, 291–92.

44 MCK, Straight.
45 MCK, Straight.
46 ECI, Gardner.
47 MCK, Straight.
48 MCK, Pierre Berton, Sept. 15, 2004.
49 MCK, Straight.
50 PB, "Vancouver's Rising Sun."
51 Charles Bruce, *News and the Southams* (Toronto: Macmillan of Canada, 1968), 352–59.
52 *SO*, 294.
53 "A Belated Account of the Great Vancouver Pig Derby," BPB, Nov. 24, 1958.
54 *SO*, 303–04.
55 *SO*, 305.
56 *SO*, 306.
57 W.A. Craik (Hon. Secretary-Treasurer, Empire Press Union, Canadian Section, Toronto) to PB, Dec. 30, 1946, acknowledging receipt of PB's letter; PBF, box 111, "Personal – Kemsley Scholarship" file.
58 PB, "Abject Confessions of a Tired Old Newspaperman," *MM*, Nov. 15, 1960.
59 ECI, Gardner; *SO*, 307–09; PB, "Abject Confessions."
60 Bruce, *News and the Southams*, 361.

CHAPTER 10: HEADLESS VALLEY

1 *SO*, 311.
2 R.A. Francis and Margaret Francis, "Nahanni . . . Valley of Mystery," undated and unattributed clipping in PBF, box 163, "Nahanni . . . Valley of Mystery" file.
3 PB, "Vallery of Mystery," *MM*, Mar. 15, 1947; Francis and Francis, "Nahanni," PBF, box 163, "Nahanni . . . Valley of Mystery" file.
4 *SO*, 311.
5 *SO*, 311–13.
6 *SO*, 313.
7 PB wrote three separate accounts of the *Vancouver Sun* Headless Valley expedition. The first is in the form of fifteen telegraphed reports to the *Sun*. With minor editing, these became the text used the *Sun* in daily articles between Feb. 3 and Feb. 19 (PBF, box 160, "Despatches from Headless Valley" file). The second account, a series of six scripts for CBC radio talks given in 1952, is rather more detailed (Headless Valley Radio Series, PBF, box 161, "North to the Nahanni" file). The third is to be found in PB's memoirs, *SO*, 310–21. Material in this paragraph is drawn from the first radio script, "The Myth of Headless Valley," Headless Valley Radio Series, no. 1.
8 PB, "The Myth of Headless Valley," Headless Valley Radio Series, no. 1, 7; *SO*, 314.
9 PB stated in his first 1952 radio talk that the decision to fly to Headless Valley was made on "a Wednesday in late January," and he repeated the claim in the second one. Straight sent his first telegram to PB at Finlay Forks, B.C., on Jan. 27. See "The Myth of Headless Valley" and "The Mad Pilot," Headless Valley Radio Series, nos. 1 and 2. Straight's telegrams to PB are in PBF, box 163, "Nahanni – Letters, telegrams, INS articles; misc." file.

10 PB, "The Mad Pilot," Headless Valley Radio Series, no. 2, 1.

11 PB, "The Mad Pilot," Headless Valley Radio Series, no. 2, 6–7.

12 Entry in PB's *Vancouver Sun* reporter's notebook, undated but written at Fort St. James. "Headless Valley," "Nahanni . . . misc." file. This delay is not noted in PB's other accounts.

13 PB, "The Mad Pilot," Headless Valley Radio Series, no. 2, 3.

14 PB, "The Mad Pilot," Headless Valley Radio Series, no. 2, 7.

15 *SO*, 273.

16 Loose sheet dated Jan. 28, 1947, "Nahanni . . . misc." file; article #3, dispatched from Finlay Forks, B.C., Feb. 3, 1947, for release on Feb. 5, 1947, PBF, box 160, "Despatches from Headless Valley" file.

17 PB, "The Great Lone Land," Headless Valley Radio Series, no. 3, 1–4.

18 PB, "The Great Lone Land," Headless Valley Radio Series, no. 3, 4–6.

19 PB, "The Great Lone Land," Headless Valley Radio Series, no. 3, 7.

20 The telegraphed reports are in PBF, box 160, "Despatches from Headless Valley" file.

21 Sidney Katz, "Pierre's adventures in Bertonland," *MM*, Oct. 6, 1962.

22 Hal Straight to PB, Jan. 29, 1947, "Nahanni . . . misc." file.

23 *SO*, 316.

24 Article #3, dispatched Feb. 3, 1947.

25 Article #10, dispatched from the South Nahanni River, N.W.T., Feb. 7, for release on Feb. 13, 1947.

26 Article #11, dispatched from Headless Valley, N.W.T., Feb. 8, for release on Fri., Feb. 14, 1947.

27 Feb. 17 is the date accompanying this text, "as told by Berton," at http://marina.fortunecity.com/reach/361/berton.htm. Rita Hayworth's telegram to Straight in PBF, however, is dated Feb. 13.

28 Article #11, dispatched Feb. 8, 1947.

29 Article #12, dispatched from Headless Valley, N.W.T., Feb. 9, for release on Sat., Feb. 15, 1947.

30 Article #13, dispatched from Watson Lake, N.W.T., Feb. 11, for release on Sat., Feb. 16, 1947. In Articles #14 and #15, dispatched from Bear Lake, PB continued telling tall tales drawn from northern life. The former told about the discovery of gold near Bear Lake; the latter, of the "strange and savage" Bear Lake Tribe – "with a history checkered by the white man's firewater and smeared with the white man's blood."

31 PB, "North to Nahanni," Headless Valley Radio Series, no. 4, 2.

32 Hal Straight to PB, Jan. 31, 1947, "Nahanni . . . misc." file.

33 Rita Hayworth to Hal Straight, Feb. 13, 1947, "Nahanni . . . misc." file.

34 A photographic negative of the award is in the "Nahanni . . . misc." file; see also *SO*, 321.

35 MCK, Pierre Berton, Sept. 15, 2004; see also *SO*, 326–27.

36 PB, "For Vancouver Sun broadcast," four-page typescript, undated, PBF, box 160, "Headless Valley Articles" file.

37 PB, "For Vancouver Sun broadcast," undated, "Headless Valley Articles" file.

38 Seymour Berkson to PB, Feb. 24, 1947, PBF, box 104, "Business Correspondence 1946–1949" file.

39 James Henle to Chester Weil, Mar. 20, 1947, PBF, box 104, "Business Correspondence 1946–1949" file.

40 PB's typescript of "Snowball in Hell" is in PBF, box 89, file 8.

41 Charles Pirie Abraham (Ottawa) to PB, Dec. 2, 1946; Russell B. Wilson (Oregon City) to Editor, *Vancouver Sun*, Mar. 14, 1947; C.G. Overhill (Revelstoke) to PB, Dec. 15, 1946; A.T. Ferguson (Yellowknife) to PB, Feb. 25, 1947; F.A. Elliott (California) to Editor, *Vancouver Sun*; all in PBF, box 163, unnamed file but with label "Jacques Egyptien Compton Correspondence" on reverse.

42 PB, "For Vancouver Sun broadcast," undated, "Headless Valley Articles" file.

43 PB, "They'll Never Believe the Truth About Headless Valley," "Headless Valley Articles" file. Typescripts on Headless Valley in this file include "The Myth of Headless Valley" and "Folklore in the Making," both undated. Internal evidence indicates that they were written after PB had returned to Toronto.

44 *SO*, 325.

45 Correspondence relating to Berton's work with the CBC, including invoices for his fees, is in PBF, box 104, "Business Correspondence, 1946–1949" file; also *SO*, 323–24.

46 "Mystery Men," *Reading: A Canadian Magazine*, vol. 1, no. 2 (Apr. 1946), 3–6.

47 PB, "Magic in Their Souls: The First Original Story of Vancouver's Jubilee," *British Columbia Digest* (July 1946), 88–95.

48 A photocopy of this sketch, with the published article, is in Elspeth Cameron Papers, TF, Ms. Coll. 337, box 81.

49 PB, "The Waiting Room," PBF, box 98, "The Waiting Room" file. After the move to Toronto, Berton used this 3,700-word short story as the basis of a half-hour play for television, the text of which is in the same location.

50 PB, "Water Hazard," PBF, box 99, "Water Hazard" file.

51 PB, "Past Imperfect," PBF, box 99, "Past Imperfect" file. It is not certain why PB chose the year 1936 rather than 1934, the year in which the movie *It Happened One Night* was released.

52 PB, "A Study in Tweed: A Vignette," PBF, box 99, "A Study in Tweed" file.

CHAPTER 11: IRWIN'S RECRUIT

1 MCK, Janet Berton, Feb. 2, 2007.

2 *SO*, 330.

3 James Lemon, *Toronto since 1918: An Illustrated History* (Toronto: James Lorimer & Company, 1985), 98–99; *MT*, 6.

4 Lemon, *Toronto since 1918*, 90.

5 ECI, Elizabeth Anglin, Dec. 9, 1986; ECI, Gerald Anglin, Dec. 12, 1986; PB to "Dear Mamma," July 29, 1947, PBF, box 237, file 36.

6 W.A. Irwin to PB, Apr. 12, 1947, PBF, box 236, file 46.

7 PB, article beginning "The First Time I Saw Toronto," *Canadian Magazine* (Canadian Airlines: Apr 1991), 37. See also PB, "Foreword" to David Mackenzie, *Arthur Irwin: A Biography* (Toronto: University of Toronto Press, 1993), ix.

8 PB to Glen Allen, Sept. 24, 1984, PBF, box 230, file 13.

9 "Irwin, Arthur," *MM*, Aug. 23, 1999; Susy Aston and Sue Ferguson, "*Maclean's Magazine*: The First 100 Years," *MM*, May 16, 2005; available electronically at http://macleans.ca/contactus/article.jsp?content=20050523_1066218_106218.

10 H. Napier Moore, "So Its Dulles Ditchwater," address to the Empire Club of Canada (Toronto), Oct. 11, 1956, in *The Empire Club of Canada: Speeches 1956–1957* (Toronto: Empire Club Foundation, 1957), 10–20; see also "Irwin, Arthur," in *The Canadian Encyclopedia*.

11 Mackenzie, *Arthur Irwin*, 3–5; J.W. Dafoe, *Canada: An American Nation* (New York: Columbia University Press, 1935).

12 *MT*, 11; PB to Glen Allen, Sept. 24, 1984.

13 James MacGowan, "Looking Back on a Legend," *Ryerson Review of Journalism*, Online content (Spring 2004), at http://www.ryerson.ca/rrj/archives/992/macgowanspr.html; *MT*, 12–14. Some of Ralph Allen's memorable wartime reports are anthologized in Christina McCall Newman, ed., *The Man from Oxbow: The Best of Ralph Allen* (Toronto: McClelland & Stewart, 1967).

14 Mackenzie, *Arthur Irwin*, 189–90; *MT*, 14.

15 MCK, Pierre Berton, Sept. 15, 2004.

16 PB to "Dear Mamma," July 29, 1947, PBF, box 237, file 36.

17 PB, "They Tempered the Whirlwind," *MM*, Sept. 15, 1947; "Tempest in a Fishbowl," *MM*, Nov. 1, 1947; "The Mayor of Atom Village," *MM*, Dec. 1, 1947; "War Dance of the Musicians," *MM*, Dec. 15, 1947; "Biggest Show on Earth," *MM*, Nov. 15, 1947.

18 PB to Glen Allen, Sept. 24, 1984.

19 MCK, Pierre Berton, Sept. 15, 2004.

20 MacGowan, "Looking Back at a Legend"; MCK, Pierre Berton, Sept. 15, 2004.

21 Mackenzie, *Arthur Irwin*, 192–93; MCK, Pierre Berton, Sept. 15, 2004.

22 Mackenzie, *Arthur Irwin*, 194.

23 PB to Glen Allen, Sept. 24, 1984.

24 ECI, Arthur Irwin, Feb. 21, 1987.

25 ECI, June Callwood and Trent Frayne, Nov. 3, 1986.

26 Anne Dublin, *June Callwood: A Life of Action* (Toronto: Second Story Press, 2006); Sandra Martin, "June Callwood, Writer, Activist and Broadcaster 1924–2007," *G&M*, Apr. 16, 2007. The following biographical passages on Callwood draw from these sources.

27 Dublin, *June Callwood*, 21.

28 ECI, Callwood and Frayne, Nov. 3, 1986.

29 *MT*, 23.

30 PB, "No Jews Need Apply," *MM*, Nov. 1, 1948.

31 David R. Davies, *The Postwar Decline of American Newspapers, 1945–1965* (Westport, Conn.: Praeger, 2006); Thomas Doherty, *Cold War, Cool Medium: Television, McCarthyism and American Culture* (New York: Columbia University Press, 2003); Erik Barnouw, *Tube of Plenty: The Evolution of American Television*. 2nd rev. ed. (New York: Oxford University Press, 1990), 112.

32 *MT*, 24–25.

33 For background, see Cheryl Krasnick Warsh, *Moments of Unreason: The Practice of Canadian Psychiatry and the Homewood Retreat, 1883–1923* (Montreal and Kingston: McGill-Queen's University Press, 1989).

34 Peter C. Newman, *The Flame of Power: Intimate Portraits of Canada's Greatest Businessmen* (Toronto: Longmans, Green, 1959).

35 MCK, Janet Berton, Feb. 2, 2007.

36 PB, "Let's Drive to Alaska," *MM*, Aug. 1, 1948; "Monsters on the Klondike," *MM*, Sept. 1, 1948; "Dan McGrew Died Here," *MM*, Sept. 15, 1948.

37 PB, "Let's Drive to Alaska."

38 PB, "Dan McGrew Died Here."

39 PB, "Dan McGrew Died Here."

40 *MT*, 58–59; MCK, Janet Berton, Feb. 2, 2007. This group evolved into the Hincks-Dellcrest Foundation. At the time this interview was conducted, Janet Berton remained involved with the group.

41 *MT*, 48–53.

42 Blair Fraser to PB, Sept. 28, 1948, PBF, box 108, "Fraser, Blair" file.

43 PB, "He Was a Love Slave," Dec. 1, 1948; *MT*, 46–47.

44 Jack Scott to PB, n.d. but December 1948, PBF, box 110, "Scott, Jack" file.

45 PB, "New Crop on Campus," *MM*, Nov. 15, 1948; PB, "He Was a Love Slave"; PB and C.G. Gifford, "The Beanery Gang," *MM*, Dec. 15, 1948. See William Foote Whyte, *Street Corner Society: The Social Structure of an Italian Slum* (Chicago: University of Chicago Press, 1943).

46 Raymond Whitehouse to PB, Oct. 29, 1948; Farrar, Straus and Company, to PB, Nov. 16, 1948, PBF, box 104, "Business Corresp. 1946–1949" file.

47 Roy MacSkimming, *The Perilous Trade: Publishing Canada's Writers* (Toronto: McClelland & Stewart, 2003), 23–41.

48 Quoted in Edward McCourt, "Canadian Letters," *Royal Commission Studies: A Selection of Essays Prepared for the Royal Commission on National Development in the Arts, Letters and Sciences* (Ottawa: King's Printer, 1951), 71.

49 *MT*, 40.

50 Quoted in Mackenzie, *Arthur Irwin*, 210.

51 ECI, Callwood and Frayne, Nov. 3, 1986. See also June Callwood, "What Makes Pierre Tear?" *Star Weekly Magazine*, Oct. 10, 1959.

52 Veronica Ross, *To Experience Wonder: Edna Staebler, A Life* (Toronto: Dundurn Group, 2003), 116–18, 131–34.

53 Anthony Reinhart, "Edna Staebler, Author, 1906–2006," *G&M*, Sept. 18, 2006. I am grateful to Susan Kent Davidson for drawing my attention to this obituary.

54 ECI, Sidney and Dorothy Katz, Jan. 6, 1987. Katz was married to the journalist Dorothy Sangster.

55 PB to John Clare, Apr. 27, 1949; quoted in Mackenzie, *Arthur Irwin*, 204.

56 PB, "The Amazing Career of George McCullagh," *MM*, Jan. 15, 1949; "Edmonton: A Boom at the Crossroads," *MM*, July 15, 1949; "Phooey on Freud!" *MM*, May 1, 1949; "Life and Loves of a Queen Bee," *MM*, May 15, 1949; "Make Way for the One-Eyed Monster," *MM*, June 1, 1949.

57 Murray Hunter to Floyd Chalmers, Sept. 12, 1949; quoted in Mackenzie, *Arthur Irwin*, 216.

58 Arthur Irwin to Floyd Chalmers, Sept. 15, 1949; quoted in Mackenzie, *Arthur Irwin*, 216–17.

59 Arthur Irwin, "What It Means to Be a Canadian," *MM*, Feb. 1, 1950; reprinted in *Canada in the Fifties: From the Archives of Maclean's*, ed. Michael Benedict (Toronto: Penguin, 2000), 151–62.

CHAPTER 12: THE ALLEN INFLUENCE

1 ECI, Gerald Anglin, Dec. 12, 1986.
2 McCall Newman, "Editor's Note" to *The Man from Oxbow*, 2.
3 "Inside Maclean's Magazine," *MM* (Oct. 1973).
4 *MT*, 28; PB, "The Amazing Career of George McCullagh."
5 *MT*, 26–28.
6 PB, "E.P. Taylor and His Empire: Part One," *MM*, Feb. 15, 1950.
7 PB, "E.P. Taylor and His Empire: Part Two," *MM*, Mar. 1, 1950.
8 PB, "The Southams," *MM*, June 15, 1950.
9 PB, "The Southams – Part Two: The Boss Who Hates to Fire People," *MM*, July 1, 1950.
10 PB, "The Southams – Conclusion: Papers, Pickets, and Profits," *MM*, July 15, 1950.
11 Clyde Gilmour to PB, Aug. 10, 1950, PBF, box 108, "Gilmour, Clyde" file.
12 As late as September 6, 1950, PB's incoming correspondence carried his Kingsway address. For example, the CBC invoice for $75 for the radio script "Creeping Green," broadcast in the *Prairie Playhouse* series on Sept. 7, is dated Sept. 6, 1950. A letter from F. Rupert Crew, dated Oct. 5, 1950, carries the address "R.R.#1, Kleinburg." PBF, box 104, "Business Correspondence 1950–1955" file.
13 The amount of the mortgage is given as $8,000 in *SO*, 57, but as $5,000 in Stephen Franklin, "Can You Make a Million Writing Canadian Books?" *Financial Post Magazine* (Oct. 1980), 88.
14 MCK, Janet Berton, Feb. 2, 2007.
15 ECI, Janet Berton, Dec. 12, 1986; *MT*, 57–59.
16 ECI, Gerald Anglin, Dec. 12, 1986.
17 June Callwood, "What Makes Pierre Tear."
18 Elspeth Chisholm (Talks, English Language Services, CBC) to PB, Mar. 1, 1950, PBF, box 104, "Business Correspondence 1950–1955" file.
19 PB, "BBC – International Service Talks," PBF, box 160, unfiled.
20 Peter McDonald to PB, Mar. 1, 1959; CBC invoice, July 5, 1950; Elspeth Chisholm to Peter Francis, Apr. 14, 1950, PBF, box 104, "Business Correspondence 1950–1955" file.
21 E.S. Hallman (Talks and Public Affairs, CBC) to PB, Aug. 2, 1950; F.W. Rowse (Department of National Health and Welfare) to PB, Aug. 14, 1950; G.F. Roll (Smith, Kline & French Laboratories) to PB, Nov. 1, 1950, PBF, box 104, "Business Correspondence 1950–1955" file.
22 A.E. McBride (Grolier Society of Canada Limited) to PB, Aug. 10, 1950, PBF, box 104, "Business Correspondence 1950–1955" file.
23 Arthur T. Lougee (Ford Motor Company) to PB, Aug. 3 and June 3, 1950; Franklin M. Reck (Ford Motor Company) to PB, Oct. 30, 1950, PBF, box 104, "Business Correspondence 1950–1955" file.
24 F. Rupert Crew to PB, Oct. 5, 1950; G. Kristjanson (Script Editor, CBC) to PB, Aug. 1, 1950; N. Alice Frick (Asst. to Supervisor of Drama, CBC) to PB, Sept. 6, 1950, PBF, box 104, "Business Correspondence 1950–1955" file.
25 F. Rupert Crew to PB, Oct. 5, 1950, PBF, box 104, "Business Correspondence 1950–1955" file.

26 E. Lewis Barton (Assistant Editor, *Everybody's*) to PB, Nov. 13, 1950, PBF, box 104, "Business Correspondence 1950–1955" file.

27 John Polwarth (Canadian Representative, BBC) to PB, Mar. 15, 1950; Tom Sloan (BBC) to PB, Aug. 14, 1950; both in PBF, box 104, "Business Correspondence 1950–1955" file.

28 "The Mystery and the Myth of Arthur Hailey," BPB, Dec. 31, 1959.

29 BPB, "Mystery and Myth"; *MT*, 40–41.

30 MCK, Pierre Berton, Sept. 15, 2004.

31 See Paul Litt, "The Massey Commission, Americanization, and Canadian Cultural Nationalism," *Queen's Quarterly*, vol. 98 (Summer 1991), 375–87; Karen A. Finlay, *The Force of Culture: Vincent Massey and Canadian Sovereignty* (Toronto: University of Toronto Press, 2004).

32 PB, "Everybody Boos the CBC," *MM*, Dec. 1, 1950.

33 MacGowan, "Looking Back on a Legend." MacGowan writes: "Ralph also got on quite well with a bottle of gin; it is said he could drink eight to ten martinis at lunch, before his food arrived, then eat his meal and go back to work as if nothing had happened." Berton's statement is from MCK, Pierre Berton, Sept. 10, 2004.

34 On bibulous *Maclean's* lunches, see *MT*, 62, and MCK, Pierre Berton, Sept. 15, 2004. Callwood quoted in Lisa Beaton, "Bad Boys, Booze and Bylines; The Rise and Demise of the Toronto Press Club," *Ryerson Review of Journalism* (Spring 2004).

35 *MT*, 94–95.

36 Ralph Allen to PB, n.d. but filed with Ralph Allen to Charles Allen (Assistant Editor, *Nation*), Oct. 17, 1951. A Canadian National telegram to Berton containing the *Nation*'s request (Oct. 16, 1951) accompanies this letter. PBF, Box 104, "Business Correspondence 1950–1955" file.

37 R.S. Lambert (Supervisor of School Broadcasts, CBC Toronto) to PB, Apr. 4, 1951; Ruth Viner (International Service, CBC Toronto) to PB, June 14, 1951; Thom Benson (International Service Representative, CBC Toronto) to PB, July 5, 1951; Elspeth Chisholm (Talks Producer, CBC International, Montreal) to PB, Aug. 24, 1951; Robert Allen (Program Division, CBC Vancouver) to PB, Dec. 17, 1951; Helen James (Producer, Talks and Public Affairs, CBC Vancouver) to PB, Dec. 28, 1951; Robert Weaver (Talks and Public Affairs, CBC Toronto) to PB, Dec. 28, 1951, all in PBF, box 104, "Business Correspondence 1950–1955" file. For "Citizens' Forum," see L.B. Kuffert, *A Great Duty: Canadian Responses to Modern Life and Mass Culture, 1939–1967* (Montreal and Kingston: McGill-Queen's University Press), 69–70.

38 Mary Richards (Associate Editor, *Ford Times*) to PB, Mar. 16, 1951; Franklin M. Reck (Managing Editor, *Lincoln-Mercury Times*) to PB, June 4, 1951; Donald Mulholland (Director of Production, NFB) to PB, Feb. 21, 1951; Paulette Poirier (Unit "A," NFB) to PB, June 20, 1951; Sidney Newman (Executive Producer, NFB) to PB, July 20, 1951, PBF, box 104, "Business Correspondence 1950–1955" file.

39 PB, "For Critically Speaking: Books," PBF, box 159, "Critically Speaking" file.

40 PB, "Critically Speaking on Books – Lifesmanship and Gamesmanship," PBF, box 159, "Critically Speaking" file.

41 Directorate of History and Heritage and Department of National Defence, *Canada and the Korean War*, Stephen J. Harris, project director: (Montreal: Editions Art Global and Department of National Defence, 2002), 19–20.

42 For overviews of Canada's involvement in the Korean War, see Desmond Morton, *A Military History of Canada: From Champlain to Kosovo.* 4th ed. (Toronto: McClelland & Stewart, 1999), 232–39; Norman Hillmer and J.L. Granatstein, *Empire to Umpire: Canada and the World to the 1990s* (Toronto: Copp Clark Longman, 1994), 213–16.

43 PB, "Rocky," *MM,* Feb. 1, 1951.

44 *Canada and the Korean War*, 42.

45 PB, "The Crisis and the Colonel," *MM*, Feb. 15, 1951.

46 PB, "How a Red Union Bosses Atom Workers at Trail, B.C.," *MM*, Apr. 1, 1951.

47 Berton refers directly to *Foreign Correspondent* in the context of the Korean War in *SO*, 68.

48 The second chapter of *MT* ends with a discussion of the camaraderie of writers at *Maclean's*; the third begins with PB on his way to Korea.

49 See the introduction to Gregory Clark, *May Your First Love Be Your Last and Other Stories* (Toronto: McClelland & Stewart, 1969), 9–45, for an overview of Clark's career written by Frank Lowe, editor of *Weekend Magazine*, Montreal; also Gregory Clark, *War Stories* (Toronto: Ryerson Press, 1964).

50 *MT*, 67.

51 ECI, Barbara Moon, Oct. 9, 1986.

52 *MT*, 68.

53 *MT*, 69.

54 PB, "Corporal Dunphy's War," *MM*, June 1, 1951; PB, "The Long Ordeal of Mrs. Tak," *MM*, June 15, 1951; PB, "This Is the Enemy," *MM*, July 1, 1951.

55 PB, "Marie Went Back to the Dark Ages," *MM*, July 15, 1951.

56 PB, field notes, "Seoul 1," PBF, box 331, file 7 ("Seoul").

57 PB, "Notes: Section Leader 1," PBF, box 331, file 3 ("Section Leaders"); PB, "Refugee 1," PBF, box 331, file 5 ("Refugees 1951").

58 PB drew attention to the movie in this context in *MT*, 70.

59 John Clare to PB, Apr. 12, 1951, PBF, box 104, "Business Correspondence 1950–1955" file.

60 *MT*, 73l; PB, "Seoul's the Saddest City in the World," *MM*, June 1, 1951.

61 *MT*, 84.

62 *MT*, 73.

63 *MT*, 84.

64 *MT*, 79.

65 William J. Lederer and Eugene Burdick, *The Ugly American* (New York: W.W. Norton, 1958); PB, *Marching as to War: Canada's Turbulent Years 1899–1953* (Toronto: Random House, 2001), 5, 553–54.

66 PB, *Marching as to War*, Lederer and Burdick, *The Ugly American*: see "A Factual Epilogue," 229.

67 *MT*, 85.

68 Ray Keitges (Stony Plain, Alberta) to Editor, *MM*, Sept. 15, 1951.

69 Stephen Brott (Montreal), C.F. Campbell (Haney, B.C.) and Maud Walherston (Toronto) to Editor, *MM*, Sept. 15, 1951.

70 Denis Stairs, *The Diplomacy of Constraint: Canada, the Korean War, and the United States* (Toronto: University of Toronto Press, 1974), xi; see esp. ch. 4, "Containing American Power." See also Hillmer and Granatstein, *Empire to Umpire*, 214–16;

Morton, *A Military History of Canada*, 237–39. For Canada's changing relations with Great Britain and the United States in these years, see J.L. Granatstein, *How Britain's Weakness Forced Canada into the Arms of the United States* (Toronto: University of Toronto Press, 1989), 43–62.

71 Stairs, *Diplomacy of Constraint*, 149; PB, *Marching as to War*, 3–5.

CHAPTER 13: WRITER, EDITOR, AUTHOR

1   PB, "There'll Always Be a Massey," *MM*, Oct. 15, 1951.

2   *MT*, 89; MCK, Patsy Berton, Feb. 21, 2006.

3   E.S. Hallman (Talks and Public Affairs, CBC) to S.M. Vinocour (Korean Pacific Press, Washington, D.C.), July 6, 1951, PBF, box 104, "Business Correspondence 1950–1955" file.

4   *MT*, 89.

5   Maurice Crompton (Chief, Commercial Division, CBC) to PB, June 22, 1951; in PBF, box 104, "Business Correspondence 1950–1955" file. The world-travelling reporter and novelist John Gunther became famous for his penetrating series of "Inside" books on the politics and societies of nations and continents. Among the more prominent of these works were *Inside Europe* (New York: Harper and Brothers, 1936), *Inside Asia* (New York: Harper and Brothers, 1939); *Inside Latin America* (New York: Harper and Brothers, 1941), *Inside USA* (New York: Harper and Brothers, 1947), and *Behind the Curtain* (New York: Harper and Brothers, 1949).

6   Elspeth Chisholm (Talks Producer, CBC) to PB, Aug. 24, 1951, in PBF, box 104, "Business Correspondence 1950–1955" file.

7   *MT*, 97.

8   PB, "The Great Vancouver Love Affair," *MM*, Nov. 15, 1951.

9   PB, "There's Always a Party at the Grahams'," *MM*, Nov. 15, 1951; PB, "From Paris to Pusan with Penny," *MM*, Jan. 1, 1952.

10 Yousuf Karsh, "Karsh Photographs the Face of Canada," *MM*, Nov. 15, 1952.

11 MCK, Penny Berton, Feb. 25, 2005.

12 PB, "A Garden in Your Mailbox," *MM*, Mar. 1, 1952.

13 PB, "The Greatest Three-Cent Show on Earth – Part One," *MM*, Mar. 15, 1952; PB, "The Greatest Three-Cent Show on Earth – Conclusion," *MM*, Apr. 1, 1952.

14 PB, "Greatest Newspaperman in Canada, Is Tribute of All Who Knew Him," *TS*, Dec. 21, 1956.

15 PB, "The Man Who's Going to Make Our TV," *MM*, May 15, 1952. The story focused on a thirty-three year-old actor turned television producer, Mavor Moore.

16 See the website of the Canada Science and Technology Museum, at http://www.sciencetech.technomuses.ca/english/collection/television2.cfm.

17 Barnouw, *Tube of Plenty*, 99–102.

18 *MT*, 90–91.

19 Robert Weaver (Talks and Public Affairs, CBC Toronto) to PB, Apr. 2, 1952, and July 31, 1952, PBF, box 104, "Business Correspondence 1950–1955" file. On PB's recycling of material, see *MT*, 97.

20 *MT*, 93.

21 Ralph Allen to editorial staff, Jan. 6, 1953, PBF, box 104, "Business Correspondence 1950–1955" file. At the time the editorial staff consisted of PB, Blair Fraser,

Ian Sclanders, McKenzie Porter, Leslie Hannon, David Macdonald, N.O. Bonisteel, Barbara Moon, Fred Bodsworth, Gene Aliman, Desmond English, and Sidney Katz. Janice Tyrwhitt, Jean Yack, and Lois Harrison were editorial assistants.

22 In 1952, single-author article production stood as follows: McKenzie Porter, 13; Fred Bodsworth, 9; June Callwood, 7; Sidney Katz, 7; Trent Frayne, 6; Barbara Moon, 3.

23 "In the Editors' Confidence," *MM*, Mar. 15, 1953.

24 For PB's address to the Empire Club of Toronto (Apr. 1, 1954), see "Addresses by Luella Creighton, Pierre Berton, and Dr. Wilder Penfield," in *The Empire Club Addresses, 1953–54* (Toronto: Empire Club Foundation, 1954), 279–98; also *MT*, 101–102.

25 PB erroneously identifies the village as "Craigie" in *MT*. It is named correctly in PB, *The Royal Family: The Story of the British Monarchy from Victoria to Elizabeth* (Toronto: McClelland & Stewart, 1954), 264.

26 PB refers to this pub as the Bag o' Nails in his 1954 address to the Empire Club, but as the Phoenix in *The Royal Family*, 266.

27 C.R. Henderson (President, Canadian Club of Canada), introduction of A. Beverley Baxter and his address, "What I Have Seen Over There and Over Here" (Oct. 6, 1941), in *The Empire Club of Canada Speeches 1941–1942* (Toronto: Empire Club of Canada, 1942), 54–69; available at http://www.empireclubfoundation. com/details.asp?SpeechID=708&FT=yes.

28 *MT*, 103.

29 *MT*, 103.

30 "Queen Mary," editorial, *G&M*, Mar. 25, 1953; "The World's Greatest Asset," editorial, *MM*, June 1, 1953, 14; "Sir Thomas White, 'Canada to Her Queen, 1953,'" *G&M*, June 2, 1953.

31 PB, "The Family in the Palace: Part One of Seven Parts," *MM*, Mar. 15, 1953.

32 PB, "The Family in the Palace: Part One," 8.

33 "Mailbag," *MM*, June 1, 1953, 86–87.

34 JGM to Hugh Kane, Nov. 6, 1953; quoted in James King, *Jack: A Life with Writers; The Story of Jack McClelland* (Toronto: Alfred A. Knopf, 1999), 56–57.

35 *MT*, 104.

36 Roger Pippett, "Mr. and Mrs. Royalty," *New York Times Book Review*, Mar. 7, 1954; Peter J. Henniker, "Spontaneity and Duty," *Christian Science Monitor*, Mar. 11, 1954; Lawrence Earl, *Kirkus Reviews*, Dec. 15, 1953, 808. For other international assessments, see *MT*, 105–06.

37 PBF, box 107, "Alfred A. Knopf – royalty statements 1954–55" file.

38 *MT*, 104.

39 St. Laurent quoted in R.A.J. Phillips, *Canada's North* (Toronto: Macmillan of Canada, 1967), 161–62.

40 See Thomas Weart, *Nuclear Fear: A History of Images* (Cambridge: Harvard University Press), 1988.

41 James King, *Farley: A Life of Farley Mowat* (Toronto: HarperCollins, 2002), 119–23; Phillips, *Canada's North*, 171; Farley Mowat, *People of the Deer* (Boston: Little, Brown, 1952).

42 Gordon Sinclair, "Radio by Gordon Sinclair," *TS*, Sept. 13, 1952.

43　PB, *The Golden Trail: The Story of the Klondike Gold Rush* (Toronto: Macmillan of Canada, 1954), illustrations by Duncan MacPherson; June Callwood, "What Makes Pierre Tear?"; *MT*, 112.

44　Blair Fraser to Ralph Allen, May 10, 1954, PBF, box 163, "Mysterious North" file.

45　*MT*, 113.

46　W.A.D. [William Arthur Deacon], "Laura's 25 Yukon Years Form Graphic Chronicle," *G&M*, Nov. 20, 1954.

47　"Buzz Sawyer," *TS*, Oct. 6, 1954; "New Hurricane Rages," *TS*, Oct. 6, 1954; also Louella Parsons, "Clifton Webb Starred as Adventurer Villain in Lord Vanity Picture," *TS*, Oct. 6, 1954.

48　"Hazel Getting Tougher," *TS*, Oct. 9, 1954; "Hazel Pounds Haiti, Jamaica; Moving North," *G&M*, Oct. 12, 1954.

49　"The Tragic Anniversary of a Night When a River Went Mad," BPB, Oct. 17, 1958.

50　*MT*, 109; BPB, "Tragic Anniversary."

51　*MT*, 110.

52　"We Haven't Done Right by Our North," editorial, *MM*, Nov. 15, 1954, 2.

53　Blair Fraser, "The Truth about Our Arctic Defence," *MM*, Nov. 15, 1954. Fraser drew this conclusion after conversations with George Jacobsen. See Fraser to Allen, May 10, 1954.

54　Robert Collins, "Keg River's One-Woman Medical Clinic," *MM*, Nov. 15, 1954; David Macdonald, "The Shaggy Saint of Labrador," *MM*, Nov. 15, 1954.

55　PB, "The Mysterious North," *MM*, Nov. 15, 1954. Quotations in the next three paragraphs are from this article.

56　Laura Beatrice Berton, "I Married the Klondike," *MM*, Apr. 15, 1954; Laura Beatrice Berton, "Down the Yukon in an Open Boat," *MM*, May 1, 1954; Laura Beatrice Berton, "The Setting of the Midnight Sun," *MM*, May 15, 1954; W.A.D., "Laura's 25 Yukon Years."

57　*MT*, 95, 115–16, 146.

58　Harold Strauss to PB, Feb. 11, 1955, PBF, box 107, "Alfred A. Knopf International 1953–1958" file. The Strauss letter is reproduced in PB, *The Joy of Writing: A Guide for Writers, Disguised as a Literary Memoir* (Toronto: Doubleday Canada, 2003), 83–89.

59　*MT*, 114.

60　Barbara Moon, "They Like Being Old-Fashioned at the Ritz," *MM*, Oct. 15, 1954; [Ralph Allen], "In the Editors' Confidence – Writers without beards," *MM*, Oct. 15, 1954.

61　ECI, Moon, Oct. 9, 1986.

62　*MT*, 114.

63　PB, "The Island That Knows No Summer," *MM*, July 23, 1955; PB, "Look What's Happening to Labrador," *MM*, Aug. 20, 1955.

64　Harold Strauss to PB, June 27, 1955, PBF, box 107, "Alfred A. Knopf International 1953–1958" file.

65　F.B. Walker to PB, letters from Oct. 1954 to June 1955; R.G. Robertson to PB, Oct. 28, 1954, Dec. 2, 1954, and Oct. 18, 1955; Svenn Orvig to PB, June 22, 1955; Cyrus S. Eaton to PB, May 12, 1955; all in PBF, box 163, "Mysterious North – Research Notes – correspondence, including various readers' reports" file.

66　PB, *The Mysterious North* (Toronto: McClelland & Stewart, 1956).

67 W.L. McGeary, "From Yukon to Labrador in Pierre Berton's Ambit," *TS*, Feb. 25, 1956.

68 W.A.D., "'The Tundra Rolled On Majestic in Its Monotony,'" *G&M*, Mar. 3, 1956.

69 Trevor Lloyd, "Polar Challenge and Assault," *New York Times Book Review*, Mar. 10, 1954.

70 See Carl Berger, "The True North Strong and Free," in Peter Russell, ed., *Nationalism in Canada* (Toronto: McGraw-Hill, 1965), 3–26.

71 See Douglas B. Holt, *How Brands Become Icons: The Principles of Cultural Branding* (Cambridge: Harvard Business School Press, 2004), 6.

CHAPTER 14: ARRIVAL

1 PB, "A Moving New Portrayal of the Nativity Story: Text by Pierre Berton," *MM*, Dec. 22, 1956.

2 A clean typescript of the article is in PBF, box 99, "A Native's Return to B.C." file.

3 Howard Boston, "The Klondike Clan," review of Pierre Berton, *Stampede for Gold: The Story of the Klondike* (New York: Alfred A. Knopf, 1955), *New York Times Book Review*, July 31, 1955.

4 Willis Kingsley Wing to PB, Apr. 23, 1956, in PBF, box 107, "Willis Kingsley Wing, N.Y. – correspondence 1956–1958" file; Alfred A. Knopf to PB, Apr. 30, 1956, PBF, box 107, "Alfred A. Knopf International 1953–1958" file. PB's proposal and sample chapters for *Klondike* are in PBF, box 155, file 1.

5 PBF, box 155, file 6 contains much of this correspondence. See especially John A. Scheel (Emporia, Kansas) to PB, Jan. 10, 1956.

6 In final form, the twenty-three-page bibliography listed 125 books and 104 magazine articles, and contained a note on government documents. MSF, box 8, file 19, contains "A Klondike Bibliography prepared by Pierre Berton, R.R.#1, Kleinburg, Ont."

7 MCK, Patsy Berton.

8 Harold Strauss to PB, May 15, 1956, PBF, box 107, "Alfred Knopf International 1953–1958" file.

9 Willis Kingsley Wing to PB, April 23 and May 14, 1956, PBF, box 107, "Willis Kingsley Wing, N.Y. – correspondence 1956–1958" file.

10 *MT*, 116; Callwood, "What Makes Pierre Tear?" In *MT*, Berton states that he went west with his family by automobile. Callwood's 1959 reference to separate travel by air and train, written only three years after the event and based on conversations with PB, is more likely the accurate one.

11 *MT*, 117.

12 At the time, the Governor General's Awards included two prizes annually for non-fiction. The second winner of the non-fiction award for 1956 was Joseph Lister Rutledge for *Century of Conflict* (New York: Doubleday, 1956), a history of the imperial struggles of England and France in colonial North America.

13 *MT*, 114–15.

14 See Barbara Wade Rose, *Budge: What Happened to Canada's King of Film* (Toronto: ECW Press, 1998), 86; also *Budge: F.R. Crawley and Crawley Films, 1939–1982*, edited by James A. Forrester (Lakefield, Ont.: Information Research Services, 1988), 100. The Forrester volume gives the title of the film as *A New Future Lies North*.

15 *MT*, 122–23; Ellen Louks Fairclough, *Saturday's Child: Memoirs of Canada's First Female Cabinet Minister*, introduction by Margaret Conrad (Toronto: University of Toronto Press, 1995). Fairclough's portfolio included responsibility for the National Film Board. By the time the Fairclough memoir was published, the politician professed no recollection of her involvement in the project. I am grateful to Dr. Margaret Conrad of the University of New Brunswick for this information (Conrad to McKillop, Mar. 16, 2007). *Women on the March* (1958), directed by Douglas Tunstell, remains available for sale by the National Film Board. PB is listed in the credits as narrator.

16 John Tibbetts, "All That Glitters," *Film Comment* (Mar. 1995), 52. I am indebted to Tibbetts's article for this account.

17 PB quoted in Tibbetts, "All That Glitters," 54.

18 In *MT*, 122, PB states that *City of Gold* won nineteen awards, including "the Grand Prix at Cannes," but I have been unable to confirm receipt of nominations or awards other than those mentioned.

19 The above description of the Berton home is drawn closely from PB's own account in "Our House," PBF, box 96, "CBC: Our House" file; MCK, Janet Berton, Feb. 2, 2007.

20 MCK, Janet Berton, Feb. 2, 2007.

21 Harold Strauss to PB, Jan. 19, 1957, and Harold Strauss to Willis Kingsley Wing, July 18, 1957, PBF, box 107, "Alfred A. Knopf International 1953–1958" file.

22 For PB's system for organizing materials, see PB, *Joy of Writing*, 178–79. Harold Strauss to PB, Nov. 14, 1957, PBF, box 107, "Alfred A. Knopf International 1953–1958" file.

23 *MT*, 122.

24 Peter Gzowski, "Ross McLean – the TV Star You Never See," *MM*, Jan. 16, 1960, 12–13.

25 Paul Rutherford, *When Television Was Young: Primetime Canada 1952–1967* (Toronto: University of Toronto Press), 227.

26 Ross McLean, "A Better Berton Makes Revisits Worthwhile," *G&M Broadcast Week Magazine*, Dec. 7, 1985; Gzowski, "Ross McLean," 42.

27 Patrick Watson, *This Hour Has Seven Decades* (Toronto: McArthur & Company, 2004), 128–29.

28 Rutherford, *When Television Was Young*, 543n45, 172.

29 Watson, *This Hour*, 132, 134.

30 Callwood, "What Makes Pierre Tear?" 46; *MT*, 133–35; Watson, *This Hour*, 137–38.

31 Watson, *This Hour*, 123; on PB's adoption of the bow tie, see *MT*, 130–31.

32 Callwood, "What Makes Pierre Tear?" 46; *MT*, 357. PB's *Close-Up* interview with Wallace took place on Jan. 5, 1958, in a "live" pickup from New York City. See "Berton vs. Wallace," *TS*, Dec. 28, 1957.

33 "The case of Mom Whyte and her empire at Bowmanville," BPB, July 31, 1959.

34 William Drylie, "Vaughan Jumped Gun on Fall Shows – CBC," *TS*, Aug. 10, 1957; Alex Barris, *Front Page Challenge: History of a Television Legend* (Toronto: Macmillan of Canada, 1999).

35 I am indebted to Professor Blaine Allan of the Department of Film Studies, Queen's University, who developed the valuable "Directory of CBC Television Series 1952–1982," available at http://www.film.queensu.ca/CBC/Index.html.

36 Barris, *Front Page Challenge*; MT, 138.
37 Harvey Hart (Producer, Special Programs TV, CBC) to PB, July 25, 1957, PBF, box 104, "Business Correspondence 1956–58" file.
38 "Barron Out? CBC Audition Stirs Wrath," TS, Aug. 31, 1957; "Hart Out," TS, Sept. 7, 1957.
39 William Drylie, "Glance" column, TS, Sept. 25 and Sept. 28, 1957; "Gordon Sinclair's Radio, TV – Comedians Still in There Pitching," TS, Oct. 24, 1957. Robins did not miss a single show during her pregnancy.
40 Barris, *Front Page Challenge*, 22–36; Rutherford, *When Television Was Young*, 235.
41 Callwood, "What Makes Pierre Tear?" 46.
42 Callwood, "What Makes Pierre Tear?" 46; MT, 141–42.
43 Barris, *Front Page Challenge*, 33. As Barris notes, Hyde was scarcely a model of tact himself: "When Indira Gandhi was a guest challenger, she was slow in getting seated, so Hyde hurried her up with: 'Put your little ass over here right now, dearie.' Another challenger Hyde 'welcomed' was Isaac Stern, the world-famous violinist, if a pudgy one. 'Sit here, Tubs,' said Steve."
44 William Drylie, "Glance" column, TS, Nov. 2, 1957, and Apr. 12, 1958.
45 Sidney Katz, "Space: Who Owns It Anyway?" (Jan. 18) and "How Mental Illness Is Attacking Our Immigrants" (Jan. 4); Peter C. Newman, "The Second Most Powerful Tory" (Jan. 4); Christina McCall, "The Brave New World of Trailer Living" (Jan. 4); Mordecai Richler, "How I Became an Unknown with My First Novel" (Jan. 19).
46 MT, 146–47.
47 MT, 146–47; Barris, *Front Page Challenge*, 31.
48 McLean, "A Better Berton."
49 MT, 148.
50 MT, 149.
51 Harold Strauss to PB, Jan. 27 and Jan. 29, 1958, PBF, box 107, "Alfred A. Knopf International 1953–1958" file.
52 Harold Strauss to PB, Apr. 4, 1958, PBF, box 107, "Alfred A. Knopf International 1953–1958" file.
53 Alfred A. Knopf to PB, June 3, 1958; Harold Strauss to PB, May 27, Aug. 25, 1958; both in PBF, box 107, "Alfred A. Knopf International 1953–1958" file.
54 PB, "The Pleasure of Writing," unidentified clipping, n.d. (1970), 4; MSF, box 9, file 10.
55 I am grateful to Robert Fulford (Fulford to author, Feb. 5, 2008) for details about the fourth-floor layout of the *Star*; regarding Beland Honderich, see Allison Vale, "Lost at Sea," *Ryerson Review of Journalism* (Spring 1994).
56 "A Binding Agreement between Two Interested Parties," BPB, Sept. 16, 1958.
57 Diefenbaker's "northern vision" as a plan for economic development originated largely with the policy adviser M.W. Menzies and the minister of northern affairs and national resources, Alvin Hamilton. See Morris Zaslow, *The Northern Expansion of Canada, 1914–1967* (Toronto: McClelland & Stewart, 1988); Patrick Kyba, *Alvin: A Biography of the Honourable Alvin Hamilton, P.C.* (Regina: Canadian Plains Research Center, 1989). The text of Diefenbaker's speech is available at http://www.northernblue.ca/canchan/cantext/speech2/1958dfnv.html.
58 MT, 124–25; William R. Morrison, *True North: The Yukon and Northwest Territories* (Toronto: Oxford University Press), 160–61.

59 PB, "Klondike! Part I," *MM*, Sept. 13, 1958; PB, "Klondike! Part II: The Strangest Gold Rush in History," *MM*, Sept. 27, 1958; PB, "Klondike! Part III: The Short Violent Reign of Soapy Smith," *MM*, Oct. 11, 1958; PB, "Klondike! Conclusion: The Rise and Fall of Dawson City," *MM*, Oct. 25, 1958.

60 Reviews of *The Klondike Fever: The Life and Death of the Last Great Gold Rush* (New York: Alfred A. Knopf, 1958): Frederick H. Guidry, "Gold, Cold, and a 'Moon at Midday,'" *Christian Science Monitor*, Oct. 27, 1958; *Library Journal*, Nov. 1, 1958; *New Yorker*, Nov. 15, 1958; Stewart H. Holbrook, "Days of Lou and Dan McGrew," *Saturday Review*, Nov. 8, 1958.

61 Richard L. Neuberger, "Where Millionaires Lived Like Galley Slaves," *New York Times Book Review*, Oct. 19, 1958.

62 Roy Minter to JGM, Sept. 23, 1958, MSF, box 8, file 19.

63 James Lovick & Company Ltd. Advertising Agency, advertising copy, Sept. 24, 1958, MSF, file 8, box 19.

64 Extensive material related to this media campaign is in MSF, box 8, file 19.

65 *MT*, 156, 230; *Charles Templeton: An Anecdotal Memoir* (Toronto: McClelland & Stewart, 1983), 188.

66 Janet Berton (as told to Marika Robert), "What It's Like to Be Married to Pierre Berton," *Chatelaine* (Dec. 1961).

CHAPTER 15: STAR CRUSADER

1 "The Fraynes" to PB, Sept. 16, 1958, PBF, box 108, "G. Correspondence Personal A-G" file.

2 Toronto-born Joe Shuster (1914–1992) delivered the *Toronto Daily Star* as a child, and his parents subscribed to the newspaper. A cousin of the comedian Frank Shuster, he moved with his family to Cleveland, Ohio, when he was about ten years old. The comic book newspaper's title was later renamed the *Daily Planet*.

3 Information on the *Star* in this and the next few paragraphs have been drawn from Ross Harkness, *J.E. Atkinson of the Star* (Toronto: University of Toronto Press, 1963) and from the following Internet sources: "Toronto Star – History of the Star," at http://www.thestar.com/aboutUs/history; Trista Vincent, "Manufacturing Concern," *Ryerson Review of Journalism* (March 1999), http://www.rrj.ca/print/293/; Sonja Miokovic, "Back When the Scoop Was King," *Ryerson Review of Journalism* (June 2005).

4 Harkness, *Atkinson of the Star*, 381–84. The purchase price of the *Star* was $25,555,021, at the time the highest amount ever paid for a newspaper.

5 A statement of these principles, which continue to guide the work of the Atkinson Charitable Foundation, may be found on the foundation's website: http://www.atkinsonfoundation.ca/about/mission.

6 June Callwood, "How Marilyn Bell Swam Lake Ontario," *MM*, Nov. 1, 1954, 51–67; reproduced in *Canada in the Fifties: From the Archives of Maclean's Magazine*, Michael Benedict, ed. (Toronto: Penguin Books, 1999). PB provided an introduction to this useful anthology.

7 Figures provided by the *Toronto Star*; see "Toronto Star – History of the Star," http://www.thestar.com/aboutUs/history.

8 See Jack Scott, *From Our Town* (Toronto: McClelland & Stewart, 1959), a collection of Scott's columns; also *MT*, 162.

9 All BPB: "An Ode to Humanity: Dedicated to the U.S. Air Force," Sept. 17, 1958; "Some Notes on a Man Who Wouldn't Be Called a Poet," Sept. 18, 1958; "Love, Love, Love Your Magic Spell Is Everywhere," Sept. 19, 1958.

10 All BPB: "A Lyric Ode to a Supermayor's Superhighway," Sept. 22, 1958; "The Curious Case of Time and John Diefenbaker," Sept. 23, 1958; "An All-Canadian Play: I Was a Teen-age Proust Addict," Sept. 24, 1958; "Memo to Ron W. Todgham: Get Yourself a New Ghostwriter," Sept. 25, 1958; "Shopping for a Coffin on a Sunny September Afternoon," Sept. 26, 1958.

11 Nicholas Dragen Bloom, *Suburban Alchemy: 1960s New Towns and the Transformation of the American Dream* (Columbus: Ohio State University Press, 2001); Dolores Hayden, *Building Suburbia: Green Fields and Urban Growth, 1820–2000* (New York: Pantheon Books, 2003).

12 Valerie J. Korinek, *Roughing It in the Suburbs: Reading* Chatelaine *Magazine in the Fifties and Sixties* (Toronto: University of Toronto Press, 2000); Doug Owram, *Born at the Right Time: A History of the Baby Boom Generation* (Toronto: University of Toronto Press, 1996); Spencer R. Weart, *Nuclear Fear: A History of Images* (Cambridge: Harvard University Press, 1989).

13 Massey Commission report quoted in Karen A. Finlay, *The Force of Nature: Vincent Massey and Canadian Sovereignty* (Toronto: University of Toronto Press, 2004), 218.

14 Robert Bothwell, *The Penguin History of Canada* (Toronto: Penguin, 2006), 365, 367.

15 Daniel Horowitz, *Anxieties of Affluence: Critiques of American Consumer Culture, 1939–1979* (Amherst and Boston: University of Massachusetts Press, 2004), 109. See also Lendol Calder, *Financing the American Dream: A Cultural History of Consumer Credit* (Princeton: Princeton University Press, 1999), and Robert D. Manning, *Credit Card Nation: The Consequences of America's Addiction to Credit* (New York: Basic Books, 2000).

16 Gary Cross, *An All-Consuming Century: Why Commercialism Won in Modern America* (New York: Columbia University Press, 2000), 140; Lizabeth Cohen, *A Consumers' Republic: The Politics of Mass Consumption in Postwar America* (New York: Alfred A. Knopf, 2003); also Benjamin R. Barber, *Consumed: How Markets Corrupt Children, Infantilize Adults, and Swallow Citizens Whole* (New York: W.W. Norton, 2007).

17 Horowitz, *Anxieties of Affluence*, 109.

18 The organization was founded as the Canadian Association of Consumers but changed its name to the Consumers' Association of Canada in 1961. The first issue of *Canadian Consumer* magazine appeared in 1963. See the CAC website at http://www.consumer.ca/1482. See also Josh Goldstein, "Public Interest Groups and Public Policy: The Case of the Consumers' Association of Canada," *Canadian Journal of Political Science*, vol. 12, no. 1 (Mar. 1979), 137–55.

19 All BPB: "One Consumer's Report on the Best and Worst in Fireworks," May 15, 1959; "Exclusive: My Own Consumer's Reports," Aug. 18, 1959; "Another Edition of My Own Consumer's Report," Sept. 4, 1959; "Another Edition of My Own Consumers' Report," Oct. 28, 1959; "Consumers Reports from My Various

Operatives," Nov. 13, 1959; "My Own Consumer's Report: Real Estate, Finishing Schools, Etc.," Jan. 11, 1960; "Some Consumer Notes on Appliances and Advertising," Feb. 9, 1960; "My Own Consumers' Reports – Drugs, Flats, Mags & HP Sauce," July 11, 1960; "Again – My Own Report on the Best and Worst in Fireworks," May 19, 1960.

20 "The Berton System for Sharks and Suckers," BPB, Apr. 5, 1960.

21 All BPB: "A Report on Door-to-Door Sales Gimmicks," Apr. 9, 1959; "Operative 81's Experiences as an Encyclopedia Salesman," July 3, 1959; "A Report on the Racket in Hot Furs," July 14, 1959.

22 "How to Sell Magazines without Ever Telling the Customer," BPB, Dec. 21, 1959.

23 PB, "Want to Be a Boss?" *MM*, June 1, 1948. On Packard, see Daniel Horowitz, *Vance Packard and American Social Criticism* (Chapel Hill: University of North Carolina Press, 1994); Horowitz, *Anxieties of Affluence*, 108–20.

24 "Operative 26 Learns How to Sell Cookware," BPB, Feb. 4, 1960.

25 "For a Columnist the Phone Is Always Ringing," BPB, June 15, 1959; *MT*, 223.

26 *MT*, 168–69; PB, "A Farewell Note about My Remarkable Secretary," *TS*, Feb. 25, 1960.

27 *MT*, 170.

28 All BPB: July 21, 1959; Dec. 9, 1959; Mar. 18, 1960; May 17, 1960; Oct. 18, 1960.

29 All BPB: "Operative 67 and the TV Repair Services," in three parts, Nov. 24, 25, 26, 1959; "Operative 67's Vain Attempts to Buy A Vacuum Cleaner," Dec. 15, 1959.

30 "Operative 67's Adventures in Arthur Murrayland," BPB, July 8, 1959.

31 "Further Adventures of Operative 67," BPB, July 16, 1959.

32 "Why Operative 67 is Quitting Arthur Murray's," BPB, July 27, 1959.

33 "Operative 107 Discovers the X-Factor at Arthur Murray's," BPB, Oct. 2, 1959; "Gosh, Miss Pupil, You Can't Leave Arthur Murray Now," BPB, Oct. 16, 1959.

34 "Yes, Mr. Murray, She Definitely Can Afford It," BPB, Nov. 6, 1959. Berton's final column used the Arthur Murray Dance Studio as a vehicle for exposing the high costs of "buy now, pay later" financing schemes. For this, Marilyn Craig became Operative 106. See "There Are Flaws in the Pay-Before-You-Play Plan," BPB, Nov. 22, 1960.

35 See "The Gospel According to Arthur Murray," ch. 8 of PB, *The Big Sell: An Introduction to the Black Arts of Door-to-Door Salesmen and Others* (Toronto: McClelland & Stewart, 1963), 196.

36 "I Reluctantly Reject a Promising Song-writing Career," BPB, Dec. 19, 1958; "The Sad Story of One Woman's Hit Songs," BPB, July 29, 1959.

37 "The Cult of the Dead as Practiced in Our Century," BPB, Jan. 7, 1959.

38 "The Cost of Dying Doesn't Have to Be So High," BPB, Feb. 26, 1960. This prompted *Canadian Funeral Service Magazine* to respond to PB's criticism of undertakers' telephone practices. See "Sequels," BPB, Apr. 22, 1960.

39 "Low Cost Funerals: What Will the Neighbors Think?" BPB, Mar. 29, 1960; "How to Sell Smart Funerals for Smart People," BPB, Aug. 2, 1960.

40 Jessica Mitford, *The American Way of Death* (New York: Simon and Schuster, 1963). Mitford's interest in funeral industry practices came through her husband, Bob Treuhaft, a labour lawyer involved in the Bay Area Funeral Society. See Mitford, *The American Way of Death Revisited* (New York: Alfred A. Knopf, 1998), xiii. Mitford died of cancer in 1996.

41 "Dear Mr. Eaton: What's a Knurled Centre Pin?" BPB, Dec. 29, 1958.
42 "The Brink of Victory: A Tragedy in Three Acts," BPB, Oct. 7, 1958. Berton became an active supporter of the Harold King Foundation, which operated a farm at Keswick for the rehabilitation of ex-prisoners. He remained involved with the charity until it wound down in 1987. See Ralph S. McCreath to David Black (Barristers and Solicitors), Sept. 16, 1987, PBF, box 236, file 50.
43 *MT*, 166; "A Report on Torture as Practiced in Modern Canada," BPB, Nov. 30, 1958.
44 "'No Blame Attached': An Instance of Legal Torture," BPB, Dec. 4, 1958.
45 "A Report on Twentieth Century Dungeons," BPB, Jan. 21, 1959.
46 "Kenneth Brymer's Experiences on a Chain Gang," BPB, Feb. 2, 1959.
47 "Are We Drifting Towards a Sadist Society?" BPB, Feb. 18, 1959.
48 ECI, Elizabeth Anglin, Dec. 9, 1986.
49 "What's Wrong at Orillia: Out of Sight – Out of Mind," BPB, Jan. 6, 1960.
50 "Orillia Charges 'True,'" *TS*, Jan. 7, 1960.
51 M.B. Dymond, M.D. (Ontario Minister of Health), to Mrs. Pierre Berton, May 24, 1960; in PBF, box 104, "Business Correspondence 1956–60"; file Pete McGarvey, "Pierre Berton Deserved Better," *Orillia Packet and Times*, Oct. 8, 1994. A brief account of the aftermath of the Berton visit to Orillia will be found in Janet Shea, "A History of the Orillia Hospital School, Orillia, 1875–1970," n.d., 186–90, unpublished manuscript in possession of Julie Harris, Ottawa.
52 "Outlaw the Hanging of Juveniles," *TS*, Oct. 2, 1959.
53 "Requiem for a Fourteen-Year-Old," BPB, Oct. 5, 1959.
54 *MT*, 166.
55 *MT*, 167. For an indication of Berton's influence on the debate over capital punishment, see Joel Kropf, "'A Matter of Deep Personal Conscience': The Canadian Death-Penalty Debate, 1957–1976" (MA thesis, Department of History, Carleton University, 2007), esp. ch. 3, "Murderers, and the Rest of Us: Moral Valuation via Statements of Contrast and Assignment of Priority," 90–122.
56 "Appeal the Steven Truscott Hanging," *TS*, Oct. 10, 1959; "In Which I Answer Some Mail," BPB, Oct. 13, 1959.
57 Isabel LeBourdais to JGM, Sept. 14, 1963, JMF, Series A, box 36, file 16.
58 Isabel Lebourdais, *The Trial of Steven Truscott* (London: Gollancz, 1966); Lebourdais's "until the duty was done" remark cited in a McClelland & Stewart press release for the book, in MSF, Box Ca4, file 51, "Isabel LeBourdais, Trial of Steven Truscott. Manuscript." M&S distributed the book in Canada. See also Patricia Clarke, "The Boy We Jailed for Life," *United Church Observer* (Jan./Feb. 1966), in McClelland & Stewart Papers, Series A, box 36, file 17.
59 "Lucky Silver's Rebellion against Certain Vital Statistics," BPB, Nov. 3, 1958.
60 "One Suburb's Vain Try to Sponsor a Sick Refugee," BPB, Dec. 11, 1959.
61 "Some Leaves from a Columnist's Notebook," BPB, Mar. 4, 1959.
62 All BPB: "Tales of the RCMP: Not Suitable for Television," Apr. 27, 1959; "The Overseas Visitors' Clubs [*sic*] Own Version of the Commonwealth," May 7, 1959; "Why Can't Vernon Lindo Keep His Apartment?" Nov. 18, 1960; "Why Vivian Petgrave Can't Join His Union," Aug. 20, 1959.
63 "South Africa and the Commonwealth Myth," BPB, Apr. 18, 1960.
64 "Why Not a Boycott of South African Goods?" BPB, Apr. 25, 1960.

65 On Kirkconnell and the humanities, see McKillop, *Matters of Mind*, 455–57.
66 "Dr. Watson Kirkconnell's Interesting Political Associates," BPB, Mar. 25, 1959.
67 BPB, "Dr. Watson Kirkconnell."
68 "Brief Comment on Various Matters at Hand," BPB, Aug. 4, 1959.
69 "Jew versus Gentile: Testing the Summer Resorts," BPB, June 16, 1960.
70 "Sequel: More Action on Summer Resorts," BPB, Aug. 24, 1960.
71 "Jew and Gentile – An Experiment in Job Hunting," BPB, Aug. 11, 1960.
72 "The Best Known Columnist of His Day," BPB, Sept. 8, 1959.

CHAPTER 16: THE DROP ON THIS WORLD

1 Jack Scott, "Our Town – Welcome Home – The Return of Pierre," *Vancouver Sun*, Sept. 18, 1958.
2 *MT*, 226.
3 All BPB: "Some Questions about Sales of Real Estate in York Township," Jan. 29, 1959; "Still More Questions on Sales of Real Estate in York Township," Mar. 13, 1959; "And Still More Questions about York Township Land Sales," Mar. 18, 1959; "Mr. J.J. Robinette, Q.C., and the York Township Council," July 19, 1959; "Some Reflections on the York Township Enquiry," May 6, 1960; "The Innocent Victims of the York Township Scandal," May 13, 1960.
4 "York Township 'Fertile for Corruption' – Judge – Back Up Berton Charges," *TS*, May 5, 1960.
5 "The Offenders Must Go," lead editorial, *TS*, May 13, 1960.
6 Gordon Minnes, "'Here's Pierre . . .' Without Even Trying, the Klondike's Berton Is Becoming Canada's Most Controversial Figure," *Mayfair* (Mar. 1959), 19.
7 Rick Salutin, "Pierre Berton, Eric Nicol: Defining the Columnist's Art," *G&M*, Apr. 27, 2001; "Notes on a Conversation with Three Typical Teenagers," BPB, Feb. 29, 1960.
8 All BPB: "The Story behind Those 'Let Me Be Your Friend' Ads," May 2, 1960; "The Moneylenders 2," June 1, 1960; "The Moneylenders 3," June 2, 1960. "The Shame of Public Charity 1: What You Don't Know about Relief," Feb. 1, 1961; "The Shame of Public Charity 2: Could You Eat on 36 Cents a Day?" Feb. 2, 1961; "The Shame of Public Charity 3: The United Appeal Didn't Make It," Feb. 3, 1961; "The Shame of Public Charity 4: They Still Can't Pay the Rent," Feb. 27, 1961. "How Gangsters Move In on Toronto's Stock Operations," Apr. 17, 1961. "Life on Skid Row: See That Shuffling Throng," Apr. 27, 1961. "How Archmount Memorial Service Exploits the High Cost of Dying," May 9, 1961.
9 "The Unexpected Aftermath of a Typical Toronto House Party," BPB, July 31, 1961. "Probe Don Jail 'Indignities' on Innocent Party Guests," *TS*, Aug. 2, 1961; "Order More Restraint in House Party Raids," *TS*, Aug. 18, 1961.
10 All BPB: "The High Cost of Money 1: One Dollar in Every Four," Jan. 9, 1962; "The High Cost of Money 2: Information You Just Can't Get," Jan. 23, 1962; "The High Cost of Money 3: Why Canadian Houses Cost More," Jan. 30, 1962; "The High Cost of Money 4: Why the O'Neils Paid Double," Apr. 5, 1962; "The High Cost of Money 5: The Costs of Auto Financing," Apr. 12, 1962; "The High Cost of Money 6: A Lesson in Gobbledygook," Apr. 23, 1962. "Why I Will Not Cross the Royal York Picket Line," Aug. 4, 1961.

11 "Why I Intend to Vote for the NDP," June 15, 1962. The CBC radio report can be heard at "Computers Predict Election Results," CBC Archives, at http://archives. radio-canada.ca/IDCC-1-75-710-4206/science_technology/computers/.

12 Minnes, "Here's Pierre." "Man of the Week: Pierre Berton – Man of Many Talents," *Park Plaza Magazine*, May 25, 1959. "Appoint Tie-Breaking Judges in Governor-General's Awards," *TS*, May 30, 1959.

13 Callwood, "What Makes Pierre Tear?"

14 *MT*, 222.

15 Budd Schulberg, *What Makes Sammy Run?* (New York: Modern Library, 1941), 21.

16 Callwood, "What Makes Pierre Tear?"

17 Sidney Katz, "Pierre's Adventures in Bertonland," *MM*, Oct. 20, 1962, 19.

18 PB, *Just Add Water and Stir* (Toronto: McClelland & Stewart, 1959).

19 See the copyright page of the first edition of *Just Add Water and Stir*.

20 Flap copy. See also typescript of front and back inside pages, PBF, box 8, file 20, "Adventures of a Columnist."

21 PB, *Adventures of a Columnist* (Toronto: McClelland & Stewart), 1960.

22 Claire Pratt reader's report, "Twelve Hundred Words a Day," n.d., PBF, box 8, file 20, "Adventures of a Columnist." Of the section called "The Twentieth Century," consisting of funny satiric and nostalgic pieces, PB wrote that he "would rather have written [it] . . . than all the stop-the-press exposés in journalism. They will not appeal to everybody but they appeal to me" (61).

23 Ellen Stafford reader's report, June 1, 1960; Ellen Stafford to JGM, June 23, 1960; both in PBF, box 8, file 20, "Adventures of a Columnist."

24 King, *Jack*, 125.

25 "I hate to admit it": "M.A.R." to Claire Pratt (memo), Mar. 23, 1960; Claire Pratt, reader's report, "Pierre Berton columns," Mar. 28, 1960, underscoring in original; in PBF, box 8, file 20, "Adventures of a Columnist."

26 "Total Sales All Editions – Pierre Berton Titles," June 1, 1970, MSF, Series 4, box 65, file 13.

27 *MT*, 174.

28 Pierre Berton, *The Secret World of Og* (Toronto: McClelland & Stewart, 1961); *MT*, 174–75.

29 Undated readers' reports, in PBF, box 107, "McClelland and Stewart – reader's reports, etc. 1961" file.

30 JGM to PB, Feb. 14, 1961, and JGM to Hugh Kane, Apr. 11, 1961, quoted in King, *Jack*, 102. King also quotes PB on the "vast conspiracy."

31 See "Pierre Berton: Book Sales to date," n.d. but marked "For Elspeth" (Elspeth Cameron, who in 1986 was preparing a feature essay on PB for *Saturday Night* magazine), Elspeth Cameron Papers, TF, box 83. "Total Sales All Editions – Pierre Berton Titles," June 1, 1970; "Berton Titles Sales to Date," July 16, 1962, MSF, Series A, box 65, file 13.

32 *MT*, 198.

33 BPB, Cairo series: "Three Misconceptions from Three World Capitals," Apr. 22, 1959; "Five Essays on Romance with Some Rude Awakenings," Apr. 23, 1959; "Some Notes about the Spread of Coca-Colism," Apr. 24, 1959. See also *MT*, 180–82.

34 BPB, Moscow series: "What It's Like to Stay at a Soviet Hotel," May 27, 1959; "A Date in Moscow: The Girl Who Liked Sarah Vaughan," May 28, 1959; "A Walk in

the Rain up the Main Drag of Moscow," May 29, 1959; "Some Notes on the Black Market in Moscow," June 1, 1959; "Five Minor Tableaux from the Land of Milk and Honey," June 2, 1959. The PB passage in the previous paragraph is drawn from *MT*, 184.

35   Callwood, "What Makes Pierre Tear?"

36   BPB, Europe series: "Scattered Notes from a European Holiday: 1 – London," Sept. 23, 1959; "Scattered Notes from a European Holiday: 2 – France," Sept. 24, 1959; "Scattered Notes from a Europe Holiday: 3 – Italy," Sept. 25, 1959; "Scattered notes on a European Holiday (Conclusion)," Sept. 26, 1959.

37   BPB, Los Angeles series, first and second of three: "Twelve Million Words but Only Scraps of News," July 14, 1960; "The Game Is Over; But Was It Ever Really Played?" July 15, 1960; *MT*, 187–92.

38   BPB, Los Angeles series, third of three: "Further adventures of a Hollywood TV Consultant," July 19, 1960; *MT*, 192–95.

39   *MT*, 193.

40   BPB, Japan series, five of six: "Just How Cheap Is Japanese Cheap Labor," Sept. 21, 1960; "How Dr. Amezawa Dispenses His Assembly Line Happiness," Sept. 22, 1960; "The City That's Built on a Graveyard," Sept. 23, 1960; "In Which We Visit a Typical Japanese Home," Sept. 26, 1960; "15 Stones Floating on a Sea of Sand," Sept. 27, 1960; *MT*, 198–205.

41   "Winkie Dolls, Rockabilly, & Beethoven," BPB, Sept. 23, 1960.

42   See, for example, "Potpourri: The Canadian Way of Life," BPB, June 8, 1962; "Potpourri: On Being Distinctively Canadian," BPB, Sept. 19, 1962; "A Glossary of Distinctive Canadian Terms," BPB, Oct. 23, 1962.

43   "I Finally Break Down and Talk about Disneyland," BPB, Aug. 12, 1960.

44   *MT*, 209; BPB, Berlin series, six parts: "Pierre Berton in Berlin – Our Adventures on the Edge of No-Man's-Land," Sept. 19, 1961; "Pierre Berton in Berlin – In Which We Take an Excursion on a Steamer," Sept. 20, 1961; "Pierre Berton in Berlin – The Schoolboy and the Armored Cars," Sept. 21, 1961; "Pierre Berton in Berlin – The Strange Familiarity of East Berlin," Sept. 22, 1961; "Pierre Berton in Berlin – Dreams, Visions, Illusions and Nightmares in the Crisis City," Sept. 25, 1961; "Pierre Berton in Berlin – Footnotes, Odd Sights & Strange Discoveries," Sept. 26, 1961.

A separate article accompanied each column, for example: "Driving by Auto to Berlin," Sept. 19, 1961; "A City Split by a Wall," Sept. 21, 1961; "Bernard Krol Makes His Decision," Sept. 22, 1961; "Where East and West Co-operate," Sept. 25, 1961; "Conversation with a Student," Sept. 26, 1961.

45   PB, "What Can a Tourist Do in Berlin?" *TS*, Sept. 20, 1961.

46   All BPB: "What Are the Hot Dogs Really Like in Wienerville?" Sept. 27, 1961; "Berton's Laws for Tourist Behaviour," Sept. 28, 1961; "Swiss Modesty, Swiss Service, Swiss Tipping," Sept. 29, 1961.

47   The manuscript of PB, *The New City: a prejudiced view of Toronto*, photographed by Henry Rossier (Toronto: Macmillan of Canada, 1961), is in box 320, Macmillan of Canada Papers, McMaster University Archives; correspondence related to the book is in box 74, file 11, "Berton, Pierre and Henri Rossier," 1958–68.

48   "Spacing – The New City Is an Old Photoblog," at http://spacing.ca/art-thenew-city-review.html. *MT*, 230.

49 *Historical Statistics of Canada*, 11-516-XIE, Noah M. Meltz, Section E: Wages and Working Conditions Series E69-70, table "Average Annual, Weekly and Hourly Earnings, Male and Female Salaried Employees, Manufacturing Industries, Canada, 1946–1969," at http://www.statcan.ca/english/freepub/11-516-XIE/sectione/sectione.htm. PB's finances are noted in Callwood, "What Makes Pierre Tear?"

50 "Beginning My Adventures as Captain of a Canal Houseboat," BPB, July 3, 1961. PB to Don Meadows, Apr. 11, 1961, and D.A. Meadows to PB, Apr. 18, 1961, in PBF, box 111, "Personal – Holiday Accommodation" file.

51 "First Dispatch from a Marooned Houseboat," BPB, July 4, 1961.

52 *MT*, 213; MCK, Patsy Berton, Feb. 21, 2006.

53 All BPB: "Life along the Warpath – 300 Years after Champlain," July 5, 1961; "Certain Ironies and Injustices in Stephen Leacock's Hometown," July 6, 1961; "The Dynasties of Balsam Lake and the Miracle of Kirkfield," July 7, 1961; "Lines Written during a Thunderstorm in Buckhorn Lake," July 10, 1961; "Oh, Susanna – How Your Backwoods Have Changed!" July 11, 1961; "Will Future Traffic Snarls Drive the Public from the Trent?" July 12, 1961; "Folly, Mystery and Poetry on the Margin of the Rice Beds," July 13, 1961.

54 "We Say Good-by to Our Floating Home on the Trent," BPB, July 14, 1961.

55 Herbert Sussan to Steve Krantz (General Manager, Screen Gems, Canada), June 8, 1961, PBF, box 104, "Business Correspondence 1961–62" file.

56 Steve Krantz to PB, Nov. 17, 1961, PBF, box 104, "Business Correspondence 1961–62" file; *MT*, 232.

57 *MT*, 232–33.

58 "The Berton Family Sets Off on a New Adventure," BPB, June 20, 1962. Correspondence concerning PB's detailed planning of the trip is in PBF, box 163, "Dawson – corresp." file.

59 PB to John Clare, n.d., PBF, box 163, "Dawson – corresp." file.

60 See the 1962 press releases of the Canadian Theatre Exchange, Stratford, in PBF, box 163, "Dawson Festival Foundation" file. Also *MT*, 215. The score for *Foxy* was by Robert Emmett Dolan; Ring Lardner Jr. provided the book. The musical opened on Broadway on Feb. 16, 1964, at the Ziegfeld Theatre. Bert Lahr went on to win a Tony Award for his performance, but the musical played for only seventy-two performances because the attention of its producer, David Merrick, had turned to his new hit, *Hello Dolly!*, which had opened the previous month. The 1962 Dawson City production, financed by the Canadian government, played for seven weeks and lost an estimated $400,000.

61 "A Preliminary Report on the Dawson City Festival," BPB, Nov. 3, 1961.

62 PB to H.R. MacMillan (Honorary Chairman of the Board, MacMillan, Bloedel & Powell River Ltd.), Nov. 2, 1961, PBF, box 163, "Dawson City Festival" file.

63 All BPB: "What We All Liked Best about Our Long Trek North," July 10, 1962; "Tales Heard Backstage at Dawson's Palace Grand," July 5, 1962; "Behind the Scenes with the World's Greatest Festival," July 4, 1962; "A Subjective Report on My Old Hometown," July 2, 1962.

64 "The Man Who Haunted My Courting Days," BPB, July 12, 1962.

65 Lotta Dempsey, "Private Line," *TS*, Feb. 2, 1962.

66 PB to JGM, June 3, 1962, MSF, box 8, file 26.

67 "Editorial Report – Fast Fast Fast Relief," June 5, 1962, MSF, box 8, file 26.

68 JGM to PB, July 18, 1962; "Schedule – Fast Fast Fast Relief: Pierre Berton. T.H. Best," July 13, 1962: both in MSF, box 8, file 26.

69 Katz, "Pierre's Adventures"; Sidney Katz to JGM, Sept. 5, 1962, MSF, box 8, file 26.

70 PB, *Fast Fast Fast Relief* (Toronto: McClelland & Stewart, 1962), 2–3. Italics in original.

71 John M. Robson, "Letters in Canada: 1962," "Light Prose" section, *University of Toronto Quarterly*, vol. 32 (July 1963), 425–26; Robson, "Letters in Canada: 1963," "Light Prose" section, *University of Toronto Quarterly*, vol. 33 (July 1964), 429–30.

72 JGM to PB, July 18, 1962; JGM to Sidney Katz, July 27, 1962; Harold Strauss to JGM, Oct. 11, 1962 (the book in Canada carried the title *The Big Sell*); all in MSF, box 8, file 26.

73 "Berton to Write on Niagara Falls" (press release), n.d.; Jim Douglas to JGM, May 25, 1962; in MSF, box 8, file 26. The Niagara book did not appear for another thirty years.

74 All BPB: "How Would the Critics Have Reviewed These Famous Works?" Nov. 5, 1962; "True Tales of Officialdom: Donald McKee's Indomitable Saga," Nov. 6, 1962; "How Would Steve McNally Have Handled This Hot Tip," Nov. 7, 1962; "Forgotten Headlines in the Case of Mrs. Tong," Nov. 8, 1962.

75 "In Which the Columnist Finally Has the Last Word," BPB, Nov. 9, 1962.

76 "Cohen, Sinclair, and Fulford; Templeton, Braithwaite and me," BPB, Nov. 19, 1959.

CHAPTER 17: JUST ADD BERTON AND STIR

1 *MT*, 234.

2 *MT*, 235.

3 Harvey Grebe, "Pierre Berton and the 47-Minute Hour," *MM*, Oct. 20, 1962.

4 Alan C. Collier to PB, Sept. 24, 1962, PBF, box 108, "Personal A–G" file; *MT*, 234–35.

5 Indecipherable to "Dear Janet [Berton]," n.d., PBF, box 111, "Personal – Family – addressed to Janet Berton (Mrs. P.B.)" file.

6 P.A.M., "Controversy Is Here to Stay," *The Performing Arts in Canada* (Spring 1963), 8, 8A, 56–57.

7 *MT*, 236–37. PB offered the turkey recipe to readers no fewer than five times during his BPB years at the *Star*: "Morton Thompson's Famous Instructions on Cooking a Turkey," Dec. 22, 1958; "And Once Again – Thompson's Famous Turkey Recipe," Dec. 18, 1959; "Now! An Easy Way to Make Morton Thompson's Famous Turkey Recipe," Dec. 19, 1960; "Once Again Morton Thompson's Turkey," Dec. 1, 1961; "That Turkey Again: A Report to the Stockholders," Dec. 27, 1961. Morton Thompson was an American writer whose bestselling novel *Not as a Stranger* (1954) was made the next year into a movie directed by Stanley Kramer and starring Olivia de Havilland, Robert Mitchum, and Frank Sinatra. Judged by Internet references, however, he is now best known for his turkey recipe.

8 P.A.M., "Controversy Is Here to Stay."

9 "Total Sales All Editions – Pierre Berton Titles," June 1, 1970, MSF, Series A, box 65, file 13; PB, *The Big Sell: An Introduction to the Black Arts of Door-to-Door*

Salesmanship & Other Techniques (Toronto: McClelland & Stewart, 1963), 109–36.
J. McCallum to Hon. W.G. Davis, Jan. 3, 1964, MSF, box 8, file 29.

10 P.C. Newman, "40 Months to Make or Break Canada," *MM*, Nov. 3, 1962; Blair Fraser, "Berlin: The False Quarrel," *MM*, Dec. 15, 1962; Ralph Allen, "A Calm Report on the Cuban Crisis," *MM*, Nov. 17, 1963; Shirley Mair, "Abortion Mills and the Law," *MM*, Nov. 3, 1962; Christina McCall Newman, "Canada's Class System," *MM*, Nov. 17, 1962.

11 "Some Background Data on Two Lonely Hearts Clubs," BPB, July 28, 1961.

12 Robert Fulford, *Best Seat in the House: Memoirs of a Lucky Man* (Toronto: Collins, 1988), 158; also Fulford to author, June 21, 2007.

13 Barbara Moon, "We Can Do Something about Fallout," *MM*, May 4, 1963.

14 PB, "It's Time We Stopped Hoaxing the Kids about Sex," *MM*, May 18, 1963.

15 *MT*, 245; Fulford, *Best Seat in the House*, 158.

16 *SO*, 245–57.

17 MCK, Penny Berton.

18 *MT*, 247; also Robert Fulford to author, June 18, 2007.

19 Fulford, *Best Seat in the House*, 160–61; *MT*, 247–48.

20 PB, "Pierre Berton's Page: The Grave Flaws in Private Medicare," *MM*, Apr. 20, 1963.

21 PB, "The Big Lie about Medical Insurance," *MM*, June 1, 1963.

22 Fulford, *Best Seat in the House*, 156–57; Sidney Katz, "Your Health and the Almighty Pill," *MM*, Dec. 1, 1962.

23 Leslie Hannon to PB, June 16 and Aug. 7, 1963, PBF, box III, "Personal – Family" file.

24 Fulford, *Best Seat in the House*, 159; Robert Fulford to author, June 18, 2007.

25 Peter Gzowski, "Editing Is Like Mixing a Martini: Everyone Thinks They Can Do It Better," *G&M*, Mar. 31, 2001, F2; Robert Fulford to author, June 18, 2007; *MT*, 249.

26 Robert E. Krug to PB, July 25, 1963, PBF, box 109, Krug file; Judith Young (Mrs. George V. Young) to Janet Berton, Aug. 7, 1963, PBF, box III, "Personal – Family – addressed to Janet Berton" file.

27 PB to Mrs. A. Robertson (Montreal), May 13, 1963, PBF, box III, "Personal – Family – re Laura" file; *MT*, 250; Bob Gardiner, "Televiews," *Ottawa Citizen*, June 6, 1963.

28 *MT*, 250.

29 *MT*, 252–55.

30 PB, *The Comfortable Pew: A Critical Look at Christianity and the Religious Establishment in the New Age* (Toronto: McClelland & Stewart, 1965), 15–25.

31 The Reverend Ernest Harrison, "Foreword: The Uncomfortable Gamble," in PB, *The Comfortable Pew*, 7–10; *MT*, 258–59.

32 *MT*, 236.

33 "Bob Shiels . . . on Television," *Calgary Herald*, Oct. 30, 1964; Helen Gurley Brown to PB, May 6, 1964, PBF, box 9, file 1.

34 Jon Ruddy quoted in *MT*, 238.

35 Robert McKenzie, "No Turning Back Now, Says Levesque," Montreal *Gazette*, Jan. 14, 1964.

36 "TCA Bilingual Progress Too Slow, Chief Says," *Peterborough Examiner*, Feb. 4, 1964; "Progress Is Too Slow," *Moncton Telegraph*, Feb. 5, 1964.

37 "Excommunication Could Have Ended Nazi Rise – Rabbi," Toronto *Telegram*, Mar. 20, 1964; "Guest on Pierre Berton Show," *Guelph Mercury*, Mar. 13, 1964; "As Jon Ruddy See it," Toronto *Telegram*, Apr. 9, 1964; "Fast Reader," *Ottawa Citizen*, Jan. 25, 1964.

38 "As Jon Ruddy Sees It," Toronto *Telegram*, May 7, 1964.

39 Pierre Maple, "Canadian Report," *TV Guide*, Canadian ed., May 9, 1964; L.N. Bronson, "Dial Turns," *London Free Press*, May 19, 1964.

40 Bill Webster, "Radio TV Review," *London Free Press*, May 30, 1964.

41 "Pierre Berton Claims 'Canadians Are Not Dull,'" *Chatham News*, May 29, 1964.

42 "Justice Dispended Today Held 'Inhuman' by Berton," *Moose Jaw Times-Herald*, Apr. 20, 1964; "Today's Justice Will Sicken Future," *Vancouver Sun*, Apr. 18, 1964; "Prisoners Support Community in U.S. Plan," *Kelowna Courier*, Apr. 28, 1964; typescript of speech on "justice in this country as seen from the point of view of a layman and a journalist," PBF, box 160, "Justice" file.

43 These figures were established using the digital archives of the *Globe and Mail* and the *Toronto Star*. Searches were made in both newspapers for mention of the specific phrase "Pierre Berton" anywhere in each newspaper.

44 Douglas B. Holt, *How Brands Become Icons: The Principles of Cultural Branding* (Cambridge: Harvard Business School Press, 2004), 3. Of various theories of branding – what marketing gurus call "mind share," "emotional," and "viral," for example – Holt's theory of "cultural branding," derived from case studies, is the one that helps best to explain how the Berton brand developed and came to possess iconic status. See David A. Acker, *Building Strong Brands* (New York: Free Press, 1996) on "mind share"; Marc Grobe, *Emotional Branding: The New Paradigm for Connecting Brands to People* (New York: Allworth Press, 2001); on viral branding, Malcolm Gladwell, *The Tipping Point: How Little Things Can Make a Big Difference* (New York: Little, Brown, 2000); also Emmanuel Rosen, *The Anatomy of Buzz* (New York: Doubleday, 2000).

45 Holt, *How Brands Become Icons*, 3–4.

46 Gerald Carson, "It Doesn't Pay to Answer the Bell," *New York Times Book Review*, Nov. 17, 1963. Berton's suggestions for resisting the hard sell, complete with scripts to use, are in ch. 9, "You, Too, Can Be a Hard Head," 229–40. "Criminal Record," *Saturday Review*, vol. 46 (Nov. 30, 1963), 40.

47 A.E., "The Dehydrated Column," SN, Dec. 5, 1959.

48 H.R. Percy, review of *Fast Fast Fast Relief*, in *Canadian Author and Bookman* (Winter 1962), 9. H.R. Percy (1920–97), a member of the Royal Canadian Navy until his retirement as lieutenant-commander in 1971, wrote short stories and novels and was editor of *Canadian Author and Bookman* from 1963 to 1966. His papers may be found in the William Ready Division of Archives and Research Collections, McMaster University Library, Hamilton.

49 JGM to D.B. Wallace, Jan. 15, 1964, MSF, box 8, file 29.

50 D.B. Wallace to JGM, Jan. 28, 1964; JGM to D.B. Wallace, Feb. 4, 1964; MSF, box 8, file 29.

51 PB, "72 Wedgewood Crescent," 233; PBF, box 190.

52 PB, "72 Wedgewood Crescent," 293.

53 "72 Wedgewood Crescent – Pierre Berton," Jan. 9, 1964; "72 Wedgewood Crescent," Jan. 20, 1964; "72 Wedgewood Crescent: A Tale of Free Enterprise," Jan. 7, 1964, in MSF, box 8, file 29.

54 Robert I. Martin to JGM, Feb. 22, 1964, MSF, box 8, file 29.

55 JGM to PB, Mar. 11, 1964, MSF, box 8, file 29. In *Jack* (Toronto: Alfred A. Knopf Canada, 1999), 146, James King quotes from this letter but erroneously links McClelland's advice to *The Comfortable Pew*.

56 Peter Israel to Miss Josephine Rogers (c/o Willis Kingsley Wing), Apr. 23, 1964, PBF, box 104, "Business Corresp. 1964" file.

CHAPTER 18: THE ELSA FACTOR

1 King, *Jack*, 142.

2 See PBF, box 102, "G. Correspondence. Business. C.C.C." file.

3 Dorothy W. Furman (Chief Social Studies Editor, Grolier Incorporated) to PB, June 19, 1964; J.W. Baillie (Supervisor of Talent Booking, CBC) to PB, June 15, 1964; PBF, box 102, "G. Correspondence. Business. C.C.C." file.

4 JGM to Rev. Ernest Harrison, May 29, 1964, PBF, box 104, "Business Corresp. 1964" file.

5 JGM to Willis K. Wing, Aug. 10, 1964, MSF, box 9, file 1; *MT*, 259.

6 PB, *Joy of Writing*, 257–58.

7 JGM to Willis K. Wing, Sept. 4, 1964, MSF, box 9, file 1. *MT*, 262. (Mrs.) M. Hodgeman (secretary to JGM) to Dr. Ernest Harrison, Sept. 15, 1964, and Ernest Harrison to JGM, Sept. 22, 1964, in MSF, box 9, file 11.

8 Bruce Ledger (Vice-President, Screen Gems Canada) to PB, July 27, 1964, PBF, box 104, "Business Corresp. 1964" file.

9 Screen Gems, "London Program Notes," week of Aug. 31 [1964]; and "Guests for Week of August 31 [1964], CFPL-TV London," PBF, box 412, "Press Coverage 1964" file.

10 Dusty Vineberg, "Berton Surveys Separatist Scene," *Montreal Star*, Sept. 15, 1964.

11 PB, "Pierre Berton Finds Honor Blackman Is a Star," Toronto *Telegram*, Nov. 7, 1964.

12 Bob Blackburn, "In Blackburn's View," Toronto *Telegram*, Sept. 30, 1964; see also "Nathan Cohen," *TS*, Oct. 16, 1964. "Berton Back from London England," Screen Gems press release, Oct. 1, 1964, PBF, box 412, "Press Coverage 1964" file. Jon Ruddy, "That Man Berton – Pierre Berton Proves Peer of Personality Probers as His Third TV Season Opens," Toronto *Telegram*, Sept. 12, 1964.

13 Pat Pearce, "Berton Monologue Refreshing Change," *Montreal Star*, Sept. 14, 1964. L.N. Bronson, "Dial Turns," *London Free Press*, Oct. 1, 1964.

14 "Saint-Vincent-de-Paul? Une honte terrible pour le Canada, selon trois députés," Montreal *Metro Express*, Oct. 8, 1964. "Prison Brutality in Montreal Penitentiary Revealed Last Night – Former Inmate Interviewed," Summerside *Journal-Pioneer*, Oct. 7, 1964.

15 Dennis Braithwaite, "Hour with Pearson," *G&M*, Nov. 18, 1964.

16 "Pearson Says Wants 'O Canada' As National Anthem," Summerside *Journal-Pioneer*, Nov. 23, 1964. "We Couldn't Survive – LBP," Calgary *Albertan*, Nov. 23, 1964. Norman Phillips, "Pearson Admits SIU Aided Some Liberals," *TS*, Nov. 23, 1964. (The story that began the SIU-Liberal Party controversy was "Banks Files Show Funds to 6 Liberals," *TS*, Nov. 6, 1964.) "Pierre Berton Special with Prime Minister Lester B. Pearson," unidentified clipping, n.d., PBF, box 412, "Press Coverage 1964" file.

17 Bob Blackburn, "In Blackburn's View," Toronto *Telegram*, Nov. 25, 1964.

18 Daisy Morant, "Phenomenon Takes Place among Young People in UK," *Guelph Mercury*, Dec. 1, 1964.

19 "TV with Frank Moritsugu," *TS*, Dec. 5, 1964. Patrick Watson, *This Hour Has Seven Decades* (Toronto: McArthur & Company, 2004), 231–34.

20 Sylvia Fraser, "Bedlam at the Bertons'," *Star Weekly*, Feb. 27, 1965. The account that follows is drawn from Fraser's article.

21 "Sylvia Fricker to Appear on TV," *Chatham News*, Dec. 23, 1964.

22 Antony Ferry, "People Will Talk – But for HOW Much?" *TS*, Oct. 17, 1964.

23 Untitled article, *Ottawa Journal*, Oct. 23, 1964.

24 McLean's professional life proceeded to disintegrate. By fall 1964, he was without work. Once the wonder child of Canadian television and still only thirty-eight, McLean had made too many enemies. "During his heyday," wrote the TV columnist Frank Moritsugu, "he was constantly accused of being arrogant, tactless, superficial and questionable in his judgement. As well as collegiate in his humor. And not without some justification." See "TV with Frank Moritsugu – What Next for Ross McLean?" *TS*, June 25, 1964.

25 *MT*, 271–72.

26 "Bob Noble – Talks of Television," *Winnipeg Free Press*, Dec. 12, 1964.

27 This biographical account is drawn from a telephone conversation and a formal interview between the author and Elsa Franklin, held on July 5, 2007, and July 11, 2007, respectively.

28 ECI, Elsa Franklin, Dec. 19, 1986; Ellie Tesher, "'I Have Infallible Taste,'" *TS*, Dec. 19, 1982.

29 Ivan Shaffer went on to write several books, three of which M&S published: *The Stock Promotion Business: The Inside Story of Canada's Mining Deals and the People behind Them* (1967), *The Midas Compulsion* (1969), and *The Sixth Day Is the Day of Death* (1978).

30 MCK, Franklin, July 11, 2007.

31 MCK, Franklin, July 11, 2007.

32 ECI, Beverley Slopen, n.d.

33 MCK, Franklin, July 11, 2007.

34 Cynthia Kelly quoted in *MT*, 275; *MT*, 274.

35 MCK, Franklin, July 11, 2007; Tesher, "'I Have Infallible Taste.'"

36 MCK, Franklin, July 11, 2007; Tesher, "'I Have Infallible Taste'"; ECI, Franklin, Dec. 19, 1986.

37 See George E. Baumann (Account Executive, McConnell, Eastman & Co.) to Elsa Franklin, Jan. 8, 1964, MSF, box 9, file 2.

38 ECI, Franklin, Dec. 19, 1986.

39 For Enright's involvement, see Joseph Stone, *Prime Time and Misdemeanors: Investigating the 1950s TV Quiz Scandal – A D.A.'s Account* (repr. New Brunswick, N.J.: Rutgers University Press, 1994). The scandal began when the program sponsor demanded a more exciting show and Enright obliged.

40 *MT*, 273.

41 MCK, Franklin, July 11, 2007.

42 M.A. Stephens, "Lenten Book by Pierre Berton," *Canadian Churchman* (Jan. 1964); A.M. Hunter, "The World Of Books," *Hamilton Spectator*, Jan. 11, 1964.

43 "Decision to Sponsor Berton Book Reaffirmed by GBRE," *Canadian Churchman* (Mar. 1964); "Anglicans Shy from Berton," *Calgary Herald*, Mar. 20, 1964; "Let Berton Write His Book, Anglican Synod Decides," *Ottawa Journal*, Apr. 24, 1964.

44 PB to JGM, Nov. 29, 1964; letters from JGM to Eric Hutton, John Clare, and Hugh Shaw, Oct. 20, 1964; memorandum from S.J. Totton to JGM re "Meeting with Reverend Jefferson, November 3rd, 1964"; "Notes from Meeting Nov. 13 at Anglican Church House, 600 Jarvis St., re promotion plans for THE UNCOMFORTABLE PEW," n.d.; all in MSF, box 9, file 1.

45 Hugh Shaw to JGM, Nov. 3, 1964; JGM to Hugh Shaw, Nov. 11 and 16, 1964, MSF, box 9, file 1.

46 Hugh Kane to JGM, Dec. 10, 1964; JGM to Elsa Franklin, Dec. 4 and 15, 1964, MSF, box 9, files 1 and 3.

47 "Promotion Report: THE COMFORTABLE PEW – from: Elsa Franklin," MSF, box 9, file 2; George E. Baumann (Account Executive, McConnell, Eastman & Co.) to Elsa Franklin, Jan. 8, 1964, MSF, box 9, file 2; Hugh Kane to David McGill (M&S memorandum), Dec. 30, 1964, MSF, box 9, file 1; Hugh Shaw (Executive Editor, *Weekend Magazine*) to JGM, Dec. 31, 1964, MSF, box 9, file 1.

48 JGM to Rev. Ernest Harrison, Jan. 15, 1965; Hugh Shaw to JGM, Jan. 20, 1965; M. Hodgeman to Josephine Rogers, Jan. 29, 1965, all in MSF, box 9, file 1.

49 "Promotion plans for THE COMFORTABLE PEW by Pierre Berton," n.d.; also "Advertising and Promotion Programme for THE COMFORTABLE PEW by Pierre Berton," Jan. 7, 1965, MSF, box 9, file 2; MCK, Franklin, July 11, 2007.

50 "Marge" [Hodgeman] to Elsa Franklin, Feb. 8, 1965, MSF, box 9, file 1.

51 *MT*, 265.

52 "Telepoll Survey – January 31, 1965. By ORC Gruneau Research Ltd.," MSF, box 9, file 2; *MT*, 263.

53 "The Pew: Phew! It's a Gold Mine," *TS*, Feb. 23, 1965; Ben Wicks, "First Call," undated *Ottawa Citizen* clipping, MSF, box 9, file 1; Dennis Braithwaite, "The Berton Era," *G&M*, Jan. 28, 1965.

54 In *MT*, 264, PB provides a sales figure of 170,000 for *The Comfortable Pew*, but a McClelland & Stewart memorandum of 1974 stated that sales had "passed the 175,000 mark." See Peter Taylor to JGM, Jan. 11, 1974, MSF, Series A, box 65, file 13. For the *Weekend Magazine* fee, see PB to Willis Kingsley Wing, n.d., PBF, box 190, group E, "The Comfortable Pew" file. On excerpt rights, see Hugh Kane to JGM, Feb. 22, 1965; JGM to Hugh Kane, Feb. 21, 1965 (handwritten note); Willis Kingsley Wing to JGM, Feb. 11, 1965, all in MSF, box 9, file 1.

The inflation calculator of the Bank of Canada was used to calculate the value of 1965 dollars; available online at http://www.bankofcanada.ca/en/rates/inflation_calc.html.

55 PB, *The Comfortable Pew: A Critical Look at the Church in the New Age* (Toronto: McClelland & Stewart, 1965), 141, 143.

56 See John A.T. Robinson, *Honest to God* (London: SCM, 1963); *The New Reformation* (London: SCM, 1965); William Kilbourn, ed., *The Restless Church: A Response to The Comfortable Pew* (Toronto: McClelland & Stewart, 1966). On the ensuing controversy, see *MT*, 265; Rev. K. James Campbell, "The Blindness of Berton," a sermon at Parkwoods United Church, Don Mills, Ont., in MSF, box 9, file 1. On translation inquiries, see George Lien to McClelland &

Stewart, Mar. 15, 1965, and E. Wedel to McClelland & Stewart, Apr. 3, 1965, MSF, box 9, file 1.

57 Michael Creal, "The Comfortable Pew Revisited," *Catholic New Times*, Jan. 16, 2005; *MT*, 266.

58 Holt, *When Brands Become Icons*, 6–12, 23–24, 28.

59 Jack Benny to PB, Sept. 8, 1964, and PB to Jack Benny, Oct. 21, 1964, PBF, box 108, "Benny" file.

60 *MT*, 248, 283; King, *Jack*, 146.

61 JGM to Mark Farrell (*Weekend Magazine*), Aug. 6, 1964, PBF, box 104, "Business Corresp. 1964" file; MacSkimming, *Perilous Trade*, 137.

62 Bob Blackburn, "In Blackburn's View," Toronto *Telegram*, Jan. 7, 1965.

63 For the text of this interview, see "The Black Vigilante," in PB, *The Cool Crazy Committed World of the Sixties* (Toronto: McClelland & Stewart, 1966), 19–28. See also the Internet site Malcolm-x.org, which contains a partial transcript.

64 Pat Pearce, "Malcolm X Riddle Unravelled a Bit," *Montreal Star*, Mar. 3, 1965.

65 Adelaide King, "Last Night's TV (A Review)," *TS*, Feb. 4, 1965.

66 On programming and outlets for the PB show, see Bob Blackburn, "In Blackburn's View," Toronto *Telegram*, May 28, 1965; L.N. Bronson, "Dial Turns," *London Free Press*, Aug. 10, 1965; "Bob Shiels . . . On Television," *Calgary Herald*, July 12.

67 Jon Margolis, *The Last Innocent Year: America in 1964; The Beginning of the "Sixties"* (New York: HarperCollins, 1999).

68 I am grateful to Elsa Franklin for providing me with lists of all guests of *The Pierre Berton Show* for the years 1965–66 to 1972–73. My brief descriptions of these shows are drawn from these documents.

69 PB, *Joy of Writing*, 262.

70 See, for example, the following BPB columns: "Sweat and Bosoms: The Startling, Uncensored Facts," Oct. 12, 1958; "A Sober Investigation into the New Cult of the Bosom," Oct. 23, 1958; "An Interview with the Man Who Started 'Playboy,'" Oct. 25, 1958; "Is It Really True That Flat Chests Mean More Brains?" Nov. 4, 1958; "The Sexless Young Ladies Who Live in the Pages of Vogue," Nov. 26, 1958; "In Which Five Frolicsome Lasses Warm a Toronto Apartment," May 12, 1959; "Talk with a Girl of Hypermammalian Development," Apr. 26, 1960; "Bawdy London Town: Mecca of the Striptease Industry," June 8, 1960.

71 On PB and the Ethos of the Sixties, see *MT*, 280. On a preoccupation with sex, see "Talk with a Girl"; "My Annual Excursion in the Land of After-hour Clubs," BPB, Mar. 28, 1962; Arnold Edinborough, "Sex, Religion and Pierre Berton," *SN* (Feb. 1965), 11–13.

72 See Gladys Taylor's novels *Pine Roots* (1956), set in Manitoba's Swan River Valley, and *The King Tree* (1958), set in the Eastern Townships at the time of the Lower Canadian Rebellion, both published by the Ryerson Press.

73 Marika Robert, "What Jack McClelland Has Done to Books," *MM*, Sept. 7, 1963.

74 MacSkimming, *Perilous Trade*, 153–54.

75 Jan Wong, "Lunch with Pierre Berton; A Canadian Historian's Remembrance of Things Past," *G&M*, Sept. 4, 1997. ECI, Jack McClelland, Nov. 11, 1986. JMF, box 10, "Sordsmen Club" file; JMF, box 26, "Sordsmen's Club – finances" file and "Sordsmen's Club – special mail file"; box 57, "Mount for award (mount only) inscribed 'Sordsmen's 1st Prize'" file. ECI, Chuck Rathgeb, Nov. 4, 1986. Rathgeb

(1921–2005) was educated at Upper Canada College and inherited his father's company, Comstock International, Inc. See his obituary in *G&M*, Sept. 2, 2005, S7.

76 Ruddy phrase quoted in Kenneth Whyte, "Last of the Red Hots," *SN*, Oct. 1996, 28.

77 Porter quoted in Whyte, "Last of the Red Hots," 28.

78 McKenzie Porter, "But I Possess Certain Powers," Toronto *Telegram*, Oct. 26, 1965.

79 *MT*, 444–45, 290.

80 Elspeth Cameron, "Once upon a Time . . .," *SN* (Aug. 1987), 28.

81 The list of names of club members is derived from McKenzie Porter's article, occasional references in Elspeth Cameron interviews cited below, from a telephone conversation between Nancy Phillips and the author on February 10, 2008, and from "Iris Nowell: Wonderful Memories of Pierre Berton," a brief tribute posted in 2004 on the Writers' Union of Canada website (and no longer available). A Sordsmen's Club attendee, Nowell became a long-time mistress of Harold Town; see her account, *Hot Breakfast for Sparrows: My Life with Harold Town* (Toronto: Stoddart, 1992). ECI, Barbara Moon, Nov. 24, 1986.

82 The author of the "raconteurs all" account is Iris Nowell; see "Iris Nowell: Wonderful Memories." ECI, William Kilbourn, Oct. 11, 1986.

83 Nowell, *Hot Breakfast*, 15.

84 ECI, Joan Taylor, Nov. 8, 1986.

85 ECI, Taylor; ECI, Kilbourn.

86 ECI, Janice Tyrwhitt, Dec. 4, 1986; ECI, Helen Simpson, Dec. 5, 1986.

87 Joan McCormack Frankel repeated this view virtually verbatim in a telephone conversation with the author, Feb. 7, 2008.

88 ECI, Joan McCormack Frankel, Jan. 8, 1987. W.O. Mitchell, *The Kite* (1962; repr. Toronto: Goose Lane Editions, 2005), 153. This is a characterization Frankel agrees is accurate. Joan Frankel, telephone conversation with author, Feb. 7, 2008.

89 ECI, McClelland; ECI, Rathgeb; ECI, Taylor. The exact wording of Cameron's notes reads: "when I pack for P – more than 3 days – French safes." ECI, Taylor.

90 Sandra Martin, "Obituary: Berton Was a Dominant Force," *G&M*, Nov. 30, 2004.

91 Joan Frankel, telephone conversation with author, Feb. 7, 2008. See John Gray, *Men Are from Mars, Women Are from Venus* (New York: HarperCollins, 1992). Berton's changing attitude toward women, assisted by his daughters, was noted in MCK, Penny Berton, Feb. 25, 2005; MCK, Patsy Berton, Feb. 21, 2006; and MCK, Pamela Berton, Feb. 22, 2006.

92 ECI, McClelland; ECI, Taylor; ECI, Charles Templeton, n.d.; ECI, Kilbourn.

93 MCK, Franklin, July 11, 2007.

94 ECI, Taylor.

95 The Porter description is in Elsa Franklin's copy of the 1964–65 guest list for *The Pierre Berton Show*.

CHAPTER 19: THE PULSE OF THE TIMES

1 Roy Shields, "Why Everybody Hates Berton," *TS*, Sept. 16, 1966.

2 PB to JGM, Mar. 10, 1967, MSF, box 9, file 5.

3 Elsa Franklin to author, Nov. 21, 2007; *MT*, 293.

4   PB to Willis Kingsley Wing, n.d. (late 1965), PBF, box 190, group E, "The Comfortable Pew" file.

5   Linda Wells, "Pierre Berton – Personality Prober," *Ryersonian*, Nov. 16, 1966; Dawn MacDonald, "Will the Real Pierre Berton Please Stand Up?" *Chatelaine* (Aug. 1970), 26–27.

6   Tesher, "I Have Infallible Taste."

7   Tesher, "I Have Infallible Taste."

8   Dawn MacDonald, "The Selling of Pierre Berton," Montreal *Gazette*, Jan. 25, 1975. MacDonald was an assistant on *The Pierre Berton Show* in 1969–70. Marilyn Craig was the daughter of a Chatham magistrate. MCK, Franklin, July 11, 2007. Bert Steel, "Celebrity Hunter Busy," *Windsor Star*, Feb. 19, 1966.

9   MCK, Janet Berton, Feb. 2, 2007; *MT*, 267. For an indication of public attitudes toward the adoption of mixed-race children in the 1960s, see Joy Huyke, as told to Anne MacDermot, "We Adopted a Negro," *MM*, Nov. 19, 1960.

10 MCK, Patsy Berton.

11 MCK, Penny Berton; MCK, Patsy Berton; MCK, Straight.

12 MCK, Straight. On Gabereau at the Bertons, see Vicki Gabereau, "As Generous a Man As Ever Lived," *G&M*, Dec. 4, 2004, R7. For general details, see *MT*, 412.

13 *Pierre Berton Show* playlist, 1966–67, in possession of Elsa Franklin. "A born shit-disturber": *MT*, 299.

14 PB to Mary Carpenter, Nov. 7, 1966, and Mary Carpenter to PB, Nov. 24, 1966, PBF, box 164, "Carpenter, Mary" file.

15 PB to O.P. Langtvet (Associate Professor, Department of Geography, University of Western Ontario), Jan. 3, 1967, and Nov. 3, 1966, PBF, box 164, "Langtvet, O.P." file. *SO*, 330.

16 Telephone conversation, Norman Kelly and the author, Jan. 13, 2005.

17 Norman Kelly to PB, May 30, 1966; Norman Kelly to PB, n.d., with clipping of "Stories Wanted from Men Who Built CPR," in *Ottawa Citizen*; PB to Norman Kelly, Oct. 13, 1966, in PBF, box 2, "Kelly, Norman" file.

18 Norman Kelly to PB, Nov. 13, 1966, PBF, box 2, "Kelly, Norman" file.

19 Norman Kelly to Ennis Halliday, May 30, 1966; Norman Kelly to PB, June 22, 1966; Norman Kelly to PB, Nov. 13, 1966; Ennis Halliday to Norman Kelly, Oct. 21, 1966 (Halliday's suggestion about weekly reports is handwritten on the bottom of the office copy of this letter); all in PBF, box 2, "Kelly, Norman" file.

20 PB to Norman Kelly, Oct. 13, 1966.

21 Peter C. Newman, "'It Could Change the Whole Direction of Canada's History,'" *TS*, Apr. 28, 1967; *MT*, 305.

22 *MT*, 304–06.

23 Ennis Halliday to Marge Hodgeman, Jan. 18, 1967, PBF, box 2, "Expo 67" file. In this letter, Halliday asks Hodgeman to "reserve the Montreal Apartment" – presumably that of M&S – from May 19 to 22, 1967.

24 *MT*, 308–09.

25 "Man of the Century," *Canadian Author and Bookman*, Centennial series – 2 (Summer 1967), 8–9.

26 Nathan Cohen, "Paradise Hill Is Lost in a Turgid Lifeless Concoction," *TS*, July 5, 1967; *MT*, 310.

27 *MT*, 309–12.

28 "Bourgault's Warning – 'Would Block Seaway,'" Toronto *Telegram*, Oct. 6, 1967. "Charges Helpful, LaMarsh Says," *Saskatoon Star-Phoenix*, Nov. 15, 1967, and also Judy LaMarsh, *Memoirs of a Bird in a Gilded Cage* (Toronto: McClelland & Stewart, 1968), 264–74; Ben Ward, "Last Straw for Ouimet," *St. John's Evening Telegraph*, Dec. 14, 1967.

29 Tony Hawke (Director, Advertising and Promotion Department, M&S) to Stephen Franklin, May 2, 1967, MSF, box 9, file 5.

30 Leslie Hannon to PB (memorandum), Sept. 14, 1967, MSF, box 9, file 5; SO, 305. For McClelland's elevation of Berton's status at M&S, see JGM to PB, Dec. 30, 1966, MSF, box 9, file 9.

31 MCK, Franklin, July 11, 2007; Elsa Franklin to author, Nov. 21, 2007.

32 Mike Boone, "NDP Back-room Dealing Focus of Duffy Coverage," Montreal *Gazette*, Nov. 29, 1989.

33 JGM to Geoff Feilding [*sic*], Oct. 2, 1967 (re J.R. Colombo), MSF, box 9, file 6. J.R. Colombo to JGM, Oct. 17, 1967, MSF, box 9, file 5. JGM to Elsa Franklin (memorandum), Nov. 7, 16, 1967; and "Berton – Smug Minority. Budget Projection," Nov. 9, 1967, all in MSF, box 9, file 6.

34 Peter Gzowski (*Star Weekly* magazine) to JGM, Nov. 13, 1967; "The Smug Minority – Pierre Berton," Nov. 22, 1967 (statement of serial rights policy sent to prospective customers), MSF, box 9, file 6.

35 W. Borden Spears to JGM, Nov. 27, 1967; Hugh Shaw to JGM, Nov. 29, 1967; Denis Harvey to JGM, Nov. 29, 1967; Peter Gzowski to JGM, Nov. 28, 1967; all in MSF, box 9, file 16.

36 (Mrs.) J. MacDougall (for JGM) to Peter Gzowski, Nov. 30, 1967, MSF, box 9, file 16.

37 Elsa Franklin to author, Nov. 21, 2007. Draft memorandum from David McGill, with recipient left blank, Jan. 5, 1968, MSF, box 9, file 16.

38 Undated press releases with letterhead "The Smug Minority" and "The Smug Minority – Promotion Campaign (Elsa Franklin)," n.d., in MSF, box 9, file 16. One press release declared that the *Star Weekly* "had paid a higher price per word [for its excerpt] than Winston Churchill received from *Life* for his memoirs."

39 PB, *The Smug Minority* (Toronto: McClelland & Stewart, 1968), 27.

40 PB, *Smug Minority*, 47.

41 PB, *Smug Minority*, 7–9. Much has been written about Gramsci and hegemony since the rise of the cultural studies movement in the 1970s, but see Carl Boggs, *Gramsci's Marxism* (London: Pluto Press, 1976), 17ff, for a start.

42 See Pierre Bourdieu, "Cultural Reproduction and Social Reproduction," in *Knowledge, Education and Social Change*, ed. R. Brown (London: Tavistock, 1973).

43 PB, *Smug Minority*, 25.

44 PB, *Smug Minority*, 84.

45 PB, *Smug Minority*, 88–90.

46 PB, *Smug Minority*, 91–92, 93.

47 PB, *Smug Minority*, 69–70.

48 PB, *Smug Minority*, 71.

49 PB, *Smug Minority*, 31; MT, 317.

50 PB, *Smug Minority*, 127–8. John Porter, *The Vertical Mosaic: An Analysis of Social Class and Power in Canada* (Toronto: University of Toronto Press, 1965).

51   PB, *Smug Minority*, 135–40. See Theodore W. Schultz, "Investment in Human Capital," *American Economic Review*, vol. 50, no. 1 (Mar. 1961), 1–17. Schultz won the Nobel Prize for Economics in 1979.

52   PB, *Smug Minority*, 157–60.

53   Robert Fulford, "The Fantastic Adventures of Super Berton," *TS*, Jan. 20, 1968. The account of the Ruddy controversy in the next two paragraphs is drawn from this source.

54   "List for Elsa – Ottawa Party," n.d. (winter 1968), MSF, box 9, file 16.

55   Charles E. Hendry to JGM, Feb. 1, 1968, MSF, box 9, file 6. See Michael Harrington, *The Other America: Poverty in the United States* (New York: Simon & Schuster, 1962).

56   Ian H. McNish to JGM, Feb. 2, 1968, MSF, box 9, file 16.

57   William C. Heine, "Bugged by Pierre Berton, the Professional Dissenter," *London Free Press*, undated clipping (before Feb. 10, 1968); Fotheringham quoted in Rina Calabrese, "Berton at 80: The Spinner Slows His Pace," *National Post*, undated clipping (July 2000), in PBF, box 286, clippings and articles about PB, 1943–88.

58   Michael Barkway (Publisher and Editor, *Financial Times* of Canada), "Still Hippy Though Fifty: Berton's Bleeding Heart Runs Away with His Head," *Financial Times*, Feb. 5, 1968; JGM to Michael Barkway, Feb. 13, 1968, MSF, box 9, file 16.

59   "Dennis Braithwaite," *G&M*, Feb. 25, 1968; PB, *Smug Minority*, 100.

60   "Dennis Braithwaite," *G&M*, Feb. 25, 1968.

61   David McGill memoranda to McClelland (cc to Elsa Franklin and Hugh Kane), Feb. 15, 26, 27, Mar. 11, 1968; JGM to Peter Gzowski, Feb. 27, 1968; JGM to Scott McIntyre, Mar. 13, 1968; all in MSF, box 9, file 16.

62   Robert Fulford, "The Small Cities Just Love Berton," *TS*, Mar. 14, 1968.

63   Conrad Black did not purchase the *Sherbrooke Record* until 1969, but the condemnation of a book about Canada's smug business tycoons and an exorbitant love affair with alliteration in this piece suggest that he may have contributed to the newspaper the previous year.

64   "Total Sales All Editions – Pierre Berton Titles," June 1, 1970, MSF, series A, box 65, file 13.

65   JGM to Scott McIntyre, Mar. 13, 1968, MSF, box 9, file 16. Several journalists inquired about the name of the "major trust company," but McClelland did not reveal it. The company was the Royal Trust Company, and its president was Conrad F. Harrington. See C.F. Harrington to JGM, Feb. 9, 1968; JGM to C.F. Harrington, Feb. 13, 1968; both in MSF, box 9, file 16. McClelland does not identify the source of his quotation from Robert Fulford.

66   Press release for *The Smug Minority*, n.d. (May 1968), MSF, box 9, file 16.

67   JGM to Dave McGill, May 27, 1968, MSF, box 9, file 16.

68   King, *Jack*, 171–73. JGM to Dave McGill, May 27, 1968, and Marge Hodgeman to Dave McGill, June 14, 1968, MSF, box 9, file 16.

CHAPTER 20: NATIONAL DREAMER

1   *MT*, 320.

2   PB to JGM, Aug. 12, 1968, MSF, box 9, file 10. As early as 1968, M&S owed Berton $22,000: $1,000 as the advance on *The Smug Minority*, $5,000 for the Preview

Book Club, and $16,000 in deferred salary. See PB to JGM, Apr. 18, 1968, MSF, box 9, file 7; also *MT*, 321. On domestic expenses, see Roy Shields, "Berton at Home Belies Tough TV Image," *Edmonton Journal*, Apr. 8, 1972.

3 *MT*, 321–22.

4 See, for example, H.T. Coleman to PB, Oct. 31, Nov. 7, 17, 1966; H.T. Coleman to Norman Kelly, Nov. 8, 1967, and Jan. 16, May 28, 1968; in PBF, box 1, "Coleman, Travers" file; related correspondence is in box 2, "Kelly, Norman" file.

5 Ennis Halliday to Norman Kelly, May 17, 1968; PB to Norman Kelly, May 14 and May 27, 1968; in PBF, box 2, "Kelly, Norman" file. The material Coleman sent included a twenty-six-page "Corporate and Historical Chronology" of the history of the CPR, compiled by Canadian Pacific News.

6 "Itinerary Mr. Pierre Berton," n.d., MSF, box 9, file 7. Norman Kelly to PB, June 22, 1968, PBF, box 2, "Kelly, Norman" file.

7 PB to H.T. Coleman, June 4, 1968; H.T. Coleman to PB (Canadian Pacific Telegram), June 10, 1968; both in PBF, box 1, "Coleman, Travers" file. *MT*, 322. By this stage in the relationship, Berton's letters began "Dear Trav."

8 PB to N.R. Crump, Mar. 7, Apr. 1, Apr. 18, Sept. 2, 1969, and Jan. 16, 1968; N.R. Crump to PB, Feb. 14, 1969; all in PBF, box 1, "Crump, N.R." file.

9 JGM to Elsa Franklin, Feb. 6, 1969, PBF, box 9, file 9.

10 *MT*, 357–58.

11 Guest List, "Pierre Berton Show – 1968–69," provided by Elsa Franklin.

12 *MT*, 323.

13 PB to N.R. Crump, Jan. 16, 1968, PBF, box 1, "Crump, N.R." file. For discussion of such "technological nationalism," beginning with Berton on the Canadian Pacific Railway, see Robert MacDougall, "The All-Red Dream: Technological Nationalism and the Trans-Canada Telephone System," Norman Hillmer and Adam Chapnick, eds., *Canadas of the Mind: The Making and Unmaking of Canadian Nationalisms in the Twentieth Century* (Montreal and Kingston: McGill-Queen's University Press, 2007), 46–62.

14 See Carl Berger, *The Writing of Canadian History: Aspects of English-Canadian Historical Writing since 1900*, 2nd ed. (Toronto: University of Toronto Press, 1986), especially the chapters on Innis and Creighton.

15 PB, "The Pleasure of Writing," n.d. (1970), 9, MSF, box 9, file 10. This article was commissioned by MM for publication at the time of the release of *The National Dream*. It appeared under the title "Stand Clear! Here Comes a Writer, Writing," in September 1970.

16 Telephone conversation between author and Norman Kelly, Jan. 31, 2005. PB, *Joy of Writing*, 258–59. *MT*, 326.

17 PB, *Joy of Writing*, 199, 220–35.

18 See John S. Moir, ed., *Character and Circumstance: Essays in Honour of Donald Grant Creighton* (Toronto: Macmillan of Canada, 1970).

19 PB, "The Pleasure of Writing," 10.

20 On rewriting, see Roy Shields, "Berton at Home with His Tribe," Vancouver *Province*, Apr. 7, 1972. Telephone conversation between Norman Kelly and author, Jan. 31, 2005. ECI, Michael Bliss, Nov. 20, 1986.

21 Michael Bliss to PB, Jan. 24, 1970, with attachment: "The Great Railway, vol. 1: The National Dream. Specific Comments," 1–10; PBF, box 1, "Bliss, Michael" file.

22 Michael Bliss, "Re: The Great Railway, v. 1: The National Dream by Pierre Berton," Jan. 24, 1970, PBF, box 1, "Bliss, Michael" file.

23 JGM to PB, Feb. 11, 1970, PBF, box 9, file 10; anthologized in Sam Solecki, ed., *Imagining Canadian Literature: The Selected Letters of Jack McClelland* (Toronto: Key Porter, 1998), 139–41. The definition of a nation is that of Frank Underhill in his Massey Lecture, *The Image of Confederation* (Toronto: CBC, 1964), 2.

24 See Stephen Azzi, "Foreign Investment and the Paradox of Economic Nationalism," in Hillmer and Chapnick, eds., *Canadas of the Mind*, 63–88.

25 George Grant, *Lament for a Nation: The Defeat of Canadian Nationalism* (Toronto: McClelland & Stewart, 1965); Al Purdy, ed., *The New Romans: Candid Canadian Opinions of the U.S.* (Edmonton: Hurtig, 1968); Robin Mathews and James Steele, eds., *The Struggle for Canadian Universities* (Toronto: New Press, 1969); Ian Lumsden, ed., *Close the 49th Parallel etc: The Americanization of Canada* (Toronto: University of Toronto Press, 1970); Kari Levitt, *Silent Surrender: The Multinational Corporation in Canada* (Toronto: Macmillan, 1970); Margaret Atwood, *Survival: A Thematic Guide to Canadian Literature* (Toronto: House of Anansi, 1972).

26 Peter C. Newman, *Here Be Dragons: Telling Tales of People, Passion and Power* (Toronto: McClelland & Stewart, 2004), 262; Stephen Azzi, *Walter Gordon and the Rise of Canadian Nationalism* (Montreal and Kingston: McGill-Queen's University Press, 173, 192–93); I am grateful to Stephen Azzi for providing information concerning these luncheon meetings.

27 A list of CIC members is attached to JGM to Elsa Franklin, Oct. 13, 1971, MSF, box 9, file 11.

28 *MT*, 344.

29 See King, *Jack*, 217–19. The quotation is at 218.

30 Press release for *The Pierre Berton Show*, Dec. 16, 1970, MSF, box 9, file 10. The transcript of the episode, which also featured the politician Tim Read as a guest, is also in this location. On JGM's appearance on the show, see King, *Jack*, 220–24. King erroneously states that McClelland's appearance was on radio.

31 *MT*, 344–45; King, *Jack*, 226–30.

32 Azzi, *Walter Gordon*, 178. The quotation is from the Committee for an Independent Canada's 1970 "Statement of Purpose." Azzi's chapter "The New Nationalism, 1968–1987" provides a useful overview of the plight of Canadian nationalism. See also "Berton Wants Code for Press," Vancouver *Province*, Mar. 31, 1970.

33 *MT*, 342–43. The account in the previous paragraph is also drawn from Berton's memoir.

34 Marge Hodgeman to Anna Szigethy and Judith Turnbull (memo), Dec. 24, 1969, MSF, box 9, file 10.

35 Anna Szigethy to Janet Craig (memo), Jan. 7, 1970, MSF, box 9, file 10.

36 JGM to Dave McGill, Geoff Matthews, Catherine Wilson, Frank Newfeld, Anna Szigethy, Peter Scaggs, Nick Milton, and Larry Ritchie (memo), Apr. 6, 1970, MSF, box 9, file 10.

37 PB, *The National Dream: The Great Railway 1871–1881* (Toronto: McClelland & Stewart, 1970). Due to television commitments, Franklin did not play a major role in promoting *The National Dream*, but she became heavily involved with *The Last Spike*. Elsa Franklin to author, Nov. 21, 2007.

38 PB to JGM, Sept. 10, 1970, MSF, box 9, file 10.

39 Hugh Kane to Peter Sypnowich; quoted in King, *Jack*, 214. Kane's conversation with Sypnowich likely took place in the first week of August 1971, since the journalist reported it in his column on Aug. 8, 1971.

40 PB to JGM, Sept. 10, 1970, MSF, box 9, file 10.

41 Bob Blackburn, "Through Fire and Flood with Dauntless Pierre," Toronto *Telegram*, undated clipping, MSF, box 9, file 10. In *MT*, PB uses Blackburn's article as an aid to memory, substituting Hamburg for Dresden (330–31).

42 PB to JGM, Sept. 17, 1970, MSF, box 9, file 10.

43 Michael Bliss to PB, Sept. 10, 1970, MSF, box 1, "Bliss, Michael" file. PB to P.B. Waite, Apr. 28, 1969, and P.B. Waite to PB, May 23, 1969, MSF, box 3, "Waite, P.B." file. Waite also answered PB's queries in 1971 on *The Last Spike* and provided extensive suggestions based on archival sources.

44 Bruce Hutchison to JGM, Aug. 3 and 7, 1970, MSF, box 9, file 10. Hugh MacLennan to JGM, June 7, 1970, MSF, box 9, file 11.

45 "The Critics Comment," MSF, box 9, file 10. W.L. Morton to JGM, n.d. (summer 1970), MSF, box 9, file 10.

46 Philip Sykes (*Maclean's*) to JGM, July 30, 1970; Frank Lowe (*Weekend Magazine*) to JGM, June 5, 1970; Michael Hanlon (*Canadian* magazine) to JGM, July 20, 1970; all in MSF, box 9, file 10. "Montreal – Berton Sales," Sept. 24, 1970; Harold Strauss (Knopf) to Pierre Berton, Feb. 11 and 26, 1970; all in MSF, box 9, file 10.

47 "Montreal-Berton Sales," Sept. 24, 1970; M.A.R. to Geoff Matthews (memo re spot check sales in Toronto), Sept. 24, 1970, in MSF, box 9, file 10.

48 "'If Any Woman Can Steal My Job, She's Welcome to,'" *Australian Women's Weekly*, Nov. 11, 1970, 10.

49 PB to Michael Bliss, Sept. 3, 1970, PBF, box 1, "Bliss, Michael" file. MCK, Elsa Franklin (July 11, 2007): "He didn't like [Kelly's] kind of research."

50 PB to JGM ("Private and Confidential"), n.d. (after Nov. 10, 1970), MSF, box 9, file 10.

51 Draft press release, n.d. (late fall 1970); Margaret Cook, "The National Dream: Berton" (books on hand and printing expected), Dec. 9, 1970; both in MSF, box 9, file 10.

52 *MT*, 327–28. Responding later to a query from a man named Basciano asking about Eric's background, Berton stated with pride, "Eric Basciano is now one of the family." PBF, box 188, "Eric" file.

53 Peter Sypnowich, "Pierre Berton's National Dream," *TS*, Aug. 27, 1970; John Rodgers, "Canadian Dream Came True," *Vancouver Sun*, Sept. 4, 1970.

54 Peter C. Newman, *Renegade in Power: The Diefenbaker Years* (Toronto: McClelland & Stewart, 1963); *The Distemper of Our Times: Canadian Politics in Transition: 1963–1968* (Toronto: McClelland & Stewart, 1968); Arnold Edinborough, "Dream, Nightmare or Insanity? All Three – But It Built a Nation," *Financial Post*, Sept. 26, 1970.

55 Harry Bruce, "Berton and the CPR: Do It for the Glory," *SN* (Nov. 1970).

56 Bruce Hutchison, "Old Tomorrow versus Young Today," unidentified source, undated clipping, MSF, box 9, file 10.

57 "Exclusive: The Times Interviews Two of Canada's Best-Known Individuals," *Queen's Times*, Jan. 18, 1971, 3.

58 "The Heroic Beginnings of a Dream," *Herald Magazine* (Newfoundland), Sept. 11, 1970; John Bassett, "Canada's Past Brought to Life," Toronto *Telegram*, Sept. 12, 1970; Peter Sypnowich, "Pierre Berton Creates a New Canadian Mythology," TS, Sept. 12, 1970.

59 Mavor Moore to PB, Apr. 15, 1971, PBF, box 109; T.C. Douglas to PB, May 18, 1971, PBF, box 108; Laurier L. LaPierre to PB, May 29, 1971, PBF, box 109; PB to Laurier LaPierre, June 4, 1971, PBF, box 109.

60 *MT*, 336–39.

61 Michael Bliss to PB, Feb. 4, 1971, with attached report: "Re: The Great Railway vol. 2: The Last Spike," MSF, box 1, "Bliss, Michael" file. See especially pages 8 and 20 of the report.

62 H.V. Nelles, "The Ties That Bind: Berton's C.P.R.," *Canadian Forum* (Nov.–Dec. 1970), 270–72.

63 Nelles, "Ties That Bind," 272. Berton responded to Nelles's review with a letter published in *Canadian Forum* (Feb. 1971, 374–75), taking issue with the reviewer's critique of Berton's "Railway Now" position. "What Mr. Nelles ignores," he wrote, "is that it would have been an equally reckless gamble not to have built the railway" (375). In response, Nelles reiterated his charge that Berton's view of Canadian nationhood represented a central Canadian bias that, for example, viewed the Riel Rebellion of 1885 "as something simply to be put down." Nelles concluded: "That is the problem with a regional state; one man's national hero is another man's rebel. That is why a National Dream (singular) is so hard to come by" (375).

64 Bliss, "Re: The Great Railway, vol. 2," MSF, box 1, "Bliss, Michael" file, 2–3.

65 PB to Michael Bliss, Feb. 15, 1971, MSF, box 1, "Bliss, Michael" file; PB, *The Last Spike: The Great Railway 1881–1885* (Toronto: McClelland & Stewart, 1971), 423.

66 JGM to P.C. Newman, Feb. 3, 1971; Lester Troob (Book-of-the-Month Club) to JGM, Mar. 17, 1971; Anna Szigethy to JGM, Mar. 8, 1971; all in MSF, box 9, file 11.

67 JGM to Bruce Hutchison, Mar. 26, 1971; Bruce Hutchison to JGM, Mar. 31, 1971; JGM to Hugh MacLennan, May 21, 1971; Hugh MacLennan to JGM, June 12, 1971; for JGM's praise, see JGM to PB, May 20, 1971; all in MSF, box 9, file 11.

68 PB to JGM, May 3, 1971, MSF, box 9, file 11.

69 Telephone conversation between Glenn Wright and author, Aug. 16, 2007.

70 Elsa Franklin, "The Last Spike Promotion – Budget Estimates," July 21, 1971, MSF, box 9, file 11.

71 Peter Taylor to JGM, Dec. 7, 1971; Elsa Franklin, "The Last Spike – Promotion – Ideas," n.d.; press release re "Last Spike Cocktail," on letterhead "from Elsa Franklin," n.d.; all in MSF, box 9, file 11.

72 John Richmond, "Behind the Pierre Berton Image," *Montreal Star*, Sept. 18, 1971. The Last Spike cocktail fortunately did not contain Geritol. Those so disposed may wish to try the official recipe: to 4 oz. of champagne (or sparkling white wine), add 1/3 oz. of Curacao, 2/3 oz. of cognac, a dash of orange bitters, and a slice of fresh orange. Stir gently and briefly. This can be turned into a Last Spike cooler by adding an equal measure of soda to the cocktail. See "An Invitation for Sunday Brunch to mark the publication of THE LAST SPIKE by Pierre Berton," MSF, box 9, file 11.

73 "The Last Spike – Ottawa Promotion," n.d. (summer 1971); Elsa Franklin to Ruth Dutton, Sept. 14, 1971; Elsa Franklin to Bertha Hanson, Sept. 14, 1971; Elsa

Franklin to Rita Kurtz (Winnipeg), Sept. 14, 1971; Carol Copeland (Saskatoon) to Elsa Franklin, Sept. 7, 1971; Elsa Franklin memorandum (no recipient specified – general publisher's representative letter), Aug. 10, 1971; all in MSF, box 9, file 11. "Mass of people": *MT*, 332.

74 See, for example, Peter Murray (Book Page Editor, *Victoria Daily Times*) to JGM, Aug. 28, 1971; Kenneth Bagnell (Editor, *Globe Magazine*), Aug. 31, 1971; both in MSF, box 9, file 11.

75 On the print run, see JGM to PB (two letters), Aug. 30, 1971; JGM to Kildare Dobbs (*Toronto Star*), Sept. 15, 1971; JGM to Elsa Franklin, Aug. 30, 1971; all in MSF, box 9, file 11.

76 Margaret Daly, "'At 51,' Says Pierre Berton, Historian, 'You Try to Do Something Lasting,'" *TS*, Sept. 11, 1971.

77 Reg Vickers, "Pierre Berton: Canada's Amazing Personality Package," *Calgary Herald*, undated clipping (fall 1971) in PBF, box 9, file 11.

78 Arnold Edinborough, "A Rage-for-Life Berton Breathes Life into a Stormy, Gutsy Epic," *Financial Post*, Sept. 25, 1971; "Books – By Donald Cameron," *MM* (Nov. 1971); Hugh A. Dempsey, review of *The Last Spike*, *Alberta Historical Review*, vol. 20 (Winter 1972), 29.

79 Bruce Hutchison, report [untitled] on *The Last Spike*, n.d., MSF, box 9, file 11.

80 Donald Swainson, review of *The Last Spike*, *Queen's Quarterly*, vol. 80 (Spring 1973), 144; "Canada's Pierre Berton Succeeds by Reinforcing a National Identity," *Wall Street Journal*, Nov. 6, 1973.

81 George F.G. Stanley, review of *The Last Spike*, *Beaver* (Summer 1972), 56–57; Harry Bruce, "The Work Has Been Done Well in Every Way," *SN* (Nov. 1971), 54–56. A notable exception was Bob Hunter, a *Vancouver Sun* critic who readily admitted that he had read only the book's first paragraph and then skimmed the rest; this did not stop him from excoriating the book or its author. *The Last Spike* was "a hot dog book," its contents utterly predictable; Berton was "the Incredible Hulk of Canadian Journalism." See Bob Hunter, "The Last Spike Is a Hot Dog Book," *Vancouver Sun*, Sept. 17, 1971, 33A–34A.

CHAPTER 21: ASTRIDE THE SUMMIT

1 *MT*, 349.

2 Ida Schneider to JGM, May 28, 1971, MSF, box 9, file 11.

3 *MT*, 339–40; McKenzie Porter, "The Self Promoters," *G&M*, Nov. 5, 1971.

4 PB is quoted on the Canadian Writers' Foundation website at http://www.canadianwritersfoundation.org/profile.html.

5 Susanne Moss to PB, Jan. 3, 1974, with attached handwritten note by Ennis Armstrong; also PB to JGM, Jan. 26, 1971, PB to JGM, Feb. 23, 1971; all in MSF, box 101, "Susanne Moss – Too Many Tears" file. PB's correspondence with or concerning Moss consists of more than fifty letters written between April 1969 and September 1974. It began when Moss sent him a thirty-two-page manuscript about her struggle as "a handicapped," and ended with publication of her memoir, *Too Many Tears* (Toronto: McClelland & Stewart, 1974).

6 Terry Mosher to author, Oct. 28, 2007; PB to JGM, Jan. 7, 1972, MSF, box 9, file 12. Mosher joined the Montreal *Gazette* in March 1973.

7   PB to Mrs. Anthony (Anahid) Swann, Aug. 16, 1971, PBF, box 110; "Swann, Anahid 1970–74" file; PB to Karl D. Jaffary (Rosedale N.D.P.), Jan. 10, 1972; PBF, box 109, "Jaffary, Karl" file; PB to Alan Innes-Taylor (Whitehorse), June 16, 1972, PBF, box 109, "Innes-Taylor, Alan" file; Laura Kinrade to PB, Mar. 28, 1972, PBF, box 109, "Kinrade, Laura" file.

8   JGM to PB (telegram), Aug. 16, 1972, and JGM to James Douglas and Scott McIntyre, MSF, box 9, file 12. Berton Woodward, "Bertons Dare Yukon River," Vancouver *Province*, July 29, 1972; *MT*, 350.

9   *MT*, 352.

10 PB, *Drifting Home: A Family's Voyage of Discovery Down the Wild Yukon* (Toronto: McClelland & Stewart, 1973), 167.

11 *DH*, 149, 12.

12 Roy Shields, "Berton at Home Belies Tough Image," *Edmonton Journal*, Apr. 18, 1972. This item, like so many others about PB, was distributed by wire service (in this case Southam) to newspapers across the country.

13 PB, "Floating Down the Yukon," photographs by Robert Holmes, *MM* (Dec. 1972), 37.

14 "Berton Wins Third National Literary Award," Vancouver *Province*, Mar. 22, 1972. "General Background – The Pierre Berton Show," PBF, box 331, file 38. On Global, see *MT*, 354. On Knopf and subsidiary rights, see Anne H. McCormick to JGM, Oct. 13, 1972, PBF, box 331, file 38.

15 On PB and the bestseller lists, see Paul King, "Pierre Berton: Still Working on the Railroad – This Time for TV," undated clipping from *MM*, MSF, box 9, file 12. Press release for *The Great Railway: Illustrated*, n.d., MSF, box 9, file 12. On the abridged paperback edition, see *MT*, 335; on sales figures, see Roy Shields, "Berton at Home with His Tribe," Vancouver *Province*, Apr. 7, 1972; Peter Taylor to JGM, Jan. 11, 1974, and David McGill to JGM (memorandum), May 30, 1974, MSF, box 65, file 13. On *Og*, see JGM to PB, Nov. 12, 1972, MSF, box 9, file 12.

16 "Author Pierre Berton Is Purposely Arrogant As Canadian Nationalist," *Brockville Recorder*, Jan. 13, 1972; "Canada 'Bloody Good' Says Berton," Vancouver *Province*, Jan. 10, 1972; "Berton Concedes He's 'Bloody Good,'" *Vancouver Sun*, Jan. 7, 1972.

17 JGM to PB, Aug. 24, 1971; PB to JGM, Aug. 30, 1971; PB to JGM, Sept. 8, 1971; all in MSF, box 9, file 11.

18 JGM to Catherine Wilson, Aug. 17, 1971, MSF, box 9, file 11.

19 "Budget Estimate – Promotion of *Klondike* and *The Great Railway*," Aug. 1, 1972; "Promotion Plans," n.d.; both in MSF, box 9, file 12. That the event took place on the weekend of September 16–17, 1972, most likely on Saturday 16, seems beyond dispute, since a letter JGM sent to Catherine Wilson explaining his actions is dated Sept. 21.

20 King, *Jack*, 247–48. Elsa Franklin has told the author that she does not know why Catherine Wilson was dismissed, but PB's correspondence with Jack McClelland about Wilson indicates clearly the degree of dissatisfaction Berton and Franklin had with her. MCK, Franklin, July 11, 2007.

21 JGM to Larry Ritchie ("Confidential"), Sept. 22, 1972, MSF, box 9, "Berton, Pierre (1964–73)" file.

22 King, *Jack*, 247–48. Robert Weaver to JGM, "Monday" (Sept. 18 or 25, 1972), MSF, box 64, file 6.

23 King, *Farley*, 291; King, *Jack*, 248; Catherine Wilson to JGM, "Wednesday" (Sept. 20, 1972), MSF, box 64, file 6.

24 PB, *Joy of Writing*, 294. JGM to Catherine Wilson, Sept. 21, 1972; JGM to Larry Ritchie, Sept. 22, 1972; Robert I. Martin (Hume, Martin & Timmins) to JGM, Sept. 26, 1972; all in MSF, box 64, file 6. JGM to Elsa Franklin, Sept. 27, 1972, MSF, box 9, file 12.

25 PB to Farley Mowat, Oct. 10, 1972, MSF, box 64, file 6.

26 Farley Mowat to PB, Oct. 12, 1972, MSF, box 64, file 6.

27 Farley Mowat to JGM, Nov. 10, 1972, MSF, box 64, file 6; also quoted in King, *Jack*, 249.

28 JGM to PB, Oct. 16, 1972, MSF, box 9, file 12.

29 Farley Mowat to JGM, May 8, 1959; quoted in King, *Farley*, 119.

30 Noted in King, *Farley*, 292.

31 Blaik Kirby, "Berton Abandons His TV Talk Show," *G&M*, Mar. 23, 1973.

32 On bestsellers, see "George Anthony," *Toronto Sun*, Mar. 1, 1972; George Anthony, "As the Voice Went, So Went the Seagull," *Toronto Sun*, Sept. 29, 1972. "Lebanon Censored Interview Tapes Pierre Berton Says," *TS*, Dec. 29, 1972. On program topics, see press releases for "The Pierre Berton Show special series," 1972–73, PBF, box 331, file 38.

33 Kirby, "Berton Abandons"; Bob Blackburn, "Pierre Berton to Quit His TV Program," *Toronto Sun*, Mar. 28, 1973; Jack Miller, "Pierre Berton Giving Up TV Talk Show," *TS*, Mar. 28, 1973.

34 George F.G. Stanley, review of *The National Dream*, in *Queen's Quarterly*, vol. 78 (Summer 1971), 327–28. Paul Rutherford, review of *The National Dream*, in *International Journal*, vol. 26 (Winter 1970–71), 278–79. P.B. Waite, review of *The National Dream*, in *Dalhousie Review*, vol. 50 (Winter 1970–71), 563–65; P.B. Waite, review of *The Last Spike*, in *Dalhousie Review*, vol. 52 (Spring 1972), 140–42.

35 The author attended both this CHA event and that of 1973. See D.G. Creighton, "The Decline and Fall of the Empire of the St. Lawrence," Canadian Historical Association *Historical Papers*, vol. 1 (1969), available on the CHA website. In 1969, Peter Waite was the association's president.

36 See Gerald Friesen, "The Western Canadian Identity," and Gregory Kealey, "Artisans Respond to Industrialism: Shoemakers, Shoe Factories and the Knights of St. Crispin in Toronto," in *Journal of the Canadian Historical Association*, vol. 8, no. 1 (1973), available online at the CHA website.

37 Terry Crowley to author (email), Dec. 2, 2004.

38 T.D. Regehr, review of *The National Dream*, in *Saskatchewan History*, vol. 24 (Winter 1971), 34–35. T.D. Regehr, review of *The Last Spike*, in *Saskatchewan History*, vol. 25 (Winter 1972), 38–40. T.D. Regehr to author, Feb. 6, 2008. I am grateful to Dr. Regehr for his recollections of the comments he and Albert Faucher made at the session, especially in his telephone conversation of April 24, 2008.

39 Allan McCullough to author (email), Dec. 3, 2004, and Mar. 20, 2008; J.R. Miller to author (email), Dec. 3, 2004, and Mar. 17, 2008; Terry Crowley to author (email), Dec. 2, 2004, and Mar. 17, 2008. McCullough retired from Parks Canada several years ago; J.R. Miller currently holds a Canada Research Chair in the Department of History, University of Saskatchewan; Terry Crowley is a professor

of history at the University of Guelph. Miller and Crowley have served as chairs of their respective departments.

40 Douglas Fisher, "Berton Maintains [remainder of title obscured in microfilm]," *Toronto Sun*, July 6, 1973. I am grateful to members of the H-Canada listserv who responded to my request to share their recollections of this event.

41 Terry Cook to author, Dec. 4, 2004. The author attended this session and experienced a similar reaction.

42 Nelles, "Ties That Bind." H.V. Nelles, review of *The Last Spike*, in *Canadian Historical Review*, vol. 53 (Dec. 1972), 453–55. Donald Swainson, review of *The National Dream*, in *Canadian Historical Review*, vol. 52 (Dec. 1971), 435–37. Swainson, review of *The Last Spike*, in *Queen's Quarterly*.

43 Fisher, "Berton Maintains"; Terry Cook to author, Dec. 4, 2004.

44 PB, *Joy of Writing*, 282–83.

45 Edinborough, "Dream, Nightmare or Insanity?" George F.G. Stanley, review of *The National Dream*, in *Queen's Quarterly*, vol. 78 (Summer 1971), 328. Nelles, "Ties That Bind." For the strength of liberal humanism, see McKillop, *Matters of Mind*.

46 Telephone conversation, Glenn Wright and author, Aug. 16, 2007.

47 "Trudeau's Use of 'Shrine' Hit," *Vancouver Sun*, June 6, 1975. Separate memoranda to JGM from B. Sayers, Nov. 23, 1973; G.E. Witmer, Nov. 26, 1973; Don Roper, Nov. 26, 1973; Eugene Henry, Nov. 27, 1973; Allan McDougall, n.d.; Rita Kurtz, Dec. 5, 1973, all in MSF, box 65, file 14.

48 *MT*, 333–35, 347. "CBC Television Presents *The National Dream*: Building the Impossible Railway," pamphlet, 1974, MSF, box 65, file 13.

49 "Change of Address – Sept. 1/75," n.d., MSF, box 73, file 17. On program subjects, see *MT*, 361, 363; also *My Country* episode list in possession of Elsa Franklin.

50 "Franklin's idea": MCK, Elsa Franklin, July 11, 2007. For PB on the Oxford team, see *MT*, 361.

51 ECI, Barbara Sears, Dec. 8, 1986; ECI, Tyrwhitt.

52 Janice Tyrwhitt believes that it may have been PB who suggested she contact Barbara Sears; Sears herself thinks it may have been Donald Brittain; Janice Tyrwhitt to author, Sept. 28, 2007; Barbara Sears to author, Sept. 4, 2007. In *Joy of Writing* (160), PB states that it was Tyrwhitt who suggested Sears.

53 PB, *Joy of Writing*, 161; PB to JGM, June 19, 1974, PBF, box 190, "Hollywood's Canada" file. ECI, Tyrwhitt.

54 Barbara Sears to author, Sept. 4, 2007.

55 ECI, Sears.

56 ECI, Sears; ECI, Tyrwhitt. The Janice Tyrwhitt papers may be found at the York University Archives and Special Collections.

57 "Reid, Berton Honored," Vancouver *Province*, Apr. 12, 1975. *MT*, 394.

58 PB to JGM, Aug. 15, 1975; Patricia Bowles to JGM, Aug. 19, 1975; JGM to Patricia Bowles, Aug. 21, 1975; all in MSF, box 73, file 17.

59 King, *Jack*, 236, 254–55.

60 On PB in Vancouver, see "Berton Speaks at Institute on Sept. 27," unidentified clipping, Vancouver Public Library clipping files; also [John] Haslett Cuff, "A Man for All Media," *Georgia Straight*, Oct. 9–16, 1975, 3–4, 24. On PB in Montreal, see "Hollywood's Canada – PB Tour," Aug. 13, 1975, MSF, box 73, file 17.

61 Scott Beaven, "Hollywood's Canada: A Place Only an Actor Could Love," *Albertan*, Sept. 4, 1975.

62 James Eayrs, "Hollywood Plays Fast, Loose with Our History, Culture," Montreal *Gazette*, Sept. 11, 1975. Roy MacSkimming, "Masterpiece from Berton in the Sociology of Trivia," *TS*, Sept. 13, 1975. Martin Knelman, "Why Berton Likes to Tell Off Hollywood," *G&M*, Sept. 16, 1975.

63 William French, "Should the Facts Ruin a Good Story?" *G&M*, Sept. 13, 1975.

64 "Alden Nowlan's Notebook," *Atlantic Advocate*, vol. 66 (Feb. 1976), 63. Peter Harcourt, review of *Hollywood's Canada*, in *Queen's Quarterly*, vol. 83 (Autumn 1976), 501.

65 Azzi, *Walter Gordon*, 179–85.

66 JGM to PB, May 19, 1977, MSF, box 190, "Hollywood's Canada" file.

67 PB to JGM, Jan. 30, 1976, and JGM to PB, Mar. 9, 1976, MSF, box 73, file 18. JGM to Anna Porter, Mar. 31, 1975; "Berton: Hollywood's Canada. Tentative Schedule," Apr. 16, 1975; JGM to Peter Taylor, Apr. 29, 1975, all in MSF, box 73, file 17.

68 *MT*, 379, 382.

69 MCK, Franklin, July 11, 2007. ECI, Tyrwhitt.

70 JGM to PB, Mar. 4, 1977; Linda McKnight to Anna Porter, Mar. 1977; both in MSF, box 73, file 20.

71 JGM to Elsa Franklin, May 2 and Apr. 7, 1977, and Peter Taylor to JGM, May 13, 1977; all in MSF, box 73, file 20.

72 PB, *The Dionne Years: A Thirties Melodrama* (Toronto: McClelland & Stewart, 1977). On PB and *Dionne* success, see James Bawden, "Dionne Success Surprises Berton," *Hamilton Spectator*, Sept. 27, 1977. For PB's complaints, see Peter Taylor to JGM, Feb. 1, 1977; PB to JGM, Feb. 3 and Mar. 2, 1977; JGM to PB, Feb. 8, 9, and 11, 1977; JGM to Linda McKnight, Mar. 21, 1977; all in MSF, box 73, file 20.

73 Jeff Greenfield, "Quint-Hype," review of *The Dionne Years*, in *New York Times Book Review* (Dec. 10, 1978), 16. Greenfield later became a popular pundit on CNN.

74 Review of *The Dionne Years*, in *New York Review of Books*, Oct. 26, 1978.

75 Margaret Atwood, "The Berton Quintuplets Meet the Dionne Quintuplets," *SN* (Oct. 1977), 60.

76 J.L. Granatstein, "Quint Essentials," review of *The Dionne Years*, in *Books in Canada* (Aug.–Sept. 1977), 12.

77 J.L. Granatstein, *Broken Promises: A History of Conscription in Canada* (Toronto: Oxford University Press, 1977); J.L. Granatstein and R.D. Cuff, *American Dollars, Canadian Prosperity: Canadian-American Economic Relations, 1945–1950* (Toronto: Samuel Stevens, 1978).

78 PB, *My Country: The Remarkable Past* (Toronto: McClelland & Stewart, 1976). PB, *The Wild Frontier: More Tales from the Remarkable Past* (Toronto: McClelland & Stewart, 1978). On McClelland's prediction for *My Country*, see JGM to PB, Apr. 11, 1978, MSF, box 73, file 22; for sales figures, see "Wild Frontier, Nov. 3, 1978," MSF, box 73, file 22; *MT*, 384.

79 For "Christmas pot-boiler," see Sandy Gage, "Pierre Berton Still Spins a Good Yarn," review of *The Wild Frontier*, in *Last Post* (Feb. 1979), 46–47; for "frostier version," see Frits Pannekoek, review of *My Country*, in *Beaver* (Spring 1977),

61–62; for British paternalism, see Alex Inglis, review of *The Wild Frontier*, in *Canadian Historical Review*, vol. 60 (Summer 1979), 364–65, and Kevin Peterson, "Pierre Berton's Romantic (and White) Heroes," review of *The Wild Frontier*, in SN (Nov. 1978), 55–56. See also Paul Rush, "Fall Again – Berton's Here," review of *My Country*, in *Financial Post*, Oct. 9, 1976.

CHAPTER 22: A WAKE OF WHISPERS

1   Rebecca Wigod, "Pierre Berton for Breakfast," Victoria *Times-Colonist*, Oct. 1, 1981; Lynda Hurst, "He's the Pierre We All Like," TS, Nov. 2, 1980; "The Berton Years," MM, Mar. 5, 1979, 5.

2   Geoff Pevere and Greig Dymond, *Mondo Canuck: A Canadian Pop Culture Odyssey* (Scarborough, Ont.: Prentice-Hall Canada, 1996), 26.

3   PB to David Crombie, Feb. 2, 1978, PBF, box 164. Box 165 contains two thick files (unnamed) of such invitations. Among speaker's fees declined were $3,500 from the Elementary School Teachers of Kent Country (Chatham, Ontario) and $1,800 from the South Peace Teachers' Convention in Grande Prairie, Alberta.

4   Carl Tapscott to PB, Dec. 3, 1973, PBF, box 110; Barry Broadfoot to PB, n.d. (1975), and PB to Barry Broadfoot, Aug. 18, 1975, PBF, box 108. Berton sent Broadfoot's letter to the Toronto psychiatrist Daniel Cappon (who had appeared on *The Pierre Berton Show*), for "any interesting comments." Cappon found the dream "unexceptional." See Dr. Daniel Cappon to PB, Aug. 27, 1975, PBF, box 108.

5   F.H. Soward to PB, Mar. 3, 1978, PBF, box 165; PB to Browni Joerin, Mar. 3, 1978, PBF, box 164; Peter Brimelow to PB, Apr. 26, 1978, PBF, box 164; Al Purdy to PB, Oct. 2, 1978, PBF, box 188; Roy MacGregor to PB, Jan. 4, 1979, PBF, box 164; Fred Taylor to PB, Apr. 9, 1979, PBF, box 165.

6   Laura Kinrade to PB, Nov. 11, 1981, PBF, box 188, and Feb. 18, 1978, PBF, box 174; Paul Hoffman (Plasti-Fab Company) to PB, Mar. 29, 1978, PBF, box 164; Edward Weil (Cuisinart) to PB, Mar. 30, 1978, PBF, box 165; Stephen Lewis to PB, PBF, box 164.

7   JGM to PB, Mar. 29, 1978, PBF, box 201.

8   Peter C. Newman to PB, Mar. 29, 1978, PBF, box 201, "McClelland and Stewart Ltd. – General – re Pierre Berton – 1978" file; PB to Martin N. Gifford, June 7, 1979, and Martin N. Gifford to PB, May 15, 1979, PBF, box 164; Sinclair Stevens to PB, Jan. 20, 1978, and PB to Sinclair Stevens, Jan. 20, 1978, PBF, box 165.

9   Justice Donald Keith to PB, Jan. 6, 1978, PBF, box 164; Ray G. [Ray Gardner] to PB, Jan. 11, 1978, PBF, box 201, "McClelland and Stewart Ltd. – General – re Pierre Berton – 1978" file; PB to [Donald A.] Keith (Supreme Court of Ontario), Jan. 12, 1978, PBF, box 164; JGM to PB, Jan. 25, 1978, PBF, box 201, "McClelland and Stewart Ltd. – General – re Pierre Berton – 1978" file; PB, *Joy of Writing*, 168.

10   Sears's report is excerpted in PB, *Joy of Writing*, 168–70; see also MT, 384–85.

11   PB, *Joy of Writing*, 168–70; MT, 384–85.

12   PB, *Joy of Writing*, 171.

13   MT, 386.

14   "Pierre Berton: Book Sales to Date," undated list marked "For Elspeth," TF, Elspeth Cameron Papers, box 83.

15 JGM to PB, Aug. 17, 1979; quoted in King, *Jack*, 335. King indicates that McClelland was referring to *My Country* in this letter, but McClelland's reference in the letter to "Washington . . . playing chicken" (336) makes clear that he meant the War of 1812 book.

16 John McClelland, "Is There an English Canadian Literature?" *Canadian Forum* (Oct. 1970), 240–41.

17 PB, *Joy of Writing*, 212; ECI, Tyrwhitt.

18 PB, *Joy of Writing*, 214.

19 Quoted in King, *Jack*, 336–37. The bestsellers, drawn from *People Entertainment Almanac*, were (1) James A. Michener's *The Covenant*, Robert Ludlum's *The Bourne Identity*, Sidney Sheldon's *Rage of Angels*, and Judith Krantz's *Princess Daisy*. See http://caderbooks.com/best80.html. PB, *The Invasion of Canada: 1812–1813* (Toronto: McClelland & Stewart, 1980).

20 Quoted in King, *Jack*, 337.

21 Doug Fetherling, "How It Really Happened," *MM*, Sept. 15, 1980, 54–55. Review of *The Invasion of Canada* in *New York Times Book Review*, Feb. 22, 1980, 18–19, Michael Bliss, "Pierre Berton's Splendid Little War," *SN* (Sept. 1980), 55.

22 Michael Power, review of *The Invasion of Canada*, in *University of Windsor Review*, vol. 16 (Fall/Winter 1981), 131–34. Keith Walden, review of *The Invasion of Canada*, in *Canadian Historical Review*, vol. 62 (Sept. 1981), 332–33; Walden's thesis was entitled "Isaac Brock: Man and Myth" (Department of History, Queen's University, 1972).

23 C.P. Stacey, "Brock's Muniments," *Books in Canada* (Aug.–Sept. 1980), 7–8. See also C.P. Stacey, *Arms, Men, and Government: The War Policies of Canada, 1939–1945* (Ottawa: Queen's Printer, 1970).

24 PB, *Joy of Writing*, 283–84; JGM quoted at 285–86. See also King, *Jack*, 337–38.

25 *Choice*, vol. 18 (Jan. 1981), 715.

26 George Woodcock, "Dismissing a Nationalist Myth," *Quill and Quire* (Sept. 1980), 64.

27 Bliss, "Splendid Little War," 55; see also PB, *Flames across the Border, 1812–1813* (Toronto: McClelland & Stewart, 1980), 314. For an indication of Bliss's views on the protectionism of the National Policy, see Michael Bliss, "Canadianizing American Business: The Roots of the Branch Plant," in Lumsden, *Close the 49th Parallel*, 26–42.

28 The author distinctly recalls that in grades eight and eleven Canadian history courses in the Winnipeg schools he attended, the War of 1812 had six causes – no more, no fewer. He cannot now recall what they were (although he could guess), but remains awestruck by the godlike certainty of textbook authors.

29 Keith Walden, review of *Flames across the Border*, in *Canadian Historical Review*, vol. 63 (June 1982), 258–59; Brereton Greenhous, review of *Flames across the Border*, in *Ontario History*, vol. 74 (Dec. 1982), 346; C.P. Stacey, "Soldiering On," *SN* (Oct. 1981), 59–60.

30 Roger Hall, "Present at the Destruction," *Books in Canada* (Dec. 1981), 23–24; Stacey, "Soldiering On."

31 Doug Fetherling, "North-South Monologue Is a Matter of Voice," *MM* (Oct. 1981), 74; Michael Bliss, "Berton Lights Up Canadian Past," *Financial Post*, Oct. 31, 1981.

32 George Woodcock, "Berton's Judgements on the Horror of War," *Quill and Quire* (Oct. 1981), 33.

33 "Berton Celebration Dinner – An Affectionate Tribute by His Friends. Toronto, Royal York Hotel, 28th February, 1979." See the minutes of several organizing meetings, the first of which (Aug. 14, 1978) ended: "These minutes were prepared by Jack McClelland. If they don't correspond to the facts, please scream." JGM Correspondence, JMF, 1975–1980, Box 73, B: "Miscellaneous 1978 to Berton, P. 1978" file; also Dinner Program, PBF, box 204, section F. This program contains written tributes by guests.

34 On PB and radio and politics, see *MT*, 339, 390–93, 397. On PB's contribution to heritage conservation in Toronto, for example, see Kate Daller, "Toronto Meets Berton's Criteria," *TS*, Mar. 7, 1982.

35 On Berton and Dawson, see "Berton Back to Beginnings," Vancouver *Province*, Nov. 15, 1982, PBF, box 188, "Beginnings – revised final script."

36 King, *Jack*, 353–59. At the time of her departure from M&S, Porter was in charge of Seal Books, a partnership between M&S and Bantam Books in the United States, established in 1977.

37 Elsa Franklin spoke of the Berton/Franklin "good cop/bad cop" negotiating tactic in MCK, Franklin, July 11, 2007. She invariably played the role of "bad cop," holding firm for the best deal. Lynda Hurst, "He's the Pierre We All Like," *TS*, Nov. 2, 1980. See also Ron Base, "The Pierre Berton Business," *Windsor Star*, Apr. 21, 1973. Gary Ross, "The Business of Being Berton – It Isn't *All* Working on the Railroad," *Canadian* magazine, Apr. 5, 1975, 2, 6, 7.

38 Zena Cherry, "Beefeater Award for Berton," *G&M*, Nov. 20, 1982.

39 "Max Wyman" (column), Vancouver *Province*, Sept. 28, 1980; "Berton Book Sets Record," Vancouver *Province*, May 14, 1980.

40 Stephen Franklin, "Can You Make a Million Writing Canadian Books?" *Financial Post Magazine* (Oct. 1980), 80, 82, 87. The conversion from 1980 dollars to 2007 dollars is from the Bank of Canada's electronic "Inflation Calculator," available at http://www.bank-banque-canada.ca/en/rates/inflation_calc.html.

41 Franklin, "Can You Make a Million," 82, 87.

42 Alex Barris's collection of anecdotes, *Front Page Challenge: The 25th Anniversary* (Toronto: Canadian Broadcasting Corporation, 1981), 109–27, provides a useful list of guest challengers. His book *Front Page Challenge: History of a Television Legend* (Toronto: Macmillan Canada, 1999) is a more coherent account of the program and its history.

43 Barris, *Front Page Challenge: The 25th Anniversary*, 110; *MT*, 377–78.

44 John D. Morrow, M.D., to Dr. Peter Granger, June 24, 1981, PBF, box 233, file "M."

45 *MT*, 394–96.

46 "Berton Recovering," Vancouver *Province*, July 22, 1983; *MT*, 396–97; "Berton Stable," *Vancouver Sun*, July 18, 1983.

47 In a letter to Mordecai Richler early in 1983, JGM had Marge Hodgeman tell the author that his own condition had been provisionally diagnosed as "hyper-senility." Hodgeman to Richler, Jan. 4, 1983; quoted in King, *Jack*, 358.

48 *MT*, 396–97.

49 Elsa Franklin noted PB's new sense of his own mortality following his hospitalization in ECI, Franklin. See also ECI, Sid and Dorothy Katz; ECI, Elizabeth Anglin.

50 On PB's projects, see "Max Wyman," Vancouver *Province*, Sept. 28, 1980; "Chaos or Paradise – Has the Past Taught Us Any Lessons? What's Ahead for Canada?" *Financial Post*, Jan. 16, 1982; "Pierre Berton: 'Somebody Has to Write History for the Average Guy . . .,'" PB interview with Paul Kennedy, *Quill and Quire* (Oct. 1986), 7; PB, *Joy of Writing*, 202; *MT*, 387.

51 PB, *Why We Act like Canadians: A Personal Exploration of Our National Character* (Toronto: McClelland & Stewart, 1982).

52 H.A.D., review of *Why We Act like Canadians*, in *Alberta History*, vol. 31 (Winter 1983), 30; Clyde Gilmour to PB, Oct. 10, 1982, PBF, box 201, "McClelland and Stewart Ltd. – General – 1981–82" file.

53 See Robert Bothwell, *The Penguin History of Canada* (Toronto: Penguin, 2006), 461–73.

54 "Pierre Berton Explains the Great White North, Eh?" *G&M*, Oct. 21, 1982.

55 See Rebecca Dube, "Sorry, But That Is So Not Me: How the Uncool Crowd Is Actually Influencing the Purchases You Make," *G&M*, Dec. 10, 2007, L1, 4. The research in question is that of Katherine White and Darren W. Dahl, "Are All Outgroups Created Equal? Consumer Identity and Dissociative Influence," *Journal of Consumer Research*, vol. 4, no. 4 (Dec. 2007), 525–36; also Katherine White and Darren W. Dahl, "To Be or Not Be: The Influence of Dissociative Reference Groups on Consumer Preferences," *Journal of Consumer Psychology*, vol. 16, no. 4 (2006), 404–13.

56 Wigod, "Pierre Berton for breakfast"; PB, *Joy of Writing*, 395, 246.

57 Letters to and from the parties to the dispute are in PBF, box 236, file 18. See especially Eugene Benson (Chairman, Writers' Union of Canada) to Mark MacGuigan (Minister of Justice and Attorney General of Canada), Jan. 9, 1984; JGM to William Ardell (President, Cole's Bookstores), Feb. 8, 1984; PB to Eugene Benson, Mar. 26, 1984.

58 Press release, n.d., beginning "If Pierre Berton and Charles Templeton . . ."; Waddington's press release, Feb. 9, 1984 (Montreal event); press release, "Everybody's Going!!!," n.d. (Toronto event); all in PBF, box 244, file 25, "Tour de Force – Promotion."

59 PB, *The Promised Land: Settling the West 1896–1914* (Toronto: McClelland & Stewart, 1984). John Herd Thompson, review of *The Promised Land*, in *Canadian Historical Review*, vol. 66 (Sept. 1985); Ramsay Cook, "How the West Was Won," *Saturday Night* (Sept. 1984), 61–63.

60 John Bemrose, "How the Canadian West Was Won," *MM*, Sept. 3, 1984, 50; Cook, "How the West Was Won," 63.

61 Michiel Horn, review of *The Promised Land*, in *Quill and Quire* (Nov. 1984), 36–37; Hugh A. Dempsey, review of *The Promised Land*, in *Alberta History*, vol. 33 (Winter 1985), 30–31; Duncan McDowall, review of *The Promised Land*, in *Canadian Geographic*, vol. 104 (Dec. 1984–85), 78–79; John G. McConnell, review of *The Promised Land*, in *Canadian Geographer*, vol. 29 (1985), 281–83.

62 David C. Jones, "Towards a New Form in the Writing of Canadian History," *Archivaria*, vol. 20 (Summer 1985), 166–71.

63 Jones, "Towards a New Form," 171.
64 Proposal from Michael Morgan & Associates (Royal Bank), PBF, box 233, file 43, "Invitations Accepted, 1984," and file 44, "Invitations – Regrets, 1984."

CHAPTER 23: ON GUARD FOR THEE

1   Stephen Franklin died on Feb. 9, 1985, after a lengthy illness, and Elsa organized a wake for four hundred friends at the family home. PB wrote an appreciation of him for the Writers' Union of Canada: "He was a good drinker, a good talker and a wonderful audience." See the draft text of his tribute, PBF, box 235, unnamed file. For Sinclair, see Doug Fetherling, "Farewell to a Cherished Curmudgeon," *MM*, May 28, 1984, 56.

2   Jay Myers to PB, May 24, 1979, and PB to Jay Myers, May 28, 1979, PBF, box 164. Ken Porteus to PB, Jan. 30, 1979; PB to Ken Porteus, Feb. 22 and May 7, 1979, PBF, box 164, "Porteus, Ken" file. Porteus's honours paper, completed under the direction of Professor Victor Batzel, was entitled "Pierre Berton's Position in Historical Writing."

3   Jennifer M. Wilson, "'History? Write On!' An Exploration of the Literary Dimension of History as Reflected in the Work of Pierre Berton" (Waterloo, Ontario, 1985), PBF, box 383, 74–81.

4   Lorna Irvine to PB, Nov. 12 and Dec. 2, 1985, PBF, box 233. Irvine gave a presentation on the paper at the 1985 Philadelphia meetings of the Canadian Studies Society of the United States. William New, editor of *Canadian Literature*, had solicited an article on Berton from her; it appeared as "The Real Mr. Canada," in *Canadian Literature*, vol. 108 (Spring 1986), 68–79.

5   Press release, "About Books & Authors," May 25, 1985, PBF, box 340, file 45.

6   Press release, "A Sporting Proposition for Jack McClelland," n.d. (summer 1985), PBF, box 340, file 45.

7   Janet Turnbull (Seal Books) to JGM, Oct. 23, 1984, PBF, box 343, file 45. The Buhasz quotation is on www.opinionatedlesbian.com, the website of Eleanor Brown; see "I Know That Masked Woman," May 23, 2005. Michael Carin, review of *Masquerade*, in Montreal *Gazette*, Oct. 2, 1985, quoted in Wilfred Cude, "Pierre Berton," in *Profiles of Canadian Literature*, ed. Jeffrey M. Heath (Toronto: Dundurn Press, 1991), 127–34.

8   William French, "Berton Revealed as Person behind Literary Deception" and "Literary Masquerade Was a Ball for Berton," *G&M*, July 12 and 13, 1985; also "Berton Unveiling Spurs Masquerade," *G&M*, July 17, 1985. "Berton Proves You Can't Judge Book by Its Author," *Vancouver Sun*, July 12, 1985. "Here's Pierre 'Lisa' Berton," Vancouver *Province*, July 14, 1985.

9   MCK, Franklin, July 11, 2007; *SO*, 405.

10 Quoted in Irvine, "The Real Mr. Canada," 70.

11 Lisa Kroniak [PB], *Masquerade: 15 Variations on a Theme of Sexual Fantasy* (Toronto: McClelland & Stewart, 1985), 96–97.

12 Kroniak, *Masquerade*, 97, 91–92. The psychiatrist in question was Daniel Cappon, who had been a guest on PB's television show in the 1960s. For PB's consulting Cappon about the meaning of his dreams, see PB to Dr. Daniel Cappon, Sept. 2,

1973; and about the meaning of Barry Broadfoot's dream (see chapter 22), PB to Dr. Daniel Cappon, Aug. 18, 1975; Cappon to PB, Aug. 27, 1975; all in PBF, box 108.

13 MacSkimming, *Perilous Trade*, 159; King, *Jack*, 367.

14 King, *Jack*, 373–75; MacSkimming, *Perilous Trade*, 162.

15 MacSkimming, *Perilous Trade*, 163–64.

16 MCK, Franklin, July 11, 2007; *MT*, 402–03.

17 Chantel Brown (Manager, Special Services, Four Seasons Hotels) to E. Armstrong, Oct. 13, 1981, PBF, box 188.

18 "Pierre Berton and Jean Marchand among 70 Named to Order of Canada," *TS*, July 1, 1986. On PB's work schedule, see Kennedy, "Pierre Berton," 7.

19 PB, *Vimy* (Toronto: McClelland & Stewart, 1986), 319.

20 ECI, Sears; Kennedy, "Pierre Berton," 4; PB, *Vimy*, 319.

21 ECI, Tyrwhitt; ECI, Sears.

22 PB, *Vimy*, 307–08.

23 PB, *Joy of Writing*, 173.

24 Dave Macdonald to PB, Dec. 30, 1985, PBF, box 306, file 12.

25 Brereton Greenhous, "War Stories to Further Our Social Mythology," *Quill and Quire* (Aug. 1986); John Bemrose, "Vimy's Bloody Victory," *MM*, Sept. 15, 1986; Desmond Morton, "Tainted Victory," *Books in Canada* (Nov. 1986); Stephen Weatherbee, "The Battle That Forged a Nation," *Alberta Report*, Sept. 1, 1986.

Robert Craig Brown's review in the *Canadian Historical Review*, vol. 68 (Dec. 1987), 626–29, noted the book's nationalist thrust, drew attention to its descriptive nature and some errors of fact, and concluded that it was "an engaging narrative of what it was like to be in the CEF before and after Vimy Ridge." In the estimation of Tim Cook, First World War historian at the Canadian War Museum, Berton's contribution to Canadian military history in *Vimy* was sound in research and placed him at the forefront of what Cook calls "the third wave of historical Great War writing." This was an approach that focused on the individual soldiers rather than military units, institutions, or the home front. Tim Cook to author, Dec. 16, 2004. See also Tim Cook, *Clio's Warriors: Canadian Historians and the Writing of the World Wars* (Vancouver: UBC Press, 2006).

26 Other important Berton contributions to historical scholarship are *Klondike, The National Dream, The Last Spike, Hollywood's Canada, The Dionne Years, The Invasion of Canada, Flames across the Border*, and *The Promised Land*. Kennedy, "Pierre Berton," 7. Berton kept files on a number of Canadian figures who held celebrity status – Fred Davis, Charles Templeton, W.O. Mitchell, and Leonard Cohen, for example. See files in PBF, box 294.

27 Kennedy, "Pierre Berton," 6; Irvine, "The Real Mr. Canada," 70.

28 "Berton Sayse" [*sic*], *Vancouver Sun*, Oct. 22, 1985.

29 Emoke Szekeres, "Pierre Berton – Not Mr. Nationalism," *A la Carte* (Sept. 1986), 12–13. See also Levitt, *Silent Surrender*; Herschel Hardin, *A Nation Unaware: The Canadian Economic Culture* (Vancouver: J.J. Douglas, 1974). Berton had written Hardin in 1975: "It is a very important book indeed. . . . It certainly confirms a great many things that I have felt for a long time." In his view, *A Nation Unaware* was the most important book published in Canada since John Porter's *The Vertical Mosaic* in 1965. He mentioned the book often on radio and recommended it to

"numberless people" he thought would be influenced by it. PB to Herschel Hardin, May 12, 1975, PBF, box 109, "Hardin, Herschel" file.

30 "M&S Speaks Out against Free Trade," *G&M*, Nov. 6, 1987, D4. Philip J. Briggs, "The Polar Sea Voyage and the Northwest Passage Dispute," *Armed Forces & Society*, vol. 16, no. 3 (1990), 437–52. "The Future of Canada Is on the Table" (advertisement), *TS*, Sept. 8, 1987, A5. Laurier LaPierre, ed., *If You Love This Country* (Toronto: McClelland & Stewart, 1987).

31 Richard Harmston (Treasurer, Group of 78) to PB, June 29, 1987, PBF, box 236, file 36; Barry Stevens (interviewer), "The Defence White Paper: Six Comments," *Peace Magazine* (Aug.–Sept. 1987), 24. Shelley Page, "Authors Issue Plea for TV Debate on Environment," *TS*, Oct. 13, 1988, 1, 2. On fundraising for the Blood Tribe, see Roland Michener (an honorary member of the tribe) to PB, May 7, 1987, PBF, box 236, file 50; also *MT*, 333. On the Nielsen Task Force, see Rich Murray to PB, Jan. 30, 1987, and PB to Flora MacDonald, Feb. 16, 1987, PBF, box 236, file 5.

32 See PB's appointments calendar for 1984, especially Sept.–Dec., PBF, box 233, file 43; PB to Dr. Allan Knight, Sept. 14, 1984, PBF, box 233. On PB's routine, see Kennedy, "Pierre Berton," 7. On the domestic scenes, see Szekeres, "Pierre Berton – Not Mr. Nationalism," 14.

33 Fulford's contract with Collins Publishers became public in September 1987; "Memoirs Bring $80,000," *G&M*, Sept. 12, 1987. "Veteran Broadcaster Ross McLean Dead," *TS*, June 2, 1987. McLean died of a heart attack.

34 John Haslett Cuff, "TV Pioneer Fondly Remembered," *G&M*, June 3, 1987. John Allan Gould, "Berton and Sinclair: Local Heroes in the Big League's Backyard," *Quill and Quire* (Nov. 1987); John Bemrose, "Prose Portrait of a National Dreamer," *MM*, Oct. 5, 1987; William French, "A Sequential Life," *G&M*, Sept. 12, 1987; Al Purdy, "Bound for Glory," *Books in Canada* (Dec. 1987).

35 On PB's lack of introspection see French, "A Sequential Life"; also Purdy, "Bound for Glory"; Gould, "Berton and Sinclair"; James Adams, "Pierre Berton's Memoirs Provide Revealing Reading," *Edmonton Journal*, Oct. 27, 1987.

36 William Closson James, review of *Starting Out*, in *Queen's Quarterly*, vol. 95 (Autumn 1988), 719.

37 James, review of *Starting Out*, 719–20.

38 Adams, "Pierre Berton's Memoirs."

39 Max Layton, "The Astonishing Story of Rochdale," *G&M*, Sept. 12, 1987: review of David Sharpe, *Rochdale: The Runaway College* (Toronto: Anansi, 1987). Nancy Wigston, "An Acute Eye Trained on a Nasty Subject," *G&M*, Sept. 12, 1987: review of Sylvia Fraser, *My Father's House: A Memoir of Incest and Healing* (Toronto: Doubleday, 1987).

40 For helpful studies of autobiography and memoir, see James B. Mitchell, "Popular Autobiography as Historiography: The Reality Effect of Frank McCourt's *Angela's Ashes*," *Biography*, vol. 26 (Fall 2003); James Olney, *Memory and Narrative: The Weave of Life-Writing* (Chicago: University of Chicago Press, 1998), and *Autobiography: Essays Theoretical and Critical* (Princeton: Princeton University Press, 1980); Sidonie Smith and Julia Watson, *Reading Autobiography: A Guide for Interpreting Lives* (Minneapolis: University of Minnesota Press, 2001); D. Jean Clandinin and F. Michael Connelly, *Narrative Inquiry: Experience and Story in Qualitative Research* (San Francisco: Jossey-Bass, 2000).

41 Burt Heward, "Pierre Berton: A New Slant on Busy and Memorable Life," *Ottawa Citizen*, Sept. 26, 1987; Douglas Sagi, "What Do People Want to Read? Pierre Thinks He Has the Answer," *Vancouver Sun*, Sept. 12, 1987.

42 William Deverell to author, Jan. 23, 2008.

43 PB, "Identity Crisis Sinks a History," *G&M*, Sept. 19, 1987.

44 William French, "Promotion Ordeal Inspires Berton to Do Even More," *G&M*, Sept. 15, 1987; Paul Taylor, "Adult-only Shelves Feared in Libraries if Porn Bill is Law," *G&M*, Aug. 4, 1987; Liam Lacey, "Book Industry Groups Protest Anti-porn Bill," *G&M*, Sept. 17, 1987; "An Open Letter to Prime Minister Brian Mulroney on Public Broadcasting" (advertisement), *G&M*, Feb. 13, 1985, 12–13. Berton's affinity for the word *unique* is noted in French, "Promotion Ordeal."

45 *MT*, 409.

46 Wilson, "'History? Write On!'" 36–76; PB, *The Promised Land*, title page. See Northrop Frye, *The Myth of Deliverance: Reflections on Shakespeare's Problem Comedies* (Toronto: University of Toronto Press, 1984).

47 Heward, "Pierre Berton: A New Slant."

48 William French, "The Lure of the Pole," *G&M*, Sept. 17, 1988.

49 Bothwell, *Penguin History*, 480–81.

50 PB, *The Arctic Grail: The Quest for the Northwest Passage and the North Pole, 1818–1909* (Toronto: McClelland & Stewart, 1988). PB quoted in Greg Heaton, "In Search of the True North," *Alberta Report*, Sept. 26, 1988, 39. See Janice Cavell, "Comparing Mythologies: Twentieth-Century Canadian Constructions of Sir John Franklin," in Hillmer and Chapnick, *Canadas of the Mind*, 15–45.

51 Heaton, "In Search of the True North," 38–39. See also Mavor Moore, "Watching Canada Flirt with the Melting Pot," *G&M*, Sept. 12, 1987, for concerns similar to those of PB.

52 Spectator, "A Literary Launch over the Beaufort," *SN*, Dec. 1988, 96.

53 "Super Launch Planned for Berton Book," *Vancouver Sun*, Aug. 13, 1988; "Berton's Book Gets Arctic Launch," *TS*, Sept. 25, 1988. Safety regulations prohibited the consumption of alcoholic beverages aboard the oil rig.

54 Daniel Francis, review of *The Arctic Grail*, in *Canadian Geographic*, vol. 108 (Dec.–Jan. 1988–89); David Todd, "Mining the Past," *MM*, Sept. 26, 1980, N6–7. For other reviews of *The Arctic Grail*, see David Gates, "Journeys to Nowhere," *Newsweek*, Oct. 31, 1988, 74; Charles Davies, "Death in the North," *Quill and Quire* (Nov. 1988), 21; M.J. Ross, *Arctic*, vol. 42 (1989), 173–74; William Barr, *Beaver* (June 1989), 51–53; I.S. Maclaren, *American Review of Canadian Studies*, vol. 20 (Autumn 1991), 365–73.

55 Christopher Moore, "Of Ice and Men," *Books in Canada* (Nov. 1988), 30.

56 Sid Adilman, "Berton's Booked Up for Years," *TS*, Sept. 24, 1988, expanded for syndication. See Adilman, "One-Man-Band Berton Keeps Busy," *Vernon Daily News*, Sept. 30, 1988. Gzowski's book was *A Private Voice: A Journal of Reflections* (Toronto: McClelland & Stewart, 1988).

57 MacSkimming, *Perilous Trade*, 322.

58 "Marie Hohtanz Talks with Pierre Berton – Canada's Story-teller," Calgary *Herald Sunday Magazine*, Jan. 10, 1988, 6–7; also Gould, "Berton and Sinclair." In *MT* (393), PB associates the first description of him as an icon with the early 1980s. No reference to PB as an "icon" appears to exist in *G&M* and *TS* prior to 1987. It appears

that Berton's memory may have been of Gould's 1987 use of the term to describe the celebrity status PB shared with Gordon Sinclair.

59 *MT*, 411–14. PB dates this get-together as August 1989 (411), but he must have meant 1988, since Hal Straight died in February 1989. See John Armstrong, "Service Set for Colourful Ex-editor," *Vancouver Sun*, Feb. 14, 1989; Mark Hume, "News Giant Laid to Rest: Straight's Legacy Relived at Service," *Vancouver Sun*, Feb. 16, 1989.

60 Jeff Boloten (Manager of Legal Affairs, Penguin Books Canada) to Elsa Franklin, Aug. 19, 1989, PBF, box 309, "Penguin Books, 1989–1991" file. See "Berton Books Focus of a New Venture," *Vancouver Sun*, Feb. 27, 1987, for the initial deal with Penguin. Avie Bennett (Chairman and President, M&S) to Elsa Franklin, Dec. 19, 1989, PBF, box 308, "McClelland and Stewart, 1989–1993" file. Michael Owen, "Aurora Online with Pierre Berton," *Aurora* (Spring 1990). The magazine is published by Athabaska University.

61 For assessments of the Reagan years, see John Ehrman, *The Eighties: America in the Age of Reagan* (New Haven: Yale University Press, 2005); Robert M. Collins, *Transforming America: Politics and Culture during the Reagan Years* (New York: Columbia University Press, 2006).

62 On the "big-box revolution," pro and con, see Richard Vedder and Wendell Cox, *The Wal-Mart Revolution: How Big Box Stores Benefit Consumers, Workers, and the Economy* (Washington: AEI Press, 2007); John Dicker, *The United States of Wal-Mart* (New York: Penguin, 2005); Bill Quinn, *How Wal-Mart Is Destroying America and the World: And What You Can Do about It* (Ten Speed Press, 1999).

63 Michael Korda, *Making the List: A Cultural History of the American Bestseller, 1900–1999* (New York: Barnes & Noble Books, 2001), esp. 166–93.

64 "The Globe and Mail National Bestseller List," *G&M*, Oct. 6, 1990.

65 See Jedediah Purdy, "Terminal Irony," *Utne Reader*, Jan. 2, 2008, at http://www. utne.com/1998-09-01/terminal-irony.aspx; Michiko Kakutani, "The Age of Irony Isn't Over After All," *New York Times*, Oct. 9, 2001.

66 Sarah Goodman, "Berton Recounts History with a Story Teller's Flair," *Vancouver Sun*, Nov. 5, 1991; Douglas Coupland, *Generation X: Tales for an Accelerated Culture* (New York: St. Martin's Press, 1991).

67 PB, *The Great Depression, 1929–1939* (Toronto: McClelland & Stewart, 1990). Barry Broadfoot, "1929 and All That," *G&M*, Sept. 8, 1990. By the time of publication, PB himself had lost interest even in promoting the book. See *MT*, 415.

68 Charles Templeton, "Silly Exercise" (letter to editor), *G&M*, Oct. 2, 1990, A14. Broadfoot was the compiler of *Ten Lost Years: Memories of Canadians Who Survived the Depression* (Toronto: Doubleday Canada, 1973).

69 Kenneth Whyte, "Pierre Berton's Depression," *Alberta Report* (Oct. 1990), 46–47, 49–50.

70 Heather Robertson, "Defining a Decade," *Books in Canada* (Nov. 1990), 34; Peter Martin, review of *The Great Depression*, in *Canadian Forum* (Nov. 1990), 52–53; Paul Axelrod, review of *The Great Depression*, in *Labour/Le Travail*, vol. 28/29 (Spring 1992), 268–69.

71 Jeffrey Boloten (Associate Publisher, Penguin Books Canada) to Elsa Franklin, Oct. 15, 1990, PBF, box 309, "Penguin Books, 1989–1991" file.

72 PB, *Niagara: A History of the Falls* (Toronto: McClelland & Stewart, 1992). John Doyle, "Over the Brink," *Books in Canada* (Oct. 1992), 46; Peeter Kopvillem,

"Made of the Mist," MM, Oct. 12, 1992, 82; Andrew Holman, review of *Niagara*, in *Ontario History*, vol. 85 (June 1993), 198–99; Patricia Jasen, review of *Niagara*, in *Canadian Historical Review*, vol. 74 (Dec. 1993), 624–26.

73 Valerie A. Jacobs (M&S) to Elsa Franklin, Feb. 6, 1991, PBF, box 308, "McClelland and Stewart, 1989–1993" file; Carol Ricketts (Royalty Department, M&S) to PB, May 4, 1993, PBF, box 308, "McClelland and Stewart, 1989–1993" file; re *Revenge of the Tribes*, see PBF, box 331, file 39; Valerie Jacobs (Publishing Manager, M&S), to PB, Oct. 25, 1993, PBF, box 308, "McClelland and Stewart, 1989–1993" file.

74 Peter Goddard, "Pierre Berton the Newspaperman Is Back," TS, Mar. 23, 1991; Sid Adilman and Pierre Berton, "Material Men Mash Madonna and Magazine; Truth Is, She Ridicules Her Friends and Fans," TS, May 18, 1991; Patrick J. Quinn, "Pierre Berton's Fluff Does Serious Harm" (letter to editor), TS, Sept. 3, 1993; and in this context, "Doesn't James Bond Realize No Means No?" in PB, *Farewell to the Twentieth Century: A Compendium of the Absurd* (Toronto: Doubleday Canada, 1996), 135–38.

75 John Herbert, "Pierre Berton Reminds Us of Writer's Worth" (letter to editor), TS, Apr. 5, 1991. Bruce DeMara, "Fight for Fort York, Pierre Berton Urges," TS, Sept. 23, 1994. Elizabeth Davis, "Pierre Berton's Pal Deserves No Handouts" (letter to editor), TS, May 16, 1992; "Roger Caron Remanded for Assessment," G&M, Apr. 4, 1992. Caron's *Go Boy! Memoirs of a Life behind Bars* (Toronto: McGraw-Hill Ryerson, 1978) won the 1978 Governor General's Literary Award for Non-Fiction, for which see "Alice Munro Wins 2nd Book Award," G&M, Mar. 21, 1979. "Travel Costs Limit Pierre Berton's Northern Exposure," TS, Oct. 20, 1993; conversation with Dave Neufeld, Parks Canada, Whitehorse, July 2004; Laszlo Buhasz, "Travel Advisory: Pierre Berton on Rail Tour," TS, June 16, 1993.

76 Anne Dublin, *June Callwood: A Life of Action* (Toronto: Second Story Press, 2006), 67–69.

77 On Callwood, see Sylvia Fraser's evocative profile "Hurricane June," *Toronto Life* (May 2005). Sandra Martin, "June Callwood, Writer, Activist and Broadcaster 1924–2007," G&M, Apr. 16, 2007, R13.

On the "culture wars" in the United States, see for example Edward T. Linenthal and Tom Engelhardt, eds., *History Wars: The Enola Gay and Other Battles for the American Past* (New York: Metropolitan Books, Henry Holt and Company, 1996); Mary Lefkowitz, *Not Out of Africa: How Afrocentrism Became an Excuse to Teach Myth as History* (New York: Basic Books, 1996); David Harlan, *The Degradation of American History* (Chicago: University of Chicago Press, 1997). On the Canadian variant, see David Bercuson, Robert Bothwell, J.L. Granatstein, "Separating the Sheep from the Goats: Politically Incorrect Thoughts," ch. 5 of *Petrified Campus: The Crisis of Canada's Universities* (Toronto: Random House Canada, 1997), 91–124. Despite the decidedly conservative views of its authors, *Petrified Campus* contains convincing evidence of a near paranoia during the first half of the 1990s, linking the decade to the 1950s of the Cold War and the 1690s of the witchcraft trials.

78 For an indication of the stance of the federal Department of Canadian Heritage prior to the "Writing Thru Race" controversy, see the "Minister's Forum on Diversity and Culture" web page, http://www.pch.gc.ca/special/dcforum/pubs/som/index_e.cfm, especially the section on background papers – for

example, Monika Kin Gagnon and Scott Toguri McFarlane, "The Capacity of Cultural Difference." See also Robert Fulford, "George Orwell, Call Your Office," *G&M*, Mar. 30, 1994; Michael Valpy, "A Nasty Serving of Cultural Apartheid," *G&M*, Apr. 8, 1994. For critical responses, see Bronwyn Drainie, "Colour Me Politically Correct and Proud of It," *G&M*, June 25, 1994; Myrna Kostash, "You Don't Check Your Colour at the Door," *G&M*, May 9, 1994.

79 *MT*, 418–19.

80 Val Ross, "Shouting Match Mars Forum on Writers Union Conference," *G&M*, May 14, 1994, C15; *MT*, 418–19; Miro Cernetig, "The Race Controversy That Fizzled," *G&M*, July 2, 1994.

81 Doug Gibson to PB, Jan. 24, 1994, PBF, box 309, "McClelland and Stewart, 1994–95" file. The picture book carried the title *Niagara Falls: A Picture Book* when first published by M&S in 1992. M&S reissued it in 1993, presumably to improve sales, as *A Picture Book of Niagara Falls* (sometimes this edition is called *Pierre Berton's Picture Book of Niagara Falls*). At 160 pages, and with 92 black-and-white archival photographs and 135 contemporary ones, it should not be confused with PB's 480-page primary study, *Niagara: A History of the Falls* (Toronto: McClelland & Stewart, 1992).

82 PB to Doug Gibson, Jan. 31, 1994, Doug Gibson to PB, Feb. 11, 1994, PBF, box 309, "McClelland and Stewart, 1994–95" file.

83 PB to Doug Gibson, Feb. 15, 1994, PBF, box 309, "McClelland and Stewart, 1994–95" file.

84 Doug Gibson to Frank Newfeld, Feb. 21, 1994, PBF, box 309, "McClelland and Stewart, 1994–95" file.

85 Frank Newfeld to PB, Feb. 28, 1994, PBF, box 309, "McClelland and Stewart, 1994–95" file; Frank Newfeld to Doug Gibson, Feb. 28, 1994; PB to Doug Gibson, Mar. 9, 1994.

86 Gibson not a "real publisher": MCK, Franklin, July 11, 2007. On dates of disbursements, see Elsa Franklin to Doug Gibson, Mar. 9, 1994, PBF, box 309, "McClelland and Stewart, 1994–95" file.

87 PB to JGM, Mar. 1, 1994; PB to JGM, Mar. 9, 1994; also JGM to PB, Aug. 12 and Sept. 8, 1994, all in PBF, box 308, "McClelland, Jack" file. McClelland made several attempts at writing his memoirs, but they remained unpublished fragments of a colourful life.

88 Beland H. Honderich to PB, Jan. 5, 1994, and John A. Honderich to PB, Oct. 11, 1994, PBF, box 308, file H.

89 Rev. James G. Macdonald to the Editor, *TS*, Oct. 1, 1994. Pete McGarvey, "Pierre Berton Deserved Better," *Orillia Packet and Times*, Oct. 8, 1994.

90 Elsa Franklin to Avie Bennett, Nov. 8, 1994, PBF, box 309, "McClelland and Stewart, 1994–95" file; PB (draft letter) to Avie Bennett, n.d., beginning, "It is with considerable regret that I find I cannot publish MY TIMES with M&S." Misfiled in PBF, box 306, file 11: "McClelland and Stewart, 1976–88."

91 Avie Bennett to Elsa Franklin, Dec. 8, 1994, PBF, box 309, "McClelland and Stewart, 1994–95" file. Val Ross, "Reader, Heal Thyself," *G&M*, June 15, 1991, C1.

92 Avie Bennett to Elsa Franklin, Dec. 8, 1994. The breakdown of unearned advances was as follows: Niagara book $136,000; Adventures series $135,000.

CHAPTER 24: ICONOCLAST AND ICON

1   PB, *My Times: Living with History 1947–1995* (Toronto: Doubleday Canada, 1995). On PB's advance, see Doubleday Canada, royalty statement, July 1998, PBF, box 410, "Correspondence – Doubleday" file. In addition, the Book-of-the-Month Club paid an advance of $22,500. Philip Marchand, "A Career Made Throwing Snowballs at Top Hats," *TS*, Sept. 9, 1995, L15.

2   Christopher Harris, "CBC Budget Cuts Kill Front Page Challenge," *G&M*, Apr. 14, 1995, A2 (under "Quiz, Hymn Shows cut").

3   Michael Valpy, "No More Front Page Challenge. No More Canada?" *G&M*, Apr. 15, 1995, D2. On the use of demographic surveys in the television industry, see Ella Taylor, *Prime-Time Families: Television Culture in Post-war America* (Berkeley: University of California Press, 1989).

4   Rick Salutin, "Some Public Thoughts on Privatization," *G&M*, May 12, 1995, D1.

5   Valpy, "No More Front Page Challenge." Michael Valpy, "Reflections on the Day of Crucifixion," *G&M*, Apr. 8, 1995.

6   Peter Buitenhuis, "Pierre Berton: Canada's Mirror Looks Back," *G&M*, Sept. 16, 1995, C26; Lynne Van Luven, "National Dreamer," *Quill and Quire* (Nov. 1995), 26; Marchand, "A Career"; Anne Denoon, "The Great Recycler," *Books in Canada* (Nov. 1995), 29, 32.

7   Denoon, "The Great Recycler," 32; Marchand, "A Career"; Van Luven, "National Dreamer"; Korda, *Making the List*, 197–99, 208–15.

8   Allen Forbes, "The 16th Annual International Festival of Authors October 11 to 21, 1995," *G&M*, Sept. 23, 1995, C23; "Festival Salutes Berton," *G&M*, Aug. 14, 1995; Val Ross, "Captain Canada at 75," *G&M*, Oct. 7, 1995.

9   Ross, "Captain Canada at 75."

10 MCK, Patsy Berton; MCK, Penny Berton.

11 *MT*, 417.

12 *MT*, 417; Nicolaas [*sic*] van Rijn, "Crowds Will Step Out for Canada," *TS*, Oct. 29, 1995, A6; Leslie Scrivener, "25,000 Cry Out to Save Country," *TS*, Oct. 30, 1995, A1, 9; "Referendum Coverage Abounds," *G&M*, Oct. 30, 1995, C2. Davies is quoted in Peter C. Newman, "Davies, Robertson: A Farewell," *MM*, Dec. 18, 1995, online at www.thecanadianencyclopedia.com. Lynda Hurst, "Why Canadians Decry the Patriot Game," *TS*, Nov. 5, 1995, F1, 4.

13 Hurst, "Why Canadians Decry"; Thomas Walkom, "Political Tomes Reflect National Malaise," *TS*, Dec. 2, 1995; "National Bestseller List," *G&M*, Nov. 11, 2005, C23.

14 Philip Marchand, "Newman Retains Competitive Edge," *TS*, Oct. 7, 1997, E7. "Temagami Battle Far from Over," *TS*, July 14, 1996, B2. Philip Marchand, "Why Criminalizing Hate Speech Aids Censorship, Not Anti-racism," *TS*, Sept. 21, 1996. Judy Stoffman, "Writers Press Chrétien," *TS*, Mar. 5, 1997; Antonia Zerbisias, "250,000 Sign Save-CBC Appeal," *TS*, Apr. 22, 1997, D5. Peter Goddard, "CBC's Revolution Has Echoes in Past," *TS*, June 28, 1997, M13. "Today's Question" (FM signal to CBC?), *TS*, Oct. 20, 1997, A17. "Eaton's as Icon No More: Berton," *TS*, Aug. 18, 1997, E1, E2.

15 Robert Wright, "A Pair of CD-ROMs That Strike Gold," *TS*, May 16, 1996, H3; "Winter Cottage Country Show" (advertisement), *TS*, Nov. 5, 1997; Christopher

Hume, "Choir Displays Canuck Heart," *TS*, June 9, 1997; Philip Marchand, "Turning History into a Great Adventure," *TS*, Jan. 12, 1997, B2.

16 Geoff Pevere, "Are You Ready for Life after Gzowski?" *TS*, May 3, 1997, K3.

17 "Journalist Ron Collister's Career Spanned 4 Decades," *TS*, June 7, 1997, A19; "Fred Davis Loved a 'Challenge,'" *TS*, July 6, 1996, A10; "Tribute to Gilmour," *TS*, Fri. Nov. 28, 1997, D10; "Book Publisher in Stable Condition," *G&M*, Nov. 27, 1996, C5; Judy Stoffman, "M&S at 90 – Jack Flash to 'Responsible' Avie," *TS*, Sept. 21, 1996, G2.

18 PB, *Farewell to the Twentieth Century: A Compendium of the Absurd* (Toronto: Doubleday Canada, 1996), epigraph at page 7; Doubleday Canada, royalty statement, Apr. 15, 2000, PBF, box 410, file 11, "Correspondence – Doubleday"; PB, *Winter* (Toronto: Stoddart, 1994); PB, *The Great Lakes* (Toronto: Stoddart, 1996); PB, *My War with the Twentieth Century* (Garden City: Doubleday, 1965).

19 PB, *Farewell to the Twentieth Century*, 40.

20 Bill Richardson, "Facing a New Era, Canadian Style," *G&M*, June 22, 1996, C22.

21 Joe Berridge, "We Are What You Like," *G&M*, June 22, 1996, C22; Stephen Smith, "Berton's Really Not Funny," *Quill and Quire* (July 1996), 50; Linwood Barclay, "Berton Takes Light Look at 20th Century," *TS*, July 13, 1996, H15.

22 Peter C. Newman, "When Politicians say, 'I Promise,'" *G&M*, Oct. 25, 1997, D19; Jeremy Mouat, "The Power without the Glory," *G&M*, Nov. 29, 1997, C1; Jeffrey Simpson, "The Men Who Made the Deal That Made Canada," *G&M*, Oct. 25, 1997, D19.

23 See Doubleday Canada, royalty statement, Apr. 15, 2000, PBF, box 410, file 11, "Correspondence – Doubleday." The advance on the paperback edition was $27,500. Peter C. Newman, "1967: More Than a Centennial," *G&M*, Sept. 6, 1997, D10 (LaMarsh quoted by Newman); PB, *1967: The Last Good Year* (Toronto: Doubleday Canada, 1997), 389–99.

24 PB, *1967: Canada's Turning Point* (Toronto: Seal Books, 1998), 385–86.

25 Judy Daniel to PB, Feb. 20, 1999, PBF, box 410, "Correspondence – D – 1999–2000" file; Marianne Ackerman, "Two Very Good Years," *Quill and Quire* (Nov. 1997), 34.

26 For sales figures of *1967*, see Doubleday Canada, royalty statement, Apr. 15, 1999, PBF, box 410, file 11, "Correspondence – Doubleday." Sales of *1967* reached 16,072 by 2000. See the April 2000 royalty statement in the same location.

27 PB, *Marching as to War: Canada's Turbulent Years 1899–1953* (Toronto: Doubleday Canada, 2001). About starting on the war book, see Brian Gorman, "Canada's Centennial Was the 'Last Good Year,'" *Ottawa Sun*, Oct. 30, 1997. For Berton's cinematic approach, see "Digging Deep," ch. 5 of PB, *Joy of Writing*, 128–51.

28 See Barbara and Ormond Mitchell, *Mitchell: The Life of W.O. Mitchell: The Years of Fame, 1948–1998* (Toronto: McClelland & Stewart, 2005), 395–98.

29 Mitchell and Mitchell, *Mitchell*, 155–56, 160–61; also conversation with Barbara Mitchell, Trent University, January 10, 2007. "The Alien" proved to be a failed novel and was not published.

30 Mitchell and Mitchell, *Mitchell*, 155–56. "Any novel will probably involve a search, and a questioning – and, in most cases, an answer," the Mitchells wrote (175).

31 "Spotlight – Canadian Walk of Fame," *TS*, Mar. 5, 1998; "Putting Stars Where No One Else Could," *TS*, June 14, 1998, B3; "Join Canada's Own Pierre Berton"

(advertisement), *TS*, Apr. 18, 1998; J19; Doug Gibson to PB, Apr. 26, 1998, and PB to Doug Gibson, Feb. 24, 1998, PBF, box 411, file 3.

32 PB to Doug Gibson, Apr. 26, May 12, May 19, 1998; Doug Gibson to PB, June 17, 1998; Elsa Franklin to Doug Gibson, June 18, 1998; Avie Bennett to PB, Feb. 17, 2000; all in PBF, box 411, file 3. The statements of royalty earnings for the period in question are also in this location.

33 Geoff Pevere, preface to PB, *Worth Repeating: A Literary Resurrection* (Toronto: Doubleday Canada, 1998), xiii–xvi.

34 Pevere, preface to PB, *Worth Repeating*, xiv–xv; Michael Holmes, review of *Worth Repeating*, in *Quill and Quire* (June 1998); Allan Levine, "Putting the Pieces Together Again," *Books in Canada* (Oct. 1998), 22, 31.

35 *Pierre Berton: Canada's Arrogant Icon* (Edmonton: Idea Factory, 1999).

36 Dave Sutherland to PB, Jan. 7, 1999, PBF, box 411, "Correspondence – S, 1999–2000" file; Jeanne Hopkins to PB, Jan. 25, 1999, box 410, "Correspondence – H, 1999–2000" file; Dinah Christie to PB, Jan. 12, 1999, PBF, box 411, "Correspondence – C, 1999–2000" file; Margaret Florczak to PB, Jan. 1999, PBF, box 410, file 13, "Correspondence – F"; Sue Parker to PB, Jan. 25, 1999, PBF, box 411, file 8, "Correspondence – P – 1999–2000."

37 On PB's evacuation from Cuba, see Warren Gerard, "Pierre Berton, 84: Canadian Icon was Outstanding Journalist," *TS*, Dec. 2, 2004. Janice Tyrwhitt to PB, Mar. 17, 1999, PBF, box 411, "Correspondence – S – 1999–2000" file; PBF; Timothy Findley to PB, Apr. 7, 1999, PBF, box 410, "Correspondence – F – 1999–2000"; Graeme Gibson to PB, Mar. 18, 1999, PBF, box 410, "Correspondence – G – 1999–2000" file.

38 On *Niagara*, see Brendan David (Product Controller, M&S) to PB, July 13, 1999, PBF, box 411, file 3, "Correspondence: McClelland & Stewart"; Lori Calham (Canadians for Medical Progress) to PB, July 21, 1999, PBF, box 410, file 2, "Correspondence – B – 1999–2000." John Herbert to PB, Sept. 13, 1999, PBF, box 410, file 17, "Correspondence – H – 1999–2000." On the Drainie Award, see John McKay, "Milgaard, DaVinci Top Gemini Winners," *Kingston Whig-Standard*, Nov. 8, 1999. Henry J. Pankratz (Chair, Canadian Club of Toronto) to PB, Nov. 8, 1999, PBF, box 410, file 2, "Correspondence – B – 1999–2000."

39 PB to Penny Dickens (Writers' Union of Canada), Feb. 11, 1999, PBF, box 410, "Correspondence – D – 1999–2000" file. On the aspiring author: PB to Stephanie Beverley, Sept. 27, 1999, PBF, box 410, "Correspondence – B – 1999–2000" file. PB to Cathy Nobleman (Research & Regional Coordinator, Honours Directorate), n.d. (Sept.–Oct. 1999), PBF, box 411, "Order of Canada" file. PB to George Powell, PBF, box 411, file 8, "Correspondence – P – 1999–2000." Heather Robertson to PB, Dec. 20, 1999, PBF, box 411, "Correspondence – R – 1999–2000" file. Emily Bradshaw to Rick Searle, Dec. 20, 1999 (enclosing fax of PB's introduction), PBF, box 411, "Correspondence – S – 1999–2000" file; also Rick Searle, *Phantom Parks: The Struggle to Save Canada's National Parks* (Toronto: Key Porter, 2000).

40 John May to PB, Aug. 18, 1999, PBF, box 411, file 1, "Correspondence – M – 1999–2009"; Vivien Bowers to PB, box 410, file 2, "Correspondence – B – 1999–2000."

41 On the purchase and early operations of Berton House, see Dan Davidson, "Berton House Is Finally Complete," *Klondike Sun*, June 23, 1998; for PB's view

of the retreat's purpose, see PB to Max Fraser, Jan. 9, 2000, PBF, box 410, file 3, "Correspondence – Berton House, 1999–2000."

42 PB to Ron Brydges (Council of Canadians, Niagara Chapter), Jan. 9, 2000, PBF, box 410, file 2, "Correspondence – B"; PB to Art Jones, Jan. 21, 2000, PBF, box 410, file 20, "Correspondence – J"; PB to Cy Porter, Jan. 23 and May 2, 2000, PBF, box 411, file 8, "Correspondence – P."

43 Warren Gerard, "A Work in Progress – Pierre Berton, Who Won a Vast Audience for Canadian History, Is Slowing Down – a Little," *TS*, June 10, 2000; Canadian Press, "Writer Pierre Berton Dead at 84," *TS*, Nov. 30, 2004, online edition; Allan Fotheringham, "A Bash to Remember," *MM*, July 17, 2000.

44 Judy Stoffman, "Top Book Firm Given to U of T," *TS*, June 27, 2000, A2; Virginia Galt, "McClelland & Stewart Gives Itself to U of T," *G&M*, June 27, 2000, A1, 6; Rod Mickleburgh, "Catamaran Takes on Arctic to Save Pieces of History," July 1, 2000, *G&M*, A6; "Eaton's as Icon."

45 Eric Reguly, "Don't Weep for CP, Canada," B1, and Guy Dixon, "Canadian Pacific's $18-billion Breakup," B1, *G&M*, Feb. 14, 2001; Martin Knelman, "The Last Chapter in McClelland's Legacy," *TS*, July 2, 2000, D2; James P. Delgado, "A Myth Begins to Melt," *G&M*, Aug. 26, 2000, A15.

46 Smith quoted in John Allemang, "The Original Canadian Idol," *G&M*, Aug. 23, 2003, F1.

47 "Russell Smith" (column), *G&M*, Aug. 12, 2000, R5; Heather Mallick, "I Hate Frank Swoonatra, Especially for That Damn Song," *G&M*, Sept. 23, 2000, R9; William Thorsell, "What Is a Duddy Kravitz to Do?" *G&M*, Aug. 27, 2001, A13.

48 Sid Adilman, "No Retirement in Sight for Pierre Berton – Captain Canada Celebrates 50 Years of Writing Books," *TS*, Mar. 24, 2001, J6; Gayle MacDonald, "When Friends Fall Out," *G&M*, May 2, 2001, R1, 7; Anthony Wilson-Smith, "Our King of Convergence," *MM*, Sept. 10, 2001, 2; Judy Stoffman, "Pierre Berton Soldiers On – Marching as to War Near Top of Bestseller List," *TS*, Oct. 7, 2001.

49 Lauren Mechling, "Iconic Author Celebrates 50-year Career with Fundraiser," *National Post*, Apr. 27, 2001, A16; "Literati Will Celebrate Pierre Berton's 50th Anniversary as a Writer," *National Post*, Apr. 25, 2001; Rick Salutin, "Pierre Berton, Eric Nicol: Defining the Columnist's Art," *G&M*, Apr. 27, 2001, A19. As was his wont, Allan Fotheringham used both occasions for top-of-the-head *Maclean's* columns on Berton in his salad days. See "A Bash to Remember"; and "Tall Teller from the Yukon," *MM*, May 2, 2001.

50 PB, *Joy of Writing*, 122ff.

51 Judy Stoffman, "Berton's New Book Filled with Errors: Historian," *TS*, Aug. 5, 2001, A2.

52 Hans Werner, "Berton Keeps Marching On," *TS*, Sept. 16, 2001, D13; Modris Eksteins, "Onward, Pierre Berton," *G&M*, Sept. 15, 2001, D5.

53 PB, *Joy of Writing*, 251; PB, *Marching as to War*, 591.

54 PB interviewed by Rudyard Griffiths for Chapters.indigo.ca, on the occasion of publication of the Anchor Canada paperback edition of *Marching as to War*. Available at: http://www.chapters.indigo.ca/books (click on the title, then scroll down to "Bookclub Guide").

55 Liane Fauler, "Prove You're Canadian, Pierre Berton Told," *Vancouver Sun*, Dec. 12, 2001; Sid Adilman, "Feds Question Whether Pierre Berton Is Canadian,"

Hamilton Spectator, Dec. 11, 2001; Canadian Press, "Pierre Berton Doesn't Have to Prove He's Canadian, Govt. Dept. Admits Error," *TS*, Dec. 13, 2001.

56 MCK, Patsy Berton. Allison Dunfield, "Shuster Farewell Left Them Laughing One More Time," *G&M*, Jan. 17, 2002, A8; "'Such Laughter and Such Superb Joy' as Friends Gather for Frank Shuster's Funeral," *National Post*, Jan. 17, 2002, 1. Francesco Contini, "Weekends: Local Diversions," *G&M*, Apr. 3, 2002, T3. "Canadian Celebrities Denounce Iraq Tension," *Calgary Herald*, Sept. 26, 2002, A2. Marcus Gee, "Stick to Your Poetry and Pianos," *G&M*, Sept. 27, 2002, A15.

57 "He's Good between the Covers" (advertisement), *G&M*, Sept. 28, 2002, D18. On the matter of who better reflected the nation's mood, see Lawrence Martin, "It's Not Canadians Who've Gone to the Right, Just Their Media," *G&M*, Jan. 23, 2003, A19: "In a middle-of-the-road country that elects Liberals as its natural governing party, it is indeed strange when the right has such preponderant weight in political commentary at the national papers"; Lawrence Martin, "Why Canadians Don't Care for the Grand Old Party," *G&M*, Jan. 24, 2008, A17. See also Thomas Frank, "Triangulation Nation: Journalism in the Age of Markets," ch. 9 of Frank, *One Market under God: Extreme Capitalism, Market Populism, and the End of Economic Democracy* (New York: Anchor Books, 2000), 307–40.

58 PB, *Cats I Have Known and Loved* (Toronto: Doubleday Canada, 2002). Elizabeth Abbott, "Cats Got Their Tongues," *G&M*, Oct. 19, 2002, D10. Also under review were cat books by the former broadcaster Pamela Wallin and the errant Freudian Jeffrey Masson. I am grateful to Patsy Berton for locating and lending me letters her father wrote to her, written mainly in the 1970s.

59 Chris Mason, "Canadian Author Speaks at Carleton," *Charlatan*, Mar. 20, 2003, 22.

60 Elsa Franklin to author, August 2002. The author conducted his first extensive interview with PB on August 12, 2002.

61 See, for example, Joel Yanofsky, "Pierre Berton and Norman Mailer on The Craft of Writing," Montreal *Gazette*, Feb. 8, 2003, H1; Nathan Whitlock, "'Suck Up to Your Editor' – Pierre Berton Explains All the Drudgery," *TS*, Mar. 16, 2003, D12; Denny Boyd, "History Maker: The Extraordinary Oeuvre – and Occasional Lapses – of a Canadian Icon," *BC Business*, Apr. 1, 2003, 21. PB's main "lapse" during his interview with Boyd was not to have remembered Boyd's name. The faux pas made for a rather churlish column.

62 Elaine O'Connor, "Good Writers Have 'an Animal Inside,'" *Ottawa Citizen*, Mar. 17, 2003, A3; Mason, "Canadian Author Speaks at Carleton." The Kesterton Lecture was named after the late Wilfred Kesterton, a Carleton professor and pioneering historian of journalism in Canada. "Charlotte Gray Wins Pierre Berton Award," *G&M*, Sept. 13, 2003, R17.

63 Sarah Hampson, "Pierre Berton: The National Dream Weaver," *G&M*, May 24, 2003, R3.

64 Allemang, "The Original Canadian Idol," F1, 2.

CHAPTER 25: LAST WORDS

1 Unless otherwise noted, details of Berton family life in this chapter are drawn from MCK: Penny Berton, Patsy Berton, Pamela Berton (Feb. 22, 2006), Janet Berton (Feb. 2, 2007), and Beverley Straight.

2 Allan Fotheringham, "Creighton Was a Newspaper Giant," *Niagara Falls Review*, Jan. 16, 2004, A4; John McKay, "'Great Wit' Entertained Canadians for Decades," *Ottawa Citizen*, Jan. 17, 2004, A9; Joan Ransberry, "Alex Barris Was TV Star," *Markham Economist & Sun*, Jan. 22, 2004, 1; Robert Fulford, "Publishing's Prince Put Writers First," *National Post*, June 15, 2004; Rebecca Caldwell, "Jack McClelland Dead at 81," *G&M*, June 15, 2004, A9; Canadian Press, "Influential Publisher Presided over Canadian Literature's Coming of Age," *G&M*, June 15, 2004, A9; also Judy Stoffman, "Publisher Who Loved Writers," *TS*, June 15, 2004, A1.

3 Kate Jaimet, "Authors Condemn 'Outrageous' Searches: Writers Decry 'Intimidation' Tactics by RCMP," *Ottawa Citizen*, Jan. 23, 2004, A6; "Celebrities Urge Prime Minister to Avoid Missile Defence Plan," St. Catharines *Standard*, Mar. 19, 2004, A6; Chris Lamb, "Berton OK with Racy Ad," *Calgary Herald*, May 13, 2004, A2.

4 MCK, Penny Berton; MCK, Patsy Berton. "That whole summer was bad for him," Patsy said.

5 The author observed PB's performance from a seat at a Berton family table, near the podium. See Allan Fotheringham, "Everything You Wanted to Know about Berton and Then Some, Too," Welland *Tribune*, Oct. 8, 2004, A6.

6 Gessell's story appeared in different forms and lengths, according to the wishes of editors of papers in the CanWest chain. See Paul Gessell, "Canadian Identity: Pierre Berton Defined This Country," *Ottawa Citizen*, Sept. 26, 2004, C11; Gessell, "Pierre Berton Closes Book on 50-year Writing Career: Esteemed Author's 50th Book Goes on Sale This Week," *Ottawa Citizen*, Sept. 26, 2004, E3; Gessell, "Pierre Berton: My Work Is Done," *Ottawa Citizen*, Sept. 28, 2004, A1, 2.

7 Kevin Bazzana, *Wondrous Strange: The Life and Art of Glenn Gould* (Toronto: McClelland & Stewart, 2003); Northrop Frye, *The Double Vision: Language and Meaning in Religion* (Toronto: University of Toronto Press, 1991); PB, *Prisoners of the North* (Toronto: Doubleday Canada, 2004), 3.

8 Pat Donnelly, "Bringing Northern History Alive," Montreal *Gazette*, Oct. 23, 2004, H4; also Alex Good, "Cultural Bondage," Kitchener-Waterloo *Record*, Nov. 6, 2004, P3. Kim Hughes, "The Obsessed: Pierre Berton Finds Fellow Romantics in Thrall to His Beloved North," *TS*, Nov. 14, 2004. For bestseller lists, see *G&M*, Oct. 30, 2004, D28; Victoria *Times-Colonist*, Oct. 10, 2004, D10; see also *Montreal Gazette*, Nov. 20, 2004, H4.

9 PB, "Survivor, the Arctic Original," *G&M*, Aug. 28, 2004, F1; PB, "King of the Gold Diggers," *G&M*, Sept. 25, 2004, F1; Pat Donnelly, "Always an Idealist," Montreal *Gazette*, Oct. 16, 2004, H5; "Readings at Roselawn," Welland *Tribune*, Sept. 29, 2004, B13; "Books," *Ottawa Citizen*, Sept. 11, 2004, N9; Lynn Peppas, "A Reading to Talk About," Welland *Tribune*, Nov. 1, 2004, B8.

10 Information in this paragraph and the two preceding it is drawn from Canadian Press, "Historian Pierre Berton Opens Library in Vaughan, Ont., Named in His Honour," *TS*, Oct. 17, 2004; Jim Wilkes, "Berton's Name Adorns New Vaughan Library," *TS*, Oct. 18, 2004, B4; Jim Wilkes, "Pierre Berton 'Mad as Hell' about Road," *TS*, Sept. 20, 2004, B2; also a telephone conversation between Elsa Franklin and the author, February 10, 2008.

11 Canadian Press, "Pierre Berton Gives Mercer Dopey Lesson," Oct. 16, 2004; Joseph Brean, "Pierre Berton Offers 40 Years of Rolling Expertise: 'Prefer Cone-shaped Joint,'" *National Post*, Oct. 16, 2004, A3; Bill Dunphy, "Cops Don't Appreciate Pierre Berton's Input," *Hamilton Spectator*, Oct. 22, 2004, A6; Pat Donnelly, "Berton's Advice," *Vancouver Sun*, Oct. 30, 2004, A8.

12 "Berton's Poetic Crusade," *TS*, Oct. 28, 2004, A27; "Another Chance for Steven Truscott," Victoria *Times-Colonist*, Oct. 29, 2004, A10.

13 PB's reading is noted in Liza Cooper, "Northern Light," *National Post*, Oct. 23, 2004, RB8. A.N. Wilson, *The Victorians* (London: Hutchinson, 2002); Richard Barber, *The Holy Grail: Imagination and Belief* (London: Allen Lane, 2004); Margaret MacMillan, *Paris 1919* (New York: Random House, 2002); Stephen Birmingham, *Duchess: The Story of Wallis Warfield Windsor* (Boston: Little, Brown, 1981); Lynn Truss, *Eats, Shoots & Leaves* (New York: Gotham Books, 2004).

14 J.L. Granatstein, "A Professor Finds That Pop History Is Trivial, Hasty, Sloppy and Demeaning," *G&M*, Jan. 29, 1977. Granatstein's statement at the ceremony: J. Kelly Nestruck, "1812, with Tiramisu: The Anti-social-historian Wins Award Won by Social Historians," *National Post*, Nov. 27, 2004, 7. On Granatstein's criticism of academic historians among other groups, see Jack Granatstein, *Who Killed Canadian History?* (Toronto: HarperCollins Canada, 1999). PB's rebuttal is reproduced in PB, *Joy of Writing*, 274–77.

In 1999, this author published a critique of Granatstein's reductionist argument, which effectively limited "real" Canadian history to the study of politics, diplomacy, and the military. That he was fully in accord with Granatstein's concern for the erasure of a sense of the Canadian past from public memory did not fall within the compass of the article. See A.B. McKillop, "Who Killed Canadian History? A View from the Trenches," *Canadian Historical Review*, vol. 80, no. 2 (June 1999), 269–99.

15 John McKay, "Author Berton Made an Impact on All Media, Not Just Printed Word," Canadian Press report, Dec. 1, 2004 online at the Friends of Canadian Broadcasting website, www.friends.ca/News/Friends_News/2004.asp: "The CBC National . . . hastily shuffled its Tuesday night lineup, giving Berton's death a good 15 minutes of lead airtime before getting to Bush coverage from Ottawa." The author watched the telecast live and timed the coverage. Several attempts by the author to contact producers at *The National* about the program's story coverage on November 30, 2004, failed to elicit a response.

16 Sandra Martin to the author, Jan. 29, 2008. A few days later, at a party in Toronto, Penny was introduced to Martin. "She told me how everyone in the newsroom was so excited that they could actually bump Bush off the front page," Penny said; MCK, Penny Berton.

17 See *G&M* (Ottawa Edition), Dec. 1, 2004, A1; *TS*, Dec. 1, 2004, A1; *National Post*, Dec. 1, 2004, A1; Joel Baglole, "Canadian Icon Dies at 84," and James Cowan, "Canada's Chronicler Spoke His Mind," *Vancouver Sun*, Dec. 1, 2004, 1, 4, 5.

18 Jack Austin, "Senators' Statements – Tributes," *Debates of the Senate* (Hansard), vol. 142, no. 21, Wednesday, Dec. 1, 2004. Cartoons by Aislin, Montreal *Gazette*, Dec. 2, 2004, A22; Brian Gable, *G&M*, Dec. 2, 2004, A20; Michael de Adder, *National Post*, Dec. 6, 2004, A17.

19 "In Memoriam – TWUC Members Remember Pierre Berton," Writers' Union of Canada website (no longer available). For a sample of letters to the editor, see "Voiced: Remembering Pierre Berton," *TS*, Dec. 1, 2004; "Proud to Be Canadian," *TS*, Dec. 3, 2004; "The Berton Legacy – 'Without Question the Greatest Canadian,'" *G&M*, Dec. 4, 2004, F8; Letters to the Editor, *London Free Press*, Dec. 4, 2004. For journalistic apologies, see Jim Chapman, "Berton Rules Pay Dividends," *London Free Press*, Dec. 4, 2004; Trevor Lautens, "Pierre Berton, a Prolific Icon Remembered," *TS*, Dec. 6, 2004, E1, 7; Farley Mowat, "As Generous a Man as Ever Lived," *G&M*, Dec. 4, 2004, R7. "Editorial: Pierre Berton, 1920–2004," *TS*, Dec. 1, 2004; Canadian Journalism Foundation advertisement, *G&M*, May 28, 2005, A8.

20 "Iris Nowell: Wonderful memories of Pierre Berton," Writers' Union of Canada website (no longer available). John Torrance to the editor, *TS*, Dec. 3, 2004; Patrick White to editor, *G&M*, Dec. 2, 2004. "Pierre Berton: True Patriot's Love," Montreal *Gazette*, Dec. 2, 2004.

21 The author was present at the event and recorded it. See also Andrew Davidson, "Family, Friends Pay Tribute to Beloved Berton," *G&M*, Dec. 8, 2004, A18; "Her Excellency the Right Honourable Adrienne Clarkson Remarks on the Occasion of a Memorial Service for Pierre Berton," http://www.gg.ca/media/doc.asp?lang=e& DocID=4347; J. Kelly Nestruck, "Who's Who Pays Tribute to 'Dynamo' Pierre Berton," *National Post*, Dec. 8, 2004, AL3; Martin Knelman, "A Glowing Farewell, Courtesy of Elsa," *TS*, Dec. 8, 2004, A3; John McKay, "In Praise of a Canuck Legend," *Toronto Sun*, Dec. 8, 2004, 38–39. The Elsa Franklin quote is in Knelman, "A Glowing Farewell."

22 PB, "Laura Secord's Candy-Coated Legend," *G&M*, Dec. 4, 2004, F8.

23 PB to "Dear Lucy," n.d. (1942), PBF, box 237, file 28.

24 *DH*, 130.

ACKNOWLEDGEMENTS

—

During the course of research for this book, and in the writing of it, I have accumulated many debts. The first of these, of course, is to Pierre Berton. He agreed to co-operate fully with a writer unknown to him, and he remained true to his word. Mr. Berton asked nothing of me except fidelity to truth, and I have tried my best to meet the request.

I am also grateful to members of the Berton family. They were perhaps wary of a stranger asking sometimes intrusive questions about their lives and that of their loved one, but each proved unfailingly co-operative and generous with time and memory. At one time or another, I have spoken to most members of Pierre Berton's immediate family, but I am especially grateful to Janet, Penny, Pamela, and Patsy Berton for their encouragement and assistance. For similar reasons, I am in the debt of Lucy Woodward and Beverley Straight. Janice Tyrwhitt and Barbara Sears kindly provided information that helped eliminate errors in the story I was trying to tell.

My research has at times led into byways of Pierre Berton's private life that his family and friends would likely have preferred I not explore, and I hope they will not conclude that I have betrayed their trust. My duty to Berton, to myself, and (not least) to readers has been to explore his life as fully as possible, and I believe that the book is richer and its subject more interesting and more fully human for my having done so. In this respect, I am especially grateful to Elsa Franklin, who provided invaluable assistance and advice throughout the duration of this project. She continued to do so even when she became aware – as surely she must have anticipated – that the book I was writing would probe into the nature of her relationship with Pierre Berton. For all this she has my profound gratitude.

Many other people came to my assistance – librarians, archivists, historians, biographers, colleagues, Berton acquaintances. They are too numerous to allow me to specify the assistance each has rendered, whether in the form of a conversation short of an interview, the provision of research assistance, a reading of parts of the manuscript, the answering of a query, a considered judgment on a Berton book, or the recounting of a favourite reminiscence. Whenever possible I have noted such contributions in the notes. At the risk of inadvertently leaving some individuals off a lengthy list, I would like to thank the following people for, variously, their information, assistance, advice, or encouragement: Gene Allen, Katherine Ashenburg, Stephen Azzi, Renu Barrett, Michael Behiels, Michael Bliss, Roberta Bonhomme, Jeanette Bosschart, Susan Burgess, Harry Campbell, Margaret Conrad, Terry Cook, Tim Cook, Terry Crowley, Dan Davidson, Joanna Dean, William Deverell, Pat Donnelly, Mary Flagg, Joan Frankel, Janet Friskney, Robert Fulford, John Gould, Madelaine Gould, Charlotte Gray, Kristina Guiguet, Roger Hall, Gerald Hannon, Barbara Hanulick, Julie Harris, Ronald Haycock, Chris Hives, Jackie Kaiser, Lulu Keating, Norman Kelly, James King, Donna Lang, Jacob Larsen, Jennifer Lehman, Jennifer Longon, Mairi MacRae, Roy MacSkimming, Yann Martel, Drew Martin, Sandra Martin, Jim Miller, Barbara Mitchell, Terry Mosher, Dave Neufeld, Sheila Nickols, Iris Nowell, Felicity Osepchook, Vaughn Palmer, Adele Petrovic, Nancy Phillips, Charlene Porsild, Anna Porter, Sean Purdy, T.D. Regehr, John Richthammer, Steve Robertson, Gary Ross, David Schlosser, Carl Spadoni, Rick Stapleton, Rosemary Sullivan, Alastair Sweeney, Cheryl Thompson, Jennifer Toews, Sheila Turcon, Keith Walden, Berton Woodward, Glenn Wright. My sincere gratitude is extended to each and all.

I must, however, single out certain people who rendered a special level of assistance. The interviews Elspeth Cameron conducted in 1986 and 1987 for her *Saturday Night* profile of Pierre Berton have proven invaluable in the writing of this book. I am grateful to her for the questions she asked of so many people (many of them no longer alive), her good sense in retaining her interview notes, and her permission to quote and publish extracts from them. Janet Berton and Lucy Woodward read the first ten chapters of the manuscript; Beverley Straight read the chapter that concerns her father, Hal Straight; and my Carleton University colleagues Sandra Campbell and Duncan McDowall, experts in Canadian literature and Canadian history respectively, read the first twelve chapters. I am very grateful to each of these kind people for comments, suggestions, and criticism.

I owe much to McClelland & Stewart, which in 2002 inherited this project from Macfarlane Walter & Ross and expressed an enthusiasm for it. Since 2004, publisher Doug Pepper has remained patient while more than one deadline passed for the delivery of the manuscript, and eventually he accepted a completed work substantially longer than the one originally agreed upon. Associate Editor Trena White has been a most cheerful point of contact with M&S, and Marilyn Biderman has led me through decisions about publication rights in her usual efficient and pleasant way.

I am especially grateful to Doug Pepper for making possible the privilege of working with Jan Walter and Barbara Czarnecki, two of the country's finest editors. When in 2001 I contacted Walter, then publisher of Macfarlane Walter & Ross, to pitch a biography of Pierre Berton, she and her partners, Gary Ross and John Macfarlane, enthusiastically embraced the idea. My only stipulation was that she and Czarnecki be my editors, as had been the case with *The Spinster and the Prophet: Florence Deeks, H.G. Wells, and the Mystery of the Purloined Past* (Toronto: Macfarlane Walter & Ross, 2000). The experience of working with such consummate professionals has once again been rewarding beyond measure. Whatever its faults may be, this book is vastly superior to the manuscript they read, and read again. I am also grateful to Barbara Czarnecki for compiling the index.

The first and the penultimate chapters of this biography were written at writers' retreats, and I would like to express my appreciation to their selection committees for choosing me as a resident author at the outset and near the conclusion of drafting the book. I spent the months of May through July 2004 living in the house in which Pierre Berton spent most of his first eleven years. Seated at the large oak desk in the old dining room, I could look up and see through the window to my right the cabin once occupied by Robert W. Service. It now seems to me inconceivable that the Yukon chapters could have been written anywhere else. I am grateful to Judith and Stephen Johnson and Susanne and Aika Saito for being such gracious hosts during my three memorable months in Dawson.

One of the books I took with me to Dawson City, and read each morning on the Berton House side porch as a source of inspiration and a substitute for Dutch courage, was Wallace Stegner's biography of the critic, novelist, columnist, and historian Bernard DeVoto, *The Uneasy Chair: A Biography of Bernard DeVoto* (Lincoln and London: University of Nebraska Press, 2001). DeVoto's brooding and reflective nature made him very different in temperament from Berton, but the two men shared a love of the history of the region from which they came (DeVoto hailed from Utah), they dedicated themselves to the writing of history for a broad readership, and they became ardent and influential conservationists. Wallace Stegner, like Berton, was marked for life by the town of his early upbringing. In Stegner's case, it was Eastend, which still guards the entrance to the Cypress Hills in southwestern Saskatchewan.

The daily presence of DeVoto and Stegner on that Dawson City porch helped channel my thinking in the weeks when I sought the arc of my narrative, so it seemed more than fitting to write the chapters in which Berton became Canada's most popular historian in the Eastend home of Stegner's childhood, now a writers' retreat. I am especially grateful to Ethel and Ken Wills for their generous hospitality during the summer of 2007. From the window of the second-floor back bedroom where Wallace Stegner once slept and where I worked, the coyotes howled in the early morning and the sun tucked in the evening behind the hills that stretched beyond Frenchman's River as it meandered past the backyard.

Finally, I wish to acknowledge debts owed to my university, colleagues, and family. Carleton University provided funding for the early stages of research on this project, and as a result I was able to employ Robbyn Gulka, one of our graduate students, to track down reviews of Pierre Berton's many books. Gulka's work was systematic and thorough, and this book has benefited a great deal from her diligence. My colleagues in the Department of History proved patient with a newly elected chair who must at times have appeared distracted, the result of engaging with Berton in the early morning hours before his "real" day began. In the evenings, my wife, Pauline, and son, Hamish, soldiered on while I dutifully maintained the bedtime schedule of a nine-year-old. They have my belated thanks and abiding love.

My eighty-six-year-old father, George McKillop, died in Winnipeg just as this biography entered the final stages of copy-editing. The letter I had just sent from Ottawa to let him know that I had dedicated the book to him arrived on the day he died, hours too late to serve as a reminder of a son's love and gratitude. In the wake of his death, the words of others have reminded me that he was a man who, quite literally to his dying day, constantly found meaning in stories about the past and worth in the detritus of the present. My father's death has made me aware not only that I owe him far more than I could possibly repay, but also that my preoccupation with history is quite possibly the most precious bequest I have inherited.

INDEX

—

A Picture Book of Niagara Falls, 620, 621–22, 643

"A Study in Tweed," 218

Abel, Alan, 487

Abel, Kerry, 34

Aboriginal people, 289, 454, 487, 598

Ackerman, Marianne, 639

ACTRA (Alliance of Canadian Cinema, Television and Radio Artists), 495, 552, 646–47

Adams, Ian, 535

Adilman, Sid, 609, 651

Adventures in Canadian History series, 613, 616, 621, 624, 625, 643

Adventures of a Columnist, 362–65

Agnes (Aggie, friend of PB), 104, 114

Aislin (Terry Mosher), 518, 567, 672

Aitken, Kate, 273, 278

Alaska Highway, 232–33, 298, 382, 386

Allan, Andrew, 220, 249, 424

Allemang, John, 659

Allen, Bob, 77

Allen, Ralph, 223–24, 225–26, 238, 241–43, 253–55, 259, 263, 273, 275, 279, 280, 293, 297, 317, 320, 392, 393

Americanization of culture, 368, 369, 374–75, 377, 491, 537, 540–42, 597

Amnesty International, 610

Angé, Denyse, 391

Anglican Church of Canada, 403–4, 416–17, 427–28, 432

Anglin, Elizabeth, 220, 249, 344, 575

Anglin, Gerald, 220, 223, 240, 242, 249, 344

anti-Communism, 258–59

anti-Semitism, 228, 229–30, 351–53

Arc Records, 449

The Arctic Grail, 591, 604, 605, 606–9, 610, 615, 642

Arctic sovereignty, 288, 293, 295, 597, 606

Arding, Jack, 154

Argus Corporation, 245

Armstrong, Ennis, 484, 487, 490, 544, 572, 591. *See also* Halliday, Ennis

Arthur Murray Dance Studio, 337–39, 363

Atkinson, Joseph E., 276, 327–29

Atwood, Margaret, 459, 492, 535, 546–47, 553, 567, 597, 598, 629, 632, 633, 656, 674

Austin, Jack, 672

Away Back in 1951 (film), 256

Axelrod, Paul, 614

Aylesworth, John, 314, 316

Bach, Richard, 528

Baird, Dorwin, 150

Baker, Russ, 197–98, 199–202, 204, 207, 209, 250

Baker, Russell, 361

Banks, Hal, 421

Barbeau, Marius, 418

Barber, James, 422

Barber, Les, 149

Barclay, Linwood, 636–37

Barkway, Michael, 475, 477

Barlow, Maude, 632, 647

Barnouw, Erik, 230, 277

Barris, Alex, 314, 315, 316, 319, 326, 635, 660

Barron, Sid, 567

Barron, Win, 314, 315

Basciano, Eric, 503

Bassett, John, 506

Bateman, Robert, 633, 656

Baum, Gregory, 486

Baum, L. Frank, 61, 365

Baxter, Beverley, 281

Bayer, Herbert, 287

BBC radio, 213, 249, 250, 251–52

Beat the Champs (radio show), 250, 272, 273

Beatty, Clyde, 187, 188

Beaverbrook, Baron, 281

Bedard, Elaine, 390

Bell, Bill, 178–79, 181

Bell, Harold, 176–77

Belli, Melvin, 405

Bemrose, John, 580, 595, 600

Bennett, Avie, 590, 607–8, 609, 610, 611, 624–25, 633, 643, 649

Bennett, Wilf, 181

Benny, Jack, 211, 434

Bergen, Edgar, 188

Berkson, Seymour, 210, 212

Berle, Milton, 361

Berlin, 375–76, 485–86

Berthon de Marigny, Marguerite, 8

Berthon de Marigny, Pierre (later Peter Berton, b. 1670s), 8

Berton, Ann, 10

Berton, Ann Street, 10

Berton, Beth, 67

Berton, Delia (née Hooke), 13, 14

The Berton Family Cookbook, 605

Berton, Frank (Francis George): childhood and youth, 12–23; employment, 30–32, 37–39, 40–42, 76–78, 86, 92, 96–97, 520–21; family and social life, 37–38, 41, 44–45, 46–49, 53–56, 63–71, 72–74, 127, 138, 146–48; military service, 19, 39–40; retirement and death, 100, 110, 174, 175, 177; seeks gold in Yukon, 19–23, 28–30, 516; unemployed in Depression, 70–76

Berton, George Duncan, 10

Berton, George Frederick Street, 10–11, 13

Berton House Writers' Retreat, 648, 652, 661–62

Berton, Jack (John Fitzgerald), 12, 13, 40, 67

Berton, Janet (née Walker), 187–88, 191, 192, 660, 666, 669, 670, 674, 676, 677; births and adoptions of children, 232, 247, 273, 307, 309, 320, 378, 452, 503; family and social life, 219–21, 224, 228, 232, 234–35, 247–49, 271, 291–93, 302, 304, 309, 321, 378–80, 382–84, 396, 417, 421–22, 451–54, 458, 459, 512, 519–22, 575, 605, 630–31, 649, 654; homes after marriage, 188, 218, 219, 232, 234 (*see also* Kleinburg, Ont., Berton home); interest in child welfare, 234, 345, 452; and PB's relationships with other women, 445, 447, 448, 630; and PB's work, 209, 225, 298, 302, 304, 321, 326, 367, 372–76, 379, 421–22, 438, 449, 526, 538, 573, 574, 654, 662. *See also* Walker, Janet

Berton, Laura (née Thompson): family and social life, 38–45, 47–48, 51, 52–56, 63–71, 73–74, 76–77, 80, 89, 91–92, 95, 104, 127, 138–39, 146–47, 175, 188, 291–92, 402, 457; writing by, 47, 48, 49, 54–55, 63, 69, 91–92, 110, 143, 153, 156, 290, 291, 295–96, 573. *See also* Thompson, Laura

Berton, Lucy (née Fox, grandmother of PB), 12, 13–15, 16, 18, 40

Berton, Lucy (sister of PB), 44, 45–46, 49, 50, 52–53, 54, 56, 64–71, 76, 77, 79, 80, 82, 96–97, 100, 101, 112, 127, 129, 143, 144, 151, 175, 177, 188, 457, 596, 648, 671, 674, 676

Berton, Maud, 67, 159

Berton, Pamela, 247, 273, 291–93, 309, 379, 383, 395, 516

Berton, Patsy, 273, 291–93, 309, 379, 380, 383, 387, 453, 471, 521, 522, 571, 605, 656, 666, 668–69, 670, 674, 676, 677

Berton, Paul, 309, 320, 379, 380, 383, 402, 519, 571, 605, 672

Berton, Peggy Anne, 378, 379, 380, 383, 452, 571, 574, 596, 605, 622, 660, 666, 670, 674, 676

Berton, Penny, 232, 234, 247–49, 273, 275, 291–93, 309, 378, 383, 395, 396, 403, 453, 458, 521, 529, 571, 660, 661–62, 666, 670–71

Berton, Perri, 452, 458, 571, 574, 598, 670, 676

Berton, Peter (b. 1670s), 8

Berton, Peter (b. 1729), 8, 9–10

Berton, Peter (son of PB), 307, 380, 383, 402, 516, 571, 574, 601, 605, 631, 670, 671

Berton, Pierre (PB):

— BOOKS BY: *A Picture Book of Niagara Falls*, 620, 621–22, 643; *Adventures of a Columnist*, 362–65; *The Arctic Grail*, 591, 604, 605, 606–9, 610, 615, 642; *The Berton Family Cookbook*, 605; *The Big Sell*, 386, 391–92, 408–9, 652; *Cats I Have Known and Loved*, 657, 658; *The Centennial Food Guide*, 449, 459; for children, 289, 301–2, 365–67 (*see also* Adventures in Canadian History series); *The Comfortable Pew*, 416–17, 426, 427–34, 440, 450, 460, 461, 652; *The Cool Crazy Committed World of the Sixties*, 439, 449; *The Dionne Years*, 545–48, 610; *Drifting Home*, 77, 519–21, 528, 611, 620, 677; *Farewell to the Twentieth Century*, 632, 635–37; *Fast Fast Fast Relief*, 384–86, 409–10, 425; *Flames across the Border*, 559, 564–67, 610, 642, 653; *The Golden Trail*, 289, 301; *The Great Depression*, 611, 612, 613–15, 616; *The Great Lakes*, 635; *The Great Railway: Illustrated*, 510, 522, 524, 620; *Hollywood's Canada*, 538–43; *If You Love This Country*, 597; *The Impossible Railway*, 510; *The Invasion of Canada*, 556–64, 566, 605, 610, 642, 653; *The Joy of Writing*, 657–58;

Just Add Water and Stir, 361–65, 409, 569; *Klondike*, 302–4, 310, 320–21, 324–26, 359, 382, 386, 483, 519, 522, 524, 545, 605, 633, 643, 652; *The Klondike Fever*, 320–21; *The Last Spike*, 488, 492, 495, 503, 507–8, 509, 510, 511–15, 521, 522–24, 530–35, 545, 605, 642, 653; *Marching as to War*, 639–40, 651, 653–54, 658; *Masquerade*, 585–89; *La minorité suffisante*, 474; *My Country*, 543, 548, 556, 611, 620, 643; *My Times*, 624–25, 626, 628–31, 632, 637; *My War with the 20th Century*, 434, 635; *The Mysterious North*, 296–302, 304–5, 309–10, 610, 652; *The National Dream*, 487–92, 495–510, 513, 514, 515, 516, 517, 521, 522–23, 530–35, 536, 545, 548, 605, 642, 653; *The New City*, 378; *Niagara: A History*, 615–16, 622, 624; *1967: The Last Good Year*, 631, 632, 637–39, 651; novels, 377, 411–14, 585–89; *Prisoners of the North*, 660, 663–64; *The Promised Land*, 579–83, 591, 605, 643; *Remembering Yesterday*, 434–35, 438; *Revenge of the Tribes*, 616; *The Royal Family*, 282–88, 652; sales figures, 288, 289, 309–10, 364–65, 367, 386, 391, 392, 430–31, 476, 477, 478–79, 503, 523, 543, 548, 556, 571, 608, 620; *The Secret World of Og*, 365–67, 386, 522, 523; serialized in magazines, 278–79, 301, 324–25, 428, 431, 463–64, 465, 502, 651; *The Smug Minority*, 461–79, 483, 652–53; *Stampede for Gold*, 302; *Starting Out*, 12, 171, 596, 599–603, 621; unpublished manuscripts, 212, 237, 410, 411–14; *Vimy*, 591–95, 605, 610, 642, 643; *Why We Act like Canadians*, 576–78, 610, 643; *The Wild Frontier*, 548, 556, 610–11; *Winter*, 635; *Worth Repeating*, 643–44

— CAREER AND PUBLIC LIFE: advocates for writers, 518, 535, 578–79, 603, 604, 617–20, 633, 647, 661; awards and honours, 304, 354, 359,

458, 552, 567, 569, 570, 583, 591, 629, 646–47, 649, 652, 655, 664–65, 673; bow tie, 313, 322; as brand, xii–xiii, 300, 331, 360, 407–9, 433–34, 464–65, 504–6, 512–15, 547–48, 549–50, 599, 609–10, 644, 651–52, 667–68; canoe quip, 151–52, 661; columns by: *see Maclean's; Toronto Star;* director of McClelland & Stewart, 434, 484, 499, 527, 540; editing skills and style, 129, 238–40, 243, 252, 275; first book, 288; first published writing, 105; net worth, 571; profiles and features about, 135, 359–61, 384, 390–91, 407, 421–22, 430, 449, 464, 472–73, 498, 499–500, 504, 512–13, 549, 570, 626, 659; research techniques and assistants, 226, 302, 304, 310, 335, 336, 450, 451, 455–56, 484–85, 487, 510–11, 534–35, 537–39, 544, 554, 556, 572, 591–92, 640, 654; scholarly studies of, 584–85; witnesses execution, 179–80, 201, 348

— FILM AND THEATRE WORK: *Away Back in 1951* (film), 256; *City of Gold* (film), 306–7; *The Decline of the Small Town* (film), 256; *The Monsters That Mine the Klondyke* (film), 256; *Paradise Hill* (musical), 458, 675; performs in school and camp concerts, 54, 67–68, 145, 160; *Quebec Industrial* (film), 256; *Spring Thaw* (revue), 305, 393; *Women on the March* (film), 305–6

— MAGAZINE WORK, 214, 215, 250, 251, 255, 305, 382. See also *Maclean's*

— MISCELLANEOUS WORK AND SKILLS, 305, 416, 449, 458, 516, 572, 579, 609, 633; cartoons, 69, 80, 97, 109, 112, 132, 150, 174, 213, 657; short stories, 214–18, 236, 249, 635; speeches, 550–51, 570, 576, 583, 647, 658; yearbooks, 95, 109, 126, 133

— NEWSPAPER WORK: camp newspapers, 97, 99, 100, 150, 153, 157; Flashbacks series for *Globe and Mail*, 664, 675; school newspapers, 74, 80, 81, 95, 227. *See also* newspapers, lore and lure of; *Toronto Star; Ubyssey;* Vancouver *News-Herald;* Vancouver *Sun*

— PERSONAL HISTORY: appearance, 50, 51, 81, 86, 115, 142, 179, 189, 322, 450; birth of, 41; books read by, 61–62, 96, 118, 146, 149, 161–62, 163, 164, 282, 416, 668; bullied as child, 51–52, 74; and cats, 92, 356, 446, 657; childhood, 42–82, 521; college years, 85, 87–90, 92–96; death of, 1, 670–77; dream life, 385; driving skills, 139, 379, 458, 519; family and social life, 219–21, 228, 232, 234–35, 247–49, 273, 291–93, 307–9, 320, 321, 365–67, 378–80, 382–84, 395–96, 417, 452–54, 458, 503, 519–22, 571, 631; family history, 7–41, 49, 353, 517; full name, 41; girls and girlfriends before marriage, 78–79, 99–100, 104, 113–16, 134, 136, 151–52, 159, 165–66, 169–71, 175–76; health, 44, 68, 81, 574–75, 578, 598, 603, 629, 646, 656, 658, 660, 662, 664, 666, 668–70; homes after marriage, 188, 218, 219, 232, 234 (*see also* Kleinburg, Ont., Berton home); marijuana use, 666–68, 675; marries Janet, 187–88; military service, 141–78; relationship with father, 30, 55, 72, 77–78, 80, 86, 97, 146–48, 171, 177, 516, 520–21; relationship with mother, 51, 53, 55–56, 146–48; religious beliefs, 118, 138, 159, 403, 570 (*see also The Comfortable Pew*); schooling, 54, 65, 74, 75–76, 79–80, 82; sexual adventures after marriage, 441–48, 630; summer jobs in Yukon, 85–87, 90–92, 96–102, 465–66; university years, 103–36; visits Ontario as child, 52–53, 63–69

— RADIO WORK: *Beat the Champs,* 250, 272, 273; *By-Line Story,* 214; campus and military stations, 109, 112, 132–33, 145–46, 155, 156; *Canadian*

Success Stories, 251; *Canadiana,* 255; *Citizens' Forum,* 255, 272; *Court of Opinion,* 272; *Creeping Green,* 251; *Critically Speaking,* 256; *Dialogue,* 499, 517, 568 (*see also* Templeton, Charles); *Eye Witness,* 250; *King of Diamonds,* 249; *March of Slime,* 132, 146, 153; *North to the Nahanni,* 279; *Past Imperfect,* 236, 249; *Pierre Berton Speaks,* 326, 360; *Prairie Playhouse,* 251; *Round the Pacific,* 250; *Sharp Edges,* 250; talks and commentaries, 199, 212, 213, 249, 255, 256, 266, 273, 289, 308, 326, 360; *The Waiting Room,* 236, 249; *Water Hazard,* 236
— TELEVISION WORK: *By Pierre Berton,* 380–81; *Close-Up,* 312–14, 319, 360, 367, 369, 381, 641; *Court of Opinion,* 272, 278, 312, 319; *Front Page Challenge,* 314–17, 319, 360–69, 459, 573–74, 626–28; *The Great Debate,* 536–37, 568; *Heritage Theatre,* 590, 591; *Horizon,* 416; *Klondike* series, 371–72; *My Country,* 536–37, 543; *The National Dream,* 522, 536; *The Pierre Berton Hour,* 389–92, 402, 404; *The Pierre Berton Show,* 381, 404–7, 417–23, 425–27, 429, 435–36, 438–41, 448, 449, 450–51, 454, 459, 485–87, 493, 497–98, 503, 507, 522, 528–29, 537, 641; *The Secret of My Success,* 609; *Tabloid,* 311–12; *Under Attack,* 460, 483, 484
Berton, William Street, 11–12, 13
Bewley, Les, 139, 144
Biezanek, Anne, 439
The Big Sell, 386, 391–92, 408–9, 652
Binder Twine Festival (Kleinburg), 459, 499, 512, 524
Birney, Earle, 493
Bishop, Billy, 594–95
Black, George, 39, 47, 67
Black, Mrs. George, 38, 47
Blackburn, Bob, 419, 421, 498, 499–500, 529
Blackman, Honor, 419

Bliss, Michael, 459, 489–91, 497, 501, 502, 507–8, 509, 560, 563, 564, 565, 566, 629
Bodsworth, Fred, 242, 535
Boloten, Jeffrey, 615
Bonanza Creek, Yukon, 20, 28, 37, 38, 325
Bonar, J.C., 484
The Book of Eve (Beresford-Howe), 572
Book-of-the-Month Club, 321, 497, 509, 522, 562, 616, 624
Borovoy, Alan, 352, 629
Bourgault, Pierre, 459
Bowles, Patricia, 540
Boy Scouts, 80–81
Boyd, Denny, 185
Brabourne, Lady, 280
Bragg, T.C., 32, 33
Braithwaite, Dennis, 430, 475–76
Braithwaite, Max, 225, 387, 388
Brand, Oscar, 405
Branden, Nathaniel, 460
Brazilian Traction, 224
Breslin, Jimmy, 451
Brimelow, Peter, 551
British Columbia Digest, 215
Broadfoot, Barry, 551, 613–14
Broadfoot, Dean, 260
Bronson, L.N., 406, 420
Brothers, Joyce, 405
Brown, Dick, 151
Brown, John (Bugs), 342
Bruce, T. Harry, 121, 401, 505, 515
Bruner, Al, 522
Buchwald, Art, 405
Buck, Tim, 405
Buckley, William F., 537
Buhasz, Laszlo, 587
Buitenhuis, Peter, 628
Burdick, Eugene, 266
Burke, Edmund, 56
Burns, Ken, 306
Burns, Skip and Cheri, 519
Bush, George W., 1, 671–72
business, 224, 231, 240, 243–47
By-Line Story (radio show), 214

"By Pierre Berton" (column). *See Toronto Star*

By Pierre Berton (TV show), 380–81

Calder, Phil, 157
Caldwell, Evelyn ("Penny Wise"), 121, 178, 189, 194, 219, 275
Callwood, June, 226–28, 239, 240, 249, 254, 313, 316, 318, 327, 329, 359–61, 391, 392, 442, 459, 486, 535, 567, 575, 579, 598, 618–19, 645, 674, 675
Cameron, Donald, 513–14
Cameron, Dorothy, 443
Cameron, Elspeth, 443–48, 489, 591
Camp Borden, Ont., 157
Canada's National History Society, 655, 658–59
Canadian Broadcasting Corporation. *See* CBC
Canadian Centennial Library, 415, 434–35, 449, 459
Canadian Historical Association, 529–35
Canadian Journalism Foundation, 673
Canadian magazine, 464
Canadian Officers' Training Corps (COTC), 104, 110, 113, 117, 126, 127–28, 137, 142
Canadian Pacific (film), 508, 509
Canadian Pacific Railway, 410–11, 434, 455–56, 484–85. *See also The Last Spike; The National Dream*
Canadian Radio League, 254
Canadian Student Assembly, 110, 112
Canadian Studies Foundation, 518
Canadian Success Stories (radio show), 251
Canadian Walk of Fame, 642
Canadian Writers' Foundation, 518
Canadiana (radio show), 255
Cann, Jeannette, 93–94
Caouette, Réal, 389–90
Capp, Al, 391, 460, 573
Carin, Michael, 587
Carmack, George, 19, 20
Carmichael, Stokely, 454
Carolan, Tom, 197
Caron, Roger, 617
Carpenter, Mary, 454, 629

Carr, Gary, 351
Carroll, Jock, 240, 260
Carson, Johnny, 451
Cats I Have Known and Loved, 657, 658
cattle business, 237–38, 250
CBC, 1, 243, 253, 278, 310–12, 421, 459, 596, 604, 626–27, 633, 638, 671. *See also* Berton, Pierre — RADIO WORK; Berton, Pierre — TELEVISION WORK
Centennial Celebration Consultants, 415–16, 458
The Centennial Food Guide, 449, 459
Central Hotel (Dawson City), 97, 99
CFCF television, 418
CFPL television, 418
CFRB radio, 273, 568
CFTO television, 389, 404, 406
Chalmers, Floyd, 223, 240–41, 279, 319, 396, 397, 400–401
Charlie, Tagish, 19
CHCH television, 590
Chesser, Eustace, 396
CHFI radio, 404
children and youth, 235, 236, 345–49, 365–67, 394–96, 421, 460, 470–72, 479, 665
Chilkoot Trail, 21, 22, 516
Chilliwack, B.C., 149–53
Chinese soldiers in Korean War, 261
Chisholm, Elspeth, 249, 273
Christie, Dinah, 443, 585, 645, 675
CHSJ television, 418
CHUM radio, 326, 360
Church, Frank, 371
Citizens' Forum (radio show), 255, 272
City of Gold (film), 306–7
civil liberties, 357–58, 471, 596, 618, 633
CJOR radio, 109, 112, 132–33
CKEY radio, 499, 568
Clare, John, 223, 226, 238, 279, 382
Clark, Gregory, 69, 259
Clark, Petula, 454
Clarkson, Adrienne, 443, 493, 609, 674, 675
Close-Up (TV show), 312–14, 319, 360, 367, 369, 381, 641

Coburn, James, 371
Coca-Colism, 368, 375, 377. *See also*
    Americanization of culture
Cohen, Leonard, 441
Cohen, Nathan, 311, 321, 387, 388, 458
Cohn-Bendit, Daniel, 486
Cold War, 189, 257, 258, 288, 332, 369,
    436
Coldwell, M.J., 155, 418
Coleman, Jim, 184, 242
Coleman, Travers, 484, 485
Coles Bookstores, 535, 578–79
Collister, Ron, 634
Colombo, John Robert, 463
Colville, Richard, 280
The Comfortable Pew, 416–17, 426,
    427–34, 440, 450, 460, 461, 652
comic strips and books, 62, 67, 68–69,
    88
Committee for an Independent Canada,
    493, 495, 543, 553, 568
Conrad, William, 372
consumerism and consumer concerns,
    331, 332–39, 341, 357, 358, 385, 391–92
Cook, Ramsay, 580–81, 604
Cook, Terry, 533
*The Cool Crazy Committed World of the
    Sixties,* 439, 449
Co-operative Commonwealth
    Federation, 155, 358–59, 462
Corio, Ann, 396
corruption, 356
Corwin, Norman, 221
Council of Canadians, 597, 632
Court of Opinion (radio and TV show),
    272, 278, 312, 319
Coward, Noel, 418
Craig, Isabel, 326
Craig, Janet, 496, 538, 539, 545, 572
Craig, Marilyn, 336–38, 339, 340–41, 398,
    451
Craigdarroch Castle, 85. *See also* Victoria
    College
Crawley, Frank Radford (Budge), 305,
    416
Creal, Michael, 432
Creeping Green (radio show), 251

Creighton, Donald G., 304, 456, 483,
    488, 489, 490, 508–9, 530–31
Creighton, Doug, 660
Crew, Rupert, 251
Crichton, Michael, 498
Critically Speaking (radio show), 256
Crombie, David, 551
Cromie, Don, 183, 184, 200, 231, 236
Cromie, Robert, 183, 231
Cromie, Sam, 183, 184, 194, 231
Crompton, Maurice, 273
Cross, Gary, 333
Crowley, Terry, 532
Crump, N.R. (Buck), 484, 485
CTV network, 389, 390, 402
Cuff, John Haslett, 541, 600
Cuisinart, 552
cultural imperialism. *See*
    Americanization of culture
Currie Barracks, Alta., 154–56
Czigler Herrndorf, Eva, 451

Dafoe, A.R., 546
Daly, Margaret, 512
Daly, Ralph, 119, 144, 178, 188
Daly, Tom, 306
D'Angelo, Ange, 350
Davidson, Joyce, 390
Davies, Robertson, 567
Davis, Fred, 315, 316, 349, 350, 442, 459,
    483, 573, 634
Davis, Jo, 349, 350, 573
Davis, Thomas, 438
Dawson City, Yukon, 20, 24–25, 29–30,
    33–35, 42–44, 46–48, 56–61, 65, 86,
    98–101, 233–34, 250, 255, 306–7,
    382–83, 520, 568, 600, 645, 647–48
Day, Dennis, 438
de Adder, Michael, 673
de Wolfe, Percy, 97
Deacon, William Arthur, 290, 295,
    299–300, 326
Dean, John, 517
The Decline of the Small Town (film), 256
Democratic Party (U.S.), 370–71
Dempsey, Hugh, 514, 577, 581
Dempsey, Jack, 438

Denham, Alice, 486
Dennett, Jack, 416
Denoon, Anne, 628, 629
DePoe, Norman and David, 486
Depression, 64–65, 68, 70, 544–48, 613–15
Deverell, William, 603
DeVoto, Bernard, 2
Dextraze, Jacques Alfred, 258
Dialogue (radio show), 499, 517, 568. *See also* Templeton, Charles
Dick, George, 640
Dickens, Penny, 647
Diefenbaker, John, 323–24, 331, 358, 359, 462
The Dionne Years, 545–48, 610
Disneyland, 375
Dominion Seed House, 275–76
Donnelly, Pat, 664
Dors, Diana, 529
Doubleday Canada, 626, 632, 636, 643, 653, 663
Doubleday New York, 434, 465, 635
Douglas, Tommy, 462, 478, 507, 597
Doyle, John, 616
Drapeau, Jean, 486
Drew, George, 235
Drifting Home, 77, 519–21, 528, 611, 620, 677
drug abuse, 230, 250
Drylie, William, 317
Dubuc, Alfred, 531
Duke, Patty, 529
Dukes, Mrs. (caregiver), 302
Dunphy, Kerry, 261, 262–63
Dunsmuir, Robert, 85
Durschmied, Erik, 369
Dymond, M.B., 344, 345, 399

Earl, Lawrence, 251, 287
Eastend, Sask., 60
Eaton, Cyrus S., 298
Eaton's, 649–50
Eayrs, James, 541
Edinborough, Arnold, 409, 504–5, 506, 513, 534

Éditions de l'Homme, 474
Edmonton, 240, 250, 255
Egypt, 367–68
eighties, 558, 577, 611–12
Eksteins, Modris, 654
Elizabeth, Princess (later Queen Elizabeth II), 274, 282, 283
Elliott, Elmina, 327
Elson, Robert T., 119, 121–22, 124, 125, 127, 138, 139, 140, 178
Empire Club of Canada, 222
Ems, Wayne, 169, 170
Enright, Dan, 426
environmental issues, 301, 466, 598, 633, 647, 665
Evans, Edith, 451
Eve Productions, 572
Everybody's magazine, 251
Expo 67, 456–58
Eye Witness (radio show), 250

Fairbanks, Douglas, Jr., 418
Fairclough, Ellen, 306, 573
Farewell to the Twentieth Century, 632, 635–37
Farquharson, Bob, 227
Farrar, John, 273
Farrar, Straus and Company, 237, 273
Fast Fast Fast Relief, 384–86, 409–10, 425
Faucher, Albert, 531
Feinberg, Abraham, 405
Fenton, Faith, 25
Fetherling, Doug, 560, 563, 564, 565–66
Feyer, George, 384, 402–3, 443
Fighting Words, 311
Filion, Harry, 156, 158, 163, 182–83, 187, 188, 189, 193, 194–95, 198, 216, 453, 610
Filion, Veryl, 156, 158, 453
Filion, Victoria (Vicki), 194, 453–54. *See also* Gabereau, Vicki
Findley, Timothy, 522, 646
First World War, 39–40, 583, 591–95
Fisher, Delia Florence, 26
Fisher, Douglas, 478, 532–33
Fisher, Yukon (Bud), 438

Flames across the Border, 559, 564–67, 610, 643, 653

Fleming, Mrs. Ian, 439

Fletcher, G.B., 352

Forbes, Bill, 443, 457, 567

Ford Motor Company, 250–51, 255

Forsey, Joan, 640

Fotheringham, Allan, 135, 475, 477, 600, 627, 649, 674, 675

Fournier, Joe, 98, 101

France, 370

Frances (wartime affair), 165, 169–71, 601, 602

Francis, Daniel, 608

Francis, R.A. and Margaret, 196

Frankel, Joan McCormack, 443, 445, 446–47

Franklin, Elsa, 423–27, 442, 447–48, 544, 567, 570, 572, 575, 579, 648, 652, 654, 657–58, 660, 661, 671, 674; and PB's books, 424–25, 428–29, 431, 450, 463, 464, 493, 498–99, 500, 510, 511–12, 524, 526, 538, 545, 559, 586, 587, 607, 608, 610–11, 615, 622, 623–25, 643; and PB's television work, 423, 425–27, 435, 436, 440, 450–51, 460, 486, 487, 497–98, 507, 528, 536–37, 539, 572, 579, 590–91, 675

Franklin, Stephen, 424, 448, 567, 570–71, 575, 584

Fraser, Blair, 235, 293, 312, 318, 330, 392, 393

Fraser, Sylvia, 421–22, 464

Frayne, Casey, 575

Frayne, Trent, 226, 227–28, 238, 242, 254, 327, 567, 575

free trade, 596–97, 606

French, William, 542, 587, 600, 601, 603, 605–6

Fricker, Sylvia, 422, 633

Friends of Public (Canadian) Broadcasting, 604, 651

Friesen, Gerald, 582

Front Page Challenge (TV show), 314–17, 319, 360, 459, 573–74, 628

The Front Page (Hecht and MacArthur, play and movie), 107, 111, 119, 194

Fulford, Robert, 388, 392, 393, 396, 400, 401, 443, 472–73, 476–77, 599, 619

funeral industry, 331, 339–41

Gabereau, Vicki, 454, 610, 661, 662, 675, 676. *See also* Filion, Victoria (Vicki)

Gable, Brian, 672–73

Gagliardi, Phil, 312

Galento, Tony, 438

Gallant, André, 635

Galloway, Virginia (Ginny), 116, 136, 152, 159, 160

gardening, 275–76

Gardiner, Bob, 389

Gardner, Ed, 201–2, 206

Gardner, Ray, 138, 140, 174–75, 178, 190, 213, 240, 554

Garner, Hugh, 184, 242, 439

Garrett, John, 117, 128

Gauvreau, Emile, 106

Gee, Marcus, 656–57

George, Henry, 27

Gerussi, Bruno, 499, 574

Gerussi, Rico, 571, 676

Gessell, Paul, 663

Gibson, Doug, 609, 615, 620–22, 624, 642–43

Gibson, Graeme, 535, 597, 646, 674

Gifford, C.G., 236

Gilmour, Barbara, 309

Gilmour, Clyde, 199, 240, 246, 567, 577, 635

Gimby, Bobby, 486

Global Television network, 522, 528, 536

Goddard, Peter, 616

Goldberg, Rube, 391

The Golden Trail, 289, 301

Goodman, Sarah, 613

Gordon, Walter, 305, 405, 474, 493

Gostick, Ron, 351

Gould, Allan, 609

Gould, Glenn, 361

Gould, John, 45, 46, 47, 49, 51, 52, 54, 59, 60, 81, 101

Gould, Lenore, 46

Governor General's Literary Awards, 304, 359, 522

Graham, Ronald and Helen, 274–75

Granatstein, Jack, 157, 547–48, 632, 653, 654, 655, 669

Grand, Ann, 158

Grand, Bill, 139, 158

Grand, Elaine, 311

Granger, Peter, 453, 503, 574–75

Granville, Yukon, 31, 36, 37

Gray, Charlotte, 655

Gray, Herb, 495, 573

Gray, John, 289

The Great Adventure (Cruise and Griffiths), 634

The Great Debate (TV show), 536–37, 568

The Great Depression, 611, 612, 613–15, 616

The Great Lakes, 635

The Great Railway: Illustrated, 510, 522, 524, 620

Grebe, Harvey (pseud. of PB), 385, 389–91

Greene, Lorne, 424

Greenfield, Jeff, 545, 546

Greenhous, Brereton, 564–65, 595

Griffiths, Muriel, 176, 188

Griffiths, Rudyard, 655

Group of 78, 597–98

Guccione, Robert, 486

Gunn, Alvin, 420

Gurley Brown, Helen, 404–5

Guthrie, Tyrone, 436

Gutteridge, Helena, 139–40

Gzowski, Peter, 242, 311, 393, 396, 401, 463, 464, 609, 634

Hailey, Arthur, 252, 417, 443, 567, 573, 629, 670

Hall, Ralph, 185

Hall, Roger, 565

Halliday, Ennis, 336, 416, 420, 435, 450, 455, 484. *See also* Armstrong, Ennis

Hallman, E.S., 250

Halton, Matthew, 259

Hambleton, Ron and Jean, 234

Hamilton, Bill, 175–76

Hampson, Sarah, 659

Hannawals, Carl, 250

Hannon, Leslie, 279, 400, 459

Hanratty, Ed, 201, 202

Harcourt, Peter, 542

Hardinge, Edward, 280

Hardy, John, 571

Harper, Lynne, 345

Harrington, Michael, 2, 474, 476

Harrison, Ernest, 403–4, 416–17, 432

Hart, Harvey, 315

Hartness, Mr. (principal), 79–80

Harvey, Denis, 464

Hays, Andy, 209

Hayworth, Rita, 208, 210

Headless Valley, 196–213, 255, 289, 298

Hearst newspapers, 203

Hecht, Ben, 107

Hefner, Hugh, 440

Hegg, Eric, 306

Heine, William C., 475

Henderson, Frank, 197

Henderson, Robert, 19

Hendrickson, Hal, 197

Hendry, Charles E., 474

Henle, James, 212

Herbert, Bill, 260

Herbert, John, 646

Heritage Canada Foundation, 536, 568

heritage issues, 382, 536, 568, 617, 649

Heritage Theatre (TV show), 590, 591

Herron, Shaun, 477

Hewitt, Foster, 574

Heyerdahl, Liv, 109–10

Heyerdahl, Thor, 109–10, 573

The Hidden Persuaders (Packard), 335

Hindmarsh, Harry, 276–77, 329

Hiroshima, 373

Hiss, Alger, 529

Hobson, Richmond P., Jr., 256

Hodgeman, Marge, 429, 496, 569

Hodgetts, J.E., 518

Hoffa, Jimmy, 529

Hoffman, Paul, 552

Holden, Dick, 78, 87

Hollywood's Canada, 538–43

Holmes, Michael, 644
Holmes, Robert, 519, 521
Holt, Douglas B., 408, 433
Holtorff, Miss, 36, 37
Honderich, Beland, 320, 322, 326, 329,
    367, 370, 493, 616, 623
Honderich, John, 623
Hope, Bob, 439
Horizon (TV show), 416
Horn, Michiel, 581
Howard, Trevor, 529
Hughes, Kim, 664
Hume, Christopher, 633
Hungary, 402–3
Hunter, Donald, 397
Hunter, Horace T., 223, 240–41
Hurricane Hazel, 291–93
Hurst, Lynda, 549, 631
Hurtig, Mel, 473, 493, 543, 553, 597
Hutchison, Bruce, 122–24, 137, 224, 304,
    317, 330, 391, 501, 505–6, 509, 514,
    567
Hyde, Steven, 317

I Married the Klondike (Laura Berton,
    book), 49, 290, 291, 295–96, 457,
    520, 568
I Married the Klondike (TV series), 468
Idea Factory, 644, 656
If You Love This Country, 597
The Illustrated History of Canada (Cook
    et al.), 604, 608
immigrants and refugees, 349–50, 535,
    578. *See also The Promised Land*
The Impossible Railway, 510
International News Service, 203, 210, 212
Inuit, 289, 454
The Invasion of Canada, 556–64, 566,
    605, 610, 642, 653
Iraq war, 593, 656, 658
Irvine, Lorna, 584, 585, 596
Irving, David, 633
Irving, John, 109
Irwin, Arthur, 200, 210, 221–24, 225–26,
    230, 232, 238, 240–41, 242, 247, 254,
    256, 567
Israel, Charles, 572

Israel, Peter, 414
It Happened One Night (film), 107,
    216–18
Italy, 370

Jackson, A.Y., 418
Jackson, Glenda, 529
Jackson, Stanley, 307
Jacobs, Ralph, 343
Jacobsen, George, 290
Jagger, Mick, 421
James, William Closson, 601–2
Japan, 372–75
Japanese Canadians, 117–18, 140,
    228–29, 261
Jasen, Patricia, 616
Jeffers, Scotty, 519
Jim, Skookum, 19
Joerin, Browni, 551
Jones, Art, 191, 198, 200, 202, 205–6,
    208, 209, 219, 648
Jones, David C., 581–82
Jones, Rachel, 486
The Joy of Writing, 657–58
Just Add Water and Stir, 361–65, 409, 569
justice system, 341–44, 345–49, 357–58,
    407

Kane, Hugh, 364, 366, 425, 428, 477,
    499
Karsh, Yousuf, 275
Kash, Linda, 675
Kash, Paula, 631
Katz, Sidney, 240, 317, 318–19, 361, 384,
    400, 575
Keatley, Pat (Patrick), 131–32, 144
Keillor, Garrison, 2, 634
Keith, Donald A., 554
Kelley, Thomas P., 235–36
Kelly, Cynthia, 425
Kelly, Fred, 438
Kelly, Norman, 455–56, 484–85, 488, 489
Kemsley Scholarship, 194, 213
Kennedy, Betty, 459, 573, 674
Kennedy, John F., 371, 437
Kennedy, Paul, 596
Kenney, Mart, 75, 116, 156, 648

Keys, David, 250
Kidd, Bruce, 422
Kilbourn, Elizabeth, 416
Kilbourn, William, 416, 432, 443, 444, 585
King, Adelaide, 436
King Features Syndicate, 212
King, James, 474, 494, 589
King of Diamonds (radio show), 249
King, W.L. Mackenzie, 155, 157, 160
Kinrade, Laura, 519, 552
Kirby, Blaik, 529
Kirkconnell, Watson, 351
Kitamura, Ken, 228–29
The Kite (Mitchell), 445, 641–42
Kleinburg, Ont.: Berton home, 7, 234–35, 247–49, 255, 273, 275–76, 307–9, 320, 378, 421–22, 484, 543, 572, 598, 676; Binder Twine Festival, 459, 499, 512, 524
Klinck, L.S., 127
Klondike (book), 302–4, 310, 320–21, 324–26, 359, 382, 386, 483, 519, 522, 524, 545, 605, 633, 643, 652
Klondike (TV series), 371–72
The Klondike Fever, 320–21
Klondike gold rush, 19–23, 28–30, 62, 255, 289, 301–4, 306–7, 372, 516
Knelman, Martin, 542, 650
Knight, Allan, 598
Knopf, Alfred A., 302, 321, 452
Knopf (publisher), 282, 286, 287, 288, 296–97, 302, 320, 386, 392, 502, 510
Koenig, Wolf, 307
Kopvillem, Peeter, 616
Korean War, 257–67, 273, 593
Koshevoy, Himie, 152, 184, 188, 189, 193, 355
Krantz, Judith, 381
Krantz, Steve, 381
Kraus, Gus and Maggie, 207
Kroitor, Roman, 307
Kroniak, Lisa (pseud. of PB), 585–86

labour movement, 26–27, 258–59, 358, 421
Ladue, Joseph, 20, 31

LaMarsh, Judy, 459, 493, 638
Lamport, Allan, 470
Landers, Ann, 405
Lantz, Walter, 497
LaPierre, Laurier, 486, 507
The Last Spike, 488, 492, 495, 503, 507–8, 509, 510, 511–15, 521, 522–24, 530–35, 545, 605, 642, 653
Laurence, Margaret, 597
Laxer, James, 491
Layton, Irving, 391, 441
Lebanon, 528
LeBourdais, Isabel, 240, 348, 438
Lederer, William J., 266
Lee, Gypsy Rose, 486
Lefolii, Ken, 392–93, 397, 400–401, 434, 449, 459
Leigh, Vivien, 418
Leja, Walter (Rocky), 418
Lemmon, Jack, 498
LeRoy, Neil, 278
Lesage, Jean, 290, 294
Lévesque, Georges-Henri, 253
Lévesque, René, 405
Levine, Allan, 644
Levison, Joe, 263
Lewis, David, 462
Lewis, Jean, 443
Lewis, J.L. Burton, 140, 141, 142
Lewis, Stephen, 552
Lightfoot, Gordon, 598
Lincoln, Evelyn, 439
Lippincott (publisher), 431
Little, Brown, 367, 562
Little Lord Fauntleroy (Burnett), 49–51
Lloyd, Trevor, 300
Lombardo, Guy, 438
London *Daily Express,* 203
London, England, 164–65, 172, 369, 418–19, 423
London Free Press, 672
London, Jack, 55
Lonergan, Wayne, 438
Low, Colin, 306
Lowe, Billy, 63
Lundstrom, Linda, 609
Lynch, Charles, 120–21, 224

Lyons, Norman, 229

MacArthur, Charles, 107
MacArthur, Douglas, 257
Macaulay, Robert, 416
Macdonald, Dave, 594
Macdonald, David, 242
MacDonald, Dawn, 450–51
MacDonald, Donald C., 344
Macdonald, John A., 456, 488, 490, 501, 505
Macdonald, Marion, 152, 153
MacDougal, Dick, 311
MacDougall, Allan, 441
MacFarlane, T.D., 36
MacGregor, Roy, 552
Maclean Hunter, 221, 223, 229, 230, 260, 319, 396–97, 400–401
Maclean, J.B., 223, 281
Maclean, J.C., 190
Maclean's, 200, 210–11, 221–26, 230, 235, 238–43, 252–55, 275, 279, 281, 283, 293, 297, 312, 317–20, 324, 463, 464, 472–73, 522; articles by PB, 199, 200, 210, 224–26, 228–34, 235–36, 237–38, 240, 243–47, 253, 255, 257–67, 271–72, 274–86, 290, 293–97, 301, 318; columns by PB, 392–400, 401–2; PB appointed articles editor, 238; PB appointed associate editor, 275; PB appointed managing editor, 279
MacLennan, Hugh, 242, 305, 501, 509
Macmillan of Canada, 286, 289, 302, 378
Macpherson, Duncan, 370–71, 567
MacSkimming, Roy, 434, 541–42, 590, 609
Mailey, Nap, 91, 100
Mair, Shirley, 393
Malcolm X, 435–36
Mallick, Heather, 650–51
Maloney, Helen, 518
Mann, Larry, 396
Mansfield, Jayne, 404, 440
Maple Leaf (army newspaper), 164, 172, 174
March of Slime (radio skits), 132, 146, 153

Marchand, Philip, 626, 628, 629, 632
Marching as to War, 639–40, 651, 653–54, 658
Margaret (aunt of Janet Walker), 151
Margeson, Helen, 452
Margeson, Jack, 128–29
Markle, Fletcher, 449, 507
Markson, Elliott, 394
Martin, Robert I., 413–14
Martin, Sandra, 446, 671, 672
Masquerade, 585–89
Massey, Vincent, 253, 271–72, 332
Masson, Hal, 223
Mather, Barry, 138, 139, 360
Mathews, Robin, 492, 493
Maugham, Somerset, xiv, 96, 118, 160, 162, 457, 585, 677
McCall, Christina, 242, 243, 317. *See also* Newman, Christina McCall
McCarter, Alex, 45, 46, 47, 48, 51–52, 64, 73, 82
McCarter, Helen, 46
McClelland & Stewart, 286, 410–11, 415, 441, 475, 490–91, 493–94, 518, 519, 554, 557, 561–62, 597, 605, 635, 649, 650; contracts and arrangements with PB, 286, 295, 320, 361, 367, 386, 416–17, 439, 463, 570, 610–11, 615, 616, 620–21, 622, 623–25, 642–43; design and production, 287, 363–64, 523, 545, 621–22; editors and free-lancers, 362, 363, 366, 377, 384, 391–92, 413–14, 463, 496, 543, 544–45, 557–58, 586, 587, 592–93; financial and management troubles, 494–95, 540, 569–70, 579, 589–90, 609; promotion and publicity, 286, 321, 325–26, 364, 384, 386, 408, 425, 427–29, 463–65, 496–97, 498–99, 500, 501, 502–3, 509–10, 511–12, 519, 524–27, 540–41, 545, 559, 586, 587, 607–8; royalties and salaries paid to PB, 288, 431, 459–60, 484, 523, 571, 608, 624, 643; series and divisions, 415, 434–35, 449, 459–60, 483, 613, 616, 625. *See also* Berton, Pierre
— BOOKS BY; McClelland, Jack

McClelland, Elizabeth, 445
McClelland, Jack, 286, 416, 441–47, 486,
    493, 553, 567, 597, 622–23, 635, 661.
    See also McClelland & Stewart
McClelland, John, 557
McClure, Robert, 493
McConachie, Grant, 197–98
McCormack, Joan, 443, 445, 446–47
McCreath, Ralph, 443
McCrow, Bill, 248
McCuish, Ronnie, 46
McCullagh, George, 240, 243–44
McCullough, Allan, 532
McDevitt, Christy, 121
McDonald, Peter, 250
McDougall, Brenda, 220–21
McDowall, Duncan, 581
McDowell, Malcolm, 528
McEachern, Ron, 401
McFarlane, Jim, 110
McGarvey, Pete, 623
McGeer, Gerald, 194–95
McGill, David, 464, 476
McGregor, Gordon, 405
McIntyre, Scott, 476
McKnight, Linda, 544, 569, 586, 589
McLean, Ross, 227, 310–14, 319, 369,
    389, 391, 423, 425, 599
McLean, Stuart, 634
McLeod, Charles, 31
McLeod, Charlie, 101
McLeod, Frank and Willie, 202, 206,
    207
McNish, Ian H., 474
Meadows, Charlie, 34
medicare, 358, 359, 397–400, 420, 666
mental health, 230, 344–45, 419
Menzies, Dorothy, 188
Mercer, Johnny, 383
Mercer, Rick, 664–65, 666–68, 675
Mew, Diane, 384, 545
Mexico, 507
Michie, Anne, 484
Mickleburgh, Bruce, 95
Middle Dominion Camp, Yukon,
    86–87, 91, 96, 97
Miki, Roy, 620

Miller, Jack, 529
Miller, Jim, 532
Miller, Max, 188
Miller, Merle, 436
Miller, Ross, 519
Mills, Charlie, 97
Mills, Charlie, Sr., 97, 99
Minnes, Gordon, 359
La minorité suffisante, 474
Minsky, Dartie, 440
Minter, Roy, 325
Mitchell, W.O., 237, 239, 242, 640–42
Mitford, Jessica, 341, 493, 573
Moir, Reg, 124, 139, 142, 176
Monday Report (TV show), 665, 666–68,
    675
The Monsters That Mine the Klondyke
    (film), 256
Montreal *Gazette*, 672, 674
Montreal Standard, 157
Moon, Barbara, 184, 242, 260, 297–98,
    312, 318, 392, 401, 443
Moore, Christopher, 608
Moore, Dora Mavor, 318
Moore, H. Napier, 222–23
Moore, Mavor, 305, 424, 458, 506–7, 567
Moore, Trevor, 470
Moreau, Pierre, 500
Moreland, Ulla, 391
Moritsugu, Frank, 421
Morton, Desmond, 595, 598, 604
Morton, W.L., 483, 493, 496, 501
Mosher, Terry (Aislin), 518, 567, 672
Moss, Susanne, 518
movies, 73–75, 88, 89, 106–7, 109, 111,
    185, 259, 262. *See also* Berton, Pierre
    — FILM AND THEATRE WORK;
    Hollywood's Canada
Mowat, Farley, 154, 242, 289, 404, 441,
    442, 525–28, 535, 569, 596, 597, 598,
    633, 673
Muggeridge, Malcolm, 391
Mulholland, Donald, 255–56
Mulroney, Belinda, 34, 43, 304
Munro, Ray, 191–93, 219
Murdoch, George, 306
Murphy, Bill, 358

Murphy, Harvey, 258–59
Murray, George (Chicago), 355
Murray, George (Fort St. John), 196
Murray, Georgina, 152
Murray, Jim, 536
Murray, Ma, 151–52
Murrow, Edward R., 2
My Country (book), 543, 548, 556, 611,
   620, 643
My Country Productions, 571–72, 609,
   646
My Country (TV show), 536–37, 543
My Times, 624–25, 626, 628–31, 632, 637
My War with the 20th Century, 434, 635
Myers, Jay, 584
Myers, Rita, 136
The Mysterious North, 296–302, 304–5,
   309–10, 610, 652
"Mystery Men," 214

Nabokov, Vladimir, 312
Nader, Ralph, 537
Nagy Innes, Eva, 451
Nahanni River valley. *See* Headless
   Valley
Nash, Knowlton, 536
Nash, Ogden, 391
The National Dream (book), 487–92,
   495–510, 513, 514, 515, 516, 517, 521,
   522–23, 530–35, 536, 545, 548, 605,
   642, 653
The National Dream (TV series), 522, 536
National Film Board, 241, 255, 305–7
National Post, 672, 673
nationalism and national identity, xiii,
   253, 305, 332, 487–88, 491–95, 504–6,
   512–14, 523, 541–45, 547–48, 553, 555,
   556–57, 576–78, 593, 595, 596, 631–32,
   644, 650–51, 655, 659
Neale, John, 632
Nelles, H.V., 508–9, 533, 534
Nellie's hostel, 618, 619
Neuberger, Richard L., 325
The New City, 378
New Democratic Party, 358–59, 461–63,
   468–69, 478, 491–92, 552, 553–54,
   570

Newfeld, Frank, 363, 434, 449, 621–22
Newlove, John, 524
Newman, Christina McCall, 393. *See
   also* McCall, Christina
Newman, Peter C., 231, 242, 317, 318,
   392, 401, 415, 457, 486, 493, 504–5,
   553, 567, 598, 637–38, 651
newspapers, lure and lore of, 94–96,
   105–12, 117, 118, 119–25, 137–41,
   185–87, 240, 254. *See also individual
   newspapers;* Berton, Pierre
— NEWSPAPER WORK
Niagara: A History, 615–16, 622, 624
Niagara Falls, 386, 611
Nicholas, Benny, 122
Nicol, Eric, 129, 130–31, 134, 567, 647
1967: The Last Good Year, 631, 632, 635,
   637–39, 651
90 Minutes Live (TV show), 552
Niven, David, 529
Noble, Bob, 423
North, Canadian: Arctic sovereignty,
   288, 293, 295, 597, 606; Berton
   family trips to, 382–83, 516–17,
   519–22; development of, 288–90,
   293–95, 298–99, 323, 324; PB identified with, 212, 290, 295–96, 299, 300,
   305, 408, 663; PB's writing and other
   work about, 198–213, 232–34, 250,
   255, 256, 279, 289–90, 293–300,
   301–7, 320–21, 323, 324, 372, 416, 438,
   454, 516–17, 519–22, 528, 599–600,
   604, 605–8, 660–63. *See also* Berton,
   Pierre — PERSONAL HISTORY;
   Dawson City
North to the Nahanni (radio talks), 279
Nowell, Iris, 444, 673–74
Nowlan, Alden, 542
nuclear energy, 250, 259

Oakville, Ont., 39, 52
O'Brien, Edna, 440
Odhams Press, 251, 287
Ontario Hospital School (Orillia, Ont.),
   344–45, 363
Ontario Royal Commission on
   Publishing, 495, 535

Orchard, Dolly, 41
Order of Canada, 539, 591, 647
Orvig, Svenn, 298
Ouimet, Alphonse, 312, 459
Oxford Union, 537

Paar, Jack, 2, 384
Packard, Vance, 2, 335
Page, Steven, 633
Palmer, Vaughn, 122
Paradise Hill (musical), 458, 675
Parkin, John C., 416, 443, 444
"Past Imperfect" (story and radio play), 216–18, 236, 249
Pastinsky, Benny, 121
Patterson, Tom, 382
Pearce, Pat, 419–20, 436
Pearson, Lester B., 322, 381, 393, 420–21, 436, 439, 462, 573
Peckinpah, Sam, 372
Penguin Books Canada, 610–11, 615
Percy, H.R., 410
Perelman, S.J., 391
The Performing Arts in Canada (magazine), 390–91
Peterson, Oscar, 188
Peterson, Roy, 474, 567
Peterson, Tom, xii
Pevere, Geoff, 643–44
Phantom Parks (Searle), 647
Philip, Prince, 274
Phillips, David Graham, 118
Phillips, Nancy, 396, 443
Phillips, Nathan, 358
Phrateres, 115, 133
Pickpocket Books, 424
Pierre Berton: Canada's Arrogant Icon (documentary), 644–46, 656
Pierre Berton Award, 655, 658–59, 669
Pierre Berton Enterprises, 378, 571–72, 646, 660
The Pierre Berton Hour (TV show), 389–92, 402, 404
Pierre Berton Resource Library (Vaughan, Ont.), 664–65
The Pierre Berton Show (TV), 381, 404–7, 417–23, 425–27, 429, 435–36, 438–41,

448, 449, 450–51, 454, 459, 485–87, 493, 497–98, 503, 507, 522, 528–29, 537, 641
Pierre Berton Speaks (radio show), 326, 360
"Pierre Berton's Page," 393–400
Pike, James, 438
Pinchi Lake, B.C., 250
Pipeline (camp newspaper), 97, 99, 100
Polanyi, John, 598
The Politics of Labor (Thompson), 26–27
polling, 231
Popper, Hans, 485
Porter, Anna, 543, 569, 609. *See also* Szigethy, Anna
Porter, Cy, 648–49
Porter, John, 471, 476
Porter, McKenzie, 240, 317, 318, 442–43, 444, 448, 517
Porteus, Ken, 584
Portman, Jamie, 501
Post, Ethel, 291
Potter, Stephen, 256
poverty, 468–70. *See also* social justice
Prairie Playhouse (radio show), 251
Pratt, Claire, 363, 364
Prince, Thomas, 201
Prisoners of the North, 660, 663–64
prisons, 342–44, 407, 420, 487
The Promised Land, 579–83, 591, 605, 643
psychology, 240, 335
"Pub" (Publications Board). *See Ubyssey*
publishing industry, 237, 494, 611–12
Purdy, Al, 493, 551–52, 600

Quebec Industrial (film), 256
Quebec politics, 405, 418, 439, 459, 568, 631–32, 638
Queen's University, 30–31

racial discrimination, 349–50, 452, 618–20
radio, 74, 75, 81, 88, 89, 434. *See also* Berton, Pierre — RADIO WORK
Radley, Don, 292
Ralston, J.L., 160
Rathbone, Basil, 188

Rathburn, Eldon, 307
Rathgeb, Charles (Chuck), 442, 443, 444, 446
Rathlou, Lee, 335–36
Reading: A Canadian Magazine, 214
Redekopp, Harold, 674
Reed, Rex, 529
Regehr, T.D., 531, 532
Reguly, Eric, 650
Reid, Dallas, 292
Reid, Margaret, 129, 134, 176
religion, 395, 403–4. *See also* Berton, Pierre — PERSONAL HISTORY, religious beliefs; *The Comfortable Pew*
Remembering Yesterday, 434–35, 438
Revenge of the Tribes, 616
reviews and criticism: by PB, 256–57, 604, 608; of PB's books, 287, 290, 295, 299–300, 301, 302, 325, 367, 378, 385–86, 408–10, 466, 474–77, 501, 506, 508–9, 513–15, 529–35, 541–42, 545–48, 558, 559–67, 577–78, 580–83, 586–87, 595, 599–600, 601–2, 606, 607, 608, 613–16, 628–29, 636–38, 644, 653–54, 664; of PB's television shows, 389–91, 404, 405, 406–7, 419–20, 421, 436, 529
Reynolds, Quentin, 419, 423
Richardson, Bill, 636
Richler, Mordecai, 317, 441
Richmond, John, 449
Ritchie, Larry, 525
Robert, Marika, 441, 442
Robertson, Gordon, 298
Robertson, Heather, 614, 647
Robertson, John Ross, 329
Robertson, Norman, 241
Robins, Toby, 314, 316, 390, 459
Robinson, Doc, 75
Robinson, John A.T., 431
Robinson, Sugar Ray, 498
Robson, J.M., 385–86
Rockingham, John, 258
Rodgers, John, 504
Rogers, Shelagh, 635
Ross, Gary, 570
Ross, Val, 620, 624, 629–30

Ross, Wanda, 78
Rossier, Henri, 377–78, 386
Rotstein, Abraham, 493
Round the Pacific (radio show), 250
Rowley, Graham, 298
Royal Bank of Canada, 583, 590
Royal Commission on National Development in the Arts (Massey Commission), 253, 271, 272, 332
The Royal Family, 282–88, 652
royal family, 274, 280–88
Royal Military College, 158–59
Rubin, Jerry, 451
Ruby, Clayton, 633
Ruddy, Jon, 405, 406, 442, 472–73
Ruscitti, Joe, 672
Russell, Bertrand, 418
Rutherford, Paul, 311, 530
Ryan, Claude, 493
Ryerson Press, 494

Sagi, Doug, 603
Sahl, Mort, 454
Saint John, N.B., 13–14
Salt, Lionel, 129, 134, 144, 176
Saltzman, Percy, 311
Salutin, Rick, 356–57, 597, 627, 652
Sanderson-Mongin, Mme (professor), 79, 93
Sangster, Dorothy, 312
Savannah, Mr. (professor), 93
Savard, Ernest, 209
Schlesinger, Arthur, Jr., 439
Schneider, Ida, 517
Sclanders, Ian, 274
Scott, Grace, 150, 158
Scott, Jack, 124–25, 126–27, 137, 139, 142, 144, 150, 152, 155, 163, 164, 165, 166, 172, 173, 178, 188, 189, 199, 224, 236, 330, 355, 568, 610
Screen Gems, 381, 389, 404, 406, 417–18, 423, 426, 460, 486, 609
Seal Books, 586, 589, 639
Searle, Rick, 647
Sears, Barbara, 537–39, 544, 554–56, 572, 576, 578, 583, 591–92, 604, 605, 608, 640, 654

Second World War, 102, 117–18, 126, 127–28, 137, 138, 140–48, 149–76, 593–94, 653

Secord, Laura, 675

The Secret of My Success (TV show), 609

The Secret World of Og, 365–67, 386, 522, 523

Service, Robert, 35, 42, 251, 312–13, 331, 361, 449, 662

"72 Wedgewood Crescent," 377, 411–14, 587

sexual issues, 240, 390, 394–96, 439–41

Shaffer, Ivan, 424

Sharp Edges (radio play), 250

Shaw, Artie, 438

Shaw, Hugh, 428, 429, 464

Shields, Roy, 449, 450

Shiels, Bob, 404

Shrum, Gordon, 137

Shuster, Frank, 656

Sifton family, 184

Silver, Ray, 349

Silvera, Makeda, 620

Simpson, Helen, 445

Sims, Don, 499

Sinclair, Alice, 234

Sinclair, Gordon, 276, 289, 314, 315, 316, 326, 330, 387, 388, 459, 465, 487, 567, 573, 584

Sinclair, Lister, 129, 131, 132, 133, 134, 172, 220, 234, 251, 256–57, 273, 278, 406, 424, 442, 507, 536, 567, 590, 629, 645, 674

Sinclair, Upton, 439

Siqueiros, David Alfaro, 507

sixties, 436–41, 461, 470–71, 491–92

Slopen, Beverley, 425

Smith, Russell, 648, 650

Smith, Stephen, 636–37

The Smug Minority, 461–79, 483, 652–53

Sniderman, Sam, 609

social justice, 138, 160, 228–30, 331, 341, 357, 393, 462, 465–72, 477–79, 487

Soles, Paul, 585, 586

Soles, Ruth Ellen, 451

Somers, Joannie, 391

Sook, Han Yung, 262

Sordsmen's Club, 441–48, 588

South Africa, 350–51

Southam family and newspaper business, 190–91, 243, 245–47

Soviet Union, 369–70

Soward, F.H., 127, 551

Spears, Borden, 463–64, 473

Spector, Phil, 439

Spring Thaw (revue), 305, 393

St. Laurent, Louis, 288, 293

St. Roch (ship), 649

Stacey, C.P., 560–62, 564–65

Stafford, Ellen, 363–64

Stairs, Denis, 267

Stampede for Gold, 302

Stanley, George F.G., 515, 530, 534

Star Weekly, 69, 382, 463, 464, 473–74

Starowicz, Mark, 2

Starting Out, 12, 171, 596, 599–603, 621

Steel, Bert, 451

Steele, James, 492

Stegner, Wallace, 60–61

Stein, David Lewis, 401

Steinberg, Sam, 405

Stevens, Sinclair, 554

Stevenson, Adlai, 371

Stewart, John William, 183

Stoddart Publishing, 635

Stoffman, Judy, 652

Stone, Jim, 260

Strachey, Lytton, 282

Straight, Beverley, 185, 186, 189

Straight, Hal, 182–83, 184–91, 193, 195, 196, 197–200, 203, 208, 209–10, 220, 224, 236, 313, 567, 610

Strauss, Harold, 296–97, 298, 303, 310, 320, 321, 386

Street, Ann, 10

Stringer, Isaac O., 33

Stronach, Frank, 609

Strong, Maurice, 598

Stursberg, Peter, 259–60

Sun Tower (Vancouver), 182, 185

Susann, Jacqueline, 440

Sussan, Herbert, 381, 389, 423

Susskind, David, 390, 460

Suzuki, David, 597, 598, 656

Swainson, Donald, 514, 533
Switzerland, 376–77
Symons, Thomas, 493
Sypnowich, Peter, 499, 501, 504
Szigethy, Anna, 496, 509, 518. *See also*
    Porter, Anna
Szilard, Leo, 312

Tabloid (TV show), 311–12
Tak, Mrs. (refugee), 261, 262
Tapscott, Carl, 551
Tate, Sharon, 486
Taylor, Elizabeth, 331
Taylor, E.P., 243, 244–45, 247
Taylor, Fred, 552
Taylor, Gladys, 396
Taylor, Joan, 443, 444, 447, 448
Taylor, Peter, 525
Teeporten murder, 193–94
Telefilm Canada, 590
television, 240, 277, 318, 371, 495. *See
    also* Berton, Pierre — TELEVISION
    WORK
Teller, Edward, 537
Templeton, Charles, 326, 361, 387, 388,
    442, 447, 462, 517, 549, 567, 568, 574,
    603, 614, 629, 645
Terkel, Studs, 2
Terry, Pat, 186
Thayer, George, 493
Thomas, Lewis G., 531
Thomas, Lowell, 211
Thomas, Norman, 438
Thompson, Delia (née Fisher), 26, 27
Thompson, Edith (née Fisher), 24, 28, 53
Thompson, Florence Clara (Florrie), 24,
    28, 64, 65, 66, 91, 104
Thompson, John Herd, 580
Thompson, Laura, 24–38. *See also*
    Berton, Laura
Thompson, Louise, 220
Thompson, Maude, 24, 28
Thompson, Phillips Whitman (Uncle
    Phil), 28, 53, 64, 66, 67, 68, 80, 157,
    220
Thompson, Thomas Phillips, 25–28, 53,
    63, 68, 353, 476

Thompson, Valerie, 589
Thomson, Roy, 418
Thorsell, William, 651
Till, Eric, 536
Time magazine, 211
Tiompkin, Dimitri, 450
Tomlin, Lily, 529
The Tonight Show, 384, 451
Too Many Tears (Moss), 518
Toronto, 64–65, 156–57, 219–21, 243,
    378
Toronto *Globe*, 26, 27, 69, 240
Toronto *Globe and Mail*, 197, 240, 407,
    664, 671–73, 675
Toronto *Mail and Empire*, 26, 27, 68,
    240
Toronto Press Club, 254
Toronto Star, 68, 197, 276–77, 321–22,
    327–30, 387–88, 407, 672, 673; "By
    Pierre Berton" column, 320, 321,
    322–23, 327, 330–32, 334–54, 355–61,
    367, 368, 369–71, 372–77, 379–81,
    382–83, 386–88; column in 1991–94,
    616–17, 623
Toronto *Telegram*, 26, 68, 240, 329, 419
The Totem (yearbook), 109, 126, 133
Tour de Force, 579
Towards the Last Spike (Pratt), 488
Town, Harold, 436, 443, 444, 493
Toynbee, Arnold, 451
Trail, B.C., 258–59
Trans-Canada Airlines, 370, 405
Trent-Severn Waterway, 378–80
The Trial of Steven Truscott (LeBourdais),
    348
Trudeau, Pierre Elliott, 418, 439, 479,
    495, 505, 577
Truscott, Steven, 345–49, 363, 438, 668
Tully, Walter, 198
Tunstell, Douglas, 305
Turnbull, Janet, 586
Turnbull, Judith, 496
Tweed, Tommy and Jean, 221
Tyrwhitt, Janice, 317, 445, 537, 538, 539,
    544, 557–58, 572, 592–93, 646, 654
Tyson, Ian, 422
Tyson, Sylvia, 422, 633

Ubyssey, 105, 108–9, 111, 112, 114, 115, 116, 127–36, 144, 150, 152, 185
The Ugly American (Lederer and Burdick), 266
Under Attack (TV show), 460, 483, 484
Underhill, Frank, 491
United Church, 403, 570
United Nations, 168, 225, 228, 257, 264
University of British Columbia, 85, 87, 103–5, 108–19, 126, 127–28
University of New Brunswick, 15–17, 31

Vallee, Rudy, 422
Valpy, Michael, 619, 627–28
Van Bibber, Alex, 97
Van Bibber, Helen, 97
Van Luven, Lynne, 628, 629
Vance, Vivian, 529
Vancouver, 69, 139–40, 215, 225, 274–75
Vancouver *News-Herald,* 110–12, 114, 117, 119–25, 126–27, 137–41, 144, 153, 159, 178–82
Vancouver *Province,* 120, 122, 124, 136, 187, 190–91, 195, 247
Vancouver Sun, 120, 123, 178, 182–95, 196, 198–200, 202–10, 214, 231, 236, 275, 672
Vancouver Women's Press Club, 191–92
Vanguard Press, 212, 237
Vaughan, Denny, 314
Vaughan, Ont., 664–65
The Vertical Mosaic (Porter), 471, 476
Vickers, Reg, 512–13
Victoria, B.C., 70, 73, 123
Victoria College, 85, 87–90, 92–96
Victoria *Times,* 122
Vienna, 376
Vietnam War, 437, 492, 493, 593
Vimy, 591–95, 605, 610, 642, 643
Visser, Helen, 446

Waisglass, Sean, 378
Waite, P.B., 501, 530, 604
"The Waiting Room" (story and radio play), 215–16, 236, 249, 635
Walden, Keith, 560, 564
Walker, Andrew, 136, 188, 308

Walker, Donald, 188
Walker, Frank B., 298
Walker, Janet, 114–16, 128, 129, 132, 134, 136, 143, 144, 150–52, 158, 159, 175–76, 177, 186. *See also* Berton, Janet
Walker, Stanley, 105–6
Wallace, D.B., 410–11
Wallace, Mike, 313, 371
War of 1812, 554–55, 593, 675. *See also Flames across the Border; The Invasion of Canada*
Ward, Max, 290
"Water Hazard" (story and radio play), 216, 236
Watkins, Mel, 491
Watson, Patrick, 313, 598
Weaver, Robert, 279, 525
Webster, Jack, 610
Weekend Magazine, 415, 428, 429, 431, 464
Weil, Chester, 212
Weil, Joseph, 405
Werner, Hans, 654
West, Evelyn, 188
W.H. Smith bookstores, 535, 587
White, Len, 198
White Pass & Yukon Route railway, 32, 41, 102, 325
Whitehead, William, 522
Whitehorse, Yukon, 40–41
Whitehouse, Raymond, 236–37
Why We Act like Canadians, 576–78, 610, 643
Whyte, Kenneth, 614
Whyte, "Mom," 314
Wicks, Ben, 430, 567, 609
Wiggins Male Orphan Institution, 13–15, 16, 48
Wilbert W. Haaze Company, 339–40
The Wild Frontier, 548, 556, 610–11
Wilde, Cornel, 529
Wilder, Thornton, 172–73
Williamson, Al, 121, 140
Willis, J. Frank, 312
Wilson, Catherine, 497, 498, 499, 500, 502–3, 524–27
Wilson, Jennifer, 584–85, 604–5
Wilson, Sir John, 280

Wilson-Smith, Anthony, 651–52
Wilson, Violet, 79
Winchell, Walter, 89
Wing, Willis Kingsley, 282, 295, 302, 303, 417, 450
Winter, 635
Winter, William, 367
Wise, Penny. *See* Caldwell, Evelyn
Wolfe, Tom, 439
Women on the March (film), 305–6
Woodcock, George, 562, 564, 566–67
Woodsworth, Mary, 114
Woodward, Berton, 519, 521, 671
Woodward, Lucy. *See* Berton, Lucy (sister of PB)
Woodward, Paisley, 671
Worth Repeating, 643–44
Worthington, F.F., 197
Wright, Glenn, 502, 510–11, 535, 578
Writers' Development Trust of Canada, 535
Writers' Trust of Canada, 535, 610
Writers' Union of Canada, 535, 567, 578–79, 603–4, 617–20, 647, 673

"Writing Thru Race" conference, 618–20
Wuorio, Eva-Lis, 240

York Township, 356
Yost, Elwy, 635
Young, Bob, 235
Young, George, 192
Young, Neil, 235, 487
young people. *See* children and youth
Young, Rassy, 221, 235
Young, Scott, 210–11, 223, 226, 235, 314, 567
Yukon College, 609, 617
Yukon Consolidated Gold Company, 86, 90, 325
Yukon Gold Company, 37, 38
Yukon gold rush. *See* Klondike gold rush
Yukon River, 22, 28, 33, 52, 53, 58, 61, 101, 519–22

Ziv Television, 371–72
Zolf, Larry, 567